COMPANY LAW

Third Edition

BRENDA HANNIGAN, MA, LLM,

Solicitor (Ireland)
Professor of Corporate Law
University of Southampton

OXFORD
UNIVERSITY PRESS

OXFORD
UNIVERSITY PRESS

Great Clarendon Street, Oxford, OX2 6DP,
United Kingdom

Oxford University Press is a department of the University of Oxford.
It furthers the University's objective of excellence in research, scholarship,
and education by publishing worldwide. Oxford is a registered trade mark of
Oxford University Press in the UK and in certain other countries

British Library Cataloguing in Publication Data
Data available

Library of Congress Cataloging in Publication Data
Library of Congress Control Number: 2012938464

ISBN 978-0-19-960802-7

Printed in Great Britain by
Ashford Colour Press Ltd, Gosport, Hampshire

Preface

The three years since the last edition of this work have not seen any slackening of the pace in the world of company law, a dynamic subject which combines a rich historic case law with a responsiveness to the business challenges of today, an environment where a moratorium on legal development is not an option, particularly not in the face of the financial crisis engulfing Europe.

One level of response to the crisis has been a flurry of corporate governance initiatives, all reflected in a completely rewritten Chapter 5. Linked to those initiatives are changes to disclosure requirements, especially to narrative reporting, accounts and audit and these changes are addressed fully in Chapter 16. The financial crisis has also meant a super-abundance of insolvency cases, some of which have had at least the incidental benefit of giving the higher courts the opportunity to review some core doctrines, such as the anti-deprivation rule, considered at length in *Belmont Park Investments Ltd v BNY Corporate Trustee Services Ltd* (S Ct, 2011), with the commercial pragmatism on view there also visible in the Supreme Court ruling in *Progress Property Co Ltd v Moorgarth Group Ltd* (2010) on unlawful distributions, and in the Court of Appeal ruling in *BNY Corporate Trustee Services Ltd v Eurosail* (2011) on the meaning of balance sheet insolvency. Less pragmatic, perhaps, was the Supreme Court approach to the definition of 'subsidiary' in *Enviroco Ltd v Farstad* (2011) while all corporate groups will look with interest, and perhaps some concern, at the recent Court of Appeal ruling in *Chandler v Cape plc* (2012): groups are discussed in Chapter 3.

On directors, there is much of interest in the finely balanced 3–2 Supreme Court decision in *Re Paycheck Services 3 Ltd* (2010) on corporate directors and in the Court of Appeal's review of the position of nominee directors in *Hawkes v Cuddy (No 2)* (2009), discussed in Chapters 6 and 9 respectively. Unsurprisingly, in the current climate, a robust approach to directors' conflicts of interest can be detected and recent important cases such as *Commonwealth Oil & Gas Co Ltd v Baxter* (CSIH, 2009), *O'Donnell v Shanahan* (CA, 2009) and *Premier Waste Management Ltd v Towers* (CA, 2011) are all discussed in detail in a reworked Chapter 11. The invaluable judgment of Lord Neuberger in *Sinclair Investments (UK) Ltd v Versailles Trade Finance Ltd* (2011) brings clarity and certainty to the difficult issue of the recoverability of secret profits and bribes and Chapter 13 has been recast to reflect this and other recent decisions.

The responsiveness of 'soft law' to business and political pressures can be seen in the significant changes to the Takeover Code prompted by the contentious takeover of Cadbury plc by Kraft in 2010. These changes are considered in Chapter 26, together with the use of schemes of arrangements for restructurings, while the merits or otherwise of pre-pack administrations are considered in Chapter 23. Shareholder remedies remain centre stage with the courts beginning to tease out the basis on which permission might be granted to bring a derivative claim. The floodgates have not opened with the availability of the statutory procedure, as some predicted, but cases such as *Iesini v Westrip Holdings Ltd* (2009), *Kiani v Cooper* (2010) and *Stainer v Lee* (2010), all discussed in Chapter 18, offer the beginnings of a judicial framework for such claims. At the same time, in *Hawkes v Cuddy (No 2)* (2009) the Court of Appeal has revived the winding up on the just and equitable ground remedy which had somewhat fallen off the radar. The decisions in

Re Sunrise Radio, Kohli v Lit (2009) and *Oak Investment Partners XII v Boughtwood* (2010) show that the unfairly prejudicial remedy still has great elastic qualities in terms of the abuses which it encompasses and the available remedies. For the traditionalist, there is even something of a resurgence of authorities on piercing the corporate veil, but in a modern commercial setting (disputes within shipping groups with assets being moved around to evade enforcement steps against particular subsidiaries): the discussion in Chapter 3 has been updated accordingly.

Hence the tradition of a rich seam of case law on topical corporate issues continues and this edition attempts to bring the reader fully up to date with these developments. These matters merely serve, however, to highlight the many interesting and challenging issues in company law which come before the courts as all stakeholders continually jostle for position. Whatever the basis of a particular dispute, a unifying theme arising from the financial crisis, and evident in both the courts and in the regulatory reviews and developments taking place, is the universal question—in whose interests are companies to be run? Many commentators have argued in recent years that the financial crisis calls for a rethinking of capitalism to make companies work for society and not just to enrich the few. Arguably, an adaptation of company law to reflect broader constituencies can already be seen in areas like takeovers, insolvency, directors' duties. Hopefully, these debates help the student reader to understand that company law is not just about the legislation, important though that is, nor about the cases, important though they are, but it is also about the role played by company law in achieving the broader political, economic and social goals of a democratic society.

I am most grateful to the OUP editorial and production teams for their attentive, professional assistance at every stage of this work.

The law is stated as of 1 February 2012.

Brenda Hannigan
Professor of Corporate Law
University of Southampton
20 May 2012

Outline contents

Contents

Part II Corporate Governance—Directors' Roles and Responsibilities

Table of statutes

Table of statutory instruments

Table of European legislation

Regulations

Table of cases

PART I

The Corporate Structure

1

Formation, classification and registration of companies

A Introduction

Registered companies

1-1 Companies registered under the Companies Act 2006 (CA 2006) and its predecessors are the focus of this book. In this initial chapter we consider the mechanics of formation and registration and the various types of companies which may be formed, as well as looking briefly at alternative vehicles for business. Before looking at these matters, an overview of the process of formation and the key players in a registered company may be helpful for the student reader at whom this book is aimed.

An overview of the formation of a registered company

1-2 To form a registered company under the CA 2006, all that is required is one person and a lawful purpose (s 7). Some brief documentation must be submitted (either electronically or on paper) to the registrar of companies (located at Companies House, Cardiff) together with a registration fee of £14 (if electronic) and £40 (if paper). Once the formalities are completed correctly, the registrar of companies issues a certificate of incorporation whereupon the company comes into existence (s 16(2)). This process typically takes less than a week (if paper-based) and it can be completed in a single day if speed is important. The process is simple, quick and inexpensive.

1-3 Imagine that A and B wish to form a registered company to run a printing business. A alone could form a company since, as noted earlier, only one person is required, but for these purposes we will assume A and B wish to form a company together. There are a few initial decisions which A and B have to make. First, they have to decide how they are going to split the ownership of the company. Assume they agree that they will split the ownership of the business 70% and 30% to reflect the contributions that they are going to make to it. The division of ownership is entirely a matter of choice for them, obviously, as is the number of shares to issue. They may decide to issue:

- 1,000 £1 shares with A taking 700 of the shares, putting £700 into the company's finances in the form of share capital, and B taking 300 shares, putting £300 into the share capital; or
- 100 £1 shares with A taking 70 (£70) and B taking 30 (£30); or
- 100 1p shares with A taking 70 (70p) and B 30 (30p); or
- 10 1p shares with A taking seven shares (7p) and B taking three shares (3p).

1-4 Share capital is considered in detail later. For the moment it suffices to appreciate that A and B have complete flexibility as to the amount of money that they put into the company in the form of share capital and the value, called the nominal value, they wish to assign to the shares. They have complete flexibility as to the number of shares they issue and the same ownership division can be achieved by issuing 10 or 100 or 1,000 shares. Shares typically carry one vote per share so, on any of the examples given in **1-3**, A has 70% of the votes and B has 30% of the votes. Most matters within a company can be decided on a simple majority vote so A has effective control of the company with B as a minority shareholder, a position which may prove uncomfortable, as we shall see. Depending on the circumstances, A and B might prefer a 60/40 split in the shareholdings, or a 90/10 split, or even a 50/50 split, but a 50/50 split has an in-built deadlock problem if the two shareholders disagree so it is not advisable. As can be seen, it is possible to form a company with very little capital, though in the case of a public company wishing to carry on business, there is a minimum share capital requirement of £50,000 (CA 2006, s 763, see **1-45**). For the moment, though, we will concentrate on private companies. The distinction between public and private status is discussed later in the chapter.

1-5 As the shareholders of the company, A and B appoint the directors who will manage the business. Given his voting control, A could impose his choice of directors, but frequently it will have been agreed that A and B will be the directors. The result is that A and B are the shareholders and A and B are also the directors of the company, a form of structure which is very common.

1-6 Equally, A and B may decide to bring other members into the business and issue further shares to them and/or appoint them to the board. With additional shares issued, the shareholders might be A, B, C and D with only A and B being directors; or A and B might be the only shareholders with the board made up of A, B, C and D; or A and B may be the only shareholders while C and D are the only directors. In other words, while uniformity of identify between the shareholders and the directors is very common in small companies, that need not be the case. Indeed one of the advantages of incorporation is that it allows the ownership of the company to be separated from the management of the business. It is possible to be a shareholder without being a director and vice versa and, of course, in the largest companies with hundreds of thousands of shareholders, there can be no question of the shareholders being the directors, and the directors usually have only minuscule shareholdings compared to the total number of shares in issue.

1-7 Now we have the key players as far as company law is concerned, the directors and the members or shareholders (for the most part, the terms 'members' and 'shareholders' are synonymous). Basically, the members or shareholders are the owners of the company with ultimate control of the company through their shareholdings while the directors provide the management of the company. Of course, many other constituencies, or stakeholders as they are often called, also have an important role to play in the company. Employees and creditors come instantly to mind, but their relationships with the company are primarily a matter of employment law, contract law and insolvency law whereas the focus of company law is the company and its shareholders and directors.

1-8 Returning to A and B, they must also decide on the type of company that they want to form. The CA 2006 provides for various types of company, but the most commonly adopted form is the private company limited by shares. A company is a company limited by shares if the liability of its members is limited by its constitution to the amount, if any, unpaid on the shares held by them (CA 2006, s 3(2)).

1-9 Let us imagine that A has taken 70 £1 shares and B has taken 30 £1 shares, the £100 company being a very common structure.[1] With only £100 of share capital, the company will initially seek to finance its activities through bank financing and so it must arrange loans and overdrafts with the bank. The company, the separate entity formed on incorporation, will acquire employees and premises, the company will enter into contracts and the company will incur debts. If the company incurs, say, debts of £25,000 and collapses into insolvency, the company owes the creditors £25,000, but the members' liability is limited to the amount unpaid, if any, on the shares held by them. The liability of A is limited to the £70 due on his shares and B's liability is limited to the £30 due on his shares. Assuming that A and B paid for their shares at the time the company issued the shares to them, as would be typical, A and B have already paid the sums due and no further payments can be required from them to meet the company's liabilities to its creditors. The only caveat being that, in some cases, A and B may have been prevailed upon by one or more creditors (typically, the company's bank) to give personal guarantees and security over personal assets which the bank can call upon in the event that, on insolvency, the company's assets are insufficient to meet the company's debts due to the bank.

1-10 For the purposes of the discussion to date, it was assumed that the parties wishing to register a company will put together the documentation and submit it to the registrar of companies, but it is also common to purchase a company from a company formation agent. Company formation agents provide ready-made companies, literally companies incorporated earlier and available for immediate use where the formalities have already been completed and the certificate of incorporation has been issued. Such companies are ready to be purchased 'off-the-shelf' by persons wishing to set up a company. There are various reasons for preferring or needing an off-the-shelf company, such as a concern not to incur any personal liabilities. As a company does not exist prior to the issue of the certificate of incorporation, any debts incurred by A and B in obtaining premises, hiring equipment, etc prior to that point are incurred personally.

1-11 For similar reasons, A and B may opt for same-day incorporation where the registrar processes all the documentation and issues the certificate of incorporation on the same day as the application for registration is made.[2] Same-day incorporation may also make sense where there is a need to secure a particular name for the company since, once registered, no other company can have the same name, or even a name considered 'too like' that name (CA 2006, ss 66, 67).

1-12 Having incorporated, A and B, as the directors and shareholders, have taken on new legal roles and responsibilities, the discharge of which is the subject of the remainder of this book. Sometimes, the ease and speed of incorporation can obscure these legal realities and it is often the case that the parties themselves have only a minimal understanding of their changed legal status and potential liabilities. In part, this lack of understanding is due to the fact that incorporation, either directly or by the purchase of a company off-the-shelf, can be achieved without any professional advice being sought or required. The result can be a failure on the part of the incorporators to appreciate the duties and responsibilities of directors including their obligations to the company's creditors, the need for the company's affairs to be run in a manner which takes account of minority shareholder

---

[1] Of the 2,498,700 companies on the register (figures for England and Wales) with an issued share capital at March 2011, 1,858,500 had an issued share capital of up to £100: see Companies House, *Statistical Tables on Companies Registration Activities 2010–11* Table A6.

[2] The same-day incorporation fee is £100 (if paper) or £30 (if electronic).

interests and does not unfairly prejudice them, and the ongoing obligations which companies have with respect to filing information with the registrar of companies so as to ensure that the public register is up to date and accurate. This is not to say that access to limited liability should be restricted, but rather that all concerned need to appreciate the legal responsibilities attached to acquiring corporate status.

1-13   Of course, A and B are not compelled to incorporate and there are some other options open to them which are worth considering before we look at the formation of registered companies.

Alternative structures to the registered company

1-14   As noted earlier, conducting a business through the mechanism of a registered company has the particular advantages of the separate legal status of the company, the limited liability of the members and the possible separation of ownership and management of the company, but where these attributes are either not important or not attainable (for example, because of the small scale of the business), then a registered limited company may not be the most appropriate legal structure for that business given that incorporation brings with it a changed set of legal roles and responsibilities which the parties may not wish to bear.[3]

A sole trader

1-15   One option is for an individual to act as a sole trader and with very large numbers of companies having no more than two members and an issued share capital of (at most) £100, it is debatable whether some of those businesses might not be conducted more appropriately as sole traders. A sole trader is simply that—an individual carrying on business as an individual. The disadvantage is that the sole trader has unlimited liability, but many shareholders in small companies obtain only partial limited liability in any event, as they may have given personal guarantees to major creditors of the company, such as banks. The main advantage in being a sole trader is privacy as there is no obligation to register any information as to the business or its financial position with a public registry.[4]

Partnership

1-16   Partnership is the relation which subsists between persons carrying on a business in common with a view of profit.[5] Partnerships are governed by the Partnership Act 1890 but most partnerships draw up their own partnership agreements which override the Act. Partnerships are not separate legal entities and partners do not have limited liability. The advantage of this structure is that the business affairs of a partnership are entirely private and there is no obligation to register financial or partnership information at a public registry.[6]

---

[3] See BIS, *Business Population Estimates for the UK and Regions 2011* (October 2011), URN 11/92A, p 1, which suggests that, at the start of 2011, 62.4% of private sector enterprises were sole proprietorships, 27.7% were companies and 9.8% were partnerships.

[4] BIS, *Business Population Estimates for the UK and Regions 2011* (October 2011), URN 11/92A, p 5, suggests that there were an estimated 2.8m sole proprietorships in the UK at the start of 2011.

[5] Partnership Act 1890, s 1.

[6] BIS, *Business Population Estimates for the UK and Regions 2011* (October 2011), URN 11/92A, p 5, suggests that there were an estimated 447,000 partnerships in the UK at the start of 2011.

Limited partnership

1-17 Limited partnerships are governed by the Limited Partnership Act 1907[7] and must be registered at Companies House. A limited partnership allows for limited partners alongside general partners with unlimited liability (though a company can be a general partner and so limited liability may be secured for the general partner in that way). The liability of a limited partner for the debts of the partnership is limited to the amount of their contribution to the partnership, but a possible disadvantage of this structure is that a limited partner must be excluded from all management functions. On the other hand, a limited partnership is a useful business vehicle for investors who are content to allow the general partners to manage the assets, particularly as financial privacy is ensured given there is no obligation to file accounts with Companies House. This structure is used throughout the venture capital investment industry and so the limited partnership has evolved into a somewhat specialised business vehicle.[8]

Limited liability partnership

1-18 Limited liability partnerships (LLPs) are something of a hybrid between a company and a partnership. A limited liability partnership is a body corporate with legal personality separate from that of its members which is formed by being registered at Companies House. LLPs are governed by the Limited Liability Partnerships Act 2000 and related regulations including, in particular, the Limited Liability Partnership (Application of the Companies Act 2006) Regulations 2009 which apply many provisions of the CA 2006 to LLPs with appropriate modifications.[9]

1-19 To register an LLP, there must be two or more persons associated for carrying on a lawful business with a view to profit.[10] Details of the registered office and of the members (an LLP does not have a share capital, so there are no shareholders) must be provided. There must be at least two designated members who are named members with particular responsibilities such as with respect to signing and delivering accounts to the registrar of companies. The constitution of the LLP, the members' internal agreement dealing with such matters as the division of management powers and profits, is not registered. To that extent, members of an LLP retain some of the essential privacy of a partnership. An LLP is required to file annual accounts and an annual return so a considerable level of financial disclosure is required. In return, the liability of the members is limited, in this case to such amount as they have agreed internally to contribute to the debts of the LLP. On insolvency, all the corporate insolvency regimes are available and applicable to an LLP which remains liable to its creditors to the full amount of its assets. As can be seen, therefore, the LLP is a hybrid creation straddling the line between partnerships and companies

---

[7] In 2008, the Government consulted on plans to modernise and simplify the law on limited partnerships in line with recommendations previously made by the Law Commission; see BERR Consultation Document, *Reform of Limited Partnership Law, Legislative Reform Order to repeal and replace the Limited Partnerships Act 1907* (August 2008), URN 08/1153 and the Law Commission Report, *Partnership Law* (Law Comm No 283), November 2003. However, these plans were dropped subsequently (some modest amendments were made to the 1907 Act by SI 2009/1940) and the governing legislation remains the Limited Partnership Act 1907.

[8] There were 18,869 on the register as of March 2011 (figures for England and Wales), see Companies House *Statistical Tables 2010–11*, Table E2.

[9] SI 2009/1804. See generally *Palmer's Limited Liability Partnership Law* (2nd edn, 2011). LLPs were introduced following intense pressure from accountancy firms which were concerned that partnership (with its unlimited personal liability of the partners) was an unattractive business vehicle for the profession. But when the legislation was enacted, it was decided to make it available to all rather than restrict it to the professions. [10] LLPA 2000, s 2(1)(a).

and, as of March 2011, 40,482 LLPs (figures for England and Wales) were registered with Companies House.[11]

An unlimited company

1-20 One other option to note is the unlimited company, i.e. a company without any limit in its constitution on the liability of its members (CA 2006, s 3(4)). This status might appear an unattractive option, given the open-ended commitment by the members to meet the company's liabilities, yet there were 5,400 on the register at 31 March 2011.[12] The advantage which an unlimited company has over other forms of registered company is that generally there is no obligation to file accounts with the registrar of companies (s 448). Where privacy is a major consideration, therefore, and the risk of insolvency is remote (for example, because the company is not trading but holding investments), unlimited liability may be attractive. On the other hand, the accounting disclosure requirements have been significantly reduced in recent years for small limited companies[13] so this advantage may not be as attractive as it once was. There may be taxation reasons, however, why an unlimited company may be advantageous.

1-21 Overall, however the popularity of these other mechanisms such as the LLP (40,482 on the register, figures for England and Wales), the limited partnership (18,869 on the register) or the unlimited company (5,400) has to be put in the context of a register of 2.3m companies,[14] the vast majority of which are companies limited by shares combining a separate legal entity with limited liability for the members.

B Company formation–companies limited by shares

1-22 The most common type of registered company is the company limited by shares so, assuming that A and B wish to register a company limited by shares, they must draw up certain documents and submit them to the registrar of companies together with the registration fee (£14 if electronic incorporation; £40 if paper-based).[15]

Memorandum of association

1-23 An application for registration must be accompanied by a memorandum of association (CA 2006, s 9(1)). The memorandum is a short prescribed document[16] stating that the subscribers wish to form a company under the CA 2006 and agree to become members of the company and, in the case of a company with a share capital, they agree to take at least one share each (s 8(1)). This form of memorandum is new and the intention is that it is to be of merely historical significance indicating the initial founding of the company. Previously, the memorandum of association was an important external-facing document telling the outside world the key facts about the company: its name, its status as a public company (if that was the case), the jurisdiction in which it was registered, the company's objects, that the members' liability was limited, and setting out the amount and division of the company's authorised share capital. Now the memorandum simply records the

---

[11] See Companies House *Statistical Tables 2010–11*, Table E4.

[12] Companies House *Statistical Tables 2010–11*, Table A2.

[13] See CA 2006, s 444 and the thresholds for this category are quite high, see s 382. See also **16–20**.

[14] Companies House *Statistical Tables 2010–11*, Table A2.

[15] The fee is low out of concerns that otherwise it might be seen as an indirect tax on capital raising, see Drury, 'The "Delaware Syndrome": European Fears and Reactions' [2005] JBL 709 at 726–7.

[16] The memorandum of a company with a share capital must be in the form set out in the Companies (Registration) Regulations 2008, SI 2008/3014, reg 2(a), Sch 1.

identity of the original founders of the company and indicates how many shares they took on formation. In many cases, the original founders will be formation agents (see **1-10**) and so the document will have no continuing relevance.

Application for registration

1-24 The company's application for registration must state:

- the company's proposed name;
- whether the registered office is to be situated in England and Wales, Wales, Scotland or Northern Ireland;
- whether the members' liability is to be limited and, if so, whether by shares or by guarantee;
- whether the company is to be a public or a private company (CA 2006, s 9(2)).

The application must contain:

- a statement of capital and initial shareholdings (if a company limited by shares) or a statement of guarantee (if a company limited by guarantee);
- a statement of the company's proposed officers, including the proposed company secretary (if the company is a public company or where a private company chooses to have a company secretary);
- a statement of the intended address of the company's registered office;
- a copy of any proposed articles of association unless the intention is to rely on the model default articles, discussed at **1-29** (CA 2006, s 9(4), (5)).

Statement of capital and initial shareholdings

1-25 The statement of capital and initial shareholdings must state:[17]

- the total number of shares and the aggregate nominal value of the shares to be taken on formation by the subscribers to the memorandum,
- for each class of shares, prescribed particulars of the rights attached to them, the total number of shares of that class and the aggregate nominal value of those shares,
- the amount to be paid up, and the amount, if any, unpaid on each share (CA 2006, s 10(2)).

1-26 The statement of capital is a useful innovation in the CA 2006 which provides important information as to the share structure of the company.[18] The share structure is important

---

[17] The statement of capital and initial shareholdings also must contain the name and address of each subscriber to the memorandum of association: CA 2006, s 10(3); the Companies (Registration) Regulations 2008, SI 2008/3014, reg 3.

[18] Unfortunately, it has proved difficult for companies with complex share capital histories to provide some of the information required and BIS has consulted on amendments which might be made to address these practical difficulties, see BIS, *Companies Act 2006: Statements of Capital, Consultation on Financial Information required* (November 2009) URN 09/1488. That consultation then revealed other difficulties, for example, with setting out the prescribed particulars of the rights attached to shares. The Government therefore stated, in May 2011, that it believes that there is a good case for simplifying the financial information requirements for all companies in all statements of capital and to simplify the information requirements concerning the rights attached to shares. The intention is to bring forward detailed proposals as soon as a suitable legislative vehicle is available.

in terms of (1) establishing how much share capital has been raised and how much is paid and unpaid and (2) identifying the rights attached to the shares where there are classes of shares. Most companies have only one type of share, an ordinary share, such as the £1 share noted at **1-9** held by A and B, and class rights are irrelevant in such a company. Class of shares are discussed at **14-16**. As from the date of incorporation, the subscribers to the memorandum become holders of the shares specified in the statement of capital and initial holdings (CA 2006, s 16(5)).

Statement of the proposed officers

1-27 Particulars of the initial director(s) of the company[19] must be delivered with the application for registration and the directors must indicate their consent to act (CA 2006, s 12(1),(3)). If the company is a public company, or where a private company chooses to appoint a secretary, particulars of the proposed secretary of the company must also be given together with his/her consent so to act. From the date of incorporation, those persons so named as directors and company secretary are deemed to have been appointed to office (s 16(6)).

Statement of the address of the company's registered office

1-28 Every company must have a registered office (CA 2006, s 86) which essentially is meant to be the administrative office of the company and all business letters, order forms and websites of the company must give the address of the registered office[20] which may be a service address. The registered office is the location at which members and others may consult the various registers which the company is obliged to maintain,[21] such as the register of members (see **14-69**). The registered office is also the place where documents must be deposited, such as the statement by the company's auditor on ceasing to hold office (s 519), and where legal documents may be served on a company. It is also the address with which the registrar of companies corresponds so it is important that any change of address of the registered office is notified promptly to the registrar.

Copy of articles of association

1-29 The application for registration must contain a copy of the proposed articles of association (CA 2006, s 9(5)) and if, on formation, articles are not registered or, if articles are registered, in so far as they do not exclude or modify the relevant model articles, the relevant model articles form part of the company's articles automatically (s 20(1)). Model forms of articles are provided for public and private companies limited by shares and for companies limited by guarantee and any company may adopt all or any of the provisions of the relevant model articles for that type of company.[22] The articles of association are a key element of the company's constitution and set out the rules governing the internal running of the company. The matters typically covered in the articles include the conduct of meetings and voting procedures; capital matters including share transfer and

---

[19] A private company must have at least one director, a public company must have at least two: CA 2006, s 154.

[20] The Companies (Trading Disclosures) Regulations 2008, SI 2008/495, reg 7.

[21] Companies may choose a single alternative inspection location as well as the registered office, see CA 2006, s 1136 and The Companies (Company Records) Regulations 2008, SI 2008/3006, reg 3.

[22] CA 2006, s 19(3). See the Companies (Model Articles) Regulations 2008, SI 2008/3229. It is the model articles in force at the time of the company's registration which apply: CA 2006, s 20(2); and subsequent amendments of the model articles do not affect a company registered before the amendment takes effect: s 19(4). Many companies on the register of companies remain subject to the 1985 Table A articles and some are still governed by the 1948 Table A articles.

transmission; the appointment and removal of directors and their powers; and the declaration of dividends. A detailed account of the articles can be found in Chapter 4.

Statement of compliance

1-30 In order to minimise the amount of checking which needs to be done by the registrar of companies, a statement of compliance (i.e. a statement that the requirements as to registration have been complied with) signed by every subscriber to the memorandum must be delivered to the registrar of companies with the registration application (CA 2006, s 13(1)). It is an offence to make a false statement of compliance (s 1112).

The company name

1-31 Care must be taken as to the choice of company name for various reasons but essentially because a name may be rejected by the registrar on a variety of grounds and there may be problems with other persons and businesses who may claim goodwill in the same or a similar name. With respect to the latter issue, the CA 2006 makes provision in ss 69–74 for a procedure whereby a person may object to a registered name on the ground that it is the same as a name associated with the applicant in which he has goodwill or that it is sufficiently similar to such a name that its use in the UK would be likely to mislead by suggesting a connection between the company and the person objecting. Objections are considered by a company names adjudicator[23] and, if an objection is upheld, the company will be required to change its name (s 73). Detailed rules as to company names are set out in CA 2006, Pt 5, ss 54–85 and related statutory instruments.[24] In addition to complying with those requirements, the directors need to consider any risk of the company being sued for passing off by other businesses and any possibility of an infringement of an existing trade mark.[25] A company may trade under a business name and, in that case, it must also comply with the business name regulations (s 82).

1-32 Essentially, the scheme governing company names is as follows:

- Certain designations or their alternatives are required unless the company meets the criteria for exemption.[26] The required designations are 'ltd' or 'limited' for a private company and 'plc' or 'public limited company' for a public company (or their Welsh equivalents).[27]

- A company must not be registered with a name if, in the opinion of the Secretary of State (i.e. the registrar of companies), its use by the company would constitute an offence or it is offensive.[28]

---

[23] See CA 2006, ss 70–74 and the Company Names Adjudicator Rules 2008, SI 2008/1738. The names adjudicator is a new role created by the CA 2006. The adjudicators are based at the UK Intellectual Property Office rather than at Companies House.

[24] See, in particular, the Company and Business Names (Miscellaneous Provisions) Regulations 2009, SI 2009/1085.

[25] It is now possible, via the Business Link advice service, to search against the companies names index and the trade-mark index so it is easy to establish whether a possible name will be a problem in either respect.

[26] CA 2006, ss 60–63.   [27] CA 2006, ss 58–59.   [28] CA 2006, s 53.

- The use of certain other 'sensitive' names requires the consent of the Secretary of State or some other designated body.[29]
- A company must not be registered with a name which is the same as another name appearing in the registrar's index of company names.[30]

1-33   A company must display its registered name at its registered office and any other location at which the company's records are available for inspection and at any other location at which it carries on business.[31] A company must also disclose its registered name on a wide range of business documentation and correspondence and on its websites.[32] The company name must be engraved on the company's seal, if it has one.[33] In addition to its name, on registration a company is allotted a registered number[34] which is important in distinguishing between companies.

1-34   A company may alter its name by special resolution or by any other means (such as an ordinary resolution or resolution of the directors) allowed by the company's articles.[35] It may be directed to change its name in certain circumstances, as where it is 'too like' an existing name.[36] There are also restrictions on the use of certain names by former directors of a company which has gone into insolvent liquidation.[37]

The certificate of incorporation

1-35   Once all the required documents are submitted together with the registration fee, and assuming there has been proper compliance with the formalities and no problems about the company name, the registrar issues a certificate of incorporation of the company which is conclusive evidence that there has been compliance with the requirements of the CA 2006 in respect of registration (CA 2006, s 15). From the date of incorporation mentioned in the certificate, the subscribers to the memorandum, together with such other persons as may from time to time become members of the company, are a body corporate (s 16(2)).

1-36   Once incorporated, the company is a separate legal entity from the shareholders which means that it is the company which conducts the business, owns property, hires employees, incurs debts, makes profits, etc. The separate existence of the company means that the membership may be constantly changing, as shareholders transfer or sell their shares, but the business of the company is unaffected. The members, as noted at **1-9**, enjoy limited

---

[29]   CA 2006, ss 54–56. 'Sensitive' words include words such as 'Royal', 'University', 'Chartered' which suggest some status or association and which could be used improperly to mislead people.

[30]   CA 2006, s 66(1).

[31]   CA 20006, s 82; Companies (Trading Disclosures) Regulations 2008, SI 2008/495, regs 3 and 4. There is an exemption for a location which is primarily used for living accommodation designed to assist small companies which carry on business from the directors' homes.

[32]   CA 20006, s 82; Companies (Trading Disclosures) Regulations 2008, SI 2008/495, reg 6. The categories of document which must disclose the registered name include business letters; bills of exchange, promissory notes, endorsements and order forms; cheques purporting to be signed by or on behalf of the company; orders for money, goods or services purporting to be signed by or on behalf of the company; and, crucially, a catch-all category of 'all other forms of its business correspondence and documentation', see reg 6(g).

[33]   CA 2006, s 45(2). A company is not required to have a company seal, s 45(1), but may choose to do so.

[34]   CA 2006, s 1066.

[35]   CA 2006, s 77(1) and see s 77(2). A special resolution requires a 75% majority while an ordinary resolution requires a simple majority: see ss 282, 283.

[36]   CA 2006, s 67; see also ss 75, 76.

[37]   See IA 1986, s 216; IR 1986, rr 4.228–4.230; see the discussion at **25–34**.

liability and are not required to participate in the management of the company which is a matter for the directors. These many advantages, in particular the separate legal status of the company, the limited liability of the members, and the separation of ownership and management of the company, ensure that the registered company limited by shares is an immensely popular and successful vehicle for the conduct of business in this jurisdiction.

C Company formation–companies limited by guarantee

1-37 A company limited by guarantee is a company having the liability of its members limited by its constitution to such amount (usually very small, £1 or £5) as the members undertake to contribute to the assets of the company in the event of its being wound up.[38] Such a company does not have a share capital (no contribution is required until winding up) and so these companies have members and not shareholders. Given the absence of share capital, such companies must necessarily be private and not public companies[39] (the distinction between private and public companies is discussed at **1-41**). While there is no prohibition on trading by companies limited by guarantee, such companies are predominantly found in the not-for-profit sector and are widely used for community and sporting groups, local associations, flat management companies and for educational and charitable purposes.[40] The advantages of incorporation for such organisations lie in legal personality and limited liability so facilitating the ownership of property and the contracting of obligations despite a fluctuating membership and without exposing the members to personal liabilities.

1-38 The incorporation process for these companies is identical in most respects to a company limited by shares, save for necessary modifications, for example, a statement of guarantee is required instead of a statement of capital and initial shareholdings (see **1-25**). Membership of a company limited by guarantee is governed by the articles of association. The model form of articles, if adopted, provides that new members may not be admitted unless approved by the directors, membership is not transferable and ceases on death and a member can withdraw on giving seven days' notice.[41]

D Private and public companies

Introduction

1-39 For those forming a company, a further choice is whether to register as a private or a public company. In practice, the vast majority of companies are formed as private companies limited by shares. As of March 2011, there were 2,287,300 companies (figures for England

---

[38] CA 2006, s 3(1), (3).

[39] See CA 2006, s 4(2). The formation of companies limited by guarantee with a share capital has been prohibited since 22 December 1980.

[40] See Companies House *Statistical Tables 2010–11*, Table A6 which shows 98,400 companies on the register with no issued share capital (figures for England and Wales). Not all of these would be companies limited by guarantee, but it could be assumed that the majority are companies limited by guarantee. Given an effective register of approximately 2.3m companies, see Table A7, clearly only a very small number opt to be a company limited by guarantee.

[41] See The Companies (Model Articles) Regulations 2008, SI 2008/3229, reg 3, Sch 2, arts 21 and 22.

and Wales) on the register of which 2,279,700 (99.7%) were private companies and 7,600 (0.3%) were public companies.[42] Even those companies which are public companies are usually formed initially as private companies and subsequently re-register as public companies (re-registration is discussed at **1-52**). As of March 2011, out of 375,700 new incorporations in the previous year, only 600 were public companies.[43]

1-40 As to the definition of a public and private company, CA 2006, s 4 states that a 'private company' is a company which is not a public company and a 'public company' is a company limited by shares or by guarantee and having a share capital,[44] whose certificate of incorporation states that it is a public company, and which has complied with the requirements of the Companies Acts in relation to public companies.

Differences between public and private companies

1-41 On many issues the CA 2006 imposes quite different requirements on public and private companies and the general regulatory approach is that the statutory requirements with respect to public companies are more onerous than those imposed on private companies. For example, public companies do not qualify for the many accounting and audit exemptions available to private companies.

1-42 CA 2006, s 4(4) draws attention to what it describes as 'the two major differences' between public and private companies, namely the prohibition on private companies offering their securities (for our purposes, essentially shares) to the public (s 755) and the requirement for a trading certificate (s 761) but it is the former which is the key distinction. Other distinctions, noted below would relate to the company name, accounting and audit requirements, officer requirements and corporate formalities.

Public offers by private companies

1-43 The key distinction between public and private companies is that a public company may offer its securities to the public (although it is not obliged to do so) and a private company is prohibited from offering its securities to the public. While there is no longer a criminal sanction attached to a breach, a private company may be subject to an order restraining a contravention of the prohibition, a requirement to re-register as a public company or even an order for the compulsory winding up of the company (CA 2006, ss 755–760).

1-44 As noted, the general approach is that the regulation of public companies is stricter than that for private companies. The reason why stricter regulation is imposed is because of the possibility that a public company may offer its shares to the public. The additional requirements (minimum capital, fuller accounts, more formal corporate governance structures, etc) could be imposed on a private company, but Parliament chooses not to do so, because a private company does not cross the threshold which would justify and require additional regulation. The threshold that does justify additional regulation is the possibility that the company may offer its shares to the public. This is not an arbitrary threshold, rather it is the precise point at which the public interest intrudes into the classification debate. Corporate self-interest in raising capital meets the public interest in the protection of investors. Investor protection requirements form a package which consists

---

[42] See Companies House *Statistical Tables 2010–11*, Table A2.
[43] See Companies House *Statistical Tables 2010–11*, Table A2.
[44] As of 22 December 1980, such companies cannot be formed: CA 2006, s 5(1), so the vast majority of public companies are companies limited by shares.

of more than mere prospectus requirements (a prospectus is the formal public document offering shares for sale) and includes the accounting requirements, the corporate governance requirements, more formal decision-making, etc which are characteristic of a public company.

Trading certificate and share capital

1-45 A public company formed as such cannot commence trading without a trading certificate issued by the registrar of companies which he may only do if satisfied that the nominal value of the company's allotted share capital is not less than the authorised minimum (CA 2006, s 761), which is £50,000 or the prescribed euro equivalent, €57,100 (s 763).[45] There is no minimum share capital for a private limited company hence the ability of A and B to set up a private company with very small amounts of capital (see the example at **1-3**) and a private company can trade immediately on incorporation without any need for a trading certificate. In general, the rules governing payment for share capital and dealings in share capital are stricter for public companies, as is discussed in Chapters 19 and 20.

Company name

1-46 The most visible distinction between a public and a private company lies in the name which, in the case of a public company, must end in 'public limited company' or its abbreviation 'plc' (or Welsh equivalent) while the name of a private company must end in 'limited' or its abbreviation 'Ltd' (or Welsh equivalent).[46] In certain circumstances, a private company may be exempted from ending its name with the word 'limited'.[47]

Accounting and audit requirements

1-47 A public company cannot qualify for the accounting exemptions (discussed in Chapter 16) available to small or medium-sized companies[48] or the audit exemption available to small companies.[49] Public companies also have a shorter period (six months rather than nine months) within which to deliver their accounts to the registrar of companies (CA 2006, s 442(2)) and the penalties for late filing are more substantial for a public company.[50]

Officers and members

1-48 A public company must have at least two directors while a private company requires only one (CA 2006, s 154). A public company must have a company secretary (ss 270, 271).

Corporate formalities

1-49 A public company must hold an annual general meeting (CA 2006, s 336) and may not use written resolutions (s 281(2)). In recognition of the informal manner in which many private companies conduct their business, private companies are not required to hold annual general meetings and are expected to use written resolutions rather than hold meetings of any sort (s 281(1)).

---

[45] See the Companies (Authorised Minimum) Regulations 2009, SI 2009/2425, reg 2.
[46] CA 2006, ss 58, 59.   [47] See CA 2006, ss 60, 61.
[48] See CA 2006, ss 384(1)(a), 467(1)(a).   [49] See CA 2006, s 478(1)(a).
[50] CA 2006, s 453(2) and the Companies (Late Filing Penalties) and Limited Liability Partnerships (Filing Periods and Late Filing Penalties) Regulations 2008, SI 2008/497, reg 2.

Publicly traded companies

1-50 Public companies can be further classified depending on whether their securities (shares for our purposes) are traded on a regulated market. A listed public company is one whose securities are included in the Official List maintained by the UK Listing Authority (UKLA)—the Financial Services Authority (FSA) when acting as the competent authority for listing is referred to as the UKLA.[51] To be accepted for listing, the securities must be admitted to trading on a recognised investment exchange market for listed securities[52] and the relevant market for this purpose is the London Stock Exchange.[53] There are 7,600 public companies on the register of companies, as noted earlier, but only 1,070 UK listed companies (as at December 2011) on the London Stock Exchange.[54] In essence, a small subset of public companies seek a listing and access to a regulated market in order to maximise the ability to offer their shares to the public. In addition to complying with the companies legislation, listed companies must comply with the Listing Rules drawn up by the FSA which cover a wide range of matters including the need for shareholder approval for major transactions, continuing disclosure obligations and provisions regulating directors and their conduct. In the event of a contravention of the Listing Rules, the FSA can impose penalties on the company and on individual directors and may issue statements of censure.[55] While the Listing Rules and the UK Listing Authority use the terminology of 'listing' and 'listed', the relevant EU Directives which apply to these types of companies commonly now define the category in terms of 'companies admitted to trading on a regulated market' hence they are often referred to as traded companies or publicly traded companies, see further at **19-99**.

1-51 Another category of public company is 'a quoted company' and this is a term used in a specific way in the CA 2006 in the context of certain disclosure requirements,[56] for example with regard to website publication of poll results (CA 2006, s 341); the directors' remuneration report (s 420); website publication of accounts (s 430); and the right of members to require publication of audit concerns on the website (s 527). This category is broader than that of listed company and is defined in s 385 as encompassing a company (incorporated in the UK) whose equity share capital is officially listed in the UK or in an EEA State or is admitted to dealing either on the NYSE or Nasdaq (i.e. the main American stock exchanges).

E Re-registration of companies

1-52 It is possible for a company to alter its status by re-registration in accordance with CA 2006, Pt 7. The most common alterations of status are when a private company decides to

---

[51] See Financial Services and Markets Act 2000, s 74. From 2013 the listing functions of the FSA will transfer to the Financial Conduct Authority: see HM Treasury, *A New Approach to Financial Regulation: the blueprint for reform* (2011), Cm 8083, para 2.122.

[52] LR 2.2.3R.

[53] Another RIE to note is Plus Markets plc: the full list is available on the FSA website.

[54] See the Main Market Factsheets published monthly by the London Stock Exchange.

[55] See FSMA 2000, s 91.

[56] The media tend to use the terms 'quoted', 'listed' and 'traded' indiscriminately whereas they have distinct legal meanings.

re-register as a public company[57] and when a public company decides to re-register as a private company.[58]

1-53 As noted at **1-39**, a private company re-registering as a public company is the most common way in which public companies are formed. A detailed re-registration procedure is laid down in the statute, but in essence the company must secure the consent of its shareholders,[59] alter its name and its articles to reflect its new status, and comply with the share capital requirements for public companies.[60] Assuming that the documentation is correct, the registrar of companies then issues a certificate of incorporation altered to meet the circumstances of the case, i.e. to show that the company is now a public company—the entity continues, but its status is changed (CA 2006, s 96). There are a number of reasons why a company might seek a change of status. The change may be driven by economic growth which the directors and shareholders feel should be reflected in the more closely regulated legal structure of a public company. It may be that the company needs to raise share capital and wants to offer its shares to the public and the original owners may wish to realise some of the value of their holding in the company by selling out to the public. It may be that the owners have no interest in raising capital, but wish simply to secure the more prestigious status of being a public company.

1-54 Just as companies may decide to move 'up' to the status of a public company, others may wish to 'retreat' from being a public company to being a private company. This change may be because the need for capital (and therefore the facility of offering their shares to the public) is no longer a priority for the company. In that situation, the company is incurring the burden of the additional regulation which is imposed as a consequence of public company status for no purpose and it makes sense to re-register. In many cases, this move backwards is achieved by the original founders of the company buying back the shares of the company in the hands of the public and returning the company to its former private status and ownership. Unless there are tangible benefits from being a public company, many directors and shareholders prefer the lighter regulation of private companies. There is also much less media attention on private companies. The detailed procedure is laid down in CA 2006, ss 97–101, but in essence the company must secure the consent of its shareholders[61] and alter its name and articles of association to reflect its new status. Assuming that the documentation is correct, the registrar of companies then issues a certificate of incorporation altered to meet the circumstances of the case, i.e. to reflect the fact that the company is now a private company (s 101).

F Groups of companies

1-55 Of course, businesses are not confined to operating through one company and it is common for larger enterprises to organise their affairs through a group of companies made up of a holding company and subsidiaries and myriad combinations thereof.

---

[57] See CA 2006, ss 90–96.

[58] See CA 2006, ss 97–101. It is also possible for a private company to re-register as unlimited (ss 102–104) and for a public company to re-register as an unlimited company (ss 109–110), but for obvious reasons of liability, those options are rarely exercised.

[59] See CA 2006, s 90(1)(a), a special resolution is required (a 75% majority, see s 283).

[60] See CA 2006, s 90(2), (3).

[61] See CA 2006, s 97(1)(a): a special resolution is required (a 75% majority, see s 283).

1-56 The CA 2006, s 1159(1) defines a company as a 'subsidiary' of another company, its 'holding company', if that other company:

  (a) holds a majority of the voting rights in it, or

  (b) is a member of it and has the right to appoint or remove a majority of its board of directors, or

  (c) is a member of it and controls alone, pursuant to an agreement with other shareholders or members, a majority of the voting rights in it, or if it is a subsidiary of a company which is itself a subsidiary of that other company.[62]

1-57 This provision identifies three mechanisms by which a company may be a subsidiary of another company so where Company A meets these criteria with respect to its control of Company B, Company B is a subsidiary of Company A. Equally, if Company B meets these criteria in respect of Company C, Company C is a subsidiary of Company B and of Company A. The effect of the definition is that, on this example, Company A is a holding company and its subsidiaries are B and C while B is also a holding company with a subsidiary, C. Each company is a separate legal entity and is formed under the CA 2006 in accordance with the formalities discussed earlier in this chapter with the only difference being the presence of corporate shareholders rather than individuals.

1-58 The requirement in CA 2006, s 1159(1)(a) is that the holding company holds a majority of the voting rights in the subsidiary company for, as noted earlier, it is voting power which gives control of a company. Equally, the person who controls the board in practice has control of the company so s 1159(1)(b) recognises that situation. Section 1159(1)(c) expands the definition further to ensure that the situation where a member does not have control of a company on paper but does have control as the result of some agreement with other shareholders or members is also encompassed by the definition. The application of the equivalent CA 1985 provision (CA 1985, s 736) was considered by the Supreme Court in *Enviroco Ltd v Farstad Supply A/S*[63] which highlights that CA 1985, s 736(1)(c), now CA 2006, s 1159(1)(c), requires that a company be a member of the subsidiary company and have control in the way outlined in the provision. In this instance, the company in question had charged its shares in the other (would-be subsidiary) company as security to a bank and, in accordance with Scots law, the company had had to register those shares in the name of the bank with the result that it was no longer a member of the other company (membership is dictated by the entries on the register of members, see **14-1**). In those circumstances, the Supreme Court ruled, as it was no longer a member of the other company, the company could not claim that the other company was its subsidiary on the basis of the application of what is now CA 2006, s 1159(1)(c).[64] A company is a 'wholly-owned subsidiary' (see s 1159(2)) where Company A is the only shareholder in Company B—B is a wholly-owned subsidiary. This is an advantageous structure for Company A for it avoids any difficulties arising from any minority interests within Company B which might otherwise affect the way in which Company A may run Company B.

---

[62] The meaning of each of the categories is expanded upon in CA 2006, Sch 6.

[63] [2011] 2 BCLC 165. The case concerned certain obligations and exemptions under a charterparty and the charterparty expressly defined the term 'subsidiary' for the purpose of the charterparty as having the meaning assigned to it by the statute (then CA 1985, s 736, now CA 2006, s 1159).

[64] The company could not rely on what is now CA 2006, s 1159(1) or (2) because it did not have control in those ways.

1-59 There are many good business reasons (and often tax reasons) why a company chooses to expand and/or divide its activities through subsidiary companies. It may be administratively convenient and economically efficient to divide activities between subsidiaries. It may make geographic sense depending on the nature of the company's business. It may be financially appropriate allowing assets and liabilities to be allocated efficiently and it may facilitate external borrowings. The business and practical reasons for proceeding through a variety of subsidiary companies within a group structure in this way are clear but the relationship between the individual companies within the group can give rise to some interesting legal issues. These are considered in Chapter 3.

G The registrar of companies and the public registry

1-60 Disclosure has always been seen as the price to be paid by incorporators in return for the conferring of limited liability which, as noted at **1-9**, insulates the shareholders' personal fortunes from the reach of the company's creditors, unless the shareholders have been persuaded to give personal guarantees. To redress the balance, Parliament has required the disclosure of information by companies in a variety of ways, of which the most important is to the registrar of companies based at Companies House in Cardiff. In addition, disclosure is required at the company's registered office and, for public companies, at annual general meetings. Traded companies are obliged by listing and stock exchange rules to keep the markets informed. Increasingly, companies make extensive use of their websites to maintain ongoing disclosure with their shareholders and, in the case of quoted companies, they are obliged to use their websites for this purpose, as noted at **1-51**. The information disclosed typically relates to the financial position of the company (for example, its annual accounts) as well as information about those persons involved with it as directors and shareholders (for example, the composition of the board and details of shareholdings). The merits of disclosure can be debated in terms of economic value but the justifications for imposing wide-ranging disclosure requirements centre particularly on the provision of information: to assist creditors in assessing the risks of dealing with a limited company; to assist shareholders to monitor the quality and conduct of the company's management and the economic performance of the company; and generally for the efficient operation of the capital markets. Disclosure is discussed in Chapter 16.

2

The framework of company law

A The statutory framework

Background

2-1 The subject of this work is the law governing registered companies, that is companies registered under the Companies Act 2006 (CA 2006) and its predecessors.

2-2 Incorporation by registration was first made possible by the Joint Stock Companies Act 1844. At that time, limited liability was unknown and it was not introduced until the Limited Liability Act 1855. The pattern of company law, thereafter, was of major consolidating legislation at regular intervals, such as the Companies Act 1908, the Companies Act 1929, the Companies Act 1948. Prior to the CA 2006, the most recent consolidation was the Companies Act 1985, subsequently amended, in particular, by the Companies Act 1989 and by the Companies (Audit, Investigations and Community Enterprise) Act 2004. More discrete material was to be found in the Company Directors Disqualification Act 1986 and the Business Names Act 1985.

2-3 Insolvency matters were hived off initially to the Insolvency Act 1985, a major piece of reforming legislation introduced in response to the Cork Committee Report on Insolvency Law and Practice (1982).[1] The Insolvency Act 1985 was then consolidated with elements of the Companies Act 1985 in the Insolvency Act 1986. Limited technical amendments to insolvency law followed in the Insolvency Act 1994 and the Insolvency (No 2) Act 1994. More significant reforms were effected by the Insolvency Act 2000 and the Enterprise Act 2002. Meanwhile, the increasing importance of cross-border insolvency issues was recognised by the EC Regulation on Insolvency Proceedings No 1346/2000[2] and the Cross-Border Insolvency Regulations 2006.[3]

2-4 In addition to these company and insolvency statutes which are of central importance to this book, there are other substantial statutes which intrude from time to time on company law matters, such as the Financial Services and Markets Act 2000, though securities regulation is very much a specialist area in its own right.

2-5 The three legislative pillars until recently then were the Companies Act 1985, the Insolvency Act 1986 and the Financial Services and Markets Act 2000. The IA 1986 and FSMA 2000 were the product of major reviews in those subject areas which left the CA 1985 as most in need of reform, especially as it was subject to much piecemeal amendment over the years. In March 1998, the Department of Trade and Industry (DTI), now

---

[1] *Report of the Review Committee on Insolvency Law and Practice*, Cmnd 8558 (1982).
[2] OJ L 160, 30.6.2000, p 1.   [3] SI 2006/1030.

the Department for Business, Innovation and Skills (BIS), decided that the time was right for a comprehensive three-year review of company law.[4]

The Company Law Review

2-6 Launching the initial consultation document,[5] the DTI acknowledged the numerous problems with the CA 1985. The legislation was drafted in excessive detail, it used over-formal language, it over-regulated some issues (such as capital maintenance) while other matters were inadequately provided for or needed legal underpinning (such as the duties of directors and the conduct of meetings).[6] The Government's intention was stated as being that new arrangements should be devised to provide a more effective, including cost-effective, framework based on principles of consistency, predictability and transparency.[7] The task of reviewing the existing arrangements and suggesting the way forward fell to the Company Law Review made up of a Steering Group, comprised essentially of businessmen and lawyers, and numerous working groups from which emerged a stream of consultation documents.[8] The Company Law Review (hereinafter CLR) produced its Final Report in 2001 which concentrated on the following issues:[9]

- For small and private companies,[10] the recommendations centred on simplified decision-making and streamlining internal administration. There should be no need for such companies to hold general meetings or to appoint a company secretary. They should have a simplified constitution; shareholders should be encouraged to use mediation and arbitration to resolve their disputes instead of litigation; the rules on share capital should be relaxed and the financial reporting and audit requirements of these companies should be reduced.[11]

- On directors, the key recommendation was for the inclusion in the statute of a statement of directors' duties.[12]

- On shareholders' rights and remedies, there were recommendations for the creation of a statutory derivative action and measures to enhance the exercise of shareholders' rights at meetings.[13]

---

[4] See DTI, *Modern Company Law for a Competitive Economy* (1998). For a comprehensive account of the Review process, see Rickford, 'A History of the Company Law Review' in De Lacy (ed), *The Reform of United Kingdom Company Law* (2002).　　　[5] DTI, *Modern Company Law for a Competitive Economy* (1998).

[6] See DTI, *Modern Company Law for a Competitive Economy* (1998), paras 3.2, 3.4, 3.7.

[7] See DTI, *Modern Company Law for a Competitive Economy* (1998), para 3.1.

[8] The most important documents, all of which go under the title *Modern Company Law for a Competitive Economy*, were *The Strategic Framework* (February 1999), URN 99/654; *Developing the Framework* (March 2000), URN 00/656; *Completing the Structure* (November 2000), URN 00/1335. Some topics were the subject of specific consultations, see *Company General Meetings and Shareholder Communication* (October 1999); *Company Formation and Capital Maintenance* (October 1999); *Reforming the Law Concerning Oversea Companies* (October 1999); *Capital Maintenance: Other Issues* (June 2000); *Registration of Company Charges* (October 2000).

[9] See CLR, *Modern Company Law for a Competitive Economy, Final Report*, vols I and II (2001), URN 01/942.

[10] Research carried out for the CLR showed that 70% of companies had only one or two shareholders and 90% had fewer than five shareholders: CLR, *Developing the Framework* (2000), URN 00/656, para 6.9.

[11] See CLR, *Modern Company Law for a Competitive Economy, Final Report*, vol I (2001), URN 01/942, Chs 2 and 4; *Completing the Structure* (2000), URN 00/1335, Ch 2; *Developing the Framework* (2000), URN 00/656, Chs 6 and 7.

[12] CLR, *Modern Company Law for a Competitive Economy, Final Report*, vol I (2001), Ch 3; *Completing the Structure* (2000), Ch 3; *Developing the Framework* (2000), paras 3.12–3.85.

[13] *Developing the Framework* (2000), Ch 4.

- On accounting and audit requirements, a significant recommendation was for larger companies to publish an operating and financial report. No changes were proposed to auditors' duties of care.[14]

2-7   The CLR considered briefly whether it would be preferable to opt for a separate free-standing limited liability vehicle for small companies with separate legislation, but it rapidly concluded that the main obstacles to that approach would be definition problems and transition difficulties as companies grow.[15] An integrated Companies Act, but one focused on small rather than larger companies, was its preferred approach.[16] On reflection, it also considered that the focus of the legislation should be on private companies, as it is the private/public distinction which is crucial,[17] as noted at **1-39**, and it was appropriate to deregulate private companies across the board rather than attempting to define some new category of small company.[18] In other words, the CLR thought that the legislation should reflect reality which is that the register of companies is made up predominantly of small private companies, though the CA 1985 envisaged a register dominated by large public companies. This 'think small first' approach has now become something of a tenet of regulation, both domestically and at the European level.

2-8   The Government responded to the CLR Report with a White Paper entitled *Modernising Company Law*[19] published in July 2002 which broadly adopted the Review's recommendations. Further progress was deferred, however, while the Government addressed what was perceived to be a more urgent matter, namely the strengthening of audit regulation in the wake of the collapse of the American energy group, Enron, with billion dollar losses. The resulting legislation, the Companies (Audit, Investigations and Community Enterprise) Act 2004, concentrated therefore on audit matters. The main reform agenda was revived by a further White Paper, *Company Law Reform*[20] in March 2005 before, at last, a Company Law Reform Bill was introduced in November 2005.

2-9   At that stage the intention was to retain substantial elements of the Companies Act 1985 alongside the CLR Bill, but eventually the Government was persuaded that the most sensible way forward was to bring those parts of the CA 1985 which were not being repealed up into the CLR Bill. As there was no time for further review, those provisions of the CA 1985 which were brought up into the Bill were merely restated so as to ensure that their drafting was consistent with the plain English used in the Bill, but no substantive changes were made to the CA 1985 provisions. The result is the CA 2006, which is a mixture of new and old, though the old has been restated in plain English so that, at least, it looks new![21] As a result of the addition of the CA 1985 provisions to the Bill, its title was changed to the Companies Bill and it received Royal Assent on 8 November 2006 as the Companies Act 2006, some eight and a half years after the launch of the Company Law Review.

---

[14] CLR, *Modern Company Law for a Competitive Economy, Final Report*, vol I (2001), Ch 8.

[15] See CLR, *Developing the Framework* (2000), URN 00/656, para 6.19; *The Strategic Framework* (1999), URN 99/654, para 5.2.   [16] See CLR, *The Strategic Framework* (1999), URN 99/654, para 5.2.

[17] See CLR, *Final Report*, vol I (2001), URN 01/942, para 2.7.

[18] See CLR, *Completing the Structure* (2000), URN 00/1335, Ch 2; *Developing the Framework* (2000), URN 00/656, Chs 6 and 7.

[19] CM 5553-I, 5553-II (2002). See Goddard, 'Modernising Company Law: The Government's White Paper,' (2003) 66 MLR 402.   [20] Cm 6456 (2005).

[21] There is always the risk when restating a provision that the result is a change in the law which may create an interpretation conundrum for the courts when faced with wording which alters the meaning of a provision but a declared legislative intent merely to restate. For example, CA 2006, s 40(1) restates CA 1985, s 35A(1), but the wording is altered and the consequence is that the law has been altered, see discussion at **8-38** et seq.

The Companies Act 2006

2-10 At the time of its enactment, the Companies Act 2006 was the largest statute ever passed by Parliament. It has 1,300 sections and 16 Schedules. The transition from the CA 1985 to the CA 2006 was slow and laborious with commencement of the legislation taking place piecemeal between 6 April 2007 and 1 October 2009. It is now fully in force (with a few very minor exceptions).[22]

2-11 Despite its length, many Parts of the Act rely on secondary legislation to supplement the statutory framework. This scheme is part of a deliberate strategy to create some flexibility to accommodate future developments since it is unlikely that Parliamentary time for further primary legislation will be available in the foreseeable future. In any event, after taking more than a decade to progress from the launch of the Company Law Review to the final commencement of the CA 2006, it is fair to say that there is no appetite for further significant change.

B The European framework

Overview of the European agenda and approach

2-12 As the limited liability company is the main vehicle for private industry across Europe, it was understood from the earliest days of the European Community that at least some measure of harmonisation of national laws would be required to ensure a common or single market, given that the legal structures of companies vary significantly across the Member States. The Treaty establishing the European Community recognised this need and imposes on the European Commission and Council an obligation to:[23]

> '…co-ordinate to the necessary extent the safeguards which, for the protection of the interests of members and others, are required by Member States of companies or firms…with a view to making such safeguards equivalent throughout the Community.'

Harmonisation

2-13 The European Commission (hereafter the Commission) proceeded initially by way of a Company Law harmonisation programme which resulted in the adoption of a series of numbered directives[24] (The First Company Law Directive, The Second Company Law Directive and so on). Some of the Directives concern relatively discrete (and technical) matters, such as the Eleventh Directive on disclosures by branches of overseas companies.[25] Others are of broader significance, such as the Second Company Law Directive

---

[22] A subsequent evaluation of the Act for the Department for Business, Innovation and Skills found relatively high levels of awareness of the legislation with small private businesses welcoming the flexibility provided for them by measures such as the removal of the requirement for private companies to hold AGMs and the greater use of written resolutions: see ORC International, *Evaluation of the Companies Act 2006* (August 2010); see also BIS Memorandum to the Business, Innovation & Skills Select Committee, *Post-Legislative Assessment of the Companies Act 2006*, January 2012, Cm 8255.

[23] Treaty Establishing the European Community (Consolidated version) OJ C 325, 24.12.2002, p 33, art 44(2)(g), now Treaty on the Functioning of the European Union (Consolidated version) OJ C 83, 30.3.2010, p 47, art 50(2)(g).

[24] Some of the proposed Directives have fallen by the wayside (for example, nos 5 and 9 and, it seems, no 14) leaving Company Law Directives numbered 1–4, 6–8, 10–13.

[25] Eleventh Council Directive (EEC) 89/666, OJ L 395, 30.12.1989, p 36.

which lays down many of the share capital rules for public limited companies.[26] The Fourth and Seventh Directives—the Accounting Directives—prescribe the content and format of company accounts and have formed the framework for accounting disclosure for the past 30 years.[27]

2-14   This harmonisation stage lasted roughly from 1968 to 1989 but it then more or less stalled, in part because other areas, such as financial services, took centre stage, in part because it was difficult to garner support for this type of highly technical harmonisation. The result was that from the mid-1990s until early 2000 there was little activity on the company law front.[28]

Modernisation

2-15   In September 2001 company law issues moved up the Commission's agenda again and a High Level Group of Company Law Experts (HLG) was formed to review the need for the modernisation of company law in Europe. The impetus for this change in attitude came in part from the need to implement the Financial Services Action Plan which aimed to ensure an integrated capital market by 2005. There were concerns that corporate scandals and collapses (including Enron in the US, but also the collapse of the Italian company, Parmalat) had damaged investor confidence which is central to the successful and efficient operation of capital markets. The collapse of Enron with billion dollar losses brought a speedy (and severe) legislative response by the American authorities, notably through the Sarbanes-Oxley Act.[29] The European authorities were anxious to show an equally positive and identifiable European response which, with an emphasis on transparency and accountability, would ensure high standards of corporate governance and restore investor confidence. Added urgency was given to the situation by the imminent accession (in May 2004) of new Member States, many of them Eastern European countries with a limited history of open corporate markets, given the post-war Soviet occupation of their countries. A further impetus for change was the general globalisation of trade and increase in cross-border economic activity and a concern that the EU had to be proactive in facilitating that trade. The HLG published a consultation document and a report in 2002[30] and the Commission responded in May 2003 with an Action Plan for Company Law which identified a number of priorities for reform.[31] The guiding criteria in drawing up the Action Plan were the need to respect subsidiarity and proportionality; the requirement for flexible application based on firm principles; and the need to shape international regulatory developments.[32]

---

[26] Second Council Directive (EEC) 77/91, OJ L 26, 31.1.1977, p 1.

[27] Fourth Council Directive (EEC) 78/660, OJ L 222, 14.8.1978, p 11; Seventh Council Directive (EEC) 83/349, OJ L 193, 18.7.1983, p 1.

[28] See generally Wouters, 'European Company Law: Quo Vadis?' (2000) 37 CMLR 257.

[29] For an interesting overview of the Sarbanes-Oxley Act 2002, see Canada, Kuhn, and Sutton, 'Accidentally in the public interest: The perfect storm that yielded the Sarbanes-Oxley Act' (2008) Critical Perspectives in Accounting 987.

[30] See Report of the High Level Group of Company Law Experts, *A Modern Regulatory Framework for Company Law in Europe* (November 2002) which was preceded by a consultation paper of the same name in April 2002.

[31] See European Commission Communication, Modernising Company Law and Enhancing Corporate Governance in the European Union—A Plan to Move Forward, COM (2003) 284, 21.5.2003. For an overview, see Baums, 'European Company Law after the 2003 Action Plan' (2007) 8 EBOR 143.

[32] See Commission Action Plan, COM (2003) 284, pp 4–5.

2-16 The short-term priorities of the Action Plan focused on securing a Shareholder Rights Directive,[33] a Recommendation on directors' remuneration and on the role of non-executive directors, the creation of a European Corporate Governance Forum and amendments to the Accounting Directives to ensure greater transparency and accountability. This phase ran (roughly) from 2001 to 2006 and was driven by a need to modernise company law across the Member States. There was less of an emphasis on harmonisation and a greater emphasis on framework Directives so leaving Member States, more leeway in addressing their particular circumstances. Such Directives may be easier to negotiate, an important consideration now that there are 27 Member States, but may encourage divergence between Member States rather than harmonisation. The Commission also made greater use of Recommendations and Communications which are not legally binding (so-called 'soft-law') with committees of experts, such as the European Corporate Governance Forum, being used by the Commission to encourage co-ordination and convergence on corporate governance measures. The advantage in proceeding in this way is that measures can be agreed swiftly by the Commission and, by identifying and setting standards of best practice, market forces can compel Member States, practices to converge, in effect, on such standards. This sudden spurt of activity from 2001 to 2005 came to a somewhat abrupt end in 2006 when, at the broader political level, it became apparent that there was some resistance to further EU integration generally (as seen in the resistance to the adoption of a European Constitution). There was more than an element of regulatory fatigue for all concerned and a backlash against what was seen as burdensome EU-derived regulation (a flame fuelled by opportunist Eurosceptics who chose to ignore the extent to which domestic Governments generated bureaucratic regulation and gold-plated European requirements).

Simplification

2-17 Though good progress was made on the short-term priorities identified in the 2003 Action Plan, the Commission decided in December 2005 to hold a further consultation to determine whether to proceed with the remaining elements of the Plan.[34] The outcome was a shift in focus from generating initiatives (other than those seen as 'enabling' measures such as the European Private Company Statute, see **2-50**) to simplification measures, a greater focus on cross-border matters and on a reduction of regulatory burdens.[35] Against this backdrop, the Commission found support for possible simplification across the whole range of Company Law Directives,[36] the goal being to create a 'simplified business

---

[33] Directive 2007/36/EC, OJ L 184, 14.7.2007, p 17.

[34] See European Commission, *Consultation on Future Priorities for the Action Plan on Modernising Company Law and enhancing Corporate Governance in the European Union* (December 2005).

[35] This move was in keeping with a broader exercise which the Commission had commenced in 2005 which had identified Company Law as one of the priority areas for simplification. See Commission Communication, *Implementing the Community Lisbon Programme: A strategy for the simplification of the regulatory environment*, COM (2005) 535, OJ C 309, 16.12.2006, pp 18–21; also Commission Communication, *Better Regulation for Growth and Jobs in the European Union*, COM (2005) 97, 16.3.2005. This strategy now is developed under the banner of 'smart regulation'.

[36] See Commission, *Communication on a simplified business environment for companies in the areas of company law, accounting and auditing*, COM (2007) 394, 10.7.2007. There was general support for simplification of the Directives rather than outright repeal which it was thought would only generate further costs and uncertainties. See Press Release 'Commission cuts unnecessary administrative burdens in EU company law', IP/08/598, 17.04.2008, announcing fast-track amendments to the First and Eleventh Directives and the Accounting Directives; followed by the announcement of fast-track amendments to the Third and Sixth Directives, see Press Release 'Commission proposes further simplification of EU rules on mergers and divisions,' IP/08/1407, 25.09.2008.

environment' starting from a 'think small first' position which recognises the central role that SMEs (small and medium-sized enterprises) play in the EU economy.[37] That goal now provides the framework for many of the EU initiatives on company law and is reflected in the Small Business Act (SBA) adopted by the Commission in 2008[38] and in the Single Market Act adopted in 2011. A review of the application of the SBA in 2011 found progress had been made, for example, on reducing the time and costs involved in forming a private limited company,[39] but continued efforts are needed to reduce disproportionate burdens on SMEs, for example, through simplifying the Accounting Directives.[40] Hence one of the 12 projects set out in the Single Market Act (which identifies projects central to an intended relaunch of the Single Market in 2012) is to simplify the regulatory environment for business and to reduce administrative burdens, especially for SMEs,[41] and, for example, from 2012 all legislative proposals will be based on the premise that micro-entities should be excluded unless a case can be made for their proportionate inclusion.[42]

2-18   As by their very nature, European measures are integral to and form part of substantive domestic law, the content of a particular measure is discussed in the chapter dealing with the substantive law on that issue, hence the capital requirements for public companies are discussed in Chapter 19; the substantive accounting and audit requirements are discussed in Chapter 16; and so on. The rest of this chapter focuses on an overview of the measures taken or planned in order to give the reader a sense of the extent of EU involvement in the development of company law. Three major (overlapping) themes emerge:

(1) an emphasis on disclosure and transparency—these are the standard regulatory tools of any jurisdiction dealing with limited entities—the aim is primarily but not exclusively creditor protection;

(2) a focus on corporate governance in publicly traded companies aimed primarily at shareholder protection and investor confidence; and

(3) a focus on structures/restructuring and corporate mobility which is consistent with the underlying rationale of the development of an integrated internal market across the European Union.

---

[37] Commission research shows that there are around 21m SMEs in the EU representing 99.8% of all enterprises and accounting for 67% of total employment: see Commission, *SME Performance Review, Annual report on EU Small and Medium-sized Enterprises, 2010/2011* (2011), Table 2.1. The position is the same in the UK where SMEs account for 99.6% of all enterprises and 98% of all enterprises employ fewer than 50 people with 88% employing fewer than 10 people: see ONS Statistics, *UK Business Activity: Activity, Size and Location 2011* (summary statement 5 October 2011).

[38] The SBA is not a piece of legislation, but a package of 10 principles intended to guide the Commission and Member States in dealing with SMEs. The 10 guiding principles relate to matters such as granting a second chance for business failures, facilitating access to finance and enabling SMEs to turn environmental challenges into opportunities. Member States are urged to ensure that the time needed to start a new company should be no more than one week, the maximum time to obtain business licences and permits should not surpass one month and that one-stop-shops should be available to assist start-ups. See '"Think Small First", A "Small Business Act" for Europe', COM (2008) 394 final, 25.6.2008.

[39] See Commission, *Review of the Small Business Act for Europe,* COM (2011) 78 final, 23.2.2011, para 2.2—the time and costs have reduced from 12 days and €485 in 2007 to seven days and €399 in 2010.

[40] See *Review of the Small Business Act for Europe,* COM (2011) 78 final, 23.2.2011, para 3.1.

[41] See Commission Communication, COM (2011) 206 final, 13.04.2011; also European Commission Press Release, IP/11/69, 13 April 2011.

[42] See European Commission, *Minimizing regulatory burden for SMEs, Adapting EU regulation to the needs of micro-enterprises,* COM (2011) 803 final, 23.11.2011, para 4, also **2-21**.

Disclosure/creditor protection

2-19 Transparency and disclosure are key themes in the domestic Member State regulation of limited liability companies and it is not surprising therefore that many of the European company law measures have focused on these issues.[43] Indeed, transparency was one of the themes of the First Company Law Directive[44] which, amongst other things, requires companies to publish certain documents (for example, the constitution and accounts) and particulars (for example, of directors) on a public register. That information must be accessible to the public and copies must be available at a price not exceeding the administrative cost of providing the information—the public register meeting these requirements is maintained here by Companies House, as discussed at **1-60**. The Eleventh Company Law Directive[45] augments these requirements by imposing disclosure requirements in respect of branches opened in a Member State by companies from another Member State. The intention is to ensure that companies cannot avoid disclosure requirements in another Member State by opening branches rather than subsidiary companies. A further Directive on the inter-connection of company registers is expected to be approved in 2012 which will improve cross-border electronic access to business information. The Commission believes this measure will be helpful to companies when setting up branches, conducting cross-border trade or providing cross-border services and also to customers dealing with such companies.[46]

2-20 Of course, the most important disclosure required of limited entities is disclosure of their financial position as evidenced by their accounts and it is with respect to accounting disclosures that the EU influence has been greatest. The accounting disclosure requirements are dominated by the Fourth and Seventh Company Law Directives. The Fourth Directive deals with the presentation and content of a company's individual accounts[47] and the Seventh Directive deals with the presentation and content of consolidated or group accounts,[48] together they are known as the Accounting Directives. The Accounting Directives have been amended on numerous occasions, especially to allow for derogations in favour of SMEs.[49] Another significant accounting step was the adoption in June 2002 of a Regulation on the application of International Accounting Standards (IAS)[50] which, from 1 January 2005, required listed companies to draw up their consolidated accounts in accordance with IAS (now IFRS—International Financial Reporting Standards) rather

---

[43] Other Directives such as the Prospectus Directive also provide for extensive financial disclosures for current and prospective shareholders, creditors and the wider securities markets: see Directive 2003/71/EC on the prospectus to be published when securities are offered to the public or admitted to trading, OJ L 345, 31.12.2003, pp 64–89, as amended by Directive 2010/73, OJ L 327, 11.12.2010, p 1.

[44] First Council Directive 68/151/EEC, OJ L 65, 14.3.1968, p 8, now codified as Directive 2009/101, OJL 258, 1.10.2009, p 11. See Edwards, *EC Company Law* (1999), Ch II.

[45] Eleventh Council Directive (EEC) 89/666, OJ L 395, 30.12.1989, p 36. See Edwards, *EC Company Law* (1999), Ch VIII.

[46] See Proposal for a Directive as regards the interconnection of central, commercial and companies registers, COM (2011) 79 final, 24.2.2011.

[47] Fourth Council Directive (EEC) 78/660, OJ L 222, 14.8.1978, p 11.

[48] Seventh Council Directive (EEC) 83/349, OJ L 193, 18.7.1983, p 1.

[49] They have also been amended, for example, to extend their application to cover general and limited partnerships where the responsible partners are themselves companies or limited companies, see Directive 90/605, OJ L 317, 16.11.1990, p 60; to allow for fair value accounting for financial instruments, see Directive 2001/65, OJ L 283, 27.10.2001, p 28; and to allow for modernisation of their requirements, see Directive 2003/51/EC, OJ L 178, 17.7.2003, p 16.

[50] Regulation (EC) No 1606/2002 of 19 July 2002 on the application of international accounting standards, OJ L 243, 11.09.2002, p 1; and see the European Commission Press Release, IP/02/827, 7 June 2002.

than standards derived from accounting practice in individual Member States.[51] This Regulation was a transformational measure which necessitated a general overhaul of the accounting framework in the EU for companies falling within the scope of the Regulation. All of these measures together (the amended Accounting Directives and the Regulation on IAS) are designed to ensure the highest standards of transparency (compatible with the economic size of the company) and comparability for accounts of companies formed in the Member States.

2-21 The next development, following a review by the Commission of the Accounting Directives, is a proposal from the Commission for their repeal and replacement with a single Directive which will introduce a modified specific regime for small companies while, for medium and large companies, the intention primarily is to reduce the number of accounting options available so as to improve the comparability of their accounts.[52] With respect to small companies, the aim is to reduce overall the regulatory burden,[53] for example, by allowing them to prepare a simpler profit and loss account and balance sheet and by limiting disclosures in the notes to the accounts and by removing any EU requirement for an audit (UK small companies are already exempt from any audit requirement, see **16-86**). It is also intended to harmonise the thresholds which define small and medium-sized companies so as to ensure that all companies across the EU are able to take advantage of the EU exemptions for that class of company.[54] Agreement has also been reached on a Directive on micro-entities which allows for minimal accounting disclosures by these companies.[55] It is likely that these proposals will be integrated into the single Directive which will replace the Accounting Directives, probably in 2012.

2-22 Of course, disclosure of accounting information alone is insufficient without assurance as to the quality of that information which comes from the requirement that the accounts be audited. Audit issues are governed by the Eighth Company Law Directive,[56] adopted in 2006, which replaced an earlier version from 1984[57] which laid down minimum requirements and qualifications for auditors. The Eighth Directive makes comprehensive provision for all matters pertaining to the statutory auditor, his qualifications, role and independence, as well as providing for disciplinary processes, quality assurance and public oversight of the audit profession. In the light of the financial crisis, the Commission has reviewed the regulation of audits and it now proposes that there should be a Regulation which will address all aspects of audit of public interest entities (i.e. entities such as listed companies, banks, insurance companies) and that the Eighth Directive should be amended to consolidate within it all the provisions on audit for all other entities,[58] see **16-33**.

---

[51] International Accounting Standards were issued by the International Accounting Standards Committee which has since been replaced by the International Accounting Standards Board (IASB) which issues International Financial Reporting Standards (IFRS).

[52] Proposal for a Directive on the annual financial statements, consolidated financial statements and related reports of certain types of undertaking, see COM (2011) 684 final, 25.10.2011.

[53] Small groups are to be exempted from the requirement to prepare consolidated accounts, see COM (2011) 684 final, 25.10.2011, para 4.6.

[54] COM (2011) 684 final, 25.10.2011, paras 3.1, 4.1.

[55] See Commission Opinion and agreement on European Parliament's amendments to a Proposal for a Directive amending Council Directive 78/660/EEC on the annual accounts of certain types of companies as regards micro-entities, COM (2012) 1 final, 11.1.2012 (2009/0035 COD). A micro-entity is a company which does not exceed at least two of the following three criteria: total assets of up to €350,000; net turnover of up to €700,000; and a maximum of 10 employees.

[56] Directive 2006/43/EC on statutory audits of annual accounts and consolidated accounts, OJ L 157, 9.6.2006, p 87.   [57] Eighth Council Directive (EEC) 84/253, OJ L 126, 12.5.1984, p 20.

[58] See Proposal for a Directive amending Directive 2006/43/EC on statutory audits of annual accounts and consolidated accounts, COM (2011) 778 final, 30.11.2011.

2-23   The Accounting Directives and the Audit Directive have a major role to play in terms of creditor protection, of course, since they are intended to ensure the provision of comparable accounts backed up by high quality audits which give creditors the information they need to assess the risk of dealing with limited companies. The other traditional protective device is the use of capital maintenance rules to ensure that companies cannot return capital to their shareholders ahead of a winding up other than in accordance with statutory procedures designed to protect creditors. Capital maintenance revolves around two types of provisions, payment rules and return of capital rules and these are found in the Second Company Law Directive which provides for the formation of public limited companies and the maintenance and alteration of their share capital.[59] Adopted in 1976, the focus was on public companies because of their economic significance and the fact that their activities could be expected to extend beyond national boundaries. Given those features, the preamble to the Directive notes the importance of ensuring minimum equivalent protection throughout the EC for both creditors and shareholders of such companies.

2-24   The Second Directive is one of the most significant European company law measures for it prescribes in detail the capital rules applicable to public companies, especially with respect to capital maintenance and the rules governing distributions to members. The drawback with the Second Directive has always been the level of prescription imposed by it and there has been pressure in the past on the Commission for reform, if not outright repeal, of the Directive.[60] However, a feasibility study conducted on behalf of the Commission on an alternative regime to the capital maintenance regime,[61] published in January 2008, concluded that in fact the Second Directive is flexible in many ways and its requirements do not cause significant operational problems for companies.[62] Subsequently, limited changes have been made to the Directive as part of the simplification programme.[63] These capital matters are discussed in detail in Chapters 19 and 20.

Corporate governance

2-25   Corporate governance is a term much in use in the past decade and it can mean different things depending on the context but essentially the focus is on how boards of companies operate and the relationship between the directors and the shareholders. The European Commission has acted relatively cautiously on these matters taking something of a back-seat role to the Member States, but it has returned to these matters in the wake of the financial crisis, with a consultation paper in 2011 on the EU corporate governance framework.[64]

---

[59] Second Council Directive (EEC) 77/91, OJ L 26, 31.1.1977, p 1, as amended; see generally, Edwards, *EC Company Law* (1999), Ch III.

[60] See BERR, Note and Consultation on European Commission Consultation on Simplification of EU Company Law etc, August 2007.

[61] See KPMG, 'Feasibility study on an alternative to the capital maintenance regime established by the Second Company Law Directive 77/91/EEC of 13 December 1976 and an examination of the impact on profit distribution of the new EU accounting regime' (January 2008).

[62] The Commission concluded therefore that 'no follow-up measures or changes in the Second Company Law Directive are foreseeable in the immediate future', see Response of the Commission to the results of the external study on the feasibility of an alternative to the Capital Maintenance regime of the Second Company Law Directive and the impact of the adoption of IFRS on profit distribution.

[63] See Directive 2006/68/EC amending Directive 77/91/EEC, OJ L 264, 25.9.2006, p 32. See Government Response to consultation on implementation of amendments to the Second Company Law Directive (2007), URN 07/1300; also DTI, 'Implementation of the Companies Act 2006' (2007), URN 07/666, Ch 6.

[64] European Commission Green Paper, *The EU Corporate Governance Framework*, COM (2011) 164, 05.04.2011. This Green Paper followed an earlier focus on financial institutions, see European Commission,

The outcome of that consultation is awaited.[64a] But it is fair to say that, so far, the direction of travel on corporate governance matters has been mainly consistent with and in the wake of UK developments (see Chapter 5).

2-26 In 2002 the Commission initiated a review of corporate governance codes across the EU, but quickly concluded that there was no need for a European corporate governance code, given that the review found that practically every Member State had at least one code and all the codes had very similar characteristics.[65] The European Commission proceeded on corporate governance issues in the following years mainly by way of Recommendations, such as its 2005 Recommendation on the role of non-executive directors[66] and its 2009 Recommendation on the remuneration of directors of listed companies.[67] Corporate governance issues have featured in various Directives, such as requirement in the Eighth Company Law Directive for certain companies to have an audit committee. The most substantive corporate governance measure adopted was the Shareholder Rights Directive,[68] implemented here by way of amendments to CA 2003, Pt 16 on Meetings (meetings are discussed in Chapter 15). The Directive sets out detailed minimum requirements with respect to the notice to be given of general meetings, the information to be provided to shareholders, the right to ask questions and receive answers at meetings, the right to add items to the meeting agenda, voting procedures including electronic participation, proxy rights etc. In other words, the focus is on the process of shareholder engagement, especially in the cross-border context.

2-27 A more controversial governance initiative involved a wide-ranging debate on voting rights in publicly traded companies, especially on proportionality between capital and control, and the principle of one share, one vote. While one share, one vote is the standard structure in this jurisdiction, many other Member States are accustomed to more complex and opaque structures with voting control commonly retained by small numbers of shareholders, often reflecting long-standing family holdings. Basically, the argument is that if a company wants to accept shareholders' capital, it should be prepared to give them voting rights proportionate to the capital contributed and allow them a say in the conduct of the company's affairs through the mechanism of the general meeting. This ensures a powerful shareholder voice as a brake on the board of directors which might otherwise enjoy a cosy relationship with the key shareholders leading to a sharing between them of private benefits not available to the other shareholders. The countervailing argument runs along the lines that these are pure contractual matters and that shareholders purchasing shares in these companies contract on the basis that they will have limited voting rights and that limitation is (a) accepted by them voluntarily and (b) reflected in the price that they pay for their shares. It is also suggested that these structures are embedded in different corporate cultures which accept and respect long-standing family control and there

---

Corporate governance in financial institutions and remuneration policies, COM (2010) 284, 02.06.2010, and accompanying Commission Staff Working Document, SEC (2010) 669.

[64a] Subsequently the Commission launched a wide-ranging (online) consultation on the future of European company law in February 2012 and the intention is that possible follow-up initiatives in corporate governance and in company law will be announced jointly in late 2012: see Commission Press Release IP/12/149, 20.02.2012, 'European Company Law: what way forward?'

[65] See Commission *Communication on Modernising Company Law*, COM (2003) 284, 21.05.2003, para 3.1; Weil, Gotshal & Manges, *Comparative Study of Corporate Governance Codes Relevant to the European Union and its Member States* (January 2002).

[66] Commission Recommendation on the role of non-executive or supervisory directors of listed companies and on the committees of the (supervisory) board (2005/162/EC), OJ L 52, 25.02.2005, p 51.

[67] C(2009) 3177, 30.4.2009.

[68] Directive 2007/36/EC on the exercise of certain rights of shareholders in listed companies, OJ L 184, 14.7.2007, p 17.

is no demand for change. If there was a concern, the market would reflect that concern by marking down the share value of companies with restricted voting rights, but no such write-downs occur which suggests it is not a matter of concern to investors. The discussion of these matters came to a slightly abrupt end in October 2007 when Commissioner McCreevy announced that, following a review of a study on proportionality in the EU [69] and an impact assessment of the issue of proportionality, no further action would be taken on the matter. In part, the decision came about because the empirical evidence available to the Commission did not provide sufficient evidence of the existence and extent of private benefit extraction resulting from a lack of proportionality.[70] There was also significant political opposition to any change, especially from the Nordic countries where such concentrated shareholdings are commonplace. If there is to be movement on the matter, it will have to come from pressure by market participants on individual companies.[71]

Corporate restructuring/mobility

2-28 A variety of measures have been adopted to facilitate mergers and takeovers as companies seek to expand through acquisitions and also to provide a range of corporate structures so as to facilitate operations across the internal market.[72]

2-29 The most significant European contribution in terms of mergers and takeovers is the Thirteenth Company Law Directive, more commonly called The Takeover Directive, which applies to takeover bids for securities of a company governed by the law of a Member State where all or some of the securities are admitted to trading on a regulated market.[73] Seventeen years elapsed from the initial proposal to the Directive coming into force on 20 May 2006.[74] The Directive lays down a framework of principles which govern takeovers and requires offers to be made to all shareholders. There are detailed rules as to the conduct of the bid and the documentation which must be provided to shareholders, though the requirements are watered down by a variety of Member State opt outs. Nevertheless, given the history of the Directive, it was an achievement at least to have secured a framework for the conduct of takeovers throughout the EU. The Directive was implemented by CA 2006, Pt 28 and has had minimal impact here given that the position under the Directive to a large extent reflects the UK position on takeovers as set out in the Takeover Code. The Directive is considered in detail in Chapter 26.

---

[69] *Report on the Proportionality Principle in the European Union* carried out by ISS Europe, ECGI, Shearman & Sterling for the European Commission (May 2007).

[70] See Commission Impact Assessment on the Proportionality between Capital and Control in Listed Companies, SEC (2007) 1705, 12.12.2007.

[71] See the interesting paper by Khachaturyan, 'Trapped in Delusions: Democracy, Fairness and the One-Share-One-Vote Rule in the European Union' (2007) 8 EBOR 335 who argues that the case for ISIV being made mandatory has not been made out and that ISIV is not as valuable as is assumed and that it is neither a sufficient nor a necessary condition for shareholder democracy in general or shareholder empowerment in the EU in particular. See also OECD Report on the issue, 'Lack of Proportionality Between Ownership And Control: Overview And Issues For Discussion' issued by the OECD Steering Group On Corporate Governance, December 2007.

[72] We can note in passing the Twelfth Company Law Directive, Directive 89/667 EEC, OJ L 395, 30.12.1989, p 40, codified as Directive 2009/102, OJ L 258, 1.10.2009, p 20, which allows for the formation of private companies having one member. It is of little significance as this is now commonplace and the CA 2006 permits public and private companies to have a single member (CA 2006, s 7).

[73] Directive 2004/25/EC on takeover bids, OJ L 142, 30.4.2004, p 12.

[74] The first proposal for a Directive on Takeovers was put forward by the European Commission in 1989: see OJ C 64/8 14.3.1989. It was revised in 1990: see OJ C 240/7, 6.9.1990; in 1996: see COM (95) 655, 07.02.1996; in 1997, see OJ C 378, 13.12.97; followed by a new proposal in 2002, see OJ C 45 E, 25.02.2003, p 1.

2-30   The Third and Sixth Company Law Directives are concerned with mergers and divisions of public companies within a single Member State.[75] They are of limited significance in this jurisdiction since they apply to mergers by way of the transfer of assets and liabilities from one company to another whereas acquisitions by purchase of the shares in the entity rather than the underlying assets is the mechanism commonly used here, see Chapter 26. The package is completed by the Tenth Company Law Directive[76] which facilitates mergers of companies from different Member States and was implemented by the Cross-Border Mergers Regulations[77] though, for similar reasons, limited use is made by UK companies of these mechanisms. For many years, there have been discussions about a proposed Fourteenth Company Law Directive on the transfer of a company's registered office from one Member State to another, but given the developing European jurisprudence on the mobility of companies, discussed at **2-31**, the Commission has not taken forward this proposal, though it is possible that it will be revived in the future.

Freedom of establishment

2-31   As discussed, there has been a measure of Commission activity in the area of corporate restructuring etc, but the greatest impetus to corporate mobility has come, not from the Commission, but from the European Court of Justice. A practice had developed of businesses from other Member States incorporating in the UK, driven by the absence of minimum capital requirements for private companies and the speed, ease and low cost of incorporation (see discussion in Chapter 1). This practice was not welcomed by the 'home' Member States of those businesses which sought to challenge or hinder such business from operating in the original home Member State. This raised issues as to freedom of establishment under arts 43 and 48 of the EC Treaty[78] which were addressed by the European Court of Justice in a series of notable cases.

2-32   In *Centros Ltd v Erhvervs-og Selskabsstyrelsen*, Case C-212/97[79] a Danish couple set up and registered a private company in England (which never carried on any activities in England) and then applied to the Danish authorities for permission to operate a branch in Denmark so circumventing the stricter minimum capital requirements imposed on Danish private companies. The Danish authorities refused to register the branch on the basis that the couple were carrying on their principal establishment in Denmark in breach of national law. The issue was referred to the ECJ which concluded that it is contrary to the right of freedom of establishment for a Member State to refuse to register a branch of a company in these circumstances.

---

[75] Third Company Law Directive 78/855/EEC concerning mergers of public limited liability companies, OJ L 295, 20.10.1978, p 36, now codified as Directive 2011/35/EU, OJ L 110/1, 29.4.2011; Sixth Company Law Directive 82/891/EEC concerning the division of public limited liability companies, OJ L 378, 31.12.1982, p 47, amended by Directive 2007/63/EC, OJ L 300, 17.11.2007, p 47 and Directive 2009/109, OJ L 259, 2.10.2009, p 14. The Commission did suggest the repeal of the Third and Sixth Directives, see Commission Communication on a simplified business environment for companies, COM (2007) 394, 10.7.2007, para 3.1, something the UK supported, but the consensus favoured their simplification rather than outright repeal.

[76] Directive 2005/56/EC on cross-border mergers of limited liability companies, OJ L 310, 25.11.2005, p 1.

[77] See The Companies (Cross-Border Mergers) Regulations 2007, SI 2007/2974.

[78] See now the Treaty on the Functioning of the European Union (Consolidated version) OJ C 83, 30.3.2010, p 47; art 49 provides for freedom of establishment and art 54 requires companies formed in a Member State to be treated in the same way as natural persons who are nationals of Member States.

[79] [2000] 2 BCLC 68, ECJ.

2-33 The Treaty provisions on freedom of establishment are intended, the court said, specifically to enable companies formed in accordance with the law of a Member State and having their registered office, central administration or principal place of business within the Community, to pursue activities in other Member States through an agency, branch or subsidiary. Member States are entitled to take measures to prevent their nationals from attempting, under cover of Treaty rights, improperly to circumvent their national legislation or from improperly or fraudulently taking advantage of Community provisions. The fact that a national of a Member State chooses to form a company in the Member State whose company law rules seem the least restrictive and to set up branches in other Member States does not, in itself, however, constitute an abuse of the right of establishment, even if no activities are then conducted in the Member State of incorporation.

2-34 This position was strengthened by the ruling in the *Uberseering*[80] case where the ECJ confirmed that Member States must recognise companies incorporated in other Member States without further formality and without any need for the Member States to enter into conventions concerning the mutual recognition of companies. In *Uberseering* the company had been incorporated in the Netherlands but came to conduct all of its activities in Germany and all its shareholders were German. When the company tried to sue on a civil matter in Germany, it was denied *locus standi* on the basis that it had no legal capacity in Germany, not having been incorporated there. The ECJ held that the failure to recognise the company's standing and effectively to require its reincorporation in Germany was an infringement of the freedom of establishment and incompatible with arts 43 and 48 of the EC Treaty.[81]

2-35 A strategy which some Member States adopted to maintain some control over these companies (sometimes described as pseudo-foreign or formally foreign companies) was not to deny recognition to the entity validly incorporated under the law of another Member State, but to impose additional constraints on them when the formally foreign company carried on all or most of their activities in their Member State (as in *Centros*). In *Inspire Art Ltd*[82] the ECJ concluded that such measures also infringe the right of freedom of establishment.

2-36 In *Inspire Art* the company was incorporated in England but its sole director was based in, and all its activities were conducted in, the Netherlands. The Dutch authorities tried to subject this formally foreign company to disclosure and minimum capital requirements which would put it on a footing similar to companies incorporated in the Netherlands. A failure to comply would result in personal liability for the directors so denying them the protection of limited liability despite the business having been incorporated as a limited liability company. The court considered this attempt to impose capital requirements to be a breach of freedom of establishment in that it made it restrictive and therefore less attractive. In so far as disclosure requirements could be imposed, the ECJ held, they were limited to the requirements of the Eleventh Company Law Directive on disclosure by branches which adequately protected the interests of creditors in the Netherlands by ensuring that they were aware of the status and nature of the foreign company.

---

[80] *Uberseering BV v Nordic Construction Co Baumanagement Gmbh (NCC)* [2005] 1 WLR 315, ECJ.
[81] See n 78.
[82] *Kamer van Koophandel en Fabrieken voor Amsterdam v Inspire Art Ltd* [2005] 3 CMLR 34.

2-37   The ECJ accepted, as it had in *Uberseering*,[83] that in certain circumstances and under certain conditions the protection of creditors, minority shareholders and employees[84] and the preservation of the effectiveness of fiscal supervision and the fairness of commercial transactions may justify measures restricting the freedom of establishment.[85] But measures restricting the fundamental freedoms must fulfil four conditions: they must be applied in a non-discriminatory manner; they must be justified by imperative requirements in the general interest; they must be suitable for securing the attainment of the objective which they pursue; and they must not go beyond what is necessary in order to attain it.[86] In *Uberseering*, however, creditor protection did not demand measures beyond disclosure.

2-38   The next stage in this jurisprudence was the decision in *Re Sevic Systems AG*[87] where the German authorities refused to register a merger between a Luxembourg company and a Germany company on the basis that the German registration provisions applied only to mergers between two German companies. The ECJ held that a difference in treatment of mergers according to whether they were internal within a Member State or of a cross-border nature between a company formed in one Member State and a company formed in another was a measure likely to hinder cross-border mergers and to deter the exercise of the freedom of establishment. The result in *Sevic* has been overtaken by the adoption of the Tenth Company Law Directive on cross-border mergers[88] which requires Member States to recognise such mergers and determines how such mergers are to be conducted. Finally, the Court of Justice ruled in *Re Cartesio Oktató*[89] that a Member State can provide that a company incorporated under the law of that Member State may not transfer its seat to another Member State whilst retaining its status as a company governed by the law of the Member State of incorporation.[90] Whereas the *Centros* line of authorities establishes the right of incorporation in a different Member State from the Member State where the company's activities are to be carried out and the requirement for the host State to recognise the entity, the *Cartesio* ruling shows that the state of incorporation is still able to determine the status of the entity incorporated under its jurisdiction. But the ruling in *Cartesio* is both limited on its facts and to some extent overtaken by the Cross-Border Mergers Directive, see **2-40**.

2-39   Side by side with these decisions upholding the right of freedom of establishment has been extensive tax litigation before the ECJ (beyond the scope of this work) where Member States have sought to restrict, in particular, the ability of large groups to structure their activities through subsidiaries etc in a way that attracts the lowest rates of corporation and other taxes. The ECJ has identified national tax measures discriminating between resident and non-resident activities and structures also as a restriction and inhibition on

---

[83] See [2005] 1 WLR 315 at 348.

[84] As to whether measures to protect employee rights of co-determination, as in Germany, might be acceptable, see Johnston, 'EC Freedom of Establishment: Employee Participation in Corporate Governance and the limits of Regulatory Competition' (2006) 6 JCLS 71.   [85] [2006] 2 BCLC 510 at 529.

[86] [2006] 2 BCLC 510 at 528; also *Gebhard v Consiglio dell'Ordine degli Avvocati e Procuratori di Milano* Case C-55/94 [1995] ECR I-4165 (para 37).

[87] [2006] 2 BCLC 510, ECJ; and see Siems, 'Sevic: Beyond Cross-Border Mergers' (2007) 8 EBOR 307.

[88] Directive 2005/56, OJ L 310, 25.11.2005, pp 1–9. See The Companies (Cross-Border Mergers) Regulations 2007, SI 2007/2974.   [89] [2010] 1 BCLC 523, ECJ.

[90] The case concerned a Hungarian partnership which wanted to transfer its seat to Italy while retaining its incorporation in Hungary when Hungarian law at the time required the seat of the company to be in Hungary. The ECJ accepted that the Hungarian authorities were entitled to refuse permission for this transfer.

the freedom of establishment.[91] The effect of these measures is to constrain the location of a company's activities and so inhibit corporate mobility. In addition therefore to the need for 'incoming' Member States to recognise the legal entity seeking to exercise its rights of freedom of establishment within that Member State, Member States must also ensure that they do not impose barriers, whether through taxation or other exit obligations, which restrict the ability of their own companies to exit the jurisdiction in exercise of their rights of freedom of establishment.[92]

2-40 The net result of this activist jurisprudence from the ECJ is that there is now a considerable measure of corporate mobility within the EU,[93] so much so that the European Commission decided in 2007 that it is no longer necessary to proceed with a proposed Fourteenth Company Law Directive allowing for the cross-border transfer of the registered office of limited companies.[94] For the moment, the same result can be achieved by other mechanisms, especially by the use of a cross-border merger whereby the company which wishes to move to another jurisdiction can now set up a company in that other jurisdiction, merge the existing company into that new company, and dissolve the first company, so effecting a transfer of the business and the registered office to the new jurisdiction.[95] It is also possible for a European Company, subject to detailed formalities (which may be simplified shortly), to transfer its registered office.[96] Critics would argue that companies should not need to use such 'detour' mechanisms but should be offered a straightforward mechanism for the transfer of the registered offices and so a Directive is still needed.[97] It may be that the Commission will revisit this issue under pressure from the European Parliament which continues to discuss it.

2-41 To sum up, businesses may choose where to incorporate and that choice may be dictated, especially for smaller companies, by considerations such as whether (and, if so, the level at which) a minimum share capital is required. Once incorporated in Member State A: (1) that company must be recognised as such in all other Member States, even if it conducts no business in the state of incorporation (*Uberseering*); (2) that company can choose to operate in another Member State either through a subsidiary, branch or agency (*Centros*);

---

[91] See, for example, *Cadbury Schweppes plc v Inland Revenue Commissioners* (C-196/04) [2007] 1 CMLR 2; *Marks & Spencer plc v Halsey (Inspector of Taxes)* (C-446/03) [2005] ECR I-10837, [2006] 1 CMLR 18, ECJ; and, generally, Barry & Healy-Rae, 'FDI Implications of Recent European Court of Justice Decisions on Corporation Tax Matters' (2010) 11 EBOR 125.

[92] See Vossestein, 'Exit restrictions on Freedom of Establishment after Marks & Spencer' (2006) 7 EBOR 863.

[93] See, generally, Johnston & Syrpis, 'Regulatory Competition in European Company Law after Cartesio' (2009) EL Rev 378; Armour & Ringe, 'European Company Law 1999–2010: Renaissance and Crisis' (2011) 48 CMLR 125.

[94] An approach now undermined, it is argued, by the ECJ decision in *Cartesio* which shows the need for a direct transfer mechanism; and see Johnston & Syrpis, 'Regulatory Competition in European Company Law after Cartesio' (2009) EL Rev 378.

[95] See Siems, 'Sevic: Beyond Cross-Border Mergers' (2007) 8 EBOR 307; Papadopoulos, 'EU Regulatory Approaches to Cross-border Mergers: Exercising the right of establishment' (2011) 36 EL Rev 71.

[96] See Council Regulation 2157/2001 on the Statute for the European Company, OJ L 294, 10.11.2001, pp 1–21, art 8. A major limitation on the process is that the SE's registered office and head office must be in the same Member State (see art 7); also Ringe, 'The European Company Statute in the Context of Freedom of Establishment' (2007) 7 JCLS 185.

[97] See Wymeersch, 'Is a Directive on Corporate Mobility needed?' (2007) 8 EBOR 161; Mucciarelli, 'Company "Emigration" and EC Freedom of Establishment: Daily Mail Revisited' (2008) 9 EBOR 267. See also Wisniewski and Opalski, 'Companies' Freedom of Establishment after the ECJ *Cartesio* Judgment' (2009) 10 EBOR 595; Lombardo, 'Regulatory Competition in Company Law in the European Union after Cartesio' (2009) 10 EBOR 627.

(3) where the choice is to act through a branch, the Member State cannot impose obligations on the branch equivalent to those imposed on businesses incorporated in that Member State (*Inspire Art*).

2-42   One consequence of the *Centros* line of authorities has been that some Member States have moved to liberalise their domestic requirements and speed up their formation processes in order to compete with this jurisdiction which is seen as having the lowest entry requirements with minimum formalities (as discussed in Chapter 1) and, of course, no minimum share capital requirement for private companies. In France, for example, the minimum capital requirement for SARLs (a type of company equivalent to a private company here) was removed while Germany modernised its law governing private limited companies (GmbH).[98]

2-43   While there have been concerns that the *Centros* jurisprudence will lead to a degree of forum shopping by businesses (most matters are determined by the law of the place of incorporation), in practice, different languages, business cultures and legal systems constrain the choice of place of incorporation which is also much influenced by tax considerations.[99] Equally, concerns that the outcome will be a 'race to laxity' or a 'race to the bottom' (i.e. that Member States in their anxiety to appear attractive to business will cease to impose protections necessary for shareholders and creditors) have failed to materialise.[100]

C European structures

2-44   In addition to facilitating movement between Member States and takeovers across jurisdictions, the Commission has also looked to create new European structures. An example is the European Economic Interest Grouping (EEIG) which can be established between two or more trading entities based in different Member States.[101] It is of limited appeal because its activities have to be ancillary to the activities of its members (so it is confined to areas such as research, marketing or training) and it cannot be profit-making in its own right. There are just 238 on the register.[102]

---

[98] The reformed GmbH Act also provides for a new category of GmbH (an UG in German), popularly known as the 'mini-GmbH', which can be started with a capital of just €1. The UG must put aside one quarter of annual profits to allow its share capital to grow to the GmbH level (€25,000). Once this level has been reached, the accumulated capital can be converted into share capital and the UG can then change its name to a GmbH. For an interesting account of the adaptation of national law to the *Centros* jurisprudence, see Bratton, McCahery and Vermeulen, 'How does Corporate Mobility affect Lawmaking? A Comparative Analysis,' in Prentice and Reisberg (eds), *Corporate Finance Law in the UK and EU* (2011).

[99] See generally Lowry, 'Eliminating Obstacles to Freedom of establishment: The Competitive Edge of UK Company Law' (2004) CLJ 331.

[100] For an interesting account of this issue, often contrasted with the Delaware syndrome (Delaware being the US State which attracts the greatest number of incorporations as a result of ensuring that its corporate law is seen as the most attractive to business), see Drury, 'The "Delaware Syndrome": European Fears and Reactions' [2005] JBL 709; also Gelter, 'The Structure of Regulatory Competition in European Corporate Law' (2005) 5 JCLS 247; Lowry, n 99.

[101] See Council Regulation EEC/2137/85, OJ L 199, 31.7.1985, p 1; and the European Economic Interest Grouping Regulations 1989, SI 1989/638. See generally Keegan, 'The European Economic Interest Grouping' [1991] JBL 457.

[102] As of 31 March 2011, see Companies House, *Statistical Tables on Companies Registration Activities 2010–11*, Table E3.

The European Company (SE)

2-45 After decades of discussion,[103] agreement was reached in 2001 on the European Company, the Societas Europaea (SE), with a Council Regulation providing for the European Company Statute[104] while a Council Directive supplements the statute and makes provision for the involvement of employees.[105]

2-46 An SE may be formed in one of four ways:

- by the merger of two or more existing public limited companies from at least two different EU Member States;
- by the formation of a holding company promoted by public or private limited companies from at least two different Member States;
- by the formation of a subsidiary of companies from at least two different Member States;
- by the transformation of a public limited company which has, for at least two years, had a subsidiary in another Member State.

2-47 An SE must have a minimum share capital of €120,000. The board of directors can be organised either on the basis of a supervisory and a management board or as a unitary board. The registered office of an SE must be in the same Member State as its head office and the registered office can be transferred to another Member State without the need to wind up the company. The provisions contained in the accompanying Directive on worker involvement are complex, given that they are the result of decades of negotiations designed to accommodate the very differing views on this issue across the Member States. Essentially, levels of worker participation in the pre-existing entities must be replicated in the SE but, if there were none, the SE need not make provision for any such participation, though there are default rules as to the provision of information to and consultation with employees.

2-48 The laws applicable to the SE are those laid down in the Regulation and Directive and where no provision is made (and no provision is made on matters such as capital maintenance, directors' duties, shareholders rights and insolvency), the matter is governed by the laws applicable to public companies of the Member State in which the SE has its registered office. The result is an element of uncertainty as to the applicable law and, given the significance of the matters governed by the law of the Member State of the registered office, these entities begin to look like national public companies which is a long way from the concept of a European company as originally envisaged.

2-49 It is also the case that the SE has been somewhat overtaken by other developments, such as the breadth of the freedom of establishment articulated by the European Court of Justice, discussed at **2-31** et seq, and the ease of transfer between Member States as a result of the Tenth Company Law Directive on Cross-Border Mergers, noted at **2-40**. The Commission has made considerable strides also in devising a package of uniform obligations with

---

[103] For the history of the proposal, see Edwards, *EC Company Law* (1999) pp 399–404. First proposed by the Commission in 1970, discussions over the years were dogged by controversy over issues such as the interface between national and European law, the appropriate taxation regime and, most particularly, by an inability to reach agreement on the provisions for employee involvement.

[104] Council Regulation (EC) No 2157/2001 on the Statute for a European Company (SE), OJ L 294, 10.11.2001, p 1. Implemented by The European Public Limited-Liability Company Regulations 2004, SI 2004/2326.

[105] Council Directive 2001/86/EC supplementing the Statute for a European Company with regard to the involvement of employees, OJ L 294, 10.11.2001, p 22.

respect to publicly traded companies, not just in terms of disclosure and corporate governance as discussed, but with regard to other matters, such as public offers of shares.[106] The result is that the existing structures may facilitate operations across the EU without the need for a European Company. Certainly, the SE has not proved attractive in this jurisdiction although it has been used to some extent in other Member States.[107] In 2010, the Commission reviewed the operation of the SE Statute.[108] It found that the positive aspects of an SE are the European image and supra-national character of the SE and the possibility it offers of transferring the registered office and using the SE to reorganise and restructure groups, but the drawbacks identified were that the process of setting up an SE is seen as costly, time-consuming and complex, especially with regard to employee participation. Overall, the Commission concluded that the application of the SE Statute poses a number of problems in practice, noting that:

> …the SE Statute does not provide for a uniform SE form across the European Union, but 27 different types of SEs. The Statute contains many references to national law and there is uncertainty about the legal effect of directly applicable law and its interface with national law. Furthermore, the uneven distribution of SEs across the European Union shows that the Statute is not adapted to the situation of companies in all Member States.[109]

In the light of these findings, the Commission is to consider bringing forward proposals for simplification of the SE Regulation by 2013.

The European Private Company (SPE)

2-50   The complexity of the European Company means that it is unlikely to prove attractive to SMEs and it was never envisaged that it might be appropriate for such entities. Instead the idea has been mooted for many years that the Commission should consider a European Private Company Statute and, as part of the Company Law Action Plan, the Commission did conduct a feasibility study on the issue in 2005.[110] The results were divided but the idea gathered momentum with support from the European Parliament and so the Small Business Act announced by the Commission in June 2008 (see **2-17**) included a proposal for a Regulation on the Statute for a European Private Company.[111]

2-51   The key elements as then envisaged of a Societas Privata Europaea (SPE) were:

- It was to be a private company limited by shares, with a minimum share capital of €1 and a name ending in 'SPE'.

---

[106] See Directive 2003/71/EC on the prospectus to be published when securities are offered to the public or admitted to trading, OJ L 345, 31.12.2003, p 64, as amended by Directive 2010/73/EU, OJ L 327, 11.12.2010, p. 1.

[107] At 31 March 2011, there were 23 SEs on the register at Companies House: see n 102. The European Commission reported that, by 2010, 595 SEs were registered in Member States with 70% of them in Germany or the Czech Republic (both jurisdictions with worker representative laws in any event). For a detailed breakdown of the figures, see Commission Staff Working Document, SEC (2010) 1391 final, 17.11.2010, section 2.

[108] See Report from the Commission to the European Parliament and the Council on the application of Council Regulation on the Statute for a European Company (SE), COM (2010) 676 final, 17.11.2010, and related Commission Staff Working Document, SEC (2010) 1391 final, 17.11.2010.

[109] See COM (2010) 676 final, 17.11.2010, section 6.

[110] See European Commission, *Feasibility Study of a European Statute for SMEs* (2005).

[111] See the *Proposal For A Council Regulation On The Statute For A European Private Company*, Com (2008) 396, 25.06.2008; also Drury 'The European Private Company' (2008) 9 EBOR 125. A leading proponent of the idea, Drury comments (at 130) that, amongst its attractions, the SPE would provide a uniform structure for a Europe-wide group of companies, would facilitate inward investment by providing a vehicle that can operate in and move to any part of the Union under a single set of rules, and would give a European identity to businesses for marketing purposes.

- It might be formed from scratch or created from another form and by one or more persons.

- It might be registered in any Member State and its registered office and centre of activities might be in different Member States. It would be able to transfer its registered office without winding up.

- It need not initially have any cross-border activities or connections.

- The legal framework for the SPE would be provided by the Statute so ensuring uniform rules across the EU, but the detailed regulation of the internal working arrangements within the SPE would be a matter for the articles.

- For matters not governed by the Statute or the articles, the law of the Member State in which the SPE is registered would apply.

2-52 As with the SE, it is not clear that there is demand for this structure given, as the Commission itself concedes, that most small businesses have no interest in cross-border trading and are reasonably content with the range of business vehicles offered by their domestic jurisdiction.[112] It might be attractive to businesses from jurisdictions with high minimum share capital requirements, especially since it need not actually engage in any cross-border activities (at least under this proposal), but as noted, many jurisdictions have already reformed their laws to abolish or significantly reduce the minimum share capital required. After some initial enthusiasm for this project, political support for the proposal has diminished and it has not progressed further.

2-53 Finally, it is worth noting a further private initiative which is underway to develop a European Model Company Law Act along the lines of the American Model Acts. The intention is to provide a model law which national legislatures would be free to adopt in whole or in part. The hope is that it will be possible to devise a structure based on broadly acceptable uniform rules, building on the common legal traditions of the Member States and the existing *acquis* and drawing on best practice in the various Member States.[113]

---

[112] The UK Government indicated that it was supportive of the proposal, but thought it was complex and that it was unlikely that many UK companies would choose to form an SPE rather than a UK private limited company, see HC, European Scrutiny Committee, 38th Report, Session 2010–12 (HC 428), paras 2.12–2.20.

[113] See Paul Krüger Andersen, 'The European Model Company Act (EMCA): A new way forward' in Bernitz and Ringe (eds), *Company Law and Economic Protectionism—New Challenges to European Integration* (2010); also Baums and Andersen, 'The European Model Company Act Project' in Tison et al (eds), *Perspectives in Company Law and Financial Regulation* (2009). Further information on this project is available at http://law.au.dk/emca.

3

Corporate personality

A A separate legal entity

The *Salomon* principle

3-1 On incorporation, a company becomes a legal entity separate and distinct from its shareholders and it is not the agent of those shareholders, not even if it is a one-man company with one shareholder controlling all its activities. This fundamental principle of company law was established by the House of Lords in *Salomon v Salomon & Co Ltd*.[1]

3-2 In this case, Mr Salomon sold his shoe business to a company which he had set up for the purpose under the Companies Act 1862. The formalities under the Act (very similar to those still required today) were completed and the members of the company were Salomon, Mrs S and five of their children (a minimum of seven members being required at that time).[2] As part of the consideration for the sale of the business to the company, Mr Salomon received fully paid-up shares and also debentures to the value of £10,000 which he subsequently assigned to another party. In effect, the debentures meant that initially Mr Salomon, and subsequently the assignee, were creditors of the business with first claim on the remaining assets should the company go into liquidation, as indeed happened. The company became insolvent and was unable to meet the full claim of the assignee or to meet at all the claims of the other (unsecured) creditors. The liquidator attempted to hold Mr Salomon liable for the debts of the company on a variety of grounds including that the whole transaction was a fraud on the company's creditors from which Salomon should not be allowed to benefit and that the company was simply his agent and therefore he should indemnify the company (and its creditors) with respect to the debts incurred by the company.

3-3 At first instance, the court agreed that the company was merely an agent of Salomon and therefore, as principal, he was liable to indemnify the agent (the company) for its debts.[3] The Court of Appeal rejected Salomon's appeal and concluded that the formation of the company and the issue of the debentures was a mere scheme to enable Salomon to carry on business in the name of a company with limited liability contrary to the true intent and meaning of the Companies Act 1862. In essence he was a sole trader screening himself

---

[1] [1897] AC 22, HL. See generally Grantham & Rickett (eds), *Corporate Personality in the 20th Century* (1998) which is an interesting collection of essays assessing the modern significance of the decision in *Salomon*.

[2] The CA 2006 permits single member private and public companies, see s 7. A public company must have two directors, however, while a private company need have only one director (s 154) who can be, and often is, the sole member.

[3] See *Broderip v Salomon* [1895] 2 Ch 323.

from liabilities and as such it was a device to defraud creditors.[4] Lopes LJ noted that 'it would be lamentable if a scheme such as this could not be defeated'.[5]

3-4 On a further appeal by Salomon, the House of Lords concluded that there was nothing untoward with the formation and operation of the company and it reversed the decision of the Court of Appeal. The company had been duly formed and registered and was not the mere alias or agent of or trustee for Mr Salomon. There was no sham or fraud, the formation and operation of the company was not contrary to the true intent and meaning of the Companies Act 1862 and Mr Salomon was not liable to indemnify the company against the creditors' claims.

3-5 Lord Macnaghten noted that when the memorandum[6] is duly signed and registered, a body corporate is formed[7] and it cannot lose that status by issuing the bulk of its shares to one person. He went on:[8]

'The company is at law a different person altogether from the subscribers to the memorandum; and, though it may be that after incorporation the business is precisely the same as it was before, and the same persons are managers, and the same hands receive the profits, the company is not in law the agent of the subscribers or trustee for them. Nor are the subscribers as members liable, in any shape or form, except to the extent and in the manner provided by the Act.'[9]

3-6 As for the description of these companies as 'one-man companies', Lord Macnaghten said that if that phrase was intended to convey that a company under the absolute control of one person was not a legally incorporated company, it was inaccurate and misleading.[10] Likewise, Lord Halsbury emphasised that the sole guide to matters was the statute which did not enact requirements as to the extent or degree of interests which may be held by the subscribers to the memorandum of association.[11] The House of Lords had little sympathy for the unsecured creditors who had only themselves to blame, having had full notice that they were no longer dealing with an individual.[12]

3-7 The result was that the House of Lords affirmed that a company is not, per se, the agent of its shareholders, even if control is concentrated in only one shareholder. The mere fact that a person owns all the shares in a company does not make the business carried on by that company his business. Once the company is legally incorporated, the company must be treated like any other independent person with rights and liabilities of its own.[13] The effect of the decision was to legitimate the one-man company and to reject the lower courts' views that such a structure was contrary to the legislation.

3-8 A further illustration of this point can be found in *Gramophone & Typewriter Co Ltd v Stanley*.[14] The shares in a German company were owned by an English company. At issue was whether the business of the German company was really the business of its English shareholder since, if it was, that exposed the shareholder to a greater tax liability. Given

[4] See [1895] 2 Ch 323 at 338–9, per Lindley LJ.   [5] [1895] 2 Ch 323 at 340–1.
[6] See CA 2006, s 8 and **1-23** as to the memorandum of association.   [7] See CA 2006, s 16(2).
[8] [1897] AC 22 at 51, HL.
[9] That liability, in the case of a company limited by shares, is limited to the amount, if any, unpaid on the shares held by them, see CA 2006, s 3(2) and **3-15**; also IA 1986, s 74(1)(d).   [10] [1897] AC 22 at 53.
[11] [1897] AC 22 at 29–30.
[12] See [1897] AC 22 at 53, per Lord Macnaghten; at 45, per Lord Herschell.
[13] [1897] AC 22 at 31, per Lord Halsbury.
[14] [1908] 2 KB 89; see also *Tunstall v Steigmann* [1962] 2 QB 593; *Ebbw Vale UDC v South Wales Traffic Area Licensing Authority* [1951] 2 KB 366.

that there was factual evidence that the German company was a real company with a real business, Buckley LJ said that the question became one of whether the German company was really the agent of the English shareholder. But, he said, it was well established that the holding of all of the shares does not establish the relationship of principal and agent between a shareholder and the company. There was no agency relationship and the business was the business of the German company.

3-9 In legitimating the one-man company, the decision in *Salomon* also legitimates the group concept with each subsidiary company being a separate and distinct entity and not the agent of its controlling or sole shareholder, its parent company.[15] The relationship between a parent and a subsidiary company is the same as between Mr Salomon and his company. The parent company (i.e. the corporate shareholder in the subsidiary) and the subsidiary company are separate legal entities and each company is entitled to expect that the court will apply the *Salomon* principle in the ordinary way and respect the separate identity of each company in the group.[16] This is so even if the subsidiary company has a small paid-up capital and a board of directors all or most of whom are also directors or executives of the parent company.[17]

An exceptional agency

3-10 Although *Salomon v Salomon & Co Ltd*[18] establishes that a company is not, per se, the agent of its shareholders, exceptionally, it may be possible to establish that an agency relationship does exist between a company and its shareholders and, in the group context, it can be advantageous sometimes for a parent company to plead that a subsidiary company is a mere agent of the parent. Of course, as a general rule, a parent company would wish to reject any agency relationship to ensure that no liability attaches to it for the subsidiary's debts, but sometimes the parent company will take a different stance.

3-11 An example of an agency relationship can be seen in *Smith, Stone & Knight Ltd v Birmingham Corp.*[19] In this case, at issue was the compensation for compulsory purchase payable by a local authority when the property of a subsidiary company was acquired. To maximise the compensation payable, the parent company on this occasion was happy to argue that the subsidiary carried on business as agent for the parent. Atkinson J said that whether there is an agency relationship is a question of fact in each case and it depends on whether the subsidiary is carrying on the business as the parent company's business or as its own.[20] Atkinson J identified a variety of factors which he thought relevant to the determination of that issue, namely who was really carrying on the business, who received the profits, who was actually conducting the business, who appointed those persons, who was the head and brains of the venture and who was in effective and constant control of

---

[15] *Salomon v Salomon & Co Ltd* [1897] AC 22; *The Albazero* [1977] AC 774 at 807, HL, per Roskill LJ; *Bank of Tokyo Ltd v Karoon* [1987] AC 45 at 64, CA; *Adams v Cape Industries plc* [1990] BCLC 479 at 519–20. The definition of holding (parent) and subsidiary company is set out in CA 2006, s 1159, and see the discussion of corporate groups at **1-55** et seq.

[16] *Adams v Cape Industries plc* [1990] BCLC 479 at 520, CA; *Ord v Belhaven Pubs Ltd* [1998] 2 BCLC 447 at 458, CA.

[17] See *Re Polly Peck International plc (No 3)* [1996] BCLC 428 at 441, per Robert Walker J (despite a subsidiary company having negligible capital, no separate management, and the most minimal role in certain bond issues, the court did not accept that it was an agent of its parent company).   [18] [1897] AC 22, HL.

[19] [1939] 4 All ER 116. See *Gramophone & Typewriter Ltd v Stanley* [1908] 2 KB 89 at 96, 100.

[20] [1939] 4 All ER 116 at 121. See Toulson J in *Yukong Line Ltd of Korea v Rendsburg Investments Corp of Liberia* [1998] 2 BCLC 485, at 495–6, who criticises this approach as coming close in effect to the approach of the Court of Appeal in *Salomon* which was rejected by the House of Lords.

the business.[21] Having reviewed the facts,[22] the court agreed that the arrangement here between the parent and subsidiary was such that the business and profits belonged as a matter of law to the parent company. Atkinson J thought the subsidiary in this instance was a legal entity and 'that is all it was'[23] so comprehensive was the parent company's control and conduct of the business. As the subsidiary was not operating on its own behalf, but on behalf of the parent company, the parent company was the party entitled to claim compensation. While the facts were exceptional, the case confirms that it is possible for an agency relationship to exist between a company (the agent) and its shareholders (the principal).[24]

3-12   In *Adams v Cape Industries plc*[25] it was argued that certain US subsidiaries were agents of an English parent company such that the English parent company was conducting business in the US. The presence of the English company in the US was necessary if a US court judgment was to be enforced against it. As is clear from the authorities, it is necessary for the court to look in detail at the relationship between the English parent company and the US subsidiaries.

3-13   With respect to one particular subsidiary, the evidence was that it leased premises, employed people and carried on activities on its own account as principal. It earned profits, paid its taxes and had its own debtors and creditors. For all the closeness of the relationship with the English parent company whose products it marketed, it had no power to bind the parent company to any contractual obligation and it never did effect a transaction in a manner such that the parent company became subject to any contractual obligations to any person. The Court of Appeal concluded that it was indisputable that a substantial part of the business carried on by the subsidiary was in every sense its own business.[26] There was no agency relationship with the parent company.

3-14   To sum up, applying *Salomon*, a registered company is not, per se, the agent of its shareholders. It is possible that, quite exceptionally, an agency relationship may arise from the facts, but it must do so from circumstances other than mere control of the company or ownership of its shares. Whether such circumstances exist involves the court in a detailed factual examination in order to determine whether the intention was to create a relationship of agency and, as Toulson J has noted, ordinarily the intention of someone who conducts trading activities through the vehicle of a one-man company will be quite

---

[21] [1939] 4 All ER 116 at 121.
[22] The parent company held all (except five) of the shares in the subsidiary company and the profits of the subsidiary were treated as the profits of the parent company. The parent company appointed the persons who conducted the business and it was in effective and constant control of the business, see [1939] 4 All ER 116 at 119–20.   [23] [1939] 4 All ER 116 at 121.
[24] See too *Re FG (Films) Ltd* [1953] 1 All ER 615. In this case a company claimed that it had made a film which was therefore a British film and so entitled to certain tax advantages. The company had a capital of £100, no premises other than its registered office and no staff. The financing of the film (some £80,000) was provided by an American company which through a nominee held 90% of the company's shares. The court concluded that it could not be said in any real sense that this 'insignificant' company had made the film, its participation was so small as to be practically negligible, and it had acted, in so far as it had acted at all, merely as the agent and nominee of the American company. See also *Firestone Tyre and Rubber Co Ltd v Llewellin* [1957] 1 All ER 561 (an assessment of tax upheld where business of parent and subsidiary carried on by the subsidiary as agent for the parent).   [25] [1990] BCLC 479.
[26] The subsidiary in this case was NAAC; see the discussion at [1990] BCLC 479 at 520–2. With regard to another subsidiary (CPC), see [1990] BCLC 479 at 523–4, the court thought the facts were even weaker in that it was not a wholly-owned subsidiary but was an independently owned company. While the English company had provided funding for it, it carried on business on its own account and not as agent for the English company.

the opposite,[27] something which could equally be said of those who set up subsidiary companies.[28]

Consequences of *Salomon*

3-15   As a legal entity, separate and distinct from its shareholders, the company must be treated like any other independent person with rights and liabilities appropriate to itself.[29] It is the company which conducts business, it is the company which enters into contracts and incurs debts. The company can own property and its property is not the property of its main shareholder (not even if he owns all the shares), who cannot insure it,[30] but who can be charged with stealing from the company.[31] The company can employ people and can employ its controlling shareholder.[32] The company has perpetual existence and succession and this continuity is important and convenient. The membership may be constantly changing but the entity continues until steps are taken to bring it to an end through winding up. Equally, the company can sue and be sued in its own name and this is advantageous to third parties who do not have to concern themselves with identifying who are the shareholders at any given moment. Most important of all, the debts are the debts of the company and not of the shareholders whose only obligation in a company limited by shares is to contribute to the company's assets such amount, if any, unpaid on the shares held by them (CA 2006, s 3(2)).[33] Ultimately, it is the company which may go into insolvency.

3-16   Sometimes the fact that the company is a distinct legal entity works to a shareholder's disadvantage and the courts are unwilling to allow a shareholder to elect to have the benefits without the disadvantages of incorporation.[34] This is particularly true with regard to

---

[27]   *Yukong Line Ltd of Korea v Rendsburg Investments Corp of Liberia* [1998] 2 BCLC 485 at 496.

[28]   See *Atlas Maritime Co SA v Avalon Maritime Ltd, The Coral Rose (No 1)* [1991] 4 All ER 769 at 779.

[29]   *Salomon v Salomon & Co Ltd* [1897] AC 22 at 30, HL, per Lord Halsbury; also *Maclaine Watson & Co Ltd v International Tin Council* [1989] 3 All ER 523 at 531.

[30]   *Macaura v Northern Assurance Co* [1925] AC 619 at 626–7, HL; '…the corporator, even if he holds all the shares, is not the corporation …' at 633, per Lord Wrenbury.

[31]   *A-G's Reference (No 2 of 1982)* [1984] QB 624, CA.

[32]   See *Lee v Lee's Air Farming Ltd* [1961] AC 12 where a controlling shareholder was a 'worker' for workers' compensation purposes when he was killed in the course of his work. A controlling shareholder of a company can be an employee of the company for the purposes of redundancy payments under the Employment Rights Act 1996, s 182, but whether such an employer/employee relationship exists in a particular case is a question of fact: the court must inquire as to whether a true contract of employment exists and the degree of an employee's shareholding and control of the company, even if total, is not ordinarily relevant to that inquiry: *Neufeld v Secretary of State for Business, Enterprise and Regulatory Reform* [2009] 2 BCLC 273.

[33]   See also IA 1986, s 74(1)(d). If the shares are fully-paid, the shareholders have no further liability as shareholders. Typically shares are issued fully-paid (see **19-16**) and the model articles for private companies, if adopted, require the shares to be fully-paid, see Companies (Model Articles) Regulations 2008, SI 2008/3229, reg 2, Sch 1, para 21.

[34]   See, for example, *Diamantides v JP Morgan Chase Bank* [2005] EWHC 263, aff'd [2005] EWCA Civ 1612, where the claimant alleged essentially that the defendant bank owed him a duty of care. Through P Ltd, he had purchased high risk investments from the bank which had proved disastrous. He was the sole shareholder and controller of P Ltd and he provided it with the funds for investment. The court struck out the claim commenting that it regarded the case as an unprincipled attempt by an individual, who chose to invest through a corporate vehicle, to pierce the veil of his own company. The purpose of doing so was to secure (under the statutory scheme as it then was) the additional protection afforded to private investors when in reality P Ltd was the customer. See also *Woolfson v Strathclyde Regional Council* (1979) 38 P & CR 521, HL, discussed at **3-22**, where the court declined to disregard the fact of incorporation so as to allow a controlling shareholder, when it suited him, to claim that the business was really his business.

attempts by shareholders to claim for what is termed reflective loss, i.e. losses suffered by shareholders which are only reflective of loss suffered by the company and in respect of which the company should sue. In keeping with the separate legal personality of the company, the rule in *Foss v Harbottle*[35] establishes that where a wrong is done to the company, the company is the proper plaintiff in respect of it. It follows that a personal claim by a shareholder in respect of the diminution in value of his shareholding as a result of a wrong done to the company (for example, where the company has a claim in negligence against a third party) is misconceived and will be struck out.[36] The shareholder's loss is merely reflective of the loss suffered by the company and that loss will be fully remedied if the company enforces its full rights against the wrongdoer.[37] This principle respects company autonomy and ensures that a party (the shareholder) does not recover compensation for a loss suffered by another (the company).[38] This issue of reflective loss is discussed in detail in Chapter 18, as is the rule in *Foss v Harbottle*.

B Disregarding the separate entity

3-17 While the fundamental principle is that a company is an entity distinct from its shareholders, sometimes a statute, typically for reasons of taxation and financial transparency, requires the separate legal entity to be disregarded. For example, the companies legislation requires parent companies to prepare consolidated group accounts showing the affairs of the parent and subsidiary undertakings.[39] More importantly, there is also a discretionary jurisdiction whereby the court may disregard the separate legal entity and look to those controlling it, a process described as piercing the corporate veil, which is considered later (see **3-21**). As the discussion of the relevant cases will show, this concept is used to encompass the approach taken by the courts in a variety of circumstances which have equally variously been described as piercing the veil, peeping behind the veil, lifting the veil, etc. Many commentators have criticised the lack of coherence, the overlap with other doctrines and indeed whether there is a concept of piercing the veil at all.[40] It is undeniable that the cases cover a wide spectrum of circumstances and that in many cases the same outcome can be reached by the application of other principles, such

---

[35] (1843) 2 Hare 461.

[36] Of course, it is possible for the defendant to owe separate obligations of care or fiduciary duty to the shareholder in respect of which he can sue, see *Johnson v Gore Wood & Co* [2003] EWCA Civ 1728; also *Conway v Ratiu* [2006] 1 All ER 571 at [78], CA; *Diamantides v JP Morgan Chase Bank* [2005] EWCA Civ 1612 at [35].

[37] *Prudential Assurance Co Ltd v Newman Industries Ltd (No 2)* [1982] 1 All ER 354 at 366–7; *Johnson v Gore Wood & Co* [2001] 1 BCLC 313, HL; see **18-59**.

[38] *Johnson v Gore Wood & Co* [2001] 1 BCLC 313 at 338, per Lord Bingham, HL.

[39] See CA 2006, ss 399, 403–406. Other provisions, such as IA 1986, s 214 (liability for wrongful trading), are sometimes described as examples of statutory piercing of the corporate veil, but in truth they are merely provisions which impose liabilities on directors as a consequence of their involvement in the running of a company.

[40] See, for example, Tham, 'Piercing the Corporate Veil: Searching for appropriate choice of law rules' [2007] LMCLQ 22; Lord Cooke of Thorndon, *Turning Points of the Common Law* (1997) Ch 1, 'A Real Thing: Salomon v A Salomon & Co Ltd'; Moore, '"A Temple Built on Faulty Foundations": Piercing the corporate veil and the legacy of Salomon v Salomon' [2006] JBL 180; Ottolenghi, 'From Peeping behind the Corporate Veil to Ignoring it Completely' (1990) 53 MLR 338. See also Davies, *Introduction to Company Law* (2010) p 33 who suggests that no single explanation of the cases will be found and that company lawyers will not often have much to contribute to these debates, essentially because the true question is what is the purpose of the rule which it is alleged requires the veil to be pierced and does it require that the corporate personality be disregarded.

as agency law or by resort to equitable remedies. To some extent, however, the criticisms ignore or predate the decision in *Adams v Cape*,[41] discussed at **3-25**, which does create a more coherent framework for the development of a distinct and certain body of law surrounding the misuse of the corporate structure as a façade to conceal some wrongdoing.

3-18 Before considering piercing the corporate veil in detail, a couple of preliminary points should be noted. First, the 'piercing' jurisdiction as devised by the English courts is narrow and used sparingly,[42] lest it create commercial uncertainty and undermine the purpose of incorporation which (coupled with limited liability) is to manage future liabilities and risk. Having incorporated, the shareholders have a legitimate expectation, as do those who deal with the incorporated entity, that the courts will respect the status of the entity and apply the principle of *Salomon v Salomon & Co Ltd* in the ordinary way.[43] Secondly, even in the limited circumstances in which the court is willing to pierce the veil, it does not pierce it for all purposes such that the company is treated as if never incorporated and the shareholders are liable for all the debts of the company. Rather, the corporate veil is pierced merely to address the particular wrong which merits the court exercising the jurisdiction. For example, when the court pierces the veil because a company is being used to evade a contractual obligation, as in *Gilford Motor Co v Horne*,[44] discussed at **3-27**, the consequence is the enforcement of that contractual obligation, or, if the veil is pierced because the company is being used to hide assets, as in *Trustor v Smallbone*,[45] discussed at 3-xx, the consequence is an order for the recovery of the assets. Actually in each of these cases the remedy was granted against the company *and* the wrongdoer so the corporate entity is accepted and noted, but a wrongful transfer is unravelled or an obligation enforced against the true defendant.[46]

3-19 Piercing is a limited operation with limited consequences rather than a wholesale disregard of the fact of incorporation.[47] The consequence of piercing will depend therefore on the nature of the wrong which warrants piercing in the first place. In *Antonio Gramsci Shipping Corp v Stepanovs*,[48] Burton J went considerably further, in terms of

---

[41] [1990] BCLC 479, CA.

[42] There is some ambiguity as to whether the jurisdiction is limited to situations where piercing is necessary in the sense that no alternative remedy exists, a view rejected by Burton J in *Antonio Gramsci Shipping Corp v Stepanovs* [2011] 1 CLC 396 at [18]–[21], who accepted that piercing is exceptional, but it is not limited by a requirement of necessity. Lord Neuberger in *Linsen International Ltd v Humpuss Transportasi Kimia* [2011] EWCA Civ 1042 at [13], an appeal on interlocutory proceedings, seems to overstate the position of Munby J in *Ben Hashem v Ali Shayif* [2009] 1 FLR 115 on this point, suggesting that Munby J held that piercing was a course which the court should take if no other remedy is possible and if certain requirements were satisfied. But it is difficult to find support for that proposition in *Ben Hashem* where Munby J made the different point that, once the requirements for piercing are satisfied, the court will pierce the veil only to the extent necessary to provide a remedy for the particular wrong which has been done, at [164].

[43] See *Adams v Cape Industries plc* [1990] BCLC 479 at 520; *Ord v Belhaven Pubs Ltd* [1998] 2 BCLC 447 at 457; *Ben Hashem v Ali Shayif* [2009] 1 FLR 115 at [221]; *Macdonald v Costello* [2011] 3 WLR 1341 at [23] and [32].

[44] [1931] Ch 935. See Tham, n 41, at 29–31 who argues that this case and also *Jones v Lipman* [1962] 1 WLR 832 should not be seen as veil-piercing cases at all but as examples of equitable relief for breaches of contract or conduct inducing breaches of contract.   [45] [2001] 2 BCLC 436.

[46] See *Linsen International Ltd v Humpuss Transportasi Kimia* [2011] 2 Lloyd's Rep 663 at [129]–[136], aff'd [2011] EWCA Civ 1042.

[47] See Munby J in *Ben Hashem v Ali Shayif* [2009] 1 FLR 115 at [164], once the requirements for piercing are satisfied, the court will pierce the veil only to the extent necessary to provide a remedy for the particular wrong which has been done. Also Warren J in *Dadourian Group International Ltd v Simms* [2006] EWHC 2973 at [682] '… if the veil is to be lifted, it is to be lifted for the purposes of the relevant transaction'.

[48] [2011] 1 CLC 396.

remedy, than previously. The case concerned an interlocutory stage in a dispute concerning the alleged siphoning of funds by executives of a shipping company. In this case the claimants had been in a position to profit from charterparties with third parties. In alleged breach of their existing duties to the claimants, executives within the claimant group of companies formed the defendant companies which were interposed between the claimant and the third parties. The interposed defendant companies entered into a head charter with the claimants and then lucrative sub-charters with the third parties so that the defendant companies reaped the rewards from those lucrative sub-charters while the benefit to the claimants from the head charter was more modest. In effect, it was alleged that the executives used the defendant companies to siphon off profits for themselves whereas, had the defendant companies not been interposed, the claimants could have entered into direct charters with the third parties and made substantial profits. These proceedings concerned the continuation of freezing orders against the defendant companies' assets and, for that purpose, the court accepted that it would be appropriate to pierce the veil of the defendant companies to reveal their controllers. Exceptionally (it was necessary for jurisdiction reasons) the court concluded that the charterparties entered into by the defendant puppet companies (with the claimant and the third parties) had been entered into personally by the controllers of the defendant companies who as parties to the charterparties were bound by their terms including a jurisdiction clause submitting to the jurisdiction of the English court. Hence the controllers too could be subject to a freezing order. Burton J concluded that '[t]here is in my judgment no good reason of principle or jurisprudence why the victim cannot enforce the agreement against both the puppet company and the puppeteer who, all the time, was pulling the strings'.[49] The distinguishing feature in *Antonio Gramsci*, arguably, is that the defendant companies were facades from the outset created specifically as vehicles for the carrying out of the alleged fraud[50] so it is easier to conclude that the charterparties which the defendant companies entered into were in fact entered into by their controllers, their puppeteers.

3-20 Opposition to the approach taken by Burton J has been swift and it is likely therefore to be limited to its exceptional facts. In *Linsen International Ltd v Humpuss Transportasi Kimia*[51] the question was whether the court should pierce the veil of a recipient company to follow assets which had allegedly been transferred to it to make them unavailable to meet claims for sums due under various charterparties. At an interlocutory stage, Lord Neuberger noted that, even if piercing was appropriate, it would be for the purpose of following the assets, not making the recipient company party to the charterparty.[52] The recipient company was merely another company in the group to which the wrongdoing company transferred assets in an attempt to make it difficult for claimants to enforce a judgment against the wrongdoers. There was no basis for treating that recipient company as a party to the charterparty, he said, though it might be appropriate to pierce the veil for the purpose of unravelling the transfers. Lord Neuberger preferred the approach of Toulson J in *Yukong Line Ltd of Korea v Rendsburg Investments Corp of Liberia*[53] that where a company properly enters into a contract, in this case a charterparty, which it

---

[49] [2011] 1 CLC 396 at [26], as was done in *Gilford Motor Co Ltd v Horne* and in *Jones v Lipman* (see **3-27**), though public policy would prevent the puppeteer from enforcing the contract, see at [23]–[27].

[50] See [2011] 1 CLC 396 at [2], [6], [8].   [51] [2011] EWCA Civ 1042, aff'g [2011] 2 Lloyd's Rep 663.

[52] [2011] EWCA Civ 1042 at [12].

[53] [1998] 2 BCLC 485 (company repudiated charterparty and the director and controller of the company immediately removed the contents of the company's bank account to another entity with a view to putting those funds beyond the reach of any claim for wrongful repudiation by the ship-owner). Incidentally, it

later repudiates, the veil cannot be pierced so as to make the controller of the company retrospectively a party to the charterparty.[54] Most recently, there has been the trenchant dismissal by Arnold J of the approach taken in *Antonio Gramsci*. In *VTB Capital plc v Nutritek International Corp*,[55] there was a claim that the veil might be pierced to make the defendants parties to a contract. Arnold J said that this is the wrong approach and that piercing the corporate veil only gives rise to equitable remedies, such as orders for account or injunctions. The approach in *Gramsci*, he thought, was not so much a decision to pierce the corporate veil as a decision to ignore privity of contract.[56] The case law does not support such an approach, he said, rather equitable relief is ordered against the puppet company to stop the puppeteer evading his own contractual obligations (as in *Jones v Lipman*[57] and *Guilford Motor Co v Horne*[58]). In his view, a contractual claim against the puppeteer on the puppet's contract is unsustainable as a matter of law.[59] He therefore dismissed the claim. It is understood that this case is going on appeal which will offer the useful prospect of hearing the Court of Appeal's views on the matter with the *Linsen*[60] case giving a considerable clue as to the likely outcome.

Piercing the corporate veil—the mere façade test

3-21   The test applied by the courts is that it is appropriate to pierce the corporate veil only where special circumstances exist indicating that it is a mere façade concealing the true facts, a principle laid down by the House of Lords in *Woolfson v Strathclyde Regional Council*.[61]

3-22   This case concerned the amount of compensation payable on the compulsory acquisition of certain land by a local authority. The land was owned by W and by S Ltd (W held 20 of the 30 issued shares in S Ltd and his wife held the remaining 10 shares). The land was occupied by C Ltd which carried on its business from there (the shares in C Ltd were held 999 by W and 1 by his wife). W argued that he, C Ltd and S Ltd should all be treated as a single entity embodied by himself who should be regarded as the owner and occupier of the land for compensation purposes.

3-23   On appeal, the House of Lords confirmed the rejection of this argument by the lower courts. It is appropriate to pierce the corporate veil only where special circumstances exist indicating that the company is a mere façade concealing the true facts.[62] In this case, there were no grounds for treating the company structure as a mere façade so that W might claim to be treated as the owner and occupier of the land. The company which carried on business from these premises which were to be compulsorily acquired, C Ltd, had no control over the owners of the land who were S Ltd and W. W held only two-thirds of the shares in S Ltd while S Ltd had no interest in C Ltd. W could not be treated as the sole owner of C Ltd since it had not been found that the one share held by his wife was held by her as his nominee. Accordingly, their Lordships held that there was no basis consonant

---

would have been appropriate to have pierced the veil in *Yukong* to follow assets which had been transferred away in that case, but that relief was not sought.

[54] See [2011] EWCA Civ 1042 at [12].
[55] [2011] EWHC 3107.   [56] [2011] EWHC 3107 at [101].   [57] [1962] 1 All ER 442.
[58] [1933] Ch 935, CA.   [59] [2011] EWHC 3107 at [102].
[60] *Linsen International Ltd v Humpuss Transportasi Kimia* [2011] EWCA Civ 1042, aff'g [2011] 2 Lloyd's Rep 663.
[61] (1979) 38 P & CR 521, HL. See generally Rixon, 'Lifting the Veil between Holding and Subsidiary Companies' [1986] 102 LQR 415.   [62] (1979) 38 P & CR 521 at 526.

with principle on which the corporate veil could be pierced to the effect of holding W to have been the true owner of the business of C Ltd or of the assets of S Ltd.[63] As the occupier of the land and the owner of the business carried on there, any direct loss as a result of the compulsory purchase fell on C Ltd and not on W whose claim for compensation was dismissed.

3-24 The mere façade test has been endorsed in numerous cases subsequently including by the Court of Appeal in *Adams v Cape Industries plc*[64] and by Sir Andrew Morritt V-C in *Trustor AB v Smallbone*,[65] both significant cases which are discussed below, while the courts have also consistently rejected any broader jurisdiction allowing the veil to be pierced merely on the basis that it is necessary to do so in the interests of justice.[66]

3-25 As Munby J noted in *Ben Hashem v Ali Shayif*,[67] there is no particular magic in the word 'façade' which, he said, is used in the sense of a deceptive front.[68] The corporate structure is being misused by the person, or persons, who control it to evade obligations or liabilities to which they are otherwise subject.[69] Control and impropriety must be established,[70] remembering that it is not improper to organise one's business affairs, in the manner of Mr Salomon, to take advantage of incorporation and limited liability. If there are a number of wrongdoers with a common purpose in material control of the company, the veil may be lifted against one or all of them.[71] The nature of the wrongdoing, the impropriety, which would merit treating the company as a façade for these purposes was examined in detail by the Court of Appeal in *Adams v Cape Industries plc*.[72] As noted at **3-12**, this case concerned jurisdictional issues relating to the enforcement of a US judgment against an English parent company and central to that issue was whether the English company had been present in the US. Subsidiary companies of the English company had been active in the US and the issue was whether their presence and activities there sufficed to render the parent company also present in the US. Applying *Salomon*, the presence of the US subsidiaries did not automatically amount to the presence of the English parent company, of course, so one line of argument was that the court should pierce the corporate veil of the subsidiaries which, it was argued, were a mere façade concealing the true facts, namely that the English company was present in the US. Following an extensive review of the authorities, the Court of Appeal accepted that the essence of those cases where piercing does occur (i.e. where the structure is a façade) is that they involve

---

[63] (1979) 38 P & CR 521 at 526.   [64] [1990] BCLC 479 at 515.   [65] [2001] 2 BCLC 436 at [20], Ch D.
[66] *Adams v Cape Industries plc* [1990] BCLC 479 at 512–13; *Trustor AB v Smallbone* [2001] 2 BCLC 436 at 444–5. See also *Ord v Belhaven Pubs Ltd* [1998] 2 BCLC 447 at 457; *Yukong Line Ltd of Korea v Rendsburg Investments Corp of Liberia* [1998] 2 BCLC 485 at 497.
[67] [2009] 1 FLR 115. This case, in the Family Division of the High Court, concerned claims in divorce proceedings that the corporate veil should be pierced to allow a wife to claim properties owned by a company (in which her husband was the dominant figure and shareholder along with several of his children) as in effect his properties and available to meet the wife's claims to his assets. Munby J emphasised that the rules on piercing the corporate veil are the same in all Divisions of the High Court and it is not the case that the Family Division applies different rules to the Chancery Division, see at [96].
[68] The cases show the use of numerous similar phrases (device, mask, cloak, stratagem, creature, puppets, sham).
[69] A company can be a façade for the purposes of the disputed conduct even if it has legitimate business activities and is carrying on business in an ordinary way, see *Ben Hashem v Ali Shayif* [2009] 1 FLR 115 at [164]–[165], though admittedly in most instances where the veil is pierced, the company will have been specifically set up as a façade (see *Gilford, Jones, Gencor, Kensington*) and in most cases where the company was pre-existing and had a business life of its own, the courts have not pierced the veil, see *Adams v Cape, Ord v Belhaven, Ben Hashem*.   [70] See *Ben Hashem v Ali Shayif* [2009] 1 FLR 115 at [163], [193], [197]–[200].
[71] *Antonio Gramsci Shipping Corp v Stepanovs* [2011] 1 CLC 396 at [16].
[72] [1990] BCLC 479 and see **3-12** where the agency arguments in this case are discussed.

situations where a corporate structure has been used by a defendant to evade (1) limitations imposed on his conduct by law; (2) such rights of relief as third parties already possess against him.[73]

Company structure used to evade limitations imposed on conduct by law

3-26 The classic examples of cases where the veil is pierced because the corporate structure is being used to evade limitations imposed on the defendant's conduct by law are *Jones v Lipman*[74] and *Gilford Motor Co Ltd v Horne*.[75]

3-27 In *Jones v Lipman*[76] the defendant, in an attempt to evade an order for specific perform-ance, transferred a property to a company which he set up and of which he and a clerk of his solicitors were the only shareholders and directors. The court made an order for specific performance against the company and the defendant noting that the company was merely a mask used by the defendant to try to evade his obligations. In *Gilford Motor Co Ltd v Horne*[77] a director of a company was subject to a restraint of trade provision on leaving the company. Subsequently, he wished to carry on a competing business in breach of that contractual provision and he did so through a company set up with his wife and an employee as directors and shareholders. The court held that the company was formed as a device to mask the carrying on of business by the defendant in breach of his pre-existing legal duty and an injunction was granted against the company and the defendant.[78]

3-28 In *Re H*[79] restraining orders were obtained by Customs and Excise preventing various individuals and companies controlled by them from dealing with their realisable property. Customs and Excise considered that the parties had been engaged in excise fraud in a sum estimated to be in excess of £100m, again evading limitations on their conduct imposed by law. The defendants argued that the receiver appointed by Customs and Excise could not treat the assets of the companies as the realisable property of the individual shareholders. The Court of Appeal held that where the defendant uses the corporate structure as a device or façade to conceal his criminal activities, the court may lift the corporate veil and treat the assets of the company as the realisable property of the defendants. Stock held in the companies' warehouses and the companies' motor vehicles could therefore be treated as the property of the defendants subject to the control of the receiver.

3-29 As the Court of Appeal emphasised in *Adams v Cape Industries plc*,[80] the motive of the defendant is a significant element for the court to consider. In the cases discussed in **3–25**, the motive behind the use of the corporate structure was patently improper, being to evade limitations on conduct imposed by law.

---

[73] [1990] BCLC 479 at 519.   [74] [1962] 1 All ER 442.   [75] [1933] Ch 935, CA.

[76] [1962] 1 All ER 442. See also *Re Bugle Press Ltd* [1961] Ch 270 where a company was formed solely to facilitate the expropriation of minority shareholders in another company by use of CA 1985, s 429, now CA 2006, s 979, which allows an offeror who has acquired 90% of the shares to compulsorily acquire the remaining 10% in certain circumstances. It was held that the incorporation was an abuse of the statutory provisions.   [77] [1933] Ch 935, CA.

[78] Likewise, *Antonio Gramsci Shipping Corp v Stepanovs* [2011] 1 CLC 396, discussed at **3-19**, can be seen as a case where executives who were subject to pre-existing fiduciary obligations which prevented them from making secret profits used companies to disguise their alleged profit-making activities, i.e. in breach of pre-existing limitations on their conduct imposed by law.   [79] [1996] 2 BCLC 500, CA.

[80] [1990] BCLC 479 at 516, 518, CA.

Company structure used to evade rights of relief which third parties already possess

3-30 In some instances, the corporate structure is simply interposed as an attempt by a defendant to evade rights of relief which third parties already possess against him. Here the
structure is not used to evade performance of an obligation, but rather to evade the consequences of non-performance of an existing obligation. For example, in *Re a Company*[81]
a chain of companies was used by the defendant to put assets out of the reach of the
plaintiffs after proceedings against the defendant for deceit and breach of fiduciary duty
had been commenced. It was held that the veil would be pierced to enable the plaintiffs
to pursue the assets.[82] In *Trustor AB v Smallbone*,[83] almost £39m had gone missing from
the claimant company with £20m ending up in a company, I Ltd, which was essentially a
front for S, the former managing director of the claimant company. The claimant sought
summary judgment that S was jointly and severally liable with I Ltd on the basis of knowing receipt which required that the corporate veil be pierced to establish that receipt by I
Ltd was receipt by S. Applying the test laid down in *Woolfson*, the court found that I Ltd
was a device or façade used for the receipt of the claimant's money which had been misapplied by S in what the court described as inexcusable breaches of his duties as a director of
the claimant company.[84] S had no defence to the claim that he had received the £20m. In
Gencor ACP Ltd v Dalby[85] a director in breach of his fiduciary duty had profited personally by diverting to himself business opportunities which came to him as a director of the
company. The company sought to recover the proceeds which had been paid direct to an
offshore company wholly owned and controlled by the director who tried to argue that he
had not profited personally. Rimer J found that the offshore company had no staff or business and its only function was to receive these profits. In essence, the court said, it was no
more than the director's offshore bank account. Rimer J considered that such a company
was quite insufficient, in his words, to prevent equity identifying it with the director and
he ordered that the company and the director were each accountable for the profits.[86] In
Kensington International Ltd v Republic of Congo[87] the court pierced the corporate veil
with respect to a variety of companies used to disguise the sale of oil by the Republic of the
Congo. Sales were conducted through a series of companies which were set up to conceal
the identity of the Congo as seller and the fact that it was the recipient of the proceeds of
sale. These structures were adopted so as to avoid, so far as possible, attachment of the
oil or of the proceeds of sale by existing creditors of the Congo in circumstances where it

---

[81] [1985] BCLC 333, CA. Although the court reached the correct conclusion in this case, it did so on the
now discredited ground that the court had jurisdiction to pierce the veil in the interests of justice (at 338):
see *Trustor AB v Smallbone* [2001] 2 BCLC 436 at [21].

[82] See also *BCCI SA v BRS Kumar Bros Ltd* [1994] 1 BCLC 211 where a company shifted assets to another
company to avoid the reach of charges granted to creditors of the first company. Held: a receiver would be
appointed over the assets of the second company which was arguably nothing more than the first company
in a new guise. No doubt piercing would have been ordered on this basis in *Yukong Line Ltd of Korea v
Rendsburg Investments Corp of Liberia* [1998] 2 BCLC 485, had the parties sought it, which strangely they
did not, see at [502].   [83] [2001] 2 BCLC 436.

[84] [2001] 2 BCLC 436 at [23].   [85] [2000] 2 BCLC 734.   [86] [2000] 2 BCLC 734 at 744.

[87] [2006] 2 BCLC 296. In *Linsen International Ltd v Humpuss Transportasi Kimia* [2011] 2 Lloyd's Rep 663,
the court would have been willing to order the piercing of the veil where a subsidiary company transferred
all its assets (value about $60m) to another subsidiary in the group which was balance sheet insolvent at the
time and which appeared never to have paid for the assets, which transfers occurred after the first subsidiary had incurred significant liabilities by repudiating certain charterparties into which it had entered. On
the facts, an interlocutory application for continuation of a freezing order, the court did not actually order
a piercing since there were jurisdictional difficulties which meant it was pointless to pierce, a position confirmed by the Court of Appeal, see [2011] EWCA Civ 1042.

was known that the creditors were taking aggressive action with a view to enforcing the Congo's debts.[88]

Rights of relief which third parties may in future acquire

3-31 Having identified the basis on which it is appropriate to pierce the corporate veil, the Court of Appeal in *Adams v Cape Industries plc*[89] was emphatic that the veil should not be pierced where the corporate structure is used to evade such rights of relief as third parties may in the future acquire, in other words where the corporate structure is set up legitimately to manage risks.[90] Slade LJ noted:[91]

> '…we do not accept as a matter of law that the court is entitled to lift the corporate veil as against a defendant company which is the member of a corporate group merely because the corporate structure has been used so as to ensure that the legal liability (if any) in respect of particular future activities of the group (and correspondingly the risk of enforcement of that liability) will fall on another member of the group rather than the defendant company. Whether or not this is desirable, the right to use a corporate structure in this way is inherent in our corporate law.'

Counsel had argued that the veil should be pierced because the purpose of the group structure in *Adams* was that the English parent company could trade in the US through subsidiaries without running the risk of tortious liability with respect to its asbestos business. Slade LJ acknowledged that this might indeed be the purpose of the structure adopted, but he went on:[92]

> '…in our judgment, Cape [the English company] was in law entitled to organise the group's affairs in that manner and…to expect that the court would apply the principle in *Salomon v Salomon & Co Ltd* [1897] AC 22 in the ordinary way.'

3-32 Likewise, on this basis, the court declined to lift the veil in *Ord v Belhaven Pubs Ltd*.[93] The plaintiffs brought an action in 1991 against the defendants alleging that the defendants had misrepresented the turnover and profitability of a public house which the plaintiffs had leased from them. Subsequently, the plaintiffs sought leave to substitute the parent company for the original defendant (subsidiary) company since, following a restructuring of the group assets in 1992, the original defendant no longer had substantial assets. The Court of Appeal held that, while the court has jurisdiction to pierce the corporate veil where a company is a mere façade concealing the true facts, no evidence existed of any such façade here, just the ordinary trading of a group of companies in circumstances where they were entitled to expect the court to apply the *Salomon* principle in the ordinary way.[94] There was no impropriety alleged in the group restructuring, no transfer away of assets of the defendant company at an undervalue and no improper motive. The restructuring was a normal attempt to rationalise the group's operating structure in the light of recessionary market circumstances and had not been undertaken in order to evade any liability towards the plaintiffs. In the absence of any

---

[88] The claimant was a judgment creditor of the Republic of the Congo and in this case sought and obtained third party debt orders so as to attach sums due to the sham companies on the basis that, once the veil was pierced, it was evident that in reality the sums were due to the Congo.

[89] [1990] BCLC 479.

[90] As Flaux J commented in *Linsen International Ltd v Humpuss Transportasi Kimia* [2011] 2 Lloyd's Rep 663 at [86], in the absence of impropriety, the court cannot declare 'open sesame' on the assets of holding companies and direct and indirect subsidiaries within a group.

[91] [1990] BCLC 479 at 520.

[92] [1990] BCLC 479 at 520.   [93] [1998] 2 BCLC 447, CA.   [94] [1998] 2 BCLC 447 at 457–8.

impropriety, sham or concealment in the restructuring of the group, it would be wrong, the court said, to lift the corporate veil in order to make the shareholders of the company (i.e. the parent company) liable instead of the (subsidiary) company.

3-33 The position is the same with respect to individuals trading through a company. A modern day Mr Salomon and family are entitled to expect the courts to apply *Salomon* in the absence of any façade.[95] In *MacDonald v Costello*[96] a couple set up a company to undertake a building contract with a construction company. At every stage of the process, it was clear that the building project was being undertaken by the company, the company hired the builders, paid the invoices etc, though of course the company was managed and run by the couple who were the only shareholders and directors. The company became insolvent and failed to pay the builders. The court accepted that the contract was between the builders and the company, but nevertheless the court made an order for restitution against the couple, on the basis that they had been unfairly enriched by being in receipt of the benefit of the building work. On appeal, the Court of Appeal quashed the order, saying it undermined the contractual arrangements entered into between the builders and the company which was the mechanism which the parties had used to allocate the risk involved in the project. Most pertinently, the Court of Appeal noted that the obligation to pay the builders was contractually confined to the company and if a claim was permitted directly against the couple (who were the shareholders and directors, it will be recalled), 'it would shatter that contractual containment' and alter the usual consequences of the company's insolvency which was one of the risks assumed by the builders in contracting with a company.[97] A direct claim against the couple would improve the builders' position over the company's other unsecured creditors.[98] Had the builders wanted to limit their risk, they could have sought personal guarantees from the couple which they had not done. In effect, the court was not prepared to let a restitution order undermine the corporate and contractual structure which the parties had transparently adopted and which the claimants had appreciated throughout.

3-34 Another interesting case is *Chandler v Cape plc*[99] which is part of the ongoing litigation involving the Cape group here and in other countries concerning liabilities to employees exposed to asbestos. In the *Chandler* case, the court concluded that a parent company and a (now dissolved) subsidiary (which had employed an injured employee) were jointly and severally liable to pay damages for breach of the duty of care which they each owed to that employee. The High Court accepted that the criteria for imposition of a duty of care between the parent company and the employee were met (forseeability, proximity and just and fair to impose a duty). On appeal, the Court of Appeal confirmed that while a parent company owes no duty of care to the employees of a subsidiary company by reason only of being the parent company, a parent company may be found to have assumed a duty of care towards the subsidiary's employees, not in all respects but, as here, a duty to advise or ensure that employees in a subsidiary company have a safe system of work. On the facts, (i) the companies were in the same line of business, (ii) the parent company's long experience in the industry gave it superior knowledge of health and safety issues; (iii) the subsidiary's system of work was unsafe as the parent company knew or ought to have known (it had previously operated from the same premises), and (iv) the parent company knew or ought to have foreseen that the subsidiary or its employees would rely on the parent company

---

[95] Hence in *Ben Hashem v Ali Shayif* [2009] 1 FLR 115 at [199], see the facts at n 67, the husband was entitled, in the absence of any impropriety, to expect that the court would respect the corporate structure which he had set up to hold various property assets.

[96] [2011] 3 WLR 1341.   [97] [2011] 3 WLR 1341 at [21].   [98] [2011] 3 WLR 1341 at [21].

[99] [2012] EWCA Civ 525, aff'g [2011] EWHC 951.

using its superior knowledge for the employees' protection. It sufficed on (iv) that there was evidence that the parent company was in the practice of intervening in the trading operations of the subsidiary and it was not necessary to show that parent company was in the practice of intervening on the health and safety policies of the subsidiary. The parent company was liable then, not as a consequence of piercing the veil, not on the basis of being an economic unit with its subsidiary, but on the basis that two separate entities each undertook obligations to the employee. The decision reinforces *Salomon* while solving for the employee the adverse consequences of the separate legal status of his (dissolved) employer distinct from its (parent company) shareholder. If the outcome reduces the value to the parent company of the separate legal status of the employing subsidiary company, it has only itself to blame since it was its own failure to observe that separate status, intervening in the trading operations of the subsidiary which gave rise to the duty of care.

C The corporate group—separate entities or single unit

Separate legal entities

3-35 As noted, the decision in *Salomon v Salomon & Co Ltd*[100] legitimated the one-man company and from that evolved the modern phenomenon of the corporate group with subsidiary companies owned by corporate shareholders, each also a separate legal entity from its shareholders.[101] Applying *Salomon*, the fact that the shares in a subsidiary are wholly within the control of one shareholder, the parent company, does not make the subsidiary company a façade nor, as discussed at **3-31**, is a group structure a façade where it is set up with a view to minimising liabilities which might arise in the future.[102]

3-36 The English courts have been robust then in their application of the *Salomon* principle in the group context. As the Court of Appeal commented in *Adams v Cape Industries plc*:[103]

'...save in cases which turn on the wording of particular statutes or contracts, the court is not free to disregard the principle of *Salomon v Salomon & Co Ltd* merely because it considers that justice so requires. Our law, for better or worse, recognises the creation of subsidiary companies, which though in one sense the creatures of their parent companies, will nevertheless under the general law fall to be treated as separate legal entities with all the rights and liabilities which would normally attach to separate legal entities...'

3-37 The clear position in this jurisdiction is that companies in a group of companies are separate legal entities and are not the agents of their controlling shareholder.

3-38 It is sometimes suggested that this adherence to a strict *Salomon* approach, affording separate legal status to each entity, is inappropriate in the modern business world where

---

[100] [1897] AC 22, HL.

[101] As the Reflection Group Report noted, the international group of companies has become *the* prevailing form of European large-sized enterprises, based on the optimal combination of central control exercised by the parent company and local autonomy granted to subsidiaries, a feature which regulation should not ignore: see *Report of the Reflection Group on the Future of EU Company Law* (April 2011) (this group of company law experts was set up by the EU Commission in December 2010 to inform the debate for a subsequent EU Commission conference on the future direction of EU Company Law).

[102] See *Adams v Cape Industries plc* [1990] BCLC 479 at 520.

[103] [1990] BCLC 479 at 513. See too Flaux J in *Linsen International Ltd v Humpuss Transportasi Kimia* [2011] 2 Lloyd's Rep 663 at [38]–[39], the closeness of companies and commonality of directors within a group are not enough to justify the disregarding of the corporate structure.

much commercial activity is carried on in corporate groups in a way which could not have been envisaged in 1897. Various alternative approaches have been proposed from time to time such as, for example, that the courts should allow the corporate veil to be pierced more freely in the group context. More fundamentally, it is argued that the law should develop a mechanism whereby obligations and responsibilities could attach to the group and not to individual companies. In this way, the law would reflect the economic reality which is that these companies trade as a group, raise capital as a group and are considered by those dealing with them to be a group.

3-39   While some support for the development of a group enterprise law was offered by Lord Denning MR in *DHN Food Distributors Ltd v Tower Hamlets LBC*,[104] it was robustly rejected by the House of Lords in *Woolfson v Strathclyde Regional Council*[105] which doubted whether the Court of Appeal had applied the correct principle in *DHN*. Generally, the English courts have shown a strong determination not to embark on any such development. In *Adams v Cape Industries plc*[106] Slade LJ noted:

> 'There is no general principle that all companies in a group of companies are to be regarded as one. On the contrary, the fundamental principle is that "each company in a group of companies (a relatively modern concept) is a separate legal entity possessed of separate legal rights and liabilities": see *The Albazero* [1975] 3 All ER 21 at 28, [1977] AC 774 at 807 per Roskill LJ.'

3-40   Slade LJ went on:[107]

> 'We agree . . . that the observations of Robert Goff LJ in *Bank of Tokyo Ltd v Karoon* [1986] 3 All ER 468 at 485, [1987] AC 45 at 64 are apposite:
>
> > "Counsel suggested beguilingly that it would be technical for us to distinguish between parent and subsidiary company in this context; economically, he said, they were one. But we are concerned not with economics but with law. The distinction between the two is, in law, fundamental and cannot here be bridged." '

3-41   Pressed to regard a group of companies as a separate economic unit in *Re Polly Peck International plc (No 3)*,[108] Robert Walker J concluded that he could not accede to that submission for it would create a new exception to the *Salomon* principle unrecognised by the Court of Appeal in *Adams v Cape Industries plc*,[109] something which was not open to the court.[110] A further rebuttal of the idea that a group of companies might be regarded as a single unit can be found in *Ord v Belhaven Pubs Ltd*,[111] discussed at **3-32**. It will be recalled that the case involved an attempt by the plaintiffs to substitute the original defendant subsidiary company with either its parent company or another wholly-owned subsidiary in the group as, following a restructuring of the group, the original defendant no longer had substantial assets. The Court of Appeal noted that the trial judge (who had permitted the substitution of the defendants) appeared to have viewed the whole group as an economic entity and therefore thought substitution was appropriate. Hobhouse LJ emphatically rejected this approach, noting:[112]

> 'The approach of the judge in the present case was simply to look at the economic unit, to disregard the distinction between the legal entities which were involved and to say: since the company cannot pay, the shareholders who are the people financially interested should be made to pay instead. That of course is radically at odds with the whole concept

---

[104] [1976] 3 All ER 462 at 467, CA. The other judges decided the case on a narrower basis.
[105] (1979) 38 P & CR 521.   [106] [1990] BCLC 479 at 508.   [107] [1990] BCLC 479 at 514.
[108] [1996] 1 BCLC 428.   [109] [1990] BCLC 479.
[110] [1996] 1 BCLC 428 at 444; and see Flaux J in *Linsen International Ltd v Humpuss Transportasi Kimia* [2011] 2 Lloyd's Rep 663 at [19], [126], the single economic unit argument forms no part of English law.
[111] [1998] 2 BCLC 447, CA.   [112] [1998] 2 BCLC 447 at 457.

of corporate personality and limited liability and the decision of the House of Lords in *Salomon v Salomon & Co Ltd* [1897] AC 22.'

3-42　The true position, Hobhouse LJ said, is that companies are entitled to organise their affairs in group structures and to expect the courts to apply the principles of *Salomon v Salomon & Co Ltd* in the ordinary way.[113]

3-43　While the legal position in this jurisdiction is therefore well established and clearly not open to change in the courts, the regulation of groups of companies continues to raise issues of concern[114] as to the position of the creditors of a subsidiary company (especially tort creditors), the duties of directors of a subsidiary, and the protection of minority interests in a subsidiary, each of which is considered briefly below.

Creditor issues

3-44　The primary legal reason for the use of a group structure is to further limit liabilities[115] since ultimately, as Templeman J memorably put it in *Re Southard Ltd*,[116] a parent company can discard the runt of the litter. He noted:[117]

> 'A parent company may spawn a number of subsidiary companies, all controlled directly or indirectly by the shareholders of the parent company. If one of the subsidiary companies, to change the metaphor, turns out to be the runt of the litter and declines into insolvency to the dismay of the creditors, the parent company and other subsidiary companies may prosper to the joy of the shareholders without any liability for the debts of the insolvent subsidiary.'

3-45　Of course, as a matter of good business practice, many parent companies will not insist on their strict legal right to walk away from the liabilities of their subsidiaries, but will meet a subsidiary's obligations, particularly if the subsidiary's creditors are also creditors and suppliers of the parent company and other companies in the group. A concern for its business reputation may also make a parent company meet a liability which legally it could otherwise disown. Once the scale of liabilities is significant, however, a parent company is unlikely voluntarily to accept the liabilities of the subsidiary since its own shareholders and creditors will be endangered by such action.

3-46　It is important therefore that creditors of a group company identify the precise subsidiary with which they are dealing and appreciate that *Salomon* will prevent their having a claim against assets elsewhere in the group. It may be the case that the subsidiary has a share capital of £100 and no assets of its own. Of course, this could equally be the position where a creditor deals with a company with individual rather than corporate shareholders, so the position is not peculiar to corporate groups.

3-47　If the creditors are to protect their position and extend their reach to the assets of the parent company and/or other companies in the group, they must use contractual devices to do so, recognising that the superior negotiating power of financial institutions may mean that the ordinary contract creditor has little bargaining power. Creditors such as banks, on

---

[113] [1998] 2 BCLC 447 at 458.

[114] See generally, Dine, *The Governance of Corporate Groups* (2000); Blumberg, *The Multinational Challenge to Corporation Law* (1993). Much of the literature focuses on the problem of group insolvency, see Mevorach, *Insolvency within Multinational Enterprise Groups* (2009).

[115] There are numerous business reasons why businesses want to use a group structure, such as diversification, geographical spread and administrative convenience.

[116] [1979] 3 All ER 556.　　　[117] [1979] 3 All ER 556 at 565.

the other hand, will be in a position to ensure that they have cross-guarantees and security from all the companies in the group. Typically, a bank will require each subsidiary company to provide security and guarantees that it will meet its own liabilities to the bank and the liabilities of any other company in the group to the bank. These contractual devices ensure that the bank is able to ignore the separate legal entities and, in effect, to lend to the group and to recover from the group. The consequence for the creditors of an individual subsidiary company may be that difficulties elsewhere in the group will force the bank to call in the cross-guarantees resulting in all probability in the collapse of the entire group.[118]

3-48 For creditors without the bargaining power to secure cross-guarantees, the most that they may be able to extract is a letter of comfort from the parent company. An illustration can be found in *Kleinwort Benson v Malaysia Mining Corp*.[119] Here a bank intended to lend several million pounds to a subsidiary company and sought some protection against the risk of default by the subsidiary from the parent company. The most the parent company was willing to give was a letter of comfort which stated: 'it is our policy to ensure that the business of the subsidiary is at all times in a position to meet its liabilities to you'. When the subsidiary collapsed, the parent company denied any liability to the creditor under the letter of comfort. The Court of Appeal agreed that this letter had no contractual effect. The court concluded that the concept of a comfort letter to which the parties had resort when the parent company refused to accept liability was known by both sides to amount to the parent assuming, not a legal liability to ensure repayment of the liabilities of the subsidiary, but a moral responsibility only.

3-49 Nevertheless, in the absence of a guarantee, creditors still seek letters of comfort in the hope that the parent company will, for business reasons, decide to honour that moral responsibility. Of course, a letter of comfort given dishonestly to induce another party to provide funding would be actionable, as would a letter of comfort which on closer analysis proves to be a binding contractual obligation, so care must be exercised in the giving and drafting of such letters.

3-50 It is also possible that, on insolvency, a liquidator may be able to establish that the parent company has exercised such control over the subsidiary as to constitute itself a shadow director of the subsidiary. This would open up the possibility of potential civil liability by the parent company as a shadow director for matters such as wrongful trading by the subsidiary company.[120] In practice, such potential liability is a remote prospect. Shadow directors are discussed at **6-17**; wrongful trading is considered at **25-18**.

3-51 As for tort creditors of a subsidiary company, it is often argued that the application of the *Salomon* principle is particularly unfair in their case since they are involuntary creditors.[121] It is clear from *Adams v Cape Industries plc*,[122] however, that the English courts see no need to regard such creditors as deserving of any particular flexibility in terms of applying the *Salomon* principle. The claimants in that case were tort creditors. They were employees of the US subsidiaries who had suffered asbestos-related illness as a result of their employment but, as discussed at **3-36**, *Adams* is a strong reaffirmation by the Court of Appeal of the *Salomon* principle. Far from showing a willingness to pierce the veil because the claimants

---

[118] For an example of these arrangements, see *Facia Footwear Ltd v Hinchcliffe* [1998] 1 BCLC 218.
[119] [1989] 1 All ER 785; a subordination agreement is another possibility for creditors to consider, see **24-76**.   [120] See *Re Hydrodam Ltd* [1994] 2 BCLC 180.
[121] See Muchlinski, 'Holding Multinationals to account: Recent Developments in English Litigation and the Company Law Review' (2002) 23 Company Lawyer 168.   [122] [1990] BCLC 479, CA.

were tort creditors, the Court of Appeal emphasised that the use of a group structure in this way to insulate the rest of the group from future liabilities of a particular subsidiary is inherent in English company law. Equally, we saw in *Chandler v Cape plc*,[123] discussed at **3-34**, that the parent company, as a separate legal entity, may owe a duty of care directly to an employee so that the parent company, in that case, was not insulated from liabilities to employees employed by a subsidiary.

Directors' duties

3-52 As far as the duties of a director are concerned, where the company is one of a group of companies, the directors must continue to act to promote the success of that company as a separate legal entity with its own separate creditors and not look solely to the overall interests of the group.[124] The directors must have regard to the interests of the company, but as Pennycuick J explained in *Charterbridge Corpn v Lloyds Bank*,[125] the absence of evidence of actual separate consideration of the interests of the company is not necessarily indicative of bad faith on their part, rather the test is whether an intelligent and honest man in the position of a director of the company concerned could, in the whole of the existing circumstances, have reasonably believed that the transaction was for the benefit of the company. Of course, at a practical level, the two issues are likely to be quite intertwined since what promotes the success of the group may be relevant to promoting the success of the company.[126]

3-53 This approach may mean that it is appropriate for a solvent subsidiary to provide financial support for the rest of a group, though the group is in financial difficulty, when the continued prosperity and the very existence of the subsidiary may depend on the group remaining in business, as is commonly the case. The problem arises because, as noted at **3-47**, modern banking arrangements typically require each subsidiary to guarantee the indebtedness of all the other companies in the group with the result that the insolvency of one company in the group can trigger the collapse of the remaining companies as well. These arrangements commonly are in the interests of the subsidiary company, as much as the interests of the group, because the subsidiary gets access to a level of borrowing and on more favourable terms than would otherwise be possible on its own account.

3-54 The difficulty in separating group interests and the company's interests is illustrated by *Facia Footwear Ltd v Hinchcliffe*[127] where a cash-rich subsidiary had entered into cross-guarantees whereby the subsidiary guaranteed the indebtedness of the group.[128] At issue were million pound payments made to other group companies by the directors of the subsidiary two months prior to the subsidiary going into administration. The administrators sought summary judgment against the directors on the grounds that making these payments in disregard of the creditors' interests (i.e. the creditors of the subsidiary

---

[123] [2012] EWCA Civ 525, aff'g [2011] EWHC 951.

[124] See *Re Polly Peck International plc (No 3)* [1996] 1 BCLC 428 at 440; *Re Capitol Films Ltd, Rubin v Cobalt Pictures Ltd* [2011] 2 BCLC 359 at [50].

[125] [1969] 2 All ER 1185 at 1194; and see *Colin Gwyer & Associates v London Wharf (Limehouse) Ltd* [2003] 2 BCLC 153 at [73].

[126] In *Nicholas v Soundcraft Electronics Ltd* [1993] BCLC 360, for example, the directors of a subsidiary company were not in breach of their duties to the company when they failed to take action to recover debts owed to it by the parent company. The parent company was the sole distributor of the subsidiary's products and was in serious financial trouble and it was in the interests of the subsidiary company that the parent should not go into liquidation.   [127] [1998] 1 BCLC 218.

[128] No challenge was made to the propriety of the decision as to the subsidiary's participation in the security arrangements: see [1998] 1 BCLC 218 at 224.

company) at that time was a breach of the directors' duties to the subsidiary company (see now CA 2006, s 172(3), discussed at **9-41**).

3-55 The application for summary judgment was refused.[129] The directors in their defence had maintained that the payments were in the normal course of implementation of group treasury arrangements and there was no suggestion that the payments were for private purposes or in breach of any statutory obligation or were otherwise than for the trading purposes of the recipient companies. Most importantly, if the group of companies collapsed, the subsidiary would collapse also under the weight of the cross-guarantees. Moreover, the court found that the directors were intent on keeping the group afloat as they believed a refinancing scheme was a serious possibility.

3-56 Sir Richard Scott acknowledged the difficulties facing the directors of the subsidiary. It was clear, he said, that in continuing trading in those final months, the directors were taking a risk; clear too that, given the parlous financial state of the group, the directors had to have regard to the interests of creditors. But, he noted, the creditors of the group, and of the subsidiary in particular, would clearly have been best served by a refinancing that could support a continuation of profitable trading. The cessation of trading followed by the disposal of the assets of the companies on a forced sale basis would lead, it was always realised, to heavy losses for the creditors. The creditors' only chance of being paid in full lay in a continuation of trading. In his opinion, it was, therefore, not in the least obvious that in continuing to trade in those final two months, the directors were ignoring the interests of the creditors of the subsidiary.[130]

3-57 The courts take a much harder line in situations where the subsidiary company is insolvent at the time of the transaction in issue, where there is less scope for consideration of the interests of the subsidiary and the group and a distinct need and legal requirement (see **9-41**) to look to the interests of the creditors of the particular company. A failure to respect the separate legal identity of a subsidiary in an insolvent situation may merit, subsequently, a finding of unfitness and disqualification as a director. For example, in *Re Genosyis Technology Management Ltd, Wallach v Secretary of State for Trade and Industry*[131] the directors of a subsidiary company entered into a settlement agreement with a defaulting creditor which involved the creditor making a significant payment to the parent company rather than to the subsidiary. The subsidiary had stood to gain €1.25m from earlier drafts of the settlement but, under the version actually signed, payment was direct to the parent company which undertook to make payments to the subsidiary amounting to £166,000. In disqualification proceedings against the two directors of the subsidiary, the court noted that the company was insolvent at the time of the agreement, therefore the interests of the creditors intruded and the directors owed a fiduciary duty to act in their interests. Instead the court found there was no evidence that the directors, who were also directors of the parent company, at any time considered the separate interests of the subsidiary and of its creditors. The directors were culpable in not doing so and were disqualified for five years. In *Re Mea Corporation Ltd, Secretary of State for Trade and Industry v Aviss*,[132] directors of three related companies were disqualified for periods ranging from seven to 11 years. At a time when each of the companies was insolvent and under pressure from creditors, the directors allowed such cash as was available to be paid out to other related companies in disregard of the interests of the creditors of the individual companies. In *Secretary of State for Business,*

---

[129] This outcome does not mean that the court would not have found against the directors in a full hearing, but simply that the case against them was not so convincing that the court would grant a summary judgment. In the event, the administrators did not pursue the case.

[130] [1998] 1 BCLC 218 at 228.   [131] [2007] 1 BCLC 208.   [132] [2007] 1 BCLC 618 at 635, 643.

Innovation and Skills v Doffman[133] the court was particularly critical of two directors who disregarded the separate interests of individual companies within a group of companies in which they were the sole shareholders and transferred assets between the companies without regard to the interests or often the solvency of the transferor. Finding the directors to be unfit and disqualifying them, the court noted that those who take advantage of the corporate entity's separate legal personality also have to recognise the concomitant duties which arise,[134] citing with approval Lewison J's comments in *Secretary of State for Trade and Industry v Goldberg*[135] that 'respect for the separate legal personality of each company, and recognition of a director's duty to exercise his powers in the best interests of the particular company of which he is a director are essential attributes of fitness to be concerned in the management of a company'.

Minority shareholders

3-58 As for the position of minority shareholders in the case of a subsidiary other than a wholly-owned subsidiary, the difficulties that they can encounter can be illustrated by *Scottish Co-operative Wholesale Society Ltd v Meyer.*[136] In this case the majority shareholder had no longer any need for the subsidiary so ran down its business to the point where it had no business. The minority shareholders petitioned for relief under CA 1948, s 210 (the precursor to CA 2006, s 994, the unfairly prejudicial remedy, discussed in detail in Chapter 17). The House of Lords concluded that the affairs of the subsidiary had been conducted by the controlling shareholder in an oppressive manner and ordered the majority to buy out the minority shareholders on a valuation basis which presupposed that no oppressive conduct had occurred. The equivalent, but more generous, jurisdiction for modern shareholders is CA 2006, s 994 which allows for petitions by a member on the basis that the company's affairs are being conducted in an unfairly prejudicial manner. The Court of Appeal in *Re Citybranch Group Ltd, Gross v Rackind*[137] accepted that, in an appropriate case, the conduct of a holding company towards a subsidiary company may constitute the conduct of the affairs of the subsidiary and can be the subject of a complaint by a shareholder in the subsidiary and, vice versa, a shareholder in a holding company may petition that the conduct of the subsidiary can be regarded as part of the conduct of the affairs of the holding company, see further at **17-25**.

Concluding points

3-59 It is clear from the authorities that there will be no significant judicial development of the law away from the *Salomon* principle and only legislative development can alter the application of that principle in the context of groups of companies. It might have been thought that this area would have been ripe for consideration by the Company Law Review (CLR) but in fact there was a reluctance to engage with this issue. Pointing out that contract creditors can protect themselves by contract terms and pricing mechanisms from the risks of trading with an insolvent subsidiary,[138] the CLR commented that it saw no merit in imposing a more integrated regime on groups which would take away flexibility and

---

[134] [2011] 2 BCLC 541.at [251].   [135] [2004] 1 BCLC 597 at [29].   [136] [1959] AC 324, HL.
[137] [2004] 4 All ER 735 at 743–4, at least where the subsidiaries are wholly owned and have boards substantially similar to the parent company, see also *Scottish Co-operative Wholesale Society Ltd v Meyer* [1958] 3 All ER 66.
[138] See Company Law Review, *Modern Company Law for a Competitive Economy, Completing the Structure* (2000) (hereinafter *Completing the Structure*), para 10.58. For a more comprehensive review, see the Report by the Australian Companies & Securities Advisory Committee, *Corporate Groups* (May 2000) which contains much of relevance to this jurisdiction.

strike at the limited liability basis of company law.[139] Furthermore, there was no evidence before it of abuse of corporate status by parent companies to avoid tort liabilities.[140] The CLR did put forward a very modest proposal for an elective regime allowing parent companies to avoid some disclosure requirements in return for accepting liability for a subsidiary's acts,[141] but the proposal was roundly criticised[142] and rejected by the Government before being dropped from the CLR's Final Report.[143]

3-60   At one time, the European Commission had ambitions for a Directive on Groups,[144] but discussions never progressed very far and in 2002 the Commission accepted the recommendation of the High Level Group of Experts on Company Law that any plans in that direction should be abandoned.[145] There has been an emphasis instead on the need for greater transparency from groups,[146] especially when they include listed companies, so ensuring that creditors are well informed as to the risks they run in contracting with such structures. There are requirements for group accounts (see **16-23**), the notes of which must give information about subsidiary companies and identify the parent and the ultimate parent company, and the Transparency and Takeover Directives respectively require disclosure of controlling shareholdings to the markets[147] and in the company's annual report.[148] The issue was revisited in the Reflection Group Report on the Future of EU Company Law which invited the EU Commission to consider whether to adopt a Recommendation recognising the interests of the group which would both allow the board of the parent company to manage the group in the interests of the group and allow the board of a subsidiary to rely lawfully on the interests of the group in reaching their decisions.[149] The Report notes that further consideration would need to be given as to how to distinguish between decisions taken when a subsidiary is solvent and when it is close to insolvency, the latter would require a modification of the principle to ensure that the interests of the creditors of the subsidiary are protected. Other issues which would require further consideration would be whether the rule would apply to all groups, or just groups with a cross-border element, and whether it would apply only to wholly-owned subsidiaries. The arguments in favour of this approach primarily rest on the fact, as noted at **3-52**, that to a considerable extent this is the position in practice in any event and a change to formal recognition of that position would bring legal clarity and certainty to current practice (especially for the directors of subsidiary

---

[139] See *Completing the Structure* (2000), para 10.20.

[140] See *Completing the Structure* (2000), paras 10.58–10.59.

[141] See *Completing the Structure* (2000), paras 10.19–10.57.

[142] For a scathing commentary, see Boyle (2002) 23 Co Law 35.

[143] Company Law Review, *Final Report*, vol 1 (2001), para 8.26.

[144] There had been some discussions in the 1970s and 1980s with respect to draft proposals for a Ninth Company Law Directive on Groups based on complex German provisions, but no progress was made, see Edwards, *EC Company Law* (1999), pp 390–1.

[145] See the Report of the High Level Group of Company Law Experts entitled *A Modern Regulatory Framework for Company Law in Europe*, 4 November 2002, Brussels, Ch V of which is devoted to Groups.

[146] See Communication from the Commission to the Council and the European Parliament, *Modernising Company Law and Enhancing Corporate Governance in the European Union—A Plan to Move Forward*, Brussels, 21.5.2003, COM (2003) 284.

[147] See the FSA Handbook, *Disclosure and Transparency Rules* (DTR), rule 5.

[148] While there are a lot of disclosure requirements which provide information on group structures, the information is scattered through a variety of documents and it remains difficult for investors and others to have a clear picture of the main features of a company's group structure. The Reflection Group Report, n 101, pp 68–75, suggests that it might be worth considering whether investors in listed companies would benefit from easily accessible information on the group structure set out in the company's corporate governance statement.

[149] See *Report of the Reflection Group on the Future of EU Company Law* (April 2011), n 101, Ch 4 on Groups of Companies.

companies) and reduce the costs of running a group. On the other hand, as the Report acknowledges, there is no strong evidence that the introduction of such a rule is needed and groups seems to function perfectly well under the current frameworks in each individual Member State. As discussed above, the UK position is not unlike that proposed by the Report; the courts appreciate that decisions by directors in a subsidiary are often taken in the group interest because the subsidiary's prospects depend on the prospects of the group and so can be justified in that way. Equally, the courts are already insistent on respect for the separate legal entities when financial difficulties loom, whether of the subsidiary or of the group, though the two are usually inextricably linked. It remains to be seen whether the EU Commission will choose to pursue this recommendation. Domestically, more modest proposals are under consideration by the Department for Business, Innovation and Skills (BIS) which is consulting on removing the audit requirement for subsidiary companies which meet certain conditions,[150] essentially that the subsidiary is not a quoted company, not involved in the financial services or insurance sector (or certain special register companies, an irrelevant category for our purposes) and provided the parent company gives a guarantee of commitments entered into by the subsidiary undertaking. The intention is that the guarantee will be irrevocable and will be in respect of the debts of the subsidiary in respect of the financial year in question.[151]

D Corporate acts and liabilities

3-61 As an artificial legal entity, of course, a company can only act through human agents and it is through their acts that a company can enter into and enforce contracts and can commit and be the victim of torts and criminal offences. On occasion, a company may attempt to disavow acts of an individual as being just that, acts of the individual, and not acts of the company for which the company should be liable. Problems are limited in respect of contract and tort where agency and statute (in the case of contracts) and vicarious liability (in the case of torts) provide the answers to questions of corporate liability. In the civil context, the rules of agency and vicarious liability suffice, for the most part, to establish liability and no further rules of attribution are required. A company is liable for the wrongful acts of an agent or employee acting within the scope of his authority or in the course of his employment,[152] as is the case with any principal or employer. Sometimes additional rules of attribution are needed in the civil context where intention or knowledge is an ingredient of the cause of action or defence, for example, if a company is to be liable for 'knowing receipt'[153] or knowingly being a party to fraudulent trading.[154] A question may arise as to whether the fraud of a controlling beneficial owner of a company can be attributed to the company so that any claim by

[150] See BIS, *Consultation on Audit Exemptions and Change of Accounting Framework,* October 2011, paras 38–70.

[151] See BIS, n 150, para 60. The proposal is to implement an exemption which exists in the 4th Company Law Directive (one of the Accounts Directives) and which the UK had not previously considered it would take advantage of, but which it is considering now because of a Government commitment to deregulation and reducing the costs for business see para 24.

[152] The term 'ordinary course of employment' has an extended scope for these purposes to include acts so closely connected with the acts that the employee was authorised to do that for the purpose of liability they can fairly and properly be said to be done by the employee while acting in the ordinary course of his employment: *Lister v Hesley Hall Ltd* [2001] 2 All ER 769, HL; *Dubai Aluminium Co Ltd v Salaam* [2003] 1 BCLC 32, HL.   [153] See *El Ajou v Dollar Land Holdings plc* [1994] 1 BCLC 464.

[154] See Re BCCI *(No 15); Morris v Bank of India* [2005] 2 BCLC 328.

the company based on that wrongdoing can be met with the defence of *ex turpi causa non oritur actio* (a defence which precludes claims based on illegality)[155] or whether the acts of a dominant manager and shareholder can be attributed to a company so as to prevent the company relying on an insurance policy which excludes liability for deliberate acts of the company,[156] or whether perjured evidence be attributed to a company so that a judgment procured by such evidence can be set aside.[157] The question of corporate responsibility is more complex in criminal matters where vicarious liability plays only a limited role and generally *mens rea* must be established ('knowingly', 'recklessly', 'intentionally', etc). Then it will be necessary to rely on rules of attribution to determine whether the mental state of an individual or individuals should be attributed to the company. As the need for specific rules of attribution is greatest in the context of criminal liability, the discussion of those rules of attribution is set out at **3-91** et seq dealing with criminal liability, but it should be borne in mind, as noted, that those rules may also be needed in a civil context. Finally it should be noted that piercing the veil and attribution are two different processes. Piercing the veil allows a claimant to set aside a façade, a deceptive front, to enforce a pre-existing obligation or to claim relief against those hiding behind that façade. Attribution involves deciding whether the acts of an individual or individuals should be attributed to the company such that they are the acts of the company.

Corporate liability in contract

3-62 Parties wishing to enforce contractual obligations entered into by companies must ensure that:

(1) the commitments made are within the capacity of the company and the authority of the executing officer or employee as agent, although much statutory protection is provided to ensure that this is the case; and

(2) any due formalities of execution have been observed (see CA 2006, ss 44 and 46). A company may enter into a contract in writing under its seal (if it has one)[158] or, more commonly, a contract may be made on behalf of the company by a person (such as a director or manager) acting under its authority, express or implied (s 43).

3-63 Issues of capacity are of ever-decreasing significance (see discussion at **4-12**) so the essential contractual issues revolve around the authority of the contracting agent and whether it suffices to bind the company. Those issues of authority involve the application of the rules of agency as to the actual or apparent authority of the agent acting for the company. These agency rules are bolstered by statutory provisions (CA 2006, ss 39 and 40) designed to minimise the risk to third parties of any lack of authority. A further complication may be that the agent has authority to enter into the transaction but is acting for an improper purpose. All of these matters are discussed in Chapter 8. A key point to note is that contractual liabilities attach to the company as the contracting party and not to the agent

---

[155] See *Stone & Rolls Ltd v Moore Stephens* [2009] 2 BCLC 563.

[156] See *KR v Royal & Sun Alliance plc* [2007] BCC 522 (company could not rely on an insurance policy which excluded liability for deliberate acts of the company; the acts in question were the acts of the company's controlling shareholder and managing director who was, the court said, the company's directing mind and will; his acts were to be attributed to it with the result that the company was unable to claim on the policy).   [157] See *Odyssey Re (London) Ltd v OIC Run-off Ltd* [2001] 1 Lloyd's Rep IR 1.

[158] Companies are not required to have a company seal and documents executed by signature in accordance with CA 2006, s 44 have the same effect as if executed under seal.

who negotiates on behalf of the company, though exceptionally an agent may be sued for breach of warranty of authority.

Corporate liability in tort

3-64 A company is entitled to sue in respect of torts committed against it and it can be sued for a tort committed by it. As the company is an artificial legal entity, all torts of a company (even torts of omission) are committed through human agents. As noted, a company is vicariously liable for the acts of an agent or employee acting within the scope of his authority or in the course of his employment.[159] The agent or employee is liable personally and the company vicariously and they are joint tortfeasors (each joint tortfeasor being liable for the entire loss caused). The position was explained in *Lloyd v Grace, Smith & Co*[160] as follows:

> '...the general rule [is] that the principal is liable to third persons in a civil suit 'for the frauds, deceits, concealments, misrepresentations, torts, negligences, and other malfeasances or misfeasances, and omissions of duty of his agent in the course of his employment, although the principal did not authorise, or justify, or participate in, or indeed know of such misconduct, or even if he forbade the acts, or disapproved of them.'

3-65 Corporate liability is straightforward and it is possible for a director who commits a wrongful act to be personally liable on this basis, as an agent acting within the scope of his authority and, as we shall see, the House of Lords now favours that straightforward approach. But there has been some debate as to whether it is more appropriate, given the company is a separate legal entity, that wrongful acts by a director should be attributed to the company so only the company is liable. This approach is sometimes referred to as the 'disattribution' theory whereby, if an act is attributed to the company on this basis, it is 'disattributed' to the director personally.[161]

3-66 This question of the personal liability of a director is particularly important where the company is a one-man company or the company is insolvent and the only person able to meet any liability in damages is the director personally (or his insurers), but there are conflicting policy issues here.[162] On the one hand, a willingness to hold a director liable personally for torts committed by the company runs the risk of disregarding the corporate entity contrary to the principle in *Salomon v Salomon & Co Ltd*[163] and, where the director is the controlling shareholder, denying the protection of limited liability conferred by incorporation.[164] The general approach is that a director is not automatically to

---

[159] As to the extended meaning of the term 'ordinary course of employment' in this context, see n 152.

[160] [1912] AC 716 at 737, HL.

[161] A leading advocate of this approach is Grantham, see, in particular, Grantham & Rickett, 'Directors' Tortious' Liability: Contract, Tort or Company Law?' (1999) 62 MLR 133, and Grantham, 'Company Director's Personal Liability in Tort' (2003) CLJ 15, but the disattribution idea is robustly rejected by Campbell & Armour, 'Demystifying the Civil Liability of Corporate Agents' (2003) CLJ 290. For a response, see Grantham, 'The Limited Liability of Company Directors' [2007] LMCLQ 362.

[162] See generally Noonan & Watson, 'Directors' Tortious Liability—Standard Chartered Bank and the Restoration of Sanity' [2004] JBL 539; Grantham (2007), n 161.   [163] [1897] AC 22, HL.

[164] See *Williams v Natural Life Health Foods Ltd* [1998] 1 BCLC 689 at 698, HL; also the dissenting judgment of Sir Patrick Russell in *Williams v Natural Life Health Foods Ltd* [1997] 1 BCLC 133, CA. But see Shapira, 'Liability of Corporate Agents: *Williams v Natural Life*' (1999) 20 Co Law 130 at 135 who makes the point that imposing liability on directors does not nullify the many other benefits of limited liability and incorporation.

be identified with his company for the purpose of the law of tort, for enterprise must not be discouraged by subjecting directors to such onerous personal obligations without due regard to the part the director plays personally in respect of the acts complained of.[165] On the other hand, the courts are concerned that an individual should not be able to avoid liability for tortious acts committed by him by sheltering behind the corporate veil.[166] For that reason, where a director commits a tort personally, his status as a director should not (and does not) confer any immunity from personal liability.[167] Of course, deciding whether the director has committed the tort personally is the difficulty, given that his argument is that he is not acting personally but acting on behalf of the company. As we shall see, the courts are working towards a pragmatic compromise between the twin policy concerns of maintaining the protection of incorporation and enforcing the personal liability of those who commit a tort.

Personal liability for torts committed by a director

3-67 The debate as to whether a director should be personally liable where he commits a tort has been clearly answered in the affirmative by the House of Lords in *Standard Chartered Bank v Pakistan National Shipping Corpn (No 2)*.[168] The facts essentially were that the managing director of a shipping company presented false shipping documents that resulted in the company obtaining payment of $1.1m from a bank. The bank subsequently sued the company and the director in deceit. The company was held liable, but the Court of Appeal allowed an appeal by the director against a finding of personal liability concluding that he had made the fraudulent representation on behalf of the company and not personally.[169] The bank appealed successfully to the House of Lords.

3-68 Lord Hoffmann noted that the director made a fraudulent misrepresentation intending the bank to rely upon it and the bank did rely on it. The fact that, by virtue of the law of agency, his representation and the knowledge with which he made it would also be attributed to the company would be of interest, Lord Hoffmann said, in an action against the company.[170] However, this did not detract from the fact that they were his representations and his knowledge.[171] Lord Hoffmann noted that the director was not being sued for the company's tort. He was being sued for his own tort and all the elements of that tort were proved against him. He was liable, not because he was a director, but because he committed a fraud.[172]

3-69 Lord Rodger, concurring, noted that someone who commits a tortious act is liable for their consequences; whether others (such as a company) are also liable depends on the circumstances.[173] All the ingredients of the tort of deceit (false statement made knowingly or recklessly intending another party to rely on it to his detriment) were made out against the director. That being so, there was no conceivable basis on which the director should

[165] *C Evans and Sons Ltd v Spritebrand Ltd* [1985] BCLC 105 at 115, per Slade LJ; see also *Rainham Chemical Works Ltd (in liq) v Belvedere Fish Guano Co Ltd* [1921] 2 AC 465 at 488; also *Trevor Ivory Ltd v Anderson* [1992] 2 NZLR 517 at 524–8.
[166] See Chadwick LJ in *MCA Records Inc v Charly Records Ltd* [2003] 1 BCLC 93 at 116.
[167] *Standard Chartered Bank v Pakistan National Shipping Corp* [2003] 1 BCLC 244 at 258, per Lord Rodger.
[168] [2003] 1 BCLC 244, HL. See Noonan & Watson, n 162; Todd, 'Assuming Responsibility for Tort' [2003] 119 LQR 199; Grantham (2003) CLJ 15.　　　[169] See [2000] 1 All ER (Comm) 1, CA.
[170] [2003] 1 BCLC 244 at 251.　　[171] [2003] 1 BCLC 244 at 251.　　[172] [2003] 1 BCLC 244 at 252.
[173] [2003] 1 BCLC 244 at 257.

not be held liable for the loss suffered by the bank.[174] His status as a director when he executed the fraud could not invest him with immunity[175] and he was liable in deceit.[176]

3-70 The decision in *Standard Chartered* shows a shift in emphasis or indeed a return to first principles.[177] Instead of approaching the issue by attributing acts to the entity so establishing a corporate liability and then looking at the possibility of some basis for a personal liability, the first consideration is to establish whether the director committed the tort. If he did, a personal liability ensues which brings with it a vicarious liability on the part of the company for the acts of its agent.

3-71 For whatever reason, perhaps because of the welcome clarity brought to these issues by the decision in *Standard Chartered*, perhaps because of the increasing availability of directors' and officers' liability insurance, perhaps because, in hard times, every avenue is worth pursuing if it increases the claimant's chances of actual recovery, there appears to be something of an increase in claims in deceit against individual directors.

3-72 In *GE Commercial Finance Ltd v Gee*[178] the executive chairman of a group of companies (who was also the 80% shareholder) and the group's finance director were liable in deceit and in conspiracy to the sum of £16m following an orchestrated and substantial fraud on the claimant involving the raising of false debts under a debt financing arrangement. The finance director knew that the figures communicated to the claimant were false, and the court found that his intention in making the false representations was to induce the claimant to make and to continue making the payments they did make. The court found that the executive chairman knew and encouraged what the finance director was doing.

3-73 In *Contex Drouzhba Ltd v Wiseman*[179] an action in deceit lay against a director who signed on behalf of the company a document containing a fraudulent misrepresentation. The Court of Appeal found that his signature was not only that of the company but also his personal signature making him a person who made a fraudulent misrepresentation. The facts were that the company entered into an agreement with a supplier that payments would be made to the supplier within 30 days of the shipment of the goods. The agreement was signed by the defendant as managing director of the company. The court found that, at the time he signed the agreement, the defendant knew that the company would be unable to make payment for the goods at all, let alone within 30 days of invoice or a reasonable period thereafter. The court found that the director had made that representation knowingly and with no reasonable belief in its truth. In these circumstances, the director was personally liable.

3-74 The Court of Appeal noted that it is clear, following the decision in *Standard Chartered Bank v Pakistan National Shipping Co*,[180] that, even if a company is liable for a deceit carried out by its director, the director also has a personal liability for his own fraud. Where a document contains a fraudulent representation made by a director, there is no reason, the court said, why his signature on the document should not render him personally liable. The court agreed that not every contract signed by a director would contain implied representations by the director. Each case would depend on its own facts. But a

---

[174] [2003] 1 BCLC 244 at 257.   [175] [2003] 1 BCLC 244 at 258.

[176] See also *Daido Asia Japan Co Ltd v Rothen* [2002] BCC 589; *Noel v Poland* [2001] 2 BCLC 645; *Edginton v Fitzmaurice* (1885) 29 Ch D 459.

[177] See Campbell & Armour, n 161; also Shapira, n 164.   [178] [2006] 1 Lloyd's Rep 337.

[179] [2008] 1 BCLC 631, CA, aff'g [2007] 1 BCLC 758. See also *UBAF Ltd v European American Banking Corp* [1984] 2 All ER 226.   [180] [2003] 1 BCLC 244.

director signing a document which contains a promise of payment on certain terms may be making an implied representation about the ability of the company to pay since there is, by implication, a representation that the company has the capacity to meet the payment terms. Here the defendant had made a fraudulent representation in writing as to the credit or ability of the company and he was liable.[181]

3-75   In cases where the claim is based on deceit, it is clear that the relevant policy considerations favour personal liability given the deliberate nature of the wrongdoing and the courts are anxious to prevent directors from avoiding this liability by hiding behind their companies.[182] On the other hand, there is possibly a greater reluctance to hold a director liable personally for negligent misrepresentations made by his company.

3-76   This issue was addressed by the House of Lords in *Williams v Natural Life Health Foods Ltd*[183] which concerned negligent advice given by what was essentially a one-man company. M was the managing director and principal shareholder of a company which held itself out as having the expertise to provide advice on running health food shops, expertise derived from M's experience in running his own shop. The plaintiffs had relied on financial projections negligently produced by the company in opening their health shop which had collapsed leaving them with significant losses. The company was liable for the negligently produced figures, but it had been dissolved. The question was whether M could be personally liable.[184] The lower courts thought so,[185] but the House of Lords disagreed.

3-77   Their Lordships agreed with the dissenting judge in the Court of Appeal that the fact that, in a one-man company, the functions of the company must necessarily be centred on this individual does not make him personally liable.[186] A director could only be personally liable to third parties for loss which they suffer as a result of negligent advice given to them by the company if he assumes personal responsibility for that advice and the plaintiffs rely on that assumption of responsibility.[187] It is not sufficient that there be a special relationship between the injured party and the company. There must be an assumption of responsibility such as to create a special relationship with the director himself and that will depend on things said and done by or on behalf of the director.[188] Moreover, the test of reliance is not simply reliance in fact but whether the plaintiffs can reasonably rely on

---

[181]   The Court of Appeal noted counsel's point that this route of suing in deceit offers creditors a possible direct remedy against directors which is more advantageous to them than liquidators bringing claims against directors for fraudulent or wrongful trading where any recovery is a collective one for the benefit of all the creditors: see [2008] 1 BCLC 631 at 633.

[182]   See Noonan & Watson, n 162, also Grantham (2007), n 161.

[183]   [1998] 1 BCLC 689, HL. There are numerous commentaries on this case, see Payne, 'Negligent Misstatement—A Healthier Decision for Company Directors' (1998) CLJ 456; Griffin, 'Company Director's Personal Liability in Tort' [1999] 115 LQR 36; Grantham & Rickett, n 161; Shapira, n 164; Todd, n 168; Reynolds, 'Personal Liability of Company Directors in Tort' (2003) 33 Hong Kong LJ 51.

[184]   It had not been pleaded that the director was a joint tortfeasor with the company, see **3-82**, but even if it had been pleaded, it would have failed since, as Lord Steyn pointed out, the basis for a claim for negligent misstatement is a special relationship between the parties giving rise to an assumption of responsibility. Joint tortfeasor liability is based on procuring etc others to act so there cannot be any special relationship between the parties and therefore joint tortfeasor liability could not be relevant to liability for negligent misstatement: see [1998] 1 BCLC 689 at 698.

[185]   The Court of Appeal decision is reported at [1997] 1 BCLC 131; the first instance judgment at [1996] 1 BCLC 288.

[186]   [1998] 1 BCLC 689 at 697. See also *Trevor Ivory Ltd v Anderson* [1992] 2 NZLR 517.

[187]   [1998] 1 BCLC 689 at 695, but see Todd, n 168.

[188]   [1998] 1 BCLC 689 at 695. See also *Noel v Poland* [2001] 2 BCLC 645.

the assumption of responsibility.[189] On the facts in *Williams*, their Lordships found that there were no personal dealings between M and the claimants, he never crossed the line to assume a personal responsibility towards them and he was not personally liable.[190]

3-78 The decision in *Standard Chartered Bank v Pakistan National Shipping Corp*[191] has clarified that where all of the elements of a tort claim can be established against an individual director, such as where fraudulent misrepresentations are made by a director, the fact that he is a director does not and should not act to bar his personal liability. There is no inconsistency between that decision and the decision in *Williams*. If the elements of negligent misstatement had been established in *Williams*, the individual director would have been liable, but they were not, and so the director was not personally liable. On the other hand, what *Williams*[192] does show is that only in exceptional cases would a claim for negligent misstatement succeed against an individual director. If in a one-man company, such as *Williams*, there was no assumption of responsibility and therefore no liability, it is difficult to imagine an assumption of responsibility by directors in other contexts.[193]

3-79 This outcome in respect of economic loss caused by negligence, reached through an application of tort law, in effect reinforces *Salomon v Salomon & Co Ltd*[194] by leaving liability to fall on the entity, if at all. Liability for economic loss from negligent misstatements is precisely the type of business risk which incorporation is used to manage. This outcome ensures the effectiveness of incorporation in those circumstances and is especially important in the context of small or one-man companies which provide advice and services.[195] On the other hand, there is no justification for allowing individuals to use corporate structures to avoid liability in tort for deliberate wrongdoing by them individually.[196]

3-80 The balance struck in *Williams* and in *Standard Chartered* can be seen as a display of judicial dexterity to resolve the uncertainties which were beginning to gain ground in this area. The decisions are welcome at every level: doctrinally it is important that tort law should apply to directors in the same way as anyone else; pragmatically because the policy issues have been resolved in a practical way which does not allow directors to evade their personal responsibilities while equally ensuring that a director is not always personally liable for all torts arising in the course of a business. The courts are essentially determining whether, as a matter of policy, in the particular context it is appropriate for the entity (negligence) or the entity and the individual (deceit) to bear the liability.

3-81 In bringing much needed clarity to this difficult area, their Lordships have taken the opportunity to assert or reassert the primacy of vicarious liability (and so reduce the

---

[189] [1998] 1 BCLC 689 at 696.

[190] See criticisms of this finding of fact by Shapira, n 164, p 133. For an exceptional case where the line was crossed, see *Fairline Shipping Corp v Adamson* [1974] 2 All ER 967 where a director involved himself personally with a customer of the company to such an extent that it was clear that he regarded himself, and not the company, as concerned with the storage of the customer's goods. The director had therefore assumed a duty of care to the customer.

[191] [2003] 1 BCLC 244, HL.   [192] [1998] 1 BCLC 689, HL.

[193] See Campbell & Armour, n 161, p 301 who make the point that this difficulty in establishing an assumption of responsibility will make it difficult to bring a successful claim against any agent acting on behalf of a principal, not just company directors.   [194] [1897] AC 22, HL.

[195] See Payne, n 183. Noonan & Watson, n 162, p 548 make the point that the very act of incorporation will often be an effective disclaimer of personal liability by a director giving advice on behalf of the company.

[196] See Grantham (2007), n 161, who makes the point that, when expressing concerns about allowing those engaged in business to shift the risk of their endeavours to others, we must not forget that that is actually the purpose of the legislation allowing for the incorporation of limited liability entities.

importance of other specific rules of attribution) in this context with their Lordships asserting in *Williams v Natural Life Health Foods Ltd*[197] and in *Standard Chartered Bank v Pakistan National Shipping Corp*[198] that the matter is an agency matter, one of the personal liability of the agent and corporate vicarious liability for the wrongs of that agent.[199]

Director's liability for procuring wrongdoing

3-82 The discussion to date has centred on the situation where a director personally commits a tort. Another way of imposing liability on a director is to hold a director liable as a joint tortfeasor with the company where the director has authorised, directed or procured the wrongful act though he has not committed the tort himself.[200] For example, if an employee of the company makes a fraudulent misrepresentation on behalf of the company, a director could be personally liable if he procured the making of the false statement.[201]

3-83 The difficulty is defining the nature and extent of the participation of the director in the tortious act which renders him personally liable on this basis. This is an elusive question, as Slade LJ described it in *C Evans and Sons Ltd v Spritebrand Ltd*,[202] but important guidance has been provided by the Court of Appeal which considered the matter at length in *MCA Records Inc v Charly Records Ltd*.[203] The facts in the case were relatively straightforward. At issue was the liability of Y who did not hold the office of director but who was described as the controller of C Ltd which had infringed the copyright vested in the claimants with respect to certain recordings. Y appealed against a finding that he was personally liable as a joint tortfeasor in respect of the infringement by the company.

3-84 The Court of Appeal emphasised that a director is not liable as a joint tortfeasor with the company if he does no more than carry out his constitutional role in the governance of the company, i.e. by voting at board meetings (likewise a controlling shareholder is not liable merely if he exercises control through use of his voting powers).[204] But, if a director or controlling shareholder chooses to exercise control otherwise than through the constitutional organs of the company, and the circumstances are such that he would be liable if he were not a director or controlling shareholder, the court thought that there was no reason why he should not be liable with the company as a joint tortfeasor.[205] The issue is whether A would be liable as a joint tortfeasor with the primary infringer B, whether or not the relationship between A and B is that A is a director of B.[206]

---

[197] [1998] 1 BCLC 689, HL.   [198] [2003] 1 BCLC 244, HL.

[199] See Lord Hoffmann in *Standard Chartered Bank v Pakistan National Shipping Corp* [2003] 1 BCLC 244 at 251–2; Lord Steyn in *Williams v Natural Life Health Foods Ltd* [1998] 1 BCLC 689 at 694.

[200] *Rainham Chemical Works Ltd (in liq) v Belvedere Fish Guano Co Ltd* [1921] 2 AC 465 at 488, HL; *Performing Right Society Ltd v Ciryl Theatrical Syndicate Ltd* [1924] 1 KB 1; *C Evans and Sons Ltd v Spritebrand Ltd* [1985] BCLC 105.

[201] See *Daido Asia Japan Co Ltd v Rothen* [2002] BCC 589 at 597.   [202] See [1985] BCLC 105 at 117.

[203] [2003] 1 BCLC 93, CA. See also *SEI Spa v Ordnance Technologies (UK) Ltd (No 2)* [2008] 2 All ER 622 (managing director and sole shareholder of a company liable as joint tortfeasor with the company having shared a common design that the acts complained of, the infringement of design rights, should take place. The director encouraged or procured the breach by the company's engineers).

[204] [2003] 1 BCLC 93 at 116–17.

[205] [2003] 1 BCLC 93 at 116–17. See also *Thames Valley Housing Association Ltd v Elegant Homes (Guernsey) Ltd* [2011] EWHC 1288 where a person found to be a company's controlling mind, though not part of its formal governance structure and not a director, was liable for inducing a breach of contract by the company and was also liable on the basis of having conspired with the company to injure by unlawful means a third party.   [206] [2003] 1 BCLC 93 at 113.

3-85   Chadwick LJ emphasised that the relevant enquiry is whether the individual has been personally involved in the commission of the tort to the extent sufficient to attract liability as a joint tortfeasor. The director must be concerned with the company in a joint act done in pursuance of a common purpose so as to attract liability.[207] But, Chadwick LJ went on:[208] 'if all that a director is doing is carrying out the duties entrusted to him as such by the company under its constitution, the circumstances in which it would be right to hold him liable as a joint tortfeasor with the company would be rare indeed.'

3-86   Returning to the facts of the dispute in *MCA Records Inc v Charly Records Ltd*,[209] the court noted that, in the context of intellectual property, liability as a joint tortfeasor might arise where the individual intends and procures and shares a common design that the infringement take place. On the facts, Y induced the company to copy the recordings and to issue them to the public, he planned the exploitation of the recordings, and intended that the company should continue to do so for as long as possible. He was rightly liable, the court held, as a joint tortfeasor.

3-87   In *Koninklijke Philips Electronics NV v Prico Digital Disc GmbH*[210] the defendant director was in charge of the day-to-day running of the defendant company. It was admitted that the company imported into the UK and kept and disposed of recordable CDs of a kind that the court previously had held infringed the claimant's patent. The director had been responsible for the decision to import the infringing CDs into the UK and for the cultivation of A as a customer for those products. The director also made a decision to indemnify A against liability for royalties when the claimant sued A for infringement. The court concluded that the director's close involvement with the day-to-day actions of the company, and his independent authority in respect of those actions, were sufficient to render him liable as a joint tortfeasor with the company.

3-88   Clearly a factual analysis of the director's conduct is needed in each instance and, in essence, where the director acts appropriately and seeks to ensure that the company's agents and employees conduct themselves in accordance with the law, personal liability is unlikely. The importance of potential liability as a joint tortfeasor, however, is that it ensures that a director cannot easily evade liability by the device of ensuring that another agent or employee carries out wrongful acts at his direction.

Criminal liability of the company

3-89   A company is subject to the criminal law in the same manner as any other person although, as an artificial legal entity, there are some offences which a company is deemed unable to commit such as bigamy or offences of assault and some offences for which it cannot be convicted as the only penalty is imprisonment, such as murder.[211] Otherwise, the requisite *actus reus* and *mens rea* can be sought in the relevant officer, agent or employee and the fact that there is a *mens rea* requirement is no obstacle to corporate liability. Thus, a company can be held liable for offences involving an intent to deceive;[212] for conspiracy to defraud[213] and for filing false tax returns.[214]

3-90   A company may be criminally liable because, for example, the offence is one for which the company may be liable vicariously as an employer or principal for the wrongful acts

---

[207]   [2003] 1 BCLC 93 at 111, applying *The Koursk* [1924] P 140.
[208]   [2003] 1 BCLC 93 at 117.   [209]   [2003] 1 BCLC 93, CA.   [210]   [2004] 2 BCLC 50.
[211]   See generally Wells, *Corporations and Criminal Responsibility* (2nd edn, 2001).
[212]   *DPP v Kent and Sussex Contractors Ltd* [1944] 1 All ER 119.
[213]   *R v ICR Haulage Ltd* [1944] 1 All ER 691.   [214]   *Moore v I Bresler Ltd* [1944] 2 All ER 515.

or omissions of its servants and agents in the course of their employment and exercise of their authority.[215] Vicarious liability has only a limited role to play in criminal law, however, mainly arising from statutory requirements, so specific rules of attribution are needed generally, if the company is to be liable. What those rules of attribution are was explored in detail by Lord Hoffmann in *Meridian Global Funds Management Asia Ltd v Securities Commission*[216] where he attempted to set the law on this issue on a new purposive basis different from the then prevailing 'directing mind and will' approach. That approach required 'the identification of the natural person or persons who are to be regarded as representing the juridical person for the purposes of the substantive rule in question',[217] those persons who are the embodiment of the company itself such that their acts are the acts of the company.[218] Before looking at the relationship between *Meridian* and the directing mind and will doctrine, it is worth remembering that, while the discussion which follows is set in the context of criminal claims, specific rules of attribution may also be needed in civil litigation if the issue cannot otherwise be resolved by agency or vicarious liability, as noted at **3-61**.

Rules of attribution

3-91 Rules of attribution are necessary then to determine whose acts count as the acts of the company and the issue is dominated by the speech of Lord Hoffmann in *Meridian Global Funds Management Asia Ltd v Securities Commission*,[219] a much cited Privy Council decision which is accepted as setting out the domestic law on this matter.[220] For Lord Hoffmann, the answer to the question of whose act is to be attributed to the company lies, not in metaphysics, not in searching for some alter ego of the company, but in the construction of the particular substantive rule. It is for the court to ask whose act or knowledge or state of mind is for the purpose of that rule intended to count as the act, knowledge or state of mind of the company, applying the usual canons of interpretation, taking into account the language of the rule (if it is a statute) and its content and policy.[221] The scope and application of the *Meridian* principle is the central issue in this area, but before exploring it, we must first to consider the metaphysics to which Lord Hoffmann alluded.

Directing mind and will

3-92 Prior to *Meridian,* the rule of attribution commonly relied on was 'the directing mind and will of the company' approach which requires the identification of the natural person or persons who are seen as the embodiment of the company such that their acts may be attributed to the company (the identification doctrine). This doctrine derives from *Lennard's Carrying Co Ltd v Asiatic Petroleum Co Ltd*[222] where Viscount Haldane famously noted:

---

[215] *Mousell Bros v London and North-Western Rly Co* [1917] 2 KB 836. See *R v British Steel plc* [1995] 1 WLR 1356; *National Rivers Authority v Alfred McAlpine Homes East Ltd* [1994] 4 All ER 286; *Re Supply of Ready Mixed Concrete (No 2), Director General of Fair Trading v Pioneer Concrete (UK) Ltd* [1995] 1 BCLC 613, HL.   [216] [1995] 2 BCLC 116, PC.

[217] *MAN Nutzfahrzeuge AG v Freightliner Ltd* [2005] EWHC 2347 (Comm), [2005] All ER (D) 357 (Oct), QBD, [154] per Moore Bick LJ.

[218] *Lennard's Carrying Co Ltd v Asiatic Petroleum Co Ltd* [1915] AC 705 at 713, HL.

[219] [1995] 2 BCLC 116, PC.

[220] *Meridian* has been relied on in numerous cases subsequently and it was cited with approval in the House of Lords in *Stone & Rolls Ltd v Moore Stephens* [2009] 2 BCLC 563, see at [39] (Lord Phillips), at [104] (Lord Scott); at [134] (Lord Walker).   [221] [1995] 2 BCLC 116 at 122.

[222] [1915] AC 705 at 713, HL; see also Lord Denning in *HL Bolton (Engineering) Co Ltd v TJ Graham & Sons Ltd* [1957] 1 QB 159 at 172, CA.

'My Lords, a corporation is an abstraction. It has no mind of its own any more than it has a body of its own; its active and directing will must consequently be sought in the person of somebody who for some purposes may be called an agent, but who is really the directing mind and will of the corporation, the very ego and centre of the personality of the corporation.'

3-93   To identify the directing mind and will of the company, it is necessary to consult the company's constitution which typically vests all powers of management in the board and there is no doubt that the board collectively represents the directing mind and will of the company. Equally, at the other end of the spectrum, it is clear that not all acts of all employees can be attributed to the company, for not all will have the status and authority which in law makes their acts in the matter under consideration the acts of the company.[223] As Lord Denning explained in *HL Bolton (Engineering) Co Ltd v TJ Graham & Sons Ltd*:[224]

'Some of the people in the company are mere servants and agents who are nothing more than hands to do the work and cannot be said to represent the mind or will. Others are directors and managers who represent the directing mind and will of the company and control what it does. The state of mind of those managers is the state of mind of the company and is treated by the law as such.'

3-94   That 'the directing mind and will' does not encompass more junior management was confirmed by the House of Lords in *Tesco Supermarkets Ltd v Nattrass*.[225] In this case, Tesco was prosecuted under the Trade Descriptions Act 1968 for the failure of one of its shop managers to ensure that goods advertised for sale at a particular price were in fact being offered for sale at that price. It was found as a fact that the company had exercised reasonable care in devising a proper system for the operation of the store. It was a defence under the 1968 Act to show that the act was due to the default of some other person. The company pleaded on appeal that the manager did not amount to the directing mind and will of the company and therefore the company could assert that the act was due to the default of some other person. The House of Lords agreed and held that the shop manager, one of several hundred, could not be treated as the embodiment of the company and his acts and defaults could not be attributed to the company. The offence was indeed due to the act or default of 'another person' and not of the company itself. As Lord Reid noted:[226]

'Normally the board of directors, the managing director and perhaps other superior officers carry out the functions of management and speak and act as the company. Their subordinates do not.'

3-95   There the law rested until Lord Hoffmann, initially in *El Ajou v Dollar Land Holdings plc*,[227] and then authoritatively in *Meridian Global Funds Management Asia Ltd v Securities Commission*,[228] set out a broader purposive approach which considers the issue of attribution not from the position in the corporate hierarchy of the defaulting agent or employee, but rather with a view to the purpose of the statutory (or other) provision and to furthering that purpose. The necessity for taking this broader approach arises from the situation

---

[223]   *R v Andrews Weatherfoil Ltd* [1972] 1 All ER 65 at 70, per Eveleigh J.
[224]   [1957] 1 QB 159 at 172, CA.   [225]   [1972] AC 153, HL.   [226]   [1972] AC 152 at 171.
[227]   [1994] 1 BCLC 464. In this case, the Court of Appeal accepted that the fraudulent intent of the non-executive chairman of a company should be imputed to the company in a 'knowing receipt' case. He was the 'directing mind and will of the company' with respect to the particular transaction at issue—the company's receipt of investment funds which the chairman knew to be the proceeds of fraud—and his knowledge was the company's knowledge.   [228]   [1995] 2 BCLC 116, PC.

where the acts in question have been carried out by, or the knowledge at issue lies with, individuals who cannot be identified as the directing mind and will of the company in circumstances where vicarious liability is not relevant. In those circumstances, unless another rule of attribution can be applied, the acts and knowledge of those individuals cannot be attributed to the company and the relevant rule cannot be applied to the company which would usually be an unsatisfactory outcome in the absence of evidence that the rule was not intended to apply to companies.

3-96 Returning to *Meridian Global Funds Management Asia Ltd v Securities Commission*,[229] in this case two employees of a Hong Kong investment management company (Meridian), one of them the company's chief investment officer, used company funds to purchase a 49% stake in a listed New Zealand company. The purchase was not disclosed by Meridian as required under the New Zealand Securities Amendment Act 1988 which essentially required the disclosure of significant shareholdings 'knowingly' acquired in public companies. The question was whether the knowledge of the employees should be attributed to Meridian so that it was in breach of the statutory requirement. The company argued that in the absence of knowledge by the directing mind and will (i.e. the board) of the acquisition of the shares, there was no breach.

3-97 The Privy Council found that, on a true construction of the relevant statute and in view of the policy of the legislation, it was appropriate to attribute the knowledge of a senior employee (the chief investment officer) to the company, since otherwise the policy of the Act would be defeated and there would be a premium on the board paying as little attention as possible to what its investment managers were doing. Accordingly, Meridian knew that it was a substantial shareholder in another company when that was known to the employee who had authority to acquire the shares. Meridian was therefore in breach of the disclosure requirement.

3-98 In a now much cited speech, Lord Hoffmann reviewed the whole question of attribution. The primary rules of attribution, he said, are to be found in the company's constitution, typically the articles, which will determine how decisions of the company are to be reached, commonly by resolution of the board of directors or of the shareholders in general meeting, and additionally company law recognises the unanimous informal assent of the shareholders as an act of the company.[230] There are also general principles of attribution, such as agency and vicarious liability, as noted, which will determine whether the acts of others count as the acts of the company. Lord Hoffmann went on :

> 'The company's primary rules of attribution together with the general principles of agency, vicarious liability and so forth are usually sufficient to enable one to determine its rights and obligations. In exceptional cases, however, they will not provide an answer. This will be the case when a rule of law, either expressly or by implication, excludes attribution on the basis of the general principles of agency or vicarious liability. For example, a rule may be stated in language primarily applicable to a natural person and require some act or state of mind on the part of that person "himself", as opposed to his servants or agents. This is generally true of rules of the criminal law, which ordinarily impose liability only for the actus reus and mens rea of the defendant himself. How is such a rule to be applied to a company?'

He noted that if the court decided that a substantive rule of law was intended to apply to a company, it then had to decide how the rule was intended to apply and whose act or knowledge or state of mind was for that purpose intended to count as the act, knowledge

[229] [1995] 2 BCLC 116, PC.   [230] [1995] 2 BCLC 116 at 121, PC.

or state of mind of the company.[231] Although in some cases that could be determined by applying the 'directing mind and will' test, that test was not appropriate in all cases. Instead, Lord Hoffmann said, it was a question of construction in each case as to whether the particular rule requires that the knowledge that an act has been done, or the state of mind with which it was done, should be attributed to the company.[232] For example, in *Tesco Supermarkets Ltd v Nattrass*[233] discussed at **3-94**, the acts or defaults of the store manager were not attributed to the company, Lord Hoffmann explained, because the purpose of the statutory provision in that case, the protection of consumers, did not require that the offence be an absolute one.[234] On the other hand, in *Re Supply of Ready Mixed Concrete (No 2), Director General of Fair Trading v Pioneer Concrete (UK) Ltd*,[235] it was necessary to attribute the acts of the employees to the company. In this case, a company was liable in contempt when its employees, while acting in the course of their employment but contrary to instructions issued by the board, carried out a deliberate act contrary to a restrictive practices order imposed on the company. The restrictive practices legislation would otherwise be worth little, Lord Hoffmann noted, if the company could avoid liability for what its employees did on the basis that the board did not know about it.[236]

3-99 In other words, to ensure the effective application of a statutory provision or other rule to a company, it may be necessary to consider a different approach to attribution. Finally, Lord Hoffmann ended with a note of caution, pointing out that their Lordships:[237]

> '...would wish to guard themselves against being understood to mean that whenever a servant of a company has authority to do an act on its behalf, knowledge of that act will for all purposes be attributed to the company. It is a question of construction in each case as to whether the particular rule requires that the knowledge that an act has been done, or the state of mind with which it was done, should be attributed to the company.'

3-100 An illustration of the use of a special rule of attribution in this way arising from the need to apply a particular statutory provision to a company can be seen in *Re Bank of Credit and Commerce International SA (in liquidation) (No 15); Morris v Bank of India*.[238] The liquidators of BCCI alleged that the defendant bank, by entering into various transactions, knowingly participated in the fraudulent trading of BCCI giving rise to a civil liability under IA 1986, s 213. The key issue was whether those at the bank responsible for entering into the transactions at issue knew that they were thereby assisting BCCI to perpetrate a fraud on its creditors and whether their knowledge should be attributed to the bank. The various transactions had been assisted and facilitated by a bank official (S) who was the general manager of the London branch of the bank.

3-101 Applying *Meridian*, the Court of Appeal looked to the construction and purpose of IA 1986, s 213 and concluded that the wording and policy behind the section indicated that it would be inappropriate to limit attribution for its purposes to the board or those specifically authorised by a resolution of the board. The crucial question was whose knowledge counted, for the purposes of IA 1986, s 213, as corporate knowledge of the bank. Given that transactions of this nature would be dealt with at a level below that of the board, it

---

[231] [1995] 2 BCLC 116 at 122.

[232] Lord Hoffmann was quite clear that the principle he was laying down was applicable to any rule and was not limited to a statutory rule, see [1995] 2 BCLC 116 at 122; see also Nourse LJ in *Odyssey Re (London) Ltd v OIC Run-off Ltd* [2001] 1 Lloyd's Rep IR 1 at 11 but Buxton LJ, dissenting in *Odyssey* makes the point (at 96) that *Meridian* was formulated, and is most easily understood, in the context of the application of statutory rules and it is much less easy to apply it to a rule of the common law.

[233] [1972] AC 153, HL.   [234] [1995] 2 BCLC 116 at 122.   [235] [1995] 1 BCLC 613, HL.

[236] [1995] 2 BCLC 116 at 123.   [237] [1995] 2 BCLC 116 at 126.   [238] [2005] 2 BCLC 328.

would in practice defeat the effectiveness of the section, the court said, if liability was limited to those cases in which the board of directors was directly privy to the fraud. Turning to the facts of the case, the court thought this was plainly an appropriate case for attribution. S had a senior position in the bank, he brought the transactions to the bank, the board relied on him in relation to them, he was given a free hand to negotiate them and they were plainly suspicious.[239] His knowledge was more relevant than that of any member of the board or of anyone else in the bank and it was necessary, given the purpose of the provision, to attribute his knowledge to the bank which was therefore liable. But the Court of Appeal was careful to emphasise (as their Lordships had done in *Meridian*) that it would be wrong to attribute to a company the knowledge of any agent irrespective of the particular facts. It is necessary in each case to look at the purpose of the statutory provision and consider whether, in those particular circumstances, the statutory purpose will be defeated unless a special rule of attribution (which may include attributing the acts of employees lower down the corporate hierarchy) is applied.[240]

3-102 Another Privy Council application of *Meridian* can be found in *Lebon v Aqua Salt Co Ltd*[241] where the issue was whether knowledge of a prior sale of land could be attributed to a company (the second purchaser) when that knowledge rested in one of its directors who was also the promoter and substantial shareholder in the company. Their Lordships considered that the substantive purpose of the relevant rule here was to prevent an inequitable trumping of the title of a first purchaser by a second purchaser with knowledge of the first transaction and the question for the court then is which rule of attribution would best serve the purpose of that rule.[242] They concluded that the substantive rule did require that the knowledge of the director, promoter and substantial shareholder be attributed to the company. He knew of the earlier sale and it should not be possible for the company to have better rights against the first purchaser than he alone would have had. Information relevant to the company's affairs in the possession of one director, however that occurs, can properly be regarded as information in the possession of the company itself.[243]

The continuing application of the 'directing mind and will' rule

3-103 Following the decision in *Meridian*, there was some uncertainty as to the continuing role of the orthodox attribution rule requiring intent to be found in the 'directing mind and will' of the company at board or 'superior officer' level. The point was addressed by the Court of Appeal in *A-G's Reference (No 2 of 1999)*[244] (a criminal case) which noted that:

> '…Lord Hoffmann's speech in the *Meridian* case, in fashioning an additional special rule of attribution geared to *the purpose of the statute* [emphasis added], proceeded on the basis that the primary "directing mind and will" rule still applies although it is not determinative in all cases. In other words, he was not departing from the identification theory but re-affirming its existence.'

3-104 The starting point in the criminal law remains therefore the application of the directing mind and will theory, applying *Tesco Supermarkets Ltd v Nattrass*.[245] The question is

---

[239] [2005] 2 BCLC 328 at 360–1.   [240] [2005] 2 BCLC 328 at 360–1.

[241] [2009] 1 BCLC 549.   [242] [2009] 1 BCLC 549 at [25]–[26].

[243] Applying Moore-Bick LJ in *Jafari-Fini v Skillglass Ltd* [2007] EWCA Civ 261 at [98].

[244] [2000] 2 BCLC 257 at 268.

[245] As a matter of precedent, but see Brooke LJ in *Odyssey Re (London) Ltd v OIC Run-off Ltd* [2001] 1 Lloyd's Rep IR 1 at 66, who accepts that that might be the case but it should not impede the development of the *Meridian* approach in civil cases, while Buxton LJ, see at 94, dissenting in that case, emphasised the importance of *Tesco v Nattrass* as binding authority on attribution in criminal law, noting that the analysis in *Meridian* is 'at best an imperfect guide to the correct approach to the rule for attribution of a crime …'. See

whether it is possible to identify someone whose acts can be equated with the direct-ing mind and will of the company such that his acts and knowledge, being the acts and knowledge which constitute the offence, are the acts and knowledge of the company. Even Lord Hoffmann in *Meridian* accepted that reference to the 'directing mind and will' is often the most appropriate description of the person designated for the purpose of the relevant attribution rule.[246] If, on the other hand, the 'guilty' party cannot be identified as the directing mind and will of the company so that route of attribution is not open, the issue is whether the purpose and policy of the rule under consideration (such as the statutory provision in *Meridian*) requires the application of a special rule of attribution in order to ensure that the particular prohibition/requirement can be applied to companies. An example of this step approach to the application of *Tesco v Nattrass* and *Meridian* can be seen in *R v St Regis Paper Company Ltd*.[247] A company operated a number of mills and it was convicted along with an employee (a technical manager) of offences under the Pollution Prevention and Control (England and Wales) Regulations.[248] The employee gave false environmental pollution readings to the Environmental Protection Agency and was convicted, as was the company, of the offence of intentionally making a false entry in the records. The company was convicted, not on the basis that the employee was the direct-ing mind and will of the company, but on the basis of a special rule of attribution to give effect to the policy of the legislation, applying *Meridian*. The Court of Appeal quashed the conviction, finding that there was no basis in law for attributing the dishonest intent of the technical manager to the company. The general rule of attribution, the directing mind and will theory, as laid down in *Tesco Supermarkets Ltd v Nattrass*[249] should be applied, the court held, and it was not appropriate in the circumstances to seek a special rule of attribution to avoid emasculating the legislation, as the trial judge had put it. The impor-tance of avoiding environmental pollution could not be overstated, but the regulations had sought to meet that danger in a carefully graduated way imposing both offences of strict liability and those which required proof of intention. As a matter of statutory con-struction of the regulations, there was no warrant for imposing liability on the company by virtue of the intentions of one who could not be said to be the directing mind and will of the company.

3-105   Despite some expectation that *Meridian* would see the demise of the 'directing mind and will' approach, it survives then, not just as a descriptive term for the person whose con-duct, applying a purposive approach, is for the specific purpose treated as the conduct of the company, but as a distinct rule of attribution.[250] Its significance may dwindle over time as Parliament seems to have taken on board these difficulties concerning attribu-tion in the criminal context and in relation both to corporate manslaughter and bribery offences has preferred to legislate specifically for the manner in which corporate liability may arise[251] rather than to leave any room for further debate as to the relevant rule of

---

too Ferran, n 256, at 258–9 who notes that any retreat from *Meridian* on the criminal side is not necessarily a matter for regret, if the alternative was unacceptable judicial activism in circumstances where often it is not possible to determine the policy and purpose behind the substantive rule.

[246]   Lord Hoffmann explains *Lennard's Carrying Co Ltd v Asiatic Petroleum Co Ltd* [1915] AC 705 on that basis—for the purpose of the statutory provision which Viscount Haldane was applying, the person who was responsible could be described as the directing mind and will of the company, see [1995] 2 BCLC 116 at 124.

[247]   [2012] 1 Cr App R 14.   [248]   SI 2000/1973.

[249]   [1972] AC 153, HL.   [250]   See Ferran, n 256, at 250.

[251]   See the Corporate Manslaughter and Corporate Homicide Act 2007, s 1 and the Bribery Act 2010, s 7, respectively.

attribution.[252] Future legislation imposing corporate liability may well commonly make clear the basis on which that liability can arise, but for the moment, especially in the context of criminal offences, the courts remain wedded to the directing mind and will approach, as laid down in *Tesco Supermarkets Ltd v Nattrass*,[253] with *Meridian* allowing an alternative approach if needed.[254]

3-106   On the civil side too, the directing mind and will approach has a lingering grip as can be seen from the controversial decision in *Stone & Rolls Ltd v Moore Stephens*,[255] a case which has attracted a lot of comment,[256] but which ultimately may be seen as limited to its facts.[257]

3-107   In this case, a company had been used as a vehicle for fraud by S, its beneficial owner. Various defrauded banks had sued the company and S in deceit and obtained judgment, but the company was insolvent and recovery could not be obtained against S. The liquidator of the company then tried to sue the company's auditors in negligence, only to be met by the defence, *ex turpi causa non oritur actio* (essentially precludes claims based on the claimants' own illegality). Essentially the auditors argued that the fraudster's conduct was to be attributed to the company such that the company itself was the fraudster and any claim by the company was therefore barred by the *ex turpi causa* principle.[258] The House of Lords divided 3–2 in favour of allowing the auditors' defence, but the judgments are 'a morass of complex reasoning'[259] and, with the majority offering differing reasons for their conclusions, it is difficult to determine the ratio of the case. The minority in the case[260] approached the problem essentially as a question of the scope of the duty owed by the auditors[261] while the majority, or at least part of the majority (Lords Walker and Brown),

---

[252] Meanwhile the Law Commission is considering the issue of attribution in the context of exploring the appropriate basis for criminal liability in regulatory contexts and central to this consideration is a review of the basis on which companies should be criminally liable. See Law Commission Consultation Paper No 195, *Criminal Liability in Regulatory Contexts* (2010).   [253] [1972] AC 153, HL.

[254] See Ferran, n 256, at 246–7, who notes that the unwillingness of the judiciary, for reasons which are unclear, to extend the more flexible approach in *Meridian* 'looks disappointing'.

[255] [2009] 2 BCLC 563, HL.

[256] See in particular, Davies, 'Auditors' Liability: No need to detect fraud' (2010) CLJ 505; Halpern, '*Stone & Rolls Ltd v Moore Stephens*: An Unnecessary Tangle' (2010) 73 MLR 487; Watts, '*Stone & Rolls Ltd v Moore Stephens*: Audit contracts and turpitude' (2010) LQR 14; Ferran, 'Corporate Attribution and the Directing Mind and Will' (2011) LQR 239.

[257] Both Lords Phillips and Walker, see [2009] 2 BCLC 563 at [18] and [193], respectively, emphasised the 'extreme' nature of the facts in this case.

[258] [2008] 2 BCLC 461 at 493, per Rimer LJ.   [259] Ferran, n 256, at 251.

[260] Lords Scott and Mance. Lord Scott (dissenting) thought the majority had in effect pierced the veil in circumstances where it was not established that the wrongdoer was the owner of the company, so there was no justification in treating him as the company, and they had applied a rule of public policy (*ex turpi causa*) in circumstances where the beneficiary of the duty owed by the auditors would have been the creditors of an insolvent company, not the wrongdoer, so there was no justification for allowing reliance on *ex turpi causa*, see [2009] 2 BCLC 563 at [116]–[122]; and see Davies, n 256. Halpern, n 256, p 491 criticises this approach as drawing a dangerous distinction between the position of a company in liquidation and prior to liquidation. Also, the case has nothing to do with piercing the veil (which involves looking behind the façade to see if it is a deceptive front for those behind it), this case is about attribution, whether the acts of an individual can be attributed to the company such that they are the (wrongful) acts of the company as well as the individual (see Halpern, n 256, at 489).

[261] Lord Mance (dissenting) particularly focused on the nature of the duty of care owed by auditors and concluded that they owed a duty to the company to have detected and reported a fraud by the top management of the company rendering the company increasingly insolvent, i.e. that their duty to the company extends beyond the interests of the shareholders in a situation where the company is insolvent at the time of each audit and increasingly so, see [2009] 2 BCLC 563 at [265]–[271]. In such circumstances, it is not open to

considered it to be an issue of attribution. Lord Phillips, also of the majority, preferred
to rest his decision on the narrow ground that the sole person for whose benefit the duty
was owed by the auditors was the person who owned and ran the company and who was
responsible for the fraud. In those circumstances, *ex turpi causa* provides a defence.[262]
Lords Walker and Brown, for their part, explicitly applied the 'directing mind and will'
rule of attribution.[263] S was the sole beneficial owner of the company,[264] he was its embodiment, he was instrumental in carrying out the frauds, his conduct was to be attributed
such that the company was the fraudster and the claim could be defeated by reliance on
ex turpi causa.[265] While there are many references in the case to *Meridian*, none of their
Lordships applied the *Meridian* approach. The fact that Lords Walker and Brown preferred to approach the problem from the perspective of identifying the directing mind
and will of the company suggests that the metaphysical still maintains a grip, even in the
civil arena. It may be that *Meridian* will prove less influential, though still useful, than
first thought.

the auditors to attribute the fraudster's knowledge to the company for the purpose of invoking against it the
maxim *ex turpi causa*, see at [275]–[277]. This approach of Lord Mance requires something of a leap from the
orthodox position on directors' duties (they have a duty to have regard to creditor interests if the company
is insolvent or doubtfully solvent, see **9-41**) to applying the same reasoning to the scope of auditors' duties,
something which is criticised by Lord Phillips, at [85], as a departure from *Caparo v Dickman* (the authority
on auditors' duties, discussed at **16-55**); and see Halpern, n 256, p 491, who describes it as a subversion of
Caparo, making the point that the wider duties of directors cannot be simply transposed from directors to
auditors.   [262] [2009] 2 BCLC 563 at [18], [86]; and see Watts, n 256, at 20.

[263] The divergence in approach between Lords Walker and Brown was that, having applied the directing
mind and will approach which attributed the fraudster's conduct and knowledge to the company, another
problem arose, namely the rule in *Hampshire Land* (*Re Hampshire Land Co* [1896] 2 Ch 743) the exact scope
of which is uncertain (see Watts, n 256, at 18–19), but the essence of which is that knowledge of a fraudulent
agent is not to be imputed to his principal. Lord Brown concluded that that rule could have no application
in circumstances where the company is a one-man company (see at [2009] 2 BCLC 563 at [198]–[203]) while
Lord Walker took the more convoluted route (an 'excursion', as Halpern describes it, see n 256, at 490) of saying there was an exception to *Hampshire Land* in the case of a one-man company (see at [167]–[168]). Either
way, they were agreed that *Hampshire Land* did not prevent the attribution to a one-man company of the
fraudster's knowledge and conduct. As Lord Phillips noted, at [32], this leaves open the question of whether
ex turpi causa will bar a claim by a company with independent shareholders where those shareholders have
been unaware that the directing mind and will of the company has involved the company in a fraud.

[264] Lord Scott did not appear to think this to be the case, but their other Lordships were agreed that this
was the position.

[265] The *ex turpi causa* rule only applies to defeat a primarily liability. Where a company is liable vicariously
only, a claim by it cannot be defended and defeated by reliance on *ex turpi causa* for the company is not the
wrongdoer, rather vicarious liability has been imposed to make it liable as if it were a wrongdoer, which is
a different matter: see *Safeway Stores Ltd v Twigger* [2011] 2 All ER 841 (a company which infringed anti-
competition provisions of the Competition Act 1998 was primarily responsible for the breach as a matter of
statutory construction and as such was precluded by the maxim *ex turpi causa non oritur actio* from recovering the amount of any penalty imposed on it by the Office of Fair Trading by suing its former directors or
employees who were themselves responsible for the infringement). They were entitled to raise the *ex turpi
causa* defence against the company as a primary wrongdoer.

4

The company constitution

A Defining the constitution

4-1 The company's constitution is defined in CA 2006, s 17 in the following terms:

> 'Unless the context otherwise requires, references in the Companies Acts to a company's constitution include—
>
> (a) the company's articles, and
>
> (b) any resolutions and agreements to which Chapter 3 applies (see section 29).'

4-2 Every company must have articles of association contained in a single document divided into paragraphs numbered consecutively.[1] Model forms of articles are provided for public and private companies limited by shares and for companies limited by guarantee and any company may adopt all or any of the provisions of the relevant model articles for that type of company.[2] Model articles are not intended to be a strait-jacket and the draftsman is free to add, subtract or vary, as the needs of the case suggest.[3]

4-3 Each company must register its articles (CA 2006, s 18(2)) and if, on formation of a limited company, articles are not registered or, if articles are registered, in so far as they do not exclude or modify the relevant model articles, the relevant model articles form part of the company's articles automatically (s 20(1)). Larger companies usually exclude all of the model articles and draw up an entire set of articles appropriate to their circumstances while drawing on the model articles in many respects. Even with smaller companies, the shareholders on formation may have matters of particular concern to them, such as issues concerning share transfers or the appointment of directors, and it is preferable for these matters to be the subject of provisions specifically drawn up to cover their individual circumstances.[4] These provisions can then be combined with the remainder of the model articles by stating that the model articles apply except to the extent that they are excluded (s 20(1)(b)).

---

[1] CA 2006, s 18(1), (3).

[2] CA 2006, s 19(3). See The Companies (Model Articles) Regulations 2008, SI 2008/3229. It is the model articles in force at the date of the company's registration which apply: s 20(2); subsequent amendments of the model articles do not affect a company registered before the amendment: s 19(4). Many companies on the register of companies remain subject to the 1985 Table A and some are still governed by the 1948 Table A. Effectively, Table A was a previous version of model articles.

[3] *Gaiman v National Association for Mental Health* [1971] Ch 317.

[4] Many small companies are purchased 'off the shelf', i.e. ready formed, however, with the result that the shareholders rarely consider or negotiate the articles, merely accepting whatever version is offered which will typically be the model articles.

4-4 While it is possible to include the model provisions by reference,[5] it is preferable and more consistent with the requirement that the articles be in a single document that the company draws up articles which include the customised matters and the matters relied on from the model articles. This approach avoids the inconsistencies which can arise from having two documents and prevents uncertainty as to the extent to which specific model provisions have been excluded or modified. At common law persons dealing with a company are deemed under the doctrine of constructive notice to have notice of the company's articles of association,[6] but the impact of this doctrine is much reduced by CA 2006, ss 39–40 (s 39 is discussed at **4-14**; s 40 is discussed at **8-27**).

4-5 The resolutions and agreements referred to in CA 2006, s 17(b) (i.e. those to which Chapter 3 applies) are resolutions and agreements listed in s 29 which must be registered with the registrar of companies (s 30). Basically there are two types of resolutions,[7] ordinary and special resolutions. An ordinary resolution is a resolution passed by a simple majority (s 282(1)) and a special resolution is a resolution passed by a majority of not less than 75% (s 283(1)). Resolutions are considered at **15-16**.

4-6 The categories of resolutions which must be registered are:

- any special resolution (s 29(1)(a));

- any resolution or agreement which to be effective should have been passed by a special resolution, but was instead agreed to by all the members (or a resolution which to be effective should have been passed by some particular majority or otherwise in some particular manner by a class of shareholders but was agreed to by all the members of the class) which resolution or agreement is nevertheless effective (and therefore should be registered) because of the *Duomatic* principle[8] that informal unanimous assent is tantamount to a resolution (s 29(1)(b) and (c));

- any resolution varying class rights (see **14-35**) which is not a special resolution (s 29(1)(d));

- other resolutions (i.e. ordinary resolutions) which are required by any enactment to be registered (s 29(1)(e)). This ensures that ordinary resolutions of importance must also be registered. For example, a resolution granting authority for an allotment of shares by the directors, though an ordinary resolution, must be registered,[9] as must an ordinary resolution granting a company authority for market purchases of its own shares,[10] and an ordinary resolution of members of a private company incorporated before 1 October 2008 allowing the directors to authorise conflicts of interest.[11] Another example of a resolution which must be registered is a resolution for voluntary winding up under IA 1986, s 84(1)(a) to which CA 2006, ss 29 and 30 apply.[12]

---

[5] See *Explanatory Notes to the Companies Act 2006*, para 76.

[6] *Ernest v Nicholls* (1857) 6 HL Cas 401; *Mahony v East Holyford Mining Co* (1875) LR 7 HL 869; *Irvine v Union Bank of Australia* (1877) 2 App Cas 366, PC; *Wilson v Kelland* [1910] 2 Ch 306.

[7] The CA 2006 abolished the category of extraordinary resolutions (essentially required 75% majority of those voting, but differed from a special resolution in that only 14 rather than 21 days' notice was required) though transitional arrangements ensure that the requirements in a company's articles or a contract for an extraordinary resolution remain effective and CA 2006, s 29 applies to any such extraordinary resolution: see SI 2007/2194, art 9, Sch 3, para 23.

[8] *Re Duomatic Ltd* [1969] 1 All ER 161, discussed at **15-73**; it was noted in the Parliamentary debates that the requirement to register resolutions based on informal unanimous assent is rarely observed.

[9] CA 2006, s 551(8), (9).   [10] CA 2006, s 701(1), (8).

[11] The Companies Act 2006 (Commencement No 5, Transitional Provisions and Savings) Order 2007, SI 2007/3495, art 9, Sch 4, Pt 3, para 47.   [12] IA 1986, s 84(3).

4-7 There has always been some uncertainty as to whether the requirement for registration extends to shareholder agreements (s 29 and its predecessors refer to resolutions or agreements) and this matter is not clarified by the Companies Act 2006. In practice, shareholder agreements are not registered and are regarded as purely private contractual documents. Anyone consulting the company's articles needs to bear in mind, therefore, the possibility (which they should enquire about) that there is a private shareholders' agreement behind the public constitution. Shareholder agreements are discussed at **4-61**.

4-8 The definition of the constitution in CA 2006, s 17 is not exhaustive ('include') and is subject to context. Beyond the articles and resolutions, the memorandum of association would also be considered to be a constitutional document. Its importance is limited by s 8 to signalling the wish of the subscribers to form a company and their agreement to become members of the company and, in the case of a company limited by shares, to take at least one share each. An indication of other documents which make up the company's constitution can be found in s 32 which, in the context of documents which must be provided to members on request, identifies the constitutional documents as including the company's articles, any resolutions and agreements that have been recorded by the registrar under s 29; a copy of the company's current certificate of incorporation, and a current statement of capital (which will give the total number of shares in the company, their aggregate nominal value, any class rights and the amount paid, or unpaid, on the shares). For the purposes of Part 10 (directors' duties), an expanded definition of the constitution is provided in s 257 to include, in addition to the matters mentioned in s 17, (a) any resolution or other decision come to in accordance with the constitution[13] and (b) any decision by the members, or by a class of members, that is treated as equivalent to a decision by the company, a reference to decisions reached on the basis of the informal unanimous assent of the members which, applying *Re Duomatic Ltd*[14] (see **15-73**), is equivalent to a decision of the company. The expanded definition means that the directors must act in accordance with the articles (s 17(a)), any special (or other) resolution registrable with the registrar of companies (s 17(b)), any resolution or other decision reached under the constitution (s 257(1)) and any decision reached by virtue of the informal unanimous assent of the members (s 257(2)).

4-9 There are therefore potentially a number of elements to the constitution depending on the context, but for most purposes, the key document is the articles of association.

B Content of the articles

Internal rules

4-10 The articles set out the internal rules and regulations which govern the relationship between the members and the company. The matters typically covered in the articles include the appointment and removal of directors, their powers, the conduct of directors' and shareholders' meetings, voting procedures, capital matters (including share transfer and transmission) and the declaration of dividends. If the company is a limited company, whether limited by shares or by guarantee, the liability of the members must be limited by the constitution (CA 2006, s 3(1)) so, for example, the model articles for private companies

---

[13] For example, the articles may require an ordinary resolution on some matter which resolution is not registrable, not being within CA 2006, s 29, and so not within the definition of the constitution in s 17.

[14] [1969] 1 All ER 161.

limited by shares provide that 'the liability of the members is limited to the amount, if any, unpaid on the shares held by them'.[15]

Provisions previously contained in a company's memorandum

4-11 Prior to the reforms effected by the CA 2006, a company's memorandum of association was an important constitutional document. Under CA 2006, s 8 it merely serves to record the agreement of the members to form an association (see **4-8**). For companies formed under the CA 1985 and its predecessors, provisions that were contained in the memorandum (including provisions for entrenchment) are treated now as provisions of the company's articles (CA 2006, s 28(1), (2)) and as such may be altered by a special resolution under s 21 (other than provisions for entrenchment which remain entrenched (s 28(3)).[16] Entrenchment is discussed at **4-17**.

Objects clauses

4-12 Prior to the CA 2006, companies were required to state their objects in the memorandum and the objects determined the company's capacity. Acts outside of the objects were ultra vires and void,[17] though the impact of that doctrine was reduced almost to obsolescence by a combination of drafting techniques, judicial interpretation and statutory reform.[18] The position has been further affected by a significant change effected by the CA 2006.

4-13 Companies are no longer required to state their objects and, unless a company's articles specifically restrict the objects of the company, a company's objects are unrestricted (CA 2006, s 31(1)). Companies formed under the CA 2006 generally do not restrict their objects (though some businesses such as charitable companies may still find it useful to do so) and therefore most companies have unrestricted capacity and no issue of ultra vires can arise. For companies formed under the CA 1985 and its predecessors, as noted, the objects clauses previously set out in the memorandum now become part of their articles and are open to alteration and deletion by way of special resolution under CA 2006, s 21 (see **4-11**). For such companies, deleting their objects puts them in the same position as companies formed under the CA 2006, their capacity is unrestricted and no issue of ultra vires can arise and it seems that many listed companies have taken the opportunity to delete their objects and so their capacity is unrestricted.

4-14 Alternatively, companies formed under the CA 1985 and its predecessors may choose to retain their objects clauses in their articles and, as mentioned, some companies formed under the CA 2006 may find it useful to restrict their objects as permitted by s 31. Strictly speaking, such companies may still enter into ultra vires transactions, i.e. acts beyond the restricted capacity limited by their objects clauses, but s 39 provides that the validity of an act done by a company cannot be called into question on the ground of a lack of capacity by reason of anything in the company's constitution.[19] The ultra vires point cannot be raised, therefore, but what can be raised within the company is the directors' failure to observe the limitation in the articles which is a failure by the directors to act in accordance with the constitution, as required by s 171. That duty is discussed in Chapter 8.

---

[15] See The Companies (Model Articles) Regulations 2008, SI 2008/3229, reg 2, Sch 1, para 2.
[16] Care must be taken not to delete the limited liability clause in the process, see text to n 15.
[17] *Ashbury Railway Carriage and Iron Co Ltd v Riche* (1875) LR 7 HL 653.
[18] Legislative intervention to protect third parties arose out of the need to implement the First Company Law Directive, Directive 68/151/EEC, 1968 OJ Spec Ed (1) 41, art 9.
[19] The application of CA 2006, s 39 is modified for charitable companies, see s 42.

C Amending the articles

The statutory power to amend the articles

4-15 A company may amend its articles of association by special resolution[20] (CA 2006, s 21(1)) and any agreement or article purporting to deprive a company of the power to amend its articles is invalid on the ground that it is contrary to the statute;[21] however, the statute does allow for the entrenchment of provisions in the articles such that they cannot be altered by a special resolution (s 22), entrenchment is discussed at **4-17**. In effect, therefore, the general power of amendment in s 21 is subject to any use of entrenched provisions as allowed by s 22. The articles may also be altered by order of a court or other authority so as to restrict or exclude the power of the company to amend its articles, in which case the company must give notice of that fact to the registrar (s 23(1)(c)).[22] An alteration cannot require a member to take more shares or in any way increase his liability to contribute to the company's share capital or otherwise to pay money to the company (i.e. payments in his capacity as a shareholder) without his consent (s 25). Furthermore, the variation of class rights set out in the articles is governed by s 630(2) and not by s 21 (class rights are discussed at **14-23**). Finally, at common law, the power to alter the articles must be exercised bona fide for the benefit of the company as a whole, see **4-20**. A member joins a company on the basis of the articles as they stand at the time he joins and on the understanding that the articles may be changed.[23] If a member wishes to protect himself against particular alterations, he will need to consider some of the protective devices which are available, mechanisms which in effect erode the principle that a company cannot be denied the power to alter the articles.

4-16 One possibility is weighted voting rights granted to a shareholder or group of shareholders to ensure that the other shareholders cannot muster the necessary votes to achieve a special resolution,[24] a result which can also be achieved by the shareholders or some of them reaching an agreement outside of the articles as to how they will exercise their

---

[20] A special resolution means a resolution passed by a majority of not less than 75%: CA 2006, s 283(1). A special resolution amending the articles must be forwarded to the registrar of companies within 15 days after it is passed or made: ss 29(1)(a), 30(1); and a copy of the articles as altered must be sent to the registrar not later than 15 days after the amendment takes effect: s 26. As to penalties for non-compliance, see s 27. The position is modified for charitable companies, see s 21(2). See also *Cane v Jones* [1980] 1 WLR 1451 and **15-30**.

[21] *Walker v London Tramways Co* (1879) 12 Ch D 705; *Malleson v National Insurance & Guarantee Corpn* [1894] 1 Ch 200; *Punt v Symons & Co Ltd* [1903] 2 Ch 506. See also *Russell v Northern Bank Development Corp Ltd* [1992] 3 All ER 161, HL. While a company cannot be precluded from altering its articles, to act on the altered articles may nevertheless be a breach of contract (giving rise to liability in damages) if the altered position is contrary to a stipulation in a contract validly made before the alteration: *Southern Foundries (1926) Ltd v Shirlaw* [1940] AC 701 at 740–1; *Cumbrian Newspapers Group Ltd v Cumberland and Westmorland Herald Newspaper and Printing Co Ltd* [1986] 2 All ER 816 at 831.

[22] The company must also give notice to the registrar if the court or other authority by order subsequently alters the articles to remove any restriction on or exclusion of the power to amend the articles: CA 2006, s 23(2)(b)(ii). If a company is subject to an order of the court or other authority restricting its power to amend the articles, on any subsequent amendment of the articles, the company must provide the registrar with a statement of compliance, certifying that any alteration has been made in accordance with the order of the court or other authority: s 24(1)–(3).

[23] *Allen v Gold Reefs of West Africa Ltd* [1900] 1 Ch 656 at 672–3, per Lindley MR; *Greenhalgh v Arderne Cinemas Ltd* [1950] 2 All ER 1120 at 1127, per Evershed MR; *Malleson v National Insurance & Guarantee Corp* [1894] 1 Ch 200 at 205, 206. See also *Peters' American Delicacy Co Ltd v Heath* (1939) 61 CLR 457 at 507, per Dixon J.   [24] See *Bushell v Faith* [1969] 1 All ER 1002.

voting rights on any resolution to alter the articles.[25] Another possibility is for the shareholder to seek to secure class rights (see **14-23**) to herself which can only be varied in accordance with s 630(2).[26] A further possibility is for the shareholders to regulate their relationship *inter se* by way of a shareholders' agreement entirely distinct from the articles, an agreement which has the merits of being a private contact which cannot be altered without consent. Shareholder agreements are discussed at **4-61**.

Provision for entrenchment

4-17   As noted, the power to amend the articles in CA 2006, s 21 is subject to any provision for entrenchment governed by s 22 which recognises that specified provisions may not be subject to alteration by special resolution. This entrenchment mechanism was provided for by s 22, in part, as a necessary consequence of the changes made to the memorandum of association demoting it from its previous role as an important constitutional document (see **4-8**). Previously, when shareholders wished to entrench provisions of the constitution, they could do so by including them in the memorandum and precluding their alteration. With the memorandum reduced to the status of a declaration of association (s 8), a new method of entrenchment is required and s 22(1) provides that:

> 'A company's articles may contain provision ("provision for entrenchment") to the effect that specified provisions of the articles may be amended or repealed only if conditions are met, or procedures are complied with, that are more restrictive than those applicable in the case of a special resolution.'[27]

The provision for entrenchment must relate to specified provisions of the articles and it is not possible to entrench all of the articles since to do so would deprive the company of the statutory power to alter the articles. A provision for entrenchment may be included in the articles from formation or it may be added by a subsequent amendment of the articles[28] and, in either case, the registrar must be informed (CA 2006, s 23(1)) so as to ensure that anyone searching the register appreciates that the articles contain such provision.[29] The requirement in CA 2006, s 22(2) that inclusion of a provision for entrenchment in the articles must be on formation or by an amendment of the articles agreed to by all the members of the company has not been brought into force[30] because of the uncertain relationship

---

[25] This type of arrangement is not caught by the prohibition on the company restricting its power to alter its articles, see *Russell v Northern Bank Development Corp Ltd* [1992] 3 All ER 161, HL.

[26] CA 2006, s 630(2) provides that rights attached to a class of a company's shares may only be varied: (a) in accordance with provision in the company's articles for the variation of those rights; or (b) where the company's articles contain no such provision, if the holders of shares of that class consent to the variation in accordance with this section; and s 630(3) provides that this is without prejudice to any other restrictions on the variation of rights (for example, from a court order).

[27] A condition might be that a 90% majority is required for alteration. The procedures to be complied with may be more restrictive than for a special resolution, for example, with regard to giving notice of the resolution. See the definition of special resolution in CA 2006, s 283 and note its application also to a special resolution of members of a class.

[28] As noted at **4-11**, provisions previously included in the old-style memorandum including provisions entrenched in the memorandum are now treated as provisions of the articles and, where a provision was previously entrenched in the memorandum, it remains as an entrenched provision in the articles, see CA 2006, s 28(2)).   [29] See *Explanatory Notes to the Companies Act 2006*, para 84.

[30] The decision not to commence CA 2006, s 22(2) is explained in the Explanatory Memorandum to The Companies Act 2006 and Limited Liability Partnerships (Transitional Provisions And Savings) (Amendment) Regulations 2009, SI 2009/2476, paras 7.5–7.7.

between s 22 and class rights (see CA 2006, ss 629–640 and **14-23**). The Department for Business, Innovation and Skills (BIS) received representations that, on one interpretation, s 22(2) could prevent the creation and variation of class rights. It is not uncommon for the articles to create class rights and to provide that they can only be varied with the consent of, say, 90% of the class, in which case, as the rights cannot be altered by a special resolution, this is a provision for entrenchment within s 22(1). If s 22(2) were in force, such class rights could only be created either on formation or with the agreement of all the shareholders. Such a limitation would be unduly restrictive of the directors' ability to manage the company's share capital structure. Therefore s 22(2) has not been commenced and class rights can continue to be created at any time and, if a variation of those class rights can only occur on terms which fall within s 22(1), the class right is entrenched. Entrenchment should be of no consequence in these circumstances since entrenchment merely means that a provision is not open to alteration by special resolution under s 21 and can be altered only in accordance with its own provisions for alteration which is the position in any event under s 630(2)(a).[31]

4-18 An entrenched provision, once included in the articles, may be altered in accordance with the method indicated in the provision for entrenchment.[32] Also, for the avoidance of doubt, s 22(3) makes clear that the fact that a provision is entrenched does not prevent amendment of the articles by agreement of all the members of the company (so even a provision which is stated to be irrevocable can be overridden, but only if all agree) or by order of the court or other authority having power to alter the company's articles.

4-19 If a company's articles are amended by the members (or altered by court or other order) so as to remove a provision for entrenchment, the registrar must be informed of that fact (s 23(2)) and the company must also provide a statement of compliance certifying that any alteration has been made in accordance with the articles (s 24(2), (3)).[33]

Common law limits to the power to amend the articles

4-20 The important common law limitation on the power to alter the articles was famously articulated by Lindley MR in *Allen v Gold Reefs of West Africa Ltd*[34] as follows:

> 'Wide, however, as the language of s 50 [CA 2006, s 21(1)] is, the power conferred by it must, like all other powers, be exercised subject to those general principles of law and equity which are applicable to all powers conferred on majorities and enabling them to bind minorities. It must be exercised, not only in the manner required by law, but also bona fide for the benefit of the company as a whole, and it must not be exceeded.'

---

[31] See n 26 for text of CA 2006, s 630(2). This lack of impact presumably explains why BIS was willing to commence the rest of s 22, but that is not to say that the relationship between s 22 and s 630 is easy to understand. There is a view that it would have been better if it had been made clear that s 22 has no application to class rights and also a view that BIS should not have commenced any of the provisions of s 22 until these issues as to the relationship between s 22 and s 630 are resolved.

[32] Initially, it was intended that an entrenched provision could not be altered or repealed, but the Government was subsequently persuaded that rendering a provision unalterable would create problems.

[33] In the Parliamentary debates, it was explained that the purpose of this requirement is to force the directors to pause and take stock and ensure that they have satisfied themselves that any necessary restrictions in the constitution have been observed; it also ensures that the public record is accurate; and if the company has overlooked any special requirements in altering the articles, the registrar of companies is able to ask the company as to the position: see 678 HL Debs GC19, 30 January 2006.   [34] [1900] 1 Ch 656 at 671, CA.

4-21   In this case the court permitted an alteration which extended a company's lien (and powers of sale) on partly-paid shares to fully paid up shares, despite the fact that the change
impacted on only one shareholder holding fully-paid shares (or rather on his estate, as he
was deceased at the time of the alteration). It was because the member had died owing
arrears on partly-paid shares that the company wanted to extend the lien to fully-paid
shares which formed part of his estate. The court agreed that it was bona fide for the benefit of the company as a whole that the company should have a lien to secure debts due to
it.[35] An alteration applicable to all members and for the benefit of the company cannot
be impeached on the grounds of bad faith merely because its practical impact is felt by
only one member.[36] As Warrington LJ put it later in *Sidebottom v Kershaw, Leese & Co
Ltd*,[37] it is commonly the case that the circumstance of an individual member may awake
the directors to the problem which the alteration is designed to resolve, but the fact that
it impacts on one shareholder of itself does not call into question the bona fides of the
shareholders.[38]

4-22   Beyond this famous dictum of Lindley MR, the judgments in *Allen v Gold Reefs of West
Africa Ltd*[39] offer little guidance as to the scope and substance of this 'bona fide for the
benefit of the company as a whole' test (hereinafter the *Allen* test) and to some extent the
courts ever since have been exercised by its meaning.

4-23   Some elaboration of the *Allen* test can be found in two subsequent Court of Appeal judgments: *Shuttleworth v Cox Bros & Co (Maidenhead) Ltd*[40] and *Greenhalgh v Arderne
Cinemas Ltd*[41] of which *Shuttleworth* is the more illuminating.[42]

4-24   In *Shuttleworth v Cox Bros & Co (Maidenhead) Ltd*[43] a provision in the company's articles
conferred life tenure on the directors unless disqualified on one of six grounds. One of
the directors failed to account for company money and property and the articles were
altered to add a further ground for disqualification, namely that any director should
resign on being asked by all his co-directors to resign. Once the articles had been altered,
the defaulting director was asked to resign. He unsuccessfully challenged the validity of
the alteration.

4-25   The Court of Appeal started by criticising the view that had been expressed in the lower
court in the earlier case of *Dafen Tinplate Co Ltd v Llanelly Steel Co Ltd*[44] that the *Allen*
test had two distinct components, bona fides and the benefit of the company.[45] The Court
of Appeal stressed that there is only one test and the proper approach was summed up by
Scrutton LJ as follows:[46]

---

[35] Vaughan Williams LJ dissented as he thought that the resolution was not passed in good faith, being
really passed merely to defeat the existing rights of an individual shareholder, see [1900] 1 Ch 656 at 677.

[36] [1900] 1 Ch 656 at 675. See also *Sidebottom v Kershaw, Leese & Co Ltd* [1920] 1 Ch 154; *Greenhalgh v
Arderne Cinemas Ltd* [1950] 2 All ER 1120; *Shuttleworth v Cox Bros & Co (Maidenhead) Ltd* [1927] KB 9.

[37] [1920] 1 Ch 154, CA.   [38] [1920] 1 Ch 154 at 171–2; and see at 166–7, per Lord Sterndale MR.

[39] [1900] 1 Ch 656 at 671, CA.   [40] [1927] 2 KB 9, CA.   [41] [1950] 2 All ER 1120, CA.

[42] The difficulties with Evershed MR's judgment in *Greenhalgh* are such (see Hannigan, n 106 at 479–80)
that it is probably best relegated to the sidelines but, of course, until overruled it stands as an authority. See
also Davies, *Gower and Davies' Principles of Modern Company Law* (8th edn, 2008), p 661 who comments
that the guidance to be gained from *Greenhalgh* is limited; and Chivers & Shaw (eds), *The Law of Majority
Shareholder Power* (2008), para 1.33 ('in many respects, a poorly reasoned decision').

[43] [1927] 2 KB 9.   [44] [1920] 2 Ch 124, Ch D.   [45] [1927] 2 KB 9 at 19, 22.

[46] [1927] 2 KB 9 at 23, cited with approval in *Citco Banking Corp NV v Pusser's Ltd* [2007] 2 BCLC 483 at
489, PC, per Lord Hoffmann.

'...when persons, honestly endeavouring to decide what will be for the benefit of the company and to act accordingly, decide upon a particular course, then, *provided* [emphasis added] there are grounds on which reasonable men could come to the same decision, it does not matter whether the Court would or would not come to the same decision or a different decision. It is not the business of the Court to manage the affairs of the company. That is for the shareholders and directors.'

4-26 The central question is whether the shareholders honestly believe the alteration to be for the benefit of the company as a whole but, in order that the test should not be wholly subjective, there is the proviso that, even if the shareholders' honesty is unchallenged, an alteration will not stand if it is such that 'no reasonable men could consider it for the benefit of the company'.[47]

4-27 The first requirement, that the shareholders exercise their power to alter the articles in good faith, is simply a reflection of the traditional equitable constraints on the ability of a majority to bind a minority, as Lindley MR said in *Allen v Gold Reefs of West Africa Ltd*.[48] It protects the minority by ensuring that alterations motivated by malice, fraud and personal benefit cannot stand while respecting the commercial judgement of shareholders acting genuinely for the benefit of the company.[49] The proviso that an alteration will not stand if it is such that 'no reasonable men could consider it for the benefit of the company' simply confirms that there are some alterations that 'cannot be regarded as being for the benefit of the company, no matter how honestly the majority believe them to be'.[50] Subjective good faith cannot be allowed to prevail where a reasonable shareholder can see no benefit to the company and the absence of such benefit would in any event cast doubt on the assertions of bona fides by the shareholders.[51]

4-28 The core element to the test (and the proviso) is the requirement that the alteration be for the benefit of the company as a whole. That is the limit to the power which 'must not be exceeded', to use Lord Lindley's words,[52] otherwise the exercise is a fraud on a power and void.[53]

---

[47] [1927] 2 KB 9 at 18, per Bankes LJ: '[an alteration must not be]...so oppressive as to cast suspicion on the honesty of the persons responsible for it, or so extravagant that no reasonable men could really consider it for the benefit of the company.'; at 24, per Scrutton LJ: '[an alteration will not stand if]...the decision of the shareholders, though honest, is such that no reasonable men could have come to it upon proper materials...'; qualifications endorsed by Atkin LJ, at 26. See Sealy, '"Bona Fides" and "Proper Purposes" in Corporate Decisions' [1989] 15 Monash U L Rev 265 at 277–8.   [48] [1900] 1 Ch 656 at 671.

[49] See *Rights & Issues Investment Trust Ltd v Stylo Shoes Ltd* [1964] 3 All ER 628 at 631; *Sidebottom v Kershaw, Leese & Co Ltd* [1927] 2 KB 9 at 23, 26, per Atkins LJ: 'It is not a matter of law for the Court whether or not a particular alteration is for the benefit of the company; nor is it the business of the judge to review the decision of every company in the country on these questions.'

[50] *Constable v Executive Connections Ltd* [2005] 2 BCLC 638 at 649–50; and see Sealy, n 47; *Hutton v West Cork Rly Co* (1993) 23 Ch D 654 at 671, per Bowen LJ: 'Bona fides cannot be the sole test, otherwise you might have a lunatic conducting the affairs of the company, and paying away its money with both hands in a manner perfectly bona fide yet perfectly irrational.'

[51] See *Shuttleworth v Cox Bros & Co (Maidenhead) Ltd* [1927] 2 KB 9 at 23.

[52] *Allen v Gold Reefs of West Africa Ltd* [1900] 1 Ch 656 at 671.

[53] See Worthington, 'Corporate Governance: Remedying and Ratifying Directors' Breaches' (2000) 116 LQR 638 at 646–50—majority shareholders are not allowed to use their powers for purposes outside the contemplation of the grant; *Vatcher v Paul* [1915] AC 372 at 378; *British Equitable Assurance Co Ltd v Bailey* [1906] AC 35 at 42, per Lord Lindley; *Re Halt Garage (1964) Ltd* [1982] 3 All ER 1016 at 1037, per Oliver J; *Peters' American Delicacy Co v Heath* (1939) 61 CLR 457 at 511–12, per Dixon J. Also note Rimer J in *Redwood Master Fund Ltd v TD Bank Europe Ltd* [2006] 1 BCLC 149 at 182 though not involving an alteration of articles, rather the variation of the terms of a loan facility.

4-29 In *Greenhalgh v Arderne Cinemas Ltd*,[54] the company's articles contained restrictive provisions governing the transfer of shares. Anyone wishing to sell their shares in the company was required to offer them first to existing members. If no member wished to purchase the shares, the shares could then be sold to an outside purchaser, but only with the consent of the board of directors. The articles were altered to allow for the direct sale of shares to an outsider without having to offer them first to the existing shareholders, provided the sale was approved by an ordinary resolution of the company in general meeting. A minority shareholder challenged the validity of this alteration. The court concluded that the alteration was merely a relaxation of the very stringent restrictions on transfer in the existing articles and as such was bona fide for the benefit of the company as a whole.[55]

4-30 As to the meaning of 'the company as a whole', while the balance of dicta in the cases can be read as interpreting the phrase as meaning the corporate entity,[56] Evershed MR in *Greenhalgh* had no doubt that the phrase 'the company as a whole' meant the shareholders as a body.[57] Regarding 'the company as a whole' as the corporators as a whole makes sense in the context of the power which is being exercised. It is a power to alter the contractual relationship between the members *inter se*[58] and between them and the company and as such should be governed by considerations as to what is in the best interests of the members as a whole and their collective interests are reflected in the commercial interests of the entity. In many of the cases, it makes little difference to the outcome, therefore, whether the meaning of 'the company as a whole' is expressed as the entity rather than the corporators or vice versa, given that it is difficult to distinguish the collective body of the shareholders from the entity. For example, it was in the interests of the corporators and the company in *Allen*[59] that the company obtained security with respect to debts owed to it; it was in the interests of the corporators and the company in *Greenhalgh*[60] that the company's strict pre-emption provisions on transfer were relaxed;[61] it was in the interests of the corporators and the company in *Sidebottom v Kershaw, Leese & Co Ltd*[62] that the articles allowed for the compulsory acquisition of the shares of members who were competitors of the company; it was in the interests of the corporators and the company in *Shuttleworth*[63] that the articles were amended to facilitate the removal of unsatisfactory directors. In fact, when the cases are considered in detail, there is evidence of considerable judicial wavering (even within a case) between viewing the company as an entity and viewing the company as the corporators.[64] Overall, in the context of these types of alterations, the community of interest between the corporators and the entity is such that

---

[54] [1950] 2 All ER 1120.

[55] [1950] 2 All ER 1120 at 1127.

[56] See Lindley MR in *Allen v Gold Reefs of West Africa Ltd* [1900] 1 Ch 656 at 671 who clearly meant the corporate entity, as did Romer LJ, at 682; as did Sterndale MR and Warrington LJ in *Sidebottom v Kershaw, Leese & Co Ltd* [1920] 1 Ch 154 at 165–6 and 171, respectively; as did Scrutton and Atkin LLJ in *Shuttleworth v Cox Bros & Co (Maidenhead) Ltd* [1927] KB 9 at 23 and 26, respectively.

[57] [1950] 2 All ER 1120 at 1126.

[58] *Peters' American Delicacy Co Ltd v Heath* (1939) 61 CLR 457 at 506, per Dixon J.

[59] *Allen v Gold Reefs of West Africa Ltd* [1900] 1 Ch 656.

[60] *Greenhalgh v Arderne Cinemas Ltd* [1950] 2 All ER 1120.

[61] The company's interest would lie in the ability to raise capital by issuing shares as a result of their increased marketability following the relaxation of the pre-emption provisions.

[62] [1920] 1 Ch 154, CA.

[63] *Shuttleworth v Cox Bros & Co (Maidenhead) Ltd* [1927] 2 KB 9.

[64] See, for example, *Sidebottom v Kershaw, Leese & Co Ltd* [1920] 1 Ch 154 at 166, 169; see too Rixon, n 77, p 454 who concluded: 'In short, "the company as a whole" is a Delphic term employed by different judges in different circumstances to signify different things…'; see also Sealy, n 47, at pp 269–70.

it matters little whether the benefit sought is expressed as the benefit of the company as a whole or the benefit of the collective body of members.

4-31   Given the general approach of the courts to the *Allen* test, it is unsurprising that it is rare for a challenge to an alteration to succeed (and the onus of proof is on the person challenging the alteration).[65] This judicial reluctance to interfere in this area was confirmed by the Privy Council in *Citco Banking Corp NV v Pusser's Ltd*.[66] In this case the company had two main shareholders, one of whom held 28% of the shares and was the company chairman, the other held 13% and was the appellant bank, and the rest of the shares were widely held. The alteration to the articles had the effect of giving the chairman voting control of the company. On the resolution to alter the articles, 1,123,665 votes were cast for the resolution and 183,000 votes against the resolution. All of the dissenting votes were cast by the appellant bank which argued that the alteration was passed in the interests of the chairman gaining control and not in the interests of the company. The Privy Council dismissed their challenge to the validity of the alteration, applied *Shuttleworth*, see **4-24,** and accepted that the test can be stated succinctly by asking whether reasonable shareholders could consider the amendment to be for the benefit of the company.[67] Stated like this, the test looks more objective than subjective,[68] but this is a condensed statement of the traditional test, i.e. could the shareholders genuinely have believed the alteration to be for the benefit of the company and was that belief one which a reasonable shareholder could have held? The authorities in any event make it difficult to determine whether the subjective or objective element is pre-eminent[69] which, of course, may be the result of a quite deliberate conflating of the issues by the courts so as to avoid criticism that the court is substituting its judgment for that of the shareholders.[70]

4-32   On the facts in *Citco*, the shareholders could have concluded in good faith that they accepted the arguments as to why the amendment would be in the interests of the company (the company needed further capital and potential investors wished the chairman to have control of the company). Just as an alteration may be for the benefit of the company though it is to the detriment of one member (as in *Allen*) so an alteration may be for the benefit of the company as a whole notwithstanding that it operates to the particular advantage of some or one shareholder.[71] In the absence of any attack on his bona fides, the Privy Council also confirmed that there is no reason why a member who benefits from an

---

[65] *Peters' American Delicacy Co Ltd v Heath* (1939) 61 CLR 457; *Citco Banking Corp NV v Pusser's Ltd* [2007] 2 BCLC 483, PC.

[66] [2007] 2 BCLC 483, PC. See Williams (2007) CLJ 500.

[67] [2007] 2 BCLC 483 at 491, PC, per Lord Hoffmann.

[68] See Kershaw, *Company Law in Context* (2009), p 602, who comments that this way of putting the test is incorrect or at least potentially misleading. On the other hand, Chivers & Shaw (eds), *The Law of Majority Shareholder Power* (2008), p 19 criticise the formulation in *Shuttleworth*, see **4-25,** as being extremely subjective and it may be that Lord Hoffmann was merely trying to remind everyone that there is a reasonable element to *Shuttleworth* which must not be overlooked.

[69] See *Sidebottom v Kershaw, Leese & Co Ltd* [1920] 1 Ch 154 at 165–6, 171–2 where the court appears to give almost equal weight to the requirement of subjective good faith and an objective benefit to the company in ridding itself of a competing shareholder.

[70] See Davies, n 42, p 654: 'The courts have hovered uncomfortably between an unwillingness to determine how businesses should be run and an equally deeply felt unease that simple majoritarianism would leave the minority exposed to opportunistic treatment.'

[71] [2007] 2 BCLC 483 at 490. See *Rights & Issues Investment Trust Ltd v Stylo Shoes Ltd* [1964] 3 All ER 628 at 631.

alteration (in this case, the chairman) should not vote, as a shareholder, in favour of that alteration.[72]

4-33   The Privy Council focus in *Citco* on *Shuttleworth v Cox Bros & Co (Maidenhead) Ltd*[73] suggests that their Lordships are content that the position now reached on the 'bona fides' test maintains a proper balance between the freedom necessary for the majority to make constitutional changes and the need to protect the minority against unfair alterations, and later courts may prefer the Hoffmann articulation of the test in terms of reasonable shareholders rather than the continued application of the somewhat empty *Allen* dicta of Lord Lindley MR. The resolutely minimalist judgment in *Citco* indicates a preference certainly for the established approach.[74]

4-34   Their Lordships in *Citco* did accept that the 'bona fides for the benefit of the company as a whole' test is not appropriate in the context of an alteration adjusting the conflicting interests of the shareholders[75] and 'some other test of validity is required',[76] but no guidance was given as to what that test might be. This point refers to the issue raised most notably in the Australian case, *Peters' American Delicacy Co Ltd v Heath*,[77] as to the inappropriateness of the *Allen* test when the alteration at issue more directly pits one section of the members against another, where those in favour of the amendment have interests directly competing or conflicting with the interests of those opposed.[78] The issue was explained by Dixon J as follows:

> 'If the challenged alteration relates to an article which does or may affect an individual, as, for instance, a director appointed for life or a shareholder whom it is desired to expropriate, or to an article affecting the mutual rights and liabilities *inter se* of shareholders or different classes or descriptions of shareholders, the very subject matter involves a conflict of interests and advantages.[79] To say that the shareholders forming the majority must consider the advantage of the company as a whole in relation to such a question seems inappropriate, if not meaningless, and at all events starts an impossible inquiry. The "company as a whole" is a corporate entity consisting of all the shareholders. If the proposal put forward is for a revision of any of the articles regulating the rights *inter se* of shareholders or classes of shareholders, the primary question must be how conflicting interests are to be adjusted, and the adjustment is left by law to the determination of those whose interests conflict, subject, however, to the condition that the existing provision can be altered only by a three-fourths majority.'

---

[72] [2007] 2 BCLC 483 at 493, citing the established principle that shareholders are free to exercise their votes in their own interests, see *Burland v Earle* [1902] AC 83 at 94.   [73] [1927] 2 KB 9, CA.

[74] Their Lordships declined the opportunity to consider further the meaning of Evershed MR's judgment in *Greenhalgh v Arderne Cinemas Ltd* [1950] 2 All ER 1120 or to explore the controversial Australian decision in *Gambotto v WCP Ltd* (1995) 182 CLR 432, discussed at **4-40.**

[75] See *Peters' American Delicacy Co Ltd v Heath* (1939) 61 CLR 457 at 512, per Dixon J; also Rixon, n 77.

[76] [2007] 2 BCLC 483 at 491.

[77] (1939) 61 CLR 457 at 507. See Rixon, 'Competing Interests and Conflicting Principles: An Examination of the Power of Alteration of Articles of Association' (1986) 49 MLR 446.

[78] On the facts in *Peters' American Delicacy*, the alteration dealt with the manner in which dividends and bonus shares were to be distributed and the change was to the advantage of those holding fully-paid shares and to the disadvantage of those holding partly-paid shares—the company had 511,000 fully-paid shares in issue and 169,000 partly-paid.

[79] Dixon J went on to give some example of issues where amendments to the articles might give rise to these sorts of conflicts between shareholders, such as amendments to voting rights, the basis of distributing profits, the basis of dividing surplus assets on a winding up, preferential rights in relation to profits or to surplus assets, or any other question affecting the mutual interests of shareholders.

In the intervening decades since that case, it would seem that the courts have had neither the opportunity nor the inclination (even when an opportunity presented itself) to devise a new test.[80] There may be a variety of reasons for the lack of development. First, even when there are competing interests, it is possible for the court to apply the traditional test and still resolve how the competing interests should be balanced, as will be seen in the expropriation cases discussed at **4-35**. In *Citco Banking Corp NV v Pusser's Ltd*,[81] it could be argued that the alteration did give rise to competing interests since most shareholders lost power while the majority shareholder's power was consolidated, yet still their Lordships were content to apply the traditional test. Secondly, minorities are well protected now by the CA 2006, s 994 which allows a member to petition for relief on the ground, *inter alia*, that an actual or proposed act or omission of the company (including an act or omission on its behalf) is or would be unfairly prejudicial to the interests of the members generally or of some part of its members including at least himself. This provision (discussed in detail in Chapter 17) allows the court considerable latitude in assessing whether conduct is unfairly prejudicial and provides a basis for challenging an alteration where there are competing interests between the majority and the minority without the need to devise a further 'alteration' test.[82]

Compulsory transfer provisions

4-35 The application of the *Allen* test in the context of compulsory transfer provisions is dominated by three decisions: *Sidebottom v Kershaw, Leese & Co Ltd*;[83] *Brown v British Abrasive Wheel Co Ltd*[84] and *Dafen Tinplate Co Ltd v Llanelly Steel Co Ltd*.[85]

4-36 In *Sidebottom v Kershaw, Leese & Co Ltd*[86] the alteration allowed the directors to require any shareholder who competed with the company's business to transfer his shares at their full value to nominees of the directors. The plaintiffs (who held 711 out of 7,620 issued shares) sought a declaration that the alteration was invalid.[87] The court accepted that such a power could be included in the articles from incorporation[88] and could be included subsequently by way of alteration of the articles, provided the exercise of the power of alteration is beyond challenge, being done bona fide for the benefit of the company as a whole.[89] It had already been established that an alteration applicable to all is not open to impeachment solely on the basis of its impact on a particular shareholder.[90] Looking at the facts in *Sidebottom*, the Court of Appeal had no hesitation in finding that the resolution had been

[80] A new test might lie along the lines of 'proper purpose' or oppression as suggested by Dixon J in *Peters' American Delicacy Co Ltd v Heath* (1939) 61 CLR 457 at 512, but the adoption of a proper purpose test in *Gambotto v WCP Ltd* (1995) 182 CLR 432, see **4-40**, attracted considerable criticism precisely on the ground that a proper purpose test is no more certain in application in this context than the 'bona fides' test, while an oppression test (also favoured in *Gambotto*) is unnecessary in the light of CA 2006, s 994 (unfairly prejudicial conduct). [81] [2007] 2 BCLC 483, PC.

[82] Using CA 2006, s 994, Mr Greenhalgh (see **4-29**) would surely have succeeded in obtaining redress, but not necessarily in getting the alteration set aside, since the remedy commonly awarded to successful petitioners under s 994 is a purchase order, see **17-79**. A shareholder who wishes to remain in the company and prevent an alteration taking place will still have to go the *Allen* route, for while the court could make an order on a successful petition requiring the company not to make any, or any specified, alterations in its articles without the leave of the court (s 996(2)(e)), such an order is unlikely to be granted, see **17-74**.

[83] [1920] 1 Ch 154, CA. [84] [1919] 1 Ch 290. [85] [1920] 2 Ch 124.

[86] [1920] 1 Ch 154, CA. [87] [1920] 1 Ch 154 at 163–5.

[88] *Phillips v Manufacturers' Securities Ltd* (1917) 116 LT 290.

[89] [1920] 1 Ch 154 at 164, per Lord Sterndale MR.

[90] *Allen v Gold Reefs of West Africa Ltd* [1900] 1 Ch 656; see also *Greenhalgh v Arderne Cinemas Ltd* [1950] 2 All ER 1120; *Shuttleworth v Cox Bros & Co (Maidenhead) Ltd* [1927] 2 KB 9.

passed bona fide for the benefit of the company as a whole. The court accepted that it was clearly for the company's benefit 'that they should not be obliged to have amongst them as members persons who are competing with them in business, and who may get knowledge from their membership which would enable them to compete better'.[91]

4-37 In *Brown v British Abrasive Wheel Co Ltd*[92] the majority shareholders held 98% of the shares and wished to alter the articles so as to permit them to acquire at fair value the shares of the remaining 2% shareholders. The majority anticipated that further capital would be required for the development of the company and they were willing to provide it only if they could acquire the 2% minority.[93] The plaintiff shareholders (who held 50 shares out of an issued share capital of 50,000) successfully sought an injunction preventing the company from altering the articles in this way. Astbury J held that the proposed alteration was merely for the benefit of the majority, enabling them to do forcibly what they were unable to effect by agreement with the minority.[94] This judgment is unsound on the law for, as the Court of Appeal pointed out in *Sidebottom*,[95] Astbury J did not apply the *Allen* test.[96] Notwithstanding that clear error, Astbury J did expressly find that the shareholders had acted for their own benefit in approving the alteration rather than honestly endeavouring to act for the benefit of the company.[97] On that basis, the Court of Appeal was agreed that the decision in the case was right.[98]

4-38 The final authority is *Dafen Tinplate Co Ltd v Llanelly Steel Co Ltd*.[99] The background was that the company had been formed on the basis of an expectation (though no legal obligation) that the shareholders would purchase supplies from the company. One shareholder who had an interest in a competing business began purchasing his supplies from that other company. Being unable to acquire his shares by agreement, the company altered the articles to provide that the majority of shareholders could determine that the shares of any member (other than one principal shareholder) should be offered for sale by the directors to anyone of their choice at a fair value to be fixed by the directors. The court refused to permit the alteration saying that it would have enabled the majority shareholder compulsorily to acquire the shares of any other member '…although there may be no complaint of any kind against his conduct and it cannot be suggested that he has done, or contemplates doing, anything to the detriment of the company'.[100] To say that such an unrestricted and unlimited power of expropriation was for the benefit of the company, Peterson J said, was to confuse the interests of the majority with the benefit of the company as a whole.[101] The approach taken by Peterson J[102] was criticised by the Court of

---

[91] [1920] 1 Ch 154 at 166, per Lord Sterndale MR.   [92] [1919] 1 Ch 290.

[93] Without further capital, the majority said the company might have to go into liquidation, see [1919] 1 Ch 290 at 295–6.   [94] [1919] 1 Ch 290 at 294.

[95] See *Sidebottom v Kershaw, Leese & Co Ltd* [1920] 1 Ch 154 at 163, 170 and 173, per Lord Sterndale MR, Warrington LJ and Eve J, respectively.

[96] Astbury J took a broad approach and asked whether the enforcement of the proposed alteration against the minority was within the ordinary principles of justice and whether it was for the benefit of the company as a whole: [1919] 1 Ch 290 at 295–6.

[97] [1919] 1 Ch 290 at 298. There was some evidence in the case that the majority had an eye to personal profit in seeking to buy out the minority. The company's position had improved, bank funding was accessible, opportunities were anticipated and the court seemed to find that there was an element of the majority seeking to ensure that the spoils of future prosperity went to them and were not shared with any minority shareholders.

[98] See *Sidebottom v Kershaw, Leese & Co Ltd* [1920] 1 Ch 154 at 167, per Lord Sterndale MR; at 172, per Warrington LJ.   [99] [1920] 2 Ch 124.

[100] [1920] 2 Ch 124 at 138.   [101] [1920] 2 Ch 124 at 141.   [102] See [1920] 2 Ch 124 at 140.

Appeal in *Shuttleworth v Cox Bros (Maidenhead) Ltd*[103] without casting doubt, however, on the outcome of the case which was clearly correct, given the finding that the majority in supporting the alteration were not honestly endeavouring to act for the benefit of the company.

4-39 On the basis of these authorities, it might be thought that the law is clear. The difficulty is that the authorities are of limited value, being two first instance decisions which have been criticised by the Court of Appeal on a point of law, and a Court of Appeal decision which is of limited value since the facts were so clear-cut. Interestingly, when the court was asked in *Constable v Executive Connections Ltd*[104] to consider the position in the more modern setting of altering the articles to include a 'drag-along' clause,[105] the court indicated some uncertainty as to the boundaries of permissible alterations to allow for compulsory transfer.[106]

4-40 It is worth digressing at this point to consider the controversial decision of the Australian High Court, *Gambotto v WCP Ltd*,[107] where the court specifically rejected the 'bona fide for the benefit of the company' test as the appropriate test governing alterations and favoured a more objective consideration of the proper purpose for the exercise of the power of alteration.[108] More specifically, the court considered that the proper purpose for the expropriation of shares is if it could reasonably be apprehended that the continued shareholding is detrimental to the company and expropriation is a reasonable means of eliminating or mitigating that detriment.[109] The court went on to note that the majority cannot expropriate the minority merely to secure for themselves some commercial advantage to be derived from a new corporate structure.[110] The court further considered that the burden in expropriation cases is on the majority to prove that the alteration is for a proper purpose and is fair in all the circumstances.[111]

4-41 In this case, the alteration (approved without the majority shareholder voting) would have enabled the majority shareholder (99.7%) to acquire the minority's shares (50,590 shares, 0.3%) at full value which would have generated tax advantages of

---

[103] [1927] 2 KB 9 at 19, 22. The court criticised the suggestion by Peterson J that where there was a conflict between the view of the shareholders and of the court as to the merits of the alteration, the court's view should prevail.

[104] [2005] 2 BCLC 638 (application for a declaration that an alteration was invalid and of no effect and an injunction preventing the company from acting on the alteration).

[105] The essence of a drag-along provision is that, on an offer for shares in a company being accepted by the majority of shareholders, the majority may require the minority to transfer their shares to the offeror on the same terms.

[106] For a detailed discussion of the issues surrounding alterations to allow for compulsory transfer provisions, see Hannigan, 'Altering the Articles to Allow for Compulsory Transfer—Dragging Minority Shareholders to a Reluctant Exit' [2007] JBL 471; Chivers & Shaw (eds), *The Law of Majority Shareholder Power* (2008), Ch 1.

[107] (1995) 182 CLR 432, noted Prentice (1996) 112 LQR 194. See generally Boros, 'Altering the Articles of Association to Acquire Minority Shareholdings' in Rider (ed), *The Realm of Company Law* (1998); and the very useful collection of essays on the case in Ramsay (ed), *Gambotto v WCP Ltd: Its Implications for Corporate Regulation* (1996), hereinafter Ramsay (ed). [108] (1995) 182 CLR 432 at 444.

[109] (1995) 182 CLR 432 at 445–6; the examples given by the court were expropriation of a competitor or if necessary to ensure that the company could continue to comply with a regulatory regime governing the principal business of the company, for example regarding foreign ownership of shares in a regulated industry. [110] (1995) 182 CLR 432 at 446.

[111] (1995) 182 CLR 432 at 447.

approximately A\$4m for the company.[112] The minority shareholders who objected held 15,898 shares, 0.1% of the issued share capital. On the facts, the court found that there was no suggestion that the continued presence of the minority was harmful to the company's business activities or that they had acted in any way to the company's detriment. All that was suggested was that there were tax and administrative advantages for the company in expropriating the minority shareholders.[113] The court did not accept that such commercial advantages of themselves could constitute a proper purpose for an alteration of the articles allowing for expropriation and so the alteration was invalid.

4-42 This decision attracted considerable criticism on a variety of grounds[114] including, so far as compulsory transfer was concerned, that the result was economically inefficient and gave too much weight to proprietary interests and too much power to the minority shareholders.[115] In fact, the approach taken by the Australian High Court on the compulsory transfer point has much to commend it[116] and is compatible with the outcome of the English compulsory transfer cases, even if the legal basis is different. *Sidebottom v Kershaw, Leese & Co Ltd*[117] was a case where the continued presence of the minority shareholder (a competitor) was detrimental to the conduct of the company's business so the alteration was rightly allowed. In *Brown v British Abrasive Wheel Co Ltd*[118] and *Dafen Tinplate Co Ltd v Llanelly Steel Co Ltd*[119] the alterations provided for the inclusion of naked compulsory transfer provisions for the benefit and advantage of the majority shareholders and rightly were not allowed. The difference is that *Gambotto* contains a clearly articulated position on the issue of what is a permissible compulsory transfer provision whereas, as *Constable v Executive Connections Ltd*[120] makes clear, the position here is more uncertain.

4-43 The Company Law Review declined to embrace *Gambotto*, preferring to leave the matter to the courts to develop.[121] As noted, their Lordships in the Privy Council in *Citco Banking Corp NV v Pusser's Ltd*[122] also considered it unnecessary to consider *Gambotto* (*Citco* did not concern compulsory transfer) but they did note that, in their view, *Gambotto* has no support in the English authorities.[123] It also looks unlikely to attract any support for it is possible to see in *Citco* a judicial unwillingness to move from reliance on the open-ended discretion of *Allen* to determine what is an acceptable alteration, even if it leaves first instance judges unsure as to the permissible limits of compulsory purchase.

---

[112] The alteration would have enabled any member entitled to 90% or more of the issued shares to acquire compulsorily the remaining shares at \$1.80 per share.

[113] The court noted that it was difficult to conceive of circumstances in which financial and administrative benefits would not be a consequence of the expropriation of minority holdings: (1995) 182 CLR 432 at 448.

[114] See generally the commentaries on the case mentioned in n 107.

[115] See Hannigan, n 106, at 488 and the commentaries cited there.

[116] See generally Hannigan, n 106, and esp at 490–2. Essentially any alteration to add a compulsory transfer provision fundamentally alters the implicit basis of the bargain made between the shareholders on coming together in the company. The essence of the association is that the investment made by each shareholder is permanent and the relationship between the shareholders *inter se* is ongoing until such time as a shareholder chooses to exercise his right of voluntary exit. The bargain can be altered by agreement of the parties or by statute, but not by the exercise of majority power to alter the articles, save where the continued presence of the minority is detrimental to the conduct of the company's business.   [117] [1920] 1 Ch 154, CA.

[118] [1919] 1 Ch 290.   [119] [1920] 2 Ch 124.   [120] [2005] 2 BCLC 638.

[121] See Company Law Review, *Modern Company Law for a Competitive Economy: Completing the Structure* (2000) paras 5.94–5.99.

[122] [2007] 2 BCLC 483.   [123] [2007] 2 BCLC 483 at 492.

D Interpreting the articles

A contract with distinctive features

4-44 The articles form a contract, but it is a statutory contract with its own distinctive features, as the Court of Appeal explained in *Bratton Seymour Service Co Ltd v Oxborough*,[124] deriving its binding force not from a bargain struck between the parties, but from the terms of the statute (see CA 2006, s 33, at **4-47**).[125] Moreover, the contract can be altered by a special resolution without the consent of all the contracting parties (s 21). Unlike an ordinary contract, it is not defeasible on the grounds of misrepresentation, common law mistake, mistake in equity, undue influence or duress and it cannot be rectified by the court even if the articles do not accord with what is proved to have been the intention of the parties.[126] Once registered, the articles are one of the statutory documents of the company open to inspection by anyone minded to deal with the company or to take shares in it, hence it is not for the court to rectify the articles, even if they do not reflect the parties' intention, rather the members must alter the articles using the procedure provided by s 21.[127]

4-45 The articles are a commercial document and, in the event of any ambiguity, the courts will construe them so as to give them reasonable business efficacy where a construction tending to that result is admissible on the language of the articles,[128] but terms cannot be implied from extrinsic circumstances. In *Bratton Seymour Service Co Ltd v Oxborough*[129] the court could not imply a term in the articles of association of a company set up to manage a block of flats that the shareholders should make a financial contribution to the upkeep of the amenity areas of the development. Such a term could not be derived from the language of the articles, but purely from extrinsic circumstances and was, the court said, a type of implication which, as a matter of law, can never succeed in the case of articles of association.[130]

4-46 The position on the implication of terms into contracts generally is now dominated by the Privy Council decision and speech by Lord Hoffmann in *AG of Belize v Belize Telecom*[131]

---

[124] [1992] BCLC 693, CA.   [125] [1992] BCLC 693 at 698, per Steyn LJ.
[126] [1992] BCLC 693 at 698, CA.
[127] [1992] BCLC 693 at 696, per Dillon LJ. See *Scott v Frank F Scott* [1940] 1 Ch 794 (articles should have included a provision on pre-emption on the death of a shareholder; the court could not rectify the articles to include such a provision).
[128] *Holmes v Keyes* [1958] 2 All ER 129 at 138; also *BWE International Ltd v Jones* [2004] 1 BCLC 406, CA; *Dashfield v Davidson* [2009] 1 BCLC 220. In *Tett v Phoenix Property and Investment Co Ltd* [1986] BCLC 149, for example, the court was able as a matter of construction to resolve difficulties surrounding the operation of a badly drafted pre-emption clause in the articles. See also *Pennington v Crampton* [2004] BCC 611.
[129] [1992] BCLC 693, CA. See also *Mutual Life Insurance Co of New York v The Rank Organisation Ltd* [1985] BCLC 11.
[130] [1992] BCLC 693 at 698, per Steyn LJ. There can be a fine line between refusing to imply terms from extrinsic circumstances and a generous construction of a provision in the articles to give effect to the obvious intention of the parties: see *Folkes Group plc v Alexander* [2002] 2 BCLC 254 where, faced with an alteration of the articles which, as a result of the misplacing of an inserted provision, gave rise to an absurd result, the court supplied five words so that the articles assumed a meaning reflecting a true sense of what was intended. Rimer J acknowledged, at [22], that his approach to the interpretation of the amended article might be regarded as close to the limits of what is permissible as a pure exercise of construction.
[131] [2009] 2 BCLC 148; see also *Mediterranean Salvage and Towage Ltd v Seamar Trading and Commerce Inc; The Reborn* [2010] 1 All ER (Comm) 1. The approach of Lord Hoffmann has been applauded for bringing clarity and certainty to this area (see Peters (2009) CLJ 513) and criticised for inappropriately affording the courts greater room to alter the bargain made (see Davies 'Recent Developments in the Law of Implied Terms' [2010] LMCLQ 140).

which concerned the implication of a term into articles of association. Essentially, the company's articles gave a particular shareholder (the C shareholder) the right where it held a special share and had 37.5% of the share capital to appoint (and remove) two directors, but the articles made no provision as to what was to happen to those appointments if the C shareholder retained the special share but the shareholding fell below the 37.5% threshold. The company had a share capital structure which was divided into differing classes with differing rights depending on the scale of the shareholdings. Lord Hoffmann concluded that, as a matter of construction—and implication is an exercise in construction of a document—it was clear that the right to appoint directors was linked to and was to reflect the size of the economic interest held by the shareholder. Therefore once C's shareholding fell below 37.5%, not only was the right to appoint lost, but those appointed would cease to be members of the board. The implication as to the composition of the board was not based upon extrinsic evidence of which only a limited number of people would have known, but upon the scheme of the articles themselves and, to a very limited extent, such background as was apparent from the memorandum and the general knowledge of the nature of the company (previously a state-owned telecoms company and now the subject of privatisation). As to the proper approach to construction, Lord Hoffmann emphasised that the court does not have power to improve the articles (or a contract or other instrument) to make them fairer or more reasonable. The court is concerned only to discover what the articles would mean to a reasonable person having all the background knowledge which would reasonably be available to the audience to whom the instrument is addressed.[132] Implication of a term is not an addition to an instrument, it only spells out what the instrument means.[133] In every case in which it is said that some provision ought to be implied, the question for the court, Lord Hoffmann said, is whether such a provision would spell out in express words what the instrument, read against the relevant background, would reasonably be understood to mean and 'business efficacy' etc are only other ways of formulating the same question, not different or additional tests.[134] Of course, the issue of implication will not arise if the plain and ordinary meaning of the words used in the articles is clear and does not give rise to a commercial absurdity.[135] In those circumstances, there is no scope for implication.

E Enforcing the articles

4-47 Generally, the courts have been reluctant to hold that an individual member has a right to have all of the articles observed, despite the wording of CA 2006, s 33(1) which provides that:

> 'The provisions of a company's constitution bind the company and its members to the same extent as if there were covenants on the part of the company and of each member to observe those provisions.'

4-48 The wording in CA 2006, s 33 is a clarification of the wording in CA 1985, s 14 ('…articles, when registered, bind the company and the members to the same extent as if they had been signed and sealed by each member…'). But, as was emphasised in the Parliamentary debates,[136] the only purpose of the amended wording is to state explicitly that the company is a party to the constitution as well as the members, as was established by *Hickman*

---

132 [2009] 2 BCLC 148 at 154.   133 [2009] 2 BCLC 148 at 154.   134 [2009] 2 BCLC 148 at 155.
135 See *Thompson v Goblin Hills Hotels* [2011] 1 BCLC 587, PC.
136 See 450 HC Debs, col 1087, 19 October 2006; 686 HL Debs, col 435, 2 November 2006.

v Kent or Romney Marsh Sheepbreeders Association[137] which is discussed at **4-51**. The new wording does not extend a member's right to enforce the articles. Likewise, the existence now of a specific statutory duty on directors to act in accordance with the constitution (CA 2006, s 171) does not alter the position (the duty is owed to the company, s 170(1)) and does not confer on members a right to enforce every provision of the constitution.

4-49 The reason for imposing limits to the enforcement of the articles is linked to the rule in *Foss v Harbottle*[138] (see **18-1**) which has two elements: first, the proper plaintiff in respect of a wrong allegedly done to a company is *prima facie* the company; secondly, where the alleged wrong is a transaction which might be made binding on the company by a simple majority of the members, no individual member of the company is allowed to bring a claim in respect of it.[139] The rule is based on two fundamental principles of company law, namely respect for the separate legal personality of the company and the principle of majority rule. In addition to reflecting those fundamental principles, the rule has certain practical advantages. It prevents multiplicity of shareholder suits and eliminates wasteful and vexatious actions by shareholders trying to harass the company. If a breach of the constitution is seen therefore as a wrong done to the company, rather than to the rights of individual members, it will fall within the rule and the majority have the option of ratifying the breach. If a breach can be regarded as an infringement of a member's personal rights, a wrong done to him personally rather than a wrong done to the company, he is untroubled by the rule in *Foss v Harbottle* and may proceed with a personal claim. It can be appreciated, therefore, that an expansive view of a member's personal rights under the articles might enable him to sidestep the rule entirely, something which the courts would regard as unacceptable, given the policies underlying the rule.

4-50 The courts have reconciled their desire to uphold the rule in *Foss v Harbottle*[140] and the fact that the statute creates a contract between the company and the members under CA 2006, s 33 by drawing a difficult distinction between: (1) provisions in the articles which do create enforceable personal rights conferred on a member qua member (not subject to the rule in *Foss v Harbottle*); and (2) provisions which relate to matters of internal management of the company. Breaches of the latter provisions amount only to internal irregularities and as such are open to ratification by the majority and are not actionable by individual shareholders.

Company may enforce the articles against a member

4-51 As noted at **4-48**, the rewording of CA 2006, s 33 has clarified that the company and the members are parties to the contract laid down in the articles, a point established in *Hickman v Kent or Romney Marsh Sheepbreeders' Association*.[141] In this case, the articles provided that disputes between the company and a member should be referred to arbitration. A member in dispute with the company commenced legal proceedings and the company brought proceedings to stop his action and require him to go to arbitration. The court held that a company is entitled as against its own members to enforce and restrain

---

[137] [1915] 1 Ch 881.   [138] (1843) 2 Hare 461.
[139] *Prudential Assurance Co Ltd v Newman Industries Ltd (No 2)* [1982] 1 All ER 354 at 357, CA; and see *Edwards v Halliwell* [1950] 2 All ER 1064 at 1066, per Jenkins LJ. As Mellish LJ explained in *MacDougall v Gardiner* (1875) 1 Ch D 13 at 25 '… if the thing complained of is a thing which in substance the majority of the company are entitled to do … there can be no use in having litigation about it, the ultimate end of which is only that a meeting has to be called, and then ultimately the majority gets its wishes.'
[140] (1843) 2 Hare 461.   [141] [1915] 1 Ch 881.

breaches of the articles. On the facts, the member was bound and the dispute was referred
to arbitration.

A member may enforce the articles against a member

4-52 It is also the case, as was accepted in *Rayfield v Hands*,[142] that a member may enforce the
articles directly against the other members. In that case, as a matter of construction of the
articles, a member wishing to transfer his shares was able to require the other members
to take the shares and the court allowed a member to enforce that provision against the
other members. Such actions are unusual and, more generally, the expectation would be
that the contract would be enforced through the company.[143]

A member cannot always enforce the articles against the company

4-53 As noted at **4-49**, a shareholder's entitlement to enforce what he perceives to be his rights
under the articles is problematic with the courts taking a restrictive approach to the issue
in order not to undermine the rule in *Foss v Harbottle*.[144]

4-54 The many conflicting authorities on this issue were reviewed in *Hickman v Kent or
Romney Marsh Sheepbreeders' Association*[145] and Astbury J concluded that the effect of
the authorities is that rights purporting to be given by the articles in a capacity other
than that of a member cannot be enforced against the company. Only membership rights
which have been conferred on the member qua member can be enforced and so, when
considering whether a provision can be enforced, it has to be asked whether it is intended
to confer rights on a member in that capacity. Provisions identified by the courts as conferring rights on the members qua members include the right of a member to have his
vote recorded,[146] to have a dividend paid in cash if the articles so specify[147] and to enforce
a declared dividend as a legal debt.[148] For example, in *Pender v Lushington*[149] the chairman
of a general meeting of shareholders improperly refused to record some of the votes cast.
This refusal was an infringement of a member's right qua member and the shareholders
were able to get an injunction restraining the company from acting on the resolutions
passed. In *Wood v Odessa Waterworks Co*[150] a member was entitled to require the company to pay a dividend in cash when the articles so provided. Rights with respect to share
transfer, for example to enforce compliance with a pre-emption provision on transfer,
may also be enforced.[151] Members qua members may also insist on the proper conduct of

---

[142] [1960] Ch 1.   [143] See *Welton v Saffery* [1897] AC 299 at 315.   [144] (1843) 2 Hare 461.
[145] [1915] 1 Ch 881 at 900.   [146] See *Pender v Lushington* (1877) 6 Ch D 70.
[147] See *Wood v Odessa Waterworks Co* (1889) 42 Ch D 636.
[148] *Re Severn and Wye and Severn Bridge Railway Company* (1896) 1 Ch 559.
[149] (1877) 6 Ch D 70. Cf *McDougall v Gardiner* (1875) 1 Ch D 13 (a member was denied relief when a chairman refused to call a poll in circumstances prescribed by the articles, the court regarding the matter as one
of internal management: this case has been much criticised and is best confined to its facts).
[150] (1889) 42 Ch D 636.
[151] *Hurst v Crampton Bros (Coopers) Ltd* [2003] 1 BCLC 304 (when a member purported to transfer shares
in breach of the pre-emption requirements in the articles, that transfer was defeasible at the suit of a member). See also *Re a company (No 005136 of 1986)* [1987] BCLC 82 where Hoffmann J took the view that a
complaint by a member about improper allotments of shares by the directors was in substance a complaint
that his contractual rights as a shareholder under the articles had been infringed and so any claim would be
a personal claim, but see Joffee, *Minority Shareholders* (4th edn, 2011), para 4.61, who notes that the decision
should be treated with caution.

meetings.[152] There are then instances in which the articles do create rights for individual shareholders which they can positively enforce. On other occasions, it is not a case that the shareholder wishes to enforce a particular right, rather he wishes to prevent the majority acting in disregard of a requirement in the articles where they have not sought first to amend the articles by a special resolution as required by CA 2006, s 21.

4-55 Certainly examples can be found where the court was prepared to restrain the company in such circumstances. In *Edwards v Halliwell*,[153] for example, two members of a trade union (similar to a company for these purposes) successfully restrained an attempt by a delegate meeting to increase the members' contribution without obtaining the two-thirds majority required under their rules. In *Quin & Axtens Ltd v Salmon*[154] the articles of association provided that certain transactions could not be entered into without the consent of both managing directors who were significant shareholders in the company. In this instance one of the directors dissented, but the company in general meeting nevertheless tried to authorise the transaction without that director's consent. The Court of Appeal rejected the purported authorisation, finding that this was an attempt to alter the terms of the contract between the parties by an ordinary rather than a special resolution, a view affirmed by the House of Lords.[155]

4-56 However, there is considerable inconsistency in the case law on these matters and in *Grant v United Kingdom Switchback Railways Co*[156] and *Irvine v Union Bank of Australia*[157] the courts permitted the majority in general meeting to ratify conduct by the directors in breach of the articles. In *Grant* the directors had entered into a particular contract with a third party although, under the terms of the articles, all of the directors bar one were prevented from voting on that contract because of a conflict of interest. The majority in general meeting passed a resolution approving and adopting the agreement and authorising the directors to carry it into effect. The court rejected an application by a shareholder for an injunction to restrain the company from proceeding with the contract. In *Irvine* the directors borrowed money in excess of a credit limit imposed by the articles and the court accepted that such an internal irregularity was ratifiable by a simple majority of shareholders. Ratification of an unauthorised act, the court said, is not the same as conferring a general power to do similar acts in the future. The shareholders' action is not so much approval of a breach of the articles, but rather the adoption or affirmation of an unauthorised act and, as such, it has no implications for the future.

4-57 These cases are supposedly distinguishable from the general principle that the majority cannot prevail where a special resolution is required on the basis that they involved only internal irregularities and were not attempts to alter for all time the terms of the contract between the members as embodied in the articles. Drawing the line between conduct which is an attempt by a simple majority to ignore the requirement for a special majority

---

[152] See *Kaye v Croydon Tramways Co* [1898] 1 Ch 358; *Tiessen v Henderson* [1899] 1 Ch 861; and *Baillie v Oriental Telephone and Electric Co Ltd* [1915] 1 Ch 503 (shareholders can prevent the company acting on resolutions improperly passed because of inadequate notice of the resolution to the shareholders).

[153] [1950] 2 All ER 1064.   [154] [1909] 1 Ch 311, aff'd [1909] AC 442.

[155] [1909] 1 Ch 311 at 319, aff'd [1909] AC 442. The Court of Appeal based its reasoning on the division of power between the board and the general meeting, governed by *Automatic Self-Cleaning Filter Syndicate Co Ltd v Cuninghame* [1906] 2 Ch 34, CA, see **8-5**, which depends on the terms of the articles but which typically precludes the general meeting interfering with management powers conferred on the directors other than by special resolution; the other side of that coin is that the members have a right to expect the division of power laid down in the articles to be observed.

[156] (1888) 40 Ch D 135.   [157] (1877) 2 App Cas 366.

and conduct which is merely the ratification of an internal management irregularity is difficult, but it is clear that the scope for ratifying internal irregularities undermines the protection afforded to the minority by the need for a special resolution to amend the articles.

4-58 In practice, a shareholder aggrieved at difficulties in enforcing his rights under the articles of association, or at non-compliance by the majority with the terms of the articles, is likely to petition for relief under CA 2006, s 994, alleging that the affairs of the company are being conducted in a manner which is unfairly prejudicial to his interests or that an act or proposed act or omission of the company is or would be so prejudicial. This route is preferable to attempting to overcome the difficulties inherent in trying to enforce the contract established by CA 2006, s 33.

The articles are not enforceable by outsiders

4-59 The articles are a statutory contract between the company and the members and do not constitute a contract between a company and an outsider (i.e. a non-member) or members claiming in a capacity other than as a member.[158] In *Eley v Positive Life Assurance Co*[159] a person named in the articles as a solicitor was unable to enforce that provision when the company employed someone else; the articles conferred no rights as between him and the company.

4-60 Any right claimed by an outsider must be conferred by a separate agreement outside the articles.[160] On occasion, that extrinsic contract may be made by the company with an outsider on the basis of the articles and such a contract may even be inferred from the conduct of the parties.[161] In *Re New British Iron Co, ex p Beckwith*[162] the articles provided for the annual remuneration of the directors. As such, of course, the articles did not constitute a contract to pay that amount of remuneration to the directors. But, the court said, where on the footing of that article, the directors were employed by the company and accepted office, the terms of that article as to remuneration were embodied in and formed part of the contract between the company and the directors.[163] An extrinsic contract derived from the articles in this way suffers from the disadvantage that the articles can be unilaterally changed by the company by special resolution under CA 2006, s 21 so altering the implied contract.[164]

F Supplementing the constitution–shareholders' agreements

4-61 In addition to the articles of association, shareholders may enter into a shareholders' agreement which is a separate contractual agreement between shareholders (or some of them) dealing with various aspects of their relationship. Matters commonly dealt with in

---

[158] *Pritchard's Case* (1873) LR 8 Ch 956; *Melhado v Porto Alegre Rly Co* (1874) LR 9 CP 503; *Eley v Positive Life Assurance Co* (1876) 1 Ex D 20, 88; *Browne v La Trinidad* (1887) 37 Ch D 1; *Hickman v Kent or Romney Marsh Sheepbreeders' Association* [1915] 1 Ch 881; *Beattie v E & F Beattie Ltd* [1938] Ch 708.

[159] (1876) 1 Ex D 20, 88.

[160] This point is confirmed by the Contracts (Rights of Third Parties) Act 1999, s 6(2) which provides that the 1999 Act does not confer any rights on a third party in the case of any contract binding on a company and its members under CA 2006, s 33.   [161] *Swabey v Port Darwin Gold Mining Co* (1889) 1 Meg 385.

[162] [1898] 1 Ch 324.   [163] [1898] 1 Ch 324 at 326.

[164] See *Swabey v Port Darwin Gold Mining Co* (1889) 1 Meg 385, where the terms as to the directors' remuneration were changed subsequently, but such alteration must not be retrospective.

a shareholders' agreement include voting rules, the provision of capital, the transfer of shares and the appointment of directors.

4-62 A shareholders' agreement has a number of advantages over articles of association:

- the agreement is a contract and binding as such and subject to all the usual contractual remedies in the event of breach. It does not involve the parties in discussions as to whether a right is conferred qua member or whether the rule in *Foss v Harbottle* applies, see **4-49**. Likewise, enforcement of outsider rights conferred by the agreement is not a problem. A disadvantage is that the agreement can only bind those party to it, of course, and so a new agreement is required where there is a change in the composition of the shareholders;

- the agreement is drawn up to address the particular position of the shareholders whereas the standard articles operate without regard to individual circumstances;

- the process of drawing up an agreement can be useful in getting the members to focus on issues of concern to them and identifying ways in which disputes might be resolved, were they to arise;

- the agreement cannot be altered by a majority of the parties, as the articles can, so a shareholder party to the agreement is assured that changes cannot occur without his consent;

- the agreement is a private contract whereas the articles are a public document registered with the registrar of companies.

4-63 These various advantages mean that a shareholders' agreement is particularly useful in certain circumstances, such as small family companies where it may help them address more fully the nature of their relationships *inter se* and with the company and, crucially, the manner of exiting from the business, given that a shareholder cannot simply demand back his capital. A shareholders' agreement is also commonly used in the quite different context of joint venture companies where commercially astute parties do not want their relationship to be governed by the vagaries of CA 2006, s 33.

PART II

Corporate Governance– Directors' Roles and Responsibilities

5

Corporate governance–board structure and shareholder engagement

A Introduction

5-1 As the number of shareholders in a company increases, it is obviously impossible for all to be involved in the management and control of the company's affairs and so a separation commonly develops between those who collectively own the company (the shareholders) and those who manage it (the directors).[1] Problems can arise from this separation of ownership and control as distance from the day-to-day running of the business makes it difficult for shareholders to restrain any managerial excesses, whether such excesses are the result of incompetence, self-dealing or outright fraud. No single mechanism can provide an answer to this so-called agency problem between shareholders and directors[2] and a variety of responses is required. Much of the focus is on internal mechanisms (such as shareholders' rights and board structures) though external mechanisms too have a role to play. Disclosure requirements are important components of governance ensuring that business is conducted in an open and transparent way. The assumption is that the full glare of publicity makes directors more circumspect in their activities and that disclosure assists shareholders in monitoring those activities and allows shareholders and creditors to assess the risks involved. To this end, much effort is being expended currently on improving the content of the annual accounts and reports and, crucially, ensuring the quality of the external audit of those accounts. Disclosure issues are considered in Chapter 16. For underperforming management in the largest companies, the markets may operate as an additional constraining force with takeovers providing a means by which to displace an existing board. That threat of displacement, it is argued, provides an incentive for efficient management – takeovers are discussed in Chapter 26. For dishonest and fraudulent management, external mechanisms lie in the hands of various regulatory authorities. The maintenance of confidence in the proper conduct of business and the protection of investors and markets may require intervention and, possibly, an investigation of the company's affairs. The exercise of investigation powers is primarily a matter for the Department for Business, Innovation and Skills acting through the Investigation and

---

[1] The theory of the separation of ownership and control originates in the famous work by Berle & Means, *The Modern Corporation and Private Property* (1932). For a modern study of the position in Europe where, unlike the UK and the US, shareholding is much more concentrated and dominant blockholders are common (giving rise to greater scope, perhaps, for conflicts between majority and minority shareholders): see Barca & Becht, *The Control of Corporate Europe* (2001).

[2] See Davies, *Introduction to Company Law* (2nd edn, 2010), pp 110–11 on the inappropriateness legally, but not factually, of this 'agency' characterisation while accepting that it is the widely adopted terminology.

Enforcement Services of the Insolvency Service (which act in respect of 'live' companies despite being part of the Insolvency Service). Listed companies can expect scrutiny by the Financial Conduct Authority (FCA) which from 2013 will perform many of the functions that the Financial Services Authority currently performs as the UK Listing Authority. Beyond these regulatory bodies lie the police and the Serious Fraud Office.

5-2   The starting point, however, is that good corporate governance primarily stems from internal structures. The classic definition of corporate governance, taken from the Cadbury Report and often cited, is that corporate governance is the system by which companies are directed and controlled with boards of directors responsible for the governance of the company while the role of the shareholders in governance is to appoint the directors and the auditors and to satisfy themselves that an appropriate structure is in place.[3] In keeping with those parameters, much of the substantive corporate governance debate[4] has centred on:

(1) the structure and role of the board of directors and, in particular, the role of non-executive directors. As a preliminary point, executive directors are those directors concerned with the day-to-day management of the company. They will have extensive management powers delegated to them by the articles and they typically have service contracts with the company which together with the articles delimit their powers and responsibilities.[5] Non-executive directors are directors without executive management responsibilities who are concerned with strategy and scrutinising the performance of the executive directors[6]—their precise role is discussed in detail later. They commonly have letters of appointment setting out their role and responsibilities. The Companies Act 2006 does not refer to or distinguish between executive and non-executive directors (these are essentially business terms) and all directors are subject to the general duties laid down in CA 2006, Pt 10 though, when considering the duty of care and skill, the different functions of the non-executive directors will be relevant, as discussed in Chapter 10.

(2) shareholder engagement—here the emphasis is on enhancing the stewardship role of the institutional investors (now the subject of a Stewardship Code) and on revitalising the general meeting as a shareholders' forum (addressed in part by the Shareholders' Rights Directive, reflected in the CA 2006 as amended) and on facilitating the engagement of the indirect investor with investee companies (addressed by CA 2006, Pt 9) in recognition of the fact that shareholdings in the largest companies are now commonly held by nominees through a chain of intermediaries, possibly even a cross-border chain.

---

[3] See *The Committee on the Financial Aspects of Corporate Governance* (1992) (known as the Cadbury Committee) para 2.5, and see **5-4**. See also the Financial Services and Markets Act 2000, s 89O(2).

[4] There is a vast literature available on corporate governance but, as a starting point, see McCahery & Vermeulen, *Corporate Governance of Non-listed Companies* (2008); Armour and McCahery (eds), *After Enron* (2006); Coffee, *Gatekeepers: The Professions and Corporate Governance* (2006); Hopt, Wymeersch et al (eds), *Corporate Governance in Context* (2005); Charkham, *Keeping Better Company: Corporate Governance Ten Years On* (2005).   [5] See *Harold Holdsworth & Co (Wakefield) Ltd v Caddies* [1955] 1 All ER 725.

[6] See, for example, Rimer J in *Re Kaytech International plc, Secretary of State for Trade and Industry v Kaczer* [1999] 2 BCLC 351 at 407; Park J in *Re Continental Assurance Co of London plc* [2007] BCLC 287 at 443. On non-executive directors generally, see Sweeney-Baird, 'The Role of the Non-executive Director in Modern Corporate Governance' (2006) 27 Co Law 67; Parkinson, 'Evolution and Policy in Company Law: The Non-executive Director' in Parkinson, Gamble and Kelly (eds), *The Political Economy of the Company* (2000).

These issues are the focus of this chapter and the debate on them sharpened following the financial crisis of 2007–08 which moved corporate governance issues back to the top of the regulatory and reform agenda.[7] Once the most acute problems in the financial sector had been addressed (stabilising the banks), attention turned to other aspects of the crisis including the failures of corporate governance across many financial institutions which enabled the banks to engage in such reckless conduct. The debate on corporate governance in the financial institutions then evolved into a debate as to whether there were improvements in corporate governance that could and should be adopted more generally.

5-3 The focus of the chapter is on publicly traded companies with widely dispersed shareholdings though corporate governance is an issue for all public companies and large private companies.

B The UK Corporate Governance Code

Introduction

5-4 The role of non-executive directors in UK companies arguably can be traced to the part-time, idle, disengaged, non-executives of mid-19th-century England, but their modern role came to the fore with the Cadbury Committee report[8] in 1992. The Committee drew up a Code of Corporate Governance based on a board structure composed of mainly independent non-executive directors involved especially on audit, remuneration and nomination committees[9] and operating on a comply or explain basis, i.e. companies were expected to comply with the Code or explain their reasons for non-compliance (see **5-7**). Over the following years, various reviews ensured the continued evolution of the Cadbury Code[10] into a Combined Code of Corporate Governance within the remit of the Financial Reporting Council (FRC).[11] In the wake of the financial crisis of 2007–2008, the FRC reviewed the content and overall effectiveness of the

---

[7] Corporate governance issues had gained prominence in the 1990s after a series of collapses in the late 1980s; and again in the late 1990s after the collapse of businesses such as Enron in the US and Parmalat in Italy with multi-billion dollar/euro losses. See Coffee, 'What Caused Enron: A Capsule Social and Economic History of the 1990s' (2004) 89 Cornell L R 269.

[8] *The Committee on the Financial Aspects of Corporate Governance* (1992) chaired by Sir Adrian Cadbury. The Committee was set up after a series of corporate collapses in the late 1980s raised concerns as to the effectiveness of the traditional board structure when dominated by powerful executive directors.

[9] Financial institutions may decide also to have a separate risk committee, see FSA, *Effective corporate governance*, CP10/3 (January 2010), para 6.25 and FSA Policy Statement in response, PS 10/15, pp 31–2 and FSA Handbook, SYSC 21.

[10] Notably as a result of the work of the Greenbury Committee chaired by Sir Richard Greenbury, see *Study Group on Directors' Remuneration* (1995); the Hampel Committee chaired by Sir Ronald Hampel, see *Report of Committee on Corporate Governance* (1998); the Higgs review, see *Review of the role and effectiveness of Non-executive Directors* (2003); and the Smith review chaired by Sir Robert Smith, see *Smith report on Audit Committees, Report to the FRC* (2003). The Higgs guidance for company chairmen and non-executive directors (in the annex to the Higgs report) developed into and has been replaced by the FRC *Guidance on Board Effectiveness* (2011) while the Smith Guidance on Audit Committees has developed into the FRC *Guidance on Audit Committees* (2010), a new edition of the Guidance is expected in 2012.

[11] The FRC took responsibility for the Combined Code in 2003 and conducted periodic reviews in 2005, 2007, and 2008 (brought forward because of the financial crisis). It will now review the Code on a two-year basis and all code changes in future will be introduced and will apply to financial years beginning on or after 1 October in any given year: see Feedback statement: *Gender Diversity on Boards* (October 2011) pp 8–9. As to the FRC, see **16-6**.

Combined Code[12] taking into account the recommendations of the Walker Report on corporate governance issues in UK banks and other financial industry entities.[13] The FRC then reissued the Code with a new name, the UK Corporate Governance Code (the UK Code), in June 2010. A further revised edition of the Code will come into effect in October 2012.

5-5   There are a number of other influential codes or guidance which have evolved alongside the UK Code. For smaller companies with a standard listing or traded companies which are not on a regulated market (i.e. companies on AIM and PLUS quoted companies, see **19-99**), the Quoted Companies Alliance has published widely accepted guidelines which reflect the requirements of the UK Code in a way which is relevant to smaller companies.[14] The Association of Investment Companies has a code which is intended to help boards of investment companies meet the requirements of the UK Code[15] and the Institute of Directors has developed corporate governance guidelines to assist unlisted companies.[16] Internationally significant instruments would include the OECD Principles of Corporate Governance (2004) and the ICGN (International Corporate Governance Network) Global Corporate Governance Principles: Revised 2009.

5-6   Developments at the European level have been very much in step with the UK, given that the Cadbury Code was the pioneer in this field. The pervasive influence of Cadbury was evident when, 10 years after Cadbury, a report commissioned by the European Commission found that most EU Member States had very similar 'comply or explain' codes to the UK.[17] In the light of that finding, the Commission concluded there was no need for a European Code as such[18] and, in keeping with that 'soft-law' approach, the European Commission proceeded on corporate governance issues in the following years mainly by way of Recommendations, such as its 2005 Recommendation on the role of non-executive

---

[12] The review was a three-stage process, see FRC, *Review of the Effectiveness of the Combined Code, Call for evidence* (March 2009); FRC, *Review of the Effectiveness of the Combined Code: Progress Report and Second Consultation* (July 2009); FRC, *Consultation on the Revised Corporate Governance Code* (December 2009).

[13] Walker, *A review of corporate governance in UK banks and other financial industry entities, Final Recommendations* (November 2009) (hereafter Walker Report), a review and report by Sir David Walker carried out at the invitation of the Government and preceded by a consultation paper of the same name in July 2009. The FRC took responsibility for the implementation of most of the Walker Report on corporate governance matters while other recommendations in Walker fell within the remit of the Financial Services Authority and were addressed by it through changes to its supervisory procedures and approach. See generally Hannigan, 'Board failures in the financial crisis—tinkering with codes and the need for wider corporate governance reforms,' Part 1 (2011) 32 Co Law 363, and Part 2 (2012) 33 Co Law 35.

[14] See QCA, *Corporate Governance Guidelines for Smaller Quoted Companies* (2010). The QCA represents traded companies outside the FTSE 350. Some provisions of the UK Code are modified in any event for smaller companies, defined as companies outside the FTSE 350 throughout the year immediately preceding the reporting year, see also n 45.

[15] See AIC, *Code of Corporate Governance* (2010) which is endorsed by the FRC as helpful to investment companies in meeting their obligations under the UK Code, see FRC, UK Corporate Governance Code, p 5; also AIC, *Corporate Governance Guidance for Investment Companies* (2010).

[16] See IOD, *Corporate Governance, Guidance and Principles for Unlisted Companies in the UK* (2010). The European Commission Green Paper, April 2011, see n 22, also explored whether thought should be given to corporate governance codes for unlisted companies, many of which may be quite large economically, just as it might be appropriate to modify the application of a code for listed companies to reflect the fact that some listed companies may be quite small economically. The UK Code already has a number of modifications which are applicable to smaller companies, defined for these purposes as outside the FTSE 350, see UK Code B.1.2, C.3.1, D.2.1 (composition of board, audit and remuneration committees, respectively)—essentially allows them to have fewer non-executive directors.

[17] See Weil, Gotshal and Manges, *Comparative Study of Corporate Governance Codes Relevant to the European Union and its Member States* (2002).

[18] See European Commission, *Modernising Company Law and Enhancing Corporate Governance in the EU—A Plan to Move Forward*, COM (2003) 284 final, 21.5.2003, para 3.1.

directors[19] which in content was very much derived from the then Combined Code. Over time, aspects of corporate governance have crept into various Directives, such as the Eighth Company Law Directive requirement for certain companies to have an audit committee and the Fourth Company Law Directive requirement for a corporate governance statement in the annual reports.[20] The financial crisis provoked a European Commission Green Paper on corporate governance in financial institutions in June 2010,[21] followed by a Commission Green Paper on the EU corporate governance framework in April 2011.[22] The outcome of that later consultation is awaited, but it is fair to say that, so far, mooted reforms have been mainly consistent with and in the wake of UK developments and the approach remains firmly on a comply or explain basis.[23]

Application and status—comply or explain

5-7 The UK Code is made up of main principles (noted as MP), supporting principles (noted as SP) and Code provisions (noted as CP) and, for the FRC, the principles (MP and SP) are the core of the Code and the way in which they are applied should be the central question for a board as it determines how it is to operate according to the Code.[24]

Comply or explain—Premium listed companies

5-8 The Listing Rules[25] require a listed company (whether incorporated in the UK or elsewhere) with a Premium listing of equity shares (see **19-100**) to include in its annual report and accounts:

(1) a statement of how the company has applied the main principles in a manner that would enable shareholders to evaluate how the principles have been applied; and

(2) a statement as to whether the company has complied with all relevant Code provisions; and identifying those provisions, if any, it has not complied with, and the period of non-compliance, and the company's reasons for non-compliance. Note that the 'comply or explain' element therefore only applies to Code provisions. The auditors must review this statement of compliance by the company[26] so far as the statement relates to:

  (i) the directors' explanation in the annual report of their responsibility for preparing the company's accounts, required by CP C.1.1;

  (ii) the directors' annual review of the effectiveness of the internal control systems, required by CP C.2.1; and

  (iii) the company's practice as to the establishment, role and responsibilities of the audit committee, required by CP C.3.1 – C.3.7.

---

[19] Commission Recommendation on the role of non-executive or supervisory directors of listed companies and on the committees of the (supervisory) board (2005/162/EC), OJ L 52, 25.02.2005, p 51. See too the Commission Recommendation on fostering an appropriate regime for the remuneration of directors of listed companies, OJ L 385, 29.12.2004, p 55.

[20] See Fourth Company Law Directive 78/660/EEC, OJ L 222, 14.08.1978, p 11, as amended by Directive 2006/46, OJ L 224, 16.08.06, p 1, art 46a(1).

[21] European Commission, *Corporate governance in financial institutions and remuneration policies*, COM (2010) 284, 2 June 2010; and accompanying Commission Staff Working Document, SEC (2010) 669.

[22] European Commission Green Paper, *The EU Corporate Governance Framework*, (April 2011), COM (2011) 164.

[23] See n 29, *Study on Monitoring and Enforcement Practices in Corporate Governance in the Member States* (2009).   [24] UK Corporate Governance Code (2010), p 4, para 2.

[25] FSA Listing Rules, LR 9.8.6R, 9.8.7R.   [26] LR 9.8.10R(2).

5-9 A failure to include the required statement is a breach of the Listing Rules and punishable as such,[27] and the FRC has stressed that this formal requirement for transparency coupled with the shareholders' ability to remove boards (where the explanations are unsatisfactory) means that a 'comply or explain' code is not self-regulation.[28] True it is not self-regulation in the sense of regulation of a trade or profession by members in their own self interest, but a code which is not mandated by law and which attracts no legal sanctions for non-compliance with the code and which is dependent on market support for its effectiveness is still some steps removed from 'hard law'. The 'comply or explain' approach was pioneered by the Cadbury Committee and it is a near universal feature now of corporate governance codes around the world. Any reaction to explanation rather than compliance is left to market participants and, depending on the circumstances and the issue, reaction may range from indifference to a significant fall in share price. In the case of egregious failures of corporate governance, in theory shareholders may be provoked into exercising their right to remove directors under CA 2006, s 168, but that would be very unusual. More commonly, institutional shareholders would expect a dialogue with the board as to the reasons for any non-compliance. There have been complaints by shareholders that the explanations provided are often inadequate and complaints by boards that shareholders pay insufficient attention to the reasons and have a mechanistic response to non-compliance.[29] Hence there is a renewed emphasis now on the quality of the explanations and the need to engage with the shareholders as to the company's reasons for non-compliance. The FRC stresses that the company should explain clearly and carefully its reasons for non-compliance to its shareholders and it should illustrate how its actual practices are consistent with the principle to which the particular provision relates and contribute to good governance.[30] In turn the shareholders must consider carefully any explanation having regard to the company's individual circumstances and shareholders should not automatically treat departures from the UK Code as breaches. It should be a process of discussion and engagement between the shareholders and the board.[31]

Comply or explain—corporate governance statements

5-10 The discussion in **5-8** relates to the requirements for companies with a Premium Listing in the UK, but all companies admitted to trading on a regulated market (which encompasses

---

[27] Listed companies must comply with the Listing Rules: Financial Services and Markets Act 2000, s 96(1); penalties may be imposed for non-compliance: s 91(1).

[28] FRC, *Response to the European Commission Green Paper on the EU Corporate Governance Framework* (2011) p 3.

[29] The EU *Study on Monitoring and Enforcement Practices in Corporate Governance in the Member States* (2009) found the overall quality of explanations to be 'unsatisfactory'. An issue is whether regulators should do more to monitor the quality of the explanations and the European Commission is considering whether regulators might actively monitor the quality of the explanations to see whether they are sufficiently informative and comprehensive (see the European Commission Green Paper, n 22, para 3.2). As from 2011 the FRC will produce an annual report on progress under the UK Code and the Stewardship Code and there may be an expanded role for the FRRP on monitoring explanations or the omission of explanations where one is required: see *FRC Response to the European Commission Green Paper* (2011), n 28, p 5. See FRC, *Developments in Corporate Governance 2011* (December 2011) which noted that on occasions explanations are perfunctory or omitted entirely, the latter being a breach of the Listing Rules, and that the FRC will continue to monitor the quality of explanations (see pp 3, 15–16). To that end, the FRC has reported further on the quality of explanation required following discussions with companies and investors, see FRC, *What Constitutes an Explanation under Comply-or-Explain? Notes of Discussions* (February 2012) (full explanations which set the context and give a convincing rationale for the action taken are what is required).

[30] FRC, *UK Corporate Governance Code* (2010) p 4, para 3. The European Commission mooted a very similar approach noting that, perhaps, codes need to be more prescriptive so that companies understand fully the need to give clear and precise explanations: see European Commission Green Paper, n 22, para 3.1.   [31] See FRC, *UK Corporate Governance Code* (2010), pp 4–5.

companies with a Premium or a Standard listing) are required by the Disclosure and Transparency Rules (DTR)[32] to include a corporate governance statement[33] either in the directors' report, or as a separate report published with the annual report, or on the company's website which must indicate which code the company is subject to (in the case of a Premium listing, obviously this will be the UK Code) and explain any non-compliance with it (DTR 7.2.3R). The corporate governance statement must also describe the main features of the company's internal control and risk management systems in relation to the financial reporting process and include a description of the composition and operation of the company's board and its committees. For companies with a Premium listing, there is a considerable degree of overlap between what is required under the DTR rules and the UK Code,[34] but the requirements are not identical, though the Department for Business, Innovation and Skills (BIS) is consulting on areas where there might be benefits from greater alignment of these requirements.[35] For example, DTR 7.2.5R requires a description of the main features of the company's internal control and risk management systems in relation to the financial reporting process whereas the UK Code requires the board to report that the annual review of the effectiveness of the internal control system has been carried out. The DTR rules are mandatory, unlike the Code, so companies must ensure that they meet the requirements of the DTR even if they choose not to comply with elements of the Code.

5-11 Though there are concerns about the effectiveness of 'comply or explain', neither the Company Law Review (see **2-6**), nor the Walker review (see **5-4**), nor the FRC found any support for putting the UK Code on a statutory basis.[36] The European Commission also seems content to retain a 'comply or explain' approach while trying to improve the calibre of explanations, though it has not ruled out the possibility that certain requirements (not identified) might need to be reinforced by legislative measures.[37] That process of movement from soft to hard law is in some ways inevitable. For example, the original requirements as to the disclosure of directors' remuneration policy etc started as a Code provision but evolved into a statutory requirement for a directors' remuneration report for quoted companies, see **5-40**. As noted at **5-10**, there is an overlap between the UK Code's requirements and binding disclosure measures in the Disclosure and Transparency Rules. A pattern is evident of issues achieving prominence initially as part of a voluntary code, then becoming widely accepted as a standard governance mechanism, and then being reinforced by legally binding measures and that process will continue. Equally, as the FRC points out, sometimes the requirements of the UK Code can be stricter than the legal requirements, such as with respect to the composition of the audit committee—all members must be

---

[32] The DTR are drawn up by the UK Listing Authority (UKLA), part of the Financial Services Authority, soon to be the Financial Conduct Authority (from 2013).

[33] Implementing the Fourth Company Law Directive 78/660/EEC on the annual accounts of certain types of companies, OJ L 222, 14.08.1978, p 11, as amended by Directive 2006/46, OJ L 224, 16.08.06, p 1, art 46a(1).

[34] Compliance with certain specified equivalent provisions of the UK Corporate Governance Code will satisfy certain requirements of the DTR, see DTR 7.2.4G, also 7.2.8G.

[35] See BIS, *The Future of Narrative Reporting, Consulting on a new reporting framework* (September 2011), URN 11/945, para 4.4. and Annex C.

[36] See Company Law Review, *Final Report*, vol 1 (2001), para 3.49; *Completing the Structure* (2000), para 12.50. The Government agreed that the Combined Code should remain as a non-statutory document: see *Modernising Company Law* (Cmnd 5553-I, 2002), paras 5.7–5.16. See too, Walker Report, n 13, paras 1.15–1.21, 2.4, 2.23, Annex 3; FRC, *Review of the Effectiveness of the Combined Code: Progress Report and Second Consultation* (July 2009) pp 3–4 (FRC shares the market's view that the flexible 'soft-law' approach remains the most appropriate way of raising standards of corporate governance in listed companies).

[37] See EU Commission Green Paper, n 22, para 3.

independent under the UK Code while the Eighth Company Law Directive on audit only requires one independent member.[38] We turn now to consider in detail the UK Corporate Governance Code (2010).

C Corporate Governance requirements—the board of directors

Composition of the board

5-12 The board should include an appropriate combination of executive and non-executive directors (including in particular independent non-executive directors) such that no individual or small group of individuals can dominate the board's decision taking (SP to B.1). At least half the board, excluding the chairman (who should be independent on appointment, CP A.3.1), should be independent non-executive directors while smaller companies (below the FTSE 350) should have at least two independent non-executive directors (CP B.1.2.). There is no prescribed size for a board, other than that the board should be of a sufficient size for the requirements of the business, and it should not be so large as to be unwieldy (SP to B.1). In terms of effectiveness, the board and its committees should have the appropriate balance of skills, experience, independence and knowledge of the company to enable them to discharge their respective duties and responsibilities effectively (MP B.1). Several of the reviews following the financial crisis highlighted the incompetence of many boards of financial institutions with the European Commission noting that the failure of boards 'to identify, understand and ultimately control the risks to which their financial institutions were exposed' lay at the heart of the origins of the crisis'.[39] In the light of these findings, the FRC was keen to make clear, by the redrafting of MP B.1 that competence is the key, not independence. The FRC commented as follows:[40] '... the [previous] drafting of [section A.3 of the 2008 code, on independence] may have encouraged the perception among some companies and investors that independence was the primary consideration in assessing the composition of the board and the respective merits of potential directors.[41] *This was not the intention. The overriding consideration should be that the board is fit for purpose* (emphasis added).' This change in stance is important and is something which needs to be focused on both by those appointing, and those seeking to take up appointments, to boards.[42] To help boards meet these requirements

---

[38] Though the intention, under current proposals for a Regulation on audit, see **16-33**, is that the audit committee will be comprised entirely of non-executive directors, a majority of whom should be independent.

[39] European Commission, *Corporate governance in financial institutions and remuneration policies*, COM (2010) 284, 2 June 2010, para 3.3.

[40] See FRC, *2009 Review of the Combined Code: Final Report*, (December 2009), para 3.17. The OECD conceded that the OECD Corporate Governance Principles too do not state as clearly as they might the importance of competence with competence often overlooked in practice in favour of an excessive focus on board independence, though an annotation to the Principles does note the importance of non-executive directors having knowledge, competencies and expertise to complement the existing skills of the board: see OECD, *Corporate Governance and the Financial Crisis, Conclusions and emerging good practices to enhance implementation of the Principles* (February 2010) para 50.

[41] See Moore, 'The Evolving Contours of the Board's Risk Management Function in UK Corporate Governance' (2010) 10 JCLS 279 who notes, at p 308, the 'significant normative influence of the directorial independence doctrine over recent years in providing companies' governance structures with an effective hallmark of legitimacy'.

[42] See FRC, n 40, para 3.18; also Walker Report, n 13, para 3.10. Both the FRC and Walker are confident that, where the requirement for expertise trumps independence in respect of a particular appointment, the shareholders will listen to and accept the company's explanation.

as to leadership and effectiveness, the FRC has issued guidance which is aimed at 'getting boards to think deeply about the way in which they carry out their role and the behaviours that they display, not just about the structures and processes that they put in place'.[43] After all, the boards of many of the failed financial institutions had all the proper corporate governance structures on paper, but it was behavioural failures by such boards which allowed the financial crisis to develop on their watch.[44]

5-13   In keeping with the need to ensure competent, fit for purpose, boards, the UK Code says there should be a formal, rigorous and transparent procedure for the appointment of new directors to the board (MP B.2) and all directors should be submitted for re-election at regular intervals (generally, intervals of no more than three years (B.7.1)), subject to continued satisfactory performance (MP B.7). In the case of directors of FTSE 350 companies, all should be subject to annual election by shareholders (B.7.1).[45] This provision was one of the major changes to come out of the FRC/Walker reviews and has the merit that, where issues arise concerning the competencies of board members, the shareholders are able to act within a relatively short time frame (assuming the chairman has not been persuaded to address the issue before it gets to the annual elections). While all appointments should be made on merit against objective criteria, due regard should be had to the benefits of diversity on the board, including gender (SP to B.2).

5-14   The European Commission has suggested a greater need to focus on diversity of skills, nationality and gender, all with a view to diluting the 'group-think' which contributes to the lack of constructive challenge within a board. The European Commission is also pursuing various initiatives concerning greater representation of women on the boards of listed companies as part of a wider strategy for gender equality.[46] The issue of gender diversity gained prominence in the UK following the publication in 2011 of the Davies Report on women on boards[47] which found that in 2010 women made up only 12.5% of the boards of FTSE 100 companies. Lord Davies recommended that the chairmen of each FTSE 350 company should set out, by September 2011, the percentage of women they aim to have on their boards in 2013 and 2015 and he recommended that FTSE 100 boards should aim for a minimum of 25% female representation by 2015.[48] In keeping with the Davies' recommendations, quoted companies are to be required to report each year on the proportion of women on the board and to disclose the proportion of female employees for those parts of the organisation for which gender information is available and an explanation of the approximate proportions of the global workforce to which the gender figures relate.[49] In addition to trying to shame boards into a more pro-active stance on gender diversity, the Davies Report also recommended that investors should pay close attention to this issue when looking at appointments to the board. In line with the Davies

---

[43]   See FRC, *Guidance on Board Effectiveness* (March 2011), Preface.

[44]   See Walker Report, n 13, Ch 4 on the behavioural failures within boards.

[45]   The FTSE 350 index is made up of the largest 350 companies by market capitalisation with a primary listing on the London Stock Exchange. Anecdotal evidence suggests that companies have complied with this change and have put their full boards up for re-election (when they could have declined and explained their non-compliance), but their willingness to do so probably reflects the reality that there is little real risk of directors in these companies being unseated by the shareholders.

[46]   See European Commission Green Paper, n 22, para 1.1.3.

[47]   Lord Davies, *Women on Boards* (February 2011), URN 13/745.

[48]   The Government is content for the moment to go along with this voluntary market-led approach to see if a voluntary approach will progress matters rather than legislation.

[49]   BIS, *The Future of Narrative Reporting, Consulting on a new reporting framework* (September 2011) URN 13/945, paras 4.10–4.18.

Report, the FRC is to amend the UK Code to require listed companies to establish and report annually on their boardroom diversity policy including gender, and on any measurable objectives which the board has set for implementing that policy, and the progress the company has made in achieving the objectives.[50] Diversity is also to become one of the factors to be considered when evaluating board effectiveness.

5-15   The board should undertake a formal and rigorous annual evaluation of its own performance and that of its committees and its individual directors (B.6) and it should report on the process in the annual report (B.6.1). FTSE 350 companies should be externally evaluated at least every three years (B.6.2). This move to external evaluation was one of the measures recommended in the Walker Report and the European Commission too is considering whether external evaluation can be of value.[51]

Core responsibilities of the board

5-16   The UK Code starts in Section A with identifying the broad responsibilities of a board noting that every company should be headed by an effective board which is collectively responsible for the long-term success of the company (MP A.1) with all directors required to act, consistent with their statutory duties, in what they consider to be the best interests of the company. The board's role is to provide entrepreneurial leadership of the company within a framework of prudent and effective controls which enables risk to be assessed and managed (SP to A.1). The board should set the company's strategic aims, its values and standards and it should review management performance (SP to A.1). The emphasis is on an informed board, acting on detailed timely information, meeting regularly under the guidance of an effective chairman, with a formal schedule of matters specifically reserved to the board (A.1.1).

5-17   Part C of the UK Code focuses more closely on some of the core responsibilities of the board. First, there is a corporate reporting principle, requiring the board to present (in the annual report and accounts) a balanced and understandable assessment of the company's position and prospects (MP C.1). As of 2010, the Code specifies that, in the annual report, the directors should include an explanation of the basis on which the company generates or preserves value over the longer term (the business model) and the strategy for delivery of the objectives of the company (CP C.1.2).[52] Also restated in 2010 is MP C.2 which provides that the board is responsible for determining the nature and extent of the significant risks it is willing to take in achieving its strategic objectives and it is for the board to maintain sound risk management and internal control

---

[50] FRC, *Consultation Document: Gender Diversity on Boards* (May 2011). These matters will be included in the report on the work of the nomination committee; the change will take effect for financial years beginning on or after 1 October 2012. The European Commission Green Paper, n 22, para 1.1.3 notes that while it should be for companies to decide whether they introduce a diversity policy, boards should at least be required to consider the matter and disclose the decisions that they have taken.

[51] See European Commission Green Paper, n 22, para 1.3.

[52] For the background, see FRC, *2009 Review of the Combined Code: Final Report* (December 2009) para 3.54. The inclusion of CP C.1.2 has been described as 'arguably the most constructive FRC reform from a risk management perspective', see Moore, 'The Evolving Contours of the Board's Risk Management Function in UK Corporate Governance' (2010) 10 JCLS 279, at 299, who considers that it will potentially assist NEDs to develop 'a panoptic vision and understanding of the company's core strategic affairs and sources of shareholder value creation' which will help them assess the riskiness and long-term sustainability of the business model adopted.

systems.[53] In turn, an audit committee should be established to consider how the board applies those two principles (on corporate reporting and on risk management and internal control) and to maintain an appropriate relationship with the company's auditor (MP C.3). Issues of corporate reporting are being addressed substantially by BIS and discussed in Chapter 16 while the FRC is focusing on improving those elements of the Code relating to risk management and internal control. Code provision C.2.1 requires the board to conduct a review, at least annually, of the effectiveness of the company's risk management and internal control systems, covering all material controls, including financial, operational and compliance controls, and they must report to the shareholders that they have done so (C.2.1).[54] This statement on internal control in the annual report is subject to a modicum of auditor review,[55] as noted at **5-8**. These principles in Part C of the Code are supplemented by further guidance, known as the Turnbull Guidance (2005) which sets out in more detail what is expected of companies in this regard.[56] The emphasis throughout the Turnbull Guidance and the UK Code is that responsibility for risk management and internal control systems rests with the board of directors. It is for the board to set appropriate policies on internal control and to seek regular assurance that enables it to satisfy itself that the system is functioning effectively. The board must further ensure that the system of internal control is effective in managing risks in the manner which it has approved.[57] An essential component of a sound system of internal control, the Turnbull Guidance emphasises, is effective monitoring on a continuous basis.[58] The FRC has indicated that it intends to undertake a limited review of the Turnbull Guidance in 2012 to bring it more into line with the shift in emphasis in the UK Code to highlight the board's responsibility for risk management.[59]

The chairman of the board

5-18 Considerable importance is attached under the UK Code to dividing the responsibilities at the head of the company between the chairman of the board who is responsible for running the board (and who should be independent on appointment, A.3.1) and the chief executive with responsibility for the running of the business (MP A.2). The UK Code position is that these roles should not be exercised by the same individual (A.2.1) and, additionally, the chief executive of a company should not move up to become chairman

---

[53] The Combined Code (2008) only required that the board should maintain a sound system of internal control to safeguard shareholders' investment and the company's assets and made no reference in the main principle to the board's responsibilities in relation to risk which the FRC now concedes was a significant omission from previous versions of the Code: see FRC, *Final Report*, n 40.

[54] Additionally, DTR 7.2.5R, noted at **5-10**, requires listed companies to describe in their corporate governance statement the main features of the internal control and risk management systems in relation to the financial reporting process.   [55] LR 9.8.10R.

[56] See FRC, *Internal Control, Revised Guidance for Directors on the Combined Code* (2005), hereinafter the Turnbull Guidance. The Guidance derived from a report under the auspices of the Institute of Chartered Accountants in England and Wales and the chairmanship of Andrew Turnbull, see ICAEW, *Internal Control: Guidance for Directors on the Combined Code* (1999).   [57] See the Turnbull Guidance, n 56, para 15.

[58] See the Turnbull Guidance, n 56, para 26.

[59] Ahead of that review the FRC has published notes on discussions which it has had with interested parties on risk management, see FRC, *Boards and Risk* (September 2011). A few key points emerge from those discussions (see pp 2–3): the need for boards to focus especially on those risks capable of undermining the strategy or long-term viability of the company or damaging its reputation; that boards are becoming more proactive in seeking to assure themselves about the risk and control culture in the company and that investors are seeking more meaningful reporting on risk.

(A.3.1).[60] The division of responsibility between the chairman and the chief executive should be clearly established, set out in writing and agreed by the board (A.2.1).[61]

5-19 Post the FRC/Walker reviews, it was decided to give greater emphasis to the role of the chairman and the UK Code now states as a main principle (previously a supporting principle) that the chairman is responsible for leadership of the board and ensuring its effectiveness on all aspects of its role (MP A.3). To emphasise his personal responsibility, the UK Code encourages the chairman to report personally in the annual report as to how the principles in the Code relating to the role and effectiveness of the board have been applied.[62] The chairman is responsible for setting the board's agenda; promoting a culture of openness and debate by facilitating the effective contribution of non-executive directors in particular; ensuring constructive relations between executive and non-executive directors; ensuring effective communication generally with shareholders (SP to A.3) and ensuring that the company maintains contact with principal shareholders in respect of directors' remuneration (SP to D.2). The chairman should also ensure that all directors are made aware of their major shareholders' issues and concerns (SP to E.1) and that the views of the shareholders are communicated to the board as a whole (E.1.1). The chairman should also discuss governance and strategy with the major shareholders (E.1.1).

5-20 In keeping with the chairman's specific responsibility for ensuring the effectiveness of the board (to which end he must ensure that the directors receive accurate, timely and clear information (SP to B.5)), the chairman must act on the evaluation of the board, recognising strengths and addressing weaknesses and, where appropriate, proposing new members or seeking resignations (SP to B.6). The chairman is also responsible for ensuring that directors keeps their skills up to date and that they have appropriate induction and training opportunities, etc (MP B.4). In turn, the non-executive directors, led by the senior independent director, should be responsible for performance evaluation of the chairman, taking into account the views of the executive directors (B.6.3). The chairman should hold meetings with the non-executive directors without executive directors being present (A.4.2).

5-21 The company chairman typically will work closely on governance matters with the company secretary[63] who is responsible for advising the board through the chairman on all governance matters (SP to B.5) and for ensuring compliance with board procedures (B.5.2). The company secretary also has responsibility for ensuring good information flows between the board and its committees and between non-executive directors and senior management (SP to B.5) which is why the appointment and removal of the company secretary is a matter for the board as a whole (B.5.2).

---

[60] If the chief executive is to move up, the matter should be discussed in advance with the major shareholders and the reasons for the move explained to the shareholders, see UK Corporate Governance Code, A.3.1. These issues can be contentious, even in well-respected companies. For example, Marks and Spencer's became embroiled in angry discussions with its shareholders on this issue when in 2008 it decided to move its chief executive, Sir Stuart Rose, to the post of executive chairman. Ultimately 22% of shareholders either voted against or abstained on his appointment (a very high percentage in this type of company). See 'Sir Stuart Rose and the thorny issue of corporate governance' *Financial Times*, 10 March 2008; 'M & S shareholders give Sir Stuart dressing down in promotion vote' *Financial Times*, 10 July 2008.

[61] On the evolving role of the chairman, see Owen & Kirchmaier, 'The Changing Role of the Chairman: Impact of Corporate Governance Reform in the UK 1995–2005' (2008) 9 EBOR 187.

[62] FRC, UK Corporate Governance Code (2010), Preface, para 7.

[63] A public company must have a company secretary: CA 2006, s 271.

The non-executive directors

5-22 At least half the board, excluding the chairman, should be independent non-executive directors while smaller companies (below the FTSE 350) should have at least two independent non-executive directors (CP B.1.2.).

The senior independent director

5-23 The board should appoint one of the independent non-executive directors to be the company's senior independent director whose role is to provide a sounding board for the chairman and to serve as an intermediary for the other directors when necessary (CP A.4.1). This senior director should meet with the non-executive directors without the chairman being present at least annually to appraise the chairman's performance and on other occasions as deemed appropriate (CP A.4.2). The senior independent director is also available to shareholders if their concerns are not resolved through normal channels (i.e. the chairman, chief executive or other executive directors) or if such contact would be inappropriate (CP A.4.1). The senior independent director should also attend sufficient meetings with a range of major shareholders to appreciate the issues and concerns of those shareholders (E.1.1). Initially this role assigned to the senior independent director was criticised as potentially divisive to a unitary board, but it has not developed in that way and the financial crisis has highlighted the need to maximise the possible leadership resource within a board. The FRC guidance also emphasises the role of the senior independent director in resolving matters when the board is in 'a period of stress'.[64]

Independence

5-24 The annual report must identify each non-executive director considered by the board to be independent[65] and it is for the board to determine whether the director is independent in character and judgement and whether there are relationships or circumstances which are likely to affect, or could appear to affect, the director's judgement (CP B.1.1). The board should state its reasons if it determines that a director is independent notwithstanding the existence of relationships or circumstances which may appear relevant to its determination, including if the director:

- has been an employee of the company or group within the last five years;
- has, or has had within the last three years, a material business relationship with the company either directly or as a partner, shareholder, director or senior employee of a body that has such a relationship with the company;
- has received or receives additional remuneration from the company apart from a director's fee, participates in the company's share option or a performance-related pay scheme, or is a member of the company's pension scheme;
- has close family ties with any of the company's advisers, directors or senior employees;
- holds cross-directorships or has significant links with other directors through involvement in other companies or bodies;
- represents a significant shareholder; or
- has served on the board for more than nine years from the date of their first election (CP B.1.1).

---

[64] See FRC, *Guidance on Board Effectiveness* (2010), para 1.10 which notes that the SID role becomes 'critically important' in that context.

[65] The Company Law Review noted that independence cannot be legislated for since 'the quality required is a state of mind and character and relevant experience, rather than some formal indication of independence', see Company Law Review, *Developing the Framework* (2000), para 3.148.

Appointment

5-25   Non-executive directors should be selected (as should all the directors) through a formal process with the terms and conditions of the appointment available for inspection at the registered office and at the annual general meeting (CP B.3.2). They should be appointed for specific terms subject to re-election (annually in the case of a director of a FTSE 350, CP B.7.1) and any proposal that someone be re-elected for a term beyond six years should be rigorously reviewed (CP B.2.3). Any non-executive who has served longer than nine years should be subject to annual re-election (CP B.7.1), if not already so subject because a director of a FTSE 350 company, and the board must state in the annual report its reasons for believing that director still to be independent (B.1.1). It has to be remembered that the Code is a reflection of market consensus to a large extent and it cannot be more prescriptive without risking a loss of support, but on some of these issues it is noticeably lax. It is difficult to believe that someone who has served for nine years could or should be regarded as independent. It would seem inevitable that there would be a tendency to identify with the executive team by that stage.

5-26   A related issue is whether non-executive directors devote enough time to their position given that, typically, each will have a number of non-executive posts. Again, reflecting market sentiment, the FRC was not willing to impose any limits on the number of other positions which a non-executive director may hold. The UK Code merely requires a non-executive director to disclose her other commitments and to undertake that she will have sufficient time to undertake what is expected of her (SP to B.3.2).[66]

Qualities of a non-executive director

5-27   As part of a unitary board (a point specifically underlined by the Code), non-executive directors should constructively challenge and help develop proposals on strategy (MP A.4). One of the key conclusions of the Walker Report (see **5-4**) was that non-executives in financial institutions had been particularly poor at providing this essential 'challenge' role.[67] Challenge is particularly difficult, of course, without a measure of understanding of the issue being discussed and Walker expressed further dismay at the lack of knowledge of the banking business displayed by the non-executive directors which made it difficult for them to make an effective contribution to governance. Without an in-depth knowledge of a company's affairs, Walker noted, it is often impossible even to articulate the issue, never mind probe the executives on the detail.[68] These concerns about a lack of company knowledge and a reluctance to challenge, in part as a result of that lack of knowledge, would not be limited to the banking sector.[69] As noted at **5-12**, following the Walker/FRC reviews, MP B.1. has been recast to emphasise that the board must have the appropriate balance of skills, experience, independence and knowledge of the company.[70] In any event, directors

---

[66]   The FRC's *Guidance on Board Effectiveness* (2011) p 6 states that a non-executive director's letter of appointment should state the minimum time required of the director and should seek the individual's confirmation that he or she can devote that amount of time to their role.

[67]   See Walker Report, n 13, p 12, which specifically found that challenge had been missing from the process of decision-making in the boards of financial institutions.   [68]   See Walker Report, n 13, para 4.3.

[69]   See, for example, the *Penrose Report of the Equitable Life Enquiry* (March 2004). On the BP/Gulf of Mexico oil well accident, the media questioned whether the non-executives of the company had the industry knowledge needed to challenge management prior to the accident on the company's safety procedures or subsequently to challenge management's response to the accident and leak, see FT, 'BP: Gloom at the top', 23 July 2010; Daily Telegraph, 'BP oil spill: the pressure grows on the company's non-executive directors', 7 July 2010.

[70]   This is a change from the 2008 Combined Code which (in Principle A.3) did require boards to have a balance of skills and experience appropriate for the requirements of the business and which did (in supporting principle A.3.1) lay down extensive requirements as to independence, but which did not specifically refer to knowledge of the company.

are under a legal duty to have sufficient knowledge and understanding of a company's business so as to enable them properly to discharge their duties as directors.[71] As every review of the Code produces ever more functions to be undertaken by the non-executive directors, as well as imposing greater board responsibility generally for risk management, we can expect to see a continued emphasis on board competence rather than formal independence[72] and this will apply especially to the non-executive directors given the importance of their 'challenge' role.

Role of the non-executive director

5-28 Turning to the specific responsibilities of non-executive directors, as mentioned, their core task is to provide a point of constructive challenge to the executive directors and to help develop proposals on strategy (MP A.4).[73] The UK Code further identifies, in SP to A.4, the non-executive director's role as being to scrutinise the performance of management in meeting agreed goals and objectives, to monitor the reporting of performance, to satisfy themselves as to the integrity of financial information and that financial controls and risk management systems are robust and defensible. They have a prime role in appointing and, where necessary, removing executive directors and they are responsible for determining appropriate levels of executive directors' remuneration and for succession planning. The Code goes on to spell out key roles for non-executive directors on the nomination, audit and remuneration committees.

D Board committees

The nomination committee

5-29 A company should have a nomination committee and a majority of the committee's members must be independent non-executive directors (B.2.1).The role of this committee has come to the fore given that the financial crisis highlighted that many boards of financial institutions did not have the combination of skills needed for the tasks at hand which raised issues about the manner in which nomination committees have approached their task in the past.[74] Since then there has been a greater focus on making sure that a board has the right balance of skills, experience, independence and knowledge of the company (MP B.1) and this is something which the nomination committee must evaluate when filling a vacancy (CP B.2.2). The committee's role is to lead the process for board appointments and make recommendations to the board but, as noted, the chairman must act on the results of the annual evaluation of the board and he should be proactive in addressing any deficiencies in its composition, given his overall responsibility for the effectiveness of the board (SP to B.6). The Code also states that the nomination committee should explain its work in the annual report and explain if neither an external search consultancy nor open advertising has been used in the appointment of the chairman or a non-executive director (CP B.2.4).

---

[71] See CA 2006, s 174; *Re Barings (No 5) plc* [1999] 1 BCLC 433.

[72] See Moore, n 52, at 307; also Hannigan, 'Board failures in the financial crisis—tinkering with codes and the need for wider corporate governance reforms,' Part 1 (2011) 32 Co Law 363, and Part 2 (2012) 33 Co Law 35.

[73] In keeping with that role, non-executive directors should be offered the opportunity to attend scheduled meetings with major shareholders, see UK Corporate Governance Code, SP E.1.1.

[74] See, generally, Hannigan, 'Board failures in the financial crisis—tinkering with codes and the need for wider corporate governance reforms,' Part 1 (2011) 32 Co Law 363, and Part 2 (2012) 33 Co Law 35.

The audit committee

5-30 The audit committee is becoming the key corporate governance committee and the FRC supplements Section C of the UK Corporate Governance Code on audit committees with the FRC *Guidance on Audit Committees*.[75] In addition, the Eighth Company Law Directive on audit requires companies admitted to trading on a regulated market to have an audit committee,[76] a requirement implemented by the FSA Disclosure and Transparency Rules (DTR) 7.1.1R–7.1.5R which apply to companies with a premium or standard listing. To minimise the overlapping requirements on this matter, it is provided that compliance with the provisions of the UK Code as to the composition and work of the audit committees also suffices for compliance with the DTR requirements (DTR 7.1.1R). The FRC Guidance emphasises that the audit committee has 'a particular role, acting independently of the executive, to ensure that the interests of shareholders are properly protected in relation to financial reporting and internal control'.[77] Details of the work of the committee must be set out in the company's annual report (C.3.3), a requirement, the Guidance notes, which 'deliberately puts the spotlight on the committee and gives it an authority that it might otherwise lack'.[78]

5-31 The UK Code recommends the establishment of an audit committee (and, as noted, listed companies must have an audit committee, DTR 7.1.1) consisting of at least three, or in the case of smaller companies (i.e. below FTSE 350) two, independent non-executive directors, at least one of whom has 'recent and relevant financial experience' (CP C.3.1).[79] In the case of smaller companies, the company chairman may be a member of the committee,[80] in addition to the two independent members, provided the chairman was considered independent on appointment as chairman (CP C.3.1). In carrying out its functions, the FRC Guidance emphasises the need for a robust committee which is well informed, well resourced, and well remunerated for the wide-ranging responsibilities which it must undertake.[81] Above all, the FRC Guidance stresses the importance of a frank, open, working relationship and a high level of mutual respect between the audit committee chairman, the board chairman, the chief executive and the finance director.[82]

---

[75] See FRC, *Guidance on Audit Committees* (2010), derived from the Smith report (Audit Committee Combined Code Guidance, Report to the FRC by group chaired by Sir Robert Smith (2003)). The Guidance is to be updated in 2012.

[76] Directive 2006/43/EC on statutory audits of annual accounts and consolidated accounts, OJ L 157, 9.6.2006, p 87, art 41. The intention is to replace this Directive with a Regulation on the audit of public-interest entities and a Directive dealing with all other aspects of audit, see **16-33**.

[77] See FRC, *Guidance on Audit Committees* (2010), para 1.4.

[78] See FRC, *Guidance on Audit Committees* (2010), para 1.6.

[79] The FRC *Guidance on Audit Committees* (2010) notes that it is desirable that the person considered to have 'recent and relevant financial experience' should have a professional qualification from one of the professional accountancy bodies, see para 2.16. The proposed EU Regulation on statutory audit of public interest entities will require audit committees to be composed solely of non-executive directors, a majority of whom should be independent, with at least one having experience and knowledge in auditing and one having experience and knowledge in accounting and/or auditing: see *Proposal for a Regulation on specific requirements regarding statutory audit of public-interest entities*, COM (2011) 779 final, 30.11.2011.

[80] This concession was introduced in 2008 and is unwelcome as the potential exists for the chairman to exert disproportionate influence over this important committee. Circumstances may arise where the audit committee is at odds with the rest of the board and the presence of the chairman of the board on the committee may result either in the committee being stifled in its endeavours or the chairman having already taken sides by the time a matter is progressed to the board. Either is unsatisfactory. The requirement that the chairman must have been considered independent on appointment offers little reassurance as to his actual independence, given he may have been on the board for some time.

[81] See FRC *Guidance on Audit Committees* (2010), paras 1.7–1.11.

[82] See FRC *Guidance on Audit Committees* (2010), para 1.7.

5-32 The main roles and responsibilities of the committee (CP C.3.2) should include:

- to monitor the integrity of the financial statements of the company, reviewing significant financial reporting judgements contained in them;
- to review the company's internal financial controls and, unless otherwise reviewed, to review the internal control and risk management systems;[83]
- to monitor and review the effectiveness of the company's internal audit function (and if there is none, annually to review the position, and to explain its absence to the shareholders, CP C.3.5);
- to make recommendations in relation to the appointment of the external auditor[84] and to approve their remuneration and terms of engagement;
- to review and monitor the external auditor's independence and objectivity, and the effectiveness of the audit process; and
- to develop and implement policy on the engagement of the external auditor to supply non-audit services.[85]

5-33 The FRC sees scope for further development of the role of the audit committee as an important intermediary between the auditors and the board and between the auditors and the shareholders, an approach also evident at EU level.[86] The FRC is consulting therefore on revising the UK Corporate Governance Code and the FRC Guidance on audit committees to extend the remit of the audit committee and to require a much fuller report from the audit committee on its work.[87] In terms of remit, it will be for the audit committee to consider the whole annual report (i.e. the financial statements and the narrative report) and to determine whether the whole report provides the information necessary for users to assess the performance and prospects of the company and for the audit committee to determine whether the annual report viewed as a whole is fair and balanced.[88] The audit committee report to the board will have to set out the significant issues which the committee considered in relation to the financial statements, and how they approached those issues and the key judgements they made, as well as explaining the basis for their conclusion that the annual report viewed as a whole is fair and balanced.[89]

---

[83] The FRC *Guidance on Audit Committees* (2010), para 4.5, defines internal financial controls as systems established to identify, assess, manage and monitor financial risks.

[84] If the board does not accept the recommendation, the board should explain in the annual report why it took a different position: UK Corporate Governance Code, CP C.3.6.

[85] If the auditor does provide non–audit services, the annual report should explain to the shareholders how auditor objectivity and independence is safeguarded: UK Corporate Governance Code, CP C.3.7.

[86] See the EU *Proposal for a Regulation on specific requirements regarding statutory audit of public-interest entities*, COM (2011) 779 final, 30.11.2011.

[87] See FRC *Revisions to the UK Corporate Governance Code and Guidance on Audit Committees* (Consultation Document, April 2012); also FRC '*Effective Company Stewardship, Next Steps* (September 2011), Ch 4, following on from FRC consultation paper, '*Effective Company Stewardship, Enhancing Company Reporting and Audit* (January 2011). See PIRC Shareholder Voting Guidelines 2011 which also favour more detailed reporting by the audit committee and an expanded audit report.

[88] In a similar manner, the proposed EU Regulation provides that the audit committee will monitor the work of the auditor and audit firm which will report to the audit committee on key matters arising from the statutory audit and, in particular, on material weaknesses in internal control in relation to the financial reporting process. The audit committee will inform the board of the outcome of the statutory audit and explain how the statutory audit contributed to the integrity of financial reporting and explain the audit committee's role in this process, see *Proposal for a Regulation on specific requirements regarding statutory audit of public-interest entities*, COM (2011) 779 final, 30.11.2011, art 24.

[89] See too the European Commission, *Proposal for a Regulation on specific requirements regarding statutory audit of public-interest entities*, COM (2011) 779 final, 30.11.2011 which envisages a longer and more

The Sharman Inquiry recommends that this extended audit committee report should be used to provide reassurance as to the robust process undertaken by the directors to evaluate whether the entity is a going concern,[90] identifying and explaining the material risks to going concern status which have been considered.[91] This proposal from the Sharman Inquiry gives the audit committee a more explicit role in relation to the consideration and reporting of going concern status than the UK Code, CP.3.2. currently provides. The audit committee report will have to be accepted by the whole board and then published in full in the annual report because, in the FRC's view, the valuable work of the committee is invisible to investors and knowledge of it will help build confidence in financial reporting.[92] The FRC also emphasises that the purpose of these changes is to reinforce the relationship between the company and its investors so as to facilitate the interaction which is crucial to making a 'comply or explain' code work. It is for this reason that the FRC favours an approach based on the dynamic between the audit committee, the board and the investors which can be specific to the individual company rather than placing greater obligations on auditors in a way which would, the FRC believes, place the auditors in a management role overseeing the content of a company's annual report.[93] The FRC's proposals will also see the audit committee report on the steps taken in respect of the appointment or reappointment of the external auditor,[94] for example, as to tendering.

5-34   The final piece of the jigsaw will be a requirement for auditors to provide the audit committee with the information needed to understand fully the factors which the auditors relied on in reaching their audit opinion and, to that end, the FRC has indicated that the relevant auditing standard is to be revised.[95] There will also be changes to the auditors' report to give greater transparency to the work carried out by the auditors in relation to the annual report as a whole which should help reassure users of financial statements that issues which are material to the financial statements have been properly disclosed.[96] Of course, the net outcome of these changes will be even more time-consuming tasks for the audit committee, especially in larger companies, and it may become increasingly difficult to recruit non-executive directors given the workloads which they are now being expected to shoulder, something which presumably will have to be reflected in their remuneration.

detailed report by auditors to the audit committee explaining in detail the results of the statutory audit carried out and which will explain any judgements about material uncertainty that may cast doubt about the entity's ability to continue as a going concern; it will assess the valuation methods applied to the various items in the accounts; provide full details of all guarantees, comfort letters, etc that have been relied upon when making a going concern assessment; and indicate whether all requested explanations and documents were provided by the audited entity, see Proposed Regulation, art 23.

[90]   The directors are required to state in the financial statements that the company is a going concern, see the UK Corporate Governance Code, CP C.1.3, and the Listing Rules, LR 9.8.6.

[91]   See Sharman Inquiry, *Going Concern and Liquidity Risks: Lessons for Companies and Auditors*, Preliminary Report and Recommendations of the Panel of Inquiry (November 2011), paras 141, 147 and Recommendation 4, p 45.

[92]   See FRC, *Effective Company Stewardship, Next Steps* (September 2011), p 12; and see FRC, No 87 (April 2012).

[93]   See FRC, *Effective Company Stewardship, Next Steps* (September 2011), pp 2, 14, 16.

[94]   See FRC, *Effective Company Stewardship, Next Steps* (September 2011), p 23; this proposal steps back from earlier proposals for greater investor involvement in auditor appointments, see FRC, *Effective Company Stewardship, Enhancing Company Reporting and Audit* (January 2011), pp 16–17; and see FRC, No 87 (April 2012) paras 7–14.

[95]   See FRC, *Effective Company Stewardship, Next Steps* (September 2011), p 19; the relevant standard which is to be reviewed is ISA (UK & Ireland) 260, 'Communication of audit matters with those charged with Governance'.

[96]   See FRC, *Effective Company Stewardship, Next Steps* (September 2011), pp 18–19; and see *FRC Consultation Paper on proposed revisions to International Standards on Auditing to give effect to FRC 'Effective Company Standardship'* (April 2012).

The remuneration committee

Background

5-35 The level of executive remuneration, especially in publicly traded companies, continues to be a source of widespread investor and political dissatisfaction[97] with the sums awarded being seen as significantly out of step with company performance and investor returns[98] and, more broadly, as creating a gross disparity between executive and employee remuneration.[99] The high profile accorded to the issue is driven then by political, business and social concerns, coupled with media interest in the topic. For investors, the key concerns include:

(1) the payment of rewards for failure, whether in the form of excessive compensation payments to departing executives who are departing because of under-performance, or excessive remuneration to executives still in post despite an uninspiring corporate performance;

(2) uncapped long-term incentive plans which permit the allocation of unlimited numbers of shares to executive directors and which are being awarded on the basis of unchallenging performance criteria;[100]

(3) awards of annual bonuses where there is a lack of transparency as to the basis on which they are being awarded; and

(4) generally, a poor alignment between corporate performance, shareholder value and executive remuneration.[101]

5-36 On the content of remuneration packages, a few specific points are addressed by the UK Code. For example, the remuneration committee must carefully consider compensation commitments in the event of early termination (D.1.4) so notice or contract periods should be set at one year or less (D.1.5)[102] which is intended to minimise the amount

---

[97] See Speech by Secretary of State for Business, Innovation and Skills, Vince Cable, to the ABI conference in June 2011 when he commented that 'ridiculous levels of remuneration are going unchallenged as the norm when there is no clear evidence of correlation with performance'. See also the 2011 report of the High Pay Commission (an independent body established with the support of the Joseph Rowntree Charitable Trust); see 'Call to end "corrosive" top pay deals', FT, 22 November 2011.

[98] For some statistics on executive remuneration, see BIS, *Executive Remuneration, Discussion Paper* (September 2011), paras 13–22 which noted that, on average, employee earnings grew 4.7% per year over the past 12 years, compared to 13.6% for FTSE 100 CEOs; also that CEOs in the UK now earn over 120 times that of the average worker (para 22). See too BIS, *A Long-term focus for Corporate Britain – a call for evidence* (October 2010) which noted (para 5.5) that FTSE 100 CEO remuneration rose annually by 13.6% on average (year-on-year) between 1999 and 2009 while, by comparison, an average annual increase in the FTSE100 index of 1% was observed across the same period. It also noted that the greatest determinant of the level of executive pay remains firm size, not executive performance (para 5.7).

[99] See generally, Villiers, 'Controlling Executive Pay: Institutional Investors or Distributive Justice' (2010) JCLS 309.

[100] The ABI has concerns in particular about uncapped LTIPs and has written to remuneration committee chairmen to tell them that they will 'red top' any company which proceeds with them without convincing explanation of the exceptional circumstances that justify their introduction: see ABI letter to remuneration committee chairman, January 2011; see n 144 as to 'red tops'.

[101] See Geiler & Renneboog, 'Managerial Compensation: Agency Solution or Problem?' (2011) JCLS 99 which discusses the component elements of the typical package and concludes that many compensation contracts 'promote managerial self-dealing and the skimming of profits' (at 138), which may not be quite what shareholders had in mind. They noted that the use of stock options raises particular difficulties involving costs, manipulation, and incentive effects, while pay for performance is problematic given the difficulty of determining valid benchmarks. See also BIS, *Executive Remuneration, Discussion Paper* (September 2011), Ch 5.

[102] See the Joint Statement on Executive Contracts and Severance by the Association of British Insurers (ABI) and the National Association of Pension Funds (NAPF), February 2008, which stresses (at para 3.5)

of compensation payable on dismissal.[103] The performance-related elements of executive directors' remuneration must be stretching and designed to promote the long-term success of the company (SP to D.1) and the Code sets out further guidance on the design of performance-related remuneration packages. BIS has been consulting extensively in an attempt to generate both debate and the emergence of a consensus as to good practice on these packages, see **5-42**.[104]

5-37   Typically, remuneration issues have been addressed in a variety of ways. For example, the UK Code advocates the use of remuneration committees to set remuneration for all executive directors and the company chairman (CP D.2.1) while, for quoted companies, the CA 2006 relies on mandatory detailed disclosure in the form of a directors' remuneration report and an advisory vote of shareholders on that report (discussed at **5-41**). The Listing Rules require prior shareholder approval by an ordinary resolution of long-term incentive plans and discounted option arrangements for directors of listed companies.[105] Some of the response is market-led. For example, the Association of British Insurers (ABI), which represents a significant section of the UK institutional shareholder community, takes a strong public stance on the need for responsible remuneration policy and practices and stresses the need for alignment with shareholder interests and sustainable value creation.[106] Executive remuneration is also very much now on the agenda for BIS which is considering additional reporting requirements as well as other measures intended to improve shareholder control of the matter, see **5-42**. The European Commission issued a non-binding Recommendation on remuneration of directors in listed companies in 2009, complementing an earlier Recommendation in 2004, the content and approach of which is very much similar to that of the UK Code, i.e. stressing the important role of independent remuneration committees and encouraging shareholders to make considered use of their votes on remuneration, but also suggesting limits on variable components, termination payments and share-based remuneration.[107] Given that a follow-up report a year later found variable implementation by the Member States,[108] the Commission may be tempted to take binding measures in future.

Composition and role of the remuneration committee

5-38   The UK Code provides that companies should have a remuneration committee made up of at least three, or in the case of smaller companies two, independent non-executive

---

that a one-year notice period should not be seen as a floor. The Statement strongly encourages boards to consider shorter periods since compensation for risks run by senior executives is already implicit in the absolute level of remuneration which they receive.

[103] This Code provision was influential in changing market practice such that practically all listed companies now set one-year periods or less. That change in practice is reflected in the CA 2006 also which requires shareholder approval for directors' service contracts longer than two years (reduced from five years in the CA 1985), see **12-8** and CA 2006, s 188.

[104] See BIS, *Executive Remuneration, Discussion Paper* (September 2011), Ch 5.

[105] See LR 9.4.1(2) and LR 9.4.4(2). For companies in parts of the financial sector, there are additional stringent requirements imposed by an FSA Remuneration Code (2011) which is beyond the scope of this work.

[106] See ABI, *Principles of Remuneration* (September 2011) p 3. See previously ABI, *Executive remuneration - guidelines on policies and practices* (December 2009) and ABI, *Position Paper on Directors' Pay* (December 2009).

[107] See Commission Recommendation 2009/385/EC on directors' remuneration; and see Ferrarini, Moloney and Ungureanu, ' Executive Remuneration in Crisis: A critical assessment of reforms in Europe' (2010) JCLS 7 which is critical of the approach adopted in the Recommendation, arguing that the Commission is moving from supporting effective incentive alignment into the muddier waters of 'fairness'.

[108] See Report on the application by Member States of the 2009 Recommendation on directors´ remuneration, COM (2010) 285 final, 2.5.2010.

directors and, in addition, the company chairman may be a member of the committee if he was considered independent on appointment as chairman (D.2.1). The UK Code stresses that levels of remuneration should be sufficient to attract, retain and motivate directors of the quality required to run the company, but a company should avoid paying more than is necessary for this purpose (MP D.1). A company should have a formal and transparent procedure for developing policy on executive remuneration and for fixing the remuneration packages of individual directors with no director being involved in deciding on his or her own remuneration (MP D.2). The committee should have responsibility for setting remuneration for all executive directors and the chairman and should recommend and monitor the level and structure of remuneration for senior management at the first tier below board level (CP D.2.2).

Criticisms of the remuneration committee

5-39 These Code provisions have been in place for some time but, as noted, concerns remain about the level of executive remuneration which raises in turn concerns about the ability of the remuneration committee to act in the shareholders' interests in this regard. A number of problems have been identified including whether the directors are sufficiently independent so as to be able to align remuneration with the long-term interests of the shareholders and whether they are sufficiently sensitive to wider factors such as pay and employment conditions elsewhere in the company or the group.[109] There are also concerns that remuneration committees are too dependent on remuneration consultants who in turn may have conflicted interests as they may well have close relationships with the company management.[110] As executive remuneration arrangements have become more complex, it is clear that remuneration committees have found the process of setting remuneration extremely challenging[111] and there may be competence issues which require addressing. Just as the audit committee requires at least one member with recent and relevant financial experience, increasingly there is an issue as to the level of expertise required on a remuneration committee.[112] It may also be that the non-executive directors are not well placed to police this issue (frequently they will hold or have held executive posts elsewhere) so they themselves may be part of a culture of high pay with the result that they are unlikely to challenge generous executive remuneration.[113] It is not easy to see a solution to these problems and while there have been suggestions that the composition of the remuneration committee might be reconsidered (for example, to include shareholder or employee representatives),[114] there is limited support for such changes which would raise a variety of legal issues as to the role of such representatives and to whom they might be held accountable.[115] The Government now appears to have moved on from the issue of specific representatives to considering more broadly whether the composition of the remuneration committees might be made more diverse and asking the FRC to amend the UK Corporate Governance Code so as to prevent serving executives in their roles as non-executives in other companies from serving on remuneration committees.[116] As the problem is predominantly one of the

---

[109] See BIS, *A Long-term focus for Corporate Britain—a call for evidence* (October 2010), para 5.11.

[110] See BIS, *A Long-term focus for Corporate Britain—a call for evidence* (October 2010), para 5.11.

[111] See BIS, *Executive Remuneration, Discussion Paper* (September 2011), para 79.

[112] The EU Commission's 2009 recommendation, see n 107, suggests that at least one member should have knowledge of and experience in the field of remuneration, see para 7.1.

[113] See BIS, *Executive Remuneration, Discussion Paper* (September 2011), paras 81–82.

[114] See Treasury Committee, 9th Report, Session 2008–09, 'Banking Crisis: reforming corporate governance and pay in the City (HC 519), para 77.

[115] See BIS, *Executive Remuneration, Discussion Paper* (September 2011), paras 84–90.

[116] See Ministerial Written Statement on Executive Pay, 24 January 2012, Secretary of State Vince Cable.

non-executive directors on the remuneration committee failing to negotiate strongly in the shareholders' interests, it may be that the best solution is for the UK Code to be amended to draw the attention of the committee to their obligations under CA 2006, s 172 to promote the success of the company for the benefit of the members as a whole. It may also be that, in addition to the advisory vote on the directors' remuneration report, it should be possible for the shareholders to pass a motion of censure of the remuneration committee. The reputational consequences of such a motion might exert sufficient pressure on the committee to focus minds on the need to negotiate remuneration packages aggressively in the company's interests.

Disclosure to and shareholder approval of executive remuneration

5-40 Quoted companies are required currently to publish a report on directors' remuneration as part of the company's annual reports and to disclose within that report comprehensive details (prescribed by regulation) of each individual director's remuneration package as well as the company's remuneration policy, the role of the board and the membership and role of the remuneration committee.[117] The main issue with the actual report is the degree of detail provided which users find difficult to understand and time-consuming to analyse and indeed there are suggestions that it contributes to a ratchet effect.[118] BIS intends therefore to make significant changes to these remuneration reporting requirements, with effect for financial years commencing from 1 October 2012, as part of a wider package of reforms of narrative reporting.[119] The main changes with regard to remuneration are that there will be a requirement for top level reporting on remuneration as part of a new Strategic Report (see **16-27**) which will require quoted companies to provide a clear statement on how executive remuneration is linked to the company strategy, performance indicators, risks and corporate governance arrangements.[120] Amongst the matters to be included in the Strategic Report, it is proposed that there will be a single aggregate figure for each director's remuneration, something which has been lacking to date.[121] In future there will be two distinct sections in the directors' remuneration report: one section will outline the proposed future remuneration policy and potential payouts; and the second section will explain how the remuneration policy was implemented in the previous financial year, including actual awards made.[122] The detailed information underpinning these calculations will be included in the Annual Directors Statement (see **16-27**).[123] The board will also have to explain how they have consulted

---

[117] CA 2006, s 420. The details of the required disclosure are set out in The Large and Medium-sized Companies and Groups (Accounts and Reports) Regulations 2008, SI 2008/410, Sch 8. A quoted company is a company listed in the UK, or officially listed in an EEA State, or admitted to dealing on either the New York Stock Exchange or Nasdaq (an American stock exchange): CA 2006, s 385. See Ferrarini et al, n 107, on the importance of disclosure as a mechanism which strengthens the board and shareholders in withstanding managerial pressures on pay.

[118] See BIS, *Executive Remuneration, Discussion Paper* (September 2011), paras 36, 60.

[119] See BIS, *The Future of Narrative Reporting* (September 2011). Also BIS, *Executive Remuneration, Discussion Paper* (September 2011), Ch 2.

[120] See BIS, *The Future of Narrative Reporting* (September 2011), Ch 5. BIS notes that shareholders had commented that in some cases the complexity of remuneration reports means that the symmetry between remuneration, shareholder returns and the long-term objectives of the company is lost, see BIS, *Executive Remuneration, Discussion Paper* (September 2011), para 45.

[121] BIS concedes that this omission was a major deficiency in the existing reporting framework, see BIS, *Executive Remuneration, Discussion Paper* (September 2011), para 43.

[122] See BIS, *Executive Pay Shareholder Voting Rights Consultation* (March 2012) para 57; also BIS, *The Future of Narrative Reporting* (September 2011), Ch 5, esp para 5.7; BIS, *Executive Remuneration, Discussion Paper* (September 2011), Ch 2. Also Ministerial Written Statement on Executive Pay, 24 January 2012, Secretary of State Vince Cable.

[123] BIS, *Executive Remuneration, Discussion Paper* (September 2011), para 39.

and taken into account the views of employees when setting executive pay and the report will have to include a distribution statement outlining how executive pay compares with other expenditure such as on dividends, business investment, taxation and general staffing costs.[124]

5-41 The directors' remuneration report must be submitted for shareholder approval (an advisory vote) by way of an ordinary resolution at the general meeting at which the company's accounts are laid (CA 2006, s 439). The shareholders are not entitled to vote on an individual director's package but vote only on the report as a whole. BIS consulted in 2011 on whether it might be desirable to move from an advisory vote to a binding vote, but found significant support from business, companies and investors for retaining merely an advisory vote which they argued still has a real reputational impact.[125] BIS then revisited the issue in 2012, suggesting raising the advisory vote threshold to something higher than a simple majority but less than 75% and consulting on whether there might be a binding vote on remuneration policy, on notice periods in excess of one year, and on exit payments,[126] see **5-42**. Certainly, the advisory vote has proved effective at the level of allowing shareholders publicly to reject remuneration deals.[127] It has galvanised shareholders into positively considering directors' remuneration packages rather than passively accepting them as a fait accompli, as was often the case in the past. An increasing number of companies in 2010 and 2011 had their reports voted down with resulting adverse publicity and leaving them with the need to renegotiate with their institutional shareholders. There does seem then to be an increasing measure of shareholder activism over remuneration packages but, as noted, shareholders have had little impact on the overall level of remuneration being rewarded[128] and remain frustrated in their attempts to link remuneration more closely to company performance or to alter the bargaining dynamic between the executive directors and the company. It might be said that the fault lies with the shareholders for failing to hold the remuneration committees to account for the committees' continued failure to address what are now well-known shareholder concerns.[129]

---

[124] See Ministerial Written Statement on Executive Pay, 24 January 2012, Secretary of State Vince Cable.

[125] See BIS, *Executive Remuneration,* Discussion Paper (September 2011), paras 61–66.

[126] See Ministerial Written Statement on Executive Pay, 24 January 2012, Secretary of State Vince Cable; see also n 130.

[127] GSK had the dubious distinction in 2003 of being the first company to have its remuneration report voted down by shareholders, see 'Investors Reject GSK executive pay policy' *Financial Times*, 20 May 2003, when shareholders refused to endorse arrangements which included a two-year notice period and munificent exit package for the company's chief executive. In 2009 a range of high-profile companies (including RBS, Shell, BP, Xstrata, and Pearson) saw significant votes against their remuneration reports, see FT, 'Floored Boards, Executive Pay', 2 June 2009; FT, 'Indignant investors flex voting muscles', 6 May 2009; FT, 'HSBC draws fire over executive remuneration', 30 May 2008. BIS reported that, while initially the average level of dissent on remuneration reports was around 5% to 6%, it had risen by 2009 (amidst the financial crisis) in some cases to dissent of 20% but has since declined, see BIS, *Executive Remuneration, Discussion Paper* (September 2011), paras 56–57. There has been evidence of increasing shareholder dissent in 2012, see FT 'Investor anger boils over', 4 May 2012, noting significant adverse votes at companies such as UBS, Citigroup, Barclays and Aviva.

[128] Sometimes companies respond by altering the components of the remuneration package, even if overall levels may remain high, see for example, FT, 'Tesco rings the changes on boardroom pay', 1 June 2011, reporting that Tesco had reduced the number of long-term incentive plans from four to one following disagreements on remuneration with shareholders the previous year, see FT, 'Investors censure Tesco on pay plans' 2 July 2010.

[129] Equally, some would argue that shareholders are not up to the task of controlling executive pay and are indeed part of the problem by permitting excessive remuneration: see Villiers, n 99, who argues for an alternative fairness approach which would take greater account of the wider social issues here. In particular, she argues for the use of CA 2006, s 172 to develop a distributive justice approach to executive pay. For a contrary position, that the issue is merely one of improving the alignment of shareholder and management

Proposed changes to shareholder approval requirements

5-42 In March 2012 the Department for Business, Innovation and Skills returned to the issue of executive pay with a further consultation on the possible levels of shareholder approval which might be required for certain elements of directors' remuneration packages and companies' remuneration policies.[130] As discussed at **5-40**, the intention for the future is to divide the remuneration report into two elements, one part setting out the executive remuneration policy for the year ahead and the other part containing a report on the remuneration actually paid to the directors in the previous year. The consultation paper asks whether the shareholder approval level needed for the remuneration policy might be raised to something higher than a majority vote so as to ensure that the policy has significant support amongst the shareholders (in the event of rejection, the company would have to revert to the last approved policy or return to the shareholders with new proposals within 90 days).[131] With respect to remuneration practice in the previous year, the requirement for a simple majority on that advisory vote would remain, but the consultation paper proposes that a company which fails to secure the support of 75% of its shareholders would have to issue a statement to the market explaining the voting position, the concerns of the shareholders and how the company proposed to address those concerns.[132] As companies would want to secure 75% support in order to avoid having to make such a market statement, the effect of this proposal would be to raise the approval threshold on the advisory vote. The consultation paper also suggests that all exit payments to directors, however categorised, will require prior shareholder approval to the extent that the payment exceeds one year's base salary,[133] a proposal which is a significant change from the current position governing exit payments, see **12-12**. All the proposed changes would be limited in application to quoted companies.

E Shareholder engagement

Introduction

5-43 As well as an effective board, good corporate governance depends on effective shareholder control of the board, but as the European Commission noted, while we tend to presume effective control by shareholders, each governance crisis shows cracks in that presumption.[134] Hence a great deal of discussion now focuses on the importance of securing, not just better shareholder participation in the annual general meeting (the orthodox forum for the exercise of shareholder power), but better shareholder engagement in the broadest sense in the interests of good corporate governance. A useful description of 'shareholder engagement' is that it involves 'actively monitoring companies, engaging in a dialogue with the company's board, and using shareholder rights, including voting and

interests, and not one of reflecting societal expectations, even if 'fairness' could somehow be captured, see Ferrarini et al, n 107.

[130] BIS, *Executive Pay, Shareholder voting rights consultation* (March 2012, URN 12/639).
[131] See n 1, para 130.   [132] See n 1, para 130.   [133] See n 1, para 130.
[134] See European Commission Green Paper, *The EU Corporate Governance Framework*, (April 2011), COM (2011) 164, para 3.5. Many of the reviews of the causes of the financial crisis criticised shareholders, not just for being passive and inactive and failing to control of the boards of financial institutions, but for implicitly supporting excessive risk taking by boards in favour of short-term profits: see Walker Report, n 13, paras 5.10–5.11; OECD, *Corporate Governance and the Financial Crisis: Key Findings and Main Messages* (June 2009), Ch 5 (shareholders in the financial crisis were ineffective, reactive, passive, there was evidence of reluctant and mechanical voting and an unwillingness to express dissent).

cooperation with other shareholders, if need be, to improve the governance of the investee company in the interests of long-term value creation'.[135]

The board and the shareholders

5-44 Under the UK Code, the board as a whole has responsibility for ensuring that a satisfactory dialogue takes place with the company's shareholders (MP E.1). It is accepted that this dialogue is mainly a matter for the chief executive and the finance director, but the company chairman and the senior independent director also have responsibility for maintaining sufficient contact with major shareholders to understand their issues and concerns (E.1.1). The chairman must also ensure that the views of the shareholders are communicated to the board as a whole (E.1.1) and that the non-executive directors have the opportunity to attend meetings with the company's major shareholders (E.1.1).

5-45 The UK Code stresses the importance of the board using the annual general meeting to communicate with investors and to encourage their participation (MP E.2). It goes on to include various recommendations as to best practice with regard to the conduct of the meeting. For example, there should be separate resolutions for each substantive matter; appropriate proxy arrangements should be in place allowing for votes to be cast for and against resolutions and for votes to be withheld; and voting outcomes should be announced and posted on a company website as soon as practical (E.2.2). The chairmen of the audit, remuneration and nomination committees should be at the annual general meeting and available to answer questions from shareholders and all directors should attend the annual general meeting (E.2.3), of which at least 20 days' notice should be given (E.2.4). Most of these matters are the subject of specific statutory requirements in any event under CA 2006, Pt 13, which governs meetings (see Chapter 15).

5-46 Another way of enhancing the importance of the general meeting is to return specific powers to the shareholders, by statute if necessary. As noted, the shareholders have an advisory vote on the directors' remuneration report, though its effectiveness is debatable, see **5-41**. It might be possible to identify other issues which could be the subject of specific approval, such as the directors' statement on risk management and internal control (see **5-17**).[136] The CA 2006 already requires shareholder approval of various actions (such as a purchase of the company's own shares)[137] or transactions (such as substantial property transactions) where directors have an acute conflict of interest[138] and, for listed companies with a Premium listing, the Listing Rules impose additional shareholder approval requirements.[139] The Takeover Code also places power firmly in the hands of the shareholders of the offeree company who must not be hindered in the exercise of their right to determine the outcome of a bid.[140] The result is a certain level of transparency and accountability and, in cases where shareholder authorisation is required, some control over these matters by the shareholders. But there is a balance to be struck between

---

[135] European Commission Green Paper, see n 134, para 2.1. The UK Stewardship Code, see **5-52**, considers engagement to include 'pursuing purposeful dialogue on strategy, performance and the management of risk, as well as issues that are the immediate subject of votes at general meetings': FRC, *UK Stewardship Code* (2010), Preface.

[136] As to the general division of power between the board and the shareholders, see **8-5** et seq.

[137] CA 2006, ss 694, 701.   [138] See CA 2006, s 190.

[139] Shareholder approval is required for class 1 (i.e. large) transactions: Listing Rules (LR) 10.5.1(2); for related party transactions: LR 11.1.7; for certain employees' share schemes or long-term incentive schemes: LR 9.4.1R; and for certain discounted option arrangements: LR 9.4.4.

[140] See Takeover Code, General Principle 3.

requiring shareholder approval of matters and unduly restricting management powers. Calling general meetings in public companies with large numbers of shareholders is a time-consuming and expensive business. Probably, the current range of matters which require shareholder approval is appropriately balanced and the issue is not so much that the general meeting's jurisdiction is too limited, but rather that procedures need to be fine-tuned to ensure effective shareholder participation at the general meeting. The rules in this regard were comprehensively overhauled by the CA 2006 and further modified to reflect the requirements of the Shareholders' Rights Directive and they are discussed in Chapter 15. It suffices to highlight a few key issues here, bearing in mind that these issues are of greatest significance in the publicly traded company.

Effective meetings

5-47 There is a greater emphasis now on electronic means of communication which offer low cost and timely disclosure to all shareholders equally: see **15-5**. The largest companies with widely dispersed shareholdings already make extensive use of their websites for instant communication with all shareholders. For example, it is common to have simultaneous webcasts of analyst and other meetings so that all shareholders, rather than just the largest, can be part of the process. Documentation can be made available to all shareholders via a website quickly and at very low cost.

5-48 Voting, attendance and participation rights at meetings have been reviewed, modified and extended so that mechanisms are available which allow shareholders flexibility as to how they engage with the company. For example, the CA 2006 confers enhanced rights on proxies to attend, speak and vote at general meetings (see **15-10**). Members representing at least 5% of the total voting rights of the members are able to require the circulation of statements concerning a matter referred to in a proposed resolution to be dealt with at a meeting or other business to be dealt with at that meeting (s 314: see **15-45**). Again, provided they meet the 5% voting rights' threshold, members can require the circulation of a written resolution in the case of a private company (s 292: see **15-29**), or the circulation of a proposed resolution to be moved at an annual general meeting of a public company (s 338: see **15-41**), and they can requisition a general meeting (s 303: see **15-46**). The costs issue (which in the past has been a deterrent to the use of such powers) has also been addressed with the company required to carry the costs of circulation in some instances. Members of a quoted company can demand an independent assessment of the outcome of a poll (s 342: see **15-15**) and can raise audit concerns on the company's website (s 527: see **16-31**). The result should be that shareholders are able to influence the agenda of the meeting rather than being dictated to by the board, though it has to be acknowledged that some of these powers have always been available and shareholders have shown little interest in exercising them.

5-49 Finally, the CA 2006 has moved to enfranchise the indirect investor or at least to acknowledge that the shareholder on the register is frequently the nominee holder for an ultimate beneficial owner who may be several steps removed. The standard position pre-2006 was that the nominee on the register was able to vote, or not, as he chose (depending on any contractual arrangement to the contrary with the ultimate beneficial owner) and did not need to pass on documentation from the company (for example, as to rights issues or annual reports etc). Often the result was that the person with the voting rights was uninterested in exercising them (being concerned only with overall shareholder returns) whereas the ultimate beneficial owner of the shares might have been interested but did not have the legal right to exert any direct influence over the company in which his money was invested. The classic example is the pension fund investment where sums are passed from the contributor through the hands of trustees and managers in an ever-lengthening chain to the company raising capital. The position of the indirect investor is discussed further at **5-60**.

Activist institutional investors

5-50 If there is to be meaningful shareholder engagement with companies, in effect it means there must be engagement between the institutional investors and the boards of directors as institutions are the most influential shareholders in listed UK companies. The latest ONS (Office of National Statistics) Share Ownership Survey (as at 31 December 2008) found that insurance companies held 13.4% of shares in UK listed companies (down from 14.7% at the end of 2006 and 21% at the end of 2000) and pension funds held 12.8% (12.7% at the end of 2006 and down from 17.7% at the end of 2000) so together they hold 27.5% which, when coupled with unit trust holdings of 1.8%, gives an aggregate institutional holding in the region of 30% with banks and other financial institutions holding a further 13.5% and individuals with 10.2%.[141] The issue is the role that such well-informed, well-financed and influential institutional investors can play and the contribution that they can make to high standards of corporate governance.[142] Their role might be seen as focused on improved corporate performance which would be reflected in shareholder value or they may be seen as having a broader role and in a position to protect wider stakeholder interests, though the two positions are not incompatible. Indeed, some would see institutional investors as effectively policing large companies for the benefit of all, adopting an almost regulatory-like role. The institutions meanwhile are concerned not to undertake a wider role, conscious that their obligations lie to their end-investors whose concern is improved shareholder returns.

5-51 Over the years, engagement typically has occurred behind the scenes,[143] but increasingly institutional investors are willing to take a more public stance,[144] fuelled in part by the need to correct what they see as erroneous comment about their apparent lack of engagement. It is still exceptional, however, for an institutional shareholder to put resolutions to the annual general meeting or to vote against the reappointment of incumbent management, though increasingly they are willing to withhold their votes on an issue. This tactic

---

[141] ONS, *Share Ownership Survey for 2008*; also BIS, *A Long-Term Focus for Corporate Britain, a call for evidence* (October 2010), Ch 4 which reviews the state of equity ownership in the UK; also ABI, *Insurance Key Facts 2011* (annual publication). See generally Cheffins, *Corporate Ownership and Control: British Business Transformed* (2008); also Dignam & Galanis, 'Corporate Governance and the Importance of the Macroeconomic Context' (2008) 28 Ox JLS 201.

[142] See Garrido & Rojo, 'Institutional Investors and Corporate Governance: Solution or Problem?' in Hopt & Wymeersch, *Capital Markets and Company Law* (2003).

[143] An interesting paper by Becht et al, 'Returns to Shareholder Activism, Evidence from a Clinical Study of the Hermes UK Focus Fund' ECGI Finance Working Paper, No 138 (2008) showed that practically all of the engagement of this fund with investee companies took place privately and without resort to mechanisms such as resolutions. This study also concluded that there were substantial effects and benefits associated with shareholder activism in the form of private engagements by an activist fund. See also Goergen et al, 'Do UK Institutional Shareholders Monitor their Investee Firms?' (2008) JCLS 39.

[144] The ABI's Institutional Voting Information System provides colour coded reports on companies on the basis of issues of corporate governance concern with the key categories being red (strong concerns) and amber (concern). This mechanism is quite effective with companies anxious to avoid being 'red topped' on any particular issue such as board composition or remuneration: see FT, 'ABI issues alert over C & W pay', 4 July 2011 (concerns about share awards to executive directors), FT, 'Thomas Cook tagged with "red-top" notice', 9 February 2011. See also Roach, 'CEOs, Chairmen and Fat Cats' (2006) 27 Co Law 297.

allows them to avoid a positive vote against a board while still expressing their disquiet about a particular matter. In so far as institutional shareholders have intervened, certainly in the past decade,[145] the focus of their engagement (at least publicly) has been mainly on narrow issues of executive pay and board composition rather than corporate performance as such. Often, intervention attracts headlines (notably concerning the rejection of remuneration packages) but does not deter other companies from subsequently offering equally unacceptable pay packages to their executives, see **5-41**. Often, because intervention tends to be reactive rather than proactive, it only comes after there has been significant destruction of shareholder value.[146] Sometimes, intervention itself is criticised, as in the case of hedge-fund activism.[147]

The Stewardship Code

5-52 Certainly, in the past decade political pressure has grown for greater engagement. Hence in 2002 the Institutional Shareholders Committee issued an influential 'Statement of Principles on the Responsibilities of Institutional Investors'[148] which by 2009 they had updated and re-designated as an ISC Code on the Responsibilities of Institutional Investors and which aimed to set out best practice guidance for investors on monitoring companies, on dialogue with boards and on voting. The ISC was reconstituted and renamed in May 2011 as the Institutional Investors Committee (IIC), a change of name which the committee considers more accurately reflects its role,[149] while the code on responsibilities has become, in effect, the UK Stewardship Code which was adopted by

---

[145] High profile events over the period ranged from preventing the appointment of Michael Green of Carlton as chairman of ITV, see FT, 'The TV Watershed: Why the clash of wills at Carlton is pushing shareholder activities to aggressive new levels', 21 October 2003; to blocking appointments or removing chief executives at companies such as Sainsbury's, see FT, 'Sainsbury's shareholders bring down the curtain on Prosser', 18 February 2004, or the Prudential, see FT, 'Investors show Bloomer who wields the power', 25 March 2005. An important landmark on remuneration was the shareholder revolt against the GSK remuneration packet for Jean-Pierre Garnier in 2003, see The Independent, 'US active investor joins revolt over Garnier's pay deal at GSK', 10 May 2003. In 2009 a range of high-profile companies saw significant votes against their remuneration reports, see FT, 'Indignant investors flex voting muscles', 6 May 2009; FT, 'Floored Boards, Executive Pay', 2 June 2009; and again in 2012, see FT, 'Investor anger boils over', 4 May 2012.

[146] As in the case of the Marconi collapse, where essentially the board of this telecommunications group spent hundreds of millions of pounds on ill-judged acquisitions which were wiped out with the bursting of the dot com bubble at the beginning of 2000, see Kam, 'Making sense of organisational failure: the Marconi debacle' (2005) 23 Prometheus 399 at 404–12.

[147] Particularly high profile was the role of hedge funds in preventing Deutsche Bourse from bidding for the London Stock Exchange, see FT, 'Funds step up pressure on Deutsche Bourse', 21 January 2005. The activism of hedge funds is often criticised and there can be a sense that more 'traditional' institutional shareholders sometimes resent the sudden appearance of hedge funds on the scene, see FT, 'Bolton attacks Cadbury split in face of activists', 11 June 2007 (well-known fund manager, Bolton, criticised Cadbury for 'giving in' to pressure from hedge funds to split its drinks and confectionery businesses) and Bolton, 'Boards must stand up to minority activists', FT, 11 June 2007. Often hedge funds are accused of acting in a way which is little more than a form of market manipulation where a fund conducts a very public campaign against a company to try to force a re-structuring or sale.

[148] The ISC was composed of the ABI and NAPF together with the Association of Investment Companies (AIC) and the Investment Management Association (IMA). In addition, some of the more prominent investors also publish their own guidelines on engagement, voting and corporate governance standards in companies in which they invest. See, for example, the NAPF, *Corporate Governance Policy and Voting Guidelines* (2011) (the National Association of Pension Funds); PIRC, *UK Shareholder Voting Guidelines* 2011 (Pensions Investment Research Consultants, a high profile independent corporate governance advisor); and Hermes, *The Hermes Responsible Ownership Principles* (2010) (Hermes, an independent institutional fund manager).

[149] The IIC is composed of the ABI and NAPF and the Investment Management Association (IMA).

the FRC in July 2010,[150] following on from recommendations to that effect in the Walker Report.[151] Walker commented, in particular, that 'those who have significant rights of ownership and enjoy the very material advantage of limited liability should see these as complemented by a duty of stewardship'.[152] An updated version of the Stewardship Code will apply from October 2012.

5-53 The Stewardship Code is addressed to asset managers, i.e. firms which manage assets on behalf of institutional investors such as pension funds, insurance companies, investment trusts and other collective investment vehicles.[153] The FRC sees the Stewardship Code (hailed as the world's first investor code)[154] as complementary to the UK Corporate Governance Code and, like the UK Code, it operates on a comply or explain basis (Stewardship Code, Preface). A statement of compliance or explanation must be put on the institutional investor's website explaining how the principles of the Stewardship Code have been applied and disclosing the specific information required by the Principles or explaining any non-compliance.[155] Adherence to the Stewardship Code is reinforced by an FSA requirement that all UK-authorised asset managers must produce a statement of commitment to the Stewardship Code or explain why it is not appropriate to their business model.[156] The FRC also urges asset owners to report if and how they have complied with the Stewardship Code and it encourages proxy voting and other advisory services to disclose how, as service providers, they carry out the wishes of their clients by applying the principles of the Code relevant to their activities. The Stewardship Code is therefore quite wide-ranging in terms of reach and application.[157]

---

[150] See FRC, *Implementation of the Stewardship Code* (July 2010), paras 7, 19 which acknowledged that the Code is little more than the ISC Statement of Principles with minor amendments. For criticism of this approach, see Roach, 'The UK Stewardship Code' (2011) JCLS 463 who notes (at 476–7) that many believe that the ISC Code did not go far enough or impose high enough standards and therefore many respondents to the FRC urged the FRC to modify/revise it rather than adopt it more or less verbatim, which is what happened. The FRC has since revised the Code for reporting periods after 1 October 2012, see FRC, *Revisions to the Stewardship Code* (April 2012).

[151] See Walker Report, n 13, Ch 5, esp recommendations 16–20.

[152] See Walker Report, n 13, para 5.7 where Walker commented that 'the potentially highly influential position of significant holders of stock in listed companies is a major ingredient in the market-based capitalist system which needs to earn and to be accorded an at least implicit social legitimacy' which it can so do at least by larger fund managers assuming obligations to attend to the performance of investee companies over the long as well as the short term.

[153] It is particularly important to focus on asset managers for, as the European Commission Green Paper, n 134, para 2.3 makes clear, there are important issues to be addressed as to their role, their remuneration and their management of conflicts of interest.

[154] There are other similar approaches, see EFAMA (European Fund and Asset Management Association) Code for External Governance Principles for the exercise of ownership rights in investee companies (April 2011) and the UN-backed Principles for Responsible Investment (2006) which now has almost 100 signatories from investment managers, asset owners and professional service providers.

[155] The institution then notifies the FRC that a statement has been posted on the institution's website and the name of the institution is published on a list maintained on the FRC's website.

[156] See FSA Handbook, COBS 2.2.3R: a firm, other than a venture capital firm, which is managing investments for a professional client that is not a natural person must disclose clearly on its website, or if it does not have a website in another accessible form: (1) the nature of its commitment to the Financial Reporting Council's Stewardship Code; or (2) where it does not commit to the Code, its alternative investment strategy.

[157] There has been a considerable take-up of the Stewardship Code with over 160 asset managers, 44 asset owners and 12 service providers having signed up by January 2012, which is not entirely unexpected given the Code's similarity to the ISC Statement of Principles—in other words, to the industry's own guidance. The FRC expects overseas institutional investors also to comply with (or explain) the Stewardship Code unless they already comply with other similar domestic or international standards; equally UK institutions investing abroad should use their best efforts to apply the Stewardship principles to their overseas holdings: Stewardship Code, Preface.

Purpose of the Stewardship Code

5-54 The Stewardship Code aims 'to enhance the quality of engagement between institutional investors and companies to help improve long-term returns to shareholders and the efficient exercise of governance responsibilities' by setting out good practice on engagement with investee companies to which the FRC believes institutional shareholders should aspire (see Preface). Crucially, there is no obligation on institutions to engage, but the decision as to whether or not to engage should be a considered one, based on the institution's investment approach.[158]

Content of the Stewardship Code

5-55 The Stewardship Code, in the manner of the UK Code, consists of Principles and Guidance on each principle. The principles of the Stewardship Code are straightforward—institutional investors should:

- publicly disclose their policy on how they will discharge their stewardship responsibilities;[159]
- have a robust policy on managing conflicts of interest in relation to stewardship and this policy should be publicly disclosed;
- monitor their investee companies;[160]
- establish clear guidelines on when and how they will escalate their activities as a method of protecting and enhancing shareholder value;
- be willing to act collectively with other investors where appropriate;[161]
- have a clear policy on voting and disclosure of voting activity (but there is no requirement to vote);[162]
- report periodically on their stewardship and voting activities.[163]

5-56 There is little about these principles which is particularly challenging for asset managers and little that is mandatory, other than a certain level of disclosure.[164] A lot of attention in the context of engagement is focused on the exercise of voting power and one of the most

---

[158] Compliance with the Code is not, in any event, an invitation to manage the affairs of the investee company nor does it preclude a decision to sell since in all matters the institutional investor must act in the best interests of the end investor (see Preface).

[159] Including disclosure of the use made, if any, of proxy voting or other voting advisory services, Stewardship Code, Guidance to Principle 1; the role played by proxy voting services is attracting some scrutiny now, see European Commission Green Paper, n 134, para 2.5. Reflecting their expanding role, some proxy voting services, such as ISS, PIRC and Manifest Information Service, have achieved considerable prominence.

[160] Institutional investors should also maintain a clear audit trail of votes cast, of reasons for voting against the investee company's management, for abstaining or for voting with the management in a contentious situation: Stewardship Code, Guidance to Principle 3.

[161] Any fears that collective action might expose institutional investors to allegations of acting in concert or engaging in market abuse have been addressed by the Takeover Panel and FSA which have tried to provide reassurance that ad hoc collective shareholder engagement will not be so categorised: see Takeover Panel, Practice Statement 2009/26, 'Shareholder Activism'; FSA letter to the Institutional Shareholders Committee, see 'FSA provides clarity for activist shareholders,' FSA/PN/110/2009, 19 August 2009.

[162] Institutional investors should seek to vote all shares held and they should not automatically support the board and they should disclose publicly voting records and if they do not, explain why: Stewardship Code, Guidance to Principle 6.

[163] The Stewardship Code, Guidance to Principle 7, states that those signing up to the Code should consider obtaining an independent audit opinion (having regard to professional standards) on their engagement and voting processes.

[164] See Roach, n 150, who notes the Stewardship Code's modest content, its weak and tentative approach in many respects and concludes that it is a product of expeditiousness rather than a well-thought-out set of principles designed to increase the current level of investor engagement.

difficult issues is whether institutional shareholders should be required to vote at general meetings, given the significant blocks of shares which they hold. The Government has threatened from time to time that it will consider introducing a legal requirement to vote if institutions do not exercise their voting rights,[165] but it would prefer that institutional investors voluntarily engage in the manner suggested by the Stewardship Code which does not impose any mandatory voting requirement. There is some evidence that the public debate on the issue of voting has resulted in a greater number of institutional votes being cast, though it is not clear to what extent this is considered voting as opposed to 'box-ticking' compliance.[166]

Challenges to shareholder engagement

5-57 The way forward appears to rest quite firmly on greater shareholder engagement, but this enthusiasm for shareholder engagement may be misplaced or at least based on unrealistic expectations.[167] As noted, shareholder engagement is not new, though it has a raised profile now, and there is little reason to believe that, once the initial flurry of activity following the financial crisis abates, anything particularly different will have emerged. For a number of reasons, the landscape may look very similar to before the crisis with some level of ongoing intervention on the issue of executive pay and board composition (these being the two issues which are easiest for shareholders to address), but without any significant change in the role played by shareholders in the largest companies. One reason for the lack of change may be that the environment in which the debate about shareholder engagement is taking place is considerably less conducive to engagement than previously. When serious discussion first started (probably about 20 years ago) of greater institutional shareholder engagement, insurance companies and pension funds did form a (relatively) homogeneous grouping of 'institutional investors',[168] but there is no such homogeneity now.[169] Insurance companies and pension funds' holdings are declining, those of sovereign wealth and hedge funds increasing and overseas investors are more visible, holding more than 40% of listed shares.[170] Encouraging engagement by those types of investors is more challenging,[171] not least because they are less susceptible to domestic

---

[165] As a first step, the Government has a power under CA 2006, s 1277 to bring in regulations to require institutions to provide information as to the exercise of their voting rights, but it has not used this power to date. See generally Schmolke, 'Institutional Investors Mandatory Voting Disclosure' (2006) 7 EBOR 767.

[166] An Investment Management Association report on adherence to the FRC's Stewardship Code in the period to September 2010 found that 80% of respondents voted 100% of their UK shares with a further 12.5% voting between 75% and 100%: nearly two-thirds of respondents publicly disclosed their voting records, see IMA, *Adherence to the FRC's Stewardship Code* at 30 September 2010 (May 2011).

[167] See generally Cheffins, 'The Stewardship Code's Achilles Heel' (2010) 73 MLR 1004.

[168] In 1981 insurance companies held 20.5% (13.4% in 2008) and pension funds 26.7% (12.8% in 2008) of listed UK shares, see the ONS *Share Ownership Survey 2008* (published January 2010), Table A.

[169] Millstein, 'Directors and Boards amidst Shareholders with Conflicting Values', Charkham Memorial Lecture, 9 July 2008. Indeed one of the problems now is the lack of clear information on who are the investors and what their strategies and priorities might be, see the *Report of the Reflection Group on the Future of European Company Law* (2011), para 3.1.4 (a report commissioned by the European Commission) which suggested that the EU Commission should undertake a regular review of the role and actions of institutional investors, say every three years, so as to start to develop an understanding of the extent to which they balance long and short-term considerations so that an appropriate regulatory response might be developed.

[170] See the ONS *Share Ownership Survey 2008* (published January 2010), Table A.

[171] These difficulties explain why, despite their declining holdings, local institutions are expected to take the lead on engagement though the FRC hopes that investors based outside the UK will commit to the Stewardship Code as their support where they have significant holdings can make a real difference, see

political pressure to engage. Even identifying shareholders, or at least those with the true economic interest, is difficult as a result of stock lending practices and long investment chains. All involved have different investment time scales and strategies. Greater engagement is being sought in an environment when it is probably unrealistic to expect much by way of common interest between these many types of investors so limiting the scope for common action.

5-58 There are also many practical issues relating to shareholder engagement which need to be considered. Improved meeting procedures and rules in the CA 2006, Pt 13, are helpful, but long-standing institutional concerns about matters such as the priority they must give to their obligations to their end-investors, the resources required for engagement, the difficulties of building a coalition of support,[172] free-rider issues, and the need to retain freedom to pursue their own investment strategies have not evaporated with the adoption of the Stewardship Code.[173] These difficulties mean that it is important to have realistic expectations of what shareholder engagement can contribute to corporate governance. That is not to deny that engagement is important for governance generally as it provides another point of intervention and scrutiny of boards, but its real value is when it is used by individual investors as a tool for limiting their risk. Selfish focused engagement could increase the possibility for some alert investors to exit from disastrous investments before all value is destroyed[174] and their exit may alert others as to the approaching calamity so bringing matters to a head rather sooner and reducing the ultimate losses. This selfish engagement does little to contribute to the long-term sustainability of the enterprise, however, and is essentially a response based on exit rather than addressing under-performance.

Long-term investment and engagement

5-59 A much broader debate then is the contribution which the institutional investors can make to the long-term success of the company. In the wake of the financial crisis, one of the issues for consideration, and on which the Department of Business, Innovation and Skills (BIS) has called for evidence, is whether there is a problem of short-termism in equity markets (i.e. a focus by investors and asset managers on short-term returns at the expense of a longer term perspective) and, if so, how it might be addressed.[175] The concern is that there is evidence of too great an obsession with the short term (holding periods for shares had shrunk to eight months by 2007 compared to in excess of five years in the 1960s)[176] with shareholders looking for instant returns and directors looking to satisfy that demand rather than focus on longer term strategies which would possibly be more beneficial to the company and its investors,

---

FRC, *Implementation of the Stewardship Code* (July 2010), para 25. The OECD would also encourage greater engagement by foreign investors, see OECD, *Corporate Governance and the Financial Crisis: Conclusions and emerging good practices*, (February 2010), para 7.6.

[172] See Keay, 'Company Directors Behaving Poorly: Disciplinary Options for Shareholders' [2007] JBL 656 at 659–62.

[173] A key practical difficulty is the chain of intermediaries which poses real difficulties for engagement, see European Commission Green Paper, see n 134, paras 2.4–2.6. See also Walker, Final Report, n 13, Ch 5.

[174] The importance of this self-interested engagement is another reason why direct shareholding by individual investors will become a thing of the past. Few individuals have the resources for the level of monitoring of their small portfolios which is necessary if they are to avoid the sort of cataclysmic losses borne by small investors in the past decade (ranging from Railtrack, to Equitable Life, to Halifax Bank of Scotland).

[175] BIS, *A Long-Term Focus for Corporate Britain, a call for evidence* (October 2010); also *Report of the Reflection Group on the Future of European Company Law* (2011), Ch 3.

[176] See BIS, n 175, para 4.19; also European Commission Green Paper, see n 134, para 2.2.

employees etc. If engagement could be shifted to a focus on long-term investment, that may be more beneficial to the economy as a whole. Following that initial call for evidence, the Government considers that there is a need 'to work out how the equity investment regime can be recalibrated to support the long-term interests of companies as well as underlying beneficiaries such as pension fund members'[177] and to that end it announced the setting up of an independent review (the Kay Review) of investment in UK equity. The Kay Review is to look at the whole investor chain and examine the role of all the players, from company boards, through pension funds, advisers and fund managers, to ultimate beneficiaries. In particular, it will examine whether the timescales considered by boards and senior management and by institutional shareholders and fund managers match the time horizons of the underlying beneficiaries and whether the markets and Government policy give sufficient encouragement to boards to focus on long-term development of their businesses. As part of that process, the review will look at the quality of engagement, building on the role of the Stewardship Code. The Kay Review is expected to publish its final report in late 2012, following on from an interim report published in February 2012.

Enfranchising the indirect investor

5-60 In keeping with the general theme of shareholder engagement, especially in larger companies, the CA 2006, Pt 9 introduces some innovative provisions with respect to the enfranchisement of indirect holders. The modern practice is that most individual investors hold shares through an intermediary and have no direct relationship with the company in which they have invested. For its part, the company looks solely to the legal owner as reflected in the register of members and does not have regard to beneficial interests (CA 2006, s 126). It is often argued that shareholder engagement demands some mechanism whereby the indirect investor, the actual provider of the capital, can engage with and be recognised by the company.[178] These enfranchisement provisions were the subject of intense debate in Parliament with various permutations being considered before agreement was finally reached on what is now CA 2006, Pt 9. The idea of enfranchising or involving the indirect investor seems attractive, but in practice it is difficult to devise a workable, cost-effective, mechanism, particularly once cross-border investors are involved. Traded companies with large numbers of registered shareholders and unquantifiable numbers of beneficial interests behind them are concerned that a liberal approach to enfranchising those beneficial interests could lead to administrative chaos and dramatically increase the costs of maintaining and operating their share registers. The CA 2006, Pt 9 is therefore a modest step forward, reflecting the numerous compromises necessary to gain Parliamentary approval, rather than a radical departure from the general rule that the company looks to the registered shareholder.

5-61 Part 9 allows for the recognition of indirect investors in two ways: (1) any company can choose to permit the registered member to nominate another person to enjoy or exercise all or any specified rights of the member in relation to the company (CA 2006, s 145); and (2)

---

[177] Speech by Secretary of State for Business, Innovation and Skill, Vince Cable, to ABI, 22 June 2011 and see Kay Review Interim Report (February 2012) URN 12/631.

[178] The Company Law Review noted the growing separation between the legal ownership and beneficial ownership and considered the grant of at least some 'control rights' to the beneficial owners while envisaging that market solutions will emerge as electronic communications make it easier for companies, intermediaries and ultimate beneficial owners to exercise these control rights: see Company Law Review, *Final Report*, vol 1 (2001), para 3.51, para 7.1; *Completing the Structure* (2000), paras 5.2–5.12; *Developing the Framework* (2000), paras 4.7–4.18.

traded companies can allow a member to nominate another person to enjoy 'information rights' so that the company must communicate with that other person directly (s 146).[179]

Nominating another to exercise rights of a member

5-62 Any company may provide in its articles that a member can nominate another person to enjoy or exercise all or any specified rights of that member in relation to the company (CA 2006, s 145). Anything which can be done by the member can then be done by the nominated person, in particular the nominated person can exercise the rights to circulate resolutions and statements (ss 292, 314, 338), to require the directors to call a meeting (s 303), to appoint a proxy (s 324) and to receive written resolutions, notice of meetings and annual accounts and reports (ss 291, 310, 423). To date, few companies, if any, appear to have chosen to alter their articles to allow for nomination in this way.

Information rights

5-63 A member in a traded company can nominate a person on whose behalf he holds shares to enjoy 'information rights' by which is meant that the nominee has the right to receive all shareholder communications and the right to receive the annual accounts and reports (CA 2006, s 146). The rights of the nominee are in addition to the rights of the registered member (s 150(5)). A registered member is not required to nominate another person for information rights and, even if nominated, the registered member can terminate the nomination at any time (s 148(2)).[180] The documents or information which the nominee is entitled to are provided by a website, unless the nominee requests the registered member to notify the company that the nominee wishes to receive hard copies and the nominee provides a postal address for that purpose (s 147(2), (5)).

5-64 Where a notice of a meeting is sent to a nominated person, the notice must state that the nominated person may have the right to be appointed as a proxy or to appoint someone else as a proxy and may be able to give his voting instructions directly to the registered shareholder, depending on the agreement between the nominee and the person by whom he was nominated (s 149). A failure by the company to recognise information rights is actionable (as a breach of the articles) only by the registered shareholder and not by the nominated person (s 150(2)).

5-65 After all the Parliamentary discussion, once enacted the provisions appear to have attracted little interest. In so far as the provisions require companies to facilitate the changes by choosing to alter their articles (to allow for nomination of another), they have shown no inclination to do so, not least because there is no pressure from shareholders for the articles to be changed. In so far as nominee shareholders may nominate the beneficial owners to enjoy information rights, it would appear they have not done so, perhaps out of inertia or a concern about the administrative burden of altering existing arrangements. In so far as the whole process depends on the indirect investors showing some interest in exercising these rights, they have not done so, probably because the rights mainly amount to a right to receive information via a website (a compromise based on the need to limit the costs involved). As much of the information on websites is anyway on open access and so in the public domain, shareholders have no particular reason to exercise these rights. The provisions are then on the statute book but they have had little impact to date.

---

[179] For detailed guidance on Part 9, see ICSA *Guidance on Part 9, Companies Act 2006, Indirect Investors—Information Rights and Voting* (2007).

[180] Furthermore, CA 2006, s 148(7) provides that a nomination can be terminated where no response is received within 28 days to a query from the company as to whether the indirect investor wishes to retain his information rights (only one such enquiry may be made per annum).

6

Board composition–appointment and removal of directors

A Appointment of directors

6-1 The directors are responsible for the management of the company's business for which purpose they may exercise all the powers of the company.[1] The expectation is that the directors act collectively as a board but the articles invariably provide that any of the powers conferred on the directors by the articles can in turn be delegated by them to smaller committees or individual directors or other persons.[2] The proceedings of the board are regulated by the articles of association which will contain detailed rules covering matters such as the manner of decision-making by the directors,[3] the calling of directors' meetings[4] and quorum requirements.[5] Minutes must be kept of all board meetings.[6]

6-2 'Director' as such is not defined in the Companies Act 2006 which provides simply that 'director' includes any person occupying the position of director, by whatever name called,[7] so making it clear that title is not the determining factor in deciding whether someone is a director. It is possible therefore for someone to be a director though described as a manager or governor. Equally, companies may describe employees as marketing or personnel directors, for example, without their occupying the position of director in law. Legally, there are three classes of director which concern us, the de jure director, the de facto director and the shadow director.

---

[1] See The Companies (Model Articles) Regulations 2008, SI 2008/3229, reg 2, Sch 1, art 3 (Ltd); reg 4, Sch 3, art 3 (Plc).

[2] See The Companies (Model Articles) Regulations 2008, SI 2008/3229, reg 2, Sch 1, art 5 (Ltd); reg 4, Sch 3, art 5 (Plc).

[3] The general rule about decision-making by the directors of a private company is that any decision must be either a majority decision of the directors at a meeting or a unanimous decision (of those eligible to vote on the matter) by written resolution: see The Companies (Model Articles) Regulations 2008, SI 2008/3229, reg 2, Sch 1, art 7 (Ltd), but see also art 16 ('subject to the articles, the directors may make any rule which they think fit about how they take decisions…'). Likewise in the case of a public company, decisions may (not 'must' as in the case of the private company articles) be taken at a directors' meeting or in the form of a directors' written resolution: see arts 7, 13, 18–19 (Plc).

[4] See The Companies (Model Articles) Regulations 2008, SI 2008/3229, reg 2, Sch 1, art 9 (Ltd); reg 4, Sch 3, art 8 (Plc).

[5] See The Companies (Model Articles) Regulations 2008, SI 2008/3229, reg 2, Sch 1, art 11(2) (Ltd); reg 4, Sch 3, art 10(2) (Plc).

[6] CA 2006, s 248. There is no provision for inspection of such minutes by the members unlike the minutes of any general meeting which are available for inspection by any member: s 358.

[7] CA 2006, s 250. See Browne-Wilkinson V-C in *Re Lo-Line Electric Motors Ltd* [1988] 2 All ER 692 at 699: 'In my judgment the words "by whatever name called" show that the subsection is dealing with nomenclature; for example where the company's articles provide that the conduct of the company is committed to "governors" or "managers".'

De jure directors

6-3 A de jure director is someone formally and validly appointed to the board. The application for registration of a company which is submitted to the registrar of companies must contain the names of the proposed first directors (first directors and company secretary if the company is a public company or is a private company which has chosen to have a company secretary)[8] and they must give their consent so to act (CA 2006, s 12(3)). On the certificate of incorporation being issued by the registrar, those persons named as directors in the application for registration are deemed to have been appointed to office (s 16(6)). Thereafter the manner of appointment is a matter for the articles which typically provide that appointments may be made by ordinary resolution or by a decision of the directors.[9] The UK Corporate Governance Code provides that all directors of FTSE 350 companies should be subject to annual election, see **5-13**, as should all non-executive directors of companies subject to the Code who have served longer than nine years, see **5-25**.[10]

6-4 A private company need have only one director whereas a public company must have at least two (CA 2006, s 154). For the first time, the CA 2006 sets a minimum age for a director which is 16 years and an appointment in breach of this requirement is void.[11]

6-5 At least one director must be a natural person,[12] otherwise corporate directors are permissible, see further at **6-13**.[13] The Government had wanted to prohibit corporate directors, but had to settle on this compromise following objections on behalf of the 64,000 corporate directors on the register.[14] The Government had concerns that corporate directors make it difficult to determine who controls a company and to apply sanctions against corporate directors. Certainly the investigation and prosecution of corporate frauds can be impeded when it is possible to have corporate shareholders and directors, often based on further layers of corporate entities, some of which may be registered in other jurisdictions.

6-6 In the case of a public company, each proposed director must be voted on individually, otherwise the resolution is void, unless those voting consent unanimously to a block resolution (CA 2006, s 160). This requirement ensures that shareholders can express their disapproval of a particular director without having to reject the entire board. The acts of a director are valid, however, notwithstanding any defect which may afterwards be

---

[8] CA 2006, s 9(4)(c).

[9] See The Companies (Model Articles) Regulations 2008, SI 2008/3229, reg 2, Sch 1, art 17 (Ltd); reg 4, Sch 3, art 20 (Plc). In the case of a public company, such an appointment is held only until the next following annual general meeting when the appointee can be re-elected: art 20(2)(a). Usefully, the model articles for private companies provide that where, as a result of death, a private company is left with no shareholders and no directors (as where the company is a sole member company and the sole member is also the sole director) the personal representative of the last shareholder to die has the right to appoint a director: see art 17(2) (Ltd).   [10] UK Corporate Governance Code (2010) B.7.1.

[11] CA 2006, s 157(1), (4), though such 'directors' remain liable for their acts: see s 157(5). Regulations may allow for exceptional cases (none have been made): s 158 (it might be appropriate to have younger directors, say, of a company operating as a youth charity). Under-age directors in office on 1 October 2008 automatically ceased to be directors (s 159(2)). A previous restriction (CA 1985, s 293) on persons aged 70 or more acting as a director of a public company has been repealed.

[12] The Secretary of State has power to direct a company to appoint the right number of directors or to ensure that at least one director is a natural person: CA 2006, s 156.

[13] CA 2006, s 155; *Re Bulawayo Market and Offices Co Ltd* [1907] 2 Ch 458. The register of directors must include the corporate name and registered office of any company holding the office of director as well as other details: CA 2006, s 164.

[14] See *Modernising Company Law* (Cmnd 5553-I, 2002), paras 3.32–3.34.

discovered in his appointment or qualification (CA 2006, s 161). This section covers the situation where there has been a breach of the requirements regarding appointment with the result that the appointment is defective, but it does not validate the acts of someone who has never been appointed at all but who simply purports to fill the office of director,[15] nor can it assist a party having knowledge of the facts giving rise to the defect or a party who is put on inquiry but does not inquire.[16]

6-7 The model articles for public companies (see **4-2**) provide for the appointment of alternate directors. Such a director is appointed by a director to exercise that director's powers and carry out that director's responsibilities in relation to the taking of decisions by the directors.[17] Except as otherwise provided, alternate directors are deemed for all purposes to be directors, are liable for their own acts and omissions and are not agents of or for their appointors.[18]

6-8 Every company must keep a register of its directors giving the following details for an individual director: name, a service address (there is no longer any requirement for residential addresses to be given), the country or state (or part of the UK) in which the director is usually resident, his or her nationality, business occupation (if any) and date of birth.[19] This register must be open to inspection at the registered office or other specified place by members of the company free of charge and by the public for such fee as may be prescribed.[20] Details of directors' service contracts must also be available for inspection at the registered office or other specified place.[21] A major change in the CA 2006 is that there is no longer a requirement for a director's usual residential address to be given in the register of directors. Instead a service address may be given and that service address may be stated as the company's registered office (s 163(5)). The residential address is available to a wide range of public authorities and others such as liquidators and creditors may seek a court order requiring disclosure of the residential address.[22] This change was introduced in order to provide additional protection for directors from harassment and threats by persons such as animal rights extremists.[23] As with the decision to limit unrestricted access to the register of members (see **14-73**), this reduction in transparency across a register of 2.3m companies is a disproportionate response to the criminal activities of a small number of extremists. The company is required to maintain a register of directors' residential addresses (s 165), but that register is not open to inspection.[24] Appointments

---

[15] *Morris v Kanssen* [1946] AC 459; *British Asbestos Co Ltd v Boyd* [1903] 2 Ch 439; *Dawson v African Consolidated Land and Travel Co* [1898] 1 Ch 6.

[16] See *Re New Cedos Engineering Co Ltd* [1994] 1 BCLC 797 at 812; *British Asbestos Co Ltd v Boyd* [1903] 2 Ch 439.

[17] See The Companies (Model Articles) Regulations 2008, SI 2008/3229, reg 4, Sch 3, arts 25–27 (Plc). As an alternate is deemed for all purposes to be a director (art 26(2)(a)), his appointment must be notified to the registrar of companies as required by CA 2006, s 167.

[18] See The Companies (Model Articles) Regulations 2008, SI 2008/3229, reg 4, Sch 3, art 26(2) (Plc).

[19] CA 2006, s 162(1), (2). There is no longer any requirement to give details of other directorships held by that director.   [20] CA 2006, s 162(3), (5); SI 2008/3006.

[21] See CA 2006, s 228(1), (2); SI 2008/3006.

[22] See CA 2006, ss 243, 244, 1088; The Companies (Disclosure of Address) Regulations 2009, SI 2009/214.

[23] Initially the Government response was to allow directors (and others, including the company secretary) at serious risk of violence or intimidation to apply to the registrar of companies for a confidentiality order: see CA 1985, ss 723B–723F; Companies (Particulars of Usual Residential Address) (Confidentiality Orders) Regulations 2002, SI 2002/912.

[24] The details contained on the company's register of residential addresses are notified to the registrar of companies on the appointment of a director (CA 2006, s 167). This information is classified as 'protected

(and resignations) of directors must be notified within 14 days to the registrar of companies (s 167) and any such notification is then publicised by the registrar in the *London Gazette*.[25]

De facto directors

6-9   Essentially, a de facto director is someone who is part of the corporate governing structure of the company and who has assumed the status and functions of a company director so as to make himself liable as if he were a de jure director.[26] The difficulty lies in distinguishing between someone who assumes that status and someone who acts for, or otherwise in the interests of, a company but is never more than, for example, a mere agent, employee or adviser.[27]

6-10   The question whether someone is a de facto director is likely to arise where a penalty or liability is imposed on a director, such as disqualification[28] or liability for wrongful trading,[29] or misfeasance[30] and the individual attempts to evade the penalty or liability by relying on the fact that he is not a de jure director (i.e. a formally and properly appointed director).[31]

6-11   The Supreme Court recently confirmed in *Re Paycheck Services 3 Ltd, Revenue and Customs Commissioners v Holland*[32] that there is no single defining and reliable test for determining whether someone is a de facto director, and indeed it is not necessary that the term 'de

information' which cannot be disclosed by the company or by the registrar of companies save to the extent permitted by the Act, for example disclosure on the order of a court: CA 2006, ss 240–246; s 1087(1)(b); also The Companies (Disclosure of Address) Regulations 2009, SI 2009/214.

[25] CA 2006, ss 1077, 1078. A company cannot rely against other persons on any change among the company's directors if that change has not been officially notified in the *Gazette* at the material time unless the other person was aware of it; and it cannot rely on any change within 15 days of the notice in the *Gazette* if the other party was unavoidably prevented from knowing of the change at that time: s 1079(1)–(3). However, the effect of s 1079 is purely negative and it does not entitle the company to treat the gazetting of an event as giving notice to all the world: *Official Custodian for Charities v Parway Estates Developments Ltd* [1984] 3 All ER 679.

[26] *Re Paycheck Services 3 Ltd, Revenue and Customs Commissioners v Holland* [2011] 1 BCLC 141 at [93]; *Re Kaytech International plc, Secretary of State for Trade and Industry v Kaczer* [1999] 2 BCLC 351 at 402–3, CA; also *Secretary of State for Trade and Industry v Tjolle* [1998] 1 BCLC 333 at 343–4; *Re Hydrodam (Corby) Ltd* [1994] 2 BCLC 180 at 183. See generally Noonan & Watson, 'Examining Company Directors through the Lens of De Facto Directorship' [2008] JBL 587.

[27] See *Secretary of State for Trade and Industry v Hollier* [2007] BCC 11 at 27 where Etherton J noted that this distinction is between someone who participates, or has the right to participate, in collective decision-making on corporate policy and strategy and its implementation, on the one hand, and others who may advise or act on behalf of, or otherwise for the benefit of, the company, but do not participate in decision-making as part of the corporate governance of the company. In that case a son in a family company was not a de facto director when he acted out of a wish to assist his father in his business, but without participating in strategic or policy decisions on a par with any other directors of the company whereas another son was a de facto director for he did exercise real control and gave instructions over a wide range of the company's activities, even though equally motivated to help his father. See also *Re Hydrodam (Corby) Ltd* [1994] 2 BCLC 180 at 183.   [28] See, for example, *Re Lo-Line Electric Motors Ltd* [1988] BCLC 698.

[29] See, for example, *Re Hydrodam (Corby) Ltd* [1994] 2 BCLC 180.

[30] See *Re Paycheck Services 3 Ltd, Revenue and Customs Commissioners v Holland* [2011] 1 BCLC 141; *Re Idessa Ltd, Burke v Morrison* [2012] 1 BCLC 80; *Primlake Ltd v Matthews Associates* [2007] 1 BCLC 666.

[31] See *Re Paycheck Services 3 Ltd, Revenue and Customs Commissioners v Holland* [2011] 1 BCLC 141 at [82], where Lord Collins explores the history of the de facto classification and concludes that the concept was significantly expanded in the 1980s to impose some particular liability on persons never appointed when previously it had been mainly used in the context of defective appointments or purported appointments.

[32] [2011] 1 BCLC 141.

facto director' be given the same meaning in all of the different contexts in which a director may be liable.[33] All the relevant factors must be taken into account, including the purpose of the rule being applied[34] and the court will look, for example, at whether the director is the sole person directing the affairs of the company (or acting with others equally lacking in a valid appointment) or acting on an equal footing with other true directors in directing its affairs;[35] whether there is a holding out by the company of the individual as a director and whether he used the title;[36] and, whether taking all the circumstances into account, the individual is part of the corporate governing structure of the company.[37]

6-12   In *Re Kaytech International plc, Secretary of State for Trade and Industry v Kaczer*,[38] for example, the Court of Appeal concluded that a person who was deeply and openly involved in the company's affairs, who devoted himself to the company's financial and property interests and who dealt with creditors, suppliers and the company's professional advisers, was not merely a consultant or company secretary but a de facto director. In *IRC v McEntaggart*[39] an undischarged bankrupt (and therefore someone automatically disqualified from being a director) who was described as the moving spirit within a construction company and whose role extended to matters such as negotiating and signing contracts, and who was involved in nearly all aspects of the management of the company's affairs, was a de facto director. In *Re Idessa Ltd, Burke v Morrison*[40] an individual who exercised real influence over the company's affairs and acted on an equal footing with the de jure director, and who had the same salary and access to the company's financial records as the de jure director, could fairly be regarded as part of the company's corporate governance and liable as a de facto director. On the other hand, in *Secretary of State for Trade and Industry v Tjolle*,[41] the court concluded that a manager employed by a holiday company who had a variety of titles including 'sales and marketing director' and even, for a period, 'deputy managing director', who sometimes attended board meetings, but who was never involved in any financial matters and who had no access to the company accounts, was not a de facto director. Likewise, in *Gemma Ltd v Davies*[42] a wife with purely clerical functions who was not involved in decision-making and who had no real influence in the governance of the company was not a de facto director.

---

[33]   [2011] 1 BCLC 141 at [93], per Lord Collins, with whom Lords Hope and Saville agreed, at [43] and [100] respectively. See also *Re Mumtaz Properties Ltd, Wetton v Ahmed* [2011] EWCA Civ 610 at [32]; *Re Idessa Ltd, Burke v Morrison* [2012] 1 BCLC 80 at [37]; also *Secretary of State for Trade and Industry v Tjolle* [1998] 1 BCLC 333 at 343–4; *Re Kaytech International plc, Secretary of State for Trade and Industry v Kaczer* [1999] 2 BCLC 351 at 423.   [34]   See [2011] 1 BCLC 141 at [39], at [93].
[35]   See *Re Richborough Furniture Ltd* [1996] 1 BCLC 507. In *Re Neath Rugby Ltd, Hawkes v Cuddy* [2008] 1 BCLC 527 the court described a wife who was a de jure director as a mere cipher for her husband such that all of her acts and omissions were his acts and omissions and he was a de facto director.
[36]   *Secretary of State for Trade and Industry v Tjolle* [1998] 1 BCLC 333.
[37]   *Re Paycheck Services 3 Ltd, Revenue and Customs Commissioners v Holland* [2011] 1 BCLC 141 at [90], [91], per Lord Collins, citing *Secretary of State for Trade and Industry v Tjolle* [1998] 1 BCLC 333 at 343–4; *Re Kaytech International plc, Secretary of State for Trade and Industry v Kaczer* [1999] 2 BCLC 351 at 423. See also *Re Mea Corporation Ltd, Secretary of State for Trade and Industry v Aviss* [2007] 1 BCLC 618 at 637; *Secretary of State for Trade and Industry v Hollier* [2007] BCC 11 at 24. A shareholder, even if acting to protect his investment, may act in a way which makes him a de facto director: see *Secretary of State for Trade and Industry v Becker* [2003] 1 BCLC 555 at 573; *Secretary of State for Trade and Industry v Hollier* [2007] BCC 11 at 27. When considering the role of the individual in the corporate governing structure, the court can look at the nature of the particular company, for example in a family company run on an informal basis, a person can be part of the governing structure without evidence of formal delegation of authority, see *Mumtaz Properties Ltd, Wetton v Ahmed* [2011] EWCA Civ 610 at [46]–[47].   [38]   [1999] 2 BCLC 351, CA.
[39]   [2006] 1 BCLC 476. See also *Re Moorgate Metals Ltd* [1995] 1 BCLC 503.   [40]   [2012] 1 BCLC 80.
[41]   [1998] 1 BCLC 333. See also *Re Red Label Fashions Ltd* [1999] BCC 308.   [42]   [2008] 2 BCLC 281.

Directors of corporate directors

6-13   As noted, the Supreme Court had the opportunity in *Re Paycheck Services 3 Ltd, Revenue and Customs Commissioners v Holland*[43] to consider some of the issues surrounding de facto directors. However, the key issue in the case was a narrow one of whether a director of a corporate director of a subject company could himself be a de facto director of the subject company.[44] The case was decided on a 3–2 ruling; Lords Hope and Collins, with whom Lord Saville agreed, delivered the majority ruling, but there is trenchant dissent from Lords Walker and Clarke.

6-14   The facts were that a number of companies (the subject companies, 42 in total) had been set up to secure certain tax advantages. The subject companies declared dividends on a regular basis at the behest of their sole corporate director, Paycheck Directors Ltd, which in turn could only act through its director, Mr Holland.[45] The Revenue Commissioners wished to establish that Mr Holland was a de facto director of the subject companies in order to sue him (under IA 1986, s 212, misfeasance procedure) for breach of fiduciary duty in misapplying subject company funds. The company had paid dividends which turned out to be improper because inadequate provision had been made for corporation tax. The subject companies had gone into insolvent liquidation leaving the Revenue, as their sole creditor, owed in the region of £3.5m for unpaid corporation tax.

6-15   Agreeing with the Court of Appeal in refusing the Revenue's claim, Lord Hope based his judgment primarily on the need to respect the status of the corporate director as a separate legal entity. Decisions of the corporate director must be treated as such and not as decisions of the person or persons who individually or collectively are the directors of the corporate director. 'So long as the relevant acts are done by the individual entirely within the ambit of the discharge of his duties and responsibilities as a director of the corporate director, it is to that capacity that his acts must be attributed.'[46] Lord Collins considered that to impose fiduciary duties on Mr Holland as a de facto director of the subject companies when all his acts could be attributed in law to the corporate director would be an unjustifiable judicial extension of the concept of de facto director.[47] If he was to be a de facto director of the subject companies simply because he was the guiding mind behind their sole corporate director, then this would be so in the case of every company with a sole corporate director and would go beyond the law as it stands and, Lord Collins said, beyond the function of the court.[48] In the context in this case of the fiduciary duty of a director not to dispose wrongfully of the company's assets (bearing in mind that 'de facto director' need not be given the same meaning in all the contexts in which a director may be liable) he agreed that the crucial question is whether the person assumed the duties of a director.[49] That person must be part of the corporate governing structure and must have assumed a role in the company sufficient to impose on him a fiduciary duty

---

[43] [2011] 1 BCLC 141. See Watts, 'De Facto directors' [2011] 127 LQR 162.

[44] See also *Secretary of State for Trade and Industry v Hall* [2009] BCC 190 (an individual may through his control of a corporate director constitute himself a de facto director of a subject company but whether or not he does so depends on what the individual procures the corporate director to do); also *Re Hydrodam (Corby) Ltd* [1994] 2 BCLC 180.

[45] Strictly speaking the corporate director had two directors, Mr and Mrs Holland, but the case proceeded on the basis that Mr Holland was the sole director of the corporate director.

[46] [2011] 1 BCLC 141 at [42] (Lord Hope), at [96] (Lord Collins), at [98] (Lord Saville), a view also taken by the Court of Appeal, see [2009] 2 BCLC 309.   [47] [2011] 1 BCLC 141 at [54].

[48] [2011] 1 BCLC 141 at [96].

[49] [2011] 1 BCLC 141 at [93], citing *Re Hydrodam (Corby) Ltd* [1994] 2 BCLC 180 and *Re Lo-Line Electric Motors Ltd* [1988] BCLC 698. See also *Re Idessa Ltd, Burke v Morrison* [2012] 1 BCLC 80 at [37].

to the company and to make him responsible for the misuse of its assets.[50] That was not the situation here. For the dissenters, Lords Walker and Clarke, the fact that Mr Holland was the only individual involved, that he took all the decisions as to the payment of the dividends that the corporate director purported to take and that he was the single guiding mind behind the corporate director meant that he was a de facto director of the subject companies as well as a de jure director of Paycheck Directors Ltd.[51] In their view, it was 'artificial and wrong' and 'arid formalism' to say that Holland was merely discharging his duties as a director of Paycheck Directors.[52] Lord Collins rejected their approach noting that the use of corporate directors had been considered by Parliament as recently as the CA 2006[53] which allows for their appointment and so, in his view, it is not for the courts to expand the category of de facto director and classify the individual directors (whether sole or multiple) of a corporate director as de facto directors of the subject companies.[54]

6-16 Whether a particular statutory provision which applies to a 'director' applies to a de facto director is a question of construction of the provision.[55] Whether a person should be subject to the fiduciary duties of a director depends, as Lord Collins said, on whether he has assumed a role in the corporate governing structure of the company sufficient to impose those obligations on him as a de facto director.[56] In *Primlake Ltd v Matthews Associates*[57] a company had sold land with significant development potential and much of the purchase money found its way into the hands of an architect involved in the sale. On the company going into liquidation, the liquidators alleged that the architect was actually a de facto director of the company who had received the money (£800,000 approx) in breach of his duties to the company. The defendant argued that he was merely a consultant to the

---

[50] [2011] 1 BCLC 141 at [93]–[94]. See also *Re Mumtaz Properties Ltd, Wetton v Ahmed* [2011] EWCA Civ 610 (a person who within an informally run family business dealt with suppliers and local authorities, who had a director's loan account on which he could make drawings for his personal benefit, and who the court found to be one of the nerve centres from which the company's activities radiated, was a de facto director for the purposes of liability under IA 1986, s 212 (misfeasance). On the totality of the court's findings as to how this company was run, he was part of the corporate governance structure of the company and was jointly and severally liable with the other directors for the misapplication of the company's funds).

[51] [2011] 1 BCLC 141 at [115], per Lord Walker; at [129], per Lord Clarke.

[52] [2011] 1 BCLC 141 at [115], per Lord Walker; at [142], per Lord Clarke. See Watts [2011] 127 LQR 162 at 163, 168 who criticises the minority for their willingness to apply a broad and undiscriminating fact-centred concept of de facto director which would have as a consequence that the individuals so classified would then be subject to the strict liability of directors with respect to the misapplication of company assets.

[53] As noted at **6-5**, the CA 2006 allows for corporate directors, but all companies must have at least one natural director (s 155) so the abuse which the minority perceived here—use of corporate structures by risk-averse individuals to insulate themselves from responsibility to unsecured creditors (see *Re Paycheck Services 3 Ltd, Revenue and Customs Commissioners v Holland* [2011] 1 BCLC 141 at [101], per Lord Walker)—will be (partially) mitigated. Only partially, since the single natural director may be a man or woman of straw and not worth holding liable, though that may be the case with any director, corporate or individual.

[54] [2011] 1 BCLC 141 at [96].

[55] See *Re Lo-Line Electric Motors Ltd* [1988] BCLC 698 at 706; *Dean v Hiesler* [1942] 2 All ER 340; and they do fall, for example, within the disqualification provisions in the Company Directors Disqualification Act 1986 (*Re Lo-Line*); the IA 1986, s 214, wrongful trading (*Re Hydrodam (Corby) Ltd* [1994] 2 BCLC 180) and IA 1986, s 212, misfeasance (*Re Paycheck Services 3 Ltd, Revenue and Customs Commissioners v Holland* [2011] 1 BCLC 141).

[56] *Re Paycheck Services 3 Ltd, Revenue and Customs Commissioners v Holland* [2011] 1 BCLC 141 at [93]. See also *Statek Corp v Alford* [2008] BCC 266 at 290 (de facto director owed fiduciary duties in respect of company assets within his control); *Shepherds Investment Ltd v Walters* [2007] 2 BCLC 207 at 214–16 (de facto director in breach of the no-conflict duty in developing a competing business and exploiting and diverting business opportunities of the company for his own benefit). See also *Secretary of State for Trade and Industry v Elms* (16 January 1997, unreported) approved in *Secretary of State for Trade and Industry v Tjolle* [1998] 1 BCLC 333 at 343–4.   [57] [2007] 1 BCLC 666.

company assisting it in finding a purchaser for the land and that the sums received had been professional fees due for his services. The court found that the individual controlled the company and ran its entire business. He negotiated the crucial contracts and made all decisions, both tactical and strategic.[58] It was only for tax reasons, the court found, that he had not actually been appointed as a director. He was a de facto director and, the court held, in breach of duty by enriching himself at the expense of the company and liable accordingly.

Shadow directors

6-17   A number of provisions in the Companies Act 2006 and the Insolvency Act 1986, particularly those requiring disclosure and regulating certain types of transactions by directors, apply to a shadow director.[59] This category is used to extend the reach of those statutory provisions to include individuals who are influential in the running of the company but who do not take up a position on the board.[60]

6-18   A shadow director is defined in CA 2006, s 251(1) as a person in accordance with whose directions or instructions the directors of a company are accustomed to act.[61] A person is not deemed to be a shadow director, however, by reason only that the directors act on advice given by him in a professional capacity (s 251(2)).[62]

6-19   In practice, the issue as to whether someone is a shadow director is most likely to arise in the context of disqualification proceedings under the Company Directors Disqualification Act 1986 brought against persons who, because they are bankrupts[63] or are already the subject of a disqualification order or undertaking, have not sought (and cannot seek) formal appointment to the board as a de jure director. The issue may also arise in the context of liability for wrongful trading under IA 1986, s 214 (discussed at **25-18**) which applies to directors and shadow directors.

6-20   The statutory definition of a 'shadow director' was considered in detail by the Court of Appeal in *Secretary of State for Trade and Industry v Deverell*[64] where Morritt LJ set out the following propositions:[65]

'(1) The definition of a shadow director is to be construed in the normal way to give effect to the parliamentary intention ascertainable from the mischief to be dealt with and the words used.

(2) The purpose of the legislation is to identify those, other than professional advisers, with real influence in the corporate affairs of the company. But it is not necessary that such influence should be exercised over the whole field of its corporate activities...

---

[58] [2007] 1 BCLC 666 at 731.

[59] See CA 2006, s 223; IA 1986, ss 206(3), 214(7). In theory, the appointment of shadow directors must be notified to the registrar of companies under CA 2006, ss 162, 167; unsurprisingly, this rarely happens.

[60] See generally Noonan & Watson, 'The Nature of Shadow Directorship: Ad Hoc Statutory Intervention or Core Company Law Principle' [2006] JBL 763.

[61] A one-off instruction or involvement is not sufficient and it is necessary to show a pattern of conduct in which the de jure director or directors are accustomed to act on the instructions of the alleged shadow director: *Secretary of State for Trade and Industry v Becker* [2003] 1 BCLC 555; see also *Ultraframe (UK) Ltd v Fielding* [2005] EWHC 1638 at [1270]–[1278].

[62] There is a further exemption for holding companies in CA 2006, s 251(3).

[63] An undischarged bankrupt is automatically disqualified from acting as a company director save with the leave of the court: CDDA 1986, s 11.

[64] [2000] 2 BCLC 133. See Noonan & Watson, n 60, who are critical of the approach taken in this case.

[65] [2000] 2 BCLC 133 at 144–5.

(3) Whether any particular communication from the alleged shadow director, whether by words or conduct, is to be classified as a direction or instruction must be objectively ascertained by the court in the light of all the evidence. In that connection I do not accept that it is necessary to prove the understanding or expectation of either giver or receiver. In many, if not most, cases it will suffice to prove the communication and its consequence....Certainly the label attached by either or both parties then or thereafter cannot be more than a factor in considering whether the communication came within the statutory description of direction or instruction.

(4) Non-professional advice may come within that statutory description. The proviso excepting advice given in a professional capacity appears to assume that advice generally is or may be included. Moreover the concepts of "direction" and "instruction" do not exclude the concept of "advice" for all three share the common feature of "guidance".

(5) It will, no doubt, be sufficient to show that in the face of "directions or instructions" from the alleged shadow director the properly appointed directors or some of them[66] cast themselves in a subservient role or surrendered their respective discretions. But I do not consider that it is necessary to do so in all cases.... Such a requirement would be to put a gloss on the statutory requirement that the board are "accustomed to act in accordance with" such directions or instructions...'

6-21 Morritt LJ also observed that 'lurking in the shadows may occur but it is not an essential ingredient to the recognition of a shadow director'.[67]

6-22 In *Deverell*, the proceedings were disqualification proceedings against two individuals who claimed that they were consultants to the insolvent company and were not therefore directors or shadow directors in respect of whom disqualification proceedings could be brought. The court found that one was concerned at the most senior level and with most aspects of the direction of the company's affairs[68] while the other's involvement went far beyond that of a consultant on matters directly affecting the company's financial affairs.[69] The court concluded that both individuals were shadow directors.[70]

6-23 In *Re Mea Corporation, Secretary of State for Trade and Industry v Aviss*[71] the evidence was that the two individuals in question (one of whom was the owner of the businesses) decided matters with regard to the recruitment of employees and the payments of creditors, they handled funding negotiations with the banks and tax matters with the Inland Revenue. The key allegation, as far as the court was concerned, was that they decided on the application within a group of companies of a group treasury policy which resulted in all companies remitting funds to the parent company which then determined how those funds were used and which creditors got paid. In particular, funds were paid to companies outside of the group in which one of the directors had a personal interest. Despite the protestations of the boards of companies in the group, this policy persisted which, the court said, showed the level of control exercised by these individuals. The court had no hesitation in finding that this ability to dictate policy in an area of corporate affairs

---

[66] See also *Ultraframe (UK) Ltd v Fielding* [2005] EWHC 1638 at [1272]—it is sufficient if the governing majority of the board is accustomed to act on the directions of the shadow director.

[67] [2000] 2 BCLC 133 at 146.   [68] [2000] 2 BCLC 133 at 150.   [69] [2000] 2 BCLC 133 at 153.

[70] Arguably, one of the defendants, given his level of involvement with the actual conduct of the company's affairs, should more accurately have been classified as a de facto director rather than a shadow director, see **6-9**. See Noonan & Watson, n 60 at p 773, who make the point that this reasoning might have been a result of a desire on the court's part to ensure that these individuals were disqualified—the Secretary of State had not claimed they were de facto directors.   [71] [2007] 1 BCLC 618.

as critical as the application of trading income and the payment of trade creditors made them shadow directors.[72]

6-24   There is a possibility that a parent company may find itself a shadow director of a subsidiary when the level of control which it exercises is such that the directors of the subsidiary are accustomed to act in accordance with its directions or instructions and it will be a question of fact in each case as to whether this level of control exists.[73] Any controlling shareholder (not just a parent company) is potentially at risk of being classified as a shadow director and it is a question of asking whether that person has exercised real influence in the conduct of the company's affairs.[74] The fact that the shareholder is so acting in order to protect his investment does not prevent him being classified as a de facto director. The courts have heard argument as to secured creditors[75] and bankers[76] being so classified, but on the facts the courts have yet to be persuaded.

6-25   While, initially, the categories of de facto and shadow director might have been seen as mutually exclusive,[77] the distinction between the categories has been eroded as the courts look to identify those with real influence in the corporate affairs of the company.[78] It is conceptually possible for a person to be both a de facto and a shadow director, certainly consecutively, but possibly even simultaneously, as where a person assumes the functions of a director as regards one part of the company's activities (say, marketing) and gives directions to the board as regards another (say, manufacturing and finance) so constituting him a de facto and a shadow director at the same time,[79] but usually they will not both be relevant.[80]

6-26   The distinction between the categories may matter given that shadow directors are a statutory creation and liable only where the statute expressly imposes a liability with it being uncertain whether shadow directors are subject to the fiduciary duties of directors. The matter was not resolved by the Delphic wording of CA 2006, s 170(5) which merely provides that the general duties apply to shadow directors where, and to the extent that,

---

[72] [2007] 1 BCLC 618 at 643.

[73] See *Re Hydrodam (Corby) Ltd* [1994] 2 BCLC 180 at 184. A limited exemption for parent companies is contained in CA 2006, s 251(3).

[74] See *Re Mea Corporation, Secretary of State for Trade and Industry v Aviss* [2007] 1 BCLC 618; also *Secretary of State for Trade and Industry v Jones* [1999] BCC 336 at 349.

[75] See *Re PFTZM Ltd, Jourdain v Paul* [1995] 2 BCLC 354, but the mere exercise of rights as a secured creditor is insufficient, see at 367.

[76] See *Re a Company No 005009 of 1987, ex p Copp* [1989] BCLC 13 at 21, a claim later abandoned, see [1990] BCLC 324 at 326.

[77] See Millett J in *Re Hydrodam (Corby) Ltd* [1994] 2 BCLC 180 at 183.

[78] *Re Paycheck Services 3 Ltd, Revenue and Customs Commissioners v Holland* [2011] 1 BCLC 141 at [91], per Lord Collins, who makes the point that the distinction is impossible to maintain with the extension of the concept of de facto director from the 1980s onwards as a mechanism for imposing liability on those assuming the office, and see at [110], per Lord Walker (…'not the case that the concepts of de facto and shadow director are fundamentally different…'); also at [127], per Lord Clarke. See *Secretary of State for Trade and Industry v Hollier* [2007] BCC 11 at 27.

[79] See *Re Mea Corporation Ltd, Secretary of State for Trade and Industry v Aviss* [2007] 1 BCLC 618 at [89], per Lewison J; *Re Paycheck Services 3 Ltd, Revenue and Customs Commissioners v Holland* [2011] 1 BCLC 141 at [127], per Lord Clarke.

[80] See, for example, *Secretary of State for Trade and Industry v Becker* [2003] 1 BCLC 555 at 564–5; *Re Kaytech International plc* [1999] 2 BCLC 351 at 424. See Noonan & Watson, n 60, who are critical of the failure to maintain clear distinctions between the categories which perform different functions.

the corresponding common law rules or equitable principles so apply.[81] At common law, the authorities are unclear and all are first instance. In *Ultraframe (UK) Ltd v Fielding*[82] Lewison J did not think that it necessarily followed from the fact that someone fell within the statutory definition of shadow director that it would be right to impose on him the same fiduciary duties as are owed by a de jure or de facto director. In his view, the indirect influence exerted by a paradigm shadow director who did not directly deal with, or claim the right to deal directly with, the company's assets would not usually be sufficient to impose fiduciary duties upon him.[83] Having said that, in *Re Mea Corporation Ltd, Secretary of State for Trade and Industry v Aviss*[84] Lewison J seems to have assumed that a shadow director owed a duty to act in the company's interests, though on the facts the persons identified as shadow directors there might as easily have been classed as de facto directors. Post-*Re Paycheck Services 3 Ltd*, it may be that where the issue is civil liability for misuse of company assets (as will commonly be the allegation in these sorts of cases), the court will look to see whether the person is part of the corporate governing structure and has assumed a role in the company sufficient to impose on him a fiduciary duty to the company and a responsibility for its assets. If so, he will be a de facto and not a shadow director. In other words, the de facto category may become the dominant avenue of civil redress with the category of shadow director limited to those situations where a statutory provision imposes a particular liability on shadow directors.

Remuneration of directors

6-27 Executive directors, at least in public companies and larger private companies, typically have a service contract with the company covering such matters as their remuneration, the duration of the appointment, and the amount of compensation payable in the event of dismissal. In public listed companies, controversy over such contracts and, in particular, over the remuneration and compensation packages contained within them, has been a central issue in the corporate governance debate, as discussed at **5-39** et seq. In smaller private companies, the directors may not have express service contracts, relying instead on more informal arrangements, but this practice should be avoided as it can be a source of subsequent disputes.[85] Non-executive directors are typically appointed on the basis of a formal letter of appointment, especially in larger companies, and this too is a formal contractual document.

6-28 In the absence of a contract, a director cannot rely on the articles as constituting a contract between himself and the company,[86] although it may be possible for a director to pursue

---

[81] See Prentice and Payne (2006) 122 LQR 558 at 564. The Explanatory Notes, *Companies Act 2006*, para 310 states that this provision means that '…where a common law rule or equitable principle applies to a shadow director, the statutory duty replacing that common law rule or equitable principle will apply to the shadow director in place of the common law rule or principle. Where the rule or principle does not apply to a shadow director, the statutory duty replacing the rule will not apply either.' In the Parliamentary debates, Lord Goldsmith commented that it is for the courts to decide if shadow directors are subject to fiduciary duties and if so which apply: HL Deb, vol 681, col 828, 9 May 2006. It is worth noting that IA 1986, s 212 (misfeasance) does not apply to shadow directors.   [82] [2005] EWHC 1638.

[83] [2005] EWHC 1638, para 1289. Noonan & Watson, n 60, argue that shadow directors should be liable to the same extent as the directors they instruct so, if the instruction makes the director liable for breach of duty, the shadow director should have a secondary liability in respect of that breach.

[84] [2007] 1 BCLC 618 at 643. See also Toulson J in *Yukong Line of Korea Ltd v Rendsburg Corp Investment* [1998] 2 BCLC 485 at 502.   [85] See, for example, *Lloyd v Casey* [2002] 1 BCLC 454.

[86] *Hickman v Kent or Romney Marsh Sheepbreeders Association* [1915] 1 Ch 881: see discussion at **4-48**.

a claim to recover payment on the basis of an implied extrinsic contract.[87] Exceptionally, a director may attempt to claim on a *quantum meruit* basis for services rendered and accepted by the company,[88] or on the basis of an equitable allowance,[89] but the courts are reluctant to allow such claims by directors.[90]

6-29   The mere holding of office by itself does not entitle a director to remuneration,[91] but the articles invariably provide, as the model articles do, that the directors are entitled to such remuneration as the directors determine both for their services as directors (i.e. for holding the office) and for any other services (i.e. as executive or non-executive directors) which they undertake.[92] Allowing the directors to determine their own remuneration gives rise to an obvious conflict of interest which in larger public companies is managed by delegating matters to a remuneration committee composed exclusively of non-executive directors, as is recommended by the UK Corporate Governance Code (see discussion at **5-35**), together with increased disclosure for quoted companies via a directors' remuneration report (see CA 2006, s 420 and **5-40**).

6-30   Where remuneration is paid, the court does not concern itself with the quantum of that remuneration and does not attempt to compare the market value of the services rendered with the amount of remuneration actually paid.[93] The court must be satisfied that the payment is genuinely remuneration, however, and not a sham transaction masking an improper return of capital to the shareholders.[94] Equally, however, as the Court of Appeal noted in *Currencies Direct Ltd v Ellis*,[95] there is no requirement that there is a specific agreement fixing the level or rate of remuneration or defining a formula for ascertaining a definite amount to be paid. Remuneration is consideration for work done or to be done and it may be paid in an infinite variety of ways and not necessarily to the person providing the consideration.[96] Excessive payments at a time when the company is in financial difficulties may be challenged by a liquidator[97] and such payments are often relied on as evidence of unfitness in disqualification proceedings (see **25-81**).

---

[87]   See *Re New British Iron Co, ex p Beckwick* [1898] 1 Ch 234.

[88]   *Currencies Direct Ltd v Ellis* [2002] 2 BCLC 482, CA; *Craven-Ellis v Canons Ltd* [1936] 2 KB 403; but there is no scope for a *quantum meruit* claim by a director when the articles have already made express provision for special remuneration for a director: *Guinness plc v Saunders* [1990] 1 All ER 652, HL.

[89]   See *Boardman v Phipps* [1967] 2 AC 46.

[90]   The position on *quantum meruit* and equitable allowance claims was restrictively stated in *Guinness plc v Saunders* [1990] 1 All ER 652, HL. Directors are precluded from contracting with their companies for their services except in the circumstances authorised by the articles of association; likewise there should be no remuneration for their services except as provided by the articles of association. To allow otherwise might encourage fiduciaries to put themselves in a position where there is a conflict between their personal interest and their duties as fiduciaries; and see *Cobbetts LLP v Hodge* [2010] 1 BCLC 30 at [118], see **13-27**.

[91]   *Hutton v West Cork Rly Co Ltd* (1883) 23 Ch D 654.

[92]   See The Companies (Model Articles) Regulations 2008, SI 2008/3229, reg 2, Sch 1, art 19 (Ltd); reg 4, Sch 3, art 23 (Plc). Equally the general meeting may resolve to pay a director for the mere holding of office, even if he undertakes no specific duties: *Re Halt Garage (1964) Ltd* [1982] 3 All ER 1016. If the articles require a specific body to determine the remuneration and the correct body has not done so, the director has no claim for payment under the articles: *Guinness plc v Saunders* [1990] 1 All ER 652, HL.

[93]   See *Re Halt Garage (1964) Ltd* [1982] 3 All ER 1016 at 1039, per Dillon J: '…assuming that the sum is bona fide voted to be paid as remuneration, it seems to me that the amount…must be a matter of management for the company to determine in accordance with its constitution which expressly authorises payment for directors' services'.   [94]   *Re Halt Garage (1964) Ltd* [1982] 3 All ER 1016.

[95]   [2002] 2 BCLC 482.   [96]   [2002] 2 BCLC 482 at 487.

[97]   For example, under IA 1986, s 212 (misfeasance); see *Re Halt Garage (1964) Ltd* [1982] 3 All ER 1016.

6-31 Long-term service contracts (essentially where the period of notice is longer than two years) require shareholder approval, subject to certain exceptions (see s 188 and **12-9**), as do payments for loss of office in certain circumstances (see **12-12**).

B Termination of appointment

Removal from office

6-32 A company may by ordinary resolution at a meeting remove a director before the expiration of his period of office, notwithstanding anything in any agreement between him and the company (CA 2006, s 168(1)).[98] There are a number of practical considerations which the company must bear in mind, however, before exercising this power of removal.

6-33 A particular issue is the amount of damages which may be payable to a dismissed director as the statutory power to remove a director does not deprive a person removed under it of compensation or damages payable in respect of the termination of his appointment as director or of any appointment terminating with that as director (CA 2006, s 168(5)). Compensation for loss of office is discussed at **12-12**.

6-34 In smaller private companies, exercise of the power of removal may trigger a petition by the sacked director/shareholder under CA 2006, s 994 alleging that his removal from the board amounts to unfairly prejudicial conduct for the purposes of that provision (see **17-56**). A shareholder/director in this type of company can protect himself to some extent against the possibility of removal by the inclusion of a provision in the articles entitling the director to weighted votes on any resolution to remove him from the board, a practice permitted by the House of Lords in *Bushell v Faith*.[99] In that case, the articles of the company provided that on a resolution to remove a particular director, his shares would carry three times the number of votes they normally carried. As a consequence, it was impossible for the other shareholders to pass the required ordinary resolution to remove him. Ungoed-Thomas J at first instance refused to permit the practice saying that it made a mockery of the Act, but the Court of Appeal and the House of Lords approved it[100] and it remains a valid method of entrenchment for directors.

Retirement

6-35 The model articles for public companies provide for the retirement of all the directors at the first annual general meeting and for the rotation of directors thereafter with a selected number retiring each year, although they remain eligible for re-election.[101]

---

[98] A written resolution may not be used: CA 2006, s 288(2)(a). At least 28 days' notice of the resolution must be given and the director concerned is entitled to be heard at the meeting where it is proposed to remove him and to have representations circulated to the shareholders, subject to certain constraints: s 169. The power to remove a director under this provision does not derogate from any power to do so by any other method: s 168(5)(b), such as a provision in the articles allowing for the removal of a director by resolution of the board. [99] [1970] 1 All ER 53, HL.

[100] See [1970] 1 All ER 53 at 57, per Upjohn LJ: 'Parliament has never sought to fetter the right of a company to issue shares with such rights or restrictions as it thinks fit.'

[101] See The Companies (Model Articles) Regulations 2008, SI 2008/3229, reg 4, Sch 3, art 21 (Plc). Private companies commonly dispense with rotation hence there is no provision for rotation in the model articles for private companies.

Resignation

6-36   A director may resign at any time by notice to the company and he will cease to be a director in accordance with the terms of that notice.[102]

Vacating office

6-37   A person ceases to be a director in the event of the occurrence of various events specified in the articles including, for example, on being prohibited by law from being a director or a bankruptcy order being made.[103] It is common to include a provision that a person ceases to be a director if he is requested in writing to resign by all his co-directors.[104]

Disqualification from office

6-38   The Company Directors Disqualification Act 1986 provides for a variety of grounds on which a person may be disqualified from being a director of a company. In practice almost all disqualification orders or undertakings are made under CDDA 1986, s 6 (unfit directors of insolvent companies).[105] A disqualification order or undertaking means that, for a specified period, a person may not be a director of a company, act as receiver of a company's property or in any way, whether directly or indirectly, be concerned or take part in the promotion, formation or management of a company unless (in each case) he has the leave of the court (CDDA 1986, s 1).[106] Disqualification is considered in Chapter 25.

---

[102] See The Companies (Model Articles) Regulations 2008, SI 2008/3229, reg 2, Sch 1, art 18(f) (Ltd); reg 4, Sch 3, art 22(f) (Plc).

[103] See The Companies (Model Articles) Regulations 2008, SI 2008/3229, reg 2, Sch 1, art 18(a), (b) (Ltd); reg 4, Sch 3, art 22(a), (b) (Plc).

[104] Such a provision is effective and the office is vacated on the service of the notice even if the directors making the request act for an ulterior motive: *Lee v Chou Wen Hsien* [1985] BCLC 45.

[105] The Insolvency Service no longer provides a detailed breakdown of disqualification statistics in terms of the section of the CDDA relied on, but previous records showed that 90% of disqualifications were under CDDA 1986, s 6 (unfit directors of insolvent companies) and there is no reason to think that that position has changed.

[106] See also The Companies (Model Articles) Regulations 2008, SI 2008/3229, reg 2, Sch 1, art 18 (Ltd), reg 4, Sch 3, art 22 (Plc) which provide that a director ceases to be a director as soon as he is prohibited from being a director by law.

7

A statutory statement of directors' duties

A Introduction

7-1 One of the most important changes implemented by the CA 2006 is the inclusion for the first time of a statutory statement of directors' general duties in Pt 10, Ch 2. The background to this change was a recommendation in 1996 from the Law Commission, following a review of directors' duties, that there should be a statement of the principal duties, but without any alteration to them.[1] From the outset, the Company Law Review (CLR) indicated that it regarded the case for a legislative statement of the general duties of directors as clearly made out.[2] It brushed aside concerns from the legal profession that such a statement would restrict the development of the law; would create uncertainty while the 'new' duties are interpreted by the courts; would encourage the courts to second-guess business decisions; and would be of little assistance to the lay director who would still need advice as to the nature of the obligations imposed.[3]

7-2 The CLR considered that a legislative statement was important for three main reasons:[4] on grounds of clarity and accessibility; to enable the law to be updated to reflect modern business practices, especially on conflicts of interest; and to address what the CLR called the 'scope' issue, i.e. in whose interests companies should be run. The CLR's clear intention was to modernise and alter the law and not merely to replicate the current position in a statutory statement. Accordingly, it recommended a full codification of directors' duties replacing the corresponding equitable and common law rules.[5]

---

[1] See Law Commission, *Company Directors: Regulating Conflicts of Interests and Formulating a Statement of Duties* (Law Comm No 261), (Cm 4436, 1999), para 4.36 and the draft statement of principles set out in Appendix A to that Report; preceded by a consultation paper of the same name, Consultation Paper No 153 (1998), Pt 13 of which surveys previous proposals for a statutory statement of directors' duties.

[2] See Company Law Review, *Developing the Framework* (2000), paras 3.14–3.19; also *Completing the Structure* (2000), paras 3.6, 3.11–3.31; *Final Report*, vol 1 (2001), paras 3.5–3.11.

[3] See Law Society Company Law Committee, *Company Law Review—Developing the Framework* Memorandum No 401 (August 2000), pp 1–22; also Memorandum No 412 (February 2001); Company Law Review, *Completing the Structure* (2000), para 3.6 (the Review noted 'we do not find these objections convincing').

[4] Company Law Review, *Final Report,* vol 1 (2001), para 3.7.

[5] See Company Law Review, *Final Report,* vol 1 (2001), paras 3.9–3.10.

B The statutory statement

7-3   The statutory statement of the general duties is set out in CA 2006, Pt 10, Ch 2 which provides for the following duties of directors:

- duty to act within their powers (s 171);
- duty to promote the success of the company (s 172);
- duty to exercise independent judgement (s 173);
- duty to exercise reasonable care, skill and diligence (s 174);
- duty to avoid conflicts of interest (s 175);
- duty not to accept benefits from third parties (s 176);
- duty to declare interest in proposed transactions with the company (s 177).

7-4   The general duties are owed by a director which includes a de jure director (i.e. one formally appointed to the office) and, it would seem, will include also a de facto director where a person has assumed a role in the corporate governing structure sufficient to impose those obligations on him[6] (see **6-11**). As discussed at **6-16** fiduciary duties may be owed by a de facto director, i.e. someone not formally appointed but who has assumed the status and functions of a director. For the avoidance of doubt, s 170(2) ensures that former directors remain subject to ss 175 and 176 as to the exploitation of property, information or opportunity (see **11-40**) and the receipt of benefits from third parties (see **11-77**) after they resign. The purpose is to prevent what would otherwise be an easy avoidance of fiduciary duty. As for shadow directors, s 170(5) provides that the general duties of directors apply to shadow directors where, and to the extent that, the corresponding common law rules or equitable principles so apply, but as it is not clear at common law that shadow directors do owe fiduciary duties to the company, this somewhat obscure provision is rather unhelpful, see the discussion at **6-26**.

7-5   The duties are cumulative as CA 2006, s 179 makes clear. It provides that 'except as otherwise provided, more than one of the general duties may apply in any given case'. For example, while directors might be able and willing to authorise a conflict of interest under s 175(4)(b), they also have to bear in mind their duty under s 172 to promote the success of the company. An exercise of the duty of care, skill and diligence (s 174) will often overlap with the need to exercise independent judgement (s 173). The duty to exercise powers for the purposes for which they are conferred (s 171(b)) will overlap with the duty to promote the success of the company (s 172) and the need to act in accordance with the constitution (s 171(a)).

7-6   Often, the overlap is quite complicated and the precise inter-relationship of the statutory duties is something which will occupy judicial time in the future. For example, CA 2006, s 175 does not apply to a conflict of interest arising in relation to a proposed transaction or arrangement with the company which is governed by s 177 while the obligation to disclose an interest in an existing transaction or arrangement with the company is governed by s 182 (which is not part of the general duties at all). It is also possible for a transaction to be governed initially by one of these provisions, for example s 182, and then to develop in ways which might subsequently attract the application of s 177 or s 175 (see the discussion at **11-102**). Furthermore, the relationship between s 176 and s 175 is unclear, in particular

---

[6] See *Re Paycheck Services 3 Ltd, Revenue and Customs Commissioners v Holland* [2011] 1 BCLC 141 at [93].

as to whether it is possible for directors to authorise (under s 175(4)(b)) the acceptance of benefits from third parties which are otherwise prohibited under s 176 (see discussion at **11-75**). Also, a director is not required to comply with s 175 or s 176 if the conflicted transaction is approved by the shareholders or is exempt from approval under CA 2006, Pt 10, Ch 4, but the other duties do continue to apply (s 180(2)). So there are numerous permutations here and the interplay between the various elements is quite complex. The relationship with other provisions must also be taken into account such as, as already mentioned, ss 182–187 (interest in existing transactions with the company), but also s 232(4) (provisions in articles dealing with conflicts of interest), s 239 (ratification of acts of directors) and Pt 10, Ch 4, ss 188–226 which deal with specific conflicts of interests. The statement of duties in CA 2006, Pt 10, Ch 2 may contain only 12 sections, but they are complex statements of the law far removed from the type of accessible statement of duties which the Law Commission originally envisaged[7] and which the CLR had asserted would be one of the main advantages of a statutory statement.

7-7   The statement of duties in CA 2006, Pt 10, Ch 2 is not exhaustive. It merely sets out the general duties and directors are subject to various other duties including duties with respect to specific conflicts of interest governed by CA 2006, Pt 10, Ch 4; statutory duties under the CA 2006 itself (such as the duty to maintain accounting records and prepare accounts, ss 386, 394), duties under the IA 1986 and duties under the general law such as employment law or health and safety legislation.

7-8   The statement does not set out the remedies for breach of duty. The Government was unable to draft a satisfactory statutory codification of the myriad remedies available for breach of fiduciary duty and so limited itself to stating in CA 2006, s 178 that breach of the statutory duties attracts the same remedies as breach of the corresponding common law or equitable rules. In most instances, this is unlikely to cause a problem since the standard remedies for breach of fiduciary duty are well established, typically a liability to account to the company for profits made or to indemnify the company for loss caused by the breach of duty. But even here the introduction of the statutory statement may be of some consequence. For example, the remedy to account for profits made has been applied strictly by the court in order to strip the disloyal fiduciary of all possible gains, an approach based on long-standing judicial opposition to any dilution of the fundamental no-conflict principle (see discussion at **11-4**). Now that duty can be avoided with the authorisation of independent directors (see s 175(4)(b)). In the event of a procedural failure with respect to authorisation (for example, it is subsequently discovered that in error an interested director participated in the granting of authorisation and the meeting would have been inquorate without him), the director is in breach of the no-conflict duty. The question is whether the courts will look to apply the full rigour of the common law in stripping the fiduciary of all his profits in those circumstances. Parliament has signalled that the duty not to profit, far from being necessary to the upholding of the highest standards of fiduciary conduct, is in fact an impediment to entrepreneurial activity, so the courts may take their cue from that legislative stance and adopt a more relaxed approach to devising an appropriate remedy.[8] However, the financial crisis and resulting concerns about standards of directors' conduct may equally push the courts in the opposite direction.

---

[7] See Law Commission Report, n 1, Appendix A.
[8] See, for example, *Murad v Al-Saraj* [2005] EWCA Civ 959, CA, at [82]–[83], per Arden LJ; at [121]–[122], per Jonathan Parker LJ.

7-9   A final concern is the uncertain relationship between the statutory statement and the pre-existing law on directors' duties, a matter addressed in CA 2006, s 170(3) and (4) which state:

> '(3) The general duties are based on certain common law rules and equitable principles as they apply in relation to directors and have effect in place of those rules and principles as regards the duties owed to a company by a director.

> (4) The general duties shall be interpreted and applied in the same way as common law rules or equitable principles, and regard shall be had to the corresponding common law rules and equitable principles in interpreting and applying the general duties.'

7-10   The difficulty is clear on the face of the provisions. Given the express statement in CA 2006, s 170(3) that these provisions apply 'in place of' the old rules, applying the usual rules of statutory interpretation, existing case law on the 'old' law should no longer be relevant and the starting point should be to interpret the language of the statute.[9] Section 170(4) states, however, that the general duties are to be interpreted and applied in the same way as common law or equitable principles and regard is to be had to the corresponding common law rules and equitable principles in interpreting and applying the general duties.

7-11   To the extent that the duties have a basis in corresponding common law or equitable principles, the existing authorities can be invoked to explain the nature of the now statutory duty, but it is not entirely clear that it is possible to identify a corresponding common law or equitable principle in all cases. Some of the provisions clearly do state the existing law or at least something quite close to it. For example, the director's duty to exercise his powers for the purposes for which they are conferred (CA 2006, s 171) is a positive statement of the common law prohibition on exercising powers for a collateral purpose. The duty to exercise care, skill and diligence in s 174 is identical to all intents and purposes to the common law duty of care and skill. Equally, some of the provisions are modified versions of the common law and equitable principles. For example, the duty to act bona fide in the interests of the company has been restated in s 172 as a duty to promote the success of the company. Other duties have been comprehensively altered, most notably, the no-conflict duty which now allows independent directors to authorise profit-making by directors in a situation of a conflict of interest (s 175(4)(b)). Identifying precisely which authorities are retained by s 170(4), therefore, is not easy.

7-12   The issue of the relationship between CA 2006, s 170(3) and (4) was considered at length in the Parliamentary debates before the Solicitor General was moved to comment as follows:[10]

> '…the courts should continue to refer to existing case law on the corresponding common law rules and equitable principles, *except where it is obviously irreconcilable with the statutory statement* [emphasis added]. The rich body of case law on and wisdom about the general duties may continue to be used—no one would benefit from abandoning the wisdom accumulated over several centuries—we do not propose to lose that.'

7-13   In practice, there may be a pragmatic judicial response to these difficulties. As the Solicitor General noted, no one is anxious to lose the accumulated wisdom of the common law and the courts will be anxious not to create unnecessary uncertainty in an area as commercially important as directors' duties. In all probability, the development of directors' duties will continue in much the same way as in the past 150 years with the main difference being that that development is now based on a statutory framework. The limited case law to date on the new provisions suggest precisely that pragmatic judicial response. There has been little evidence of any radical change, just the onward development of directors'

---

[9] See *Bank of England v Vagliano Brothers* [1891] AC 107 at 144–5, per Lord Herschell.
[10] HC Debs, Session 2005–06, Standing Committee D, column 536 (6 July 2006).

duties in an incremental fashion. Certainly, the concerns expressed in **7-2** have not materialised, though the costs of implementation should not be overlooked. The benefits are that the statement of directors' duties has been modernised and, as part of that drafting process, the scope issue has been thoroughly debated (see Chapter 9). It can be seen, however, that the resulting statutory statement is more lawyers' law than a statement of duties that is accessible to the average director.

C Duties owed to the company

7-14 Directors owe their general duties to the company and not to the shareholders, individually or collectively,[11] nor do they owe any duties directly to the company's creditors, individually or collectively.[12] This common law principle[13] is expressed in CA 2006, s 170(1). It follows that enforcement of the general duties is a matter for the company, a point which the Government was keen to emphasise in the Parliamentary debates whenever concerns were expressed that the inclusion of a statutory statement exposed directors to a greater risk of being sued, particularly in the light of the introduction of the statutory derivative claim in CA 2006, Pt 11 (see Chapter 18).

7-15 An application of the principle can be seen in *Peskin v Anderson*.[14] A dispute arose out of the sale by the Royal Automobile Club Ltd (RACL) of its motoring services business which essentially resulted in the shareholders in RACL receiving £34,000 each in respect of the sale. The claimants were all former shareholders whose membership had ceased before the sale and so they did not receive any part of the benefits flowing from the sale. They brought an action against the directors of RACL claiming damages for breach of fiduciary duty by the directors in failing to disclose to the shareholders the proposals relating to the sale of the business. The Court of Appeal dismissed the claim for directors do not, solely by virtue of the office of director, owe fiduciary duties to the shareholders, collectively or individually.

7-16 The shareholders may specifically appoint the directors as their agents in any matter, of course, in which case the directors will owe them the fiduciary duties arising from that agency relationship.[15] Directors may also find themselves liable to shareholders under ordinary legal principles, for example in misrepresentation, if they give misleading advice or abuse their position.[16] Liability issues under this heading may be an issue in the context of takeovers where shareholders rely on the advice of the directors as to the merits of any bid before them. Where a takeover bid has been made, the directors must give sufficient information to the shareholders and refrain from misleading them.[17] In the case of competing bids, the

---

[11] Not even if appointed as the nominee of a particular shareholder or class of shareholders: *Scottish Co-operative Wholesale Society Ltd v Meyer* [1958] 3 All ER 66, HL; *Boulting v ACTT* [1963] 1 All ER 716, CA; *Re Neath Rugby Ltd (No 2), Hawkes v Cuddy* [2009] 2 BCLC 427. As to the position of the nominee director, see **9-18**.

[12] *Multinational Gas and Petrochemical Co v Multinational Gas and Petrochemical Services Ltd* [1983] 2 All ER 563; *Yukong Line Ltd of Korea v Rendsburg Investments Corp of Liberia* [1998] 2 BCLC 485. Where a company owes fiduciary obligations to a client or joint venturer, it is possible for a director of the company also personally to owe fiduciary obligations to that client or joint venturer: see *Satnam Investment Ltd v Dunlop Heywood & Co Ltd* [1999] 1 BCLC 385, CA; *JD Wetherspoon plc v Van de Berg & Co Ltd* [2007] PNLR 28, Ch D; *Ross River Ltd v Waveley Commercial Ltd* [2012] EWHC 81, Ch D.

[13] See *Percival v Wright* [1902] 2 Ch 421.   [14] [2001] 1 BCLC 372.

[15] *Allen v Hyatt* (1914) 30 TLR 444; *Briess v Woolley* [1954] 1 All ER 909.

[16] *Gething v Kilner* [1972] 1 All ER 1166; *Dawson International plc v Coats Paton plc* [1989] BCLC 233, CS (OH); *Platt v Platt* [2001] 1 BCLC 698.

[17] *Re a Company* [1986] BCLC 382; *Gething v Kilner* [1972] 1 All ER 1166.

directors must do nothing to prevent the shareholders from choosing to take the best price,[18] but the courts do not accept that the board must inevitably be under a positive duty to recommend and take all steps within its power to facilitate whichever is the highest offer.[19] If directors take it on themselves to give advice to current shareholders, they have a duty to advise in good faith and not fraudulently and not to mislead, whether deliberately or carelessly.[20] If a director misrepresents the financial position of the company so as to induce the shareholders to transfer their shares to him for a nominal consideration, he is liable in damages for negligent misrepresentation in the usual way.[21]

7-17 Exceptionally the courts may consider that the relationships within the company do give rise to fiduciary duties as between the directors and their shareholders. The leading authority is *Coleman v Myers*,[22] a decision of the New Zealand Court of Appeal which has been cited with approval by the English courts. In this case, the court held that the directors did owe fiduciary duties to the shareholders including a duty not to mislead them on the sale of their shares. The court thought the fiduciary obligation arose from the nature of the relationships within this family company where the minority shareholders habitually looked to the directors for guidance on matters affecting their interests.[23]

7-18 The approach in *Coleman v Myers* was endorsed in *Re Chez Nico (Restaurants) Ltd*[24] by Browne-Wilkinson V-C who agreed that fiduciary duties can arise between the directors and the shareholders which might include a duty of disclosure where directors are purchasing shares in the company from shareholders.

7-19 In *Peskin v Anderson*,[25] noted at **7-15**, the claimants failed to establish that the directors owed duties to the shareholders so the claimants attempted to argue in the alternative that their circumstances brought them within the *Coleman v Myers* qualification, i.e. that special circumstances existed which brought the directors into a fiduciary relationship with the shareholders. The Court of Appeal agreed that a fiduciary duty may be owed by a director to a shareholder personally where a special factual relationship exists between the parties in the particular case. As Mummery LJ noted, events may take place which bring a director into direct and close contact with the shareholders in a manner capable of generating fiduciary obligations.[26] On the facts in *Peskin*, however, the court found that there were no relevant dealings, negotiations, communications or other contact directly between the directors and the shareholders. The actions of the directors had not caused the shareholders to leave the company when they did. Most important of all, prior to being approached by a bidder for the business, there was nothing sufficiently concrete and specific, either in existence or in contemplation, for the directors to disclose to the shareholders.[27] The court concluded that there was nothing special in the factual relationship between the directors and the shareholders to give rise to a fiduciary duty of disclosure.[28]

---

[18] *Heron International Ltd v Lord Grade* [1983] BCLC 244.
[19] *Re a Company* [1986] BCLC 382; and see **26-44**.
[20] *Dawson International plc v Coats Paton plc* [1989] BCLC 233, CS (OH).
[21] See *Platt v Platt* [2001] 1 BCLC 698, CA.   [22] [1977] 2 NZLR 225.
[23] See also the interesting decision of the New South Wales Court of Appeal in *Brunninghausen v Glavanics* (1999) 46 NSWLR 538, noted Goddard (2000) 116 LQR 197.   [24] [1992] BCLC 192 at 208.
[25] [2001] 1 BCLC 372.   [26] [2001] 1 BCLC 372 at 379.   [27] [2001] 1 BCLC 372 at 384.
[28] [2001] 1 BCLC 372 at 384. See also *Platt v Platt* [1999] 2 BCLC 745 where, at first instance, the court was prepared to find that a fiduciary relationship had arisen between a director and two shareholders (his brothers). The director had acquired their shareholdings on the basis of a misrepresentation and, the court found, in breach of a fiduciary duty owed to them. The Court of Appeal confirmed the finding as to a liability in misrepresentation, but expressly declined to comment on the correctness of the finding of a breach of a fiduciary duty: see [2001] 1 BCLC 698.

8

Duty to act within constitution and powers

A Introduction

'A director of a company must—

(a) act in accordance with the company's constitution, and

(b) only exercise powers for the purposes for which they are conferred.'(CA 2006, s 171)

8-1 At common law the equivalent obligation was stated in terms of a duty to act bona fide in the interests of the company and a requirement for directors to exercise their powers for a proper purpose and not for any collateral (i.e. personal or sectional) purpose. The CA 2006 splits that duty into distinct obligations: to act in accordance with the constitution (defined s 257) and to exercise powers for the purposes for which they are conferred in s 171 and to act to promote the success of the company in s 172. This demarcation clarifies the elements of these obligations, but there remains a degree of overlap between them, as we shall see. This chapter concentrates on s 171 while s 172 is discussed in Chapter 9.

8-2 Turning to the distinct components of CA 2006, s 171. First, s 171(a) is concerned with ensuring that the directors respect the division of power agreed within the company as between the shareholders and the directors. As we shall see, the typical division of power is that, subject to the articles and any directions given by the shareholders by special resolution,[1] the directors are 'responsible for the management of the company's business for which purpose they may exercise all the powers of the company'.[2] The issues under s 171(a) are the scope of the authority given to the directors by the constitution (see **4-8** as to the definition) and the implications, internally and externally, when they ignore or breach the terms of that mandate, whether collectively or individually.

8-3 Secondly, CA 2006, s 171(b) sets out the duty to exercise powers for the purposes for which they are conferred, i.e. to promote the success of the company and not, say, to advance the personal interests of a director or directors. In the past it was considered that the issue of an abuse of authority by the exercise of a power for an improper purpose was distinct from the agency issue presented by an absence of authority,[3] but it is now clear, as is discussed in detail later, and as s 171 implicitly acknowledges, that the two issues are more

---

[1] See The Companies (Model Articles) Regulations 2008, SI 2008/3229, reg 2, Sch 1, art 4 (Ltd); reg 4, Sch 3, art 4 (Plc).

[2] See The Companies (Model Articles) Regulations 2008, SI 2008/3229, reg 2, Sch 1, art 3 (Ltd); reg 4, Sch 3, art 3 (Plc).

[3] See Millett J in *Macmillan Inc v Bishopsgate Investment Trust plc (No 3)* [1995] 3 All ER 747 at 753, relying on *Bowstead on Agency,* but the *Bowstead* position on this has changed, see *Bowstead and Reynolds on Agency* (19th edn, 2010), para 3–008.

directly intertwined.[4] The issues under s 171(b) include determining whether a power has been exercised for an improper purpose and the implications, internally and externally, of such an abuse of power.

8-4 The overall picture is complex but progress is being made to a more coherent framework based solidly on agency law.[5] A lack of authority and the exercise of authority for an improper purpose are distinct issues as CA 2006, s 171 makes clear, but there is considerable overlap between them with each problem being addressed in much the same way (as a matter of agency law), bringing much needed coherence to this important aspect of directors' duties. Unfortunately, the opportunity was not taken in the CA 2006 to expressly state that framework nor indeed to address some of the recognised uncertainties with regard to the scope of CA 2006, s 40 which, as we shall see at **8–27**, has an important role to play in terms of protecting third parties against any want of authority on the part of the directors.

B The constitutional division of power within a company

Authority conferred

8-5 Before considering problems of a want of authority, it is useful to consider the authority normally conferred by the constitution (as defined in CA 2006, s 257). As determined by the Court of Appeal in *Automatic Self-Cleansing Filter Syndicate Co Ltd v Cuninghame*,[6] the relationship between a board and the shareholders is a contractual relationship based on the articles which determine the extent of the management powers conferred on the board. The model articles provide (and this provision is common to practically all companies) that 'subject to the articles, the directors are responsible for the management of the company's business for which purpose they may exercise all the powers of the company',[7] but the shareholders may by special resolution direct the directors to take, or refrain from taking, specified action.[8] In addition, the shareholders do have a common law residual power of management, but this exceptional power only arises if the board is unable to act,[9]

---

[4] See *Criterion Properties plc v Stratford UK Properties LLC* [2006] 1 BCLC 729, HL; also the valuable analysis of these issues in Payne & Prentice, 'Company Contracts and Vitiating Factors: Developments in the Law on Directors' Authority' [2005] LMCLQ 447. Payne and Prentice go on to comment (at 455) that 'the distinction between an act being an abuse of authority and one being in excess of authority is wafer thin, but nevertheless they are conceptually distinct and explicit in [CA 1985] s 35A (now CA 2006 s 40).' That provision addresses a want of authority, not an abuse of power, but as an abuse of power gives rise to a want of authority, the overlap is clear: see **8-19**.

[5] See *Criterion Properties plc v Stratford UK Properties LLC* [2006] 1 BCLC 729, HL; and Payne & Prentice, n 4.

[6] [1906] 2 Ch 34, CA; *Gramophone and Typewriter Ltd v Stanley* [1908] 2 KB 89 at 98, CA; *Salmon v Quin & Axtens Ltd* [1909] 1 Ch 311, CA; aff'd sub nom *Quin & Axtens Ltd v Salmon* [1909] AC 442, HL; *Howard Smith Ltd v Ampol Petroleum Ltd* [1974] AC 821 at 837, PC; see also *Breckland Group Holdings Ltd v London & Suffolk Properties Ltd* [1989] BCLC 100.

[7] See The Companies (Model Articles) Regulations 2008, SI 2008/3229, reg 2, Sch 1, art 3 (Ltd); reg 4, Sch 3, art 3 (Plc). In turn the directors may delegate any of the powers conferred on them to any committee or any director or any other person, as they think fit: art 5 (Ltd); art 5 (Plc). The extent of the delegated powers will depend on the terms of the delegation, but also on the implied authority arising from the office held, see *Smith v Butler* [2012] EWCA Civ 314 at [36]; also *Mitchell & Hobbs (UK) Ltd v Mill* [1996] 2 BCLC 102; externally, a third party may be able to rely on the appearance of authority, see discussion at **8-16**.

[8] See The Companies (Model Articles) Regulations 2008, SI 2008/3229, reg 2, Sch 1, art 4 (Ltd); reg 4, Sch 3, art 4 (Plc).   [9] *Foster v Foster* [1916] 1 Ch 532.

or is deadlocked or for all practical purposes has ceased to exist.[10] The shareholders may resolve the situation by appointing another director and, once a functioning board is in operation, the powers of management revert to it.

8-6 The division of power is predominantly in favour of the board then at the expense of the shareholders and the CA 2006 has shifted the balance further in favour of the board. The CA 1985 permitted certain corporate actions when authorised by the shareholders by resolution or by the articles (such as an allotment of shares (CA 1985, s 80), or purchase of the company's own shares (CA 1985, s 162)), but the position regarding these matters under the CA 2006 is that the company (and therefore the directors in the exercise of their management powers) has the particular power unless prohibited by the articles. In other words, now there must be a positive decision via the articles to subject a power to shareholder control, otherwise the power vests in the directors. For example, a company has power to purchase its own shares unless restricted by the articles (CA 2006, s 690) and the directors of a private company with one class of shares (which is almost invariably the case) have the power to allot shares unless prohibited by the articles (s 550).

8-7 The division of power is not entirely one-sided, however, and some matters are reserved for the shareholders by statute, such as the right to amend the articles (CA 2006, s 21), to reduce the share capital[11] (s 641) and to petition for a voluntary winding up (IA 1986, s 84(1)(b)). As noted at **8-5**, the delegation of power to the directors is also subject to the articles and to any directions given, on an ad hoc basis, by way of a special resolution.[12] Constraints which might be imposed via the articles might include monetary limits on powers to borrow, or a requirement for the consent of named directors to the exercise of a particular power,[13] or constraints in the form of procedural requirements, for example with respect to the calling of meetings, quorum requirements or procedures for the execution of documents. If the directors ignore a requirement of the articles, a shareholder cannot force compliance unless the article in question confers a right on the shareholder qua member, see discussion at **4-54**, though if the shareholder knew of the matter in advance, the shareholder may seek injunctive relief. On the other hand, any director who fails to act in accordance with the constitution is in breach of s 171(a) and it is open to any shareholder to bring a derivative claim for breach of duty against him. In this way, a balance is achieved, the business of the company is not disrupted by numerous personal claims by individual shareholders, but in an egregious case the possibility exists of any shareholder, not just the affected shareholder, bringing a claim for breach of duty and that possibility operates to deter directors from casually ignoring requirements of the constitution. In smaller companies, the preference will be for redress via a petition alleging unfairly prejudicial conduct under CA 2006, 994.

8-8 There are other constraints too. As discussed in Chapter 4, companies may restrict their objects under the CA 2006, s 31 and companies formed under previous legislation may choose to retain their objects clauses in the articles. In either case, the objects act as a constraint on directors' authority (third parties are protected against issues of lack of capacity by s 39). The articles also normally confer on the shareholders a power to appoint directors

---

[10] *Barron v Potter* [1914] 1 Ch 895.

[11] A reduction must be confirmed, however, by the court or supported by a solvency statement by the directors, see CA 2006, s 641(1).

[12] See The Companies (Model Articles) Regulations 2008, SI 2008/3229, reg 2, Sch 1, art 4 (Ltd); reg 4, Sch 3, art 4 (Plc). Giving directions on an ad hoc basis tends to be difficult because shareholders lack the necessary information to intervene at an early stage and typically only find out about events after they have happened.   [13] See *Quin & Axtens Ltd v Salmon* [1909] 1 Ch 311, CA, aff'd [1909] AC 442, HL.

though the directors usually also have a power to appoint.[14] If the company is a listed company, the Listing Rules require shareholder approval of certain transactions,[15] as does CA 2006, Pt 10, Ch 4 (discussed in Chapter 12) and shareholders in quoted companies have an advisory vote on the directors' remuneration report (s 439). Most crucially, the shareholders have power to remove a director (s 168) and the shareholders retain ultimate control of the company through their ability to sell their shares to new owners.[16]

8-9 Notwithstanding the existence of these various powers vested in shareholders, and assuming that the company has articles in the form of the model articles, the practical position is that all the powers of the company are vested in the directors. Having said that, it is worth noting that there is a considerable variation in practices within companies, especially as between the largest public companies and the small private company.

8-10 In a small private company, a formal division of power between the directors and the shareholders is often meaningless as they are frequently the same individuals acting as shareholders and as directors without differentiating particularly between those capacities. This reality is recognised by the CA 2006 which dispenses with many of the formal decision-making mechanisms which otherwise operate. For example, private companies need not hold an annual general meeting (agm) of shareholders, unless they want to, while public companies must hold an agm (CA 2006, s 336). The expectation is that, in a private company, many if not all decisions will be taken by written resolution rather than through formal meetings (see s 281). To that end, the procedures for written resolutions have been modified and, in particular, the require- ment for unanimity dropped (ss 282(2), 283(2)). In their day-to-day activities, it can be said that these companies are untroubled by any formal division of responsibilities between the directors and the shareholders. Nevertheless, even in such companies, it is important for the persons involved to appreciate their respective roles as directors and as shareholders because of the consequences which may attach to failing to act in the way required by the appropriate capacity. For example, directors are subject to fiduciary duties which do not apply to shareholders. Equally, on occasion a decision may need to be taken or a transaction authorised by the shareholders rather than the directors, for example on an alteration of the articles (s 21) or approval of a substantial property transaction in which a director has an interest (s 190).

8-11 In large private and public companies, on the other hand, there is a distinct division of power and responsibility between the board of directors and the shareholders with all powers of management firmly vested in the board and very little power retained by the shareholders. The board's role in practice is supervisory rather than managerial with extensive powers delegated to individual directors and to professional executive managers operating just below board level, a group largely ignored by the legal structure.[17] The issue in these companies is trying to ensure shareholder engagement so that the shareholders act as an effective counterbalance to all powerful directors. As discussed in Chapter 5, shareholders have increased rights in terms of controlling and influencing the conduct of

---

[14] See The Companies (Model Articles) Regulations 2008, SI 2008/3229, reg 2, Sch 1, art 17 (Ltd); reg 4, Sch 3, art 20 (Plc). In the case of a public company, a director appointed by the directors must retire at the next annual general meeting, though he may be reappointed: art 21(2)(a) (Plc).

[15] See UKLA, *Listing Rules*, LR 10 Significant transactions.

[16] See *Howard Smith Ltd v Ampol Petroleum Ltd* [1974] AC 821 at 837–8.

[17] See Berle and Means, *The Modern Corporation and Private Property* (1932); Eisenberg, *The Structure of the Corporation* (1976); Parkinson, *Corporate Power and Responsibility* (1993), Ch 2.

business at general meetings and listed companies, in particular, are expected to engage fully with their major shareholders, whatever the strict legal division of powers.

C Types of authority

Actual authority

8-12 Actual authority may be express or implied actual authority. As noted at **8-5**, the directors collectively have extensive actual authority. For an individual director, express actual authority arises from an explicit conferring of authority on a director which would typically be recorded in the board minutes. Implied actual authority arises from the position which the individual holds. For example, if an individual is appointed as a managing director, implied authority authorises him to do all such things as fall within the usual scope of that office.[18] In *Hely-Hutchinson v Brayhead Ltd*[19] the chairman of the company also acted as its de facto managing director.[20] He entered into contracts on the company's behalf on his own initiative and subsequently reported them to the board which acquiesced in this practice. Later the board refused to honour certain undertakings which the director had given. The Court of Appeal found that the director lacked express actual authority and he had no implied actual authority as the office of chairman did not carry authority to enter into contracts without the sanction of the board. As de facto managing director, however, he did have implied actual authority. This authority would be implied from the circumstance that the board by its conduct over many months had acquiesced in his acting as managing director and committing the company to contracts without the necessity of sanction from the board.[21]

8-13 It is clear that a managing director or, in modern terminology, a chief executive officer (CEO) by virtue of his position has actual or apparent authority co-extensive with the power of the board to manage the business. It is likely that the courts would also consider a finance director, or chief financial officer (CFO), certainly in a large company, to have extensive authority, actual and apparent, with respect to matters within the usual scope of the office of a finance director.[22] These individual directors by virtue of their management positions are seen, therefore, as having extensive authority to bind the company. The position is different with respect to the company chairman, for his main responsibility is running the board, not running the business of the company,[23] so his actual authority to bind the company is limited, likewise his apparent authority. Beyond these CEO and CFO offices, individual directors will have such actual authority as is delegated to them expressly and such implied actual authority as arises from any position they hold as an executive director, i.e. they are impliedly authorised to do such things as fall within the usual scope of that executive office.[24] They may have considerable apparent authority also, as is discussed below.

8-14 There is then a hierarchy of authority where the board has the greatest actual and apparent authority to manage the business, with CEOs and CFOs having extensive authority in

---

[18] *Hely-Hutchinson v Brayhead Ltd* [1967] 3 All ER 98, CA; *Hopkins v TL Dallas Group Ltd* [2005] 1 BCLC 543. *Smith v Butler* [2012] EWCA Civ 314 at [28] (implied authority is subject to the articles and any express agreements—on the facts, the managing director did not have implied authority to dismiss the chairman of the board).

[19] [1967] 3 All ER 98, CA.   [20] As to de facto directors, see **6-9**.

[21] [1967] 3 All ER 98 at 103, CA.

[22] See *Harold Holdsworth & Co v Caddies* [1955] 1 All ER 725.

[23] See the UK Corporate Governance Code (2010), A.2, and **5-18**.

[24] *Hely-Hutchinson v Brayhead Ltd* [1967] 3 All ER 98.

respect of matters within the usual scope of their offices. Individual directors as such may have the least express actual authority to bind the company, though they have implied actual authority consistent with the scope of their office and, possibly, apparent authority.

8-15 The limits to actual authority were succinctly expressed by the court in *Re Capitol Films Ltd, Rubin v Cobalt Pictures Ltd*:[25]

> '… it is implicit that a director of a company only has actual authority to act in a manner which is in the interests of his company. If he acts in a manner which is contrary to the interests of his company, his actions will be without authority, and the agreement which he purports to make will not bind the company unless the third party can rely upon the doctrine of apparent authority.'

Apparent authority

8-16 Apparent (or ostensible) authority is the authority of an agent as it appears to others[26] and it can operate to enlarge actual authority or to create authority where no actual authority exists,[27] but it cannot be relied on if the third party knows that the agent has no actual authority or is put on inquiry as to an absence of authority.[28] Its use in the company context is primarily to provide authorisation for the individual director who does not hold one of the executive posts (such as CEO or CFO) which the law recognises as conferring considerable actual authority, as discussed earlier, and so has no or limited actual authority to bind the company on the basis of the position which he holds.[29] The leading authority is *Freeman and Lockyer v Buckhurst Park Properties (Mangal) Ltd*[30] where the director in question managed the company's property and acted on its behalf. The board had been aware of his conduct and had acquiesced in it. In that role the director employed the plaintiff architects to draw up plans for the development of land held by the company. The development ultimately collapsed and the plaintiffs sued the company for their fees. The company denied that the director had any authority to employ the architects. The court found that, while he had never been appointed managing director (and therefore had no actual authority, express or implied), the company had held him out as being the managing director which conferred on him an ostensible authority which would bind the company.[31] The architects were entitled to rely on that ostensible or apparent authority and the company was liable for the fees.

---

[25] [2011] 2 BCLC 359 at [53], per Richard Snowden QC, sitting as a Deputy Judge of the High Court.

[26] *Hely-Hutchinson v Brayhead Ltd* [1967] 3 All ER 98 at 102, CA, per Lord Denning.

[27] See *First Energy (UK) Ltd v Hungarian International Bank Ltd* [1993] BCLC 1409 at 1422–3.

[28] *A L Underwood Ltd v Bank of Liverpool* [1924] 1 KB 775, CA; *B Liggett (Liverpool) Ltd v Barclays Bank Ltd* [1928] 1 KB 48; *Morris v Kanssen* [1946] 1 All ER 586, HL; *Rolled Steel Products (Holdings) Ltd v British Steel Corpn* [1985] 3 All ER 52, CA; and see *Criterion Properties plc v Stratford UK Properties LLC* [2006] 1 BCLC 729 at 741, per Lord Scott.

[29] See *Bowstead & Reynolds on Agency* (19th edn, 2010), paras 3–00 et seq: the distinction essentially is between actual authority arising from the consensual relationship between the principal and agent and authority as it appears to third parties. 'The link is that the authority which the third party is entitled to assume the agent has is in most situations the authority which would normally be implied between principal and agent in the circumstances. The actual and apparent authority will therefore normally coincide' (para 3–005); see also *Smith v Butler* [2012] EWCA Civ 314 at [29].

[30] [1964] 1 All ER 630, CA.

[31] This case must be distinguished from *Hely-Hutchinson* (see **8-12**). In *Hely-Hutchinson*, the director was found to have been a de facto managing director and it was from that position that the court found that the director did have implied actual authority. The director in *Freeman & Lockyer* did not hold such a position and therefore there was less scope for finding implied actual authority as opposed to looking for some apparent authority. See also n 29 as to the relationship between implied actual and apparent authority.

8-17 For apparent authority to arise, the agent must have been held out by someone with actual authority[32] to carry out the transaction and an agent cannot hold himself out as having authority.[33] The acts of the principal must constitute a representation that the agent has a particular authority and must be reasonably so understood by the other party who deals with the agent on the faith of the representation. In determining whether a principal has represented his agent as having authority to enter into the particular transaction, the court has to consider the totality of the principal's conduct.[34] The commonest form of holding out is permitting the agent to act in the conduct of the principal's business[35] and in many cases the holding out consists solely of the fact that the company has invested the agent with a particular office, e.g. 'managing director' or 'secretary'.[36] The very act of appointing someone as a director is a representation that they have the usual authority of someone in that position. The holding out may also come from a course of conduct where the agent has a course of dealing with a particular contractor and the principal acquiesces in the practice and honours transactions arising out of it.[37] For these reasons, an individual director may acquire considerable apparent authority.

8-18 The problem with apparent authority is that it cannot be relied upon if the other party knows or is put on inquiry as to some limitation which prevents the authority arising.[38] This may be knowledge, including constructive notice,[39] of the company's articles which might clearly indicate a lack of authority, for example, where the articles state that no individual director may enter into a transaction in excess of £1m. A third party is deemed (by the doctrine of constructive notice) to be aware of that limitation even if the third party has not actually read the articles, though if he can rely on CA 2006, s 40, discussed in detail later, the third party is unaffected even by actual knowledge of such a limitation.

---

[32] Although the courts have also accepted the following principle set out in *Bowstead and Reynolds on Agency* (19th edn, 2010), para 8–021: 'It seems correct in principle to say that an agent can have apparent authority to make representations as to the authority of other agents, provided that his own authority can finally be traced back to a representation by the principal or to a person with actual authority from the principal to make it', but see further para 8–021. See *Re Ing (UK) Ltd v Verischerung* [2007] 1 BCLC 108, esp at 127.

[33] *Freeman and Lockyer v Buckhurst Park Properties (Mangal) Ltd* [1964] 1 All ER 630, CA; *British Bank of the Middle East v Sun Life Assurance Co of Canada (UK) Ltd* [1983] BCLC 78, HL; *Armagas Ltd v Mundogas SA* [1986] 2 All ER 385, HL. See too *Hudson Bay Apparel Brands LLC v Umbro International Ltd* [2011] 1 BCLC 259 at [53].

[34] *Egyptian International Foreign Trade Co v Soplex Wholesale Supplies Ltd, The Raffaella* [1985] BCLC 404 at 411, CA, per Browne-Wilkinson V-C.

[35] *Freeman and Lockyer v Buckhurst Park Properties (Mangal) Ltd* [1964] 1 All ER 630 at 645, per Diplock LJ.

[36] *Egyptian International Foreign Trade Co v Soplex Wholesale Supplies Ltd, The Raffaella* [1985] BCLC 404 at 411, CA, per Browne-Wilkinson V-C. As Toulson J commented in *Re Ing (UK) Ltd v Verischerung* [2007] 1 BCLC 108 at 128: '…many instances of ostensible authority arise by implication from acts of a quite general nature, typically putting an agent in a position which may normally be expected to carry a certain level of authority', see also at 132–3.

[37] See *Armagas Ltd v Mundogas SA* [1986] 2 All ER 385 at 389–90, HL, per Lord Keith.

[38] *A L Underwood Ltd v Bank of Liverpool* [1924] 1 KB 775, CA; *B Liggett (Liverpool) Ltd v Barclays Bank Ltd* [1928] 1 KB 48; *Morris v Kanssen* [1946] 1 All ER 586, HL; *Rolled Steel Products (Holdings) Ltd v British Steel Corpn* [1985] 3 All ER 52, CA; *Criterion Properties plc v Stratford UK Properties LLC* [2006] 1 BCLC 729, HL. See, for example, *Hudson Bay Apparel Brands LLC v Umbro International Ltd* [2011] 1 BCLC 259 at [54], where there could not be apparent authority when the third party dealing with the company knew (from previous negotiations) that the company representative in the US did not have authority to execute agreements on behalf of the company which could only be executed by a senior employee in the UK.

[39] Constructive notice does not affect anyone able to rely on CA 2006, s 40, but it has not been abolished otherwise. CA 1985, s 711A which would have done so was never brought into force and was repealed by CA 2006, s 1295, Sch 16.

8-19   It may be that the third party is put on inquiry as to the authority of the agent by the very nature of the proposed transaction which may indicate that a director is acting for an improper purpose. As Lord Scott commented in *Criterion Properties plc v Stratford UK Properties LLC*[40] (see **8-63**):

> '…if a person dealing with an agent knows or has reason to believe that the contract or transaction is contrary to the commercial interests of the agent's principal, it is likely to be very difficult for the person to assert with any credibility that he believed the agent did have actual authority. Lack of such a belief would be fatal to a claim that the agent had apparent authority.'

8-20   In *A L Underwood Ltd v Bank of Liverpool*[41] a bank was put on inquiry when a director paid cheques drawn in favour of the company into his personal bank account. If put on inquiry by the circumstances, the third party should make such inquiries as ought reasonably to be made to ensure the agent's authority is sufficient to bind the principal.[42] In *Hopkins v TL Dallas Group Ltd*[43] a third party was unable to hold a company to undertakings given by a deputy managing director (who had subsequently been dismissed for dishonesty) when the recipient of the undertakings had been on the clearest notice that the transactions were abnormal and suspicious. In those circumstances, the court said, the recipient should have sought confirmation of the propriety and regularity of the transaction from the managing director of the company. The director had no actual authority to execute the undertakings[44] and the recipient could not rely on any apparent authority on the director's part in the light of his failure to inquire. Accordingly, the undertakings were not binding on the defendant company and could not be enforced against it.

8-21   In *Wrexham AFC Ltd v Crucialmove Ltd*[45] the company was a football club. A director and the company secretary executed a declaration on behalf of the company that the freehold of the football ground (which had been purchased with funding provided by a third party) was held on trust for the third party. However, what was not disclosed was that the director and the third party had entered into a joint venture agreement for the redevelopment of the ground to their personal advantage. Clearly, in those circumstances, the third party knew that the director had a conflict of interest between his personal interests and his duty to the company. The ownership of the freehold was subsequently challenged by the club which disputed the authority of the director (who was company chairman and an executive director) to execute the declaration of trust.

8-22   The court found that this was a highly unusual case where the third party was not dealing with company officers of whom he knew nothing. Because of the joint venture agreement, the third party knew of all the circumstances that meant that the director had a conflict of interest in securing the freehold of the land and in making the declaration of trust. The third party was on notice that the director was entering into the transaction for an

---

[40] [2006] 1 BCLC 729 at 741, HL.
[41] [1924] 1 KB 775, CA. A third party can only rely on apparent authority provided he does not know that the director has no actual authority; *Re Capitol Films Ltd, Rubin v Cobalt Pictures Ltd* [2011] 2 BCLC 359 at [55], applying Lord Scott in *Criterion*; also *Hopkins v TL Dallas Group Ltd* [2005] 1 BCLC 543 at [88].
[42] *Hopkins v TL Dallas Group Ltd* [2005] 1 BCLC 543.   [43] [2005] 1 BCLC 543.
[44] The director had no express actual authority for this transaction. Equally, despite the title of deputy managing director, he had no implied actual authority because the giving of undertakings of this nature did not fall within the usual scope of the office of deputy managing director. He was subordinate to an executive chairman and to an executive managing director and had no responsibility in relation to these types of undertakings.
[45] [2008] 1 BCLC 508, CA. See too *Rolled Steel Products (Holdings) Ltd v British Steel Corpn* [1984] BCLC 466 at 497, 507–8, 517–18, CA.

improper purpose and in breach of his fiduciary duty to the company and he was bound to inquire whether the transaction had been authorised or approved by the company or its board. Given the third party was on notice and had failed to inquire, the Court of Appeal held that he could not rely on any apparent authority of the director as a matter of agency law nor on the statutory protection provided for third parties by CA 2006, s 40[46] (this latter point is discussed further at **8-27**). The court upheld a declaration by the lower court that the freehold of the land was held on trust for the company, subject to a charge in favour of the third party in respect of the purchase price.

8-23 Another example of the third party being on notice can be found in *Re Capitol Films Ltd, Rubin v Cobalt Pictures Ltd*.[47] In this case, the company was in severe financial difficulties and the director assigned most of the company's main assets (distribution rights in films) to the third party for an undefined consideration (the provision of 'certain services' and a 'certain amount' of financing to the company). In those circumstances, the court held, the third party knew that the director was acting contrary to the commercial interests of his company and could have no actual authority which meant, applying the dictum of Lord Scott in *Criterion Properties*, cited at **8-19**, that the third party equally could not rely on the doctrine of apparent authority. A clinching consideration here was that the director who acted for the company was also the director of the third party and he signed the assignment documents on behalf of the company and the third party. As the court noted, if the same person purports to act as a director on behalf of both parties to a transaction, it is self-evident that the other contracting party is to be taken to have known of the lack of authority of that person to act for the company.[48]

8-24 As can be seen from these cases, the courts have reached a very settled position on the position of the third party. He may rely on the actual authority of the director, if such is found to exist, and, if not, he is able to rely on apparent authority provided he has not been put on inquiry and failed to inquire. Crucially, if the third party knows or has reason to believe that the transaction is contrary to the commercial interests of the director's company, then he cannot believe that the director has actual authority to enter into the transaction and that knowledge is fatal to any reliance on apparent authority.

D Statutory protection for third parties

8-25 As discussed at **8-5**, the directors' mandate to manage the business, their authority to act on the company's behalf, is derived from the constitutional division of power within the particular company set out primarily (but not exclusively) in the articles[49] as well as the authority conferred on them by agency law. A failure to act within the scope of their authority is a breach by the directors of CA 2006, s 171(a) and leaves persons dealing with the company through them as parties to an unauthorised transaction. The problem here is a want of authority. This risk of being party to an unauthorised transaction would seem to require third parties to scrutinise carefully the company's constitution and the limits to the directors' authority, collectively and individually. But that type of scrutiny is time-consuming and expensive in the context of commercial operations and, therefore, both

---

[46] [2008] 1 BCLC 508 at [45], [47].   [47] [2011] 2 BCLC 359.
[48] [2011]2 BCLC 359 at [53]–[55].
[49] The constitution is defined more broadly than the articles, see CA 2006, s 17; and see **4-8**. It is also possible that the directors' powers may be limited by directions given by the shareholders by special resolution: see The Companies (Model Articles) Regulations 2008, SI 2008/3229, reg 2, Sch 1, art 4 (Ltd); reg 4, Sch 3, art 4 (Plc).

domestically and as a result of EU requirements, the policy balance here favours, exter-nally, commercial certainty and the protection of the third party over any need, inter-nally, to protect shareholders by upholding constitutional constraints on the authority of the directors. That policy is reflected in CA 2006, s 40 and, at common law, by agency law, as discussed at **8–16**, and the rule in *Turquand's* case, discussed at **8-45**.

8-26   As far as third parties are concerned, the practical context in which a problem is likely to arise is where a company wishes to disown a transaction (usually as a result of a change in circumstances which makes the transaction disadvantageous) by alleging that the director or directors responsible had no authority to enter into it. A third party may have an action for damages for breach of an implied warranty of authority against a director in such circumstances,[50] but he is usually more concerned with holding the company to the transaction. The answer to this problem of a want of authority lies in a combination of agency law and company law, common law and statute.

Companies Act 2006, s 40

8-27   Statutory protection for third parties dealing with the company is provided by CA 2006, s 40 which implements the requirements of the First EC Company Law Directive in this regard.[51] Section 40(1) states:

> 'In favour of a person dealing with a company in good faith, the power of the directors to bind the company, or authorise others to do so, is deemed to be free of any limitation under the company's constitution.'

The statutory provision operates only 'in favour of' a person dealing with a company in good faith so the company needs to authorise the transaction if it wants to hold the other party to it.

8-28   Before looking in detail at the application of s 40, note in particular that s 40 has effect subject to CA 2006, s 41 where the parties to the transaction include a director of the company or of its holding company or a person connected (as defined in s 252) with such a director.[52] In that situation, the transaction is voidable at the instance of the company subject to the possibility that the right to avoid may be lost in the usual ways (*restitutio impossible*, rights of bona fide third parties for value intervene, etc: see s 41(4)). Further, the director and connected person and any director who authorised the transaction (sub-ject to the defence in s 41(5)) may be civilly liable under s 41(3) and under any other rule of law such as for breach of duty (s 41(1)). The application of s 41 may give rise to the

---

[50] *Hely-Hutchinson v Brayhead Ltd* [1967] 3 All ER 98, CA.

[51] The relevant provision is art 9 of the First Council Directive on Company Law, 68/151/EEC, OJ Spec Edn 1968, p 41 which provides as follows: '(1) Acts done by the organs of the company shall be binding upon it even if those acts are not within the objects of the company, unless such acts exceed the powers that the law confers or allows to be conferred on those organs. However, Member States may provide that the company shall not be bound where such acts are outside the objects of the company, if it proves that the third party knew that the act was outside those objects or could not in view of the circumstances have been unaware of it; disclosure of the statutes shall not of itself be sufficient proof thereof. (2) The limits on the powers of the organs of the company, arising under the statutes or from a decision of the competent organs, may never be relied on as against third parties, even if they have been disclosed.' See the detailed account of art 9 by Edwards, *EC Company Law* (1999), Ch 1, pp 33–45, though some of the difficulties in implementation iden-tified there (see pp 42–4) appear to have been addressed by subtle changes in the drafting of CA 2006, s 40, see discussion in text.

[52] CA 2006, ss 40(6), 41(2). Section 40 also has effect subject to s 42 where the company is a charity: s 40(6).

situation where a transaction is valid with respect to one party under s 40(1), because they are unaffected by the application of s 41 (see s 41(6)), and voidable with respect to another party to the same transaction if they are a director or connected person under s 41(2). In that situation, the court has wide powers to affirm, sever or set aside the transaction on such terms as appears to be just (s 41(6)).

A person dealing in good faith

8-29 An issue which has arisen is whether a director can be a 'person' for these purposes so as to rely on the protection of CA 2006, s 40. In *Smith v Henniker-Major & Co*,[53] while agreed that, as a matter of ordinary language, 'person' may include a director, the majority in the Court of Appeal did not accept that a director could rely on the statutory provision with respect to an error as to authority when he was the author of his own mistake.[54] The judicial reluctance to accept that a director (where he is the author of and hopes to be the beneficiary of the lack of authority) can rely on the protection of the statutory provision is understandable. As Schiemann LJ commented, there should be no difficulty in excluding from 'person' the very directors who overstepped the limitations in the company's constitution. But the case is not a very useful authority for the facts were exceptional,[55] as the court stressed, and there are three difficult judgements agreeing and conflicting with one another in almost equal measure.[56] There is no need to consider it further for the position has been clarified, it is suggested, by the rewording of CA 2006, s 40(6) which now states expressly that s 40 has effect subject to s 41.[57] In other words, when a director is a party (or one of the parties) to the transaction, his position is governed by s 41, not s 40. The starting point as regards a director is that the transaction is voidable under s 41 (s 41(2)), see **8-28**.

8-30 In *EIC Services Ltd v Phipps*,[58] the Court of Appeal was also robust in rejecting, obiter, a first instance finding that a shareholder could rely on CA 2006, s 40 as a 'person' dealing in good faith. The case concerned an unauthorised bonus issue to shareholders in breach of the articles and the question was whether the shareholders could rely on s 40 so as to be able to hold on to the shares which had been erroneously allocated (and which had increased in value significantly). As discussed at **8-31**, the court held in any event that a bonus issue does not amount to a 'dealing' with the company, but had there been a dealing, the court did not accept that a shareholder could be a 'person' for these purposes. Peter Gibson LJ, with whom Sedley LJ and Newman J agreed, thought the answer lay in the First Company Law Directive, art 9, which is implemented by CA 2006, s 40 and

---

[53] [2002] 2 BCLC 655, CA.

[54] See [2002] 2 BCLC 655 at 684, per Carnwath LJ, who stressed that the director here was also the chairman and the person entrusted with ensuring that the constitution was observed; also at 687, per Schiemann LJ. Robert Walker LJ dissented on the basis of the relationship between what is now CA 2006, s 40 and s 41, but the basis of his dissent has been eroded by the fact that s 40(6) now states expressly that s 40 has effect subject to s 41.

[55] The facts were that a 30% shareholder and director, Smith, at an inquorate board meeting (attended only by himself) had the company assign to him what was in effect its sole asset, namely a claim against a firm of solicitors for damages in respect of a sale of land. The validity of the assignment was challenged by the solicitors. Mr Smith claimed that, as he was a person dealing with the company in good faith, he could rely on the statutory protection and was unaffected by any (quorum) limitation on the powers of the board. He lost.

[56] See Walters, 'Section 35A and Quorum Requirements: Confusion Reigns' (2002) 23 Co Law 325.

[57] The previous wording was that CA 1985, s 322A (now CA 2006, s 41) had effect notwithstanding CA 1985, s 35A (now CA 2006, s 40): CA 1985, s 35A(6).   [58] [2004] 2 BCLC 589, CA.

which is intended to protect 'third parties'.[59] While noting that the Directive does not define 'third parties', Peter Gibson LJ thought it tolerably clear from the Directive itself that the term 'third parties' does not include the company or its members and there was no reason to think that a provision intended to implement the Directive had gone further than the Directive in the absence of any other known mischief which the section was intended to counteract.[60]

8-31   For the purpose of CA 2006, s 40, a person 'deals with' a company if he is a party to any transaction or other act to which the company is a party.[61] In *EIC Services Ltd v Phipps*,[62] noted at **8-30**, the Court of Appeal did not accept that an issue of bonus shares by a company to its shareholders, an internal arrangement involving no change in proportionate shareholdings and a consequence of a single resolution applicable to all shareholders, could amount to a 'dealing' with the company for these purposes.[63] Peter Gibson LJ noted that, as a matter of ordinary language, the section contemplates a bilateral transaction between the company and the person dealing with the company or an act to which both are parties.[64]

8-32   As to the good faith requirement in s 40(1), the statute goes to great lengths to ensure that it is difficult for a person dealing with a company to be in bad faith, in particular, by imposing a presumption of good faith and absolving the third party from an obligation to inquire to a certain extent. The key provision is CA 2006, s 40(2)(b) which provides as follows:

'(2) For this purpose—...

(b) a person dealing with a company—

(i)   is not bound to enquire as to any limitation on the powers of the directors to bind the company or authorise others to do so,

(ii) is presumed to have acted in good faith unless the contrary is proved, and

(iii) is not to be regarded as acting in bad faith by reason only of his knowing that an act is beyond the powers of the directors under the company's constitution.'

8-33   As is clear from (iii), the statutory protection extends even to providing that a person cannot be regarded as acting in bad faith by reason *only* of his knowing that an act is beyond the powers of the directors under the company's constitution (i.e. beyond their authority). At common law, persons dealing with a company are deemed under the doctrine of constructive notice to have notice of the company's articles of association and various public documents (and this doctrine has not been repealed)[65] but this deemed knowledge is irrelevant under CA 2006, s 40 since even actual knowledge of a constitutional limita-

---

[59] The full text of art 9 is set out at n 51.

[60] [2004] 2 BCLC 589 at 660–1. Nor did he think that any inference as to the application of CA 2006, s 40 to shareholders could be drawn from the fact that the legislature dealt specifically with transactions with directors in s 41.

[61] CA 2006, s 40(2)(a). This wording ensures that the provision applies to gratuitous as well as commercial transactions.   [62] [2004] 2 BCLC 589, CA.

[63] See Payne and Prentice, n 4, p 463, who cogently criticise this finding and point out that at the very least a bonus issue amounts to an act to which the company is a party: see CA 2006, s 40(2)(a). See also *Cottrell v King* [2004] 2 BCLC 413 at [29] where it was doubted, obiter, whether the operation of pre-emption provisions in the articles requiring notice to be given by a member to the other members who might then purchase the member's shares could be said to be 'dealing with the company' for these purposes.

[64] [2004] 2 BCLC 589 at 660.

[65] See *Ernest v Nicholls* (1857) 6 HL Cas 401; *Mahony v East Holyford Mining Co* (1875) LR 7 HL 869; *Irvine v Union Bank of Australia* (1877) 2 App Cas 366, PC. The doctrine of constructive notice was to have been

tion does not establish bad faith. To establish bad faith, it is necessary to show something additional such as knowledge of, or being put on inquiry as to, an improper purpose on the part of the directors, or some collusion by the third party in a breach by the directors of their duties.[66]

8-34 The circumstances needed to rebut the presumption of good faith were considered in *Wrexham AFC Ltd v Crucialmove Ltd*,[67] discussed at **8-21**, where the third party knew that the director executing a particular agreement on behalf of the company had a conflict of interest. As discussed, the Court of Appeal held that the third party who knows of, or is on inquiry as to, an improper purpose and who fails to inquire cannot rely on apparent authority and, as a matter of agency law, cannot hold the company to the transaction.[68] The Court of Appeal also held that CA 2006, s 40 was of no assistance to the third party as the statutory provision does not absolve a person dealing with the company from any duty to inquire when the circumstances are such as to put that person on inquiry.[69] This case provides important clarification of the limits to the good faith presumption in s 40(2)(b)(ii). The section operates to negate any knowledge (actual or constructive) of *constitutional* limitations on the powers of the directors to bind the company and to relieve the third party from the obligation to inquire as to such limitations. But if a third party is put on inquiry by the circumstances of the transaction (which must be by something other than knowing of a lack of authority) and fails to inquire, then he cannot rely on s 40. The policy objectives of securing commercial certainty and the protection of the third party against constitutional limitations do not extend to protecting a third party with notice of a wider problem.

8-35 To sum up, if the problem facing the third party is merely a want of authority on the part of the directors because of some constitutional limitation, CA 2006, s 40 offers full protection to the third party acting in good faith assuming the various statutory requirements ('dealing', etc) are met. But where the third party is put on inquiry by something other than merely knowing of a lack of authority (such as knowledge, actual or constructive, of an improper purpose) and fails to inquire, the statutory presumption of good faith

---

abolished by CA 1985, s 711A but that provision was never brought into force and it was repealed by CA 2006, s 1295, Sch 16. This deemed notice can prevent apparent authority arising at common law; see **8-18**.

[66] See *Barclays Bank Ltd v TOSG Trust Fund Ltd* [1984] BCLC 1 (on the earlier but similarly worded provision, European Communities Act 1972, s 9); *International Sales and Agencies Ltd v Marcus* [1982] 3 All ER 551. Driving a hard bargain does not point to bad faith, but secretly working with a director to rob the company of its assets would point to a lack of good faith, see *Ford v Polymer Vision Ltd* [2009] 2 BCLC 160 at [92]–[93].   [67] [2008] 1 BCLC 508, CA.

[68] [2008] 1 BCLC 508 at 523.

[69] [2008] 1 BCLC 508 at 523. This approach is consistent with *International Sales and Agencies Ltd v Marcus* [1982] 3 All ER 551, at 559–60, where Lawson J (addressing the European Communities Act 1972, s 9, an earlier version of CA 2006, s 40) decided that a third party who received from a director sums of money which the recipient knew came improperly from the company's funds was liable applying constructive trust principles as a recipient of company money knowingly paid in breach of trust. The statutory purpose, he said, was to protect innocent parties who entered into transactions which the companies might otherwise seek to avoid but the statute did not affect the operation of a constructive trust if the facts gave rise to such a trust. This position also means that the complication of a person being within the statutory protection with respect to a lack of authority, but beyond the section with respect to an improper purpose cannot arise. A third party who is put on inquiry as to a proper purpose is not in good faith. A position reinforced by *Cooperatieve Rabobank 'Vecht en Plassengebied' BA v Minderhoud* [1998] 2 BCLC 507, ECJ where the court agreed that the provisions of the First Company Law Directive (which are reflected in CA 2006, s 40) are intended to protect innocent parties dealing with the company but they do not prevent the application of national laws on matters such as conflicts of interests to any agreement purportedly entered into by a company. See also Edwards, *EC Company Law* (1999), Ch 1 at pp 38–9.

in CA 2006, s 40(2)(b)(ii) is rebutted and the protection of the section is not available to him.[70]

8-36 If for some reason (for example, no 'dealing' for these purposes) a third party cannot bring himself within CA 2006, s 40 in the first place, then he must rely on agency law if he is to bind the company when faced with a want of authority on the part of a director or directors. The difficulty is that, as a matter of agency law, even constructive notice of a want of authority puts him on inquiry and a failure to inquire means that he cannot rely on any apparent authority. In that regard, the statute offers greater protection since, under the statute, a third party is not put on inquiry merely by knowing of a lack of authority (CA 2006, s 40(2)(b)(iii)). Equally, if a person dealing with a company is on notice that the directors are exercising the relevant power for purposes other than the purposes of the company, he cannot rely on the ostensible authority of the directors and, on ordinary principles of agency, cannot hold the company to the transaction.[71] Being put on inquiry as to the directors' purposes removes any credible belief in the directors' actual authority which, as Lord Scott commented in *Criterion Properties plc v Stratford UK Properties LLC*,[72] is fatal to any claim that the agent had apparent authority, see **8-63**.

Constitutional limitations may be disregarded

8-37 Assuming these thresholds in terms of 'a person' 'dealing' and 'good faith' can be met, limitations imposed by the company's constitution on the powers of the directors to bind the company or their powers to delegate to others may be disregarded. For example, if the articles limit the power of the directors to borrow to £5m, a bank which lends in excess of that amount to the company is unaffected by the limitation, assuming the bank deals in good faith. Constitutional limitations are found primarily in the company's articles (CA 2006, s 17) but s 40(3) broadens the application of the section to include limitations deriving from a resolution of the company or any class of shareholders, or from any agreement between the members of the company or of any class of shareholders.[73] Such limitations on the powers of the directors do not affect a person dealing with the company in good faith.

8-38 The wording of CA 2006, s 40(1) (see at **8-27**), 'the power of the directors', differs slightly but significantly from its predecessor, CA 1985, s 35A. The 1985 wording referred to constitutional limitations on 'the power of the board of directors' which led to debate as to whether requirements such as quorum requirements for a valid board meeting were limitations on the power of the board (and so within the section) or addressed the logically prior question of what constitutes a board of directors (and so were not within the section). A majority in the Court of Appeal in *Smith v Henniker-Major & Co*,[74] obiter,

---

[70] Of course there is an element of linkage here as to how a person is put on inquiry as to an improper purpose. While knowledge of a constitutional limitation (i.e. of a lack of authority) does not affect a person dealing in good faith with the company (CA 2006, s 40(2)(b)(iii)), that knowledge might put the third party on inquiry as to an exercise of a power for an improper purpose. A failure then to inquire will negate this presumption of good faith: see *Wrexham AFC Ltd v Crucialmove Ltd* [2008] 1 BCLC 508; Payne and Prentice, n 4, at p 455.

[71] *Rolled Steel Products (Holdings) Ltd v British Steel Corpn* [1984] BCLC 466 at 508, per Slade LJ.

[72] [2006] 1 BCLC 729 at 741, HL.

[73] Resolutions of the company would include either resolutions of the board or the shareholders which addresses a concern raised by Edwards, n 51, pp 43–4, as to the improper implementation of the First Directive, art 9.   [74] [2002] 2 BCLC 655 at 668, 687. See **8-29** and n 55.

favoured the former view, though the latter view had been favoured at first instance.[75] By removing the reference to 'the board', the wording expands the scope of the section and eliminates, it would seem, any scope for further debate as to whether procedural limitations are included. The section applies to any constitutional limitations on the powers of the directors to bind the company which must include quorum or other procedural requirements as these are matters that limit the powers of the directors to act.[76] In *Ford v Polymer Vision Ltd*[77] the court accepted that specific provisions concerning the holding of board meetings (a requirement for notice to certain directors and a requirement that meetings be held outside the UK, neither of which were observed in this instance) were limitations under the constitution for the purposes of s 40(1). The alternative interpretation leaves us with the sort of contorted categorisation of provisions in the articles evident in the judgments in *Smith v Henniker-Major & Co*[78] ('constitutional limitations', 'procedural requirements' and 'nullities'). Rather than indulge in such debate, it is preferable to adopt a generous approach to the section and the protection of third parties in line with the purpose of the First Directive.[79]

8-39 The wording of CA 2006, s 40(1) (see **8-27**) also raises a question which had arisen under a previous version of the provision,[80] namely as to the meaning of 'the directors' in this context. Having changed the wording from the 'board of directors' to 'the directors', it is clear that the section covers acts of the board and of any director authorised (in the sense of having actual authority to bind the company) to represent the company (i.e. the act need not be the act of the board collectively).[81] Support for interpreting 'directors' in accordance with that approach can be found in *Criterion Properties plc v Stratford UK Properties LLC*[82] which concerned the authority of two only of the directors and the court accepted that CA 1985, s 35A (now CA 2006, s 40) might be relevant and in *Wrexham AFC Ltd v Crucialmove Ltd*[83] which likewise concerned two only of the directors (the company chairman and the managing director) and where again the court considered s 35A to be relevant. In *International Sales & Agencies Ltd v Marcus*[84] too the court was content that the statutory protection might apply to acts of someone who was only one of a number of directors, in this case the sole effective director to whom all actual authority to act for the company had been delegated.

8-40 The result is a statutory provision which increases significantly the security of third parties dealing in good faith with the company. The downside for the company, i.e. the shareholders, is that the company does not have the option of disowning unauthorised transactions. But the shareholders are not entirely powerless, see **8-41**, and, as noted, a third party on inquiry as to an improper purpose is not protected by the section, nor

---

[75] See [2002] BCC 544 where Rimer J had concluded that, as the board was inquorate, there was no act of the board of directors to which CA 1985, s 35A might apply.

[76] See *TCB Ltd v Gray* [1986] 1 All ER 587 at 597 where Browne-Wilkinson V-C thought that any provision in the articles as to the manner in which the directors can act as agents of the company (such as rules governing the affixing of the company seal) is a limitation on their power to bind the company.

[77] [2009] 2 BCLC 160 at [74], [78], Blackburne J noting that there is every good reason why such defects should be within the purview of s 40. [78] [2002] 2 BCLC 655 at 668, 687.

[79] See Payne & Prentice, n 4, pp 457–8; and see *Ford v Polymer Vision Ltd* [2009] 2 BCLC 160 at [78].

[80] i.e. under s 9 of the European Communities Act 1972 which referred to transactions decided on by the directors: see Farrar & Powles (1973) MLR 270; Collier & Sealy (1973) CLJ 1.

[81] To be within the section, the directors must have actual (express or implied) authority to bind the company since the purpose of the provision is to prevent limits imposed on an existing authority from affecting a third party. See Edwards, *EC Company Law* (1999), pp 43–4. [82] [2006] 1 BCLC 729 at 740, HL.

[83] [2008] 1 BCLC 508 at 523. [84] [1982] 3 All ER 551 at 560.

can directors or connected persons rely on the statutory scheme (CA 2006, s 40(6)), so a balance is struck between commercial certainty and shareholder protection.

Possible redress for shareholders

8-41 A member may obtain an injunction to restrain 'the doing of an act which is beyond the powers of the directors although no such proceeding may lie in respect of an act to be done in fulfilment of a legal obligation arising from a previous act of the company' (CA 2006, s 40(4)). An injunction cannot be obtained, therefore, to restrain the execution of an executory contract. Given that s 40 prevents the shareholders from disowning an unauthorised transaction, it might be thought that shareholders have an incentive to monitor the conduct of the directors in order to prevent such transactions by injunctive relief. The practical difficulties of doing this, and the natural inertia of many shareholders, mean that this is unlikely to occur. In practice the members simply never find out about transactions in time to seek injunctive relief so making this provision somewhat irrelevant.

8-42 Shareholders are not without redress, however, for while a third party dealing with the company in good faith is able to hold a company to a transaction entered into in disregard of constitutional limitations on the powers of the directors, the directors responsible are in breach of the duty imposed by CA 2006, s 171(a) to act in accordance with the constitution and liable to indemnify the company for any loss suffered as a consequence. That the director is liable for breach of duty is confirmed by CA 2006, s 40(5) which provides that the protection afforded by s 40(1) does not affect any liability incurred by the directors, or any other person, by reason of the directors exceeding their powers. Note that this provision applies not just to directors, but to 'any other person' who may also be liable to the company on the basis of involvement in the breach of duty by the director.[85]

8-43 If the person dealing with the company cannot bring himself within the statutory protection in s 40, the unauthorised transaction is void[86] and not binding on the company though it is always open to the board or the shareholders, as appropriate, subsequently to decide not to treat the unauthorised transaction as a nullity but to affirm or adopt it,[87] if they so choose. If the company does not adopt or affirm the transaction, it remains a void transaction and the third party is liable, on the basis of a total failure of consideration, to account for any benefits obtained.[88]

8-44 Regardless of affirmation or adoption of the transaction, the directors responsible remain liable for breach of their duties under s 171. Whether the shareholders would wish to relieve a director from liability for breach of duty in these circumstances is a separate matter and the limits to the shareholders' powers to ratify breaches of duty are discussed in Chapter 18.

---

[85] See n 69.

[86] For example, in *EIC Services Ltd v Phipps* [2004] 2 BCLC 589 the board's failure to observe the requirements of the articles governing the issue of bonus shares meant that the share issue was void and the shareholders could not claim title to the allocated shares. See also *Guinness plc v Saunders* [1990] BCLC 402, HL (a committee of the board purported to award remuneration to an individual director when it had no power to do so under the articles. The contract in question was void for want of authority.) See also *Clark v Cutland* [2003] 2 BCLC 393, CA.

[87] An act in excess of the board's authority can be affirmed or adopted by an ordinary resolution even though an alteration to the board's powers for all time would require a special resolution: *Irvine v Union Bank of Australia* (1877) 2 App Cas 366, PC; *Grant v United Kingdom Switchback Railways Co* (1888) 40 Ch D 135, CA.   [88] *Guinness plc v Saunders* [1990] BCLC 402.

The indoor management rule

8-45 In addition to the protection afforded by apparent authority and the CA 2006, s 40, a third party may look to the common law rule in *Royal British Bank v Turquand*[89] which provides that persons dealing with a company are not obliged to inquire into the internal proceedings of a company but can assume that all acts of internal management have been properly carried out, save where an outsider knows or is put on inquiry as to the failure to adhere to procedures.[90] Insiders, i.e. persons holding positions within the company, are prevented from relying on the rule as they are in a position to know whether there has been compliance with the internal requirements.[91]

8-46 In *Royal British Bank v Turquand*[92] the board of directors had borrowed money without having the transaction authorised by a resolution of the company in general meeting as required by the deed of settlement (i.e. their articles). The court held that the company was bound by the borrowing as the resolution was a matter of internal management which the third party could assume had been correctly carried out.[93] In *Mahony v East Holyford Mining Co*[94] a bank was entitled to accept cheques drawn and signed by the directors in the manner authorised by the articles and was not obliged to query whether the individuals signing the cheques were validly appointed as directors.

8-47 The question is whether any role remains for the rule in *Turquand's* case in the light of CA 2006, s 40 and provisions such as s 161 precluding challenges to the acts of a director on the basis of a defect in his appointment (see **6-6**). For example, the situation in *Royal British Bank v Turquand*[95] would now be within s 40 as it involved a limitation on the board's authority to act. The scope of CA 2006, s 40 is broader in that it applies to any constitutional limitation on the powers of the directors whereas the rule in *Turquand* is limited to internal procedural irregularities. The circumstances in which the protection of the section and of the rule are lost are similar (party is put on inquiry and fails to inquire) but it may be possible to resort to the rule where a third party cannot bring themselves within the thresholds set by CA 2006, s 40 (for example, as to 'dealing with the company') though insiders are precluded from relying on the rule (as they are from relying on s 40, see **8-29**). All of which makes it difficult to envisage circumstances in which it would still be necessary to have recourse to the rule. It might conceivably be of some

---

[89] (1856) 6 E & B 327.

[90] *B Liggett (Liverpool) Ltd v Barclays Bank Ltd* [1928] 1 KB 48; *Morris v Kanssen* [1946] 1 All ER 586, HL; *Rolled Steel Products (Holdings) Ltd v British Steel Corpn* [1985] 3 All ER 52, CA; *Wrexham AFC Ltd v Crucialmove Ltd* [2008] 1 BCLC 508 at 523, CA. A further refinement to the rule is that it does not apply if the document which the outsider seeks to rely on is a forgery: see *Ruben v Great Fingall Consolidated* [1906] AC 439, HL; also *Kreditbank Cassel GmbH v Schenkers Ltd* [1927] 1 KB 826, CA; but this limitation has been criticised, see *Lovett v Carson Country Homes* [2009] 2 BCLC 196 at [92]–[95] (*Ruben's* case does not mean that a forged document can in no circumstances have any effect whatsoever, for a party may be estopped from disputing the validity of a forged document. The principle of apparent authority is a broad reflection of the principles of estoppel, the court said, and it is accepted that, in appropriate circumstances, a principal may be bound by the fraudulent acts of an agent (and forgeries are no different to other fraudulent acts) in circumstances where there is ostensible authority).

[91] *Morris v Kanssen* [1946] 1 All ER 586, HL; *Howard v Patent Ivory Manufacturing Co* (1888) 38 Ch D 156; cf *Hely-Hutchinson v Brayhead Ltd* [1967] 3 All ER 98.   [92] (1856) 6 E & B 327.

[93] The court noted that the party here, on reading the deed of settlement, would find not a prohibition from borrowing but a permission to do so on certain conditions. Finding that the authority might be made complete by a resolution, he would have a right to infer the fact of a resolution authorising that which on the face of the document appeared to be legitimately done.   [94] (1875) LR 7 HL 869.

[95] (1856) 6 E & B 327.

assistance with respect to reliance on the apparent authority of an individual director (where apparent authority can be established, but there is then some additional internal management requirement which has not been complied with), but it does not enable a party to hold the company to an unauthorised transaction entered into by a director. It allows a third party to assume that a transaction within the authority of the directors has been properly carried out, but it requires the third party to establish the fact of authority, actual or apparent, in the first place.

E Exercise of a power for an improper purpose

8-48 The duty to exercise a power for the purposes for which it is conferred, set out in CA 2006, s 171(b) (see **8-1**), applies to the exercise by the directors of any of their powers, be it the power to make allotments of shares;[96] to make calls on shares;[97] to refuse to register share transfers;[98] to order the forfeiture of shares;[99] to alienate the property of the company;[100] to expel a member;[101] to enter into agreements with third parties.[102] The wider the power conferred, the more difficult it may be to restrain the directors,[103] but the duty brings an objective measure of control to the exercise of a power in contrast to s 172 which, see Chapter 9, is primarily subjective (a director must act in the way he considers, in good faith, is most likely to promote the success of the company for the benefit of the members as a whole).

The substantial purpose for exercise

8-49 The leading authority on the proper purpose duty is the Privy Council decision in *Howard Smith Ltd v Ampol Petroleum Ltd*.[104] The leading speech was given by Lord Wilberforce who explained that the proper approach to an exercise of a power is:[105]

'...to start with a consideration of the power whose exercise is in question...Having ascertained, on a fair view, the nature of this power, and having defined as can best be done in the light of modern conditions the, or some, limits within which it may be exercised, it is then necessary for the court, if a particular exercise of it is challenged, to examine the substantial purpose for which it was exercised, and to reach a conclusion whether that purpose was proper or not.'

8-50 The first step is to construe the article conferring the power in order to ascertain the nature of the power and the limits within which it may be exercised. In theory, the article

---

[96] See *Punt v Symons & Co Ltd* [1903] 2 Ch 506; *Piercy v S Mills & Co Ltd* [1920] 1 Ch 77; *Hogg v Cramphorn Ltd* [1966] 3 All ER 420; *Bamford v Bamford* [1969] 1 All ER 969; *Howard Smith Ltd v Ampol Petroleum Ltd* [1974] 1 All ER 1126.

[97] *Galloway v Halle Concerts Society* [1915] 2 Ch 233; *Alexander v Automatic Telegraph Co* [1900] 2 Ch 56.

[98] *Re Smith & Fawcett Ltd* [1942] 1 All ER 542; *Re Bede Steam Shipping Co Ltd* [1917] 1 Ch 123.

[99] *Re Agriculturalist Cattle Insurance Co, Stanhope's Case* (1866) 1 Ch App 161.

[100] See *Bishopsgate Investment Management Ltd v Maxwell* [1993] BCLC 1282; *Ford v Polymer Vision Ltd* [2009] 2 BCLC 160.

[101] See *Gaiman v National Association for Mental Health* [1970] 2 All ER 362; noted Prentice (1970) 33 MLR 700.

[102] See *Lee Panavision Ltd v Lee Lighting Ltd* [1992] BCLC 22, CA.

[103] See *Re Smith & Fawcett Ltd* [1942] 1 All ER 542; *Gaiman v National Association for Mental Health* [1970] 2 All ER 362, noted Prentice (1970) 33 MLR 700.   [104] [1974] AC 821, PC.

[105] [1974] AC 821 at 835.

could be limitless, permitting the exercise of the power in question for any purpose,[106] but even an apparently limitless power is inherently limited by a need to exercise it in order to promote the success of the company. Of course, in many cases, there may not be a specific power as such, rather the directors will be exercising their powers of general management conferred on them by the articles (see **8-5**).[107]

8-51 Having established the limits, if any, to the power, the second step is to determine the substantial purpose or purposes for which it was exercised. This is not always easy to decide and may involve a detailed examination of the facts. Here Lord Wilberforce noted that:[108]

> '…the court…is entitled to look at the situation objectively in order to estimate how criti-
> cal or pressing, or substantial or, per contra, insubstantial an alleged requirement may
> have been. If it finds that a particular requirement, though real, was not urgent, or critical,
> at the relevant time, it may have reason to doubt, or discount, the assertions of individuals
> that they acted solely in order to deal with it, particularly when the action they took was
> unusual or even extreme.'

8-52 In keeping with the reluctance of the judiciary to review the business decisions of directors, Lord Wilberforce accepted that there are difficulties of proof here which will require crediting the bona fide opinion of the directors, if such is found to exist, and respecting their judgement as to matters of management.[109] Having done so, he went on, the ultimate conclusion must be as to the side of a fairly broad line on which the case falls.[110]

8-53 Having carried out this exercise and identified the actual purpose for which the power was exercised, that actual purpose then has to be measured against the range of permissible purposes for the exercise of that power, as indicated by the articles or ascertained by the court, in order to decide whether that actual exercise was proper. Provided that the substantial purpose for which the power was exercised is a proper purpose, the exercise of the power is not invalidated by the presence of some other improper, but insubstantial, purpose. For example, some incidental benefit obtained by a director does not invalidate the exercise of the power unless his self-interest was the substantial purpose for the exercise of the power.[111] Equally, if the substantial purpose was improper, a director's honest belief that he was acting in the interests of the company is insufficient to validate the exercise of the power.[112]

---

[106] See *Re Smith & Fawcett Ltd* [1942] 1 All ER 542 at 545, per Lord Greene; also Prentice (1970) 33 MLR 700.

[107] See, for example, *CAS (Nominees) Ltd v Nottingham Forest FC plc* [2002] 1 BCLC 613; also The Companies (Model Articles) Regulations 2008, SI 2008/3229, reg 2, Sch 1, art 3 (Ltd); reg 4, Sch 3, art 3 (Plc).

[108] *Howard Smith Ltd v Ampol Petroleum Ltd* [1974] AC 821 at 832.   [109] [1974] AC 821 at 832.

[110] [1974] AC 821 at 835.

[111] *Ngurli v McCann* (1954) 90 CLR 425 at 440; *Mills v Mills* (1938) 60 CLR 150 at 164–5; *Hirsche v Sims* [1894] AC 654 at 660–1. See also *Whitehouse v Carlton Hotel Pty Ltd* (1987) 5 ACLC 421 at 427 where the Australian High Court added the refinement that where there are competing permissible and impermissible purposes, the preferable view is that regardless of whether the impermissible purpose was the dominant one or but one of a number of significant contributing causes, an allotment will be invalidated if the impermissible purpose was causative in the sense that but for its presence the power would not have been exercised (citing Dixon J in *Mills v Mills* (1938) 60 CLR 150).

[112] *Howard Smith Ltd v Ampol Petroleum Ltd* [1974] AC 821; *Re a company, ex p Glossop* [1988] BCLC 570 at 577; *Lee Panavision Ltd v Lee Lighting Ltd* [1992] BCLC 22 at 31; *Extrasure Travel Insurances Ltd v Scattergood* [2003] 1 BCLC 598 at 619.

8-54 Turning to the facts in *Howard Smith Ltd v Ampol Petroleum Ltd*,[113] the case concerned a takeover battle for a company where the directors favoured a particular bidder and made an allotment of shares to that bidder with a view to diluting the holdings of the potential rival bidders (who were the existing majority shareholders) for the company.[114] It was accepted that the directors were not motivated by any purpose of personal gain or advantage or desire to retain their posts. The Privy Council agreed with the trial judge that, although the directors had acted honestly, it was unconstitutional for the directors to use their fiduciary powers over the shares in the company for the purpose of destroying an existing majority or creating a new majority. As the directors' primary objective was to alter the majority shareholding, the directors had improperly exercised their powers and the allotment was invalid.

8-55 The Privy Council did accept in *Howard Smith Ltd v Ampol Petroleum Ltd*[115] that, as far as a power to allot shares is concerned, that power is not restricted to cases where the company requires additional capital. Such a power may be used (unless the articles otherwise provide), for example, to foster business connections,[116] to ensure that the company has the requisite number of shareholders to exercise its statutory functions[117] and to reach the best commercial agreement for the company, even if this has the effect of defeating a takeover bid.[118]

8-56 As is clear from *Howard Smith Ltd v Ampol Petroleum Ltd*[119] the courts are alert to attempts by the directors to manipulate control of the company by the improper exercise of the power to allot shares and this case is but one of a long line of authorities on this issue. In *Punt v Symons & Co Ltd*[120] an injunction was granted to prevent the company from holding a meeting when an improper allotment had been made for the purpose of securing the passing of a resolution at that meeting; in *Piercy v S Mills & Co Ltd*[121] an allotment made for the purpose of destroying the voting control of the existing majority shareholders was held to be invalid; in *Hogg v Cramphorn Ltd*[122] an allotment was invalid where its primary purpose was to ensure control of the company by the directors and their supporters; likewise in *Bamford v Bamford*[123] an allotment was invalid when made with an eye primarily on the exigencies of a takeover and not with a single eye to the benefit of the company.

8-57 It should be noted that, in addition to the constraints imposed by CA 2006, s 171, improper allotments of shares to manipulate the control position within a company are constrained now by a variety of statutory requirements (see **19-30** et seq). Directors must have authority to allot either via the articles or by resolution (s 551) and generally allotments must be on a rights basis subject to certain exceptions, exclusions and disapplications.[124] The CA 2006 does allow directors of a private company with only one class of shares to allot shares without shareholder approval (s 550), a power which is potentially open to abuse as the

---

[113] [1974] AC 821.

[114] Briefly, the company had majority shareholders A+B who together held 55% of the shares and they were interested in acquiring total control of the business. The company did need additional capital and the directors made an allotment of 4.5m shares to H which was also interested in acquiring control of the business. The allotment to H had the effect of reducing A+B's control to 36.6% and put H in a position to take over the company.   [115] [1974] AC 821 at 835.

[116] See *Harlowe's Nominees Pty Ltd v Woodside Oil Co* (1968) 121 CLR 483, H Ct Aust.

[117] See *Punt v Symons & Co Ltd* [1903] 2 Ch 506.

[118] See *Teck Corpn Ltd v Millar* (1972) 33 DLR (3d) 288, S Ct BC; noted Ziegel [1974] JBL 85.

[119] [1974] AC 821.   [120] [1903] 2 Ch 506.   [121] [1920] 1 Ch 77.   [122] [1966] 3 All ER 420.

[123] [1970] Ch 212.

[124] A rights issue requires that shares are offered to existing shareholders in proportion to their existing holdings; the mechanics of rights issues are discussed at **19-35**.

cases discussed above illustrate, but the requirement for a rights issue remains, subject to the statutory exceptions. Further, shareholders can challenge allotments, even an allotment on a rights basis, as being unfairly prejudicial conduct[125] (the unfairly prejudicial jurisdiction is discussed in Chapter 17). In larger public companies, the directors' ability to manipulate control in takeover situations is subject also to the constraints imposed on defensive actions by incumbent management by the Takeover Code (see **26-52**).

8-58 As noted, the duty to exercise a power for the purposes for which it is conferred applies to all the powers which directors possess and is not limited to the exercise of the power to allot shares. In *Extrasure Travel Insurances Ltd v Scattergood*,[126] for example, two directors transferred funds from the company to another company in the group in order to meet the demands of a pressing creditor of that other company. Applying *Howard Smith v Ampol*, the court concluded that:[127]

- the power in question was the directors' ability to deal with the assets of the company in the course of trading;
- the purpose for which that power was conferred on the directors was broadly to protect the company's survival and to promote its commercial interests in accordance with its objects;
- the substantial purpose for which the power was actually exercised was to enable the recipient company to meet its liabilities and not to preserve the transferor company;
- it followed that the purpose for which the transfer was made was plainly improper.

8-59 In *Lee Panavision Ltd v Lee Lighting Ltd*[128] the court found that it was unconstitutional and beyond the powers of outgoing directors, however much they thought it in the company's interests, to commit the company to a management agreement with a third party (with whom the outgoing directors were closely associated) which would have deprived the incoming directors of all management powers. The court refused to assist the third party to enforce the agreement. In *Bishopsgate Investment Ltd v Maxwell (No 2)*[129] the court found a director in breach of his fiduciary duty when he gave away the company's assets for no consideration to a private family company of which he was a director. This was an exercise of the power to alienate property of the company for an improper purpose and the director was liable to indemnify the company for its loss.[130] In *Criterion Properties plc v Stratford UK Properties LLC*[131] the court questioned whether it could be a proper exercise of the directors' powers to commit the company in effect to a poison pill arrangement which deterred takeover bidders and protected the interests of certain directors,[132] see **8-63**.

---

[125] CA 2006, s 994. See *Re Sunrise Radio Ltd, Kohli v Lit* [2010] 1 BCLC 367 (rights issue at par unfairly prejudicial, for even if the substantial purpose of the rights issue was to raise capital, a failure to give proper consideration to the price of the issue (so benefiting those who took up the offer and disadvantaging those who did not) would ordinarily be a breach of the duty to act fairly as between the shareholders as required by CA 2006, s 172(1)(f)); *Dalby v Bodilly* [2005] BCC 627 (allotment made by the company's sole director and 50% shareholder which had the effect of diluting the other 50% shareholder to a 5% shareholder was the plainest possible breach by the director of his fiduciary duty); see **17-46**.

[126] [2003] 1 BCLC 598.   [127] [2003] 1 BCLC 598 at 633.   [128] [1992] BCLC 22 at 30.

[129] [1993] BCLC 1282.   [130] [1993] BCLC 1282 at 1286.   [131] [2006] 1 BCLC 729, HL.

[132] See too *Ford v Polymer Vision Ltd* [2009] 2 BCLC 160 where the court had concerns about an option agreement entered into by two directors to sell the business to F. The court looked at the one-sided nature of the agreement and thought that the terms agreed, especially as to the price and the time frame (a 10-year option), seemed much more favourable to F than to the company. It was at least arguable, the court said, that

8-60 The criticism levied at these authorities is that the courts are imposing limits on powers which have not been so limited, either expressly or impliedly, by the shareholders (the articles commonly grant all powers to the directors without limit, see **8-5**) and that the courts are using this doctrine to do what they consistently say they do not do, namely review business decisions reached by the directors. Of course, there is an element of the courts reviewing business decisions according to their perception of the standards expected of a fiduciary office holder,[133] reflecting in essence objective judgements as to the conduct expected of directors,[134] but the approach is not unduly interventionist[135] and it has to be set against the more subjective test in CA 2006, s 172.

8-61 It is useful to contrast the approach in *Extrasure Travel Insurances Ltd v Scattergood*,[136] and in *CAS (Nominees) Ltd v Nottingham Forest FC plc*.[137] In *Extrasure*, see **8-58**, the directors allowed company funds to be transferred away to assist companies with which the directors were connected and which were in financial difficulty. The directors had no regard to the company's interests (or its creditors) in so acting and they were held liable. In *CAS (Nominees) Ltd v Nottingham Forest FC plc*[138] the directors of a parent company had a choice as to whether to sell shares in a subsidiary directly to an outsider in order to raise much needed funds for the subsidiary or to raise funds via the parent company shareholders. This was not a case where there was an issue as to diluting the existing shareholders' interests, as was the scenario in the cases discussed at **8-56**. Instead a good faith business decision was taken to sell shares directly to an outsider and bypass the shareholders in the parent company. The shareholders of the parent company argued that the board of the parent company had exercised its powers for an improper purpose. The court dismissed the shareholders' petition finding that the directors were exercising their powers of management of the business (in this case managing an asset, the investment in the subsidiary) and, given a genuine desire to raise capital, they had not exercised their powers to manage for a purpose foreign to their proper ambit. At issue ultimately was a business choice as to how to solve a funding problem in a subsidiary. In the absence of a breach of any statutory requirements or bad faith on the part of the directors, the court was content to let their business judgement stand.

Consequences of exercise for improper purpose

8-62 As a matter of agency law, it is clear that 'unless otherwise agreed, authority to act as agent includes only authority to act for the benefit of the principal'.[139] A failure so to act negates any actual authority and the transaction is void as regards the principal.[140] The exercise

committing the company to the disposal of all its assets and undertaking on such terms was an improper exercise of power, see at [89].

[133] See Nolan, 'The Proper Purpose Doctrine and Company Directors' in Rider (ed), *The Realm of Company Law* (1998), pp 20–2.

[134] See Sealy, ' "Bona Fides" and "Proper Purposes" in Corporate Decisions' (1989) 15 Mon ULR 265 at 276: 'the courts are in truth making naked value judgments'; and see Sealy, 'Directors' Duties Revisited' (2001) Co Law 79 at 82.

[135] See Lord Wilberforce in *Howard Smith Ltd v Ampol Petroleum Ltd* [1974] AC 821 at 832 cautioning against second-guessing the business judgement of directors.   [136] [2003] 1 BCLC 598.

[137] [2002] 1 BCLC 613.   [138] [2002] 1 BCLC 613.

[139] See *Bowstead and Reynolds on Agency* (19th edn, 2010), para 3-007; *Hopkins v TL Dallas Group Ltd* [2005] 1 BCLC 543 at 572; see *Criterion Properties plc v Stratford UK Properties LLC* [2006] 1 BCLC 729 at 741.

[140] See *Bowstead and Reynolds on Agency* (19th edn, 2010), para 8–218; *Hopkins v TL Dallas Group Ltd* [2005] 1 BCLC 543 at 573; *Criterion Properties plc v Stratford UK Properties LLC* [2006] 1 BCLC 729 at 741;

by a director (the agent) of a power for an improper purpose is clearly not for the benefit of the company (the principal) and so negates the director's actual authority to act. A third party can still rely on the agent's apparent authority, but the ability to do so is lost if the third party knows or is put on inquiry as to the exercise of the power for an improper purpose.[141]

8-63 These issues were central to the House of Lords decision in *Criterion Properties plc v Stratford UK Properties LLC*.[142] The question was whether a managing director of a company and another director could commit the company to an arrangement known as a poison pill (which has the effect of warding off takeover bidders and deterring them from making a bid to shareholders) which in this case was drafted in extremely wide and onerous terms but which was beneficial to the directors concerned. There had been considerable confusion in the lower courts as to the proper approach to this issue,[143] but their Lordships were resolutely clear that the matter is one of agency law.[144] The issue which needed to be resolved was whether the directors had actual or apparent authority to enter into such an arrangement, a factual matter which was remitted to trial. Lord Scott explained the position succinctly:

> '...if a person dealing with an agent knows or has reason to believe that the contract or transaction is contrary to the commercial interests of the agent's principal, it is likely to be very difficult for the person to assert with any credibility that he believed the agent did have actual authority. Lack of such belief would be fatal to a claim that the agent had apparent authority.'

8-64 Further, as *Wrexham AFC Ltd v Crucialmove Ltd*[145] makes clear, the third party in this situation is equally unable to rely on CA 2006, s 40 because the section imposes the same duty to inquire as agency law.[146] In this case (the facts are given at **8-21**), the third party knew that the director executing a particular agreement was in breach of his fiduciary duties to the company. In those circumstances, the third party was bound to inquire whether the transaction had been authorised or approved by the company or its board. Given he was on notice and had failed to inquire, the Court of Appeal held that the third party could not rely as a matter of agency law on any apparent authority of the director, nor could he rely on CA 2006, s 40 for the statutory provision, the court said, does not absolve a person dealing with the company from any duty to inquire when the circumstances are such as to put that person on inquiry.[147] Where the third party knows or is put on inquiry as to the improper purpose and fails to inquire, the outcome is the same

---

Re Capitol Films Ltd, Rubin v Cobalt Pictures Ltd [2011] 2 BCLC 359 at [53]–[55]; *GHLM Trading Ltd v Maroo* [2012] EWHC 61 at [171].

[141] *Rolled Steel Products (Holdings) Ltd v British Steel Corpn* [1985] 3 All ER 52, CA.

[142] [2006] 1 BCLC 729, HL.

[143] See [2003] 2 BCLC 129, CA, [2002] 2 BCLC 151, Ch D. In error, the lower courts had approached the matter essentially on the basis of the unconscionability of the conduct of the third party and issues of 'knowing receipt', see [2006] 1 BCLC 729 at 739, HL, a 'faulty elision of the issues' as Lord Nicholls commented (at 732). [144] [2006] 1 BCLC 729 at 740.

[145] [2008] 1 BCLC 508, CA.

[146] It is arguable that CA 2006, s 40 has no application here as it deals only with constitutional limitations on an authority which the director otherwise possesses (as discussed at **8-37** et seq) and does not apply to an exercise of power for an improper purpose. But, even if the exercise of a power for an improper purpose can be classed as a constitutional limitation (and s 171 might support that argument) the position is the same whether or not s 40 applies. A third party put on inquiry with respect to the exercise of a power for an improper purpose and who fails to inquire cannot rely on either apparent authority or the statute for protection. [147] [2008] 1 BCLC 508 at 523–4.

then under agency law or the Companies Act. The third party is not protected and if in receipt of assets/benefits under the contract must account for them,[148] for the transaction is void and the company is not bound.[149] A third party who is not aware and is not put on inquiry as to an improper purpose is able to hold the company to the transaction relying on the apparent authority of the directors to act in the way they have (assuming there are no other problems with the transaction).

8-65 It is open to the shareholders to affirm a transaction though entered into for an improper purpose, provided the transaction is not open to challenge on other grounds. Here it is necessary to consider *Bamford v Bamford*[150] where the Court of Appeal decided that an exercise of powers for an improper purpose (in that case an allotment of shares made to manipulate control within the company) was voidable and open to ratification by the shareholders by ordinary resolution. That decision looks to be wrong now, given that an improper purpose negates any authority to act so there is nothing for the shareholders to ratify (as indeed Plowman J considered at first instance in *Bamford* before being overruled by the Court of Appeal).[151] Actually, *Bamford* is still correct, even if the language of voidability is wrong. As discussed earlier, the exercise of a power for an improper purpose renders the transaction void in the sense that the directors have no authority to enter into it. A transaction void for want of authority can be subsequently authorised or affirmed by the shareholders as a matter of ordinary agency law. This is an affirmation of an exercise of a power not a ratification of the director's breach of duty which remains a separate matter though shareholders can ratify a good faith exercise of power for an improper purpose as in *Bamford*. The limits to ratification are considered at **18-31**.

8-66 Where the shareholders choose not to ratify the director's breach of duty,[152] the director is liable to account for any gain or to indemnify the company for any loss caused by the exercise of the power for an improper purpose and, in an appropriate case, the exercise of powers for an improper purpose is evidence of unfitness justifying disqualification.[153]

---

[148] See *Guinness v Saunders* [1990] BCLC 402, HL; and see *Criterion Properties plc v Stratford UK Properties LLC* [2006] 1 BCLC 729 at 732, HL; *Rolled Steel Products (Holdings) Ltd v British Steel Corpn* [1985] 3 All ER 52, CA.

[149] *Rolled Steel Products (Holdings) Ltd v British Steel Corpn* [1985] 3 All ER 52, CA.

[150] [1969] 1 All ER 969, CA.

[151] See also *Hogg v Cramphorn* [1967] Ch 254. See Nolan, 'The Proper Purpose Doctrine and Company Directors' in Rider (ed), *The Realm of Company Law* (1998), p 32 who comments that there is no good reason why a majority of shareholders should be able to ratify a colourable allotment of shares, while also noting that *Hogg* and *Bamford* are out of line with earlier authorities that an exercise of a power for an improper purpose is void: see *Punt v Symons & Co Ltd* [1903] 2 Ch 506; *Piercy v S Mills & Co Ltd* [1920] 1 Ch 77.

[152] See *Bishopsgate Investment Ltd v Maxwell (No 2)* [1993] BCLC 1282; also *Extrasure Travel Insurances Ltd v Scattergood* [2003] 1 BCLC 598 at 619.

[153] See, for example, *Re Looe Fish Ltd* [1993] BCLC 1160.

9

Duty to promote the
success of the company

A Introduction

9-1 At common law, directors were under a duty to act bona fide in what they considered to be in the interests of the company, interpreted as meaning in the interests of the shareholders as a general body, balancing the short-term interests of present members against the long-term interests of future members.[1] There was also a statutory obligation on directors to 'have regard in the performance of their functions to the interests of the company's employees in general as well as the interests of its members' (CA 1985, s 309). Additionally, the courts developed the duty to include within it a requirement for directors to have regard to the interests of creditors where the company is insolvent or of doubtful solvency and it is the creditors' money which is at risk.[2] Further control over the directors was imposed by the obligation to exercise their powers for a proper purpose and this proper purpose doctrine is retained by CA 2006, s 171 (discussed in Chapter 8) and continues to constrain directors in the exercise of their powers.

9-2 The duty to act bona fide in the interests of the company is restated in s 172(1) as a duty to act[3] to promote the success of the company,[4] as follows:

'(1) A director of a company must act in the way he considers, in good faith, would be most likely to promote the success of the company for the benefit of its members as a whole, and in doing so have regard (amongst other matters) to—

(a) the likely consequences of any decision in the long term,

(b) the interests of the company's employees,

(c) the need to foster the company's business relationships with suppliers, customers and others,

---

[1] *Re Smith & Fawcett Ltd* [1942] Ch 304 at 306; Second Savoy Hotel Investigation, Report of the Inspector (1954) HMSO; *Gaiman v National Association for Mental Health* [1971] Ch 317 at 330.
[2] *West Mercia Safetywear Ltd v Dodd* [1988] BCLC 250, CA. See also *Colin Gwyer & Associates Ltd v London Wharf (Limehouse) Ltd* [2003] 2 BCLC 153 at [74]; *Re MDA Investment Management Ltd, Whalley v Doney* [2004] 1 BCLC 217 at [70].
[3] The provision applies to 'acts' and is not limited to decision-making, formal or informal, nor to business conducted at board meetings
[4] In *Re Southern Counties Fresh Foods Ltd* [2008] EWHC 2810 at [52], Warren J noted that the old and the new formulations 'come to the same thing' with the modern formulation giving 'a more readily understood definition of the scope of the duty'. The obligation in CA 2006, s 172 is qualified by s 247 (restating CA 1985, s 719) which permits the directors to make provision for the benefit of the employees or former employees on the cessation or transfer of the business, even though such acts are not to promote the success of the company.

    (d) the impact of the company's operations on the community and the environment,

    (e) the desirability of the company maintaining a reputation for high standards of business conduct, and

    (f) the need to act fairly as between members of the company.'

This duty has effect 'subject to any enactment or rule of law requiring directors, in certain circumstances, to consider or act in the interests of creditors of the company' (s 172(3)), see **9-41**. The duty is also modified in application where the purposes of the company include purposes other than for the benefit of the members (s 712(2)), as discussed at **9-15**. As a result, those wishing to form companies with objectives other than or in addition to increasing shareholder value, such as charitable ventures, may find it useful to include objects clauses in their articles to ensure that the constitution reflects the company's priorities and guides the directors as to what constitutes 'success' in their context.

9-3 In the Parliamentary debates on the CA 2006, the Government stressed that there are not two duties in s 172—a duty to act in good faith and to have regard to the factors listed—there is only one duty: it is for directors to decide as a matter of business judgement what would be most likely to promote the success of the company for the benefit of its members as a whole and the factors are subordinate to that overriding duty.[5] In this way, it was hoped also to curb the scope for allegations of breach of duty arising from a supposed failure to have regard to one or more of the factors. For the purposes of discussion, the duty is separated in this chapter into its component elements, but this general point, that there is only one duty in s 172(1), must not be overlooked.

B Duty to act in good faith

9-4 The first point about the duty in CA 2006, s 172(1) is that it is a subjective test. A director must act in the way he considers (not what a court may consider), in good faith, would be most likely to promote the success of the company[6] for the benefit of its members and the duty applies to all acts of a director. The position was explained by Jonathan Parker J in *Regentcrest plc v Cohen*[7] as follows:

> 'The question is not whether, viewed objectively by the court, the particular act or omission which is challenged was in fact in the interests of the company; still less is the question whether the court, had it been in the position of the director at the relevant time, might have acted differently. Rather, the question is whether the director honestly believed that his act or omission was in the interests of the company. The issue is as to the director's state of mind.'

9-5 In *Regentcrest plc v Cohen*[8] the directors of a property development company waived a clawback claim (valued at £1.5m) which the company had under an agreement with the vendors of certain property to it. The vendors (S and F) were members of the board of the company and the clawback payment was waived at a meeting which took place 12 days before a petition for winding up the company was presented by a creditor. In return for

   [5] Originally, the drafting of this provision required that the directors 'must' have regard to these factors, but the Bill was amended to remove the second 'must', as it was suggested that using 'must' twice might have implied a separate duty: see HL Deb, vol 681, cols 845, 883–4 (9 May 2006).
   [6] *Re Smith & Fawcett Ltd* [1942] Ch 304 at 306.   [7] [2001] 2 BCLC 80 at 105.
   [8] [2001] 2 BCLC 80. See also *Re Welfab Engineers Ltd* [1990] BCLC 833.

waiving the claim, S and F undertook to work for the company for no remuneration for a period of years. The interested directors declared their interest and took no part in the proceedings nor did they vote in respect of the resolution to waive the clawback.

9-6 On winding up, the liquidators claimed that the directors who waived the clawback claim had acted in breach of their duty to the company and were liable to make good the loss to the company. It was alleged that the directors did not honestly believe that the waiver was in the interests of the company and that the sole reason for agreeing to it was to protect the vendors (their fellow directors) from liability.

9-7 Applying the subjective approach, the court found that the board had acted bona fide. The decisive consideration in the minds of the directors in agreeing to waive the clawback claim had been the need to maintain a united board and not to create a situation in which two of the directors were being sued by the company and were contesting the claim. The company was in difficult negotiations with its creditors at that time and suing two of its directors would have given rise to the gravest misgivings on the part of anyone concerned in trying to save the company. In voting in favour of the waiver, the court concluded that the directors honestly believed that they were acting in the best interests of the company. Accordingly, the claim for breach of duty failed.

9-8 This test does give a director considerable leeway—his duty is to act in the way he considers most likely to promote the success of the company, but if he is to establish his honest belief to that effect, then necessarily there must be some evidence that he has actually considered the matter. As the court noted in *Extrasure Travel Insurances Ltd v Scattergood*[9] (see facts at **8-58**):

> 'The fact that his alleged belief was unreasonable may provide evidence that it was not in fact honestly held at the time but, if having considered all the evidence, it appears that the director did honestly believe that he was acting in the best interests of the company, then he is not in breach of his fiduciary duty merely because that belief appears to the trial judge to be unreasonable, or because his actions happen, in the event, to cause injury to the company.'

9-9 In *Extrasure*,[10] however, the court did not believe that the defendant directors had ever formed any opinion at all,[11] never mind an honest belief, that a transfer of moneys from one company to another company in a group to enable that second company to pay a pressing creditor was in the interests of the transferor company. The court found that the directors made the transfer simply because the second company needed the money, the transferor company had the money and the creditor of the second company was pressing.

9-10 Deferring to the honest belief of the directors, if that is found to exist, reflects the traditional view that the courts must not get involved in reviewing the exercise of business judgement by the directors and, in particular, must avoid reviewing a situation with the

---

[9] [2003] 1 BCLC 598 at 619.   [10] [2003] 1 BCLC 598.

[11] [2003] 1 BCLC 598 at 632–3. See also *Re McCarthy Surfacing Ltd, Hequet v McCarthy* [2009] 1 BCLC 622 (board had not reached a bona fide decision not to pay dividends in the interests of the company, rather the board consistently failed to consider whether to declare dividends in breach of their duties). See too *Roberts v Frohlich* [2011] 2 BCLC 625 where Norris J was prepared to find that directors had acted in good faith when entering into an arrangement without a good deal of thought (preliminary stages of a property development project); he thought their conduct might call into question their competence, but did not demonstrate a lack of honest belief, see at [89].

benefit of hindsight.[12] That approach has long been summed up by the famous dictum of Lord Eldon LC in *Carlen v Drury*[13] to the effect that the court is not to be required 'to take the management of every playhouse and brewhouse in the kingdom'. As Lord Wilberforce put it:[14]

> 'There is no appeal on merits from management decisions to courts of law: nor will courts of law assume to act as a kind of supervisory board over decisions within the powers of management honestly arrived at.'

9-11   On the other hand, while the test is essentially subjective, there are clearly some limits to it[15] (not least the other duties, especially the duty in CA 2006, s 171 to act for a proper purpose), and the court will not accept in an unquestioning way a director's assertion that he acted bona fide when the facts might appear to suggest otherwise, bearing in mind Bowen LJ's comments in *Hutton v West Cork Rly Co*[16] to the effect that bona fides cannot be the sole test, for a lunatic may act perfectly bona fide yet perfectly irrationally.

9-12   The limits to the subjective test lie along the boundaries of unreasonableness and detriment to the company. In considering whether a director did act bona fide in the interests of the company, the question can be asked in terms of whether an intelligent and honest director could in the whole of the circumstances reasonably believe the transaction to be for the benefit of the company.[17] As Jonathan Parker J noted in *Regentcrest plc v Cohen*,[18] where it is clear that the act or omission under challenge resulted in substantial detriment to the company, the director will have difficulty in persuading the court that he honestly believed it to be in the company's interest. For example, in *Re Genosyis Technology Management Ltd, Wallach v Secretary of State for Trade and Industry*[19] two directors were disqualified for entering, on behalf of the company, into a settlement agreement with a customer under which the company gave up a claim for €1.25m (which was instead paid to its parent company) and gained a maximum of £166,000. Even if it was accepted that the directors honestly believed this settlement to be in the interests of the company (because the subsidiary would continue to benefit from the support of the parent), the court said they had no reasonable grounds for that belief and were in breach of their duties.[20]

9-13   Often the bad faith of the director is relatively evident. In *Neptune (Vehicle Washing Equipment) Ltd v Fitzgerald (No 2)*[21] the court had little difficulty in concluding that a sole director was not acting in the interests of the company, but was acting exclusively to further his own personal interests, when he procured an ex gratia payment to him by the company of £100,000 on termination of his service contract with the company.[22] Likewise,

---

[12] See *Regentcrest plc v Cohen* [2001] 2 BCLC 80 at 106–7; also *Facia Footwear Ltd v Hinchcliffe* [1998] 1 BCLC 218 at 228.   [13] (1812) 1 Ves & B 154 at 158.
[14] *Howard Smith Ltd v Ampol Petroleum Ltd* [1974] 1 All ER 1126 at 1131; see also *Burland v Earle* [1902] AC 83 at 93, per Lord Davey.
[15] See *Re a Company, ex p Glossop* [1988] BCLC 570 at 577, per Harman J ('It is vital…to remember that actions of boards of directors cannot simply be justified by invoking the incantation 'a decision taken bona fide in the interests of the company'').   [16] (1993) 23 Ch D 654 at 671.
[17] See *Charterbridge Corp Ltd v Lloyds Bank Ltd* [1969] 2 All ER 1185 at 119; also *Re Southern Counties Fresh Foods Ltd* [2008] EWHC 2810 at [53], per Warren J.   [18] [2001] 2 BCLC 80 at 105.
[19] [2007] 1 BCLC 208.   [20] [2007] 1 BCLC 208 at 213.
[21] [1995] BCC 1000. Cf *Runciman v Walter Runciman plc* [1992] BCLC 1084 where the court accepted that the directors had acted bona fide and in the interests of the company in extending a director's service contract for five years.
[22] See [1995] BCC 1000 at 1017 for a discussion of the evidence which showed a lack of bona fides on the part of the director which included, for example, the furtive and secretive manner in which he acted and the fact that he knew the shareholders would not have approved the payment.

a director who pays away significant sums of the company's money either knowing that the recipient is not entitled to it, or at the very least, without regard to the entitlement of the recipient, cannot be said to have an honest belief that payment was in the interests of the company.[23] Similarly, a director who releases a significant quantity of stock to a customer (who already owes the company money in circumstances where there is no real prospect of recouping it) without prepayment cannot reasonably believe the transaction to be in the interests of the company.[24]

C The success of the company for the benefit of the members as a whole

9-14 The duty in CA 2006, s 172 is expressed in terms of promoting the success of the company and 'success' is a matter for the members to determine, they define the objectives of the company and then it is for the directors to promote the success of the company in those terms.[25] The directors will be guided by their business judgement and their knowledge of the nature and purpose of the company, reinforced by anything in the company's constitution.[26] In practice, directors will probably prefer not to have anything specific on this issue in the articles so as to give themselves maximum flexibility to determine the direction of the company's business, safe in the knowledge that the courts will not second-guess their business judgement (see **9-10**). In some circumstances, such as where there are different classes of shareholders so decisions of the directors may adversely affect the interests of one class and benefit another, it is accepted that the question is not so much one of the interests of the company as one of what is fair as between different classes of shareholders.[27] Indeed, regardless of whether there are different classes as such, directors must be mindful of the need to act fairly as between members of the company (s 172(1)(f)).[28]

9-15 For most companies, 'success' is usually defined in economic terms, looking to a long-term increase in shareholder value,[29] but success may be measured in other ways. For example, where the company is formed to acquire a business or carry out a joint venture, success is measured against those objectives. Some companies also exist for purposes other than the benefit of the members and CA 2006, s 172(2) envisages that companies may have a combination of purposes, not all of which are commercial or

---

[23] See *Primlake v Matthews Associates* [2007] 1 BCLC 666 at 731 (de jure director paid out in excess of £800,000 from the company's funds to a de facto director when neither director had an honest belief that the de facto director was entitled to payment).

[24] See *Simtel Communications Ltd v Rebak* [2006] 2 BCLC 571 at 596 (an intelligent and honest man in the position of the director could not in all the circumstances have reasonably believed that the transaction was for the benefit of the company).   [25] See HL Deb, vol 678, GC258 (6 February 2006).

[26] CA 2006, s 171(a) requires a director to act in accordance with the constitution and the constitution is broadly defined for the purposes of directors' general duties as including the articles and all binding decisions of the members, whether formal or informal (ss 17, 257), so the directors may have to take into account any guidance in ordinary resolutions of the shareholders in determining what can be regarded as 'success' in a particular company: see HL Deb, vol 678, GC 255–8 (6 February 2006).

[27] *Mills v Mills* (1938) 60 CLR 150 at 164, per Latham CJ; *Howard Smith Ltd v Ampol Petroleum Ltd* [1974] 1 All ER 1126 at 1134.

[28] *Mutual Life Insurance Co of New York v Rank Organisation Ltd* [1985] BCLC 11; *Re BSB Holdings Ltd (No 2)* [1996] 1 BCLC 155.   [29] See HL Deb, vol 678, GC 258 (6 February 2006).

profit-orientated.[30] The application of s 172(1) in such circumstances is modified by s 172(2) in the manner explained in *Stimpson v Southern Private Landlords Association*.[31] In this case, concerning permission to continue a derivative claim (see **18-24**), the respondent company was not a trading company, but a not-for-profit organisation formed as a company limited by guarantee rather than a company limited by shares. It operated essentially as a trade association where the members did not have any interest in its assets and remained members only for so long as they paid their subscriptions. The court noted that CA 2006, s 172(2) contemplates two different situations: where the objects of the company consist of purposes other than the benefit of its members (in which case the director's duty is to achieve those purposes) and where the purposes of the company include purposes other than the benefit of its members. In the latter case, a director must act in a way that he considers in good faith would be most likely to promote the success of the company for the benefit of its members as a whole whilst at the same time achieving these other purposes and, if there is a conflict between those dual purposes, a balancing exercise is required of the director in the exercise of his honest business judgement.[32]

9-16 The duty is to promote the success of the company and, for most purposes, this means promote the interests of the entity which typically calls for a balancing of the short and long-term interests of the shareholders[33] but promoting the interests of the entity also calls for a wider perspective as is evident in the factors listed in s 172 and this is so even in the context of a takeover bid when it might be thought that the only relevant interest is the interests of the current shareholders.[34] Not only must the focus be on the entity under this duty, but the Government is looking for a greater focus by companies and boards and shareholders on the long-term prospects of the entity[35] rather than short-term returns, a focus on the latter having been identified as one of the contributory factors to the financial crisis of 2007–08. In that spirit, the Department for Business, Innovation and Skills has consulted on this issue of whether there is a sufficient long-term focus in UK companies and equity markets or whether shareholders are unduly focused on short-term profitability and share prices and whether boards too take a short-term view, driven in part by pressure from the shareholders, but also by executive incentive plans where bonuses, for example, might be determined by short-term gains.[36]

---

[30] CA 2006, s 172(2) provides that where or to the extent that the purposes of the company consist of or include purposes other than the benefit of its members, sub-s (1) has effect as if the reference to promoting the success of the company for the benefit of its members were to achieving those purposes.

[31] [2010] BCC 387.

[32] [2010] BCC 387 at 398–399; *Explanatory Notes to the Companies Act 2006*, para 330.

[33] This was very much the position at common law, see n 1.

[34] This point is reinforced by amendments to the Takeover Code in 2011 which clarified that, despite market perceptions to the contrary, the offer price is not the determining factor for the board of the offeree company when giving its opinion on any takeover offer (Takeover Code, note 1 to rule 25.2) and the board is not precluded from taking into account any other factors which it considers relevant and these would certainly include the interests of the employees. For the background to this change, see **26-44** Consultation Paper, Code Committee of the Takeover Panel, 'Review of Certain Aspects of the Regulation of Takeover Bids', Proposed Amendments to the Takeover Code', PCP 2011/1, March 2011, paras 4.1–4.3.

[35] See generally Keay who has explored the difficulties in adopting either a shareholder or stakeholder model and who argues cogently for greater consideration of the sustainability of the entity, see Keay 'Ascertaining the Corporate Objective: An Entity Maximisation and Sustainability Model' (2008) 71 MLR 663; Keay, 'The Ultimate Objective of the Company and the Enforcement of the Entity Maximisation and Sustainability Model' (2010) JCLS 35.

[36] See BIS, 'A Long-term Focus for Corporate Britain, A call for evidence' (October 2010) paras 4.24 and 6.5. The majority of respondents thought that boards did focus on long-term strategy but had to deal with increasing short-term pressures from investors, analysts and markets focused on short-term returns; they also thought

9-17 Where the company is one of a group, the requirement remains that the directors must act to promote the success of the separate legal entity, the individual company, and not look solely to the overall interests of the group, indeed to disregard the interests of the particular company is grounds for possible disqualification, see **3-57**. It may be, of course, that the most effective way to promote the success of the company is to promote the success of the group. For example, it may be appropriate for a subsidiary to provide financial support for the rest of a group, though the group is in financial difficulty, when the continued prosperity and the very existence of the subsidiary may depend on the group remaining in business, as is commonly the case.[37] A decision of the directors of a subsidiary company to continue lending to the group could then still be a decision taken bona fide in the interests of the company, see **3-54**.

The nominee director and the interests of his appointor

9-18 The obligation to promote the interests of the company also raises issues about the role of nominee directors appointed to represent particular interests.[38] It is common commercial practice for directors to be appointed to represent, for example, the interests of the venture capitalist who may be a significant but not majority shareholder and who wants some protection for his investment, or the joint venture partner who wants to ensure the company properly pursues that joint venture, or the lender who wants to keep the company's activities under close scrutiny. The issue also arises with respect to group companies where the holding company appoints nominee directors to the boards of subsidiary entities. As noted earlier, the director must act in the interests of the subsidiary, not the group, though their interests may coincide.

9-19 The position under the CA 2006 (which makes no specific mention of nominee directors) is that all directors owe their general duties to the company (s 170(1)) and, as discussed, s 172 requires a director to act in a way most likely to promote the success of the company. The theoretical position then is clear, once appointed the nominee director's obligations lie to the company and its interests, not to the appointor and his interests. In practice the position is more complicated with the appointor expecting that his interests will be safeguarded, his voting intentions carried out, and even, perhaps, that he will have access to information from the company's boardroom. But these commercial expectations raise several legal difficulties. For example, a nominee director (or any director) must respect the company's confidential information and is not entitled to convey such information to his appointor without the consent of the company. A director is required to exercise independent judgement under s 173 and so a nominee director cannot vote automatically in accordance with the wishes of his appointor, though the position may be modified by the company's constitution, a point discussed at **10-50**. Another duty likely to cause difficulties for the nominee director is the no-conflict duty (s 175(1)), though that duty can be managed in that s 175(4)(b) allows for the authorisation of conflicts of interest by disinterested directors and s 177 merely requires conflicts between a director and his company in respect of proposed transactions to be disclosed to the other directors. At the practical

that CA 2006, s 172 and the UK Corporate Governance Code were positive influences on a more long-term approach by boards, see BIS, 'A Long Term Focus for Corporate Britain', Summary of responses, March 2011, paras **10–11**. There findings prompted BIS to set up the Kay Review of Equity Markets and Long-term Decision Making which published an interim report in February 2012 (URN 12/631), see Chapter 3 especially.

[37] See *Facia Footwear Ltd v Hinchcliffe* [1998] 1 BCLC 218 at 225–6, 228–9, see **3-54**; also *Nicholas v Soundcraft Electronics Ltd* [1993] BCLC 360.

[38] See Ahern, 'Nominee Directors' Duty to Promote the Success of the Company: Commercial pragmatism and legal orthodoxy' [2011] 127 LQR 118.

level, what probably matters most for nominee directors is this ability to be released from the no-conflict duty and they are probably less concerned about any general release (and, possibly, have no expectation that they could or should be released) from their core obligations under s 172. The problems of a nominee director with respect to conflicts are no different from any director with a conflict of interest, the main difference being that the nominee's conflict will usually be evident from the outset. As conflicts of interest are discussed in detail in Chapter 11, that discussion is not repeated here.

9-20 The main issue to be considered here is the extent to which the nominee director is required by s 172 to promote the success of the company when his appointor may expect, wish, even demand, that the nominee act to promote the interests of the appointor. The issue came before the Court of Appeal recently in *Re Neath Rugby Ltd (No 2), Hawkes v Cuddy*[39] where the court confirmed that:[40]

- the fact that a director has been nominated by someone does not, of itself, impose a duty on the director owed to his nominator;

- though the nominated director may owe duties to his nominator arising from some other relationship (such as being an officer or employee of the nominator) or by reason of a formal or informal agreement, that cannot detract from the director's duty to the company when he is acting as director;[41]

- the director may take the interests of his appointor into account, provided that his decisions as a director are in what he genuinely believes to be the best interests of the company.

To a large extent this ruling confirms the pre-existing position, noted earlier in the context of groups, that the director's duty is to the company and the overriding duty is to act in the interests of the company, but that a nominee director may have regard to the interests of the appointor so long as those interests are consistent with promoting the success of the company.[42] As the duty to promote the success of the company is a (predominantly) subjective duty, that combination of obligation to the company with the subjective belief of the director may offer some leeway for the nominee director to accommodate his duty to the company and the commercial expectations of his appointor.

9-21 Turning to CA 2006, s 173(2) and the permitted modification of the duty to exercise independent judgement, and bearing in mind the cumulative nature of a director's duties (s 178), the constitution could make provision for the nominee director to consult his

---

[39] [2009] 2 BCLC 427, CA at [32]–[33], affirming on this point Lewison J's ruling in [2007] EWHC 2999, [2008] BCC 390.

[40] Cuddy had been appointed a director of O Ltd by N, a 50% shareholder in O Ltd. Cuddy was also a de facto director of N. At issue was the extent of the obligations owed by Cuddy to N when acting as a director of O Ltd.

[41] See *Scottish Cooperative Wholesale Society v Meyer* [1959] AC 324 at 366–7; *Kuwait Asia Bank EC v National Mutual Life Nominees Ltd* [1990] BCLC 868 at 892.

[42] Ahern, n 38, sees this positive statement of the position as evincing some pragmatism in mediating between strict legal principle and commercial reality (p 131) while acknowledging that there is no great distance between the old absolutist approach and this stance which Ahern labels as a 'corporate primacy approach'. It is possible to find some evidence of this approach in earlier cases too, see, for example, *Nicholas v Soundcraft Electronics Ltd* [1993] BCCLC 360 at 366–7. The board of a subsidiary company which included nominees appointed by the parent company was not in breach of duty in failing to sue the parent company for sums due to the subsidiary, a decision which the court considered to be a sensible business judgement on the board's part in the interests of both companies, given that the subsidiary's continued existence depended on the group remaining afloat and the parent company could not afford to pay the subsidiary the amount due.

appointor and to suspend his independent judgement in favour of his appointor's views and to vote in accordance with the appointor's view, but only to the extent that this is consistent with his duty under s 172 to promote the success of the company.[43] Section 172 is a statement of the fundamental obligation of loyalty of the fiduciary to the company and a modification of s 173(1) cannot negate the obligation to comply with s 172, a point reinforced by *Re Southern Counties Fresh Foods Ltd, Cobden Investments Ltd v RWM Langport Ltd.*[44] In this case counsel unsuccessfully argued that a nominee director may advance the interests of his appointor rather than the company if the shareholders unanimously so agree. While accepting that certain directors' duties can be qualified by the unanimous assent of the shareholders, Warren J thought, rightly it is suggested, that it was doubtful whether, as a matter of English law, it is possible to release a director from his general duty to act in the best interests of the company.[45]

D Having regard to various factors

9-22 One of the initially controversial elements of CA 2006, s 172 is the list of factors in s 172(1) (a)–(f), set out at **9-2**, to which a director must have regard (amongst other matters) when acting in the way he considers, in good faith, would be most likely to promote the success of the company for the benefit of the members as a whole.

Background–the pluralist debate

9-23 The issue for the Company Law Review (CLR) was whether directors should be required to adopt a more inclusive approach and consider the interests not just of the company's shareholders, employees and creditors, as was the position at common law, but broader constituencies such as its suppliers, customers and the community at large.[46] The CLR defined the issue as one of the scope of company law, meaning for what purposes and in whose interests should companies be run, which for the CLR essentially involved a choice between enlightened shareholder value and a pluralist approach.[47]

9-24 The enlightened shareholder value approach is based on the idea that maximising shareholder value is in principle the best means of securing overall prosperity.[48] The pluralist approach is based on the idea that a company should serve a wider range of interests not subordinate to, or as a means of achieving, shareholder value, but as valid in their own

---

[43] To the extent that his conduct is inconsistent with the interests of the company, i.e. where a director favours the interests of his appointor, it may be grounds for an unfairly prejudicial petition under CA 2006, s 994, see *Scottish Cooperative Wholesale Society v Meyer* [1959] AC 324 at 366–7.

[44] [2008] EWHC 2810.

[45] [2008] EWHC 2810 at [67]. Warren J did think it might be possible, where the nominee is acting as negotiator for his appointor in agreeing a deal with the company, that the shareholders by unanimous agreement might relieve the nominee in those negotiations from an obligation to act to promote the success of the company, assuming that the nominee is excluded from board discussions or votes on the matter. But it is not clear that such a scenario should be regarded as a relief from the application of s 172, rather the duty engaged in that situation is primarily the no-conflict duty and the application of that duty can be tempered by shareholder authorisation under s 180(4)(a) or by independent directors under s 175(4)(b).

[46] See Goldenberg, 'Shareholders v Stakeholders: The Bogus Argument' (1998) 19 Co Law 34; Plender, *A Stake in the Future: the Stakeholding Solution* (1997); RSA Inquiry, *Tomorrow's Company* (1995); Parkinson, *Corporate Power and Responsibility* (1993) Ch 9.

[47] Company Law Review, *Completing the Structure* (2000), para 3.1; also *Strategic Framework* (1999), Ch 5; *Developing the Framework* (2000), Chs 2 and 3; *Completing the Structure* (2000), Ch 3.

[48] Company Law Review, *Strategic Framework* (1999), para 5.1.11.

right, i.e. the interests of a number of constituencies should be advanced without the interests of a single constituency (shareholders) prevailing.[49] This approach would enable, and indeed require, the directors to override shareholders' interests in circumstances where this would be in the interests of the company as widely defined by those stakeholders.

9-25   As the enlightened shareholder value approach is essentially the status quo, the argument for the CLR centred on whether the pluralist approach should be adopted. Following consultation, the CLR found that there were strong philosophical arguments against such an approach on the grounds that:

- it would not necessarily achieve its objective and would have the effect of leaving the directors with a broad (and largely unpoliced) managerial discretion;

- it was unnecessary since broader interests such as employees and creditors are included within the range of interests to which directors had to have regard at common law and it would suffice simply to clarify the legal position;

- the pluralist approach would achieve external benefits through company law which are better served by specific legislation applicable to all businesses (and not just registered companies) on planning, environmental and competition law, etc;

- there was a risk that the pluralist approach (by diluting the obligation owed to shareholders) would enable directors to frustrate takeovers against the wishes of the shareholders and so distort the operation of the market for corporate control which is an important mechanism in holding directors to account.[50]

9-26   More generally, there were concerns that any alteration to a pluralist approach would turn directors away from being business decision-makers and into moral, political and economic arbiters.[51]

9-27   A number of technical difficulties with the pluralist approach were also identified including:[52]

- the need to decide which interest should prevail if there was a conflict;

- the need to frame directors' duties differently to take account of the shift in approach;

- the need to alter board composition to reflect the differing interests;

- the need to rethink the division of power between the board and the general meeting as well as the ability of one interest group (the shareholders) to appoint and remove the board; and

- the proper approach to the enforcement of such a duty (a key objection as far as the CLR was concerned).[53]

9-28   Following consultation, the CLR found support for and duly recommended retaining the existing common law duty on directors to operate companies for the benefit of their shareholders,[54] but that the duty should be framed in an inclusive way which would give due recognition to the importance of considering the long-term implications of decisions

---

[49] Company Law Review, *Strategic Framework* (1999), paras 5.1.12–5.1.13.
[50] Company Law Review, *Developing the Framework* (2000), para 3.24; see also *Strategic Framework* (1999), paras 5.1.25–5.1.29; also HL Deb, vol 678, GC273 (6 February 2006).
[51] See Company Law Review, *Developing the Framework* (2000), para 2.21.
[52] Company Law Review, *Developing the Framework* (2000), paras 3.26–3.31; and Ch 2.
[53] See Company Law Review, *Completing the Structure* (2000), para 3.5.
[54] Company Law Review, *Developing the Framework* (2000), para 2.11.

and of fostering effective relationships over time with employees, customers and suppliers and in the community more widely.[55] The CLR rejected the pluralist approach as neither workable nor desirable[56] and it considered that a more inclusive statement, while it would make little difference to the common law position, would have a major influence on changing behaviour and the climate of decision-making.[57] The Government was in favour of this type of approach which it considered would also make the law clearer to directors than any duty defined in terms of acting bona fide in the interests of the company.[58] The result is a broad, aspirational, statement of the core obligation of loyalty owed by a company director.[59]

The inclusive statement of relevant factors

9-29 As part of their duty to promote the success of the company, the directors are then required by CA 2006, s 172(1) to have regard to all of the factors on the list (set out at **9-2**),[60] but they are not precluded from considering other matters ('amongst other matters'). For example, the list makes no reference to short-term considerations, only long-term consequences, but this does not preclude directors considering short-term matters. Likewise, there is no mention of pension matters, but this issue would fall within the requirement to have regard to the interests of the employees. Some of the factors merely reflect the pre-existing position—for example, the directors' obligation to have regard to the likely consequences of any decision in the long term (s 172(1)(a));[61] to have regard to employees' interests (s 172) (1)(b));[62] and the need to act fairly as between members of the company (s 172(1)(f)).[63]

9-30 This duty to act fairly between members is a significant protection for minority shareholders. The leading authority is *Mutual Life Insurance Co of New York v Rank Organisation Ltd*[64] where the company decided to make an issue of shares to its existing ordinary shareholders excluding any ordinary shareholders from the United States and Canada. The exclusion was imposed in order to avoid the onerous regulatory requirements of those

---

[55] Company Law Review, *Developing the Framework* (2000), para 2.11, Ch 2, paras 3.17–3.31; *Completing the Structure* (2000), paras 3.1–3.24; *Final Report*, vol 1 (2001), paras 3.5–3.10.

[56] Company Law Review, *Completing the Structure* (2000), para 3.5.

[57] See Company Law Review, *Developing the Framework* (2000), para 3.58, but see Worthington, 'Reforming Directors' Duties' (2001) 64 MLR 439 at 445–8.

[58] The White Paper *Modernising Company Law* (Cm 5553-I, 2002), paras 3.3–3.5.

[59] See the discussion in Hannigan, 'Reconfiguring the No Conflict Rule, Judicial Strictures, a Statutory Restatement and the Opportunistic Director' (2011) 23 SAcLJ 714 at 723–6 as to whether this duty is a fiduciary duty, as it is commonly described.

[60] See comments by Minister Margaret Hodge, HC Official Report, SC D (Company Law Reform Bill), 13 July 2006, col 591—the duty is not a pluralist duty: directors are required to have regard to the factors laid out when promoting the success of the company for the benefit of its members but a director who puts one of those factors ahead of his overarching duty to promote the success of the company acts in breach of that duty to the company.

[61] Second Savoy Hotel Investigation, Report of the Inspector (1954) HMSO; *Gaiman v National Association for Mental Health* [1971] Ch 317 at 330, per Megarry J.

[62] Previously CA 1985, s 309. In the context of a takeover bid for the company, the obligation to have regard to employee interests is underscored by changes in 2011 to the Takeover Code which require the board of the offeree company when giving its opinion to the shareholders of the offeree company on the takeover offer to include its views on the effect of implementation of the offer on all the company's interests, including, specifically, employment and its views on the offeror's strategic plans for the offeree company and their likely repercussions on employment: Takeover Code, rule 25.2.

[63] *Mutual Life Insurance Co of New York v Rank Organisation Ltd* [1985] BCLC 11.

[64] [1985] BCLC 11; see also *Re BSB Holdings Ltd (No 2)* [1996] 1 BCLC 155 at 249.

jurisdictions. The excluded shareholders' objections were rejected by the court. Goulding J ruled that the directors' powers were subject to two limitations, that their powers must be exercised in good faith in the interests of the company *and* that they must be exercised fairly as between different shareholders. Both elements were satisfied on the facts. The directors honestly believed that raising capital in this way was advantageous to the company and gave a prospect of continuing benefit to all the shareholders. The exclusion of the North American shareholders did not affect their shares nor the rights attached to them and was due to a difficulty resulting only from their own personal situation. The law does not require the interests of the company to be sacrificed to the particular interests of a group of shareholders, as *Mutual Life Insurance v Rank* makes clear, but it does require the director to consider the particular position within the company. In *Re BSB Holdings Ltd (No 2)*[65] this duty required the directors (when undertaking a complex financing agreement) to have considered the effect of the proposals on the different groups of shareholders within the company and a failure to do so was a breach of duty, but on the facts, the failure did not amount to unfairly prejudicial conduct[66] for the purposes of (now) CA 2006, s 994.

9-31   The significance of this obligation to act fairly as between the shareholders was highlighted in *Re Sunrise Radio Ltd, Kohli v Lit*[67] where a rights issue was made by a company for the genuine purpose of raising capital, though it was made at a time when it was likely that the minority shareholder would not take up the shares and therefore faced dilution (from a 15% holding to 8.33%). Furthermore, the rights issue was priced at par when the evidence was that the shares, which were taken up by the majority shareholder, could have been issued for a significantly higher price so the minority shareholder suffered a dilution in the value as well as in the size of her holding. The court held that, even if the directors had acted in accordance with the duty to exercise their powers for a proper purpose (s 171), they were in breach of their duty to act fairly between shareholders (s 172(1)(f)). The court noted that what is the proper price for shares will necessarily fall within a range of possibilities, but the board is required to consider all these matters fairly in the interests of all groups of shareholders and having regard to the foreseeable range of responses from the shareholders to the rights issue. Where it is known or foreseen that the minority may not be able or wish to subscribe, the directors in the interests of even-handedness and fairness must consider the price which can be extracted from those who are willing to subscribe or be in breach of their duties to the company.[68] On the facts, issuing the shares at par without considering any alternative, particularly when the directors (as the majority shareholders) benefited appreciably from the issue at par, was a breach of duty and unfairly prejudicial to the petitioner.[69]

9-32   The remaining factors: the need to foster business relationships, (s 172(1)(c)); the impact of operations on the community and the environment (s 172(1)(d)); and the desirability of maintaining a reputation for high standards of business conduct (s 172(1)(f)) are new in the sense that they have not previously been explicitly articulated in this way and, as noted at **9-28**, they are intended to give effect to the desire for a more inclusive definition of this duty. On the other hand, as was pointed out in the Parliamentary debates, these factors are matters which any well-informed and conscientious director would have regard to in

---

[65] [1996] 1 BCLC 155.   [66] See [1996] 1 BCLC 155 at 251.   [67] [2010] 1 BCLC 367.
[68] [2010] 1 BCLC 367 at [95].
[69] See also *Re McCarthy Surfacing Ltd, Hequet v McCarthy* [2009] 1 BCLC 622 (distribution of profits via a bonus scheme for management so denying the minority shareholders any opportunity to participate was a breach of the duty to act fairly between the shareholders).

any event.[70] The difference now is that there is a duty on directors to have regard to each of these factors when acting on behalf of the company.

9-33 There is the possibility, even a probability, that in any given scenario there will be a conflict between two or more of the factors. An example would be where there is a possible take-over bid for the company which will give the shareholders a significant financial return, but which will result in job losses, or where a decision to continue with opencast mining might be to the advantage of the shareholders and the employees, but to the detriment of the environment, and so on. The resolution of such conflicts is a matter for the business judgement of the directors, acting in good faith and exercising appropriate care and skill[71] as was made clear in *Shepherd v Williamson*.[72] In this case, a whistle-blowing director had to balance, the court said, the deleterious consequences of his conduct as far as relations with the company's major customer was concerned (disclosing anti-competitive behaviour to them) and the potential for damage to the company's employees if a contract with that customer was not gained (s 172(1)(a), (b) and (c)), against the company's reputation as a whole (s 172(1)(e)) in the light of the fact that the company had given the OFT earlier undertakings about its conduct which it was at risk of breaching. Balancing those considerations was a matter for the director's subjective judgement in compliance with his duty to promote the success of the company.[73] The court concluded that the director could not be criticised for wanting to ensure that a contract was not obtained by the use of collusive activities (so avoiding a problem with the OFT), irrespective of whether it meant that the company might lose the contract altogether (and so cause a loss of business).

Honest and careful regard to the factors

9-34 There was some criticism in the Parliamentary debates as to the limited nature of the requirement 'to have regard' to the factors and the Government was careful to emphasise that that standard must be measured against the overall requirements for directors to act in good faith and with care and skill which means that directors cannot pay mere lip service to the statutory requirements.[74] There were also initial concerns that directors, in their anxiety to demonstrate that they had complied with s 172(1), would look to document every step in the decision-making process, something which would be particularly problematic, given that not every decision is taken at a board meeting and given that the section is not limited in application to formal decision-making. Indeed the converse is the position with relatively few matters decided formally by the board compared to the large variety of matters decided upon every day by the directors.

---

[70] See DTI, *CA 2006, Duties of Company Directors, Ministerial Statements* (June 2007), p 2: '…pursuing the interests of shareholders and embracing wider responsibilities are complementary purposes, not contradictory ones' (Minister Margaret Hodge).

[71] Lowry suggests that an effect of the requirement to have regard to constituencies outside the narrow realm of members' interests is that it will allow directors to defend almost any bona fide decision aimed at promoting the success of the company, see Lowry, 'The Duty of Loyalty of Company Directors: Bridging the accountability gap through efficient disclosure' (2009) CLJ 607 at 621. Far from restricting directors' decision-making, the effect of CA 2006, s 172 may be to free up their discretion.

[72] [2010] EWHC 2375 at [103]–[104].

[73] The court was considering the director's conduct in the context of an unfairly prejudicial petition brought by him based in part on his exclusion from the company following his whistle-blowing to the customer.

[74] What is required is a 'proper consideration' of the issues, that the directors think about them rather than merely tick boxes, according to Minister Margaret Hodge: see HC Deb, vol 450, col 789, (17 October 2006). See also *Explanatory Notes to the Companies Act 2006*, para 328; HL Deb, vol 681, GC 846 (9 May 2006).

9-35 The Government's position was that nothing new or additional is required, just the normal documentation which would accompany any decision of the directors, since CA 2006, s 172(1) merely identifies the factors which a reasonable director exercising care and skill in the carrying out of his functions would consider anyway.[75] This position is reinforced by advice from the influential GC100 group which from the outset advised companies not to adopt the practice of referring to CA 2006, s 172 in the board minutes.[76] The GC100 advice made the point that, prior to the CA 2006, board minutes did not record that the directors, in reaching decisions, had complied with their duties and nothing in the CA 2006 requires a change to that practice. That advice appears to have been heeded and there is little evidence of companies compiling copious documentation to ensure compliance with s 172(1). No doubt, on occasion, in the largest companies and for the most complex or contentious matters, directors may want to make sure that formal board decisions are challenge-proof so board minutes may refer to the s 172 factors. In that type of context, directors may want to bolster those decisions with references to internal papers, perhaps even consultants' reports and advice from outside experts, so as to show, not only that they had regard to the factors, but that they exercised appropriate care and skill in considering them. That practice would be the exception rather than the norm,[77] however, and post-implementation, decision-making by directors appears to have continued much as before. As discussed below, the duty set out in s 172 is not enforceable by any of the stakeholder groups, only by the company or shareholders bringing a derivative claim on behalf of the company, so litigation is likely to be rare and that too reinforces the status quo. Honest decision-making based on reasonable grounds is what is required. Assuming the directors reach that standard, they are at no greater risk of liability under s 172 than they were under their previous obligation to act bona fide in the interests of the company. It also has to be borne in mind that the courts will not second-guess business decisions of directors, see **9-10**, and that remains the position under s 172.

9-36 Some of the early concerns surrounding the possible impact of CA 2006, s 172 related to the fact that CA 2006, Pt 11 provides, for the first time, for a statutory derivative claim (see Chapter 18). Part 11 allows for claims by any member against any director for a breach of any duty owed by a director to the company (s 260(3)).[78] Recovery is solely for the benefit of the company and not for the individual claimant. The concern was that shareholder activists would look to use the combination of the new derivative procedure and s 172 to challenge business decisions of directors on the basis of an alleged failure to have regard to the factors set out in the section. A derivative claim could be used to seek judicial

---

[75] See HL Deb, vol 681, GC 841 (9 May 2006) where Lord Goldsmith, speaking for the Government, refused to accept that anything about CA 2006, s 172 makes it is necessary to have some particular form of paper trail. See also HC Official Report, SCD (Company Law Reform Bill), cols 591–2.

[76] The GC100 group essentially represents general counsel and company secretaries of the FTSE 100 companies.

[77] For an interesting consideration of whether lawyers' advice to corporate clients on the scope and implementation of CA 2006, s 172 may change boardroom practice in this way, see Loughrey, Keay, Cerioni, 'Legal Practitioners, Enlightened Shareholder Value and the Shaping of Corporate Governance' (2008) 8 JCLS 79.

[78] A member needs the permission of the court to bring the claim and various thresholds are set in CA 2006, Pt 11. In particular, when considering applications for permission the court has to consider whether a person acting in accordance with his duty under CA 2006, s 172 would seek to continue the claim and the importance which he would attach to continuing the claim (see ss 263(2)(a), 263(3)(b)). In applying those provisions, the courts have been clear that directors, when weighing up the factors in s 172, are essentially reaching a commercial decision which the courts are ill-equipped to take and that some directors could legitimately conclude one way on an issue whereas others, equally legitimately, could take the opposite view: see *Iesini v Westrip Holdings Ltd* [2011] 1 BCLC 498 at [85]–[86], and the discussion at **18-30**.

review, in effect, of a commercial decision of management. As discussed at **18-11**, in practice there has not been any significant use of the derivative claim, especially not in relation to traded companies where activist litigation of this nature (if it was to occur) would be most likely and these concerns about the combined effect of s 172 and the introduction of a statutory derivative claim have proved unfounded to date.

9-37 Of course, even if shareholders brought a derivative claim and could establish a failure to consider a particular factor or factors, it is not clear what an appropriate remedy might be or how any loss might be quantified. For example, if it was established that the directors failed to take into account the interests of the employees in a particular matter and 50 of them had lost their jobs, there would be a breach of duty on the part of the directors but no loss suffered by the company to which the duty is owed.

The link to the business review

9-38 The proper place to refer to the CA 2006, s 172 factors is in the business review part of the directors' report[79] and a business review is required of all companies other than small companies (s 417(1)), see **16-25**.[80] The purpose of the review is expressly stated to be 'to inform members of the company and help them assess how the directors have performed their duty under section 172' (see s 417(2)).[81]

9-39 The business review must contain a fair review of the company's business and a description of the principal risks and uncertainties facing the company. It must provide a balanced and comprehensive analysis of the development, performance and position of the company's business during and at the end of the financial year, consistent with the size and complexity of the business. More detailed requirements are imposed on quoted companies which must include in the business review, to the extent necessary for an understanding of the development, performance or position of the company's business, information on, *inter alia*, environmental matters (including the impact of the company's business on the environment), the company's employees, and social and community issues, all of which are reflected in s 172 as factors to which the directors must have regard.

9-40 The role assigned to the business review by CA 2006, s 417 reflects the Government's intention that the restated duty in s 172 should bring about a cultural change in how companies perceive their responsibilities,[82] rather than generate pointless bureaucratic

---

[79] The Department for Business, Innovation and Skills has indicated that it intends to replace the directors' report with a more focused Strategic Report, with these business review disclosures being retained and appearing in that report: see BIS, *The Future of Narrative Reporting, Consulting on a new reporting framework* (September 2011), URN 11/945, para 2.9, also discussion at **16-27**.

[80] The CLR was keen to require large public and private companies to report widely on the business and its affairs as part of their annual reporting requirements. See Company Law Review, *Final Report*, vol 1 (2001), paras 3.28–3.45; *Completing the Structure* (2000), paras 3.7–3.10; 3.32–3.42; *Developing the Framework* (2000), paras 2.19–2.26, 3.85, 5.74–5.100; *Strategic Framework* (1999), paras 5.1.44–5.1.47.

[81] That disclosure is an integral element in reinforcing s 172, while also helping shareholders fulfil their stewardship role, is highlighted by the suggestion from the Sharman Inquiry that the directors' assessment of whether the entity is a going concern should be addressed also in the proposed Strategic Report (which will replace the business review) as part of the discussion of the business strategy and the principal risks facing the entity. Sharman sees addressing these issues of risk and the solvency of the entity as integral to the directors' duty under s 172, see The Sharman Inquiry, *Going Concern and Liquidity Risks: Lessons for Companies and Auditors, Preliminary report and recommendations of the Panel of Inquiry* (November 2011), paras 7, 13.

[82] See Minister Margaret Hodge, n 70, '...s 172 is a "radical departure" from the previous law which catches a cultural change...': see Introduction to Ministerial Statements.

procedures restricting decision-making. The focus on disclosure of the company's conduct in the business review is designed to force companies to acknowledge and respond to the interests of the stakeholders affected by their activities. Of course, corporate social responsibility (CSR) is now an important issue in its own right to which large companies, in particular, pay considerable regard. To some extent, therefore, this aspect of s 172 has been overtaken by events. Ideas which seemed radical (e.g. the disclosure of CSR-type activities) when the Company Law Review was set up (in March 1998) are now commonplace and that is the difficulty in trying to assess the significance of the changes effected by CA 2006, s 172. At one level, it may be said that the law is playing catch-up with a developing business culture which does look to a much wider agenda and broader constituencies than merely a company's own shareholders. In the years since the Company Law Review focused on these issues, large companies, especially multinational companies, have attached ever-increasing importance to the value of their reputations and their brands and arguably have done so quite independently of any legal obligations arising by virtue of s 172.

E Considering the creditors' interests

9-41 A director's duty to act in the way he considers, in good faith, would be most likely to promote the success of the company for the benefit of its members as a whole has effect 'subject to any enactment or rule of law requiring directors, in certain circumstances, to consider or act in the interests of creditors of the company' (CA 2006, s 172(3)). The obligation in s 172(1) is qualified ('subject to'), but only 'in certain circumstances' and it may only require 'consideration' of the creditors' interests as opposed to an obligation to act in their interests ('to consider or act').[83]

9-42 The relevant enactments which require directors to consider or act in the interests of creditors are the Company Directors Disqualification Act 1986 and the Insolvency Act 1986. Trading to the detriment of creditors' interests warrants a finding of unfitness and disqualification under the CDDA 1986, s 6 (see **25-87**) and potential liability for wrongful trading under IA 1986, s 214, i.e. continuing to trade after a point in time when a director knew or ought to have known that there was no reasonable prospect of avoiding insolvent liquidation, see **25-18**[84] The IA 1986 also regulates transactions which adversely affect creditors' interests such as transactions at an undervalue (IA 1986, s 238, see **25-37**) and preferences (IA 1986, s 239, see **25-50**). It should be said that the duty to have regard to creditors' interests in certain circumstances does not mean that the company must cease trading when the company is in financial difficulties. The directors are entitled to continue to trade if they honestly believe it is possible that the company can trade its way out of the financial difficulties (an outcome that would most protect creditors), but if the company continues to trade past a point in time when the directors knew or ought to have concluded that there was no reasonable prospect of avoiding insolvent liquidation,[85] the directors may be personally liable for wrongful trading under IA 1986, s 214.

---

[83] For a detailed analysis of this issue, see Keay, *Company Directors' Responsibilities to Creditors* (2007) which draws on numerous articles by the author on this topic.

[84] It is a defence for a director to show that he took every step with a view to minimising the potential losses to the company's creditors as he ought to have taken: IA 1986, s 214(3).

[85] See *Secretary of State v Creggan* [2002] 1 BCLC 99 at 101, CA; cf *Secretary of State v Gill* [2006] BCC 725.

The development of the requirement

9-43 At common law, the requirement to consider or act in creditors' interests had its origins in influential Australian and New Zealand decisions to this effect.[86] This approach was endorsed by the Court of Appeal in *West Mercia Safetywear Ltd v Dodd*[87] where Dillon LJ approved the following statement by the New South Wales Court of Appeal in *Kinsela v Russell Kinsela Pty Ltd*:[88]

> 'In a solvent company the proprietary interests of the shareholders entitle them as a general body to be regarded as the company when questions of the duty of directors arise...But where a company is insolvent the interests of the creditors intrude. They become prospectively entitled, through the mechanism of liquidation, to displace the power of the shareholders and directors to deal with the company's assets. It is in a practical sense their assets and not the shareholders' assets that, through the medium of the company, are under the management of the directors pending either liquidation, return to solvency, or the imposition of some alternative administration.'[89]

9-44 In the *West Mercia* case a director had arranged for his company to partially repay a debt due from the company to its parent company. The reason he had organised the payment of £4,000 was that he had personally guaranteed the debts of the parent company and the part-payment of the debt reduced his personal liabilities to that extent. The court found that the director in causing the company, which he knew to be insolvent, to make this payment at that time had acted in disregard of the interests of the general creditors of the company and in breach therefore of his duty to the company. He was ordered to repay £4,000 with interest.

9-45 This obligation to have regard to the interests of creditors in this way, though initially the subject of some criticism,[90] is now a well-recognised element of a director's duties.[91] It might have been expected therefore that the obligation would have been developed and reflected in the statutory statement of directors' duties, but this turned out to be a matter on which, surprisingly, the Company Law Review had little of substance to say.[92] For its part, the Government is content to leave the matter to develop at common law,[93] as CA 2006, s 172(3) provides.

---

[86] Especially *Walker v Wimborne* (1976) 50 ALJR 446 and *Nicholson v Permakraft (NZ) Ltd* [1985] 1 NZLR 242. See Dawson, 'Acting in the Best Interests of the Company—For whom are Directors "Trustees"?' (1984) 11 NZULR 68.

[87] [1988] BCLC 250. See also *Brady v Brady* [1988] 2 All ER 617, HL; *Re Horsley & Weight Ltd* [1982] 3 All ER 1045 at 1055–6.

[88] (1986) 4 ACLC 215 at 223, per Street CJ.   [89] [1988] BCLC 250 at 252.

[90] See Sealy, 'Directors' Duties—An Unnecessary Gloss' (1988) CLJ 175 at 177.

[91] For example, see *Yukong Line Ltd of Korea v Rendsburg Investments Corp of Liberia* [1998] 2 BCLC 485 (removal of funds by a director from insolvent company's bank account with a view to putting those funds beyond the reach of the company's sole creditor was a clear breach of the director's fiduciary duties); also *Re Capitol Films Ltd, Rubin v Cobalt Pictures Ltd* [2011] 2 BCLC 359 at [49].

[92] Initially the CLR was not inclined to include any specific obligation to creditors though there was concern that, without some reference to creditors, the statutory statement of directors' duties would not be exhaustive. Some limited proposals were included belatedly in the Final Report, but rejected in any event by the Government which preferred to proceed as set out in CA 2006, s 172(3). See Company Law Review, *Developing the Framework* (2000), paras 3.72–3.73; also the draft statutory statement of directors' duties in Company Law Review, *Final Report*, vol 1 (2001), Annex C, paras 8 and 9; and, *Final Report*, vol 1 (2001), paras 3.12–3.20.   [93] See *Modernising Company Law* (Cm 5553-I, 2002), paras 3.8–3.14.

Trading at the creditors' risk

9-46 The main issue of concern to directors is the point in time at which this obligation to consider or act in the interests of the creditors supplements or displaces the duty to act for the benefit of the members as a whole. Clearly, where the company is solvent, there is no need for directors to consider or act in the interests of the creditors who will get paid in the usual way or who can otherwise enforce their contractual rights to payment. Clearly, where the company is insolvent, the interests of the creditors should be the focus of the directors' decisions and conduct. The difficult area is when the company is under financial pressure so it may weave in and out of 'doubtful solvency' or 'near insolvency'. For example, a company may lose a major customer and endure a difficult period before subsequently gaining a new order when its finances improve. In some sectors, such as the airline industry, companies may flirt with insolvency because of extraneous circumstances such as soaring oil prices. Depending on the duration of the problem, companies may survive or may collapse. Yet the imposition of an obligation to have regard to creditors' interests in precisely that 'zone of insolvency' or in the 'vicinity of insolvency', to use the American terminology, is essential to curb the incentives for directors at that stage to take on excessive risks (basically because as far as they are concerned all is probably lost).[94]

9-47 In one of the influential New Zealand decisions, *Nicholson v Permakraft (NZ) Ltd*,[95] Cooke J thought creditors were entitled to consideration if the company was insolvent, or near-insolvent, or of doubtful solvency, or if a contemplated payment or other course of action would jeopardise its solvency. In *Re MDA Investment Management Ltd, Whalley v Doney*,[96] the court thought the obligation to have regard to creditors' interests arose where the company was in 'a dangerous financial position' or the company was 'in financial difficulties to the extent that its creditors are at risk'.[97] In *Facia Footwear v Hinchcliffe*,[98] Sir Richard Scott thought that, given 'the parlous financial state of the company', the directors had to have regard to the interests of the creditors when paying out company's funds (at a time when it was hopelessly insolvent) to support the continued trading of other companies in the group.[99] Much discussion has centred on trying to refine these thresholds into a defined point in time when this duty to consider creditors' interests arises, but it is difficult to devise a precise legal test which will identify that point in time and instead, as we shall see, directors must maintain a degree of vigilance about the company's financial position and respond accordingly.

Potential liabilities of directors

9-48 As a practical matter, the issue of whether the directors did trade in disregard of creditors' interests is always an exercise in hindsight since the duty in CA 2006, s 172(3) only has an impact if the company actually becomes insolvent and goes into either liquidation or

---

[94] See generally Davies, 'Directors' Creditor—Regarding Duties in Respect of Trading Decisions in the Vicinity of Insolvency' (2006) 7 EBOR 301. Also Milman, 'Strategies for Regulating Managerial Performance in the Twilight Zone: Familiar Dilemmas, New Considerations' [2004] JBL 493.

[95] [1985] 1 NZLR 242 at 249, 250.   [96] [2004] 1 BCLC 217 at 247–8.

[97] See too *Colin Gwyer & Associates Ltd v London Wharf (Limehouse) Ltd* [2003] 2 BCLC 153 at [74] (where the company is insolvent or of doubtful solvency or on the verge of insolvency and it is the creditors' money which is at risk, the directors must consider the interests of the creditors as paramount).

[98] [1998] 1 BCLC 218.

[99] [1998] 1 BCLC 218 at 228; and note the comments by Sir Richard Scott on the importance of not applying hindsight in judging the directors' conduct and of recognising that the interests of the creditors sometimes lie in conduct which ensures a continuation of trading, see also **3-54** et seq.

administration. Only then will the question of whether the directors had sufficient regard for creditor interests come to the fore as a liquidator or administrator looks to see if he can establish a liability on the directors' part in respect of the dissipation of company assets in breach of that duty (imposing a personal liability may be helpful to the creditors collectively, especially if the directors have liability insurance).

9-49 The reason why it is a matter only for a liquidator or administrator is that directors' duties are owed to the company (CA 2006, s 170(1), see **7-14**) and this duty is not owed directly to the creditors.[100] An individual creditor is not entitled to sue for breach.[101] Enforcement occurs indirectly (if at all) through misfeasance proceedings (for breach of duty) by liquidators under IA 1986, s 212 (see **25-3**), or wrongful trading proceedings under IA 1986, s 214 (see **25-18**) or challenges to transactions on the basis of their being a preference (see **25-50**) or at an undervalue (see **25-37**). In *Roberts v Frohlich*,[102] for example, liability for wrongful trading and misfeasance (on the basis of failing to act in the interests of the company) arose where the court found that the directors' wilful blindness to the company's mounting financial problems meant that they could not have had an honest belief that continued work on a development site (the company's business was property development) was in the company's interests meaning, the court said, given the parlous state of its finances, the paramount interests of the company's creditors. Disqualification proceedings under the CDDA 1986 may also ensue (see **25-87**). For example, in *Re Mea Corporation Ltd, Secretary of State for Trade and Industry v Aviss*[103] directors were disqualified in essence for causing or allowing each of three companies to trade to the detriment of creditors. At a time when those companies were under increasing pressure from creditors and were each unable to pay their debts as they fell due (i.e. were insolvent), the directors allowed such cash as was available to be paid out to other companies in which one of the directors had a substantial personal interest. In *Re Genosyis Technology Management Ltd, Wallach v Secretary of State for Trade and Industry*[104] two directors were disqualified for entering, on behalf of the company, into a settlement agreement with a customer under which the company gave up a claim for €1.25m (which was instead paid to its parent company) and gained a maximum of £166,000. Given the company was insolvent at the time of the settlement, the court found the directors in breach of their duty to have regard to the creditors' interests.

9-50 A director must focus on whether the company is insolvent[105] or whether a contemplated payment or other course of action would jeopardise its solvency and put its creditors at risk[106] so administration or liquidation (and therefore actions against the directors by administrators or liquidators) is likely. In either scenario (insolvent or transaction would jeopardise solvency), if the directors are to diminish the risk of subsequent personal liability, they must act in a way consistent with their obligations under CA 2006, s 172(3) to consider or act in the creditors' interests rather than the interests of the members as a whole. Where creditor interests are relevant, the director's duty is to have regard to the interests of the

---

[100] *Multinational Gas and Petrochemical Co v Multinational Gas and Petrochemical Services Ltd* [1983] 2 All ER 563 at 585; *Yukong Line Ltd of Korea v Rendsburg Investments Corp of Liberia* [1998] 2 BCLC 485. See also *Kuwait Asia Bank EC v National Mutual Life Nominees Ltd* [1990] 3 All ER 404, PC.

[101] *Yukong Line Ltd of Korea v Rendsburg Investments Corp of Liberia* [1998] 2 BCLC 485.

[102] [2011] 2 BCLC 625 at [94], [112]–[113]. See also *Re Oxford Pharmaceuticals Ltd* [2009] 2 BCLC 485.

[103] [2007] 1 BCLC 618 at 635, 643.

[104] [2007] 1 BCLC 208.

[105] See IA 1986, s 123: a company may be insolvent on a cash flow basis (being unable to pay its debts as they fall due) or on a balance sheet basis (liabilities exceed assets).

[106] See *Nicholson v Permakraft (NZ) Ltd* [1985] 1 NZLR 242 at 249, 250, per Cooke J.

creditors as a class and, if a director acts to advance the interests of a particular creditor, without believing the action to be in the interests of creditors as a class, he will commit a breach of duty, regardless of whether any of the specific provisions of the Insolvency Act 1986, such as s 239 (preferences), are in point and the fact that the conditions laid down by a section such as s 239 are not met does not, of itself, preclude a finding of breach of duty, but may have a bearing on the remedy available for breach of that duty.[106a] To determine whether the company is insolvent or whether a contemplated payment or course of action would jeopardise its solvency, the directors need to know or be aware of the company's financial position. This should not be a problem for them since a variety of obligations ensure that the directors do indeed know and appreciate the company's financial position.

9-51 First, every company must keep adequate accounting records sufficient to disclose, with reasonable accuracy, at any time, the financial position of the company at that time (CA 2006, s 386(1), (2)(b)). Directors must prepare annual accounts and large and medium-sized companies must have those accounts audited which should ensure an appreciation of the company's position.[107] Secondly, the directors are obliged under s 174 to exercise care, skill and diligence in the performance of their functions as directors which requires, *inter alia*, an appropriate level of knowledge of the company's affairs and its financial position at any time (see **10-24**).[108] Thirdly, it is implicit in many of the factors to which directors must have regard under s 172(1) that the directors need to be aware of the company's financial position. In considering any matter and in order to have proper regard to the interests of the employees, or to the need to foster business relationships with suppliers, or to the impact of the company's operations on the community, a director needs to know the company's financial position. Indeed, more broadly, it is difficult to see how any director could honestly fulfil his duty to promote the success of the company if he is unaware of the company's financial position (at least in general terms).

9-52 Against the backdrop of these various obligations, a reasonable director acting in accordance with the requirements of CA 2006, s 174 as to care and skill should be able to form a view as to whether the company is insolvent or whether a contemplated payment or other course of action would jeopardise its solvency. That consideration determines whether the director should continue to look to his obligations under s 172(1) or whether s 172(3) comes into play.

[106a] *GHLM Trading Ltd v Maroo* [2012] EWHC 61, Ch D.

[107] Small companies are exempt from an audit (CA 2006, s 477, see **16-36** et seq) unless they choose to have one and the downside to the exemption may be that the directors do not have outside accounting/audit advice which would draw their attention to the company's financial position. The risk of directors breaching the obligation to have regard to creditors' interests may therefore be greater in an audit exempt company, but whether a liquidator or administrator would pursue a remedy is another matter. Disqualification is the most likely sanction.

[108] See *Re Westmid Packing Services Ltd, Secretary of State for Trade and Industry v Griffiths* [1999] 2 BCLC 704; *Re Galeforce Pleating Co Ltd* [1999] 2 BCLC 704; *Re Landhurst Leasing plc, Secretary of State for Trade and Industry v Ball* [1999] 1 BCLC 286; *Re Park House Properties Ltd* [1997] 2 BCLC 530.

10

Duty of care, skill and independent judgement

A Introduction

10-1 It is important that, in addition to their fiduciary obligations, directors should be subject to duties of care and skill appropriate to the modern commercial world, bearing in mind the increased emphasis on higher standards of corporate governance. The duty of care, skill and diligence is not a fiduciary duty, as CA 2006, s 178(2) makes clear. It is a statutory statement of a common law duty of care governed by the normal common law rules as to liability for negligence. The most often cited explanation of the distinction between fiduciary and other duties is that given by Millett LJ in *Bristol & West Building Society v Mothew*[1] where he emphasised that fiduciary duties are duties peculiar to fiduciaries, breach of which attracts legal consequences different from those consequent upon the breach of other duties. Breach of fiduciary duties attracts equitable remedies which are primarily restitutionary or restorative rather than compensatory, as would be the case on a breach of a duty of care. Millett LJ went on to make the point that the core of fiduciary duties is loyalty and a breach of fiduciary duty is primarily about disloyalty, so mere incompetence is not enough.[2] The duty of care and skill in CA 2006, s 174 is therefore a reflection of the common law duty of care and liability for breach may lie in tort or additionally in contract where a director has a contract of employment as it is an implied contractual term that an employee will exercise reasonable care and skill in the performance of his duties.[3]

10-2 Prior to the CA 2006, the courts had looked to IA 1986, s 214(4) as an accurate statement of the general standard of care and skill expected of directors,[4] applying it beyond the confines of that section (which concerns wrongful trading).[5] Section 214(4) requires the conduct of a director to be measured against the standard of a reasonably diligent person having both the general knowledge, skill and experience that may reasonably be expected of a person carrying out the same functions as are carried out by that director in relation to the company, and the general knowledge, skill and experience that that director has.

---

[1] [1996] 4 All ER 698 at 711–12.

[2] [1996] 4 All ER 698 at 711–12. See also *Extrasure Travel Insurances Ltd v Scattergood* [2003] 1 BCLC 598 at 618: 'Fiduciary duties are concerned with concepts of honesty and loyalty, not with competence' (Deputy Judge Jonathan Crow). [3] *Lister v Romford Ice & Cold Storage Ltd* [1957] 1 All ER 125.

[4] See *Re D'Jan of London Ltd, Copp v D'Jan* [1994] 1 BCLC 561; *Norman v Theodore Goddard* [1991] BCLC 1028; *Re Landhurst Leasing plc, Secretary of State for Trade and Industry v Ball* [1999] 1 BCLC 286 at 344; *Cohen v Selby* [2001] 1 BCLC 176 at 183.

[5] Liability for wrongful trading arises where a director is found to have continued trading after a point in time when he knew or ought to have concluded that there was no reasonable prospect of the company avoiding insolvent liquidation, see **25-18**.

That approach was endorsed by the Law Commission,[6] the Company Law Review[7] and the Government[8] and is reflected in CA 2006, s 174 which, with minimal changes,[9] reproduces the wording of IA 1986, s 214(4). The standard of care, skill and diligence therefore remains as previously established and the existing case law remains relevant (CA 2006, s 170(4)).

10-3 Though the standard expected is now clearly identified, the content of this duty is still under development by the courts and it is not always easy to draw from the cases a comprehensive and coherent statement of what is required of directors. To some extent there is a dearth of authority. For a period, much valuable guidance on the duty of care and skill was found in the large number of reported cases on disqualification proceedings brought against a director of an insolvent company on the ground that his conduct has shown him to have fallen below the standards of probity and competence (i.e. care and skill) expected of a director.[10] But disqualification is now mainly dealt with by administrative undertakings (see **25-72**) with the result that this source of authorities on care and skill has largely dried up.

10-4 The importance of the disqualification authorities reflects the fact that, in practice, directors are rarely sued for negligence in the management of a company's affairs. As with the other duties of directors, enforcement of the duty of care and skill takes place, if at all, when the company goes into insolvent liquidation or administration where a liquidator or administrator may consider it worthwhile to pursue a director for misfeasance (see **25-3**) or wrongful trading under IA 1986, s 214 (see **25-18**). As noted, disqualification proceedings may also be brought on the grounds of unfitness, though here the relevant standard is more frequently described as a standard of 'probity and competence', rather than stated in the traditional terms of care and skill,[11] but if the allegation is incompetence without dishonesty, it must be incompetence to a high degree[12] (see **25-84**).

10-5 Of course, for many small companies, family ties are usually stronger than concerns about standards of care and skill. For solvent private companies, in so far as allegations of negligence arise, they tend to do so in the context of unfairly prejudicial petitions under CA 2006, s 994 and with limited success (see **17-48**). In part there is a judicial view that directors are elected by the shareholders and if the shareholders choose to appoint poor managers then, short of insolvency, that is a matter for them and, of course, in many small companies the directors and the shareholders are the same people. Another constraint on judicial enthusiasm for negligence claims against directors is their long-held view that the courts should not interfere or second-guess directors on matters of business judgement (see **9-10**) and frequently what is presented as a claim in negligence is merely a disagreement on business strategy or decisions. Furthermore, as the courts point out, directors

---

[6] Law Commission, *Company Directors: Regulating Conflicts of Interests and Formulating a Statement of Duties* (Law Comm No 261), 1999, Ch 5.

[7] Company Law Review, *Final Report,* vol 1 (2001), p 346 and Annex C; and see *Developing the Framework* (2000), pp 40–3.   [8] See *Modernising Company Law* (Cm 5553-I, 2002), paras 3.2–3.7.

[9] 'Diligence' is expressly included in the section but the case law had already established the need for a director to exert and apply himself in the conduct of the company's affairs and the courts do penalise those found to be inattentive to their duties: see, for example, *Re Park House Properties Ltd* [1997] 2 BCLC 530, discussed at **10-18**.   [10] CDDA 1986, s 6.

[11] See *Re Landhurst Leasing plc, Secretary of State for Trade and Industry v Ball* [1999] 1 BCLC 286 at 344; *Secretary of State for Trade and Industry v Gray* [1995] 1 BCLC 276 at 286.

[12] *Re Sevenoaks Stationers (Retail) Ltd* [1991] 1 BCLC 325 at 337; *Re Barings plc (No 5)* [1999] 1 BCLC 433 at 483–4, aff'd [2000] 1 BCLC 523, CA.

are not trustees and they are appointed precisely in order to take risks in an environment of risk which is, after all, the purpose of the limited company.

10-6 Issues of competence are central, however, to corporate governance concerns in respect to public companies, especially in the wake of the financial crisis.[13] The UK Corporate Governance Code emphasises the need for an effective board with an appropriate balance of skills, experience, independence and knowledge of the company to enable the directors to discharge their duties and responsibilities effectively (see **5-12**).[14] Also, the board is expected to undertake an annual evaluation of its own performance and that of its committees and individual directors.[15] Reminding the shareholders that it is for them to remove directors if not satisfied with their performance, the UK Code now recommends that all directors of FTSE 350 companies be subject to annual election,[16] so ensuring that shareholders have frequent opportunities to address competence issues.

10-7 Occasionally and exceptionally, a public company with a new board in place may sue the company's former directors for negligence and such litigation can have an impact on directors,[17] even if the litigation is rarely prosecuted to fruition, and non-executive directors in particular are exercised by the reputational damage done even by threatened litigation. There were some concerns that the statutory derivative claim under CA 2006, Pt 11 (which for the first time allows derivative claims to be brought on the basis of negligence) would encourage litigation but, as discussed at **18-11**, this has not occurred. Any attempt to pursue a claim in negligence faces the difficulty of establishing that a duty of care was owed in respect to the kind of loss which has occurred,[18] something which can be problematic in this context where the line is frequently blurred, as noted, between poor commercial judgements and actual negligence.[19] The net result is that it is rare for directors to be sued directly for breach of the duty of care and skill. However, the general duties imposed on directors under CA 2006, Pt 10, Ch 2, are cumulative (s 179) and conduct which is in breach of care and skill may equally be open to challenge on other grounds such as that the director has acted for an improper purpose in breach of s 171, or has failed to promote the success of the company in breach of s 172, or failed to exercise independent judgement as required by s 173. In *Re Bradcrown Ltd, Official Receiver v Ireland*,[20] for example, a finance director was in breach of his duty of care in abdicating all responsibility for a complex transaction whereby the company transferred away its assets valued at £3.7m for no consideration. In so acting the director also failed to act bona fide in the interests of the company and he used his powers for an improper purpose in divesting

---

[13] See Hannigan, 'Board Failures in the Financial Crisis – Tinkering with Codes and the Need for Wider Corporate Governance Reforms,' Part 1 (2011) 32 Co Law 363; Part 2 (2012) 33 Co Law 35.

[14] FRC, UK Corporate Governance Code (2010) Main Principle B.1, and see **5-12**.

[15] FRC, UK Corporate Governance Code (2010) Main Principle B.6, and see **5-15**.

[16] FRC, UK Corporate Governance Code, CP B.7.1.

[17] See, for example, the *Equitable Life* case. For the story of this litigation which was ultimately dropped, see *Equitable Life Assurance Society v Bowley* [2004] 1 BCLC 180; Reed (2006) 27 Co Law 170.

[18] See *Re Continental Assurance Co of London plc* [2007] 2 BCLC 287 at 437, 445; see also *Bishopsgate Investment Management Ltd v Maxwell (No 2)* [1993] BCLC 814 at 829–30. Generally see *Customs and Excise Commissioners v Barclays Bank* [2006] 4 All ER 256; *MAN Nutzfahrzeuge AG v Freightliner Ltd* [2008] 2 BCLC 22, CA; also Arden LJ in *Johnson v Gore Wood & Co* [2003] EWCA Civ 1728 at [91]; [2003] All ER (D) 58 (Dec).

[19] See, for example, *Roberts v Frohlich* [2011] 2 BCLC 625—directors of property development company made poor business decisions and misjudged the level of risk which is not the same as negligence, at [108], but continuing on with the business in circumstances where there was mounting evidence of significant financial difficulties was not the conduct of reasonably competent directors and was a breach of the duty of care and skill, at [102].   [20] [2001] 1 BCLC 547 at 561.

the company of its assets for no consideration. In many cases therefore where liability is established in respect of a breach of fiduciary duty, it would also have been possible to have brought a claim for breach of care and skill. As noted at **10-1**, there are certain practical advantages in pursuing a breach of fiduciary duty rather than a claim in negligence.

B The statutory standard of care, skill and diligence

Collective and individual responsibilities

10-8 The starting point is the collective responsibility of the board for the management of the company's affairs, but equally directors' duties are 'personal and inescapable' duties,[21] and so within that collective responsibility, each director must meet the appropriate standard of care, skill and diligence. Much cited on this point is the statement of Lord Woolf MR in *Re Westmid Packing Services Ltd, Secretary of State for Trade and Industry v Griffiths* as follows:[22]

> '…the collegiate or collective responsibility of the board of directors of a company is of fundamental importance to corporate governance under English company law. That collegiate or collective responsibility must however be based on individual responsibility. Each individual director owes duties to the company to inform himself about its affairs and to join with his co-directors in supervising and controlling them.'

10-9 The standard expected is laid down in CA 2006, s 174:

> '(1) A director of a company must exercise reasonable care, skill and diligence.
>
> (2) This means the care, skill and diligence that would be exercised by a reasonably diligent person with—
>
> > (a) the general knowledge, skill and experience that may reasonably be expected of a person carrying out the functions carried out by the director in relation to the company, and
> >
> > (b) the general knowledge, skill and experience that the director has.'

10-10 The standard set is an objective minimum standard, that of a reasonably diligent person who has taken on the office of director, set in the context of the functions undertaken, with that objective minimum standard capable of being raised (but not lowered) in the light of the particular attributes of the director in question.[23] For example, if a director is a professional person, such as a chartered accountant, s 174(2) requires him to meet the standard to be expected of a reasonably diligent director carrying out the functions carried out by him in that company and having that personal attribute. The personal attributes of the director cannot lower the standard set in s 174(2)(a) for that would mean that a subjective standard would always apply, determined by those personal attributes. On the other hand, the standard set is of the reasonably competent director in the position undertaken and with those personal attributes and the courts will not allow the

---

[21] See *Secretary of State for Trade and Industry v Goldberg* [2004] 1 BCLC 557 at 608, per Lewison J, relying on *Re Westmid Packing Services Ltd, Secretary of State for Trade and Industry v Griffiths* [1998] 2 BCLC 646 at 654.

[22] [1998] 2 BCLC 646 at 653, a view endorsed by the courts on many subsequent occasions: see, for example, *Re Kaytech International plc, Secretary of State for Trade and Industry v Kaczer* [1999] 2 BCLC 351 at 425, CA; *Re Landhurst Leasing plc* [1999] 1 BCLC 286 at 346; *Re Barings plc (No 5)* [1999] 1 BCLC 433 at 486.

[23] See *Re Brian D Pierson (Contractors) Ltd* [2001] 1 BCLC 275 at 302.

test to be used to impose unrealistically high levels of skill. For example, non-executive directors of an insurance company can be expected to appreciate the general accounting requirements applicable to insurance companies, but cannot be required to be specialists in sophisticated accounting issues pertaining to insurance companies, even if they possess accounting qualifications.[24]

Functions undertaken

10-11 Flexibility in the application of the statutory standard is maintained by the obligation to have regard to the functions carried out by the director in relation to the company in question. This point was emphasised by Jonathan Parker J in *Re Barings plc (No 5), Secretary of State for Trade and Industry v Baker (No 5)*[25] where he stressed that the competence of the director must be assessed in the context of and by reference to the role in the management of the company which was in fact assigned to him or which he in fact assumed and by reference to his duties and responsibilities in that role.[26] He went on:[27]

> 'Thus the existence and extent of any particular duty will depend upon how the particular business is organised and upon what part in the management of that business the respondent could reasonably be expected to play (see *Bishopsgate Investment Management Ltd (in liq) v Maxwell (No 2)* [1993] BCLC 1282 at 1285 per Hoffmann LJ). For example, where the respondent was an executive director the court will assess his conduct by reference to his duties and responsibilities in that capacity. Thus, while the requisite standard of competence does not vary according to the nature of the company's business or to the respondent's role in the management of that business—and in that sense it may be said that there is a 'universal' standard—that standard must be applied to the facts of each particular case.'

10-12 By focusing on the functions which an individual undertakes or which are entrusted to him, the court is able to calibrate the content of the duty in the light of the size and complexity of the business and the position of the individual director.[28] In this way, it is possible to accommodate within the same legal standard the managing director of a multi-million pound banking company, the non-executive director of an insurance company and a teenage director of a family company carrying on business in a limited way. It is clear that there are certain minimum functions expected of any director who takes on the office of director which include compliance with the statutory requirements with regard to the maintenance of proper accounting records and the preparation of accounts.[29] The relevant functions beyond the minimum will depend on the post held, the tasks assigned and how the company organises its affairs. It is also necessary to consider the exercise of the functions in the context of the company's financial position and the care and skill required and the acts which might justifiably be undertaken in a solvent company might

---

[24] See *Re Continental Assurance Co of London plc* [2007] 2 BCLC 287 at 401–2.

[25] [1999] 1 BCLC 433, aff'd [2000] 1 BCLC 523, CA.

[26] [1999] 1 BCLC 433 at 484, aff'd [2000] 1 BCLC 523 at 535, CA. See also *Re Continental Assurance Co of London plc, Secretary of State for Trade and Industry v Burrows* [1997] 1 BCLC 48 at 57–8; *Re Produce Marketing Consortium Ltd (No 2)* [1989] BCLC 520 at 550; *Re Vintage Hallmark Ltd, Secretary of State for Trade & Industry v Grove* [2007] 1 BCLC 788 at 793.   [27] [1999] 1 BCLC 433 at 484.

[28] See *Re Produce Marketing Consortium Ltd (No 2)* [1989] BCLC 520 at 550.

[29] See *Re Produce Marketing Consortium Ltd (No 2)* [1989] BCLC 520 at 550; *Re Queens Moat Houses plc, Secretary of State for Trade and Industry v Bairstow (No 2)* [2005] 1 BCLC 136.

be quite different from what would be appropriate in relation to a company of doubtful solvency.[30]

The functions of an executive director

10-13 If a director is an executive director, his conduct must be considered against what could be expected of a reasonably diligent person carrying out his duties and responsibilities as an executive director in that company. A managing director, for example, would have general responsibility to oversee the activities of the company.[31] An executive director would normally have responsibility (subject to any appropriate delegation) for common management tasks such as signing cheques. A reasonably diligent director in that position would not sign blank cheques,[32] nor cheques of such a large amount in the context of the company's business as would put him on inquiry without first seeking a full explanation as to their purpose,[33] nor sign a simple insurance proposal form without checking the accuracy of its contents.[34] If the director performs a special function, such as a 'finance director', the special skills expected of a person in that capacity are to be expected of him[35] and a failure to meet those standards will be a breach of his individual responsibilities. In *Re AG (Manchester) Ltd, Official Receiver v Watson*[36] the court was particularly critical of a finance director who allowed an inner group of directors to take key decisions on dividends and other financial matters without reference to the board as a whole. Such conduct fell below the standard expected of a finance director who, in a private company, is often an essential brake, the court said, on the financial ambitions of the shareholders. It was the finance director's duty, whatever the conduct of the other directors, the court said, to ensure that the company was run in accordance with the articles and the Companies Act.[37]

The functions of a non-executive director

10-14 Much of the interest in this area concerns the standards expected of non-executive directors in public companies where the courts must balance the need to promote higher standards of corporate governance against concerns that too high a standard will deter able people from accepting directorships. The functions of non-executive directors in public companies are considered in detail in Chapter 5 where it was noted that the non-executive directors play particularly important roles on matters such as risk management and internal controls (see at **5-28**) and in constructively challenging the executive directors, all of which will permeate judicial perceptions of the standards expected of them.[38]

---

[30] See *Roberts v Frohlich* [2011] 2 BCLC 625 at 659.

[31] See *Re Continental Assurance Co of London plc* [2007] 2 BCLC 287 at 443.

[32] *Dorchester Finance Co Ltd v Stebbing* [1989] BCLC 498. When signing cheques, a director is only required to satisfy himself that the cheque has been authorised by the board. He need not verify that the money is in fact required for the particular purpose specified or is indeed expended on that purpose, assuming that the cheque comes before him for signature in the regular way having regard to the usual practice of that company: *Re City Equitable Fire Insurance Co Ltd* [1925] Ch 407 at 452.

[33] *Secretary of State for Trade and Industry v Swan* [2005] BCC 596 at 617–18, see **10-39**.

[34] *D'Jan of London Ltd, Copp v D'Jan* [1994] 1 BCLC 561 (the effect of the lack of care in this instance was to deprive the company of insurance cover when the policy was invalidated because of inaccuracies in the proposal form).   [35] *Re Brian D Pierson (Contractors) Ltd* [2001] 1 BCLC 275 at 310.

[36] [2008] 1 BCLC 321.   [37] [2008] 1 BCLC 321 at 373–4.

[38] See *Re Continental Assurance Co of London plc* [2007] 2 BCLC 287 at 443, where Park J accepted that one of the duties of non-executive directors is to monitor the performance of the executive directors; also *Re Kaytech International plc, Secretary of State for Trade and Industry v Kaczer* [1999] 2 BCLC 351 at 407 (Rimer J): 'The functions of a non-executive lie in the monitoring of the manner in which the executives are

10-15 For example, a non-executive director of a listed company approached by senior executives about possible financial wrongdoing within the company was not acting as a reasonably careful and diligent director if he merely discussed the concerns with the chief executive and the finance director and took no further steps in the matter, as happened in *Secretary of State for Trade and Industry v Swan*,[39] a disqualification case. In this case, the non-executive director was also the deputy chairman of the company and a member of the company's audit committee, the company was a listed company, and the matter concerned financial impropriety involving significant sums of money. The allegations were serious, the sources reliable and merely consulting the finance director was an inadequate response, the court thought, in a situation where 'decisive, courageous and independent action' (including consulting his fellow non-executives and the auditors) was required of a non-executive director. The director's want of competence, the court said, related to a failure to pursue an enquiry with sufficient vigour.[40] Given that his conduct fell below that expected of someone in his position and with his experience, he was disqualified.

Functions in a family business

10-16 As to the extent of a director's functions, of course, it is not the case that all directors must be involved in all of the company's affairs. A director is not under any obligation to undertake a definitive part in the conduct of the company's business and roles vary according to the size and business of the particular company.[41] Equally, a director cannot reduce his role to such an extent that he is in effect making no or only the most minimal contribution to the collective responsibility of the directors to supervise and control the company's business,[42] not even if it is a family company.

10-17 In such businesses, there is a tendency for a spouse or offspring to take on a directorship without ever playing any role (or indeed intending to play any role) in the management of the company's affairs. Typically such individuals regard themselves as simply having a nominal or honorific title. The courts do not accept that a director may have such a role. As was noted in *Re Brian D Pierson (Contractors) Ltd*:[43]

> 'The office of director has certain minimum responsibilities and functions, which are not simply discharged by leaving all management functions, and consideration of the company's affairs to another director without question, even in the case of a family

---

conducting the affairs of the company'; also Langley J in *Equitable Life Assurance Society v Bowley* [2004] 1 BCLC 180 at 189 '…plainly arguable that a company may reasonably at least look to non-executive directors for independence of judgment and supervision of executive management'.

[39] [2005] BCC 596.   [40] [2005] BCC 596 at 625.

[41] See *Re Barings plc (No 5), Secretary of State for Trade and Industry v Baker (No 5)* [1999] 1 BCLC 433 at 436.

[42] See *Re Westmid Packing Services Ltd, Secretary of State for Trade and Industry v Griffiths* [1998] 2 BCLC 646 at 653. An incentive to act may be found in the many provisions of the CA 2006 which impose criminal sanctions on the company and on any 'officer in default'. An officer is in default if he authorises or permits, participates in *or fails to take all reasonable steps* to prevent the contravention: s 1121(3). On this basis (the definition is different from that which previously applied, CA 1985, s 730(5), which was limited to officers who knowingly and wilfully authorised or permitted the contravention), the inactive, ill-informed, director may find it difficult to escape liability for contraventions by others.

[43] [2001] 1 BCLC 275 at 309–10. The case concerned a director's wife who though also a director and drawing remuneration as such had only a very limited clerical role in the company. The court found that Mrs Pierson, in ignoring the signals of financial difficulties and failing to appreciate even the questions that ought to have been asked about the company's affairs, was instrumental in the company continuing to trade and therefore was liable for wrongful trading under IA 1986, s 214.

company...One cannot be a "sleeping" director; the function of "directing" on its own requires some consideration of the company's affairs to be exercised.'

10-18   In *Re Park House Properties Ltd*[44] the directors of a company were a husband, his wife and his two teenage children. The husband was responsible for the conduct of the affairs of the company and he was disqualified as unfit on the grounds of continuing to trade in disregard of creditors' interests, non-filing of company accounts and allowing the company to expend £173,000 on an extension to a property, the benefit of which would go to the director personally rather than the company. His wife played no part whatever in the affairs of the company and his son and daughter played only very marginal roles in its affairs. None of them received any remuneration as directors. Nevertheless, all three were disqualified. The court held that each of them, by virtue of sheer inactivity over the period of their respective directorships, had been guilty of conduct which made him or her unfit. Neuberger J emphasised that:[45]

> 'The law imposes statutory and fiduciary duties on directors of companies and even where, as here, the respondents received no payment, and any advice given to [the husband] would have been unlikely to have been acted on, they cannot escape from those duties. [Their] complete inactivity in relation to, and complete uninvolvement with, the running of the company, the financial problems of the company, the preparation and filing of the accounts, and the decision to spend a substantial sum on the construction of the extension...lead to the conclusion that, in the absence of special circumstances, they are unfit.'

10-19   In *Re Galeforce Pleating Co Ltd*[46] a textile company collapsed with losses of approximately £438,000. The directors of the company included a husband and wife and one other. In the disqualification proceedings brought against the wife, she pleaded that she had 'a most negligible actual involvement in the running of the company'.[47] Disqualifying her for a period of five years, the court emphasised that it was not a sufficient discharge of a director's responsibilities to maintain 'a negligible actual involvement' in the affairs of the company. So long as an individual continues to hold office as a director and, in particular to receive remuneration from it, it is incumbent upon that person, the court said, to inform himself as to the financial affairs of the company and to play an appropriate role in the management of its business. If a director is not prepared to discharge his responsibilities properly, the appropriate course is to resign. Furthermore, the court stressed that it is not an excuse for a director to say that the running of a company is left to his or her spouse.[48]

10-20   For the same reasons, the courts are unwilling to accept that someone can be a professional nominee director acting for hundreds, if not thousands, of companies in return for an annual fee.[49] Such a person cannot realistically be carrying out any functions with regard to those companies.

---

[44] [1997] 2 BCLC 530. See also *Re Westminster Property Management Ltd (No 2), Official Receiver v Stern (No 2)* [2001] BCC 305 at 352–5.   [45] [1997] 2 BCLC 530 at 555–6.
[46] [1999] 2 BCLC 704.   [47] [1999] 2 BCLC 704 at 716.   [48] [1999] 2 BCLC 704 at 716.
[49] See *Official Receiver v Vass* [1999] BCC 516. See also *Re Kaytech International plc, Secretary of State for Trade and Industry v Kaczer* [1999] 2 BCLC 351 (director claimed to be a director of 1,000 Isle of Man companies, see at 414). The court noted in *Kaytech* that the law should give no encouragement to the notion that if a man takes on so many directorships that he cannot remember them, he is thereby released from the heavy responsibilities which he has undertaken: [1999] 2 BCLC 351 at 426, per Robert Walker LJ.

C The content of the duty

10-21 While the statute identifies the standard of care, skill and diligence required, it remains for the courts to add content to the duty. Unfortunately most of the authorities to date are first instance decisions and there has been little opportunity for the higher courts to explore these issues. A leading authority is the decision of Jonathan Parker J in *Re Barings plc (No 5) Secretary of State for Trade and Industry v Baker (No 5)*[50] where he identified certain propositions, now widely cited, with which the Court of Appeal subsequently agreed without further elaboration.

10-22 In the *Barings* case a number of senior directors of an investment bank were found to be unfit (though there was no question as to their honesty and integrity) and disqualified as a result of their failure to supervise a 'rogue trader' within the bank whose unauthorised trading resulted in losses of £827m and the collapse of the bank. Jonathan Parker J summarised the duties of directors as follows:[51]

(1) Directors have, both collectively and individually, a continuing duty to acquire and maintain a sufficient knowledge and understanding of the company's business to enable them properly to discharge their duties as directors.

(2) Whilst directors are entitled (subject to the articles of association of the company) to delegate particular functions to those below them in the management chain, and to trust their competence and integrity to a reasonable extent, the exercise of the power of delegation does not absolve a director from the duty to supervise the discharge of the delegated functions.

(3) No rule of universal application can be formulated as to the duty referred to in (2) above. The extent of the duty, and the question whether it has been discharged, must depend on the facts of each particular case, including the director's role in the management of the company.

10-23 For ease of discussion, we will consider each of these elements separately, though in practice they overlap and cannot be regarded as discrete elements. Most complaints will involve all of them: a lack of understanding of the business, a failure to participate and supervise, an absence of knowledge which prevents a director from exercising independent judgement, all of which make it difficult for a director to assert that he is acting in a way likely to promote the success of the company. It is a cumulative picture of incompetence and breach of other duties which typically emerges.

Knowledge of the company's affairs

10-24 The importance of sufficient knowledge and understanding of the company's business, both collectively and individually, in order to supervise and control the conduct of the company's affairs, is highlighted by the *Barings* case itself. As noted at **10-22**, the Barings group of companies collapsed in 1995 with losses of £827m following the unauthorised trading activities of a single 'rogue trader' in Singapore. The disqualification proceedings reported in *Re Barings plc (No 5), Secretary of State for Trade and Industry v Baker (No 5)*[52] concerned three of the directors, all of whom were found to be unfit and they were disqualified for periods ranging from four to six years. In essence, the court concluded

---

[50] [1999] 1 BCLC 433, aff'd [2000] 1 BCLC 523, CA.
[51] [1999] 1 BCLC 433 at 489, [2000] 1 BCLC 523 at 535, CA.
[52] [1999] 1 BCLC 433, aff'd [2000] 1 BCLC 523.

that the directors had little understanding of the nature of the rogue trader's activities and were not therefore in a position to exercise the requisite level of supervision.[53] The court noted with respect to the most senior director that his failures in this regard amounted 'not so much to bad management but non-management'. Jonathan Parker J commented that 'it is a truism that if a manager does not properly understand the business which he is seeking to manage, he will be unable to take informed management decisions in relation to it'.[54]

10-25   As noted at **10-17**, in a family business, it is not uncommon for family members to be directors without having anything to do with the running of the business and so they have no knowledge of the company's affairs. The courts have consistently found such directors to be unfit.[55] This is not to say that each director must have detailed knowledge of the day-to-day conduct of a company's affairs, for their role depends on the way in which the company's business is organised. The question is whether they have knowledge sufficient to exercise their collective and individual responsibility to supervise and monitor the conduct of the company's affairs.[56]

10-26   The court assesses a director's level of knowledge against the standard set in CA 2006, s 174 (see **10-9**). In *Re Queens Moat Houses plc, Secretary of State for Trade and Industry v Bairstow (No 2)*[57] dividends had been declared improperly on the strength of accounts which were misleading and did not give a true and fair view of the company's affairs. In disqualification proceedings, the court assessed the defendant director's knowledge on the basis of objectively considering (as required by CA 2006, s 174(2)(a)) what could be expected of a reasonably diligent person who was the chairman and senior executive director of the company and subjectively considering (as required by s 174(2)(b)) what could be expected of that director, given his wide business experience and knowledge of the company's affairs (he had been a director for 20 years) while also acknowledging that he had no formal accountancy qualifications. The court accepted that, given the preparation of the accounts had been properly delegated to the finance director, the director was not in breach of his duty in failing to appreciate that the accounting treatment of certain items in the accounts (i.e. technical specialist information beyond his competence) was misleading. Because of his business experience and knowledge of the company's affairs, he ought to have been aware, however, that the accounts showed inflated turnover and profits (i.e. business information within his comprehension) and were therefore misleading. He was in breach of duty and disqualified for six years.

10-27   In *Re Westmid Packing Services Ltd, Secretary of State for Trade and Industry v Griffiths*,[58] also disqualification proceedings, the court found that the directors did not know that

---

[53] See [1999] 1 BCLC 433 at 528–9, 574–5, 600.

[54] See [1999] 1 BCLC 433 at 528. All of this remained true of the boards of the banks which collapsed in the financial crisis in 2007–08; the subsequent Walker review (see **5-4**) found there had been a lack of banking knowledge within the boards which made it difficult, if not impossible, for there to be any challenge to the business strategy; see also Hannigan, n 13.

[55] See, for example, *Re Brian D Pierson (Contractors) Ltd* [2001] 1 BCLC 275; *Re Park House Properties Ltd* [1997] 2 BCLC 530; *Re Galeforce Pleating Co Ltd* [1999] 2 BCLC 704, discussed at **10-18** et seq. Likewise courts do not accept that someone can be a professional nominee director of hundreds of companies for it is impossible for the nominee to have a sufficient knowledge of the companies to discharge his duties as a director of them, see **10-20**.

[56] See *Re Vintage Hallmark, plc, Secretary of State for Trade & Industry v Grove* [2007] 1 BCLC 788 at 810—what is required is a good general knowledge of the business.   [57] [2005] 1 BCLC 136.

[58] [1998] 2 BCLC 646 at 652.

the dominant director had used company assets to support other businesses of his own and did not know that he had the company cross-guarantee the borrowings of those businesses. This failure to keep themselves properly informed about the company's financial position was sufficient to justify their disqualification though it was the sole allegation of unfitness established against them. In *Re Kaytech International plc, Secretary of State for Trade and Industry v Kaczer*,[59] Rimer J thought that a non-executive director has to ensure that he is informed about the company's constitution, its board membership, the nature and course of its business and its financial position from time to time so that he is in a position to monitor the manner in which the executives are conducting the company's affairs.

10-28 On the other hand, the law does not require an unreasonable level of knowledge, as was made clear in *Re Continental Assurance Co of London plc*.[60] This case concerned the collapse of a small insurance company in 1992. Large and unexpected losses had arisen which came to the board's attention in June 1991. In this litigation the liquidators sought contributions to the company's assets from the directors on the grounds of wrongful trading and/or misfeasance (see **25-18**). A particular issue was an allegation that the company applied inappropriate accounting policies which showed the company to be solvent in July 1991 when, had an appropriate accounting policy been adopted by the company, the directors would and should have appreciated that the company was insolvent and they should have taken steps to stop trading. The court found that for the directors to have reached that conclusion would have required of them knowledge of accounting concepts of a particularly sophisticated nature. Declining to hold the directors liable, Park J rejected any idea that the law imposes such an unrealistically high standard of skill. He noted:[61]

> '...In my view, [the directors] would have been expected to be intelligent laymen. They would need to have a knowledge of what the basic accounting principles for an insurance company were.... They would be expected to be able to look at the company's accounts and, with the guidance which they could reasonably expect to be available from the finance director and the auditors, to understand them. They would be expected to be able to participate in a discussion of the accounts, and to ask intelligent questions of the finance director and the auditors. What I do not accept is that they could have been expected to show the sort of intricate appreciation of recondite accounting details possessed by a specialist in the field...'

10-29 On the facts, Park J found that the directors took a wholly responsible and conscientious attitude both to the company's position and to their own responsibilities as directors at all times from and after the first crisis board meeting in 1991 when the unexpected losses were reported to them. The directors did not ignore the question of whether the company could properly continue to trade; on the contrary, the court found that they considered it directly, closely and frequently.[62] The case against them was dismissed.

---

[59] [1999] 2 BCLC 351 at 407. In *Lexi Holdings plc v Luqman* [2008] 2 BCLC 725, reversed on other grounds, see [2009] 2 BCLC 1, the court did not accept that non-executive directors of a company engaged in the business of making loans secured on real property had a duty to appraise themselves of the detailed provisions of the loan facility agreement which the company had with Barclays Bank (that task could properly be delegated to one of the executive directors with banking experience), but they did have a duty to have made some study of the company's loan book since that lay at the heart of understanding the company's business.

[60] [2007] 2 BCLC 287.   [61] [2007] 2 BCLC 287 at 402–3.   [62] [2007] 2 BCLC 287 at 360.

Delegation and the residual duty of supervision

10-30 It has long been accepted that an intelligent devolution of labour must be possible[63] and a company could not hope to run its business in an efficient manner if the directors were required to do everything themselves and were not permitted to delegate on a wide scale, though the extent to which they can do so depends on the provisions of the company's articles.[64] At the same time, some matters must remain the collective responsibility of the board of directors, such as the responsibility of the board to approve the company's annual accounts.[65]

10-31 Having permitted delegation, and in the absence of grounds for suspicion, the law does not require that the directors should distrust and constantly supervise those to whom tasks have been delegated for this would defeat the whole purpose. Directors do retain a residual duty of supervision, however, as was made clear by Jonathan Parker J in *Re Barings plc (No 5), Secretary of State for Trade and Industry v Baker (No 5)*,[66] see **10-22**. The key point is that it is delegation, not abdication, which is permissible. A number of common scenarios emerge from the authorities.

10-32 First, there is the dominant member syndrome, where directors defer to a particular individual on the board such that in effect they delegate all power to him, abdicate their own responsibilities and exercise no residual supervision. The dominant director(s) may be someone on whom the other directors are unduly reliant and therefore they are reluctant to challenge or question him. They may owe him their positions on the board, particularly if they are former employees promoted by him to the board. The courts are clear, however, that a board must not permit one individual to dominate and use the other directors in this way. In *Re Westmid Packing Services Ltd, Secretary of State for Trade and Industry v Griffiths*,[67] for example, the court disqualified two of the executive directors for breach of their inescapable personal responsibilities by allowing themselves to be manipulated and deceived by another member of the board who was the dominant and controlling influence in the business. Their failure to act allowed the dominant director to use the company's assets to fund his other businesses by way of interest-free unsecured loans which ultimately proved irrecoverable and brought the company to ruin.[68]

10-33 In *Re Landhurst Leasing plc, Secretary of State for Trade and Industry v Ball*[69] the court disqualified two executive directors who had taken a relatively subordinate role (reflecting the fact that they had been promoted to the board from the ranks of the employees) vis-à-vis the conduct of the affairs of the company by two forceful joint managing directors who were convicted of criminal offences in respect to their management of the company. The disqualified directors had failed to draw the board's attention to sham transactions

---

[63] *Dovey v Cory* [1901] AC 477 at 485; also *Huckerby v Elliott* [1970] 1 All ER 189.

[64] The model articles provide that, subject to the articles, the directors are responsible for the management of the company's business, for which purpose they may exercise all the powers of the company and they may delegate any of the powers conferred on them under the articles. See The Companies (Model Articles) Regulations 2008, SI 2008/3229, reg 2, Sch 1, arts 3, 5 (Ltd); reg 4, Sch 3, arts 3, 5 (Plc).

[65] CA 2006, s 414. See *Re Landhurst Leasing plc, Secretary of State for Trade and Industry v Ball* [1999] 1 BCLC 286 at 346, relying on *Re City Equitable Fire Insurance Co Ltd* [1925] Ch 407.

[66] [1999] 1 BCLC 433, aff'd [2000] 1 BCLC 523, CA.   [67] [1998] 2 BCLC 646.

[68] [1998] 2 BCLC 646 at 653.

[69] [1999] 1 BCLC 286. See also *Re Bradcrown, Official Receiver v Ireland* [2001] 1 BCLC 547 where a finance director (who had been promoted from being an employee) was found to have exercised no independent judgement and to have deferred in all matters to the managing director. The court noted that this was the clearest case of accepting office as a director but intending from the outset to act as a loyal employee.

of which they were aware and to ensure that the accounts made adequate provision for bad debts and credit risks.[70] As to the boundaries of delegation, Hart J concluded that a director might rely on his co-directors to the extent that (1) the matter in question lay within their sphere of responsibility given the way in which the particular business was organised, and (2) that there existed no grounds for suspicion that that reliance might be misplaced.[71] However, Hart J continued, even where there were no reasons to think the reliance was misplaced, a director might still be in breach of duty if he left to others matters for which the board as a whole had to take responsibility, for example the responsibilities of the board to approve the company's annual accounts.[72]

10-34 Sometimes the dominant element is not an individual but an inner group of directors, as in *Re AG (Manchester) Ltd, Official Receiver v Watson*.[73] In this case, the court disqualified for six years a finance director and subsequent chief executive who acquiesced in a system under which members of an inner group of directors took all the key decisions without reference to the board as a whole with the result that the other directors were effectively reduced to the role of departmental managers with no serious input at board meetings on issues affecting the running of the company.[74]

10-35 A second scenario is the abdication of responsibility to other directors without exercising any residual supervision by an inactive director of a family business.[75] In *Re Westminster Property Management Ltd, Official Receiver v Stern (No 2)*[76] a property development company had collapsed with multi-million pound losses and the two directors before the court in disqualification proceedings were a father and son. With respect to the son, the court considered that 'he was not conscious of his position or duties as a director, that he never undertook those duties except as dictated by his father (for example, to sign cheques or accounts) and that he applied his mind barely, if at all, to the consequences of his position as a director'. He was disqualified for four years for this abrogation of his duties as a director.[77] As well as disqualification, inactivity on the part of a director can lead to a personal liability. A failure to act, and often the claims in respect of breach of the duty of care do concern inactivity, with the result that the director did not do something he ought to have done, means he is liable for the consequences of not doing it. In *Lexi Holdings plc v Luqman*[78] two directors (they were sisters) of a company were in breach of their duties in not informing the other directors and the auditors of the criminal convictions for fraud of another director (their brother) and that he was operating a fictitious directors' loan account (a mechanism which they knew he had employed in previous frauds). Had they informed the auditors or the incoming directors of what they knew, i.e. had they performed their duties as directors of the company, controls would have been imposed on him or he would have been removed from office so the subsequent misappropriation of the company's funds by the fraudulent director would not have occurred. In such

---

[70] See [1999] 1 BCLC 286 at 349 and 353.

[71] [1999] 1 BCLC 286 at 346; see also *Cohen v Selby* [2001] 1 BCLC 176 at 185.

[72] [1999] 1 BCLC 286 at 346, relying on *Re City Equitable Fire Insurance Co Ltd* [1925] Ch 407.

[73] [2008] 1 BCLC 321.   [74] See [2008] 1 BCLC 321 at 373–4.

[75] See *Re Brian D Pierson (Contractors) Ltd* [2001] 1 BCLC 275; *Re Galeforce Pleating Co Ltd* [1999] 2 BCLC 704; *Re Park House Properties Ltd* [1997] 2 BCLC 530, discussed at **10-18** et seq.

[76] [2001] BCC 305 at 354–5.

[77] See also *Re AG (Manchester) Ltd, Official Receiver v Watson* [2008] 1 BCLC 321 where a director who was the wife of the controlling shareholder was disqualified. Though a director, she left all financial and strategic decisions to an inner group of directors (including her husband) and was content to take substantial dividends from the company regardless of how and whether they could be paid. The court found her conduct in failing to act independently and in the interests of the company amounted to an abdication of responsibility and justified her disqualification for four years (see at 374–5).   [78] [2009] 2 BCLC 1.

circumstances, the Court of Appeal held, they were liable for the losses (the full amount of the misappropriations) caused by their failure to perform their duties as directors of the company.[79]

10-36 Equally, a director who knowingly allows a practice of improper loans to directors to continue is to be treated as having authorised the payments, even though he does not have actual knowledge of each individual payment at the time when it is made, and so is jointly and severally liable therefore for their repayment.[80] In such circumstances, the Court of Appeal considers also that it is the duty of a director aware of the improper payments, not merely to ensure that a stop is put to the practice, but that steps are taken to recover the indebtedness outstanding to the company.[81]

10-37 A third scenario is where financial and accounting matters are delegated to a finance director. When a problem subsequently emerges, the other directors tend to claim that they had no responsibility in the matter, given that it was properly delegated to another. Again the issue is their failure to exercise any residual supervision.

10-38 The situation can be illustrated by *Re Queens Moat Houses plc, Secretary of State for Trade and Industry v Bairstow (No 2)*,[82] the facts of which are at **10-26**. In this case the court agreed that, with regard to the preparation and content of the financial statements, the chief executive was entitled to delegate those matters to the finance director. Such matters were properly within the finance director's area of responsibility and competence and the chief executive had no reason to doubt that the functions properly delegated had been properly performed. But many of the matters in the accounts were matters that it should have been apparent to the chief executive, given his business experience and knowledge of the company, were of doubtful accuracy and propriety. He was in breach of his duties, not for having improperly delegated the task of preparing the financial statements, but for failing to exercise his residual duty of supervision when those financial statements came to the board for approval.[83] The position can be contrasted with that in *Re Continental Assurance Co of London plc*,[84] the facts of which are at **10-28**. Park J there concluded that the board of an insurance company was entitled to rely on the advice of the finance director and the company's auditors as to whether the company was solvent and the appropriateness of the company's accounting policies and systems. The directors did not blindly accept what was put before them, but engaged in detailed and critical consideration of the company's accounts,[85] while looking for detailed guidance on technical matters to the finance director and the auditors as they were perfectly entitled to do.[86]

10-39 Another example of a failure to supervise can be found in *Secretary of State for Trade and Industry v Swan*[87] where a chief executive of a listed company was disqualified for signing large cheques (two for £1m each, two for £4m each) without enquiring what they were for, though the court considered that (because of their size in the context of the company's business) they called out for comment and enquiry.[88] His defence (that he relied on his

---

[79] [2009] 2 BCLC 1 at [38], [48]–[53].

[80] *Queensway Systems Ltd v Walker* [2007] 2 BCLC 577; *Neville v Krikorian* [2007] 1 BCLC 1, CA.

[81] *Neville v Krikorian* [2007] 1 BCLC 1, CA. The director's liability on this basis is for the difference between the amount which the company could have recovered at the date when the director became aware of the improper loans and the amount recoverable at the time of the claim.   [82] [2005] 1 BCLC 136.

[83] See [2005] 1 BCLC 136 at 158.   [84] [2007] 2 BCLC 287.   [85] [2007] 2 BCLC 287 at 444.

[86] [2007] 2 BCLC 287 at 410–11, 444. See also *Secretary of State for Trade and Industry v Gill* [2006] BCC 725.   [87] [2005] BCC 596.

[88] [2005] BCC 596 at 612.

finance director and finance department to verify the cheques) was rejected as an abdication of his responsibilities. His duty of supervision should have been triggered by the size of the cheques and the unusual nature of the transactions.[89] His unfitness in this case lay, the court said, in an absence of vigilance.[90]

10-40 Clearly, the extent of the residual duty to supervise depends on a variety of factors including the nature of the business; the nature and extent of the delegation; the standing and status of the person to whom the matter is delegated; the remuneration of the director;[91] the nature of the transaction and the potential risk/losses involved.[92] In larger companies with complex businesses, whether a director has discharged his individual role involves an examination of the systems for which he personally has responsibility while, at board level, the collective responsibility of the directors is to satisfy themselves that the task delegated and the system instituted is appropriate to the level of risk involved—hence the emphasis in the UK Corporate Governance Code on the collective responsibility of the board for maintaining sound risk management and internal control systems.[93]

10-41 The final variation on the delegation/abdication point comes with reliance on professional advisers. Of course, there are many circumstances in which reliance on professional advisers, such as auditors, is perfectly proper, as was noted in *Re Continental Assurance Co of London plc*.[94] Similarly in *Re Stephenson Cobbold Ltd, Secretary of State for Trade and Industry v Stephenson*[95] where it was alleged that a non-executive director (who was a cheque signatory) should be disqualified as unfit on the grounds, *inter alia*, that he had allowed an executive director to use company funds for personal expenditure. The court found that the non-executive director had queried the transactions at issue with the company's auditors and, in those circumstances, he was entitled to rely on the explanations given by the auditors (that the payments were part of the director's usual remuneration arrangements) as reassurance that the financial side of the company was being run properly.

10-42 On the other hand, excessive reliance amounting to a total abrogation of responsibility can be seen in *Re Bradcrown Ltd, Official Receiver v Ireland*[96] where a finance director relied entirely on professional advisers in respect of a complex transaction, the net effect of which was that the company transferred away its main assets for no consideration. In

---

[89] [2005] BCC 596 at 618, 621–2. There was no supporting documentation with the cheques which were matching cheques of equal and extraordinary amounts related to the company's practice of cheque-kiting, a practice which generates brief false balances in bank accounts and which the court described as, at the very least, commercially improper and unacceptable. On the other hand, it was not unreasonable for the chief executive to delegate and rely on the finance director and other accounting personnel to deal with and confirm details in a circular to shareholders in the absence of anything to alert him to some discrepancy.

[90] [2005] BCC 596 at 622.

[91] On this, see *Re Barings plc (No 5)* [1999] 1 BCLC 433 at 488. Even an unpaid director has obligations which they accept when they become director: see *Re Park House Properties Ltd* [1997] 2 BCLC 530 at 555–6.

[92] The more critical the risk or the more extensive the potential losses (for example, from unauthorised derivatives trading where the losses can run out of control very quickly), the greater the duty of residual supervision.   [93] FRC, The UK Corporate Governance Code (2010), Main Principle C.2, see **5-17**.

[94] [2007] 2 BCLC 287. See too *Green v Walkling* [2008] 2 BCLC 332.

[95] [2000] 2 BCLC 614. See also *Norman v Theodore Goddard* [1991] BCLC 1028 where it was reasonable for a director to rely on information regarding the company's investments supplied to him by a solicitor who was a partner in an eminent firm of City solicitors. It turned out that the solicitor had misappropriated the company's money. Looked at in the light of how standards have developed since this decision, the case seems close to the borderline with the director almost abrogating his responsibilities to the company.

[96] [2000] 1 BCLC 547.

terms of reliance on professional advisers, the court noted that the issue is essentially one of degree. In the instant case, although the director was entitled to rely on professional advice, he had asked no questions and simply did what he was told, abdicating all responsibility. In those circumstances, the court held that he could not seek refuge in the fact that professional advisers were involved in the transactions and he was disqualified for two years.

10-43 There is a risk that if too great a reliance on professional advisers is permitted then, in larger companies especially, directors will expend the shareholders' money in having professional advisers approve their every move in order to reduce the individual risk to themselves. A line needs to be drawn therefore between justified reliance and abrogation of responsibility and these lines depend on the nature of the company and its business and the position of the director. Essentially, the issue is whether it is reasonable in all the circumstances for the director to rely on the professional adviser. A director of a small family company may be entitled to put greater reliance on professional advisers than a highly paid and qualified finance director at an international bank; conversely, the complexity of transactions in the latter situation may justify greater reliance on advisers in certain circumstances.

D Duty to exercise independent judgement

10-44 The CA 2006, s 173 states that a director must exercise independent judgement.

> '(1) A director of a company must exercise independent judgment.
>
> (2) This duty is not infringed by his acting—
>
> > (a) in accordance with an agreement duly entered into by the company that restricts the future exercise of discretion by its directors, or
> >
> > (b) in a way authorised by the company's constitution.'

10-45 As was explained in the Parliamentary debates, this obligation in s 173(1) to exercise independent judgement does not restrict a director's ability to take advice or to rely on advice (to the extent permissible under the duty of care and skill, as discussed above) nor does it require the director himself to be independent.[97]

10-46 Section 173(2)(a) reflects long-standing common law authorities on the directors' obligation not to fetter their discretion. An important authority on this issue is *Thorby v Goldberg*[98] where the directors of a company agreed as part of a broader restructuring transaction to allot shares in a particular manner at a later date. They then failed to do as they had promised. In an action to force them to make the allotment of the shares, they pleaded that the undertaking was an invalid fettering of their discretion on their part. The court rejected this argument, holding that the time for exercising their discretion was at the time of entering into the agreement. Provided they had considered the interests of the company at that time, the agreement was valid. It was not the case that the directors had wrongly fettered their discretion, rather that they had already exercised it.[99]

---

[97] HC Official Report, SC D (Company Law Reform Bill), 11 July 2006, col 598.
[98] (1964) 112 CLR 597, H Ct of Australia. See Prentice (1977) 89 LQR 107 at 111–13.
[99] (1964) 112 CLR 597 at 618, per Owen J.

10-47 In *Fulham Football Club Ltd v Cabra Estates plc*[100] the Court of Appeal emphatically endorsed the approach taken in *Thorby v Goldberg*.[101] In this case, the directors of a company had entered into undertakings to support, and to refrain from opposing, planning applications by another party for the development of certain land in return for the receipt by the company of large sums of money. The directors subsequently wanted to give evidence to a planning inquiry opposing the development and sought a declaration that they were not bound by the undertakings and were entitled to give such evidence to the inquiry as they considered to be in the interests of the company.

10-48 The Court of Appeal held that they were bound by the undertakings. As the undertakings given by the directors were part of contractual arrangements which conferred substantial benefits on the company, the directors had not improperly fettered the future exercise of their discretion by giving those undertakings. Nor was there any scope for the implication of a term into those undertakings that the directors would not be required to do anything that would be inconsistent with their fiduciary duties to the company.[102] The distinction which must be drawn, the court said, is between directors fettering their discretion (which is prohibited) and directors exercising their discretion in a way which restricts their future conduct (which is permissible). The directors had exercised their independent judgement at the time when they gave the undertakings not to oppose the planning application and therefore it was not a case of fettering their discretion, but rather a case that they had already exercised it. Certainly there will be many transactions where the proper time for the exercise of the directors' judgement is the time of the negotiation of the contract rather than the time when the contract is to be performed.[103]

10-49 The duty to exercise independent judgement is not infringed by a director acting in a way authorised by the company's constitution: CA 2006, s 173(2)(b) (and constitution is as defined in s 257). As already noted (see **10-30**), it is accepted that directors may delegate their powers to the extent permitted by the company's articles and, to the extent that the articles allow for delegation, the directors can be relieved of the obligation to exercise independent judgement. The model articles for public and private companies provide that, subject to the articles, the directors may delegate any of the powers conferred on them under the articles.[104] As discussed, this right to delegate is subject to the obligation to maintain a residual duty of supervision (see **10-31**).

10-50 One possibility raised in the Parliamentary debates is that this provision makes it possible for the status of the nominee director to be enshrined in the constitution.[105] It has always been the position that a nominee once appointed owes his duty to the company, as is the case with any director (CA 2006, s 170(1)), and the nominee is not able to, nor required to, follow the instructions of the person nominating him, though in practice

---

[100] [1994] 1 BCLC 363; noted Griffiths [1993] JBL 576.

[101] (1964) 112 CLR 597.

[102] To the extent that earlier authorities (*John Crowther Group plc v Carpets International plc* [1990] BCLC 460 and *Rackham v Peek Foods Ltd* [1990] BCLC 895—directors' undertakings to use best endeavours to secure shareholder consent to transactions were subject to directors' duties to act in interests of the company) could be read as laying down a general proposition that directors can never bind themselves as to the future exercise of their fiduciary powers, the Court of Appeal considered they were wrong and the decisions should be limited to the particular facts: [1994] 1 BCLC 363 at 393.

[103] See *Thorby v Goldberg* (1964) 112 CLR 597 at 605–6.

[104] See The Companies (Model Articles) Regulations 2008, SI 2008/3229, reg 2, Sch 1, arts 3, 5 (Ltd); reg 4, Sch 3, arts 3, 5 (Plc).   [105] HC Official Report, SC D (Company Law Reform Bill), 11 July 2006, col 601.

the legal position is no doubt often ignored, see the discussion at **9-18**. Section 173(2)(b), set out at **10-44,** allows the position to be regularised in that the articles may relieve a nominee director from this obligation to exercise independent judgement, but it applies only to that duty and the nominee director remains subject to all the other general duties, in particular his duty under s 172 to act in the way he considers, in good faith, would be most likely to promote the success of the company, see the discussion at **9-20**. A nominee director continues therefore to have a somewhat uncomfortable role in terms of managing the conflicting demands of duties to the company and the expectations of his nominating shareholder.

11

Duty to avoid a conflict of interest

A Introduction

11-1 Central to a director's duties is the long-established equitable rule precluding a fiduciary from entering, without consent, into engagements in which he has, or can have, a personal interest conflicting, or which possibly may conflict, with the interests of those whom he is bound to protect (the no-conflict rule),[1] and the equally inflexible rule that, without consent, a person in a fiduciary position is not entitled to profit from that position[2] (the no-profit rule). Together the no-conflict and no-profit rules express the duty of undivided loyalty owed by a fiduciary to his principal.[3] The rationale for the two strands is that the no-conflict rule is designed to prevent the judgement of the fiduciary being swayed by self-interest and the no-profit rule is designed to strip the disloyal fiduciary of gains made in breach of duty.[4] In most instances, both rules will be relevant, as where a director profits personally in a situation where his personal interests conflict with the company's interests and his duty to promote those interests.[5] The no-conflict duty generally ceases to apply, however, once a director resigns[6] since the duty is intended to prevent a director, in the exercise of his powers, from being swayed by his self-interest,[7] but a former director continues to be subject to the no-conflict rule as regards the exploitation of property, information or opportunity of which he became aware at a time when he was a director (CA 2006, s 170(2)(a)).

11-2 As far as these fundamental no-conflict and no-profit rules are concerned, the key statutory provision is CA 2006, s 175 which provides as follows:[8]

> '(1) A director of a company must avoid a situation in which he has, or can have, a direct or indirect interest that conflicts, or possibly may conflict, with the interests of the company.

---

[1] *Aberdeen Rly Co v Blaikie Bros* (1854) 1 Macq 461 at 471–2, per Lord Cranworth; *Imperial Mercantile Credit Assoc v Coleman* (1873) LR 6 HL 189; '… human nature being what it is, there is danger, in such circumstances, of the person holding a fiduciary position being swayed by interest rather than by duty, and thus prejudicing those whom he was bound to protect': *Bray v Ford* [1896] AC 44 at 51, per Lord Herschell. See Farrar and Watson, 'Self-dealing, Fair Dealing' (2011) JCLS 495 on the history of this rule.

[2] *Regal (Hastings) Ltd v Gulliver* [1942] 1 All ER 378, HL; also *Parker v McKenna* (1874) 10 Ch App 96; *Boardman v Phipps* [1967] 2 AC 46, HL.

[3] *Bristol and West BS v Mothew* [1996] 4 All ER 698 at 712. See *Ultraframe (UK) Ltd v Fielding* [2005] EWHC 1638 at [1306]–[1322]; *Quarter Master UK v Pyke* [2005] 1 BCLC 245 at [53]–[56] for useful overviews of the rules.

[4] See *Chan v Zacharia* (1984) 154 CLR 178 at 198; and see *King Productions Ltd v Warren* [2000] 1 BCLC 607.   [5] See, for example, *Bhullar v Bhullar* [2003] 2 BCLC 241; see **11-11.**

[6] See *Quarter Master UK Ltd v Pyke* [2005] 1 BCLC 245 at 264; *CMS Dolphin Ltd v Simonet* [2001] 2 BCLC 704 at 733; *A-G v Blake* [1998] 1 All ER 833 at 841.

[7] See *Ultraframe (UK) Ltd v Fielding* [2005] EWHC 1638 at [1309]–[1310], per Lewison J; also *Wilkinson v West Coast Capital* [2007] BCC 717 at [251].

[8] The application of CA 2006, s 175 to charitable companies is modified in accordance with s 181.

(2) This applies in particular to the exploitation of any property, information or opportunity (and it is immaterial whether the company could take advantage of the property, information or opportunity).'

While now expressed in the statute, the courts will interpret and apply this duty in the light of the corresponding common law rules and equitable principles (s 170(4), see **7-9**) so the existing case law on these matters remains relevant, but it must be read in the light of the statute. The statutory scheme clearly adopts the no-conflict rule, set out in s 175(1), as the core obligation with the no-profit rule, reflected in s 175(2), as a subset of that broader obligation.[9] This approach ends the debate as to whether there is one rule or two and is a valuable clarification of the law.[10] There is one rule, a no-conflict rule, and a prohibition on profiting when in a position of conflict.

11-3 The strictness of the duty imposed by CA 2006, s 175(1) and (2) (and note the application to indirect interests, not defined) is tempered by the disapplications set out in s 175(3)–(4) and by the possibility of authorisation in accordance with s 180, all of which are discussed later in the chapter. Furthermore, s 175 does not apply to a conflict of interest arising in relation to a proposed transaction or arrangement with the company (s 175(3)) which is governed by a separate duty of disclosure under s 177 (see **11-83**). The obligation to disclose an interest in an existing transaction or arrangement with the company is governed by s 182 (see **11-101**). Further, a director is not required to comply with s 175 if the conflicted transaction is approved or is exempt from approval under CA 2006, Pt 10, Ch 4 which requires shareholder approval of specific transactions with directors (s 180(2)). If the transaction is exempt under Pt 10, Ch 4, it is because Parliament considered that the particular conflict of interest is not a matter of concern, and if the shareholders have approved the conflict of interest under Pt 10, Ch 4, there is no need to impose a further requirement of compliance with s 175. Part 10, Ch 4 is discussed in Chapter 12.

11-4 Traditionally the courts have applied the no-conflict, no-profit, rules with unyielding strictness, regarding it as of fundamental importance that a company is entitled to the undivided loyalty of its directors.[11] As Rix LJ noted in *Foster Bryant Surveying Ltd v Bryant*,[12] these duties are 'exacting requirements, exactingly enforced'. Two main justifications are put forward for such a strict approach. First, the deterrent argument, i.e. the duties must be rigorously applied so as not to offer any encouragement to fiduciaries (in this context, directors) to pursue their own interests at the expense of their beneficiaries (in this context, the shareholders).[13] Secondly, a strict approach is an efficient way of

---

[9] See *Boardman v Phipps* [1966] 3 All ER 721 at 756, per Lord Upjohn; *New Zealand Netherlands Society 'Oranje' Inc v Kuys* [1973] 2 All ER 1222. See *Quarter Master UK Ltd v Pyke* [2005] 1 BCLC 245 at 263–4 for a useful discussion of the overlap between these obligations; also generally Conaglen, 'The Nature and Function of Fiduciary Loyalty' (2005) 121 LQR 452. The distinguished Australian judge and author, PD Finn, described the no-profit rule as a 'loose end' to the general no-conflict rule: see Finn, *Fiduciary Obligations* (1977), p 246.

[10] On the one or two rule debate, for example, see *Chan v Zacharia* (1984) 154 CLR 178 at 198; *Ultraframe (UK) Ltd v Fielding* [2005] EWHC 1638 at [1305]–[1306]; *Don King Productions Inc v Warren* [2000] 1 BCLC 607 at 629–30, CA; *Gencor ACP Ltd v Dalby* [2000] 2 BCLC 734 at 741. See generally Hannigan, 'Reconfiguring the No Conflict Rule—Judicial Strictures, a Statutory Restatement and the Opportunistic Director' (2011) 23 SAcLJ 714.

[11] See *Parker v McKenna* (1874) 10 Ch App 96 at 124, per James LJ; *New Zealand Netherlands Society 'Oranje' Inc v Kuys* [1973] 2 All ER 1222 at 1225, per Lord Wilberforce; *Industrial Development Consultants Ltd v Cooley* [1972] 2 All ER 162 at 173–4, per Roskill J; *Premier Waste Management Ltd v Towers* [2012] 1 BCLC 67 at [9].   [12] [2007] 2 BCLC 239 at 266.

[13] See, for example, *Lindsley v Woodfull* [2004] 2 BCLC 131 at 140; *Murad v Al-Saraj* [2005] EWCA 959 at [74]; also generally Conaglen, 'The Nature and Function of Fiduciary Loyalty' (2005) 121 LQR 452. See too Grantham,

addressing the agency problem within companies, by which is meant the difficulty which shareholders have in monitoring the conduct of their directors.[14] Holding fiduciaries to exacting obligations reduces the need for such monitoring. As Mummery LJ stated in *Premier Waste Management Ltd v Towers*:[15] 'The rationale and the justice of the [no-conflict] principle lie in its strict regard for the protection of those interests potentially at risk from a director who does not give his undivided loyalty to the company.'

11-5 Notwithstanding that starting point, the position is not one of unremitting severity for the emphasis on the fact-specific nature of these fiduciary obligations has always allowed a certain amount of judicial flexibility in the application of the duties[16] and, as Arden LJ noted, 'equity has been able skilfully to adapt remedies against defaulting fiduciaries to meet the justice of the case'.[17] Also, a fiduciary who wants relief from the strict application of the law always has the option of seeking the informed consent of the shareholders after full and frank disclosure of all relevant matters,[18] an option retained by CA 2006, s 180(4)(a) (see **11-69**).

11-6 From time to time, there have been judicial suggestions (and academic comment) that the unrelenting application of the no-profit rule, in particular, might be relaxed, out of concerns that its unyielding application may operate harshly and unduly restrict entrepreneurial freedom to compete with companies.[19] Those concerns were addressed by the Companies Act 2006 which modifies the strict application of the no-conflict duty to permit disinterested directors to authorise conduct which would otherwise be a breach of duty (see s 175(4)(b) and discussion at **11-49**). It remains to be seen whether this change in position might encourage the courts to take a more relaxed view of whether there is a conflict of interest in a particular case on the basis that Parliament no longer supports the idea of 'exacting obligations, exactingly applied'. Equally, given the (easier) availability

---

'Can Directors Compete with the Company?' (2003) 66 MLR 109 who comments (at 112) that equity imposes such rigorous obligations because of the beneficiary's vulnerability to the fiduciary, the need to maintain the sanctity of relationships of trust and confidence and the difficulty of actually proving breach of duty.

[14] See *Item Software (UK) Ltd v Fassihi* [2005] 2 BCLC 91 at 110.   [15] [2012] 1 BCLC 67.

[16] See *Foster Bryant Surveying Ltd v Bryant* [2007] 2 BCLC 239 at 266, per Rix LJ; *Wilkinson v West Coast Capital* [2007] BCC 717 at [245]; *In Plus Group Ltd v Pyke* [2002] 2 BCLC 201 at 222, per Sedley LJ; *Henderson v Merrett Syndicates* [1995] AC 145 at 206, per Lord Browne-Wilkinson; *Boardman v Phipps* [1966] 3 All ER 721 at 756–7, per Lord Upjohn. But see *Premier Waste Management Ltd v Towers* [2012] 1 BCLC 67 at [9], '... flexibility in the application of the no conflict rule does not undermine the strict nature of the liability enshrined in the principle where it applies', per Mummery LJ.

[17] See *Murad v Al-Saraj* [2005] EWCA 959 at [81].

[18] *New Zealand Netherlands Society 'Oranje' Inc v Kuys* [1973] 2 All ER 1222; *Gwembe Valley Development Co Ltd v Koshy* [2004] 1 BCLC 131 at 151; *Crown Dilmun v Sutton* [2004] 1 BCLC 468 at 511; *Murad v Al-Saraj* [2005] EWCA 959 at [71]; *Quarter Master (UK) Ltd v Pyke* [2005] 1 BCLC 245 at 269. There must be actual disclosure and consent; what the beneficiaries might have done, if there had been disclosure, is irrelevant: *Murad v Al-Saraj*, at [70]–[71] and the disclosure must be of all material facts: see Mummery LJ in *Gwembe Valley Development*, at 151; *Newgate Stud Co v Penfold* [2008] 1 BCLC 46 at 102; *FHR European Ventures LLP v Mankarious* [2011] EWHC 2308 at [77]-[83].

[19] See, for example, *Murad v Al-Saraj* [2005] EWCA 959 at [82]–[83], per Arden LJ; at [121]–[122], per Jonathan Parker LJ, but see criticism by Conaglen 'The Extent of Fiduciary Accounting and the Importance of Authorisation Mechanism' (2011) CLJ 548 who robustly and rightly argues that 'it would subvert the incentive structure of fiduciary doctrine if fiduciaries were encouraged to think that they can make a profit in breach of fiduciary duty and then proceed to court (if caught) to argue about how much of it they ought to be able to keep', at 577. For academic comment in favour of modernising the no-conflict, no-profit rules, see Lowry & Edmunds, 'The No Conflict-No Profit Rules and the Corporate Fiduciary: Challenging the Orthodoxy of Absolutism' [2000] JBL 122, and criticisms by Kershaw, 'Lost in Translation: Corporate Opportunities in Comparative Perspective' (2005) 25 Ox JLS 603.

of authorisation by disinterested directors, the courts may take the view that the director who chooses not to seek authorisation should continue to be subject to the full rigour of the law, and given post-financial crisis concerns about standards in corporate boardrooms, it is suggested that the latter view is more likely to find judicial favour.

B Scope of the duty to avoid conflicts of interest

S 175(1)–Avoiding a conflict or possible conflict of interest

11-7 The CA 2006, s 175(1) provides that a director of a company must avoid a situation in which he has, or can have, a direct or indirect interest that conflicts, or possibly may conflict, with the interests of the company. This requirement largely mirrors the equitable no-conflict rule famously laid down by Lord Cranworth in *Aberdeen Railway Co v Blaikie Bros*[20] where he noted that:

> '…it is a rule of universal application, that no one, having [fiduciary] duties to discharge shall be allowed to enter into engagements in which he has or can have a personal interest conflicting or which possibly may conflict with the interests of those whom he is bound to protect.'

11-8 The no-conflict duty applies (CA 2006, s 175(7)) whether the conflict is between 'interest' and 'duty', i.e. between the direct or indirect interests[21] of a director and the interests of the company and his duty to advance those interests and also where there is a conflict or possible conflict between 'duties' (for example, where a director is a director of two or more companies and has a separate duty to advance the interests of each company). The holding of multiple posts is discussed at **11-25**.

11-9 Liability under CA 2006, s 175(1) arises from a situation of conflict or of possible conflict with 'possible' being limited in the manner explained by Lord Upjohn in *Boardman v Phipps*:[22]

> 'The phrase "possibly may conflict" requires consideration. In my view it means that the reasonable man looking at the relevant facts and circumstances of the particular case would think that there was a real sensible possibility of conflict; not that you could imagine some situation arising which might, in some conceivable possibility in events not contemplated as real sensible possibilities by any reasonable person, result in a conflict.'

In statutory form, the limitation is negatively expressed in s 175(4)(a) so as to exclude from the ambit of the no-conflict duty situations that cannot reasonably be regarded as likely to

---

[20] (1854) 1 Macq 461 at 471.

[21] See *Transvaal Lands Company v New Belgium (Transvaal) Land and Development Company* [1914] 2 Ch 488 where a director of the plaintiff company voted in favour of a resolution for the purchase of shares from the defendant company. It turned out that, as a trustee, he held 0.5% of the shares in the defendant company. This conflicting interest was held sufficient to found a claim to avoid the transaction.

[22] [1966] 3 All ER 721 at 756; and see his earlier comments to similar effect in *Boulting v ACTAT* [1963] 2 QB 606 at 637–8: '…a broad rule like this must be applied with common sense and with an appreciation of the sort of circumstances in which over the last 200 years and more it has been applied and thrived. It must be applied realistically to a state of affairs which discloses a real conflict of duty and interest and not to some theoretical or rhetorical conflict.' See *Aberdeen Railway Co v Blaikie Bros* (1854) 1 Macq 461 at 471–2, per Lord Cranworth; *Transvaal Lands Company v New Belgium (Transvaal) Land and Development Company* [1914] 2 Ch 488; also *Cowan de Groot Properties Ltd v Eagle Trust plc* [1991] BCLC 1045 at 1116; *Re Dominion International Group plc (No 2)* [1996] 1 BCLC 572 at 597.

give rise to a conflict of interest, with 'likely' continuing to be defined, it can be expected, as 'a real sensible possibility'[23], so there is no change in the law. References hereafter to 'possibly may conflict' or 'not reasonably likely' should be read, respectively, in the light of and by reference to s 175(4)(a). Obviously, much of the case law discussed in this chapter, given its vintage, refers only to a 'real sensible possibility of conflict'.[24]

Conflict of interest and duty

11-10 Jonathan Parker LJ noted in *Bhullar v Bhullar*[25] that the no-conflict rule (now s 175(1)) is essentially a simple rule 'albeit it may in some cases be difficult to apply'. The problem lies in identifying that a conflict exists and directors are poor at realising when they are in a position of conflict or, perhaps, they recognise the conflict but choose to ignore it or, perhaps, the courts surprise them with the breadth of the rule. The existing case law continues to provide essential guidance on the application of s 175(1), but it must be read, as noted in **11-2**, in the light of the change to a no-conflict rule with a no-profit subset to that rule.

11-11 An important modern authority on the no-conflict rule is *Bhullar v Bhullar*[26] where two directors of a family company were found to be in breach of the rule when they acquired property adjacent to the company without telling the company that the property was available for purchase. They had come across the information that the property was for sale quite by chance and in circumstances which had nothing to do with their directorships. The company was a family business which was deadlocked and it had been agreed by the shareholders that the company would not acquire further properties. The intention was that the parties would go their separate ways but they had not actually taken any formal steps to bring that about.[27] The court found that the directors' personal interest in acquiring the land was in conflict with their duty to promote the company's interests which required them to communicate the existence of the opportunity to the company[28] which could then have considered whether to acquire it. There was a real sensible possibility of conflict, the court said, and they were in breach of their duty when they acquired the property for themselves.

11-12 The case highlights the breadth of the no-conflict duty. A director can be in breach of the no-conflict rule though he does not exploit his fiduciary position or information or opportunity acquired in that capacity although, of course, that feature may be and often is present. The application of the no-conflict rule is not dependent on the information being obtained by a director in the exercise of his functions as a director or on it being information which the director was 'tasked' to obtain,[29] it depends on whether the information places the director in a situation of conflict or possible conflict. There is likewise no need to show the exploitation of property 'belonging' to the company—there is no proprietary element to it[30]—merely a need for a real sensible possibility of conflict and the fiduciary's

---

[23] See, for example, *Eastford Ltd v Gillespie* [2010] CSIH 12 at [7], [11].

[24] The Government considered that CA 2006, s 175(4)(a) introduces a requirement of reasonableness, see HL Deb, vol 678, GC293 (6 February 2006), but it is not clear that the provision does much other than reflect the limitation already identified by Lord Upjohn.

[25] [2003] 2 BCLC 241 at 253. See *Wilkinson v West Coast Capital* [2007] BCC 717 at [252]–[253] on the difficulty in identifying in any given situation whether the relevant element of conflict is present.

[26] [2003] 2 BCLC 241, noted Armour (2004) CLJ 33; Prentice & Payne [2004] 120 LQR 198.

[27] See [2003] 2 BCLC 241 at [10], [22].

[28] As to the duty to communicate information to the company, this point is considered further at **11-46**.

[29] *Commonwealth Oil & Gas Co Ltd v Baxter* [2009] CSIH 75, [2009] SLT 1123 at [11], [79].

[30] A point reflected in the absence of any reference to property, information or opportunity *of the company* in CA 2006, s 175(2) (set out at **11-2**). This wording was deliberately chosen as it is for the courts to determine

exploitation of an opportunity in such circumstances.[31] As the company is entitled to the undivided loyalty of its directors, the very act of a director putting himself in a position of conflict or possible conflict is a breach of duty, without more, as was explained in *Quarter Master (UK) Ltd v Pyke*:[32]

> 'It is not because he has made a profit from trust property or a profit from his fiduciary position that the director is liable under the conflict rule. Rather, it is because, being in a fiduciary position, he has entered into a transaction, inconsistent with his fiduciary duty of loyalty to the company, which has yielded the profit and he has thereby misused his position. The opportunity to make the profit may not arise from the director's fiduciary position; he might just as well have had the opportunity if he had not been in that position but even so, his liability in respect of the profit arises because of the conflict of interest. In many cases, where the conflict rule applies, the director will also have taken advantage of the property of the company or of his fiduciary position but this will not always be so.'

11-13   An older authority is *Cook v Deeks*[33] where two of the three directors of a Canadian railway company diverted a contract in which the company was interested to another company which they had formed. The Privy Council found that, while they were directors and with their duties to the company entirely unchanged, they had proceeded to negotiate in reality on their own behalf.[34] There was a clear conflict between their personal interests in securing the contract and their duty to secure it for the company. The court held that the benefit of the contract belonged in equity to the company and the directors were bound to hold it on behalf of the company.[35]

11-14   Another important authority is *Industrial Development Consultants Ltd v Cooley*,[36] where Cooley had been employed as managing director by the company (IDC) and was actively involved in negotiations with the Eastern Gas Board to secure certain construction contracts for IDC.[37] It became clear that the Gas Board was not prepared to contract with IDC. A year later, the Gas Board approached Cooley and indicated a willingness for him personally to take on the management of these construction projects. He promptly resigned from IDC (giving the company the misleading impression that he was ill) and took the contracts offered by the Gas Board which were in substance the work that the company had unsuccessfully attempted to obtain the previous year.

11-15   Roskill J held that, as a director, Cooley occupied a fiduciary position which subjected him to an obligation to avoid possible conflicts between his personal interests and his fiduciary duty. Information which came to him while he was managing director (i.e. the knowledge that the Gas Board was back in the market and looking to place these

---

whether the exploitation of the property, information or opportunity has given rise to a conflict of interest, see HL Deb, vol 681, GC864 (9 May 2006). *Bhullar v Bhullar* [2003] 2 BCLC 241 at 252. See also Lewison J in *Ultraframe (UK) Ltd v Fielding* [2005] EWHC 1638 at [1355]: 'The application of the no-conflict rule does not depend on establishing that the company has a proprietary interest in the business opportunity that has been diverted'; and see Kershaw, 'Does it Matter how the Law Thinks about Corporate Opportunities?' (2005) 25 Legal Studies 533.

[31] [2003] 2 BCLC 241 at [27]–[28].
[32] [2005] 1 BCLC 245 at [54]–[55], per Paul Morgan QC, sitting as a Deputy Judge.
[33] [1916] 1 AC 554, PC. See *Ultraframe (UK) Ltd v Fielding* [2005] EWHC 1638 at [1334], per Lewison J; *Wilkinson v West Coast Capital* [2007] BCC 717 at [264], per Warren J.   [34] [1916] 1 AC 554 at 559–60.
[35] [1916] 1 AC 554 at 564.   [36] [1972] 2 All ER 162.
[37] It is also important that it was Cooley who was conducting the negotiations: see *Furs Ltd v Tomkies* (1936) 54 CLR 583; *Framlington Group plc v Anderson* [1995] 1 BCLC 475.

construction contracts) and which was of concern to the company and was relevant to the company to know was information which it was his duty, because of his fiduciary position, to pass on to the company.[38] Instead he embarked upon what was, the court found, a deliberate policy and course of conduct which put his personal interest in direct conflict with his pre-existing and continuing duty as managing director of the company.[39]

11-16 The statute in s 175(1) reflects this line of authority by focusing on the question of whether the director's interests are in conflict with his duty to the company and it is not suggested that the outcome under the statute would have been any different in these cases, not even in *Bhullar*, where a reasonable man would have thought there was a real sensible possibility of conflict between the directors' personal interest in acquiring a property adjacent to the company and their duty to promote the interests of the company.

Identifying the company's interests

11-17 One of the advantages of the 'bright line' approach, favoured in *Bhullar* and reflected in the statute, of asking the simple question of whether there is a conflict or possible conflict of interest, is that it avoids any need for a corporate opportunities doctrine which looks to whether the director has appropriated an opportunity or a maturing business opportunity *of* the company. This approach typically involved a consideration of the factors identified by Laskin J in *Canadian Aero Service Ltd v O'Malley*[40] such as 'the position or office held, the nature of the corporate opportunity, its ripeness, its specificness and the director's relation to it, the amount of knowledge possessed, the circumstances in which it was obtained, etc'. None of this is required under the statute,[41] but it is still necessary to have some regard to the nature of the opportunity etc vis-à-vis the scope of the company's business since the scope of the business determines the extent of the company's interests (and the director's duty to promote those interests) and therefore whether there is a conflict for the director.[42]

11-18 Usually, there is little difficulty in deciding whether a situation/opportunity is within the scope of the business for in many of the cases, such as *Cook v Deeks* and *IDC v Cooley*, the company has been actively pursuing the contract which the director has secured for himself. In *Bhullar*, however, we see the court holding that a company had an interest in acquiring an adjacent property though the company was deadlocked and had effectively decided not to pursue any further acquisitions. In keeping with the courts' view of the exacting nature of the duty of loyalty owed by a fiduciary, it is clear that the courts take a generous view of the range of activities in which the company may have an interest and so it can be said that the courts favour a strict, possibly over-inclusive, version of the duty. The approach can be illustrated by two recent cases, *Commonwealth Oil & Gas Co Ltd v*

---

[38] [1972] 2 All ER 162 at 173–4, but see the discussion of this 'duty' to pass on information at **11-46**.

[39] [1972] 2 All ER 162 at 173–4.   [40] (1973) 40 DLR (3d) 371 at 391.

[41] See also *Island Export Finance Ltd v Umunna* [1986] BCLC 460 at 481–2.

[42] See generally Hannigan, 'Reconfiguring the No Conflict Rule—Judicial Strictures, a Statutory Restatement and the Opportunistic Director' (2011) 23 SAcLJ 714.

Baxter[43] and *Re Allied Business and Financial Consultants Ltd, O'Donnell v Shanahan,*[44] hereafter *O'Donnell v Shanahan.*

11-19 In *Commonwealth Oil & Gas Co Ltd v Baxter*[45] the company's business[46] lay in onshore oil and gas exploration in Azerbaijan and it was anxious to secure additional opportunities of that nature to which end it needed to secure the agreement of the Azerbaijan authorities, especially of a body called SOCAR. The defendant director secured an agreement concerning possible offshore exploration with SOCAR for another company of which he was also a director and significant shareholder. He did not inform the company of the possibility of securing this agreement, considering that it had no interest in offshore activities which it had never undertaken. The court found that the company probably would have been interested, given its desire to secure new opportunities and develop a relationship with SOCAR, had it known the details of the situation.[47] In those circumstances, the court said, a reasonable man in the director's position would have known that such an agreement with SOCAR would have been of interest to the company and the director was in breach of the no-conflict rule. In effect, offshore exploration, though not within the company's past or current interests, was sufficiently proximate to the fundamental nature of its activities to fall within the scope of the company's business.

11-20 This issue of the scope of the business was also central to *O'Donnell v Shanahan*[48] where the trial judge favoured, though the Court of Appeal did not, a more pragmatic assessment of what is a 'possible' conflict looking in detail at what the company is actually doing rather than what might conceivably be possible. The central allegation of breach of duty in this case concerned the involvement by two (of the three) directors of a company[49] with a client of the company in the acquisition of an investment property. The directors had been approached by a third party to find a purchaser for the property and, after an initial deal fell through, the directors found a client who was willing to proceed, but only on the basis, which they agreed to, that he would share the deal 50/50 with the two directors and that he would not pay a commission to the company (a commission to the company had been integral to the initial failed deal).[50] The court also found, as a fact, that had the

---

[43] [2009] CSIH 75, [2009] SLT 1123. A Scottish case, but the views of the Scottish courts will be of increasing interest as the CA 2006 applies to the UK, see CA 2006, 1299, though the facts of this case pre-date the commencement of CA 2006.

[44] [2009] 2 BCLC 666; and see Ahern, 'Guiding Principles for Directorial Conflicts of Interest: *Re Allied Business*' (2011) 74 MLR 596.

[45] [2009] CSIH 75, [2009] SLT 1123.

[46] In fact, the company was a wholly owned subsidiary within a group and the court noted that they tended to ignore the separate legal entities, but nothing turns on that: [2009] CSIH 75, [2009] SLT 1123 at [64].

[47] The site was offshore but in shallow water, it was in an established oilfield and SOCAR was disposed to grant an exclusive agreement to negotiate with respect to the project, see [2009] CSIH 75, [2009] SLT 1123 at [55]–[58].

[48] [2009] 2 BCLC 666, reversing [2009] 1 BCLC 328. For a detailed discussion of this case, see Hannigan, 'Reconfiguring the No Conflict Rule—Judicial Strictures, a Statutory Restatement and the Opportunistic Director' (2011) 23 SAcLJ 714.

[49] [2009] 2 BCLC 666 at [32]. The company was a quasi-partnership formed originally between four individuals, but subsequently involving only these three shareholder/directors, each holding 2,525 shares; the fourth shareholder retained 25 shares but had left the business many years earlier.

[50] [2009] 2 BCLC 666 at [23]–[24]. Had the company received a £30,000 commission, it would have been divided equally between the three director/shareholders as was their custom. In fact there was no loss to the shareholders here for the two defendant directors paid the third director the amount of commission which she would otherwise have received.

opportunity to acquire the property been presented to the company, the company would not have been willing or able to accept the opportunity.[51] At first instance, the court found no breach of the no-conflict rule or of the no-profit rule, but, on appeal, the decision was reversed on both grounds.[52]

11-21 At first instance, the court thought there could not be a real sensible possibility of conflict in the circumstances because the company's business was the provision of financial advice and assistance, and though property investment could have fallen within its open-ended objects, actually it was not within the scope of the company's business, even taking an extended view of the scope of that business (i.e. considering the likelihood of the company extending its business into other areas).[53] The Court of Appeal rejected that conclusion finding that, while the company's business initially was the provision of financial advice and assistance, it had diversified into a variety of property and investment roles.[54] In the acquisition at issue, it acted essentially as an estate agent, something which it had not done previously and which, the court thought, indicated that its categories of activities were not closed.[55] The court was not willing then to limit the scope of the company's interests by reference to what it was actually doing. It went on to find that in failing to secure a commission for the company on the second deal in which the directors participated, they had preferred their own interests to the company's interests in breach of the no-conflict rule.[56]

11-22 Of course, the more generous the approach taken to the scope of a company's interests (so, as discussed earlier, an onshore oil company has an interest in offshore exploration, a company which has decided against further acquisitions has an interest in acquiring an adjacent property and a company which has never acquired investment properties has an interest in acquiring one after all) the wider the no-conflict duty and the greater the limitations on a director's conduct. Hence the Court of Appeal in applying a strict version of the no-conflict rule is giving the greatest protection to the company against the opportunistic director.

11-23 *Wilkinson v West Coast Capital*,[57] on the other hand, is an unusual example of the court agreeing that there was no possible conflict. Here the dispute centred on whether a company could have an interest in an opportunity which its constitution prevented it from

---

[51] [2009] 2 BCLC 666 at [35].

[52] It may be felt that the result here was unfair. The company would not have taken the opportunity, if it had been offered; at most the company lost a commission on the deal which would have been divided between the three directors and the third director was paid her share of that missed commission; she knew all along that the defendants had their own property investment company and she knew almost immediately of their involvement in the 1999 transaction which they conducted largely in front of her. She also waited six years before making any allegation of breach of duty.

[53] [2009] 1 BCLC 328 at [208], [212]. Sheldon QC (sitting as a Deputy Judge) did take into account that the company had branched (in the very transaction under scrutiny) into estate agency, but that was some way removed, he said, from contemplating property investment by the company itself.

[54] [2009] 2 BCLC 666 at [5]–[7] (its activities included arranging the purchase and sale of properties, acting as agents for banks and building societies, placing investments for clients, and providing advice on financial and business restructuring).

[55] [2009] 2 BCLC 666 at [53]; 'there was no bright line marking off what it did and did not do', at [71].

[56] Despite finding that the company's interests were not closed, and despite noting that the 'opportunity led the respondents straight into a breach of the no conflict rule', see [2009] 2 BCLC 666 at [54], which might have led to the conclusion that taking the opportunity was itself a breach of the no-conflict rule, the court limited its finding on the no-conflict rule to the directors' failure to secure a commission for the company, see at [75].

[57] [2007] BCC 717.

pursuing. In this case it was alleged that two of the directors of a company had acted in breach of their duties when they acquired another business on their own account rather than on account of the company.[58] There was a shareholders' agreement to which all (including the company) were party whereby the consent of 65% of the shareholders was required for any further acquisitions by the company. The two directors owned 50% of the shares and, as shareholders, were opposed to the company acquiring any further businesses.

11-24 Warren J held that, in these circumstances, where the shareholder-directors were in a position as shareholders to block any further acquisitions by the company, there was no possibility of the company having an interest in the acquisition.[59] When the two directors took the opportunity personally, therefore, there was no conflict of interest to which the rule could apply. Warren J considered that the position of a non-shareholder director would have been different[60] and the no-conflict rule would have applied, presumably because, for that director, there still would be a possible conflict[61] and, if he wanted to exploit the situation, that director would have needed the informed consent of the company.[62] But for the shareholder-directors there was no chance of there being a real sensible possibility of conflict.

Conflict of duty and duty—multiple directorships

11-25 As noted, the prohibition extends not just to a conflict of interest and duty, but a conflict of duty and duty (s 175(7)). In theory, there is no rule that a director cannot be a director of another company, even a company which is wholly or partly engaged competitively in the same trade.[63] In practice, there is significant potential for conflicts of interest, for example, where a director of company A is also a director of Company B which is a customer or supplier of Company A or where a director is a director of Company A and Company B and each company is seeking business from Company C. Disclosure and consent is the key to this conflict and the director who holds two directorships in situations of potentially conflicting interests is in breach of the obligation of undivided loyalty which he owes to each company unless he secures the informed consent of each company.[64] Even then, the

---

[58] The issue arose in the context of a shareholder's petition under CA 1985, s 459 (now CA 2006, s 994) alleging unfairly prejudicial conduct.

[59] It was the impossibility of the trust acquiring the shares in *Boardman v Phipps* [1967] 2 AC 46 which so persuaded the minority in that case that there was no liability to account when the fiduciaries acquired the shares in question (see Lord Upjohn, at 119, 'of cardinal importance'; Viscount Dilhorne, at 88, 89, 92, trustee was clear that he would not support the trust acquiring any shares under any circumstances), but the majority favoured liability on the basis of breach of the no-profit rule.

[60] See [2007] BCC 717 at [301]–[303].

[61] The shareholders' agreement might be flawed, the shareholders might abandon it, the company might see the merits of diversification, etc. The non-shareholder director in that situation could not be sure what attitude the shareholders and therefore the company might take to further acquisitions.

[62] [2007] BCC 717 at [302].

[63] *London and Mashonaland Exploration Co Ltd v New Mashonaland Exploration Co Ltd* [1891] WN 165, approved in *Bell v Lever Bros* [1932] AC 161, HL by Lord Blanesburgh, but see n 65. See Christie, 'The Director's Fiduciary Duty not to Compete' (1992) 55 MLR 506.

[64] See *Bristol and West BS v Mothew* [1996] 4 All ER 698 at 712, per Millett LJ.

director will find it difficult to serve two masters without being in breach of his obligation to one or the other.[65] As Millett LJ commented in *Bristol and West BS v Mothew*:[66]

> 'Even if a fiduciary is properly acting for two principals with potentially conflicting interests he must act in good faith in the interests of each and must not act with the intention of furthering the interests of one principal to the prejudice of those of the other...He must not allow the performance of his obligations to one principal to be influenced by his relationship with the other. He must serve each as faithfully and loyally as if he were his only principal.'

11-26 This issue of multiple competing directorships is important in practice and it has given rise to concerns as to how the duty in CA 2006, s 175(1) can be met. As already noted, the first stage is to disclose the potential conflict and seek the consent of each company to the director holding multiple posts. Large companies commonly adopt articles which allow for the exclusion of the conflicted director from receipt of information, participation in discussions and/or exempt him from any obligation to disclose confidential information belonging to the other company, etc, but practical difficulties persist in managing day-to-day issues which give rise to possible conflicts. Resignation may prove to be the only possible course and, in practice, multiple competing posts are difficult, if not impossible, to maintain.[67]

S 175(2) Exploiting property, information or opportunity

11-27 In addition to avoiding a situation of conflict as required by CA 2006, s 175(1), the no-profit rule in s 175(2), set out at **11-2**, particularly prohibits the exploitation of any property, information or opportunity in circumstances where there is a conflict, or possible conflict, of interest. As already noted, the prohibition is not limited to the exploitation of the director's position or of property, etc, of or belonging to the company ('any property'), see **11-12**.

11-28 At common law, the no-profit duty has its origins in the leading trust case of *Keech v Sandford*,[68] but the most famous application of the rule in company law is *Regal (Hastings) Ltd v Gulliver*.[69] In this case a company could not finance the acquisition of additional cinemas which it wished to acquire. It was unable to put up sufficient share capital for the acquiring subsidiary and instead that capital was put up by the directors who then profited personally on the sale of the shares in the subsidiary. The new controllers of the company successfully sued the former directors to recover those profits.

11-29 The House of Lords found that the directors had obtained their profits by reason of and in the course of the execution of their office as directors of Regal.[70] They had entered into the

---

[65] See *In Plus Group Ltd v Pyke* [2002] 2 BCLC 201 at 222, CA, where Sedley LJ made clear that he thought the position of a competing director is almost unsustainable and it was clear that all three judges in the case believed the *Mashonaland* principle, see n 63, to be of very limited application, as where in effect the position of the director in one company is purely nominal to such an extent that the director attracts no fiduciary obligations from that position; see Grantham (2003) 66 MLR 109. In *Commonwealth Oil & Gas Co Ltd v Baxter* [2009] CSIH 75 at [5], [76]–[77], the Scottish court was equally sure, obiter, that little weight should be given to *Mashonaland*. See too *Scottish Co-operative Wholesale Society Ltd v Meyer* [1959] AC 324 at 367–8, HL.

[66] [1996] 4 All ER 698 at 713.

[67] See *Bristol and West BS v Mothew* [1996] 4 All ER 698 at 713, per Millett LJ.

[68] (1726) Sel Cas Ch 61.   [69] [1942] 1 All ER 378, HL.

[70] [1942] 1 All ER 378 at 389, per Lord Russell.

transaction in the course of their management and in utilisation of their opportunities and special knowledge as directors.[71] They were thus liable to account, notwithstanding the fact that they had acted bona fide throughout. As directors, they were in a situation of conflict between their personal interests and their duty to the company and they exploited the conflict to their own advantage. In such circumstances, the court said, 'the profiteer, however honest and well-intentioned, cannot escape the risk of being called upon to account'.[72]

11-30 A ringing endorsement of this approach can be found in *O Donnell v Shanahan*,[73] the facts of which are discussed at **11-20**. The opportunity to acquire an investment property came to the directors' attention in their capacity as directors of the company acting on the company's business and the information which they relied on in deciding to participate in the acquisition (various financing and valuation reports) was also obtained in the course of so acting.[74] The situation justified, the Court of Appeal concluded, the straightforward and rigorous application of the no-profit rule,[75] as exemplified by *Regal (Hastings) Ltd v Gulliver*.[76]

11-31 Examples of undisclosed profiting in a situation of conflict abound. In *Gencor ACP Ltd v Dalby*[77] a director had in effect been running a parallel competing business for many years, diverting contracts for the company's products to companies which he controlled in breach of the no-conflict and no-profit duties. In *Crown Dilmun v Sutton*[78] the director of a property development company was liable when he took for himself a development opportunity despite the clear conflict of interest between him and the company. In *Quarter Master UK Ltd v Pyke*[79] the directors, at a time when the company was in significant financial difficulties, engaged in a strategy to salvage for themselves a major ongoing contract with a customer. There was a conflict of interest between their seeking to obtain the contract for themselves, to which end they exploited the company's customer database and goodwill for their own benefit, and their duty to the company to seek ways to maximise the value of the contract for the company and its creditors (even if the company was no longer in a position to continue the contract itself). The court held that they acted in breach of the no-conflict and the no-profit rule and were liable to account for the profits which they made as a result of their breach of fiduciary duty.

11-32 These cases would still be decided the same way today under the statute, but they would be decided on the basis of the application of CA 2006, s 175(1) and (2), that the defendant directors in these cases, while still in post, had allowed a clear conflict to arise between their personal interests and their duty to their companies and they had sought to exploit the conflict for their personal advantage. The main change here is that the terminology and unhelpful focus on profiting 'by reason of and in the course of their management'

---

[71] [1942] 1 All ER 378 at 392, per Lord Macmillan.

[72] [1942] 1 All ER 378 at 386, per Lord Russell. The actual decision in *Regal* has been criticised: see Davies, *Gower and Davies' Principles of Modern Company Law* (8th edn, 2008), para 16–66: '…equitable principles were taken to inequitable conclusions'; also Jones (1968) 84 LQR 472 at 497. But see Sullivan (1979) 42 MLR 711 who points out that the directors had a would-be purchaser in mind throughout and that there were other shareholders in *Regal* who could have put up some of the money required but who were not invited to do so. See also *Boardman v Phipps* [1966] 3 All ER 721, HL.   [73] [2009] 2 BCLC 666.

[74] [2009] 2 BCLC 666 at [52], [54], [60].   [75] [2009] 2 BCLC 666 at [54]–[60].

[76] [1942] 1 All ER 378, HL.   [77] [2000] 2 BCLC 734.   [78] [2004] 1 BCLC 468.

[79] [2005] 1 BCLC 245.

as per *Regal*, is dispensed with.[80] In an important clarification of the law, s 175(2) is not expressed in those terms.

Liability regardless of the company's position

11-33 This strict liability to account applies regardless of whether the company could take advantage of the property, opportunity or information (CA 2006, s 175(2)). It suffices that the director has profited from a situation of conflict and it is better to apply a strict rule than to attempt to investigate whether, in fact, the company could or would have exploited the opportunity.[81] That is a particularly difficult matter to investigate given that many of the factors relevant to it may lie within the director's control (such as the company's ability to borrow money) which the director may have manipulated precisely in order to show that the company could not or would not have exploited the opportunity. For these reasons, the courts prefer the strict approach (reflected in s 175(2)) that the company's position is not a relevant issue when considering the liability of a director who has exploited a conflict of interest. In this context, the courts commonly cite the famous dictum by Lord Russell in *Regal (Hastings) Ltd v Gulliver*[82] that:

> '[t]he rule of equity which insists on those, who by use of a fiduciary position make a profit, being liable to account for that profit, in no way depends on fraud, or absence of bona fides; or upon such questions or considerations as whether the profit would or should otherwise have gone to the plaintiff, or whether the profiteer was under a duty to obtain the source of the profit for the plaintiff, or whether he took a risk or acted as he did for the benefit of the plaintiff, or whether the plaintiff has in fact been damaged or benefited by his action. The liability arises from the mere fact of a profit having, in the stated circumstances, been made. The profiteer, however honest and well-intentioned, cannot escape the risk of being called upon to account.'

11-34 In *Regal*, discussed at **11-28**, the inability of the company to fund the acquisition of additional cinemas was irrelevant to the directors' liability for breach of the no-profit rule. There are numerous cases where the fact that the company might not have wished or been able, typically for financial reasons, to have taken the opportunity, or where the third party might not have been willing to deal with the company, is disregarded by the court in determining the liability of the director who has exploited a conflict of interest. In *Industrial Development Consultants Ltd v Cooley*,[83] see **11-14**, the fact that the company only had a 10% chance of securing the construction contracts at issue was irrelevant to the liability of the director.[84] In *Crown Dilmun v Sutton*,[85] see **11-31**, it was irrelevant whether the company would/could have taken the major contract which the director diverted to a company that he had formed.[86] In *Quarter Master UK Ltd v Pyke*,[87] see **11-31**, the fact that a key client had indicated that it was not likely to renew a contract with the company (which was in significant financial difficulties) was irrelevant to the directors' liability to account when they took the contract on their own behalf. In *O'Donnell v Shanahan*,[88] see **11-20,** it was irrelevant that the company would not have taken the opportunity to

---

[80] It was still used in *Re Allied Business & Financial Consultants Ltd, O'Donnell v Shanahan* [2009] 2 BCLC 666, but it is a pre-2006 Act case.

[81] See *Regal (Hastings) Ltd v Gulliver* [1942] 1 All ER 378 at 392; also *Furs Ltd v Tomkies* (1936) 54 CLR 583 at 592, approved in *Gwembe Valley Development Co v Koshy* [2004] 1 BCLC 131 at 146; and *Wilkinson v West Coast Capital* [2007] BCC 717 at [255]. But for criticism of the view that investigation of these matters is too difficult, see *Murad v Al-Saraj* [2005] EWCA 959 at [82], [155].

[82] [1942] 1 All ER 378 at 386.   [83] [1972] 2 All ER 162, CA.   [84] [1972] 2 All ER 162 at 176.

[85] [2004] 1 BCLC 468.   [86] [2004] 1 BCLC 468 at 511.   [87] [2005] 1 BCLC 245.

[88] [2009] 2 BCLC 666.

acquire the investment property had it been offered to the company. Likewise in *Bhullar v Bhullar*,[89] see **11-11**, where two directors bought a property adjacent to the company's premises without telling the company that it was for sale. Jonathan Parker LJ noted that 'whether the company could or would have taken that opportunity, had it been made aware of it, is not to the point'.[90] Having acquired the property in circumstances where there was a real sensible possibility of conflict between their personal interests and their duties to the company, the court had no doubt that the directors were liable to account.

The no-conflict rule and the departing director

11-35 A director may resign at any time even though such resignation may damage or harm the company.[91] Equally, there is nothing to stop a person forming the intention, while a director, to set up in competition with his company after his directorship ceases (subject to any contractual constraints) for the no-profit rule is not intended to hinder directors in the exploitation of the general fund of knowledge and expertise acquired while a director.[92] A director is also able to take preliminary steps to investigate or forward that intention to compete, provided he does not engage in any actual competitive activity[93] and so does not reach the situation where there is a conflict or possible conflict between his interests and his duty to the company.

11-36 The problem is that it is difficult to identify the point in time when the mere intention to compete turns into a conflict of interest[94] and, by and large, the case law shows that directors in that situation commonly overstep the mark.

11-37 The discussion is limited to liability for breach of fiduciary duty but many directors will have service agreements with express provisions governing the solicitation of customers and use of confidential information post-resignation.[95] In many cases, therefore, the director may also face claims based on a breach of contract or common law obligations of confidence.

Intending to resign

11-38 In *Colman Taymar Ltd v Oakes*[96] a director was liable when he failed to disclose his intention to compete with the company and, while still a director, used confidential information and the company's staff to assist him in securing leases and hiring equipment for his new business. In *Shepherds Investments Ltd v Walters*[97] the defendant directors were liable when, while still directors and without disclosing their plans, they took very active steps to promote a competing business to be carried on by them in the future. They

---

[89] [2003] 2 BCLC 241, CA.   [90] [2003] 2 BCLC 241 at 256.

[91] See *CMS Dolphin Ltd v Simonet* [2001] 2 BCLC 704 at 729.

[92] See *Island Export Finance Ltd v Umunna* [1986] BCLC 460 at 482–3; *Balston Ltd v Headline Filters Ltd* [1990] FSR 385 at 412. As noted in *Berryland Book Ltd v BK Books Ltd* [2009] 2 BCLC 709 at [25] (reversed in part for reasons which are irrelevant here, [2010] EWCA Civ 1440), the court has to be astute to ensure that litigation is not used as an illegitimate trade protection exercise so as to stifle legitimate competition; it must respect personal freedom to compete where that does not intrude on the misuse of the company's maturing business opportunities.

[93] See *Balston Ltd v Headline Filters Ltd* [1990] FSR 385 at 412, per Falconer J; also *Framlington Group plc v Anderson* [1995] 1 BCLC 475 at 495–6, 498.

[94] See *Shepherds Investments Ltd v Walters* [2007] 2 BCLC 202 at 223–4; *Balston Ltd v Headline Filters Ltd* [1990] FSR 385 at 412, per Falconer J; also Watts, 'The Transition from Director to Competitor' (2007) 123 LQR 21.

[95] See, for example, *Kingsley IT Consulting Ltd v McIntosh* [2006] BCC 875.   [96] [2001] 2 BCLC 749.

[97] [2007] 2 BCLC 202.

drew up business plans and financial projections, contacted advisers, sought backers and drafted complicated documentation relating to the new company's financial products. In *Simtel Communications Ltd v Rebak*[98] the defendant director was liable when, while still a director and employee of the company and without disclosing his plans, he set up a competing company, diverted contracts to that company, solicited the company's customers, removed information and destroyed computer files, all to the advantage of his new business. In *Berryland Books Ltd v BK Books Ltd*[99] Judge Hodge summarised matters in the following terms (and a director's obligations are more onerous in this regard than an employee):

> 'I am satisfied from the authorities cited…that, when drawing the line between legitimate preparation for future competition and undertaking illegitimate competitive activity before an employee has left his employment, the law regards it as unlawful to undertake the following: (1) working for a competitor while still employed; (2) personally competing while still employed; (3) concealing or diverting matured or maturing business opportunities; (4) misusing the employer's property, including confidential information and assets; and (5) taking the steps necessary to establish a competing business so that it is "up and running" or "ready to go" as soon as the employee leaves his employment.'

11-39 As these cases show, practically any preparatory steps to form a competing business will give rise to a possible conflict of interest[100] with the result, given the obligation to disclose and seek authorisation for that conflict (see discussion below),[101] that the director is propelled towards resignation at the earliest possible moment.[102] This approach provides maximum protection for the company by ensuring, in effect, that a director cannot remain in post without disclosing his intention to resign and to compete. This forced early disclosure allows a company to manage the process, for example by requiring that the director leaves immediately or, where a period of notice is enforced, ensuring that the departing director no longer has access to customer data or commercially valuable information.

Resignation

11-40 By resigning, as Hart J noted in *British Midland Tool Ltd v Midland International Tooling Ltd*,[103] a director 'puts an end to his fiduciary obligations to the company so far as concerns any future activity by himself, provided it does not involve any exploitation of confidential information or business opportunities available to him by virtue of his directorship'. As noted at **11-1**, the no-conflict duty generally falls away on resignation,[104] but a former director remains subject to the no-conflict rule (CA 2006, s 175) as regards the exploitation of property, information or opportunity of which he became aware at a time when he was a director (s 170(2)(a)).

---

[98] [2006] 2 BCLC 571.

[99] [2009] 2 BCLC 709, reversed on other grounds [2010] EWCA Civ 1440.

[100] See *British Midland Tool Ltd v Midland International Tooling Ltd* [2003] 2 BCLC 523 and *Shepherds Investments Ltd v Walters* [2007] 2 BCLC 202 as to what may be permissible, but the courts are reluctant to give precise guidance as the circumstances vary so much from case to case.

[101] *Industrial Development Consultants Ltd v Cooley* [1972] All ER 162; *Bhullar v Bhullar* [2003] 2 BCLC 241; *Item Software (UK) Ltd v Fassihi* [2005] 2 BCLC 91; see also *Crown Dilmun v Sutton* [2004] 1 BCLC 468 at 511; *Shepherds Investments Ltd v Walters* [2007] 2 BCLC 202 at 229–30; and Watts (2007) 123 LQR 21.

[102] See *British Midland Tool Ltd v Midland International Tooling Ltd* [2003] 2 BCLC 523; *Coleman Taymar Ltd v Oakes* [2001] 2 BCLC 749.   [103] [2003] 2 BCLC 523.

[104] See *Ultraframe (UK) Ltd v Fielding* [2005] EWHC 1638 at [1310], per Lewison J; also *Wilkinson v West Coast Capital* [2007] BCC 717 at 768, per Warren J.

11-41   This duty obviously comes with a built-in expiry date in the sense that the longer the period post-resignation, the less likely it is that it can be established that the former director is exploiting property etc of which he became aware when he was a director. This prohibition does not extend to *any* property, information, or opportunity of which the director became aware during that period for such a restriction would be contrary to public policy.[105] There must be some link between the exploitation of the property, information or opportunity and the fiduciary position which the director held (as s 170(2)(a) indicates). The link is to the exploitation of property, information or opportunity acquired in circumstances where the director had a conflict, or possible conflict, of interest. As the no-profit duty in s 175(2) is an element of the broader no-conflict duty in s 175(1), there can be no liability under the no-profit rule in the absence of an exploitation of a conflict of interest. The intention in s 170(2)(a) is to prevent the easy evasion of the no-conflict rule by resignation rather than to inhibit unduly the entrepreneurial activities of individuals merely because they once held a directorship.

11-42   For example, in *CMS Dolphin Ltd v Simonet*[106] a director of the claimant company, an advertising agency, left the company and set up a new business. All the staff of the company subsequently joined him as did the principal clients of the company. The company successfully brought an action against him claiming breach of fiduciary duty and seeking an account of profits made by him. The court found that the former director took away from the company the benefit of contracts with existing clients and the business opportunities it had with those clients.[107] Another example of exploitation by a former director of property, information or opportunities in a situation of conflict can be found in *Industrial Development Consultants Ltd v Cooley*,[108] *see* **11-14**, where the director resigned in order to take a contract with the Gas Board which the company was anxious to secure for itself. In *Kingsley IT Consulting Ltd v McIntosh*[109] a company had secured two contracts from a client and had just signed a third contract when the director resigned. The client then terminated the third contract with the company and awarded it to a company set up by the director prior to his resignation.[110] The court found that the former director had acquired the third contract in circumstances where he was bound to carry it out for the benefit of the company if he was to carry it out at all. In all these cases, the directors are liable for exploiting, post-resignation, an opportunity of which they became aware when they were directors and in respect of which they had a conflict of interest.

11-43   The circumstances of resignation can vary greatly, however, as Rix LJ noted in *Foster Bryant Surveying Ltd v Bryant*,[111] and, while the cases discussed here are clear examples of directors resigning in order to exploit property, information or opportunity in a situation of a conflict of interest, other cases are less clear-cut and require careful consideration by the courts. Sometimes resignation is as a result of a breakdown in relations within a company rather than an intention to exploit a conflict of interest. In that scenario, when the defendant does resign and subsequently secures a contract with the company's main customer, the courts have been content (in the absence of use of actual company property,

---

[105] See *Island Export Finance Ltd v Umunna* [1986] BCLC 460 at 482–3; *Murad v Al-Saraj* [2005] EWCA Civ 959 at [62].   [106] [2001] 2 BCLC 704.

[107] See also *Berryland Books Ltd v BK Books Ltd* [2009] 2 BCLC 709 at [32] (reversed in part for reasons which are irrelevant here, see [2010] EWCA Civ 1440).   [108] [1972] 2 All ER 162.

[109] [2006] BCC 875.

[110] No explanation was given as to why the client terminated the contract, but the court concluded that it happened because the director asked the client to transfer the contract to his new company.

[111] [2007] 2 BCLC 239, CA.

such as customer data or technical drawings) to find there is no liability to account.[112] Examples can be found in *Island Export Finance Ltd v Umunna*,[113] *In Plus Group Ltd v Pyke*,[114] and *Foster Bryant Surveying Ltd v Bryant*,[115] but it must be noted that the facts of these cases are exceptional.[116]

11-44 In *Island Export Finance Ltd v Umunna*,[117] following a breakdown in relations within the company, a director (whom the court considered to be the managing director only in name)[118] resigned and within a few months obtained orders from the Cameroon postal authorities for his new company (this was business which previously the company had secured). At the time of his resignation, the court found the company was not actively pursuing further business with the Cameroon authorities. The court rejected a claim for breach of duty finding that there was no conflict of interest at the time he resigned (given the company had moved on to new activities) and, even if there was, the director did not resign in order to exploit it, hence there was no liability to account.[119] In *In Plus Group Ltd v Pyke*[120] the director in question had been excluded from all aspects of running the company for almost 15 months before his resignation which he had delayed to protect his interests as a shareholder in the company. In the absence of a fiduciary relationship (as a result of his exclusion) and any misuse of company property, he was not liable to account on contracts which he subsequently obtained from the company's main customer. In *Foster Bryant Surveying Ltd v Bryant*[121] the period was shorter, the director had ceased to act in any role as a director three months before his formal resignation, but the scenario was the same. Personal relations within the company had broken down and after a period effectively of isolation the director resigned and subsequently secured contracts from the company's main customer.[122] The Court of Appeal upheld the trial judge's finding that there was no breach of fiduciary duty by the director. His resignation had been innocent of any disloyalty or conflict of interest, i.e. he had not resigned to exploit a conflict of interest, there was no finding that any property or opportunity of the company has been taken or exploited by him and he was not liable.[123]

Disclosure and authorisation by independent directors

Disclosure of the conflict

11-45 The cases highlight, as Sedley LJ explained in *In Plus Group Ltd v Pyke*,[124] that not only must the fiduciary not place himself in a position of conflict or possible conflict, 'if, even accidentally, he finds himself in such a position, he must regularise or abandon it', i.e.

---

[112] See Rix LJ in *Foster Bryant Surveying Ltd v Bryant* [2007] 2 BCLC 239 at 271: 'As for the innocence of [the director's] resignation, although the matter may not be free of doubt, it seems well arguable on the authorities that it is critically opposed to liability to account [in the case of a retiring director] where there is no active competition or exploitation of company property while the defendant remains a director.'

[113] [1986] BCLC 460.   [114] [2002] 2 BCLC 201, CA.   [115] [2007] 2 BCLC 239, CA.

[116] See Lowry and Sloszar, 'Judicial Pragmatism: Directors' Duties and Post-resignation Conflict of Duty' [2008] JBL 83.   [117] [1986] BCLC 460; see Grantham (2003) 66 MLR 109.

[118] [1986] BCLC 460 at 468.

[119] [1986] BCLC 460 at 482.   [120] [2002] 2 BCLC 201, CA.

[121] [2007] 2 BCLC 239, see Lowry and Sloszar [2008] JBL 83.

[122] The contracts came as a result of an initiative by the customer, not by the resigning director. A feature of this case was that the company's major client was willing to continue to use the company for as much work as it could handle but wished also to continue to work with the departing director and to that end offered to (and did) set him up in business following his departure from the company.   [123] [2007] 2 BCLC 239 at [89].

[124] [2002] 2 BCLC 201 at 225.

regularise or abandon the conflict. On the latter point, if the director in the *Bhullar*-type situation (see **11-11**) drives past the property for sale and does nothing about it, his inactivity eliminates the conflict of interest, actually a conflict never arises because his personal interests are never engaged (we consider later in the chapter whether he has any duty of disclosure in those circumstances). On the other hand, if the director does want personally to exploit a situation where there is a conflict of interest, he must regularise the position, i.e. he must disclose the conflict of interest and seek authorisation (discussed later). He has the option also of resigning his position, of course, but resignation will not allow him to exploit property, information or opportunity of which he became aware as a director in circumstances in which he had a conflict or possible conflict of interest, as discussed at **11-40** (CA 2006, s 170(2)(a)). Disclosure then is a consequence of being in a position of conflict which the director wishes to exploit personally and part of the process by which he must seek the informed consent of the company.[125]

11-46   A difficult issue is whether there is any general duty of disclosure by directors to the company. In *Bhullar v Bhullar*,[126] Jonathan Parker LJ (with whom Brooke and Schiemann LJJ agreed) concluded that 'the existence of the opportunity [to acquire an adjacent property] was information which it was relevant for the company to know', and, he went on, 'it follows that the appellants [directors] were under a duty to communicate it to the company',[127] applying Roskill J in *Industrial Development Consultants Ltd v Cooley*.[128] This approach was developed, controversially, in *Item Software (UK) Ltd v Fassihi*[129] by Arden LJ (with whom Holman and Mummery LJJ agreed) into a prescriptive obligation on a director to disclose his own misconduct to his company,[130] not as a result of some free-standing duty of disclosure,[131] but, as Arden LJ saw it, as part of the fundamental duty of loyalty to which a director is subject, that is the director's duty to act in what he in good faith considers to be the best interests of his company.[132] More recently, this approach was rejected, correctly it is submitted, by the Scottish Court of Session, Inner House (equivalent to the English Court of Appeal) in *Commonwealth Oil & Gas Co Ltd v Baxter*,[133] see **11-19**, with the court emphasising that the no-conflict rule does not create any obligation on the part of a director to communicate an opportunity of which he becomes aware to the company, rather the no-conflict duty merely bars the director from personally exploiting the opportunity in the absence of informed consent[134] and so the 'duty' to disclose

---

[125]   See *Commonwealth Oil & Gas Co Ltd v Baxter* [2009] CSIH 75, [2009] SLT 1123 at [78], [82].
[126]   [2003] 2 BCLC 241.
[127]   [2003] 2 BCLC 241 at [41].   [128]   [1972] 2 All ER 162 at 173–174.
[129]   [2005] 2 BCLC 91, especially at [40]–[41], [63]–[68].
[130]   See also *Crown Dilmun v Sutton* [2004] 1 BCLC 468 at [181]; *British Midland Tool Ltd v Midland International Tooling Ltd* [2003] 2 BCLC 523 at [89]. It is not entirely clear whether Arden LJ was limiting the duty to disclosure of misconduct rather than the wider category of 'information which it is relevant for the company to know', but, as she bases the disclosure obligation on the duty to act in the best interests of the company, it must also extend to the wider category where such disclosure is in the best interests of the company, see [2005] 2 BCLC 91 at [44]; Etherton J in *Shepherds Investments Ltd v Walters* [2007] 2 BCLC 202 at [132] clearly sees it as extending to the wider category; see also *GHCM Trading Ltd v Maroo* [2012] EWHC 61 at [195] (no reason to restrict the disclosure that can be necessary to misconduct).
[131]   Arden LJ expressly stated that she did not consider it correct to infer from *Bhullar* or *IDC v Cooley* that a fiduciary owes a *separate* and independent duty to disclose his own misconduct or more generally information of relevance and concern to his principal: see [2005] 2 BCLC 91 at [41].
[132]   [2005] 2 BCLC 91 at [41]. For a fuller discussion of the issue, see Hannigan, 'Reconfiguring the No Conflict Rule—Judicial Strictures, a Statutory Restatement and the Opportunistic Director' (2011) 23 SAcLJ 714.   [133]   [2009] CSIH 75, [2009] SLT 1123.
[134]   [2009] CSIH 75, [2009] SLT 1123 at [13], [82]. The President of the Inner House, Lord Hamilton, reserved his position on the analysis adopted by Arden LJ and stated that he was not to be taken as agreeing

arises only where a director seeks the informed consent of the company to a conflict of interest.[135] Apart from disclosure in that context, and in the absence of some contractual provision otherwise requiring disclosure, or a situation where a failure to disclose information amounts to a breach of another duty, such as the duty to exercise care and skill,[136] there is no prescriptive duty on directors to communicate information to the company. The case law supports this approach. In *Commonwealth Oil & Gas Co Ltd v Baxter*[137] the director's involvement in securing an exploration agreement for a second company which his company also had an interest in securing placed him in a position of conflict which he could only have regularised by disclosing to the company his activities with regard to the second company (incidentally the case highlights the difficulty of holding multiple competing directorships) and seeking the informed consent of the company to those activities. He failed to seek that consent, there was no disclosure and so he was in breach of the no-conflict rule. In *Shepherds Investments Ltd v Walters*,[138] which purported to apply *Item Software*, a director who remained in post while developing and selling his own directly competing products was in a position of conflict so that he was required to disclose his activities and get the company's informed consent to what he was doing. In that sense, there was a duty to communicate information to the company. In *Item Software (UK) Ltd v Fassihi*[139] itself the defendant director should have disclosed that, while the company was negotiating with a client (and he was part of the negotiating team) for the renewal of an important distribution contract, he was negotiating to secure the contract for his personal benefit. He could only have regularised that conflict by disclosing his plan to acquire the distribution contract for himself and seeking consent.[140] Again, for the purpose of regularising that conflict, he had a duty to communicate information to the company which it was relevant for it to know.

11-47 Hence there is no free-standing prescriptive duty imposed on a director to disclose or communicate information to a company, only a proscriptive duty on a director not to exploit a conflict or possible conflict of interest without the informed consent of the company.

11-48 In effect, given that in these circumstances a director will be unwilling to disclose his plans and seek authorisation to resolve his conflict and the company equally would be unlikely to consent, the requirement of disclosure forces the director to resign and then s 170(2)(a) applies (see **11-40**) so as to preclude the director from profiting from information of which he became aware as a director in circumstances in which he had a conflict of interest.

---

with the reasoning of the Court of Appeal in *Bhullar*, though he agreed with the result: [2009] CSIH 75, [2009] SLT 1123 at [14]. Lord Nimmo Smith likewise noted that he would not go so far as *Bhullar* or *Item Software* to the extent that they appeared to support a positive duty to disclose or communicate information to the company which it was relevant for it to know, rather, he said, 'there is simply the need for disclosure at the stage when informed consent is sought': [2009] CSIH 75, [2009] SLT 1123 at [82]. Lady Paton, the other member of the court, agreed with Lords Hamilton and Nimmo Smith, at [98].

[135] [2009] CSIH 75 at [81], [82]; and see Hannigan, 'Reconfiguring the No Conflict Rule—Judicial Strictures, a Statutory Restatement and the Opportunistic Director' (2011) 23 SAcLJ 714. See too *Boardman v Phipps* [1967] 2 AC 46; *New Zealand Netherlands Society v Kruys* [1973] 1 WLR 1126.

[136] See, for example, *Lexi Holdings plc v Luqman* [2009] 2 BCLC 1, see **10-35**.

[137] [2009] CSIH 75, [2009] SLT 1123.

[138] [2007] 2 BCLC 202.

[139] [2005] 2 BCLC 91, noted Berg (2005) 121 LQR 213 who is critical of the imposition of a duty to disclose misconduct; see also Ho and Lee, 'A Director's Duty to Confess: A Matter of Good Faith' (2007) CLJ 348.

[140] [2005] 2 BCLC 91 at 104.

Authorisation by directors

11-49 Prior to the CA 2006, a fiduciary who wanted relief from the strict application of the no-conflict duty had to seek the informed consent of the shareholders after full and frank disclosure of all relevant matters,[141] although the articles typically allowed for certain conflicts (essentially interests in transactions with the company and related companies) to be dealt with by disclosure to the board.[142]

11-50 The major change in the CA 2006 is that the directors (other than interested directors) may authorise a conflict of interest and profiting therefrom (s 175(4)(b)). Of course, this might mean no more than authorising multiple directorships, but the section is not so limited and so a conflicted director may be authorised to act, whatever the nature of the conflict, including in theory authorised to start or participate in a competing business.[143] Authorisation by the directors overrides any common law requirement for shareholder approval *unless* (and this is an important qualification in terms of shareholder protection) an enactment[144] or the company's constitution imposes a requirement for shareholder approval (see s 180(1)). But broad though s 175(4)(b) is, there are some constraints on this power to authorise. It must be exercised by the directors acting in accordance with their duties, such as the duty to act in a way most likely to promote the success of the company (s 172). The conflicted director seeking authorisation remains subject to his duties (other than s 175) and he needs also to consider whether he is acting in accordance with s 172.[145] The example given earlier of authorising a director to start or participate in a competing business is unlikely to meet these requirements. Of course, whether anyone would subsequently be in a position to challenge either the authorised director or the authorising directors as to their compliance with their duties is another matter, so these constraints may be more theoretical than real.

11-51 As Lord Wedderburn, the distinguished company lawyer, commented in the House of Lords, to alter from a position of shareholder approval to a point where only the authorisation of the board is required is to enter uncharted territory[146] and the Government accepted in the Parliamentary debates that this is a significant change to the law.[147]

---

[141] *New Zealand Netherlands Society 'Oranje' Inc v Kuys* [1973] 2 All ER 1222; *Gwembe Valley Development Co Ltd v Koshy* [2004] 1 BCLC 131 at 151; *Crown Dilmun v Sutton* [2004] 1 BCLC 468 at 511; *Murad v Al-Saraj* [2005] EWCA Civ 959 at [71].

[142] The Companies (Tables A to F) Regulations 1985, SI 1985/805, Table A, art 85 provided as follows: 'Subject to the provisions of the Act, and provided that he has disclosed to the directors the nature and extent of any material interest of his, a director notwithstanding his office—(a) may be a party to, or otherwise interested in, any transaction or arrangement with the company or in which the company is otherwise interested; (b) may be a director or other officer of, or employed by, or a party to any transaction or arrangement with, or otherwise interested in, any body corporate promoted by the company or in which the company is otherwise interested; and (c) shall not, by reason of his office, be accountable to the company for any benefit which he derives from any such office or employment or from any such transaction or arrangement or from any interest in any such body corporate and no such transaction or arrangement shall be liable to be avoided on the ground of any such interest or benefit.'

[143] See HL Deb, vol 678, GC288 (6 February 2006).

[144] For example, CA 2006, Pt 10, Ch 4 requires shareholder approval in many instances, and see **11-63** as to the overlap between that chapter and s 175.

[145] See GC100 Guidance, para 2.10. The GC100 group essentially represents general counsel and company secretaries of the FTSE 100 companies and it has issued guidance on conflicts: GC100: *Companies Act 2006—Directors' Conflicts of Interest*, 18 January 2008 (hereinafter the GC100 Guidance), available at www.practicallaw.com/6–378–7923.

[146] HL Deb, vol 678, GC321–322, and 324 (9 February 2006). See generally De Mott, 'The Figure in the Landscape: A Comparative Study of Directors' Self-interested Transactions' (1999) CfiLR 190.

[147] See HL Deb, vol 678, GC337 (9 February 2006): 'This is an area where the statutory statement of the general duties of directors will have made changes—I do not shrink from saying that they are significant

11-52 The change originates from a recommendation of the Company Law Review (CLR) that 'the statute should (subject to any stricter rule in the company's constitution, or adopted by agreement) allow the company's rights to be waived by the board, acting independently of any conflicted director'.[148] The justifications suggested by the CLR for such a change (while acknowledging the possibility of board collusion) included that requiring shareholder approval is impractical and onerous; it is inconsistent with the principle that it is for the board to make business assessments; and it stifles entrepreneurial activity.[149] The CLR concluded that allowing disinterested board approval would 'strike the right balance between…encouraging efficient business operations and the take-up of new business opportunities…and providing effective protection against abuse'.[150] The Government agreed that it was important that the no-conflict duty did not 'impose impractical and onerous requirements which stifle entrepreneurial activity'.[151]

11-53 The argument that the no-conflict duty stifles entrepreneurial activity ignores the fact that the duty merely prevents a director in a situation of a conflict of interest from exploiting that situation. It does not mean that an economic opportunity is discarded. The opportunity will be exploited instead by someone other than a fiduciary with a conflict of interest. The central concern of the CLR and the Government initially seems to have been the narrow issue of liability in circumstances where the company could not or would not have taken the opportunity (a matter which, as discussed at **11-33**, is irrelevant to the application of the duty). The initial question was whether that element of the duty might be relaxed. The final broader change to the law arose because the CLR concluded, as the courts have done, that requiring a director to prove that the company could not have exploited the opportunity would raise major factual uncertainties. The solution, as far as the CLR and the Government was concerned, was to provide for board authorisation (excluding the interested directors).[152]

11-54 It is difficult to justify this change in the law even if it is accepted, as is sometimes argued, that the application of the no-conflict duty can be somewhat harsh (though in fact it is difficult to identify cases where the outcome could be so described).[153] In any event, the harshness of the application of fiduciary duties has always been an integral element of their deterrent effect, see **11-4**, and the harshness can be mitigated in terms of the remedies which the court is prepared to grant.[154] Far from 'encouraging efficient business operations' as the Company Law Review envisaged,[155] this shift to board authorisation may encourage the type of conduct which was criticised in earlier times. Instead of directors avoiding situations of possible conflict, they have the option of considering situations

changes—to the common law rules and equitable principles concerning conflicts of interest' (Lord Goldsmith for the Government). It is because of the significance of the change that companies formed under the CA 1985 are only able to take advantage of the new provisions if they pass a resolution allowing for independent authorisation in accordance with s 175(5), see n 157 and **11-55**.

[148] Company Law Review, *Final Report*, vol 1 (2001), para 3.24.
[149] Company Law Review, *Final Report*, vol 1 (2001), para 3.23.
[150] Company Law Review, *Final Report*, vol 1 (2001), para 3.27.
[151] DTI, *Company Law Reform* (Cm 6456, 2005), para 3.3.
[152] Company Law Review, *Final Report*, vol 1 (2001), para 3.24.
[153] *Regal (Hastings) Ltd v Gulliver* [1942] 1 All ER 378, is commonly cited as an example, but see n 72. The outcome in *O'Donnell v Shanahan* [2009] 2 BCLC 666 seems harsh, see n 52, but the court did not have evidence before it as to the extent of any profit made by the defaulting fiduciaries which might alter the perception of the case.
[154] See *Murad v Al-Saraj* [2005] EWCA Civ 959 at [81], per Arden LJ ('… equity has been able skilfully to adapt remedies against defaulting fiduciaries to meet the justice of the case').
[155] See Company Law Review, *Final Report*, vol 1 (2001), para 3.27.

with a view to exploiting them personally, assuming they can get authorisation. They will be tempted to consider opportunities with half an eye to the personal exploitation of the opportunity rather than looking at it solely in terms of their duty to promote the success of the company in the interest of the members as a whole.

11-55   For a public company to take advantage of this authorising power, the company's constitution must include an enabling provision allowing directors to exercise this power: CA 2006, s 175(5)(b).[156] Vice versa, in the case of private companies formed under the CA 2006, the directors have the power to authorise conflicts in accordance with s 175(4) so long as there is nothing in the constitution which invalidates authorisation by the directors: s 175(5)(a). In the case of a private company incorporated before 1 October 2008, the members must pass an ordinary resolution permitting authorisation to be given by the directors.[157]

Public companies

11-56   With regard to public companies, it is difficult to see why directors in such companies would ever authorise private profit-making by a director in a situation of possible conflict between his personal interests and his duty to the company, especially in the light of the remuneration arrangements commonly available to directors of such companies. The shareholders in these companies rightly demand and expect single-minded loyalty of their highly paid directors.[158] It might be argued that shareholders in public companies have a choice on this matter, given that they need to agree to the inclusion of an authorisation provision in the articles (CA 2006, s 175(5)(b)). In practice, the widely dispersed nature of shareholdings in public companies means that shareholders exercise little influence over the content of the constitution. Here, as on other matters, it is for institutional shareholders to take the lead, but they are not opposed to the adoption of authorisation provisions by public companies.[159] Presumably they take the view that their presence and influence ensures that most boards of public companies will be circumspect in their use of this power.

11-57   Also, in public companies, the authorising directors may be wary of granting authorisation as they remain bound by their general duties including the duty to exercise care and skill, the duty to act within their powers and, in particular, the duty to act in the way most likely to promote the success of the company.[160] They will also have an eye to protecting their own

---

[156]   Public companies formed under the CA 1985 must change their articles to allow for authorisation and it is thought that many have altered their articles to allow for authorisation. Public companies formed under the CA 2006 may choose to have an authorisation provision in their articles from formation and, again, it seems it has become a standard provision in public company articles. The model articles do not make any provision for authorisation so it cannot arise by default: see The Companies (Model Articles) Regulations 2008, SI 2008/3229, art 14 (Ltd); art 16 (Plc).

[157]   The Companies Act 2006 (Commencement No 5, Transitional Provisions and Savings) Order 2007, SI 2007/3495, art 9, Sch 4, Pt 3, para 47. Note that this requirement for shareholders to pass a resolution permitting the directors to authorise in accordance with CA 2006, s 175(5)(a) is not a transitional arrangement—it applies indefinitely to private companies formed before 1 October 2008. Each such private company must obtain a resolution of its shareholders before its directors are in a position to exercise these authorisation powers.

[158]   See *Bristol & West BS v Mothew* [1996] 4 All ER 698 at 712, per Millett LJ.

[159]   The GC100 Guidance, see n 145, para 1.8 notes that shareholders (i.e. institutional shareholders) are unlikely to raise objections to the exercise of these authorisation powers provided the company has a sound governance structure, effective procedures for exercising the powers and confirms compliance with such procedures.

[160]   See HL Deb, vol 678, GC326 (9 February 2006). The authorising directors will need to consider how allowing the conflict would promote the success of the company, (the GC100 Guidance (n 145) suggests, for

reputations. The net result may be that in public companies, certainly large public companies, the power may be used for little other than authorising multiple directorships.

Private companies

11-58 The greatest concern about the change from shareholder approval to board authorisation must lie with regard to the private company with a small number of shareholder/directors. In such companies, the exclusion of the interested director(s) from the board for the purposes of authorisation will do little to turn the board into an independent arbiter of this issue. In all probability the remainder of the board will be family members or close business colleagues who are likely to be incapable of exercising any independence on the issue of a director personally exploiting an opportunity in circumstances where he has a conflict between his personal interests and his duty to promote the interests of the company. It will be difficult to assess the motives of the authorising directors in such small companies and in any event the courts have always been sceptical (or realistic) about their ability to determine directors' motives in the face of an assertion that the directors honestly considered the interests of the company.[161]

11-59 The diversion and exploitation of corporate opportunities, information etc is central to the many disputes in these companies[162] which end up in court as petitions alleging unfairly prejudicial conduct under CA 2006, s 994 (see Chapter 17). Prior to the CA 2006, the courts regarded the exploitation of property, information or opportunity in circumstances of a conflict of interest as conduct clearly in breach of fiduciary duty and conduct of the company's affairs in an unfairly prejudicial manner (see **17-44**). With this change in the law, the position alters significantly. It is now possible (with a little ingenuity and bearing in mind that the courts will not second-guess the business judgement of directors) for directors to approve at a board meeting the diversion of assets and opportunities to one of their number, assuming a quorate board of disinterested directors can be assembled. Of course, as mentioned at **11-50,** all the authorising directors remain subject to their individual fiduciary duties, including the duty to promote the success of the company (s 172) and therein lies the protection of the minority shareholder. But, enforcing those duties is problematic, not least for the difficulties which the court would face in determining the motives behind authorisation. The result may be that the minority shareholder finds himself in a company with dwindling assets and business. The difference is that, following the change in the law, the diversion of contracts and the exploitation of information and opportunities etc becomes approved profit-making by a director and there is no breach of duty constituting unfairly prejudicial conduct. A petitioner would need to show therefore that the exercise of the power to authorise (or possibly even seeking authorisation) was contrary to understandings between the shareholders such that it amounted to conduct of the company's affairs in an unfairly prejudicial manner.[163] That argument may be difficult to make given that, in the case of a private company, an exclusion of the power

---

example, that allowing directors to accept other directorships could be seen as gaining access to industry or sector expertise which could be valuable to the company), but there is some difficulty in seeing the benefit to the company where a director seeks authorisation to pursue and profit from an opportunity in circumstances where he has a conflict of interest.

[161] See *Regal (Hastings) Ltd v Gulliver* [1942] 1 All ER 378 at 392, HL, per Lord Wright; *Ex p James* (1803) 8 Ves 337 at 345: 'no court is equal to the examination and ascertainment of the truth in these cases'.

[162] See for example, *Re Little Olympian Each-Ways Ltd (No 3)* [1995] 1 BCLC 454; *Re Full Cup International Trading Ltd* [1995] 1 BCLC 636; *Lloyd v Casey* [2002] 1 BCLC 454; *Allmark v Burnham* [2006] 2 BCLC 437; *Re Baumler (UK) Ltd, Gerrard v Koby* [2005] 1 BCLC 92.

[163] See **17-51**; *O'Neill v Phillips* [1999] 2 BCLC 1, HL.

to authorise must be contained in the constitution, essentially in the articles (CA 2006, s 175(5)(a)), so it might be difficult to argue reliance on an understanding in those circumstances. Also, as noted at **11-55**, private companies formed before 1 October 2008 must pass a resolution allowing their directors to exercise these authorisation powers, in which case that resolution, arguably, would negate any suggestion that there was an understanding that the powers would not be exercised. Evidence of such a resolution will point the other way, to a taking of a power, not a resiling from it. It may not be possible therefore to challenge an authorisation using CA 2006, s 994.

11-60 It is also possible to envisage situations where the risk is to the company's creditors as where the directors (in a mutually beneficial way) divert business away from the company, as part of authorised conflicts, until eventually the company is left with insufficient assets to meet the claims of creditors. Again, theoretically, a claim for misfeasance under IA 1986, s 212 could lie against the interested director (not for breach of CA 2006, s 175, but possibly for breach of s 172) or against the authorising directors (again, possibly for breach of s 172 or even s 171), but whether a claim would be brought is problematic, given the costs issues involved in funding litigation by a liquidator, even before considering the difficulties of establishing the substantive case of breach of duty.

Obtaining authorisation

11-61 Authorisation by disinterested directors is required. It is not clear whether authorisation by committee is possible, but it seems unlikely. Of course, it may be very practical to use a committee (especially for large companies with a number of directors needing authorisation at any time) and it is common for many management matters to be delegated to committees rather than being dealt with by the full board. It is difficult to accept, however, that Parliament, having effected such a radical change in the law and conferred a statutory power on 'the directors', intended that these matters would and could be dealt with by a committee.[164] The trust of the provision is consideration of 'the matter' by the directors as a board.

11-62 Authorisation may be unconditional or subject to any restrictions which the disinterested directors choose to impose. Authorisation is required with regard to specific transactions ('the matter') and it is not possible for a director to give a general notice of matters giving rise to a conflict of interest in contrast with the position under CA 2006, s 177(2) (see **11-98**). The explanation given in the Parliamentary debates for the difference in approach was that s 177 deals with transactions where the company is a party to the transaction and will know the matters surrounding it, but the type of conflict of interest governed by s 175 will necessarily relate to things of which the company knows nothing and in respect of which a general notice would not suffice.[165]

11-63 There is no prescribed level of disclosure by a director and the court will be guided, no doubt, by the common law requirement of full and frank disclosure as to the nature of the opportunity so that the other directors can see what the director's interest is and how far it extends.[166] A director will have every incentive to make maximum disclosure for the

---

[164] Interestingly, the GC100 Guidance, see n 145, envisages companies using a reviewing committee to review annually the exercise of the power, but the power should be exercised by the board (see Guidance para 4.10).

[165] See HL Deb, vol 678, GC328 (9 February 2006) where Lord Goldsmith noted that a general notice in this context would leave the company too much in the dark.

[166] *Movitex Ltd v Bulfield* [1988] BCLC 104 at 121; *Imperial Mercantile Credit Association v Coleman* (1873) LR 6 HL 189 at 205.

consequence of inadequate disclosure is that authorisation is not validly obtained and the director would be in breach of the no-conflict duty.

11-64 Authorisation is only effective if the director in question and any other 'interested directors' are excluded from the quorum[167] (but they do not have to be excluded from participation in the discussion, though the articles may so provide)[168] and the matter must be agreed without their voting or the matter would have been agreed to even if their votes had not been counted (CA 2006, s 175(6)). There is no definition of who is an 'interested' director for these purposes and so is excluded. Many family companies have husbands and wives as directors and the question is whether a husband (as a disinterested director for the purpose of s 175(4)) could authorise an interested director, his wife, to exploit a situation on her own account.[169] The CA 2006 does not expressly address this point,[170] but if it is possible for a spouse to be treated as a disinterested director for these purposes, the risk of board collusion is significantly increased.

11-65 The answer lies not in definitions of family relationships for there is always a risk that the exercise of fiduciary duty may be influenced by any personal relationship.[171] The proper approach is to focus on the substance of the transaction (which in this context is the granting of authorisation) and ask whether the authorising director, though not having a personal interest in the transaction, has a conflict of interest with regard to the granting of authorisation (i.e. a conflict between a personal interest in facilitating the other director by granting authorisation and his duty to promote the interests of the company). If so, that (different) conflict would mean that the director would have to step aside by virtue of his obligations under CA 2006, s 175(1), unless the shareholders consent to his acting despite that conflict or, possibly, the articles so provide, relying on s 180(4)(a) and (b).

11-66 This same approach would apply to business associates on the board who may be close personal friends of the director seeking authorisation, though not related by family connection. As discussed at **11-60**, there is a risk of mutually supportive collusion between the interested director and such associates who may divide up opportunities between themselves and the company on a basis which favours their personal interests rather than the interests of the company as a whole. The risk from such collusion lies on the minority shareholders and the creditors. As appropriate, such directors too should be treated as having a conflict of interest and excluded from the quorum and voting, unless the shareholders otherwise resolve.

11-67 In small private companies, these exclusions may mean that there are no disinterested directors capable of forming a quorum or voting and so authorisation by the directors may

---

[167] The Government emphasised that compliance with the requirements of CA 2006, s 175(6) (quorum and voting position) does not of itself guarantee that it is a valid authorisation, but non-compliance with these elements renders it automatically invalid and the constitution may impose additional requirements: see HL Deb, vol 678, GC326 (9 February 2006).

[168] See Clark, 'UK Company Law Reform and Directors' Exploitation of "Corporate Opportunities"' (2006) ICCLR 231 at 239 who notes that, given the degree of influence that directors may exert on fellow directors, the interested directors should have been excluded from participation.

[169] See Prentice & Payne (2004) 120 LQR 198 at 201.

[170] Many provisions of CA 2006, Pt 10, Ch 4 (for example, s 190) extend the application of various provisions to directors and connected persons (defined in s 252) but this categorisation is not used for the purposes of s 175(5).

[171] See David Richards J on this issue in *Newgate Stud Co v Penfold* [2008] 1 BCLC 46 at 105–6.

not be possible,[172] which solves the problems identified at **11-59**. Of course, in any type of company, there may be occasions when all the directors are conflicted.[173] In these situations, the common law option, retained by CA 2006, s 180(4)(a), of seeking the informed consent of the shareholders (to the director's personal exploitation of the relevant opportunity, etc) following full disclosure of all relevant information[174] would then be useful, see **11-69**.

11-68   Finally, given the significance of this change in the law on authorisation, it is curious that there is no provision for shareholders to be notified of any authorisations granted under CA 2006, s 175(4)(b), whether in a public or in a private company (bearing in mind that shareholders do not have access to board minutes). The CLR had indicated that disclosure of the transaction in the annual accounts and reports would be an important safeguard,[175] but the Government was not persuaded that any additional protection was required other than the measures in s 175(6) re quorum and voting etc and the duties imposed on authorising directors.[176] It is impossible therefore for shareholders to gauge the extent to which these powers are being exercised and in what circumstances. Given the absence of any transparency, shareholders should consider imposing a disclosure requirement via the articles and larger companies may want to find a disclosure mechanism which is appropriate in their context.[177] The conflicted directors will also wish to ensure that there is an accurate record internally so that there is no ambiguity about the authorisation granted, its date, terms and any restrictions, etc. Likewise, it is in the company's interests to maintain a detailed record in case of future disputes and possible litigation.

Authorisation/ratification by the company

11-69   All the general duties imposed on directors, including CA 2006, s 175, are subject to any rule of law enabling the company to give authority for anything to be done or omitted by the directors, or any of them, that would otherwise be a breach of duty (s 180(4)(a)).[178] Full and frank disclosure is required for authorisation to be effective.[179]

11-70   Where there are difficulties in securing authorisation by disinterested directors, it may be possible to look for shareholder authorisation or ratification. But there are a number of issues to consider. The ill-defined common law limits to the power of the shareholders to

---

[172]   In more dubious cases, we can expect to see people appointed to the board for short time periods precisely to provide a quorum of 'disinterested' directors who can authorise the matter and the courts will need to be alert to this possibility, as they were in a different context in *Re In a Flap Envelope Ltd* [2004] 1 BCLC 64.   [173]   See, for example, *Lee Panavision Ltd v Lee Lighting Ltd* [1992] BCLC 22.

[174]   See *New Zealand Netherlands Society 'Oranje' Inc v Kuys* [1973] 2 All ER 1222; *Gwembe Valley Development Co Ltd v Koshy* [2004] 1 BCLC 131 at 151; *Crown Dilmun v Sutton* [2004] 1 BCLC 468 at 511; *Murad v Al-Saraj* [2005] EWCA Civ 959 at [71].

[175]   Company Law Review, *Final Report*, vol 1 (2001), para 3.24.

[176]   See HL Deb, vol 678, GC325–6 (9 February 2006).

[177]   See GC100 Guidance, n 145, which suggests including information in the annual corporate governance element of the directors' report and, perhaps, a register of authorisations, see para 4.7.

[178]   Only actual consent will obviate the liability to account, it is not enough to assert that the shareholders would have consented had they been asked, see *Murad v Al-Saraj* [2005] EWCA Civ 959 at [71].

[179]   See *New Zealand Netherlands Society 'Oranje' Inc v Kuys* [1973] 2 All ER 1222; *Gwembe Valley Development Co Ltd v Koshy* [2004] 1 BCLC 131 at 151; *Crown Dilmun v Sutton* [2004] 1 BCLC 468 at 511; *Murad v Al-Saraj* [2005] EWCA 959 at [71]. If the shareholders are informed as to the nature and extent of the conflict and all assent informally, applying *Re Duomatic Ltd* [1969] 1 All ER 161, that unanimous informal assent suffices to waive the conflict and permit a director to profit, see *Lee v Futurist Developments Ltd* [2011] 1 BCLC 653 at [46], assuming no fraud on creditors. As to the *Duomatic* principle, see **15-73**.

authorise in advance or ratify subsequently conduct that would otherwise be a breach of duty are preserved by s 180(4)(a) and s 239(7). The limits to shareholder power are drawn at illegal or ultra vires conduct, fraud on creditors and fraud on the minority, see the discussion at **18-31**. The fraud on the minority category prevents shareholders from ratifying acts which amount to the misappropriation of 'money, property or advantages which belong to the company or in which the other shareholders are entitled to participate',[180] though *Regal (Hastings) Ltd v Gulliver*[181] suggests that bona fide incidental profit-making is ratifiable.[182] The CA 2006 s 239(7) retains the common law as to acts that are incapable of being ratified and therefore limits the possibility for seeking ratification of a conflict of interest which falls into the fraud on the minority category. Further, even with respect to ratifiable wrongs, s 239 imposes voting restrictions so that on any resolution to ratify a (ratifiable) breach of duty, the votes of the interested director (if a member of the company) and any member connected with him must be disregarded.[183] That statutory voting limitation applies only to ratification and, therefore, it might seem that there may be tactical advantage in seeking prior shareholder authorisation rather than relying on subsequent ratification. But it is not necessarily the case that a shareholder/director can seek prior shareholder authorisation for a conflict of interest and then vote to secure that authorisation. The general position is that a shareholder has a right to vote on any matter though he has a personal interest opposed to or different from the interests of the company, but that right is subject to some ill-defined constraints which preclude its use in what can be described as an oppressive, unfair and improper manner.[184] Given an appropriate set of facts, that common law position may preclude a majority shareholder voting as a shareholder to authorise his exploitation of a situation where the shareholder, as a director, has a conflict of interest. There is not necessarily therefore a voting advantage in seeking authorisation rather than ratification. The difference is that the extent of the common law limitations on self-interested voting in cases of authorisation is unclear whereas there is a clear statutory prohibition on interested voting on ratification.

Authorisation via the articles

11-71 A company may make provision in its articles for conflicts of interest and the general duties owed by a director are not infringed by anything done or omitted to be done in accordance with those provisions (CA 2006, s 180(4)(b)). The extent to which such provision may be made is limited, however, by s 232 which prohibits provisions exempting directors from liability for breach of duty, save such provisions in the articles 'as has previously been lawful for dealing with conflicts of interest' (s 232(4)). There is uncertainty as to how much leeway this gives with respect to modifying the application of s 175 via provisions in the articles. It is unlikely that the courts will accept anything in the nature of a universal authorisation via the articles, for example with regard to conflicts arising

---

[180] *Burland v Earle* [1902] AC 83 at 93, per Lord Davey; *Cook v Deeks* [1916] 1 AC 554; *Daniels v Daniels* [1978] 2 All ER 89. [181] [1942] 1 All ER 378.

[182] See [1942] 1 All ER 378 at 389, per Lord Russell; also at 394, per Lord Wright.

[183] CA 2006, s 239(3), (4); connected persons are defined in ss 252–255.

[184] See *North-West Transportation Co Ltd v Beatty* (1887) 12 App Cas 589, at 583–94, per Sir Richard Baggallay, PC (director was able to vote as a shareholder to ratify his own undisclosed conflict of interest in a transaction with the company, but the transaction in that case was fair, the price market based and the company benefited from the transaction); also *Burland v Earle* [1902] AC 83 at 94, PC; *Cook v Deeks* [1916] AC 554 at 564, PC (majority shareholders cannot make a present to themselves of an asset belonging in equity to the company). See generally Hannigan, 'Limitations on a Shareholder's Right to Vote—Effective Ratification Revisited' [2000] JBL 493.

from a particular class of transactions. Indeed when it is considered that Parliament has already significantly modified the no-conflict duty via s 175(4)(b), it seems unlikely that the courts will see much scope for further dilution of the duty in s 175 by provisions in the articles,[185] a point confirmed by the wording of s 232(4) ('such provision as has previously been lawful').

11-72 Measures 'previously lawful' included provisions such as 1985 Table A, art 85[186] (now reflected to a certain extent in CA 2006, s 177, discussed at **11-83**) and provisions dealing with quorum and voting requirements for board meetings where a conflicted transaction with the company was being considered.[187] Those provisions were relatively modest pragmatic provisions dealing with the reality of business relationships, situations which would fall primarily within s 177 rather than s 175. That background would further support the view that there is little scope for provisions in the articles with respect to the broader conflicts governed by s 175. Typically, the articles will be used to deal with multiple directorships, particularly with the practical issues such as limiting access to confidential information and allowing for the director's exclusion from certain meetings etc, see **11-26**. Sometimes the articles may identify certain transactions as not being transactions which can reasonably be regarded as likely to give rise to a conflict of interest for the purposes of CA 2006, s 175(4)(a) (and therefore exempt from the application of s 175), but such provisions cannot be determinative of the scope of the duty—it is for the courts ultimately to determine whether a conflict cannot reasonably be regarded as likely to give rise to a conflict of interest.

11-73 Of course, it is also possible to use the articles to tighten, not to loosen, the requirements of CA 2006, s 175 by requiring shareholder approval in addition to authorisation by the directors (see s 180(1)). In some companies shareholders may be more comfortable with the protection of shareholder approval rather than director approval, however disinterested.

C Benefits from third parties

Introduction

11-74 The CA 2006, s 176 makes provision for a distinct aspect of the no-conflict duty, namely the acceptance of benefits from third parties which would include the acceptance of bribes,[188] the law looking broadly to any payment or benefit or bribe which puts the recipient in a position of conflict in breach of his duty of loyalty. The civil liability of a director

---

[185] The Government emphasised in the debates that it did not want a return to the old practice of widely drafted exemption clauses: see HL Deb, vol 682, cols 721–2 (23 May 2006).

[186] The text of art 85 is set out at n 142.

[187] Again, the type of provision previously found in the 1985 Table A, see arts 94 and 95, and see SI 1985/805.

[188] Both the giver and the recipient of a bribe would be guilty of an offence under the Bribery Act 2010, ss 1 and 2. See *Fiona Trust & Holding Corp v Privalov* [2010] EWHC 3199 at [70]–[73] where Andrew Smith J notes that English law takes a broad view of what constitutes a bribe for the purposes of civil claims and it is a question of fact where the line is to be drawn between 'a little present' and a bribe and the court will look at the bribe or gift or benefit to see if it is sufficient to create a real possibility of a conflict of interest. See also *Daraydan Holdings Ltd v Solland International Ltd* [2005] Ch 119 at [52]–[53].

is the same with respect to bribes, benefits and secret profits (see **13-16**), but additionally bribery is a criminal offence under the Bribery Act 2010.[189]

11-75 The relationship between CA 2006, s 176 and s 175 is unclear, in particular as to whether it is possible for directors to authorise (under s 175(4)(b)) the acceptance of benefits from third parties (obviously there is no question of authorising the acceptance of bribes). On the one hand, there seems no reason why benefits cannot be authorised since, as the Explanatory Notes make clear,[190] a situation where a director benefits from his position will fall into both sections, as a conflict and exploitation of a conflict within s 175 (there must be a conflict for s 176 to apply, see s 176(4)) and an acceptance of a benefit under s 176 (and the duties are cumulative in any event, s 179). If s 175 also applies, then s 175(4)(b) must apply in the absence of any provision excluding its particular application in the context of s 176. It would also be strange that under s 175 a director could be authorised by disinterested directors to exploit an opportunity for his personal benefit while his acceptance of a benefit conferred by reason of his position (which while generating a conflict may be quite a modest benefit) cannot be so authorised. Further support for the view that s 175 does apply is that s 180 deals with specific overlaps and exclusions between ss 175, 176, 177 and Pt 10, Ch 4. It would have been easy for Parliament to have added a clause excluding the application of s 175 in cases where s 176 applies, but it did not do so.

11-76 On the other hand, it could be argued that the reason why benefits were singled out in CA 2006, s 176 is precisely to ensure that they cannot be so authorised, supported by the fact that the Explanatory Notes appear to rule out the possibility of board authorisation.[191] This provision, s 176, is distinguishable from the broad brush of s 175 as it focuses on benefits conferred by reason of being a director or doing or not doing anything as a director, i.e. the focus is on the office of director. It is payments with respect to the office and the conduct of the office which are caught by this provision. Looked at in that light, and given that such payments undoubtedly undermine the duty of loyalty of the office-holder to the company, it is right that authorisation by the board should not be permitted, though it would have been better if the statute had made that clear.

The scope of the duty

11-77 Section 176 imposes a duty on directors not to accept benefits from a third party conferred *by reason of* his being a director, or *by reason of* his doing or not doing anything as a director,[192] again the underlying rationale for the prohibition being that accepting the benefit raises the possibility of a conflict between the director's duty to the

---

[189] Bribery is an evil practice which threatens the foundations of any civilised society: *Attorney General for Hong Kong v Reid* [1994] 1 All ER 1 at 4, per Lord Templeman. See too *Fyffes Group Ltd v Templeman* [2000] 2 Lloyd's Reports 643.　　[190] See Explanatory Notes to the Companies Act 2006, para 344.
[191] See Explanatory Notes to the Companies Act 2006, para 344, though the statement in that paragraph is not entirely free from ambiguity, stating first that the acceptance of a benefit giving rise to an actual or potential conflict of interest will fall within s 175 as well as s 176 before then stating that s 176 is not subject to any provision for board authorisation. Of course, if s 175 applies, then s 175(4)(b) applies.
[192] The provision is limited to benefits accepted by the director, leaving some apparent scope for evasion by way of benefits conferred on persons connected with the director. For example, a third party might pay the university fees of the director's children in return for the director's support in ensuring that the company awards a contract to that third party. Leaving aside the difficulty in discovering such arrangements, the director would be in a position of conflict and CA 2006, s 175(1) would apply so such arrangements would be caught.

company and his interest in accommodating the giver of the benefit.[193] As with s 175, liability is not dependent on establishing that the director acted to advantage the giver or that the company suffered loss as a consequence, it suffices that a conflict has arisen.[194] The benefit must be conferred as a consequence, by reason of, the office so to bring a conflict within this section rather than s 175 (which may be desirable so as to exclude the possibility of a benefit being authorised), so it will be necessary to show that the benefit was conferred because of the office or something done or omitted in that office.[195] The prohibition extends to a former director who may not accept benefits from third parties conferred by reason of things done or omitted by the director before he ceased to be a director (s 170(2)(b)). 'Benefit' for these purposes is to be given its ordinary dictionary meaning, of 'a favourable or helpful factor, circumstance, advantage or profit' and, in particular, 'benefit' is not limited to a tangible corporeal advantage.[196] All benefits, whether in cash or kind, such as appointing the director to another position, are included.[197]

11-78 In *Premier Waste Management Ltd v Towers*[198] a director borrowed machinery for personal use from one of the company's customers.[199] The parties did not know one another, it seems, but a company employee asked the customer whether he could assist. Arguably, the benefit was conferred on the director by reason of his being a director with the customer assuming, presumably, that there would be some advantage to him in doing the favour, even if he did not know the director personally. The director did not disclose the arrangement (which he considered to be an entirely private matter) to the company which subsequently sued him for breach of the no-conflict rule. The equipment consisted of an excavator and dumper truck which were old, dilapidated and in poor condition and which were used by the director for a period of about six months while renovating a farmhouse—the value to the director was assessed at £5,000, approximately. Having lost at first instance, the director appealed unsuccessfully. Giving judgment, Mummery LJ emphasised the simple, strict and salutary duties of loyalty and no conflict to which directors are subject (the transaction preceded the CA 2006 so there is no reference to the statutory provisions). There was a real possibility of conflict since the director was potentially involved in approving transactions involving the customer. The fact that the company would not have been interested in this transaction with the customer, the absence of any finding of bad faith on the part of the director, the absence of quantifiable loss suffered by the company, the fact that the benefit to the director was small and that the customer received no benefit from it, were all irrelevant and, in Mummery LJ's view, missed the point.[200] A director's liability for disloyalty in office does not depend on proof of fault or proof that a conflict of interest has in fact caused the company loss. Accordingly, the director was in breach of his duties and liable to account for the benefit received. Applying the statute, the situation could be interpreted either as the

---

[193] See *Fiona Trust & Holding Corp v Privalov* [2010] EWHC 3199 at [73].

[194] See *Daraydan Holdings Ltd v Solland International Ltd* [2005] Ch 119 at [52]–[53] with regard to bribes, but equally applicable to benefits obtained in a situation of conflict, see *Premier Waste Management Ltd v Towers* [2012] 1 BCLC 67, discussed at **11-78**.

[195] See Lord Goldsmith who commented in the debates that the clause applies 'only to benefits conferred because the director is a director of the company or because of something that the director does or doesn't do as director': see HL Debs, GC col 330, 9 February 2006.

[196] See HC Official Report, SC D (Company Law Reform Bill) 11 July 2006, col 622 (Solicitor General).

[197] See HL Deb, vol 678, GC330 (9 February 2006).   [198] [2012] 1 BCLC 67.

[199] See [2012] 1 BCLC 67 at [20].

[200] [2012] 1 BCLC 67 at [48], [51].

straightforward application of s 175 or as a benefit conferred on the director by reason of his being a director and a breach of s 176.

Limits to the duty

Benefits from related companies or service agreements

11-79 There are exemptions for benefits received from the company or associate companies or from persons acting on their behalf or from companies which provide services to the company via the director (CA 2006, s 176(2)). These exemptions are designed to ensure that directors' remuneration and service contract agreements, especially the common arrangement for the provision of a director's services via a management company, are not within the prohibition (see s 176(3)).

Acceptance not likely to give rise to conflict

11-80 There is no de minimis financial threshold with the Government choosing instead to limit the scope of the provision by reference to the risk of a conflict of interest[201] and so the duty is not infringed if the acceptance of the benefit cannot reasonably be regarded as likely to give rise to a conflict of interest[202] (CA 2006, s 176(4)). This limitation means that 'ordinary' commercial hospitality (meals, gifts, tickets for entertainment or sporting events) is not caught.[203] Guidance as to benefits which 'cannot reasonably be regarded as likely to give rise to a conflict of interest' may be provided in the articles (see **11-82**).

Benefits approved or exempt under Part 10, Ch 4

11-81 A director is not required to comply with CA 2006, s 176 if the transaction in respect of which the benefit arises is approved by the shareholders or is exempt from approval in accordance with CA 2006, Pt 10, Ch 4 (s 180(2)). Part 10, Ch 4, is discussed in Chapter 12.

Authorised by the company or via the articles

11-82 The shareholders may authorise the acceptance of benefits from third parties (CA 2006, s 180(4)(a)) and may ratify a breach of s 176 (subject to s 239), subject to the common law limits on authorisation and ratification, discussed at **11-69**. Acceptance of a bribe would be a breach of s 172 and s 176 and a criminal offence under the Bribery Act 2010 and cannot be authorised or ratified by the shareholders, not even unanimously. As noted, the articles may make provision for the acceptance of benefits from third parties

---

[201] See HC Official Report, SC D (Company Law Reform Bill) 11 July 2006, cols 622–4 (Solicitor General). The Government considered that any financial thresholds would be purely arbitrary.

[202] See *Fiona Trust & Holding Corp v Privalov* [2010] EWHC 3199 at [73], where Andrew Smith J noted that some gifts or benefits are too small and amount only to 'a little present' so that the question, as ever, is whether the benefit or bribe is sufficient to create a real possibility of a conflict between interest and duty. In *Premier Waste Management Ltd v Towers* [2012] 1 BCLC 67, discussed at **11-78**, a benefit what might have appeared to be 'de minimis' nevertheless, did give rise to a real possible conflict and the fact that the benefit gained by the director was small made no difference to the breach of duty.

[203] The 'value' of some of these benefits, such as tickets to prestigious events, may be greater than their financial value and hospitality over a long period of time may be cumulatively valuable so it may be difficult to determine at what point 'hospitality' crosses over into a conflict of interest prohibited by s 176.

(s 180(4)(b)), subject to s 232(4)), see **11-71**, but for the reasons given there, which would be equally applicable to s 176, the scope for use of the articles is limited.

D Proposed transactions with the company

Introduction

11-83 The distinct situation where a director is in any way directly or indirectly interested in a proposed transaction or arrangement *with the company* is governed by CA 2006, s 177, not by s 175.[204] The director must disclose the conflict of interest to the board before the transaction is entered into so enabling the board to decide how to proceed in the light of this information.[205] In essence, what s 177 addresses is a situation which necessarily creates a possible conflict of interest, but rather than leave it to fall within s 175 (which would be commercially inconvenient), s 177 sets out the manner of dealing with the conflict, in this case by prior disclosure to the company, via the board, whose decision to proceed with the transaction in the light of the conflict can be seen as a consent by the company to the conflict. Hence the prohibition in s 175(1) does not apply to a conflict arising in relation to a proposed transaction or arrangement with the company which is managed instead in accordance with s 177. It is a duty of disclosure consequent on what would otherwise be a duty to avoid a conflict of interest.

11-84 The provision is limited to proposed transactions with the company and does not extend to proposed transactions with a subsidiary or holding company of the company which will fall within CA 2006, s 175 and which must therefore be authorised by the directors under s 175(4)(b) or possibly dealt with under the articles (see **11-71**).

11-85 Compliance with s 177 overrides the common law requirement for shareholder approval unless the company's constitution imposes a requirement for shareholder approval (see s 180(1)).[206] Disclosure under s 177 does not obviate the need for compliance with Pt 10, Ch 4 where the transaction or arrangement falls within one of the categories regulated by that chapter and which may require disclosure and approval by the shareholders in addition to disclosure to the directors under s 177 (s 180(3)). Though not required to comply with s 175, a director subject to the disclosure obligations of s 177 remains subject to all the other general duties (s 179). Particularly relevant in this context is his duty (under s 171) to act within his powers and (under s 172) to promote the success of the company.

---

[204] Of course, a situation under CA 2006, s 175 of potential conflict may evolve into a situation which then is governed by s 177 when that conflict gives rise to an actual transaction or arrangement with the company, for example, the director who is a potential supplier to the company (so within s 175) and who then secures a supply contract with the company for his business (and so is within s 177): see the GC100 Guidance, n 145.

[205] The company can consider whether to enter into the transaction, on what terms and with what safeguards, see HL Deb, vol 678, GC334 (9 February 2006).

[206] A listed company with a Premium Listing must comply with the Listing Rules (LR) requirements (see LR 11) with respect to related party transactions ('related party' is defined in LR 11.1.4. and includes directors and substantial shareholders) which, subject to certain exceptions, require the transaction to be notified to the market, a circular sent to the shareholders (including a statement by the board that the transaction or arrangement is fair and reasonable as far as the shareholders are concerned and that the directors have been so advised by an independent adviser) and prior approval of the shareholders obtained (with the related party and associates required to abstain from voting)—there are modifications for smaller transactions, see LR 11.1.10.

11-86 The leading authority on conflicts of interest in transactions with the company is *Aberdeen Rly Co v Blaikie Bros*[207] where a company was entitled to set aside a contract for the purchase of railway equipment entered into between it and a partnership when it transpired that the chairman of its board of directors was also a partner in the partnership. The conflict of interest is obvious: the director is obliged to act in the interests of the company, in this case, to purchase goods on behalf of the company at the lowest possible price while, as a member of the partnership, he wishes to sell the goods at the highest price. Where such a conflict exists, the law recognises that the director, despite his best intentions, may be swayed by his own self-interest.[208] The fact that the director is only one member of the partnership which is contracting with the company does not affect the application of the no-conflict rule nor does the fact that the transaction is fair.[209] All that is relevant is the existence of a possible conflict of interest and duty.

11-87 A director's conflict of interest in a proposed transaction with the company may arise in all sorts of direct and indirect ways. In *Aberdeen Rly Co v Blaikie Bros*,[210] as noted, the director was effectively on the side of both the purchaser and the seller of goods. In *Movitext Ltd v Bulfield*[211] the directors leased property which they owned to the company and took security from the company with respect to its obligations under the lease. As the owners of the property, the directors were the lessors while, as directors of the company, they were acting for the tenant. In *Gwembe Valley Development Co Ltd v Koshy*[212] the company purchased foreign currency from another business controlled by the company's managing director. In these transactions, the director is on both sides of the relationship, acting on behalf of the company and acting on his own behalf and so in a position of conflict between his personal interest and his duty to promote the interests of the company.

11-88 Of course, the mere existence of a conflict of interest is not necessarily to the company's disadvantage and the application of a strict no-conflict duty with regard to transactions with the company can be commercially inconvenient. The director may be willing to give the company a favourable deal and the prohibition of dealings between a director and his company may force a company to incur costs in contracting with an outsider when an insider is the sole or most favourable source of the goods or services which the company requires.[213] The director may have been appointed to the board precisely in order to foster certain business relationships and so possible conflicts may exist from the outset. Prohibiting all conflicts might simply drive these matters underground with directors going to some lengths to hide their involvement in particular transactions. At common law, the commercial inconvenience typically was overcome by a provision in the articles (usually in the form of Table A, art 85) permitting directors to be interested in contracts with the company or in which the company was otherwise interested, provided the nature and extent of that interest was disclosed to the board of directors.[214]

Scope of the duty under s 177

11-89 The significant change effected by the CA 2006 is that the disclosure regime previously imposed by the Table A articles has become the statutory regime[215] imposed on a director

---

[207] (1854) 1 Macq 461; and see Farrar and Watson (2011) JCLS 495 on its significance.
[208] (1854) 1 Macq 461 at 471–2.   [209] (1854) 1 Macq 461 at 471–2.
[210] (1854) 1 Macq 461.   [211] [1988] BCLC 104.   [212] [2004] 1 BCLC 131.
[213] See *Boulting v Association of Cinematograph, Television and Allied Technicians* [1963] 2 QB 606 at 637.
[214] See n 142 for the text of art 85.
[215] The Company Law Review took the view that if, in practice, all companies opted out of the rule in *Aberdeen Rly Co v Blaikie Bros* (1854) 1 Macq 461 and substituted disclosure requirements instead, the law

who is in any way, directly or indirectly, interested in a proposed transaction or arrangement with the company and requiring him to declare the nature and extent of that interest to the other directors,[216] before the company enters into the transaction or arrangement (s 177(1), (4)). Disclosure of the conflict of interest is required, not approval. As the disclosure is before the company enters into the transaction, the board has the choice whether or not to proceed. If not, that ends the matter. If, following compliance with s 177, the company does proceed, the transaction is not voidable at the option of the shareholders, unless an enactment[217] or the articles require shareholder approval (s 180(1)).

11-90   In the event of a failure to disclose as required, any resulting contract with the company is voidable (because of the undisclosed conflict of interest in breach of duty) and may be set aside at the instance of the company without any enquiry as to the fairness or otherwise of the transaction.[218] The company has a choice whether to affirm or avoid the contract.[219] The right to avoid the contract is lost if: (1) the company delays unduly before rescinding; or (2) *restitutio in integrum* becomes impossible; or (3) the rights of bona fide third parties intervene.[220] If the company wishes to rescind the contract, the decision to rescind must be communicated clearly and promptly and until then the contract is valid and binding and continues in existence.[221] The contract cannot be rescinded if has been fully performed.[222]

11-91   The company may hold the director to account for any profit which he has made from the transaction or require him to indemnify the company against any loss incurred and liability is not dependent on the company rescinding the contract.[223] A liability regardless of rescission is also consistent with the statutory remedies in CA 2006, ss 195(3) and 213(3). The director is not liable, however, for losses which the company would probably have suffered even if the director had complied with the rules on disclosure of interests.[224]

should reflect that practice and the rule should be disclosure.

[216] This provision does not apply to shadow directors unlike CA 2006, s 182 which is specifically applied to shadow directors by s 187.

[217] For example, CA 2006, Pt 10, Ch 4 requires shareholder approval in many instances.

[218] CA 2006, s 178(1); *Hely-Hutchinson v Brayhead Ltd* [1967] 3 All ER 98, CA; *Guinness plc v Saunders* [1990] BCLC 402 at 417.

[219] A contract can be affirmed even if the company is in liquidation: *Ultraframe (UK) Ltd v Fielding* [2005] EWHC 1638 at [1441]. An unqualified demand for payment of sums due under a voidable contract amounts to an election to affirm the contract: *Ultraframe (UK) Ltd v Fielding* [2005] EWHC 1638 at [1449].

[220] *Hely-Hutchinson v Brayhead Ltd* [1967] 3 All ER 98.

[221] See *Re Marini Ltd* [2004] BCC 172 at 196.   [222] See *Re Marini Ltd* [2004] BCC 172.

[223] See *Gwembe Valley Development Co Ltd v Koshy* [2004] 1 BCLC 131 at 150–1 (director liable to account for profit made on undisclosed conflict of interest in transaction with the company despite the contract having long been performed and therefore incapable of being set aside); also *Re MDA Investment Management Ltd, Whalley v Doney* [2004] 1 BCLC 217 at 260 where likewise the conflicted transaction could no longer be set aside but the director was liable to account for profit gained by him personally on the transaction; also dissenting judgment of Bowen LJ in *Re Cape Breton* (1885) 29 Ch D 795. This position clarifies the confusion which arose from the majority decision in that case which was that the company could not affirm the contract *and* hold the director to account: *Re Cape Breton Co* (1885) 29 Ch D 795; *Burland v Earle* [1902] AC 83.

[224] *Gwembe Valley Development Co Ltd v Koshy* [2004] 1 BCLC 131 at 174–5. See also *Bishopsgate Investment Management Ltd v Maxwell (No 2)* [1993] BCLC 1282 at 1285, per Hoffmann J who noted that, in cases where the alleged breach of duty is an omission, the plaintiff must prove that compliance with the duty would have prevented the damage; also *Galoo v Bright Grahame Murray* [1995] 1 All ER 16; *Re Continental Assurance Co of London plc* [2007] 2 BCLC 287 at 445–6; *Cohen v Selby* [2001] 1 BCLC 176 at 183, 186; *Lexi Holdings Ltd v Luqman* [2009] 2 BCLC 1.

11-92 The duty of disclosure in s 177 applies only to proposed transactions with the company whereas s 182 imposes a statutory duty of disclosure where the director has an interest in an existing transaction. As was explained in the Parliamentary debates, the reason for the distinction is that where it is a proposed transaction, the company is still in a position to decide whether it wishes to proceed with the transaction in the light of the conflict of interest whereas, if the conflict has arisen subsequently in respect of an existing transaction, the company has limited options in terms of responding to the conflict.[225] In the latter case, it is still important for disclosure to be made so that the company is aware of the director's conflict of interest, but it will probably be too late for the company to avoid the transaction. Section 182 is discussed at **11-101**. The distinction initially appears helpful, but the position in practice may be more complex than this neat division may suggest, see **11-102**.

Interests which must be disclosed

11-93 The disclosure obligation applies to any interest, direct or indirect, of the director so a disclosure obligation may arise even though the director is not actually a party to the transaction with the company. It is not clear whether there is a duty on a director to disclose an interest in transactions or arrangements between the company and a connected person (as defined in CA 2006, s 252), but it seems implicit in the statutory scheme that such disclosure is required. Section 177(2)(b)(ii) allows for the giving of a general notice of interests for the purposes of s 177 and s 185(2)(b) provides that a general notice may indicate that the director is to be regarded as interested in any transactions between the company and a specified connected person which rather supposes that such interests are within the indirect interests of a director.[226] This seems the most practical interpretation of the provision which would otherwise be open to easy invasion, but it would have been helpful had the legislation spelt out that that is the position.

11-94 The disclosure requirement extends to any transaction within CA 2006, Pt 10, Ch 4 so that transaction still requires formal disclosure to the directors[227] in accordance with s 177. Of course, given that Pt 10, Ch 4 requires shareholder approval (unless the transaction is exempt under that Part), it may be possible to establish that the directors 'knew or ought to have been aware' of the transaction and so disclosure is not required (s 177(6)(b)), but rather than rely on that provision, it is preferable, and easy, to make a formal declaration under s 177.

Interests excluded from disclosure

11-95 The expansive scope of CA 2006, s 177(1) is modified by certain exclusions in s 177(5) and (6). Disclosure is not required of the following interests:

- an interest of which the director is not aware or where the director is not aware of the transaction or arrangement in question, which might be the case in respect of

---

[225] See HL Deb, vol 678, GC334 (9 February 2006).

[226] This interpretation is supported by the Explanatory Notes to the Companies Act 2006 which state (at para 347): 'An interest of another person in a contract with the company may require the director to make a disclosure under this duty, if that other person's interest amounts to a direct or indirect interest on the part of the director.'

[227] The exemption in CA 2006, s 180(4)(b) for transactions approved or exempt under Pt 10, Ch 4 applies only to ss 175 and 176 and not to s 177.

indirect interests (the director is treated, however, as being aware of matters of which he ought reasonably to be aware)[228] (s 177(5));

- an interest that cannot reasonably be regarded as likely to give rise to a conflict of interest (s 177(6)(a)). The company may use the articles to identify 'de minimis' transactions which fall within this category and do not require disclosure under s 177. In a case of doubt, of course, it is preferable to make a declaration;

- an interest if and to the extent that the other directors are already aware of it (for these purposes, the other directors are treated as aware of anything of which they ought reasonably to be aware)[229] (s 177(6)(b)). The problem with this exemption is that, given that the consequence of non-disclosure is a breach of duty, few directors will want to rely on this exclusion and the safest course of action is to make a formal declaration;

- an interest in the terms of a director's service contract which terms have been or are to be considered by a meeting of the directors or a committee of the directors appointed for the purpose under the company's constitution,[230] an exclusion which addresses an issue which had arisen in the case law (s 177(6)(c)).[231]

Manner and timing of disclosure

11-96 The courts require strict compliance with the requirements of CA 2006, s 177 as it is the means by which a conflict of interest is addressed and the burden of proof is on the director to show that he made full disclosure before the company entered into the transaction or arrangement (s 177(3)). The disclosure required is full and frank disclosure of the nature and extent of the director's interest so that the other directors can see what the director's interest is and how far it extends.[232] Once made, further disclosure may be needed where a declaration proves to be, or becomes, inaccurate or incomplete (s 177(3)), but there is no need to update the original disclosure unless the transaction is still a 'proposed transaction' for these purposes. If it is not, s 182 would then apply.

---

[228] Although this issue as to what the director ought reasonably to be aware of was the subject of some debate in Parliament, the Government's view was that the requirement reflected the current law. On the equivalent wording in CA 2006, s 182, the Solicitor General commented that 'this is an objective test so that it will take into account any relevant circumstances relating to that director; it will focus on the individual director. This is the question that will be asked: what is it reasonable to expect a director in those circumstances to have been aware of? For example, a non-executive director might be expected generally to be less aware of the individual transactions or arrangements entered into by a company': see HC Official Report, SC D (Company Law Reform Bill) 11 July 2006, col 628.

[229] For a situation where the directors were aware or ought reasonably to have been aware of the nature and extent of a conflict, see *Re Marini Ltd* [2004] BCC 172. Previously, there were conflicting views as to whether formal disclosure was required even though all of the directors were aware informally of the conflict of interest: see *Lee Panavision Ltd v Lee Lighting Ltd* [1992] BCLC 22 at 33.

[230] The requirement that the committee be 'appointed for the purpose under the company's constitution', suggests that it must be a formal appointments/remuneration committee rather than an ad hoc management committee.

[231] See *Runciman v Walter Runciman plc* [1992] BCLC 1084.

[232] *Movitex Ltd v Bulfield* [1988] BCLC 104 at 121; *Imperial Mercantile Credit Association v Coleman* (1873) LR 6 HL 189 at 205. See also *Ultraframe (UK) Ltd v Fielding* [2005] EWHC 1638 at [1432]. See also *Stainer v Lee* [2011] 1 BCLC 537 at [43]–[46], shareholder approval of a loan agreement but court did not accept that it was informed consent when there was no evidence that the shareholders knew the purpose of the agreement or the close relationship between the recipient of the loan and the company's controlling shareholder and director).

11-97 Disclosure must be to the other directors[233] and it would seem that disclosure to a committee of directors is insufficient[234] other than where the committee is merely the mechanism by which information is conveyed to all the directors. As disclosure has to be made to the other directors, there is no requirement of disclosure in the case of a private company with a sole director, but the director in that case must have regard to his obligations under CA 2006, s 171 (to act in accordance with the constitution), and s 172 (to promote the success of the company).[235]

11-98 The declaration may (but need not) be made at a meeting of the directors[236] or it can be by notice to the directors in writing[237] or by way of a general notice.[238] There are detailed requirements in ss 184 and 185 as to what is a notice in writing or a general notice for these purposes.

11-99 A further issue is whether a director, having made a declaration of a conflict of interest, is able to participate in the meeting which considers the transaction. The model articles provide that the director is not to be counted for quorum or voting purposes, subject to (1) a decision of the company by ordinary resolution to allow him to be counted, or (2) where the director's interest cannot reasonably give rise to a conflict (which is somewhat pointless since the section does not apply when the interest cannot reasonably give rise to a conflict, see s 177(6)(a)), or (3) where the director's conflict of interest arises from a permitted cause which in the model articles includes transactions of benefit to the company such as guarantees, indemnities and subscriptions for securities.[239]

---

[233] There is no mechanism for shareholders to be notified of disclosures made under CA 2006, s 177. Large companies must disclose, in notes to their accounts, particulars of transactions which the company has entered into with related parties if such transactions are material and have not been concluded under normal market conditions: see SI 2008/410, Sch 1, Pt 3, para 72. The Listing Rules (LR) require disclosure to and prior shareholder approval of certain related party transactions, see LR 11 and n 206.

[234] See *Guinness plc v Saunders* [1988] BCLC 607 at 611; also *Gwembe Valley Development Co Ltd v Koshy* [2004] 1 BCLC 131 at 150; *Re MDA Investment Management Ltd, Whalley v Doney* [2004] 1 BCLC 217 at 255. For the same reasons, disclosure to the company secretary is insufficient unless the secretary is the mechanism by which information is relayed to all the directors: see comments by Solicitor General, HC Official Report, SC D (Company Law Reform Bill) 11 July 2006, col 630.

[235] To require a sole director to make disclosure to himself is a nonsense, see HL Deb, vol 678, GC343 (6 February 2006).

[236] There are merits in a formal declaration at a board meeting, see Lightman J in *Neptune (Vehicle Washing Equipment) Ltd v Fitzgerald* [1995] 1 BCLC 352 at 359: all the directors are reminded of the interest; it is an occasion for a statutory pause for thought about the existence of the conflict of interest and the duty to prefer the interests of the company; and the disclosure should be a distinct happening at a meeting and be recorded in the minutes.

[237] In accordance with CA 2006, s 184: s 177(2)(b)(i). A notice in writing under CA 2006, s 184 is deemed to form part of the proceedings of a meeting of directors and therefore must be formally recorded in the minutes (applying s 248): see s 184(5).

[238] In accordance with CA 2006, s 185: s 177(2)(b)(ii). A general notice must be given at a meeting or it must be brought up and read at the next board meeting after it is given, to ensure that it forms part of the minutes of the meeting: ss 185(4), 248. A general notice may be to the effect that the director is a member of a specified company or firm and is to be regarded as interested in any contract which may, after the date of the notice, be made with that company or firm; or that the director is connected with a specified person and is to be regarded as interested in any contract which may, after the date of the notice, be made with that person: s 185(2).

[239] See The Companies (Model Articles) Regulations 2008, SI 2008/3229, art 14 (Ltd); art 16 (Plc). Taking their lead from the model articles, it is not uncommon for companies to include a more extensive list of permitted causes (such as conflicts arising where the director has a conflict solely by virtue of a shareholding in the company or in the other party to the transaction) when the conflicted director is not excluded for quorum/voting purposes.

Authorisation by the shareholders or articles

11-100 All the general duties imposed on directors, including CA 2006, s 177, are subject to any rule of law enabling the company to give authority, for anything to be done or omitted by the directors, or any of them, that would otherwise be a breach of duty (s 180(4)(a)), the constraints on that power are discussed at **11-69.** As also noted it is possible for a company to include provisions in its articles to deal with conflicts of interest, and the general duties owed by a director are not infringed by anything done or omitted to be done in accordance with those provisions (s 180(4)(b)). The potential breadth of any provision in the articles is limited by CA 2006, s 232(4) to such provision in the articles 'as has previously been lawful for dealing with conflicts of interest'. As noted at **11-89,** the previous standard provision in the articles on conflicts, Table A, art 85 is now reflected in CA 2006, s 177 so obviously there is no point in including that provision in the articles. Table A also included provisions on quorum and voting requirements for board meetings and provisions on these matters are in the model articles which companies may choose to adopt.[240] Other possible provisions in the articles might be provisions dealing with group company relationships as these relationships may result in a director (through his other directorships within the group) having a direct or indirect interest in a proposed arrangement with the company. Finally, the articles can require shareholder approval in addition to compliance with s 177 (see s 180(1)).

E   Existing transactions with the company

11-101 Section 182 provides that a director (and a shadow director)[241] who is in any way, directly or indirectly, interested in a transaction or arrangement that has been entered into by the company, must declare the nature and extent of the interest to the other directors[242] as soon as is reasonably practicable.[243]

11-102 A number of possible scenarios will attract the application of CA 2006, s 182. One possibility is that the director had an interest in a proposed transaction with the company which he neglected to disclose under s 177, in which case he is in breach of s 177 and also in breach of s 182, assuming that the transaction has been entered into and he has not disclosed his interest. Another possibility is that the director had no interest in the transaction for the purpose of s 177 at the time it was entered into, but subsequently becomes interested, directly or indirectly, in the transaction or becomes aware of an interest in the transaction (assuming it was not one which he ought reasonably to have been aware of, see s 177(5)). On this basis, he need comply only with s 182. A third scenario is where he becomes interested in a transaction after it has been entered into (for example, he becomes a shareholder in a company which has secured a supply contract from the company) and so must disclose his interest under s 182. Time passes and the renegotiation of the contract arises, in which case it is arguable that the contract becomes a proposed transaction again and he now comes under a duty to disclose his interest under s 177, unless he chooses to rely on the defence in s 177(6)(b) that the other directors are aware or ought reasonably to be aware of his interest. Section 175 does not apply in this scenario

---

[240] See The Companies (Model Articles) Regulations 2008, SI 2008/3229, art 14 (Ltd); art 16 (Plc).
[241] CA 2006, s 187: in this case notice in writing is required in accordance with s 184: s 187(4).
[242] As to the required disclosure where there is only one director though there should be more, see s 186.
[243] CA 2006, s 182(1), (4). Failure to make a declaration as soon as is reasonably practicable does not affect the underlying duty to make the declaration.

(see s 175(3)), but there is potential here for the application of that provision as where the company in which the director now has an interest competes with his company in respect of some transaction, for example both look to win a contract from the same customer. In that case, the director now falls within s 175 again. It is important therefore in every scenario to remember that more than one duty may apply and the various duties may apply in different ways at different stages of what in business terms might be seen as all one transaction (such as an ongoing supply relationship).

11-103 The wording of s 182 reflects that of CA 1985, s 317 and the nature of that section was considered by the Court of Appeal in *Hely-Hutchinson v Brayhead Ltd*[244] which concluded that s 317, now CA 2006, s 182, merely created a statutory duty of disclosure.[245] The only sanction for non-compliance with s 182 is that a director is liable to a fine and a breach of s 182, or indeed compliance with it, has no effect on the validity of any contract entered into

by the company. Likewise, non-compliance with s 182 does not give a company a separate right of action for damages against a director; any right of action must arise from a breach of fiduciary obligation by a director and not from a contravention of the section.[246]

11-104 The disclosure requirements under CA 2006, s 182 are identical to those outlined at **11-98** with respect to s 177. Disclosure may be at a meeting or by notice in writing or a general notice (s 182(2)). If the declaration proves to be or becomes inaccurate or incomplete, a further declaration must be made (s 182(3)). A declaration is not required if the interest has already been declared under s 177 (i.e. when it was merely a proposed transaction); or if the interest cannot reasonably be regarded as likely to give rise to a conflict of interest; or is an interest that the other directors are already aware of or ought reasonably to be aware; or the interest concerns the director's service contract which has been or is to be considered by a meeting or committee of directors appointed for that purpose (s 182(1), (6)).

---

[244] [1967] 3 All ER 98; endorsed by Lord Goff in *Guinness plc v Saunders* [1990] 1 All ER 652 at 665.
[245] See [1967] 3 All ER 98 at 109, per Lord Pearson.
[246] *Coleman Taymar Ltd v Oakes* [2001] 2 BCLC 749; *Movitex Ltd v Bulfield* [1988] BCLC 104 at 125.

12

Specific conflicts—CA 2006, Part 10, Ch 4

A Introduction

12-1 Following the discussion in Chapter 11 of the general duties governing conflict of interests, we turn in this chapter to consider CA 2006, Pt 10, Ch 4, which regulates transactions with directors where the conflict of interest between the director's personal interests and his duty to the company is thought to be particularly acute such that it is appropriate to seek shareholder approval for the following transactions, namely:

- directors' service contracts;
- payments for loss of office;
- substantial property transactions; and
- loans and similar financial transactions.

12-2 To a large extent, the provisions of Ch 4 reflect the long-established position on these transactions previously set out in CA 1985, Pt X. Such changes as have been made are a result, primarily, of a Law Commission review of CA 1985, Pt X,[1] the recommendations of which were generally adopted[2] and reflected in CA 2006, Pt 10, Ch 4. The result is a number of mainly technical changes to the provisions and a closer alignment of their requirements so as to give greater consistency of approach. The criminal penalties imposed by CA 1985, Pt X were also removed on the basis that the civil consequences of breach provide sufficient deterrence.[3] The overall effect is that the CA 2006, Pt 10, Ch 4 generally relaxes the constraints previously imposed on these particular transactions. Given that approach, it is important that directors, whether beneficiaries of these arrangements or instrumental in authorising them,[4] remember their general duties under ss 171–177. Minority shareholders and creditors may have to rely on those general duties for protection against abuse of the now more permissive provisions of Pt 10, Ch 4.

---

[1] See Law Commission, *Company Directors: Regulating Conflicts of Interests and Formulating a Statement of Duties* (Law Comm No 261), 1999, esp Section B (hereinafter Law Commission Report); preceded by a consultation paper of the same title, see Law Comm No 153, 1998.

[2] See *Modernising Company Law* (2002) Cm 5553-I, paras 3.19–3.20; *Company Law Reform* (2005) Cm 6456, para 3.3; also the Company Law Review, *Developing the Framework* (2000), paras 3.86–3.89 and Annex C; also *Completing the Structure* (2000) paras 4.8–4.21; and the *Final Report* (2001), paras 6.8–6.14.

[3] See 678 HL Official Report (5th Series) GC359 (9 February 2006).

[4] Those directors who authorise the arrangements in breach of the statute are commonly also made jointly and severally liable with the beneficiary of the arrangement, see CA 2006, s 195(3), (4); s 213(3), (4) and s 222(1), subject to the defence of not knowing the relevant circumstances surrounding the contravention, see, for example, s 195(7). The burden of proof is on the company to show authorisation by the director, but for the authorising director to prove the absence of knowledge which founds the statutory defence: *Lexi Holdings plc v Luqman* [2008] 2 BCLC 725 at [171], [182], rev'd on other grounds [2009] 2 BCLC 1.

12-3 In respect of these transactions, therefore, directors must comply with their general duties under CA 2006, Pt 10, Ch 2 *and* seek shareholder approval under Pt 10, Ch 4 (s 180(3)), but if a transaction is approved by the shareholders under Ch 4, or is exempt from approval under Ch 4, it is not necessary for the director also to comply with s 175 (duty to avoid conflicts of interest) or s 176 (duty not to accept benefits from third parties): s 180(2). These are the only duties disapplied in these circumstances and compliance with the rest of the general duties remains a requirement.

Overview of the general scheme of Part 10, Ch 4

12-4 The provisions apply to directors including shadow directors (CA 2006, s 223(1)). In many instances, the provisions extend also to transactions with connected persons, a category defined at length in ss 252–256. Essentially, the key categories of persons connected with a director are:

- members of his family;[5]
- a body corporate with which he is connected;[6]
- trustees of a trust the beneficiaries of which are the director or members of his family or companies with which he is connected;
- any partner of the director or a partner of any person who by virtue of any of the other categories is connected with that director; and
- certain firms with which the director is connected (s 252(2)).

12-5 The overall scheme adopted in CA 2006, Pt 10, Ch 4 is that, for each class of conflicted transaction, prior shareholder approval is required by an ordinary resolution unless the articles specify a higher majority.[7] Failure to secure approval typically makes the transaction or arrangement voidable, subject to the usual defences, with the beneficiary liable to account for the gain made and jointly and severally liable with the authorising director to indemnify the company against any resulting loss. In some cases, affirmation after the event is possible,[8] in which case the transaction or arrangement may no longer be avoided under the statute. Where the director is a director of the company's holding company, the transaction must also be approved by the members of the holding company.[9] Shareholder approval is not required in respect of these transactions where the company is not a UK-registered company[10] or where the company is a wholly-owned subsidiary of another body corporate.[11]

---

[5] Defined in CA 2006, s 253 and includes a director's spouse, parents, his children or step-children of whatever age (previously, the category was limited to minor children), any cohabiting partner and minor children of the cohabitant if they live with the director.

[6] Defined in CA 2006, s 254. Essentially, a director is connected with a body corporate if the director and persons connected with him together are interested in at least 20% of the equity share capital of that company or are entitled to exercise or control the exercise of more than 20% of the voting power at any general meeting. See also s 255.

[7] References in the provisions to a resolution are to an ordinary resolution: CA 2006, s 281(3). Informal unanimous consent also suffices, at least under s 188 (shareholder approval of a director's service contract): *Wright v Atlas Wright (Europe) Ltd* [1999] 2 BCLC 301; and s 190 (shareholder approval of certain substantial property transactions): *NBH Ltd v Hoare* [2006] 2 BCLC 649 at [43]; the position with respect to improper loans may be more problematic, given the risk they could pose to creditors, see **15-76**.

[8] See CA 2006, s 196 (property transactions); s 214 (loans, etc.).

[9] CA 2006, ss 188(2), 190(2), 197(2), 198(3), 200(3), 210(3), 203(2), 217(2), 218(2).

[10] Defined CA 2006, s 1158; the effect is to exclude companies not formed and registered under the CA 2006 or its predecessors.

[11] CA 2006, ss 188(6), 190(4), 197(5), 200(6), 201(6), 217(4), 218(4), 219(6).

12-6 Where approval in a private company is by way of the written resolution, a memorandum setting out particulars of the proposed transaction/payments etc[12] must be circulated to the members eligible to vote on the resolution at or before the time at which the proposed resolution is sent to the members.[13,14] Where approval is by way of a resolution at a meeting, a like memorandum must be made available for inspection by the members for not less than 15 days before the meeting and at the meeting itself.[15]

12-7 A transaction which falls within more than one provision (for example a director may obtain a loan from the company and enter into a substantial property transaction at the same time) requires approval under each applicable provision (which should not prove a problem in practice since they are relatively uniform in approach) but it is not necessary to pass a separate resolution for the purposes of each provision.[16]

B Directors' long-term service contracts: CA 2006, ss 188–189

12-8 The length of directors' service contracts, particularly in public companies, has been controversial because of the level of compensation payable in the event of early termination of the contract.

12-9 CA 2006, s 188 requires shareholder approval of any provision under which the guaranteed term of a director's employment[17] with the company (or where he is the director of a holding company, within the group consisting of that company and its subsidiaries) is, or may be, longer than two years.[18] This applies to all companies, not just public companies. The 'guaranteed term of a director's employment' has a distinct statutory meaning. It is the period during which the director is employed if that employment cannot be determined by the company by notice or it can be so terminated only in specified circumstances (CA 2006, s 188(3)(a)) or, in the case of a contract which is terminable by the company by notice, the period of notice required to be given is longer than two years

---

[12] Other than in the case of a substantial property transaction within CA 2006, s 190 where there is no requirement of a memorandum, but the company still needs to ensure that the shareholders have sufficient information if they are to pass a resolution approving the transaction.

[13] CA 2006, ss 188(5), 197(3), 198(4), 200(4) 203(3), 217(3), 218(3), 219(3).

[14] An accidental failure to send a memorandum to one or more members is disregarded for the purposes of determining whether this requirement has been met, subject to any contrary provision in the articles (CA 2006, s 224); this provision was added for the avoidance of doubt, but it does seem generously drafted, see 681 HL Official Report (5th Series), col 872 (9 May 2006). In small private companies, especially, it may be difficult to prove that an opportune omission was anything other than accidental. When coupled with the ability to pass a written resolution by a majority (CA 2006, s 282) rather than unanimity, as was previously the case, minority shareholders may find themselves ill-informed and unable to prevent approval being given.

[15] CA 2006, ss 188(5)(b), 197(3)(b), 198(4)(b), 200(4)(b) 203(3)(b), 217(3)(b), 218(3)(b), 219(3)(b).

[16] CA 2006, s 225. See 678 HL Official Report (5th Series) GC360 (9 February 2006).

[17] 'Employment' is defined as including any employment under a director's service contract which is then broadly defined in CA 2006, s 227, see **12-10** et seq.

[18] CA 2006, s 188(1); the period was reduced from five years under the CA 1985. As before, rolling contracts, where the contract is novated daily so that on any day there is always a two-year period of notice to run, remain an option. The Law Commission was critical of the use of such devices to circumvent the statutory policy (see Law Commission Report, n 1, paras 9.31–9.33) but the Company Law Review took the position that such rolling contracts are consistent with the policy objective of limiting the maximum period of notice in respect of which the director can receive compensation on termination: see Company Law Review, *Developing the Framework* (2000), paras 3.86–3.89 and Annex C.

(s 188(3)(b)).[19] A provision included in contravention of s 188 and without the approval of the members is void and the contract is deemed to contain a term entitling the company to terminate the contract at any time by the giving of reasonable notice (s 189).

12-10 Directors' service contracts are defined in CA 2006, s 227 as including contracts of service, contracts for services *and,* for the first time, letters of appointment as directors (commonly used for non-executive appointments)[20] and details of these service contracts must be available for inspection by any member at the company's registered office or other specified place.[21]

'**Directors' service contracts**

(1) For the purposes of this Part a director's "service contract", in relation to a company, means a contract under which—

(a) a director of the company undertakes personally to perform services (as director or otherwise) for the company, or for a subsidiary of the company, or

(b) services (as director or otherwise) that a director of the company undertakes personally to perform are made available by a third party to the company, or to a subsidiary of the company.

(2) The provisions of this Part relating to directors' service contracts apply to the terms of a person's appointment as a director of a company.

They are not restricted to contracts for the performance of services outside the scope of the ordinary duties of a director (CA 2006, s 227).'

12-11 The scope of CA 2006, s 227 was explained by Lord Sainsbury in the Parliamentary debates in the following terms:[22]

'Subsection (1)(a) covers contracts of service such as any employment contract that the director may hold with a company or a subsidiary of the company of which he is director, for example, as executive director, or any contract for services that he personally undertakes to perform as such.

Subsection (1)(b) covers the case where those services are made available to the company through a third party such as a personal services company. In either case, the contract must require the director personally to perform the service or services in question.

Subsection (2) brings within the definition of a service contract letters of appointment to the office of director. Many directors will have no contract of service or for services with the company. The second sentence of subsection (2) ensures that the definition of "service contracts" includes arrangements under which the director performs duties within the

---

[19] Where the guaranteed term falls partly within CA 2006, s 188(3)(a) and (3)(b), the periods are aggregated: s 188(3). For listed companies with a premium listing, the Listing Rules require that the directors' annual report to the shareholders includes details of any directors' service contract with a notice period in excess of one year or with provisions for pre-determined compensation on termination which exceeds one year's salary and benefits in kind, giving the reasons for such notice period, together with details of the unexpired term of any director's service contract of a director proposed for election or re-election at the next annual general meeting, and, if any director proposed for election or re-election does not have a service contract, a statement to that effect: Listing Rules, LR 9.8.8(8) and 9.8.8(9).

[20] See 678 HL Official Report (5th Series) GC361–2 (9 February 2006); and Law Commission Report, n 1, paras 9.9–9.11.

[21] CA 2006, s 228. The 'specified place' is a single alternative location situated in the same part of the UK as the company's registered office: s 1136; The Companies (Company Records) Regulations 2008, SI 2008/3006, reg 3. Members have rights to inspect and to take copies of any service contract: CA 2006, s 229; SI 2008/3006, Pt 3. These disclosure requirements extend to shadow directors (s 230) but they are unlikely to have service contracts.   [22] 678 HL Official Report (5th Series) GC361–2 (9 February 2006).

scope of the ordinary duties of the director, as well as contracts to perform duties outside the scope of the ordinary duties of the director. Without that, the term "service contract" might be interpreted as applying only to the latter type of contract.'

C Payments for loss of office: CA 2006, ss 215–221

12-12 Directors' remuneration arrangements typically make provision for payments to the director as compensation for the loss of office or on retirement from office. Problems most commonly arise when the company attempts to dismiss an executive director with a service contract. If, say, the finance director, is appointed by contract for a fixed term and the company exercises its power to remove him as a director before that term expires, the company will be liable in damages as the courts will imply a term that the company undertakes to do nothing of its own accord (for example, by terminating his post as a director) to bring to an end the circumstances necessary to enable a person to act as finance director.[23]

12-13 Compensation payments (sometimes dubbed 'rewards for failure') are often controversial, particularly in listed public companies where the size of such payments has attracted media attention and investor anger, especially as resignations or retirements may arise as a result of poor performance.[24] As discussed at **12-8**, in certain circumstances, directors' service contracts with a guaranteed term of employment in excess of two years must be approved by the shareholders (CA 2006, s 188), a measure designed at least to draw the shareholders' attention to the compensation which may be payable should the director be dismissed. The UK Corporate Governance Code (see **5-4**) states that notice or contract periods should be set at one year or less,[25] the purpose being to reduce the compensation payments which would otherwise be payable: see **5-36**. The Code also states that remuneration committees should carefully consider the compensation commitments which would arise if a director's contract is terminated early and that the remuneration committee should take a robust line on reducing compensation to reflect the obligation on a departing director to mitigate his or her loss,[26] an obligation which in practice seems frequently to be overlooked. To address these concerns, the statutory controls on payments for loss of office were tightened in the CA 2006 (when compared with CA 1985, ss 313–316) with an emphasis on anti-avoidance provisions.

Payments requiring approval

12-14 The basic scheme is that a company may not make a payment for loss of office (or on retirement) to a director of the company or to a director of its holding company unless the

---

[23] *Shindler v Northern Raincoat Co Ltd* [1960] 2 All ER 239; *Southern Foundries (1926) Ltd v Shirlaw* [1940] 2 All ER 445, HL. Where a director does not have a separate service contract and has simply been appointed under the articles, his position can be terminated at any time and he cannot recover any damages: *Read v Astoria Garage (Streatham) Ltd* [1952] 2 All ER 292. Indeed the company may specifically alter its articles to facilitate the removal of such a director and he will not be entitled to any relief: *Shuttleworth v Cox Bros & Co (Maidenhead) Ltd* [1927] 2 KB 9. It would be unusual now for a director, certainly in larger companies, not to have a service contract.

[24] See discussion at **5-39**; also West, 'Challenging the "golden goodbye"' [2009] JBL 447.

[25] FRC, UK Corporate Governance Code, D.1.5. There is some anecdotal evidence that, if anything, this limitation has had an upward effect on compensation agreements with directors requiring even larger sums to compensate for the insecurity, as they perceive it, of one-year contracts.

[26] FRC, UK Corporate Governance Code, D.1.4.

proposed payment is approved by a resolution of the members of the company and, if necessary, the members of the holding company (CA 2006, s 217(1)–(3)). Similar provisions apply: (1) where a payment for loss of office is made in connection with the transfer of the whole or any part of the undertaking or property of the company (s 218); and (2) where a payment for loss of office is in connection with a transfer of shares in the company, or in a subsidiary of the company, resulting from a takeover bid[27] (s 219). In a clarification of the law, if a payment is made in contravention of the requirement for member approval, the payment is held by the recipient on trust for the company making the payment and any director who authorised the payment is jointly and severally liable to indemnify the company that made the payment for any loss resulting from it.[28]

12-15 The key to the statutory scheme is the expanded definition of 'payment for loss of office' in CA 2006, s 215 which includes payments for loss of office or on retirement as a director but also for loss of or in connection with retirement from any other office or employment in connection with the management of the company's affairs or the affairs of a subsidiary. The Law Commission had recommended this change in order to address a gap in the protection afforded to shareholders which had been revealed by the decision of the Privy Council in *Taupo Totara Timber Co Ltd v Rowe*[29] (interpreting the equivalent New Zealand section). The Privy Council had concluded that the then statutory disclosure requirement did not apply to any payment made to a director in respect of his executive position with the company. That loophole is closed by CA 2006, s 215(1).

12-16 The definition extends to payments to directors or past directors (CA 2006, s 215(1)); payments in cash and in kind (s 215(2)); payments by other persons at the direction of the company (s 215(4)); payments to connected persons and to other persons at the direction or for the benefit of the director or connected person (s 215(3));[30] and payments to directors of holding companies.[31] All these payments need shareholder approval unless they fall within the exempt categories.

Payments not requiring approval

12-17 Approval is not required for a payment made in good faith:

(1) in discharge of an existing legal obligation,[32]

(2) by way of damages for breach of such an obligation,

---

[27] The purpose of the provision is to avoid the risk that directors may obtain advantageous payments from persons launching a takeover bid which should in fact go to the members in return for their shares, see comments by Lord Sainsbury, 678 HL Official Report (5th Series) GC358 (9 February 2006).

[28] CA 2006, s 222(1); s 222(2)–(5) set out the permutations where more than one requirement is breached. In particular, the claims of the offeree shareholders under s 219 have priority over those of the company under s 217; see *Explanatory Notes to the Companies Act 2006*, para 413.

[29] [1978] AC 537, [1977] 3 All ER 123. See Law Commission Report, n 1, paras 7.38–7.48.

[30] The Law Commission considered that the provision should not be extended to connected persons, but the Company Law Review disagreed on the basis that other provisions of this Part apply to connected persons and therefore this loophole should also be closed: see the Company Law Review, *Developing the Framework* (2000), Annex C, para 5.

[31] CA 2006, ss 217(2), 218(2). The Law Commission had recommended this change to reflect the reality that many companies are today organised in groups and to prevent avoidance: see the Law Commission Report, n 1, paras 7.68–7.71.

[32] The 'existing legal obligation' must arise independently (for example, from a contract of employment) of the event giving rise to the payment for loss of office. It will not suffice if, as part of the event giving rise to the loss of office, a legal obligation is entered into to pay compensation: CA 2006, s 220(2), (3). The exemption allows payments to be made by associated companies (see s 220(2)) so a subsidiary may make a payment to a director in respect of a legal obligation of its holding company: see 678 HL Debs, GC350 (9 February 2006).

(3) by way of settlement or compromise of any claim arising in connection with the termination of a person's office or employment, or

(4) by way of pension in respect of past services[33] (CA 2006, s 220(1)).

12-18 The exemption for payments in discharge of existing legal obligations gives statutory effect to the interpretation of the previous provision adopted by the Privy Council in *Taupo Totara Timber Co Ltd v Rowe*[34] and so merely states what was considered to be the law in any event.[35] Overall, the exceptions are wide enough (especially the exemption for payments in discharge of existing legal obligations and that for pension payments) to ensure that few payments need the approval of the general meeting hence the significant level of shareholder dissatisfaction in listed public companies with these payments. In the light of these shareholder concerns, BIS is consulting (at the time of writing) on a proposal that all exit payments to directors, however categorised, will require prior shareholder approval to the extent that the payment exceeds one year's base salary, see **5-42**. As can be seen from the discussion above, this would be a radical change from the current position.

12-19 For all companies, details of the total amount of the directors' remuneration, any compensation paid for loss of office and payments to third parties for directors' services must be included in notes to the company's annual accounts.[36] Quoted companies[37] must draw up a detailed directors' remuneration report,[38] see discussion at **5-40**.

D Substantial property transactions: CA 2006, ss 190–196

12-20 Substantial property transactions are governed by CA 2006, s 190 (previously CA 1985, ss 320–322) which provides in subsection (1) that, subject to certain exceptions, a company may not enter into an arrangement under which:

'(a) a director of the company or its holding company, or a person connected with such a director,[39] acquires or is to acquire from the company (directly or indirectly) a substantial non-cash asset [see **12-23**]; or

(b) the company acquires or is to acquire a substantial non-cash asset (directly or indirectly) from such a director or a person so connected;

---

[33] A further (and it would seem pointless) exception is provided for small payments which do not exceed £200: CA 2006, s 221.

[34] [1977] 3 All ER 123 (interpreting the equivalent New Zealand provision). The Law Commission had recommended that, as that decision was likely to be followed, the statutory provision should be amended to make the position clear: Law Commission Report, n 1, paras 7.6–7.16.

[35] This exception for payments in discharge of legal obligations is something of a major loophole in the requirement for shareholder approval, given that most golden parachutes are paid as a result of a legal obligation, see also **5-42** for the latest reform proposals.

[36] CA 2006, s 412; The Small Companies and Groups (Accounts and Directors' Report) Regulations 2008, SI 2008/409, reg 5, Sch 3; The Large and Medium-sized Companies and Groups (Accounts and Reports) Regulations 2008, SI 2008/410, reg 8, Sch 5.

[37] A quoted company is a company whose equity share capital (a) has been included in the official list in accordance with the provisions of the Financial Services and Markets Act 2000, Pt 6; or (b) is officially listed in an EEA State (EU with Norway, Iceland and Liechtenstein); or (c) is admitted to dealing on either the New York Stock Exchange or Nasdaq: CA 2006, s 385.

[38] See CA 2006, ss 420–422; the content is prescribed by The Large and Medium-sized Companies and Groups (Accounts and Reports) Regulations 2008, SI 2008/410, reg 11, Sch 8.

[39] Defined CA 2006, s 252 and see **12-4**.

unless the arrangement has been approved by a resolution of the members of the company or is conditional[40] on such approval being obtained.'[41]

12-21   If the arrangement is with a director of the company's holding company or a person connected with such a director, the arrangement must also be approved by a resolution of the members of the holding company.[42] If approval is required, but not obtained, the transaction is voidable (s 195(2)) but it is possible for the members (and, if necessary, the members of the holding company) to affirm the arrangement within a reasonable period (s 196) in which case it can no longer be avoided under the statute.

12-22   The purpose of requiring prior shareholder approval is to provide the members of a company with an opportunity to check on any potential abuse of position by directors and it allows a matter to be more widely considered and a more objective decision reached.[43] The section does not prohibit the interested director from voting as a shareholder in favour of the arrangement at the general meeting,[44] but there are common later limitations on voting which will need to the considered, see **11-70**.

12-23   Approval is required only if the value of the non-cash asset,[45] at the time the arrangement is entered into, exceeds 10% of the company's asset value and is more than £5,000 or exceeds £100,000 (s 191); and the onus is on the person alleging the contravention of the statutory provision to prove that the value of the non-cash asset exceeds the requisite value.[46]

12-24   The application of the statutory provision can be illustrated by *Re Duckwari plc (No 1)*,[47] where a company (Offerventure) entered into a contract to purchase a property for £495,000. Having paid the deposit, Offerventure agreed to pass the property on to Duckwari in return for Duckwari repaying the deposit to Offerventure and undertaking

---

[40] Allowing a company to enter into a conditional arrangement is new and follows a Law Commission recommendation that companies should have that commercial freedom and flexibility: see the Law Commission Report, n 1, paras 10.8–10.10. If the transaction is conditional on approval which is not secured, the company is not subject to any liability by reason of the failure to obtain the required approval: CA 2006, s 190(3).

[41] Previously, the transaction would have had to be disclosed in the notes to the company's accounts, see CA 1985, s 232, Sch 6, Pt II, para 15(c), but this is no longer a requirement. A substantial property transaction might in some circumstances have to be recorded in the notes to the accounts as a related party transaction, see The Large and Medium-sized Companies and Groups (Accounts and Reports) Regulations 2008, SI 2008/410, Sch 1, para 72. Disclosure to the directors is required under CA 2006, s 177 so the item will be recorded in the board minutes (s 248(1)). For listed companies with a premium listing, there are extensive disclosure and approval requirements for related party transactions in Listing Rules, LR 11.

[42] CA 2006, s 190(2). For an example of the importance of securing the approval of the holding company (where necessary), see *British Racing Drivers' Club Ltd v Hextall Erskine & Co* [1997] 1 BCLC 182.

[43] See *British Racing Drivers' Club Ltd v Hextall Erskine & Co* [1997] 1 BCLC 182 at 198. Informal unanimous assent suffices: see *NBH Ltd v Hoare* [2006] 2 BCLC 649, but see **15-76**.

[44] The limitations on a director voting in CA 2006, s 239(4) apply only to voting to ratify a breach of duty.

[45] 'Non-cash asset' is defined in CA 2006, s 1163 as meaning 'any property or interest in property, other than cash'; see *Ultraframe (UK) Ltd v Fielding* [2005] EWHC 1638 at [1367]–[1410]. A new anti-avoidance provision requires a series of arrangements or transactions to be aggregated: see s 190(5). A company's 'asset value' means the value of the company's net assets determined by reference to its most recent statutory accounts or, if no such accounts have been so prepared, the amount of the company's called-up share capital: s 191(3).

[46] *Niltan Carson Ltd v Hawthorne* [1988] BCLC 298. See also the Scottish case *Micro Leisure Ltd v County Properties and Developments Ltd* [2000] BCC 872 where the court concluded that the value should be determined in the context of the particular transaction which might include taking into account the value of the property to the director which may be different from the market value.   [47] [1997] 2 BCLC 713.

to pay the remaining purchase price. The shareholders in Offerventure were C and his wife and C was a director of Duckwari. The transaction was an agreement therefore by a company (Duckwari) to acquire a non-cash asset[48] from a person (Offerventure) connected with one of its (Duckwari's) directors. The acquisition was of a non-cash asset within the statutory threshold[49] and the approval of the shareholders of Duckwari was required under what is now CA 2006, s 190. Given that such approval had not been obtained, the transaction was in contravention of the statutory requirements. The liabilities arising from this contravention are discussed at **12-45**.

12-25   Approval is not required for a transaction between a company and a person in his character as a member of the company whether the acquisition is by a member from the company,[50] or, and this is a new element, by the company from a member (s 192(a)). It is not clear why the provision was extended to cover acquisitions by the company from a member qua member and there may be some potential for abuse in that situation.

12-26   Approval is not required in the case of a transaction between a holding company and its wholly-owned subsidiary, or between two wholly-owned subsidiaries of the same holding company (CA 2006, s 192(b)). This exemption is designed to facilitate intra-group activities which might otherwise be affected because one of the companies is a connected person of a director[51] and so the transaction would be within the general provision.

12-27   Approval is not required (either of the members of the company or of the holding company) for an arrangement entered into by a company which is being wound up (unless it is a members' voluntary winding up[52]) or is in administration (CA 2006, s 193).[53] The purpose is to ensure that a liquidator or administrator is not hampered in the execution of his duties when the directors may be the only possible purchasers of the assets of the company in liquidation or administration.

12-28   For the avoidance of doubt, CA 2006, s 190(6) makes clear that approval is not required in respect of a transaction so far as it relates to anything to which a director of the company is entitled under his service contract (as defined in s 227, see **12-10**) or to payments for loss of office (as defined in s 215).[54]

---

[48]   Millett LJ noted that the asset acquired could be described either as the benefit of the purchase contract (i.e. the right of Offerventure to call for completion of the contract and conveyance of the property on the payment of the purchase price) or as Offerventure's beneficial interest in the property which was subject to an unpaid vendor's lien for the balance of the purchase money: see [1997] 2 BCLC 713 at 724–5.

[49]   Millett LJ noted that on whatever view was taken of the nature of the non-cash asset, see n 48, the asset was worth at least £49,500, see [1997] 2 BCLC 713 at 725. The trial judge had established that 10% of the company's asset value in this case was £44,399 and therefore the case fell within the relevant financial thresholds: see [1997] 2 BCLC 713 at 715, 721.

[50]   Lord Sainsbury noted that the intention in providing an exemption for members is to ensure that transactions such as a dividend in specie, the distribution of assets to a member on a winding up in satisfaction of his rights qua member, a duly sanctioned return of capital other than in cash, and issues of shares are clearly within the exemption and do not require shareholder approval: see 678 HL Debs, GC347 (9 February 2006). All these examples are of acquisitions by the members from the company, not vice versa.

[51]   See CA 2006, s 252 and **12-4**.

[52]   In that case, the members retain an interest in the disposal of the company's assets.

[53]   See 681 HL Official Report (5th Series), col 870 (9 May 2006). The exemption was not extended to receivers or administrative receivers apparently for fear of abuse of the provision, see HC Official Report, SC D (Company Law Reform Bill) (11 July 2006), col 632; also *Demite Ltd v Protech Health Ltd* [1998] BCC 638.

[54]   See the Law Commission Report, n 1, paras 10.11–10.13.

12-29 As the consequences of contravention of the substantial property provisions (see CA 2006, s 195) and the consequences of contravention of loan, quasi-loan, etc provisions (see s 213) are essentially identical, the matter is discussed at **12-45**.

E Loans, quasi-loans and credit transactions: CA 2006, ss 197–214

12-30 The CA 2006 significantly alters the position on loans from that which applied under the CA 1985. That Act prohibited (on pain of criminal sanctions) loans to directors and to connected persons and further prohibited quasi-loans and credit transactions in the case of relevant companies (essentially public companies or companies part of a group which contained a public company).

Shareholder approval required

12-31 Under the CA 2006, in the case of private companies (other than private companies associated with public companies, see below), loans[55] to directors[56] and directors of the holding company are permissible with the approval of the members (though there are a number of exemptions when approval is not required) and, if necessary, the members of the holding company and there are no criminal sanctions. Shareholder approval is also required, subject to certain exemptions, if the company is to give guarantees or provide security in connection with a loan made by any person to a director of the company or of its holding company. There are no restrictions on loans to connected persons (other than the need for the directors to adhere to their general duties when entering into such arrangements) nor on loans to directors of subsidiary companies provided that the director is not also a director of the holding company.

12-32 Public companies and companies associated with a public company[57] require shareholder approval for loans and also for quasi-loans;[58] credit transactions;[59] and for the giving of guarantees and the provision of security, in this case whether the arrangement is for a director of the company or a director of its holding company or a person connected with such a director, but again subject to certain exemptions discussed at **12-37**.

---

[55] 'Loan' is not defined by the statute but the essence of a loan is a requirement for repayment: see *Champagne Perrier-Jouet SA v HH Finch Ltd* [1982] 3 All ER 713 at 717; *First Global Media Group Ltd v Larkin* [2003] EWCA Civ 1765, para 41. Frequently, there is a dispute as to whether the sum paid has been paid as a loan (subject to repayment) or as an advance on remuneration (not subject to repayment): see, for example, *Currencies Direct Ltd v Ellis* [2002] 2 BCLC 482, CA, but, in any event, liability for unauthorised payments may arise for breach of the statute or a misapplication of company money and a breach of duty, see *Queensway Systems Ltd v Walker* [2007] 2 BCLC 577.

[56] 'Director' includes shadow directors: CA 2006, s 223(1)(c).

[57] 'Associated company' is defined in CA 2006, s 256 which replaces a more complex definition of a relevant company in CA 1985, s 331. A holding company is associated with all its subsidiaries and a subsidiary is associated with its holding company and all the other subsidiary companies of its holding company: see *Explanatory Notes to the Companies Act 2006*, para 406.

[58] CA 2006, s 199(1): a quasi-loan is a transaction whereby payments are made by a creditor (the company) on behalf of the borrower (the director), or the company reimburses expenditure incurred by another party for the director, on terms that the director or a person on his behalf will reimburse the company or in circumstances giving rise to a liability on the part of the director to reimburse the company.

[59] CA 2006, s 202(1): a credit transaction is a transaction under which one party (the creditor): supplies any goods or sells any land under a hire-purchase agreement or a conditional sale agreement, leases or hires any land or goods in return for periodical payments, or otherwise disposes of land or supplies goods or services on the understanding that payment, in whatever form, is to be deferred.

12-33 If prior approval is not obtained, the arrangement is voidable, but it is possible for the members (and, if necessary, the members of the holding company) to affirm the arrangement within a reasonable period (CA 2006, s 214).

12-34 In addition to shareholder approval, details of advances and credits granted by the company to its directors and of guarantees of any kind entered into by the company on behalf of its directors, must be included in the notes to the company's accounts (CA 2006, s 413).[60]

12-35 This change from prohibition to shareholder approval may have a significant impact (and some potential for abuse) in private companies where the members and the directors are mostly the same people. In small private companies, shareholder approval would be easy to secure, though shareholders are constrained by common law limits to voting power, see **11-70**. Directors remain subject to their general duties in CA 2006, ss 171–177 and, as creditors are possibly most at risk from these transactions, s 172(3) may be particularly relevant (need to consider or act in the interests of creditors in certain circumstances, see **9-41**).

12-36 As before, in order to reduce the possibility of transactions being constructed in a way which circumvents the requirements for approval, arrangements such as back-to-back transactions (whereby another person enters into a transaction which, if it had been entered into by the company, would have required approval) and the assignment and assumption by the company of rights and obligations which if entered into directly by the company would require shareholder approval, also require shareholder approval (CA 2006, s 203(1)).

Shareholder approval not required

12-37 There are a variety of exemptions when approval by the members is not required. Generally the CA 2006 increased the scope of the exemptions and, in some cases, modified their application, for example to extend them to directors of holding companies and connected persons. Exemptions under more than one heading may apply.

Expenditure incurred on company business

12-38 This generous exemption, being the most general in application, is important in practice for directors. Approval is not required for anything done by a company to provide a director of the company, or of its holding company, or a person connected with any such director with funds to meet expenditure incurred or to be incurred by him for the purposes of the company or for the purpose of enabling him properly to perform his duties as an officer of the company, or to enable any such person to avoid incurring such expenditure (CA 2006, s 204). In this case, the aggregate value of the transactions must not exceed £50,000.

Expenditure on defending proceedings or in connection with regulatory action or investigation

12-39 Approval is not required for anything done by a company to provide a director of the company, or of its holding company, with funds to meet expenditure incurred or to be

---

[60] BIS consulted on minor changes to these disclosure requirements and, in that context, raised for consideration whether the requirements of CA 2006, s 413 might be extended, for example to apply to a wider range of transactions or to arrangements with connected persons: see BIS, *Disclosure of Loans to Directors in Company Accounts* (August 2009), URN 09/1139. Subsequently, the Government made some minor amendments, but concluded that amendments to clarify and/or extend the scope of s 413 could only be done after a fuller consultation, see URN 09/1475, and there has been no further movement on the matter.

incurred by him in defending any criminal or civil proceedings in connection with any negligence, default, breach of duty or breach of trust by him[61] in relation to the company or an associated company or in connection with an application for relief[62] or to enable any director to avoid incurring such expenditure (CA 2006, s 205), see **13-41**. The terms of the loan must provide for the loan to be repaid, or any liability of the company incurred in connection with any such loan to be discharged, in the event that the director is convicted in the proceedings or judgment is given against him (s 205(2)) though the company could decide to extend this requirement of repayment in the interests of the company, for example, to cover the settlement of any claim without a conviction or judgment.

12-40 A new provision, added for the avoidance of doubt,[63] is an exception from the need for shareholder approval for anything done by the company to provide a director of the company or of its holding company with funds to meet expenditure incurred or to be incurred by him in defending himself in an investigation by a regulatory authority or against action proposed to be taken by a regulatory authority in connection with any alleged negligence, default, breach of duty or breach of trust by him in relation to the company or an associated company or to enable any such director to avoid incurring such expenditure (CA 2006, s 206), see **13-42**. In this instance, notably, there is no requirement that the funds be repaid but, again, the directors authorising the provision of funds may wish to impose requirements as to repayment in the interests of the company.

Small amounts

12-41 A company may make a loan or quasi-loan or give a guarantee or provide security (whether to or for a director of the company or of a holding company or even to a connected person) provided the aggregate of the relevant amounts does not exceed £10,000 (CA 2006, s 207(1)). Approval is not required for credit transactions where the aggregate value does not exceed £15,000 (s 207(2)). There is also an exemption for credit transactions if the company enters into the transaction in the ordinary course of its business and the value of the transaction is not greater and the terms are not more favourable than those which it is reasonable to expect the company to have offered to a person of the same financial standing but unconnected with the company (s 207(3)).

Loans to associated companies

12-42 Approval is not required for loans or quasi-loans to, or credit transactions for, an associated body corporate or the giving of a guarantee or provision of security in connection with a loan or quasi-loan to an associated body corporate (CA 2006, s 208). The definition of associated body corporate in s 256 means that this exemption has been extended in scope to allow in essence for any transactions within a group.

Money-lending companies

12-43 A company which is a money-lending company (defined CA 2006, s 209(2)) may make a loan or quasi-loan to any person provided the loan is made in the ordinary course of the company's business and the amount of the loan is not greater, and the terms are not

---

[61] This exemption was narrowed from the equivalent provision in CA 1985, s 337A which applied to expenditure incurred in defending 'any criminal or civil proceedings'.

[62] i.e. an application under CA 2006, s 661 (acquisition of shares by innocent nominee) or, more commonly, an application under s 1157 (general power of court to grant relief).

[63] In the Government's opinion such expenditure is already included within the exemption for defence expenditure: see 678 HL Official Report (5th Series) GC351–2 (9 February 2006); 681 HL Official Report (5th Series), col 871 (9 May 2006).

more favourable, than that or those which it is reasonable to expect the company to have offered to a person of the same financial standing but unconnected with the company (s 209). There is no monetary limit.

12-44　A money-lending company may also make a loan to a director or a director of its holding company or one of its employees to enable such a person to purchase their only or main residence, to improve their dwelling house, or in substitution for a loan provided by a third party for any of those purposes, provided that loans of that type are ordinarily made by the company to its employees on terms no less favourable (s 209(3),(4)).

Consequences of contravention of loan or substantial property provisions

12-45　One of the aims of the restatement of these provisions in CA 2006, Pt 10, Ch 4, was to align the remedies more closely so the consequence of breach are practically identical[64] in s 195 (consequence of contravention of substantial property provisions) and s 213 (consequence of contravention of loan, quasi-loan, etc, provisions). The abolition of the criminal sanctions attached to improper loans further clarifies the position regarding remedies since there is no longer any issue of recovery on an illegal contract.[65]

12-46　Any arrangement or any transaction entered into in pursuance of the arrangement (and in the case of a substantial property transaction, whether by the company or by any other person) without members' approval in contravention of the relevant statutory requirement is voidable at the instance of the company unless:

(1) restitution of any money or other asset that was the subject matter of the arrangement or transaction is no longer possible, or

(2) the company has been indemnified for the loss or damage suffered by it; or

(3) rights acquired in good faith, for value and without actual notice of the contravention by a person who is not a party to the arrangement or transaction would be affected by its avoidance (CA 2006, ss 195(2), 213(2)).

12-47　Regardless of whether the arrangement has been avoided, and without prejudice to any liability which might otherwise arise,[66] any director with whom the company entered into the arrangement; any connected person who entered into the arrangement with the company; the director with whom any such person is connected; and any other director who authorised the transaction or arrangement[67] is liable as follows (CA 2006, ss 195(4), 213(4)), subject to certain defences:[68]

---

[64] There is a slight difference in the wording as between CA 2006, s 195(2)(b) and s 213(2)(b) but it is difficult to see that it makes any practical difference.

[65] See *Currencies Direct Ltd v Ellis* [2002] 1 BCLC 193, appealed on other grounds; *Tait Consibee (Oxford) Ltd v Tait* [1997] 2 BCLC 349.

[66] CA 2006, ss 195(8), 213(8).

[67] A director who knowingly allows a practice of improper loans to directors to continue is to be treated as having authorised the payments, even though he does not have actual knowledge of each individual payment at the time when it is made, and is jointly and severally liable therefore for their repayment: *Queensway Systems Ltd v Walker* [2007] 2 BCLC 577; *Neville v Krikorian* [2007] 1 BCLC 1, CA. It is the duty of a director not merely to ensure that a stop is put to the practice, but that steps are taken to recover the indebtedness outstanding to the company: *Neville v Krikorian* [2007] 1 BCLC 1, CA.

[68] If the arrangement is between a company and a connected person, the director to whom he is connected is not liable if he shows that he took all reasonable steps to secure the company's compliance with the statutory requirements: CA 2006, ss 195(6), 213(6). In any case, a person so connected and any director who authorised the transaction are not liable if he can show that, at the time the arrangement was entered into, he

(1) to account to the company for any gain that he has made directly or indirectly by the arrangement or transaction; and

(2) jointly and severally with any other person so liable to indemnify the company[69]for any loss or damage resulting from the arrangement or transaction (ss 195(3)(a) and (b), 213(3)(a) and (b)).[70]

12-48 The scope of the obligation to indemnify the company was considered in *Re Duckwari plc (No 2)*,[71] the facts of which are discussed at **12-24**. The company, Duckwari, acquired a non-cash asset (a property) from a person connected with one of its directors in 1989 for £495,000. There was no evidence that the property had been under or over-valued at the time of purchase. By May 1993, however, when the property was valued for the purposes of the proceedings, and following the collapse of the property market, it was valued at £90,000. As it was no longer possible to avoid the transaction, the company sought an indemnity for the loss suffered by it. This hearing revolved around the point in time at which the loss or damage caused by the transaction should be measured.

12-49 The Court of Appeal held that the loss recoverable is the difference between the cost of the unauthorised acquisition and the amount realised on the sale of the asset and not the difference between the cost of the acquisition and the market value of the acquisition at that date. In other words, the full risk of the depreciation in value of the asset (which in fact occurred here) falls on the director or connected person who are treated as trustees liable to make good the misapplication of the company's money.[72] Such liability to account for the amount of the company's loss is strict and no question of foreseeability or remoteness, in particular, the foreseeability of a depreciation in value, arises.[73]

---

did not know the relevant circumstances constituting the contravention: ss 195(7), 213(7). See *Lexi Holdings plc v Luqman* [2008] 2 BCLC 725 at 771, rev'd on other grounds [2009] 2 BCLC 1.

[69] See *Re Broadside Colours and Chemicals Ltd, Brown v Button* [2011] 2 BCLC 597 (improper loans made to three directors—their liability is personal with respect to individual loans received by them and a claim in respect of the recovery of those loans is for the recovery of trust property and therefore no limitation period applies, but their joint liability to indemnify the company with respect to improper loans arises when the loan is made and is statute barred after six years).

[70] In the case of a substantial property transaction in contravention of CA 2006, s 190(1)(a) (acquisition from the company at an undervalue), the liability of the director etc is to account under s 195(3)(a) and, in the case of a contravention of s 190(1)(b) (acquisition by the company at an overvalue), the liability of the director etc is to indemnify the company against loss under s 195(3)(b): see *Re Duckwari plc (No 2), Duckwari plc v Offerventure Ltd* [1998] 2 BCLC 315 at 320; *NBH Ltd v Hoare* [2006] 2 BCLC 649 at 667; CA 2006, s 190(1) is set out at **12-20**. In either case, it must be a gain made *by* or loss resulting *from* the arrangement or transaction.   [71] [1998] 2 BCLC 315, CA.

[72] See [1998] 2 BCLC 315 at 322.

[73] *Re Duckwari plc (No 3)* [1999] 1 BCLC 168 at 171. At this subsequent hearing, the Court of Appeal clarified that the indemnity extends only to the loss resulting from the acquisition and does not extend to the means by which the acquisition was brought about. Duckwari could not recover, therefore, for costs incurred when it borrowed to fund the acquisition. But see *Murray v Leisureplay plc* [2005] EWCA Civ 963, [2005] IRLR 946 at [98], [117] where doubts are expressed as to this ruling in *Duckwari (No 3)*.

13

Directors' liabilities for breach of duty

A Introduction

13-1　Having reviewed the nature and extent of directors' duties to the company in Chapters 8 to 12, we turn in this chapter to consider the extent of the potential liabilities of directors for breach of those duties.

13-2　As the duties of directors are owed to the company (CA 2006, s 170(1), see **7-14**), it is for the company to sue, though in limited circumstances a shareholder may sue derivatively on behalf of the company under CA 2006, Pt 11 (see Chapter 18). While it is for the company to sue, a claim may not be brought, despite an apparent breach of duty, for a number of reasons. The decision to litigate is a management matter for the board which must weigh up the time, costs, and adverse publicity involved and the likelihood of success and of recovery from the defaulting director. All things considered, the board may legitimately decide that it is not in the company's interests to sue.[1] Of course, in reaching that decision, the directors have to bear in mind their own duties, especially under s 172 to promote the success of the company and under s 174 to exercise care and skill. Frequently, a quiet resignation and possibly some agreement as to the repayment of sums to the company is preferable and justifiable. Litigation may be resorted to on a change of control following a takeover when an incoming board may consider it has grounds for complaint against the former directors, or on liquidation where a liquidator may consider pursuing misfeasance (breach of duty) claims against the former directors in the hope of recovering some funds for the company's creditors.

13-3　As far as the shareholders collectively are concerned, they too may choose to settle or waive or compromise a claim against a director for breach of duty[2] and they may also choose to ratify a breach of duty (subject to certain limits to ratification, discussed at **18-31**). As noted, individual shareholders may bring a derivative claim, but such claims are still unusual. Shareholders are more likely to make use of the broad unfairly prejudicial jurisdiction under CA 2006, s 994 (see Chapter 17), though the purpose there usually is to force the majority shareholders to buy out the minority rather than to seek recovery for the company in respect of any breach of directors' duties.

13-4　In addition or as an alternative to a claim for breach of fiduciary duty, a claim may be made in negligence for breach of s 174 (the duty of care and skill). Another possibility is

---

[1]　See CA 2006, s 239(6)(b) which confirms that the directors have the power to agree not to sue or to settle or release a claim made by them on behalf of the company.

[2]　See, for example, *Smith v Croft* [1986] BCLC 207.

a claim for breach of the director's contract of employment, if he has one,[3] but a company cannot claim for an account of profits for breach of duty and for damages for breach of contract arising out of the same actions, but must elect as to which remedy to pursue.[4] It may also be that the breaches of duty and of contract complained of (especially where business is diverted to another company set up by a director) amount to the tort of conspiracy to injure the company's business by unlawful means enabling the claim to be brought against the fiduciary and those who are accessories to the breach.[5] Claims may be on multiple grounds, subject to the court being alert to attempts at double recovery.

13-5 In addition to civil claims, there is a possibility of criminal prosecution, for example, for fraud under the Fraud Act 2006, or receipt of a bribe under the Bribery Act 2010, and a dishonest agreement by directors to impede a company in the exercise of its right to recover secret profits made by them may constitute a conspiracy to defraud.[6] Disqualification proceedings post-insolvency are also a possibility, essentially on the basis that the breaches of duty establish that a person is unfit to be involved in the management of a company (disqualification is discussed in Chapter 25).

13-6 There are then a variety of possible consequences where directors are found to have acted in breach of duty, but the focus of this chapter is the extent of a director's civil liability for breach of fiduciary duty and the liability of third parties involved in some way in that breach of duty.[7] The ability to mitigate liability through indemnity provisions, insurance and by application to the court for relief is also considered.

B Claim for breach of fiduciary duty

Introduction

13-7 It had been hoped that it would be possible to complement the statutory statement of directors' duties in the CA 2006 with a statement of remedies for breach of duty, see **7-8**, but it proved impossible to devise a coherent and comprehensive statement of the multiple options available and so CA 2006, s 178 merely preserves the existing law and allows for its continued development in the normal way. Section 178 provides that:

'(1) The consequences of breach (or threatened breach) of sections 171 to 177 are the same as would apply if the corresponding common law rule or equitable principle applied.

(2) The duties in those sections (with the exception of section 174 (duty to exercise reasonable care, skill and diligence)) are, accordingly, enforceable in the same way as any other fiduciary duty owed to a company by its directors.'

---

[3] See, for example, *Simtel Communications Ltd v Rebak* [2006] 2 BCLC 571; *Shepherds Investments Ltd v Walters* [2007] 2 BCLC 202; *Aerostar Maintenance International Ltd v Wilson* [2010] EWHC 2032. As to whether a third party who engages with the defaulting fiduciaries in a new venture is liable in damages in tort for having induced or procured a breach of contract on their part, see *Mainstream Properties Ltd v Young* [2007] 4 All ER 545, HL; *Aerostar Maintenance International Ltd v Wilson* [2010] EWHC 2032 at [163]–[166].

[4] *Coleman Taymar Ltd v Oakes* [2001] 2 BCLC 749; and see *Dranez Anstalt v Hayek* [2002] 1 BCLC 693, reversed in part [2003] 1 BCLC 278, CA; *CMS Dolphin Ltd v Simonet* [2001] 2 BCLC 704.

[5] *OBG Ltd v Allan* [2007] 4 All ER 545, HL. See *Simtel Communications Ltd v Rebak* [2006] 2 BCLC 571; *British Midland Tool Ltd v Midland International Tooling Ltd* [2003] 2 BCLC 523; *Aerostar Maintenance Intenational Ltd v Wilson* [2010] EWHC 2032 at [172]–[177], [189]–[191].

[6] *Adams v R* [1995] 2 BCLC 17, PC.

[7] See, generally, the valuable analysis of the remedies awarded against defaulting fiduciaries by Elliott & Mitchell, 'Remedies for Dishonest Assistance' (2004) 67 MLR 16, esp at 23–36.

13-8 A fiduciary was defined by Millett LJ in *Bristol & West BS v Mothew*[8] as someone who has undertaken to act for or on behalf of another in a particular matter in circumstances which give rise to a relationship of trust and confidence. Given that typically directors have all powers of management over the company and its assets, directors are indisputably fiduciaries.[9] Whether the general duties owed by directors (other than the duty of care and skill) are fiduciary duties is a moot point.[10] Some of the duties certainly are, such as the no-conflict provisions in ss 175 and 176 and the complementary provision in s 177, while the duty in s 171 prohibiting the exercise of powers for an improper purpose can be seen as a manifestation of the broader doctrine of fraud on a power,[11] others are not fiduciary duties, such as s 174 which reflects the common law on negligence, others arguably are not, such as s 172 which merely states the obligation of loyalty which is the distinguishing overarching obligation of a fiduciary.[12] There are advantages in obligations being categorised as fiduciary obligations, primarily with respect to the availability of what has been described as 'more elastic' remedies in the event of breach.[13] For example, claims for breach of fiduciary duty may be subject to more generous limitation periods than if the claim was for breach of a common law obligation;[14] a claim can be made for profits made by the fiduciary though the company itself could not have made the profits;[15] and the obligation to make good losses suffered by the company applies on a more generous basis (designed to deter) than a common law obligation to pay damages (issues of foreseeability and remoteness are, in general irrelevant), though the loss must still be shown to have been caused by the breach of fiduciary duty.[16] Liability for breach of duty is an individual liability and, as between defaulting directors, liability is joint and several.[17] An innocent

---

[8] [1996] 4 All ER 698 at 711. See generally Millett, 'Equity's Place in the Law of Commerce' (1998) 114 LQR 214.

[9] See Finn, *Fiduciary Obligations* (1977), Ch 1; Finn, 'The Fiduciary Principle' in Youdan (ed), *Equity, Fiduciaries and Trusts* (1989), Ch 1; *Regal (Hastings) Ltd v Gulliver* (1942) 1 All ER 378 at 395.

[10] See generally Conaglen, *Fiduciary Loyalty* (2010), esp Ch 3. In the much cited words of Millett LJ: 'The expression "fiduciary duty" is properly confined to those duties which are peculiar to fiduciaries and the breach of which attracts legal consequences differing from those consequent upon the breach of other duties. Unless the expression is so limited it is lacking in practical utility. In this sense it is obvious that not every breach of duty by a fiduciary is a breach of fiduciary duty': *Bristol & West BS v Mothew* [1996] 4 All ER 698 at 710.

[11] See Conaglen, *Fiduciary Loyalty* (2010), pp 44–50; Worthington, 'Corporate Governance: Remedying and ratifying directors' breaches' (2000) 116 LQR 638.

[12] See further Hannigan, 'Reconfiguring the No Conflict Rule, Judicial Strictures, a Statutory Restatement and the Opportunistic Director' (2011) 23 SAcLJ 714 at 723–6; Conaglen, *Fiduciary Loyalty* (2010), pp 54–8.

[13] See *Swindle v Harrison* [1997] 4 All ER 705 at 732, per Mummery LJ. See the interesting dissenting judgment of Kirby J (Aust H Ct) in *Pilmer v Duke Group Ltd* [2001] 2 BCLC 773 at [149]–[160] where he considers the benefits of claiming remedies for breach of fiduciary duty.

[14] See the Limitation Act 1980, s 21: no period of limitation prescribed by this Act applies to an action by a beneficiary under a trust in respect of any fraud or fraudulent breach of trust to which the trustee was a party or privy; or to recover from the trustee trust property or the proceeds of trust property in the possession of the trustee, or previously received by the trustee and converted to his use. See *JJ Harrison (Properties) Ltd v Harrison* [2002] 1 BCLC 162; *Gwembe Valley Development Co Ltd v Koshy* [2004] 1 BCLC 131. But the limitation issues here are complex, see Mather, 'Fiduciaries and the Law of Limitation' [2008] JBL 344; Mitchell, 'Dishonest Assistance, Knowing Receipt and the Law of Limitation' [2008] Conv 226.

[15] See, for example, *Industrial Development Consultants Ltd v Cooley* [1972] 2 All ER 162; *Regal (Hastings) Ltd v Gulliver* [1942] 1 All ER 378, HL; *Quarter Master UK v Pyke* [2005] 1 BCLC 245.

[16] *Swindle v Harrison* [1997] 4 All ER 705 at 732–3, per Mummery LJ, noted (1998) 114 LQR 181; also *Target Holdings Ltd v Redferns* [1995] 3 All ER 785; *Nocton v Lord Ashburton* [1914] AC 932. See *United Pan-Europe Communications NV v Deutsche Bank AG* [2000] 2 BCLC 461 at 484, CA, per Morritt LJ, 'comparison with the remedy in damages is unhelpful'. See Elliott & Mitchell, n 6, at 28–30.

[17] See *Re Lands Allotment Co* [1894] 1 Ch 616; also *Bishopsgate Investment Management Ltd v Maxwell (No 2)* [1993] BCLC 1282. See also *Re Broadside Colours Ltd, Brown v Button* [2011] 2 BCLC 597.

director is not liable unless he is in breach of his duty of care and skill in allowing the wrongdoing to occur.

Directors as trustees and accountable in equity

13-9   As directors are fiduciaries and as the most common class of fiduciaries are trustees, it is common to describe directors as trustees and to describe breaches of duty by them as breaches of trust or of fiduciary duty and, in particular, to equate directors with trustees for the purpose of measuring their liability to make good any misapplication of the company's assets.[18] The classic statement of their position comes from Lindley LJ in *Re Lands Allotment Co*:[19]

> 'Although directors are not properly speaking trustees, yet they have always been considered and treated as trustees of money which comes to their hands or which is actually under their control; and ever since joint stock companies were invented directors have been liable to make good moneys which they have misapplied upon the same footing as if they were trustees.'

It is common in this context of claims and remedies to talk of directors being liable as constructive trustees, but this use should be avoided as it is misleading. As Millett LJ explained in *Paragon Finance plc v D B Thakerar & Co*,[20] the term 'constructive trustee' is used in two entirely different ways, first, in the sense of someone who is really a trustee (class 1 *Paragon*) and, secondly, where a constructive trust is imposed as a remedy consequent to some unlawful transaction (class 2 *Paragon*). He went on to describe the class 1 case as arising by operation of law whenever the circumstances are such that it would be unconscionable for the owner of property to assert his own beneficial interest in the property and deny the beneficial interest of another whereas the second class of case arises when a person sufficiently implicated in a fraud is rendered accountable in equity.[21] Describing the latter as a constructive trustee is unfortunate, Millett LJ said, since such a person is not in fact a trustee at all and the phrase 'constructive trust' is being used as nothing more than a formula for equitable relief.[22] The terminology for this class of case, he subsequently said, should be 'accountable in equity'.[23]

13-10   At first instance in *Sinclair Investments (UK) Ltd v Versailles Trade Finance Ltd*,[24] Lewison J crisply explained that the distinction between the two *Paragon* classes turns on:

> '... whether the defendant has assumed pre-existing fiduciary duties in relation to the specific item of property in issue. The expression "pre-existing" means duties which precede the events of which complaint is made. If he has, then the case falls within the first class. If he has not, and in particular if the fiduciary duty in relation to the specific item of property arises only as a result of the transaction being impugned, the case falls within the second class.'

Where the breach of duty by a director involves a misappropriation of company assets by the director, the company's claim is a class 1 *Paragon* claim that the director (the trustee)

---

[18]   The analogy is not entirely accurate as directors, unlike trustees, are risk takers and appointed as such.

[19]   [1894] 1 Ch 616 at 631; *Re Duckwari plc (No 2)* [1998] 2 BCLC 315 at 321. See also *Great Eastern Railway Co v Turner* (1872) LR 8 Ch App 149.

[20]   [1999] 1 All ER 400. See generally Smith, 'Constructive Trusts and Constructive Trustees' (1999) CLJ 294.   [21]   [1999] 1 All ER 400 at 409.

[22]   [1999] 1 All ER 400 at 409.   [23]   *Dubai Aluminium Co Lt v Salaam* [2003] All ER 97 at [142].

[24]   [2011] 1 BCLC 202 at [80], aff'd [2011] 2 BCLC 501.

restore the trust assets and, at the company's choice,[25] it may pursue a proprietary claim where it can trace the asset or an identifiable substitute (so if the director still has the asset, the court can order the director to transfer it *in specie* to the company[26]) or, if that is not possible, a personal claim that the director compensate (i.e. pay a sum of money to) the company for the loss.[27] In practice, a personal claim will often produce the same result in value as a proprietary claim, but the disadvantage of a personal claim is that it ranks *pari passu* with the claims of the other unsecured creditors of the defaulting fiduciary so the bankruptcy of the fiduciary may affect the ability of the claimant company to recover.[28] A proprietary claim, assuming the asset or its traceable proceeds can be identified, prevails against all the world other than a bona fide purchaser for value without notice of the breach of duty, even where there have been numerous successive transactions, so long as the tracing exercise is successful and no bona fide purchaser for value without notice has intervened.[29] Where a proprietary claim exists and the moneys beneficially owned by the company can be traced to, but have been inextricably mixed with, funds of the defaulting fiduciary, the proprietary claim is not lost, rather the onus is on the defaulting fiduciary to establish, on the balance of probabilities, which part of the mixed fund is his property.[30] Further, on a proprietary claim, the company can require that the director make good the trust property *and* any benefit derived therefrom.[31] In respect of a class 2 *Paragon* claim, the claim is a personal claim for an account of profits made by the fiduciary in breach of duty or an indemnity in respect of loss arising from the breach of duty. In that case, on the bankruptcy of the defendant, the claimant company is left to compete as an unsecured creditor with the other unsecured creditors of the defendant.

Claims against directors

13-11 A breach of duty by a director can give rise to claims under either class of *Paragon* (see **13-9**) depending on the type of breach which has occurred. Taking class 1 *Paragon* claims first, as noted, a director is treated as a trustee of the company's assets and any claim in

---

[25] The beneficiary will choose whichever option is most advantageous in the circumstances, see *Foskett v McKeown* [2000] 3 All ER 97 at 122.

[26] See *Foskett v McKeown* [2000] 3 All ER 97 at 120. As Lord Millett emphasised in *Boscawen v Bajwa* [1995] 4 All ER 769 at 777, this is only one of the proprietary remedies which is available to a court of equity. If the plaintiff's money has been applied by the defendant, for example, not in the acquisition of property but in its improvement, then the court may treat the land as charged with the payment to the plaintiff of a sum representing the amount by which the value of the defendant's land has been enhanced by the use of the plaintiff's money. If the plaintiff's money has been used to discharge a mortgage on the defendant's land, the court may achieve a similar result by treating the land as subject to a charge by way of subrogation in favour of the plaintiff, see, for example, *Primlake Ltd v Matthews Associates* [2007] 1 BCLC 666.

[27] *Target Holdings Ltd v Redferns* [1995] 3 All ER 785 at 793–4; *Foskett v McKeown* [2000] 3 All ER 97 at 122; *Sinclair Investments (UK) Ltd v Versailles Trade Finance Ltd* [2011] 2 BCLC 501 at [40].

[28] See *Sinclair Investments (UK) Ltd v Versailles Trade Finance Ltd* [2011] 2 BCLC 501 at [46], per Lord Neuberger.

[29] *Foskett v McKeown* [2000] 3 All ER 97 at 122, per Lord Millett; also *Re Lehman Brothers International (Europe) (No 2)* [2010] 2 BCLC 301 at [331].

[30] *Sinclair Investments (UK) Ltd v Versailles Trade Finance Ltd* [2011] 2 BCLC 501 at [138]-[141], per Lord Neuberger, who explained that the burden should not be other than the normal civil standard of proof out of principle and out of fairness to the other creditors of the defaulting fiduciary. So if, after considering the evidence, the court concludes that it is more probable than not that a particular sum of money held by the defaulting fiduciary is not attributable to the funds (or the identifiable substitute of the funds) of the beneficiary, the court should refuse a tracing remedy.

[31] *JJ Harrison (Properties) Ltd v Harrison* [2002] 1 BCLC 162 at [52]; *CMS Dolphin Ltd v Simonet* [2001] 2 BCLC 704 at [96]–[97].

respect of any misapplication of those assets is a class 1 situation meriting a proprietary claim.[32] The director's possession of the asset 'is coloured from the first by the trust and confidence by means of which he obtained it, and his subsequent appropriation of the property to his own use is a breach of that trust'.[33] The Court of Appeal applied Millett LJ's analysis in *Paragon* in *JJ Harrison (Properties) Ltd v Harrison*[34] where a director acquired land at an undervalue from his company in circumstances which amounted to a breach of his duty to act in the interests of the company (now CA 2006, s 172). The director subsequently sold that land for a substantial gain. The Court of Appeal concluded that his possession of the land was subject to his pre-existing obligations as a trustee of that land, derived not from the transaction by which he came to possess the property, but from his appointment as a director. Chadwick LJ agreed that if a director, in breach of his fiduciary duties to the company, comes into possession of the company's property, his obligations as a trustee in relation to the property do not arise from the transaction by which he obtains it, but predate it and arise out of his pre-existing duties as a director.[35] Therefore he holds the property on trust (i.e. as a trustee, class 1 *Paragon*) for the company. In this instance, the director was in breach of his fiduciary duty to the company in allowing the land to be sold to him without insisting that the company receive up-to-date information on the planning position and the development potential of the site. In effect, the director sought personally to exploit the commercial opportunities relating to the land of which he, but not the company, was aware. The director held the land as trust property on behalf of the company. The land having been sold, the company was entitled to the entire proceeds of sale, subject only to an allowance to the director limited to the purchase price paid by him and any expenditure incurred by him for the preservation or enhancement of the value of the land.[36]

13-12 This liability to reinstate the trust (company) assets can be seen in cases such as *Bairstow v Queens Moat Houses plc*[37] where the former directors of a company were liable to repay the entire amount of unlawful dividends which they had declared, regardless of whether the company might through other mechanisms have lawfully declared such dividends with the result that there was no loss to the company. The issue is not whether the company has sustained a loss, but the strict liability of directors/trustees who have acted in breach of duty to make good any misapplication by them of the company's assets.[38] Another example of a director's liability to reinstate the company's assets can be seen in *Primlake Ltd v Matthews Associates*[39] where a de facto director paid himself £836,500 out of company funds in breach of duty. The company had a proprietary claim to the

---

[32] *JJ Harrison (Properties) Ltd v Harrison* [2002] 1 BCLC 162 at 175; *Re Lands Allotment Co* [1894] 1 Ch 616 at 631, 638, 657; *Cook v Deeks* [1916] AC 554 at 564; *Keech v Sandford* (1726) Sel Cas Ch 61; *Sinclair Investments (UK) Ltd v Versailles Trade Finance Ltd* [2011] 2 BCLC 501 at [88]. See generally Goode, 'The Recovery of a Director's Improper Gains: Proprietary Gains for Infringement of Non-Proprietary Rights' in McKendrick (ed), *Commercial Aspects of Trusts and Fiduciary Obligations* (1992).

[33] *Paragon Finance plc v D B Thakerar & Co* [1999] 1 All ER 400 at 409.   [34] [2002] 1 BCLC 162.

[35] [2002] 1 BCLC 162 at 175. See too *Belmont Finance Corp Ltd v Williams Furniture Ltd (No 2)* [1980] 1 All ER 393 at 405 (improper financial assistance); *Bishopsgate Investment Management Ltd v Maxwell (No 2)* [1993] BCLC 1282 (director gave away the company's assets for no consideration to a private family company of which he was a director); *Bairstow v Queens Moat Houses plc* [2001] 2 BCLC 531 (unlawful distributions by directors); see also *Rolled Steel Products v British Steel* [1985] 3 All ER 52 at 88.

[36] See [2002] 1 BCLC 162 at 182–3.   [37] [2001] 2 BCLC 531, CA.

[38] [2001] 2 BCLC 531, CA; this strict liability to make good the entire amount of an improper dividend regardless of loss was endorsed, obiter, by the Supreme Court and the Court of Appeal in *Re Paycheck Services 3 Ltd, Revenue and Customs Commissioners v Holland* [2011] 1 BCLC 141 at [49], [124], [146], agreeing with Rimer LJ [2009] 2 BCLC 309 at [98]. See also Elliott & Mitchell, n 7, at 24–5.   [39] [2007] 1 BCLC 666.

company's funds or their traceable proceeds.[40] That proprietary claim enabled the company to recover funds from the director's wife, a volunteer with no knowledge of the circumstances, to the extent that she still had control of funds which were identifiable as the property or the substitute for the property of the company. But, in the absence of any knowledge on her part, no personal claim lay against her with respect to funds which had passed through their joint account.[41] In *Clark v Cutland*[42] misappropriated company funds were diverted to the director's pension fund with the result that the trustees of the pension fund, though no personal claim lay against them, held the property on behalf of the company.[43] An innocent volunteer in possession must yield to the proprietary claim, but no personal claim arises against the volunteer in the absence of participation in some way in the breach of duty.[44]

13-13 As discussed in Chapter 11, there are endless ways in which directors can profit in a situation of conflict in breach of their fiduciary duties and it will depend on the facts whether profiting in a situation of conflict does fall into a class 1 *Paragon* giving rise to a proprietary claim, or is an unauthorised profiting in breach of duty, a class 2 *Paragon* case, making the director accountable in equity for the profit made from the breach of duty, see **13-9**. An example of unauthorised profit-making in a class 2 *Paragon* situation can be found in *Gwembe Valley Development Co Ltd v Koshy*[45] where a director profited from certain currency transactions by his company in circumstances which involved an undisclosed conflict of interest on his part in breach of what is now CA 2006, s 177. The company was aware that the director had an interest in currency transactions entered into by the company, but he failed to disclose that he stood to make almost $5m from the transactions. The Court of Appeal concluded that he had no pre-existing trust-like responsibilities in relation to the sums and so did not fall within class 1 *Paragon* (**13-9**), but was within class 2 and the company could pursue a personal claim holding him to account for his gains.[46] Applying the *Paragon* classification, at first instance in *Sinclair Investments*

---

[40] [2007] 1 BCLC 666 at [334]. The couple also used some of the company's money to repay the mortgage on their home and release it from a bank security. The court held that the company was entitled to be subrogated to the bank's position to the extent that the company's money had been used to discharge the debt and redeem the charge, see at [340]. See also *Boscawen v Bajwa* [1995] 4 All ER 769.

[41] [2007] 1 BCLC 666 at [336].   [42] [2003] 2 BCLC 393, CA.

[43] The company was entitled to trace the asset (the payments made into the pension fund) and to seek proprietary relief in the form of a charge over the pension fund assets to secure the sum due to the company, see [2003] 2 BCLC 393 at 404.

[44] See *Foskett v McKeown* [2000] 3 All ER 97 at 120; also *Clark v Cutland* [2003] 2 BCLC 393, CA. The company is able to assert its title to the property against any third party in whose hands it is, even if the recipient is not aware that it is trust property, but the recipient is not personally liable to account as trustee. If the recipient has the requisite knowledge, he can be liable on the basis of knowing receipt: see *Re Diplock's Estate* [1948] 2 All ER 318; *Re Montagu's Settlement Trusts* [1992] 4 All ER 308; *Westdeutsche Landesbank Girozentrale v Islington LBC* [1996] 2 All ER 961 at 990, per Lord Browne-Wilkinson.

[45] [2004] 1 BCLC 131. See too *Halton International v Guernroy* [2006] EWCA 80 at [22]–[26], aff'g [2006] 1 BCLC 78 at [163]–[164] where, on the basis of an assumption of a fiduciary relationship, the Court of Appeal was agreed that any liability for unauthorised profit-making by the fiduciary, in the absence of use of trust assets, would be a personal claim for him to account for the profits and did not give rise to any proprietary relief. 'The dividing line drawn by the cases is between a trust which arises "before the occurrence of the transaction impeached" and one which arises "only by reason of that transaction"', a view endorsed in *Sinclair Investments (UK) Ltd v Versailles Trade Finance Ltd* [2011] 2 BCLC 501 at [87]–[88].

[46] The case was a limitation case, so the distinction mattered in terms of limitation periods, see n 14. See [2004] 1 BCLC 131 at 165, per Mummery LJ: '...it is clear in our view that any trust imposed on [the director] is a class 2 trust within Millett LJ's classification.' (for Millett LJ's classification, see **13-9**). See criticism of the decision by Elliott & Mitchell, n 7, at 32; also Hayton, n 49, at 490, who queries whether *Gwembe* could not be seen as a class 1 *Paragon* case.

(UK) Ltd v Versailles Trade Finance Ltd[47] Lewison J considered that a claim in relation to unauthorised profits made by a company director otherwise than by acquiring and subsequently exploiting property formerly owned (or treated as owned) by the company itself falls within the second class of case.[48] This important case requires close consideration. In *Sinclair Investments (UK) Ltd v Versailles Trade Finance Ltd*[49] a company (TPL) raised funds from investors for a trade finance business to be carried on on TPL's behalf by another company (VTFL). In fact, VTFL was just a vehicle for an enormous fraud by its two directors (including C) who were also the directors of TPL. A consequence of the fraud was the artificial inflating of the value of shares held by C in another company (VGP) which was the parent company of VTFL. C sold those shares for £28.6m before the fraud was discovered and the companies collapsed into insolvency. The proceeds of sale were in the hands of or had been distributed by the receivers appointed to VTFL who had reached a settlement with C. The essence of the case is a claim by TPL for breach of duty[50] by its director C who allowed the company's funds to be misused in this fraudulent way and TPL asserted that it had a proprietary claim to the proceeds of sale of the shares as an unauthorised gain made by C in breach of duty.[51] As other parties, specifically a number of creditor banks, had received varying amounts of the sale proceeds from the receivers, whether the claim was a proprietary claim was a crucial question, since a proprietary claim prevails against all the world save bona fide purchasers for value without notice. The issue then would have been whether the recipient banks had notice. On the other hand, if the claim was merely a personal claim against C for profiting in breach of his fiduciary duties, then TPL's claim would rank *pari passu* with the rest of C's unsecured creditors.[52]

13-14 The Court of Appeal agreed with Lewison J in the lower court that the claim was a personal claim. The money received by C from the proceeds of sale of the shares was derived from his fiduciary position and in plain breach of his fiduciary duties, but it was not money which was part of the assets of TPL subject to those duties, or derived from such assets.[53] A beneficiary has a proprietary claim in respect of any money or asset acquired by a fiduciary in breach of his duties to the beneficiary where the asset or money is or has been beneficially the property of the beneficiary or the trustee acquired the asset or money by taking advantage of an opportunity or right which was properly that of the beneficiary, otherwise a beneficiary cannot claim a proprietary interest, but is entitled to an equitable account of profits made or compensation for losses incurred.[54] A claimant cannot claim proprietary ownership of an asset purchased by the defaulting fiduciary

[47] [2011] 1 BCLC 202.
[48] [2011] 1 BCLC 202 at [80], endorsed by Lord Neuberger at [2011] 2 BCLC 501 at [92].
[49] [2011] 2 BCLC 501, CA, aff'g [2011] 1 BCLC 202. For notes on the CA decision, see Virgo, 'Profits Obtained in Breach of Fiduciary Duty: Personal or Proprietary Claim' (2011) CLJ 502; and Hayton, 'Proprietary Liability for Secret Profits' (2011) 127 LQR 487; for notes on the first instance decision, see Nolan, 'Bribes: a reprise' (2011) 127 LQR 19; Hicks, 'Constructive Trusts of Fiduciary Gains: Lister revived' (2011) Conv 62.
[50] The claims of TPL had been assigned to the claimant, Sinclair, see [2011] 2 BCLC 501 at [23].
[51] See [2011] 2 BCLC 501 at [25], where the claim is summarised and see [32]. TPL also had a more straightforward claim in respect of TPL funds held by VTFL—it was accepted that VTFL owed TPL fiduciary duties with respect to those funds. In those circumstances, the misappropriation of those funds by VTFL gave rise to a clear proprietary claim, a class 1 *Paragon* constructive trust, which could only be defeated by a bona fide purchaser for value without notice. However, much of the remaining funds had been distributed to creditor banks of VTFL at a time when the banks were bona fide purchasers for value without notice so defeating the proprietary claim, though TPL did have a proprietary claim with respect to funds held by VTFL after the point when the banks had notice of that proprietary claim, see at [142]–[148].
[52] See [2011] 2 BCLC 501 at [48].   [53] [2011] 2 BCLC 501 at [55].
[54] [2011] 2 BCLC 501 at [88], per Lord Neuberger.

with funds which, although they could not have been obtained if he had not enjoyed his fiduciary status, were not beneficially owned by the claimant or derived from opportunities beneficially owned by the claimant.[55] TPL did not have a proprietary claim to the proceeds of sale, therefore, and consequently the issue of whether the banks were bona fide purchasers for value without notice did not arise.[56]

13-15 Two important aspects of breach of the no-conflict duty require further examination in the light of the ruling in *Sinclair Investments*. The first issue, directly addressed in the case, is whether a claim in respect of benefits, secret commissions, or bribes received by a director in breach of duty give rise to proprietary or personal claims and, secondly, whether, applying the analysis in *Sinclair Investments*, the exploitation of 'corporate opportunities' gives rise to proprietary or personal claims, something which was not directly at issue in the case.

Recovery of secret profits and bribes

13-16 As discussed in Chapter 11, a director may secretly profit in a variety of ways which may be in breach of CA 2006, ss 175–177. They may profit by exploiting opportunities or information in a situation of conflict (s 175), or receive benefits from third parties by reason of being a director (s 176) or they may exploit transactions with the company (s 177). In *Sinclair Investments (UK) Ltd v Versailles Trade Finance Ltd*[57] the Court of Appeal made clear that secret profit-making and bribes should be treated the same and the issue is the nature of the claim, a matter which has been extensively discussed in the context of bribes.[58]

13-17 The question of whether a bribe received by a fiduciary could be the subject of a personal or of a proprietary claim by a beneficiary was problematic until this decision in *Sinclair Investments* because of the divergence of opinion which existed as to whether the courts should follow *Lister v Stubbs*[59] (long-standing Court of Appeal decision that there was only a personal liability to account for a bribe and there was no scope for proprietary remedies) or *Attorney General for Hong Kong v Reid*[60] (persuasive, more recent, Privy Council

---

[55] [2011] 2 BCLC 501 at [89], see also [50].

[56] Nevertheless, the court considered, obiter, that once a person knows certain facts, he should only be treated as appreciating the legal consequences if he actually knew of the consequences or if in all the circumstances he ought reasonably to have appreciated those consequences. The Court of Appeal took a rather generous approach in this case being reluctant to hold that the banks were on notice for many months (though eventually they were on notice of the proprietary claim of the claimants) even when the transactions at issue were entered into 'in the shadow of insolvency and fraud', the court noting the importance of not interpreting or developing the law of notice in such a way as to interfere unacceptably with ordinary and honest commerce. See [2011] 2 BCLC 501 at [98]–[112].   [57] [2011] 2 BCLC 501.

[58] [2011] 2 BCLC 501 at [55]–[56].

[59] (1890) 45 Ch D 1, CA. For example, in *Daraydan Holdings Ltd v Solland International Ltd* [2005] 4 All ER 73 at 92–3, Lawrence Collins J indicated that, if necessary, he would have followed *AGHK v Reid* and not *Lister v Stubbs*. On the facts in *Daraydan*, he considered it possible to distinguish *Lister v Stubbs* as the price paid by the company for the services obtained had been increased by the suppliers by the amount of the bribes which the suppliers had had to pay to secure the contract. The bribes were derived directly from the claimants' property therefore and the claimants were entitled to proprietary relief. See *Cadogan Petroleum plc v Tolley* [2011] EWHC 2286 at [36], where Newey J doubts this analysis, though he notes that the position may be different if the contact pursuant to which the bribes are paid is rescinded by the claimant, relying on Millet J in *El Ajou v Dollar Land Holdings plc* [1993] 3 All ER 717 at 734 (who suggested that rescinding the transaction revests an equitable title to the purchase money in the claimants).

[60] [1994] 1 All ER 1, PC.

decision that *Lister v Stubbs* was wrongly decided and a proprietary remedy is entirely appropriate to ensure that the fiduciary cannot benefit from his breach of duty).[61]

13-18 In *Sinclair Investments (UK) Ltd v Versailles Trade Finance Ltd*[62] the Court of Appeal did not agree that it was open to the court to follow the decision in *AGHK v Reid*.[63] As a matter of precedent, the court concluded that, save where there are powerful reasons to the contrary, the Court of Appeal should follow its own previous decisions until they are overruled and there are five previous domestic Court of Appeal decisions on this matter.[64] On that ground alone, it was not open to the courts to follow *Attorney General for Hong Kong v Reid*. In any event, on the specific issue, Lord Neuberger MR considered that the decision in *AGHK v Reid* is unsound for a bribe could not possibly be said to be an asset which the fiduciary is under a duty to take for the beneficiary. He noted that a fundamental distinction exists between a fiduciary (the director) enriching himself by depriving a claimant beneficiary (the company) of an asset and a fiduciary enriching himself by doing a wrong to the beneficiary.[65] The receipt of a bribe is the same as unauthorised profit-making by a director; in each case, there is a breach of duty which entitles the company to bring a personal claim for the amount of the bribe or the unauthorised profit.[66] Lord Neuberger acknowledged that limiting the claim to a personal claim means that the faithless fiduciary will not be accountable for further gains which he derives from the benefit or bribe.[67] In that regard, Lord Neuberger thought that concerns about the (deterrent) need to strip the defaulting fiduciary of all of his gain could be met, with less damage to the law and greater flexibility, by expanding the equitable compensation jurisdiction rather than by creating a proprietary claim with possibly untoward effects on other creditors of the fiduciary.[68]

Misappropriation of 'corporate opportunities'

13-19 The second issue, post-*Sinclair Investments*, is whether the 'corporate opportunity' cases, using that phrase as shorthand for cases where a director exploits some property,

---

[61] See [1994] 1 All ER 1 at 9, per Lord Templeman. In *Reid*, the bribes had been invested in a number of properties which had increased in value substantially. The fiduciary had to account not just for the bribe but for the increased value of the property representing the bribe since otherwise he would receive a benefit from his breach of duty. See Nolan, 'Bribes: a reprise' (2011) 127 LQR 19 who notes that the policy arguments do not speak uniformly in favour of one outcome to this debate and comments that, given the social importance of an appropriate civil remedy for bribery, it may be that a proprietary claim is appropriate, though it may require Parliamentary action to achieve that outcome.   [62] [2011] 2 BCLC 501.

[63] [1994] 1 All ER 1, PC.

[64] [2011] 2 BCLC 501 at [73]. The exceptional cases would be where it is a foregone conclusion that the Supreme Court would follow the Privy Council, as has happened on two occasions, see at [74]; see also *Re Spectrum Plus Ltd, National Westminster Bank plc v Spectrum Plus Ltd* [2005] 2 BCLC 30 at [58].

[65] [2011] 2 BCLC 501 at [80].

[66] See *Cadogan Petroleum plc v Tolley* [2011] EWHC 2286 (summary judgment could be given dismissing a proprietary claim in relation to the alleged receipt of bribes and secret commissions since, even if the alleged facts were established, having regard to the decision in *Sinclair*, such a proprietary claim would fail).

[67] [2011] 2 BCLC 501 at [89].

[68] [2011] 2 BCLC 501 at [90]. Lord Neuberger considered that Lord Templeman in *AGHK v Reid*, in allowing a proprietary claim in respect of the bribe, may have given insufficient weight to the potentially unfair consequences to other creditors of the defaulting fiduciary, see at [83]. See too Lord Neuberger's earlier comments to similar effect in *Re BA Peters plc* [2010] 1 BCLC 142 at [21]. Nolan, n 49, at 23 also suggests that some reformulation of the personal claim to recover any uplift in value of the bribe and capture any gain generated by the bribe would improve the effectiveness of the personal claim without having to address the perceived problems of allowing proprietary claims in this context (i.e. the impact of proprietary claims on other creditors on the bankruptcy of the fiduciary).

information or opportunity in a situation of conflict of interest in breach of s 175(1) and (2) (see **11-27** et seq), will give rise to proprietary claims. Certainly, in some instances, the court treats the opportunity as if it were property of the company so that the director who exploits an opportunity on his own behalf holds the opportunity, the contract diverted from the company, as a class 1 *Paragon* trustee on behalf of the company.[69] For example, in *CMS Dolphin Ltd v Simonet*[70] a director of the claimant company, an advertising agency, left the company and set up a new business. All the staff of the company subsequently joined him as did the principal clients of the company. The court found that the director took away from the company the benefit of contracts with existing clients and the business opportunities the company had with those clients. The director was held liable to account for the profits derived from those contracts/opportunities which he had diverted from the company to his new business, together with a sum to take account of other benefits derived from those contracts, for example, other contracts might not have been won, or profits made on them, without the opportunity or cash-flow benefit which flowed from the contracts unlawfully obtained.[71] Lawrence Collins J stated:

> 'In my judgment the underlying basis of the liability of the director who exploits after his resignation a maturing business opportunity of the company is that the opportunity is to be treated *as if it were* [emphasis added] property of the company in relation to which the director had fiduciary duties. By seeking to exploit the opportunity after resignation he is appropriating for himself that property. He is just as accountable as a trustee who retires without properly accounting for trust property. In the case of the director he becomes a constructive trustee of the fruits of his abuse of the company's property which he has acquired in circumstances where he knowingly had a conflict of interest, and exploited it by resigning from the company.'[72]

13-20 The advantage of requiring the director to account for the opportunity as a trustee, in the sense of class 1 *Paragon*, see **13-9**, is that the director would hold any gain resulting or derived from it, i.e. other contracts gained on the back of it, also on trust for the company so maximising the return to the company and enhancing the deterrent effect of the prohibition. An example of this approach can be found in *Lindsley v Woodfull*[73] (the case concerned a partnership but the same principles apply) where a partner who diverted to his own business a contract which the partnership had been pursuing had to account for the profits from the contract *and* the profits from its subsequent renewal[74] as those profits are consequent upon the breach of duty. Likewise in *Kingsley IT Consulting Ltd v McIntosh*[75] the director's liability to account extended from the profit derived from the contract which he had diverted from his company to the profit derived from two subsequent extensions of that contract.

---

[69] See, for example, *Cook v Deeks* [1916] 1 AC 554 where the Privy Council held that the benefit of a contract (which the company had been pursuing but which the directors secured on their own behalf) belonged in equity to the company and the directors were bound to hold it on behalf of the company, at 564.

[70] [2001] 2 BCLC 704.

[71] [2001] 2 BCLC 704 at 733–4, subject to taking into account the expenses connected with those profits and a reasonable allowance for overheads.

[72] [2001] 2 BCLC 704 at [96]; the analysis was endorsed in general terms by the Court of Appeal in *In Plus Group Ltd v Pyke* [2002] 2 BCLC 201 at 220; and in *Foster Bryant Surveying Ltd v Bryant* [2007] 2 BCLC 239 at 245–6; see also *Shepherds Investments Ltd v Walters* [2007] 2 BCLC 202 at 231.

[73] [2004] 2 BCLC 131.

[74] See [2004] 2 BCLC 131 at [28]. There will come a point, of course, as Jonathan Parker LJ noted in *Murad v Al-Saraj* [2005] EWCA Civ 959 at [115], when it can safely be said that profits of a business are not attributable to the opportunity taken from the original company and are not tainted by the conflict in which the defaulting directors had placed themselves.   [75] [2006] BCC 875.

13-21 This approach is reinforced by the ruling in *Sinclair Investments (UK) Ltd v Versailles Trade Finance Ltd*.[76] Having reviewed the authorities, Lord Neuberger there concluded, as noted at **13-14**, that there is a consistent line of reasoned decisions stretching back to the 19th century 'which appear to establish that a beneficiary cannot claim a proprietary interest, but is entitled to an equitable account in respect of any money or asset acquired by a fiduciary in breach of his duties to the beneficiary, unless the asset or money is or has been beneficially the property of the beneficiary or the trustee acquired the asset or money by taking advantage of an opportunity or right which was properly that of the beneficiary'.[77] The situation where a director exploits property, information or opportunity in circumstances of a conflict of interest can fall within the latter category, but it is limited by whether the opportunity or right was 'properly that of the beneficiary'. This would be the case in respect of the diversion of existing contracts of the company[78] (as in *Quarter Master UK Ltd v Pyke*,[79] see **11-31**, or *CMS Dolphin Ltd v Simonet*,[80] see **11-42**) and in the case of contracts or opportunities which the company is actively pursuing (as in *Cook v Deeks*,[81] see **11-13**, or *IDC v Cooley*,[82] see **11-14**), but the line would be drawn at the exploitation of opportunities by a director in a situation of conflict, as in *Commonwealth Oil & Gas Co Ltd v Baxter*,[83] see **11-19**, where the company had no pre-existing interest in the opportunity.[84] Profit-making by a director in those circumstances in breach of his duties, in the manner akin to which the director in *Gwembe Valley Development Co Ltd v Koshy*,[85] see **13-13**, profited in breach of his duties, gives rise only to an accounting in equity for the gain made, but not a proprietary claim.[86]

The liability to account

13-22 As to the extent of a fiduciary's duty to account for a profit made, the court is inclined to order the widest possible accounting limited only by the need for a reasonable connection between the breach of duty and the profit for which the fiduciary is accountable.[87] The purpose of a liability to account for secret profits is to strip the defaulting fiduciary of his profit[88] and the burden of proof is on the defaulting fiduciary to show that the profit is not one for which he should account.[89]

---

[76] [2011] 2 BCLC 501, aff'g [2011] 1 BCLC 202.

[77] *Sinclair Investments (UK) Ltd v Versailles Trade Finance Ltd* [2011] 2 BCLC 501 at [88], per Lord Neuberger.

[78] See *Commonwealth Oil & Gas Co Ltd v Baxter* [2009] CSIH 75, [2009] SLT 1123 at [18], [94], [98].

[79] [2005] 1 BCLC 245.   [80] [2001] 2 BCLC 704.

[81] [1916] AC 554 (contract belonged in equity to the company).   [82] [1972] 2 All ER 162.

[83] [2009] CSIH 75, [2009] SLT 1123.

[84] See *Commonwealth Oil & Gas Co Ltd v Baxter* [2009] CSIH 75, [2009] SLT 1123 at [17]–[18], per Lord Hamilton.   [85] [2004] 1 BCLC 131.

[86] See *Commonwealth Oil & Gas Co Ltd v Baxter* [2009] CSIH 75, [2009] SLT 1123 at [16]-[19], [94], [95]. It would seem that the remedy granted in *Bhullar v Bhullar* [2003] 2 BCLC 241, see **11-11**, was the wrong remedy—the court ordered the company which had acquired the property held it on 'constructive trust' for the directors' company when they acted in breach of the no-conflict duty in acquiring it—the proper remedy should have been an accounting in equity by them for the benefit made in breach of duty and the company should have been liable on the basis of knowing assistance, but the property should not have been held on trust for the company since it had no pre-existing interest in the asset.

[87] *CMS Dolphin Ltd v Simonet* [2001] 2 BCLC 704 at 733–4; *Ultraframe (UK) Ltd v Fielding* [2005] EWHC 1638 at [1588]. But see *Murad v Al-Saraj* [2005] EWCA Civ 959 where Clarke LJ (dissenting) was disposed to be more flexible on the accounting.

[88] See *Murad v Al-Saraj* [2005] EWCA Civ 959 at [56], per Arden LJ; at [108], per Jonathan Parker LJ; *United Pan-Europe Communications NV v Deutsche Bank AG* [2000] 2 BCLC 461 at 484, CA.

[89] See *Murad v Al-Saraj* [2005] EWCA Civ 959 at [77].

13-23   If a director diverts contracts, opportunities, etc to a partnership where he is only one of the number of partners, he is liable to account to the full extent of the profit made, even if his partners are entitled to a share of those profits and are ignorant of his breach of duty, but to the extent that a number of the partners are implicated in the breach of duty, they are jointly and severally liable.[90]

13-24   If the improper profit is made through a company used by the director as a device to mask his breach of fiduciary duty, the courts have no hesitation in piercing the corporate veil and treating the company's gain as the director's gain.[91] In *Gencor ACP Ltd v Dalby*[92] a director had for some time diverted business opportunities away from the company to another company which he owned and controlled. The court found that the other company had no staff or activities and its only function was to make and receive payments. The court concluded that it was little other than the director's offshore bank account in a nominee name and the veil should be pierced in such circumstances, see **3-30**. In *Trustor AB v Smallbone*[93] two directors had misappropriated significant sums of money from their company with some of the money ending up in the hands of a company controlled by one of the directors. The court held that receipt by the company was receipt by the director where the company was merely a device or façade to conceal the true facts and was being used to avoid or conceal any liability of an individual, see **3-30**.

13-25   Apart then from where the company is a mere façade so it is appropriate to pierce the corporate veil and to treat receipt by the company as receipt by the director,[94] the fact that the fiduciary has a substantial or even a controlling interest in a company[95] which knowingly receives trust property does not make the fiduciary personally accountable for that receipt,[96] rather the director remains liable for his own breach of duty and must account for the profits made by him and the company (as a recipient) may be liable on the basis of knowing receipt.[97] An example can be seen in *Quarter Master UK v Pyke*[98] where directors who obtained a contract for themselves in breach of the no-conflict rule when the contract should have been obtained for their company (see **11-31**), were liable to

---

[90]   *Imperial Mercantile Credit Association v Coleman* (1873) LR 6 HL 189 at 208–9.

[91]   See *Ultraframe (UK) Ltd v Fielding* [2005] EWHC 1638 at [1576].   [92]   [2000] 2 BCLC 734.

[93]   [2001] 2 BCLC 436; and see *Lindsley v Woodfull* [2004] 2 BCLC 131 at 140.

[94]   *Woolfson v Strathclyde Regional Council* [1978] SC (HL) 90, see **3-22**. See *Aerostar Maintenance Intenational Ltd v Wilson* [2010] EWHC 2032 at [205] (court declined to pierce the corporate veil so as to recognise receipt of corporate opportunity by a company formed and controlled by a defaulting director to be receipt by the director personally; the company was formed to carry out a new business rather than to be the creature of the director and to disguise the director's breach of duty, distinguishing *Trustor* and *Gencor*. Note too *Law Society of England & Wales v Isaac* [2010] EWHC 1670 at [40], where Norris J cautioned that a claim for piercing the corporate veil should not become a routine adjunct to any claim against a company for dishonest assistance or knowing receipt.

[95]   See *Crown Dilmun v Sutton* [2004] 1 BCLC 468 where the defaulting director held 49% of the company which secured the contract diverted by the director from his own company. The recipient company was liable on the basis of knowing receipt because the director's knowledge of his breach of duty was attributed to the company with serious consequences for the majority shareholder of the recipient company who had no knowledge of the breach of fiduciary duty (see at 515).

[96]   *Ultraframe (UK) Ltd v Fielding* [2005] EWHC 1638 at [1576]. See *Quarter Master UK Ltd v Pyke* [2005] 1 BCLC 245 at 172; *Aerostar Maintenance Intenational Ltd v Wilson* [2010] EWHC 2032 at [202].

[97]   *Ultraframe (UK) Ltd v Fielding* [2005] EWHC 1638 at [1576], per Lewison J—each party should be liable for his own gain (followed by *National Grid v McKenzie* [2009] EWHC 1817 at [117]; *Aerostar Maintenance International Ltd v Wilson* [2010] EWHC 2032 at [202]–[206]) in preference, rightly, to the suggestion by Lawrence Collins J in *CMS Dolphin Ltd v Simonet* [2001] 2 BCLC 704 at [98]–[104] that the director and the company might be jointly and severally liable though the director personally had not received the profit.

[98]   [2005] 1 BCLC 245.

account for the personal profits made by them. The company to which they diverted the contract was also liable to account for the profits derived by it from the arrangements on the basis of knowing receipt.[99] The director's liability is to account for all of *his* gain and where his gain is indirect through, for example, an increase in value of his shareholding in a company which exploited the opportunity etc, he must still account for that gain, but as part of his personal liability to account for all of his profits.[100] Where there is an overlap between the recipient company's liability and the director's liability to account, the court is careful to prevent double recovery.

13-26 This extensive liability to account applies even though it can result in a windfall to the company and can appear unduly harsh to the faithless fiduciary, as in *Regal (Hastings) Ltd v Gulliver*[101] (where the company could not put up the funding required, see **11-28**) or, as in *Industrial Development Consultants Ltd v Cooley*[102] (see **11-14**) where the court thought that the company only had a 10% chance of getting the contract secured by the director for himself yet the director had to account for all the gain made by him from carrying it out.[103] This response is justified on the basis of the need to deter fiduciaries from breach of fiduciary duty,[104] though concern has been expressed that 'the liability of the fiduciary should not be transformed into a vehicle for the unjust enrichment of the plaintiff'.[105]

13-27 In keeping with this strict approach, the courts are reluctant to exercise their discretion to grant an equitable allowance to the fiduciary for his work and skill[106] in generating the profits so as to ensure that fiduciaries are denied any incentive to act in breach of fiduciary duty, though an allowance will be made for costs incurred in securing the profit.[107] An allowance will only be granted then if it can be given without undermining the fiduciary obligation to avoid conflicts of interest and doubts were expressed in *Guinness plc v Saunders*[108] as to whether such an allowance could ever be permitted in the case of company directors

---

[99] See [2005] 1 BCLC 245 at [79].

[100] *Gwembe Valley Development Co Ltd v Koshy* [2004] 1 BCLC 131 at 172.

[101] [1942] 1 All ER 378. Many of the cases have a windfall element to them, for example, see *Crown Dilmun v Sutton* [2004] 1 BCLC 468 (not clear company could or would have pursued the opportunity diverted by the director to himself); *Quarter Master UK v Pyke* [2005] 1 BCLC 245 (company could not have obtained the contract diverted by the directors as the third party was not willing to deal with the company due to its financial position).   [102] [1972] 2 All ER 162.

[103] As already discussed, the inability of the company to exploit the opportunity has no bearing on the breach of duty, see **11-33**.

[104] See *Guinness plc v Saunders* [1990] BCLC 402; *Lindsley v Woodfull* [2004] 2 BCLC 131 at 140; *Murad v Al-Saraj* [2005] EWCA Civ 959 at [74]–[75]; also *Quarter Master UK v Pyke* [2005] 1 BCLC 245 at 269 where the court made the point that a director can always free himself from the obligation to account by obtaining the informed consent of the company. Now, there is the other option of obtaining the authorisation of independent directors under CA 2006, s 175(4)(b).

[105] *Warman International Ltd v Dwyer* (1995) 182 CLR 544 at 561, Aust HC; a point taken on board by Lewison J in *Ultraframe (UK) Ltd v Fielding* [2005] EWHC 1638 at [1588]. See also *Fyffes Group Ltd v Templeman* [2000] 2 Lloyd's Rep 643 at 672; *Crown Dilmun v Sutton* [2004] 1 BCLC 468 at 517.

[106] *Phipps v Boardman* [1966] 3 All ER 721. See *FHR European Ventures LLP v Mankarious* [2011] EWHC 2308 (not appropriate to make any allowance for work done by an agent who received a secret €10m commission on a hotel deal—he had opportunities to disclose the fee to his principals, but failed to do so).

[107] For example, in see *CMS Dolphin Ltd v Simonet* [2001] 2 BCLC 704 at 733, see **11-42**, an allowance was possible for overheads and expenses connected with exploiting the corporate opportunities which the wrongdoer had diverted to his own business, but not for a salary for the wrongdoer; in *Cobbetts v Hodge* [2010] 1 BCLC 30 an allowance was made for the costs of acquiring shares from which the fiduciary profited personally, but no allowance was made for his work and skill to enhance their value; in *Lee v Futurist Developments Ltd* [2011] 1 BCLC 654, a director had to account for a secret commission which he obtained subject to an allowance limited to legitimate expenses incurred in securing the commission.

[108] [1990] 1 All ER 652.

acting in breach of their fiduciary obligations. In *Quarter Master UK Ltd v Pyke*,[109] applying *Guinness plc v Saunders*, the court refused any allowance for the directors who diverted a contract away from the company to themselves. There was no evidence that they had exercised any special skills or taken unusual risks and the fact that the company could not have obtained the contract (it was in severe financial difficulties) did not make the facts sufficiently special to persuade the court to exercise its discretion, see **11-31**.

13-28   Many of the cases concern a liability to account for a profit made by the director in breach of duty, but the claim may equally be one to indemnify the company in respect of losses incurred. Where an asset has been misapplied and there has been a subsequent loss in value of the asset, that loss must be made good by the director/trustee, not in the sense of a liability for loss at common law, but as part of the process of reinstating that trust asset.[110]

13-29   In *Re Duckwari plc (No 2), Duckwari plc v Offerventure Ltd (No 2)*[111] the company had acquired an asset which had subsequently fallen in value in part due to the collapse of the property market. The transaction by which the company had acquired the asset was in contravention of the statutory provisions governing substantial property transactions between a company and a director or person connected with a director, see **12-20** and now CA 2006, s 190. The court held the director was liable to make good the full amount of the misapplication of the company's funds so the loss arising from the acquisition (including the loss as a result of the fall in the property market) fell on the director/trustee, see **12-48**. Imposing liability, Nourse LJ noted: 'it is well recognised that the basis on which a trustee is liable to make good a misapplication of trust moneys is strict and sometimes harsh, especially where, as here, there has been a huge depreciation in the value of the asset acquired'.[112] He also noted that, given the failure to obtain shareholder approval as required, it was not unfair for the loss to fall on the director.

C Liability of third parties

13-30   Third party liability may arise on one of two main grounds and in many cases on both:[113] (1) on the basis of 'dishonest assistance' where the third party has participated or assisted in the breach by the director of his duties; (2) on the basis of 'knowing receipt' of company funds. Another possibility is to seek to hold the third party liable in damages as party to a conspiracy to injure by unlawful means,[114] or on the basis of procuring or inducing a breach of contract by the director.[115] However, liability under the respective headings is not cumulative[116] and a payment, for example, under a personal liability to account

---

[109] [2005] 1 BCLC 245 at 271–2.

[110] See Millett, 'Equity's Place in the Law of Commerce' (1998) 114 LQR 214 at 227.

[111] [1998] 2 BCLC 315, see **12-24**.   [112] [1998] 2 BCLC 315 at 324.

[113] See, for example, *Crown Dilmun v Sutton* [2004] 1 BCLC 468.

[114] *OBG Ltd v Allan* [2007] 4 All ER 545, HL. See *Simtel Communications Ltd v Rebak* [2006] 2 BCLC 571; *British Midland Tool Ltd v Midland International Tooling Ltd* [2003] 2 BCLC 523; *Aerostar Maintenance International Ltd v Wilson* [2010] EWHC 2032 at [172]–[177], [189]–[191]. See too the cautionary words of Morgan J in *Aerostar*, at [170], as to the undesirability, where accessory liability is being determined both on the basis of equitable liability (dishonest assistance and knowing receipt) and on the basis of the tort of conspiracy to injure by unlawful means) of differing principles governing accessory liability.

[115] See *Mainstream Properties Ltd v Young* [2007] 4 All ER 545, HL; *Aerostar Maintenance International Ltd v Wilson* [2010] EWHC 2032 at [163]–[166].

[116] Note comments by Norris J in *Law Society of England & Wales v Isaac* [2010] EWHC 1670 at [99], where Norris J cautioned against the temptation to advance multiple analyses of the same facts in terms of differing

in equity will discharge *pro tanto* damages awarded in respect of the same conduct on the grounds of unlawful means conspiracy and liability under dishonest assistance and knowing receipt in respect of the same breach of duty will simply provide a different basis for recovery for the sums in question.[117]

Dishonest assistance

13-31 As Lord Millett noted in *Twinsectra Ltd v Yardley*,[118] liability in knowing assistance claims is fault-based and the remedy is compensatory (to compensate the beneficiary for the wrongful interference with the due performance of the fiduciary duties) and he went on:

> 'The cause of action is concerned with attributing liability for misdirected funds. Liability is not restricted to the person whose breach of trust or fiduciary duty caused their original diversion. His liability is strict. Nor is it limited to those who assist him in the original breach. It extends to everyone who consciously assists in the continuing diversion of the money. Most of the cases have been concerned, not with assisting in the original breach, but in covering it up afterwards by helping to launder the money.'

13-32 This liability in equity to make good to the company any resulting losses attaches to any third party who dishonestly procures or assists a director in a breach of fiduciary duty to the company.[119] It seems that, alternatively, the dishonest assistant may be held to account for any profit which he himself makes from his dishonest assistance.[120] There is no requirement that the breach of duty, in which the third party has dishonestly assisted, should involve property held on trust or its misapplication or appropriation.[121]

13-33 The Privy Council in *Royal Brunei Airlines v Tan*[122] established that, in this context, acting dishonestly means simply not acting as an honest person would in the circumstances and, for the most part, dishonesty is to be equated with conscious impropriety.[123] The court, when deciding whether a person is acting honestly, looks at all the circumstances known to the third party at the time and has regard to the personal attributes of the third party such as his experience and intelligence and the reason why he acted as he did.[124] It is

causes of action unless it is anticipated to produce a significantly different outcome in terms of ultimate recovery, having regard to a defendant's means. For an example of multiple causes of action being brought on the same facts, see *Aerostar Maintenance International Ltd v Wilson* [2010] EWHC 2032.

[117] See *Law Society of England & Wales v Isaac* [2010] EWHC 1670 at [100].

[118] [2002] 2 All ER 377 at 405; see also *Royal Brunei Airlines v Tan* [1995] 3 All ER 97 at 104, PC, per Lord Nicholls.

[119] *Royal Brunei Airlines v Tan* [1995] 3 All ER 97, PC; *Barnes v Addy* (1874) LR 9 Ch App 244. As to the nature of the liability for dishonest assistance, see the valuable analysis of Elliott and Mitchell, 'Remedies for Dishonest Assistance' (2004) 67 MLR 16. For a critical account of the case law and the debates as to the scope of the jurisdiction, see *Attorney General of Zambia v Meer Care & Desai* [2007] EWHC 952 at [332]–[371], per Peter Smith J (reversed on other grounds, [2008] EWCA Civ 1007).

[120] See *Fiona Trust & Holding Corp v Privalov* [2010] EWHC 3199 at [63]–[66] and the authorities cited there; also *Ultraframe (UK) Ltd v Fielding* [2005] EWHC 1638 at [1594], per Lewison J. See Prentice & Payne (2006) 122 LQR 558 at 563 who note that this extension to an accounting for profits made is a substantial extension of the remedies available to the beneficiary beyond the classic compensation claim. In *Fiona Trust*, Andrew Smith J approved of the recovery of profit made on the basis that it deters other persons from knowingly assisting a fiduciary to violate his duties, see at [66].

[121] See *Fiona Trust & Holding Corp v Privalov* [2010] EWHC 3199 at [61], agreeing with *JD Weatherspoon v Van de Berg* [2009] EWHC 639 at [518]–[520], per Peter Smith J.   [122] [1995] 3 All ER 97, PC.

[123] [1995] 3 All ER 97 at 106, PC.

[124] [1995] 3 All ER 97 at 107, PC.

not necessary for the third party to know every element of the breach of duty, but he must know that the fiduciary is doing something which he is not entitled to do.[125]

13-34 The House of Lords in *Twinsectra Ltd v Yardley*[126] muddied the waters somewhat by supporting what was interpreted as a two-prong test for dishonesty—whether what is done is dishonest by the standards of ordinary people[127] and whether the defendant knows that his conduct is dishonest by the ordinary standards of honest and reasonable men.[128] The second element of this test proved problematic and their Lordships, in the guise of the Privy Council, sought to clarify the position in *Barlow Clowes International Ltd v Eurotrust International Ltd* [129] where Lord Hoffmann (regretting the ambiguity which was generated by *Twinsectra*) commented:[130]

> 'Although a dishonest state of mind is a subjective mental state, the standard by which the law determines whether it is dishonest is objective. If by ordinary standards a defendant's mental state would be characterised as dishonest, it is irrelevant that the defendant judges by different standards.'

13-35 In *Abou-Rahmah v Abacha*[131] Arden LJ considered that this position can be accepted also as a statement of the law of England and Wales,[132] a position also adopted by the Court of Appeal in *Starglade Properties Ltd v Nash*.[133] The issue is dishonesty and it is to be assessed on an objective basis, deciding whether the conduct complained of is dishonest according to the standards of ordinary people, regardless of whether the defendant himself considered it to be dishonest.[134] In *Starglade*, a director did not consider it dishonest to prefer some creditors of the company over another—he paid off all the creditors out of money which he was required to hold on trust for the one creditor who was not paid.[135] The Court

---

[125] *Ultraframe (UK) Ltd v Fielding* [2005] EWHC 1638 at [1505]–[1506]. For examples of dishonest assistance, see *Simtel Communications Ltd v Rebak* [2006] 2 BCLC 571 (former employee dishonestly assisted in director's breach of duty as contracts diverted from the company to a new business set up by the director and former employee); *Statek Corpn v Alford* [2008] BCC 266 (individual dishonestly assisted two directors misappropriate $19.8m from a company by passing company money from its accounts through his bank accounts and on to the two directors).   [126] [2002] 2 All ER 377.

[127] [2002] 2 All ER 377 at 382–3, 'a consciousness that one is transgressing ordinary standards of honest behaviour', per Lord Hoffmann.   [128] [2002] 2 All ER 377 at 387, per Lord Hutton.

[129] [2006] 1 All ER 333, PC, see comments by Conaglen & Gaymour (2006) CLJ 18; Yeo (2006) 122 LQR 171.

[130] [2006] 1 All ER 333 at [10], see also at [15]–[16]. See too *Attorney General for Zambia v Meer Care & Desai* [2007] EWHC 952 at [334], [339], per Peter Smith J—the test of dishonesty is essentially a question of fact whereby the state of mind of the defendant has to be judged in the light of his subjective knowledge, but by reference to an objective standard of honesty (reversed in part [2008] EWCA Civ 1007 on other grounds).

[131] [2007] 1 Lloyd's Rep 115; see comments by Ryan [2007] Conv 168, Lee [2007] JBL 209.

[132] See [2007] 1 Lloyd's Rep 115 at 129–30. Rix LJ (at 119, 120) still seemed to suggest there is some element of subjectivity to it while Pill LJ (at 133) thought it unnecessary to enter the debate. Arden LJ was able to resolve the difficulty involved in preferring a decision of the Privy Council to domestic authorities by deciding that the statement of the Privy Council in *Barlow Clowes* represented the law of England and Wales as set down in *Twinsectra* so that it was possible to follow the guidance given by the Privy Council without departing from the House of Lords ruling. In *Sinclair Investments (UK) Ltd v Versailles Trade Finance Ltd* [2011] 2 BCLC 501 at [74], the Court of Appeal cited, without disapproval, *Abacha* as an example of the exceptional circumstances in which the Court of Appeal could follow the Privy Council decision (i.e. because it was a foregone conclusion that the Supreme Court would).

[133] [2010] EWCA Civ 1314; see too *Attorney General for Zambia v Meer Care & Desai* [2007] EWHC 952 at [332]–[371] (reversed in part [2008] EWCA Civ 1007 on other grounds).

[134] See also *Aerostar Maintenance International Ltd v Wilson* [2010] EWHC 2032 at [184], [198].

[135] The claimant company had a negligence claim against a surveyor which it assigned to L Ltd and the defendant, the sole director and member of L, undertook in writing on behalf of L to pay to the claimant

of Appeal ruled that the lower court had applied the wrong test of dishonesty (the trial judge had considered that not everyone would have considered that preferring some creditors would be dishonest). The relevant standard to apply is the ordinary standard of honest behaviour and, ultimately in civil proceedings, it is for the court to determine what that ordinary standard is and to apply it to the facts of the case.[136] The deliberate removal of the assets of an insolvent company so as to entirely defeat the just claim of a creditor was not in accordance with the ordinary standards of honest commercial behaviour, nor could a man in the position of the defendant have thought otherwise, notwithstanding a lack of understanding as to the legal position.[137]

Knowing receipt

13-36 The claim in the case of knowing receipt is receipt-based, there must be a receipt by one person of assets from another, and primarily restitutionary—whether the asset can be recovered depends on whether it or its traceable proceeds can be identified and, if it has been disposed of or dissipated, then there is no longer a proprietary claim but monetary restitution must be made.[138] The claim is a claim against the knowing recipient for any benefit which he has received or acquired as a result of the knowing receipt.[139] A much cited statement of the position on knowing receipt by a third party is that of Buckley LJ in *Belmont Finance Corp v Williams Furniture Ltd (No 2)*:[140]

'…if the directors of a company in breach of their fiduciary duties misapply the funds of their company so that they come into the hands of some stranger to the trust who receives them with knowledge (actual or constructive) of the breach, he cannot conscientiously retain those funds against the company unless he has some better equity. He becomes a constructive trustee for the company of the misapplied funds.'

13-37 In order to bring a claim on the basis of knowing receipt, Lord Hoffmann stated in *El Ajou v Dollar Land Holdings plc*[141] that it is necessary for the plaintiff to show:

'… first, a disposal of his assets in breach of fiduciary duty; secondly, the beneficial receipt by the defendant of assets which are traceable as representing the assets of the plaintiff; and thirdly, knowledge on the part of the defendant that the assets he received are traceable to a breach of fiduciary duty.'

---

half of the net money received from the claim and to hold all money so received on trust. L having become insolvent, the defendant director used the money received to pay off numerous creditors of L, but did not pay the claimant the amount due under the agreement. The director was sued as a dishonest assistant in the breach of trust by L Ltd.

[136] [2010] EWCA Civ 1314 at [32].   [137] [2010] EWCA Civ 1314 at [39].

[138] See *Twinsectra Ltd v Yardley* [2002] 2 All ER 377 at 404, per Lord Millett; *Ultraframe (UK) Ltd v Fielding* [2005] EWHC 1638 at [1486]; and see *Commonwealth Oil & Gas Co Ltd v Baxter* [2009] CSIH 75, [2009] SLT 1123 at [20], per Lord Hamilton.

[139] See *Ultraframe (UK) Ltd v Fielding* [2005] EWHC 1638 at [1577], per Lewison J and see at [1520]: 'But the proprietary remedy does not depend on profit. It is not a claim for unjust enrichment. As Lord Millett explained [in *Foskett v McKeown* [2000] 3 All ER 97 at 121–122] …: "Conversely, a plaintiff who brings an action like the present must show that the defendant is in receipt of property which belongs beneficially to him or its traceable proceeds, but he need not show that the defendant has been enriched by its receipt. He may, for example, have paid full value for the property, but he is still required to disgorge it if he received it with notice of the plaintiff's interest."'

[140] [1980] 1 All ER 393 at 405, CA. See also *JJ Harrison (Properties) Ltd v Harrison* [2002] 1 BCLC 162; *Bairstow v Queens Moat Houses plc* [2001] 2 BCLC 531; *Re Duckwari plc (No 2), Duckwari plc v Offerventure Ltd (No 2)* [1998] 2 BCLC 315 at 321, per Nourse LJ. See Sealy, 'The Director as Trustee' (1967) CLJ 83.

[141] [1994] 1 BCLC 464 at 478.

Looking, first, at the degree of knowledge required, the nature of 'knowing receipt' liability was comprehensively reviewed and the current state of the law is as stated by the Court of Appeal in *Bank of Credit and Commerce International (Overseas) Ltd v Akindele*[142] which adopted a markedly different approach to the basis of liability than the earlier authorities which had focused on liability arising from (increasingly convoluted) degrees of knowledge. The Court of Appeal held that dishonesty is not an essential ingredient of a claim for knowing receipt, and the test for knowledge in such a claim is simply whether the defendant's knowledge makes it unconscionable for him to retain the benefit of the receipt. Although such a test cannot avoid difficulties of application, the court thought it preferable to the complexity of the previous categorisations of knowledge for these purposes.[143] Moreover, Nourse LJ thought, this approach should better enable the courts to give common-sense decisions in the commercial context in which claims in knowing receipt are now frequently made, paying equal regard, on the one hand, to the need to avoid the mischief of paralysing trade and, on the other hand, to the realisation that there are cases in which a commercial man should not be allowed to shelter behind the exigencies of commercial life.[144]

13-38 The pragmatic response to the commercial realities evident in *BCCI v Akindele*[145] is also evident in the robust approach taken by the courts as to what is to be regarded as property or funds of the company for these purposes, bearing in mind that a key requirement is that assets of the company are transferred and received with knowledge of the breach of trust by the recipient (see Hoffmann LJ in *El Ajou*, see **13-37**). Liability in knowing receipt depends on the prior existence of an asset which is the subject of a trust in favour of a beneficiary.[146] Clearly, property vested in the company prior to the breach of fiduciary duty can be the subject of claim,[147] but it may also encompass property in the form of business opportunities so the recipient of a contract diverted away from a company by a director in breach of duty may be liable on the basis of knowing receipt of company property.[148] In *Crown Dilmun v Sutton*[149] the court found that the defendant company had received the claimant company's property (in the form of a contract which was a business opportunity of the claimant, see **11-31**) and

---

[142] [2000] 4 All ER 221, applying *Belmont Finance Corporation Ltd v Williams Furniture Ltd (No 2)* [1980] 1 All ER 393; see also *Charter plc v City Index Ltd* [2008] 3 All ER 126 at 130; also *El Ajou v Dollar Land Holdings plc* [1994] 1 BCLC 464 at 478.

[143] The older authorities had established that a third party who received company funds might be liable to the company if he received the funds with *knowledge* of the directors' breach of duty, whether it be actual knowledge, or knowledge in the sense that he wilfully shut his eyes to the obvious, or wilfully and recklessly failed to make the type of inquiries which an honest and reasonable man would have made: see *Selangor United Rubber Estates Ltd v Cradock (No 3)* [1968] 2 All ER 1073; *Eagle Trust plc v SBC Securities Ltd* [1992] 4 All ER 488; *Re Montagu's Settlement Trusts* [1992] 4 All ER 308; *Polly Peck International plc v Nadir (No 2)* [1992] 4 All ER 769; *Cowan de Groot Properties Ltd v Eagle Trust plc* [1992] 4 All ER 700.

[144] [2000] 4 All ER 221 at 236.   [145] [2000] 4 All ER 221.

[146] *Commonwealth Oil & Gas Co Ltd v Baxter* [2009] CSIH 75, [2009] SLT 1123 at [94]–[95], per Lord Nimmo Smith: 'It is the disposal of that asset, in breach of fiduciary duty, and receipt of that asset by the recipient in knowledge of that breach, which together give rise to a constructive trust over that asset in the hands of the recipient', citing *Barnes v Addy* (1874) LR 9 Ch App 244 at 251–2 and *El Ajou v Dollar Land Holdings plc* [1994] 1 BCLC 464 at 478.

[147] See, for example, *JJ Harrison (Properties) Ltd v Harrison* [2002] 1 BCLC 162; *Ultraframe (UK) Ltd v Fielding* [2005] EWHC 1638 at [1488].

[148] See *Ultraframe (UK) Ltd v Fielding* [2005] EWHC 1638 at [1487]–[1493]; *CMS Dolphin Ltd v Simonet* [2001] 2 BCLC 704 at 733.   [149] [2004] 1 BCLC 468.

the defendant company had knowledge of the director's breach of duty.[150] Accordingly, it was unconscionable for the defendant company to retain the benefits of the contract and it was liable to account for the profits it had made (even though this was disadvantageous to the majority shareholder in the company who was an innocent party to the breach of fiduciary duty). However, there are limits to the extent to which business opportunities can be regarded as property of the company in this way, as the Court of Session Inner House noted in *Commonwealth Oil & Gas Co Ltd v Baxter*,[151] see **11-19**. A key consideration is whether the contracts which are diverted are existing contracts of the company[152] (as in *Quarter Master UK Ltd v Pyke*,[153] see **11-31**, or *CMS Dolphin Ltd v Simonet*,[154] *see* **11-42**) or contracts or opportunities which the company is actively pursuing (as in *Cook v Deeks*,[155] see **11-13**, or *IDC v Cooley*,[156] see **11-14**) or just opportunities which a director has exploited in a situation of conflict (as in *Commonwealth Oil & Gas Co Ltd v Baxter*,[157] see **11-19**). In the former two situations, diversion of an existing contract or of an opportunity which the company is actively pursuing, there is a pre-existing asset or property of the company so as to give rise to potential 'knowing receipt' liability, but the latter case, exploitation of an opportunity which is not property of the company nor treated as property of the company, does not give rise to any liability on the basis of 'receipt' for, in these circumstances, an asset is created, rather than transferred, in breach of trust,[158] though it may be possible to establish dishonest assistance in such circumstances.[159] This approach in *Commonwealth Oil & Gas Co Ltd v Baxter*[160] is consistent with the Court of Appeal ruling in *Sinclair Investments UK Ltd v Versailles Trade Finance Ltd*[161] where the court limited trust assets to assets which were or had been beneficially the property of the beneficiary or had been acquired by the fiduciary taking advantage of an opportunity or right 'which was properly that of the beneficiary',[162] see **13-14**. If an opportunity has never been 'properly that of the beneficiary', though the taking of it is a breach of the no-conflict rule, knowing receipt is not the appropriate basis for accessory liability which should instead be on the basis of knowing assistance.

D Claims for negligence

13-39 A director's duty of care and skill (CA 2006, s 174) is not a fiduciary duty, as s 178 makes clear, and a breach of this duty gives rise to the standard common law liability in damages for negligence. Claims against directors in negligence are rare for the reasons discussed at **10-4** et seq to which the reader is referred.

---

[150] The sole director of the company knew of the defaulting director's breach of fiduciary duty and that knowledge was attributed to the company with the result that the company was liable on the basis of knowing receipt of the benefit of the contract diverted from the claimant company by the faithless fiduciary: see [2004] 1 BCLC 468 at 515.   [151] [2009] CSIH 75, [2009] SLT 1123.
[152] See *Commonwealth Oil & Gas Co Ltd v Baxter* [2009] CSIH 75, [2009] SLT 1123 at [18], [94], [98].
[153] [2005] 1 BCLC 245.   [154] [2001] 2 BCLC 704.
[155] [1916] AC 554 (contract belonged in equity to the company).   [156] [1972] 2 All ER 162.
[157] [2009] CSIH 75, [2009] SLT 1123.
[158] See *Commonwealth Oil & Gas Co Ltd v Baxter* [2009] CSIH 75, [2009] SLT 1123 at [17], per Lord Hamilton, and see at [94]–[96], per Lord Nimmo Smith.
[159] See *Commonwealth Oil & Gas Co Ltd v Baxter* [2009] CSIH 75, [2009] SLT 1123 at [19].
[160] [2009] CSIH 75, [2009] SLT 1123.   [161] [2011] 2 BCLC 501, CA.
[162] [2011] 2 BCLC 501 at [88].

E Managing potential liabilities

13-40 Given that a director is potentially liable on the various grounds, as discussed, the next issue is the extent to which it is possible for directors to manage those potential liabilities through mechanisms such as contractual clauses excluding or limiting liability or through insurance cover. Another option is to seek authorisation or ratification from the shareholders, as discussed at **18-31**. Liability is also reduced in some contexts by the provision of 'safe harbours,' for example in the context of misleading statements in the directors' report (see **16-28**). Another possibility is that the amount of the liability might be reduced or waived where the director successfully applies for relief under CA 2006, s 1157 which requires the director to satisfy the court that he has acted honestly and reasonably and ought fairly to be excused, see **13-53**.

13-41 Quite apart from any potential liability for breach of duty, a major concern for any director is the potential litigation costs involved if he is sued whether by the company or by a third party such as a shareholder or creditor. Commercial litigation tends to be lengthy and directors are concerned that funding an expensive and lengthy defence may exhaust their personal resources so that by the time they win (if they do) and the case is dismissed, they are personally bankrupt, although able to recover their costs. This particular issue is addressed by CA 2006, s 205 whereby companies are permitted (but not required) to provide a director of the company or of a holding company with funds to meet expenditure incurred or to be incurred by a director in defending any criminal or civil proceedings in connection with any alleged negligence, default, breach of duty or breach of trust by him in relation to the company (which would include any derivative claim) or in connection with any application by him to the court for relief under s 1157. Of course, the decision to grant such funding must be taken by the other directors in accordance with their fiduciary duties, in particular the duty to exercise their powers for a proper purpose and the duty to promote the success of the company (ss 171 and 172). If funding is provided, it must be repaid if the director is convicted in criminal proceedings, or judgment is given against him in any civil proceedings, or the court refuses him relief on an application under s 1157 (s 205(2)), save to the extent that the director has a qualifying third party indemnity, discussed at **13-48**, which indemnifies the director in respect of liabilities incurred in civil proceedings brought by third parties.

13-42 Directors of larger companies are almost equally concerned about becoming embroiled in a regulatory investigation or disciplinary proceeding which can also be a lengthy process requiring legal representation. To address such concerns, a company may provide a director or a director of its holding company with funds on a similar basis as discussed above to meet expenditure incurred in defending himself in an investigation by a regulatory authority, or against action proposed to be taken by a regulatory authority, such as the Financial Services Authority (soon to be the Financial Conduct Authority), in connection with any alleged negligence, default, breach of duty or breach of trust by the director in relation to the company or an associated company (CA 2006, s 206). In this instance, strangely, there is no express requirement for the funding to be repaid in the way provided by s 205(2), noted above. Interestingly, in neither case is shareholder approval required for the provision of this funding.

Exemption provisions

13-43 Historically, companies included in their articles widely drafted exemption clauses relieving their officers from liability arising from breaches of their duties save in the case of wilful negligence or default,[163] but the Greene Committee on Company Law recommended that the practice be prohibited.[164] The current prohibition is set out in CA 2006, s 232(1) which provides that any provision, whether contained in the articles or in any contract with the company or otherwise,[165] that purports to exempt a director of a company (to any extent) from any liability that would otherwise attach to him in connection with any negligence, default, breach of duty or breach of trust in relation to the company is void.[166]

13-44 An important qualification to the prohibition is that it does not prevent the company from including in its articles 'such provision as has previously been lawful for dealing with conflicts of interest' (s 232(4)). Unfortunately the extent to which companies can lawfully include provisions in their articles in respect of conflicts is unclear, see the discussion at **11-71**.

Indemnity provisions

13-45 As in the case of exemption provisions, CA 2006, s 232(2) provides that any direct or indirect provision by a company of an indemnity (to any extent) for a director of the company, or of an associate company,[167] against any liability in connection with any negligence or breach of duty etc in relation to the company of which he is a director, is void though this prohibition does not rule out the provision of insurance cover for a director nor the provision of qualifying indemnities under CA 2006, ss 234 and 235.

13-46 The background to the introduction of indemnities (by the Companies (Audit, Investigations and Community Enterprise) Act 2004) was that there had been several high-profile cases, including in particular litigation involving the non-executive directors of Equitable Life,[168] which generated a sense that directors are subject to significant litigation risks which may deter able people from accepting posts unless they are protected against that risk. Domestically, there were concerns about the length of possible proceedings; the difficulty of funding legal representation (which of course is a general problem, not particular to company directors); and the enormous sums being claimed which are likely to far outstrip any available insurance. For larger companies with operations in the US, there were concerns that their directors were exposed to even greater litigation risks

---

[163] See *Re Brazilian Rubber Plantations and Estates Ltd* [1911] 1 Ch 425; *Re City Equitable Fire Insurance Co Ltd* [1925] Ch 407.

[164] The Greene Committee on Company Law (Cmnd 2657, 1929), paras 46–47. The prohibition was introduced by CA 1929, s 152.

[165] CA 2006, s 232(3). The words 'or otherwise' are to be construed *eiusdem generis* with the preceding words 'whether contained in the company's articles or in any contract with the company', the genus being any arrangement between the company and its officers: *Burgoine v London Borough of Waltham Forest* [1997] 2 BCLC 612.

[166] CA 2006, s 232(2): see generally *Burgoine v London Borough of Waltham Forest* [1997] 2 BCLC 612. The equivalent provision with respect to the liability of auditors is CA 2006, s 532(1), but it is subject to s 532(2) which allows certain indemnity provisions and liability limitations agreements, see **16-69**. As to 'default', see *Customs & Excise Commissioners v Hedon Alpha Ltd* [1981] 2 All ER 697; and n 175.

[167] A parent company cannot indemnify the directors of its subsidiary and the subsidiary cannot indemnify the directors of its parent company. It used to be the practice in some groups that one group company would indemnify the director of another group company and so circumvent the rule that a company could not indemnify its own directors. This loophole was closed by the CAICE Act 2004.

[168] For the story of this litigation, see *Equitable Life Assurance Society v Bowley* [2004] 1 BCLC 180; also Reed (2006) 27 Co Law 170. In a nutshell, the new owners of Equitable Life sued the previous board essentially alleging that the company's acute financial difficulties arose as a result of incompetence on the part of the directors—the claim was ultimately dropped.

because of features of the US legal system such as the common use of shareholder class actions and, possibly, more activist regulators. There was also a sense of more activist shareholders with some, such as aggressive hedge funds, perhaps more attuned to using litigation than had previously been the case. It was also argued that the availability of a statutory derivative action, now enacted in CA 2006, Pt 11, coupled with the statutory statement of directors' duties, would encourage and facilitate litigation though this concern has not been vindicated, to date at least, see **18-11**.

13-47   There is no doubt an element of truth in these concerns, but no doubt too that they were exaggerated in order to extract the maximum possible concessions from the Government. The result is that, despite the initial impression given by CA 2006, s 232(2) prohibiting indemnities (see **13-45**), companies may provide extensive indemnities protecting their directors against personal liability in a wide range of circumstances, though not where the liability is to the company itself. There, Parliament did draw the line.

Qualifying third party indemnity provisions

13-48   In essence, a company may indemnify a director against liability incurred (including costs) by the director to a third party (i.e. someone other than the company or an associated company, defined CA 2006, s 256), such as a shareholder or regulator provided certain conditions are met (s 234).[169] These indemnities are known as qualifying third party indemnity provisions (QTPIPs).

13-49   A company (likewise an associated company) cannot provide an indemnity in respect of:

- any liability of a director to the company or to an associated company;
- any criminal penalties;
- any regulatory penalties;
- any liability incurred by the director in defending criminal proceedings in which he is convicted, or civil proceedings brought by the company or associated company in which judgment is given against him, or in respect of an unsuccessful application for relief [170] (CA 2006, s 234(2)).

13-50   The existence of any QTPIP must be disclosed in the directors' report (s 236) and copies of the qualifying indemnity provision must be available for inspection by any member (s 237), but shareholder approval of the QTPIP is not required.

13-51   As with decisions on defence costs funding (see **13-41**), the decision to grant indemnities to directors must be taken by the other directors in accordance with their fiduciary duties, in particular the duty to exercise their powers for a proper purpose and the duty to promote the success of the company (ss 171 and 172). In practice, for large companies, the granting of indemnities has become routine with annual reports commonly recording that the company has provided indemnities to their directors to the extent permitted by law.[171]

---

[169] A failure to meet the conditions means that the indemnity is void since it then falls back within the prohibition in CA 2006, s 232(2), see **13-45**. Equivalent indemnity provision is available for directors of corporate trustees of occupational pension schemes: see s 235.   [170] i.e. under CA 2006, s 1157.
   [171] See also The Companies (Model Articles) Regulations 2008, SI 2008/3229, reg 2, Sch 1, art 52 (Ltd); reg 4, Sch 3, art 85 (Plc) and note the width of the drafting.

Insurance provision

13-52 A company is not prevented from purchasing and maintaining for a director of the company, or of an associate company, insurance against any liability attaching to a director in connection with any negligence, default, breach of duty or breach of trust in relation to the company of which he is a director (CA 2006, 233). It is commonplace for public companies to purchase directors and officers' liability insurance,[172] though concerns remain as to its cost and coverage.

Application to court for relief

13-53 The court has power under CA 2006, s 1157 to relieve an officer[173] of the company from liability[174] where the officer is or may be liable in respect of negligence, default,[175] breach of duty or breach of trust, if the court is satisfied that he has acted honestly and reasonably and that, having regard to all the circumstances of the case, he ought fairly to be excused.[176] The scope of the provision is limited to relief in cases where the company or someone on its behalf (such as a liquidator) is seeking to enforce the personal duties that directors owe to the company.[177] The provision does not apply to proceedings by a third party (i.e. a creditor) to recover a debt owed by the director.[178]

13-54 It is an absolute precondition to the grant of relief that the director has acted honestly and reasonably and the burden of proving honesty and reasonableness is on those who ask for relief.[179] Whether the director has acted honestly and reasonably is essentially an objective

---

[172] For an overview of the insurance issues, see Deane, 'D & O Insurance' (2008) PLC 23. See also The Companies (Model Articles) Regulations 2008, SI 2008/3229, reg 2, Sch 1, art 53 (Ltd); reg 4, Sch 3, art 86 (Plc).

[173] Defined CA 2006, s 1173 as including a director, manager or secretary. It does not extend to shadow directors in the absence of an express provision to that effect: see *Ultraframe (UK) Ltd v Fielding* [2005] EWHC 1638 at [1452].

[174] Including a liability to account for profits, see *Coleman Taymar Ltd v Oakes* [2001] 2 BCLC 749; but not a liability to repay sums paid to a director under a void contract: *Guinness plc v Saunders* [1990] 2 AC 663 at 695, 702; or, it seems, a liability to make a contribution for wrongful trading under IA 1986, s 214: *Re Produce Marketing Consortium Ltd* [1989] 3 All ER 1.

[175] By 'default' is meant some fault or misconduct by a director or officer in their capacity as such in the discharge of their obligations under the companies legislation, see *Customs & Excise Commissioners v Hedon Alpha Ltd* [1981] 2 All ER 697. It was accepted, obiter, in *Re Duckwari plc (No 2)* [1998] 2 BCLC 315 at 325 that 'default' includes the personal liability of directors to indemnify the company under the statutory provisions governing conflicts of interest, now set out in CA 2006, Pt 10, Ch 4 (specific conflicts); and see *Queensway Systems Ltd v Walker* [2007] 2 BCLC 577 at 595.

[176] The CA 2006, s 1157 restates CA 1985, s 727 without substantive amendment. The CLR proposed, but the Government rejected, that the 'reasonableness' requirement be dropped. For a valuable analysis of the provision and the CLR proposals, see Edmunds & Lowry (2003) 66 MLR 195 who note, *inter alia*, the importance of the section in the context of directors of small family companies where directors' liability insurance is not feasible.

[177] *Customs & Excise Commissioners v Hedon Alpha Ltd* [1981] 2 All ER 697; *IRC v McEntaggart* [2006] 1 BCLC 476.

[178] For that reason, relief is not available with respect to liability incurred under the 'phoenix' name prohibition in IA 1986, ss 216, 217: *First Independent Factors & Finance Ltd v Mountford* [2008] 2 BCLC 297; or in proceedings under CDDA 1986, s 15 (liability of disqualified person for debts incurred when acting though disqualified): *IRC v McEntaggart* [2006] 1 BCLC 476; or in proceedings to recover taxes: *Customs & Excise Commissioners v Hedon Alpha Ltd* [1981] 2 All ER 697 (no relief in respect of liability for unpaid betting and gaming tax).

[179] *Bairstow v Queens Moat Houses plc* [2001] 2 BCLC 531, CA; and see *Re In a Flap Envelope Ltd* [2004] 1 BCLC 64. It is not reasonable for directors to fail to make provision in the accounts for the possibility that

test.[180] In applications under this section, the court tends to take a broad look at all the circumstances of the case[181] in order to determine whether the director ought fairly to be excused, rather than seek for these purposes to impose discrete thresholds as to 'honesty' and 'reasonableness',[182] and conduct may be reasonable for this purpose despite amounting to a lack of reasonable care at common law. In *Re D'Jan of London Ltd*[183] a director in breach of his duty of care had signed an insurance form without reading it. Had he done so, he would have discovered the inaccurate information which subsequently caused the insurance company to repudiate liability under the policy. Although he was careless, the court granted him partial relief, finding that he had acted honestly and reasonably and Hoffmann LJ thought that what had happened could have happened to any busy man.[184]

13-55 Ultimately, the court has considerable discretion under this provision for, once a director establishes that he has acted honestly and reasonably, the court must still be satisfied that the director 'ought fairly to be excused'. The court is very unlikely to exercise its discretion to relieve a director from liability if the director has obtained a material personal benefit through a breach of duty,[185] or if the director gains at the expense of the creditors, as where he seeks to be relieved of a liability to repay money to the company which would be available to meet the creditors' claims.[186]

13-56 There is some potential for a director to obtain relief under IA 1986, s 212(3), even in circumstances where relief has been refused under CA 2006, s 1157. Section 212 is discussed in detail at **25-3** and it suffices for present purposes to note that it provides a summary mechanism whereby an order of the court can be obtained for repayment, contribution, accounting, etc by a director who has been guilty of any misfeasance or breach of any fiduciary or other duty in relation to the company. Crucially, IA 1986, s 212(3) provides that the court may make such an order for restoration, accounting, contribution etc 'as the court thinks just'. The extent to which that discretionary power can be used to relieve

---

tax relief might not be forthcoming on a particular scheme with the result that improper dividends are paid: *Re Loquitur Ltd* [2003] 2 BCLC 442.

[180] See *Bairstow v Queens Moat Houses plc* [2001] 2 BCLC 531 at 550 (criticising *Coleman Taymar v Oakes* [2001] 2 BCLC 749 which seemed to suggest to the contrary).

[181] See *Ultraframe (UK) Ltd v Fielding* [2005] EWHC 1638 at [1451]: 'the expression "the circumstances of the case" does not mean the litigation, it primarily means the circumstances in which the breach took place but it may include a review of the director's stewardship of the company, but not a more wide ranging inquiry into the director's character and behaviour'.

[182] Sometimes the court finds that the director has acted honestly but not reasonably and sometimes that he has acted honestly and reasonably but in the circumstances ought not to be excused, though the section envisages that 'honesty' and 'reasonableness' are threshold requirements which trigger the court's discretion to look at the fairness of the situation: see Edmunds & Lowry, n 176, on the mingling of these elements by the courts.

[183] [1994] 1 BCLC 561. See also *Inn Spirit Ltd v Burns* [2002] 2 BCLC 780 at 787–8.

[184] [1994] 1 BCLC 561 at 564; see Edmunds & Lowry, n 176, 207–10, as to the approach adopted by Hoffmann LJ in this instance.

[185] *Re In a Flap Envelope Co Ltd* [2004] 1 BCLC 64 (director as a shareholder was a beneficiary of improper financial assistance given by the company in breach of CA 1985, s 151); *Re Marini Ltd* [2004] BCC 172 (receipt of improper dividends—it would not be fair if the director benefited and the creditors suffered).

[186] See *Inn Spirit Ltd v Burns* [2002] 2 BCLC 780 at 788: '...I cannot see that the court could or should excuse [the directors] from liability at the expense of the creditors of the company...' (Rimer J) (improper dividend paid to directors/shareholders which amounted to an improper misapplication of almost the entire assets of the company); also *First Global Media Group Ltd v Larkin* [2003] EWCA Civ 1765 (improper drawings by directors...out of the question, the Court of Appeal said, that the directors could be fairly excused from repaying the money when the people out of the money were the creditors of the company); also *Queensway Systems Ltd v Walker* [2007] 2 BCLC 577 at 596.

the director of liability was discussed, obiter, in *Re Paycheck Services 3 Ltd, Revenue and Customs Commissioners v Holland*[187] by both the Court of Appeal and Supreme Court which were agreed that, whatever the scope of the discretion under IA 1986, s 212(3), it is as to the order that should be made once liability has been established, i.e. as to how much the director must pay. The section is not intended to replicate or extend the court's power to grant relief against liability under CA 2006, s 1157 and therefore it is not permissible in the exercise of that discretion under the IA 1986, s 212(3) to order that the director need make no payment at all.[188]

---

[187] [2011] 1 BCLC 141, SC, affirming [2009] 2 BCLC 309.

[188] [2011] 1 BCLC 141 at [51], per Lord Hope, agreeing with Rimer LJ [2009] 2 BCLC 309 at [108]–[110], with whom Lords Walker and Clarke also agreed, see [2011] 1 BCLC 141 at [124] and [146], respectively.

PART III

Corporate Governance– Shareholders' Rights and Remedies

14

Membership and the incidents of membership

A Becoming a member

14-1 Membership of a company is governed by CA 2006, s 112 which provides: (1) that the subscribers of a company's memorandum of association (discussed at **1-23**) are deemed to have agreed to become members of the company and on its registration become members and must be entered as such in its register of members; and (2) that every other person who agrees[1] to become a member of a company, and whose name is entered in its register of members, is a member of the company.[2] The fundamental importance of entry on the register was highlighted by the Supreme Court decision in *Enviroco Ltd v Farstad Supply A/S*[3] where the dispute related to claims under a charterparty. For the purpose of that dispute, the issue was whether a company (B) was a subsidiary of another company (A) within the definition in CA 1985, s 736(1)(c), now CA 2006, s 1159(1)(c), which requires that A be *a member* of B and have control in the way outlined in that provision (see **1-56**). In this case, A did own shares in B, but A had charged those shares in B as security to a bank and, in accordance with Scots law, A had had to register those shares in the name of the bank's nominee with the result that the register of members showed the bank's nominee as the member of Company B, not Company A. As Lord Collins put it, essentially the question was whether the putative holding company remained a 'member' notwithstanding that the shares were registered in the name of the nominee.

The Supreme Court ruled that it is a fundamental principle of English law, reflected in CA 1985, s 22, now CA 2006, s 112, that, except where express provision is made to the contrary,[4] the person on the register of members is the member to the exclusion of any other person, unless and until the register is rectified.[5] This has been the position since the Companies Act 1862 and the companies legislation would be unworkable, the court said, if that were not so.[6] On this basis, A was no longer a member of B and could not claim that B was its subsidiary on the basis of the application of what is now CA 2006, s 1159(1)(c).[7]

---

[1] This requirement of agreement is satisfied when a person assents to become a member and it does not require that there should be a binding contract between the person and the company: *Re Nuneaton Borough Association Football Club Ltd* [1989] BCLC 454, CA.

[2] See *Re Florence Land and Public Works Co, Nicol's Case, Tufnell and Ponsonby's Case* (1885) 29 Ch D 421, CA.   [3] [2011] 2 BCLC 165.

[4] For example with regard to bearer shares, see CA 2006, s 122(3).

[5] [2011] 2 BCLC 165 at [37], per Lord Collins with whom the rest of the court agreed.

[6] [2011] 2 BCLC 165 at [38].

[7] Also, while the statute does make provision (CA 1985, s 736A(6) and (7), now CA 2006, Sch 6, paras 6 and 7) attributing rights held by a nominee to another person and attributing rights attached to shares

While there has been criticism of the outcome,[8] there is no dispute that the law required this conclusion, given the role assigned to entry on the register of members.

14-2 Typically, entry on the register is a matter for the directors and routine entries are dealt with by the company secretary (where there is a company secretary). Listed public companies use the services of professional registrars to maintain their share registers. Inspection of the register and its rectification is discussed in detail at **14-94**. For the most part, entry on the register of members happens without any difficulty and so, having acquired some shares, the shareholder becomes a member of the company. In general, the shareholders are the members of the company and the terms 'shareholders' and 'members' may be used interchangeably.[9]

14-3 As practically all the companies on the register of companies are companies limited by shares, the initial stage in the process of becoming a member of a company involves becoming a shareholder and there are four methods of becoming a shareholder:

  (1) by subscribing to the memorandum of association;

  (2) by taking up an allotment of shares by the company;

  (3) by a transfer of shares from an existing member;

  (4) by a transmission of shares on the death or bankruptcy of a member.

14-4 As noted at **14-1**, the subscribers to the company's memorandum are deemed to have agreed to become members and on registration of the memorandum they must be entered as such in the company's register of members (CA 2006, s 112(1)). The memorandum states that each subscriber agrees to become a member and undertakes, in the case of a company having a share capital, to take at least one share (s 8(1)). It is unusual for any problems to arise with regard to subscribers.

14-5 The allotment of shares by the company to existing or new investors is a matter for the directors, subject to certain statutory constraints. The duties of directors in this regard (to exercise their powers for a proper purpose) are discussed in Chapter 8 while the statutory constraints and mechanics of allotment are discussed in Chapter 19. Following an allotment, the company issues share certificates to the shareholders, unless the shares are being held in uncertificated form, discussed at **14-7**, and the shareholders' names are entered on the register of members. Few problems with entry on the register of members occur in these cases since, obviously, the company has decided to allot more shares and is willing to accept new members.

14-6 Problems are most likely to arise on the transfer and transmission of shares. Here the company is a bystander to transactions (in the case of transfers) and dispositions (in the

---

held by way of security to the person providing the security, those provisions are concerned with rights, not membership, and refer to voting rights and the right to appoint the board for the purposes of the definitions (of holding company and subsidiary) in CA 1985, 736, now CA 2006, s 1159, see [2011] 2 BCLC 165 at [41]–[43], [64].

  [8] Even their Lordships seemed doubtful of the outcome, Lord Clarke commenting that 'on any sensible view of the facts', B was throughout a subsidiary of A, see [2011] 2 BCLC 165 at [72], and see Lord Collins at [5].

  [9] Exceptional cases are: (1) where the company is a company limited by guarantee without a share capital, in which case the company has members but no shareholders; (2) where a company limited by shares has issued bearer share warrants, in which case the holders of the bearer share warrants are shareholders, but not members, because their names have not been entered on the register of members, subject to any provision in the articles deeming the bearer to be a member: see CA 2006, s 122(1), (3).

case of transmission) which alter the membership of the company. On occasion, particularly in private companies, the directors may be unhappy at a change in the membership and this can give rise to problems for the transferees with respect to securing the entry of their names on the register of members.

14-7 In terms of the process of transfer, for most companies the process involves a proper instrument of transfer (i.e. a paper form) and a (paper) share certificate. The company gives effect to the transfer or transmission by removing the transferor from the register of members and inserting the name of the transferee. The company cancels the share certificate in the name of the transferor and issues a new certificate in the name of the transferee. Larger publicly traded companies have uncertificated shares which are transferred electronically[10] and in this case there is no requirement for a proper instrument of transfer and share certificates are not issued, instead the member's shareholding is recorded electronically. The majority of private investors hold their shareholdings in certificated form while institutional and professional investors hold their shareholdings in uncertificated form.

Share certificates

14-8 Unless the conditions of issue of the shares otherwise provides, within two months after the allotment of any shares, or within two months after a transfer of any shares being lodged with a company, the company must complete and have ready for delivery the relevant share certificates.[11] This requirement to issue a share certificate does not apply where the shares are in uncertificated form.[12]

14-9 The certificate is *prima facie* (not conclusive) evidence of title (CA 2006, s 768(1)) and the presumption arising from it can be rebutted, but the company may be estopped from denying the facts stated in the certificate. In *Re Bahia and San Francisco Rly Co*[13] the court noted:

> 'The power of giving certificates is...for the benefit of the company in general; and it is a declaration by the company to all the world that the person in whose name the certificate is made out, and to whom it is given, is a shareholder in the company, and it is given by the company with the intention that it shall be so used by the person to whom it is given, and acted upon in the sale and transfer of shares.'

14-10 For example, if the company issues certificates which describe shares as fully paid up when they are not and a third party relies on the certificate, the company is estopped from

---

[10] For such companies, the company's register of members means the company's issuer register of members and the Operator register of members: SI 2001/3755, as amended, reg 20(4). The 'Operator' is the electronic settlement platform for shares and other securities known as CREST which is operated by Euroclear UK and Ireland. The legal underpinning of electronic settlement is provided by CA 2006, Pt 21, Ch 2 and related regulations, i.e. The Uncertificated Securities Regulations 2001, SI 2001/3755, as amended by Companies Act 2006 (Consequential Amendments) (Uncertificated Securities) Order 2009, SI 2009/1889. The CA 2006, ss 786(1)(b) makes provision for regulations requiring companies to adopt electronic holdings, but no such regulations have been made.

[11] CA 2006, ss 769(1), 776(1), subject to the exemptions in ss 769(2), 776(3).

[12] See The Uncertificated Securities Regulations 2001, SI 2001/3755, as amended, reg 38(2).

[13] (1868) LR 3 QB 584 at 595. See also *Cadbury Schweppes plc v Halifax Share Dealing Ltd* [2007] 1 BCLC 497 where the company was estopped from denying the validity of share certificates issued to fraudsters (and subsequently sold by them) who had stolen the identities of genuine shareholders.

denying that they are fully-paid.[14] In *Bloomenthal v Ford*[15] a lender to a company took shares in the company as collateral security. The certificate stated that he was the holder of 10,000 fully-paid ordinary shares when the shares were not in fact fully-paid. It was held by the House of Lords that the company was estopped from denying the certificate. The lender could have found out the true position by enquiry but there was no actual notice and he had acted in good faith.

14-11 If a share certificate is issued following the presentation of a forged transfer, the company is not estopped from denying its validity. This is because the person presenting the transfer impliedly warrants the authenticity of the transfer.[16] A purchaser from such a person is in a better position and can claim compensation from the company if he is displaced by the true owner since the purchaser relies not on the forged transfer but on the certificate issued by the company.[17] A forged share certificate is said to be a nullity and does not bind the company,[18] but, arguably, the extent to which a third party can rely on a forged share certificate might be better approached as a question of the apparent authority of the agent to bind his principal.[19]

Restrictions on membership

14-12 As a general rule, anyone may be a member but there are restrictions imposed on some classes of persons.

Minors

14-13 There is no prohibition on minors[20] being shareholders although the company may refuse to accept a minor as a shareholder.[21] Applying ordinary contract law rules, a contract to purchase shares is voidable by a minor before or within a reasonable time of attaining his majority. If the minor repudiates the contract, he is not liable for future calls but he cannot recover the purchase price unless there has been a total failure of consideration,[22] which is unlikely to be the case. Given that shares are normally issued as fully-paid, there

---

[14] See *Burkinshaw v Nicolls* (1878) 3 App Cas 1004. Where there is a subsequent transfer and the transferor had acquired a good title by estoppel, the transferee acquires a good title even if he had actual notice that the shares were only partly-paid: *Re Stapleford Colliery Co, Barrow's Case* (1880) 14 Ch D 432, CA. Cf *Re London Celluloid Co* (1888) 39 Ch D 190 at 197, CA.   [15] [1897] AC 156, HL.

[16] The presentor of the improper transfer must indemnify the company against liability arising from the company acting on the invalid transfer: *Sheffield Corporation v Barclay* [1905] AC 392; *Yeung Kai Yung v Hong Kong & Shangai Banking* [1980] 2 All ER 599.

[17] *Re Bahia and San Francisco Railway Co* (1868) LR 3 QB 584; *Balkis Consolidated Co v Tomkinson* [1893] AC 396; *Dixon v Kennaway & Co* [1900] 1 Ch 833. See also *Cadbury Schweppes plc v Halifax Share Dealing Ltd* [2007] 1 BCLC 497.   [18] *Ruben v Great Fingall Consolidated* [1906] AC 439.

[19] See *Lovett v Carson Country Homes* [2009] 2 BCLC 196 at [92]–[95] (*Ruben's* case does not mean that a forged document can in no circumstances have any effect whatsoever, for a party may be estopped from disputing the validity of a forged document. The principle of apparent authority is a broad reflection of the principles of estoppel, the court said, and it is accepted that, in appropriate circumstances, a principal may be bound by the fraudulent acts of an agent (and forgeries are no different to other fraudulent acts) in circumstances where there is ostensible authority); and see Sealy & Worthington, *Cases and Materials in Company Law* (9th edn, 2010), p 540.

[20] That is anyone under 18 years of age in England and Wales: Family Law Reform Act 1969, s 1; anyone under 16 in Scotland.

[21] *Re Asiatic Banking Corpn, Symon's Case* (1870) Ch App 298. For companies with uncertificated shares, the power to refuse to register a transfer to a minor is retained, see The Uncertificated Securities Regulations 2001, SI 2001/3755, as amended, regs 27(4)(b), 28(4)(b).

[22] *Steinberg v Scala (Leeds) Ltd* [1923] 2 Ch 452, CA.

is little reason now for repudiation and it is rare for problems with minors to arise, unlike in the late nineteenth century when there were many cases of heirs and heiresses seeking to repudiate contracts for shares. Until the minor repudiates, he has full rights of membership.

Subsidiary companies

14-14 A company cannot be a member of itself, a point originally established in *Trevor v Whitworth*[23] and stated in CA 2006, s 658 which provides that any purported acquisition by a company of its own shares other than in accordance with the provisions of the Act is void (see **20-17**) and an offence by the company and any officer in default. The Act further provides that, subject to certain exceptions, a body corporate cannot be a member of its holding company and any allotment or transfer of shares in a company to its subsidiary is void (s 136).[24] The policy behind this prohibition is to reinforce the rule in *Trevor v Whitworth*[25] and prevent any reduction of capital whereby capital provided by a parent company to a subsidiary is returned by the subsidiary to the parent company. The prohibition cannot be avoided by using a nominee for the prohibition applies to a nominee acting on behalf of a subsidiary as to the subsidiary itself (s 144).

14-15 There are a number of exceptions, however, when a subsidiary may hold shares in its holding company, for example where the subsidiary holds the shares only as a personal representative or trustee (CA 2006, s 138)[26] or in the ordinary course of its business as an authorised dealer in shares (s 141). Equally, where a company acquired shares in circumstances where it would not have been within the prohibition on a subsidiary being a member of its holding company, but would now fall within the prohibition, the company may remain as a member of the holding company (and receive bonus issues in respect of its holding) but it has no right to vote those shares on a written resolution or in general or class meetings (s 137).

B Classes of shares

14-16 It is common for the articles of association to give a company complete freedom to issue shares with such rights and restrictions as the company may by ordinary resolution determine[27] although most companies (public and private) limit their structures to ordinary shares. Where a more sophisticated share structure is required (for example, to facilitate a division of control in a joint venture company), the company may have more classes of shares, typically ordinary and preference shares, and possibly several forms of each. The London Stock Exchange encourages public listed companies to restrict themselves to one class of shares, favouring the equality of treatment and the transparency of rights which such a capital structure ensures. The nature of ordinary and preference shares is now considered, but it must be stressed that the particular rights in any given company depend on the terms of issue.

---

[23] (1887) 12 App Cas 409, HL.
[24] 'Holding company' and 'subsidiary' are defined in CA 2006, s 1159 and Sch 6.
[25] (1887) 12 App Cas 409, HL.
[26] Unless the holding company or a subsidiary of it is beneficially interested under the trust, see CA 2006, s 138(1).
[27] See The Companies (Model Articles) Regulations 2008, SI 2008/3229, reg 2, Sch 1; art 22 (Ltd), reg 4, Sch 3, art 43 (Plc).

Ordinary shares

14-17   Ordinary shares (often loosely described as equities) carry the residual rights of participation in the income and capital of the company which have not been granted to other classes. Ordinary shareholders have no right to any fixed dividend (i.e. a return on their investment usually expressed as so many pence per share) on their shares, but after the payment of any dividends to preference shareholders, the ordinary shareholders enjoy the remainder of the surplus profits actually distributed as dividend by the directors. Distributions are considered in detail in Chapter 20.

14-18   In difficult times, the ordinary shareholders run the risk that the profits available for distribution will be inadequate and will not extend beyond (or indeed to) the payment of the dividend due on the preference shares. In prosperous times, however, the preference shareholders are restricted to their fixed dividend and the ordinary shareholders enjoy all of the surplus distributable profits. For example, if the company has distributable profits of £30,000 and the fixed dividend payable to preference shareholders costs £20,000, then the ordinary shareholders share a fund of £10,000. On the other hand, if the company has distributable profits of £300,000, the preference shareholders remain entitled as before to their dividend of £20,000 and the ordinary shareholders share the remaining £280,000. The ordinary shareholders run the risk of no dividend or a small dividend, as we can see, but they also stand to scoop the pool in the event that the company makes significant profits. Preference shareholders take less risk and so are entitled to less return.

14-19   Ordinary shareholders have a right to a return of capital ranking after the preference shares but, as with dividends, ordinary shares claim the pool of surplus assets in a solvent winding up after the return of capital to all other shareholders.

14-20   Ordinary shares usually carry one vote per share although companies may attach such voting rights as they choose. For example, a company may provide that ordinary shares carry 10 votes per share or it may divide its ordinary shares into two classes of ordinary shares, one voting and one non-voting class. Non-voting ordinary shares are not common and are disapproved of by the Stock Exchange. Preference shareholders generally have limited voting rights so it is the ordinary shareholders who have voting control in general meetings.

Preference shares

14-21   Typically, a preference share has a fixed preferential cumulative dividend[28] and a priority as to a return of capital on a winding up which ensures that the preference shareholders get their capital back ahead of the ordinary shareholders although, as shareholders, the preference shareholders rank after secured and unsecured creditors. Preference shareholders are non-participating as to surplus both while the company is a going concern (i.e. with respect to any further distributions of profits) and on a winding up (i.e. with respect to any surplus assets remaining after the creditors have been paid and capital has been returned to the shareholders). To ensure participation in any such surpluses, preference shares may be issued as participating preference shares, i.e. participating as to dividend and/or capital which means that the shares carry additional rights to participate in

---

[28]   The payment of dividends is still dependent on the company having distributable profits as required by CA 2006, Pt 23, but if there are such profits then the terms of issue of preference shares usually require the payment of a dividend on fixed dates.

profits or assets. Preference shares usually have restricted voting rights limited to matters which affect their rights such as when their dividends are in arrears.

14-22 In some ways, the position of preference shareholders is akin to that of creditors and preference shares are often regarded as a hybrid category of investment between equity or share capital and loan capital. The fixed dividend payable to preference shareholders resembles the fixed interest payable on loan capital and the priority to a return of capital in a winding up resembles a creditor's right to a return of the capital sum. Equally, preference shares can carry rights quite similar to ordinary shares and the company may issue preference shares which are convertible into ordinary shares either on a set date or at the option of the shareholders or, in some circumstances, at the option of the company. As with all shares, the precise nature of a preference share depends on the terms of issue.

C Class rights

Identifying a class right

14-23 As noted at **14-16**, it is common for the articles of association to provide that a company may issue shares with such rights and restrictions as the company may by ordinary resolution determine. Class rights may be set out in the articles or in the resolution creating them. In practice, they are usually set out in the articles.[29] If all the shares fall within one class, there are no class rights, only shareholder rights.[30] Where particular rights (such as the right to a dividend or to a return of capital on a winding up) are attached to certain shares, these are described as class rights.

14-24 In *Cumbrian Newspapers Group Ltd v Cumberland and Westmorland Herald Co Ltd*,[31] Scott J broadened the classification of class rights to include rights conferred on a member of a company in his capacity as a member which rights are not attached to any particular class of shares. The member in this case had acquired 10% of the shares in the company in 1968 and, at the same time and as part of the arrangement under which the shares were issued, the company adopted articles which gave this member, by name, certain rights of pre-emption, the right to appoint a director and rights to transfer shares (the purpose being to enable the member to obstruct an attempted takeover). In 1985, the directors made clear that they proposed to call a general meeting to cancel the articles conferring these special rights on this member. The value of a right being classified as a class right is that a variation of rights attached to a class of shares is subject to statutory constraints, now in CA 2006, s 630, which essentially provides that such rights cannot be varied or abrogated other than in accordance with a variation provision in the articles or, if the articles make no provision for variation, with the consent of the class in accordance with s 630(4). Scott J concluded that the shares for the time being held by this member did constitute a class for the purposes of the statutory procedure for variation of class rights, saying:[32]

---

[29] The statement of capital which accompanies a return of allotment of the shares must give, for each class, the prescribed particulars of the rights attached to the shares, and the total number of shares of that class: CA 2006, s 555(3),(4). The registrar must also be notified of the assignment of a new name or designation to any class of members and of variations of class rights: ss 636, 637.

[30] See *Union Music Ltd v Watson* [2003] 1 BCLC 453 at 464, where there are no rights conferred on one shareholder which have not also been conferred on the other shareholder(s), there are no classes of shares.

[31] [1986] 2 All ER 816.

[32] [1986] 2 All ER 816 at 830. Cf *Re Blue Arrow plc* [1987] BCLC 585 at 590 (a right conferred on an individual by the articles (to remain president of the company) unrelated to any shareholding in any way cannot

'In my judgment, a company which, by its articles, confers special rights on one or more of its members in the capacity of member or shareholder thereby constitutes the shares for the time being held by that member or members a class of shares for the purposes of s 125 [now CA 2006, s 630, variation of class rights]. The rights are class rights.'

As the rights conferred in *Cumbrian* were class rights, the company could only alter them in accordance with the statutory procedure and the court made a declaration to that effect. Provisions which are classified as class rights therefore confer greater security on the beneficiary than rights conferred merely by the articles which are open to the risk of alteration by a special resolution under CA 2006, s 21(1). Class rights can therefore form a valuable element in the protection of minority shareholders[33] or any other special interests.[34] It is for this reason that the broad approach taken in *Cumbrian* is important and the decision can be justified on its facts, though not everyone agrees with it.[35] It is also possible now to protect minority or other interests through the use of entrenched provisions in the articles and, as discussed at **4-17,** where a variation of class rights can only occur on terms which fall within CA 2006, s 22(1), the class right is an entrenched provision. Entrenchment should be of no consequence in these circumstances since entrenchment merely means that a provision is not open to alteration by special resolution under s 21 and can be altered only in accordance with its own provisions for alteration which is the position in any event under s 630(2)(a) on the variation of class rights, see **14-34.**

14-25   The application of CA 2006, s 630(1) must not be confused by reference to s 629 which addresses a quite distinct issue. Section 629 provides that 'for the purposes of the CA 2006, shares are of one class if the rights attached to them are in all respects uniform'.[36] This section defines when 'shares are of one class' rather than what is a class of shares (the heading to the section is misleading in this regard).[37] This definition is needed for the application of various provisions such as s 550 (directors' power to allot when private company has only one class of shares) and s 569 (disapplication of pre-emption rights when private company has only one class of shares).[38]

---

be described as a class right—a class right, Vinelott J said, is a right attaching, in some way, to a category of shares in the company).

[33] For example, the courts will not exercise their discretion under CA 2006, s 306 to call a general meeting if to do so would override a class right with respect to the calling of meetings: see *Harman v BML Group Ltd* [1994] 2 BCLC 674, see **15-53.**

[34] In the past the Government has used class rights to retain control of privatised companies by way of a so-called 'golden share', typically nothing more elaborate than a single £1 special preference share. The extent to which the use of golden shares to retain control in this way is permissible under European Law has been addressed by the European Court of Justice which essentially concluded that such measures are contrary to the free movement of capital, but may in some circumstances be permissible in the protection of the public interest, provided the measures adopted are proportionate, objective and non-discriminatory. See *Commission v Portugal* (Case C-367/98), *Commission v France* (Case C-483/99), *Commission v Belgium* (Case C-503/99) [2003] QB 233.

[35] See Polack [1986] CLJ 399; Morse [2008] JBL 96 at 98 who variously describes it as an unwise and an unfortunate decision.

[36] For these purposes, the rights attached to shares are not regarded as different from those attached to other shares by reason only that they do not carry the same rights to dividends in the 12 months immediately following their allotment: CA 2006, s 629(2).

[37] A point confirmed by the Explanatory Notes to the Companies Act 2006, para 934 which points out that the statute does not define what amounts to a class which remains a matter for the common law.

[38] See also CA 2006, s 725(1) (Treasury shares: maximum holding); s 974(2)(b) (Meaning of 'takeover offer').

Rules of construction

14-26 Certain rules of construction have been developed by the courts to assist them in identifying the rights attaching to each class of shares, given that they vary from company to company. It must be stressed, however, that each case ultimately turns on the particular terms of issue.

A presumption of equality

14-27 There is a presumption of equality as between shareholders with all shareholders being deemed to be entitled to the same proportionate part in the capital of the company.[39] This presumption is easily rebutted by an issue of shares on terms which gives special rights with respect to matters such as dividends, the return of capital or to voting at meetings of the company. As noted earlier, preference shareholders typically have a preferential right to a dividend and to a return of capital on a winding up.

Rights granted are deemed to be exhaustive

14-28 There is a presumption that any rights attached to a share are deemed to be exhaustive.[40] The position was clearly expressed by Sargant J in *Re National Telephone Co*[41] as follows:

> '...the weight of authority is in favour of the view that, either with regard to dividend or with regard to the rights in a winding up, the express gift or attachment of preferential rights to preference shares, on their creation, is, prima facie, a definition of the whole of their rights in that respect, and negatives any further or other right to which, but for the specified rights, they would have been entitled.'

14-29 In *Will v United Lankat Plantations Co*[42] the attachment of preferential dividend rights to preference shares was presumed to be exhaustive as to their dividend rights. This had the effect of negating any right to further participation in any surplus profits of the company. This presumption of exhaustive rights can be rebutted by expressly declaring the shares to be participating preference shares with a right of participation in surplus profits after a certain percentage of dividend has been paid to the ordinary shareholders.[43]

14-30 Likewise where preference shares are given an express priority to a return of capital on a winding up, this negates any right to participate in surplus assets in a winding up.[44] Again, the terms of issue may enable preference shareholders to share in surplus assets with the other shareholders after their capital had been repaid, but it is for preference shareholders to show that they are entitled to participate further in this way.[45]

A cumulative dividend

14-31 *Prima facie*, preference shares are entitled to a cumulative dividend, even in the absence of any such provision in the terms of issue.[46] This means that the preference shareholders are entitled to have any deficiencies in a given year made up from the profits of subsequent years before anything is distributed to other shareholders. Alternatively, preference

---

[39] *Birch v Cropper, Re Bridgewater Navigation Co Ltd* (1889) 14 App Cas 525 at 543, per Lord Macnaghten, HL.   [40] *Re National Telephone Co* [1914] 1 Ch 755.
[41] [1914] 1 Ch 755 at 774.   [42] [1914] AC 11.
[43] See *Re Isle of Thanet Electric Supply Co Ltd* [1950] Ch 161.
[44] *Scottish Insurance Corpn Ltd v Wilsons and Clyde Coal Co Ltd* [1949] 1 All ER 1068; *Prudential Assurance Co Ltd v Chatterley-Whitfield Collieries Ltd* [1949] 1 All ER 1094, HL.
[45] *Re Isle of Thanet Electric Supply Co Ltd* [1950] Ch 161, CA; *Scottish Insurance Corpn Ltd v Wilsons and Clyde Coal Co Ltd* [1949] 1 All ER 1068, HL.   [46] *Webb v Earle* (1875) LR 20 Eq 556.

shares may be issued as non-cumulative, but this must be clearly stated to ensure that the presumption does not apply.[47]

14-32 On a winding up, if the company is solvent, a question concerning the payment of arrears of dividend may arise. There is a *prima facie* presumption that dividends and arrears thereof are only payable while the company is a going concern and are no longer payable once winding up has begun.[48] That inference is rebuttable where there are express words in the terms of issue to the contrary or a definition in the right to dividend which is inconsistent with it.[49]

14-33 The net effect of these rules of construction is that class rights are usually spelt out in great detail in the terms of issue to avoid falling foul of one or other presumption.

Variation or abrogation of class rights

14-34 The statutory scheme for variation of class rights was simplified on the recommendation of the Company Law Review and it is intended to provide a comprehensive code setting out the manner in which rights attached to a class of shares can be varied.[50]

14-35 A variation or abrogation[51] must be carried out in accordance with a variation provision in the articles or, if no provision is made in the articles, in accordance with the scheme in CA 2006, s 630(4)[52] which requires the consent in writing of the holders of not less than three-quarters in nominal value of the issued shares of that class or a special resolution of the class passed at a class meeting sanctioning the variation.[53] At a class meeting

---

[47] *Staples v Eastman Photographic Materials Co* [1896] 2 Ch 303, CA (the terms of issue referred specifically to dividends paid out of the profits of each year).   [48] *Re Crichton's Oil Co* [1902] 2 Ch 86.
[49] *Re E W Savory Ltd* [1951] 2 All ER 1036 (reference to the ranking of the preference shares must have been a reference to what would happen on winding up); *Re Walter Symons Ltd* [1934] Ch 308.
[50] See Company Law Review, *Final Report*, vol 1 (2001), URN 01/942, para 7.28; *Completing the Structure* (2000), URN 00/1335, paras 5.42–5.44; *Developing the Framework* (2000), URN 00/656, paras 4.147–4.151. A major change effected by the CA 2006 is to extend the statutory provisions on variation of class rights to companies without a share capital, see s 631.
[51] References to variation include reference to abrogation: CA 2006, s 630(6). An alteration of an existing variation provision or the insertion of a variation procedure is itself a variation of class rights: s 630(5). The Court of Session in *Re House of Fraser plc* [1987] BCLC 293 at 301 noted that 'variation' presupposes the continuance of rights in a varied state while 'abrogation' presupposes the termination of rights without satisfaction or fulfilment.
[52] Note CA 2006, s 630(3) which provides that the mechanisms for variation provided by s 630(2) (variation in accordance with a provision for variation in the company's articles or, in the absence of any such provision, in accordance with the statutory scheme in s 630(4)) are without prejudice to other restrictions on variation. Paragraph 937 of the *Explanatory Notes to the CA 2006* states that s 630(3) has two consequences: (a) the company must comply with any more onerous regime in its articles for the variation of class rights (but s 630(2)(a) says that in any event); and (b) if the rights are entrenched, that protection cannot be circumvented by varying the rights using this (s 630) provision. But if the rights are entrenched, it is because there is a provision dealing with their amendment which is more restrictive than a special resolution (s 22(1)) and, if there is a provision dealing with their amendment, then s 630(2)(a) requires that procedure to be followed in any event. It is not clear then what purpose is served by CA 2006, s 630(3).
[53] The test is different under s 630(4)(a) and (b), (a) being of the total issued shares of that class while (b) is of the votes cast at the meeting by those entitled to vote and the difference may dictate which route is used in a particular case. As to the application of CA 2006, Pt 13, Ch 3 (meetings) to class meetings, see s 334. Note in particular that the quorum requirement for a variation of class rights meeting is two persons present holding at least one-third in nominal value of the issued shares of the class in question: s 334(4)(a). This provision overrides any provision in the company's articles.

so held, the shareholders must have regard to what is in the interests of the class.[54] In practice provisions in the articles are generally drafted in broadly similar terms to the statutory scheme, but it is possible for the articles either to impose a stricter scheme or a less onerous one (for example, requiring an ordinary resolution). In either case, the provision in the articles must be obeyed and the statutory scheme in s 630(4) only applies in the absence of provision in the articles.[55]

14-36 As noted, a class right may be an entrenched provision where the variation of those rights can only occur on terms which fall within CA 2006, s 22(1). Entrenchment should be of no consequence in these circumstances since entrenchment merely means that a provision is not open to alteration by special resolution under s 21 and can be altered only in accordance with its own provision for alteration which is the position in any event under s 630(2)(a). Entrenchment is discussed at **4-17**.

14-37 Where a class has consented to a variation, the holders of not less in total than 15% of the issued shares of that class, provided that they did not consent to or vote for the variation, may apply to the court within 21 days to have the variation cancelled, in which case the variation does not take effect until it has been confirmed by the court (CA 2006, s 633(2)–(4)). If the court is satisfied that the variation would unfairly prejudice the shareholders of the class represented by the applicant, it may disallow the variation; otherwise, it must confirm it and the court's decision is final (s 633(5)). In practice, this provision is rarely used, not least because it is unlikely that a court will overturn a variation which has been agreed to by three-quarters of the class.

Judicial interpretation of 'variation or abrogation'

14-38 The restrictions on variation or abrogation in CA 2006, s 630 only apply if what has occurred amounts to a variation or abrogation of the rights attached to a class (CA 2006, s 630(1), (6)) and the courts have restricted the protection afforded by the statute by interpreting 'variation' and 'abrogation' restrictively.

14-39 In approaching the question of whether a variation or abrogation has occurred, the courts have drawn a distinction between matters affecting the rights attached to each share and matters affecting the enjoyment of those rights. Only variations or abrogations affecting the rights attached to a class of shares attract the protection of CA 2006, s 630(2). Where only the enjoyment of the right is affected, the shares may be commercially less valuable but their rights remain what they always were and the shareholders cannot demand the protection of the section.[56]

14-40 A typical case is *White v Bristol Aeroplane Co Ltd*[57] where an issue of preference shares which would dilute the control of the existing preference shareholders was held not to be a variation. The new shares were to be issued to the existing ordinary shareholders and paid for out of the company's reserves. The company's articles provided that all or any of the rights or privileges attached to any class of shares might be affected, modified, varied, dealt with or abrogated in any manner with the sanction of an extraordinary resolution

---

[54] *British America Nickel Corpn Ltd v O'Brien* [1927] AC 369; *Re Holders Investment Trust Ltd* [1971] 2 All ER 289.   [55] See Explanatory Notes to the CA 2006, paras 936, 937.

[56] The Company Law Review considered the provision of a specific remedy for shareholders in this situation but concluded that if shareholders in a class wish protection for their broader economic interests (as well as their rights) then they should contract for that protection: Company Law Review, *Completing the Structure* (2000), URN 00/1335, para 5.81, and see discussion at **14-50** of contractual protection for class interests.   [57] [1953] Ch 65, CA. See also *Re John Smith's Tadcaster Brewery Co Ltd* [1953] 1 All ER 518.

passed at a separate meeting of the members of that class. It was argued by the plaintiff preference shareholder that the word 'affect' was wide and must be taken to cover a transaction which, though not necessarily modifying or varying rights, would in some way otherwise affect them. On this basis, it was argued, the proposed allotment was a variation requiring the consent of the existing preference shareholders.

14-41 The Court of Appeal disagreed. Evershed MR concluded that the new issue did not affect the rights or privileges of the existing preference shareholders which remained exactly as they were before. The preference shareholders might be affected as a matter of business by reason of the new preference shares which would be in the possession of the ordinary shareholders and which would have a majority over the existing preference shares. This outcome would only affect the enjoyment of the rights, however, and not the rights themselves and so the consent of the existing preference shareholders was not required. Romer LJ drew a distinction between rights on the one hand and the result of exercising the rights on the other hand. He noted:[58]

> 'The rights, as such, are conferred by resolution or by the articles, and they cannot be affected except with the sanction of the members on whom those rights are conferred; but the results of exercising those rights are not the subject of any assurance or guarantee under the constitution of the company, and are not protected in any way.'

14-42 Similarly, in *Greenhalgh v Arderne Cinemas Ltd*[59] a subdivision of a class of 10 shilling ordinary shares into two shilling shares was held not to vary the rights of Mr Greenhalgh, a holder of the existing two shilling ordinary shares, although the result of the sub-division was to alter control of the company. The court accepted that the effect was to alter his position as a matter of business but, as a matter of law, his rights were quite unaltered.[60]

Reduction of capital and variation of class rights

14-43 Schemes for the reduction of capital (see **20-56 et seq**) may involve paying off preference shareholders who are often reluctant to be 'expelled' from the company in this way, particularly when it means an end to high dividend returns which are no longer available in the market. The issue for the court is whether such a reduction of capital amounts to a variation or abrogation of the class rights of the preference shareholder so requiring the consent of the class.

14-44 The approach of the courts is to look at what the class rights would be in a winding up and to compare that position with the position which would arise under the proposed reduction. If what is proposed on reduction is in accordance with the class rights on a winding up, there is no variation requiring the consent of the class.[61]

14-45 For example, if the reduction is because capital has been lost or is unrepresented by available assets and the classes rank *pari passu* (equally), then *prima facie* the loss should be borne equally;[62] but if there are preference shares which have priority as to a return of capital on a winding up, the ordinary shares must bear the loss as they would do if the company was being wound up.[63] Alternatively, if the reduction of capital involves the

---

[58] [1953] Ch 65 at 82, CA.   [59] [1946] 1 All ER 512, CA.   [60] [1946] 1 All ER 512 at 518, CA.

[61] *Re Saltdean Estate Co Ltd* [1968] 3 All ER 829; *House of Fraser v ACGE Investments Ltd* [1987] AC 387, HL.

[62] See *Bannatyne v Direct Spanish Telegraph Co* (1886) 34 Ch D 287, CA where the preference shareholders had no preference as to capital, but only as to dividend.

[63] *Re Floating Dock Company of St Thomas Ltd* [1895] 1 Ch 691.

return of surplus capital, that return will normally be to the preference shareholders who will usually have priority as to repayment of capital in a winding up.[64]

14-46   These issues were considered in *House of Fraser plc v ACGE Investments Ltd*[65] where the ordinary shareholders passed a special resolution approving the paying off of the whole of the preference share capital of the company as being in excess of the wants of the company. No class meeting of the preference shareholders was held to approve the reduction. The company's articles provided that the special rights attached to any class of shares could only be modified, commuted, affected or dealt with, with the consent of the holders of the class of shares. The preference shareholders argued that the failure to obtain their consent meant that the court could not confirm the reduction of capital.

14-47   The House of Lords accepted that this issue was definitively addressed by Buckley J in *Re Saltdean Estate Co Ltd*,[66] a case on almost identical facts. In a much cited judgment Buckley J confirmed the long-established position that, where capital is to be repaid, that class of capital should first be repaid which would be returned first in a winding up of the company.[67] If the preference shareholders are entitled to prior repayment of capital in a winding up, the first class of capital to be repaid should *prima facie* be the preferred shares. Such a proposed cancellation is not an abrogation of the rights attached to those shares when it is in accordance with the right and liability to prior repayment of capital attached to their shares. The liability to prior repayment on a reduction of capital, corresponding to their right to prior return of capital in a winding up, forms an integral part of the definition or delimitation of the bundle of rights which make up the preferred share. Giving effect to it does not involve the variation or abrogation of any rights attached to such shares. Buckley J concluded that this vulnerability to prior repayment in this way is, and has always been, a characteristic of preferred shares.[68]

14-48   Applying that approach in *House of Fraser plc v ACGE Investments Ltd*,[69] the House of Lords found that the proposed reduction of capital involved the extinction of the preference shares in strict accordance with the contract embodied in the articles of association to which the preference shareholders were party. The preference shareholders had a right to a return of capital in priority to other shareholders and that right was not affected, modified, dealt with or abrogated, but was given effect to by the proposed reduction with the result that the consent of the preference shareholders was not required.[70]

14-49   This is the position in any instance where the preference shareholders have priority as to a return of capital, even if they also have further rights of participation as regards dividend.[71] It is not clear whether preference shares which are participating as to surplus on a winding up could be dealt with in this way although *Re William Jones & Sons Ltd*[72] suggests that they can.

---

[64]   *Re Chatterley-Whitfield Collieries Ltd* [1948] 2 All ER 593, aff'd sub nom *Prudential Assurance Co Ltd v Chatterley-Whitfield Collieries Ltd* [1949] 1 All ER 1094, HL; *Scottish Insurance Co Ltd v Wilsons & Clyde Coal Co Ltd* 1948 SC 360, aff'd [1949] 1 All ER 1068, HL; *Re Fowlers Vacola Manufacturing Co Ltd* [1966] VR 97; *Re Saltdean Estate Co Ltd* [1968] 3 All ER 829; *House of Fraser v ACGE Investments Ltd* [1987] AC 387, HL.   [65]   [1987] AC 387, HL.

[66]   [1968] 3 All ER 829.   [67]   See especially [1968] 3 All ER 829 at 831–2.

[68]   [1968] 3 All ER 829 at 833–4. See also *Bannatyne v Direct Spanish Telegraph Co* (1886) 34 Ch D 287, CA; *Scottish Insurance Co Ltd v Wilsons & Clyde Coal Co Ltd* 1948 SC 360, aff'd [1949] 1 All ER 1068 at 1077–8, per Lord Simonds, HL.   [69]   [1987] AC 387, HL.

[70]   [1987] AC 387 at 393.   [71]   *Re Saltdean Estate Co Ltd* [1968] 3 All ER 829.

[72]   [1969] 1 All ER 913. In that instance, however, the preference shareholders raised no objection to being paid off, probably because they were to be paid off in full although the shares stood at less than par. Moreover,

Deemed variations or abrogations—a contractual solution

14-50 The decisions in cases such as *White v Bristol Aeroplane Co Ltd*,[73] *Greenhalgh v Arderne Cinemas Ltd*[74] and *House of Fraser plc v ACGE Investments Ltd*[75] highlight the limits to the protection which can be conferred by class rights when it is left to the courts to determine whether a variation or abrogation has occurred.

14-51 A class of shareholders can avoid the risk of a restrictive interpretation by the courts of what constitutes a variation of their class rights by identifying in the terms of issue matters (such as a reduction or an increase in capital) which are deemed to be a variation or abrogation of the rights attached to that class and so will require the consent of the class. In that way, the scope for judicial determination of whether a variation or abrogation has occurred is reduced.

14-52 The courts will give effect to such provisions and will interpret them in the light of their protective purpose. In *Re Northern Engineering Industries plc*[76] the articles stated that the rights of any class were to be deemed to be varied by the reduction of the capital paid up on those shares. The company proposed to reduce its capital by paying off its preference shares and cancelling them without obtaining the consent of the class. The company argued that the provision in the articles only applied to a 'reduction', i.e. something which involved a diminution or lessening from one number to a smaller number. It did not apply to a reduction to zero.

14-53 The Court of Appeal rejected this argument finding that the provision in the articles must be construed in the light of its purpose, namely the protection of the shareholders of the class affected. It applied both where there was a piecemeal reduction of capital and where there was complete repayment of their investment. A reduction of capital without the consent of the class affected could not be confirmed.

14-54 Given that reductions of capital by private companies need not require court confirmation where the directors are willing to make a solvency statement (see CA 2006, s 641(1) and discussion at **20-65**), those investing in a class of shares should take care to: (a) specify the rights attached to the class, (b) provide a mechanism for the variation of those rights in the articles and (c) identify matters of concern which are to be deemed to be variations so triggering that variation mechanism.

D   Share transfer and transmission

Introduction

14-55 Shares are personal property (CA 2006, s 541) and are transferable in the manner provided by the company's articles (s 544(1)), subject to the Stock Transfer Act 1963 which overrides any requirements in the articles to allow fully-paid shares to be transferred by a simplified process and to regulations[77] which allow for the electronic transfer of shares (CA 2006, s 544(2)).

---

there was no present prospect of the company being wound up so the enjoyment of any surplus on a winding up would not occur for many years.

[73] [1953] Ch 65, CA.   [74] [1946] 1 All ER 512, CA.   [75] [1987] AC 387, HL.

[76] [1994] 2 BCLC 704.

[77] See The Uncertificated Securities Regulations 2001, SI 2001/3755, as amended by Companies Act 2006 (Consequential Amendments) (Uncertificated Securities) Order 2009, SI 2009/1889; also *Mills v Sportsdirect.com* [2010] 2 BCLC 143 at 147.

14-56 A company may not register a transfer of shares unless a proper instrument of transfer has been delivered to the company (s 770(1)). A proper instrument of transfer for these purposes is an instrument appropriate or suitable for stamp duty purposes[78] and this restriction is imposed to facilitate the raising of taxation. The requirement as to a proper instrument of transfer is subject to exceptions where the transfer is an exempt transfer within the Stock Transfer Act 1982 or is in accordance with regulations dealing with uncertificated securities (CA 2006, s 770(1)).

A *prima facie* right to transfer shares

14-57 A shareholder has a *prima facie* right to transfer his shares and directors have no discretionary powers, independent of any powers given to them by the articles, to refuse to register a transfer.[79] Any restriction of this right to transfer must be clearly stated in the articles and the right to transfer is not to be cut down by uncertain language or doubtful implications.[80] If restrictions on transfer are laid down by the articles, they must be complied with. The directors have no power to authorise registration in circumstances where there has been a breach of the articles and any purported transfer in breach of the articles is defeasible at the suit of a member.[81]

Restrictions on the transfer of shares

14-58 In practice, it is customary for the articles of a private company (and private companies make up 99.6% of the register of companies) to impose restrictions on the transfer of shares.[82] These restrictions are usually justified on the basis that many such companies are small family concerns or quasi-partnership-type ventures where it is important to the existing members to retain control over the membership of the company. It is unusual for public companies to impose any restrictions on transfer while shares in listed public companies must be freely transferable.[83] A provision commonly included in the articles is one to the effect that the directors may, in their absolute discretion and without assigning any reason therefor, decline to register any transfer of any share, whether or not it is a fully-paid share.[84] The CA 2006 modified that type of provision by requiring the company to give reasons for a refusal to register a transfer (s 771(1)), though this does not affect the right to refuse.

14-59 In addition to a discretion conferred on directors to refuse to register transfers, pre-emption provisions are commonly included to ensure that existing members have the opportunity to buy any shares that may be for sale before they are offered outside the company. For example, a member wishing to sell is often permitted to transfer his shares to an existing member without restriction, but where he seeks to transfer to an outsider, a pre-emption provision comes into effect. This provision normally requires the intending

---

[78] *Nisbet v Shepherd* [1994] 1 BCLC 300.

[79] *Re Smith, Knight & Co, Weston's Case* (1868) 4 Ch App 20.

[80] *Re Smith & Fawcett Ltd* [1942] 1 All ER 542; *Stothers v William Steward (Holdings) Ltd* [1994] 2 BCLC 266, CA. See also *BWE International Ltd v Jones* [2004] 1 BCLC 406 at 413; *Re Coroin Ltd, McKillen v Misland (Cyprus) Investments Ltd* [2011] EWHC 3466.

[81] *Hurst v Crampton Bros* [2003] 1 BCLC 304; *Tett v Phoenix Property and Investment Co Ltd* [1986] BCLC 149, CA. See also *Curtis v J J Curtis & Co* [1986] BCLC 86, NZCA.

[82] Until 1980 it was mandatory for private companies to include a restriction on the transfer of their shares in the articles: see CA 1948, s 28 repealed by CA 1980, Sch 4.

[83] See Listing Rules LR 2.2.4R, subject to limited exceptions which are irrelevant for our purposes.

[84] This provision was contained in the 1948 Table A, see CA 1948, Sch 1, Table A Pt II, reg 3.

transferor[85] to give notice to the company secretary or other nominated person who must notify the other members that there are shares available for purchase.[86] If the other members make an offer for the shares, the transferor may accept or reject their offer but, if he rejects it, he is precluded normally from proceeding with the transfer of the shares to an outsider. If the shares are not taken up by the other shareholders, the transferor is usually entitled at that stage to offer his shares to an outside purchaser, subject to the proviso that the directors may refuse to register a transfer in such circumstances.[87]

Absolute discretion to refuse registration

14-60 With regard to an absolute discretion, as noted, a common provision is one which states that the directors may, in their absolute discretion, decline to register any transfer of any share. The leading authority is *Re Smith & Fawcett Ltd*[88] where the Court of Appeal accepted that where the articles contain a provision such as this, drafted in the widest possible terms, there is no limitation on the exercise by directors of that power other than the standard requirement that, as a fiduciary power, it must be exercised bona fide in what the directors consider—and not what a court may consider—to be in the interests of the company, and not for any collateral purpose.[89] In reaching their decision, the directors are *prima facie* presumed to have acted in good faith and the onus of proof is on those challenging their decision.[90] Now the limitation on their powers would be expressed in terms of the directors' duty in CA 2006, s 171 to exercise their powers for the purpose for which they are conferred which, given it is an absolute power, means (applying s 172) it must be exercised in the way the directors consider most likely to promote the success of the company having regard, in this instance, to the need to act fairly as between members of the company (s 172(1)(f)). Given the judicial acknowledgement of the importance of these provisions in private companies, as exemplified by the Court of Appeal in *Re Smith & Fawcett*,[91] the courts are likely to be still quite generous in the amount of leeway which they give directors exercising an absolute power of this nature, in the absence of evidence of bad faith.

14-61 It may be easier in future to find evidence of bad faith (or at least material which might be relevant to a petition alleging unfairly prejudicial conduct) because of the obligation now for the company to give reasons for a refusal to register a transfer (CA 2006, s 771(1)).[92] It remains to be seen whether this will be a significant change or whether a standard

---

[85] Disputes as to whether these types of provisions have been triggered are common and arise in a variety of situations depending on the wording of the articles, see *Lyle & Scott Ltd v Scott's Trustees* [1959] 2 All ER 661; *Safeguard Industrial Investments Ltd v National Westminster Bank Ltd* [1982] 1 All ER 449; *Theakston v London Trust plc* [1984] BCLC 390; *Re Sedgefield Steeplechase Co (1927) Ltd, Scotto v Petch* [2000] 2 BCLC 211, Ch D, aff'd [2001] BCC 889, CA; *Hurst v Crampton* [2003] 1 BCLC 304; *Re Coroin Ltd, McKillen Misland (Cyprus) Investments Ltd* [2012] EWCA Civ 179.

[86] Notice to the members of a pre-emption right having been triggered amounts to an option conferred on the other members to purchase the shares at the price determined by the articles—that option creates an equitable interest which prevails over the interest of a donee of the shares incorrectly registered as the holder of the shares: *Cottrell v King* [2004] 2 BCLC 413; *Tett v Phoenix Property and Investment Co Ltd* [1984] BCLC 599 at 619 revd on other grounds [1986] BCLC 149.

[87] These pre-emption provisions tend to be lengthy and complex and the courts sometimes have to interpret them purposefully to give them business efficacy: see *Pennington v Crampton* [2004] BCC 611; *Tett v Phoenix Property and Investment Co Ltd* [1986] BCLC 149, CA.   [88] [1942] 1 All ER 542.

[89] [1942] 1 All ER 542 at 543. See *Re Bell Brothers, ex p Hodgson* (1891) 7 TLR 689; *Re Coalport China Co* [1895] 2 Ch 404; also *Popely v Planarrive Ltd* [1997] 1 BCLC 8.

[90] See *Village Cay Marina Ltd v Acland* [1998] 2 BCLC 327 at 335–6, PC, per Lord Hoffmann, citing *Charles Forte Investments Ltd v Amanda* [1963] 2 All ER 940; see also *Re Coalport China Co* [1895] 2 Ch 404; *Popely v Planarrive Ltd* [1997] 1 BCLC 8 at 16.   [91] [1942] 1 All ER 542.

[92] Reversing the long standing common law position that the directors could not be required to give reasons: *Re Gresham Life Assurance Society, ex p Penney* (1872) 8 Ch App 446.

formula of words emerges which is less than illuminating. The transferee can ask for further information as to the reasons for the refusal though the company is not required to hand over board minutes (s 772(1)(b)).

A limited power to refuse registration

14-62 The directors' power to refuse to register may be a more limited power and such provisions vary greatly from company to company. For example, the articles may provide that the directors may refuse to register any transfer: (1) where the company has a lien on the shares; (2) where it is not proved to their satisfaction that the proposed transferee is a responsible person; (3) where the directors are of the opinion that the proposed transferee is not a desirable person to admit to membership.[93]

14-63 In *Re Bede Steam Shipping Co*[94] the articles provided that the directors might decline to register a transfer of any shares if, in their opinion, it was contrary to the interests of the company that the proposed transferee should be a member thereof. The directors admitted that no inquiry had been made as to the fitness of the transferees. The transfers in question had been rejected because a majority of the board objected to the transferor disposing of single shares or small lots of shares to individuals with a view to increasing the number of shareholders who would support him. The Court of Appeal found that the articles required the directors to focus on the qualities of the transferee and identify reasons why he was unsuitable.[95] The particular objections which the directors had focused on were more concerned with the motives and attitudes of the transferor. These were not grounds provided for by the articles and so the transferees were entitled to be registered.

Time-limits

14-64 Registration may be secured as a result of the failure of the directors to exercise their discretion to refuse registration within the requisite time period. The directors must register the transfer or decide to refuse and notify the transferee of the refusal and give reasons for the refusal as soon as practicable and, in any event, within two months of the transfer being lodged with the company (CA 2006, s 771(1)). Once the two-month period has elapsed, the directors are no longer able to exercise their discretion[96] and an application may be made under s 125 to have the register rectified by the inclusion of the name of the transferee.

---

[93] See *Re Coalport China Co* [1895] 2 Ch 404. Other examples can be found in *Re Gresham Life Assurance Society, ex p Penney* (1872) 8 Ch App 446; *Berry and Stewart v Tottenham Hotspur Football & Athletic Co* [1935] Ch 718.

[94] [1917] 1 Ch 123. See also *Re Bell Brothers, ex p Hodgson* (1891) 7 TLR 689; *Re The Ceylon Land & Produce Co, ex p Anderson* (1891) 7 TLR 692.

[95] See also *Holman v Adams Securities Ltd* [2010] EWHC 2421, where the court refused to strike out a petition alleging unfairly prejudicial conduct (see CA 2006, s 994) where central to the dispute was the operation of a provision in the articles allowing the directors to refuse to register any transfer of any shares to any person whom they considered to be undesirable. The court noted that it was at least arguable that the blanket operation of such a policy without consideration by the directors of the merits of each individual application for transfer could be unfairly prejudicial, particularly against the background of use of the provision to persuade minority shareholders to sell their shares to the company and the non-exercise of the policy when it came to the transfer of the majority shareholders' shares to a new holding company.

[96] This outcome is not required by CA 2006, s 771 which simply imposes a fine for default (s 771(3)) but it was accepted in *Re Swaledale Cleaners Ltd* [1968] 3 All ER 619 that this can be the only consequence of requiring the power to be exercised within two months; also *Re Inverdeck Ltd* [1998] 2 BCLC 242. Where the directors decide to refuse to register a transfer within the time-frame, but fail to notify the transferee of the refusal, the failure to notify (while it attracts a fine) does not nullify the decision: *Popely v Planarrive Ltd* [1997] 1 BCLC 8.

Position as between the vendor and purchaser when registration refused

14-65 Where the directors have correctly exercised their discretion so making the decision to refuse registration unimpeachable, the vendor and the purchaser of the shares are left in the position that they cannot now complete the transaction by having the purchaser registered. The position on a sale of shares is that the equitable title to the shares passes to the purchaser once the contract is made (assuming the contract can be specifically enforceable—if not, no equitable title passes), and the legal title passes on completion and registration by the company.[97] The vendor provides the purchaser with a duly signed transfer form and the share certificates for submission to the company for registration. Unless the contract so provides, the vendor does not promise to secure registration and, if the directors do refuse to register the transfer, the vendor is not liable in damages for breach although he will hold the shares as bare trustee for the purchaser.[98] Where the parties are agreeable to such an outcome, they can negate the effect of the directors' refusal to register.

14-66 An imperfect gift of shares will take effect in equity if the donor has done everything necessary to enable the donee to enforce a beneficial claim to the shares without further assistance from the donor[99] (typically the donor will have delivered the share transfer form and the relevant certificates to the donee, but no registration has taken place). In those circumstances, the donor remains the legal owner, but having done all in his own power to transfer the shares, beneficial ownership will pass to the donee pending registration as the legal owner. In *Curtis v Pulbrook*[100] an attempt by a donor to gift part of his shareholding in a family company to his wife and daughter failed when he merely delivered new share certificates to them (he was one of the directors of the company) without executing any share transfer forms and without delivering his own share certificates from which their interest was to be carved.[101] A gift also failed in *Kaye v Zeital*[102] where the donor merely gave a blank transfer form (undated and unsigned) to the donee without any share certificate. In neither case had the donor done all in his power to procure the transfer of the shares to the donee so the gifts failed as imperfect gifts. Sometimes, in these cases, it is possible to construe the situation as giving rise to a trust because of some detrimental reliance by the donee upon the imperfect gift in such a way as to bind the conscience of the donor[103] or to find that a shareholder has made an effective declaration of trust in favour of another. For example, where a shareholder signed a letter indicating that he was holding certain shares for another and delivered the letter together with a signed blank share transfer form to that other, though no share certificates were delivered, the court held it was an effective declaration of trust in favour of that other.[104]

---

[97] *Societe Generale de Paris v Walker* (1886) LR 11 App Cas 20; see also *Roots v Williamson* (1888) 38 Ch D 485; *Ireland v Hart* [1902] 1 Ch 522. See Lewison J in *Mills v Sportsdirect.com Retail Ltd* [2010] 2 BCLC 143 at [74]–[75], [86]–[87] as to whether a contract for the sale of shares is specifically enforceable.

[98] *Re Rose, Rose v IRC* [1952] 1 All ER 1217. As to the position of the vendor under an uncompleted contract for the sale of shares, see *Musselwhite v Musselwhite & Son Ltd* [1962] 1 All ER 201; *JRRT (Investments) Ltd v Haycraft* [1993] BCLC 401; *Michaels v Harley House (Marylebone) Ltd* [1999] 1 BCLC 670, CA.

[99] *Re Rose* [1949] Ch 78; *Re Rose, Rose v IRC* [1952] 1 All ER 1217. See Luxton [2012] Conv 70 at 75: intention, even a fervent desire, is not sufficient, the donor must have done everything necessary.

[100] [2011] 1 BCLC 638, see Luxton [2012] Conv 70.

[101] See [2011] 1 BCLC 638 at [45]; and see the critical comments by Briggs J about the lack of any identifiable or rational policy objective in the rules governing the circumstances when equity will and will not perfect an imperfect gift of shares, at [47].   [102] See [2010] 2 BCLC 1 at [43].

[103] See *Pennington v Waine* [2002] 2 BCLC 448 (gift effective, though no delivery of a stock transfer form, nor of the share certificates though the court thought nothing turned on the absence of share certificates since throughout they had been held by the company and therefore could not be delivered by the donor).

[104] See *Shah v Shah* [2010] EWCA Civ 1408.

Transmission of shares

14-67 Transmission arises by operation of law on the death or bankruptcy of a member. On the death of a shareholder, the shares are transmitted to his personal representative and the production of the grant of probate of the will or letters of administration of the estate or confirmation as executor of a deceased person must be accepted by the company as sufficient evidence of the grant (CA 2006, s 774).

14-68 The position on transmission is generally governed by the articles and the model articles provide that a person becoming entitled to a share in consequence of death or bankruptcy may choose either to become a holder of the share or to have someone else registered as the transferee.[105] Usually, the election by the personal representative or trustee in bankruptcy to be registered or to have someone else registered has the effect of triggering any pre-emption provisions which may exist and will be subject to any discretion vested in the directors to refuse to register any transfer.[106]

E The register of members

Status and contents of the register of members

14-69 Every company must maintain a register of members (CA 2006, s 113) and entry on the register is essential to membership in all cases save that of subscribers to the memorandum (s 112), as noted at **14-1**.[107] A company registered in England and Wales is not concerned with trusts over its shares and no notice of any trust, expressed, implied or constructive, is to be entered on the register or be receivable by the registrar.[108] The register is *prima facie*, but not conclusive,[109] evidence of any matters directed or authorised by the Companies Act to be inserted in it (s 127).

14-70 The register must include details of the names and addresses (which need not be residential addresses) of the members of the company (s 113(2)). The register of members must disclose the date of entry on the register as a member and the date of ceasing to be a member (s 113(2)), dates which affect voting and dividend rights and the right to participate in corporate actions such as a rights issue. If the number of members of a limited company falls to one or increases from one to two or more members, the register of members must include a statement that the company has only one member, or has ceased to have only one member, as the case may be, and must give the dates of these occurrences (s 123).

---

[105] See The Companies (Model Articles) Regulations 2008, SI 2008/3229, reg 2, Sch 1, art 27(2) (Ltd), reg 4, Sch 3, art 66(2) (Plc). An instrument of transfer of a share of a deceased member may be made by his personal representative (though not himself a member) and it is as effective as if he had been a member at the time of execution of the instrument: CA 2006, s 773. See also *Scott v Frank F Scott (London) Ltd* [1940] Ch 794.

[106] See, for example, the provisions at issue in *Re Benfield Greig Group plc, Nugent v Benfield Greig Group plc* [2000] 2 BCLC 488 at 497 and *Dashfield v Davidson* [2009] 1 BCLC 220 at [8], and see comments of Lewison J at [53] as to the mandatory nature of the obligations in that case and at [54] on the benefits of having these provisions in a private company.

[107] If the company holds shares as treasury shares (see **20-38**), the company must be entered in the register as the member holding those shares: CA 2006, s 124(2).

[108] CA 2006, s 126; *Société Générale de Paris v Walker* (1885) 11 App Cas 20.

[109] See *Reese River Silver Mining Co v Smith* (1869) LR 4 HL 64 at 80, per Lord Cairns; also *Re Briton Medical and General Life Association* (1888) 39 Ch D 61 at 72, per Stirling J.

14-71 The register of members must be available for inspection at the registered office or other place specified by the regulations[110] and the registrar of companies must be notified of that place (s 114). Larger public companies do not maintain their own registers, but use professional registrar services instead, hence the need to permit the register to be inspected other than at the registered office. In an age of computerised records, the physical location of the register becomes less important, provided it is not outside the country of registration.

14-72 The register of members helps creditors and investors identify those behind the company which may affect any decision to invest or provide credit. The register of members is also constantly monitored by public companies in order to detect bidders building up a stake with which to launch a takeover bid.

Inspection of the register

14-73 The register of members is open to inspection and any person seeking to exercise the right either to inspect the register or to obtain a copy thereof or a copy of any part of the register must make a request to the company to that effect (CA 2006, s 116(3)). The request must:

(1) identify the name and address of the individual making the request or the name and address of the individual responsible for making a request on behalf of an organisation;

(2) specify the purpose for which the information is to be used;

(3) indicate whether the information is to be disclosed to any other person; if so, full details must be given of that other person and the purpose for which the information is to be used by that person (s 116(4)).

14-74 It is an offence for a person knowingly or recklessly in making a request to include a statement which is misleading, false or deceptive in a material particular (s 119(1)). It is also an offence for a person in possession of information following a request to inspect the register to disclose the information obtained to another person knowing or having reason to suspect that that person may use the information for a purpose which is not a proper purpose (s 119(2)).

14-75 The company has five working days either to comply with the request or to apply to the court for an order that the company need not comply with the request. If following an application the court does not so order, the company must immediately comply with the request to inspect the register (s 117(5)). It is an offence for the company to fail to do so in the absence of a court order allowing it to refuse and the court can compel disclosure if need be (s 118(3)).[111] If the court is satisfied that the inspection is not for a proper purpose, it can direct the company not to comply with the request and can extend the order to preclude compliance with similar requests (s 117(4)) so ensuring that a company cannot be bombarded with like requests and forced to go to court every time to get an order justifying non-compliance. In addition, where the court concludes that the purpose is not a proper purpose, the court can order that the company's costs of the application be paid in whole or in part by the person who made the inspection request, even if he is not party to the application to the court (s 117(3)(b)).

---

[110] See CA 2006, s 1136 and see SI 2008/3006.
[111] The court's power to compel inspection is discretionary, see *Pelling v Families Need Fathers Ltd* [2002] 1 BCLC 645.

14-76   In addition to the information on the members contained in the company's register of members, all companies are required to deliver an annual return to the registrar of companies (CA 2006, s 854) giving the address of the company's registered office, the prescribed particulars of the directors and the company secretary (if there is one), identifying the type of company and its business activities (s 855), providing information about its share capital (s 856) and including the names of the members. A full list of members is required in the first annual return following incorporation and then every third year.[112] In the case of non-traded companies, only the shareholders' names (not addresses) and details of shareholdings are required.[113] In the case of traded companies, disclosure in the annual return is only required of a limited category of traded companies[114] and only in respect of members who hold 5% or more of the issued shares of any class of the company who are required to give their names, addresses and details of their shareholdings,[115] but they are very unlikely to be individuals as opposed to institutional shareholders and their (corporate) addresses are probably matters of public record in any event. The Company Law Review had considered reducing this requirement for an annual return, particularly with respect to small private companies, but after consideration concluded that it is in the public interest to retain this requirement, thus ensuring that a public record is available as well as the company's register of members.[116] In many instances, existing and potential investors and creditors may prefer to inspect the public record discreetly rather than approach the company to inspect the register of members, but the public record may not be as up to date as it should be which is why access to the company register may well be desirable.

Rectification of the register of members

14-77   The details in the register of members can be challenged, for instance, on the grounds of mistake, but any shareholder wishing to challenge an entry must act promptly.[117] Rectification of the register is governed by CA 2006, s 125 which provides that if:[118]

'(a) the name of any person is, without sufficient cause, entered in or omitted from the company's register of members; or

(b) default is made, or unnecessary delay takes place in entering on the register the fact of any person having ceased to be a member;

---

[112]   In the intervening years the company need only provide information on those who become members, or cease to be members, or any share transfers: CA 2006, s 856(3), (5). Larger companies prefer to provide a full list of members every year rather than attempt to track changes in the intervening two years.

[113]   CA 2006, s 856A.

[114]   See CA 2006, s 856B(1). Essentially, disclosure is limited to companies that are not DTR5 issuers; a DTR5 issuer (see s 855(4)) is a company subject to Chapter 5 of the Disclosure and Transparency Rules of the UKLA which requires disclosure of major shareholders to the market in any event. Therefore the Government has removed the need for such issuers to include duplicate information in their annual returns, hence the category of traded company which must provide information is limited to those which are not DTR5 companies.   [115]   CA 2006, s 856B(3).

[116]   See Company Law Review, *Final Report*, vol 1 (2001), para 11.45; *Completing the Structure* (2000), para 8.15; *Developing the Framework* (2000), paras 10.45–10.52.

[117]   *Re Scottish Petroleum Co* (1883) 23 Ch D 413 at 434, CA.

[118]   The directors of a company may rectify the register of members without any application to the court if there is no dispute about the matter and the circumstances are such that the court would order rectification: *Reese River Silver Mining Co v Smith* (1869) LR 4 HL 64 at 74; *Hartley's Case* (1875) 10 Ch App 157; *First National Reinsurance Co Ltd v Greenfield* [1921] 2 KB 260 at 279; but ordinarily the protection of the court's order is essential to any rectification by the removal of the name of a registered holder of shares: *Re Derham and Allen Ltd* [1946] Ch 31 at 36.

the person aggrieved, or any member of the company, or the company may apply to the court for rectification of the register.'

14-78   The court has a discretion to refuse the application or to order rectification and the payment by the company of any damages sustained by any party aggrieved (s 125(2)). There is no necessity to show any wrongdoing by the company and any question of omission by error or entry by error can be raised.

14-79   The power to rectify has been exercised where there was no valid allotment of shares;[119] or the allotment was irregular;[120] or where a transfer of shares was improperly registered or registration was refused.[121]

14-80   The nature of the jurisdiction to rectify the register was considered in *Re Piccadilly Radio plc*.[122] In this instance, shares in a radio company were transferred without obtaining the consent of the Independent Broadcasting Authority (IBA) as required by the articles of association. Other shareholders in the company, with a view to preventing certain proposals being agreed to at a general meeting, sought rectification of the share register by deleting the names of the transferees and restoring the name of the original transferor. Millett J, despite finding that there had been a breach of the articles, refused rectification. In his opinion, the statutory procedure provided a discretionary remedy and the court must consider the circumstances in which and the purpose for which the relief was sought. The circumstances here did not warrant rectification for a number of reasons. The applicants had no interest in the shares and were not seeking to have their own names restored to the register. They were seeking to disenfranchise opposition to certain proposals to be put to the general meeting and had seized on a breach of an article of which the IBA itself did not complain. Moreover, the transferor did not seek rectification and the company itself did not support the application.

---

[119]   See *Re Homer District Consolidated Gold Mines, ex p Smith* (1888) 39 Ch D 546 at 551; *Re Portuguese Consolidated Copper Mines Ltd* (1889) 42 Ch D 160, CA.

[120]   See *Re Homer District Consolidated Gold Mines, ex p Smith* (1888) 39 Ch D 546; *Re Cleveland Trust plc* [1991] BCLC 424 (register rectified by deletion of bonus shares after bonus issue mistakenly made); *Re Thundercrest Ltd* [1995] 1 BCLC 117 (register rectified by cancellation of improper allotment to two members).

[121]   See *Re Copal Varnish Co Ltd* [1917] 2 Ch 349; *Welch v Bank of England* [1955] 1 All ER 811 (restoration of status quo after forged transfers); *International Credit and Investment Co (Overseas) Ltd v Adham* [1994] 1 BCLC 66 (restoration of status quo: no proper share transfers were executed merely entries made in share register purporting to deprive the true owner of his entire holding); *Re New Cedos Engineering Co Ltd* [1994] 1 BCLC 797 (on their true construction, a right to be registered existed under the articles); *Stothers v William Steward (Holdings) Ltd* [1994] 2 BCLC 266 (directors purported to exercise discretion to refuse registration which power, on the true construction of the articles, they did not possess).   [122]   [1989] BCLC 683.

15

Decision-making and company meetings

A Introduction

15-1 As discussed in Chapter 8, the typical division of power within a company is that the power to manage the company is vested in the board of directors with very limited powers retained by the shareholders (see **8-5**). Those powers include statutory rights, such as the right to alter the articles (CA 2006, s 21), or to increase or reduce the share capital,[1] and other powers, such as the power to appoint the directors, customarily given to the general meeting by the articles.[2] In some instances, the statute requires shareholder approval of various transactions, such as any purchase of the company's own shares[3] or transactions where directors have an acute conflict of interest.[4] Previously, the forum for the shareholders to exercise such powers as they possess was the general meeting of the company and the mechanism was by resolutions of the shareholders passed at such meetings. The Companies Act 1985 therefore provided a basic framework for meetings while allowing matters of detail to be determined by the company's articles.

15-2 For private companies, given the small numbers of shareholders commonly involved, it is accepted now that a formal general meeting is not a significant or appropriate forum for most decision-making. Instead, it should be possible for shareholders in such companies to reach decisions in any manner which is appropriate to their circumstances. In keeping with the 'think small first' philosophy (see **2-7**), the CA 2006 therefore provides that a resolution of the members of a private company may be passed as a written resolution or at a meeting (s 281(1)) and the underlying expectation is that the members will act through written resolutions and meetings will be the exception.[5] It is also possible for the shareholders unanimously to agree on any matter informally (see **15-73**).

15-3 For public companies, the scheme is quite different. In a public company, decisions must be made at a meeting of the members or a class of members, as the case may be (CA 2006, s 281(2)) and the CA 2006 precludes public companies from using written

---

[1] See CA 2006, ss 617–619 (increasing share capital) and s 641 (reduction of share capital).
[2] The Companies (Model Articles) Regulations 2008, SI 2008/3229, reg 2, Sch 1, arts 17–18 (Ltd); reg 4, Sch 3, arts 20–22 (Plc).   [3] CA 2006, ss 690–701.
[4] For example, substantial property transactions governed by CA 2006, s 190.
[5] For single member companies, details of decisions which have effect as if agreed to by the company in general meeting (for example, where the statute requires a shareholder resolution on some matter, such as a reduction of capital: CA 2006, s 641) must be provided to the company (unless the decision is reached by a written resolution) so as to ensure there is a record of the decision and it can be seen that there is compliance with the statutory requirements: CA 2006, s 357.

resolutions.[6] Moreover, public companies must hold an annual general meeting within six months of the financial year end (s 336(1)). For these companies, the annual general meeting of shareholders is intended to provide an opportunity for the shareholders not only to take decisions but to hold the directors to account for their stewardship of the company. Too often, the reality is that the shareholders are a remote dispersed group with individually little influence and collectively lacking a unified voice on matters of substance. The emphasis in recent years therefore has been on trying to ensure that the general meeting does act as an effective counterbalance to the board and considerable attention is now paid to this issue in the interests of good corporate governance, see **5-45**.

15-4 As discussed previously, shareholders in traded companies range from individual shareholders with a few hundred shares to institutional shareholders with millions of shares and it is not unusual to find that 80% of the company's shareholders are individuals but they hold only 20% of the shares (and the votes attached) while 20% of the shareholders are institutions holding 80% of the shares and the votes. The effectiveness of shareholder control through the general meeting to a large extent will be determined therefore by the willingness of the institutional investors (typically insurance companies and pension funds) to exercise their voting power (see the discussion of these corporate governance issues at **5-50**). In this chapter, we look at the mechanisms for meetings. If the general meeting is to assume its intended role as an important component of our corporate governance structures, the legal requirements set out in the CA 2006 must enhance its effectiveness and ensure that shareholders are heard and the rules must facilitate all shareholders, whether individual or institutional, in the exercise of their voting power.[7] The Shareholder Rights Directive (reflected in the CA 2006, as amended) also focused on improving the mechanisms of participation, especially cross-border participation, so as to facilitate and encourage shareholder engagement in traded companies.[8] In keeping with the general theme of shareholder engagement, the CA 2006 Pt 9 introduced measures aimed at engaging with indirect shareholders and that aspect is considered at **5-60**. Before proceeding, it should be noted that, while the CA 2006 provisions on decision-making concentrated on private, public and quoted companies,[9] implementation of the Shareholder Rights Directive required provision for traded companies[10] which is a slightly narrower category than quoted companies (though the essence of both is that the companies are admitted to trading on a regulated market) so the statute now

---

[6] There is some debate as to whether the prohibition applies only to resolutions required by the Companies Act 2006 as opposed to resolutions required by the company's articles, see **15-26**.

[7] Many of these issues were addressed in detail by the Company Law Review which favoured incremental reform of meeting procedures rather than wholesale changes: see Company Law Review, *Modern Company Law for a Competitive Economy, Final Report*, vol 1 (2001) URN 01/942, paras 7.5–7.16; *Completing the Structure* (2000) URN 00/1335, paras 5.18–5.40; *Developing the Framework* (2000) URN 00/656, paras 4.24–4.64; *Company General Meetings and Shareholder Communication* (1999) URN 99/1144.

[8] Directive 2007/36/EC on the exercise of certain rights of shareholders in listed companies, OJ L 184, 14.7.2007, p 17, implemented by The Companies (Shareholders' Rights) Regulations 2009, SI 2009/1632, with effect from 3 August 2009.

[9] Defined CA 2006, ss 361, 385 as a company whose equity share capital: (a) has been included in the official list in accordance with the provisions of FSMA 2000, Pt VI; or (b) is officially listed in an EEA State (i.e. EU with Norway, Iceland and Liechtenstein); or (c) is admitted to dealing on either the New York Stock Exchange or Nasdaq (an American stock exchange).

[10] Defined CA 2006, s 360C, as a company any shares of which carry rights to vote at general meetings and are admitted to trading on a regulated market in an EEA State (see n 9) by or with the consent of the company.

contains a sometimes confusing mix of provisions applicable to these distinct categories of companies.

15-5 Another change effected by the CA 2006 is a significant shift in emphasis in terms of the use of electronic communications.[11] Large companies have always been concerned about the costs involved in communicating with a widely dispersed shareholder base and electronic communication offers low cost and speedy methods of overcoming those problems. Likewise in small companies, the ease of electronic communication can and should be used to facilitate and expedite decision-making. The intention in the CA 2006 is to move more purposefully to greater use by companies (and greater uptake by shareholders) of electronic processes, for example by giving companies power to opt for website communication (if so authorised by the shareholders) with shareholders being deemed to assent unless they positively opt to have hard copies (see **15-6**). Companies may be deemed also to have accepted electronic communications from shareholders. For example, if a company gives an electronic address in a notice calling a meeting, or in an instrument of proxy sent out by the company, or in an invitation to appoint a proxy issued by the company, it is deemed to have agreed that any document or information relating to the meeting may be sent by electronic means to that address (s 333) and the largest companies are using this method to deal, for example, with proxy appointments.

15-6 The overall communications scheme (CA 2006, ss 1143–1148 and Schs 4 and 5) is somewhat complex, but essentially the Act allows companies to communicate with shareholders by hard copy, electronically or via a website or any other mechanism agreed with the recipient.[12] Hard copy documents may be handed to the shareholder or posted and hard copies are always available to shareholders free of charge even if they opt for other methods of communication.[13] Electronic communications such as email may be used if the shareholder opts in to such use and provides an email address.[14] Websites can be used to communicate with shareholders if the company's articles or a shareholder resolution allow for such use.[15] Where a company has that power, it must ask the shareholder individually whether he consents to website communication, but crucially if the shareholder declines to answer, he is deemed to have assented to website use.[16] In this way, shareholder inertia is turned into assent to website communication though any shareholder, at any time, can require communications in hard copy. Where shareholders have assented or have been deemed to have assented, the company must still send them a notification, either by letter or email, alerting them to the fact that information has been posted on the website.[17]

15-7 The largest companies already make extensive use of their websites as a means of communicating with their investors and this is both facilitated (as noted in **15-6**) and required by the legislation. The CA 2006 requires quoted companies to use their website to publish their annual accounts and reports (s 430); to report the results of polls taken at a general meeting and any independent assessor's report on such polls (ss 341, 351); and members of the company holding a certain percentage of the shares can require a statement to be put on the website setting out any audit concerns which they may have (s 527). A traded company must publish on a website a wide variety of information in advance of a meeting

---

[11] The use of electronic communication had been endorsed by the Companies Act 1985 (Electronic Communications) Order 2000, SI 2000/3373, but only to a limited extent and effect.

[12] CA 2006, Sch 5, paras 2, 5, 8, 15.   [13] CA 2006, s 1145(1), (3), also Sch 5, para 3.

[14] CA 2006, Sch 5, paras 6, 7.   [15] CA 2006, Sch 5, para 10(2).   [16] CA 2006, Sch 5, para 10(3).

[17] CA 2006, Sch 5, para 13.

including the contents of the notice of the meeting, details of the share capital and voting rights, as well as of members' statements, resolutions and matters of business received by the company (where not already included in the notice of the meeting) and that information mainly must be available on or before the date on which notice of the meeting is given and kept available for a period of two years after that date (s 311A).

B Voting entitlement

Voting in person

15-8 Subject to any provision in the company's articles, on a vote on a resolution on a show of hands at a meeting each member present in person has one vote and on a poll taken at a meeting (where the actual votes cast by each member are counted) every member has one vote for each share held by him (CA 2006, s 284(2), (3)). In practice, voting rights are spelt out expressly in the articles. The CA 2006 recognises that a member may hold shares on behalf of a number of beneficial owners and s 152 provides that a member holding shares in a company on behalf of more than one person is not required to exercise all the rights attached to the shares (which would include voting rights) in the same way.[18] A member is able therefore to cast votes for and against a resolution in accordance with the instructions of the beneficial owners.

15-9 Certain classes of shares may carry restricted voting rights; for example, it is commonly the case that preference shareholders may only vote on matters of direct concern to them, see **14-21**. Equally, the articles may confer enhanced rights; for example, a shareholder may be given three times the number of votes on a particular matter than is otherwise the case.[19]

Voting by proxy

15-10 Proxies are instruments executed by voting members of a company in favour of another person enabling that person to exercise the member's voting rights at a meeting. The position with respect to proxy rights was clarified and improved by the Companies Act 2006 and the company's articles can confer even more extensive rights (s 331). Any member of a company who is entitled to attend and vote at meetings (including class meetings) of the company may appoint another person, whether a member or not, as his proxy to exercise all or any of his rights to attend and to speak and vote at a meeting of the company (s 324). A proxy must vote in accordance with any instructions given by the member who appointed him (s 324A). A proxy is entitled to vote on a show of hands and on a poll (s 285) and a proxy can demand a poll and his demand is the same as a demand by a member (s 329). It is common to appoint the company chairman as a proxy, but given the right of a proxy to speak at a meeting, that may not be entirely appropriate since it could result in the chairman having to speak against a resolution. In the case of a company having a share capital, a member may appoint more than one proxy in relation to a meeting provided

---

[18] Nothing in CA 2006, s 284 is to be read as restricting the effect of s 152 (exercise of rights by nominees) or s 285(voting by proxy) or s 323 (voting by corporate representatives): s 284(5).

[19] See *Bushell v Faith* [1969] 1 All ER 1002 (shareholder had three times the number of votes he usually had on any resolution calling for his removal from the board, so giving him an effective veto on his own removal).

that each proxy is appointed with respect to different shares (s 324(2)). This flexibility is particularly important in larger companies where the registered shareholder is frequently a nominee for a number of beneficial owners and the ability to appoint multiple proxies allows their differing interests to be individually represented at the meeting.

15-11 The instrument appointing a proxy may be in writing or contained in an electronic communication.[20] The proxy must be lodged with the company ahead of the meeting and the company's articles may not contain any requirement that it be received by the company more than 48 hours before a meeting in order that the appointment be effective.[21] This is to ensure that the shareholders have flexibility and are not forced at an early date to decide whether they will attend or appoint a proxy. At the same time, the 48-hour window allows the company enough time to determine who is to attend and in what capacity. The notice of the meeting must draw attention to the rights to appoint a proxy (CA 2006, s 325). Termination of the appointment is governed by s 330.

Voting by corporate representatives

15-12 Companies may hold shares in other companies and such corporate shareholders may attend meetings through corporate representatives and a corporate representative is entitled to exercise the same powers as if the corporation were an individual member of the company (CA 2006, s 323 (1), (2)). It is also possible for a corporation to appoint multiple corporate representatives though the voting position can become difficult in that situation and they must be careful to vote on a poll in respect of different shareholdings. If, on a poll, they purport to exercise voting powers in respect of the same shares and they exercise that power in different ways, the power is treated as not having been exercised at all (s 323(4)). A better solution is not to appoint corporate representatives, given the uncertainties and ambiguities in s 323, but to appoint multiple proxies.[22] The problem with using proxies is that notice of the appointment must be given to the company not later than a clear 48 hours before the meeting (s 327(2)) which in some circumstances may be impractical.

Polls

15-13 Resolutions at meetings can be and in smaller companies are normally passed on a show of hands but a poll (where the votes cast are counted) may be demanded in a meeting to obtain a more accurate picture reflecting the members' shareholdings.[23] Increasingly

---

[20] Notice of the appointment of a proxy may be by electronic communication where the company is agreeable to appointments being made in this way and has provided an address for this purpose: CA 2006, s 333. As to the content and form of a proxy, see The Companies (Model Articles) Regulations 2008, SI 2008/3229, reg 2, Sch 1, art 45 (Ltd); reg 4, Sch 3, art 38 (Plc); and see the specific requirements re notice of appointment of a proxy in the case of a traded company: CA 2006, s 327(A1) . The Listing Rules, LR 9.3.6R, require a proxy to be a three way (for, against, withheld) in keeping with the requirements of the UK Corporate Governance Code, E.2.1.

[21] CA 2006, s 327(2)(a). Non-working days are excluded when calculating the earliest deadline that can be specified in the articles: s 327(3).

[22] That solution is suggested by the Explanatory Notes to the Companies Act 2006 which state 'If a corporation wishes to appoint people with different voting intentions or with authority to vote different blocks of shares, they should appoint proxies' (para 569).

[23] The model articles provide that a resolution put to a vote at a general meeting must be decided on a show of hands unless a poll is duly demanded: see The Companies (Model Articles) Regulations 2008, SI 2008/3229, reg 2, Sch 1, art 43 (Ltd), reg 4, Sch 3, art 34 (Plc).

larger companies vote only on a poll so as to avoid complexities in counting votes on a show of hands where multiple proxies or corporate representatives are present.

15-14   The company's articles cannot exclude the right to demand a poll at a general meeting, save in respect of the election of the chairman and the adjournment of the meeting.[24] Furthermore, the articles cannot make ineffective a demand for a poll which is made either by not less than five voting members, or by a member or members representing not less than 10% of the total voting rights of all members having the right to vote on the resolution, or by a member or members holding shares conferring a right to vote on the resolution, being shares on which an aggregate sum has been paid up equal to not less than 10% of the total sum paid up on all the shares conferring that right (CA 2006, s 321(2)). On a poll taken at a general meeting of the company, a member entitled to more than one vote need not, if he votes, use all his votes or cast all the votes he uses in the same way (s 322).

15-15   Where a poll is taken at a general meeting of a quoted company or a traded company the company must ensure that information on the outcome of the poll is made available on a website (CA 2006, s 341). In particular, the number of votes cast in favour and the number of votes cast against the resolution must be set out and, in the case of a traded company, more detailed voting information is required (s 341(1A)). Further provision is made for the proper scrutiny of polls of quoted companies in the light of concerns expressed as to the accuracy of polls.[25] Members of a quoted company representing not less than 5% of the total voting rights of all the members who have the right to vote on the matter, or not less than 100 members having the right to vote on the matter and holding shares paid up on average per member of not less than £100,[26] may require the directors to obtain an independent report on any poll taken or to be taken at a general meeting of the company (s 342). Any report made by the independent assessor on a poll must be made available on the company's website (s 351). This mechanism may prove valuable to companies where the resolution is controversial or the margin of victory, or defeat, narrow. For example, there is considerable interest in the precise voting pattern on the advisory vote on the directors' remuneration report in the case of quoted companies (see **5-41**). It is also now possible for the company's articles to make provision that voting on a resolution on a poll in a meeting may include votes cast in advance[27] and, in the case of a traded company, such provision can be subject only to such requirements and restrictions as are necessary to verify the identify of the person voting (s 322A).

---

[24]   CA 2006, s 321(1)(a) and (b). The Companies (Model Articles) Regulations 2008, SI 2008/3229, reg 2, Sch 1, art 45(2) (Ltd), reg 4, Sch 3, art 36(2) (Plc) allow a poll to be demanded by the chairman, the directors, two or more persons having the right to vote on the resolution or a person or persons representing not less than one-tenth of the total voting rights of all shareholders.

[25]   There has been concern about 'lost' votes, i.e. that the chain of intermediaries is now so long from beneficial owner through to the registered shareholder that voting instructions and/or votes get lost along the way so that either votes are not cast in accordance with instructions, or votes are not counted because of a confusion of instructions, or agents are not acting on instructions. The matter was the subject of a series of reports by Paul Myners, see Myners, *Review of Impediments to Voting UK Shares* (2004) with follow-up reports in 2005 (twice) and in 2007. The hope is that this new procedure will help provide greater assurance as to the accuracy of polls.

[26]   Indirect investors, subject to the requirements of CA 2006, s 153 being met, may count towards the 100 figure: CA 2006, s 342(2).

[27]   As to the time constraints, see CA 2006, s 322A(3)—essentially the company cannot impose a cut-off point for casting a vote in advance any earlier than 48 hours before the meeting or if the poll is not taken for 48 hours after it is demanded, 24 hours before the time for taking the poll.

C Resolutions

15-16 Resolutions fall into two categories, ordinary and special,[28] and, in the case of a private company, may be passed either in writing or at a meeting (CA 2006, s 281(1)). A public company may not use written resolutions and must pass resolutions (including resolutions of a class of members) at a meeting (s 281(2)), but see **15-26**. A resolution at a meeting is validly passed if notice of the meeting and of the resolution is given and the meeting is held and conducted in accordance with the provisions of the CA 2006 governing the conduct of meetings and annual general meetings (i.e. Pt 13, Chs 3 and 4) and the company's articles (s 301).

Ordinary resolutions

15-17 If the Companies Act requires 'a resolution' and does not specify what type of resolution, this means an ordinary resolution unless the articles require a higher majority or unanimity (CA 2006, s 281(3)), but if the statute specifies an ordinary resolution or a special resolution, that requirement is mandatory and the articles cannot impose a different majority requirement than that specified in the Act,[29] though anything that may be done by an ordinary resolution may equally be done by a special resolution (s 282(5)).

15-18 An ordinary resolution is a resolution passed by a simple majority of the members or a class of members (s 282(1)). A written resolution is passed by a simple majority if it is passed by members representing a simple majority of the total voting rights of eligible members (s 282(2)).[30] A resolution passed at a meeting on a show of hands is passed by a simple majority if it is passed by a simple majority of the votes cast by those entitled to vote (s 282(3)). A resolution passed on a poll is passed by a simple majority if it is passed by members representing a simple majority of the total voting rights of members who being entitled to do so vote in person, by proxy or in advance (see **15-15**) on the resolution (s 282(4)).

15-19 There are no specific notice requirements for a resolution and the company will give notice of the resolution to the shareholders at the same time as it gives notice of the meeting (see **15-56**). In a few instances, the statute requires that special notice is given *to* the company of an ordinary resolution, for example on any resolution to remove a director [31] or an auditor.[32] A company's articles may also make provision for special notice. Special notice, for the purposes of the CA 2006, requires that notice of the intention to move the resolution is given to the company at least 28 days before the meeting (s 312(1)).

---

[28] Previously, there were also extraordinary and elective resolutions. Elective resolutions were used by private companies to elect to opt out of certain provisions of the companies legislation: CA 1985, s 379A. Extraordinary resolutions required a 75% majority and 14 days' notice—they remain effective where a company's articles or a contract make provision for them: see the Companies Act 2006 (Commencement No 3, Consequential Amendments, Transitional Provisions and Savings) Order 2007, SI 2007/2194, art 9, Sch 3, para 23.

[29] See Explanatory Notes to the Companies Act 2006, para 523.

[30] 'Eligible members' in relation to a written resolution of a private company is defined by CA 2006, s 289 as the members who would have been entitled to vote on the resolution on the circulation date (defined s 290 as the date on which the written resolution is sent to the members).

[31] CA 2006, s 168(2), or to appoint someone in his stead at the meeting at which he is removed.

[32] CA 2006, s 511(1). Special notice is also required of a resolution to appoint as auditor a person other than the retiring auditor: s 515(2).

Special resolutions

15-20 A special resolution means a resolution passed by a majority of not less than 75% (CA 2006, s 283(1)) and it is required by the legislation on a number of occasions typically involving a matter of some significance, such as constitutional changes,[33] changes to the capital structure of the company[34] or where the company resolves to go into winding up.[35]

15-21 A special resolution which is passed as a written resolution must be passed by a majority of not less than 75% of the total voting rights of eligible members (s 283(2)).[36] Where a resolution of a private company is passed as a written resolution, the resolution is not a special resolution unless it is stated that it was proposed as a special resolution and, if the resolution so states, it may only be passed as a special resolution (s 283(3)).

15-22 A resolution passed at a meeting on a show of hands must be passed by a majority of not less than 75% of the votes cast by those entitled to vote (s 283(4)). A resolution passed on a poll is passed by a majority of not less than 75% if it is passed by members representing not less than 75% of the total voting rights of members who being entitled to do so vote in person, by proxy or in advance on the resolution (s 283(5)).

15-23 A resolution passed at a meeting is not a special resolution unless the notice of the meeting includes the text of the resolution and specifies the intention to propose the resolution as a special resolution and, if the notice of the meeting so states, the resolution may only be passed as a special resolution (s 283(6)). If the resolution is to be validly passed, it must be the same resolution as that identified in the notice of the meeting.[37]

Written resolutions

15-24 As noted at the beginning of this chapter, the emphasis in the CA 2006 is on the use of written resolutions by private companies which is intended to expedite decision-making in such companies and to enable them to avoid the formalities involved in calling a meeting. The key advantages are speed (no notice of a meeting is required) and costs (likely to be minimal). Subject to two exceptions, any resolution may be passed as a written resolution (CA 2006, s 281(1)) and any provision in the company's articles precluding the use of written resolutions is void (s 300). The exceptions are that written resolutions may not be used (s 288(2)): (1) to remove a director under s 168; and (2) to remove an auditor from office under s 510 since, in these instances, the directors and auditors have the right to make representations at, or to, a general meeting.[38]

15-25 A major change effected by the CA 2006 is that written resolutions need no longer be unanimous, as was the case under the CA 1985. A written resolution requires the same majority (simple or not less than 75%) as is required for an ordinary or special resolution passed at a meeting. The change means that in many private companies (depending on

---

[33] For example, a special resolution is required on an alteration of the articles of association: CA 2006, s 21(1); on a change of name: s 77(1); on the re-registration of a public company as a private company: s 97(1).

[34] For example, a special resolution is required on disapplying the statutory pre-emption rights: CA 2006, s 570; on a reduction of share capital: s 641; on the occasion of an off-market purchase of a company's own shares: s 694.

[35] For example, a special resolution is required where a company resolves that it be wound up voluntarily: IA 1986, s 84(1)(b); and where a company resolves that the company be wound up by the court: s 122(1)(a).

[36] As to the definition of 'eligible members' see n 30.

[37] *Re Moorgate Mercantile Holdings Ltd* [1980] 1 All ER 40.   [38] See CA 2006, ss 169, 511(3), (5).

shareholder composition, of course) the resolution will effectively be passed before it is even circulated since minority shareholders by definition cannot block an ordinary resolution and may not (depending on their percentage holding) be in a position to block a special resolution. Of course, the same would be true of a resolution proposed at a meeting, but at least a meeting requires the majority to put forward some case for the action being undertaken and to hear opposing views. The minority may find it doubly frustrating to be outvoted and not heard. Some balance is restored, however, as members representing at least a 5% holding can require a written resolution of their own to be circulated (see CA 2006, s 292 and **15-29**) and can require a meeting to be held (see s 303 and **15-46**).

15-26 The statutory scheme for written resolutions for private companies is mandatory with CA 2006, s 288(1) stating that a written resolution is a resolution proposed and passed in accordance with Pt 13, Ch 2 which means that companies must follow the statutory scheme rather than any written resolution provisions which companies may have in their articles. The CA 2006 no longer permits public companies to use written resolutions (s 281(2)), at least for resolutions required by the Act. This is a change to the previous law which permitted public companies to include provisions for written resolutions in their articles though their practical use was limited by the requirement that such resolutions had to be passed unanimously. Nevertheless in some circumstances they were of use to public companies. There seems no reason why public companies cannot use written resolutions for matters other than statutory requirements, if their articles so provide. In so far as it is permissible and practicable, public companies can rely also on informal unanimous shareholder assent (see **15-73**).

15-27 Given the obligation to follow the statutory scheme on written resolutions, the key points to note are:

- A copy of the resolution must be sent to every eligible member (i.e. every member entitled to vote on the resolution, CA 2006, s 289);[39] accompanied by a statement as to how the member may signify agreement and a date by which the resolution must be passed otherwise it lapses under s 297 (s 291(4)).[40] If the resolution is to be a special resolution, it must so state (s 283(3)).

- The resolution may be circulated in hard copy or electronically or by way of a website, subject to compliance with the rules on electronic communications noted at **15-6**, and it must be sent at the same time (so far as reasonably practical) to all members.[41]

- Certain statutory schemes, such as those relating to a purchase by a company of its own shares (see **20-9**), require documents to be available for inspection by shareholders at the general meeting. Where a written resolution is used, copies of such documents as would otherwise be available at a general meeting must be circulated to the members at or before the time when the resolution is supplied for signature.[42]

---

[39] A copy of the proposed resolution must be sent to the company's auditors: CA 2006, s 502, but merely for information. The auditor cannot delay the process and is not required to assent in any way to it so a failure to provide a copy has no consequence.

[40] But note that the validity of the resolution, if passed, is not affected by a failure to comply with these requirements, see CA 2006, s 291(7).

[41] If the resolution is sent via a website, it is not validly sent unless it is available on the website throughout the period from the circulation date (defined CA 2006, s 290) to the date on which the resolution lapses under s 297: s 299.

[42] For examples, see disapplication of pre-emption rights (CA 2006, 571(7)); off-market purchases of own shares (s 696(2)); redemption or purchase of own shares out of capital (s 718(2)); approval of directors' long-term service contracts (s 188(5)).

- A written resolution lapses if the time-limit imposed by the articles elapses or, if there is no such limit, within 28 days of the circulation date (i.e. the date when the resolution is first sent to any member: s 290): s 297.

15-28 A written resolution of a private company is passed when the required majority of eligible members signify their agreement to it (CA 2006, s 296(4)) and they do so when the company receives an authenticated document,[43] whether in hard copy or electronic form, identifying the resolution and indicating agreement to it (s 296(1), (2)).[44] Once a member has signified his agreement to a written resolution, he may not revoke his agreement (s 296(3)). A written resolution of a private company has effect as if passed by the company in general meeting or by a meeting of a class of members (s 288(5)). The company must keep a copy of all written resolutions for at least 10 years (s 355(1), (2)).

Circulation of members' written resolutions

15-29 Directors may circulate a written resolution at any time (s 291) but an important innovation in the CA 2006 is that members holding 5% of the total voting rights of members entitled to vote on the resolution (or such lesser figure as specified in the articles) may require the company to circulate a proposed written resolution and with it a statement of not more than 1,000 words on the subject matter of the resolution (s 292). Such matter is to be circulated at the members' expense, however, unless the company otherwise resolves (s 294(1)). If the company has not so resolved, it need not circulate the resolution and statement until the members deposit or tender a sum reasonably sufficient to meet the company's expenses in circulating it (s 294(2)). However, the costs may be modest if the shareholders have agreed to electronic or website communications and non-existent if the company has few members.

15-30 The company, or any person aggrieved, may apply to the court for an order that the company is not bound to circulate any statement on the ground that the right to have a resolution and statement circulated are being abused (s 295(1)) and there is potential for the members concerned to be penalised in costs (s 295(2)), a possibility that should prevent vexatious use of these provisions.

15-31 If the company fails to comply with the requirement to circulate the resolution and statement when otherwise required to do so, every officer in default is liable to a fine (s 293(1), (5)).

Registering resolutions

15-32 The resolutions and agreements listed in CA 2006, s 29 must be registered with the registrar of companies under s 30, see discussion at **4-6**. Essentially this applies to any special resolution; any resolution or agreement whether of the company or of a class of shareholders which is effective because of the *Duomatic* principle[45] that informal unanimous assent is tantamount to a resolution, see **15-73**; any resolution varying class rights which is not a special resolution; and other resolutions (i.e. ordinary resolutions) which are required by statute to be registered (s 29).

---

[43] If the company gives an electronic address in the document containing or accompanying the written resolution, it is deemed to have agreed to a response being made to that address: see CA 2006, s 298.
[44] There is no requirement for a signature, merely that agreement is signified which could be by email or even a text message, where electronic communications are permitted.
[45] *Re Duomatic Ltd* [1969] 1 All ER 161.

15-33 A copy of the resolution (or, if not in writing, a memorandum setting out its terms) must be registered with the registrar of companies within 15 days after it is passed. A failure to comply with the registration requirement is an offence (CA 2006, s 30(2)).

D General meetings

Meeting convened by the directors

15-34 The directors may at any time convene a meeting of the company (CA 2006, s 302) and, in the case of a public company, the directors must call an annual general meeting and they must also call a general meeting when a public company suffers a serious loss of capital (s 656) though this latter requirement is sometimes ignored in practice. Under the CA 1985 and the 1985 Table A, all general meetings other than the annual general meeting were called extraordinary general meetings,[46] but that terminology is not carried forward to the CA 2006 which describes company meetings as general meetings or the annual general meeting, as the case may be.

Annual general meeting

15-35 A public company must hold an annual general meeting within six months of its accounting reference date, i.e. the financial year end (CA 2006, s 336(1)). Non-compliance is an offence.[47] Private companies (unless they are a traded company[48]) are not required to hold an annual general meeting, but may do so if they choose or if their articles require.

15-36 Convening a general meeting is a matter for the directors (s 302) and, in the appropriate case, the notice calling the meeting must specify that it is the annual general meeting (s 337(1)). The notice requirements for general meetings are discussed at **15-56.**

15-37 The statute does not dictate the business to be conducted at an annual general meeting but the typical business of such a meeting includes:

- laying the annual accounts, the directors' report, the auditors' report and, if the company is a quoted company, the directors' remuneration report, before the meeting;[49]
- re-electing retiring directors and electing new directors;[50]
- appointing an auditor, if required to do so,[51] and setting the auditor's remuneration[52] although in practice that matter is often delegated to the board; and
- declaring a dividend.[53]

---

[46] See, for example, CA 1985, s 368; Table A, reg 36.

[47] CA 2006, s 336(4). Repeated failures to hold annual general meetings may amount to unfairly prejudicial conduct under what is now CA 2006, s 994: see *Re a company (No 00789 of 1987), ex p Shooter* [1990] BCLC 384.

[48] A private company which is a traded company must hold an annual general meeting within nine months of the year end: CA 2006, 336. This provision derives from the implementation of the Shareholders' Rights Directive, see n 8, but it would be exceptional here for a private company to be a traded company.

[49] CA 2006, ss 437(1), 471(2).

[50] CA 2006, s 160. See The Companies (Model Articles) Regulations 2008, SI 2008/3229, reg 2, Sch 1, art 17 (Ltd); reg 4, Sch 3, arts 20–22 (Plc).   [51] See CA 2006, ss 485(1), 489(1).

[52] CA 2006, s 492(1).

[53] See The Companies (Model Articles) Regulations 2008, SI 2008/3229, reg 2, Sch 1, art 30 (Ltd); reg 4, Sch 3, art 70 (Plc).

15-38 Any other matter may be included in the business of a general meeting provided proper notice of the matter is given. Public companies typically include resolutions relating to the allotment of shares, disapplying to a certain extent the statutory pre-emption rights and allowing a company to purchase its own shares.[54] It is now common also to include a resolution authorising the calling of general meetings, other than an annual general meeting, on not less than 14 clear days' notice, a consequence of changes effected by the Shareholders' Rights Directive, see **15-56**, However, institutional shareholders, while willing to grant authority for meetings on 14 days' notice, caution against routine use of the power which can prevent shareholders having sufficient time to consider the issues before them. Quoted companies must submit the directors' remuneration report for shareholder approval by way of an ordinary resolution (s 439), see **5-41**.

15-39 Notice of the meeting must state the intention to propose any special resolution and must set out the text of any special resolution to be considered at the meeting. For other matters, a difficult issue is the degree of detail which must be given with respect to matters other than the standard matters of business for, if the notice given is misleading, the court can restrain the holding of the meeting[55] and resolutions incorrectly notified are invalid and not binding on the company.[56] The key requirement is that the notice must disclose all relevant facts so that a member can exercise an informed business judgement as to whether he ought to attend the meeting[57] and this requires a fair, candid and reasonable explanation of the purpose or purposes for which the meeting is summoned.[58] Particular attention must be given to full and frank notice of any resolution involving a personal advantage to a director.[59] For example, a notice to the shareholders of an agreement to sell the business which failed to disclose the substantial payments which would be made to the directors personally as part of the agreement was invalid.[60]

15-40 Members holding a certain size of shareholdings have various rights as to the circulation of resolutions and statements and the inclusion of matters on the agenda for a meeting.

Circulation of resolutions, inclusion of agenda matters at an annual general meeting

15-41 Members of a public company representing not less than 5% of the total voting rights of all the members entitled to vote on the resolution or not less than 100 members[61] having the right to vote on the resolution holding shares paid up to the sum, per member, of at least £100 (CA 2006, s 338(3)), may require the company to give notice of a resolution to be moved at the next annual general meeting. It must be a resolution that may properly be moved and is intended to be moved at the annual general meeting so excluding resolutions which would be ineffective (because inconsistent with an enactment, the company's constitution or otherwise), defamatory, frivolous or vexatious (s 338(1), (2)). The request to give notice of the resolution may be in hard copy or electronic form, must identify the

---

[54] See CA 2006, ss 551, 571, 701 respectively.

[55] *Jackson v Munster Bank* (1884) 13 LR IR 118.

[56] *Baillie v Oriental Telephone and Electric Co Ltd* [1915] 1 Ch 503.

[57] *Tiessen v Henderson* [1899] 1 Ch 861.

[58] *Kaye v Croydon Tramways Company* [1898] 1 Ch 358 at 373, per Rigby LJ.

[59] *Baillie v Oriental Telephone and Electric Co Ltd* [1915] 1 Ch 503; *Tiessen v Henderson* [1899] 1 Ch 861; *Kaye v Croydon Tramways Company* [1898] 1 Ch 358.

[60] *Kaye v Croydon Tramways Company* [1898] 1 Ch 358.

[61] Indirect investors, subject to the requirements of CA 2006, s 153 being met, may count towards the 100 figure.

resolution of which notice is to be given and it must be authenticated by the persons making it (CA 2006, s 338(4)). The request must be received by the company not later than six weeks before the annual general meeting to which it relates or, if later, the time at which notice is given of that meeting (s 338(4)).

15-42 In addition to this right to require the circulation of a resolution, in the case of a traded company, there is a right to request the inclusion of any matter in the business to be dealt with at an annual general meeting which may properly be included in the business, again excluding the defamatory, frivolous and vexatious, and subject to the same membership thresholds as outlined in 15–41 (s 338A). The request in this case must be accompanied by a statement setting out the grounds for the request.

15-43 The company must carry the costs of circulation if the notice of the resolution, or the request to add to the agenda, is received before the end of the financial year preceding the annual general meeting (CA 2006, ss 340(1), 340B(1)) and, if not, the members must bear the costs of circulation unless the company otherwise resolves. If the company has not so resolved, it need not circulate the resolution or request until the members deposit or tender a sum reasonably sufficient to meet the company's expenses of circulation (ss 340(2), 340B(2)) and that potential expense may be an inhibiting factor, depending on the size of the company. Of course, if the company is using electronic or website communication, the costs may be modest, being limited in effect to circulating hard copies to those who have opted for that mode of delivery.

15-44 If the company fails to comply with the requirement to circulate the resolution or request when otherwise required to do so, every officer in default is liable to a fine (s 339(4), (5) and s 340A(3), (4)).

Circulation of statements, right to answers, at any general meeting

15-45 Subject to certain thresholds being met, members have a right under CA 2006, s 314 to circulate a statement of not more than 1,000 words to any general meeting of any company, public or private. This statement may be in addition to a resolution which the members (or other members) wish to circulate, it may be in respect of a resolution which the directors have given notice of or it may be in respect of any other business to be conducted at the meeting. The same requirements are imposed, as discussed at **15-41** et seq, with regard to the percentage of members required to trigger the right (s 314(2)), the restrictions on statements which are defamatory, vexatious etc (s 317), the position on costs so far as they apply to a public company (s 316) and that it is an offence by each officer in default if the company fails to circulate a statement when otherwise required to do so (s 315(3)). Further, at any general meeting of a traded company, the company must answer any question relating to the business being dealt with at the meeting put by a member subject to certain exceptions, as where to answer would be prejudicial to the good order of the meeting, would involve the disclosure of confidential information, would be undesirable in the interests of the company, etc (s 319A).

Meeting requisitioned by the members

15-46 The directors are required to call a general meeting once requested to do so by members representing at least 5% of the paid-up capital of the company as carries the right to vote in general meetings (CA 2006, s 303(2)). The obligation to convene the meeting can only arise if the request is valid and where it is ineffective because of a defect in its form then, despite the threshold requirements being met, the directors are not obliged to call a meeting.[62]

15-47   A request must state the general nature of the business to be dealt with at the meeting and must be authenticated by the persons making it.[63] It may include the text of a resolution that may properly be moved and is intended to be moved at the meeting (CA 2006, s 303(4)) excluding resolutions which would be ineffective (because inconsistent with an enactment, the company's constitution or otherwise), defamatory, frivolous or vexatious (s 303(5)). If the resolution is a special resolution, the notice of the meeting must so state (s 283(5)). Notice of any resolution included in the request must be included in the notice of the meeting.[64]

15-48   If within 21 days of becoming required to do so the directors do not call a meeting, to be held on a date not more than 28 days after the date of the notice convening the meeting, the members may themselves call a meeting (CA 2006, s 305(1)).

Meeting convened by the court

15-49   The court has a discretionary power under CA 2006, s 306 (previously CA 1985, s 371) to order a general meeting to be held in such manner as it thinks fit if it is impracticable to call a meeting in the normal way or to conduct the meeting in the manner prescribed by the company's articles or the CA 2006. The court may exercise this power either of its own motion, or on the application of any director, or on the application of any member of the company who would be entitled to vote at the meeting.[65] The court may direct, in particular, that one member of the company present be deemed to constitute a meeting (s 306(4)).

15-50   The intention behind the power is to allow a company 'to get on with managing its affairs without being frustrated by the impracticability of calling or conducting a general meeting in the manner prescribed by the articles and the Act'.[66] This power may be invoked, for example, where a company finds itself without directors able to convene a meeting, or there is uncertainty as to who are the members, or the members are overseas and the company is unable to serve notice on them.[67] Occasionally, the power of the court is invoked because of the potential for violence. In *Re British Union for the Abolition of Vivisection*,[68] for example, it was impractical to call a general meeting of all 9,000 members of the BUAV

---

[62]   *Rose v McGivern* [1998] 2 BCLC 593; *Isle of Wight Railway Co v Tahourdin* (1883) 25 Ch D 320; see also *PNC Telecom plc v Thomas* [2003] BCC 202.

[63]   CA 2006, s 303(4) and (6). A meeting convened on requisition cannot transact any business other than that covered by the terms of the requisition: *Ball v Metal Industries Ltd* 1957 SC 315, together with any resolutions which the directors might put forward and of which due notice has been given, see *Rose v McGivern* [1998] 2 BCLC 593.   [64]   CA 2006, ss 303(4)(b), 304(2), (3).

[65]   CA 2006, s 306(2). The mere fact that a petition alleging unfairly prejudicial conduct has been presented under s 994 does not automatically oust the court's jurisdiction, but it may be a relevant factor in determining whether the court should exercise its discretion to call a meeting: *Harman v BML Group Ltd* [1994] 2 BCLC 674, CA; *Re Whitchurch Insurance Consultants Ltd* [1993] BCLC 1359; cf. *Re Sticky Fingers Restaurant Ltd* [1992] BCLC 84.

[66]   *Vectone Entertainment Holding Ltd v South Entertainment Ltd* [2004] 2 BCLC 224 at 231; and see *Wheeler v Ross* [2011] EWHC 2527.

[67]   See *Harman v BML Group Ltd* [1994] 2 BCLC 674 at 677. It is not sufficient that the meeting is to be chaired by a director whom some of the shareholders wish to remove from office—this does not render it 'impracticable' to call a meeting: *Might SA v Redbus Interhouse plc* [2004] 2 BCLC 449; see also *Monnington v Easier plc* [2006] 2 BCLC 283.   [68]   [1995] 2 BCLC 1.

when a previous meeting had degenerated into near riot and had been stopped by the police.

15-51 This power of the court to convene a meeting is often used to resolve cases where shareholders have refused to attend meetings so rendering them inquorate. By absenting themselves, the shareholders hope to prevent the majority shareholders from exercising their voting powers on a particular issue, typically the removal of the absent shareholders from office as directors.[69] The courts have generally refused to allow absent shareholders to gain an effective veto over company business in this way and so will order a meeting to be held which is quorate despite the absence of those shareholders.[70]

15-52 In *Re Opera Photographic Ltd*,[71] for example, the company had an issued share capital of 100 hundred shares, divided 51/49 between the two parties who were also the directors. The articles provided that the quorum for a meeting of the directors or the shareholders was two. The parties fell out and the 51% shareholder wanted to hold a general meeting in order to remove the 49% shareholder from office as a director, but no meeting could be held because of the lack of a quorum. The court granted an application to convene a meeting of the company, taking the view that the quorum requirements in the articles of association could not be treated as conferring on the 49% shareholder a form of veto to prevent the holding of a meeting to consider removing him from office as a director. Likewise in *Re Whitchurch Insurance Consultants Ltd*[72] where a husband and wife were the only directors of the company and held 666 and 334 of the 1,000 issued shares of the company respectively: the personal and business relationship between them broke down and the husband wanted to hold a general meeting to pass a resolution removing his wife as a director. The quorum requirement was set at two members so no meeting could be held. The court agreed that an order convening a meeting should be made to allow a board of directors to be appointed.

15-53 There are limits to the discretion of the court under CA 2006, s 306, however, and there are two clear categories of cases where the discretion will not be exercised. In *Harman v BML Group Ltd*[73] the company's capital was divided into A and B shares and no shareholders' meeting was quorate without a B shareholder or proxy being present. The parties fell out and the other shareholders applied for an order under what is now CA 2006, s 306, allowing them to hold meetings without B. The Court of Appeal refused the application as the effect of ordering meetings without B would be to override a quorum requirement which, the court found, constituted a class right conferred on B so as to protect him from removal from office as a director. In *Ross v Telford*[74] a husband and wife were the directors of two companies and they were also equal shareholders of one of the companies. The quorum for board and general meetings of both companies was two with the result that both companies were potentially deadlocked at board and general meeting levels. The Court of Appeal refused an application by the husband for a court order convening a meeting with the view to appointing an additional director. It concluded that what is now CA 2006, s 306, is not an appropriate vehicle for resolving deadlock between two equal shareholders. It is a procedural section and is not designed to affect substantive voting rights or to shift the balance of power between shareholders by permitting a

---

[69] See *Re El Sombrero Ltd* [1958] Ch 900; also *Re HR Paul & Son* (1973) 118 Sol Jo 166.

[70] See, for example, *Smith v Butler* [2012] EWCA Civ 314 at [54]; *Vectone Entertainment Holding Ltd v South Entertainment Ltd* [2004] 2 BCLC 224.

[71] [1989] BCLC 763.   [72] [1993] BCLC 1359.   [73] [1994] 2 BCLC 674.

[74] [1998] 1 BCLC 82.

50% shareholder to override the wishes of the other 50% shareholder. The shareholders had agreed that power would be shared equally and potential deadlock was a matter which they must be taken to have been agreed on with the consent and for the protection of each of them.

15-54 The limits to the court's discretion therefore are that the court will not order a meeting under CA 2006, s 306 where to order a meeting would negate a class right conferred on a shareholder [75] or where it would shift the balance of power in a company which is deadlocked 50/50 by virtue of the parties' agreement. The Court of Appeal confirmed these limitations in *Union Music Ltd v Watson*[76] where the shareholdings were split 51% and 49% and the two shareholders were the only directors. A shareholders' agreement provided that the consent of both shareholders was required for any meeting of the shareholders and the quorum for board meetings was set by the articles at two. Once the parties fell out, this meant that the company was deadlocked at board and general meeting level.

15-55 Overruling the first instance decision, the Court of Appeal ordered that a general meeting be held for the sole purpose of appointing another director which meeting was to be attended by the 51% shareholder only. The court considered that the case was distinguishable from *Harman v BML Group Ltd*[77] and *Ross v Telford*.[78] Outside of the circumstances in those cases, the court said, a provision as to the consent of the shareholders to a meeting could be overridden by a court order so as to enable a company to have an effective board in a position to manage its affairs properly. One side or other has to prevail and Peter Gibson LJ could not see that the contractual provisions in the shareholders' agreement provided a sufficient reason why the power to order a meeting should not be exercised given that, on the facts in *Union Music*, neither of the exceptional circumstances limiting the court's discretion was applicable.

E Meeting procedures

Notice of meetings

Minimum periods of notice

15-56 In the case of an annual general meeting of a public company (or a traded company), the minimum notice period is at least 21 clear days (CA 2006, s 307(2)(a), s 307A(1)(b)).[79] In the case of a general meeting, whether of a private or public company, at least 14 clear days' notice must be given (s 307(1), (2)(b)). A traded company may only call general meetings on at least 14 days' notice if (a) the meeting is not an annual general meeting, (b) the company offers the facility for shareholders to vote by electronic means accessible to all

---

[75] See also *Alvona Developments Ltd v The Manhattan Loft Corporation (AC) Ltd* [2006] BCC 119 where, although there was no class right as such, the court did not think it would be appropriate to make an order (for a meeting to appoint further directors) when it would override an agreement between the parties that there would be one jointly appointed director. *Cf Smith v Butler* [2012] EWCA Civ 314.

[76] [2003] 1 BCLC 453, CA.

[77] [1994] 2 BCLC 674.   [78] [1998] 1 BCLC 82.

[79] The periods of notice prescribed must be clear both of to the day of notice and of to the day of the meeting: CA 2006, s 360. The UK Corporate Governance Code (see **5-14**) requires that notice of an annual general meeting be sent to the shareholders at least 20 working days before the meeting, see E.2.4.

shareholders,[80] and (c) shareholders have passed, at the preceding annual general meeting or a general meeting held since that meeting, a special resolution approving the calling of meetings on at least 14 days' notice (s 307A).[81] All these periods of notice are minimum periods and the articles may provide for longer periods (ss 307(3), 307A(6)). Failure to give timely notice invalidates the meeting and nullifies the proceedings.[82]

15-57 It is possible for general meetings (other than for traded companies) to be called at shorter notice (s 307(4)) with the consent of a majority in number of the members having the right to attend and vote at the meeting and holding at least 95% in nominal value of the shares carrying voting rights in public companies and 90% in private companies,[83] but an annual general meeting of a public company which is not a traded company can only be called on short notice if the shareholders are unanimous (s 337(2)). There is no statutory provision for traded companies to hold general meetings on shorter notice than the minimum prescribed (s 307A). Once there is agreement to short notice, there is no minimum period of notice which is required and it can be as brief as the members choose. Short notice can be particularly useful if the company needs to remove a director, approve a major transaction or authorise changes to the capital structure, but some institutional shareholders, as a matter of policy, oppose attempts to shorten notice periods.

Manner of notice

15-58 Notice of a general meeting must be given in hard copy form, electronically or by means of a website, or partly by one such means and partly by another (CA 2006, s 308).

Persons entitled to notice

15-59 Subject to any provision of the company's articles and any enactment, notice of a general meeting must be given to every member (including any person entitled to a share in consequence of the death or bankruptcy of a member, if the company has been notified of their entitlement) and every director (CA 2006, s 310). Notice of a general meeting must be given to the company's auditor who is entitled to attend and to be heard on any part of the business which concerns him as auditor, a potentially very wide category (s 502).

15-60 An omission (other than an accidental omission within CA 2006, s 313) to give notice to any person entitled to it invalidates the meeting and nullifies the proceedings.[84] Failure to give notice because of an error on the part of directors, for example where they were under the erroneous impression that someone had ceased to be a member of the company, is not an accidental omission for these purposes.[85]

---

[80] It suffices for these purposes if members can appoint a proxy by means of a website: CA 2006, s 307A(3).

[81] This position is a consequence of the implementation of the Shareholders' Rights Directive, article 3, **n 8**, which requires at least 21 days' notice for all general meetings of traded companies but gives Member States the option to allow traded companies to call meetings on 14 days' notice subject to these conditions. Hence a resolution of this nature has become a standard part of the business of an annual general meeting of traded companies so ensuring that they always have an existing authority to call general meetings on at least 14 days' notice, but there is some evidence of institutional shareholder opposition to these short notice resolutions on the basis that the time period is too short for shareholders to engage fully with the business of the meeting.

[82] *Smyth v Darley* (1849) 2 HLC 789. See too CA 2006, s 301.

[83] Private companies can increase that 90% threshold to 95% by their articles: CA 2006, s 307(6).

[84] CA 2006, s 301; *Smyth v Darley* (1849) 2 HLC 789.

[85] *Musselwhite v C H Musselwhite & Son Ltd* [1962] Ch 964.

Contents of notice

15-61 The notice must specify the time and date and place of the meeting and, subject to the company's articles (other than a traded company), must state the general nature of the business to be dealt with at the meeting (CA 2006, s 311(2)).[86] Every notice calling a meeting of a company (or of any class of the members) must contain a reasonably prominent statement that the member is entitled to appoint a proxy or proxies (see **15-10**) to attend and vote instead of him and that a proxy need not be a member (s 325). Where the meeting is the annual general meeting of a public company, the notice calling the meeting must so state (s 337). A quoted company, when giving notice of an accounts meeting, must draw attention to the right of the members to use the company website to draw attention to audit concerns.[87] A traded company which is required under s 388 to include any matter in the business to be conducted at the annual general meeting at the request of shareholders must give notice of the matter in the same manner and at the same time, or as soon as reasonably practicable thereafter, as it gives notice of the meeting (s 340A(1)). It must also publish the matter on the website which the company uses to publish information (as required by s 311A) in advance of the general meeting (s 340A(1)). There are very detailed requirements as to the content of the notice to be given by a traded company with respect to matters such as setting out the website address used by the company to communicate with the shareholders, the manner of attending and voting (including voting in advance), the formalities for appointing proxies and the right to ask questions at the meeting (see s 311(3)).

Location of meetings

15-62 In order for a meeting of members to be validly constituted, it is not necessary for all the members to be physically present in the same room. A valid meeting can be held using overflow rooms provided that all due steps are taken to direct those unable to get into the main meeting into the overflow room, and that there are adequate audio-visual links to enable those in all the rooms to see and hear what is going on in the other rooms and that there is appropriate opportunity to participate in the debate.[88]

Chairman of meetings

15-63 Subject to any provision in the articles stating who may or may not be chairman, any member may be elected to be chairman by a resolution passed at the meeting (CA 2006, s 319).[89] The articles commonly provide that the chairman of the board of directors or, in his absence, some other director nominated by the directors, is to act as the chairman of the meeting.[90] It is the chairman's duty to preserve order, to conduct proceedings

---

[86] A company whose shares are admitted to trading on a regulated market must provide information to holders on: (1) the place, time and agenda of meetings; (2) the total number of shares and voting rights; and (3) the rights of holders to participate in meetings: DTR 6.1.1.12R.

[87] See CA 2006, s 529; for the definition of 'quoted company,' see n 9; and for the 'accounts meeting' see CA 2006, s 437(3), essentially the general meeting of a public company at which the company's accounts are laid.

[88] *Byng v London Life Association Ltd* [1989] BCLC 400, CA.

[89] See The Companies (Model Articles) Regulations 2008, SI 2008/3229, reg 2, Sch 1, art 40 (Ltd); reg 4, Sch 3, art 31 (Plc).

[90] There is no requirement that the chairman be 'neutral' and he may occupy the chair even though the matter for discussion is the removal of all of the directors including himself and the appointment of a new board: *Might SA v Redbus Interhouse plc* [2004] 2 BCLC 449.

regularly, to deal with the business of the meeting and to take care that the sense of the meeting is properly ascertained with regard to any question before it.[91] In the case of a vote on a resolution by show of hands, a declaration by the chairman that the resolution has/has not passed or passed with a particular majority is conclusive evidence of that fact without proof of the number or proportion of the votes in favour of or against the resolution (s 320(1)).[92] In the event of a dispute, the solution is to demand a poll[93] (see **15-13**).

Adjournment of meetings

15-64 The chairman must adjourn if directed to do so by the meeting or if, within half an hour before the start, a quorum is not present, or if at any time during the meeting a quorum ceases to be present.[94]

15-65 The chairman may adjourn a meeting if the meeting consents to the adjournment or if it appears necessary to do so to protect the safety of any person attending the meeting or to ensure that the business of the meeting is conducted in an orderly manner.[95]

15-66 A chairman's decision to adjourn is invalid not only if it is taken in bad faith but also if he fails to take into account relevant factors, or takes into account irrelevant factors, or reaches a conclusion which no reasonable chairman could have reached, having regard to the purpose of his power to adjourn which is to ensure that the members have a proper opportunity to debate and vote on resolutions.[96]

15-67 In *Byng v London Life Association Ltd* [97] the Court of Appeal found that, in deciding to adjourn an overcrowded general meeting from the morning to the afternoon, the chairman had failed to take into account relevant factors. The court thought that there must be very special circumstances to justify a decision to adjourn the meeting to a time and place where, to the knowledge of the chairman, it could not be attended by a number of the members who had taken the trouble to attend the original meeting and who could not even lodge a proxy vote because it was too late to do so.[98]

15-68 No business is to be transacted at an adjourned meeting other than business which might properly have been transacted at the meeting from which the adjourned meeting took place. Resolutions passed at an adjourned meeting take effect from the date on which they are in fact passed and are not deemed passed on any earlier date (CA 2006, s 332).

---

[91] *National Dwelling Society v Sykes* [1894] 3 Ch 159. It appears (the wording is unclear) that the chairman has a casting vote at a general meeting on a resolution on a show of hands, see CA 2006, s 282(3) and s 283(4), but not on a poll, whereas under the 1985 Table A, reg 50, the chairman had a casting vote on a show of hands or on a poll. A saving provision in the Companies Act 2006 (Commencement No 3, etc) Order 2007, SI 2007/2194, art 9, Sch 3, para 23A allows companies (other than traded companies) which, immediately before 1 October 2007, had such a provision with respect to ordinary resolutions in their articles to retain it or reinsert it, if they have removed it from their articles.

[92] See The Companies (Model Articles) Regulations 2008, SI 2008/3229, reg 2, Sch 1, art 45(2) (Ltd); reg 4, Sch 3, arts 35 and 36(2)(Plc).

[93] A chairman may call a poll: see The Companies (Model Articles) Regulations 2008, SI 2008/3229, reg 2, Sch 1, art 42 (Ltd); reg 4, Sch 3, art 33 (Plc).

[94] See The Companies (Model Articles) Regulations 2008, SI 2008/3229, reg 2, Sch 1, art 42 (Ltd), reg 4, Sch 3, art 33 (Plc); *Salisbury Gold Mining Co Ltd v Hathorn* [1897] AC 268, PC.

[95] See The Companies (Model Articles) Regulations 2008, SI 2008/3229, reg 2, Sch 1, art 42 (Ltd), reg 4, Sch 3, art 33 (Plc).

[96] *Byng v London Life Association Ltd* [1989] BCLC 400, CA.   [97] [1989] BCLC 400.

[98] As to when a proxy must be lodged, see CA 2006, s 327 and **15-10**.

Quorum for meetings

15-69 Subject to the articles, two qualifying persons present at a meeting are a quorum,[99] but not if the two persons present are corporate representatives or proxies for the same member.[100] In other words, the requirement is that two separate members are represented. Any resolution passed at a meeting which is inquorate is void.[101]

15-70 One shareholder cannot form a meeting,[102] except:

- if there is only one shareholder in a class of shareholders, the assent of that shareholder is the equivalent of a meeting of the class;[103]
- if the company is a single member company (whether public or private, limited by shares or by guarantee), one qualifying person present is a quorum (CA 2006, s 318(1)); and
- where the court convenes a meeting under s 306 (see **15-49**), a direction may be given that one member present may constitute a quorum (s 306(4)).

Minutes of meetings

15-71 Every company is required to keep minutes of general meetings (CA 2006, s 355(1)(b)) and of directors' meetings (s 248). Any minute purporting to be signed by the chairman of the meeting at which such proceedings took place or by the chairman of the next succeeding meeting is evidence of those proceedings (s 356(4)). Where a sole member takes any decision which has effect as if agreed by the company in general meeting, he must provide the company with details of the decision (s 357(2)).

15-72 The minutes of general meetings are open to inspection by any member without charge, and a member is entitled, on payment of a small fee, to copies (s 358(3),(4)). Where inspection is refused, the court may by order compel inspection (s 358(7)).

F The *Duomatic* principle—informal unanimous assent

15-73 Recognising that shareholders do not always observe all of the formalities of meetings and resolutions as envisaged by the legislation, the courts accept that the informal unanimous assent of all shareholders who have a right to attend and vote at a general meeting of the company is as binding as a resolution of the company in general

---

[99] See The Companies (Model Articles) Regulations 2008, SI 2008/3229, reg 2, Sch 1, art 39 (Ltd); reg 4, Sch 3, art 30 (Plc). As to the quorum for a variation of class rights meetings, see CA 2006, s 334(4).

[100] CA 2006, s 318(2). The wording is unclear because it appears to provide that neither of the two representatives or proxies can count towards the quorum (neither being a qualifying person), as opposed to allowing them to count as one member personally present.

[101] *Re Cambrian Peat, Fuel and Charcoal Ltd, De La Mott's Case and Turner's Case* (1875) 31 LT 773; *Re Romford Canal Co, Pocock's Claims* (1883) 24 Ch D 85.

[102] *Sharpe v Dawes* (1876) 2 QBD 25; *Re London Flats Ltd* [1969] 2 All ER 744.

[103] *East v Bennett Bros* [1911] 1 Ch 163; *Re RMCA Reinsurance Ltd* [1994] BCC 378. The case of a single member of a class is exceptional. Otherwise the ordinary meaning of the word 'meeting' is the coming together of two or more persons: *Re Altitude Scaffolding Ltd, Re T & N Ltd* [2007] 1 BCLC 199 (court refused to sanction a scheme of arrangement under what is now CA 2006, s 899 which provided for class meetings requiring the attendance in person or by proxy of one member of a class only).

meeting provided the persons assenting are competent to effect the act to which they have assented.[104]

15-74   This principle that unanimous assent is tantamount to a resolution of a properly convened general meeting[105] is known as the *Duomatic* principle[106] and companies and shareholders often need to resort to it to validate actions which are otherwise not in conformity with the requirements of the articles,[107] or the Companies Act[108] (discussed at 15–76), or a shareholders' agreement.[109]

15-75   Assent by the shareholders[110] for these purposes may be given formally or informally (i.e. without any meeting at all) and it need not be given simultaneously but at different times.[111] Assent need not be in writing, it may be oral, or tacit, in the form of acquiescence by the shareholders with knowledge of the matter,[112] but a mere internal decision by a shareholder cannot constitute assent, there must be material from which assent can be objectively ascertained or (in the case of acquiescence) inferred.[113] The principle cannot apply where the assent of the shareholders has never been sought[114] or where there is no evidence of any discussion or knowledge of the facts to enable them to assent.[115] It is not enough for *Duomatic* purposes to show that assent would probably have been given if asked, there has to be an actual assent,[116] an unqualified agreement, objectively established.[117] Also, the persons assenting must be competent to effect the act to which they have assented,[118] i.e. it must be an act which the general meeting could have carried into effect and, as shareholders

---

[104] *Re Express Engineering Works Ltd* [1920] 1 Ch 466; *Re Oxted Motor Co Ltd* [1921] 3 KB 32; *Parker & Cooper v Reading* [1926] Ch 975; *Re Duomatic Ltd* [1969] 1 All ER 161 at 168, per Buckley J; *Re New Cedos Engineering Co Ltd* [1994] 1 BCLC 797. Strictly speaking, registration of such assent is required in certain cases, see CA 2006, s 29(1)(b) and s 30, but this registration requirement is rarely, if ever, observed.

[105] Or of a class of shareholders: *Re Torvale Group Ltd* [1999] 2 BCLC 605. The principle also applies to informal decisions of directors, see *Runciman v Walter Runciman plc* [1992] BCLC 1084 at 1092.

[106] Though, as is frequently pointed out, the origins of the principle are much earlier than the *Duomatic* decision, see n 104.   [107] See *Re Duomatic Ltd* [1969] 1 All ER 161.

[108] See *Wright v Atlas Wright (Europe) Ltd* [1999] 2 BCLC 301, CA.

[109] See *Re Euro Brokers Holdings Ltd v Monecor (London) Ltd* [2003] 1 BCLC 506, CA (shareholders had accepted as valid and were bound by a call for capital made by email though a shareholders' agreement provided for capital calls to be made by formal notice from the board).

[110] It is debatable whether the assent of beneficial (as opposed to registered) owners will suffice. Lindsay J thought (probably) not in *Domoney v Godinho* [2004] 2 BCLC 15 at [44]–[45], but Mann J, obiter, in *Shakar v Tsitsekkos* [2004] EWHC 2659 at [67] thought there was no reason why the assent of the beneficial shareholders might not suffice, for example, where the nominee shareholder leaves all decisions to his beneficiary, and Newey J, obiter, in *Re Tulsesense Ltd, Rolfe v Rolfe* [2010] 2 BCLC 525 at [42]–[43] was willing to assume, without deciding, that the assent of all the beneficial owners meets the *Duomatic* requirement.

[111] *Parker & Cooper Ltd v Reading* [1926] Ch 975.

[112] See *EIC Services Ltd v Phipps* [2004] 2 BCLC 589; *Re Ravenhart Service (Holdings) Ltd* [2004] 2 BCLC 376 at [89], [93]; *Re Torvale Group Ltd* [1999] 2 BCLC 605; *Re Bailey Hay & Co Ltd* [1971] 3 All ER 693.

[113] *Schofield v Schofield* [2011] 2 BCLC 319 at [32] approving Newey J *in Re Tulsesense Ltd, Rolfe v Rolfe* [2010] 2 BCLC 525 at [41].

[114] *EIC Services Ltd v Phipps* [2004] 2 BCLC 589 at 623–4, Ch D, per Neuberger J (appealed on unrelated grounds). Shareholder authorisation was required for the capitalisation of reserves and an allotment of bonus shares and, while the shareholders knew of the proposed bonus issue, their consent to the issue was neither sought nor given so, the court concluded, there could be no reliance on *Duomatic* to cure the omission of the necessary shareholder resolutions.   [115] *Queensway Systems Ltd v Walker* [2007] 2 BCLC 577.

[116] *EIC Services Ltd v Phipps* [2004] 2 BCLC 589 at 627; and see *Re D'Jan of London Ltd* [1994] 1 BCLC 561 at 564; see *Secretary of State for Business, Innovation and Skills v Doffman (No 2)* [2011] 2 BCLC 541 at [40]: cannot rely on *Duomatic* if the shareholders have never addressed their minds to the matter.

[117] *Schofield v Schofield* [2011] 2 BCLC 319.

[118] *Re New Cedos Engineering Co Ltd* [1994] 1 BCLC 797; and see *Wright v Atlas Wright (Europe) Ltd* [1999] 2 BCLC 301 at 314–15, CA.

cannot approve, even unanimously, an ultra vires distribution,[119] or an act in fraud of the creditors,[120] the principle can have no application in such circumstances.

15-76 A particular issue is the extent to which statutory requirements as to how a transaction or scheme might be carried out can be overridden by informal consent in this way. The principle cannot apply where the statutory requirement is clearly strict and mandatory.[121] In cases where the position is less clear, the court will consider the purpose and underlying rationale of the statutory formality in question and will refuse to allow reliance on the *Duomatic* principle to override statutory provisions where that rationale extends beyond the protection of the class which has purported to waive the provision.[122]

15-77 Hence the court has accepted that unanimous informal assent may suffice in place of the statutory requirement, now in CA 2006, s 188, for shareholder approval of a director's service contract for the purpose of that provision does not extend beyond the benefit and protection of the shareholders of the company,[123] likewise CA 2006, s 190 which requires shareholder approval of certain substantial property transactions between a director and his company.[124] In these cases the statutory formality of a resolution in general meeting is open to waiver by the class for whose protection it is designed. With respect to the statutory scheme for the purchase of a company's own shares, the courts have allowed informal unanimous shareholder assent to override some of the procedural requirements surrounding such purchases, but not where the relevant procedural requirement was intended to protect a wider class of persons, in particular the company's creditors, rather than merely the shareholders.[125]

15-78 The Company Law Review concluded that the *Duomatic* principle should be codified,[126] but the Government rejected that recommendation on the grounds that the common law position is very flexible (as can be seen from the case law) and codification would lead to rigidity and restrictions on the operation of this very beneficial principle.[127] Hence the Companies Act 2006 confirms that nothing in the provisions governing resolutions and meetings affects any enactment or rule of law as to things done otherwise than by passing a resolution (CA 2006, s 281(4)(a)).[128]

---

[119] *Re Exchange Banking Company, Flitcroft's Case* (1882) 21 Ch D 519; *Aveling Barford Ltd v Perion Ltd* [1989] BCLC 626 at 630–1; *Bairstow v Queens Moat Houses* [2001] 2 BCLC 531 at [36], *Secretary of State for Business, Innovation and Skills v Doffman (No 2)* [2011] 2 BCLC 541 at [41].

[120] *Rolled Steel Products (Holdings) Ltd v British Steel Corp* [1985] 3 All ER 52 at 86; *Secretary of State for Business, Innovation and Skills v Doffman (No 2)* [2011] 2 BCLC 541 at [44].

[121] For example, in *Re Oceanrose Investments Ltd* [2008] EWHC 3475, [2009] Bus LR 947, Richards J considered a requirement in the Companies (Cross-Border Mergers) Regulations 2007, SI 2007/2974, reg 13, for a meeting of the members to approve the terms of a proposed merger to be a mandatory requirement, given that the regulations expressly provided for certain limited exceptions, none of which applied on the facts, and so left no room for the operation of the *Duomatic* principle. A meeting was required, therefore, even in the case of a company with only one (informed) shareholder who could not rely on *Duomatic*.

[122] *Wright v Atlas Wright (Europe) Ltd* [1999] 2 BCLC 301.

[123] *Wright v Atlas Wright (Europe) Ltd* [1999] 2 BCLC 301.

[124] *NBH Ltd v Hoare* [2006] 2 BCLC 649 at [43].

[125] *Kinlan v Crimmin* [2007] 2 BCLC 67 at 82; *Dashfield v Davidson* [2008] BCC 222; *BDG Roof-Bond Ltd v Douglas* [2000] 1 BCLC 401 at 417; *Re Torvale Group Ltd* [1999] 2 BCLC 605. Cf. *Re R W Peak (Kings Lynn) Ltd* [1998] 1 BCLC 193.

[126] Company Law Review, *Modern Company Law for a Competitive Economy, Final Report*, vol 1 (2001) URN 01/942, paras 7.17–7.26; also *Completing the Structure* (2000) URN 00/1335, paras 5.13–5.17; *Developing the Framework* (2000) URN 00/656, paras 4.21–4.23.

[127] See *Modernising Company Law* (Cm 5553-I, 2002), paras 2.31–2.35.

[128] See also CA 2006, s 239(6)(a) (ratification of acts of directors—nothing in the section affects the validity of a decision taken by unanimous consent of the members of the company).

16

Informed shareholders and stakeholders—disclosure and the limited company

A Introduction

The role of disclosure

16-1 Disclosure has always been seen, in part, as a price to be paid by those forming a company in return for the conferring of limited liability which insulates shareholders' personal wealth from the reach of the company's creditors (unless the shareholders have been persuaded to give personal guarantees).[1] Against that general backdrop, the key purposes of disclosure would include:[2]

(1) to assist creditors to assess risk. Historically, disclosure requirements have been seen as a mechanism to assist creditors in assessing the risks of dealing with a limited company. The company puts forward information about itself and the creditor decides in the light of that information whether to deal with the company and on what terms (for example, as to price, interest and security required). In that context, financial information in the form of timely, independently audited, publicly available, annual accounts is particularly important, at least for the largest companies and their creditors, together with narrative reporting by directors on the activities and performance of the business.[3] These requirements are the focus of this chapter. Smaller companies are often heavily dependent on bank finance and will have a direct relationship with their bank (which will usually demand regular management accounts) and, probably, a small number of trade creditors who form

---

[1] Given that disclosure is designed primarily to protect creditors and others dealing with a limited liability company, an unlimited company (subject to certain exceptions) need not deliver accounts to the registrar of companies: CA 2006, s 448, though unlimited companies must prepare accounts for their shareholders: s 394.

[2] On the possible overuse of disclosure as a regulatory technique, see Sorensen, 'Disclosure in EU Corporate Governance—A Remedy in need of Adjustment?' (2009) 10 EBOR 255; also generally Villiers, *Corporate Reporting and Company Law* (2006).

[3] See BIS, *Consultation on Audit Exemptions and Change of Accounting Framework* (October 2011), URN11/1193, which discusses the possibility of exempting qualifying dormant subsidiaries from preparing and filing accounts, but limits the possible exemption to that category rather than all qualifying subsidiaries, noting, *inter alia*, that to extend the category would result in significant potential loss of public information of use to creditors, employees and other interested parties, see para 52. The document also notes that accessing company accounts and checking financial information were among the top reasons given by customers for obtaining company information held by Companies House and that they used that information to make business decisions, undertake credit assessments, due diligence and to assess customers/suppliers, see para 52(c).

a view as to the company's creditworthiness from their dealings with it rather than as a consequence of any mandated disclosure.

(2) to assist shareholders and others to hold management to account. The establishment of high standards of corporate governance requires quality financial and non-financial disclosure to enable shareholders and future investors to assess the company's management and profitability. Disclosure promotes efficient management as directors appreciate that their actions are subject to scrutiny. That transparency linked to concerns for their own business reputations can help to maintain appropriate standards of conduct. In Chapter 5, we discussed the importance of shareholders actively engaging in the governance of their companies. To do this effectively, shareholders require detailed accessible information, detailed enough for the sophisticated investor to appreciate the company's position without having to expend disproportionate time and resource in identifying key information and accessible enough so that all investors have the opportunity to understand the state of the company's affairs.

(3) to facilitate the operation of the capital markets. Investors need appropriate information to facilitate informed investment choice and the efficient allocation of capital by them. The role of disclosure in the capital markets is beyond the scope of this book, but an example of its importance can be seen in the context of capital raising where the Prospectus Directive[4] (implemented by FSMA 2000, ss 64–87R and by the Prospectus Rules of the UK Listing Authority, UKLA) requires a detailed prospectus to be prepared and published when a company wishes to offer its shares to the public and/or seeks admission to a regulated market (see **19-105**). Other Directives of note would include the Transparency Directive[5] (implemented mainly via the Disclosure and Transparency Rules (DTR) of the UKLA) which requires frequent financial disclosures by traded companies and disclosure of major shareholdings and the Takeover Directive[6] (implemented mainly by the Takeover Code) which requires disclosure of control structures within a publicly traded company, see **26-64**.

Disclosure may occur in a variety of ways, for example, through filing information such as the annual accounts at a public registry (the role of Companies House, the public registry, is discussed in Chapter 1), or by making certain company documents available for inspection at the company's registered office, or by discussing matters at annual general meetings (if a public company), or by making announcements to the markets (if a traded company). Increasingly, companies make extensive use of their websites to maintain ongoing disclosure with their shareholders and quoted companies are obliged to post information on their websites in certain circumstances.[7] Finally, the media also plays an important role in bringing corporate information to the attention of the public.

---

[4] Directive 2003/71/EC, OJ L 345/64, 31.12.2003, as amended by Directive 2010/73/EU, OJ L 327/1, 11.12.2010.

[5] Directive 2004/109/EC, OJ L 390/38, 31.12.2004. There is currently a proposal for the modification of the Transparency Directive, see COM (2011) 683 final, 25.10.2011, 2011/0307, following a review of its operation, see COM (2010) 243 final, 27.5.2010.   [6] Directive 2004/25/EC, OJ L 142/12, 30.4.2004, see art 10.

[7] See CA 2006, s 341 (obligation to post poll results on website); s 430 (obligation to publish annual accounts and reports on website); s 527 (ability of members to post audit concerns on the website). 'Quoted company' is defined in CA 2006, s 385 as a company whose equity share capital—(a) has been included in the official list in accordance with the provisions of Part 6 of the Financial Services and Markets Act 2000; or (b) is officially listed in an EEA State (EU with Norway, Iceland and Liechtenstein); or (c) is admitted to dealing on either the New York Stock Exchange or Nasdaq.

16-2 Most disclosure comes in the form of accounts and reports focusing on the financial position and the activities of the company, but mandated disclosure can extend in all directions so as to include, for example, health and safety issues, political and charitable donations, environmental concerns and general corporate social responsibility. Most disclosure is addressed to shareholders and/or creditors, present and future, but it can extend to a wide variety of stakeholders who may have an interest in the company's affairs, such as employees and customers, local communities and the wider public, as well as local and national authorities.[8] Many of the obligations are modified for the smallest companies with public companies subject to more onerous obligations than private companies and with the greatest transparency required of traded companies.

The regulatory framework on accounting requirements

16-3 The statutory framework on accounts is laid down in CA 2006, Pt 15 augmented by a number of statutory instruments as a result of the decision to remove much of the accounting detail from the CA 2006 in the interests of clarity and to allow for ease of amendment in future. The key instruments which need to be read together with Part 15 are the Small Companies and Groups (Accounts and Directors' Report) Regulations 2008, SI 2008/409 and the Large and Medium-sized Companies and Groups (Accounts and Directors' Report) Regulations 2008, SI 2008/410 which, respectively, set out the detailed requirements. The legislative framework reflects the requirements of the Fourth and Seventh Company Law Directives which deal, respectively, with the presentation and content of a company's individual accounts[9] and consolidated or group accounts.[10] These Directives are known as the Accounting Directives and they have been the subject of a process of constant amendment and updating to reflect modern accounting standards over the years since their adoption in 1978 and 1983 respectively. Following a period of review of the Directives, the European Commission has now proposed their repeal and replacement with a single Directive which will introduce a modified specific regime for small companies while, for medium and large companies, the intention primarily is to reduce the number of accounting options available so as to improve the comparability of their accounts.[11] With respect to small companies, see current thresholds at **16-120**, the aim is to reduce overall the regulatory burden,[12] for example, by allowing them to prepare a simpler profit and loss account and balance sheet and by limiting disclosures in the notes to the accounts to five items (though including, for the first time, a requirement for disclosure of related party transactions)[13] and by removing any EU requirement for an audit (UK small companies are already exempt from any audit requirement, see **16-36**). It is also intended to harmonise the thresholds which define small and medium-sized companies so as to ensure that all companies across the EU are able to take advantage of the

---

[8] See Company Law Review, *Developing the Framework* (2000), para 5.4; also *The Strategic Framework* (1999), paras 5.144–5.147.

[9] Fourth Council Directive (EEC) 78/660, OJ L 222, 14.8.1978, p 11.

[10] Seventh Council Directive (EEC) 83/349, OJ L 193, 18.7.1983, p 1.

[11] *Proposal for a Directive on the annual financial statements, consolidated financial statements and related reports of certain types of undertaking*, COM (2011) 684 final, 25.10.2011.

[12] Small groups are to be exempted from the requirement to prepare consolidated accounts, see n 11, COM (2011) 684 final, 25.10.2011, para 4.6.

[13] The Commission notes that the reduction in the information available to creditors is balanced by the information required by the notes concerning related party transactions and also guarantees and commitments entered into by the company, see n 11, COM(2011) 684 final, 25.10.2011, para 3.3.

EU exemptions for that class of company.[14] The EU Parliament meanwhile has approved a new Directive on micro-entities[15] which allows for further reductions on the disclosures required of companies which meet the threshold for a micro-entity, namely a company which does not exceed at least two of the following three criteria: total assets of up to €350,000; net turnover of up to €700,000; and a maximum of 10 employees (it is thought that approximately 75% of EU companies fall into this category). In effect, the changes allow Member States at their choice to remove the micro-entities from the Accounting Directives and the UK Government has already consulted on how the disclosure requirements of micro-entities might be drastically simplified.[16]

16-4 The accounting measures are designed to ensure the highest standards of transparency (compatible with the economic size of the company) and comparability for the accounts of companies formed in the Member States. For larger companies, the key development in the past decade has been the adoption, not just within the EU, but globally, of international accounting standards drawn up by the IASB[17] rather than standards derived from national accounting practice, again a move designed to enhance the transparency and comparability of accounts.[18]

16-5 The move within the EU to international accounting standards started with the adoption in 2002 of a Regulation on the application of International Accounting Standards (IAS)[19] which, since 1 January 2005, requires listed companies (see **19-100**) to draw up their consolidated accounts in accordance with IAS, now known as IFRS (International Financial Reporting Standards),[20] in which case the directors must state in the notes to the accounts that the consolidated accounts have been prepared in accordance with IAS (CA 2006, s 406).[21] A company (other than a charity) has the option of preparing its individual accounts either in accordance with IAS or the CA 2006,[22] but a parent company must ensure that its individual accounts and the individual accounts of its undertakings are prepared using the same framework, whether that is IAS or CA 2006, except to the extent that in the directors' opinion there are good reasons for not doing so (CA 2006, s 407). If a company prepares either its consolidated or individual accounts according to

---

[14] See n 11, COM(2011) 684 final, 25.10.2011, paras 3.1, 4.1.

[15] See Proposal for a Directive amending Council Directive 78/660/EEC on the annual accounts of certain types of companies as regards micro-entities, COM (2009) 83 final (2009/0035 (COD)). The provisions of this proposed Directive are likely to be integrated into the proposed single Directive replacing the Accounting Directives.

[16] See BIS, *Simpler Reporting for the Smallest Businesses, Discussion Paper*, August 2011, URN 11/1100.

[17] See n 20.

[18] The requirement to use IAS was intended to end, what the then European Commissioner Bolkestein described as 'the current Tower of Babel' in financial reporting. See Commission Press Release, IP/02/827, 7 June 2002.

[19] Regulation (EC) No 1606/2002, OJ L 243/1, 11.09.2002; and see the European Commission Press Release, IP/02/827, 7 June 2002.

[20] International Accounting Standards were issued by the International Accounting Standards Committee which has since been replaced by the International Accounting Standards Board (IASB), an independent standard-setting body which issues IFRS.

[21] See BIS, *Consultation on Audit Exemptions and Change of Accounting Framework* (October 2011), URN 11/1193, para 71, which states that an estimated 7,300 UK companies use IFRS.

[22] Accounts prepared under the CA 2006 (called Companies Act accounts) either apply full UK GAAP or a modified version of UK GAAP for smaller entities, namely the Financial Reporting Standards for Smaller Entities (FRSSE). See BIS, *Consultation on Audit Exemptions and Change of Accounting Framework* (October 2011), para 71, which states that an estimated 50,000 UK companies use full UK GAAP and 1.9m companies use FRSSE.

IAS for a financial year, it cannot switch back to the CA 2006 requirements in subsequent years (s 395(3)), subject to a limited number of exceptions (ss 395(4), 403(5)).[23]

Towards a new disclosure framework

16-6 Clearly, both domestically and at the EU level, disclosure requirements have become the regulatory tool of choice. But the financial crisis (from 2007 onwards) revealed that even extensive disclosure did not alert shareholders, or regulators, or Governments, to the impending crisis. Consequently, a public debate has arisen between providers, users and regulators as to the value, relevance and effectiveness of much of the required disclosure with a consensus quickly emerging of the need for more focused, targeted, effective disclosure. The lead in the debate has been taken by the Financial Reporting Council (FRC) which has responsibility for promoting high standards of corporate reporting and corporate governance and which acts through a number of important operating bodies especially, for our purposes, the Accounting Standards Board (ASB) which issues accounting standards; the Auditing Practices Board (APB) which establishes auditing standards and the Financial Reporting Review Panel (FRRP) which keeps a watching brief on the annual accounts of public companies and large private companies to verify that they are complying with the requirements of the Companies Act 2006 and applicable accounting standards.[24] All of these bodies have established standing as important regulators in their respective areas and are actively involved in the maintaining and raising of standards in corporate reporting, accounting and auditing and hence in the public debate. However, it is accepted by the FRC and Government that this structure is overly complex and a simplified structure is to be created. The FRC retains responsibility for setting or promulgating standards for governance, accounting and audit and actuarial work in the interests of investors in the corporate sector, concentrating on publicly traded companies and the largest private companies and will do so through three FRC Board Committees (one for Codes and Standards, a Conduct Committee and an Executive Committee) rather than the current seven operating bodies.[25]

The audience and manner of disclosure

16-7 An important issue in any disclosure policy is to whom disclosure should be addressed, given it is now accepted that accounts and reports are aimed at too many types of users. The FRC considers that it is appropriate for providers to refocus on the primary purpose of corporate disclosures which is 'providing investors with information that is useful for

---

[23] The intention originally was to prevent a company confusing users of the accounts by constantly changing between accounting frameworks. The Government has indicated that that is no longer a major concern and that it is minded to significantly deregulate the process of moving from IFRS to UK GAAP so as to give companies and groups more flexibility, see BIS, *Consultation on Audit Exemptions and Change of Accounting Framework* (October 2011), URN 11/1193, paras 77–90. The proposal is to allow companies to change, as now, if there is a change of circumstances (CA 2006, s 395(3), (4)), but also to change for 'any other reason', though this new category will be restricted to a move from IFRS to UK GAAP no more frequently than once every five years.

[24] Additionally, there is the Professional Oversight Board (POB) which provides independent oversight of the regulation of the accounting and auditing professions; the Accountancy and Actuarial Discipline Board (AADB) which is an independent investigation and disciplinary body for accountants and actuaries and the Board for Actuarial Standards (BAS).

[25] BIS, *Proposals to Reform the Financial Reporting Council, a Joint Government and FRC Response* (March 2012), URN 12/700; BIS, *Proposals to Reform the Financial Reporting Council, a Joint BIS and FRC Consultation* (October 2011), URN 11/1250. It is also proposed that the FRC should have greater independence from the accountancy professional bodies and a greater range of proportionate sanctions.

making their resource allocation decisions and assessing management's stewardship',[26] i.e. those who provide capital whether it be equity or loan capital. That approach works for large and for small companies, for even in the smaller companies, shareholders have to look to the effective use of their capital and have a legitimate interest in monitoring and reviewing the management of the company.[27] Having identified the target audience, the FRC has adopted four regulatory principles governing disclosure, namely that the disclosures required should be targeted (a focus on the mischief to be addressed), proportionate (the requirements should be appropriate in extent and impact to the mischief and the type of company involved), coordinated (so as to avoid overlaps, for example, between UK and EU requirements and between differing bodies such as UKLA and the FRC) and clear (more accessible, more useful for the user).[28] Other principles which guide the FRC's approach include that all material issues must be reported in a manner that is complete, neutral, free from error, fair and balanced.[29] Finally, in terms of the manner of communication, the FRC has adopted four communication principles which require that the information disclosed be communicated in a focused, open and honest, clear and understandable, interesting and engaging way.[30]

The content of disclosure

16-8 As to content, for financial statements, the content of the disclosure is dictated in large part by the need to prepare the statements in accordance with either domestic (UK GAAP) or international accounting standards (IFRS) with the latter being mandatory only in respect of listed companies preparing consolidated accounts.

16-9 The ASB had signalled that, in the long term, it sees merit in shifting all companies, other than the smallest, to IFRS so ensuring a uniform approach, less complexity and reduced costs,[31] but it has encountered a degree of resistance on the basis that such a move itself would introduce complexity and increase costs. It has therefore now issued revised proposals[32] for essentially three tiers of regulation with the largest companies (those already required to use IFRS, as adopted by the EU) continuing to be subject to IFRS. Companies not within that category, i.e. not required to and not wanting to adopt IFRS, will apply UK Financial Reporting Standards and a new single financial reporting standard will be

---

[26] FRC, *Louder than Words: Principles and actions for making corporate reports less complex and more relevant* (FRC Discussion Paper, June 2009) (hereafter FRC *Louder than Words*), p 5.

[27] The FRC approach is consistent with the view taken by the Company Law Review that there must be 'sufficient information to support the management process and to enable monitoring and review of management on behalf of those with a legitimate interest', see Company Law Review, *Developing the Framework* (2000), para 8.3.

[28] The FRC and the ASB have been pursuing a project to reduce clutter in annual reports ('clutter' being defined essentially as immaterial disclosures and repetitive explanatory information): see FRC, 'Cutting Clutter: Combating Clutter in Annual Reports' (FRC Discussion Paper, April 2011).

[29] FRC, *Effective Company Stewardship, Next Steps* (September 2011), p 3.

[30] FRC, *Louder than Words*, n 26, pp 16–17, 40–1. In the light of support for these principles, the FRC has adopted them (see Feedback Statement—*Louder than Words*, October 2010, paras 3.6, 3.14).

[31] See ASB, The Future of Financial Reporting in the UK and Republic of Ireland. FRED 43: Application of Financial Reporting Standards. FRED 44: Financial Reporting Standard for Medium-size entities (October 2010).

[32] See ASB, FRED 46, Application of Financial Reporting Requirements (January 2012). Also 'ASB issues revised proposals for the Future of Financial Reporting Standards in the UK and Republic of Ireland', ASB PN 366, 30 January 2012.

drafted to cover these companies.[33] The smallest companies will continue to apply FRSSE (domestic Financial Reporting Standard for Smaller Entities),[34] as now. The aim is to have a new structure in place for accounting periods beginning after 1 January 2015.

16-10 As to the narrative content which sits alongside the financial statements, the Department for Business, Innovation and Skills (BIS) found that, while companies generally comply with the legal requirements, there were concerns that lengthy and complex directors' reports militated against presentation of a clear, coherent and relevant picture of a business.[35] In particular, respondents to a BIS consultation suggested that narrative reporting could be unfocused and inaccessible with social and environmental reporting poorly integrated with the strategy and risks of the business and overly-long and complex remuneration reports.[36] The FRC and FRRP also identified the disclosure of risk and the management of risk as a weak element of the directors' report.[37] These initial findings prompted a greater focus on narrative reporting with the aim of improving the quality (rather than the quantity) of disclosure, mainly to facilitate stronger and more effective shareholder engagement.[38] To that end, the intention is that the reporting framework will be simplified 'to enable quoted companies to provide clear and relevant information to investors about strategy, performance and risk, in a simpler and more concise report with supporting information on the company's website'.[39]

16-11 BIS has consulted on a new approach therefore which will require companies (other than small companies) to produce a Strategic Report setting out the strategy, direction and challenges facing the company,[40] evidenced by high-level financial and remuneration information, together with an Annual Directors' Statement essentially containing all other information required by law, including the directors' remuneration report, corporate governance statement and audit committee report, but presented in a more structured, comparable, way (these documents are discussed further at **16-27**). For small companies, the changes are expected to be purely cosmetic with the directors' report renamed as the Annual Directors' Statement. For medium companies there may be some simplification and the business review part of the directors' report becomes part of the Strategic Report. The most significant changes will affect quoted companies, especially with respect to the coverage of risk etc in the Strategic Report, and there are likely to be significant changes to the directors' remuneration report, see **5-40**.

---

[33] See ASB, FRED 48, The Financial Reporting Standard applicable in the UK and Republic of Ireland (draft FRS 102) (January 2012).

[34] The ASB will re-consult on the content of FRSSE in the light of the proposal from the European Commission for the replacement of the Accounting Directives, see n 11, which makes clear that mandatory adoption of IFRS for SMEs is not going to be pursued at the EU level, see COM (2011) 684 final, 25.10.2011, para 3.3.

[35] BIS, The Future of Narrative Reporting: A Consultation (August 2010).

[36] BIS, The Future of Narrative Reporting: Consulting on a new reporting framework (September 2011), URN 11/945, para 2.7. See the Government Response (March 2012) URN 12/588.

[37] See FRRP Statement, February 2011 'Better reporting of risk'.

[38] BIS, The Future of Narrative Reporting: A Consultation (August 2010); and see FRC, Effective Company Stewardship, Next Steps (September 2011), p 3.

[39] BIS, The Future of Narrative Reporting: A Consultation (August 2010).

[40] The FRC is to work with BIS to support implementation of this change and the FRC too believes that narrative reports should focus primarily on strategic risks rather than operational risks that arise naturally and without action by the company and that companies should disclose the risks inherent in their business model and their strategy for implementing that business model: see FRC, Effective Company Stewardship, Next Steps (September 2011), pp 4, 10.

B The statutory scheme

16-12 The statutory provisions governing company accounts are lengthy and complex and it is not intended to provide a detailed accounting treatment in this chapter, but rather an overview of the requirements so as to appreciate the obligations on directors and the level and type of disclosure which is available to shareholders and stakeholders.

Accounting records

16-13 Every company must keep adequate accounting records sufficient to show and explain the company's transactions and to disclose with reasonable accuracy at any time its financial position at that time and to enable the directors to ensure that any accounts required to be prepared comply with the CA 2006 and, where applicable, IAS requirements.[41] A failure to maintain records is an offence by every officer in default[42] and prosecutions for breach of this requirement are (relatively) common. Also, non-compliance with this requirement will often be one of the grounds (evidencing unfitness) relied on against a director in disqualification proceedings,[43] see **25-70**.

Prepare accounts

16-14 Having maintained the required accounting records, the directors must prepare for the shareholders:

(1) individual accounts for each financial year (CA 2006, s 394) and, in the case of companies admitted to trading on a regulated market, half-yearly financial reports are required[44] together with interim management statements if the company does not also prepare quarterly reports (though the European Commission has proposed that the requirement for quarterly reports be abolished);[45]

(2) a directors' report reviewing the company's activities (s 415), see **16-24**. For financial years from 1 October 2012 onwards, it is proposed that the directors' report will be renamed the Annual Directors' Statement, see **16-27**.

(3) a directors' remuneration report (s 420), if the company is a quoted company[46], see **5-40**; and

(4) an auditors' report (ss 475, 495), though many companies are audit exempt, see **16-43**.

---

[41] CA 2006, s 386; and see ICAEW Tech 01/11, *Guidance for Directors on Accounting Records under the CA 2006* (February 2011). Records must be maintained (for three years in the case of a private company and six years, if a public company, (s 388(4)) at the company's registered office or such other place as the directors think fit and must be available for inspection by the officers of the company (s 388(1)) and by the auditors (s 499(1)(a)). Inspection of company records is governed by The Companies (Company Records) Regulations 2008, SI 2008/3006.

[42] CA 2006, s 387(1); unless the officer can show that he acted honestly and that in the circumstances the default was excusable: s 387(2).

[43] For example, see *Re Galeforce Pleating Co Ltd* [1999] 2 BCLC 704; *Secretary of State for Trade and Industry v Arif* [1997] 1 BCLC 34.

[44] These additional reporting requirements beyond the annual statements are derived from the Transparency Directive 2004/109/EC, OJ L 390/38, 31.12.2004, which was implemented by the UKLA Disclosure and Transparency Rules, DTR, see DTR 4, especially DTR 4.2 and 4.3.

[45] A proposal has been put forward by the European Commission for the modification of the Transparency Directive which will remove this requirement for quarterly or interim reporting for all listed companies, see COM (2011) 683 final, 25.10.2011, para 2.2.   [46] Defined CA 2006, s 385 and see n 7.

16-15 The directors must prepare individual accounts for the company for each financial year.[47] A company's individual accounts consist of a balance sheet and a profit and loss account and notes thereto.[48] The format is determined by whether the company is a small or other company and is dictated by the regulations noted at **16-3**. In all cases, the applicable accounting principles are that the company is presumed to be carrying on business as a going concern, the accounting policies adopted must be applied consistently, the amount of any item in the accounts must be determined on a prudent basis and the accounts prepared on an accruals basis, reflecting transactions in the year to which they relate without regard to the date of receipt or payment.[49]

16-16 If a company's individual accounts are prepared as IAS individual accounts, the directors must state in a note to the accounts that the accounts have been prepared in accordance with international accounting standards (CA 2006, s 397). If the individual accounts have been prepared in accordance with the CA 2006, the accounts must give a true and fair view of the state of the affairs of the company as at the end of the financial year and its profit or loss for the financial year (s 396(2)). The significance of the 'true and fair view' is reinforced by s 393(1) which states that directors must not approve accounts unless they are satisfied that they give a true and fair view of the assets, liabilities, financial position and profit or loss of the company and this requirement applies to all accounts whether prepared in accordance with the CA 2006 or IAS requirements.[50]

A true and fair view

16-17 The ASB is the prescribed body[51] with responsibility for determining domestic accounting standards, known as FRSs, Financial Reporting Standards. Accounting standards are authoritative statements of how particular types of transactions and other events should be reflected in financial statements and accordingly, compliance with the appropriate accounting standards is normally necessary if the accounts are to give a true and fair view.[52] Only recently, the FRC and ASB reaffirmed that it would be 'extremely rare' for it to be necessary to depart from an accounting standard in order to give a true and fair view.[53]

16-18 Given the importance of the 'true and fair view' principle underpinning the accounting requirements and that financial statements prepared to IAS requirements must present fairly the financial position of the company[54] rather than give a 'true and fair view', the FRC sought Counsel's opinion in 2008 as to the 'true and fair' requirement.[55] A key conclusion of Counsel was that the requirement set out in international accounting

---

[47] CA 2006, s 394: a company's financial year is determined in accordance with s 390.

[48] CA 2006, s 396(1), (3). For traded companies, the annual financial report must include audited financial statements, management reports and responsibility statements, see DTR (n 44) 4.1.5.

[49] SI 2008/409, Sch 1, paras 11–14 (small companies); SI 2008/410, Sch 1, paras 11–14 (large and medium-sized companies).

[50] Note also CA 2006, s 393(2) which requires the auditor to have regard to this duty of the directors when carrying out his functions as auditor.

[51] Prescribed under CA 2006, s 464; see The Accounting Standards (Prescribed Body) Regulations 2008, SI 2008/651; see also **16-6**.

[52] Accounting Standards Board, *Foreword to Accounting Standards* (June 1993), para 16.

[53] FRC, 'True and Fair' (July 2011), p 3. See too Accounting Standards Board, *Foreword to Accounting Standards* (June 1993), para 18 (only in special circumstances would departure from an accounting standard be necessary in order for accounts to give a true and fair view).   [54] See IAS 1, para 13.

[55] The Opinion of Martin Moore QC is posted on the FRC website. Previous legal opinions on this issue, written by Hoffmann and Arden in 1983 and 1984 and by Arden in 1993 and commissioned by the ASB are also available on the website. Martin Moore refers to the 'almost iconic status' achieved by those Opinions (see para 7 of his Opinion).

standards that the accounts present fairly the position of the company is not a different requirement to that of showing a true and fair view but is a different articulation
of the same concept. Further, the preparation of financial accounts is not a mechanical process where compliance with the accounting standards automatically ensures that
the accounts give a true and fair view or a fair presentation; while highly likely to have
that outcome, it does not guarantee it. Directors must consider whether, taken in the
round, the financial statements that they approve are appropriate. Similarly, auditors
are required to exercise professional judgement before expressing an audit opinion. As a
result, Counsel's Opinion confirms that it is not sufficient for either directors or auditors
to reach such conclusions solely because the financial statements are prepared in accordance with applicable accounting standards. Objective professional judgement must be
applied to ensure that the statements give a true and fair view or achieve a fair presentation.[56] These aspects of Counsel's Opinion were further stressed in 2011 in a joint note
from the FRC and ASB on 'true and fair', highlighting the need for professional and
considered judgement at all stages of preparation of the accounts and confirming that
'the true and fair requirement remains of fundamental importance in both UK GAAP
and IFRS',[57] noting that in the vast majority of cases, compliance with the accounting
standards will result in a true and fair view.[58]

16-19 Ultimately, however, the question whether the accounts do give a true and fair view is
a matter of law for the courts to decide.[59] Recently the Court of Appeal considered the
matter in *Macquarie Internationale Investments Ltd v Glencore UK Ltd*[60] where a dispute
arose between the parties to the sale and purchase of a business. M had purchased the
entire share capital of a number of subsidiaries of G on terms which included, *inter alia*,
a warranty by the seller that the statutory accounts were prepared in accordance with relevant accounting standards and gave a true and fair view of assets and liabilities. M was
subsequently liable for £3.1m in unexpected charges (as a result of an error by a supplier to
one of the subsidiaries which had gone undetected by the supplier until after the sale). The
question was whether G was in breach of the warranty when the existence of that liability
had remained unknown and not reasonably discoverable by G at the time of the sale.
Affirming the decision at first instance, the Court of Appeal agreed that where statutory
accounts are properly prepared in accordance with published professional standards, that

---

[56] See Martin Moore Opinion, n 55, paras 41–46.

[57] FRC, 'True and Fair' (July 2011). The note stresses that all involved in preparing the accounts, the directors and the auditors, must stand back at the end of the process of preparation and ensure that the accounts
as a whole do give a true and fair view and, crucially, ensure that the consideration that they give to these
matters is evident in their deliberations and documentation, see at p 4.

[58] FRC, 'True and Fair' (July 2011), p 3; the note goes on to say that in those 'extremely rare' circumstances
where directors and auditors do not believe that following a particular accounting policy will give a true
and fair view, they are legally required to adopt a more appropriate policy, even if this requires a departure
from an accounting standard; and where a proper explanation is given of the reason for the departure and its
effects, the FRRP (see **16-6**) will be reluctant to substitute its own judgement for the company's board unless
it is not satisfied that the board has acted reasonably (pp 3–4).

[59] See Accounting Standards Board, *Foreword to Accounting Standards* (June 1993), esp paras 16–19, and
Counsel's Opinion annexed thereto; see also Evans, '"True and fair" Revisited' [1990] LMCLQ 255; McGee,
'The True and Fair View Debate: A Study in the Legal Regulation of Accounting' (1991) 54 MLR 874. It is
possible that there may be more than one 'true and fair view', hence the reference to 'a true and fair view' see,
Lord Neuberger in *BNY Corporate Trustee Ltd v Eurosail* [2011] 3 All ER 470 at [61]: 'Clearly, the fact that
the figures have been audited and are said to convey a "true and fair" view of the company's position in the
opinion of its directors should normally have real force. However, the figures will inevitably be historic, they
will normally be conservative, they will be based on accounting conventions, and they will rarely represent
the only true and fair view.'   [60] [2011] 1 BCLC 561, CA.

is strong evidence that the accounts in question do present a true and fair view. This was so here, despite the absence of any provision for the missing charges. The court agreed with the trial judge that it was difficult to see how the absence of provision for something which the seller did not know about, and could not reasonably have discovered, could mean that the accounts failed to give a true and fair view.[61]

Small companies

16-20 Exemptions are available as to the detail of the accounts to be prepared and delivered by small companies which meet certain statutory eligibility criteria. To qualify as a small company, a company must satisfy two or more of the following criteria in relation to the relevant year: the company's turnover must not exceed £6.5m; the balance sheet total must not exceed £3.26m; the number of employees must not exceed 50 (CA 2006, s 382);[62] and the company must not be excluded by s 384 from the small companies regime (i.e. must not be a public company, certain financial services companies or a member of an ineligible group, for example, because the group contains a public company).

16-21 The accounts (i.e. balance sheet, profit and loss accounts and accompanying notes) prepared for the members of a small company must comply with the required form and content and information to be provided in the notes as prescribed (CA 2006, s 396(3)).[63] The directors of a company subject to the small companies regime are only required to deliver the balance sheet to the registrar of companies (s 444(1)). A further refinement is that the directors of a small company can choose to deliver a modified balance sheet in which case the accounts are referred to as abbreviated accounts (s 444(3)).[64] Small companies which wish to take advantage of this exemption therefore need to prepare two sets of accounts, one for their members and one for the registrar of companies. As the main benefit is the provision of minimal information to the public registry, some companies are happy to bear the additional cost though those searching the public registry may be less happy with this level of disclosure. If a company delivers abbreviated accounts and it is not exempt from the requirement to have an audit (see at **16-36**), or it has chosen not to take advantage of audit exemption, it must deliver a special auditors' report (s 449(1)). This report does not state that the accounts give a true and fair view (the auditors would not be willing so to state with regard to abbreviated accounts) but states that, in the auditor's opinion, the company is entitled to deliver abbreviated accounts and that the abbreviated accounts are properly prepared (s 449(2)).

---

[61] On the same basis, the court rejected a claim for breach of equivalent warranties with respect to management accounts that had been provided to the purchaser and which had been prepared in accordance with relevant accounting standards while noting that a lesser degree of accuracy may be expected from management accounts than from statutory accounts subject to audit, see [2011] 1 BCLC 561 at [67], [86].

[62] When replacing the Accounting Directives, see **16-3**, the EU proposes to increase the current thresholds, but also to harmonise fully the size criteria for the different categories of companies. Previously the Member States could choose whether or not different sizes of undertaking should be recognised within their jurisdiction and, within limits, the relevant size criteria, see now the Proposal for a Directive on the annual financial statements, consolidated financial statements and related reports of certain types of undertakings, COM (2011) 684 final, para 4.1.

[63] See The Small Companies and Groups (Accounts and Directors' Report) Regulations 2008, SI 2008/409, Sch 1.

[64] See The Small Companies and Groups (Accounts and Directors' Report) Regulations 2008, SI 2008/409, Sch 4. The Company Law Review had recommended that this facility for filing abbreviated accounts be abolished: Company Law Review, *Final Report*, vol 1 (2001), para 4.38; also *Developing the Framework* (2000), paras 8.32–8.34. The Government initially accepted this recommendation, see *Modernising Company Law*, Cmnd 5553-I, (2002), para 4.26, but later changed its position and abbreviated accounts are retained by CA 2006, s 444(3).

Medium-sized companies

16-22 To qualify as a medium-sized company, a company must satisfy two or more of the following criteria in relation to the relevant year: the company's turnover must not exceed £25.9m; the balance sheet total must not exceed £12.9m; and number of employees must not exceed 250 (CA 2006, s 465); and the company must not be excluded by s 467 from the medium-sized companies regime (i.e. must not be a public company, certain financial services companies or a member of an ineligible group). For medium-sized companies, the accounting exemptions available are modest, allowing some information to be aggregated or omitted from the profit and loss account delivered to the registrar of companies, but a balance sheet, profit and loss account and a directors' report must be delivered in the usual way.[65]

Group accounts

16-23 A parent company (other than a small parent company[66] or a company otherwise exempt[67]) must prepare its own individual accounts *and* prepare group accounts (s 399(2)), namely, a consolidated balance sheet and consolidated profit and loss account for the whole group (s 404). In some cases consolidated accounts must be prepared in accordance with IAS (s 403(1)), see **16-5**, otherwise group accounts may be prepared in accordance with IAS or CA 2006 requirements (s 403(2)). The content and format are as prescribed by regulations.[68] Companies Act group accounts must give a true and fair view of the state of affairs of the group and the profit or loss of the group.[69] If the group accounts are prepared as IAS group accounts, the directors must state in a note to the accounts that the accounts have been prepared in accordance with international accounting standards (s 406).

The directors' report

16-24 Every company must prepare, have approved and (save in the case of a small company) deliver a directors' report for each financial year (CA 2006, s 415).[70] If the company is a small company, it need not deliver a directors' report though the company may choose to deliver it (s 444(1)). The content of the directors' report is prescribed by regulation,[71] but must include the directors' names, the principal activities of the company, information on political and charitable donations,[72] on employment policies (if number of employees

---

[65] CA 2006, s 445, see the Large and Medium-sized Companies and Groups (Accounts and Directors' Report) Regulations 2008, SI 2008/410, para 4.

[66] A parent company is not required to prepare and deliver group accounts if it heads a group which qualifies as a small group and it is not an ineligible group: CA 2006, ss 399(1), 383, 384(2). A group qualifies as a small group if it meets two of the following criteria in the relevant year: turnover must not exceed £6.5m net; the balance sheet total must not exceed £3.26m net; and the number of employees must not exceed 50: ss 381, 383 and see s 384(2) as to an ineligible group.

[67] i.e. a company within the exemptions in CA 2006, ss 400–402.

[68] See The Large and Medium-sized Companies and Groups (Accounts and Reports) Regulations 2008, SI 2008/410, reg 9, Sch 6, Pt 1.

[69] CA 2006, s 404(2); there is provision for the exclusion of some subsidiary undertakings from the group accounts: see s 405; and a parent company need not provide its individual profit and loss account to the registrar though it must still be approved by the directors: s 408(3).

[70] For delivery requirements, see CA 2006, ss 445–447.

[71] See The Small Companies and Groups (Accounts and Directors' Report) Regulations 2008, SI 2008/409, reg 7, Sch 5; The Large and Medium-sized Companies and Groups (Accounts and Reports) Regulations 2008, SI 2008/410, reg 10, Sch 7.

[72] There is a proposal to remove this disclosure requirement with effect for financial years after 1 October 2012, see BIS, *The Future of Narrative Reporting*, n 36, para 4.3, Table 1.

exceed 250),[73] on payment of creditors,[74] details of the directors' shareholdings and, save in the case of small companies, the amount recommended for a dividend payment (s 416). In the case of companies admitted to trading on a regulated market, the report must include information on the company's voting and control structures (required by the Takeover Directive, see **26-64**) and a corporate governance statement (see **5-10**).[75]

16-25 Save for companies entitled to the small companies exemption,[76] the directors' report must include a business review (CA 2006, s 417) which is a fair review of company's business and a description of the principal risks and uncertainties facing the company. The purpose of the review is specifically stated to be 'to inform members of the company and help them assess how the directors have performed their duty under s 172 (duty to promote the success of the company) (s 417(2) and see **9-38**). The review must provide a balanced and comprehensive analysis of the development and performance of the company's business during the financial year, and the position of the company's business at the end of that year, consistent with the size and complexity of the business. More extensive disclosure is required of quoted companies to the extent necessary for an understanding of the development, performance or position of the company's business, including information on: the main trends and factors likely to affect the future development, performance and position of the company's business; environmental and employment matters; social and community issues; together with information about supply and other arrangements which are essential to the business of the company (a requirement of somewhat uncertain breadth).[77]

16-26 Where the company's accounts are subject to audit, (see **16-34**), the directors' report must also contain a statement by the directors that there is no relevant audit information (i.e. information needed by the auditor in connection with the preparation of his report) of which the auditor is unaware and there are criminal sanctions for false statements to this effect (CA 2006, s 418). A director exercising care and skill needs to make such necessary enquiries of his fellow directors and otherwise as to enable him to meet his obligations under this provision (s 418(4)). In turn, the company's auditors (where the company's accounts are subject to audit) must state in their report whether the information contained in the directors' report is consistent with those accounts (s 496).

A new narrative reporting framework

16-27 As noted at **16-10**, there is a considerable degree of dissatisfaction amongst users that much of the narrative reporting is inaccessible, unfocused and too complex while the FRC and FRRP are also concerned that companies are not addressing risk issues properly.[78] Changes have been proposed therefore to the directors' report which is to be renamed

---

[73] See n 72.   [74] See n 72.

[75] The requirements for listed companies are set out in the UKLA Disclosure and Transparency Rules (DTRs), see DTR 7.2 and n 44. There is an option to provide a separate corporate governance statement.

[76] See CA 2006, s 415A.

[77] See 'The Financial Reporting Review Panel highlights challenges in the reporting of principal risks and uncertainties', FRRP, PN 130, 1 February 2011.

[78] See 'The Financial Reporting Review Panel highlights challenges in the reporting of principal risks and uncertainties', FRRP PN 130, 1 February 2011 which expressed concern about how companies were reporting the principal risks and uncertainties facing their business, and noted complaints that many companies were making inadequate or generic disclosures which mean that the business review was not performing its function and members were not being informed as to how the company was managing the principal risks facing the business.

the Annual Director's Statement (ADS) with key information about the company's strategy, risks and business model contained in a separate Strategic Report. The ADS will be
the repository for all narrative reporting requirements other than those matters required
to be included in the Strategic Report.[79] Essentially this means that the ADS will include
all the disclosure requirements otherwise required by the CA 2006 and related statutory
instruments, requirements imposed by other legislation, and by the Listing Rules and
the UK Corporate Governance Code. The layout and content will be prescribed to ensure
comparability between companies, but companies will also be able to add information to
it, if they choose. It is also possible that, to reduce the length of the ADS, provision may be
made for information to be posted on the company website rather than repeated year on
year in the statement. The Strategic Report will provide the essential information about
the business (its strategy, its business model, its performance and key financial data, any
significant changes to governance and principal risks)[80] as well a forward-looking analysis by the directors of the challenges and opportunities facing the company.[81] In the
case of quoted companies, key elements of the director's remuneration report (see **5-40**)
will be included, particularly the link between company performance and remuneration.[82] The Strategic Report is intended to be clear and concise and will cross-reference
to more detailed information in the ADS though the expectation is that, for most users,
the Strategic Report will provide enough information for them to make an assessment
of the company's historic performance and future prospects.[83] In order to ensure that
the board of directors takes responsibility for and ownership of the Strategic Report, the
Government is proposing that the report should be signed by each individual director as
well as the company secretary.[84] As is currently the case with the directors' report, the
company's auditors (where the company's accounts are subject to audit) will be required
to state in their report whether the information contained in the Strategic Report and the
ADS is consistent with those accounts.[85]

Directors' liabilities for disclosures

16-28 Given the level of disclosure required in the directors' report, directors have become
increasingly concerned about potential liabilities arising from erroneous statements,
especially in the context of the business review requirements which for quoted companies require the inclusion of forward-looking statements. To address those concerns, a
safe-harbour provision is included in CA 2006, s 463 which imposes liability on directors to compensate the company (only) for loss suffered by it as a result of any untrue or

---

[79] BIS, The Future of Narrative Reporting, n 36, paras 3.23–3.31, Annex B.

[80] The UK Corporate Governance Code, C.1.3, and the Listing Rules LR 9.8.6(3) require directors to
state in the annual financial statements that the company is a going concern. The preliminary report of the
Sharman Inquiry (set up by the FRC in 2011) recommends that the FRC integrates going concern reporting
into the discussion of strategy and principal risks and therefore it would be appropriately contained in the
Strategic Report, see The Sharman Inquiry, *Going Concern and Liquidity Risks: Lessons for Companies and
Auditors; Preliminary Report and recommendations of the Panel of Inquiry* (November 2011), paras 15, 21,
and Ch 5. See also FRC, *Going Concern and Liquidity Risk: Guidance for Directors of UK Companies* (2009).

[81] BIS, The Future of Narrative Reporting, n 36, paras 2.9–2.12, 3.16–3.19, Annex B.   [82] See n 81.

[83] BIS, The Future of Narrative Reporting, n 36, para 3.23 which is why it is also proposed that summary
financial statements can be replaced with the Strategic Report, see para 3.20. At the moment, companies
may provide summary financial statements (derived from the annual accounts and the directors' report) to
their shareholders instead of the full annual accounts and reports (CA 2006, s 426). The form and content is
governed by The Companies (Summary Financial Statements) Regulations 2008, SI 2008/374.

[84] BIS, The Future of Narrative Reporting, n 36, para 3.21.

[85] BIS, The Future of Narrative Reporting, n 36, para 6.9.

misleading statement in the directors' report (or in the directors' remuneration report) but a director can only be liable if he knew the statement was untrue or misleading or was reckless as to whether it was untrue or misleading. In other words, liability can only arise in deceit (which is quite unlikely) and not in negligence and liability can only be to the company (which is quite unlikely to sue) and only for loss suffered as a result of the statement (which it would be difficult to identify). A further indirect safe harbour is provided by FSMA 2000, s 90A and Sch 10A in respect of damage or loss suffered as a consequence of false and misleading information disclosed by issuers of securities that are, with the consent of the issuer, admitted to trading on a securities market (where the market is situated or operating in the UK or the UK is the issuer's home State).[86] FSMA 2000, Sch 10A sets out the circumstances in which an issuer (only) is liable to pay compensation[87] to a person who has acquired, sold or continues to hold securities in reliance on published information to which the Schedule applies[88] (which includes the company's financial statements and reports) and who has suffered loss as a result of an untrue or misleading statement in that published information.[89] Despite these safe harbours, directors remain concerned about their potential liabilities in respect of narrative reporting (particularly, it is thought, directors of companies with a US listing or about to issue a prospectus), so BIS is considering further whether there are other measures which might be taken which would encourage fuller and more meaningful disclosures.[90]

The directors' remuneration report

16-29 Quoted companies are required to draw up a detailed directors' remuneration report containing a full explanation of the company's policy on directors' service contracts and on notice periods and termination as well as comprehensive details of the remuneration (and compensation) packages of each individual director and the membership and role of the remuneration committee (CA 2006, s 420).[91] The remuneration report must be submitted to the annual general meeting for shareholder approval of the report by way of an

---

[86] These provisions were the result of the Davies Review instigated by the Treasury, see HM Treasury, *Extension of the statutory regime for issuer liability* (July 2008); *Davies Review of Issuer Liability: Final Report* (June 2007).

[87] See *Davies Review of Issuer Liability: Final Report* (June 2007), paras 54–59 as to why liability should not be extended to the directors individually—essentially because there are other sanctions etc which deter directors from making fraudulent or negligent statements such as the threat of FSA censure and the possibility that the company will sue the director where a director's conduct/statements have caused loss to the company and that liability of the director to the company is retained by FSMA 2000, Sch 10A, para 7(2) (a person other than the issuer is not subject to any liability, other than to the issuer, in respect of any loss).

[88] The category of information which is within the provision is very broadly defined as all information published by, or the availability of which is announced by, a regulatory information service, see FSMA 2000, Sch 10A, para 2, so it is much wider than merely periodic financial information.

[89] The statutory liability of the issuer is deceit based and an issuer within this provision is exempt from other forms of liability in respect of loss suffered as a result of misstatements, omissions etc, but the exemption does not affect certain other specified liabilities, such as liability under FSMA s 90 (misleading statements in prospectus or listing particulars, see **19-110**) or liability for breach of contract or liability under the Misrepresentation Act 1967 or liability to a civil penalty or criminal liability: FSMA 2000, Sch 10A, para 7(3)—the width of these liabilities is such as to cast doubt on the value of this 'safe harbour'.

[90] See BIS, *The Future of Narrative Reporting*, n 36, paras 4.19–4.21.

[91] The details of the required disclosure are set out in The Large and Medium-sized Companies and Groups (Accounts and Reports) Regulations 2008, SI 2008/410, para 11, Sch 8. Part of the report is subject to review by the auditors who must state whether that part of the report has been properly prepared in accordance with the requirements of the CA 2006: see CA 2006, s 421(1); SI 2008/410, reg 11, Sch 8, Pt 3. As to 'quoted company', see n 7 and CA 2006, s 385.

ordinary resolution (s 439). For a discussion of this report and its impact, see **5-40**. The safe harbour discussed at **16-28** applies also to untrue or misleading statements in the directors' remuneration report.

Approving accounts

16-30 The accounts must be approved by the board and signed on the balance sheet on behalf of the board by a director (CA 2006, s 414), likewise, the directors' report (s 419) and the directors' remuneration report (s 422). The directors must not approve the accounts unless they are satisfied that the accounts give a true and fair view of the company's assets, liabilities, financial position and profit or loss (s 393(1)). Provision is made for the revision of defective accounts or reports, either voluntarily by the directors (s 454),[92] or on the intervention of the Secretary of State (s 455), whose powers in this respect with regard to public and large private companies are exercised by the Financial Reporting Review Panel (see **16-9**).[93]

Circulating, laying and filing accounts

16-31 A copy of the accounts and reports must be sent to each member[94] and, if the company is a public company, laid by the directors before a general meeting known as the 'accounts meeting' (CA 2006, s 437(1), (3)). The accounts may be sent to the members in hard copy or electronic form, subject to the rules governing electronic communications (see **15-5**). A copy of the accounts and reports must be delivered by the directors to the registrar of companies.[95] A quoted company must publish its accounts and reports on its website as soon as reasonably practicable (s 430) and is required to publish its financial statements within four months of the end of the financial year.[96] Members of a quoted company holding a certain percentage of the shares may require a company to put a statement on the company's website setting out any audit concerns which they may have (s 527) and the company when giving notice of the accounts meeting must draw attention to the right of the members to use the company website in this way (s 529).

16-32 In the case of a private company, a copy of the accounts must be sent to the members not later than nine months from the end of the financial year or, if earlier, the date on which the company actually delivers its accounts to the registrar (CA 2006, s 424(2)(a), s 444(2)). Nine months is a lengthy period which means that the accounts are of limited value when they finally appear on the public record. Public companies must send the accounts to the members at least 21 days before the accounts meeting (s 424(3)), see **16-31**, and must deliver the accounts to the registrar of companies within six months from the end of the financial year (s 442(2)(b)). The effect of these long lead-in times for delivery to the registrar of companies means that, even with respect to compliant companies, the information provided to the public registry is quite dated. Despite these generous timescales, there are significant levels of non-compliance by companies, though a failure to deliver accounts to

---

[92] See also The Companies (Revision of Defective Accounts and Reports) Regulations 2008, SI 2008/373.

[93] See Companies (Defective Accounts and Directors' Reports) (Authorised Person) and Supervision of Accounts and Reports (Prescribed Body) Order 2008, SI 2008/623.

[94] CA 2006, s 423(1)(a); and also to the holders of the company's debentures and to every person entitled to receive notice of the company's meetings: s 423(1)(b),(c).

[95] CA 2006, s 441 subject to small company exemptions, see **16-21**. Unlimited companies are exempt: see s 448.

[96] FSA, Disclosure and Transparency Rules, DTR 4.1.3; for 'quoted company', see n 7.

the registrar of companies is a criminal offence by the directors (s 451(1)) and late filing penalties apply (s 453).[97]

C The auditors' role

The regulatory framework for audit

16-33 Disclosure of accounting information alone is insufficient without assurance as to the quality of that information which comes from the requirement that the accounts be audited. The regulatory framework for company audits and auditors is provided by CA 2006, Pt 16 (Audits) and Pt 42 (Statutory Auditors). Part 16 is our main concern, the requirements as to audit, Part 42 concentrates on the regulation of the audit profession and public oversight issues. The origin of many of the provisions lies in domestic reforms enacted post-Enron,[98] now reflected in CA 2006, Pt 16, and the requirements of the Eighth Company Law Directive[99] adopted in 2006 which replaced an earlier version from 1984. The Eighth Directive makes comprehensive provision for all matters pertaining to the statutory auditor, his qualifications, role and independence, as well as providing for disciplinary processes, quality assurance and public oversight of the audit profession. In the light of the financial crisis, the European Commission in 2010 issued a Green Paper on audit policy[100] followed in 2011 by proposals for reform with the stated objectives of clarifying the role of the auditor, reinforcing the independence and professional scepticism of the auditor,[101] making the top end of the audit market more dynamic while reducing the audit burdens on SMEs, improving the supervision of auditors and facilitating the cross-border provision of audit services.[102] The Commission has therefore proposed a Regulation which will address all aspects of audit of public interest entities[103] (such as listed companies, banks, insurance companies) and an amended Eighth Directive that will consolidate the provisions

---

[97] See Companies (Late Filing Penalties) and Limited Liability Partnerships (Filing Periods and Late Filing Penalties) Regulations 2008, SI 2008/497. The penalty imposed varies in amount depending on the type of company and the period of the delay. Fines run from £150 for a private company which is not more than one month late filing up to £1,500 if more than six months late; equivalent figures for public companies are £750 and £7,500; penalties double if the offence is repeated in two consecutive years. See *R (on the application of Pow Trust) v Chief Executive and Registrar of Companies* [2003] 2 BCLC 295 where the court rejected a claim that such penalties infringe the European Convention on Human Rights.

[98] See the Companies (Audit, Investigations and Community Enterprise) Act 2004.

[99] Directive 2006/43/EC on statutory audits of annual accounts and consolidated accounts: OJ L 157, 9.6.2006, p 87. See also the Commission Recommendation of 6 May 2008 on external quality assurance for statutory auditors and audit firms auditing public interest entities: OJ L 120, 7.5.2008, p 20.

[100] See EU Commission, *Audit Policy: Lessons from the Crisis*, COM (2010) 561, 13.10. 2010; and the UK Government Response (December 2010), URN 10/1346.

[101] On auditor scepticism, see FSA, *Enhancing the Auditor's Contribution to Prudential Regulation* (June 2010), Discussion Paper (DP) 10/3, and Feedback Statement, FS11/1 (March 2011). Auditing standards require that auditors should plan and perform an audit with professional scepticism which essentially involves a challenging, questioning mindset, particularly regarding areas which are heavily reliant on management judgements, but there is little agreement on a definition, see FRC/APB Discussion Paper, *Auditor scepticism: raising the bar* (2010) and the Feedback Statement on it, FRC/APB (March 2011), where the APB indicated that further work is needed to achieve a more consistent understanding, both for auditors and audit committees, of the nature of professional scepticism and its role in the conduct of an audit.

[102] See European Commission, 'Reforming the Audit Market', Memo 11/856, 30.11.2011.

[103] See Proposal for a Regulation on specific requirements regarding statutory audit of public-interest entities, COM (2011) 779 final, 30.11.2011.

on audit for all other entities.[104] Two particular elements to note in respect of the Directive are that (a) Member States are to ensure that statutory auditors carry out audits in accordance with international auditing standards and (b) the intention is that the audit requirements imposed at Member State level should reflect the size of the audited entity and auditing standards should be modified to ensure proportionate and simplified audits for SMEs. As for the measures of note in the proposed Regulation governing public interest entities, there are additional restrictions on the provision of certain non-audit services, in some cases outright prohibition, in others dependent on the consent of the audit committee or the competent authority responsible for the supervision of auditors; there is also an emphasis on the need for professional scepticism in performing an audit, and a requirement for mandatory rotation of audit firms after a maximum engagement period of six years (subject to some exceptions) with a four-year cooling off period.[105] There are also proposals for an expanded audit report and for the auditors to provide a longer and more detailed report to the audit committee (an approach also favoured by the FRC, see **5-33**) and a requirement that the audit committee be composed solely of non-executive directors (already a requirement under the UK Corporate Governance Code, see **5-31**) and that at least one member of the committee should have experience and knowledge in auditing and another should have experience in accounting and/or auditing (more onerous than existing requirements, see **5-31**).

Appointment of auditors

16-34 Every company must appoint an auditor or auditors unless, for each financial year, the directors reasonably resolve otherwise on the ground that audited accounts are unlikely to be required (CA 2006, ss 485(1), 489(1)).[106] In the case of public companies, where an auditor is to be appointed (which will be in all cases other than where the company qualifies as dormant, see **16-39**), the appointment must be made at the accounts meeting (s 489(2) and see **16-31**). Auditors may be individuals or firms and they must be appropriately qualified (s 1219). They must be members of recognised supervisory bodies (s 1212)[107] and meet independence requirements (s 1214).

16-35 In addition to their role as the company auditor, auditors frequently provide the company (especially larger companies) with additional non-audit services, such as advice on taxation matters, on corporate restructuring, information technology and on human resources. Large companies must give details of any remuneration received by the auditor or an associate of an auditor in respect of non-audit services in a note to the company's accounts[108] while small and medium-sized companies must disclose the audit fee paid to

---

[104] See Proposal for a Directive amending Directive 2006/43/EC on statutory audits of annual accounts and consolidated accounts, COM (2011) 778 final, 30.11.2011.

[105] There will also be a prohibition on 'Big Four' contractual clauses which restrict a company to having its audit conducted by the one of the 'Big Four' audit firms (PwC, Ernst & Young, Deloittes and KPMG) and requirements for mandatory tendering for audit contracts.

[106] Auditors appointed as such are officers of the company for the periods for which they are appointed: *Mutual Reinsurance Co Ltd v Peat Marwick Mitchell & Co* [1997] 1 BCLC 1; *Re London and General Bank* [1895] 2 Ch 166; *Re Kingston Cotton Mill Co* [1896] 1 Ch 6. The CA 2006 gives the Secretary of State power by regulations to make provision for the disclosure of the terms on which a company's auditor is appointed, remunerated or performs his duties (s 493). This power has not been exercised to date.

[107] For example, they may be members of the Institute of Chartered Accountants of England and Wales (ICAEW) or the Institute of Chartered Accountants of Scotland (ICAS) or the Association of Chartered Certified Accountants (ACCA).

[108] CA 2006, s 494 and The Companies (Disclosure of Auditor Remuneration and Liability Limitation Agreements) Regulations 2008, SI 2008/489, as amended by SI 2011/2198, reg 5(1). The audit fee and all

their auditors.[109] The concern about the provision of non-audit services, which are typically much more lucrative than the statutory audit, is that the value of the services may compromise the independence of the auditor.

Exemption from obligation to appoint auditors

16-36 It might be expected that all companies' accounts should be audited, but small companies are audit-exempt. The argument against the need for a statutory audit for these companies is essentially one of the costs involved particularly when, it is argued, it is difficult to identify a real need for, or benefit from, the statutory audit. In many small companies, the shareholders typically are also the directors and often all concerned are members of one family so there is no shareholder need for an audit. Equally, the company's creditors in many cases consist of the company's bank (which would have its own picture of the company's finances) and a small number of trade creditors providing limited amounts of credit on short timescales. Hence, it is argued, there is no identifiable creditor need for an audit either.

16-37 The arguments in favour of retaining the audit centre on the value to these small companies of obtaining professional assistance with their accounts at least once a year. Many of these companies are woefully unaware of their obligations with respect to a variety of accounting and taxation matters and the annual audit offers an opportunity for some professional advice. It also means that the auditors are in a position to draw the directors' attention to matters such as a drift towards insolvency (and their corresponding duties to creditors, see **9-41**) and the risk of possible liability for wrongful trading (see **25-18**) and disqualification (see **25-69**). Filing unaudited accounts with the registrar reduces the value of the public registry as searchers are unable to assess the reliability of the (minimal) information being presented by the company (remember small companies need only deliver a balance sheet to the registrar). Finally, given that not all small companies are wholly owned by the directors or their families, minority shareholders who are not directors and who do not have access to the company's records may need the reassurance of an annual independent review of the accounts, though this point is met, at least in part, by a provision whereby shareholders representing more than 10% in nominal value of the issued share capital may require the company to have an audit (CA 2006, s 476).

16-38 The requirement for an audit was abolished in 1994 initially for companies with a turnover below £90,000;[110] now the threshold stands at £6.5m.[111] In 2010–11, 71% of the companies on the register for England and Wales (1.33m companies) filed audit-exempt accounts.[112]

16-39 There are two main ways in which companies may be exempt from the audit requirement:[113]

> (1) where the company is a small company which qualifies as a small company in relation to that year under s 382 (see **16-20**) and its turnover in that year is not more

---

other fees receivable by the auditors for services supplied by them and their associates to the company, its subsidiaries and associated pension schemes must be disclosed, subject to certain exceptions. This level of disclosure was part of the quid pro quo for the introduction of liability limitation agreements, see **16-70**.

[109] SI 2008/489, reg 4(1).

[110] See The Companies Act 1985 (Audit Exemption) Regulations 1994, SI 1994/1935. For background to the change, see generally, Freedman and Godwin, 'The Statutory Audit and the Micro Company—An Empirical Investigation' [1993] JBL 105.   [111] CA 2006, s 477(1), as amended.

[112] See Companies House, *Statistical Tables on Companies Registration Activities 2010–11*, Table F2.

[113] There is also a limited exemption in respect of non-profit-making companies subject to public sector audit, see CA 2006, s 482.

than £6.5 million, and its balance sheet total for that year is not more than £3.26 million (s 477), and it is not an excluded company within s 478.[114]

The Government has indicated that it will amend the criteria in s 477 merely to provide that a company which qualifies as a small company under s 382 is audit-exempt, so bringing the small company accounting criteria and audit exemption criteria into line, but the excluded categories will remain;[115]

(2) where the company is a dormant company within s 480. A company is a dormant company if it has no significant accounting transaction during the period in question, i.e. no transaction that requires to be entered in the company's accounting records (s 1169). A dormant company may be either a public or a private company, provided it is not otherwise ineligible (ss 480, 481). A company may be dormant for a variety of reasons. For example, it may have been incorporated to protect a company name; or it may be part of a group of companies where activities have been transferred to other parts of the group; or it may have been incorporated to carry out a venture which never got off the ground.

16-40 In either case (small or dormant), a company is not entitled to the audit exemption unless the balance sheet contains a statement by the directors to the effect that:

(1) the company is entitled to the exemption (CA 2006, s 475(2));

(2) shareholders holding 10% of the shares have not sought an audit (s 475(3)(a));

(3) the directors acknowledge their responsibility for keeping accounting records and the preparation of the accounts (s 475(3)(b)).

If that statement is false, criminal penalties may arise for approving accounts which do not comply with the statutory requirements (s 414(4), (5)).

16-41 The Department for Business, Innovation and Skills has proposed that non-dormant qualifying subsidiaries should be exempt from an audit requirement provided various conditions are met (there is no size threshold if a company would otherwise qualify). The conditions are:[116]

(1) the parent company must be subject to the laws of an EU Member State;

(2) the parent company must be willing to guarantee all of the subsidiary's debts in the particular financial year and a declaration to this effect must be filed by the subsidiary with the registrar of companies (probably included in its annual return);

(3) the shareholders of the subsidiary must unanimously approve of the exemption and a declaration to that effect must be filed with the registrar; the parent company

---

[114] Excluded categories essentially are public companies or certain financial services or special register companies, see CA 2006, s 478; special rules apply to small companies which are part of a group, see s 479.

[115] See BIS, *Consultation on Audit Exemptions and Change of Accounting Framework* (October 2011), URN11/1193, para 31.

[116] See BIS, *Consultation on Audit Exemptions and Change of Accounting Framework* (October 2011), paras 38–53, 57–59. The suggestion is that 83,000 companies would fall into this category and between 75% and 100% would take up this option. The document also acknowledges that the key factor will be the nature of the guarantee which the Government proposes will be irrevocable, in respect of all debts of the subsidiary in respect of that financial year and, until an audited set of account for the subsidiary is filed, it will also be in respect of future debts incurred by the subsidiary—the Government will issue guidance on an acceptable form of such a guarantee, see paras 60–68. The changes, if adopted, would apply to accounting years ending on or after 1 October 2012.

must include the subsidiary in its consolidated audited accounts and must disclose in the notes to those accounts that the subsidiary is audit exempt; and the subsidiary must be unquoted and not in the banking or finance sector.

Removal and resignation of auditors

16-42 A company may by ordinary resolution at any time remove an auditor from office (CA 2006, s 510), but removal of the company's auditor from office on grounds of divergence of opinions on accounting treatments or audit procedures, or on any other improper grounds, is treated as being unfairly prejudicial to the interests of some part of the company's members so as to enable a member (not the auditor) to petition for relief in those circumstances (CA 2006, s 994(1A)).[117] An auditor who is not re-appointed after expiry of his term of office may require the company to allow him to make representations to the members (s 514). An auditor may resign his office at any time by depositing a notice in writing to that effect at the company's registered office (s 516) and the company must send a copy of that notice to the registrar of companies (s 517). In the case of an unquoted company, where an auditor ceases for any reason to hold office (i.e. removal or failure to re-appoint or resignation), he must deposit at the company's registered office a statement of any circumstances connected with his ceasing to hold office which he considers should be brought to the attention of the members or creditors of the company or, if he considers that there are no such circumstances, a statement that there are none (s 519).[118] An auditor who deposits a statement about the circumstances of his departure can require the directors to call a meeting to discuss those circumstances (s 518) and he must send notice of his resignation to the registrar of companies (s 521). An auditor of a major audit[119] who ceases to hold office for any reason must notify the appropriate audit authority,[120] as must an auditor in any other case who leaves office before the expiry of his term of office (s 522). The appropriate audit authority must in turn notify the Secretary of State and the appropriate accounting authorities (s 524).[121] As is obvious, there is now quite an elaborate degree of notification required which is designed to eliminate practices which may have existed in the past whereby disagreements between management and auditors were resolved by timely resignations or failures to re-appoint which left the shareholders (and the regulators) unaware of any audit concerns or tensions at the root of the departures.[122]

---

[117] As noted in *Re Sunrise Radio Ltd, Kohli v Lit* [2010] 1 BCLC 367 at [9], the board may genuinely and correctly disagree with accounting treatments, but removal of the auditors on those grounds is unfairly prejudicial conduct, even though the conduct complained of may have no necessary impact on the value of the complaining shareholder's investment.

[118] The auditor must make up his own mind as to whether there are circumstances which need to be brought to the attention of the mentioned parties and the court will presume that the auditors are acting in faithful discharge of their duty and not in pursuit of any private or collateral interest, unless the contrary is shown: *Jarvis plc v PricewaterhouseCoopers* [2000] 2 BCLC 368.

[119] Defined as an audit of a listed company or another entity where there is a major public interest: CA 2006, s 525(2).

[120] The 'appropriate audit authority' means, in the case of a major audit, the Professional Oversight Board (see **16-6**); for audits other than major audits, it means the relevant supervisory body: CA 2006, s 525; the Statutory Auditors (Delegation of Functions etc) Order 2008, SI 2008/496, art 5.

[121] The appropriate accounting authorities are the Secretary of State and the FRRP: CA 2006, s 524(2).

[122] BIS is aware of the complexity and has consulted as to how to streamline the procedures, see BIS, *Notices of Auditors Leaving Office, Consultation on Simplification for Companies and Auditors* (November 2009), URN 09/1485, and the subsequent BIS response indicating support for simplification, but noting that primary legislation will be needed so the matter has been shelved until a legislative opportunity arises.

The auditor's report

16-43   An auditor's primary task is to make a report to the company's members on the annual accounts of the company (CA 2006, s 495(1)). As Lord Oliver commented in *Caparo Industries plc v Dickman*:[123]

> '…the primary purpose of the statutory requirement that a company's accounts shall be audited annually is almost self-evident. The structure of the corporate trading entity, at least in the case of public companies whose shares are dealt with on an authorised stock exchange, involves the concept of a more or less widely distributed holding of shares rendering the personal involvement of each individual shareholder in the day to day management of the enterprise impracticable, with the result that management is necessarily separated from ownership. The management is confided to a board of directors which operates in a fiduciary capacity and is answerable to and removable by the shareholders who can act, if they act at all, only collectively and only through the medium of the general meeting. Hence the legislative provisions requiring the board annually to give an account of its stewardship to a general meeting of shareholders.'

16-44   The auditor's report must identify the accounts and the financial reporting framework that has been applied (CA 2006, s 495(2)) and it must describe the scope of the audit. The report must state whether in the auditor's opinion the accounts give a true and fair view:

(1)   in the case of an individual balance sheet, of the state of affairs of the company as at the end of the financial year;

(2)   in the case of an individual profit and loss account, of the profit or loss of the company for the financial year;

(3)   in the case of group accounts, of the state of affairs as at the end of the financial year, and the profit or loss for the financial year, of the undertakings included in the consolidation as a whole, so far as concerns members of the company (s 495(3)(a)).

The report must also state whether the annual accounts have been properly prepared in accordance with the relevant financial reporting framework and the requirements of the CA 2006 and, where applicable, IAS (s 495(3)(b), (c)). The report can be qualified or unqualified and the auditor may draw attention to matters by way of emphasis without qualifying the report (s 495(4)).[124]

16-45   The auditor's report must state whether the directors' report is consistent with the accounts (s 496) and, if the company is a quoted company, whether that part of the directors' remuneration report which is subject to review by the auditors has been properly prepared (s 497). If the auditor is of the opinion that adequate accounting records have not been kept; or the accounts are not in agreement with the accounting records; or the auditable part of the directors' remuneration report is not in agreement with the accounting records, he must so state in the audit report (s 498(2)). If an auditor fails to obtain the information necessary for the purposes of the audit, he must so state in the audit report (s 498(3)); if the directors have claimed to be entitled to use the small companies regime

---

[123]   [1990] 1 All ER 568 at 583. The FRC sees the fundamental purpose of the audit in narrower terms: '… to carry out an independent check into whether a company's financial statements, including the decisions, judgements and estimates involved, have been properly prepared and are fair and balanced,' see FRC, *Effective Company Stewardship, Next Steps* (September 2011), pp 5, 18.

[124]   An auditor's report may be modified by adding an emphasis of matter paragraph to highlight a matter affecting the financial statements which is included in a note to the financial statements that more extensively discusses the matter: ISA 700 (Revised), para 46, see n 125.

and, in the auditor's opinion, they are not so entitled, he must so state in the audit report (s 498(5)). If certain information is not disclosed as to directors' benefits and remuneration when it is required to be disclosed, the auditor must include the particulars in his report (s 498(4)). The report must state the auditors' names and be signed and dated by them (s 503).

16-46 Clearly, the statute now dictates much of the content of the auditors' report, but its form and content is also the subject of extensive professional guidance in an auditing standard, ISA 700 (Revised), updated most recently in 2011.[125] The revised standard was the result of a consultation initiated by the APB in 2008 in response to concerns that so much information was being included in the auditors' report that the key elements of it were in danger of being swamped by the surrounding information and that more concise reports would be welcomed by users. Under the revised standard, the emphasis is placed on reporting on whether the accounts have been properly prepared in accordance with the applicable financial reporting framework, including with the applicable law, and this includes evaluating whether the auditors have obtained sufficient appropriate audit evidence as to whether the financial statements as a whole are free from material misstatement, whether due to fraud or error, and whether they give a true and fair view,[126] rather than, for example, lengthy descriptions of the scope of the audit.[127] The standard also requires that the report include a statement that those charged with governance, the directors for our purposes, are responsible for the preparation of the financial statements while the responsibility of the auditor is to audit and express an opinion on the financial statements in accordance with applicable legal requirements and International Standards on Auditing (standards which require the auditor to comply with the APB's Ethical Standards for Auditors).[128] The APB notes that an appreciation of the interrelationship between the responsibilities of those who prepare financial statements and those who audit them facilitates an understanding of the nature and context of the opinion expressed by the auditor hence the need to include this statement in the report.[129] The APB goes on to point out that the preparation of financial statements requires those charged with governance to make significant accounting estimates and judgements, as well as to determine the appropriate accounting principles and methods used in preparation of the financial statements, something which the FRC also has emphasised in its guidance on the 'true and fair' requirement, discussed at **16-18**, whereas it is the auditor's responsibility to audit the financial statements in order to express an opinion on them.[130]

16-47 The significance of the audit report is enhanced by a requirement that the senior statutory auditor sign the report (ss 503, 504). In other words, the audit engagement partner must sign his own name as well as the name of the firm which does not increase his personal liability in any way (s 504(3)), but is designed to reinforce his appreciation of his personal professional responsibilities with regard to the audit. It is also a criminal offence to knowingly or recklessly cause an auditor's report on the annual accounts to include any matter

---

[125] Standards on auditing are determined by the Auditing Practices Board in the form of ISAs (International Standards on Auditing). The current ISA on the auditor's report is ISA (UK and Ireland) 700 (Revised), *The Auditor's Report on Financial Statements* (updated February 2011). The FRC has indicated that ISA 700 is to be further reviewed, see FRC, *Effective Company Stewardship, Next Steps* (September 2011), p 19.

[126] See ISA 700 (Revised), n 125, para 8.

[127] Indeed ISA (UK and Ireland) 700 (Revised), n 125, para 16 allows for the report to refer the reader to the APB website for further information on scope rather than clutter up the report with the information, but this is an optional method of disclosure which has not proved popular and little use has been made of this website option.   [128] See ISA 700 (Revised), n 125, para 15.

[129] ISA 700 (Revised), n 125, para A6.   [130] ISA 700 (Revised), n 125, para A7.

that is misleading, false or deceptive in a material particular or to omit statements otherwise required to be included (CA 2006, s 507).[131]

16-48 Many corporate collapses in the past have revealed significant fraudulent activity by the directors and/or other employees, indeed often long-running wrongdoing on a massive scale. The financial crisis has revealed huge losses by banks built up over periods when they continued to secure 'clean' audit reports. That loss-making on the scale which has afflicted European banks as well as losses from corporate frauds has gone undetected by the companies' auditors raises issues as to: (1) the manner in which the auditors conduct an audit; and (2) their liabilities in the event that the audit fails to detect wrongdoing or significant poor performance by the company such that the accounts give an erroneous picture of the company's business.

The conduct of the audit

16-49 As noted at **16-46**, an audit involves obtaining evidence about the amounts and disclosures in the financial statements sufficient to give reasonable assurance that the financial statements are free from material misstatement, whether caused by fraud or error.[132] There are a number of older authorities which establish that an auditor is not an insurer,[133] nor is he required to approach his work with suspicion or with a foregone conclusion that something is wrong, and he is justified, in the absence of suspicion, in believing employees in whom confidence is placed by the company.[134] An auditor should approach his work with an inquiring mind,[135] however, and once put on inquiry, he is under a duty to get to the bottom of the matter in question.[136] These older authorities must be treated with some caution for the courts are likely to expect higher standards from today's highly paid, professional, auditors but they do provide some basic pointers as to what is expected of auditors.

16-50 In *Sasea Finance Ltd v KPMG*[137] the Court of Appeal concluded that where a company's auditors discover that a senior employee is defrauding the company on a massive scale, and that employee is in a position to continue doing so, the auditors would normally have a duty to report the discovery to the management immediately, not merely when rendering their report and, if the management are implicated in the wrongdoing, the auditors would have to report directly to a third party without the management's knowledge or consent.

16-51 To assist the auditors in their task, they have a right of access at all times to the company's books and accounts and they are entitled to require a wide range of persons, in particular the company's officers and employees, to provide them with such information and explanations as they think necessary for the performance of their duties (CA 2006, s 499).

---

[131] i.e. a failure to include a statement that the accounts do not agree with accounting records, or that necessary information has not been included, or that the directors are wrongly using the small companies exemption: see CA 2006, s 507(2).

[132] ISA 700 (Revised), n 125, para 8; and see *Barings plc v Coopers & Lybrand* [1997] 1 BCLC 427.

[133] See *Re London and General Bank Ltd (No 2)* [1895] 2 Ch 673.

[134] *Re Kingston Cotton Mill Co (No 2)* [1896] 2 Ch 279.

[135] See Lord Denning in *Fomento (Sterling Area) Ltd v Selsdon Fountain Pen Co Ltd* [1958] 1 WLR 45 at 61.   [136] *Re Thomas Gerrard & Son Ltd* [1967] 2 All ER 525.

[137] [2000] 1 BCLC 236.

Criminal sanctions apply where the information or explanation is misleading, false or deceptive in a material particular (s 501).[138] Auditors of a parent company with overseas subsidiaries can require the parent company to obtain from the subsidiary, its officers etc, such information or explanations as the auditor reasonably requires for the purposes of his duties as auditor and the parent company must take all such steps as are reasonably open to it to obtain that information etc (s 500). An auditor is entitled to receive all communications relating to a proposed written resolution of a private company and also has the right to be notified of and to attend any general meeting and to speak on any part of the business of the meeting which concerns him as auditor (s 502(2)). In practice, auditors rarely need to rely on their statutory rights in this regard since an auditor who is dissatisfied with his access to information or to the shareholders has other mechanisms at his disposal, most notably the ability to qualify his report (s 495(4)(a)), to add statements short of qualification (s 495(4)(b)) or to resign (s 516).

D Auditors' liability and limitation of liability

Duty of care of auditors

16-52 One of the most contentious issues is the extent of any duty of care owed by the company's auditors to the company, the shareholders and others who read and rely on the audited accounts. While there is much case law on the matter involving auditors (and other professionals), the general trend is a reluctance to find that a professional adviser owes a common law duty of care to a non-client.[139]

16-53 There are two possible types of claims:

(1) claims by clients against their auditors which would be straightforward claims in contract (since the auditors owe the company appointing them a duty to exercise reasonable care and skill in performing their contractual obligations) and in tort;[140] and

(2) claims in tort by third parties who are not in any direct relationship with the auditors but who claim damages for losses arising from reliance on negligently audited accounts. The extent of any duty of care in tort to such users of the company's accounts is problematic. A duty of care may arise between an auditor and another under two different but interrelated approaches:[141] because of an assumption of

---

[138] There is a right against self-incrimination: see CA 2006, s 499(3).

[139] See *Bank of Credit and Commerce International (Overseas) Ltd v Price Waterhouse* [1998] BCC 617 at 636, per Sir Brian Neill; *BDG Roof-Bond v Douglas* [2000] 1 BCLC 401 at 420, per Park J. The Company Law Review made no recommendation for any statutory extension of auditors' duties of care, preferring to leave the issue to the development of the law of negligence in the normal way: see *Final Report* (2001), paras 8.134–8.135.

[140] As the payment of improper dividends or bonuses is the natural and probable result of the false picture which the auditors have allowed the accounts to present, the auditors are liable for those amounts: *Re Thomas Gerrard & Son Ltd* [1967] 2 All ER 525 (auditors aware of discrepancies but failed to investigate further); *Re London and General Bank (No 2)* [1895] 2 Ch 673 (auditors omitted information from report to shareholders); and see *Barings plc v Coopers & Lybrand (No 1)* [2002] 2 BCLC 364; *Equitable Life Assurance Society v Ernst & Young* [2003] 2 BCLC 603.

[141] There is possibly a third approach—the incremental approach approved by Lord Bridge in *Caparo Industries plc v Dickman* [1990] 1 All ER 568 at 576 where he stated that it is preferable that 'the law should develop novel categories of negligence incrementally and by analogy with established categories, rather than by a massive extension of a *prima facie* duty of care restrained only by indefinable "considerations which

responsibility for the task/advice in question or because of meeting the three-fold test (foreseeability, proximity and fairness) established in *Caparo Industries plc v Dickman*.[142] In practice the courts apply one or other or both approaches depending on the circumstances. The House of Lords in *Customs and Excise Commissioners v Barclays Bank*[143] made it clear that it is not possible to force the law into a single test.

As Hamblen J commented in *Standard Chartered Bank v Ceylon Petroleum*:[144]

'... recent case law has emphasised the importance of a pragmatic approach which concentrates on the exchanges and dealings between the parties considered in their context rather than the application of high level statements of principle. Attention should be concentrated on "the detailed circumstances of the particular case and the particular relationship between the parties in the context of their legal and factual situation as a whole,"—per Lord Bingham in *Commissioners of Customs & Excise v Barclays Bank...*'[145]

An assumption of responsibility for the task/advice in question

16-54   Where the parties have a contractual or 'almost contractual'[146] relationship (for example, a client relationship or a relationship between an auditor and a regulatory authority[147]) and so fall clearly within the *Hedley Byrne & Co Ltd v Heller & Partners Ltd*[148] principle, the matter is relatively straightforward. This assumption of responsibility rests upon a relationship between the parties, which may be general or specific to the particular transaction, and which may or may not be contractual in nature.[149] Whether there is such an assumption of responsibility is a matter to be considered objectively.[150] Accountants who carry out specific reporting obligations under a statutory requirement to do so owe a duty of care to the regulatory authority to whom they report;[151] likewise, auditors may assume a duty of care to a regulatory authority.[152]

Meeting the three-fold test established in *Caparo*

16-55   Most disputes arise where there is no relationship between the auditor and the claimant but the claimant alleges that the parties are sufficiently proximate to give rise to a duty of care on the part of the auditor. The leading authority on auditors' liability is *Caparo*

---

ought to negative, or to reduce or limit the scope of the duty or the class of person to whom it is owed"'. But the value of this approach has been doubted, see *Customs and Excise Commissioners v Barclays Bank* [2006] 4 All ER 256 at [7] ('little value as a test in itself'), per Lord Bingham; also Mitchell and Mitchell, 'Negligence Liability for Pure Economic Loss' (2005) 121 LQR 194.   [142] [1990] 1 All ER 568.

[143] [2006] 4 All ER 256, HL.   [144] [2011] EWHC 1785 at [478].   [145] [2006] 4 All ER 256 at [8].

[146] As Lord Bingham said, the paradigm situation being a relationship having all the indicia of contract save consideration, see *Commissioners of Customs & Excise v Barclays Bank* [2006] 4 All ER 256 at [4].

[147] See *Andrew v Kounnis Freeman* [1999] 2 BCLC 641.   [148] [1963] 2 All ER 575.

[149] *Henderson v Merrett Syndicates Ltd* [1994] 3 All ER 506 at 520, HL, per Lord Goff.

[150] *Commissioners of Customs & Excise v Barclays Bank* [2006] 4 All ER 256 at [5]; *Electra Private Equity Partners v KPMG Peat Marwick* [2001] 1 BCLC 589; *Henderson v Merrett Syndicates Ltd* [1994] 3 All ER 506 at 518–21; *Spring v Guardian Assurance plc* [1994] 3 All ER 129; *Williams v Natural Life Health Foods Ltd* [1998] 1 BCLC 689; *Peach Publishing Ltd v Slater & Co* [1998] BCC 139. See Jackson LJ's comments that, in his view, the conceptual basis upon which the concurrent (as in contract and tort) liability of professional persons in tort to their clients now rests is assumption of responsibility, noting that it is perhaps understandable that professional persons are taken to assume responsibility for economic loss to their clients. They expect their clients and possibly others to act in reliance upon their work product, often with financial or economic consequences, see *Robinson v PE Jones (Contractors)* [2011] 3 WLR 815 at [74]–[75].

[151] See *Law Society v KPMG Peat Marwick* [2000] 4 All ER 540.

[152] See *Andrew v Kounnis Freeman* [1999] 2 BCLC 641.

Industries plc v Dickman[153] where, having reviewed the authorities, the House of Lords concluded that in order for a duty of care to arise, there must be:[154]

(1) a reasonable foreseeability of damage;

(2) a relationship of sufficient 'proximity' between the party owing the duty and the party to whom it is owed; and

(3) the imposition of the duty of care contended for should be just and reasonable in all the circumstances.

16-56 It is relatively easy to establish the first element, a foreseeability of damage if accounts are negligently audited, but that is not sufficient of itself. The third element, the 'just and reasonable' consideration, was imposed by the court in order to prevent foreseeability alone giving rise, in the famous words of Cardozo CJ in *Ultramares Corpn v Touche*,[155] to 'liability in an indeterminate amount for an indeterminate time to an indeterminate class'.

16-57 Most discussion has focused on the second element as to whether, on a particular set of facts, there is a relationship of sufficient proximity for a duty of care to arise. In *Caparo*, Lord Oliver identified the circumstances which should exist in order to establish the necessary relationship of proximity between the person claiming to be owed the duty (the advisee) and the adviser:[156]

(1) the advice is required for a purpose, whether particularly specified or generally described, which is made known, either actually or inferentially, to the adviser at the time the advice is given;

(2) the adviser knows, either actually or inferentially, that his advice will be communicated to the advisee, either specifically or as a member of an ascertainable class, in order that it should be used by the advisee for that purpose;

(3) it is known, either actually or inferentially, that the advice so communicated is likely to be acted upon by the advisee for that purpose without independent inquiry; and

(4) it is so acted upon by the advisee to his detriment.

16-58 The key elements then are that the auditor knows (whether actually or inferentially) that his report will be communicated to a person (whether individually or as a member of a class) specifically for a particular purpose and that there would be reliance on it. It is because these are the key elements which may give rise to a duty of care with respect to third parties that professional guidance to auditors encourages the use of disclaimers in an attempt to minimise the potential for these elements being present.[157] Hence the auditors' report commonly includes a paragraph to the effect that the report is made solely to the company's members in accordance with the CA 2006 and solely for the purposes of the CA 2006 and 'to the fullest extent permitted by law, we [the auditors] do not accept or

---

[153] [1990] 1 All ER 568; noted [1990] LQR 349; [1990] MLR 824.

[154] [1990] 1 All ER 568 at 573–4, per Lord Bridge, though as Lord Bingham acknowledged in *Commissioners of Customs & Excise v Barclays Bank* [2006] 4 All ER 256 at [6], this threefold test itself provides no straightforward answer to the question whether or not a party owes a duty of care.

[155] (1931) 255 NY 170 at 179.   [156] [1990] 1 All ER 568 at 589.

[157] The practice arises from the decision of the Scottish courts in *RBS plc v Bannerman* [2006] BCC 148 where the court considered that the absence of a disclaimer of liability to a third party could be a relevant circumstance pointing to an assumption of liability in respect of that third party's use of information provided by the auditor.

assume responsibility to anyone other than the company and the company's members as a body for our audit work, for this report, or for the opinions we have formed'.[158]

16-59 In *Caparo*, as noted at **16-43**, the House of Lords concluded that the purpose of the audit is to enable the shareholders as a body to exercise informed control of the company.[159] It follows that auditors do not owe a duty of care to members of the public at large who rely on the audited accounts to buy shares; nor to an individual shareholder in the company who wishes to buy more shares in the company since an individual shareholder is in no better position than a member of the public at large;[160] nor to possible takeover bidders,[161] nor do they owe a duty of care to existing or future creditors who extend credit on the strength of the audited accounts.[162] In none of these cases is the relationship proximate enough, without more, to give rise to a duty of care. Returning to the facts in *Caparo*, the House of Lords found the auditors owed no duty of care to an existing shareholder in the company who purchased additional shares and took over the company in reliance on the audited accounts only to discover that the accounts were inaccurate. The auditors owed their duty to the shareholders as a body and not to an individual investor.

16-60 These issues can be illustrated by considering *Barings plc v Coopers & Lybrand (No 1)*.[163] This case arose out of the collapse of the Barings Bank group of companies as a result of the unauthorised activities of a rogue trader in the Far East who accumulated losses of about £800m. The parent company (P1) had a subsidiary (S1) which had a subsidiary (S2) and the rogue trader was an employee of S2. Following the collapse of the group, an action in contract and tort was brought by S2 against its auditors (D&T) in respect of their allegedly negligent audits of the company. An action in tort was also commenced against the auditors by P1 and S1. Essentially, these companies argued that, had the audit been conducted properly, the wrongdoing would have been uncovered, these companies would not have continued to advance funding to S2, and the group would not have collapsed. The court granted an application for the claim to be struck out.

16-61 Turning to the criteria established by *Caparo*, Evans-Lombe J pointed out that, in the case of a claim in tort against an auditor, it is necessary to plead and prove that at the time the auditor undertook his services, he must have had in contemplation that they would be relied on by the claimant for the purpose of a particular transaction or class of transactions. That reliance then must have resulted in the loss for which compensation was claimed. Evans-Lombe J noted that these limitations (reliance on the audit for a contemplated purpose) were necessary to control the scope of claims in this area of the law. He went on:[164]

'To the outsider it would seem far-fetched that the negligence of a subsidiary auditor of one of the minor subsidiary companies of a complex and substantial banking group should

---

[158] See ICAEW, *The Audit Report and Auditors' Duty of Care to Third Parties*, Technical release, Audit 01/03, as updated.   [159] See [1990] 1 All ER 568 at 583–4, 606–7.

[160] [1990] 1 All ER 568 at 581, 601, 607.

[161] *Caparo Industries plc v Dickman* [1990] 1 All ER 568; see also *James McNaughton Papers Group Ltd v Hicks Anderson & Co* [1991] BCLC 163; though the position may be different where representations are made after an identified bidder has emerged; see *Morgan Crucible Co plc v Hill Samuel Bank Ltd* [1991] BCLC 18; *Galoo Ltd v Bright Grahame Murray* [1994] 2 BCLC 492; where it may be possible, on the facts, to establish that a duty of care has been assumed: see *ADT v BDO Binder Hamlyn* [1996] BCC 808; also *Electra Private Equity Partners v KPMG Peat Marwick* [2001] 1 BCLC 589.

[162] *Al Saudi Banque v Clark Pixley* [1989] 3 All ER 361; *Berg Sons & Co Ltd v Mervyn Hampton Adams* [1993] BCLC 1045.   [163] [2002] 2 BCLC 364, Ch D.

[164] [2002] 2 BCLC 364 at [88].

expose that auditor to liability for massive damages flowing from the collapse of the entire group, notwithstanding that it can be said that but for his negligence that collapse would not have taken place.'

16-62 As the auditors of S2, the auditors never had it in contemplation that their report would be used by the other companies in the group when deciding to meet the trader's funding requests through S2.[165] Equally, no transactions made by P1 which resulted in the loss of the entire group could be identified as transactions which had been embarked upon in reliance on the audit and which the auditors had in contemplation when they undertook that audit.[166]

16-63 This case highlights another issue, causation (but see below). Even if a duty of care can be established, the alleged breach of duty must be the effective or dominant cause of the claimants' loss as opposed to merely the occasion for the loss. In determining that issue, the court applies its common sense to the issue. In *Galoo Ltd v Bright Grahame Murray*[167] the court struck out a claim for losses arising from continued trading after a negligent audit. It was argued that, had the audit been conducted properly, the companies involved would not have continued to trade and therefore the claim was for the losses arising from the continued trading. The court rejected the claim. The breach of duty gave the companies the opportunity to continue and to incur losses, but it did not 'cause' the loss in the sense that 'cause' is used in law. This point was reinforced recently in *Haugesund Kommune v Depfa ACS Bank*[168] where the issue was the extent of a law firm's liability for loss in respect of negligent advice given to a bank. The advice resulted in the bank making ultra vires loans to local authorities which could not be recovered. The local authorities were liable in restitution to make full repayment to the bank, but could not do so as they were insolvent. The Court of Appeal ruled that the extent of the lender's loss that falls within the adviser's duty has to depend on the reason for that loss. If it is due to the invalidity of the transactions, the loss plainly falls within the scope of the adviser's duty, but if the loss is due in reality to the impecuniosity of the borrower who cannot meet the restitutionary claim, that loss does not fall within the scope of the adviser's duty.

16-64 More recently the authorities have moved away from a focus on causation and *Galoo* is better analysed now in terms of the scope of the duty of care. The overall approach was summed up by Arden LJ in *Johnson v Gore Wood & Co*[169] in the following way:

> 'Starting with *Caparo v Dickman*, the courts have moved away from characterising questions as to the measure of damages for the tort of negligence as questions of causation and remoteness. The path that once led in that direction now leads in a new direction. The courts now analyse such questions by enquiring whether the duty which the tortfeasor owed was a duty in respect of the kind of loss of which the victim complains. Duty is no longer determined in abstraction from the consequences or vice-versa. The same test applies whether the duty of care is contractual or tortious. To determine the scope of the duty the court must examine carefully the purpose for which advice was being given and generally the surrounding circumstances. The determination of the scope of the duty thus involves an intensely fact-sensitive exercise. The final result turns on the facts, and it is likely to be only the general principles rather than the solution in any individual case that are of assistance in later cases.'

---

[165] [2002] 2 BCLC 364 at [75]–[76].   [166] [2002] 2 BCLC 364 at [85].

[167] [1994] 2 BCLC 492. Cf *Sasea Finance Ltd v KPMG* [2000] 1 BCLC 236, where the court accepted that where the auditors failed in breach of duty to 'blow the whistle' on fraudulent and dishonest activities of senior staff, it was arguable that that failure caused continued losses brought about by such frauds.

[168] [2011] 3 All ER 655.   [169] [2003] EWCA Civ 1728 at [91].

16-65 Two key points emerge: first, these issues are intensely fact-sensitive and, secondly, the focus is on the scope of the duty in terms of whether there was a duty in respect of the kind of loss of which the victim complains. As Lord Phillips commented in *Stone & Rolls Ltd v Moore Stephens*,[170] it is questionable whether it is sensible in this context to attempt to distinguish between duty, breach and actionable damage, noting Lord Oliver's comment in *Caparo*[171] that 'it is not a duty to take care in the abstract, but a duty to avoid causing to the particular plaintiff damage of the particular kind which he has in fact sustained'. The position can be illustrated by *MAN Nutzfahrzeuge AG v Freightliner Ltd*[172] where the Court of Appeal dismissed a claim by a parent company for breach of duty by an auditor of a subsidiary company.

16-66 Essentially, the facts were that a subsidiary company (S1) was sold by its parent company (P1) to M by way of a share purchase agreement. It later transpired that for some time previously the accounts of S1 had been persistently manipulated by its financial controller, E, who was responsible for a systematic VAT fraud. E had played a prominent role in the negotiations for the sale and made dishonest representations to M as to the accuracy of the accounts. P1 settled a claim in deceit against it by M and the issue before the Court of Appeal was whether P1 could look for a contribution from S1's auditors who accepted that, if the audit had been conducted with due care and skill, the defects in the accounts would have been identified. The auditors were aware of the importance of the accounts in the negotiations with M.

16-67 The Court of Appeal accepted that it was within the scope of the auditors' duty of care to protect S1 from the consequences of decisions taken by S1 or by its shareholders in relation to the affairs of S1 on the basis that the accounts were free from material misstatement. Though it was not necessary to decide the point, the court considered that it would also have been within the scope of a special duty of care owed by the auditors to protect P1 from the consequences of representations and warranties made in the share purchase agreement with M. But the auditors could not be held to have assumed responsibility for the fraudulent use which the dishonest employee made of the subsidiary's accounts in the negotiations for the sale of S1 since that would impose on the auditors a liability greater than they could reasonably have thought they were undertaking. P1's losses (its liability in deceit) were the direct result of the dishonesty of S1's employee (which resulted in a vicarious liability for fraudulent misrepresentation) rather than the inaccuracy of the accounts themselves and the auditors did not undertake a special audit duty to P1 in respect of representations made by E as to the accuracy of the accounts. For all those reasons the auditors were not liable for the loss which P1 had suffered.

16-68 Auditors will also take heart from the decision of the House of Lords in *Stone & Rolls Ltd v Moore Stephens*[173] where, by a 3–2 majority, their Lordships confirmed that auditors sued in negligence by an insolvent audit client, a one-man company under the sole control of S, a fraudster, could rely on the maxim *ex turpi causa non oritur actio* which precludes claims based on the claimant's own illegality. In this case, a company had been used as a vehicle for fraud by S, its beneficial owner. Various defrauded banks had sued the company and S in deceit and obtained judgment, but the company was insolvent and

---

[170] [2009] 2 BCLC 563 at [81].   [171] [1990] BCLC 273 at 311.   [172] [2008] 2 BCLC 22, CA.

[173] [2009] 2 BCLC 563, aff'g [2008] 2 BCLC 461, CA. See generally Davies, 'Auditors' Liability: No need to detect fraud' (2010) CLJ 505; Halpern, '*Stone & Rolls Ltd v Moore Stephens*: An Unnecessary Tangle' (2010) 73 MLR 487; Watts, '*Stone & Rolls Ltd v Moore Stephens*: Audit contracts and turpitude' (2010) LQR 14; Ferran, 'Corporate Attribution and the Directing Mind and Will' (2011) LQR 239.

recovery could not be obtained against S. The liquidator of the company then sued the company's auditors in negligence only to be met by the defence *ex turpi causa non oritur actio*. Essentially the auditors argued that the fraudster's conduct was to be attributed to the company such that the company itself was the fraudster and any claim by the company was therefore barred by the *ex turpi causa* principle.[174] The House of Lords divided 3–2 in favour of allowing the auditors' defence. Lords Walker and Brown (of the majority) considered the issue to be one of attribution. S was the sole beneficial owner of the company, he was its embodiment, he was instrumental in carrying out the frauds, his conduct was to be attributed to the company such that the company was the fraudster and the company's claim could be defeated by reliance on *ex turpi causa*.[175] Lord Phillips, also of the majority, preferred to rest his decision on the narrow ground that the sole person for whose benefit the duty was owed by the auditors was the person who owned and ran the company and who was responsible for the fraud. In those circumstances, *ex turpi causa* provides a defence.[176] He noted what while it might be arguable that the duty of care of auditors should extend to protecting the interest that creditors have in the preservation of the company's assets, that would involve a departure or extension of *Caparo*, something not required by the issue before the court which was the application of the *ex turpi causa* maxim.[177] On the other hand, Lord Mance (dissenting) did focus particularly on the duty of care owed by auditors[178] and he concluded that they did owe a duty to the company to have detected and reported a fraud by the top management of the company rendering the company increasingly insolvent, i.e. their duty to the company extends beyond the interests of the shareholders in a situation where the company is insolvent at the time of each audit and increasingly so.[179] Such an approach is not inconsistent, in his view, with *Caparo* since a situation of insolvency was not before the court in that case.[180] Lord Mance concluded by stating that the approach taken by the majority in the case would have the effect of weakening the value of an audit and diminishing auditors' exposure in relation to precisely those (one-man) companies most vulnerable to management fraud. It is in relation to exactly such companies that auditors ought to be encouraged to exercise the skill and care anyway due, he thought, rather than to let them feel that the risks of incurring liability to the company for a negligent audit are reduced.[181] While some have found this reasoning compelling,[182] and certainly the issue in the case would have been better approached in terms of the scope of the duty rather than the contortions indulged in as a result of treating the issue as one of attribution,[183] this approach of Lord Mance requires too great a leap from the orthodox position on directors' duties (they have a duty to have regard to creditors' interests if the company is insolvent or doubtfully solvent, see **9-41**)

---

[174] [2008] 2 BCLC 461 at 493, per Rimer LJ.   [175] For a discussion of the attribution issues, see **3-106**.

[176] [2009] 2 BCLC 563 at [18], [86]; and see Watts, n 173, at 20.

[177] [2009] 2 BCLC 563 at [85] and see Watts n 173, at pp 15–16—the audit contract (and therefore any duty of care) extends only to shareholder interests because it is to the shareholders that the auditors report, otherwise auditors would be exposed to indeterminate liability measured by the extent of the company's creditors.

[178] Lord Scott also dissented; he thought that the majority had in effect pierced the veil in circumstances where it was not established that the wrongdoer was the owner of the company so there was no justification in treating him as the company, and they had applied a rule of public policy (*ex turpi causa*) in circumstances where the beneficiary of the duty owed by the auditors would have been the creditors of an insolvent company, not the wrongdoer, so there was no justification for allowing reliance on *ex turpi causa*, see [2009] 2 BCLC 563 at [116]–[122], but see Davies, n 173. Halpern, n 173, p 491 criticises this approach as drawing a dangerous distinction between the position of a company in liquidation and prior to liquidation.

[179] [2009] 2 BCLC 563 at [265]–[271].   [180] [2009] 2 BCLC 563 at [267]–[268].

[181] [2009] 2 BCLC 563 at [276].   [182] See Ferran, n 173, at 253–4.

[183] See Watts, n 173, also Halpern, n 173, and **3-107**.

to applying the same reasoning in the quite different context of the scope of auditors' duties.[184] It is also not necessary to make such a dramatic leap, rather the question of duty can be asked in the manner suggested by Lord Oliver in *Caparo* who stated that 'it is not a duty to take care in the abstract, but a duty to avoid causing to the particular plaintiff damage of the particular kind which he has in fact sustained'.[185] If the issue is approached in the pragmatic terms favoured by the courts, see **16-53,** and in the light of the scope of duty identified in *Caparo*, and the question is asked whether an auditor has a duty to avoid causing to a company's creditors damage arising from the fraud of the company's sole shareholder and director, the answer is clearly no, there is no such duty unless the law is expanded to create one. Of course, many cases where the auditor fails to discover a fraud will fall within the scenario in *Moore Stephens*, i.e. in the context of frauds committed by a sole director and shareholder through the medium of the company and it is easy to agree with Lord Mance that it is unappealing at one level that the auditors in such circumstances should be able to raise the defence of *ex turpi causa*. On the other hand, the answer to fraud in one-man companies probably lies elsewhere than in imposing a duty of care on auditors owed to the creditors of the insolvent, fraudulently run, company. Arguably, it is those who do business with such companies without pursuing their own checks as to the creditworthiness of the company and the integrity of those running it that allow fraudsters to perpetrate frauds in the first place. To make the auditors responsible for the subsequent losses would be disproportionate. As Lord Phillips commented in *Moore Stephens*, in the circumstances of that case, to have held the auditors liable would have required the duty of care undertaken by them to extend to taking reasonable care that the company was not used as a vehicle for fraud and that this duty was owed for the benefit of those that the company might defraud.[186] His verdict on that: 'I see no prospect that such a duty could be established.'[187]

Limiting auditors' liabilities

16-69 Faced with concerns as to the extent of their possible liability for negligent audits though, as discussed, there are considerable limitations to that liability and it is not as open-ended as auditors would have us believe, the auditing profession has been anxious to secure some safe harbours against liability. The starting point is CA 2006, s 532 which provides (subject to exceptions for indemnities and liability limitation agreements, discussed at **16-70**) that any provision, whether contained in a company's articles or in any contract with the company or otherwise, for exempting an auditor of a company (to any extent) from any liability that would otherwise attach to him in connection with any negligence, default, breach of duty or breach of trust in relation to the company occurring in the course of the audit of accounts, is void. Despite this restriction, there are a number of ways in which auditors successfully manage or limit their potential liabilities for negligent audits:[188]

    (1) Audit firms may incorporate as companies with limited liability or they may register as limited liability partnerships (LLPs) under the Limited Liability Partnerships Act 2000 (see **1-18**). Indeed LLPs were originally conceived as a mechanism to pro-

---

  [184] See Halpern, n 173, at 491, who describes Lord Mance's approach as a subversion of *Caparo*, making the point that the much wider duties of directors cannot be simply transposed from directors to auditors.

  [185] [1990] BCLC 273 at 311.   [186] [2009] 2 BCLC 574 at [85].   [187] [2009] 2 BCLC 574 at [85].

  [188] More generally, accountants providing services will try to limit their risk by managing the terms of their engagement, see ICAEW, 'Managing the Professional Liability of Accountants' Tech 02/11, though contractual terms are not so effective with respect to the audit engagement where the audit requirements are dictated by statute and professional standards.

tect auditors from limitless personal liability, but on enactment they were made available to all businesses.[189]

(2) Insurance—auditors may purchase insurance to protect themselves, but insurance is expensive and adequate cover may not be available, at any price. If a claim is for hundreds of millions of pounds, there is likely to be a significant shortfall between the cover (which might be for, say, £50m) and the amount claimed.

(3) Indemnities—a company may indemnify its auditor against any liability incurred by him in defending proceedings (whether civil or criminal) in which judgment is given in his favour or he is acquitted, or in connection with an application under CA 2006, s 1157 in which relief is granted to him by the court (s 533).[190]

(4) Court relief—auditors are amongst those entitled to apply to the court for relief under CA 2006, s 1157 (power of court to grant relief in case of honest and reasonable conduct), see **13-53**.

(5) It is possible for companies and their auditors to enter into liability limitation agreements (LLAs).

Liability limitation agreements

Background

16-70 The background to LLAs is the long-running concern of auditors, already noted, that they risk catastrophic losses in the event of liability in negligence, a concern fuelled by the implosion in 2002 of Arthur Andersen (then one of the world's largest audit firms), following the collapse of the American energy company, Enron, which had been audited by Andersen. The particular concern of auditors is that joint and several liability in English law means that, following a corporate collapse, there is no one left to sue who is worth suing other than the auditors who are treated as the deep pockets to meet the entire losses though the directors and others may also be culpable. As is clear from the case law, the legal position is somewhat more complex with the law limiting the auditor's liability to the company rather than to third parties and with liability in turn limited by the scope of the duty of care imposed. Nevertheless, the auditing profession has been relentless in its pursuit of legal protection against claims.

16-71 The collapse of Arthur Andersen also increased concerns amongst regulators and national authorities that with the 'Big Five' auditing firms now reduced to the 'Big Four' (PwC, Deloitte, Ernst & Young, KPMG), a further collapse would mean very limited audit choice for the largest companies and indeed a risk that the largest companies would find it very difficult to appoint an auditor at all.

16-72 This last aspect sufficiently concerned the European Commission that it concluded that unlimited liability for auditors combined with insufficient insurance cover poses significant problems for the development of a competitive audit market. Hence in 2008 it issued a Recommendation to Member States that Member States should take national measures to limit audit firms' liabilities save in the case of an intentional breach of duty by an

---

[189] For a critical review of this response to auditors' concerns, see Freedman & Finch, 'Limited Liability Partnerships: Have Accountants Sewn up the "Deep Pockets" Debate?' [1997] JBL 387.

[190] Indemnities are excluded from the application of s 532(1) see **16-69**.

auditor.[191] The Recommendation suggested three possible limitation methods: a financial cap, a mechanism for proportionate liability or a contractual limitation approved by the shareholders and left it to Member States to decide on the appropriate method for limiting liability. The Recommendation also sets out the key principles to be followed by Member States when they select a limitation method including that a limitation of liability should not apply in the case of an intentional breach of duty by an auditor; and it should not prevent injured parties from being fairly compensated (in other words, only a limitation and not an exemption from liability should be provided), but a limitation should apply to limit claims by the company and by any third party entitled under national law to bring a claim for compensation.[192] In the event, the UK had already made provision for auditor LLAs in the CA 2006, ss 532–538, which came into force on 6 April 2008 and which the Government thought would address the concerns of individual auditors about their liability. It was also thought that the availability of LLAs would help to expand the pool of audit services available (new entrants would be willing to enter the market if they could manage their potential liabilities effectively) and that this would lead to a more competitive market and a reduction in costs.

16-73 Given the novelty of allowing auditors to limit their liability, the FRC issued guidance on the content of LLAs and the issues which the directors should bear in mind when considering an LLA. The FRC Guidance includes specimen clauses and explains the process to be followed to obtain shareholder approval together with specimen shareholder resolutions.[193] While there are concerns (also expressed about the EU Recommendation) that there is an insufficient balance between the protection of auditor interests and shareholder interests, the FRC comments that these concerns must be assessed in the light of the efforts being made to improve audit quality, the need for LLAs to be approved by shareholders and that, under CA 2006, s 537, the court has the power to disapply the LLA unless it is satisfied that the agreement is fair and reasonable. At the same time the Institutional Shareholders Committee issued a statement indicating that institutional investors will expect companies to employ the specimen principal terms for agreements laid out in the FRC's Guidance.[194] This position suggests that the FRC Guidance will become in effect a code to be followed by the largest companies when considering entering into an LLA.

Agreeing a liability limitation agreement

16-74 A 'liability limitation agreement' is an agreement that purports to limit the amount of a liability owed to a company by its auditor in respect of any negligence, default, breach of duty or breach of trust, occurring in the course of the audit of accounts, of which the auditor may be guilty in relation to the company (CA 2006, s 534(1)). Each company must negotiate its own LLA and there cannot be group-wide agreements. A liability limitation

---

[191] Commission Recommendation of 5 June 2008 concerning the limitation of the civil liability of statutory auditors and audit firms, OJ L 162, 21.06.2008, p 39.

[192] The Recommendation follows an earlier consultation on liability, see DG Internal Market Commission Staff Working Paper: *Consultation on Auditors' Liability and its Impact on the European Capital Markets* (January 2007); also London Economics, *Report on Economic Impact of Auditors' Liability Regimes* for EC-DG Internal Market and Services (September 2006); also an earlier study commissioned by the European Commission: *A study on systems of civil liability of statutory auditors in the context of a Single Market for auditing services in the European Union* (2001).

[193] See FRC, *Guidance on Auditor Liability Limitation Agreements* (June 2008).

[194] See Institutional Shareholders' Committee (ISC) Statement on Auditor Liability Limitation Agreements (June 2008). Membership includes the Association of British Insurers and National Association of Pension funds, the two most influential institutional investor groups; in May 2011, the ISC was reconstituted and renamed as the Institutional Investors Committee.

agreement cannot apply to more than one financial year so, for example, auditors cannot negotiate five-year deals and the agreement must specify the financial year in relation to which it applies (s 535(1)). Shareholder authorisation is required by an ordinary resolution unless the articles require a higher majority.[195] A private company can pass a resolution waiving the need for approval, or pass a resolution before entering into the agreement approving its principal terms,[196] or it can pass a resolution approving the (entire) agreement after the company has entered into it (s 536(2)); likewise for a public company, but a public company cannot waive the need for approval (s 536(3)). Authorisation may be withdrawn by the company passing an ordinary resolution to that effect at any time before the company enters into the agreement, or if the company has already entered into the agreement, before the beginning of the financial year to which the agreement relates (s 536(5)). A company which has made a liability limitation agreement must disclose in a note to the accounts its principal terms and the date of the approval resolution (or resolution waiving the need for approval, in the case of a private company) passed by the company's members.[197]

16-75 There are limits to what can be agreed and an auditor cannot limit its liability in an unreasonable way and a significant safeguard imposed is that a liability limitation agreement is not effective to limit the auditor's liability to less than such amount as is fair and reasonable in all the circumstances of the case having regard (in particular) to the auditor's responsibilities under CA 2006, Pt 16, the nature and purpose of the auditor's contractual obligations to the company and the professional standards expected of him (s 537(1)).[198] A liability limitation agreement that purports to limit the auditor's liability to less than an amount that is fair and reasonable in all the circumstances takes effect as if so limited so the court will simply adjust the limitation downwards when it is set too high (s 537(2)).[199] In determining what is fair and reasonable in all the circumstances of the case no account is to be taken of matters arising after the loss or damage in question has been incurred, or matters (whenever arising) affecting the possibility of recovering compensation from other persons liable in respect of the same loss or damage (s 537(3)). For example, the fact that the liability is shared with an employee who is not worth suing is ignored.[200]

16-76 The legislation does not impose a limitation mechanism and, in particular, the limit on the amount of the auditor's liability need not be a sum of money or a formula specified in the agreement (s 535(4)). It is clear from the Institutional Shareholders Committee's statement on LLAs (**16-73**) that institutional shareholders will only accept agreements providing for proportionate liability (liability based on the auditor's share of the responsibility for the company's loss) or a liability expressed in terms of what is fair and reasonable, but they will not support fixed caps.[201] Proportionate liability is likely therefore to become

---

[195] CA 2006, ss 534(2)(b); 281(3).

[196] The 'principal terms' of an agreement are terms specifying or relevant to the determination of the kind (or kinds) of acts or omissions covered by the LLA, the financial year to which the LLA relates, or the limit of the auditor's liability: CA 2006, s 535(4).

[197] CA 2006, s 538; The Companies (Disclosure of Auditor Remuneration and Liability Limitation Agreements) Regulations 2008, SI 2008/489, reg 8.

[198] The Government has a power by regulations to prescribe specific provisions or to prohibit certain provisions (CA 2006, s 535(2)), but it does not intend to exercise the power at the moment.

[199] In other words, auditors risk nothing by overreaching in an LLA for the LLA does not become void, but is merely rewritten by the court. This may seem favourable to the auditors but it reflects the fact that all concerned will have made arrangements, such as insurance cover, on the basis of a liability limitation being in place. Note the UCTA 1977, ss 2(2), 3(2) do not apply to LLAs: CA 2006, s 534(2)(b).

[200] See *Explanatory Notes to the Companies Act 2006*, para 828.   [201] See n 194 as to the ISC.

the norm for large companies.[202] For smaller companies, in time, other limitation options will emerge possibly based on a multiple of the audit fee or other variations.

16-77 Though these provisions on LLAs came into force in April 2008, there has been only a modest uptake with, it seems, no listed companies entering into an LLA[203] and little evidence of any large companies agreeing them with their auditors. There is no reason for such companies to take the initiative in agreeing something that restricts the ability of the company to recover losses and, at that end of the market, there appears to be little pressure from the audit firms for these agreements, presumably because the audit firm is anxious to retain high value clients (bearing in mind the level of non-audit services which the client may well be purchasing from the auditor). The position may be different lower down the corporate hierarchy with some evidence that LLAs have been agreed in medium and small companies where the audit price seems to have been the leverage used by auditors to secure agreement.[204] In essence, companies seem to have signed up to agreements in order to ensure that they could retain a particular audit firm and/or because they secured the audit at a lower price than would be the case without the agreement.

16-78 The issue for any directors contemplating entering into an LLA is the need to have regard to their duty to promote the success of the company (s 172, see **9-2**) and the ISC Statement stresses, for example, that the directors must look to see what the company will get out of the arrangement in terms of assurances that audit quality will be preserved and enhanced by the auditors and that 'other benefits' (not defined) might be secured for the company.[205] The directors will also need to weigh up the fact that the auditors may refuse to act for the company at an acceptable price without an LLA and so the use of an LLA may be necessary to help the company secure the audit firm of choice, a point acknowledged in the FRC Guidance.[206] An alternative point of view is that these changes are too favourable to auditors and too unfavourable to shareholders who pay large fees to auditors in the expectation that they will do a careful and skilful job. Auditors are able to operate through LLPs and manage their liabilities in that way, after all, and the duty of care owed by them is carefully circumscribed by the courts.

---

[202] The ABI and NAPF have indicated that their members should vote against any LLA drawn up on any other basis.

[203] It appears that the American Securities and Exchange Commission has indicated that it will not accept the entry into LLAs by UK companies which also have to register with it, a stance which would explain why LLAs are not a realistic option at the listed company level.

[204] The evidence comes from an evaluation conducted on behalf of the Department of Business, Skills and Innovation following the implementation of the CA 2006, see BIS, *Evaluation of the CA 2006 (2010)*, vol 1, para 6.13 .

[205] See ISC Statement, n 194, p 2.

[206] See FRC Guidance, n 193, Section 3 'What Issues should the Directors consider?', para 3.6.

17

The unfairly prejudicial remedy and the minority shareholder

A Introduction

17-1 The most important shareholder remedy in practice is the ability of a member to petition for relief on the ground that the affairs of the company are being or have been conducted in a manner which is unfairly prejudicial to the interests of members generally, or of some part of its members, under CA 2006, s 994, previously CA 1985, s 459.

17-2 Before examining the unfairly prejudicial remedy in detail, it may be useful to draw attention to some background considerations which should be borne in mind.

Disputes in private companies

17-3 The vast majority of companies registered under the CA 2006 and its predecessor, the CA 1985, are private companies. These companies typically have only a small number of shareholders,[1] most if not all of whom are also the directors, and many of whom are also employees of the company. Often the shareholders will be members of the same family and, even if they are not, the relationships involved tend to be personal as well as commercial. Disputes too tend to be personal and bitter and settling such cases can be difficult.

17-4 A typical scenario would involve the initial enthusiastic participation of all the shareholders in the company as directors and employees rapidly followed by disagreements among the participants, perhaps about the direction of the company, or the respective merits of the contributions made by each participant, or the extent to which the parties are benefiting financially from the business, and culminating in the majority shareholder or shareholders voting to remove the minority shareholder from his position as a director and dismissing him as an employee. Voluntary exit by the minority shareholder from the company at this point is the desirable option but it may be difficult to achieve.

17-5 Finding a purchaser for a minority stake in a private company is not easy and, even if a purchaser is found, the minority shareholder may find that the company's articles of association constrain him as to whom he can sell. For example, the articles may require him to offer the shares initially to the existing members and may require the price to be determined by the company's auditor and not by the vendor. It is commonly the case that the board of directors has a power in any event to refuse to register any transfer of any shares (see discussion at **14-58**). Voluntary exit can be difficult to achieve, therefore, and legal action, or at least the threat of legal action, may be necessary.

---

[1] Research carried out for the Company Law Review showed that 70% of the companies on the register had only one or two shareholders and 90% had fewer than five shareholders: Company Law Review, *Developing the Framework* (2000), para 6.9. The position is unlikely to have changed significantly since then.

17-6   The position of minority shareholders once they are in disagreement with the majority is exacerbated by difficulties in obtaining accurate information about the company's affairs,[2] especially where the shareholder has been removed from the board and no longer has access to management accounts and minutes of board meetings[3] although shareholders are entitled to the annual accounts.[4]

Disputes in public companies

17-7   Disputes in public companies do not have the focus on personal participation and remuneration which characterises disputes in private companies. Instead there may be complaints about the standard of management and the level of their remuneration. A variety of mechanisms can be deployed to address these issues with litigation and legal redress generally low on the shareholders' range of options. Management under-performance may be addressed by setting contractual targets and linking remuneration to performance. Many of the shareholders in these companies are institutional shareholders who are able to exercise influence by voicing their concerns directly to the board and, of course, now the emphasis is very much on shareholder engagement with the board, as discussed at **5-43**. In the worst cases of mismanagement, a declining share price may mean that the company becomes a target of a takeover and so under-performing management may be replaced through the market for corporate control. Takeovers are discussed in Chapter 26. Of course, for shareholders with a grievance in a public company, the best option is often to exit the company by selling their shares, something which is particularly easy in the case of a traded public company with shares admitted to trading on a market.

Majority and minority shareholders

17-8   Most disputes necessarily involve minority shareholders seeking redress as the majority can secure redress for themselves through the exercise of their voting power.[5] It should be borne in mind, however, that minority shareholders too can behave in an obstructive and damaging way with a view to forcing the majority to buy them out at an inflated value simply to rid themselves of the nuisance.[6]

Anticipating and preventing disputes

17-9   As Professor Prentice has commented, a feature of shareholder disputes particularly in smaller private companies is the parties' chronic failure to anticipate the nature, extent

---

[2]   A point recognised by the court as a problem in *Harborne Road Nominees Ltd v Karvaski* [2011] EWHC 2214.

[3]   Shareholders have no right of access to board minutes, only to minutes of general meetings: see CA 2006, s 358; but they can obtain details of directors' service contracts: s 228; and inspect statutory registers such as the register of members, s 116, subject to the company's ability to refuse permission under s 117. As to a petitioner's entitlement to disclosure of company documents, see *CAS (Nominees) Ltd v Nottingham Forest FC plc* [2002] 1 BCLC 613; *Arrow Trading & Investment Est 1920 v Edwardian Group Ltd* [2005] 1 BCLC 696.

[4]   The accounts may be quite dated, however, since a private company has nine months from the end of the financial year in which to send the accounts to each member: see CA 2006, ss 423–424, 442.

[5]   See *Re Legal Costs Negotiators Ltd* [1999] 2 BCLC 171; *Re Baltic Real Estate Ltd (No 2)* [1993] BCLC 503.

[6]   The courts are alert to this possibility, see *Re a Company (No 007623 of 1984)* [1986] BCLC 362 at 367, per Hoffmann J: '…the very width of [the unfairly prejudicial] jurisdiction mean that unless carefully controlled, it can become a means of oppression'.

and consequences of a breakdown in their relationship.[7] He identified a variety of reasons for this stance including an unwillingness to contemplate breakdown of the relationship at the beginning of the venture; an inability in any event to anticipate all future contingencies; and the fact that the costs of trying to so anticipate may simply not be justified.[8]

17-10 These difficulties are compounded by the practice in this jurisdiction whereby a substantial percentage of companies incorporated annually are shelf companies (i.e. purchased from a formation agent as a ready-made company, see **1-10**), with the result that those incorporating in this way are likely to have had minimal, if any, advice and the company's articles of association will simply be a standard version which do not address future breakdown.[9]

Governing principles

17-11 Shareholder remedies were the subject of a detailed review[10] by the Law Commission in 1996–97 and that work was considered and generally adopted by the Company Law Review[11] which did not devote much time to this issue. The Law Commission in its report identified what it considered to be the governing principles appropriate to this area, principles which we encounter throughout our consideration of company law, namely the proper plaintiff rule, the principle of majority rule in matters of internal management, non-interference by the courts in commercial decisions, recognition of the sanctity of contract and freedom from unnecessary shareholder interference.[12]

17-12 The proper plaintiff rule means that normally the company should be the only party entitled to enforce a cause of action belonging to it, reflecting the fact that the company is a separate legal entity. Accordingly, a member should be able to maintain proceedings about wrongs done to the company only in exceptional circumstances. The majority rule reflects the basic mechanism for decision-making in companies which has its corollary that an individual member should not be able to pursue proceedings on behalf of the company about matters of internal management, that is, matters which the majority are entitled to regulate by ordinary resolution. These two principles are central to the derivative claim which is discussed in Chapter 18.

17-13 The importance of the courts having proper regard for the decisions of directors on commercial matters, provided the decision is made in good faith, on proper information and in the light of the relevant considerations, and appears to be a reasonable decision for the directors to have taken, is a central theme in judgments for a century or more.[13]

17-14 The principle of freedom from unnecessary shareholder interference is reflected in the tight judicial control of the derivative claim, discussed in Chapter 18. The intention is

[7] Prentice, 'Protecting Minority Shareholders' Interests' in Feldman & Meisel (eds), *Corporate and Commercial Law: Modern Developments* (1996) at p 80.

[8] Prentice, n 7, at pp 89–93.

[9] See Prentice, n 7, at p 90.

[10] See Law Commission, *Shareholder Remedies* (Law Comm No 246) (Cm 3769, 1997).

[11] Company Law Review, *Developing the Framework* (2000), paras 4.70–4.71; *Completing the Structure* (2000), para 5.106.

[12] See Law Commission Report, n 10, para 1.9.

[13] The courts' reluctance to interfere in commercial decisions is long standing: see *Carlen v Drury* (1812) 1 Ves & B 154, 35 E.R.61 at 63: 'This Court is not to be required on every Occasion to take the Management of every Playhouse and Brewhouse in the Kingdom …' (per Lord Eldon); also *Burland v Earle* [1902] AC 83 at 93, per Lord Davey; *Hogg v Cramphorn Ltd* [1966] 3 All ER 420 at 428, per Buckley J; and *Shuttleworth v Cox* [1927] 2 KB 9 at 23: 'It is not the business of the court to manage the affairs of the company.'

that, in keeping with the right of directors to manage the company's affairs, shareholders should not be able to involve the company in litigation without good cause.

17-15   The principle of sanctity of contract means that a member is taken to have agreed to the terms of the constitution when he became a member, whether or not he appreciated what it contained at the time. In the interests of commercial certainty, the law should continue to treat him as so bound unless he shows that the parties have come to some other agreement or understanding which is not reflected in the constitution. The basis of the parties' relationship, whether it be restricted to the articles or the subject of wider agreements or understandings, is central to the judicial approach to the unfairly prejudicial remedy which is the subject of this chapter.

B Petitioning on the grounds of unfair prejudice

17-16   The most valuable shareholder remedy is that contained in the Companies Act 2006, s 994(1), previously CA 1985, s 459, which provides that:

'A member of a company may apply to the court by petition for an order on the ground

(a) that the company's affairs are being or have been conducted in a manner which is unfairly prejudicial to the interests of members generally or of some part of its members (including at least himself), or

(b) that an actual or proposed act or omission of the company (including an act or omission on its behalf) is or would be so prejudicial.'[14]

17-17   Where the court is satisfied that a petition under s 994 is well founded, it may make such order as it thinks fit for giving relief in respect of the matters complained of (s 996(2)). In practice, relief is most commonly sought in respect of private company disputes and the remedy most commonly sought is a purchase order requiring the respondents to purchase the shares of the petitioner (s 996(2)(e)). The nature of these companies and of these disputes is such that the only possible resolution, usually, is that the minority shareholder must leave the company and a purchase order under CA 2006, s 996 ensures that she or he exits at a fair value. Often there is no dispute over the exit of the minority shareholder, but a protracted dispute over the valuation of the minority shareholding which itself requires resolution by the court.[15] To encourage the parties to settle (so saving themselves time and costs and freeing up court time), given the outcome of these disputes is so predictable (a purchase order), a petition will usually be struck out if the respondents make the petitioner a fair offer[16] (see **17-66**) which gives her/him everything which she/he could reasonably expect to achieve under CA 2006, s 994.

17-18   In *Fulham Football Club (1987) Ltd v Richards*[17] the Court of Appeal resolved the uncertainty which had been created by conflicting first instance decisions[18] as to whether it is

---

[14] See generally Joffe, *Minority Shareholders* (4th edn, 2011), Chs 7, 8; Hollington, *Shareholders' Rights* (5th edn, 2010), Chs 7–9; Payne, 'Sections 459–461 Companies Act 1985 in flux: the future of shareholder protection' (2005) CLJ 647; Boyle, *Minority Shareholders' Remedies* (2002).

[15] See, for example, *Re Southern Counties Fresh Foods Ltd* [2010] EWHC 3334 (Ch) where a purchase order was made in January 2009 and by December 2010 the parties were still arguing, without an end in sight, about the proper valuation method to be adopted.

[16] See *O'Neill v Phillips* [1999] 2 BCLC 1, also *Harborne Road Nominees Ltd v Karvaski* [2011] EWHC 2214, discussed at **17-71**.   [17] [2012] 1 All ER 414.

[18] See *Re Vocam Europe Ltd* [1998] BCC 396 (unfair prejudice petition was stayed by the court as a shareholders' agreement provided for disputes to go to arbitration); *Re Exeter City AFC v Football Conference Ltd*

possible for shareholders to contract out of their right to petition under CA 2006, s 994 and to agree instead to refer their disputes to arbitration. The court concluded that there is no express or implied statutory preservation of a right of access to the court and nothing in the nature of these disputes which requires the exclusive jurisdiction of the court. Unlike a winding-up order which an arbitrator cannot award, it being a class remedy, s 994 relief cannot be categorised as a class remedy. While orders under the section have some potential to affect third parties, that point has consequences for the remedies which an arbitrator can award but, as Patten LJ put it, these jurisdictional limitations on what an arbitration can achieve are not decisive of the question whether the subject matter of the dispute is arbitral. In the unanimous view of the Court of Appeal, these disputes can be subject to arbitration agreements.[19] Notwithstanding this ruling, minority shareholders would be ill-advised to give up their right to petition under CA 2006, s 994, given that it is an expansive jurisdiction with flexible remedies which has proved invaluable to shareholders aggrieved at the unfairly prejudicial manner in which a company's affairs are being conducted, as we shall see.

The petitioner

17-19 Only members[20] have a right to petition and the definition of 'member' is extended to include persons to whom shares have been transferred or transmitted by law (CA 2006, s 994(2)) which extends standing to petition to persons such as personal representatives and trustees in bankruptcy.[21] A petition may be brought by a nominee shareholder. In *Atlasview Ltd v Brightview Ltd*[22] the court refused to strike out a petition holding that it was arguable that the 'interests' of a nominee shareholder were capable of including the economic and contractual interests of the beneficial owners of the shares. To hold otherwise, the court said, would produce the arbitrary result that the registered shareholder would have standing to petition as a member but no 'interests' for these purposes, while the beneficial owner would have an interest but no standing to present a petition, not being a member. A petition can be brought by a member even though the company is insolvent and will remain insolvent (meaning that the petitioner cannot benefit in his

---

[2005] 1 BCLC 238 (shareholders' right to petition was an inalienable right which could not be limited by agreement and an arbitration agreement could not be invoked to require a stay of a petition).

[19] It is noteworthy that the authorities on the issue, see n 18, had unusual facts; two concerned disputes between football clubs and football bodies (*Exeter City AFC* and *Fulham Football Club*) and the other involved a company where the majority shareholders were Australian companies and the shareholders' agreement provided for arbitration in Melbourne (*Vocam*). None presented the more usual scenario of persons within the jurisdiction engaged in a business venture together.

[20] In certain circumstances, the Secretary of State may petition on the same grounds under CA 2006, s 995, but this power is never used.

[21] See *Re McCarthy Surfacing Ltd* [2006] EWHC 832 where the court allowed a petition by two shareholders (who had executed a transfer of their shares) and the transferee (whose request for registration had been refused by the directors), noting that the transferee has to have standing to petition for a period of time after the transfer and before registration, otherwise CA 2006, s 994(2) would have no effect. The court also considered that there was nothing to prevent the three petitioners having concurrent standing as long as care was exercised on any relief being ordered to prevent double recovery. See also *Harris v Jones* [2011] EWHC 1518 at [36], [149] (share transferred by one shareholder to another shareholder to be held on trust, the shareholder trustee executed an undated share transfer form back in favour of the original transferor which made the original transferor a transferee for the purposes of CA 2006, s 994(2) and therefore entitled to petition under s 994(1)).

[22] [2004] 2 BCLC 191. The court noted with some surprise that this precise point as to the standing of a nominee shareholder had not previously been determined, but it also noted that numerous successful proceedings have been brought by nominee shareholders.

capacity as a shareholder) so long as the petitioner derives some real financial benefit from the petition.[23]

17-20   There is nothing to preclude a majority shareholder from petitioning, but the court would normally expect a majority shareholder to exercise his control of the company to bring to an end the conduct complained of.[24]

17-21   While there is no requirement that a petitioner should come to the court with clean hands, the conduct of the petitioner may, depending on the seriousness of the matter and the degree of its relevance, lead the court to refuse relief, even if the conditions for the exercise of the discretion in his favour are otherwise satisfied.[25]

Conduct of the company's affairs

17-22   The conduct complained of must relate to the conduct of the affairs of the company and it can relate to a course of conduct or a specific act or omission. It must be concerned with acts done or left undone by the company or those authorised to act as its organ, typically the directors, but a resolution of the company in general meeting is also an act of the company. While individual shareholders exercising their rights to vote are not acts of the company, or part of the conduct of the company's affairs, the resolution consequent on the exercise of their voting rights is an act of the company and part of the conduct of the company's affairs.[26] On the other hand, as Harman J noted in *Re Unisoft Group Ltd (No 3)*:[27]

> '...the vital distinction between acts or conduct of the company and the acts or conduct of the shareholder in his private capacity must be kept clear. The first type of act will found a petition under s 459 [s 994]; the second type of act will not.'

Shareholders' disputes between themselves in their private capacities are not part of the conduct of the company's affairs and not within the section. For example, in *Re Legal Costs Negotiators Ltd*[28] the complaint was about the failure of a shareholder to sell his shares. The company had been set up by four individuals with equal shareholdings. All the shareholders were directors and employees of the company. Three of the directors fell out with the fourth who was dismissed as an employee and resigned from the board just prior to being removed as a director. Having failed to persuade the fourth member to sell his shareholding to them, the majority shareholders petitioned for an order that he should transfer or sell his shares to them. In essence, they were unhappy with his continued presence as a shareholder in the prosperous business that they were creating. The Court of

---

[23] *Gamlestaden Fastigheter AB v Baltic Partners Ltd* [2008] 1 BCLC 468, PC, noted Walters (2007) 28 Co Law 289; Singla (2007) 123 LQR 542, and see discussion at **17-76**. Their Lordships rejected the argument that, as on a winding-up petition, the petitioner under CA 2006, s 994 needs to show a tangible interest in the winding up (essentially that surplus funds would be available) on the basis that the public interest considerations which underlie that requirement in winding up do not apply to unfairly prejudicial petitions: see [2008] 1 BCLC 468 at 478.   [24] See *Re Legal Costs Negotiators Ltd* [1999] 2 BCLC 171 at 199, 201.
[25] *Richardson v Blackmore* [2006] BCC 276; *Re London School of Electronics Ltd* [1985] BCLC 273; *Re R A Noble & Sons (Clothing) Ltd* [1983] BCLC 273. If the conduct of the petitioner is neither sufficiently serious nor sufficiently closely related to the respondents' unfairly prejudicial conduct, however, it is not appropriate for the court to refuse its discretion to grant relief: *Richardson v Blackmore*.
[26] See *Re Unisoft Group Ltd (No 3)* [1994] 1 BCLC 609 at 611.   [27] [1994] 1 BCLC 609 at 623.
[28] [1999] 2 BCLC 171l; see also *Re Astec (BSR) plc* [1998] 2 BCLC 556 (statements by the majority shareholder which allegedly depressed the share price could not amount to conduct of the company's affairs since the statements were made on behalf of the shareholder and not on behalf of the company: petition dismissed).

Appeal rejected the petition for complaint about the respondent's retention of his shares is not a complaint about the conduct of the company's affairs or an act or omission of the company.[29] In *Arrow Nominees Inc v Blackledge*[30] the Court of Appeal dismissed a petition based on allegations against the majority shareholders who were significant lenders and suppliers to the company. The court noted that the complaints against the majority related to the terms of those loan and supply contracts which, even if established, related to the majority's conduct as a lender and supplier to the company and did not relate to the conduct of the company's affairs by the majority. A decision to lend to the company at a certain rate of interest or to supply goods at a particular price could not amount to unfairly prejudicial conduct of the company's affairs. That would only arise if the majority used their position to compel the company to accept the funds/supplies at that rate of interest/price by preventing it securing other, more favourable, funding/suppliers.

17-23 Leaving aside those types of disputes which fall outside the scope of CA 2006, s 994, in *Hawkes v Cuddy*[31] the Court of Appeal stressed that the requirement for the conduct to be of the 'affairs of the company' should be liberally construed for the purposes of the section and may extend to matters which are capable of coming before the board, rather than restricted to matters that actually come before the board. Likewise, in *Oak Investment Partners XII v Boughtwood*[32] the Court of Appeal endorsed taking an expansive view of whose conduct might amount to the conduct of the company's affairs for this purpose, agreeing with the approach taken by Sales J in the lower court.[33] Sales J had concluded that it is possible for the conduct of a shareholder or director who acts in the carrying out of the company's affairs, but not through any company organ, to attract relief under CA 2006, s 994. In this case, the complaint was that the respondent shareholder (he held a majority of the ordinary shares) and director had persistently failed to adhere to his agreed management role and tried to dictate and ultimately did seize control of the management of the company. This behaviour was in breach of the constitutional arrangements agreed between him and a venture capital firm (the other significant shareholder in the company) as to the conduct of the company's affairs.[34] Sales J held, and the Court of Appeal agreed, that the respondent's conduct did amount to conduct of the company's affairs in an unfairly prejudicial manner, though the conduct was not that of the board or of the directors. Sales J had noted that the jurisdiction under CA 2006, s 994 is a broad jurisdiction which allows the court to take into account the myriad ways in which the affairs of a company may in practice be carried on, accepting that the precise distribution of management decision-making authority in any particular company might be a matter of chance.[35] It was difficult to see, Sales J said, why the application of CA 2006, s 994 should turn upon such fortuitous matters. If a significant shareholder, appointed to the management, engages in the course of that role in a way that improperly asserts rights of control over the conduct of the company's affairs, such conduct is capable of being conduct of the company's affairs for the purposes of s 994.

---

[29] See too *Re Leeds United Holdings plc* [1996] 2 BCLC 545 where the court dismissed a petition arising from a disagreement between shareholders as to the manner of the disposal of their shares. Again, the matter did not relate to the conduct of the company's affairs. [30] [2000] 2 BCLC 167.

[31] [2009] 2 BCLC 427 at [50]. [32] [2010] 2 BCLC 459. [33] See [2010] 2 BCLC 459 at [120], [122].

[34] The company had been formed as an engineering joint venture with the respondent providing technical expertise and the venture capital firm providing the necessary funding. The respondent subsequently ousted, in effect, the management team which the parties had jointly agreed on and took control of the business when the parties had agreed that he would no longer have overall management control, see [2010] 2 BCLC 459 at [150]. [35] See [2010] 2 BCLC 459 at [77].

17-24   Generally, the petitioner's complaints will be of the past conduct of the company's affairs,[36] but proposed acts of the company (such as resolutions of the general meeting) which, if carried out or completed, would be prejudicial to the interests of the petitioner may be the subject of a petition.[37] The petitioner must not be too hasty, however, in seeking relief. In *Re Astec (BSR) plc*[38] the petition was premature when it was brought at a time when the majority had only made statements as to steps which they would or might take in the future, but they had not taken any of those steps at the time of the petition.

17-25   In keeping with the judicial view that the ambit of CA 2006, s 994 should not be artificially constrained,[39] the Court of Appeal accepted in *Re Citybranch Group Ltd, Gross v Rackind*[40] that, in an appropriate case, the conduct of a holding company towards a subsidiary company may constitute the conduct of the affairs of the subsidiary and can be the subject of a complaint by a shareholder in the subsidiary and, vice versa, a shareholder in a holding company may petition that the conduct of the subsidiary can be regarded as part of the conduct of the affairs of the holding company,[41] especially where the subsidiary is wholly owned and the directors of the holding company also represent a majority of the directors of the subsidiary.[42]

Conduct unfairly prejudicial to the interests of the members

17-26   The conduct complained of must be conduct which is unfairly prejudicial to the interests of the member as a member as opposed to any other interests which the member might possess,[43] but here too the courts have emphasised that this requirement that the prejudice be suffered as a member must not be too narrowly construed and the courts take a broad view of what may properly be regarded as a petitioner's interests as a member.[44]

---

[36] Past acts of the company which have been remedied may be the basis of a petition if they are likely to recur but, if they are unlikely to recur, the court would have no scope to give relief. See *Re Kenyon Swansea Ltd* [1987] BCLC 514 at 521; *Re Legal Costs Negotiators Ltd* [1999] 2 BCLC 171 at 198.

[37] See *Re Kenyon Swansea Ltd* [1987] BCLC 514; *Re a Company (No 00314 of 1989), ex p Estate Acquisition and Development Ltd* [1991] BCLC 154.

[38] [1998] 2 BCLC 556; see also *Re a Company (No 005685 of 1988), ex p Schwarcz (No 2)* [1989] BCLC 427 at 451 (concerns about what might happen if the company was re-registered as a private company were premature).

[39] See *O'Neill v Phillips* [1999] 2 BCLC 1 at 15; *Gamlestaden Fastigheter AB v Baltic Partners Ltd* [2007] 4 All ER 164 at 175–6, PC; *Re Macro (Ipswich) Ltd* [1994] 2 BCLC 354 at 404; *Re Little Olympian Each-Ways Ltd* [1994] 2 BCLC 420 at 429.   [40] [2004] 4 All ER 735 at 743–4.

[41] See, for example, *Oak Investment Partners XII v Boughtwood* [2010] 2 BCLC 459 at [8], where it was agreed that the conduct of the business of a wholly owned subsidiary qualified as conduct of the affairs of the holding company for the purposes of CA 2006, s 994, the court noting that the reality was a single business conducted through a combined corporate structure.

[42] See also agreement on this point in *Re Ravenhart Service (Holdings) Ltd, Reiner v Gershinson* [2004] 2 BCLC 376 and in *Irvine v Irvine (No 1)* [2007] 1 BCLC 349 at 418. Note that, in each case, the subsidiaries were wholly owned and had boards substantially similar to the parent company. See Goddard & Hirt, 'Section 459 and Corporate Groups' [2005] JBL 247 which criticises the court's failure to respect the separate legal entities involved and also considers that this approach gives an unnecessarily wide interpretation to the statutory provision.

[43] *Re a Company (No 004475 of 1982)* [1983] 2 All ER 36 at 44; *Re a Company (No 00314 of 1989), ex p Estate Acquisition & Development Ltd* [1991] BCLC 154 at 160. For example, in *Re J E Cade & Son Ltd* [1992] BCLC 213 the petition was struck out when the petitioner was protecting his interests as a freeholder of a farm rather than his interests as a member of the company running the farm; also *Re Unisoft Group Ltd (No 3)* [1994] 1 BCLC 609 at 626 where the allegations concerned the relationship of the parties as landlord and tenant rather than as members of the company.

[44] See *O'Neill v Phillips* [1999] 2 BCLC 1 at 15: 'the requirement that prejudice must be suffered as a member should not be too narrowly or technically construed', per Lord Hoffmann; *Gamlestaden Fastigheter AB*

17-27 In particular, the courts have consistently held that if the terms on which a person became or continues as a member in a small private company include his participation in the management of the company, his removal *as a director* without cause is a prejudice suffered in his capacity as a member[45] entitling him to petition for relief under CA 2006, s 994. This point is important in practice for removal as a director is the most common basis for petitions.

17-28 A broad approach to what constitutes the interests of a member as a member may also allow the court to take account of the members' interests as creditors in certain circumstances. In *R & H Electrical Ltd v Haden Bill Electrical Ltd*[46] there were four equal shareholders and directors. The petitioner was one of the shareholders and he provided the company with its working capital through loans from another company wholly owned by him. These loans formed an essential part of the arrangements between him and his fellow shareholders who regarded it as immaterial whether the funding came from the petitioner or through his other company. The relationship between the parties broke down and the others attempted to remove the petitioner from office as a director. He petitioned for relief and the respondents argued that, in so far as he had concerns, they related to his role as a creditor of the company rather than matters affecting his interests as a member. In the circumstances, however, Robert Walker LJ considered the loan arrangements were sufficiently closely associated with his membership of the company[47] to be within the scope of the statutory provision. It was unfairly prejudicial to his interests as a member, therefore, to remove him from management of the company while he was a significant creditor of the company and he was entitled to relief.

17-29 That approach was endorsed by the Privy Council in *Gamlestaden Fastigheter AB v Baltic Partners Ltd*[48] (see further at **17-76**) where similarly a joint venture company was funded primarily by loans by the petitioner (again via a company associated with the petitioner) and the court considered it would be appropriate to take into account the member's interest as a creditor of the company when considering whether to grant relief. Lord Scott, giving the ruling of the Privy Council, emphasised the importance of the funding arrangements being part of, or in pursuance of, the joint venture arrangements between the parties (as was the case in *Haden Bill*, see **17-28**).

17-30 In *Re Woven Rugs Ltd*[49] the shareholders had funded the company through large scale, interest-free, subordinated debt so they were creditors of the company. The director and majority shareholder organised a restructuring of the company's finances in a way which left the petitioners as creditors, but the majority shareholder's debt was repaid and replaced by bank loans which were much more expensive for the company. The court held that the restructuring was unfairly prejudicial to the petitioners' interests as members and as creditors, positions which were in substance indistinguishable.[50] It is clear in each of these cases that the key element bringing the petitioners within the section is this close association and intertwining of their roles as members and creditors such that it is

---

v Baltic Partners Ltd [2007] 4 All ER 164 at [35], PC; see too *Shepherd v Williamson* [2010] EWHC 2375 at [105].

[45] See *O'Neill v Phillips* [1999] 2 BCLC 1 at 14–15 ('It is the terms, agreement, or understanding on which [the petitioner] became associated as a member which generates the restraint of the power of expulsion', per Lord Hoffmann); see also *R & H Electric Ltd v Haden Bill Electrical Ltd* [1995] 2 BCLC 280 at 292–3.

[46] [1995] 2 BCLC 280.   [47] [1995] 2 BCLC 280 at 293–4.

[48] [2008] 1 BCLC 468, [2007] 4 All ER 164, PC; noted Walters (2007) 28 Co Law 289; Singla [2007] 123 LQR 542.   [49] [2010] EWHC 230.

[50] [2010] EWHC 230 at [96].

possible to assert that what has occurred, though it impacts on their position as creditors, is unfairly prejudicial to their interests as members.

17-31   Finally, it should be noted that the removal of the company's auditor from office on grounds of divergence of opinions on accounting treatments or audit procedures, or on any other improper grounds, is treated as being unfairly prejudicial to the interests of some part of the company's members so as to enable a member (not the auditor) to petition for relief in those circumstances (CA 2006, s 994(1A)).[51] This provision gives effect to art 38 of Directive 2006/43/EC on statutory audit[52] which requires Member States to ensure that statutory auditors may only be dismissed on proper grounds and is intended to safeguard the independence of auditors from undue pressure by the company's directors.

Unfairly prejudicial conduct

17-32   Whether the company's affairs are being or have been conducted in a manner which is unfairly prejudicial to the petitioner's interests is an objective, and not a subjective, matter.[53] The prejudice must be real, rather than merely technical or trivial,[54] and the petitioner does not have to show that the persons controlling the company have acted deliberately in bad faith or with a conscious intent to treat him unfairly.[55] The conduct complained of must be prejudicial in the sense of causing prejudice or harm to the relevant interest of the member (usually, but not limited to, reducing the value of the petitioner's shareholding) and also unfairly so (usually connoting some breach of company law or the constitution, but not limited to that) and it is not sufficient if the conduct satisfies only one of these tests.[56] The conduct may be prejudicial but not unfair, for example, if the petitioner has acquiesced in the breaches of which he now complains,[57] or it may be prejudicial to remove a member from his post as a director but not unfairly so, if his conduct merited removal.[58] It can be prejudicial not to consult a minority shareholder, but not unfair, if the petitioner has chosen to withdraw from active involvement in the business,

---

[51] As Judge Purle QC commented in *Re Sunrise Radio Ltd, Kohli v Lit* [2010] 1 BCLC 367 at [9], the effect of this mandatory section is to classify conduct by the board which may have been the result of a good faith genuine disagreement with the auditors as unfairly prejudicial conduct and it is unfairly prejudicial though it may have no necessary impact on the value of the petitioner's shareholding.

[52] See OJ L 157, 9.06.2006, p 87.

[53] *Re Saul D Harrison & Sons plc* [1995] 1 BCLC 14, CA.

[54] *Re Saul D Harrison & Sons plc* [1995] 1 BCLC 14, CA. See *Re Sunrise Radio Ltd, Kohli v Lit* [2010] 1 BCLC 367 at [7], [8] (in judging unfair prejudice, isolated trivial complaints, even when in breach of some legal requirement, having no impact on the value of the petitioner's shares or on any realistic objective assessment of the integrity and competence of the board, will be ignored, unless that requirement is an absolute standard imposed by the statute or constitution and, even then, minor inadvertent departures can be ignored as will irregularities which can be set right at any moment).

[55] See *Re R A Noble & Sons (Clothing) Ltd* [1983] BCLC 273 at 290–1.

[56] *Re Saul D Harrison & Sons plc* [1995] 1 BCLC 14 at 31, CA; *Re Sunrise Radio Ltd, Kohli v Lit* [2010] 1 BCLC 367 at [4]; *Re R A Noble (Clothing) Ltd* [1983] BCLC 273.

[57] If the shareholders are agreed that the company should be run in disregard of the obligations imposed by the Companies Act, none of them can complain that such conduct by another shareholder is unfair on that ground alone, see *Croly v Good* [2010] 2 BCLC 569 at [94]; also *Hawkes v Cuddy* [2009] 2 BCLC 427 at [72]: a shareholder who had been a party to the other shareholder's unlawful participation in the management of the company (in breach of IA 1986, s 216), could not then found a petition under CA 2006, s 994 on that unlawful conduct. But a shareholder who has agreed or acquiesced for a period of years in the company being run quite informally in disregard of the requirements of the statute and constitution is entitled subsequently, on giving reasonable notice, to revive reliance on her strict entitlements under the articles: see *Fisher v Cadman* [2006] 1 BCLC 499.   [58] See, for example, *Grace v Biagioli* [2006] 2 BCLC 70.

as in *Re Metropolis Motorcycles Ltd, Hale v Waldock*.[59] Vice versa, conduct may be unfair but not prejudicial, as in *Irvine v Irvine (No 1)*[60] where the court found that there had been a failure to meet the statutory requirements as to approving the accounts and holding of annual general meetings, but the failures could not be said to have caused the petitioner any material prejudice.

17-33 The leading authority on the scope of the unfairly prejudicial jurisdiction is *O'Neill v Phillips*,[61] the sole House of Lords authority on the provision, and the speech by Lord Hoffmann is definitive as to the approach to be taken when assessing allegations of unfair prejudicial conduct of the affairs of a company.[62]

17-34 The petitioner, O, joined the company as a manual worker in 1983. In 1985, the respondent, P, impressed by O's abilities, gave him 25% of the issued shares and appointed him a director. Between 1985 and 1990, P retired from the board, leaving O as sole director. The company prospered and O was credited with half of the profits. There were discussions with a view to O obtaining a 50% shareholding, but no agreement was concluded. In 1991 P became concerned about the company's financial position and O's management so he resumed personal command and gave O the option of managing, under him, the UK or the German branches of the business. O decided to go to Germany and remained on the board as a director. Later that year P determined that O would no longer receive 50% of the profits but would be paid only his salary and any dividends payable upon his 25% shareholding. O decided to sever his links with the company and petitioned the court claiming that the company's affairs were being conducted in a manner 'unfairly prejudicial' to his interests.

17-35 Following a difference of opinion in the lower courts, the matter reached the House of Lords where Lord Hoffmann (who gave the sole speech) concluded that a member will not ordinarily be entitled to complain of unfairness unless there has been:

(1) some breach of the terms on which the member agreed that the affairs of the company should be conducted; or

(2) some use of the rules in a manner which equity would regard as contrary to good faith—i.e. cases in which equitable considerations make it unfair for those conducting the affairs of the company to rely upon their strict legal powers.[63]

Each of these grounds is considered in detail later.

17-36 As P had not acted in breach of the terms upon which it was agreed that the affairs of the company should be conducted and there was no ground, consistent with the principles of equity, for any belief that O was entitled to half the profits and half the shareholding, O could not bring his claim within either basis for relief and his petition was dismissed.

17-37 If the company is purely a commercial relationship, as would usually be the case where the company is a public company, and is often the case in private companies, a petitioner

---

[59] [2007] 1 BCLC 520.

[60] [2007] 1 BCLC 349. Likewise in *Oak Investment Partners XII v Boughtwood* [2010] 2 BCLC 459 at [121], there was some evidence of unfair conduct by the petitioners (non-disclosure of information) but it had caused no prejudice.

[61] [1999] 2 BCLC 1; noted Prentice and Payne, 'Section 459 of the Companies Act 1985—The House of Lords View' [1999] 115 LQR 587; Goddard, 'Taming the Unfair Prejudice Remedy: Sections 459–461 of the Companies Act 1985 in the House of Lords' (1999) CLJ 487; Boyle (2000) 21 Co Law 253.

[62] See *Oak Investment Partners XII v Boughtwood* [2010] 2 BCLC 459 at [118], per Rimer LJ.

[63] [1999] 2 BCLC 1 at 8.

is confined to allegations under (1), see **17-35**, of breaches of the articles (or other contractual arrangements governing the shareholders' relationship), or of the statute, i.e. CA 2006, which would include breaches of directors' duties. In the case of a public company, the expectation generally would be that the entire relationship of the parties is exhaustively determined by the constitution[64] and there is no scope for equitable considerations to arise and therefore no basis for relying on (2), see **17-35**. This is particularly so if the company is a listed public company, a point made forcibly in *Re Astec (BSR) plc*[65] by Jonathan Parker J:

> 'If the market in a company's shares is to have any credibility members of the public dealing in that market must, it seems to me, be entitled to proceed on the footing that the constitution of the company is as it appears in the company's public documents, unaffected by any extraneous equitable considerations and constraints.'

17-38   Likewise, where the relationship of the parties is spelt out in detailed agreements, especially agreements drafted and advised upon by professional advisers, there is little scope for arguing that the relationship is other than a purely commercial one.[66] It is possible therefore to use carefully drafted agreements as a method of limiting the opportunities to invoke the unfairly prejudicial jurisdiction.

17-39   On the other hand, if the company has the characteristics of a quasi-partnership (see **17-52**) such that equitable considerations arise, the petitioner may bring his claim under heading (1) and/or (2), see **17-35**, so CA 2006, s 994 applies more broadly in that context and, as we shall see, the remedy awarded may be more generous if the company is a quasi-partnership, see **17-84**.

17-40   The issue is the nature of the relationship at the time of the unfairly prejudicial conduct, not whether the company was from the outset a commercial association or a quasi-partnership,[67] for the parties' relationship may change over time. A company may start out on a purely commercial footing, but by the time of the conduct complained of, may have become one where equitable considerations come into play, as was the case in *O'Neill v Phillips*.[68] The petitioner initially was an employee of the company, but the relationships within the company changed over the years as he became a shareholder and a director such that the company became a quasi-partnership, a not uncommon scenario. Another example can be seen in *Croly v Good*[69] where the court again found that the relationship had changed from being that of employee to that of quasi-partner. The key factors were that the petitioner, who had initially been employed as a salesman, subsequently became a shareholder, participated in management to a significant degree, was held out to outside parties as a principal in the business and reached agreement with effectively the only other shareholder on an equal division of profits. The court noted that the totality of the arrangements between the parties must be considered with no single element conclusive either way[70] and, in this instance, the result was a relationship requiring the qualities of trust and confidence found in a quasi-partnership.

---

[64]   See *Re Saul D Harrison & Sons plc* [1995] 1 BCLC 14.

[65]   [1998] 2 BCLC 556 at 589. See also *CAS (Nominees) Ltd v Nottingham Forest FC* [2002] 1 BCLC 613 at 627; *Re Tottenham Hotspur plc* [1994] 1 BCLC 655 (the shareholders are entitled to expect that the entire relationship between the company and the chief executive is set out in his service agreement and the constitution).

[66]   See *Re a Company (No 005685 of 1988), ex p Schwarz (No 2)* [1989] BCLC 427.

[67]   See *Croly v Good* [2010] 2 BCLC 569 at [88]; *Re Sunrise Radio Ltd, Kohli v Lit* [2010] 1 BCLC 367 at [306].   [68]   [1999] 2 BCLC 1.

[69]   [2010] 2 BCLC 569.   [70]   [2010] 2 BCLC 569 at [89]–[92].

17-41 Equally, a relationship which begins on a quasi-partnership footing may become a more commercial venture, as in *Re a Company (No 005134 of 1986), ex p Harries*.[71] In that case, the parties did operate initially as a quasi-partnership but, as the business developed, the petitioner withdrew into the role of a passive shareholder with the result that the relationship moved on to a purely commercial footing. In *Re McCarthy Surfacing Ltd, Hequet v McCarthy*[72] the relationships originally were that of quasi-partners, but the minority shareholders had destroyed that quasi-partnership, the court found, by unfounded legal action some years earlier, after which they ceased to be involved in the running of the company and the position reverted to a formal commercial relationship.[73]

17-42 Finally, note that in *O'Neill v Phillips*[74] Lord Hoffmann expressly rejected reliance on 'legitimate expectations' as a basis for a petition. This reliance had become a prominent element of the case law prior to this decision with petitions being brought effectively on the basis that a petitioner was aggrieved that (what he perceived to be) his legitimate expectations as to the conduct of the company's affairs had not been met. For example, in *O'Neill* the petitioner (who held 25% of the shares) felt that he had 'legitimate expectations' to 50% of the shares in the company and 50% of the profits although he could establish no entitlement in law or equity to such equality. Lord Hoffmann in *O'Neill* noted that he himself had used the phrase 'legitimate expectations' in *Re Saul D Harrison & Sons plc*,[75] but he conceded that this use was a mistake.[76]

Breach of the terms on which the affairs of the company should be conducted

17-43 In considering the scope of the unfairly prejudicial jurisdiction, Lord Hoffmann emphasised in *O'Neill v Phillips*[77] the need to appreciate the business context in which the section operates. Companies are associations of persons for economic purposes where the terms of association are contained in the articles and perhaps in shareholder agreements.[78] It follows that a member is not ordinarily able to complain of unfairness unless there has been some breach of the terms on which he has agreed that the affairs of the company should be conducted, i.e. primarily some breach of the legislation and/or the constitution which governs the company. For example, in *Oak Investment Partners XII v Boughtwood*,[79] the facts of which are given at **17-23,** the Court of Appeal held that the destructive conduct of the respondent shareholder and director in overriding the constitutional arrangements (as to board composition and division of management tasks) governing the operation of the business (in effect he seized control of the business) was unfairly prejudicial conduct. Breaches of the CA 2006 will be central to many petitions, usually involving allegations of breaches of directors' duties (for example, the misappropriation of corporate assets and improper allotments of shares) and breaches of the requirements governing disclosure (for example, failures to call meetings or provide accounts). Each is considered in more detail later. It is common for petitions to include allegations on numerous grounds, not least because the court will look at the cumulative picture in assessing whether the company's affairs have been conducted in an unfairly prejudicial manner.

---

[71] [1989] BCLC 383.

[72] [2009] 1 BCLC 622; see also *Fowler v Gruber* [2010] 1 BCLC 563 where the company started as a quasi-partnership, but became a commercial relationship when the petitioner sold some of his shares and subsequently a local authority also became a shareholder.

[73] [2009] 1 BCLC 622 at [93]–[96].   [74] [1999] 2 BCLC 1.   [75] [1995] 1 BCLC 14.

[76] [1999] 2 BCLC 1 at 11.   [77] [1999] 2 BCLC 1.

[78] See [1999] 2 BCLC 1 at 7; *Re Saul D Harrison & Sons plc* [1995] 1 BCLC 14 at 17–18.

[79] [2010] 2 BCLC 459.

Breach of the no-conflict duty

17-44   It is a common feature of many of these disputes that, when the majority and minority shareholders fall out, the majority look to use the company's assets as their own and they often appropriate, without authorisation and for their own benefit, opportunities and contracts which properly belong to the company. Typically they extract from the company benefits beyond their strict entitlements and run down the business of the company (so reducing the value of the minority's holding) while transferring business to another entity wholly owned by them. Such clear breaches of the no-conflict duty (CA 2006, s 175, see **11-27**) amount to conduct of the company's affairs in an unfairly prejudicial manner.

17-45   Illustrations of such breaches of duty amounting to unfairly prejudicial conduct can be found in the following cases:

- In *Re Little Olympian Each-Ways Ltd (No 3)*[80] the assets of the company were transferred at an undervalue to another company wholly owned by the majority shareholders. The assets were then sold on at their market value to a third party.

- In *Re Full Cup International Trading Ltd*[81] the respondents were found to have stifled the business of the company. They deprived it of its stock and business which was transferred to another entity in which they, but not the petitioner, had an interest.

- In *Re Brenfield Squash Racquets Club Ltd*[82] the majority shareholders and directors caused the company's assets to be used as security for debts of their businesses and transferred to those businesses assets that rightfully belonged to the company.

- In *Lloyd v Casey*[83] a director arranged a variety of transactions for his own ultimate benefit including payments to a company controlled by him and additional contributions to his own pension fund.

- In *Allmark v Burnham*[84] the majority shareholder and director opened a competing business in the same street as the company's main retail outlet, failed to consult the minority shareholder and director on management matters and doubled his own salary once he had removed the minority shareholder from the board.

- In *Re Baumler (UK) Ltd, Gerrard v Koby*[85] the company was split 49% and 51% between two shareholders who were also the two directors. An opportunity to acquire the company's premises and adjoining land from their landlord was taken up by a third party acting on information provided to him by the 51% respondent with the expectation of a secret profit. The court found that the underhand conduct of the respondent in procuring the acquisition of the properties was a breach of duty by him and conduct unfairly prejudicial to the petitioner.

- In *Irvine v Irvine (No 1)*[86] the respondent director in breach of the articles awarded himself excessive and unauthorised remuneration without reference to the board or the minority shareholders. A consequence of this conduct was that the petitioner received less by way of dividend than should have been received consistent with the company's historic policy of maximum profit distribution. Conducting the company's affairs in this manner was unfairly prejudicial to the interests of the petitioner.

---

[80]   [1995] 1 BCLC 636.   [81]   [1995] BCC 682.   [82]   [1996] 2 BCLC 184.
[83]   [2002] 1 BCLC 454. See also *Fowler v Gruber* [2010] 1 BCLC 563 (director had the company lend him money to purchase shares from an existing shareholder which purchase made the director the majority shareholder; he had the company write off the loan and awarded himself excessive remuneration as well as making substantial payments to his pension fund).   [84]   [2006] 2 BCLC 437.
[85]   [2005] 1 BCLC 92.   [86]   [2007] 1 BCLC 349.

- In *Grace v Biagioli*[87] the respondent directors consciously and deliberately failed to pay a dividend which had been declared with the available profits distributed instead in the guise of management fees to the respondents. The non-payment of the declared dividend was unfairly prejudicial conduct.

- In *Re McCarthy Surfacing Ltd, Hequet v McCarthy*[88] a bonus agreement was deliberately designed to benefit the directors (and majority shareholders) and to ensure that none of the profits made on a particular project would be available to the other shareholders. In such circumstances, the making of the bonus agreement was a breach of the duty to act fairly and of the no-conflict rule and was unfairly prejudicial, as was a persistent failure by the board to consider whether or not to declare dividends and a failure by the board to have regard to the company's interests when negotiating transactions with the majority shareholder.

- In *Re Woven Rugs Ltd*[89] the respondent director in breach of duty refinanced the company in a way which favoured the interests of the majority shareholders over the interests of the minority shareholders for no purpose other than to benefit the majority at the expense of the company. He also was responsible for the extraction of funds from the company in the form of unauthorised remuneration and management charges. All of these matters amounted to the conduct of the company's affairs in an unfairly prejudicial manner.

Breach of duty to act for a proper purpose and fairly between shareholders

17-46 A common ploy in these disputes is for the directors to make an allotment of shares, nominally to raise capital, but really for the purpose of diluting the petitioner's interest in the company, something which is in breach of the directors' duty to act in accordance with the constitution and to exercise their powers for the purposes for which they are conferred (CA 2006, s 171). The ability of directors to manipulate allotments is limited to some extent by the statutory requirement (subject to certain exceptions) for shares to be allotted on a rights basis (i.e. to existing shareholders in proportion to existing holdings, CA 2006, s 561, see **19-35**). Allotting in breach of the rights requirement, so diluting the holdings of the minority shareholder, is unfairly prejudicial conduct. For example, in *Re Coloursource Ltd, Dalby v Bodilly*[90] an allotment made in breach of the rights requirement by the company's sole director and 50% shareholder had the effect of diluting the other 50% shareholder to a 5% shareholder. There were allegations of other misconduct, but Blackburne J thought it was sufficient to look at the allotment of shares which was the plainest possible breach by the director of his fiduciary duty and unfairly prejudicial conduct.[91]

17-47 In some circumstances even a rights issue can be unfairly prejudicial, as in *Re Regional Airports Ltd*[92] where the ulterior motive for a proposed rights issue, the court found, was to enhance the majority's position and to increase pressure on the (now to be diluted)

---

[87] [2006] 2 BCLC 70.   [88] [2009] 1 BCLC 622.   [89] [2010] EWHC 230.

[90] [2005] BCC 627. See also *Re a Company (No 005134 of 1986), ex p Harries* [1989] BCLC 383 (majority shareholder and director made an allotment of shares in breach of the statutory requirements for a rights issue for the purpose of increasing his shareholding and decreasing the petitioner's holding from 40% to 4%). However, where there was a genuine desire to raise capital, a scheme proposed by the directors, although devised so as to avoid the need for a rights issue, was not conduct which was unfairly prejudicial to those shareholders who were thereby denied the possibility of taking up additional shares: see *CAS (Nominees) Ltd v Nottingham Forest FC plc* [2002] 1 BCLC 613 at 627–32.

[91] [2005] BCC 627 at 631. In the circumstances, it was irrelevant that no dividend had been declared on any of the additional shares and that no use had been made of the additional shareholding. See too *Harris v Jones* [2011] EWHC 1518 at [152] (dilution from 50% to 0.1% shareholding was unfairly prejudicial).

[92] [1999] 2 BCLC 30.

minority to sell their shares at a discounted valuation.[93] Other examples of an improper purpose behind an apparently fair rights issue which would justify a finding of unfairly prejudicial conduct are if it is known that a particular shareholder does not have sufficient funds to take up the rights offer and it is made for that reason, or where a shareholder is engaged in litigation with the majority and the offer is designed to deplete the resources available to him to finance that litigation.[94]

It is even possible for a rights issue which is made for a proper purpose, i.e. genuinely to raise capital, to be unfairly prejudicial if the directors do not also act fairly when determining the price of the shares. In *Re Sunrise Radio Ltd, Kohli v Lit*[95] the court accepted that a rights issue had been made for the genuine purpose of raising capital though it was made at a time when it was likely that the minority shareholder would not take up the shares and therefore faced dilution (from a 15% holding to 8.33%). But the shares had also been issued at par when the evidence was that the shares, which were taken up by the majority shareholder, could have been issued for a significantly higher price, so the minority shareholder suffered a dilution in the value, as well as the size, of her holding. The court held that, even if the directors had acted in accordance with the duty to exercise their powers for a proper purpose (s 171), they were in breach of their duty to act fairly between shareholders (s 172(1)(f)).[96] The court noted that what is the proper price for shares will necessarily fall within a range of possibilities, but the board is required to consider all these matters fairly in the interests of all groups of shareholders and having regard to the foreseeable range of responses from the shareholders to the rights issue. Where it is known or foreseen that the minority may not be able or wish to subscribe, the directors in the interests of even-handedness and fairness must consider the price which can be extracted from those who are willing to subscribe or be in breach of their duties to the company.[97] On the facts, issuing the shares at par without considering any alternative, particularly when the directors (as the majority shareholders) benefited appreciably from the issue at par, was a breach of duty and unfairly prejudicial to the petitioner.[98]

Breach of duty of care and skill

17-48 The courts are reluctant to accept that disagreements over managerial decisions can amount to conduct of the company's affairs in an unfairly prejudicial manner.[99] The judicial view, essentially, is that differences as to commercial judgement are not for the courts to adjudicate upon, especially not with the benefit of hindsight which shows that the decisions were not in the company's interest.[100] After all, the directors are appointed by the shareholders and, if they are disappointed with the quality of the management provided,

---

[93] It was obvious to the majority shareholder that the minority shareholders either could not or would not take up the rights issue—it had been made clear to them that their continued presence as investors was not welcome—therefore their holdings were bound to be diluted as a consequence of the issue, see [1999] 2 BCLC 30 at 72–3, 80.

[94] See *Re a Company (No 002612 of 1984)* [1985] BCLC 80 (injunction granted to restrain a proposed rights issue which had followed immediately on the presentation by the minority shareholder of a petition. Had it gone ahead, it would have reduced the petitioner's shareholding in the company from 33% to 0.33%); also *Re a Company (No 007623 of 1984)* [1986] BCLC 362.   [95] [2010] 1 BCLC 367.

[96] See *Mutual Life Insurance Co of New York v The Rank Organisation* [1985] BCLC 11; also *Re McCarthy Surfacing Ltd, Hequet v McCarthy* [2009] 1 BCLC 622 at [77]–[81] (the directors in adopting a bonus agreement designed to ensure that profits were not available to all the shareholders acted for an improper purpose and contravened their duty to act fairly between the shareholders).   [97] [2010] 1 BCLC 367 at [95].

[98] A subsequent increase in authorised share capital and a disapplication of the rights issue requirement was also unfairly prejudicial, though no shares had been issued pursuant to that authority, when the petitioner had been misled as to the calling of the general meeting where these matters were agreed, see [2010] 1 BCLC 367 at [135].

[99] See *Re Elgindata Ltd* [1991] BCLC 959 at 993–4; *Re Saul D Harrison & Sons plc* [1995] 1 BCLC 14 at 31, CA.   [100] See *Oak Investment Partners XII v Boughtwood* [2010] 2 BCLC 459 at [8].

the remedy lies in the shareholders' power to dismiss the directors. In *Re Elgindata Ltd*,[101] for example, the complaint was a broad complaint where the shareholder was simply disappointed as to the poor quality of the management of the business.[102] That was insufficient, the court said, as a basis for an allegation of unfairly prejudicial conduct.

17-49 If the decisions taken cause actual financial loss to the company, however, the petition is more likely to succeed since, in essence, the allegation then is of a failure to exercise reasonable care, skill and diligence as required by CA 2006, s 174. In *Re Macro (Ipswich) Ltd*,[103] for example, it was possible to point to specific failures repeated over many years which caused financial loss to the company. The company had a substantial portfolio of properties which had been mismanaged by the sole director who was 83 years of age and the father of the petitioners in this case. He had failed to institute a proper maintenance system for the properties or to ensure that they were properly let and rents duly paid with the result that the value of these assets had been depleted. Such conduct was unfairly prejudicial conduct. On the other hand, in *Fisher v Cadman*[104] the court rejected complaints from a shareholder about the inactive management of a property company's assets by its directors. It was the practice of the company to hold properties in the hope of realising capital gains without expending large sums of money on repairing and letting the properties. The court thought that the decision to manage the assets in that way was within the range of reasonable business decisions available to the directors as managers and did not amount to mismanagement.

Breach of statutory rights

17-50 A breach of members' statutory rights, for example, repeated failures to hold annual general meetings and to lay accounts before the members (when required to do so[105]) so depriving members of their right to know and consider the state of the company's affairs,[106] may merit a petition, subject to the general qualification that trivial infringements will not found a petition.[107]

Use of the rules in an inequitable manner

17-51 The second basis for a petition under CA 2006, s 994 identified by the House of Lords in *O'Neill v Phillips*[108] is that there has been some use of the rules in a manner which equity would regard as contrary to good faith. As noted at **17-42**, care must be taken in relying on this ground and vague assertions that some legitimate expectations of the petitioner have not been met will be rejected by the court.

17-52 The correct approach is to start by establishing whether equitable considerations have arisen to affect or constrain the exercise of legal powers. The type of company which will typically give rise to such equitable constraints on the exercise of legal powers is a company which has one or probably more of the characteristics identified by Lord Wilberforce in *Ebrahimi v Westbourne Galleries Ltd*,[109] namely:

    (1) an association formed or continued on the basis of a personal relationship involving mutual confidence;

---

[101] [1991] BCLC 959.   [102] [1991] BCLC 959 at 993–4.   [103] [1994] 2 BCLC 354.

[104] [2006] 1 BCLC 499.

[105] Only public companies are required to hold annual general meetings or to lay accounts before such meetings: see CA 2006, ss 336, 437.

[106] See *Re a Company (No 00789 of 1987), ex p Shooter* [1990] BCLC 384; *Fisher v Cadman* [2006] 1 BCLC 499.

[107] See *Re Saul D Harrison & Sons plc* [1995] 1 BCLC 14 at 18, CA; also *Irvine v Irvine (No 1)* [2007] 1 BCLC 349. See *Re Sunrise Radio Ltd, Kohli v Lit* [2010] 1 BCLC 367 at [7]–[8] as to trivial infringements, but even a trivial infringement may amount to unfairly prejudicial conduct if the requirement infringed is imposed as an absolute requirement by the statute.   [108] [1999] 2 BCLC 1.

[109] [1972] 2 All ER 492 at 500, the case is discussed in detail at **18-83**.

(2) an agreement, or understanding, that all or some (for there may be 'sleeping' members) of the shareholders shall participate in the conduct of the business; and

(3) restrictions on the transfers of shares so that a member cannot take his stake and go elsewhere.

17-53 These companies are commonly described as 'quasi-partnerships' though 'it is clear that Lord Wilberforce was not intending to set out an exhaustive list of factors, and that the term quasi-partnership is only intended as a useful shorthand label'.[110]

17-54 Where these elements or some of them are present, the company is something more than the usual commercial association and there is a common understanding on all sides that the articles of association do not represent a complete and exhaustive statement of the parties' relationships.[111] In addition to the articles, there are understandings and promises (though not contractually binding) between the parties, typically about matters such as participation in the management of the company, financial returns, and, more broadly, the nature of the venture on which the parties have embarked. While these understandings etc will usually be found at the time of entering into the association, there may be later promises, by words or conduct, which it may be unfair to ignore,[112] given that relationships are not static but evolve over time. As Arden LJ explained in *Strahan v Wilcock*:[113] 'In determining what equitable obligations arise between the parties, the court must look at all the circumstances, including the company's constitution, any written agreement between the shareholders and the conduct of the parties.'

17-55 If the company is of this nature, i.e. something broader than a commercial association,[114] equitable considerations enable the court to hold the majority shareholders to the mutual agreements, promises or understandings which form the basis of the relationship. Complaints on this ground therefore have to show that the conduct of the company's affairs, while not necessarily a breach of the statute or of the constitution, is a breach of the understandings which form the basis of the association. A useful test, as Patten J explained in *Grace v Biagioli*,[115] is to 'ask whether the exercise of the power or rights in question would involve a breach of an agreement or understanding between the parties which it would be unfair to allow a member to ignore'.

Understandings as to participation in management

17-56 Complaints about removal from office are central to most unfairly prejudicial petitions. If the parties in a small private company have come together as members on the basis that all or some of them shall participate in the management of the company, the exclusion of a shareholder from management by removing him without cause as a director (a power open to the majority by ordinary resolution under CA 2006, s 168) is unfairly prejudicial

---

[110] *Fisher v Cadman* [2006] 1 BCLC 499 at 526. In this case the court noted that the family relationship between the parties (two brothers and a sister) was as important as the relationship defined by the articles of association and the company was a quasi-partnership though the petitioner had never taken any role in the management of the company and had contributed no capital, having been given or inherited her shares from her parents.   [111] *Fisher v Cadman* [2006] 1 BCLC 499 at 528.

[112] *O'Neill v Phillips* [1999] 2 BCLC 1 at 10–11.   [113] [2006] 2 BCLC 555 at 565.

[114] A company can be of this nature, thought it may look a very commercial venture. For example, in *Oak Investment Partners XII v Boughtwood* [2010] 2 BCLC 459, though the relationship was a joint venture between a large US venture capital firm and an individual entrepreneur and inventor, there was no dispute that their relationship was of a quasi-partnership nature giving rise to mutual obligation of good faith and trust, see at [119].   [115] [2006] 2 BCLC 70 at 92.

to his interests as a member in the absence of a fair offer by the majority to buy the petitioner's shares or to make some other fair arrangement.[116]

17-57 A typical example is *Brownlow v G H Marshall Ltd* [117] where the company was a family business built up over a long period of time and with the shares now held equally by a brother and two sisters, all of whom were directors. Following various disagreements and the breakdown of the personal relationships involved, an attempt was made to exclude one of the sisters from the board. The court held that attempting to exclude her without a fair offer for her shares amounted to the conduct of the company's affairs in a manner which was unfairly prejudicial to her interests so entitling her to relief.

17-58 An issue which has arisen is whether the fact that the director complaining of removal has a service agreement undermines his case, i.e. by suggesting that the relationship is a commercial one rather than a broader association based on mutual understandings. The courts have been reluctant so to conclude if when viewed overall the relationship is broader than a mere commercial association. In *Brownlow v G H Marshall Ltd*,[118] for example, the directors did have service agreements with the company but the court found that there was nothing in the arrangements reached which altered the basis on which the company operated, i.e. that it was a quasi-partnership. The service agreements were not designed, the court thought, to affect the shareholders' position as shareholders or to preclude any potential remedy which a shareholder might have under CA 2006, s 994, but were designed to ensure fair arrangements for the working directors.[119] A similar approach can be found in *Quinlan v Essex Hinge Co Ltd* [120] where the court agreed that the existence of a service agreement between the director and the company did not prevent the company having the characteristics of a quasi-partnership.

17-59 The position would be different if, as in *Re a Company (No 005685 of 1988), ex p Schwarz (No 2)*[121] the entire relationship between the parties is spelt out in detailed agreements, drafted and advised upon by professional advisers. The more detailed the agreements, the more likely it is that the company is being operated on a purely commercial basis and does not have the characteristics of a quasi-partnership.

17-60 In the absence of these personal quasi-partnership elements, every director is subject to the possibility of removal and has no right to remain in office.[122] Of course, removal of a director for cause will not merit a petition for, while such removal is prejudicial to the petitioner, it is not unfair.[123] If, as in *O'Neill v Phillips*,[124] and despite a changing relationship between the parties, the respondent chooses to continue to work with the petitioner without attempting to remove him from office, no grounds for complaint exist.

---

[116] *O'Neill v Phillips* [1999] 2 BCLC 1 at 14 ('It is the terms, agreement, or understanding on which [the petitioner] became associated as a member which generates the restraint of the power of expulsion', per Lord Hoffmann).

[117] [2000] 2 BCLC 655. See also *Shepherd v Williamson* [2010] EWHC 2375 at [131]; *Fowler v Gruber* [2010] 1 BCLC 563 at [129].   [118] [2000] 2 BCLC 655.

[119] [2000] 2 BCLC 655 at 669.   [120] [1996] 2 BCLC 417.   [121] [1989] BCLC 427, esp at 440–1.

[122] *Re Estate Acquisition and Development Ltd* [1995] BCC 338; *Re Tottenham Hotspur plc* [1994] 1 BCLC 655; *Re a Company (No 005134 of 1986), ex p Harries* [1989] BCLC 383; *Re a Company (No 005685 of 1988), ex p Schwarcz (No 2)* [1989] BCLC 427; *Re Blue Arrow plc* [1987] BCLC 585.

[123] See *Grace v Biagioli* [2006] 2 BCLC 70 (not unfairly prejudicial conduct to remove a director when he had been negotiating secretly to acquire a company dealing in the same line of business as the company and had put himself in a position of actual or potential conflict with his duties as a director). See also *Hussain v Cooke* [2009] EWHC 3690.   [124] [1999] 2 BCLC 1.

Understandings as to participation in financial returns

17-61 Dividend issues can loom large in disputes in small companies. A common problem is that the company does not declare any dividends while continuing to amass reserves with the majority shareholders rewarded via directors' remuneration.[125] Of course, the mere absence of dividends to shareholders cannot of itself constitute unfairly prejudicial conduct, even if the situation continues for years on end, since the declaration of dividends is a matter within the discretion of the directors. If the directors consider that no dividends should be paid for any particular period, and do so bona fide in the interests of the company, it is not for the court to second-guess the directors' reasoning or substitute its own view of what the directors ought fairly to have done. But if, as in *Re McCarthy Surfacing Ltd, Hequet v McCarthy*,[126] the board of directors fails even to consider the payment of any dividends,[127] that breach of duty is itself unfairly prejudicial conduct. Even if the circumstances are not quite as blatant as in *Re McCarthy Surfacing Ltd*, a failure to declare dividends may be unfairly prejudicial conduct if it can be shown to be contrary to the understandings of the parties as to how the financial rewards are to be shared.[128] In *Croly v Good*[129] the court found that the quasi-partners had an agreed remuneration strategy for an equal division of available funds between them.[130] The intention was that a scheme would be operated whereby each of them would draw money from the company as required during the year (so giving rise to a debt to the company) and a dividend would be declared at the end of the year which would reduce that debt as much as possible. In fact, no dividends were declared with the result that, when the parties subsequently fell out, there was a considerable debt due from the petitioner to the company on his loan account which debt would have been reduced had dividends been declared. Given the understanding as to the manner of remuneration, the court found that the failure to declare dividends (when funds were available) with the result that the directors' debts to the company continued to mount was unfairly prejudicial to the petitioner's interests as a member.[131] But, if, as in *Re Metropolis Motorcycles Ltd, Hale v Waldock*,[132] the company's financial situation prevents the company declaring dividends, the minority shareholder has no grounds for complaint, even if the majority shareholder as a director is able to continue drawing a salary. It would

---

[125] See, for example, *Quinlan v Essex Hinge Co Ltd* [1996] 2 BCLC 417 (non-declaration of dividends, despite the company having substantial reserves, with profits distributed by bonus payments to working directors or retained in the company). It is unfairly prejudicial conduct for the majority shareholders and directors to pay themselves remuneration when the understanding of the parties is that remuneration will not be paid, see *Fisher v Cadman* [2006] 1 BCLC 499 where the directors provided only limited services to the company which merely held properties for investment purposes and it was the understanding of all concerned that they would not be paid. It was unfairly prejudicial conduct, therefore, for them to award themselves remuneration in excess of £50,000.   [126] [2009] 1 BCLC 622.

[127] In this instance, the directors and majority shareholders were in a long-running dispute with the other shareholders and the majority received remuneration in other ways.

[128] See *Irvine v Irvine (No 1)* [2007] 1 BCLC 349; *Quinlan v Essex Hinge Co Ltd* [1996] 2 BCLC 417; *Re a Company (No 004415 of 1996)* [1997] 1 BCLC 479; *Re Sam Weller & Sons Ltd* [1990] BCLC 80. In *Re a Company (No 004415 of 1996)* Sir Richard Scott noted that, if it is established at trial that dividends have been kept at an unreasonably low level, that fact would be reflected in the price which would be set for the petitioner's shares if a purchase order is made under CA 2006, s 996.   [129] [2010] 2 BCLC 569.

[130] [2010] 2 BCLC 569 at [65]. The company had a 60/40 shareholding split with the 40% shareholder having moved from being an employee to being a quasi-partner, see **17-40**.

[131] Further, given the agreement as to equal division of spoils, drawings by the respondent director in excess of that received by the petitioner also amounted to unfairly prejudicial conduct, see [2010] 2 BCLC 569 at [96] and [99].

[132] [2007] 1 BCLC 520. In this case, the court found that the situation which had occurred—the inability of the company to make payments to the minority shareholder—had not been contemplated by the parties when they had set up the company so, in the absence of anything in the nature of a promise of payments to the minority shareholder, there was no basis for an order that he be bought out.

not necessarily be fair for this position to go on forever, however, and the majority would have to recognise, the court said, that the minority could be said to have a legitimate claim to some form of return, see **17-65**. In *Grace v Biagioli*[133] a dividend had been declared, but the respondents (aggrieved by the conduct of the petitioner) then deliberately chose not to pay it and instead distributed the available profits as management fees to themselves. This non-payment, the court held, was unfairly prejudicial conduct.

Understandings as to the basis of the relationship

17-62   In *O'Neill v Phillips*[134] Lord Hoffmann also considered that relief will be available under CA 2006, s 994 where some event has occurred which puts an end to the basis on which the parties entered into association with each other, so making it unfair that one shareholder should insist on the continuance of the association (a frustration-type situation).[135] But something more is needed than merely an assertion by the petitioner that the association should be brought to an end. Returning to *O'Neill v Phillips*,[136] it will be recalled that the House of Lords found that there was no unfairly prejudicial conduct. The minority shareholder had not been removed from office and there was no basis for his complaints that he should have received 50% of the shares and of the profits of the company, see **17-33**. It was argued by counsel that, even if nothing unfair had occurred, the trust and confidence between the parties had broken down to such an extent that there had to be a parting of the ways and it would be unfair to leave the petitioner locked into the company as a minority shareholder. Lord Hoffmann noted that the argument essentially was that, in a quasi-partnership company, one partner ought to be entitled at will to require the other partner to buy his shares at a fair value where he considered that trust and confidence between the partners had broken down. Lord Hoffmann rejected the argument, noting that he could find no support in the authorities for such a stark right of unilateral withdrawal where the member had not been dismissed or excluded from the company.[137] The purpose of the statutory provision (CA 2006, s 994) is 'to provide relief for shareholders who have been unfairly prejudiced, not to enable a locked-in minority shareholder to require the company to buy him out'.[138] It is quite clear then that a mere situation of deadlock between the parties who have lost trust and confidence in one another is insufficient to merit relief under CA 2006, s 994, a point affirmed by the Court of Appeal in *Re Phoenix Office Supplies Ltd*.[139] In that case, the court rejected a claim by a shareholder that his co-shareholders and directors were obliged to purchase his shares when he decided (for purely personal reasons) to leave the company. The Court of Appeal ruled that a quasi-partnership company relationship does not give rise to an entitlement to a 'no-fault divorce' enabling one member at will to require the other members to buy his shares at fair value. More recently, in *Hawkes v Cuddy*[140] the Court of Appeal confirmed that deadlock alone is insufficient to found a petition under CA 2006, s 994 (though it would suffice for winding up on the just and equitable ground, see **18-90**) even if it shows a breakdown of trust and confidence between the parties which makes it impossible for the company to conduct its affairs as originally contemplated. It is still necessary to establish unfair prejudice which may lie in the manner in which the other party reacts to the deadlock or the

---

[133]   [2006] 2 BCLC 70.   [134]   [1999] 2 BCLC 1.
[135]   [1999] 2 BCLC 1 at 11 where Lord Hoffmann noted that the analogy of contractual frustration suggested itself.   [136]   [1999] 2 BCLC 1.
[137]   [1999] 2 BCLC 1 at 13.
[138]   *Re a Company* [1983] BCLC 126 at 136. See, for example, *Re Abbington Hotel Ltd, DiGrado v D'Angelo* [2012] 1 BCLC 410 at [105].
[139]   [2003] 1 BCLC 76. See also *Re Jayflex Construction Ltd, McKee v O'Reilly* [2004] 2 BCLC 145.
[140]   [2009] 2 BCLC 427 at [108].

misconduct which created the deadlock and the resulting irrevocable breakdown in trust and confidence between the parties.[141] In *Re Abbington Hotel Ltd, DiGrado v D'Angelo*[142] one of the two effective shareholders tried to sell the business (a hotel) behind the back of the other shareholder in breach of an understanding that they would run the business for some time before selling. That conduct was a breach of the agreed basis on which the business was to be conducted, hence there was fault and unfairly prejudicial conduct. That fault destroyed the essential relationship of trust and confidence between the shareholder resulting in deadlock and relief under s 994, but it was not relief because of deadlock, it was relief as a consequence of the wrongful conduct of the respondent.

17-63   Given the clear authority that deadlock and a mere desire to bring to an end the association is not a sufficient basis for a petition, and that unfairly prejudicial conduct is required, it is difficult to see exactly what this category as envisaged by Lord Hoffmann adds to the preceding categories identified as the basis for petitions, i.e. a breach of the statute or the constitution or a use of legal powers in an inequitable way contrary to the understandings which form the basis of the association. Any of these elements would be the 'something more' required in addition to deadlock,[143] but they would in any event found the court's jurisdiction so rendering this 'category' unnecessary.

17-64   The nature of Lord Hoffmann's quasi-frustration category was considered by Mann J in *Re Metropolis Motorcycles Ltd, Hale v Waldock*[144] where he noted that:

> '....Lord Hoffmann was demonstrating that unfairness does not arise only out of a failure to comply with prior agreements or to fulfil prior expectations. The relationships between shareholders are more subtle than that, and Lord Hoffmann was recognising that unfairness can come out of a situation *where the game has moved on* [emphasis added] so as to involve a situation not covered by the previous arrangements and understanding. In those circumstances the conduct of the affairs of the company can be unfairly prejudicial within the section notwithstanding the absence of the prior arrangements, and the court can thus intervene. However, for the court to intervene the change in circumstances must be such that it is not reasonable or fair to require the former association to remain as it was, and such that the court's intervention is required to adjust matters. Lord Hoffmann's words have to be borne in mind: "[circumstances] making it unfair that one shareholder should insist upon the continuance of the association".'[145]

17-65   The need for the 'game to have moved on' and the 'quasi-frustration' analogy suggest that the change in circumstances which would bring a case within Lord Hoffmann's category

---

[141]   [2006] 2 BCLC 70 at [77]. See also *Re Neath Rugby Ltd, Hawkes v Cuddy* [2009] 2 BCLC 427 at [108]; *Oak Investment Partners XII v Boughtwood* [2010] 2 BCLC 459 at [8], [120] (there the parties were deadlocked but misconduct lay in the respondent's underhand, destructive and unconstitutional usurping of management power within the company which destroyed the relationship between the quasi-partners); *Re Sunrise Radio Ltd, Kohli v Lit* [2010] 1 BCLC 367 at [32] (no-fault divorce is not available, the failure of trust and confidence must be justified by reference to some unfair conduct on the part of those in control—in that case an improperly priced rights issue).

[142]   [2012] 1 BCLC 410. Deadlock too can be seen in *Shepherd v Williamson* [2010] EWHC 2375, but created by the unfairly prejudicial conduct of the respondent in excluding the petitioner from participation in the management of what was a quasi-partnership.

[143]   Examples can be seen in *Re Coloursource Ltd, Dalby v Bodilly* [2005] BCC 627 where the court found the trust and confidence between the parties had been destroyed by the willingness of the majority shareholder to make manipulative allotments of shares (so a breach of the statute) and in *Irvine v Irvine (No 1)* [2007] 1 BCLC 349 where the court found a breach of trust and confidence as a result of excessive remuneration awarded to himself by the majority shareholder.   [144]   [2007] 1 BCLC 520.

[145]   [2007] 1 BCLC 520 at 560.

would have to be a change which arose independently of the conduct of either party (so there would be no breach of the statute, constitution or understandings), but which would nevertheless render the continuation of the association unfair. Such cases must be rare and, unsurprisingly, in *Re Metropolis Motorcycles Ltd*[146] the court did not feel that the case fell into this 'quasi-frustration' category. The parties had an understanding that only the majority shareholder would be a director. The minority expected to be able to make monthly drawings from the company on account of profits, but the parties failed to antici-pate that circumstances might arise which would prevent the minority having any return on his substantial investment in the company. The company fell into financial difficulties and, while the majority shareholder continued to get a financial return as a director, the company was not in a position to declare a dividend to the minority. The court concluded that that was a failure by the parties to anticipate what had occurred rather than a change in the circumstances requiring court intervention to bring the association to an end. Mann J indicated, however, that it might be appropriate for the minority to come back to court at a later date if the majority did not respond to the changed circumstances and make some provision for a financial return to the minority shareholder.[147] In those cir-cumstances, it would then be open to the minority to rely on the frustration analogy and to argue that circumstances were such that it would be unfair for the majority shareholder to insist upon the continuation of the association on a basis that gave a return to him but none to the minority shareholder. Even on that scenario, that would essentially involve an allegation that understandings as to financial participation had not been met, or perhaps a breach of the duty to act fairly between shareholders, something would found the s 994 jurisdiction in any event. It seems unlikely that this 'quasi-frustration' category is of any great significance, even more so now that there appears to be a resurgence in the just and equitable winding-up jurisdiction which will give relief in cases of deadlock in quasi-partnerships, see further at **18-90**.

A fair offer—striking out the petition

17-66 As noted, a petition under CA 2006, s 994 may be brought either on the basis of a breach of the terms on which the affairs of the company should be conducted or use of the rules in an inequitable manner, as per *O'Neill v Phillips*.[148] However, while those are the grounds on which a petition may be based, it is not necessarily the case that the petition can pro-ceed for, in some circumstances, the petition may be struck out by the court. Generally, the court will strike out a petition if an offer has been made to the petitioner (whether as required by the articles or otherwise) that gives the petitioner all the relief that he could realistically expect to obtain on the petition and it would therefore be an abuse to con-tinue with the litigation.[149]

17-67 Tactically, therefore, it is important for the respondent to consider answering a legitimate complaint by a minority shareholder with a fair offer. A failure to make an offer where the petitioner has legitimate grievances means that ultimately the court will force the respondent to make a fair offer (through a purchase order under CA 2006, s 996) and all that has been achieved is that time and resources have been expended in litigation and the

---

[146] [2007] 1 BCLC 520.   [147] See [2007] 1 BCLC 520 at 561.   [148] [1999] 2 BCLC 1.

[149] *O'Neill v Phillips* [1999] 2 BCLC 1. See also *Wilkinson v West Coast Capital* [2007] BCC 717 at [329]–[331]. Typically the offer will be to buy out the petitioner, but it need not be, see *Music Sales Ltd v Shapiro Bornstein & Co Inc* [2006] 1 BCLC 311. See also *Re a Company (No 007623 of 1984)* [1986] BCLC 362; *Re a Company (No 004377 of 1986)* [1987] BCLC 94; *Re a Company (No 003843 of 1986)* [1987] BCLC 562; *Re a Company (No 006834 of 1988), ex p Kremer* [1989] BCLC 365; *Re Castleburn Ltd* [1991] BCLC 89; *Re a Company (No 00836 of 1995)* [1996] 2 BCLC 192.

respondent will be liable in costs. Likewise, a petitioner must be careful not to reject a fair offer for the court will not allow a petition to proceed in those circumstances. In effect, the fair offer/strike out rule is used to force the parties to the negotiating table.

17-68   In a quasi-partnership, to be a fair offer, the offer typically has to be an offer to purchase the minority shares on a pro-rata basis, see **17-82**, on a valuation made by an independent valuer.[150] The valuer must be independent and, while this does not automatically rule out the company's auditors, the nature of the auditors' relationship with the majority share-holders and their past involvement in matters which will affect the valuation means that in many instances the court will agree that the petitioner need not accept such a valuation and the petition can continue.[151]

17-69   Valuable guidance on what is a fair offer, such that a petition should be struck out, was given, obiter, by Lord Hoffmann in *O'Neill v Phillips*[152] as follows and this now provides the basic benchmark for a fair offer:

'i)   the offer must be to purchase the shares at a fair value.

ii)   the value, if not agreed, should be determined by a competent expert;

iii)   the offer should be to have the value determined by the expert as an expert. It is not required that the offer should provide for the full machinery of arbitration or the half-way house of an expert who gives reasons. The objective should be economy and expedition, even if this carries the possibility of a rough edge for one side or the other (and both parties in this respect take the same risk) compared with a more elaborate procedure;

iv)   the offer should provide for equality of arms between the parties. Both should have the same right of access to information about the company which bears upon the value of the shares and both should have the right to make submissions to the expert; and

v)   when the offer is made after a lengthy period of litigation, it cannot serve as an inde-pendent ground for dismissing the petition, on the assumption that it was otherwise well founded, without an offer of costs. But this does not mean that payment of costs need always be offered. If there is a breakdown in relations between the parties, the majority shareholder should be given a reasonable opportunity to make an offer (which may include time to explore the question of how to raise finance) before he becomes obliged to pay costs.'

17-70   An example of an offer which did not amount to a fair offer (and so it was possible to continue with the petition) can be seen in *North Holdings Ltd v Southern Tropics Ltd*[153] concerning alleged misuse by the respondents of the company's assets and goodwill to develop the business of another company in which they were interested. The court thought that valuation of the petitioner's shares in this case raised serious questions of law (as to the extent of the first company's interest in the second company, given the alleged misuse of the first company's assets) which it was not appropriate to leave to a valuer and the petition should not be struck out. Another example is *Allmark v Burnham*[154] where the

---

[150]   See *Re a Company (No 00836 of 1995)* [1996] 2 BCLC 192.

[151]   See *North Holdings Ltd v Southern Tropics Ltd* [1999] 2 BCLC 625 at 639; *Re Rotadata Ltd* [2000] 1 BCLC 122 at 132–3; *Re Benfield Greig Group plc* [2002] 1 BCLC 65, CA; also *Re Belfield Furnishings Ltd, Isaacs v Belfield Furnishings Ltd* [2006] 2 BCLC 705 at 722.   [152]   [1999] 2 BCLC 1 at 16.

[153]   [1999] 2 BCLC 625.

[154]   [2006] 2 BCLC 437. See also *Re Woven Rugs Ltd* [2010] EWHC 230 (offers made did not make provi-sion or redress for the dissipation of the company's funds which had been found to be unfairly prejudicial conduct); *Rahman v Malik* [2008] 2 BCLC 403 (offers did not make provision for the under-declaration of profits by the company and unpaid dividends); *Hussain v Cooke* [2009] EWHC 3690 at [74] (offer 'subject to

court found that the purported 'offers' did not offer the petitioner a satisfactory alternative remedy which he ought reasonably to have accepted. There were a variety of defects in the 'offers' including an absence of equality of arms between the parties with the respondent, but not the petitioner, being allowed to influence the valuation; an absence of detail on matters such as the fair value to be paid (i.e. whether a minority discount would apply) and the date of valuation and the absence of proper accounts in relation to the company.

17-71 The role of 'O'Neill' offers was considered in detail recently in *Harborne Road Nominees Ltd v Karvaski*[155] where HHJ David Cooke was anxious to stress that the guidance given by Lord Hoffmann does not have the status of legislation.[156] Lord Hoffmann was not prescribing a system whereby someone is protected from a petition, despite behaving in an unfairly prejudicial manner, provided an offer is then made in the specified form. It would be a cardinal error, the court said, to assume that if an offer complied with the guidance, any petition would inevitably be struck out.[157] Also, HHJ Cooke noted that the guidance was given in the context of a majority shareholder buying out a minority, not in the context of equal shareholders where it is not always clear which of the shareholders should exit from the company.[158] In that situation, it would be unjust, he said, if one of them was able to seize control of the company and then effectively force the other to accept an offer.[159]

17-72 The question for the court in all cases is whether it is appropriate to strike out the petition because its continued prosecution is an abuse or bound to fail which will always be highly sensitive to the facts of each case.[160] In particular, the offer must give the petitioner all that he could reasonably achieve at trial[161] and it may be difficult to determine that this is the case where, for example, the petitioner has had limited access to information about the company and so cannot determine whether the offer reflects the true value of his shares.[162] There is also the difficulty that if the petition alleges wrongdoing, such as a diversion of business or misappropriation of assets, the determination of that claim by the court would have a direct bearing on the value of the shares and would be reflected in any order a court might make, but a valuer would only be able to express an opinion as to the impact of the potential claim on the value of the shares.[163] Often the relief sought is wider than a purchase order[164] and so an offer which is limited to an offer to purchase the petitioner's shares would not give the petitioner all the relief which he could reasonably expect to achieve from the proceedings and therefore the petition would not be struck out. On the facts in *Harborne*, there were a number of factors (a failure to resolve all the disputes between the parties, ambiguity as to whether the company would declare certain dividends and a lack of information about the company's affairs) which meant that it would be wrong to dismiss the petition given that the petitioner might well obtain from the court an offer which would be more advantageous to him in material respects than the offer made.[165]

---

affordability' did not meet the requirements of a fair offer); *Shepherd v Williamson* [2010] EWHC 2375 (various defects in the offers made including no equality of arms, no provision for independent valuation and deferred consideration, all of which meant, the court said, that these were not 'O'Neill' type offers).

[155] [2011] EWHC 2214.   [156] [2011] EWHC 2214 at [24].   [157] [2011] EWHC 2214 at [26].
[158] [2011] EWHC 2214 at [27].   [159] [2011] EWHC 2214 at [27].   [160] [2011] EWHC 2214 at [26].
[161] [2011] EWHC 2214 at [35].   [162] [2011] EWHC 2214 at [31].   [163] [2011] EWHC 2214 at [30].
[164] [2011] EWHC 2214 at [35]. Often the petition will ask for other matters such as adjustments to directors' loan accounts, or provision to be made for any company property which the petitioner used or may seek to keep, see Joffee et al, *Minority Shareholders* (4th edn, 2011), paras 8.108–8.116.
[165] [2011] EWHC 2214 at [40], [43]–[47].

17-73 The court also considered the effect of refusing the offer (in *Harborne* no offer remained on the table) and the consequences if the court then strikes out the petition as an abuse. HHJ Cooke considered that if a fair offer is made which clearly and finally cures the alleged prejudice and it is rejected, the petitioner cannot complain that he is left without an exit mechanism and has to remain as a minority shareholder in an unhappy situation, for he is not entitled to insist on a standing offer that he can accept at any time.[166] This does not mean that he is forever without a remedy, for subsequent unfairly prejudicial conduct may occur which would allow him to petition.[167]

Court's power to grant relief

17-74 Where the court is satisfied that a petition under CA 2006, s 994 is well founded, it may make such order as it thinks fit for giving relief in respect of the matters complained of (CA 2006, s 996(1)).[168] Without prejudice to the generality of the court's powers, CA 2006, s 996(2) indicates certain types of orders which the court may make,[169] such as regulating the conduct of the company's affairs in the future, or requiring the company to refrain from doing or continuing an act complained of by the petitioner, or to do an act which the petitioner has complained it has omitted to do. The remedy most commonly sought and obtained, as noted, is a purchase order requiring the respondents to purchase the petitioner's shares at a fair value which normally requires the shares to be valued as if the wrongdoing had not occurred so ensuring that the shareholder recovers any diminution in the value of his shares caused by the wrongdoing.[170]

17-75 The courts have consistently taken the view that the wording of CA 2006, s 996 ('such order as the court thinks fit') offers the widest possible discretion to grant relief. In making an order under CA 2006, s 996, the court must consider the whole range of possible remedies and it is not limited merely to reversing or putting right the immediate conduct which justifies the order, but it must also look to cure for the future the unfair prejudice suffered by the petitioner[171] so any likelihood of the conduct recurring is a relevant consideration. In determining what is the appropriate remedy, as Patten J noted in *Grace v*

---

[166] [2011] EWHC 2214 at [34].

[167] [2011] EWHC 2214 at [34]. Also, where it is a quasi-partnership, he may be in a position to petition for a winding up on the just and equitable ground on the basis of the breakdown of the relationship of trust and confidence between the parties, see **18-90**.

[168] The court's power extends to granting relief which the petitioner has not sought or agreed to: *Hawkes v Cuddy* [2009] 2 BCLC 427 at [88]–[91], though in practice all petitions specify the relief sought as well as asking for 'such other order as the court thinks fit'. The making of any order is ultimately a discretionary exercise by the court which in a case where there is unfairly prejudicial conduct by both parties (see, for example, *Re Abbington Hotel Ltd, DiGrado v D'Angelo* [2012] 1 BCLC 410) involves a more complicated balancing exercise as to how to exercise the discretion, see *Oak Investment Partners XII v Boughtwood* [2010] 2 BCLC 459 at [119].

[169] In the exceptional case where a member petitions with respect to the improper removal of an auditor under CA 2006, s 994(1A), see **17-31**, presumably any order would relate to the re-appointment of the original auditors, the appointment of new auditors, or any other remedy which the court deems appropriate. In practice, it is unlikely that much use will be made of this provision.

[170] See, for example, *Re Little Olympian Each-Ways Ltd (No 3)* [1995] 1 BCLC 636.

[171] *Re Bird Precision Bellows Ltd* [1985] BCLC 493 at 499–500; *Grace v Biagioli* [2006] 2 BCLC 70. See, for example, *Re Woven Rugs Ltd* [2010] EWHC 230 where in addition to the usual purchase order—the majority to purchase the shares of the minority—the court also ordered the majority to repay a loan made by the minority to the (now insolvent) company on the basis that the majority had procured the repayment of their equivalent loan and the loan was inextricably bound up with the shareholders' membership of the company.

Biagioli,[172] the court is 'entitled to look at the realities and practicalities of the overall situation, past, present and future'.[173]

17-76 Interim remedies are available[174] and the court may make an order against third parties where they are involved, innocently or knowingly, in the prejudicial conduct[175] and orders may be made for the benefit of the company,[176] a point discussed further later. In *Gamlestaden Fastigheter AB v Baltic Partners Ltd*[177] the Privy Council (considering the Jersey statutory equivalent[178] of CA 2006, s 996) accepted that the court could order that damages be paid by the wrongdoers to the company.[179] Indeed the Privy Council was prepared in that case to accept that, given the width of the jurisdiction to give relief, exceptionally, the court might grant relief though the company was insolvent.

17-77 The petitioners in *Gamlestaden* were minority shareholders in a joint venture and the essence of their allegation was that the directors had negligently allowed the bulk of the company's assets to be lost rendering it insolvent (allegedly the assets were withdrawn from the business for no consideration by the majority shareholders). The minority shareholder had lent the company DM165.5m and an award of damages payable by the majority shareholders to the company, while it would not restore the company to solvency, would at least offer some prospect for the minority as creditors to recover some of these loans.[180] The respondent directors unsuccessfully applied to have the petition struck out on the basis that relief had to be of benefit to the petitioner in his capacity as a member rather than for the benefit of the creditors. The Privy Council concluded that, given the width of the jurisdiction to give relief under what is now CA 2006, s 996, exceptionally the court may grant relief though the company is insolvent and will remain insolvent so long as the petitioner derives some real financial benefit from the petition.[181] The exceptional element in *Gamlestaden* was that the company was a joint venture formed on the basis of

---

[172] [2006] 2 BCLC 70 at 90.

[173] For example, in *Fowler v Gruber* [2010] 1 BCLC 563, the court rejected the successful petitioner's request that he be appointed managing director of the company. Given the level of disagreement between the parties, the court thought that would be neither sensible nor practical and the court ordered instead that the petitioner's shares be purchased by the respondent.

[174] See *Pringle v Callard* [2008] 2 BCLC 505, where Arden LJ gives useful guidance on the role of interim remedies in this context; also *Re Ravenhart Service (Holdings) Ltd, Reiner v Gershinson* [2004] 2 BCLC 376.

[175] See, for example, *Clark v Cutland* [2003] 2 BCLC 393 (order addressed to pension fund trustees—the petition was based on unauthorised payments of company money (£145,000) by a director to his pension fund—the court ordered that the company was entitled to a charge over the pension fund cash reserves to secure the sum of £145,000 (set off by £100,000 owed by the company to the pension fund). See also *Lowe v Fahey* [1996] 1 BCLC 262 at 268; *Re a Company (No 005287)* [1986] BCLC 68 at 71.

[176] See *Clark v Cutland* [2003] 2 BCLC 393; *Bhullar v Bhullar* [2003] 2 BCLC 241; *Anderson v Hogg* [2002] BCC 923, SC, but these cases should be seen as confined to their exceptional facts, see Hannigan, 'Drawing boundaries between derivative claims and unfairly prejudicial petitions' [2009] JBL 606 at 620–6.

[177] [2008] 1 BCLC 468, PC, noted Walters (2007) 28 Co Law 289; Singla (2007) 123 LQR 542 and discussed in detail in Hannigan, n 176, [2009] JBL 606 at 620–6.   [178] See Companies (Jersey) Law 1991, art 141.

[179] See also *Atlasview Ltd v Brightview Ltd* [2004] 2 BCLC 191 at [55].

[180] The loans had been provided by the petitioner's parent company, though procured by the petitioner pursuant to its obligations to do so under the joint venture agreement. Their Lordships agreed with Robert Walker J in *R & H Electric Ltd v Haden Bill Electrical Ltd* [1995] 2 BCLC 280 at 294, where there was a similar arrangement, that this feature should not bar the petitioner from relief, see [2008] 1 BCLC 468 at 480 and discussion at **17-28,** though in that case the company was solvent.

[181] Their Lordships rejected the argument that, as on a winding-up petition, the petitioner under CA 2006, s 994 needs to show a tangible interest in the winding up (essentially that surplus funds would be available) on the basis that the public interest considerations which underlie that requirement in winding up do not apply to unfairly prejudicial petitions: see [2008] 1 BCLC 468 at 478. It is difficult to see much difference between a 'real financial benefit' and a tangible interest, but the tangible interest must accrue to the shareholder as such whereas a real financial benefit can arise more broadly as *Gamlestaden* demonstrates.

an agreement between the joint venturers that the company be funded through share and loan capital. These funding arrangements were so closely connected to the petitioner's membership of the joint venture that if the relief sought was of real value to the joint venturer in recovering some part of his investment, then, in their Lordships' opinion, he ought not to be precluded from relief on the ground that it would benefit him as a loan creditor and not as a member.[182]

17-78   This issue of corporate relief on an unfairly prejudicial petition requires further consideration in the light of the statutory derivative claim under CA 2006, Pt 11. Where in essence a petitioner is seeking corporate relief for breach of directors' duties, the petition should be dismissed and the petitioner required instead to seek permission to bring a derivative claim (see Chapter 18), other than in the rare case where the petitioner seeks personal and corporate relief and it is convenient and appropriate to deal with the corporate claim on the petition.[183] In a different but still relevant context (unfairly prejudicial conduct of a company's affairs in administration) Millett J in *Re Charnley Davies Ltd (No 2)*,[184] having commented that it is a matter of perspective, explained that there is a distinction between cases where the unlawfulness of the conduct complained of is the whole gist of the complaint and it may be adequately addressed by the remedy provided by the law for that wrong and cases where the burden is of alleging and proving that the acts or omissions complained of evidence or constitute unfairly prejudicial conduct of the company's affairs and wider relief may be sought. In essence, instances of misconduct should be the subject of a derivative claim under CA 2006, Pt 11 while unfairly prejudicial mismanagement of the company's affairs should be the subject of a petition under CA 2006, s 994.

Purchase orders

17-79   As noted, in practice, a petitioner typically requests an order under CA 2006, s 996(2) (e), requiring the respondents to purchase the shares held by the petitioner[185] and, as the Court of Appeal commented in *Grace v Biagioli*,[186] in most cases of unfairly prejudicial conduct nothing less than a clean break between the parties is likely to be required. In this case the respondents consciously and deliberately failed to pay a dividend which had been declared and the available profits were distributed instead as management fees to the respondents. At first instance, the trial judge considered that the appropriate relief was to order the company to pay the petitioner the missing dividend plus interest. On appeal, the Court of Appeal concluded that the judge had erred as to the scope of the discretion to order relief, in particular as to the need to cure the problem for the future. In this case, there was some evidence of changes in trading arrangements which would reduce the profits available to be distributed as dividends, a change which the court noted 'does not

---

[182]   [2008] 1 BCLC 468 at 479.

[183]   For a detailed consideration of the issue of corporate relief on an unfairly prejudicial petition, see Hannigan, 'Drawing boundaries between derivative claims and unfairly prejudicial petitions' [2009] JBL 606.

[184]   [1990] BCLC 760 at 783. This approach was supported by Lord Scott sitting in the HK Court of Final Appeal in *Re Chime Corp* [2004] HKFCAR 546 at [63], discussed in Hannigan, n 176.

[185]   On occasion, the petitioner asks for and obtains an order entitling him to purchase the respondent's shares at a fair value, see, for example, *Re Abbington Hotel Ltd, DiGrado v D'Angelo* [2012] 1 BCLC 410; *Oak Investment Partners XII v Boughtwood* [2010] 2 BCLC 459 at [123]; *Re Hedgehog Golf Co Ltd, Lantsbury v Hauser* [2010] EWHC 390; *Clark v Cutland* [2003] 2 BCLC 393; *Re Brenfield Squash Racquets Club Ltd* [1996] 2 BCLC 184. Where there is an equality of shareholdings, the court may order the persons responsible for the unfairly prejudicial conduct to sell their shares to the petitioner: see *Re Planet Organic Ltd* [2000] 1 BCLC 366.   [186]   [2006] 2 BCLC 70.

bode well for future relations between the parties'.[187] Taking everything into account, the Court of Appeal thought that nothing short of a purchase order would provide appropriate protection for the petitioner.[188] A purchase order, the court said, frees the petitioner from the company and enables him to extract his share of the value of the business and assets in return for forgoing any future right to dividends.[189] It also preserves the company and its business for the benefit of the respondents, free from the petitioner's claims and removes the possibility of future difficulties between the shareholders.[190]

17-80   In *Re Coloursource Ltd, Dalby v Bodilly*[191] the unfairly prejudicial conduct was an improper allotment of shares which had the effect of diluting a 50% shareholder to a 5% shareholder. The respondent argued that the appropriate relief was a reversal of the allotment, rectification of the register of members and an undertaking by him not to make further allotments of shares. The court refused to limit the relief in that way and granted the purchase order sought by the petitioner. A buy-out order was an entirely appropriate order, the court said, when the respondent had conducted himself in such a way as to forfeit the other shareholder's confidence in the respondent's ability to conduct the company's affairs in a proper way.

17-81   Once the court determines that a purchase order is the appropriate relief, it is not required to add to the order an 'escape clause', i.e. an order for alternative relief in the event that the respondent is unable to raise the necessary funds to purchase the shares. That approach was rejected as wrong in principle by the Court of Appeal in *Re Cumana Ltd*[192] for a purchase order is a reflection of the amount of compensation due to the petitioner for the wrong (the unfairly prejudicial conduct) done to him by the respondent and the fact that the respondent is impecunious is no reason for not giving judgment for the amount due to the victim.[193] For the same reason, it is irrelevant that the shares which the respondent is ordered to buy are worthless, as where the company is in administration, for the payment is compensation to the petitioner for the damage caused by the wrongful conduct.[194]

Valuation issues

17-82   The basic approach to the valuation of the shares to be acquired was established in *Re Bird Precision Bellows Ltd*[195] which has been followed in numerous cases. The key considerations are:

(1) The price fixed by the court must be fair,[196] so the valuation must be adjusted to take into account the unfairly prejudicial conduct, for example, any misappropriation

---

[187]   [2006] 2 BCLC 70 at [82].

[188]   [2006] 2 BCLC 70 at [83]. The court also noted that it would not have been appropriate in any event to order the company, as opposed to the respondents, to pay the missing dividend, see at [86].

[189]   [2006] 2 BCLC 70 at [75].   [190]   [2006] 2 BCLC 70 at [75].

[191]   [2005] BCC 627. See also *Irvine v Irvine (No 1)* [2007] 1 BCLC 349, the unfairly prejudicial conduct was the payment of excessive and unauthorised remuneration, but the court considered that the breakdown in trust between the parties had gone too far to be rectified by an order requiring the respondent to repay the excessive amount and fixing the level of his remuneration as to the future. A purchase order requiring him to purchase the minority's shares was the only appropriate remedy.   [192]   [1986] BCLC 430.

[193]   [1986] BCLC 430 at 436–7; *Re Scitec Group Ltd, Sethi v Patel* [2011] 1 BCLC 277 at [34].

[194]   *Re Woven Rugs Ltd* [2010] EWHC 230 at [175]. The company going into administration may itself be suspect, see *Re Scitec Group Ltd, Sethi v Patel* [2011] 1 BCLC 277 where the court was suspicious of the fact that the company's value declined rapidly before going into administration whereupon it was sold, by way of a pre-pack (see **23-5**), back to the respondent shareholder; likewise in *Shepherd v Williamson* [2010] EWHC 2375, see at [151]–[152].   [195]   [1984] BCLC 195, aff'd [1985] BCLC 493.

[196]   For example, the valuation of ordinary shares, where there are also preference shares in the company with a priority to a return of capital on a winding up, should reflect that liquidation preference which is an integral feature of the respective rights of the ordinary and preference shares and likely to have an impact on

of assets or opportunities or usage of company funds by the respondents for their personal benefit, etc which will have had the effect of diminishing the value of the shares.[197] The regular practice of the court is to value the shares 'not as they are, but as they would have been if events had followed a different course',[198] i.e. if the unfairly prejudicial conduct had not occurred.

(2) There is no rule that the shares have to be bought on a pro-rata basis, but nor is there a general rule that they have to be bought on a discounted basis to reflect the fact that they are a minority holding. It all depends on the circumstances of the case.

(3) In general, however, the court would distinguish between two types of shareholding in small private companies: (a) where the holding is in what is essentially a quasi-partnership and the sale is being forced on the holder because of the unfairly prejudicial manner in which the majority have conducted the affairs of the company; and (b) where the company is not a quasi-partnership.

(4) Where the sale is of a holding acquired in what is essentially a quasi-partnership and the sale is being forced on the holder because of the unfairly prejudicial manner in which the majority have conducted the affairs of the company then, as a general rule, the correct course would be to fix the price pro rata according to the value of the shares as a whole and without any discount.

17-83 As already explained, the majority of petitions do relate to quasi-partnerships and therefore the general approach is to require a pro-rata valuation. The offer should be on a pro-rata basis because, as Lord Millett explained in *CVC/Opportunity Equity Partners Ltd v Demarco Almeida*,[199] the matter should be approached as a sale of the whole business to an outside purchaser. In order to be free to manage the business without regard to the relationship of trust and confidence which formerly existed between the parties, the majority must buy the whole business, 'part from themselves and part from the minority, thereby achieving the same freedom to manage the business as an outside purchaser would enjoy'.[200]

17-84 Classifying a relationship as a quasi-partnership (see **17-52**) will then have a significant impact on valuation. In *Strahan v Wilcock*[201] it was argued that this general rule (pro-rata valuation in a quasi-partnership) should be set aside. In that case the parties' relationship had developed from one of employer/employee into a quasi-partnership, but the acquisition of shares in the business by the petitioner had also been the subject of commercial option agreements. The question was whether such commercial aspects to the relationship meant that a pro-rata basis should be set aside in favour of a discounted value. The Court of Appeal concluded that the relationship overall was correctly classified as a quasi-partnership when the petitioner's employment, his rights under the option agreements (the terms of which did not suggest a purely commercial relationship) and his participation in the management of the business were all taken into account. Given all the

---

the valuation of the ordinary shares, but the court might have a discretion to order otherwise in the circumstances of a particular case: *Oak Investment Partners XII v Boughtwood* [2010] 2 BCLC 459 at [129].

[197] See, for example, *Re Scitec Group Ltd, Sethi v Patel* [2011] 1 BCLC 277; *Croly v Good* [2010] 2 BCLC 569; *Re Little Olympian Each-Ways Ltd (No 3)* [1995] 1 BCLC 636.

[198] *Profinance Trust SA v Gladstone* [2002] 1 BCLC 141 at [31], per Robert Walker LJ. It is not open to the respondent to argue that the shares are valueless if they are so because of his own conduct, see *Croly v Good* [2010] 2 BCLC 569 at [118].   [199] [2002] 2 BCLC 108.

[200] [2002] 2 BCLC 108 at 119, per Lord Millett.   [201] [2006] 2 BCLC 555, CA.

circumstances of the relationship, on the petitioner's exclusion from the management of the company, fairness required that his shares be purchased on a non-discounted basis.

17-85 Where the company is not a quasi-partnership, different considerations apply and the price fixed will normally be discounted to reflect the fact that it is a minority holding held essentially as an investment. For example, in *Re Elgindata Ltd*[202] a discounted value was appropriate for the shares had been acquired by the petitioners for investment purposes. In *Re McCarthy Surfacing Ltd, Hequet v McCarthy*[203] the relationships originally were that of quasi-partners but, after previous disputes, the position had reverted to a formal commercial relationship so a purchase order on a discounted basis was appropriate.[204] In *Re Planet Organic Ltd*[205] the purchase order related to preference shareholders and the court concluded that, as they were investors rather than active participants in the running of the company, they should be bought out at a discount. A discounted valuation applies, even if the minority holding is substantial, as in *Irvine v Irvine (No 2)*.[206] In this case, the petitioners tried to persuade the court that their 49.96% shareholding was so substantial that the holding should be valued on a pro-rata, non-discounted basis, though the company was not a quasi-partnership. The court rejected their claim and ruled that a minority shareholding, even where the extent of the minority is slight, is to be valued as a minority shareholding unless a good reason exists (i.e. that the company is a quasi-partnership or some other exceptional circumstance) to attribute to it a pro-rata share of the overall value of the company. In the instant case, the company was not a quasi-partnership and there was no good reason or exceptional circumstance to order anything other than a discounted valuation. Indeed, in *Strahan v Wilcock*,[207] Arden LJ considered it difficult to conceive of circumstances in which a pro-rata valuation would be appropriate where there was no quasi-partnership relationship.

17-86 But, an example can be found in *Re Sunrise Radio Ltd, Kohli v Lit*[208] where the court did order a pro-rata valuation despite the company not being a quasi-partnership, noting that there is no inflexible rule of universal application excluding a pro-rata valuation.[209] The unfairly prejudicial conduct in this case (see **17-47**) essentially involved improper allotments of shares at par (when a significant premium might have been obtained) which diluted both the petitioner's shareholding in the company and the value of her shares. In the circumstances, the court thought that there were a variety of reasons why a pro-rata value was appropriate.[210] First, the petitioner was an original shareholder who did not obtain her shares at a discounted value and she was not a willing seller, rather her exit was occasioned by the unfairly prejudicial conduct of the respondents. Secondly, the company had not declared dividends as the strategy was to look for capital growth and, though not in itself a ground for complaint,[211] it was unfair that she would be deprived of any part of the fruits of that capital growth. Thirdly, a solvent winding up of the company would have been open to her on the just and equitable ground (see **18-74**) whereby she would have received a rateable proportion of the realised assets. The court saw no reason why she

---

[202] [1991] BCLC 959.   [203] [2009] 1 BCLC 622.

[204] See also *Fowler v Gruber* [2010] 1 BCLC 563 (company started as a quasi-partnership, but became a commercial relationship when the petitioner sold part of his shares and a local authority became a shareholder—discounted value appropriate); *Re a Company (No 005134 of 1986), ex p Harries* [1989] BCLC 383 (company started as a quasi-partnership but had reverted to a more commercial footing when the petitioner withdrew from the business—discounted value appropriate).   [205] [2000] 1 BCLC 366.

[206] [2007] 1 BCLC 445.   [207] [2006] 2 BCLC 555 at 561, CA.   [208] [2010] 1 BCLC 367.

[209] [2010] 1 BCLC 367 at [291]–[297].

[210] The reasons are summarized in [2010] 1 BCLC 367 at [308].

[211] See [2010] 1 BCLC 367 at [136]–[142].

should be in a worse position under a s 994 petition than she would be under a winding-up petition,[212] given that her choice of remedy kept the company alive for the benefit of the remaining shareholders. Fourthly, the court considered that the particular value of the shares to the respondents might be a very material factor.[213] The company was very successful and was likely to be floated on the stock exchange in the near future, something which the petitioner would have benefited from, had the unfairly prejudicial conduct of the respondents not made her into an unwilling seller of her shares. There was a risk that the respondents would end up unjustly enriched by the acquisition of her shares which had been triggered by their wrongful conduct which was especially unjust if there was reason to suspect that their conduct was influenced by a desire to buy out or worsen the position of the minority.[214] The first three reasons given by the court seem insufficiently compelling to justify a pro-rata valuation and they would be present in many cases so, if they are the determining factors, then the categories of petitioner entitled to a pro-rata valuation would be greatly expanded. The fourth factor, however, appears to be a genuinely exceptional element which merits a pro-rata valuation though the company was not a quasi-partnership. Exceptionally, fairness did require a different outcome in this case from the normal discount and fairness, as noted in *Re Bird Precision Bellows Ltd*,[215] is the key objective in valuing the shares.

17-87   In addition to disputes as to the basis of valuation, it is common for there also to be disagreements as to the appropriate date for valuation for this may have a significant bearing on the outcome. The starting point is that the shares should be valued at the date of the court's order for purchase, as that is the time when the unfairly prejudicial conduct is brought to an end, and an interest in a going concern should be valued at the date when it is ordered to be sold.[216] As the overriding criterion is fairness, in the circumstances of a particular case, fairness may require that the valuation be directed to take place at an earlier date,[217] such as the date of the petition, or the date of improper exclusion from participation in the management of the company if exclusion has been established. In relation to the latter possibility, the court is particularly so disposed to value the shares as at the date of exclusion if, as in *Croly v Good*,[218] the value of the company declines significantly after the exclusion in circumstances which raise suspicions as to how that decline has occurred. A feature of a number of cases recently has been that, by the time of the judgment, the company is in administration, sometimes dubiously so.[219] The fact that the

---

[212] [2010] 1 BCLC 367 at [301]. It is interesting given, as discussed later, that there has been something of a revival of the just and equitable winding-up jurisdiction, see **18-90**, that the court thought that the potential availability of relief through the winding-up process should be taken into account, in an appropriate case, in fashioning the remedy under CA 2006, s 996.   [213] [2010] 1 BCLC 367 at [305].

[214] [2010] 1 BCLC 367 at [305].   [215] [1984] BCLC 195, aff'd [1985] BCLC 493.

[216] *Profinance Trust SA v Gladstone* [2002] 1 BCLC 141.

[217] Guidance as to the circumstances in which an earlier valuation might be called for was given by the Court of Appeal in *Profinance Trust SA v Gladstone* [2002] 1 BCLC 141. In determining the date, the Court of Appeal emphasised that the date of valuation may be heavily influenced by the parties' conduct in making and accepting or rejecting 'O'Neill offers' (see **17-66**) either before or during the course of the proceedings. In *Re Scitec Group Ltd, Sethi v Patel* [2011] 1 BCLC 277 the petitioner chose the (earlier) date of his resignation from the company which then worked to his disadvantage when his shares would possibly have been given a higher value at the date of the court order, see at [42].   [218] [2010] 2 BCLC 569 at [113], [117].

[219] See also *Shepherd v Williamson* [2010] EWHC 2375 (significant decline in value of the company after the petitioner's exclusion followed by the company being placed into administration and sold by way of a pre-pack (see **23-5**) to persons connected with the original company and therefore with the respondent—the court ordered that the valuation date would be the date of exclusion).

company is in administration is not a bar to making a purchase order, but it does suggest that the valuation date should not be the date of the order.[220]

Relationship with other shareholder remedies

17-88 The range of conduct covered and the flexibility of the relief offered means that petitioning for relief under CA 2006, s 994 is almost invariably the most attractive solution for an aggrieved shareholder, but there are other options available, including various statutory rights under the CA 2006, see **18-69**, which may be relevant in some circumstances and the option of seeking a winding up of the company on the just and equitable ground or bringing a derivative claim on behalf of the company.

Winding up on the just and equitable ground

17-89 In addition to petitioning for relief under CA 2006, s 994, a petitioner may petition in the alternative for a winding-up order on the just and equitable ground under IA 1986, s 122(1)(g), there being no power to make a winding-up order under CA 2006, s 996. The effect of petitioning under the winding-up jurisdiction is to oblige the company to seek a validation order[221] under IA 1986, s 127 which otherwise avoids dispositions of company property made after the commencement of the winding up (i.e. after the presentation of the petition), see **24-32**. The requirement of a validation order under IA 1986, s 127 means that presenting a winding-up petition alongside the unfairly prejudicial petition maximises the pressure that the petitioner can bring to bear on the respondents. The courts are alert to the oppressive possibilities of this tactic, however, and a Practice Direction makes clear that a petitioner should not seek relief under CA 2006, s 994 and winding up unless winding up is the relief which the petitioner prefers or it is thought that it may be the only relief to which he is entitled.[222] In practice, it is unlikely that a petitioner does want a winding-up order. As discussed, the successful petitioner is able under CA 2006, s 996 to obtain a purchase order and exit the company and has no reason to pursue a winding-up order. Moreover, the very availability of relief under s 994 means that the court may refuse to exercise its discretion to make a winding-up order: see IA 1986, s 125(2), discussed at **18-78**. Having said that, there may be circumstances, such as deadlock, in which a claim cannot be brought within CA 2006, s 994 (see **17-62**), but which would fall within the just and equitable winding-up jurisdiction. For a fuller discussion of the overlap between the remedies, see **18-90**.

A derivative claim

17-90 As is evident from the authorities discussed in this chapter, breaches of directors' duties are classic examples of conduct of the company's affairs in a manner which is unfairly prejudicial to the interests of members[223] and therefore within the unfairly prejudicial jurisdiction. But such breaches are also wrongs done to the company, of course, in respect of which the company may sue or a derivative claim may lie under CA 2006, Pt 11. Where the derivative claim and the petition raise substantially the same issues, the court may want to look at what is the whole gist of the complaint and the relief sought before

---

[220] See, for example, *Re Woven Rugs Ltd* [2010] EWHC 230 at [173] (company in administration—earlier date appropriate, a date which preceded the damaging conduct and dissipation of company funds by the majority shareholder).

[221] A validation order permits the company to make dispositions of its property after the commencement of the winding up.

[222] See CPR, PD 49B which contains a standard form IA 1986, s 127 validation order.

[223] See *Atlasview Ltd v Brightview Ltd* [2004] 2 BCLC 191 at 207–8.

determining which proceedings would be most appropriate, see **17-78**.[224] The mere fact that the conduct would merit a derivative claim is not a reason to strike out the petition;[225] also if a petition would give the petitioner all the relief which he is seeking, the court is likely to refuse permission to continue a derivative claim.[226] If the only substantive relief sought on the petition is a claim on behalf of the company against a third party, however, the court will not necessarily allow the claimant to proceed by petition instead of by derivative claim.[227] The advantage of proceeding by way of a petition under CA 2006, s 994 is that it avoids the procedural obstacles surrounding the derivative claim which require a claimant to obtain the permission of the court to continue the claim. A petition also secures a personal remedy for the petitioner rather than a remedy for the company, as is the case with a derivative claim. On the other hand, a derivative claim may be attractive where the shareholder does not wish to have his shares purchased by the respondents, but wants a remedy for misconduct and the recovery of assets belonging to the company[228] and he wishes to take advantage of the indemnity for costs which is available with respect to a derivative claim.[229] As discussed at **18-44**, the courts may be expected now to establish clearer jurisdictional boundaries between claims under CA 2006 Pt 11 and petitions under s 994.[230]

---

[224] See *Cooke v Cooke* [1997] 2 BCLC 28; see also *Clark v Cutland* [2003] 2 BCLC 393 at 396.

[225] See *Re a Company (No 005287)* [1986] BCLC 68; *Lowe v Fahey* [1996] 1 BCLC 262; *Re Little Olympian Each-Ways Ltd (No 3)* [1995] 1 BCLC 636 at 665.

[226] See *Kleanthous v Paphitis* [2011] EWHC 2287 (permission refused: evidence suggested that the remedy that the applicant really wanted was to be bought out and was pursuing the derivative claim because of the availability of a costs indemnity); also *Mission Capital plc v Sinclair* [2010] 1 BCLC 304 (permission refused: the court did not consider that the claimants were seeking anything which could not be recovered by means of an unfair prejudice petition); *Franbar Holdings Ltd v Patel* [2009] 1 BCLC 1 (permission refused: claims by the member for breach of a shareholders' agreement as well as under CA 2006, s 994 should give the applicant all the relief sought).

[227] *Lowe v Fahey* [1996] 1 BCLC 262.

[228] See, for example, *Wishart v Castlecroft Securities Ltd* [2009] CSIH 615, [2009] SLT 812, see **18-44**.

[229] There was some blurring of the lines on this issue in *Clark v Cutland* [2003] 2 BCLC 393 at 405 where it was accepted that where, exceptionally, corporate relief is ordered on a petition, the petitioner is entitled to an indemnity for costs.

[230] See Hannigan, 'Drawing boundaries between derivative claims and unfairly prejudicial petitions' [2009] JBL 606.

18

The derivative claim and the rule in *Foss v Harbottle*

A Corporate claims for wrongs done to the company

The rule in *Foss v Harbottle*

18-1 At common law shareholders' remedies are dominated by the rule in *Foss v Harbottle*[1] which has two elements: first, the proper plaintiff in respect of a wrong allegedly done to a company is *prima facie* the company; secondly, where the alleged wrong is a transaction which might be made binding on the company by a simple majority of the members, no individual member of the company is allowed to bring a claim in respect of it.[2] As Mellish LJ explained in *MacDougall v Gardiner*:[3] '...if the thing complained of is a thing which in substance the majority of the company are entitled to do...there can be no use in having litigation about it, the ultimate end of which is only that a meeting has to be called, and then ultimately the majority gets its wishes'. In *Foss v Harbottle*[4] the court refused to permit two shareholders to bring an action on behalf of the company against the directors and promoters who had allegedly sold property to the company at an inflated value. On the facts, the court was not convinced that there was anything to prevent the company suing in its corporate character. In those circumstances, it was not open to individual members to assume to themselves the right of suing in the name of the company. The company was the proper person to sue and while the court acknowledged that the rule could be departed from, it should not be, save for very urgent reasons. Moreover, the alleged transactions were matters which the court considered might be decided by the majority of the shareholders who might ratify them and so render any litigation pointless.

18-2 The rule is based then on two fundamental principles of company law, namely respect for the separate legal personality of the company and the principle of majority rule. In addition to reflecting those fundamental principles, the rule has certain practical advantages. It is convenient and efficient that the company should sue in respect of a wrong done to it rather than have a multiplicity of shareholder suits. It eliminates wasteful litigation where the only outcome can be that the majority pass a resolution approving the 'wrongdoing'. It prevents vexatious actions started by troublesome shareholders trying to harass the company. It ensures a process that is for the collective benefit of the shareholders and, where there is any issue as to the solvency of the company, the creditors.

---

[1] (1843) 2 Hare 461.
[2] *Prudential Assurance Co Ltd v Newman Industries Ltd (No 2)* [1982] 1 All ER 354 at 357, CA; and see *Edwards v Halliwell* [1950] 2 All ER 1064 at 1066, per Jenkins LJ.   [3] (1875) 1 Ch D 13 at 25.
[4] (1843) 2 Hare 461.

The common law derivative claim

18-3   Where the wrong done to the company has been committed by a third party, the directors in the exercise of their management powers will decide whether the company should sue.[5] This is not a matter which is within the remit of the shareholders, at least where the company's articles include the standard delegation of all powers of management to the board.[6]

18-4   Where the wrong is committed by those in control of the company, however, it is inappropriate that the first element of the rule (that the company is the proper plaintiff) should prevent an action in respect of that wrongdoing (because the wrongdoer in control will ensure that the company does not claim). Hence the development of an exception to the rule whereby, in limited circumstances consistent with respect for the second element of the rule, a shareholder may sue derivatively, i.e. on behalf on the company to obtain a remedy for the company. The circumstances meriting a derivative claim were explained as follows in *Burland v Earle*:[7]

> 'The cases in which the minority can maintain such an action are, therefore, confined to those in which the acts complained of are of a fraudulent character or beyond the powers of the company. A familiar example is where the majority are endeavouring directly or indirectly to appropriate to themselves money, property, or advantages which belong to the company, or in which the other shareholders are entitled to participate, as was alleged in the case of *Menier v. Hooper's Telegraph Works*.[8] It should be added that no mere informality or irregularity which can be remedied by the majority will entitle the minority to sue, if the act when done regularly would be within the powers of the company and the intention of the majority of the shareholders is clear.'

18-5   As a preliminary matter, at common law, the court required the claimant in a derivative claim to establish a *prima facie* case that the company was entitled to the relief claimed and that the action fell within the proper boundaries of the exception to the rule in *Foss v Harbottle*, namely: (1) that the wrong was a fraud on the minority, in the sense of an unratifiable wrong not capable of 'cure' by the majority; and (2) that wrongdoer control of the company prevented the company itself bringing an action in its own name.[9] Further, even when a *prima facie* case existed, the court would not permit a derivative action to proceed where the majority of the shareholders who were independent of the wrongdoers, for disinterested reasons, did not wish the proceedings to continue.[10]

18-6   In practice, derivative actions were rare which was unsurprising given the difficulty in establishing standing to sue as a result of the restrictive rule in *Foss v Harbottle*. The derivative jurisdiction was also less attractive, given the absence of personal relief, than pursuit of a personal remedy under the generous unfairly prejudicial jurisdiction which evolved under what is now CA 2006, s 994 and which is discussed in Chapter 17.

---

[5]   See *Breckland Group Holdings Ltd v London and Suffolk Properties Ltd* [1989] BCLC 100.
[6]   See The Companies (Model Articles) Regulations 2008, SI 2008/3229, art 3 (Ltd); art 3 (Plc), previously SI 1985/805, Table A, reg 70; *Automatic Self-Cleansing Filter Syndicate Ltd v Cunninghame* [1906] 2 Ch 34.
[7]   [1902] AC 83 at 93–4, per Lord Davey.
[8]   (1874) LR 9 Ch App 350.
[9]   *Prudential Assurance Co Ltd v Newman Industries Ltd (No 2)* [1982] 1 All ER 354 at 366; *Smith v Croft (No 2)* [1987] 3 All ER 909 at 945.
[10]   *Smith v Croft (No 2)* [1987] 3 All ER 909.

Statutory reform

18-7 A report on shareholders' remedies by the Law Commission in 1997 concluded that: (1) the rule in *Foss v Harbottle* was complicated and unwieldy; (2) the scope of the exception to the rule (i.e. the circumstances when a derivative claim could be brought) was uncertain; and (3) the procedural difficulties were such that simply establishing standing to sue could amount to a mini-trial.[11] The Law Commission recommended that the common law action be replaced with a statutory derivative procedure with more modern, flexible and accessible criteria for determining whether a shareholder may bring a claim.[12] The intention was to put a derivative claim on a clearer and more rational basis which would give the courts flexibility to allow cases to proceed in appropriate circumstances while giving guidance to advisers as to the matters which the court would take into account in deciding whether to grant leave to bring a claim.[13] The Law Commission thought that a statutory procedure would give greater transparency to the requirements for a claim; it would alert interested parties to the availability of a derivative claim; and it would ensure that the Companies Act constituted a more complete code (with the unfairly prejudicial remedy) with regard to shareholders' remedies.[14] The Law Commission also thought that, in an age of international business, it was important to set out the rules in the statute in keeping with other jurisdictions.[15] The Law Commission's recommendations were endorsed by the Company Law Review without much further deliberation[16] and the statutory derivative claim, now found in CA 2006, Pt 11, is modelled largely on the Law Commission's proposals. It replaces the common law derivative claim, see **18-16**.

18-8 Not everyone welcomed the introduction of a statutory derivative claim and, while it has not unleashed the torrent of litigation which its critics feared, it is important to appreciate their concerns since they were influential in shaping the eventual legislation. A particular issue was the juxtaposition of a 'new' shareholder remedy alongside the statutory statement of directors' duties, specifically the obligation in CA 2006, s 172 requiring directors to promote the success of the company having regard to the factors set out in that section, see **9-2**. The concern was that shareholder activists might use the combination of the derivative claim and s 172 to challenge business decisions of directors on the basis of an alleged failure to have regard to the factors set out in that section, see **9-36**. A derivative claim, it was argued, could be used to seek judicial review, in effect, of a commercial decision of management. There was also a perception that the jurisdiction under CA 2006, Pt 11 was very wide, given that the statute swept aside the common law thresholds (requiring fraud on the minority and wrongdoer control) and allowed derivative claims in respect of a breach of any duty owed by a director to the company including, for the first time, in

---

[11] Law Commission, *Shareholder Remedies* (Law Com No 246) (Cm 3769, 1997) ('Law Commission Report'), para 6.4. The Report was preceded by a Consultation Paper of the same name: Con Paper No 142 (1996). For comments on the Law Commission's proposals, see Boyle, *Minority Shareholders' Remedies* (2002), Ch 3; Poole & Roberts, 'Shareholder Remedies—Corporate Wrongs and the Derivative Action' [1999] JBL 99.   [12] Law Commission Report, n 11, para 6.15.

[13] Law Commission Report, n 11, para 6.14.   [14] Law Commission Report, n 11, paras 6.16–6.18.

[15] Law Commission Report, n 11, para 6.9. See the Canadian Business Corporations Act 1975, s 239, and Cheffins, 'Reforming the Derivative Action: The Canadian Experience and British Prospects' [1997] Company, Financial and Insolvency Law Review 227; the New Zealand Companies Act 1993, ss 165–168, and Watson, 'A Matter of Balance: The Statutory Derivative Action in New Zealand' (1998) 19 Co Law 236; the Australian Corporations Act 2001, ss 236–242, and Ramsay and Saunders, 'Litigation by Shareholders and Directors: An Empirical Study of the Australian Statutory Derivative Action' [2006] 6 JCLS 397.

[16] See Company Law Review, *Developing the Framework* (2000), paras 4.112–4.139 for the main discussion of the issues; also *Completing the Structure* (2000), paras 5.82–5.89; and *Final Report* (2001), paras 7.46–7.51.

respect of alleged negligence by a director (s 260(3)). Furthermore, the CA 2006 changed the rules on ratification to preclude directors, as shareholders, voting to ratify their own wrongdoing (see s 239). As the critics saw it, the result was more grounds for a derivative claim and less possibility of ratification.

18-9 At a practical level, there were concerns that there is more scope for speculative or vexatious litigation now for a variety of reasons: the availability of conditional fee agreements;[17] the rise of activist shareholders ranging from those representing a particular 'lobby' (such as environmentalists) to hedge funds with deep pockets; and the increased presence of US shareholders and lawyers in London who may be more attuned to vindicating investor rights through the courts rather than a discreet market exit and for whom derivative actions are merely another mechanism for holding underperforming directors to account.

18-10 The Government responded to these concerns by amending CA 2006 Pt 11 to enhance the protection for directors[18] by (1) strengthening the judicial controls of derivative claims (discussed later), and (2) restating the duty of directors to act to promote the interests of the company (s 172(1)) to emphasise that the overriding obligation of directors remains to promote the success of the company for the benefit of its members as a whole (see **9-38**) so curbing, it was hoped, the scope for allegations of a breach of duty arising from a supposed failure to have regard to one or more of the factors set out in that section.

18-11 To date at least, it is clear that the fears of the critics that a combination of factors (expanded duties, the availability of a statutory derivative claim; and activist shareholders) would create a threat of litigation which would deter people from taking up directorships of public companies have not been realised. There is no noticeable increase in derivative claims, there are no noticeably litigious shareholders or shareholder groups, and no evidence that anyone has been deterred from taking a lucrative position with a public company board because of derivative claims. In that respect, the Government position throughout the Parliamentary debates, that CA 2006, Pt 11 does not introduce any major change of principle and that there was no reason to expect any significant increase in the number of derivative actions, has been vindicated. The Government view was that the derivative claim is a well-established mechanism which has certain inherent characteristics which limit the potential for speculative litigation, notably that a claim can only be brought on behalf of the company with any sums recovered going to the company and not to the claimant who runs the risk of incurring substantial costs.[19] The balance to be struck in Part 11 is between protecting directors from vexatious and frivolous claims[20] so allowing them to take business decisions in good faith while protecting the rights of shareholders to bring meritorious claims.[21]

---

[17] There is some debate as to whether conditional fee agreements are possible with respect to derivative claims: see the differing views of Payne, 'Sections 459–461 Companies Act 1985 in Flux: The Future of Shareholder Protection' (2005) CLJ 647 at 665; Reisberg, 'Funding Derivative Actions: A re-examination of costs and fees as incentives to commence litigation' (2004) 4 JCLS 345 at 380.

[18] See 681 HL Official Report (5th series), cols 883–4, 9 May 2006.

[19] See 679 HL Official Report (5th series), cols GC4–5, 27 February 2006; HC Official Report, SC D (Company Law Reform Bill), 13 July 2006, col 665.

[20] 679 HL Official Report (5th series), col GC6, 27 February 2006.

[21] See 681 HL Official Report (5th series), col 883, 9 May 2006.

Impact on the rule in *Foss v Harbottle*

18-12 Before discussing CA 2006, Pt 11 in detail, it is worth emphasising that the rule in *Foss v Harbottle*[22] has not been swept aside. As noted at **18-1**, there are two elements to the rule: the proper plaintiff element and the majority rule element.

18-13 As regards the proper plaintiff aspect, the position remains that the proper plaintiff in respect of a wrong allegedly done to a company is *prima facie* the company. If therefore the company is in a position to pursue a claim vested in it, it is for the company to do so, not the shareholders.[23]

18-14 The majority rule element meant that, at common law, a shareholder could not bring a derivative claim in respect of an act which was capable of being confirmed by the majority.[24] Under CA 2006, Pt 11, actual authorisation or ratification is required to bar a claim (s 263(2)(b), (c)), see **18-28**. Otherwise, the possibility of authorisation or ratification is a matter to be taken into account by the court when deciding whether to give permission for a claim to proceed (s 263(3)(c) and (d)), see **18-42**. The position is therefore clearer under the statute in that actual authorisation or ratification is required to bar a claim, but it makes no substantive change to the general principle of majority rule in that if the majority chooses to authorise or ratify the conduct in question, assuming it is ratifiable, then that ends the matter (though s 239 impacts on who can vote, see **18-36**). Derivative claims, though facilitated by the new procedural mechanism of Part 11, remain subject to the general principle of majority rule.[25]

18-15 What has altered is that the derivative claim (i.e. the procedural mechanism) invented by the courts as an exception to the rule in *Foss v Harbottle* (based on wrongdoer control and unratifiable wrongs) is replaced by the statutory mechanism and thresholds laid down in CA 2006, Pt 11,[26] which came into force on 1 October 2007.

B The derivative claim—CA 2006, Part 11

18-16 A derivative claim is a claim by a member of a company in respect of a cause of action vested in the company and seeking relief on behalf of the company (CA 2006, s 260(1)) and it may only be brought under Part 11 or in pursuance of an order of the court in unfairly prejudicial proceedings under s 994 (s 260(2)); the latter is in practice unlikely and for our purposes can be disregarded. The limitation that derivative claims may *only* be brought under CA 2006, Pt 11 reflects the Law Commission recommendation that the statutory derivative claim supersede the common law derivative action in order to allow for the development of a coherent body of law based on the statute alone.[27] This approach means

---

[22] (1843) 2 Hare 461.   [23] See *Cinematic Finance Ltd v Ryder* [2010] EWHC 3387 at [9], [11].

[24] *MacDougall v Gardiner* (1875) 1 Ch D 13 at 25, CA; *Burland v Earle* [1902] AC 83 at 93–4, see **18–4**.

[25] *Burland v Earle* [1902] AC 83 at 93–4.

[26] See, generally, Lightman, 'Two Aspects of the Statutory Derivative Claim' [2011] LMCLQ 142; Keay & Loughrey, 'Derivative Proceedings in a Brave New World for Company Management and Shareholders' [2010] JBL 151; Hannigan, 'The Derivative Claim—An Invitation to Litigate?' in Hannigan & Prentice, *The Companies Act 2006—A Commentary* (2nd edn, 2009); Nessen, Goo and Low, 'The Statutory Derivative Action: Now Showing Near You' [2008] JBL 627; Keay & Loughrey, 'Something Old, Something New, Something Borrowed: an Analysis of the New Derivative Action under the Companies Act 2006' (2008) 124 LQR 469; Reisberg, 'Derivative Actions and Corporate Governance (2007).

[27] See Law Commission Report, n 11, paras **6.51–6.55**.

that there is no scope for multiple derivative claims (i.e. a claim by a member of a parent company in respect of wrongs done to a subsidiary company) since such a claim does not fall within s 260(1) (a claim by a member in respect of a wrong done to the company) though it would have been possible, it seems, at common law.[28] An alternative view is that this interpretation of s 260(2) as replacing all common law derivative claims is misplaced in the absence of an express statutory statement that the common law derivative claim has been abolished.[29] On this view, the word 'only' in s 260(2) merely means that a derivative claim as defined in s 260(1) (a claim by a member in respect of a wrong done to the company) can only be brought under Part 11, but that other derivative claims, such as a multiple derivative claim, may still be brought at common law. Given the background to the enactment of Part 11 and the Law Commission's intention that the courts should start with a clean sheet to develop a statutory derivative claim, this argument, while having merit (the wording could have been more explicit in s 260(2)), is inconsistent with the purpose of the reforms which was to create a single route for derivative claims.[30] It is also not necessary to allow a common law multiple derivative claim in order to overcome the difficulties of uncorrected wrongdoing in a subsidiary. A member could formulate the claim as a derivative claim by alleging a breach of duty by the directors of the parent company in not seeking redress for the wrongs committed in respect of the subsidiary company. Another option may be to bring a petition under CA 2006, s 994 alleging that the affairs of the parent company are being conducted in an unfairly prejudicial manner, the Court of Appeal having accepted in *Re Citybranch Group Ltd, Gross v Rackind*[31] that conduct of a company's affairs can extend to the conduct of the affairs of a subsidiary of that company, see **17-25**. As relief on a successful petition, the court could order the directors of the parent company to take steps to address the wrongdoing in the subsidiary (using its wide discretionary powers in CA 2006, s 996).

Bringing a derivative claim

18-17 A derivative claim may be initiated by a member[32] who then requires the permission of the court to continue with it (CA 2006, s 261(1)).[33] The claimant must be a member at the time of the proceedings, but it is immaterial whether the cause of action arose before or after the claimant became a member of the company.[34] No minimum shareholding is required which, in theory, means that litigious parties could purchase one share with a view to bringing a case against the directors, but whether the court would give permission

---

[28] See *Waddington Ltd v Chan Chun Hoo Thomas* [2009] 2 BCLC 82, HKCFA, noted by Prentice & Reisberg [2009] 125 LQR 209; also Koh, 'Derivative Actions Once Removed' [2010] JBL 101; Goo, 'Multiple Derivative Actions and the Common Law Derivative Action Revisited: A Tale of Two Jurisdictions' (2010) 10 JCLS 255.   [29] See Lightman, 'Two aspects of the Statutory Derivative Claim' [2011] LMCLQ 142.

[30] Admittedly, another type of derivative claim is permitted under CA 2006, s 370 in respect of directors' liability under s 369 for unauthorised political donations and expenditure, but a claim under s 370 must be brought by an authorised group (defined in s 370(3)) and the section regulates a form of group litigation and does not undermine the interpretation of s 260(2) as requiring that a derivative claim by a member may only be brought under Pt 11.   [31] [2004] 4 All ER 735 at 743–4.

[32] References to a 'member' include a person who is not a member but to whom shares in the company have been transferred or transmitted by operation of law: CA 2006, s 260(5)(c).

[33] See CPR 19.9(4), 19.9A(4) and Practice Direction on Derivative Claims; also *Portfolios of Distinction Ltd v Laird* [2004] 2 BCLC 741. It is also possible for a member to apply for permission to continue as a derivative claim a claim commenced by the company or by another member (CA 2006, ss 262(1), (2), 264), but these scenarios are somewhat unlikely.

[34] CA 2006, s 260(4). See Law Commission Report, n 11, para 6.98; 679 HL Official Report (5th series), col GC15, 27 February 2006; *Seaton v Grant* (1867) LR 2 Ch App 459.

to such a claimant to proceed is another matter.[35] In any event, there is little advantage in a person acquiring a single share with a view to bringing a derivative claim since any recovery is for the benefit of the company and the claimant runs the risk that he will be penalised in costs. While the section refers to 'a member', it will be a minority member for, as the court noted in *Cinematic Finance Ltd v Ryder*,[36] only in very exceptional circumstances (which the court thought difficult to envisage) would it be appropriate to permit a shareholder in control of a company to bring a derivative claim. A controlling shareholder has other options open to him or her, such as appointing a new board of directors, and then the claim can be brought by the company in the usual way so respecting the rule in *Foss v Harbottle* that a claim vested in the company should be pursued by the company, see **18-1**.

18-18 A derivative claim may be brought against a director (including a shadow director) or another person or both (CA 2006, s 260(3)). Former directors are included[37] (s 260(5)(a)) and claims against such directors might arise, for example, where directors have resigned in order to exploit an opportunity which came to their attention while they were directors in a situation of a conflict of interest (see **11-2**).

18-19 The intention behind permitting derivative claims against 'another person' is to allow a claim to be made against a person who has assisted a director in a breach of duty or who is a recipient of corporate assets in circumstances where he knows the director is acting in breach of his duties.[38] The basis for suing them derivatively is their involvement in the director's breach of duty and a derivative claim cannot be brought where the breach of duty etc is solely that of the third party, such as a negligent auditor. As the Law Commission noted, the decision whether to sue a third party (i.e. someone who is not a director and where the claim is not closely connected with a breach of duty by a director) is one for the board.[39]

18-20 A derivative claim may be brought only in respect of a cause of action arising from an actual or proposed[40] act or omission involving negligence, default,[41] breach of duty or

---

[35] Concerns were raised that vulture funds, environmentalists, animal rights activists and US lawyers, amongst others, would seek to take advantage of the absence of any minimum shareholding: see 679 HL Official Report (5th series), cols GC11–13, 27 February 2006. But, as Lord Cairns explained in *Seaton v Grant* (1867) LR 2 Ch App 459 at 465, the quantum of the claimant's interest is irrelevant, if the claim is one which should otherwise be brought, for the aggregate interest of all the shareholders is amply sufficient to sustain the claim.   [36] [2010] EWHC 3387 at [14].

[37] Their inclusion avoids the problem that they would otherwise be classed as third parties whom the current board would be expected to sue on behalf of the company, see Ford's *Principles of Corporations Law* (11th edn, 2003), para 11.250.

[38] See Law Commission Report, n 11, paras 6.35, 6.36; 679 HL Official Report (5th series), cols GC9–10, 27 February 2006; HC Official Report, SC D (Company Law Reform Bill), 13 July 2006, col 666.

[39] See Law Commission Report, n 11, paras 6.34, 6.35. A derivative claim may lie, however, where the board's decision not to pursue a claim against a third party is itself a breach of duty by the directors, subject to difficulties of causation and quantification in such circumstances, see Law Commission Report, n 11, para 6.32.

[40] The ability to bring claims with respect to proposed acts may offer some scope for shareholders to take pre-emptive action, as where the directors make known their intention, say, to make certain acquisitions or look to expansion overseas. Shareholders might look to bring a claim alleging that such actions would be in breach of s 172 (promote the success of the company) or s 174 (exercise care and skill) and seeking an injunction to prevent the directors proceeding. It is difficult to envisage the court encouraging that type of behaviour which would likely amount to little more than a challenge to the business judgement of the directors, but the possibility is there because the section covers 'proposed' acts.

[41] 'Default' enables claims to be brought in respect of breaches of statutory obligations imposed by the companies legislation: *Customs and Excise Commissioners v Hedon Alpha Ltd* [1981] 2 All ER 697.

breach of trust by a director of the company (s 260(3)).[42] The significant change here is that a claim may be brought in respect of any breach of duty by a director. At common law the conduct complained of had to amount to an unratifiable wrong not capable of 'cure' by the majority i.e. acts of an ultra vires, illegal or fraudulent character which typically involved the misappropriation of money, property, or advantages belonging to the company, and which are generally described as a fraud on the minority.[43] All other breaches of duty, being ratifiable, could not be the subject of a derivative action at common law, even if the breaches had not actually been ratified.[44] Now any breach of duty is potentially actionable and mere ratifiability no longer suffices to dismiss a claim, but if the majority are able to and do ratify the wrongdoing, the court must dismiss a derivative claim (s 263(2)(c)). Authorisation or ratification remain as a complete bar to a claim so a claim will only proceed if the wrong is not capable of authorisation or ratification (as was the case with claims at common law) or, where the wrong may be authorised or ratified, the majority chooses not to do so or cannot do so, as s 239 prevents a director who is a member (and members connected with him) from voting to ratify his own wrongdoing, see **18-36**. Authorisation and ratification are discussed at **18-31**.

18-21 The extension of the derivative claim to negligence[45] was recommended by the Law Commission which noted that, while investors take the risk that those who manage companies may make mistakes, they do not have to accept that directors will fail to comply with their duties,[46] a view endorsed by the Company Law Review.[47] Of course, while negligence will found a derivative claim, the courts will continue to distinguish between commercial misjudgements and negligent conduct (and negligence is ratifiable[48]).

18-22 To sum up, a derivative claim may be brought:

- by any member (however few shares he holds and however recently acquired, though not ordinarily by a majority shareholder[49]);

- against any director (including former and shadow directors) and other persons implicated in the breach;[50]

- in respect of negligence, default, breach of duty and breach of trust by a director of the company.

---

[42] The claim must be based on a breach by the directors and, for example, a claim asserting that assets of the company are held by some other person on trust for the company will not merit a derivative claim unless there is a failure by the directors, in breach of duty, to assert or pursue that trust claim against that other person, see *Iesini v Westrip Holdings Ltd* [2011] 1 BCLC 498 at [104]–[109].

[43] *Burland v Earle* [1902] AC 83 at 93–4, per Lord Davey, see **18-4**; and see *Menier v Hooper's Telegraph Works* (1874) LR 9 Ch App 350; *Cook v Deeks* [1916] 1 AC 554; *Daniels v Daniels* [1978] 2 All ER 89; see **18-34**.

[44] *MacDougall v Gardiner* (1875) 1 Ch 13 at 25; *Burland v Earle* [1902] AC 83 at 93–4.

[45] At common law, mere negligence from which the director did not benefit personally could not found a derivative claim (ratifiable): *Pavlides v Jensen* [1956] 2 All ER 518, and it was necessary to show that the negligence was of the self-serving variety (unratifiable) seen in *Daniels v Daniels* [1978] 2 All ER 89 where the board sold an asset at a gross undervalue to one of the directors.

[46] See Law Commission Report, n 11, para 6.41.

[47] Company Law Review, *Developing the Framework* (2000), para 4.127.

[48] *Pavlides v Jensen* [1956] 2 All ER 518.

[49] *Cinematic Finance Ltd v Ryder* [2010] EWHC 3387.

[50] The company is also made a defendant in order that it be bound by the outcome so that, if the claim proceeds and is unsuccessful, the directors are not exposed to the risk of another claim based on the same matter, see *Roberts v Gill & Co* [2010] 4 All ER 367 at [58]–[61].

18-23 While it is possible to commence a derivative claim on this basis and therefore Part 11 looks to be a much broader jurisdiction than the common law derivative claim, the statutory claim may not proceed very far, however, for the claimant must obtain the permission of the court to continue the claim.

Judicial control of a derivative claim

18-24 There are two stages involved once a derivative claim has been commenced. At the first stage, done entirely on the papers without the company being represented, the court must be satisfied that there is a *prima facie* case for giving permission to continue a derivative claim, otherwise the court must dismiss the claim (CA 2006, s 261(2)). At the second stage, when the company can appear and put in evidence,[51] a variety of factors must be considered, some of which oblige the court to dismiss the claim (s 263(2)), otherwise the court has a broad discretion to give or refuse permission or adjourn the proceedings and give such directions as it thinks fit (s 263(3)).

18-25 The first stage requires the court to dismiss the claim if the application and the evidence filed by the applicant in support of it do not disclose a *prima facie* case for giving permission (CA 2006, s 261(2)).[52] The Government was initially reluctant to set any particular threshold requirement, preferring to let the matter progress to a hearing when the court would consider the factors set out in s 263(3). The intention was to avoid turning the preliminary stages of a claim into an expensive and time-consuming mini-trial and to let the courts develop appropriate thresholds for these claims.[53] Following criticisms that there were inadequate filters to prevent vexatious litigation, the Government was persuaded that the court should have a specific power to dismiss unmeritorious cases at an early stage without involving the company and this *prima facie* threshold was included for that purpose.[54]

18-26 It was always likely that the courts would be reluctant to throw out a remotely plausible case at this first threshold,[55] given that this is a new remedy introduced to facilitate shareholder claims, and that they would be inclined to allow shareholder claimants the opportunity for a second-stage consideration of their concerns, bearing in mind that it is still possible for the court to stop the proceedings at that stage.[56] Indeed, there is some evidence

---

[51] As can the defendant director, see *Kleanthous v Paphitis* [2011] EWHC 2287 at [44].

[52] See *Iesini v Westrip Holdings Ltd* [2011] 1 BCLC 498 at [78], where Lewison J noted that this threshold (a *prima facie* case 'for giving permission') entails a decision by the court that there is a *prima facie* case both that the company has a good cause of action and that the cause of action arises out of a director's breach of duty etc, which he describes as 'precisely the decision that the Court of Appeal required in *Prudential v Newman* [1982] 1 All ER 354', see **18-5**. This position is criticised rightly by Keay & Loughrey as setting a higher threshold that is warranted by the statutory scheme (and the background to the introduction of the two stages, discussed at **18-10**); see Keay & Loughrey, 'Derivative Proceedings in a Brave New World for Company Management and Shareholders' [2010] JBL 151 at 156.

[53] See 679 HL Official Report (5th series), col GC22, 27 February 2006; Law Commission Report, n 11, paras 6.4, 6.71.

[54] The provision was added at Report Stage in the House of Lords, see 681 HL Official Report (5th series), cols 883–4, 9 May 2006. The court's power to dismiss the application at this stage is reinforced by CA 2006, s 261(2)(b) which enables the court to penalise an applicant with costs orders or deter a nuisance applicant with a civil restraint order (restraining a person from making any application to a civil court without the consent of a judge).   [55] See 679 HL Official Report (5th series), col GC14, 27 February 2006.

[56] See Cheffins, n 15, at 244 who noted that the Canadian courts, while not granting leave as a matter of course, were unwilling to impose particularly onerous thresholds at the equivalent stage in a statutory derivative claim. Instead they were content to restrict their enquiry to whether the complainant had raised fair questions which should properly be considered in an action.

of the parties themselves consenting to the merging of the stages,[57] but in *Langley Ward Ltd v Trevor*[58] the court was critical of the bypassing of the *prima facie* stage, noting that this undermines the scheme specified by the statute which contemplates a preliminary examination of the matter by the court solely on the papers. The unfortunate outcome in that case, the court said, was a much greater expenditure of costs and time by the parties when, had the first stage been observed, the claim or at least some of the allegations might have been dismissed so making any second stage more efficient.

18-27 If the case is not dismissed at this *prima facie* threshold, the court may grant an adjournment, for example, to allow the company to seek authorisation or ratification of the conduct in question which will then act as a complete bar to the claim proceeding (see CA 2006, s 261(4)) or to enable the company to take some other steps which may have a bearing on whether a derivative claim is needed and appropriate.[59]

Absolute bars to a derivative claim proceeding

18-28 Permission to continue a claim must be refused if the court is satisfied that:

> (1) a director acting in accordance with CA 2006, s 172 (duty to promote the success of the company) would not seek to continue the claim; or
>
> (2) the act or omission has been authorised by the company or ratified by the company (CA 2006, s 263(2)).

The hypothetical director

18-29 The issue under (1) is not what conclusion the court would come to nor what a reasonable director would conclude. The court must ask itself whether a director acting in the way he considers, in good faith, would be most likely to promote the success of the company would not seek to continue the claim.[60]

18-30 As a director's obligations under s 172 are written in quite expansive terms, see **9-2**, the courts are reluctant to conclude under s 236(2)(a) that a director, faced with a *prima facie* case justifying a derivative claim (which there must be for the application to have reached the second stage) would not seek to continue the claim. It is accepted by the courts that, frequently, a decision either way might be one which a hypothetical director might reach, given the range of factors to which he must have regard under s 172,[61] with the result that s 263(2)(a) only applies if the court is satisfied that no director would seek to continue the

---

[57] See *Franbar Holdings Ltd v Patel* [2009] 1 BCLC 1 at [24]; *Mission Capital plc v Sinclair* [2010] 1 BCLC 304 at [36]; *Stimpson v Southern Private Landlords Association* [2010] BCC 387 at [3].

[58] [2011] EWHC 1893 at [6]–[7] and [61]–[63].

[59] See *Iesini v Westrip Holdings Ltd* [2011] 1 BCLC 498 (proceedings adjourned to allow the board to consider whether it wished to assert a claim on behalf of the company against third parties in relation to the ownership of certain assets which would obviate the need for a derivative claim against the board for not securing those assets); also *FanmailUK.com Ltd v Cooper* [2008] BCC 877 (proceedings adjourned to allow dispute as to ownership of the company to be determined as a preliminary issue since that would have a bearing on the appropriateness of a derivative claim).

[60] See *Regentcrest plc v Cohen* [2001] 2 BCLC 80; HC Official Report, SC D (Company Law Reform Bill), 13 July 2006, col 678. As the Law Commission noted, 'this does not mean that the court is bound to accept the views of the director—the existence of a conflict of interest may affect the weight to be given to those views and the court would give no weight to views which no reasonable director could hold': see Law Commission Report, n 11, para 6.79.

[61] There is an inevitable tendency in the cases to combine this test in s 263(2)(a) and that in s 263(3)(b)— the importance which a hypothetical director would attach to continuing the claim, see *Stimpson v Southern Private Landlords Association* [2010] BCC 387 at [40]; *Iesini v Westrip Holdings Ltd* [2011] 1 BCLC 498 at [86]; *Langley Ward Ltd v Trevor* [2011] EWHC 1893 at [45].

claim.[62] For example, in *Kiani v Cooper*[63] the court considered that a hypothetical director would seek to continue a claim as there was some strong evidence of breach of fiduciary duty by the defendant director involving, *inter alia*, an improper payment of £296,000 to a company controlled by the defendant. It was therefore appropriate to give permission to continue the claim, but the court (using its broad powers with respect to the terms of permission, see s 261(4)) limited the permission to continue to the point of disclosure only which would give the defendant director the opportunity to produce the documentation which he said supported the payment.

Authorisation and ratification by the company

18-31 Actual authorisation or ratification provides a complete defence to a derivative claim.[64] Authorisation ensures that there is no breach of duty (and the right to authorise what would otherwise be a breach of duty, to the extent permitted by the law, is retained by CA 2006, s 180(4)(a)) while ratification cures any breach that previously existed. Authorisation or ratification by the company may mean by the shareholders or by the directors or may be via a provision in the articles. For most purposes it will be by the shareholders, though by virtue of CA 2006, s 175(4)(b) directors may authorise what would otherwise be a conflict of interest and, by virtue of s 173(2)(b), the articles may authorise what would otherwise be a breach of the duty to exercise independent judgement and otherwise may make provision for dealing with conflicts of interest (s 180(4)(b)). Looking at the shareholders' powers, whether a derivative claim is an option will be determined by the ability (and willingness) of the shareholders to authorise the conduct at issue or to ratify a breach of duty. There are two issues to be considered: (1) whether the wrong is capable of authorisation or ratification; and (2) whether there is sufficient support amongst the shareholders to secure authorisation or ratification.

18-32 The ability of shareholders to authorise or ratify acts of the directors is limited by common law restrictions which are preserved by s 180(4)(a) (authorisation) and by s 239(7) (ratification).[65]

18-33 Shareholders cannot authorise or ratify acts which are illegal or acts which are ultra vires[66] in the sense of transactions which constitute a return of capital to shareholders other than with the sanction of the court or in accordance with a statutory scheme.[67] Such ultra vires transactions can be described as a fraud on the creditors and are incapable of

---

[62] *Iesini v Westrip Holdings Ltd* [2011] 1 BCLC 498 at [86]; *Kiani v Cooper* [2010] 2 BCLC 427 at [13]; *Franbar Holdings Ltd v Patel* [2009] 1 BCLC 1 at [30]; also *Kleanthous v Paphitis* [2011] EWHC 2287. For an example of a case where no director would seek to continue the claim, see *Langley Ward Ltd v Trevor* [2011] EWHC 1893 (unparticularised speculative complaints, much of which did not disclose a cause of action, or involved small amounts, and from some of which the company benefited; it was clear that the court would probably have dismissed these claims at the *prima facie* stage, had the parties not skipped it).

[63] [2010] 2 BCLC 427.

[64] This is a change from the common law where a derivative action did not lie in respect of an act which was capable of being confirmed by the majority: *Burland v Earle* [1902] AC 83 at 93–4, PC; *MacDougall v Gardiner* (1875) 1 Ch D 13, CA.

[65] See generally Hannigan, 'Limitations on a Shareholder's Right to Vote—Effective Ratification Revisited' [2000] JBL 493.

[66] Ultra vires is used in another sense to mean transactions beyond the company's objects. For companies with objects clauses (see Chapter 3), a restriction will operate only to limit the authority of the directors (see CA 2006, s 39) and a breach of a restriction is a breach of the duty to act in accordance with the constitution (s 171) which is capable of ratification or, more accurately, authorisation by the shareholders, see discussion in Chapter 8, especially **8-65**. [67] *Trevor v Whitworth* (1887) 12 App Cas 409.

ratification[68] and it is not also open to the shareholders to authorise or ratify a breach of duty by the directors at a time when the directors are required by virtue of the company's circumstances to look to the creditors' interests,[69] see **9-41**. Shareholders cannot authorise or ratify acts in breach of the company's constitution where the matter is a breach of a shareholder's substantive rights.[70] Shareholder rights are derived essentially from the articles and, since the articles can only be amended by a special resolution (CA 2006, s 21), there should be no question of the majority being able to ratify breaches of the articles. The position is not that clear-cut, however, for the extent to which the articles confer substantive rights on the shareholders is problematic and the distinction drawn in the case law (see **4-53** et seq) between matters of internal management[71] (within the control of the majority: *MacDougall v Gardiner*[72]) and rights conferred by the constitution qua member (not within the control of the majority: *Pender v Lushington*[73]) remains. The net result is that some breaches of the articles are ratifiable, others are not, with the dividing line being drawn between matters of internal management and matters affecting rights conferred qua member.

18-34   Shareholders cannot authorise or ratify acts which amount to the misappropriation of 'money, property or advantages which belong to the company or in which the other shareholders are entitled to participate', a category usually described as a fraud on the minority[74] though, as Sealy notes, a fraud on the company would be a more accurate description.[75] This limitation remains, as CA 2006, s 239(7) preserves any rule of law as to acts that are incapable of being ratified by the company. Many of the more egregious breaches of the no-conflict rule will fall within this 'fraud on the minority' category amounting to a misappropriation of money, property or advantage etc. It remains the case therefore that such a breach of duty cannot be ratified. Of course, now, directors can avoid a breach of the duty in the first place by seeking authorisation from disinterested directors in accordance with CA 2006, s 175(4)(b). If they do not use that mechanism, a breach of the no-conflict rule amounting to a fraud on the minority cannot be ratified.

18-35   Apart from that 'fraud on the minority' constraint, many breaches of duty by directors are ratifiable, such as the non-disclosure of a conflict of interest in a transaction with the company, as in *Aberdeen Rly Co v Blaikie Bros*;[76] or mere negligence, as in *Pavlides v Jensen*;[77] or the exercise of powers bona fide but for a collateral purpose, as in *Bamford v Bamford*,[78] while *Regal (Hastings) Ltd v Gulliver*[79] suggests that bona fide incidental profit-making

---

[68]   *Trevor v Whitworth* (1887) 12 App Cas 409; *Ridge Securities Ltd v IRC* [1964] 1 All ER 275; *Re Halt Garage (1964) Ltd* [1982] 3 All ER 1016; *Aveling Barford Ltd v Perion Ltd* [1989] BCLC 626; also *Barclays Bank plc v British and Commonwealth Holdings plc* [1996] 1 BCLC 1 at 7. See *Rolled Steel Products (Holdings) Ltd v British Steel Corp* [1985] 3 All ER 52 at 86, per Slade LJ.

[69]   See CA 2006, s 172(3); *West Mercia Safetywear Ltd v Dodd* [1988] BCLC 250, approving *Kinsela v Russell Kinsela Pty Ltd* (1986) 4 ACLC 215 at 223; *Rolled Steel Products (Holdings) Ltd v British Steel Corp* [1985] 3 All ER 52 at 86, per Slade LJ; *Secretary of State for Business, Innovation and Skills v Doffman* [2011] 2 BCLC 541 at [39]–[45].

[70]   See *Pender v Lushington* (1877) 6 Ch D 70; *MacDougall v Gardiner* (1875) 1 Ch D 13 at 25, CA.

[71]   See *Grant v United Kingdom Switchback Railways Co* (1888) 40 Ch D 135; *Irvine v Union Bank of Australia* (1877) 2 App Cas 366.   [72]   (1875) 1 Ch D 13.

[73]   (1877) 6 Ch D 70.

[74]   *Burland v Earle* [1902] AC 83 at 93, per Lord Davey; *Atwool v Merryweather* (1867) LR 5 Eq 464n; *Menier v Hooper's Telegraph Works* (1874) 9 Ch App 350; *Cook v Deeks* [1916] 1 AC 554; *Daniels v Daniels* [1978] 2 All ER 89.   [75]   Sealy & Worthington, *Cases and Materials in Company Law* (9th edn, 2010), p 620.

[76]   (1854) 1 Macq (HL) 461.   [77]   [1956] 2 All ER 518.

[78]   [1969] 1 All ER 969, see also *Hogg v Cramphorn* [1966] 3 All ER 420; and see **8-65**.

[79]   [1942] 1 All ER 378.

is ratifiable.[80] Of course, drawing the line between misappropriation amounting to a fraud on a minority and the incidental self-serving conduct of *Regal* is not easy but it is a type of exercise undertaken by judges every day[81] with an inexact line being drawn depending on the degree of damage to the company and the degree of benefit to the wrongdoer.[82] As Professor Boyle has noted: 'It is ultimately an ethical judgment (as to the degree of directorial misbehaviour for which ratification is permissible) in the guise of legal principle'[83] so some blurring of the boundaries to ratification is inevitable. However, even where a breach of duty is ratifiable, the CA 2006 has altered the position significantly by imposing limits on the ability of the wrongdoing directors, as shareholders, to vote on that ratification.

18-36 Assuming then that the wrongdoing is capable of authorisation or ratification, the second issue is whether there is sufficient shareholder support to secure it.[84] Here the CA 2006 makes a significant change by providing that, on any resolution to ratify a (ratifiable) breach of duty, the votes of the interested director (where he is a member of the company) and any member connected with him (as defined in ss 252–255) must be disregarded (see s 239(3), (4)),[85] so securing the necessary majority to ratify may not be possible in any given case. The limitation on voting in CA 2006, s 239 applies only to ratification of a breach of duty and does not apply to prior authorisation so it might be tempting for the wrongdoer to use his voting power ahead of time to seek authorisation for the breach of duty, but while as a rule shareholders are entitled to exercise their votes as they please, the position is more nuanced than that with respect to wrongdoers voting to benefit themselves.[86] Finally, in a widely held company, authorisation or ratification may not be a realistic option, either in terms of the time and costs involved in holding shareholder meetings, or indeed in terms of the wider dissemination of information on the matter which would then occur.

18-37 Looking at the absolute bars in s 263(2) to a derivative claim proceeding, there is some potential for discussion of these matters to be lengthy and costly, but it would seem that practice is evolving in a way that suggests that there is limited scope for dismissing a claim under this provision. As noted at **18-30**, the courts will only dismiss a claim for permission under s 263(2)(a) if no director would continue the case so a plausible case cannot be dismissed on this basis. It is also quite likely that there is no evidence of actual authorisation or ratification which would mean the refusal of permission under s 263(2)(b) or (c) for, had there been, the shareholder would not have considered bringing a derivative

---

[80] See [1942] 1 All ER 378 at 389, per Lord Russell; also at 394, per Lord Wright.

[81] See Sealy (1981) CLJ 29 at 32; Baxter, 'The True Spirit of *Foss v Harbottle*' [1987] 38 NILQ 6 at 42–5.

[82] See Hannigan, 'Limitations on a Shareholder's Right to Vote—Effective Ratification Revisited' [2000] JBL 493 at 504–7.

[83] See Boyle, 'The Private Law Enforcement of Directors' Duties' in Hopt and Teubner (eds), *Corporate Governance and Directors' Liabilities* (1984), p 265; also Sealy (1981) CLJ 29.

[84] It is also possible for the shareholders to vote to waive the company's claim rather than to ratify the wrongdoing and that vote is not subject to the restrictions in s 239, but see n 86. See also s 239(6)(b) as to the powers of the directors to agree not to sue.

[85] Determining whose votes must be disregarded will not be straightforward, given the breadth of the definition of a connected person.

[86] See *North-West Transportation Co Ltd v Beatty* (1887) 12 App Cas 589, esp at 593–4 (director was able to vote as a shareholder to ratify his own undisclosed conflict of interest in a transaction with the company, but the transaction in that case was fair, the price market-based and the company benefited from the transaction); *Burland v Earle* [1902] AC 83 at 94, PC; *Cook v Deeks* [1916] AC 554 at 564, PC (majority shareholders cannot make a present to themselves of an asset belonging in equity to the company). See generally Hannigan, 'Limitations on a Shareholder's Right to Vote—Effective Ratification Revisited' [2000] JBL 493; also **11-70**.

claim (unless he wishes to dispute whether the matter was capable of authorisation or validly ratified). The result is that, in most instances, there will be no basis on which to dismiss the claim under s 263(2)[87] and the court will proceed to consider the matter under s 263(3). In practice, successful reliance on s 263(2) will probably only arise where the court adjourns the proceedings and the company uses the adjournment to authorise or ratify the breach of duty which means the court must dismiss the case. On the other hand, just because permission cannot be refused under s 263(2), it does not necessarily follow that a derivative claim can be brought.[88] The question then becomes one of the exercise of the court's discretion as to whether the claim can proceed which it must exercise in the light of the factors set out in CA 2006, s 263(3).

Discretion to allow a claim to proceed

18-38   In considering whether to give permission for a claim to proceed, the court must take into account, in particular, a number of factors which are set out in CA 2006, s 263(3) as follows:

  (a) whether the member is acting in good faith in seeking to continue the claim;

  (b) the importance that a director acting to promote the success of the company would attach to continuing it;

  (c) whether the act or omission (still to occur) would be likely to be authorised or ratified by the company or,

  (d) where the cause of action arises from an act or omission that has already occurred, whether the act or omission could be, and in the circumstances would be likely to be, ratified by the company;

  (e) whether the company has decided not to pursue the claim;

  (f) whether the act or omission in respect of which the claim is brought gives rise to a cause of action that the member could pursue in his own right rather than on behalf of the company.

18-39   The factors listed in s 263(3) are not exhaustive and so, while the court must take them into account 'in particular', it can also consider any other matter which it considers to be relevant such as the position of the company's employees,[89] or the issue of costs,[90] or the solvency of the company,[91] or indeed the fact that much of any money recovered from the defendants would be returned to them subsequently by way of distribution (they being

---

[87] As noted in n 62, in *Langley Ward Ltd v Trevor* [2011] EWHC 1893, the claim was dismissed on this basis, but only because the parties skipped the *prima facie* stage when the claims would probably have been dismissed.

[88] See, for example, *Mission Capital plc v Sinclair* [2010] 1 BCLC 304; *Franbar Holdings Ltd v Patel* [2009] 1 BCLC 1 where, in each case, the court quickly concluded that there were no grounds for dismissing the application under the mandatory requirements of CA 2006, s 263(2), but equally quickly dismissed the application under the discretionary jurisdiction in s 263(3) instead.

[89] *Stimpson v Southern Private Landlords Association* [2010] BCC 387 at [37].

[90] See *Iesini v Westrip Holdings Ltd* [2011] 1 BCLC 498 at [126], where Lewison J, obiter, thought that the potential liability of the company for costs is a proper consideration for the court in deciding whether to allow a derivative claim to continue.

[91] A derivative claim should not normally be brought on behalf of a company in liquidation or administration for then the liquidator or administrator is in a position to act on behalf of the company, see *Barrett v Duckett* [1995] 1 BCLC 243; *Cinematic Finance Ltd v Ryder* [2010] EWHC 3387; and this would also apply if the company is insolvent, but not in liquidation or administration: *Cinematic Finance Ltd v Ryder* at [22].

the majority shareholders).[92] There is no threshold test on the merits of the claim, but the merits are implicitly relevant to many of the factors in s 263(3), especially (3)(a), (b) and (e).[93] The court is expected to take into account all of the factors together and in no particular order and how important each is in any case is for the court to determine having regard to all the circumstances,[94] but the courts are conscious of the need to avoid a mini-trial at this stage.[95] In weighing up the overall position, the court is likely to be guided by the purpose of a derivative claim, namely to give a remedy for a wrong which would otherwise escape redress.[96]

Member acting in good faith—s 263(3)(a)

18-40 The motives of the claimant will be an important filter used by the courts to deal particularly with speculative litigation. It is for the shareholder seeking permission to establish to the satisfaction of the court that he is a person acting in good faith and should be allowed to sue on behalf of the company,[97] but once there is a real purpose in bringing the claim, the court is unlikely to consider the claimant to be in bad faith.[98] An interest in the commercial benefits to be gained from the litigation would not necessarily rule out a claim if the court otherwise thinks it is in the company's interests.[99] A claimant will not be in good faith, however, if motivated to litigate by personal considerations rather than in the interests of the company.[100]

Importance a director would attach to continuing the claim—s 263(3)(b)

18-41 Accepting that a director would seek to continue the claim for the purpose of s 263(2)(a) (otherwise the case would not have reached this stage), the court moves on to assessing the importance which a director would attach to continuing it. The court may be as reluctant to refuse permission to continue the claim on this basis as under s 263(2)(a).[101]

---

[92] See *Kleanthous v Paphitis* [2011] EWHC 2287 (main defendant director held 72% of the shares and the company did not require additional funds so the court thought that much of any money recovered from the directors for an alleged breach of duties, after the payment of costs, would be returned to the directors, as shareholders, by way of distribution).

[93] *Wishart v Castlecroft Securities Ltd* [2009] CSIH 615, [2009] SLT 812 at [40]; *Kleanthous v Paphitis* [2011] EWHC 2287 at [40]–[42].

[94] See 679 HL Official Report (5th series), col GC26, 27 February 2006. Boyle, n 11, suggests that the factors are ill-suited to the circumstances likely to arise in public listed companies. Keay & Loughrey, 'Derivative Proceedings in a Brave New World for Company Management and Shareholders' [2010] JBL 151, at 168, criticise the unnecessary proliferation of factors which the courts are considering which only prolong proceedings and create uncertainty as to the basis on which permission is being given or refused.

[95] *Wishart v Castlecroft Securities Ltd* [2009] CSIH 615, [2009] SLT 812; and see the criticisms expressed in *Langley Ward Ltd v Trevor* [2011] EWHC 1893 at [61].

[96] See *Burland v Earle* [1902] AC 83 at 93–4; *Prudential Assurance Co Ltd v Newman Industries Ltd* [1982] 1 All ER 354 at 357–8; *Smith v Croft (No 2)* [1987] 3 All ER 909 at 945.

[97] *Barrett v Duckett* [1995] 1 BCLC 243 at 250. It may be helpful to show that the claimant has the support of other minority shareholders, see *Stainer v Lee* [2011] 1 BCLC 537 at [49] (applicant for permission could show letters of support and a financial contribution from 35 other small shareholders).

[98] *Mission Capital plc v Sinclair* [2010] 1 BCLC 304 at [42].

[99] The mere fact that the claimant is also a creditor and so would benefit from any recovery by the company does not make his claim one for a collateral purpose and lacking in good faith: *Parry v Bartlett* [2011] EWHC 3146 at [94]. See also *Franbar Holdings Ltd v Patel* [2009] 1 BCLC 1 at [33]; Law Commission Report, n 11, para 6.76.

[100] *Barrett v Duckett* [1995] 1 BCLC 243 (claimant not pursuing claim bona fide in the interests of the company, but for personal reasons associated with the divorce of the company's sole director and the claimant's daughter); and see Payne, ' "Clean Hands" in Derivative Actions' (2002) CLJ 76 at 81.

[101] In *Iesini v Westrip Holdings Ltd* [2011] 1 BCLC 498 at [85], Lewison J suggested that, as the weighing of the considerations is essentially a commercial decision for the hypothetical director, the court is ill-equipped

The same type of task is required—the court has to look at the matter from the perspective of the hypothetical director acting in the way he considers would be most likely to promote the success of the company. The court must assess the commercial considerations (time and costs involved, the distraction of management, damage to reputation, likelihood of success and recovery, size of the loss) which the director would regard as relevant in assessing the importance of continuing the claim.[102] A hypothetical director may consider it appropriate to continue a claim where the case against the director seems very strong, even if the likely level of recovery is not so large, since the claim may provoke a settlement or summary judgment and, likewise, a director may consider it appropriate to continue a claim where the case is less strong, but the amount of the potential recovery is very large.[103] Clearly, it would be influential if independent non-executive directors whose conduct is not the subject of the claim were opposed to the claim proceeding as their position might be seen as somewhat akin to that of the hypothetical director.[104] The fact that the potential claim might more naturally be the subject of a petition for relief under CA 2006, s 994 (unfairly prejudicial conduct) is also something which a hypothetical director would consider.[105]

Authorisation/ratification—s 263(3)(c) and (d)

18-42 Two issues arise under these provisions. First, whether the breach of duty can be authorised or ratified—the position on authorisation and ratification was discussed at **18-31**—and this will involve an assessment not just as to whether the breach is capable of authorisation or ratification, but also whether ratification is possible given the voting constraints in s 239(3), (4). Secondly, the question whether an act or omission is likely to be authorised or ratified requires the court to consider the factual position within the individual company, bearing in mind that it is always open to the court to adjourn the proceedings (under s 261(4)(c)) to allow a meeting to be called for the purposes of authorisation or ratification.[106]

Company has decided not to pursue the claim—s 263(3)(e)

18-43 The decision of the company not to pursue the claim (as opposed to authorising or ratifying the breach) may be taken by the directors or the shareholders.[107] If the company has not actually considered the matter, the court may use its powers to adjourn proceedings to allow

to take this decision, save in clear cases. See Keay & Loughrey, 'Derivative Proceedings in a Brave New World for Company Management and Shareholders' [2010] JBL 151 at 161–2, who criticise the comment, noting that if judges were to follow this thinking, it would render the derivative claim virtually redundant.

[102] *Franbar Holdings Ltd v Patel* [2009] 1 BCLC 1 at [36].

[103] *Stainer v Lee* [2011] 1 BCLC 537 at [29]; and see *Kleanthous v Paphitis* [2011] EWHC 2287; *Parry v Bartlett* [2011] EWHC 3146 (hypothetical director would attach considerable importance to continuing the claim, giving a strong *prima facie* case of breach of duty).

[104] See *Kleanthous v Paphitis* [2011] EWHC 2287, discussed **18-33**. CA 2006, 263(3)(b), provides a mechanism by which the court may have regard to the views of the independent directors while s 263(3)(e) requires the court to have regard to the views of the company and s 263(4) requires the court to have regard to the views of disinterested members. The cumulative effect is to require the court to consider all possible constituencies within the board and the shareholders.

[105] See *Franbar Holdings Ltd v Patel* [2009] 1 BCLC 1 at [37]; *Mission Capital plc v Sinclair* [2010] 1 BCLC 304 at [43], [46].

[106] See 679 HL Official Report (5th series), cols GC27–8, 27 February 2006; HC Official Report, SC D (Company Law Reform Bill), 13 July 2006, col 679. If it is clear that the breach will be ratified, it is pointless to call a meeting, and the court can simply refuse permission to continue the claim: *Smith v Croft (No 2)* [1987] 3 All ER 909 at 957; see also Law Commission Report, n 11, para 6.84.

[107] 679 HL Official Report (5th series), cols GC8, 29–30, 27 February 2006. As was noted in *Prudential Assurance Co Ltd v Newman Industries Ltd (No 2)* [1982] 1 All ER 354 at 365, a board might conclude that to pursue the claim would not be to the company's advantage and to allow someone to do so might result in the company being 'killed by kindness'; and see CA 2006, s 239(6)(b).

for that consideration. As Knox J explained in *Smith v Croft (No 2)*,[108] the purpose of the adjournment is to obtain for the court a realistic assessment of the practical desirability of the claim going forward made by the organ that has the power and ability to take decisions on behalf of the company. In *Kleanthous v Paphitis*,[109] refusing permission to continue, the court was influenced by the fact that the company had set up a committee made up of the two directors who were not defendants to the claim and they had concluded that it would not be in the company's commercial interests (in terms of management disruption, damage to the company's performance as a result of the loss of experienced and high profile directors, damage to reputation and to the brand) to continue the claim against the company's major shareholders and directors, factors which would also be relevant to the importance which a director would attach to continuing the claim under s 263(3)(b), see **18-41**.

A cause of action that a member could pursue in his own right—s 263(3)(f)

18-44 The focus of this provision is on whether there is a cause of action that a member could pursue as a personal claim, but the existence of an alternative personal claim arising from the same act or omission is not a bar to a derivative claim, rather it is just one of the factors to be considered by the court.[110] It requires the court to look broadly at the particular complaint and the most appropriate redress for it rather than merely at the existence of an alternative remedy for that claimant.[111] Of course, in most cases, the issue is whether the potential availability of relief under the broad unfairly prejudicial jurisdiction in CA 2006, s 994 is 'a cause of action' that a member could pursue in his own right[112] so that a derivative claim is inappropriate and permission to continue the claim should be refused.[113] Typically the court will refuse permission where all the relief which the applicant is seeking is available to him under CA 2006, s 994.[114] There may be reasons, however, why, despite the possibility of a successful petition under CA 2006, s 994, a shareholder wishes to bring a derivative claim. The claimant may wish to remain a member of the company and so would prefer a corporate remedy rather than a personal remedy under s 994 which would typically see him exit from the company with his shares being

---

[108] [1987] 3 All ER 909 at 956.   [109] [2011] EWHC 2287, also nn 101, 138.

[110] *Iesini v Westrip Holdings Ltd* [2011] 1 BCLC 498; *Kiani v Cooper* [2010] 2 BCLC 427 at [38], [41]; *Franbar Holdings Ltd v Patel* [2009] 1 BCLC 1 at [50].

[111] The wording is quite deliberate for, during the Parliamentary debates, the Government declined to adopt an Opposition amendment which would have required the court to consider specifically the availability of an alternative remedy. It did so on two grounds: (1) that an alternative remedy in the form of an offer to buy the claimant's shares is not an appropriate remedy in the circumstances of a derivative claim; and (2) that this approach might encourage vulture funds to tell companies that they must either buy them out or face a possible derivative claim: see 682 HL Official Report (5th series), cols 726–8 (23 May 2006).

[112] As was noted in *Langley Ward Ltd v Trevor* [2011] EWHC 1893 at [13], the language of 'cause of action' is not very apt for petitions under CA 2006, s 994, but since the factors listed in s 263(3) are not exhaustive, the court can have regard to the availability of relief under s 994 regardless of whether, strictly speaking, it falls within a 'cause of action' and s 263(3)(f).

[113] See *Jafari-Fini v Skillglass Ltd* [2005] BCC 842, CA, permission to bring a derivative claim at common law refused when, on the same grounds, the claimant could and was bringing a claim for breach of contract. The court concluded that it was better for that contractual claim to be determined first than for the company to be put to the cost of funding a derivative claim in respect of the same issues.

[114] See *Kleanthous v Paphitis* [2011] EWHC 2287 (permission refused: evidence suggested that the remedy that the applicant really wanted was to be bought out and was pursuing the derivative claim because of the availability of a costs indemnity, see **18-51**); also *Mission Capital plc v Sinclair* [2010] 1 BCLC 304 (permission refused: the court did not consider that the claimants were seeking anything which could not be recovered by means of an unfair prejudice petition); *Franbar Holdings Ltd v Patel* [2009] 1 BCLC 1 (permission refused: claims by the member for breach of a shareholders' agreement as well as under CA 2006, s 994 should give the applicant all the relief sought).

purchased by the respondents to the petition.[115] The other advantage to pursing a derivative claim, assuming personal relief is not required, is the possibility of obtaining an indemnity for costs (see **18-51**). There is also the possibility that the claimant is not able to meet the requirement under s 994 that the company's affairs are being or have been conducted in a manner which is unfairly prejudicial to the interests of the member or members generally when the complaint relates to an issue of misconduct by a director.[116] These points were all considered relevant by the court in *Wishart v Castlecroft Securities Ltd*[117] where the allegations concerned the alleged exploitation of a corporate opportunity by a director personally to the detriment of the company. The claimant was another director and shareholder in the company and, while the court considered that a petition under CA 2006, s 994 might have given him a satisfactory remedy, that availability is not conclusive on whether permission to continue a derivative claim should be given. In this case, a derivative claim was preferable and the availability of relief under s 994 was not a compelling consideration for the court for a variety of reasons, especially that:

(1) the complaint was not that the company's affairs were being conducted in an unfairly prejudicial manner, but that the director had acted in breach of duty with the knowing assistance of a third party;

(2) the relief sought was that the company's position be restored to what it should have been, rather than that the claimant be bought out;

(3) a purchase order for the claimant's shares under CA 2006, s 994 would not have been an attractive remedy in what was a declining market, while a derivative claim would allow the misappropriated opportunity to be held on trust for the company which remedy might be a more valuable relief as markets recover; and

(4) a derivative claim would allow the matter to be pursued against a third party also so allowing for direct relief for the company in respect of that party's knowing assistance in the director's breach of duty.

18-45 Another issue is whether winding up is a more appropriate outcome in the circumstances rather than a derivative claim. Again, this issue is not strictly a case of 'a cause of action which the member could pursue in his own right',[118] but the availability of that option is another factor which the courts take into account. In *Langley Ward Ltd v Trevor*,[119] the company was not only deadlocked, but had run its course (its business was property development which had been completed) and it was, the court thought, a natural candidate to be wound up on the just and equitable grounds under IA 1986, s 122(1)(g), see **18-74**. In those circumstances, the court thought it was appropriate to consider the comparative merit of

---

[115] See Law Commission Report, n 12, paras 6.10–6.12. See, for example, *Airey v Cordell* [2007] BCC 785, where the claimant wished to use a common law derivative claim (essentially founded on a diversion of corporate assets to another entity) to recover those assets for the company (so that he could participate in the long-term gains to be expected from their exploitation) rather than be bought out of the company; also *Kiani v Cooper* [2010] 2 BCLC 427 at [38], [41], claimant wanted the company to pursue various development projects as planned and wanted to remain a member of it; *Stainer v Lee* [2011] 1 BCLC 537 at [52], claimant wanted the company to pursue a claim against two directors for misconduct and an order for restitution to the company, he did not want to be bought out.

[116] See *Re Charnley Davies Ltd (No 2)* [1990] BCLC 760, discussed at **17-78**; and *Stainer v Lee* [2011] 1 BCLC 537 at [52]; *Parry v Bartlett* [2011] EWHC 3146 (not clear that CA 2006, s 994 petition was a realistic alternative on the facts).

[117] [2009] CSIH 615, [2009] SLT 812 (a Scottish decision, but the provisions on derivative claims in Scotland, set out in CA 2006, Pt 11, Ch 2, are in substance identical to those applicable to the rest of the UK, though there are procedural differences as the CPR do not apply in Scotland).   [118] See n 112.

[119] [2011] EWHC 1893.

leaving all or some of the disputes to be dealt with by a liquidator rather than by a derivative claim. On balance, the court found that a liquidation would be the best forum for the claims to be investigated and so refused permission for the continuation of a derivative claim.

Views of disinterested shareholders—s 263(4)

18-46　Distinct from the factors listed in s 263(3), there is a mandatory requirement in s 263(4) for the court to have particular regard to any evidence before it as to the views of members of the company who have no personal interest, direct or indirect, in the matter.[120] This requirement is intended to reflect the position adopted by Knox J in *Smith v Croft (No 2)*[121] as to the weight to be given to the influential views of those shareholders who are independent of the wrongdoers.[122] Knox J was unconvinced that a just result is achieved by a single minority shareholder having the right to involve a company in an action for recovery of compensation for the company if all the other minority shareholders are, for disinterested reasons, satisfied that the proceedings will be productive of more harm than good.[123]

18-47　It was also suggested in the Parliamentary debates that this provision allows the opinions of shareholders in a major quoted company to be taken into account while acknowledging that it is not practicable or desirable in such companies to ask shareholders formally to approve directors' commercial decisions.[124] Ratification or authorisation may not have taken place, nor be likely to, likewise, there may not be an actual decision of the company not to continue the claim, but it may nevertheless be possible to show that the shareholders are content to support the directors in respect of what has occurred.[125]

18-48　A practical concern, particularly in widely-held companies, is how to identify 'persons who have no personal interest, direct or indirect' in the matter[126] and how to obtain evidence as to their views on the claim.[127] This point was echoed by Lewison J in *Iesini v Westrip Holdings Ltd*[128] where he commented, obiter, as to the difficulty of applying this provision since, in theory, all shareholders have an obvious interest in any claim brought on the company's behalf. He thought it was probably intended by this provision that the court must have regard to the views of the members not implicated in the wrongdoing and who do not stand to benefit otherwise than in their capacity as members of the company.

18-49　Even when identified, there must also be a question mark over whether such persons would be willing to become involved in a claim, even in this minimal way. A scenario may be envisaged where institutional shareholders make known to the court their view that a claim should not continue and the court refuses permission for the claim to continue. If it later emerged that the claim was well founded, the institutions would face criticism for

---

[120]　See *Stainer v Lee* [2011] 1 BCLC 537 at [46], but their views must be based on knowledge of all the facts.　　　[121] [1987] 3 All ER 909 at 957.

[122]　See 681 HL Official Report (5th series), cols 883–4, 888, 9 May 2006. This provision was part of the package of amendments introduced to meet concerns that there were inadequate filters to deter vexatious claims (see **18-10**).　　　[123] [1987] 3 All ER 909 at 956.

[124]　See 681 HL Official Report (5th series), col 884, 9 May 2006.

[125]　See 681 HL Official Report (5th series), col 884, 9 May 2006.

[126]　The Law Commission had considered this issue in terms of seeking the opinion of an independent organ (see Law Commission Report, n 11, paras 6.88–6.89), a term derived from *Smith v Croft (No 2)* [1987] 3 All ER 909 at 957–60, but it was criticised as being unclear. The formulation in the statute has avoided that problem, but may be difficult to apply in a widely-held company.

[127]　On the latter point, in *Stimpson v Southern Private Landlords Association* [2010] BCC 387, though not a traded company, it had a large (and fluctuating) number of members, a questionnaire was circulated by order of the court to the members to determine their views on permitting the claim to proceed, but it was an unusual not-for-profit company which was essentially a trade association.

[128]　[2011] 1 BCLC 498 at [129]–[130].

the role they played in preventing the claim proceeding. Independent shareholders may prefer to remain on the sidelines rather than risk being put in such a position. Where the institutions positively favour a claim being pursued, a derivative claim will probably be unnecessary for the institutions will be able to effect board changes which ensure that the company pursues the matter.

18-50 Having reviewed all the factors in s 263(3) and considered the views of the disinterested shareholders under s 263(4), the court may grant permission for the claim to proceed,[129] refuse permission, or adjourn the proceedings and give such directions as it thinks fit, but even if permission is given, it is merely permission to continue the claim,[130] and costs will be an important consideration at this stage.

Costs of bringing a derivative claim

18-51 The CA 2006, Pt 11 makes no specific provision for costs and the Law Commission's position was that the court's power to make costs indemnity orders in derivative actions should remain unchanged. The position is governed by the Court of Appeal decision in *Wallersteiner v Moir (No 2)*[131] which held that where a shareholder has, in good faith and on reasonable grounds, sued as plaintiff in a minority shareholder's action, the benefit of which if successful will accrue to the company and only indirectly to the plaintiff as a member of the company, and which action it would be reasonable for an independent board of directors to bring in the company name, the court may order the company to pay the plaintiff's costs.[132]

18-52 The ability to secure an indemnity from the company is an important consideration for a shareholder contemplating a derivative action,[133] but concerns that the very possibility of obtaining an indemnity order will encourage vexatious claims are misplaced.[134] Claimants cannot be sure that the court will exercise its discretion and make an indemnity

---

[129] The court can grant permission on a limited basis. For example, in *Stainer v Lee* [2011] 1 BCLC 537 at [37], [55], permission was granted to continue just to the conclusion of disclosure which would give a clearer picture of the strength of the case and the quantum of loss. In *Kiani v Cooper* [2010] 2 BCLC 427 at [42], permission was given to continue down to disclosure which would give the defendant director the opportunity to produce the documentation which he said he possessed and which would refute allegations of improper payments to a company controlled by him. In each case, the applicant must then return to the court to seek further permission to continue the claim.

[130] Once permission to continue a claim is given, the court may order that the claim cannot be discontinued, or settled, or compromised without the court's permission, see CPR 19.9F; Practice Direction 19C—Derivative Claims, para 7.   [131] [1975] 1 All ER 849.

[132] [1975] 1 All ER 849 at 868–9, per Buckley LJ; see also CPR 19.9E (the indemnity may cover the costs incurred in obtaining permission to continue and in the claim itself). In *Smith v Croft* [1986] 2 All ER 551, Walton J took a restrictive view of the jurisdiction to make an indemnity order, but this restrictive approach was not followed in *Jaybird v Greenwood Ltd* [1986] BCLC 318. For examples of situations where an indemnity order was refused, see *Halle v Trax BM Ltd* [2000] BCC 1020 (in effect asking company to fund dispute between two partners in a joint venture); *Mumbray v Lapper* [2005] BCC 990 (essentially a partnership break-up); also *Watts v Midland Bank plc* [1986] BCLC 15 (no indemnity order where company hopelessly insolvent). See generally Reisberg, 'Funding Derivative Actions: A Re-Examination of Costs and Fees as Incentives to Commence Litigation' [2004] 4 JCLS 345; Quigxiu Bu, 'The Indemnity Order in a Derivative Action' (2006) 27 Co Law 2.

[133] See Reisberg, 'Derivative Actions and the Funding Problem: The Way Forward' [2006] JBL 445 who argues that, until US-type contingency fee agreements are introduced in this jurisdiction, financing the litigation will remain a major obstacle to use of the derivative claim.

[134] See 679 HL Official Report (5th series), col GC13, 27 February 2006.

order or it may order only a limited indemnity[135] so a claimant does have a potential exposure to significant costs and the indemnity does not act as an actual incentive to bring a claim.[136]

18-53 Companies may fund costs incurred by a defendant director in derivative proceedings, but those costs must be refunded if the director loses the case (CA 2006, s 205(1), (2)). In larger companies, directors will also have insurance cover against personal liability (paid for by the company) and they will want to ensure that those policies cover derivative claims and associated legal costs. It is possible therefore that companies may end up funding the claimant (under a *Wallersteiner* order) and the defendant directors (through insurance and by way of loans to meet defence costs) and so a derivative claim may be expensive for the company.

Potential for derivative claims

18-54 At first glance, CA 2006, Pt 11 looks as if it dramatically alters the landscape of shareholders' remedies, allowing any member (regardless of size of shareholding or length of membership) to bring a derivative claim in respect of any breach of duty (including negligence) or default by any director, but many caveats must be added to that picture of open-ended liability.

18-55 First, derivative claims, though facilitated by the new mechanism of Part 11, remain subject to the general principle of majority rule, see **18-12**. Moreover, the newly available power of disinterested directors to authorise conflicts of interests in advance significantly reduces the potential for the type of 'fraud on the minority' conduct which in the past formed the basis of typical derivative actions.

18-56 Secondly, the threshold tests are sufficient, cumulatively, to deter many would-be claimants, especially when costs issues are factored in, not to mention the informational disadvantages facing a claimant.[137] In the Parliamentary debates, there was much emphasis on the expectation that the courts will maintain the long tradition of not second-guessing directors' business judgement which may curb any judicial enthusiasm for a liberal approach to the derivative jurisdiction. The judiciary remain anxious not to open the doors here to the sort of speculative litigation sometimes seen in the US and tight judicial control is imposed, as is evident in the small number of reported cases to date (generally permission has been refused or where granted, has been granted on a limited basis and on limited indemnities).[138] There remain some concerns, nevertheless, about the length and costs of the 'satellite' litigation involved when permission is sought.[139]

18-57 Thirdly, the position remains that recovery is for the benefit of the company, not the individual claimant who can only benefit to the extent that benefit to the company is reflected

---

[135] See, for example, *Kiani v Cooper* [2010] 2 BCLC 427 at [48]–[49], indemnity awarded but not against any adverse costs order—in a dispute between two directors and shareholders in a company, where there were no significant unsecured creditors whose interests came into the equation, the court thought the claimant should be required to assume part of the risk of the litigation; see also *Stainer v Lee* [2011] 1 BCLC 537 at [56], given the uncertainty as to likely recovery, the court limited the indemnity to £40,000, with permission to apply later for an extension of the indemnity.

[136] Reisberg, n 132, argues that the only real incentive for shareholders to bring derivative actions would be if the courts could order some element of personal recovery for them when the claim is successful; see also Cheffins, n 15, 256–60.

[137] See Kosmin, 'Minority Shareholders' Remedies: A Practitioner's Perspective' [1997] Company, Financial and Insolvency Law Review 211.

[138] See *Kiani v Cooper* [2010] 2 BCLC 427; *Stainer v Lee* [2011] 1 BCLC 537. See also *Wishart v Castlecroft Securities Ltd* [2009] CSIH 615, [2009] SLT 812.

[139] See *Langley Ward Ltd v Trevor* [2011] EWHC 1893 at [61]–[63].

in the value of his shares, so there is no incentive to litigate via a derivative claim. Save where a claimant is determined to remain as a member of the company, it continues to be preferable to petition for relief under CA 2006, s 994 (unfairly prejudicial conduct) without the need for any permission of the court and with the prospect of personal recovery.

18-58   When all these factors are considered, it is difficult to conclude that the mere introduction of the statutory derivative claim dramatically increases the litigation risk to directors, at least to the level that it would deter people from acting as a director of a public company. Overall, few cases are likely to proceed to full-blown trials of the issues and this has been the experience of other jurisdictions which have introduced statutory derivative actions.[140] Derivative claims have always been uncommon and, to date, that position has not changed under CA 2006, Pt 11. Occasionally, there may be a high profile case pursued as much for the publicity as recovery and settled long before trial, but there is no expectation, and no evidence, of any significant increase in the number of derivative claims being brought as a result of the introduction of Part 11.

C Corporate loss and reflective loss

18-59   The decision of the Court of Appeal in *Prudential Assurance Co Ltd v Newman Industries Ltd (No 2)*[141] establishes that a personal claim by a member against another in respect of the diminution in value of his shareholding as a result of a wrong done to the company is misconceived and should be struck out, for the shareholder's loss is merely reflective of the loss suffered by the company and that loss will be fully remedied if the company enforces its full rights against the wrongdoer.[142] The wrongdoer may be a director[143] or a third party, such as a solicitor or other adviser to the company.[144] The no reflective loss principle was affirmed by the House of Lords in a complex judgment in *Johnson v Gore Wood & Co*[145] and has been the subject of further analysis by the Court of Appeal, particularly in *Giles v Rhind*[146] and *Gardner v Parker*.[147]

---

[140]   The evidence from Canada, New Zealand and Australia is that the statutory derivative procedures in those jurisdictions have been used to an insignificant degree and mainly in respect of private companies (not public companies as might have been anticipated): see Ramsay and Saunders, n 16, 420; Cheffins, n 15, 241. There is nothing about CA 2006, Pt 11 which suggests that the experience here will be any different. See also Hannigan, 'Drawing Boundaries between Derivative Claims and Unfairly Prejudicial Petitions' [2009] JBL 606.   [141]   [1982] 1 All ER 354.

[142]   [1982] 1 All ER 354 at 366–7; see also *Stein v Blake* [1998] 1 All ER 724. It matters not whether the shareholder's claim is for breach of contract, in tort, or for breach of fiduciary duty: *Gardner v Parker* [2004] 2 BCLC 554; *Shaker v Al-Bedrawi* [2003] 1 BCLC 517. The *Prudential* principle does not apply where a duty is owed only to the shareholder so that the company has no claim or where there is a separate duty owed to the shareholder breach of which causes a loss distinct and separate from that suffered by the company (and which is not remedied therefore by recovery by the company): *Giles v Rhind* [2003] 1 BCLC 1 at 14; *Day v Cook* [2002] 1 BCLC 1 at 16, 25; *Johnson v Gore Wood & Co* [2001] 1 BCLC 313 at 338, per Lord Bingham; and see *Pearce v European Reinsurance Consultants* [2005] 2 BCLC 366 where the shareholder did have a distinct claim; also *Jafari-Fini v Skillglass Ltd* [2005] BCC 842 at 848.

[143]   See *Gardner v Parker* [2004] 2 BCLC 554, CA; *Giles v Rhind* [2003] 1 BCLC 1, CA; *Shaker v Al-Bedrawi* [2003] 1 BCLC 517, CA.

[144]   See *Johnson v Gore Wood & Co* [2001] 1 BCLC 313, HL; *Day v Cook* [2002] 1 BCLC 1.

[145]   [2001] 1 BCLC 313, HL. See Ferran, 'Litigation by Shareholders and Reflective Loss' (2001) CLJ 245; Watts, 'The Shareholder as Co-promisee' (2001) 117 LQR 388; Mitchell, 'Shareholders' Claims for Reflective Loss' (2004) 120 LQR 457; also Mukwari, 'The No Reflective Loss Principle' (2005) 26 Co Law 304; Lee Suet Lin, 'Barring Recovery for Diminution in Value of Shares on Reflective Loss Claims' (2007) CLJ 533.

[146]   [2003] 1 BCLC 1.

[147]   [2004] 2 BCLC 554, affirming the decision of Blackburne J, see [2004] 1 BCLC 417.

18-60 The result is that no action lies at the suit of a shareholder suing to make good a diminution in value of his shareholding (including loss of dividends and all other payments which the shareholder might have obtained from the company had it not been deprived of its funds,[148] and whether those payments would have been received in the capacity of shareholder or otherwise[149]) where that claim merely reflects the loss suffered by the company and that loss would have been made good if the company had enforced in full its rights against the defendant wrongdoer. No action by a shareholder lies even if the company acting through its constitutional organs declines or fails to make good that loss.[150] However, if the company has been disabled by the wrongdoer by the very act of which complaint is made from pursuing the loss, as opposed to choosing not to sue or settling the claim disadvantageously,[151] the shareholder can maintain a claim for what is reflective loss, a qualification established by *Giles v Rhind*.[152] That qualification from *Giles v Rhind* was criticised by Lord Millett sitting as a member of the Hong Kong Court of Final Appeal in *Waddington v Chan Chun Hoo* Thomas[153] who considered that *Giles v Rhind* was wrongly decided and had the effect of allowing recovery by the wrong party to the prejudice of the company and its creditors. Subsequently, in *Webster v Sanderson*,[154] the Court of Appeal robustly rejected that criticism, noting that the decision in *Giles v Rhind* is binding on the Court of Appeal and only the Supreme Court can overrule it, but also noting that the decision was considered in detail and without dissent by the Court of Appeal in *Gardner v Parker*.[155] The critical point in *Giles v Rhind*, the court noted, was that the company was disabled from bringing the claim by the very wrongdoing complained about by the shareholder.[156]

18-61 This rule against the recovery of reflective loss is not concerned with debarring causes of action as such, but with barring recovery of certain types of loss.[157] The foundation of the rule is the need to avoid double recovery.[158] As Lord Millett explained in *Johnson v Gore Wood*: 'If the shareholder is allowed to recover in respect of such loss, then either there will be double recovery at the expense of the defendant or the shareholder will recover at the expense of the company and its creditors and other shareholders. Neither course can be permitted.'[159] He went on: 'Justice to the defendant requires the exclusion of one claim or the other; protection of the interests of the company's creditors requires that it is the company which is allowed to recover to the exclusion of the shareholder.'[160] As Arden LJ put it in *Day v Cook*,[161] '…the company's claim, if it exists, will always trump that of the shareholder's', subject now to the 'disability' exception in *Giles v Rhind*.[162] Given that

---

[148] See *Johnson v Gore Wood & Co* [2001] 1 BCLC 313 at 370, per Lord Millett.

[149] For example, as a creditor or employee of the company, see *Johnson v Gore Wood & Co* [2001] 1 BCLC 313 at 370, per Lord Millett; *Gardner v Parker* [2004] 2 BCLC 554 at 572, per Neuberger LJ.

[150] See *Johnson v Gore Wood & Co* [2001] 1 BCLC 313 at 337, per Lord Bingham.

[151] See *Gardner v Parker* [2004] 2 BCLC 554 at 570, per Neuberger LJ; *Johnson v Gore Wood & Co* [2001] 1 BCLC 313 at 369, per Lord Millett.

[152] [2003] 1 BCLC 1, noted Hirt [2003] JBL 420. As the Court of Appeal noted in this case, it was the defendant director's wrong (essentially he 'stole' the company's business reducing it to insolvency) that had disabled the company from pursuing any claim for damages against him which wrong he then compounded by an application for security for costs against the company when his own breach made it impossible for the company to provide such security: see [2003] 1 BCLC 1 at 25, 28. The Court of Appeal considered that *Johnson v Gore Wood & Co* [2001] 1 BCLC 313 had no application to that situation which had not been in the contemplation of the House of Lords. See also *Perry v Day* [2005] 2 BCLC 405.

[153] [2009] 2 BCLC 82 at [81]–[88].   [154] [2009] 2 BCLC 542 at [36].   [155] [2004] 2 BCLC 554.

[156] [2009] 2 BCLC 542 at [38].   [157] *Gardner v Parker* [2004] 2 BCLC 554 at 567, per Neuberger LJ.

[158] *Johnson v Gore Wood & Co* [2001] 1 BCLC 313; *Gardner v Parker* [2004] 2 BCLC 554.

[159] [2001] 1 BCLC 313 at 365.   [160] [2001] 1 BCLC 313 at 366.   [161] [2002] 1 BCLC 1 at 15.

[162] [2003] 1 BCLC 1.

foundation, a claim will be barred even where there is a breach of duty to the company *and* the shareholder and even if the claim is brought in another capacity, for example as a creditor of the company. If the substance of the claim is the same, though the cause of action is different, the no reflective loss rule applies.[163]

18-62 In *Gardner v Parker*[164] a company had suffered significant losses and gone into administrative receivership as a result of breaches of duty by the company's sole director. Receivers had been appointed to the company and they had settled the company's claims against the director. A claim against the director by the minority shareholder in the company for losses suffered in its capacity as a shareholder in and creditor of the company (the shareholder had made a substantial loan to the company) was rejected for its losses would have been made good if the company had enforced its rights against the defendant. The rule against recovery of reflective loss therefore applied and the claim was dismissed.

18-63 The position now reached on the recovery of reflective loss is clear [165] and it is a position based on a combination of policy and practical considerations. The principle reflects the first limb of the rule in *Foss v Harbottle*.[166] It looks to company autonomy and ensures that the interests of the company are respected and that a (shareholder) party does not recover compensation for a loss suffered by another (the company).[167] It protects the interests of the company's creditors and ensures they are not prejudiced by an action by an individual shareholder.[168] At a practical level, it prevents a multitude of cases being brought by shareholders (with the courts being required to act as referee between the different claimants and with an eye to the need to protect the company's creditors). In the circumstances, it is procedurally efficient to exclude all claims other than those of the company, save where the company has been disabled by the wrongdoer from bringing its claim. It also facilitates settlements of claims for, in the absence of the prohibition of recovery of reflective loss, wrongdoers will be unwilling to compromise or settle claims with the company for fear of being met by a further claim by a shareholder.[169]

18-64 One question is whether the availability now of a statutory derivative claim helps the shareholder get around the no reflective loss principle. If the problem in many instances is that the company has not pursued its remedy against the wrongdoer director, the solution may lie in the shareholder pursuing the claim for the company via a derivative claim. Of course, usually the reason the company has not pursued the wrongdoer is that the company is in liquidation and the question then is whether a derivative claim can be brought when a company is in liquidation. The common law answer was no[170] and while there are suggestions that, as CA 2006, Pt 11 is new, the courts should not be bound by

---

[163] *Gardner v Parker* [2004] 2 BCLC 554 at [49], applying *Shaker v Al-Bedrawi* [2003] 1 BCLC 157. That is not to say, Neuberger J noted, that a creditor is without remedies. The creditor may sue the company for repayment if it is solvent (leaving the company to pursue the wrongdoing director) and, if the company is insolvent, the creditor can either fund an action by the liquidator against the director or take an assignment of the company's claim against him, see [2004] 2 BCLC 554 at [74]; also *Johnson v Gore Wood & Co* [2001] 1 BCLC 313 at 369.   [164] [2004] 2 BCLC 554.

[165] Even if there is some criticism of the courts for not having adopted a more nuanced approach to these issues rather than the bright line approach of Lord Bingham and Lord Millett in *Johnson v Gore Wood & Co*, see Mitchell (2004) 120 LQR 457 at 464–5.   [166] (1843) 2 Hare 461, see **18-1**.

[167] See *Johnson v Gore Wood & Co* [2002] 1 BCLC 313 at 338, per Lord Bingham; at 365, per Lord Millett.

[168] See *Johnson v Gore Wood & Co* [2002] 1 BCLC 313 at 338, per Lord Bingham; at 366, per Lord Millett.

[169] See *Johnson v Gore Wood & Co* [2002] 1 BCLC 313 at 370, per Lord Millett; *Giles v Rhind* [2003] 1 BCLC 1 at 30, per Chadwick LJ.

[170] See *Fargro v Godfroy* [1986] BCLC 370; *Barrett v Duckett* [1995] 1 BCLC 243, see n 91.

their previous position,[171] initial indications are that the courts see no reason to diverge from the existing principle. Despite the enactment of Part 11, the company remains the proper plaintiff in respect of a wrong done to it and where the company is in liquidation or administration, it is for the liquidator or administrator to sue on the company's behalf and no derivative claim will lie.[172] A derivative avenue to circumventing the no reflective loss principle is not then an option.

18-65 Of course, a breach of a director's duties to the company often forms the basis of a petition under CA 2006, s 994 alleging unfairly prejudicial conduct of the company's affairs and the standard relief for the successful petitioner is a purchase order at a price which reflects the value of his shares as if the unfairly prejudicial conduct had not occurred (see **17-79**). Such a purchase order does in effect allow the petitioner to recover for reflective loss and, while the company is not compensated for the wrong done to it, the diminution in value of the petitioner's shares as a consequence of that wrong is made good.[173] The court in *Atlasview Ltd v Brightview Ltd*[174] was unconcerned about such an outcome, merely noting that the court would be careful to ensure no double recovery by the company and the petitioners.[175]

D Personal actions at common law

18-66 It may be that a shareholder wishes to remedy not a wrong done to the company but a wrong done to him personally. Such a personal action is unaffected by the rule in *Foss v Harbottle*.[176] A shareholder may bring a personal claim to obtain an injunction to restrain proposed illegal or ultra vires acts,[177] but this option is of limited significance since it is rare for shareholders to be aware of a proposed illegal or ultra vires act in time to seek an injunction.

18-67 When considering the possibility of a personal claim, typically the issues revolve around the enforcement of the articles of association with a shareholder looking either to enforce what he perceives to be his rights under the articles or to prevent breaches by the majority of the articles, or even to prevent the articles from being altered. All these issues are considered in detail in Chapter 4 to which the reader is referred. Trying to enforce particular rights or to prevent the majority from acting in breach of particular provisions is not a

---

[171] See Keay, 'Can Derivative Proceedings be Commenced when a Company is in Liquidation' (2008) 21 Insolv Int 49 who was cautiously optimistic that, given the new procedure, the courts would be willing to entertain applications by members when the company is in liquidation.

[172] In *Cinematic Finance Ltd v Ryder* [2010] EWHC 3387, the court considered this also to be the position if the company is insolvent, though not in liquidation or administration.

[173] See *Re Cumana Ltd* [1986] BCLC 430 at 437.

[174] [2004] 2 BCLC 191 at [60]–[64].

[175] For more detailed discussion of this issue, see Hannigan, 'Drawing Boundaries between Derivative Claims and Unfairly Prejudicial Petitions [2009] JBL 606 at 615–20.   [176] (1843) 2 Hare 461.

[177] See *Simpson v Westminster Palace Hotel Co* (1860) 8 HL Cas 712; *Parke v Daily News* [1962] 2 All ER 929; *Smith v Croft (No 2)* [1987] BCLC 206. It had been thought that shareholders could bring a personal action with respect to losses arising from illegal or ultra vires acts, but in *Smith v Croft (No 2)* Knox J took the view that such actions are to recover corporate losses arising from the transaction and, as such, should be the subject of an action by the company, or by the shareholders on a derivative basis, but no personal action will lie.

straightforward matter with the courts generally taking a restrictive approach to these issues, precisely in order not to undermine the rule in *Foss v Harbottle*, see **18-33**.

18-68 In practice, a shareholder aggrieved at difficulties in enforcing his rights under the articles of association, or at non-compliance by the majority with the terms of the articles, is likely to petition for relief under CA 2006, s 994, alleging that the affairs of the company are being conducted in a manner which is unfairly prejudicial to his interests.

E Statutory remedies

18-69 As already noted, the preferred statutory remedy for shareholders with general grievances about the unfairly prejudicial manner in which the affairs of the company are being conducted is to bring a petition for relief under CA 2006, s 994, which is discussed in detail in Chapter 17. The CA 2006 also provides a number of specific statutory remedies and rights which shareholders may be able to invoke in an appropriate case to which we now turn. Finally, the IA 1986, s 122(1)(g) provides a shareholder remedy in the form of a right to seek a winding-up order on the just and equitable ground, see **18-74**.

Statutory rights under the CA 2006

18-70 A number of provisions in the CA 2006 are designed to enhance shareholders' rights of engagement (e.g. rights of access to information, rights of participation in meetings, right to circulate resolutions etc) and are particularly of interest in larger companies. In each case, the relevant section sets a threshold which needs to be met to exercise the particular right and these vary from provision to provision. A typical requirement would be that the support of holders of not less than 5% of the total voting rights of all the members who have the right to vote is needed. Of particular value are the following rights:

- the right to obtain copies of the company's constitutional documents: CA 2006, s 32, see **4-8**;
- the right to inspect the register of members, subject to the company's right to go to court to refuse access: CA 2006, s 117, see **14-73**;
- the right to require the holding of a general meeting: CA 2006, s 303; and where the directors fail to call the meeting, the right of shareholders to call it themselves: s 305, see **15-48**;
- the right of members of a private company to require the circulation of a written resolution; CA 2006, s 292, see **15-29**; and, for public companies, the right to require the circulation of resolutions for annual general meetings: s 338, see **15-41**; and, for all companies, the right to require the circulation of statements with respect to proposed resolutions or business to be conducted at a general meeting: s 314, see **15-45**;
- the right of members of a quoted company[178] to require an independent report on any poll taken, or to be taken, at a general meeting of the company: CA 2006, s 342, see **15-15**;
- the right of members to copies of the company's accounts and reports: CA 2006, ss 431 and 432, see **16-31**;

---

[178] 'Quoted company' is defined in CA 2006, s 385: see s 361.

- the right of members of a quoted company to require the company to publish on a website a statement setting out audit concerns that the members propose to raise at the next accounts meeting of the company:[179] CA 2006, s 527, see **16-31**.

18-71 Other provisions allow shareholders to object to a particular corporate act, such as the variation of class rights. Again, the statutory provision will set a minimum threshold for invoking the particular remedy (for example, the holders of not less than 15% of the class who have not agreed to the variation of the class rights: CA 2006, s 633) and possibly a time-limit within which the relief must be sought (for example, within 21 days of the consent to the variation). Examples of these provisions would be:

- the right to object to the re-registration of a public company as a private company: CA 2006, s 98;
- the right to challenge a variation of class rights: CA 2006, s 633, see **14-37**;
- the right to apply for rectification of the register of members: CA 2006, s 125, see **14-77**;
- the right to require the company to exercise its powers under CA 2006, s 793 requiring information about the holders of interests in the company's shares: s 803;
- the right of a minority shareholder to be bought out by an offeror where there has been a takeover offer for all the shares in the company: CA 2006, s 983, see **26-80**.

18-72 Other statutory schemes do not provide a specific shareholder remedy as such, but the ability of the company to proceed with the scheme is dependent on court confirmation, as in the case of a reduction of capital by special resolution confirmed by the court under CA 2006, ss 645–651, see **20-70**, or a scheme of arrangement under CA 2006, s 899, see **26-99**, and the protection of the minority in such instances lies in the requirement for court sanction.

18-73 Finally, shareholders have the right to remove a director by an ordinary resolution under CA 2006, s 168, although exercise of this power may itself give rise to further problems, see **6-32**. Issues to bear in mind include any entitlement to damages which may arise (see CA 2006, s 168(5)); the possibility that the director in question can command a sufficient majority of votes to prevent his removal and, most importantly, the possibility in quasi-partnerships that removal (without a fair offer for the dismissed director's shares) may trigger a petition for unfairly prejudicial conduct under CA 2006, s 994: see **17-56**.

Winding up on the just and equitable ground

18-74 A member may petition under IA 1986, s 122(1)(g) for a winding-up order on the just and equitable ground,[180] a provision which has traditionally provided the court with a wide discretionary jurisdiction.[181] It had been thought that this jurisdiction was all but superseded by the unfairly prejudicial jurisdiction (CA 2006, s 994) but, as discussed at **18-90**, in some circumstances relief may not be available under s 994, but will merit a winding up. The main situation within the latter jurisdiction, but not the former, is deadlock between the parties in a quasi-partnership which will not amount to unfairly prejudicial

---

[179] 'Accounts meeting' is defined in CA 2006, s 437(3), see **16-31**.

[180] Various other parties (including the directors and creditors) may also petition for a winding up: see **24-20**. Here we deal only with petitioning shareholders.

[181] See *Re Yenidje Tobacco Co* [1916] 2 Ch 426; *Loch v John Blackwood Ltd* [1924] AC 783; *Ebrahimi v Westbourne Galleries Ltd* [1972] 2 All ER 492; *Re Zinotty Properties Ltd* [1984] 3 All ER 754; *Re A & BC Chewing Gum Ltd* [1975] 1 All ER 1017.

conduct for the purpose of s 994 (see **17-62**), but will merit a winding up on the just and equitable ground. Equally, misconduct by an individual director may not amount to the conduct of the company's affairs in an unfairly prejudicial manner,[182] but may amount to a lack of probity which merits a winding up on the just and equitable ground, see **18-90**.

Procedural matters

18-75   An application to the court for a winding-up order may be made by a contributory,[183] defined as every person liable to contribute to the assets of a company in the event of its being wound up.[184] For example, a partly paid-up shareholder who remains liable to contribute the amount unpaid on his shares in the event of the company being wound up is a contributory, but it is rare now for shareholders to be partly-paid. A fully paid-up member must establish that he has a tangible interest in the winding up, defined as a *prima facie* probability of surplus assets remaining after the creditors have been paid for distribution amongst the shareholders.[185] In other words, in an insolvent company, a fully paid-up member has no *locus standi* to seek a winding up.

18-76   A further condition is that a contributory is not entitled to present a winding-up petition unless the number of members is reduced below two; or the shares held by him, or some of them, either were originally allotted to him, or have been held by him and registered in his name for at least six months during the 18 months before the commencement of the winding up, or have devolved on him through the death of a former holder (IA 1986, s 124).

18-77   A petitioner seeking a winding-up order on the just and equitable ground must come with clean hands.[186] If the breakdown in the conduct of the company's affairs is a result of the petitioner's own misconduct,[187] or the petitioner has acquiesced in the conduct of which he now complains,[188] the court will refuse the application. If the petitioner can establish sufficient grounds for petitioning, however, the fact that he also has an ulterior, perhaps personal, motive for pursuing the matter does not render those grounds insufficient.[189]

18-78   The court has a discretion under IA 1986, s 125(2) to refuse to make a winding-up order where there is some alternative remedy available to the petitioner and he is acting unreasonably in seeking to have the company wound up instead of pursuing that other remedy. An obvious alternative remedy is the ability to petition for relief on the unfairly prejudicial ground under CA 2006, s 994. In *Re a company (No 001363 of 1988), ex p S-P*[190] the court accepted that the availability of relief, possibly wider relief, under the unfairly prejudicial remedy does not of itself make it plainly unreasonable to seek a winding-up order so as to justify striking out the petition. However, winding up is a remedy of last resort and, given

---

[182]   See *Re Charnley Davies Ltd (No 2)* [1990] BCLC 760 at 783, also **17-78**.   [183]   IA 1986, s 124(1).

[184]   IA 1986, s 79(1); every present and past member is included in the definition: s 74(1). In the case of a company limited by shares, no contribution is required from any member exceeding the amount (if any) unpaid on the shares in respect of which he is a liable as a present or past member: s 74(2)(d).

[185]   *Re Rica Gold Washing Co* (1879) 11 Ch D 36; *Re Expanded Plugs Ltd* [1966] 1 All ER 877; *Re Othery Construction Ltd* [1966] 1 WLR 69; *Re Bellador Silk Ltd* [1965] 1 All ER 667. See also *Re Chesterfield Catering Co Ltd* [1976] 3 All ER 294 at 299 where Oliver J suggested that 'tangible interest' is not limited to surplus assets but could cover where, as a member of the company, the shareholder will achieve some advantage or avoid or minimise some disadvantage which would accrue to him by virtue of his membership of the company.   [186]   *Ebrahimi v Westbourne Galleries Ltd* [1972] 2 All ER 492 at 507, per Lord Cross.

[187]   *Ebrahimi v Westbourne Galleries Ltd* [1972] 2 All ER 492 at 507, per Lord Cross.

[188]   *Re Fildes Bros Ltd* [1970] 1 All ER 923.   [189]   *Bryanston Finance Ltd v De Vries* [1976] 1 All ER 25.

[190]   [1989] BCLC 579.

the width of the jurisdiction under CA 2006, s 994, generally the courts would expect a petitioner to seek alternative relief under the unfairly prejudicial jurisdiction.[191]

18-79 Another option which may be open to the aggrieved shareholder is to exit from the company by selling his shares via a purchase mechanism provided by the articles of association or pursuant to an offer to acquire his shares made by the other shareholders. The courts initially took quite a strict line and regarded a refusal to use such mechanisms as unreasonable and ground for striking out the winding-up petition.[192] This approach was somewhat harsh, given that in many instances the mechanism in the articles or offer requires the petitioner to accept a valuation of his shares as determined by the company's auditor. Petitioners often feel that such valuations are arbitrary and biased in favour of the majority shareholder hence their preference for obtaining a winding-up order from the court.

18-80 The strict position altered with the decision in *Virdi v Abbey Leisure Ltd*[193] which established that there is no hard-and-fast rule that a petitioner who declines to utilise an exit mechanism in the articles or to accept an offer to acquire his shares is necessarily acting unreasonably in pursuing a winding-up order.[194] It depends on the fairness of the purchase mechanism and in *Virdi* the Court of Appeal found that the petitioner's refusal to use the mechanism was not unreasonable, given that the value of his shares might be discounted under that scheme though on the facts a discount was inappropriate.[195] But where a fair offer is available,[196] a petitioner will be acting unreasonably in seeking to have the company wound up rather than pursuing that alternative: he is not entitled to his day or month in court.[197]

Grounds for the petition

18-81 The courts have been reluctant to limit the just and equitable jurisdiction by categorising the grounds on which a petition might be brought but certain recognised (and overlapping) categories have developed over the years which centre on quasi-partnerships (see **18-87**, though the jurisdiction is not limited to quasi-partnerships) and on the breakdown in relations between the parties and/or a lack of probity in the conduct of the company's affairs.[198] In *Re Yenidje Tobacco Co Ltd*[199] the relationship between the two shareholders (who were also the directors) had completely broken down. They refused to talk to one another and all communications were through a third party. The court found that the company was in essence a partnership and that there was such a state of animosity between

---

[191] See, for example, *Re a Company (No 004415 of 1996)* [1997] 1 BCLC 479.

[192] See *Re a Company (No 002567 of 1982)* [1983] 2 All ER 854; *Re a Company (No 004377 of 1986)* [1987] BCLC 94 at 103; *Re a Company (No 003843 of 1986)* [1987] BCLC 562; *Re a Company (No 003096 of 1987)* (1988) 4 BCC 80; *Re a Company (No 005685 of 1988), ex p Schwarcz (No 2)* [1989] BCLC 427 at 452.

[193] [1990] BCLC 342, CA.

[194] See *Re a Company (No 00330 of 1991), ex p Holden* [1991] BCLC 597 at 604.

[195] [1990] BCLC 342 at 349. See also *Re a Company (No 001363 of 1988), ex p S-P* [1989] BCLC 579 where the petitioner's refusal to accept an offer for his shares under the articles was not unreasonable when there was a dispute as to the number of shares to which he was actually entitled.

[196] The guidance as to what is a fair offer provided in *O'Neill v Phillips* [1999] 2 BCLC 1 at 16–17, see **17-66**, will be influential on this point.   [197] See *Fuller v Cyracuse Ltd* [2001] 1 BCLC 187 at 193.

[198] See Chesterman, 'The Just and Equitable Winding Up of Small Private Companies' (1973) 36 MLR 129; Prentice, 'Winding up on the Just and Equitable Ground' (1973) 89 LQR 107.

[199] [1916] 2 Ch 426. See also *Symington v Symington Quarries Ltd* 1906 SC 121; *Re Davis and Collett Ltd* [1935] Ch 693; *Re Wondoflex Textiles Pty Ltd* [1951] VLR 458; *Re Worldhams Park Golf Course Ltd, Whidbourne v Troth* [1998] 1 BCLC 554; *Jesner v Jarrad Properties Ltd* [1993] BCLC 1032; *Langley Ward Ltd v Trevor* [2011] EWHC 1893 at [15].

the parties as to preclude all reasonable hope of reconciliation or friendly co-operation.[200] In such circumstances, it is just and equitable that the company be wound up. But the jurisdiction is not limited to situations of deadlock[201] and in looking at a lack of probity in the conduct of the company's affairs, the court looks for conduct 'which substantially impairs those rights and protections to which shareholders, both under statute and contract, are entitled'.[202] In *Loch v John Blackwood Ltd*[203] the directors failed to hold general meetings or submit accounts or recommend a dividend. Instead the majority shareholder treated the business as if it was his own business and ran it down with a view to forcing the minority shareholder to sell out at an undervalue. Though the company was not deadlocked, the lack of probity in the conduct of the company's affairs merited a winding-up order.[204]

18-82 It was also possible to get a winding-up order if it was or became impossible or illegal to achieve the main objectives for which a company was formed.[205] These loss of substratum cases, as they were known, are obsolete now as modern drafting techniques ensure that companies have many and varied objects such that loss of substratum is not an issue and, in any event, companies formed under the CA 2006 have unrestricted objects unless the parties choose to restrict them (see s 31).

The modern jurisdiction

18-83 The landmark modern authority on the just and equitable jurisdiction is the decision of the House of Lords in *Ebrahimi v Westbourne Galleries Ltd*[206] which established that, where a company has the characteristics of a quasi-partnership, as described by Lord Wilberforce, see **18-87**, the court may subject the exercise of legal rights to equitable considerations, i.e. considerations of a personal character arising between one individual and another which may make it unjust or inequitable to insist on strict legal rights or to exercise them in a particular way. It may therefore be just and equitable to wind up a company where the majority have acted in disregard of those equitable considerations.

18-84 In this instance, two shareholders (E and N) had formed a company which operated on a quasi-partnership basis including an understanding that both would be involved in the management of the company. N's son later joined the company. The majority shareholders (N and his son) were entitled in those circumstances subsequently to exercise their undoubted legal power to remove the minority shareholder (E) as a director and, having done so, the House of Lords concluded that the only just and equitable course was to dissolve the association and to grant E a winding-up order under IA 1986, s 122(1)(g).

18-85 The House of Lords found that, as a matter of law, the majority shareholders had acted completely within their rights, within the provisions of the articles, and the Companies Act in removing E as a director. But the just and equitable jurisdiction was not limited

---

[200] [1916] 2 Ch 426 at 430, per Cozens Hardy MR.
[201] See *Ebrahimi v Westbourne Galleries Ltd* [1972] AC 360 at 376.
[202] *Loch v John Blackwood Ltd* [1924] AC 783 at 788, per Lord Shaw.   [203] [1924] AC 783.
[204] See also *Re Worldhams Park Golf Course Ltd, Whidbourne v Troth* [1998] 1 BCLC 554; see *Re Sunrise Radio Ltd, Kohli v Lit* [2010] 1 BCLC 367 at [308] (lack of probity indicated by improper allotments of shares would have merited a winding-up order); see also *Re Internet Investment Corporation Ltd* [2010] 1 BCLC 458.
[205] The doctrine originated in *Re Suburban Hotel Co* (1867) 2 Ch App 737. See also *Re Haven Gold Mining Co* (1882) 20 Ch D 151; *Re German Date Coffee Co* (1882) 20 Ch D 169; *Re Red Rock Gold Mining Co Ltd* (1889) 61 LT 785; *Re Baku Consolidated Oilfields Ltd* [1944] 1 All ER 24; *Re Kitson & Co Ltd* [1946] 1 All ER 435.
[206] [1972] 2 All ER 492, HL.

to proven cases of mala fides and the legal correctness of their conduct did not make it unassailable.

18-86 The words 'just and equitable' were:

'…a recognition of the fact that a limited company is more than a mere judicial entity, with a personality in law of its own: that there is room in company law for recognition of the fact that behind it, or amongst it, there are individuals, with rights, expectations and obligations inter se which are not necessarily submerged in the company structure. That structure is defined by the Companies Act 1948 and by the articles of association by which shareholders agree to be bound. In most companies and in most contexts, this definition is sufficient and exhaustive, equally so whether the company is large or small. The "just and equitable" provision does not, as the respondents suggest, entitle one party to disregard the obligation he assumes by entering a company, nor the court to dispense him from it. It does, as equity always does, enable the court to subject the exercise of legal rights to equitable considerations; considerations, that is, of a personal character arising between one individual and another, which may make it unjust, or inequitable, to insist on legal rights, or to exercise them in a particular way.'[207]

18-87 As to when these equitable considerations will arise, Lord Wilberforce noted:

'Certainly the fact that a company is a small one, or a private company, is not enough. There are very many of these where the association is a purely commercial one, of which it can safely be said that the basis of association is adequately and exhaustively laid down in the articles. The superimposition of equitable considerations requires something more, which typically may include one, or probably more, of the following elements: (i) an association formed or continued on the basis of a personal relationship, involving mutual confidence—this element will often be found where a pre-existing partnership has been converted into a limited company; (ii) an agreement, or understanding, that all, or some (for there may be "sleeping" members), of the shareholders shall participate in the conduct of the business; (iii) restriction on the transfer of the members' interest in the company—so that if confidence is lost, or one member is removed from management, he cannot take out his stake and go elsewhere. It is these, and analogous, factors which may bring into play the just and equitable clause, and they do so directly, through the force of the words themselves.'[208]

18-88 Lord Wilberforce went on to note that such companies are commonly, if confusingly, called quasi-partnerships, a term which must not obscure the fact that the parties are members in a company.[209]

18-89 The position then is that a winding-up order on the just and equitable ground may be sought where there is deadlock, or a lack of probity in the conduct of the company's affairs, or the inequitable use by the majority of their legal powers, subject to the court's discretion to refuse relief where there is some alternative available, etc, see **18-78**. It has already been noted that this judgment in *Ebrahimi* plays a key role in determining the scope of the unfairly prejudicial jurisdiction, as Lord Hoffmann acknowledged in *O'Neill v Phillips*,[210]

---

[207] [1972] 2 All ER 492 at 500.

[208] [1972] 2 All ER 492 at 500. See also *CVC/Opportunity Equity Partners Ltd v Demarco Almeida* [2002] 2 BCLC 108 at 117.

[209] [1972] 2 All ER 492 at 500. Though Lord Wilberforce cautioned against the use of that term, it has entered common parlance, especially in the context of the unfairly prejudicial jurisdiction, and it is too late now to limit its use.   [210] [1999] 2 BCLC 1.

see **17-51.** The question is whether there is any role left to be played by the winding-up remedy, given the availability of relief under s 994.

Relationship with the unfairly prejudicial remedy

18-90 The Court of Appeal made clear in *Hawkes v Cuddy*[211] that the winding-up jurisdiction remains an important shareholder remedy in its own right and there are cases where it will be the more appropriate remedy, and possibly the only remedy, available to a shareholder. A situation where relief will be available under IA 1986, s 122(1)(g), but not under the unfairly prejudicial jurisdiction, is where there is deadlock between the parties involving a breakdown in mutual trust (such as *Re Yenidje Ltd*,[212] see **18-81**) where winding up is warranted but where there is no objective unfairness to support a petition under CA 2006, s 994, see **17-62.** Equally, there may be cases of misconduct which will amount to a breach of probity within the *Lock v John Blackwood*[213] category, see **18-81**, but which do not amount to a carrying on of the company's affairs in an unfairly prejudicial manner. Again winding up on the just and equitable ground is an option in those circumstances.

18-91 Notwithstanding the clarification provided by *Hawkes v Cuddy*,[214] the width of the unfairly prejudicial jurisdiction and the attractiveness of a personal buy-out order, often on a pro-rata basis,[215] see **17-82**, and the effect of IA 1986, s 125(2), see **18-88**, mean that generally petitioners will continue to look to the unfairly prejudicial remedy rather than seek a winding-up order, but clearly the winding-up option remains available and may be desirable depending on the particular circumstances.

---

[211] [2009] 2 BCLC 427, overruling a controversial decision by Jonathan Parker J in *Re Guidezone Ltd* [2000] 2 BCLC 321 to the effect that the jurisdiction under IA 1986, s 122(1)(g) was, at the very least, no wider than CA 2006, s 994. The decision was much criticised as a unnecessary conflation of the two jurisdictions, not required by anything said by Lord Hoffmann in *O'Neill v Phillips*, see Boyle, *Minority Shareholders' Remedies* (2002), pp 96–100; Acton, 'Just and Equitable Winding up: the Strange Case of the Disappearing Jurisdiction' (2001) 22 Co Lawyer 134.   [212] [1916] 2 Ch 426.

[213] [1924] AC 783.   [214] [2009] 2 BCLC 427.

[215] As was pointed out in *Re Sunrise Radio Ltd, Kohli v Lit* [2010] 1 BCLC 387 at [303], a winding-up order will often be at break-up value and therefore will not necessarily be advantageous to the petitioning shareholder though it produces a pro-rata distribution of the realised assets for all shareholders.

PART IV

Corporate Finance—Share and Loan Capital

19

Share capital–capital raising and payment

A Introduction

19-1 This chapter considers the statutory rules governing share capital requirements, especially those relating to the allotment of, and payment for, shares. The share capital measures, while statutory, frequently reflect long-established common law rules.

19-2 The general approach is that the capital rules are stricter for public companies than for private companies.[1] This position is a reflection of the general policy that public companies with their greater exposure to investors and creditors should be subject to a more rigorous regime than private companies. More specifically, the stricter capital rules with respect to public companies reflect the requirements of the Second EC Company Law Directive (hereafter the Second Directive) with regard to the establishment and maintenance of share capital in public companies.[2] The requirements of the Directive limited the extent to which amendments could be made in the CA 2006 to the capital rules as they apply to public companies.

19-3 In 2007, the European Commission consulted on possible simplification (including repeal) of a broad sweep of company law, accounting and audit requirements including the Second Directive.[3] The overall response to the consultation, however, was that the focus should be on simplification rather than repeal of the Directives on the basis that they bring legal certainty and repealing them would involve additional costs, though the UK's preference was for outright repeal of the Second Directive, see **2-24**. However, a feasibility study conducted on behalf of the Commission on an alternative regime to the capital maintenance regime,[4] published in February 2008, concluded that in fact the Second Directive is flexible in many ways and its requirements do not cause significant

---

[1] As 99.7% of the companies on the register are private companies, the stricter rules have limited application, but they may influence the choice of type of company. The CA 2006 also significantly relaxes the regime for private companies so it is unsurprising that it is the preferred type of company for most businesses, unless they have some specific need for public company status, see **1-41**. At 31 March 2011, there were 2,279,700 private companies (99.7% of all companies) and 7,600 public companies (0.3%), figures for England and Wales, see Companies House, *Statistical Tables on Companies Registration Activities*, Table A2.

[2] Directive 77/91/EEC, OJ L 26/1, 31.1.1977. See generally Edwards, *EC Company Law* (1999), Ch III.

[3] See Communication from the Commission on a simplified business environment for companies in the areas of company law, accounting and auditing: COM (2007) 394, 10.7.2007.

[4] See KPMG, *Feasibility study on an alternative to the capital maintenance regime established by the Second Company Law Directive 77/91/EEC of 13 December 1976 and an examination of the impact on profit distribution of the new EU accounting regime* (January 2008).

operational problems for companies.[5] Subsequently, limited changes have been made to the Directive as part of the simplification programme.[6]

19-4 As far as private companies are concerned, their capital requirements are a domestic matter not subject to the Second Directive and there is room for a more laissez-faire approach. In fact, most companies on the register are rarely troubled by the statutory requirements as to share capital with 77% of all companies (1.8m companies) having an issued share capital of £100 or less and 92% approximately having a share capital of £10,000 or less (all figures are for 2010/11, England and Wales).[7] For those companies with less than £100, many of these are £2 companies with an issued share capital of two £1 pound shares. In such companies no share capital is ever issued subsequent to the initial two shares on incorporation and for these companies the rules governing share capital are irrelevant. Even outside the £100 category, share capital is relatively insignificant with only 4.2% of the register having between £10,000 and £100,000 issued share capital and 2.3% having between £100,000 and £1m. Only 1.6% of the register, some 37,500 companies, had an issued share capital in excess of £1m. That final statistic also cautions us against assuming that only public companies have significant share capital. There were only 7,600 public companies on the register in 2010/11 so the 37,500 companies with an issued share capital in excess of £1m must include a large number of private companies. Given this overall position as to share capital, it is not surprising that the Company Law Review noted that: 'our limited enquiries tend to indicate that creditors and potential creditors do not any longer regard the amount of a company's issued share capital as a significant matter when it comes to deciding whether or not to extend credit'.[8] This absence of significant equity (share) funding means that such companies must fund their activities in other ways, primarily, but not exclusively, through loan capital (typically term loans and bank overdrafts) which may mean that the company is subject to greater economic pressures than would be the case if it had more substantial equity funds. Larger companies increasingly look to the bond markets for capital rather than seek to raise equity capital. At the lowest end of the scale, where there is the greatest reliance on bank finance, directors/shareholders in these companies may have to commit themselves to personal guarantees to secure bank lending so reducing the value to them of limited liability. Overall, the absence of significant equity funding acts as a brake on the development of these businesses though obviously many of the micro-businesses are content to remain at that level. For those with an interest in expanding their business, once they have exhausted their own personal resources, attracting equity funding to smaller companies can be a problem.[9] Equally, for many entrepreneurs, the risk of losing control of the company as their holdings are diluted by further issues of shares acts as a deterrent in any event to seeking further equity investment. It is also a form of capital

---

[5] The Commission concluded therefore that 'no follow-up measures or changes in the Second Company Law Directive are foreseeable in the immediate future', see Response of the Commission to the results of the KPMG study mentioned in n 4.

[6] See Directive 2006/68/EC amending Directive 77/91/EEC, OJ L 264, 25.09.2006, p 32. See Government Response to consultation on implementation of amendments to the Second Company Law Directive (2007), URN 07/1300; also DTI, 'Implementation of the Companies Act 2006' (2007), URN 07/666, Ch 6.

[7] See Companies House, *Statistical Tables on Companies Register Activities 2010–2011*, Table A6.

[8] Company Law Review, *Strategic Framework* (1999), para 5.4.3.

[9] For the difficulties faced by SMEs in raising equity capital, see BIS, *The Provision of Growth Capital to UK Small and Medium Sized Enterprises* (2009) (the Rowlands Review on behalf of BIS and HM Treasury); and see HM Treasury/BIS, *A Plan for Growth* (March 2011), paras 2.88–2.114, setting out Government plans for tax and other incentives and measures to ensure a supply of debt and equity capital for businesses. It is accepted that the equity gap is acute for investments between £250,000 and £2m, but the Rowlands review also highlighted the difficulties where funding between £2m and £10m is sought.

raising which is less familiar to them than debt finance, though the difficulties now in accessing debt finance may force a re-think on their part.

B Share capital requirements

Nominal value of shares

19-5 Shares must have a fixed nominal (or par) value (CA 2006, s 542(1)) and this figure is settled on incorporation (it may change thereafter as and when new classes of shares are created or capital restructuring takes place). As discussed at **1-3,** A and B may form a company with shares with a nominal value of £1, equally they may have shares with a nominal value of 1p. Typically, the figure is set quite low, for example, £1, 25p and 1p are quite common nominal values. The relevance of par value to the shareholder is that the company may not issue its shares for less than the par value, see **19-24.** Of course, once the company has been trading for a while and is prospering, A and B will not be willing to sell further shares at £1. They will want a higher figure to reflect the increased value of the company. For example, they might consider that £2 is more appropriate in which case C who buys at £2 is said to contribute £1 of share capital and £1 of share premium, premium being any sum which is obtained above the nominal or par value.

19-6 Companies used to have shares of a high par value but today low par values are the norm as they are seen to increase the marketability of the shares and are preferred by investors. Many jurisdictions allow shares of no par value[10] and the issue was considered by the Company Law Review which noted that the requirement of a nominal value is an anachronism which is confusing for the layman. It initially favoured the mandatory introduction of no par shares for all companies while recognising that the requirements of the Second Directive preclude such a change for public companies.[11] On consultation, a variety of concerns emerged about these proposals, not least regarding the transitional difficulties which would arise given the many contracts and agreements which make express reference to par values. The major obstacle, however, was that par values would have to be retained for public companies so there would be different requirements in this regard for public and private companies. This outcome would make transition from one classification to the other difficult which would be a serious drawback in practice. In the light of these concerns, the Company Law Review reluctantly concluded that the obligation for all companies to have shares with a nominal or par value should be retained,[12] hence CA 2006, s 542(1) requires shares to have a fixed nominal value.[13]

19-7 Nominal or par values may be denominated in any currency and different classes of shares may be denominated in different currencies (CA 2006, s 542(3)). The minimum authorised allotted share capital for a public company (see **19-10**) may be in sterling (£50,000) or

---

[10] The Gedge Committee in 1954 (Cmnd 9112) and the Jenkins Committee in 1962 (Cmnd 1749) recommended that no par value shares be permitted in the UK but an attempt to introduce such reforms in the Companies Act 1967 failed.

[11] See Company Law Review, *Strategic Framework* (1999), paras 5.4.26–5.4.33; *Company Formation and Capital Maintenance* (1999), para 3.8; *Capital Maintenance: Other Issues* (2000), paras 8–23.

[12] Company Law Review, *Completing the Structure* (2000), paras 7.2–7.3; *Final Report,* vol I (2001), para 10.7.

[13] An allotment of a share that does not have a fixed nominal value is void: CA 2006, s 542(2); and the company and any officer in default commits an offence: s 542(4), (5).

euros (€57,100, the prescribed euro equivalent)[14] but it cannot be partially in sterling and partially in euros.[15]

19-8 On formation, a company with a share capital provides the registrar of companies with a statement of capital and initial holdings (CA 2006, s 9(4)(a)), see **1-25**. That statement of capital contains the following information:

(1) the total number of shares of the company to be taken on formation by the subscribers to the memorandum (see s 8(1));

(2) the aggregate nominal value of those shares;

(3) for each class of shares,[16] the number of shares of that class, their aggregate nominal value; and the prescribed particulars of the rights attached to those shares; and

(4) the amount to be paid up[17] and the amount (if any) to be unpaid on each share[18] (s 10(2)).

Thereafter, every time the company makes a further allotment of shares, it must deliver to the registrar a return of allotment[19] and a statement of capital setting out the total capital position of the company[20] so ensuring that the public record always contains an up-to-date statement of the position.[21]

Issued and allotted share capital

19-9 While the terms 'issued' and 'allotted' with respect to shares are often used interchangeably, they refer to distinct processes.[22] For the purposes of the Companies Acts, shares are taken to be allotted when a person acquires the unconditional right to be included in the company's register of members in respect of those shares.[23] An allotment creates an enforceable contract for the issue of the shares and the shares are issued when an application to the company has been followed by allotment and notification to the purchaser and completed by entry on the company's register of members.[24]

---

[14] CA 2006, s 763 and The Companies (Authorised Minimum) Regulations 2009, SI 2009/2425, reg 2.

[15] CA 2006, ss 763(1), 765(1).

[16] Most companies have only one type of share, ordinary shares, and a company with only one type of share does not have classes of shares and so this information is not required.

[17] The amount to be paid up includes any share premium.

[18] Most shares are issued fully paid up now so usually there is no amount unpaid, see **19-17**.

[19] See CA 2006, s 555(2); also see The Companies (Shares and Share Capital) Regulations 2009, SI 2009/388, as to the prescribed contents of the return of allotment.

[20] CA 2006, s 555(3); and see s 555(4) as to the prescribed contents of the statement of capital.

[21] Unfortunately, it has proved difficult for companies with complex share capital histories to provide some of the information required in the statement of capital and BIS has consulted on amendments which might be made to address these practical difficulties, see BIS, *Companies Act 2006: Statements of Capital, Consultation on Financial Information required* (November 2009), URN 09/1488. The intention in due course is to simplify the financial information requirements for all companies in all statements of capital and the Government is waiting for a suitable legislative vehicle to become available.

[22] See *Clarke's Case* (1878) 8 Ch D 635 at 638, CA; also CA 2006, s 546(1). It would seem that the meaning of 'issue' depends on the context of the enactment in which the word occurs: *National Westminster Bank plc v Inland Revenue Commissioners* [1994] 3 All ER 1, HL.

[23] CA 2006, s 558; see also s 546. The company must maintain a register of its members: s 113, see **14-69**.

[24] *National Westminster Bank plc v Inland Revenue Commissioners* [1994] 3 All ER 1, HL (tax relief to investors in shares was altered in respect of shares 'issued' after 16 March 1993: here shares had been allotted prior to that date but registration took place after the date: held (3–2 majority) shares were 'issued' after 16 March 1993). See also *Clarke's Case* (1878) 8 Ch D 635 at 638, CA.

Minimum capital requirements

Public companies

19-10 Public companies are required by the Second Directive to have a minimum share capital and the authorised minimum in relation to the nominal value of a public company's allotted share capital is £50,000 or €57,100 (the prescribed euro equivalent).[25]

19-11 A company registered as a public company on its original incorporation may not do business or exercise any borrowing powers unless the registrar of companies has certified under CA 2006, s 761 that he is satisfied that the nominal value of the company's allotted share capital is not less than the authorised minimum.[26] A trading certificate to this effect is conclusive evidence that the company is entitled to do business and exercise any borrowing powers.[27] Once a public company has this trading certificate, it can redenominate the minimum capital into any currency, subject to any prohibition or restriction in the company's articles.[28]

19-12 If a company does business or exercises any borrowing powers without this trading certificate, the company and any officer in default is liable to a fine (CA 2006, s 767(1)), but the validity of any transaction entered into by the company is not affected (s 767(3)). If, however, a company enters into a transaction in contravention of this requirement and fails to comply with its obligations in that connection within 21 days of being called upon to do so, the directors of the company who were the directors at the time the company entered into the transaction are jointly and severally liable to indemnify the other party to the transaction in respect of any loss or damage suffered by him by reason of the company's failure to comply with those obligations.[29]

19-13 This requirement of a trading certificate is of limited practical significance as most companies are formed as private companies and subsequently re-register as public companies (see **1-52**), a process which requires them to have the minimum share capital,[30] but does not require them to obtain a trading certificate.

19-14 In addition to requiring public companies to have a minimum allotted share capital, the Second Directive also provides that where a public company has suffered a serious loss of capital so that its net assets are half or less of its called-up share capital, the directors must call a general meeting to consider whether any, and if so what, steps should be taken to deal with the situation.[31]

Private companies

19-15 There is no minimum share capital required for private companies, hence approximately 77% of all private companies have an issued share capital of £100 or less, as noted at **19-4**. As discussed in Chapter 2, the lack of a minimum share capital for private companies has encouraged businesses in other Member States to incorporate here which has given

---

[25] CA 2006, ss 763, 765. See The Companies (Authorised Minimum) Regulations 2009, SI 2009/2425, reg 2; Second Directive 77/91/EEC [1977] OJ L 26/1, art 6.

[26] The application for a trading certificate must be accompanied by a statement of compliance that the company meets the requirements for a trading certificate and the registrar may accept that statement as sufficient evidence of the matters stated in it: CA 2006, s 762(2), (3).

[27] CA 2006, s 761(4). A public company registered as such on its original incorporation which has not obtained a trading certificate and more than a year has expired since it was registered as a public company may be wound up by the court: IA 1986, s 122(1)(b).   [28] CA 2006, ss 617(4), 622(1), (7).

[29] CA 2006, s 767(3), (4), although it would be difficult to establish such loss or damage.

[30] See CA 2006, ss 90(2)(b), 91(1)(a).

[31] CA 2006, s 656; and Second Directive 77/91/EEC, OJ L 26/1, 31.1.1977, art 17.

rise to considerable jurisprudence from the European Court of Justice on the freedom of establishment and corporate mobility, see the discussion at **2-31** et seq.

Paid-up share capital

19-16 Shares may be fully or partly paid-up. In the latter case, the company can make calls on the shareholder up to the amount of the share price which has not been paid. For example, a share may be issued at £3.50 of which only £1.50p is paid up on allotment leaving the company later to call up the remaining £2. It is uncommon today to find companies with partly-paid shares as they prefer to obtain from the outset the capital which they have raised and so avoid the administrative burden of making calls on shareholders. Also any company which adopts the model articles for private companies (see **4-2**) is restricted to issuing fully paid shares[32] which is not a problem given that the amount of issued share capital in private companies is very small, as noted at **19-4**.

19-17 As for public companies, they must not allot a share except as paid up at least as to one-quarter of its nominal value and the whole of any premium, i.e. any amount in excess of the nominal value of the share (CA 2006, s 586(1)).[33] Given the insignificance of the nominal value in respect of the market value of shares in most public companies, the effect of this requirement that the whole of the premium be paid up is that shares in public companies are issued fully paid and, for listed companies, it is in any event a condition of listing that all share capital be fully paid up.[34]

C Issuing shares at par, premium or a discount

19-18 A company may issue its shares:

(1) at par, i.e. for the nominal or par value set by the company (nominal value is discussed at **19-5**); or

(2) at a premium, i.e. for a figure in excess of the nominal or par value; but

(3) it must not issue its shares at a discount, i.e. for a figure less than the nominal or par value.

Issue at a premium

19-19 While the initial subscribers to the memorandum may take their shares at the nominal or par value, it is common thereafter for shares to be issued at a premium, i.e. at more than par value. For example, a share with a par value of £1 may be issued for £1.30, £1.50 or any higher figure which the market will bear.

19-20 There is no requirement for companies to issue shares at a premium.[35] It depends on the circumstances of each case whether it is prudent or possible to do so and this is a matter

---

[32] See Companies (Model Articles) Regulations 2008, SI 2008/3229, reg 3, Sch 1, art 21(1) which provides that no share is to be issued for less than the aggregate of its nominal value and any premium to be paid to the company in consideration for its issue.

[33] In the event of a breach, the allotment is still valid, but the allottee is liable to pay the company the minimum amount which should have been received in respect of the shares less any consideration actually paid: CA 2006, s 586(3).   [34] See Listing Rules, LR 2.2.4(2).

[35] *Hilder v Dexter* [1902] AC 474; *Lowry v Consolidated African Selection Trust Ltd* [1940] 2 All ER 545.

for the directors to decide.[36] An example of a situation where the company may forgo some of the available premium is where the company makes a rights issue[37] to raise further capital from its shareholders and does so, as is normally the practice, at a price which is at a discount to the market price. In this instance, the company forgoes the maximum available premium, but the discount ensures (usually) that the shares are taken up and, in some cases, this may mean that the company saves on the expense of having the issue underwritten (see **19-26**). In some circumstances, however, directors may be in breach of their duties to the company in not obtaining the greatest financial return from an issue of shares.[38] In *Re Sunrise Radio Ltd, Kohli v Lit*,[39] which is discussed in detail at **17-47**, the court concluded that issuing shares at par in circumstances where they could have been issued for a significant premium, particularly when the directors (as the majority shareholders who took up the shares—the minority not being in a position to do so) benefited appreciably from the issue at par, was a breach of duty and unfairly prejudicial to the petitioner.[40]

19-21 A premium may arise whether shares are issued for cash or for a non-cash consideration. Shares issued for a consideration other than cash are issued at a premium if the value of the assets in consideration of which they are issued is more than the nominal value of the shares. The point arose in *Henry Head & Co Ltd v Ropner Holdings Ltd*[41] where there was an amalgamation of two shipping companies through the formation of a new holding company. There was a one-for-one exchange of shares by the shareholders of the two companies for shares in the holding company. The assets of the companies were undervalued and were worth £5m more than the nominal value of the shares in the new holding company. The question was whether it was correct for the holding company to transfer £5m to a share premium account. The court found that it was necessary for a transfer to be made to the share premium account and this decision was followed in *Shearer (Inspector of Taxes) v Bercain Ltd*.[42]

19-22 When a company issues shares at a premium, whether for cash or otherwise, a sum equal to the aggregate amount or value of the premiums on those shares must be transferred to a share premium account (CA 2006, s 610). There are some exceptions to this requirement set out in ss 611–614 which identify certain circumstances when either a share premium account is not required or only a limited amount need be transferred to such an account. These provisions were introduced in response to the decisions in *Henry Head & Co Ltd v Ropner Holdings Ltd*[43] and *Shearer (Inspector of Taxes) v Bercain Ltd*,[44] noted above, and the net effect is to allow certain group reconstructions and mergers to take place without a transfer (or only a limited transfer) to a share premium account so releasing certain assets which may be distributed to the members as a dividend.

---

[36] *Hilder v Dexter* [1902] AC 474 at 480, per Lord Davey.

[37] Essentially, an offer of further shares to the company's existing shareholders, see the discussion at **19-35**.

[38] *Hilder v Dexter* [1902] AC 474 at 481, per Lord Davey, an allotment at par when a premium is available may be open to challenge as improvident or an abuse or in excess of the powers of management committed to the directors. See also *Lowry v Consolidated African Selection Trust Ltd* [1940] 2 All ER 545 at 565.

[39] [2010] 1 BCLC 367.

[40] A subsequent increase in authorised share capital and a disapplication of the rights issue requirement was also unfairly prejudicial, though no shares had been issued pursuant to that authority, when the petitioner had been misled as to the calling of the general meeting where these matters were agreed, see [2010] 1 BCLC 367 at [135].   [41] [1951] 2 All ER 994.

[42] [1980] 3 All ER 295.   [43] [1951] 2 All ER 994.   [44] [1980] 3 All ER 295.

19-23 Share premium is treated in most respects as share capital and its use is restricted to writing off any expenses incurred or commission paid on the issue of the shares in respect of which the premium has arisen and to paying up new shares to be allotted to members as fully paid bonus shares (see **19-55**).[45]

Prohibition on issue at a discount

19-24 A company's shares must not be allotted at a discount, i.e. for less than the nominal or par value (CA 2006, s 580(1)). If shares are allotted in contravention of this requirement, the allottee is liable to pay the company an amount equal to the amount of the discount, with interest at the appropriate rate.[46] The company and any officer in default is liable on conviction to a fine (s 590). This statutory rule reflects the long-established common law to this effect laid down in *Ooregum Gold Mining Co of India Ltd v Roper*.[47]

19-25 In this case, a company purported to issue £1 preference shares credited with 15 shillings paid up, leaving only five shillings to be paid on allotment. The House of Lords held that there was no power under the Companies Acts to do this and the allotment was ultra vires with the allottees liable to pay the full amount of £1 on each of their shares.[48] As Lord Macnaghten noted, in a limited liability company shareholders purchase immunity from liability beyond the amount due on their shares, but they do so on the basis that they remain liable up to that limit.[49]

19-26 As a limited exception to the no-discount rule, companies are permitted to pay underwriting commissions, provided such payments are authorised by the articles and the amount involved does not exceed specified limits (CA 2006, ss 552–553). Underwriting involves the use of professional intermediaries (such as investment banks and institutional investors) which undertake, in return for a fee, to subscribe or procure subscriptions for shares to the extent that the public or other persons do not subscribe for them. This fee could be prohibited as a discount on the shares were it not for s 553 expressly permitting such payments.

19-27 Finally, it should be noted that, while a company may not allot shares at a discount to the nominal value, payment for shares may be in the form of money or money's worth (CA 2006, s 582(1)). Where money's worth is received and the company is a private company, the courts will not inquire into the adequacy of the consideration unless it is illusory or manifestly inadequate.[50] In such circumstances, it is possible that the issue of shares for a

---

[45] CA 2006, s 610(2). The CA 2006 tightened the rules on use of share premium. It is no longer possible to use the share premium account to write off (1) the company's preliminary expenses on formation, or (2) the expenses incurred, commission paid or discount allowed on any issue of debentures or in providing for the premium payable on redemption of debentures of the company, as was the case under CA 1985, s 130.

[46] CA 2006, s 580(2). Directors who allot shares at a discount are guilty of a breach of duty to the company and are liable to pay the amount of the discount and interest to the company if that amount cannot be recovered from the allottee or holder of the shares, as where the shares have passed into the hands of a bona fide purchaser for value from the original allottee: *Hirsche v Sims* [1894] AC 654, PC.

[47] [1892] AC 125, HL. See also *Re Eddystone Marine Insurance Co* [1893] 3 Ch 9; *Welton v Saffery* [1897] AC 299. The rule cannot be evaded by issuing convertible debentures at a discount which are capable of being immediately converted to ordinary shares: *Mosely v Koffyfontein Mines Ltd* [1904] 2 Ch 108.

[48] Allowing the company to allot at a discount is unfair to shareholders who paid the full amount and misleading for creditors who rely on the stated par value as indicating the minimum price at which the company has issued and will issue its shares.

[49] [1892] AC 125 at 145. Equally, the company cannot thereafter increase the member's liability to contribute to the company's share capital without his consent: CA 2006, s 25(1)(b).

[50] *Re Wragg Ltd* [1897] 1 Ch 796.

non-cash consideration disguises what is, in effect, an issue of shares at a discount. This matter is considered at **19-62**.

D Alteration of share capital

19-28 A company needs flexibility in dealing with its share capital to enable it to react to changing business circumstances and so the statute allows a company to alter its share capital in the following ways, subject to any prohibition or restriction in the company's articles. Authorisation from the shareholders is also required, usually by an ordinary resolution of the shareholders (a special resolution, if it is a reduction of capital). A company may (CA 2006, s 617):

(1) increase its share capital by allotting new shares (discussed at **19-30**);

(2) reduce its share capital (discussed at **20-56**);

(3) sub-divide or consolidate all or any of its share capital into shares of smaller/larger amount than its existing shares. Sub-division involves dividing a share into a number of new shares (for example, £1 shares can be sub-divided into four 25p shares or ten 10p shares) and may be done to increase the marketability of shares where companies feel the nominal value is too high. It may also be necessary if the company wants to issue new shares at a nominal value lower than the current nominal value since the company cannot issue shares at a discount to the nominal value, as noted at **19–24**. Consolidation involves combining a number of shares into a new share of commensurate nominal value. For example, 10 £1 shares may be consolidated into one £10 share. This process is less common now as investors prefer shares of lower rather than higher nominal value, but it is sometimes used when a capital reorganisation leaves the company with shares of an unwieldy nominal value, for example, 12.5p shares may be consolidated into 50p or £1 shares. This exercise has no financial impact on a shareholder who now holds fewer shares of greater nominal value but representing the same percentage interest in the company as the shareholder held previously;

(4) reconvert any stock into paid-up shares of any denomination. It is rare for UK companies to have stock (which arises from a conversion of fully paid shares) but this power is retained to allow any company which still has stock to convert it back into shares (CA 2006, s 620). Companies are no longer able to convert shares into stock;

(5) redenominate all or any of its share capital into another currency. The ability to redenominate shares into another currency was introduced by the CA 2006, ss 622–628. It is intended to facilitate companies in changing their capital structures without the need for more complex schemes involving a reduction or purchase of shares followed by the cancellation of those shares and a new allotment in a different currency. It is open to any company, public or private, to redenominate its shares into any currency or into multiple currencies.

19-29 Notice of any of these alterations must be given to the registrar of companies typically within one month of the alteration (within 15 days, if a reduction of capital).[51] In each

---

[51] CA 2006, s 555(2) (allotment of shares), s 619(1) (sub-division and consolidation), s 621(1) (redenomination). In the case of a reduction of capital, notice must be given within 15 days of the passing of the resolution for reduction: ss 627(1), 644(1).

case the notice must be accompanied by a statement of capital.[52] In the event of default in complying with any of these disclosure requirements, the company and any officer in default is liable to a fine.[53]

E Allotment of shares

19-30 Quite apart from the ability to raise money for the company, the authority granted to the directors to make an allotment of shares is important because an allotment will affect the balance of power within the company, given that shares typically carry one vote per share. An allotment may be used improperly to prejudice minority shareholders by diluting their holdings, or to alter the voting position so as to ensure that the directors cannot be voted out of office or that opponents cannot be appointed to the board, or to prevent a takeover of the company. Statutory controls are imposed therefore to restrain directors from acting improperly in this regard and these are discussed at **19-32**.

19-31 The statutory framework also operates against a backdrop of other constraints which should prevent improper allotments. First, directors are under a duty to exercise their powers for the purpose for which they are conferred, CA 2006, s 171, and a power to allot shares is primarily, though not exclusively, conferred in order that the company may raise capital, see **8-55** et seq. Secondly, the directors must also be mindful of their duty to act to promote the success of the company under s 172(1), having regard (amongst other matters) to the need to act fairly as between the members (s 172(1)(f)), see **9-30** et seq. Thirdly, in an appropriate case, minority shareholders may petition for relief under CA 2006, s 994, alleging that the allotment amounts to the conduct of the company's affairs in an unfairly prejudicial manner, see **17-46** et seq.

Authorisation to allot

19-32 As a general rule, directors may exercise the power to allot shares only if authorised to do so by the articles or by an ordinary resolution (CA 2006, s 551(1)).[54] Authorisation may be general or particular, conditional or unconditional, and must specify the maximum number of shares and may be for a period of up to five years (s 551(2)–(3)). Public companies typically seek authority to allot at successive annual general meetings and, for listed companies, they are mindful of the influential guidelines on allotment issued by the Association of British Insurers (ABI).[55] On allotment, ABI members will regard as routine (and therefore as shareholders will usually support) requests by the company for authorisation to allot new shares in an amount up to one-third of a company's existing issued share capital. They will also regard as routine requests for authorisation to allot a further one-third (by reference to the company's existing share capital so two-thirds

---

[52] CA 2006, ss 555(3), 619(2), 621(2), 625(2), 627(2), 644(1).

[53] CA 2006, ss 557(1), 619(4), 621(4), 625(4), 627(7), 644(9).

[54] Allotments must be notified to the registrar of companies within one month of the allotment: CA 2006, s 555; companies must register an allotment in the register of members within two months of the allotment: s 554.

[55] See ABI, *Guidelines on directors' powers to allot share capital and disapply shareholders' pre-emption rights*—the latest version was drawn up in 2008 and amended in November 2009. The intention is to allow companies greater flexibility, especially in the context of rights issues, see **19-53**.

in all) where the allotment (of that further one-third) is purely on a rights basis (rights issues are discussed below).[56]

19-33 An important exception to the general rule that authorisation is required is that, in the case of a private company with only one class of shares[57] (and most private companies fall into this category), the directors may allot shares of that class, without the need for any express authorisation, *unless* they are prohibited from doing so by the company's articles (CA 2006, s 550). This general permission to allot was introduced by the CA 2006 following a recommendation by the Company Law Review that the requirement for authorisation to allot shares should not apply to private companies.[58] In many private companies, the directors and the shareholders are the same people so the Review considered it an unnecessary complication to require A and B, as shareholders, to authorise A and B, as directors, to allot shares. In so far as there is potential for abuse of this power, it is constrained, as noted at **19-31**, by the requirements of the directors' duties in CA 2006, Pt 10, and the potential for minority relief under s 994. Furthermore, the requirement for authorisation remains if:

(1) the articles prohibit the exercise of the power to allot;

(2) the directors are to allot shares of a different class; or

(3) the private company has more than one class of shares.

19-34 A further constraint is that, while the directors have a power to allot, the statutory framework dictates to whom the shares must be allotted. A rights issue is required unless the shareholders choose to exclude or disapply that rights requirement.

Rights issues

19-35 A rights issue requires a company to offer a new issue of shares to existing shareholders in proportion to their existing shareholdings. Such pre-emption rights, if taken up, enable the existing shareholders to retain their proportionate shareholdings in the company and prevent the dilution of their holdings which would otherwise occur if a fresh issue of shares was offered to only some of the existing shareholders or to outside investors. As public companies usually offer a fresh issue of shares at a (usually substantial) discount to the market price, the obligation to offer the shares on a rights basis to the existing shareholders means not only that they can protect their percentage holding in the company, but also that they, rather than outside investors, get the benefit of any discount to the market price.

19-36 The statutory scheme is set out in CA 2006, Pt 17, Ch 3, s 560 et seq and reference must be made to the precise wording of the somewhat complicated provisions which, as regards public companies, implement the requirements of the Second Company Law Directive.[59]

---

[56] If that rights issue exceeds one-third of the company's existing issued share capital and the monetary proceeds realised exceed one-third of the pre-issue market capitalisation, the Guidelines indicate that all members of the board should then stand for re-election at the next annual general meeting of the company. For FTSE 350 companies, this latter element irrelevant now that the UK Corporate Governance Code recommends that FTSE 350 companies put all their directors up for re-election by their shareholders on an annual basis in any event, see **5-13**.   [57] See CA 2006, s 629, as to when shares are of one class; and **14-25**.

[58] Company Law Review, *Developing the Framework* (2000), paras 7.28–7.32; *Completing the Structure* (2000), para 2.16; *Final Report*, vol I (2001), para 4.5.

[59] Directive 77/91/EEC, OJ L 26/1, 31.01.1977, art 29. For companies with a premium-listing of securities, see LR 9.3.11R which imposes pre-emption requirements, but these too fall away if there is a statutory disapplication under the CA 2006, see LR 9.3.12.

The overall scheme is that a company (including a private company) proposing to make an allotment of shares must do so on a rights basis (i.e. to existing shareholders in proportion to their existing holdings) unless the case falls within one of the exceptions, exclusions or disapplications permitted by the statute.

19-37 A company proposing to allot equity securities[60] (essentially ordinary shares[61] but including a sale of treasury shares held by the company[62]) must first make an offer to each person who holds ordinary shares in the company to allot to him on the same or more favourable terms a proportion of those shares that is as nearly as practicable equal to the proportion in nominal value held by him of the ordinary share capital of the company (CA 2006, s 561(1)(a)).[63]

19-38 The offer may be made in hard copy or electronic form and must state a period of not less than 14 days during which the offer may be accepted[64] and the offer must not be withdrawn before the end of that period.[65] The company cannot allot any of those shares to any person unless the period during which any such offer to the existing holders may be accepted has expired or the company has received notice of the acceptance or refusal of every offer so made (CA 2006, s 561(1)(b)).

19-39 In the event of a contravention of the requirement to make an allotment on a rights basis, or of the provisions concerning the communication of pre-emption offers, the company, and every officer of it who knowingly authorised or permitted the contravention, are jointly and severally liable to compensate any person to whom an offer should have been made for any loss, damage, costs or expenses which the person has sustained or incurred by reason of the contravention.[66] A failure to comply with the pre-emption requirement may be grounds for a petition alleging unfairly prejudicial conduct under CA 2006, s 994, see the discussion of the cases at **17-46** et seq.

19-40 These requirements are subject to a variety of exceptions and exclusions and may be disapplied by the shareholders in certain circumstances. Again, reference should be made to the detailed wording of the provisions.

Exceptions

Allotment of bonus shares

19-41 The pre-emption requirement does not apply in relation to an allotment of bonus shares (CA 2006, s 564). Bonus shares are discussed at **19-55**.

---

[60] See the definition of 'allotment of equity securities' in CA 2006, s 560(2).

[61] See CA 2006, s 560(1). 'Equity securities' means ordinary shares in the company or a right to subscribe for, or to convert securities into, ordinary shares in the company; and 'ordinary shares' means shares other than shares that as respects dividends and capital carry a right to participate only up to a specified amount in a distribution.

[62] CA 2006, s 560(2)(b). The effect is that a sale of treasury shares held by a company must be on a rights basis unless that requirement is excluded or disapplied. Institutional shareholders insisted on this requirement for fear that otherwise directors would use sales of treasury shares as an easy way of evading the pre-emption requirements. See CA 2006, s 724(5) as to when shares are treasury shares; also **20-38**.

[63] The right to subscribe in itself has a value which shareholders can sell (known as nil paid rights).

[64] The period was reduced from 21 days to 14 calendar days amidst concerns that rights issues take too long, especially in volatile market conditions; the Listing Rules state 10 business days, see LR 9.5.6R, see **19-53**.

[65] CA 2006, s 562(2), (4)–(5); in certain circumstances, a notice in the *Gazette* suffices: s 562(3).

[66] CA 2006, s 563(1), (2), subject to a two-year limitation period: s 563(3). No provision is made for allotments in breach of these requirements to be set aside, but see *Re Thundercrest Ltd* [1995] 1 BCLC 117 where the court did set aside an allotment by directors in their own favour which was made in breach of the statutory requirements.

Allotments other than for cash

19-42 The pre-emption requirement does not apply to a particular allotment if the shares are, or are to be, wholly or partly paid-up otherwise than in cash (CA 2006, s 565). This exception is a common method of avoiding the requirement to have a rights issue.[67]

Allotments held under an employees' share scheme

19-43 The pre-emption requirement does not apply to an allotment that would (apart from any renunciation or assignment) be held under an employees' share scheme (CA 2006, s 566).

Exclusions

Exclusion by private companies

19-44 All or any of the requirements as to pre-emption (or the provisions governing communication of pre-emption offers to shareholders) may be excluded by a private company by a provision contained in the articles (CA 2006, s 567).[68] As noted earlier, the pre-emption requirements for public companies are mandatory as they are required by the Second Company Law Directive, art 29.

Allotments to a class

19-45 The pre-emption requirement does not apply where a company is required by its articles to make an allotment on a rights basis to a class of shares in pursuance of a class right to that effect (CA 2006, s 568(1)). If a member of the class (or anyone in whose favour he has renounced his right to the allotment) does not accept the shares offered to him, any subsequent offer of those shares is on a pre-emption basis to the rest of the shareholders rather than to the general public unless, in the case of a private company, the articles exclude the need for a rights issue in this situation[69] or the requirement for a rights issue is disapplied.[70]

Disapplication of pre-emption rights

Private company with only one class of shares

19-46 The directors of a private company that has only one class of shares may be given power by the articles, or by a special resolution of the company, to allot ordinary shares of that class as if the pre-emption requirement does not apply or applies with such modifications as the directors may determine (CA 2006, s 569(1)).

Disapplication by other companies

19-47 Any public or private company may disapply the statutory scheme of pre-emption, either by way of a general disapplication or by way of a limited disapplication done with regard to a specified allotment. These provisions are complicated and reference should be made to their precise wording. Their application is linked to the authority to allot shares granted to the directors under CA 2006, s 551 (see **19-32**) and listed companies must have regard to the Pre-emption Group statement which limits the extent of disapplication, see **19-54**.

---

[67] See *Siemens AG v Nold: Case C-42/95* [1997] 1 BCLC 291. As to when a share is deemed paid up in cash or allotted for cash, see CA 2006, s 583 and **19-60**.

[68] The pre-emption rights may be excluded generally or in relation to allotments of a particular description: CA 2006, s 567(2); and see s 567(3). [69] CA 2006, s 568(2), (3).

[70] i.e. under CA 2006, ss 570, 571 or 573.

A general disapplication

19-48 Where the directors of a company have a general authority to allot shares under CA 2006, s 551, they may be given power by the articles, or by a special resolution of the company, to allot ordinary shares pursuant to that authority as if the requirement for a rights issue does not apply or as if it applies to the allotment with such modifications as the directors may determine (s 570(1)).

A specific disapplication

19-49 Where the directors of a company have an authority to allot shares under CA 2006, s 551 (whether generally or otherwise), the company may by special resolution resolve either that the rights requirement does not apply to a specified allotment of shares to be made pursuant to that authority or that the rights requirement applies to the allotment with such modifications as may be specified in the resolution (s 571(1)). This special resolution must be recommended by the directors who must circulate to the shareholders a written statement setting out their reasons for making the recommendation, the amount to be paid to the company in respect of the shares to be allotted and the directors' justification of that amount.[71]

19-50 As the disapplication in each case is linked to the authority to allot shares granted to the directors under CA 2006, s 551, the disapplication ceases when that authority under s 551 is revoked or expires, but if the authority to allot is renewed, the disapplication can also be renewed by a special resolution.[72]

Disapplication on sale of treasury shares

19-51 As noted in **19-37**, the pre-emption requirement applies on a sale of treasury shares,[73] but this requirement can be the subject of a general or specific disapplication. The directors may be given power by the articles, or by a special resolution of the company, to sell treasury shares as if the requirement for a rights issue does not apply or as if it applies to the sale with such modifications as the directors may determine (CA 2006, s 573(1)). Alternatively, the company may by special resolution resolve either that the rights requirement does not apply to a specified sale of treasury shares or that that rights requirement applies to a specified sale with such modifications as may be specified in the resolution (s 573(4)).

Institutional investors and pre-emption rights

19-52 As noted at **19-35**, pre-emption rights are a protective device ensuring that existing shareholders cannot have their percentage holdings diluted without their having an opportunity to acquire additional shares. Pre-emption rights are also valuable commercially because existing shareholders get the benefit of any discount to market price so that the value of the company is transferred to them and not to outside investors. Pre-emption rights also ensure that long-term shareholders cannot suddenly find control of the company has passed to new investors. It is unsurprising, therefore, that institutional investors (the most significant shareholders in listed public companies) see considerable value in the statutory requirement (reflecting the Second Directive) for rights issues.[74]

---

[71] CA 2006, s 571(5)–(6); and see s 572 as to penalties for misleading, false or deceptive statements. Where the resolution is proposed as a written resolution, the statement must be supplied to every eligible member at or before the time at which the resolution is sent or submitted to him for signature; where the resolution is to be at a meeting, the statement must be circulated with the notice of the meeting: s 571(7).

[72] CA 2006, ss 570(3), 571(3).   [73] CA 2006, s 560(2)(b).

[74] See Association of British Insurers (ABI), 'Rights Issues and Capital Raising—An ABI Discussion Paper' (July 2008).

19-53 Equally, on occasion, companies may wish to avoid the administrative burden of a rights issue (which can be costly[75] and time-consuming to conduct—a prospectus is usually required, see **19-105** et seq). hence the statutory provisions for exceptional cases and the ability to disapply the provisions on a more general basis. For many years, there have been concerns that the insistence on pre-emption rights limits the flexibility of smaller listed companies, in particular, and makes it more complicated and expensive for such companies to raise equity capital.[76] Following a joint Treasury and FSA review and report in November 2008,[77] some changes have been made both to process (the 21-day period during which the rights issue must remain open has been reduced to 14 days,[78] as noted at **19-38**) and to market practice (the ABI relaxed its guidelines on allotment and pre-emption to ensure companies have greater flexibility in terms of authorisation to allot so reducing the need to call further general meetings to seek authorisations, see **19-32**). Amendments to the Prospectus Directive,[79] which are to be implemented by July 2012, should also bring increased flexibility by providing for a proportionate disclosure regime which will allow a short form prospectus to be used on a rights issue,[80] see **19-104**.

19-54 Equally important in terms of addressing these issues are voluntary guidelines on pre-emption drawn up by the Pre-Emption Group which is made up of representatives of listed companies, institutional investors and intermediaries. Originally introduced in 1987, the latest guidance was issued in 2008 as a Statement of Principles which addresses the factors which should be taken into account by a company when considering making a request to the shareholders to disapply the statutory pre-emption rights.[81] The Statement of Principles primarily relates to issues of equity securities for cash other than on a pre-emptive basis by all UK companies with a listing on the Main Market of the London Stock Exchange.[82] The Statement reiterates that the overarching principle remains that pre-emption rights are a cornerstone of company law and protect shareholders against inappropriate dilution of their investments but it is also accepted that a degree of flexibility is appropriate in circumstances where new issues of shares on a non-pre-emptive basis would be in the interests of companies and their owners.[83] Disapplication is considered

---

[75] A particular concern is the underwriting costs, a matter which was addressed by the Institutional Investor Council, see *Report of the Rights Issue Fees Inquiry* conducted by the Institutional Investor Council (December 2010) and also by the Office of Fair Trading. The OFT considered whether to launch a market investigation, but concluded that it would not be appropriate in this instance, rather companies and their boards need to be more proactive in negotiating underwriting fees and shareholders need to hold them to account over the matter, see OFT, *Equity underwriting and associated services* (January 2011), OFT 1303. To assist boards, the Institutional Investor Committee issued a *Best Practice Guidance for Issuers when Raising Equity Capital* (May 2011) which seeks to give practical guidance on how boards should approach capital issues and matters they need to consider with respect to the fees payable.

[76] See, for example, the Myners review: DTI, *Pre-emption rights: Final Report*, URN 05/679, (February 2005); also HM Treasury, *Smaller Quoted Companies—a Report to the Paymaster General* (November 1998) paras 46–47.

[77] See HM Treasury, *A Report to the Chancellor of the Exchequer by the Rights Issue Review Group* (November 2008).   [78] See FSA, *Rights Issue Subscription Periods*, CP 09/4, (January 2009).

[79] See Amending Directive 2010/73/EU, OJ L 327/1, 11.12.2010.

[80] See FSA, *UK Implementation of Amending Directive 2010/73/EU, Simplifying the EU Prospectus and Transparency Directives*, CP11/28, (December 2011). Rights issues require a prospectus and the amendments will allow issuers to produce a shorter prospectus which should encourage them in turn to have rights issues.

[81] See *Disapplying Pre-emption Rights, A Statement of Principles* which is is supported by the Association of British Insurers, the National Association of Pension Funds and the Investment Managers Association representing owners and investment managers.

[82] Companies on AIM (see **19-101**) are encouraged to apply the Statement of Principles but it is recognised that greater flexibility is likely to be justified in such companies, see Statement of Principles, para 5.

[83] Statement of Principles, paras 1 and 2.

a routine matter (and therefore shareholders would expect to agree) where the company seeks authority to issue shares on a non-rights basis up to no more than 5% of the company's ordinary share capital in any one year and no more than 7.5% of the company's ordinary capital in any rolling three-year period. Any discount at which ordinary shares are issued for cash other than to existing shareholders is of major concern so companies should restrict the discount to a maximum of 5% of the immediately preceding market price. Disapplication requests which exceed these percentage levels are not ruled out but would be considered by shareholders in the light of the business case made by the company on a case-by-case basis.[84]

Bonus issues

19-55 A bonus issue of shares occurs where a company capitalises profits or revenue reserves or some other permissible fund[85] and applies the proceeds in paying up bonus shares which go to existing members in proportion to their entitlement to dividend so providing the shareholders with additional fully paid shares in the company.[86] It is essentially an accounting exercise as the company's reserves are reduced but its share capital fund is increased.

19-56 From the point of view of the shareholders, calling the issue a bonus issue is somewhat misleading for the company is still worth the same as before the bonus issue and the total value of their shareholding has not altered.[87] All that has happened is that each shareholder holds more shares but each share is worth less than before.

19-57 One advantage so far as the company and shareholders are concerned is that a bonus issue is not a distribution[88] for the purposes of the distribution rules in CA 2006, Pt 23 so funds which would not be available for distribution as dividends may be used for this purpose. Distributions are discussed in Chapter 20: see **20-84**.

F Payment for shares

19-58 Having considered the requirements as to the issuing of shares, we turn now to the rules concerning payment for share capital and, by way of background, the reader is referred to the discussion of the doctrine of capital maintenance at the beginning of Chapter 20.

Payment for shares in money or money's worth

19-59 A company cannot make a gratuitous allotment of its shares nor an allotment at a discount.[89] The allottee must pay in full at least the nominal value of the shares and will

---

[84] Statement of Principles, paras 14–15.

[85] The company may use its share premium account (CA 2006, s 610(3)), redenomination reserve (s 628(2)) or capital redemption reserve (s 733(5)) to finance a fully paid bonus issue. See *Re Cleveland Trust plc* [1991] BCLC 424 where a bonus issue was declared void on the ground of common mistake when the directors and shareholders were mistaken as to the availability of profits which could be capitalised; also *EIC Services Ltd v Phipps* [2004] 2 BCLC 589, CA (bonus issue in breach of articles void).

[86] As this appears to be a case of the company allotting shares without receiving money or money's worth, it would seem to fall foul of CA 2006, s 582(1), but s 582(2)(a) provides that this requirement does not prevent the company from allotting bonus shares.

[87] Of course, it is not strictly accurate to say that there is no difference in value before and after a bonus issue, for the market may respond favourably to a bonus issue so the shares may gain a little in value but essentially the shareholder's position does not alter.   [88] CA 2006, s 829(2)(a).

[89] CA 2006, s 580; *Re Wragg Ltd* [1897] 1 Ch 796; *Ooregum Gold Mining Co of India Ltd v Roper* [1892] AC 125; *Re Eddystone Marine Insurance Co* [1893] 3 Ch 9.

possibly pay a premium as well. The sum due may be paid up in money or money's worth including goodwill and know-how (CA 2006, s 582).[90]

19-60 An extended definition of an allotment for cash is set out in CA 2006, s 583 which provides that a share in a company is deemed paid up (as to its nominal value or any premium on it) in cash or allotted for cash if the consideration received for the allotment or payment up is a cash consideration. A cash consideration for these purposes means (s 583(3)):

(a) cash received by the company;

(b) a cheque received by the company in good faith which the directors have no reason for suspecting will not be paid;

(c) a release of a liability of the company for a liquidated sum;

(d) an undertaking to pay cash to the company at a future date;[91] or

(e) payment by any other means giving rise to a present or future entitlement (of the company or person acting on the company's behalf) to payment, or credit equivalent to payment, in cash.[92]

19-61 Category (c) requires a little explanation. This provision reflects the decision in *Re Harmony and Montague Tin and Copper Mining Co, Spargo's Case*[93] which illustrates how an allotment which appears to be on a non-cash basis may in fact be regarded as being for cash. It is necessary to regard the transaction as being in two stages: first, an individual sells assets to the company and the company becomes indebted to him for a stated amount (a liquidated sum); secondly, the company allots fully paid shares to him and in return the company is released from the liability to pay the liquidated sum. In *Spargo's Case*, Sir W M James LJ explained that it is not necessary that the formality should be gone through of the money being handed over and taken back again. If the two demands are set off against each other (the demand for payment for the shares and the liability for a liquidated sum), the shares have been paid up in cash.[94]

19-62 The possible inconsistency between prohibiting the allotment of shares at a discount (CA 2006, s 580(1)), but allowing payment in money's worth (s 582(1)) which may disguise an allotment at a discount, was noted by Lindley LJ in *Re Wragg Ltd*[95] who accepted that the difference between issuing shares at a discount and issuing them at a price put upon property or services by the vendor and agreed to by the company may not always be very apparent in practice. In the court's opinion, however, the two transactions were essentially different and a company is entitled to issue fully paid-up shares in return for a non-

---

[90] Details of any non-cash consideration is given in the return of allotment to the registrar of companies: CA 2006, s 555; and The Companies (Shares and Share Capital) Regulations 2009, SI 2009/388, reg 14(c). Shares taken by a subscriber to the memorandum of a public company in pursuance of an undertaking of his in the memorandum, and any premium on the shares, must be paid up in cash: CA 2006, s 584.

[91] An assignment of a debt is not an undertaking to pay cash at a future date for these purposes, see *System Control plc v Munro Corporate plc* [1990] BCLC 659.

[92] Category (e) is intended to clarify uncertainty which had existed as to whether payments within a computerised share settlement system, such as CREST, are a cash consideration. These automated systems provide for assured payment obligations which are to be treated as equivalent to cash: see *Explanatory Notes to the Companies Act 2006*, para 880. The Secretary of State has power to expand category (5) by statutory instrument: CA 2006, s 583(4).   [93] (1873) 8 Ch App 407.

[94] (1873) 8 Ch App 407 at 412.   [95] [1897] 1 Ch 796.

cash consideration provided it does so honestly and not colourably, and provided that it has not been so imposed upon as to be entitled to be relieved from its bargain.[96]

19-63 The question whether the consideration is colourable is one of fact in each case[97] and, as Lord Watson noted in *Ooregum Gold Mining Co of India Ltd v Roper*,[98] 'so long as the company honestly regards the consideration given as fairly representing the nominal value of the shares in cash, its estimate ought not to be critically examined'.

19-64 It is only where the consideration is illusory or it is manifest on the face of the instrument that the shares are issued at a discount that the court will be prepared to consider the adequacy of the consideration.[99] This judicial attitude is in keeping with the courts' traditional reluctance to interfere in business matters.

Payment rules applicable to public companies

19-65 The common law approach to non-cash consideration, discussed above, is rather lax and applied to public companies issuing shares for a non-cash consideration would not be acceptable in view of the general policy to regulate such companies more strictly in the public interest[100] nor would it meet the requirements of the Second Company Law Directive,[101] art 10 of which requires an independent valuation of any non-cash consideration for the issue of shares by a public company, though these provisions have been relaxed to a limited extent (see **19-72**). Hence the need for further controls on the consideration which may be accepted by public companies as payment for their shares.

Valuation of non-cash consideration

19-66 A public company must not allot shares as fully or partly paid-up (as to their nominal value or any premium on them) otherwise than in cash[102] unless:

(1) the consideration for the allotment has been independently valued;[103]

(2) the valuer's report has been made to the company during the six months immediately preceding the allotment of the shares; and

(3) a copy of the report has been sent to the proposed allottee.[104]

---

[96] Lindley LJ cautioned against being misled by talking of value: 'The value paid to the company is measured by the price at which the company agrees to buy what it thinks it worth its while to acquire. Whilst the transaction is unimpeached, this is the only value to be considered': [1897] 1 Ch 796 at 831. The consideration in this case for the allotment of the shares was the transfer of a business comprising land, stock and goodwill.   [97] *Re Innes & Co Ltd* [1903] 2 Ch 254 at 262.

[98] [1892] AC 125 at 137.

[99] See *Re White Star Line Ltd* [1938] 1 Ch 458 (certificates, essentially credit notes, equal in nominal amount to the sum due on the shares were accepted which, to the knowledge of all the parties, were always worth less than the nominal value).

[100] It has already been noted that public companies must have a minimum allotted capital (CA 2006, ss 761, 763), see **19-10**, and must call a general meeting in the event of a serious loss of capital (s 656), see **19-14**.   [101] Directive 77/91/EEC, OJ L 26/1, 31.01.1977.

[102] See CA 2006, s 583(3) (set out at **19-60**) as to when a share in a company is deemed paid up in cash or allotted for cash.

[103] Detailed rules as to the independent valuation and report are in CA 2006, ss 1150–1153. Any person who knowingly or recklessly makes a statement which is misleading, false or deceptive in a material particular in connection with the preparation of such report commits an offence: s 1153(2).

[104] CA 2006, s 593(1); bonus issues are not caught by these provisions: s 593(2). These requirements for independent valuation do not apply to an allotment of shares in connection with: (1) a share exchange for all or some of the shares in another company or of a particular class of shares in another company; or (2) a proposed merger of the company with another: ss 594–595.

19-67 If a company allots shares in contravention of these requirements and either the allottee has not received the valuer's report, or there has been some other contravention of the requirements as to the independent valuation and report which the allottee knew or ought to have known amounted to a contravention, the allottee is liable to pay the company an amount equal to the aggregate of the nominal value of the shares and the whole of any premium or, if the case so requires, so much of that aggregate as is treated as paid up by the consideration with interest at the appropriate rate.[105]

19-68 A copy of the valuation report must be filed by the company with the registrar of companies at the same time as it files the return of allotment of those shares by the company.[106]

19-69 The valuation of the non-cash consideration and the report required thereon must be made by an independent person ('the valuer'), that is to say a person eligible to be the statutory auditor of the company and who meets the independence criteria set out in CA 2006, s 1151.[107]

19-70 The valuer's report must state:

(1) the nominal value of the shares to be wholly or partly paid for by the consideration in question;

(2) the amount of any premium payable on the shares;

(3) the description of the consideration, the method used to value it and the date of the valuation;

(4) the extent to which the nominal value of the shares and any premium are to be treated as paid up by the consideration or in cash (CA 2006, s 596(2)).

19-71 The report must also state that:

(1) the method of valuation (and any delegation of responsibility) was reasonable in all the circumstances;

(2) it appears to the valuer that there has been no material change in the value of the consideration since the valuation; and

(3) on the basis of the valuation, the value of the consideration (together with any cash by which the nominal value of the shares or any premium payable on them is to be paid up) is not less than so much of the aggregate of the nominal value and the whole of any such premium as is treated as paid up by the consideration and any such cash (CA 2006, s 596(3)).

19-72 The Second Directive has been amended to allow public companies to allot shares for a non-cash consideration without the need to go through these formalities for independent valuation in cases where there is some other method of valuing the asset in question.[108]

---

[105] CA 1985, s 593(3). The effect is to create an immediate liability as if the allottee had agreed to take up the shares for cash: *Re Bradford Investments Ltd* [1991] BCLC 224 at 233. These penalties can be onerous, see *Re Ossory Estates plc* [1988] BCLC 213; *Re Bradford Investments plc (No 2)* [1991] BCLC 688, but may be mitigated by the court's powers under CA 2006, s 606 to give relief, see **19-86.**

[106] CA 2006, s 597. A return of allotment is required within one month of the allotment: s 555.

[107] CA 2006, s 1150. To be independent, the person must not be an officer or employee of the company or of an associate or a partner or employee of such a person. The company's existing auditor is not included in the categories of excluded persons and so may act as the valuer for these purposes: s 1151. The valuer may also delegate the valuation to another person: s 1150(2).

[108] Directive 2006/68/EC amending Directive 77/91/EEC, OJ L 264/32, 25.09.2006. For example, where the assets are financial instruments traded on a regulated market, the valuation can be taken to be the

The UK decided against adopting this option as there is no de-regulatory advantage since another valuation method is required in any event.[109]

Transfers to public company of non-cash assets

19-73 Further controls are imposed on agreements for:

(1) any transfer of non-cash assets[110] to the company (or another) by a subscriber to the memorandum of association of a public company incorporated as such within two years from the date of the company being issued with a trading certificate[111] (CA 2006, s 598);

(2) any such transfers by a member of a private company within two years of the company re-registering as a public company (s 603);

(3) for a consideration equal in value to 10% or more of the company's issued share capital[112] at that time.

19-74 In practice, transactions within (1) are unusual and the statutory provisions apply mainly to transactions within (2). Not all agreements within these provisions (ss 598, 603) will involve an allotment of shares but, as many do, it is convenient to consider these matters here.

19-75 The company must not enter into the agreements outlined at **19-73** unless the following conditions are met:

(1) the consideration to be received by the company,[113] and any consideration other than cash to be given by the company, must be independently valued by a valuer in the same way[114] as outlined at **19-70** with respect to CA 2006, s 596 (shares allotted for a non-cash consideration) and the valuer's report must be made to the company during the six months immediately preceding the date of the agreement;[115]

(2) the terms of the agreement must be approved by an ordinary resolution of the company;[116] and

(3) copies of the valuer's report must be circulated to the members, where a written resolution is used, at or before the time when the resolution was submitted to the members and, if a meeting is held, the report must be circulated no later than the date on which notice of the meeting is given and the report must be circulated to the other party to the agreement if not then a member of the company.[117]

---

average market valuation during the relevant period; or where an asset has already been the subject of a fair valuation by an independent expert in the previous six months; or the fair value can be determined from the statutory accounts, duly audited. In each case, shareholders holding at least 5% of the company's issued capital may demand a valuation by an independent expert.

[109] See DTI, *Implementation of the Companies Act 2006* (2007), URN 07/666, Ch 6, esp paras 6.10–6.16, 6.23–6.26.

[110] 'Non-cash asset' is defined in CA 2006, s 1163 as meaning any property or interest in property other than cash; and see s 1163(2) as to the transfer of a non-cash asset.

[111] i.e. a certificate of entitlement to do business required by CA 2006, s 761, see **19-11**. In most cases, this will mean within two years of incorporation.　　　　　[112] See definition in CA 2006, s 546.

[113] See CA 2006, ss 599(2), 603.　　　[114] See CA 2006, ss 600, 603.

[115] CA 2006, ss 599(1)(b), 603. The contents of the report are set out in s 600 and are essentially the same as those required under s 596, outlined at **19-70** et seq.　　　　　[116] CA 2006, ss 601, 603.

[117] CA 2006, ss 599(1), 601(3), 603. Copies of the valuer's report and the resolution must be delivered to the registrar of companies within 15 days of passing the resolution: ss 602, 603.

19-76 These requirements do not apply where it is part of the company's ordinary business to acquire such assets as are to be transferred and the agreement is entered into in the ordinary course of business of that company, a potentially wide category (CA 2006, 598(4)).[118]

19-77 In the event of contravention of these valuation requirements, the company is entitled to recover from the other party any consideration given by it under the agreement, or an amount equal to the value of the consideration at the time of the agreement; and the agreement, so far as not carried out, is void.[119]

19-78 There is clearly a degree of overlap between the requirement for a non-cash consideration to be valued before an allotment of shares (CA 2006, s 593), discussed at **19-66**, and these provisions governing the transfer to a public company of non-cash assets in the initial period (ss 598–603), but it is important to appreciate the different scope of the provisions.

19-79 Section 593 applies whenever a public company accepts a non-cash consideration from anyone as consideration for an allotment of shares. Section 598 applies to any transfer of a non-cash asset from a subscriber or member to the company whether the consideration for the transfer is an allotment of shares or something else. There are also different exceptions to each provision.

19-80 It is possible for the provisions to be applicable in the same instance since the provisions are not mutually exclusive. Any allotment of shares for a non-cash consideration to a subscriber or member within the two-year period is potentially within CA 2006, s 593 and ss 598–603, which is not unduly burdensome as the requirements for an independent valuation and report are similar. The major difference is that ss 598–603 require the relevant agreements to be approved by an ordinary resolution. On the other hand, ss 598–603 do not apply where it is part of the company's ordinary business to acquire such assets as are to be transferred and the agreement is entered into in the ordinary course of that business.[120] The type of transaction which is within ss 598–603 but not within s 593 is where the transaction does not involve an allotment of shares but is simply a transfer of non-cash assets by a subscriber or member within the relevant time-frame to a public company or a company re-registered as a public company.

Undertakings to do work or perform services

19-81 A public company must not accept at any time, in payment up of its shares or any premium on them, an undertaking given by any person that he or another should do work or perform services for the company or any other person (CA 2006, s 585(1)). If a public company accepts such an undertaking, the holder of the shares when they or the premium are treated as paid up (in whole or in part) by the undertaking is liable to pay the company in respect of those shares an amount equal to their nominal value, together with the whole of any premium or, if the case so requires, such proportion of that amount as is treated as paid up by the undertaking, together with interest (s 585(2)). In the event of a contravention, the company and any officer in default is liable on conviction to a fine (s 590). Despite any contravention, any undertaking given by any person to do work or perform services or to do any other thing remains enforceable by the company.[121]

---

[118] Nor do they apply to agreements entered into as a result of a court order or under court control: CA 2006, s 598(5). [119] CA 2006, s 604(1), (2).

[120] CA 2006, ss 598(4), 603. [121] CA 2006, s 591, subject to s 589.

Restriction on long-term undertakings

19-82 A public company must not allot shares as fully or partly-paid (as to their nominal value or any premium on them) otherwise than in cash if the consideration for the allotment is or includes an undertaking which is to be, or may be, performed more than five years after the date of the allotment.[122] In the event of breach, the allottee is liable to pay the company an amount equal to the aggregate of the nominal value and the whole of any premium due.[123]

Consequences of breach of the payment rules

19-83 The consequences of breach of any of the statutory payment and valuation rules are relatively uniform.

19-84 As a general rule, the allottee remains liable to pay an amount equal to the nominal amount and any premium due together with interest.[124] Subsequent holders are jointly and severally liable unless they are purchasers for value and did not have actual notice of the contravention or they took from a holder who was not himself liable under these provisions.[125]

19-85 These penalties can be quite onerous. In *Re Ossory Estates plc*[126] property was sold to a company and the vendor received as part of the consideration 8m shares in the company. As this was an allotment of shares for a non-cash consideration, an independent valuation and report was required. No such report was ever made with the result that the allottee, despite having transferred his property to the company, was liable to pay the company £1.76m as the price of the shares. Not surprisingly, this was described by Harman J as a somewhat startling conclusion.[127]

19-86 It is possible for a person so liable to make an application to the court to be exempted in whole or in part from the liability (CA 2006, ss 589(1), 606(1)). If such liability arises in relation to payment in respect of any shares, the court may exempt the applicant from the liability only if and to the extent that it appears to the court just and equitable to do so having regard to the matters mentioned (CA 2006, ss 589(3), 606(2)). The matters to be taken into account by the court are:

(1) whether the applicant has paid, or is liable to pay, any amount in respect of any other liability arising in relation to those shares under any of the relevant provisions, or of any liability arising by virtue of any undertaking given in or in connection with payment for those shares;

(2) whether any person other than the applicant has paid or is likely to pay (whether in pursuance of an order of the court or otherwise) any such amount; and

(3) whether the applicant or any other person has performed, in whole or in part, or is likely so to perform any such undertaking, or has done or is likely to do any other thing in payment or part payment for the shares.[128]

---

[122] CA 2006, s 587. The provision also applies to a contract which did not originally contravene this provision but is subsequently varied and results in a contravention. In such cases, the variation is void. Equally caught is the situation where an undertaking was to have been performed within five years but was not: s 587(3) and (4).   [123] CA 2006, s 587(2).

[124] The effect is to create an immediate liability as if the allottee had agreed to take up the shares for cash: see *Re Bradford Investments plc* [1991] BCLC 224 at 233.   [125] CA 2006, ss 588(1), (2), 605(3).

[126] [1988] BCLC 213.   [127] [1988] BCLC 213 at 214.

[128] CA 2006, s 589(3). See *Re Bradford Investments plc (No 2)* [1991] BCLC 688 at 693 where Hoffmann J thought that, in the light of what is now CA 2006, s 589(5) (see **19-87**), these matters are not intended to be an exhaustive statement of the matters to which the court should or may have regard.

19-87 In determining whether it should exempt the applicant in whole or in part from any liability, the court must have regard to the following overriding principle,[129] namely that a company which has allotted shares should receive money or money's worth at least equal in value to the aggregate of the nominal value of those shares and the whole of any premium or, if the case so requires, so much of that aggregate as is treated as paid up (CA 2006, ss 589(5), 606(4)).

19-88 In *Re Ossory Estates plc*,[130] noted at **19-85**, relief was granted as the company had sold some of the property transferred to it in consideration for the allotment at a substantial profit and had undoubtedly received at least money or money's worth equal in value, and probably exceeding, the aggregate of the nominal value of the shares and any premium. It was just and equitable that the allottee should be relieved from any further liability.

19-89 This outcome can be contrasted with that in *System Control plc v Munro Corporate plc*[131] where the court said there was no prospect of relief being granted when there was absolutely no evidence that the company had received the minimum amount; likewise in *Re Bradford Investments plc (No 2)*[132] where the applicants failed to discharge the burden of showing that the company had received value for its shares.

19-90 Where a person is liable under CA 2006, s 604(2) to a company as a result of the transfer to a public company of a non-cash asset in the initial period,[133] the court may, on application, exempt him in whole or in part from that liability if and to the extent that it appears to the court just and equitable to do so having regard to any benefit accruing to the company by virtue of anything done by him towards the carrying out of the agreement for transfer (s 606(6)).

19-91 In addition to the civil consequences, where there is a breach of these provisions, the company and officers in default are also guilty of an offence and liable to a fine.[134] Directors may also be in breach of duty, for example the duty to exercise their powers for a proper purpose (CA 2006, s 171(b)) and to promote the success of the company (s 172), and liable to make good any damage suffered by the company as a result of the breach.[135]

G Capital raising

Introduction

19-92 The basic function of companies is to provide a vehicle for entrepreneurial activity. Large-scale entrepreneurial activity may require amounts of capital which can only be provided by inviting outside investors to pool their resources and invest in an enterprise over which they may have relatively little control. To persuade such investors to come forward two incentives are needed. One is limited liability and that is provided by the companies legislation.[136] The other is an active stock market to provide a means by which investors can realise their investment. Without such a market investors will require a higher return

---

[129] See *Re Bradford Investments plc (No 2)* [1991] BCLC 688 at 694 where Hoffmann J thought that the designation 'overriding principle' did not oblige the court to refuse relief unless the company had received at least the nominal value of the allotted shares and any premium: had that been the intention, the requirement would have been framed as a rule.

[130] [1988] BCLC 213.   [131] [1990] BCLC 659.   [132] [1991] BCLC 688.

[133] The restrictions on such transfers are discussed at **19-73** and see CA 2006, ss 598, 603.

[134] CA 2006, ss 590, 607.   [135] *Hirsche v Sims* [1894] AC 654.

[136] As to the importance of limited liability to investors, see Easterbrook and Fischel, *The Economic Structure of Corporate Law* (1991), Ch 2; Halpern, Trebilcock and Turnbull, 'An Economic Analysis of Limited Liability in Corporation Law' (1980) 30 Univ of Toronto Law Jo 117.

on their investment to compensate for the lack of liquidity. The existence of a market for shares thus not only makes it possible for companies to raise external funding but makes it cheaper for them to do so as well. A stock market meets these needs of the company and the investors by providing a primary market through which the company can offer its shares to the public and so raise capital and a secondary market where investors can trade in those shares. For the original owners, admission to a market offers the opportunity to realise their investment in the business and to sell out to new owners. Once admitted to trading, the company may use the stock market to raise further capital in all manner of ways. It may make further public offers of its shares[137] from time to time and, with a broader shareholder base, it may find that a rights issue (i.e. the offer of new shares to existing shareholders in proportion to their existing holdings: see **19-35**) is an appropriate way of raising additional capital. As well as the ability to issue shares to investors to raise capital, traded companies commonly offer their shares as consideration for a takeover or in consideration for the acquisition of an asset where the shares are offered, respectively, to the target company's shareholders or to the vendors of the asset (and in some instances immediately resold on their behalf). These offers are described as acquisition or merger issues or vendor consideration or vendor placings. This ability to fund acquisitions and mergers by offering shares instead of cash is one of the main advantages of being a traded company and it is only available to a public company as a private company is prohibited from offering its shares to the public (CA 2006, s 755), see below.

19-93 In terms of raising capital, the choice typically lies between a public offer (often referred to as an IPO, initial public offer) or a placing (though sometimes companies combine a public offer with a placing) with IPOs being restricted by cost to the larger companies looking to raise significant sums of money while placings are typically used to raise more modest sums. A placing allows the securities to be marketed to specified persons or clients of the sponsor or any securities house assisting in the placing.[138] Where the company itself offers to the public shares not yet in issue or allotted, this is known as an offer for subscription[139] and persons who acquire the shares directly from the company are known as subscribers. Where the offer of shares to the public is not by the company itself, but by a third party holding shares already in issue or allotted (such as an investment bank), it is called an offer for sale and persons who acquire the shares are known as purchasers.[140]

Private companies and public offers

19-94 A private company is prohibited from offering to the public any securities (i.e. shares or debentures) of the company (CA 2006, s 755(1), (5)).[141] A company proposing to contravene this prohibition can be restrained by court order (s 757)[142] and, if the contravention

---

[137] It is also possible to issue debt securities, typically corporate bonds, to raise loan capital. For large companies, debt securities are a much more important source of funding than equity securities (shares). For example, for the year to December 2011, UK companies raised £11.7 bn in equity issues, but £196 bn in Eurobond issues: see London Stock Exchange, *Main Market, Market Statistics*, Market Summary Table (December 2011).

[138] Listing Rules, App 1.1. Relevant Definitions, see 'placing'.

[139] Listing Rules, App 1.1. Relevant Definitions, see 'offer for subscription'.

[140] Listing Rules, App 1.1. Relevant Definitions, see 'offer for sale'.

[141] This prohibition on public offers in CA 2006, s 755 restates the prohibition in CA 1985, s 81, but it removes the criminal sanction which the 1985 Act imposed. The prohibition extends to allotments to third parties with a view to the securities being offered to the public, see CA 2006, s 755(2), and note the presumption that this is the case in certain circumstances.

[142] An application can be made by any member, creditor or the Secretary of State and note the unusual requirement that an order must be made by the court where, in unfairly prejudicial proceedings under CA

has already occurred, on an application being made, the court must require the company to re-register as a public company, save where it is impracticable or undesirable to so order (s 758(2)).[143] If re-registration is not an option, the court may still make a remedial order[144] or a winding-up order or both (s 758(3)).[145] A breach of the prohibition does not affect the validity of any allotment or sale of any securities (s 760).

19-95 An offer is not to be regarded as an offer to the public if it can properly be regarded, in all the circumstances:

(1) as not being calculated to result, directly or indirectly, in the shares or debentures becoming available to persons other than those receiving the offer; or

(2) as being a private concern of the person receiving and making it (s 756(3)).

Furthermore, an offer is presumed to be of a private concern of the person making and receiving it if the company offers the shares to its existing members, employees and their families, or an existing debenture holder, or a trustee of a trust where the principal beneficiary of the trust is within these categories, or if the offer is an offer under an employees' share scheme;[146] and, if the offer is renounceable, it is renounceable only to these restricted groups (s 756(4), (5)). The intention with these exceptions is to ensure that a private company may still raise equity capital, but from a limited circle of people.

19-96 This prohibition on the offer of shares to the public is not always clearly understood by private companies and they may offer their shares to a wider audience than that permitted which has a number of consequences. First, it is a breach of the prohibition in CA 2006, s 755, as noted. Secondly, it is unlawful for a company to offer transferable securities to the public without first publishing an approved prospectus (Financial Services and Markets Act 2000 (FSMA 2000), s 85, see **19-105**). Depending on the circumstances, there may also be a breach of the rules governing financial promotion.[147] Each of these provisions apply to different categories of offers and different types of securities and compliance with one set of requirements does not necessarily mean compliance with the others so private companies need to be alert to the various consequences if, inadvertently, they make an offer to the public.

19-97 The prohibition on public offers by private companies is not an arbitrary barrier, as the CA 2006 makes clear,[148] rather it is the precise point at which the public interest intrudes. Corporate self-interest in raising capital meets the public interest in the protection of

2006, Pt 30 (see Chapter 17), it appears to the court that the company is proposing to act in contravention of this prohibition on public offers by private companies: s 757(1).

[143] See CA 2006, s 758(4) for the categories of persons who can apply for an order in this case.
[144] Defined in CA 2006, s 759 as an order for the purpose of putting a person affected by the contravention in the position he would have been in had there not been the contravention.
[145] This power is discretionary because it may be that the prohibition has been breached but the company has not allotted the shares or the company has withdrawn the offer and undertaken not to make a further offer so a remedial order is unnecessary: see *Explanatory Notes to the Companies Act 2006*, para 1061.
[146] Defined CA 2006, s 1166.
[147] Financial promotion is governed by FSMA 2000, s 21 and The Financial Services and Markets Act 2000 (Financial Promotion) Order 2005, SI 2005/1529, as amended. Extensive guidance on the application of s 21 is found in the FSA *Perimeter Guidance Manual*, PERG 8, Financial Promotion. Essentially, it is a criminal offence for persons other than authorised persons, in the course of business, to communicate an invitation or inducement to engage in investment activity. See *Re UK-Euro Group plc* [2007] 1 BCLC 812 (compulsory winding up on public interest grounds when company raised its share capital in clear breach of FSMA 2000, s 21).
[148] The CA 2006, s 4(4) identifies the two major differences between private and public companies as being those set out in Part 20 of the Act, namely this prohibition on public offers by private companies (s 755) and

investors. A company which wishes to offer shares to the public must submit to the greater regulation imposed on public companies in the interests of investors by the CA 2006 and by the FSMA 2000. The mischief at which CA 2006, s 755 (see **19-94**) is aimed is companies making offers to the public without complying with the range of regulatory requirements (in respect of company accounts and disclosure, capital and corporate governance requirements) imposed on public companies in the interests of investor protection—hence the leeway allowed to private companies which are technically in breach of s 755 but which are in the process of re-registering and do so re-register (s 755(3)). The presumption in s 758 is therefore that private companies in breach of the prohibition on public offers should be made to re-register as public companies and so be subject to the appropriate level of regulation.

Publicly traded companies

19-98 Being a public company is not synonymous with being listed on a stock market nor are all markets for listed securities. Technology now allows markets to operate in a much more segmented way than previously which gives rise to a somewhat complex picture as exchanges attempt to meet the demands of investors and issuers (companies looking to raise equity or loan capital). The result is that exchanges are no longer single-tier markets for listed companies but instead offer a variety of markets with differing entry requirements. The law relating to the operation of these markets and the trading of securities is beyond the scope of this work[149] and the discussion here is limited to an overview of the ways in which public companies use the markets and the regulatory requirements which govern them.

19-99 The questions for public companies are: (a) whether they wish to offer their shares to the public at all (they are not required to do so); (b) whether they wish also to be admitted to trading (which usually goes hand in hand with a desire to offer their shares to the public since the public will only be willing to buy the shares if they can then trade them); and (c) whether they wish to trade through a regulated market or an exchange regulated market. Admission to trading on a regulated market is the standard threshold for the application of EU Directives,[150] such as the Prospectus and Transparency Directives, so companies whose securities are traded on such markets are subject to those EU requirements. Exchange regulated markets are more lightly regulated and companies look to trade on them precisely in order to escape the reach of Directives such as the Prospectus Directive.[151] The common position in the UK is that larger established public companies look for a listing on a regulated market, typically on the Main Market run by the London Stock Exchange (LSE), while newer, smaller, more speculative companies look

the requirement for a minimum share capital (s 761, see **19-10**), but it is the former requirement which is the significant difference.

[149] Readers are referred to specialist texts such as Gulliver & Payne, *Corporate Finance Law* (2011); Hudson, *Securities Law* (2008); Moloney, *EC Securities Regulation* (2nd edn, 2008).

[150] The FSA maintains on its website the register of regulated markets required by art 47 of the Markets in Financial Instruments Directive (2004/39/EC) (Mifid). The most relevant regulated market for our purposes is the Main Market of the London Stock Exchange. The PLUS-listed market run by PLUS Markets plc gained regulated market status in 2007 but has failed to challenge the dominance of the listed sector by the LSE.

[151] In 2004, the London Stock Exchange altered the status of the Alternative Investment Market from a regulated market to an exchange regulated market in order that companies trading on it did not have to meet the requirements of the Prospectus Directive once it came into force in 2005.

to be admitted to trading on an exchange regulated market, typically the Alternative Investment Market (AIM) also run by the LSE. Of course, these decisions are not irreversible and companies can move up to the Main Market and down to AIM depending on their circumstances.

19-100 Securities are listed when the security (not the issuer) is admitted to the Official List maintained by the FSA which is the competent authority for these purposes and in this context is known as the UK Listing Authority (UKLA).[152] To be admitted to the Official List, equity securities must be admitted to trading on a regulated market for listed securities operated by a recognised investment exchange[153] which in practice means admitted to trading on the Main Market of the LSE. The Listing Rules drawn up by UKLA govern listing and the LSE's Admission and Disclosure Standards govern trading on the Main Market of the LSE. There are then differing roles for the UKLA and the LSE, but the steps are linked and an application to UKLA for listing and to the LSE for admission to trading will be made simultaneously. With effect from April 2010, UKLA restructured the listing regime to clarify the choices available to companies seeking listing and to provide greater transparency for those investing as to the standards to which the company adheres.[154] Now there are two listing segments, Premium and Standard, and companies can migrate between them. Companies with premium-listed securities are subject to 'super-equivalence' requirements, i.e. they are subject to the requirements of the EU Directives and other 'super' UK requirements imposed by the Listing Rules, hence this category is synonymous with the highest standards of investor protection.[155] Only equity securities are eligible for a premium listing and all other listings of securities are standard listings. The Listing Rules in respect of a standard listing are based on (though sometimes go beyond) the minimum standards imposed by the EU Directives governing securities admitted to trading on a regulated market (i.e. the Prospectus, Transparency and Market Abuse Directives). In the event of any breach of any provision of the Listing Rules, UKLA can impose a penalty of such amount as it considers appropriate or it may publish a statement of censure with respect to the issuer and any director knowingly concerned in the contravention (FSMA 2000, s 91).

Listing Rule (LR) 2 sets out the basic requirements for admission to listing for all types of securities[156] and LR 14 sets out the additional eligibility and ongoing requirements where a company seeks a standard listing of equity shares.[157] LR 6 sets out additional eligibility

---

[152] FSMA 2000, s 74(1). [153] Listing Rules, 2.2.3.

[154] For the background, see FSA, *Listing Regime Review*, PS 10/02 (February 2010); FSA, *Listing Regime Review: Consultation on changes to the listing categories consequent to CP09/24*, CP 09/28 (November 2009); FSA, *Listing Regime Review*, CP 09/24 (October 2009); FSA, CP 08/21, feedback on DP 08/01; FSA, *A Review of the Structure of the Listing Regime*, DP08/1, (January 2008).

[155] See FSA, *Amendments to the Listing Rules*, etc, CP 12/2, January 2012 where the FSA notes the importance of these super-equivalent requirements to the reputation and 'quality' of the market, notes also renewed debate about the nature of premium listing and invites views on whether the premium listing standard remains correctly positioned as a benchmark of high standards or whether specific enhancements to the Listing Rules may be desirable in terms of providing additional protections to investors, see paras 1.8–1.23. Depending on responses, the FSA expects to consult further in 2012.

[156] The requirements for admission to listing include that the issuer is validly incorporated; equity securities are admitted to trading on a regulated market for listed securities operated by a recognised investment exchange; the securities must be freely transferable, fully paid, with an expected market value of at least £700,000; and there must be an approved prospectus or listing particulars: LR 2 and 3.

[157] In particular, a sufficient number (usually at least 25%) of the shares being listed must be distributed to the public and the company must comply with various disclosure obligations under the FSA Disclosure and Transparency Rules (DTR).

requirements where a company seeks a premium listing[158] and LR 7–13 set out a range of additional requirements which apply to a premium listing. LR 9 includes the continuing obligations which apply to a company with a premium listing of equity shares[159] and LR 10 (significant transactions) and LR 11 (related party transactions) are also significant obligations applicable to premium listings. There are also a series of high-level Listing Principles set out in LR 7 which are intended to guide the conduct of a listed company with a premium listing stating, for example, that a listed company must take reasonable steps to enable its directors to understand their responsibilities and obligations as directors; to establish and maintain adequate procedures, systems and controls to enable it to comply with its obligations; and it must act with integrity towards holders and potential holders of its listed equity shares.

19-101 Of course, a company need not seek a listing and it can be (and most public companies are) unlisted, i.e. its securities are not admitted to the Official List maintained by UKLA, but such a company can still be admitted to trading and unlisted public companies are commonly traded on AIM, the Alternative Investment Market which is an exchange regulated market operated by the LSE. Companies trading on AIM are subject to a simpler regime (most Directives do not apply) and with more relaxed criteria for entry to the market. Companies are not required to have reached a certain size, or to have a defined percentage of shares in public hands, or to provide a lengthy trading history.[160] All companies must produce an admission document making certain disclosures about such matters as their directors' backgrounds, their promoters and business activities.[161] Once admitted to AIM, a company has to accept certain ongoing requirements, mainly disclosure requirements with respect to financial matters and company and related party transactions and changes in the business and the management structures.[162]

19-102 There were 7,900 UK public companies on the register of companies as at 31 March 2011.[163] At the same date, there were 1,003 UK listed companies so approximately 13% of public companies were listed companies[164] while 87% were unlisted. There were 1,173 UK companies trading on AIM at that date so more companies were traded on AIM than on the Main Market though, of course, the companies on the Main Market are more significant

---

[158] Requirements in LR 6 include a requirement for a three-year trading record with published audited accounts over that period; an independent auditor; unqualified working capital statement; the appointment of a sponsor; a sufficient number (usually at least 25%) of the shares being listed must be in the hands of the public; and the securities must be capable of electronic settlement.

[159] Crucially these obligations require compliance with the DTR requirements, with the Listing Rules Model Code on directors' dealings, with various obligations with respect to allotments of shares, with disclosure and transparency obligations, with detailed requirements as to the contents of the annual report and accounts, and with corporate governance obligations.

[160] The company must be judged to be appropriate to join AIM by a nominated adviser (generally known as a nomad) who must be on a register of nomads maintained by the LSE. The company must retain a nomad at all times and the nomad is responsible for guiding and helping the company to comply with the market rules: AIM Rules, r 1.   [161] AIM Rules, r 3 and Sch 1.

[162] AIM Rules, rr 10–36.

[163] See Companies House, *Statistical Tables on Companies Registration Activities 2010–11*, Table A2. Public companies make up only 0.3% of the effective register, see Table A2.

[164] Monthly statistics on listed companies can be found on the LSE website. Another term commonly used in the media as synonymous with listed company is 'quoted company.' UKLA uses it to describe companies traded on an exchange regulated market as opposed to listed companies traded on a regulated market. In the CA 2006, the term 'quoted company' has a precise meaning (see s 385) where it is used in the context of certain disclosure requirements (see **16-1**, n 7) and is defined as encompassing a company whose equity share capital is officially listed in the UK or in an EEA State or is admitted to dealing either on the NYSE or Nasdaq (i.e. the main American stock exchanges).

economically. The numbers of companies on the respective markets are a result, in part, of a flight in recent years from regulation and from the high costs of listing, a reaction reflected in the decline, for essentially the same reasons (regulatory burdens and costs), in the numbers of public companies on the register over the past decade.[165] These market statistics also show that more than 70% of public companies are not traded on any market. For those businesses, being a public company is about status and credibility with suppliers and customers rather than any need or desire to raise share or loan capital, but it is clear that many companies no longer think the benefits justify the burdens and costs associated with public company status, hence the ongoing decline in the number on the register.

Public offers of securities

19-103 Much of the law relating to securities regulation generally and including public offers of shares derives from EU Directives which shape the domestic legislation on these matters. The objectives with respect to EU securities regulation (as broadly reflected in the preambles to the various Directives) would include:

- to establish an equivalent level of securities disclosure and investor protection throughout the EU;
- to contribute to the correct functioning and development of securities markets and to the maintenance of confidence in those markets;
- to facilitate cross-border listings and offers of shares in order to promote greater inter-penetration of national securities markets with a view to ensuring a genuine EU capital market;
- to prevent forum shopping by companies seeking jurisdictions within the EU with the lowest regulatory requirements.

19-104 The key Directive in the context of public offers is the Prospectus Directive[166] which was adopted in 2003 and came into force on 1 July 2005. It was amended by Directive 2010/73/EU[167] following a review by the European Commission[168] which concluded that generally the Prospectus Directive has functioned well and efficiently since its introduction, but that some clarifications and improvements are desirable, particularly to ease the administrative burdens on SMEs.[169] The Amending Directive must be implemented by July

---

[165] There were 11,200 public companies on the register in 2006/07 and 7,900 in 2010/11, (figures for Great Britain): Companies House, *Statistical Tables on Companies Registration Activities 2010–11*, Table A2.

[166] Directive 2003/71/EC on the prospectus to be published when securities are offered to the public or admitted to trading and amending Directive 2001/34/EC, OJ L 345, 31.12.2003, p 64. There is an associated Prospectus Directive Regulation 2004/809/EC, OJ L 149, 30.04.2004, p 1, which provides the technical detail as to the content and format of prospectuses; much of the technical detail was overseen by the Committee of European Securities Regulators (CESR) which is now replaced by the European Securities Market Authority (ESMA) and ESMA will provide technical input on the adoption of the Amending Directive 2010/73/EU.

[167] OJ L 327/1, 11.12.2010. As to the associated Regulation, see C (2012) 2086 final.

[168] The background to the amendments can be found in the following documents, see *Study on the Impact of the Prospectus Regime on EU Financial Markets, Final Report* (June 2008) which was followed by a Commission consultation in 2009 on a proposal for a draft Directive amending the Prospectus Directive which was followed by a proposal for an amending Directive, see COM (2009) 491 final, 23.09.2009.

[169] The main changes proposed were to subject some public offers to less comprehensive disclosure requirements (for example, with respect to small companies and for rights issues); to improve the format and content of the prospectus summary; to clarify the exemption from the obligation to publish a prospectus

2012.[170] The governing framework domestically is FSMA 2000, Pt VI (ss 72–103) and the FSA Prospectus Rules (PR) which contain the core rules governing the content and delivery of prospectuses and breach of either Part VI or the PR attracts the penalties specified in FSMA 2000, s 91(1A) and (3), i.e. monetary penalties and public censure.

19-105 The basic scheme is that it is unlawful for transferable securities[171] to be offered to the public in the UK unless an approved prospectus (approved by UKLA) is available to the public before the offer is made (FSMA 2000, s 85(1)) and, likewise, it is unlawful to request the admission of transferable securities[172] to trading on a regulated market situated or operating in the UK unless an approved prospectus is publicly available before the request is made (s 85(2)). The consequence of the dual prohibition is that even though an offer may be exempt from the requirement for a prospectus, if the securities are the subject of a request for admission to a regulated market, then an approved prospectus is required,[173] and vice versa. A breach of either prohibition is a criminal offence and attracts civil liability for breach of statutory duty (s 85(3), (4)).

19-106 There are exemptions from the requirement to provide a prospectus which vary depending on whether an offer to the public or admission to trading is being sought. If both steps are being taken, an offer to the public and admission to trading is sought, then any exemptions relied on must extend to each of those steps. In each case, the requirement for a prospectus is limited by the definition of 'transferable securities' with the categories of excluded securities (for example, government and public securities) being set out in FSMA 2000, Sch 11A and the PR, but note that the categories differ depending on whether the step being taken is an offer to the public or an admission to listing.[174] With respect to an offer to the public, the requirement for a prospectus does not apply, for example, to transferable securities included in an offer where the total consideration of the offer is less than €5m, an exemption which is important in practice as it allows companies to raise small but useful sums of money without the need for an approved prospectus.[175] With respect to admission to trading, there is an exemption (no prospectus is required) with respect to the admission of shares representing, over a period of 12 months, less than 10% of the number of shares of the same class already admitted to trading on the same regulated market.[176] As to what is an offer to the public, FSMA 2000, s 102B offers the widest possible definition. For these purposes, there is an offer of transferable securities to the public if there is a communication in any form or by any means to any person which presents sufficient information on the transferable securities to be offered and the terms

when companies sell through intermediaries ('retail cascades') and for employee share schemes; and to address overlapping disclosure requirements with the Transparency Directive.

[170] See FSA, *UK Implementation of Amending Directive 2010/73/EU, Simplifying the EU Prospectus and Transparency Directives*, CP11/28, December 2011.

[171] 'Transferable securities' is defined in FSMA 2000, s 102A(3). The requirement for a prospectus applies for the purposes of this provision to all transferable securities other than those excluded by s 85(5), i.e. those listed in FSMA 2000, Sch 11A or excluded by the Prospectus Rules, see PR 1.2.2.

[172] 'Transferable securities' is defined in FSMA 2000, s 102A(3). The requirement for a prospectus for the purposes of this provision applies to all transferable securities other than those excluded by s 85(6), i.e. those listed in FSMA 2000, Sch 11A, Pt 1, or excluded by the Prospectus Rules, see PR 1.2.3.

[173] It was for this reason that the Alternative Investment Market (AIM) run by the London Stock Exchange altered its status in October 2004 to an exchange regulated market ahead of the implementation of the Prospectus Directive. Most companies using AIM could frame an offer in a way which is an exempt offer, but a prospectus would still have been required to gain admission to AIM as long as AIM remained a regulated market, hence the change in status.   [174] See nn 171 and 172.

[175] FSMA 2000, s 85(1), (5), Sch 11A, para 9 (the threshold was raised in 2011 from €2.5m).

[176] PR 1.2.3R(i).

on which they are offered to enable an investor to decide to buy or subscribe for the securities in question (s 102B(1), (3)).[177] Certain categories of exempt offers (where an approved prospectus is not required) are set out in s 86, namely offers to qualified investors,[178] to fewer than 150 members (recently raised from 100 members), or where the total consideration payable for the securities cannot exceed €100,000; the minimum consideration which may be paid by any person is at least €50,000; or the securities are denominated in amounts of at least €50,000. In these situations, the investor protection goals which drive the requirement for the publication of a prospectus are of less significance either because of the nature of the securities (low value) or the nature of the would-be purchaser (qualified) or the scale of the would-be purchase (high denomination securities).

19-107 A prospectus must be submitted to UKLA for approval and must be formally approved before publication.[179] The UKLA must be satisfied that it is the home state authority in relation to the issuer; that the prospectus contains the necessary information (discussed at **19-108**); and all other requirements relating to a prospectus have been complied with.[180] The UKLA merely satisfies itself that these requirements are met by the issuer; it does not investigate or verify the accuracy of the information in the prospectus. A key feature of EU requirements is 'passporting' whereby a document approved in one Member State must be accepted by other Member States without the imposition of any further substantive requirements. UKLA must accept incoming prospectuses approved in EEA States provided they are accompanied by a certificate of approval from the home competent authority and, if requested, a translation of the summary of the prospectus (FSMA 2000, s 87H). UKLA also provides a facility whereby UK companies can request that a prospectus be approved by UKLA so that it may be used in another Member State even though there is to be no public offer or request for admission to trading in the UK.[181] A prospectus must be made available free of charge to the public as soon as possible after approval at various locations including the offices of the relevant exchange or the issuer or any intermediary involved in selling the securities, or it must be published in a newspaper widely circulated in the state where the offer is made, or made available on the issuer's website or the exchange's website.[182]

19-108 There are detailed requirements with regard to the content and form of the prospectus[183] in keeping with its status as a critically important document intended to ensure that investors are in a position to make an informed decision as to the acquisition of any securities. The necessary information which must be contained in a prospectus if it is to be approved by UKLA is the information necessary to enable an investor to make an informed assessment of the assets and liabilities, financial position, profits and losses, and prospects of the issuer of the securities and of any guarantor and the rights attaching to the

---

[177] Furthermore, to the extent that an offer of transferable securities is made to a person in the UK, it is an offer of transferable securities to the public in the UK: FSMA 2000, s 102B(2) which means it will fall within the requirement in s 85(1) for an approved prospectus.

[178] Qualified investors may be individuals or small or medium-sized firms and, assuming they meet the criteria laid down in the Prospectus Directive, n 166, art 2(1)(e), (2), they must apply for entry on the register of qualified investors which is maintained by the FSA: see PR 5.4.   [179] PR 3.1.1R.

[180] FSMA 2000, s 87A(1). 'Home state authority' is defined in s 102C.

[181] See UKLA Factsheet No 4, *Passporting Factsheet* (October 2008) as to the process. The home authority generally is the authority where the company has its registered office but there are some exceptions to that general principle.   [182] PR 3.2.4R.

[183] See PR 2; the key document as to contents and format is the Prospectus Directive Regulation (No 2004/809/EC), see n 166; also C (2012) 2086 final for proposed replacement Regulation.

securities.[184] In determining whether information is required to be included by virtue of this general duty of disclosure, regard is to be had to the particular nature of the securities and of the issuer (FSMA 2000, s 87A(4)). Essentially, detailed information must be provided as to the business, its performance, its future plans and development, any risks to which it might be subject, its financial statements, its working capital position, its directors and management, its major shareholders, and details of the offer being made and the share capital structure together with a summary of the information. The information must be presented in a form which is comprehensible and easy to analyse (FSMA 2000, s 87A(3)). A supplementary prospectus is required where a significant new factor arises or a material mistake or inaccuracy arises in the prospectus (FSMA 2000, s 87G).

19-109   A prospectus may be made up of one document (including a summary) or several and where there are separate documents, the information must be divided between a registration document which concentrates on the issuer; a securities note which concentrates on the securities being offered or listed; and, save in certain circumstances, a summary note.[185] The summary must, briefly and in non-technical language, convey the essential characteristics of, and risks associated with, the issuer, any guarantor and the transferable securities to which the prospectus relates (FSMA 2000, s 87A(6)). Different formats of prospectus reflecting different types of securities, issuers and investors may be drawn up and it is possible to include information by reference to other previously published documents (such as the annual accounts or the company's constitution).[186] The prospectus must be in the language of the home Member State and, where it is to be used in other Member States, it must be in the language of that other state or in a language customarily used in international finance although the competent authority of the Member State may require the summary to be translated into its language.[187]

Responsibility and liability for a misleading prospectus

19-110   Compensation is payable by any person responsible for a prospectus when any person has acquired securities[188] and suffered loss in respect of them as a result of any untrue or misleading statements in, or the omission of any required information from, the prospectus (FSMA 2000, s 90).[189] The persons responsible for the prospectus where the offer is of equity securities are the issuer (and the offeror, if different); each director;[190] any person who accepts responsibility for all or part of the prospectus and any person who authorised the contents of the particulars.[191] There are a number of defences set out in FSMA 2000,

---

[184]   FSMA 2000, s 87A(2). There are exceptions to the disclosure requirements, for example, on the grounds of public interest, serious detriment to the issuer and matters of minor importance: see s 87B(1). There is no longer any reference to the reasonable investor unlike in the previous law: see Hudson, *Securities Law* (2008), paras 12–56 et seq on this point. See *Secretary of State for Business Enterprise and Regulatory Reform v Sullman* [2009] 1 BCLC 397, an interesting disqualification case where the court considered that, whatever the position about a breach of a precise statutory obligation, non-disclosure or partial disclosure to investors is culpable conduct meriting a finding of 'unfitness' and is conduct below the expected standards of commercial probity which the law is entitled to expect.

[185]   As to when a summary is not required, see FSMA 2000, s 87A(5); PR 2.1.3R.   [186]   See PR 2.4.1R.

[187]   See PR 4.1.

[188]   Relief is not restricted to subscribers and purchasers in the market can claim compensation.

[189]   The measure of compensation is the tort measure rather than the contract measure.

[190]   Save in the unlikely situation where the prospectus is published without the director's knowledge or consent and, on becoming aware of its publication, as soon as practicable, he gives reasonable public notice that it was published without his knowledge or consent: PR 5.5.6R.

[191]   PR 5.5.3R. The 'persons responsible' for a prospectus are defined in PR 5.5.

Sch 10; most crucially it is a defence if a person can satisfy the court (and the burden is on him) that he reasonably believed any statement for which he was responsible to be true and not misleading or that any information omitted was properly omitted.[192] Liability is imposed therefore for negligent or fraudulent false statements. A person is also not liable if he satisfies the court that a timely correction was made of any false statements; that the false statement arose from the accurate and fair reproduction of an official statement or document; that the plaintiff was aware of the falsehood or the omitted information; or that he reasonably believed that a change in circumstances was not such as to warrant a supplementary prospectus.[193] This statutory liability under FSMA 2000, s 90(1) does not preclude other remedies such as rescission of the contract by which shares were acquired, or claims for damages for deceit, or damages for untrue or innocent misrepresentation under the Misrepresentation Act 1967.[194] Proceeding under the statute is the most straightforward claim, however, especially as it imposes what Professor Davies has described as a strong version of liability, for it is for the defendant to prove that he was not negligent rather than for the claimant to prove that he was.[195]

19-111 This potential liability under FSMA 2000, s 90 can be contrasted with the 'safe harbours' with respect to untrue or misleading statements in directors' reports[196] or in periodic or ad hoc disclosures published to the market.[197] In each case, liability arises only in cases of deceit which is unlikely to be established.[198] That this trend to restrict liability has not embraced prospectuses underlines the central role of this document in terms of investor protection.

---

[192] This defence applies not only to directors (who basically accept responsibility for the whole prospectus) but also to those experts who have contributed reports etc to the prospectus for which they must accept responsibility (but who are able to limit their potential liability in any event to the part for which they accept responsibility). In addition, any person who authorised the inclusion of an expert's statement is not liable for that statement if he reasonably believed that the expert was competent and had consented to the inclusion of the report: FSMA 2000, Sch 10, para 2(2).   [193] FSMA 2000, Sch 10, paras 3–7.

[194] See also *Secretary of State for Business Enterprise and Regulatory Reform v Sullman* [2009] 1 BCLC 397, as to potential disqualification on the grounds of unfitness in a case of non-disclosure or incomplete disclosure.

[195] See Davies, *Review of Issuer Liability, Liability for Misstatements To The Market*: A Discussion Paper by Professor Paul Davies QC (HM Treasury, March 2007), para 28. Prof Davies also noted that it is accepted that the standard of accuracy in prospectuses is high and that this could be attributed in part to the imposition of a negligence standard (see at para 71).

[196] See CA 2006, s 463 (directors liable only to company and only in deceit with respect to untrue or misleading statements in the directors' report, the remuneration report or any summary financial statement derived therefrom).

[197] See FSMA 2000, s 90A; only the issuer can be liable and only in deceit. See the discussion of s 90A at **16-28**. For the background to the modification of issuer liability under FSMA 2000, s 90A (the scope of the provision was extended in the light of the recommendations of the Davies review), see HM Treasury *Extension of the statutory regime for issuer liability* (July 2008); Davies, *Review of Issuer Liability, Final Report* (June 2007) and an earlier discussion paper of the same name, (March 2007).

[198] Further, while there is potential for an overlap between liability under FSMA 2000, s 90 and s 90A, it is provided that the application of s 90A does not limit any liability arising under s 90: Sch 10A, para 7(3) (a)(i). This ensures that claims under s 90 are protected and can be pursued rather than have the claimant constrained by the limitations of s 90A.

20

The doctrine of capital maintenance

A An overview of the doctrine of capital maintenance

20-1 With the advent of limited liability in 1855, the courts' concern turned to the protection of creditors. To that end there developed the doctrine of capital maintenance which essentially is a collection of rules designed to ensure, first, that a company obtains the capital which it has purported to raise (hence the rules governing payment for share capital which are discussed at **19-58**) and, secondly, that that capital is maintained, subject to the exigencies of the business, for the benefit and protection of the company's creditors and the discharge of its liabilities. In particular, the doctrine of capital maintenance precludes the return of capital, directly or indirectly, to the shareholders ahead of a winding up of the company.[1]

20-2 The landmark case on the doctrine of capital maintenance is the decision of the House of Lords in *Trevor v Whitworth*[2] which established the fundamental principle that there can be no return of capital to the members other than on a proper reduction of capital duly sanctioned by the courts. At issue in the case was whether a company could purchase its own shares. The House of Lords rejected any such possibility, holding that a company had no such power under the Companies Acts, even if so authorised by its articles of association. Creditors had to be protected from a reduction of capital in this way without the company adhering to the statutory provisions on reduction of capital which required any reduction to be confirmed by the court.[3] Their Lordships noted that creditors took the risk of a company losing its capital in trading, but they also had a right to rely on the company not diminishing its capital by returning any part of it to its shareholders.[4] Lord Watson explained the position as follows:[5]

---

[1] For an interesting overview of this doctrine, see the judgment of Harman J in *Barclays Bank plc v British & Commonwealth Holdings plc* [1996] 1 BCLC 1 at 6–10, Ch D, aff'd on different grounds [1996] 1 BCLC 27, CA. See also *Aveling Barford Ltd v Perion Ltd* [1989] BCLC 626 at 630–3. Of course, on a winding up of the company, shareholders can retrieve their capital only if all the creditors have been paid.

[2] (1887) 12 App Cas 409. See also *Re Exchange Banking Co, Flitcroft's Case* (1882) 21 Ch D 519 at 533; *Ooregum Gold Mining Co of India Ltd v Roper* [1892] AC 125 at 133, per Lord Halsbury LC, HL. See generally Gullifer & Payne, *Corporate Finance Law* (2011), Ch 4, 'Legal Capital'; Micheler, 'Disguised Returns of Capital—An Arm's Length Approach' (2010) CLJ 151; Armour, 'Share Capital and Creditor Protection: Efficient Rules for a Modern Company Law' (2000) 63 MLR 355; Ferran, 'Creditors' Interests and "Core" Company Law' (1999) 20 Co Law 314.

[3] See CA 2006, s 641(1). It is possible now for private companies to reduce capital without court approval: see ss 642–644, see **20-65**.   [4] See (1887) 12 App Cas 409 at 415, per Lord Herschell.

[5] (1887) 12 App Cas 409 at 423, 424.

'Paid-up capital may be diminished or lost in the course of the company's trading; that is a result which no legislation can prevent; but persons who deal with, and give credit to a limited company, naturally rely upon the fact that the company is trading with a certain amount of capital already paid, as well as upon the responsibility of its members for the capital remaining at call; and they are entitled to assume that no part of the capital which has been paid into the coffers of the company has been subsequently paid out, except in the legitimate course of its business.'

20-3 Within the limits then of what the law can achieve, the courts set about developing a set of rules concerning the establishment and maintenance of capital, rules now reflected in the provisions of the CA 2006 governing payment for share capital, the purchase of a company's own shares including financial assistance for such purchases, the reduction of capital and, crucially, distributions to shareholders. Although in the earliest cases, such as *Trevor v Whitworth*,[6] the term 'return of capital' did mean an actual return of share capital subscribed, over the years the capital maintenance doctrine has broadened into a prohibition on any payment out of or transfer of company assets to a shareholder other than by way of a distribution (typically a dividend) lawfully made, an authorised reduction of capital or other lawfully authorised procedure.[7]

20-4 Linked to the prohibition on the return of capital to the members is an equal prohibition on giving away the company's capital to non-members through a gratuitous disposition of the company's assets other than in furtherance of the company's objectives.[8] As Nourse LJ explained in *Brady v Brady*:[9]

'... the principle is that a company cannot give away its assets. So stated, it is subject to the qualification that in the realm of theory a memorandum of association may authorise a company to give away all its assets to whomsoever it pleases, including its shareholders. But in the real world of trading companies, charitable or political donations, pensions to widows of ex-employees and the like apart, it is obvious that such a power would never be taken. The principle is only a facet of the wider rule, the corollary of limited liability, that the integrity of a company's assets, except to the extent allowed by its constitution, must be preserved for the benefit of all those who are interested in them, most pertinently its creditors.'

20-5 From *Trevor v Whitworth*[10] onwards, the approach of the courts has been consistently to the effect that a company cannot, without the leave of the court or the adoption of a special procedure, return its capital to its shareholders nor give away its capital in the case of dispositions to non-shareholders. Such transactions or dispositions are ultra vires and void and cannot be ratified, not even by the shareholders unanimously.[11]

20-6 Statutory reinforcement of the protection afforded to creditors by the CA 2006 and the common law can be found in the IA 1986 which allows transactions which prove

---

[6] (1887) 12 App Cas 409.

[7] See Harman J on this point in *Barclays Bank plc v British & Commonwealth plc* [1996] 1 BCLC 1 at 14–15. See also Sealy & Worthington, *Cases and Materials* in *Company Law* (9th edn, 2010), p 514 who note that, for example, the 'capital' returned in *Re Halt Garage (1964) Ltd* [1982] 3 All ER 1016 was several thousand pounds whereas the shareholder had only contributed £1 (and retained that £1 after the 'return' of capital); and the recipient of 'capital' in *Aveling Barford Ltd v Perion Ltd* [1989] BCLC 626 was not a shareholder but a corporate vehicle used by a shareholder.

[8] *Ridge Securities Ltd v IRC* [1964] 1 All ER 275; and see Hannigan, 'Limitations on a Shareholder's Right to Vote—Effective Ratification Revisited' [2000] JBL 493 at 495–9.

[9] [1988] BCLC 20 at 38; reversed on other grounds [1988] BCLC 579, HL.   [10] (1887) 12 App Cas 409.

[11] See Hannigan, n 8.

injurious to creditors to be challenged, for example, on the ground that the transaction is at an undervalue (IA 1986, s 238: see **25-37**) or is a preference (IA 1986, s 239: see **25-50**). Directors also run the risk of personal liability for wrongful trading under IA 1986, s 214, see **25-18**, if they allow the company to continue trading past a point when they know or ought to know that there is no reasonable prospect of avoiding insolvent liquid-ation. The capital maintenance doctrine and the rules which comprise it are broader in application than the provisions of the IA 1986 for there is no requirement that the com-pany actually be insolvent at the time of the transaction or be rendered insolvent by the transaction.[12]

20-7 It would be fair to say that the doctrine of capital maintenance has its critics. Doubts have been expressed, for example, as to whether the rules on distributions are too restrictive and too costly to apply, whether the rules on financial assistance are part of the doctrine of capital maintenance at all (though this issue is less significant now that the prohibition on financial assistance applies only to public companies[13]), and, more fundamentally, as to whether the rules achieve their aim of creditor protection.

20-8 There is little doubt that the doctrine of capital maintenance can appear complex, not least because (and despite the statutory interventions) so much of the law has developed from those early cases such as *Trevor v Whitworth*[14] which the courts continue to cite. The result has probably been to obscure (because of the reliance on the language of pre-1900 cases) rather than clarify the modern doctrine. Initially, there was a self-contained and relatively narrow doctrine about the inability of a company to return share capital to its members intended to provide some protection for creditors dealing with companies with limited liability. More than a century later there is a multi-faceted (and therefore untidy) doctrine, still concerned (in part) with the protection of creditors, but also operating to constrain directors and to reinforce their duty to exercise their powers for the purposes for which they are conferred and to act to promote the success of the company (CA 2006, ss 171, 172). In this modern guise, these rules offer protection to creditors, but also to shareholders, against improper conduct by the directors and the unauthorised dissipation of the company's assets. The label 'capital maintenance' may have a dated ring to it, but the mischief at which it is aimed, unauthorised depletion of the company's assets, remains relevant. It is also the case that when an independent review of the capital maintenance doctrine was undertaken for the European Commission (in the context of a review of the Second Company Law Directive which in effect applies the doctrine of capital mainten-ance to public companies) the result was a finding that the costs arising from the applica-tion of the doctrine are not excessive and the doctrine does not unduly hinder companies in the conduct of their affairs.[15] The same is probably true in the domestic context with the notable exception of the rules governing financial assistance which were complex and costly and time consuming to apply, but which have now been repealed in respect of pri-vate companies (99.7% of the register). It is possible that the perception of the costs and complexity of the capital maintenance regime does not quite match the business reality. It is also the case that a change to any new system also would involve costs and uncertainty[16]

---

[12] See *Aveling Barford Ltd v Perion Ltd* [1989] BCLC 626 at 633 where Hoffmann J refutes any such limita-tion; also *Ridge Securities v IRC* [1964] 1 All ER 275.   [13] See CA 2006, s 678.

[14] (1887) 12 App Cas 409.

[15] KPMG, 'Feasibility Study on an alternative to the capital maintenance regime established by the Second Company Law Directive, etc' (January 2008); and see **2-24**.

[16] See Gullifer and Payne, n 2, which suggests allowing contract law and the IA 1986 to fill any gap in creditor protection arising from abolishing the doctrine of capital maintenance, but that in itself would involve costs for creditors (so far as they would need to adopt new contractual tools or refine their existing

which may be a reason for continuing the existing settled position which is well understood by company advisers. The one area which remains controversial, perhaps, is with respect to distributions, a matter which is considered at the end of this chapter.

B Purchase and redemption of a company's own shares

Introduction

20-9 As noted at **20-2**, the landmark decision of the House of Lords in *Trevor v Whitworth*[17] established the fundamental principle that there can be no return of capital to the members other than one duly sanctioned by the courts. At issue in the case was whether a company could purchase its own shares. The House of Lords rejected any such possibility holding that a company had no such power under the Companies Acts, even if so authorised by its articles of association. Creditors had to be protected from a reduction of capital in this way without the company adhering to the statutory provisions on reduction of capital which required any reduction to be confirmed by the court. The capital maintenance principle established by this case remains a foundation stone of company law but modern business needs have persuaded Parliament that some aspects of the doctrine may be relaxed, in particular with respect to the issue in the case, namely the purchase by a company of its own shares. More recently, the CA 2006 also relaxed the requirement for court confirmation of a reduction of capital, see **20-65**.

20-10 The relaxation of the prohibition on a company acquiring its own shares came initially in the Companies Act 1981 which permitted companies to issue redeemable shares (i.e. shares redeemable at the option of the company or the shareholder),[18] to purchase back their own shares and, in the case of private companies, to purchase back out of capital, so effecting the very reduction of capital which concerned the House of Lords in *Trevor v Whitworth*.[19]

20-11 This statutory change was just one of a series of measures (including tax and other incentives) introduced in the early 1980s designed to make it easier for small companies to raise equity (share) capital. The difficulties which small companies face in trying to raise equity investment are well documented, see **19-4**. Many small businesses are family concerns where the individuals concerned, much as they might welcome an injection of capital, are reluctant to raise it through an issue of shares for fear of losing control of the business to an outsider. Equally, outside investors are reluctant to contribute their capital to an enterprise when the shares are not easily marketable and where they risk being locked in. Any scheme to assist such companies has to be flexible enough to increase the marketability of the shares without necessarily depriving the existing owners of control and without jeopardising the position of the company's creditors.

---

ones) and while it would protect the large creditors in a position to use these mechanisms, smaller creditors typically find it difficult to exercise any contractual power. As for reliance on the IA 1986, the relevant creditor protection provisions are currently underused because of problems in their drafting and application and crucially the lack of funding for liquidators who have primary responsibility for pursuing these matters, see discussion in Chapter 25.

[17] (1887) 12 App Cas 409.

[18] The power to issue redeemable shares was not new in 1981 as companies had been able from 1929 to issue redeemable preference shares but the power was extended to any type of redeemable shares.

[19] (1887) 12 App Cas 409.

20-12 Allowing a company to have complementary powers to issue redeemable shares and to purchase back its own shares was thought to meet these requirements and give companies the flexible equity capital structure they wanted.[20] A company may issue redeemable shares envisaging from the outset that the shareholder's commitment is to be a short-term one or at least for a definite period. The company has the use of the capital for this period while the investor knows that he is not locked in. The purchase powers, on the other hand, enable the company at some point in the future to buy back shares without having to anticipate that eventuality at the time of issue. As far as investors are concerned, the possibility that the company will purchase the shares reduces the chances of their being locked into the company.

20-13 It was thought that these new powers might accommodate family re-arrangements, for example by enabling founding shareholders to resign and realise their investment without the remaining family members being required personally to fund the purchase back of their shares. The provisions might offer a means of dealing with the holdings of deceased members, or buying out discontented shareholders, or buying employee shareholdings when the employment is terminated.

20-14 All of these factors pointed towards these powers being of greatest use in private companies, but the powers are also available to public companies and commonly used by them. Indeed, it is standard practice for listed public companies to seek authority from their shareholders each year to purchase back their own shares. Obviously, the use of the powers by such companies is not driven by concerns about any lack of marketability of their shares, rather they see a variety of other advantages in having this flexibility.[21] For example, buy-backs, as purchase schemes are commonly called, may be a means of enhancing earnings per share when market conditions otherwise make this difficult. In addition, cash-rich companies may want to return capital to shareholders to enable the shareholders to make their individual investment decisions with regard to that capital rather than have the company use it in unsuitable and wasteful ways simply to reduce the company's cash holdings. Buy-backs can also prove attractive to institutional shareholders who because of the size of their holdings find it difficult to offload their holdings in the market in the normal way. On occasion, concerns have been voiced that listed companies might use these powers, for example as a defensive mechanism against takeover bids (by buying up shares in the market) or might in effect be insider dealing in their own shares. The general constraints on such conduct (the Takeover Code, the Listing Rules, the criminal law) are sufficient to address any such concerns, however, and there has been no evidence of any such abuses occurring.

20-15 A final point to remember is that the exercise of these powers may have tax consequences for both the company and the shareholders involved and that factor weighs heavily in any decision to use these provisions.

The statutory framework

20-16 Given the fundamental shift away from the prohibition on the purchase of a company's own shares as laid down in *Trevor v Whitworth*,[22] Parliament surrounds the exercise of these redemption and purchase powers with stringent procedural requirements designed

---

[20] See DTI, *The Purchase by a Company of its Own Shares, A Consultative Document* (Cmnd 7944, 1980).
[21] See Pettet, 'Share Buy-Backs' in Rider (ed), *The Corporate Dimension* (1998).
[22] (1887) 12 App Cas 409.

to ensure that the powers can only be exercised in certain circumstances, using certain funds and in the full glare of publicity. The question is whether such requirements are effective to minimise the erosion of the doctrine of capital maintenance. A broader question, as noted earlier, is whether the doctrine itself is an effective way of protecting creditors.

20-17 The starting point is CA 2006, s 658(1) which, reflecting the rule in *Trevor v Whitworth*,[23] provides that a limited company may not acquire its own shares[24] whether by purchase, subscription or otherwise[25] except in accordance with the statutory provisions of CA 2006, Pt 18, i.e. redemption in accordance with ss 684–689 or purchase under ss 690–737. This prohibition on a company acquiring its own shares does not apply to:

(1) the acquisition of shares in a reduction of capital duly made (discussed later);

(2) the purchase of shares in pursuance of a court order under certain statutory provisions[26] (which rarely occurs); or

(3) the forfeiture of shares, or the acceptance of shares surrendered in lieu, in pursuance of the articles, for failure to pay any sum payable in respect of the shares (which rarely occurs) (s 659(2)).

20-18 The statutory provisions on redemption and purchase are complex and the procedures, while similar, are not identical. On issues of detail, therefore, the precise wording of the statutory provisions should be consulted.

20-19 Strict adherence to the statutory procedures is required[27] for it is only redemption or purchase in accordance with the statutory provisions which is permissible (CA 2006, s 658(1)). The courts may allow some dispensing with or waiver of some procedural requirements when agreed to informally but unanimously by the members,[28] but not if the provision in question is intended to protect a wider class of persons, in particular the company's creditors rather than merely the current shareholders.[29] In the event of a contravention, the company is liable on conviction to a fine, every officer of the company who is in default is liable to imprisonment or a fine, and the purported acquisition is void.[30]

Redemption of own shares

20-20 A private limited company may issue shares that are to be redeemed or are liable to be redeemed, subject to any exclusion or restriction in the company's articles, while a public

---

[23] (1887) 12 App Cas 409.

[24] See also CA 2006, s 136 which generally prohibits a company from being a member of its holding company and ss 660–661 (shares held by company's nominee are treated as held by the nominee on his own account). The prohibition on the acquisition of its own shares does not prevent a company (A) from acquiring the shares of another company (B) in circumstances where the sole asset of the acquired company (B) is shares in the acquiring company (A): *Acatos & Hutcheson plc v Watson* [1995] 1 BCLC 218.

[25] A company may acquire its fully-paid shares other than for valuable consideration: CA 2006, s 659(1).

[26] i.e. under CA 2006, s 98 (objections to resolution for public company to be re-registered as private); s 721(6) (objection to redemption or purchase out of capital); s 759 (breach of prohibition of public offers by private company) or Part 30 (relief on the grounds of unfair prejudice to members): s 659(2).

[27] *Re R W Peak (Kings Lynn) Ltd* [1998] 1 BCLC 193.

[28] *Kinlan v Crimmin* [2007] 2 BCLC 67 at 81; *Dashfield v Davidson* [2008] BCC 222; *BDG Roof-Bond Ltd v Douglas* [2000] 1 BCLC 401 at 417; *Re Torvale Group Ltd* [1999] 2 BCLC 605, applying the *Duomatic* principle which is discussed at **15-73**.

[29] *Kinlan v Crimmin* [2007] 2 BCLC 67 at 81; *Dashfield v Davidson* [2008] BCC 222; *BDG Roof-Bond Ltd v Douglas* [2000] 1 BCLC 401 at 417; *Re Torvale Group Ltd* [1999] 2 BCLC 605.

[30] CA 2006, s 658(2), (3); *Trevor v Whitworth* (1887) 12 App Cas 409.

company may only issue redeemable shares if it is authorised to do so by its articles (CA 2006, s 684(1)–(3)). Redeemable shares cannot be issued unless the company has other shares in issue which are not redeemable (s 684(4)).

20-21 The directors may determine the terms, conditions and manner of redemption if they are authorised to do so by the articles or by an ordinary resolution of the company,[31] otherwise the terms, conditions and manner of redemption must be stated in the articles.[32] The directors, if so authorised, must determine those terms etc before the shares are allotted and details of the terms etc must be included in the statement of capital which must be provided to the registrar of companies when the shares are allotted.[33]

20-22 Shares to be redeemed must be fully paid-up (otherwise the creditors would lose a valuable asset on liquidation, namely uncalled capital) and payment must be made at the time when the shares are redeemed unless the terms of redemption provide for deferred payment[34] by agreement between the company and the holder (CA 2006, s 686). It had been thought that 'payment' had to be in cash, but in *BDG Roof-Bond Ltd v Douglas*[35] the court considered that a non-cash consideration may be agreed—the CA 2006 does not clarify this point. The funds which may be used for payment are restricted to distributable profits and the proceeds of a fresh issue made for the purposes of the redemption (s 687(2)), save in the case of a private company which may redeem out of capital (s 687(1)), see **20-42**.

20-23 Shares acquired are cancelled on redemption so reducing the company's issued capital by the nominal value of the shares redeemed (CA 2006, s 688). Because of the requirement to establish a capital redemption reserve (s 733, see **20-35** et seq), a reduction of capital does not occur save in the exceptional case where a private company redeems out of capital. Within one month of the redemption, notice must given to the registrar of companies specifying the shares redeemed together with a statement of capital (s 689(1), (2)).

20-24 If, having agreed to do so, a company fails to redeem shares, the company is not liable in damages in respect of any such failure.[36] Specific performance may still be available but not if the company shows that it is unable to meet the costs of redeeming the shares in question out of distributable profits.[37]

Purchase of own shares

20-25 Any company (public or private) may purchase its own shares (including redeemable shares) in accordance with the statutory scheme, subject to any restrictions in the company's articles, and provided that the company is not left with only redeemable shares or

---

[31] CA 2006, s 685(1). Details of the earliest and latest dates on which the company has power to redeem the shares; whether the shares are redeemable in any event or liable to be redeemed at the option of the company or of the shareholder; and whether any (and if so, what) premium is payable on redemption must be included in the notes to the accounts: s 396(3); The Large and Medium-sized Companies and Groups (Accounts and Reports) Regulations 2008, SI 2008/410, Sch 1, Pt 3, para 47(2).

[32] CA 2006, s 685(4); and see *Dashfield v Davidson* [2008] BCC 222 where the contract was contained in the articles. [33] CA 2006, s 685(3); see also s 555(3)(b).

[34] Allowing for deferred payment is new in the CA 2006, previously deferred payment rendered the transaction void, see *Kinlan v Crimmin* [2007] 2 BCLC 67. [35] [2000] 1 BCLC 401.

[36] CA 2006, s 735(2). The section is concerned with direct claims for damages as a result of a breach by the company of its obligation to redeem or purchase the shares. It does not preclude the recovery of damages claimed by a plaintiff against the company for breach of a financing agreement even though the measure of damages for that breach may well be the equivalent of damages for failure to redeem: *Barclays Bank plc v B & C Holdings plc* [1996] 1 BCLC 1, CA.

[37] CA 2006, s 735(3). As to the position where the company goes into winding up, see s 735(4)–(6).

shares held as treasury shares (see **20-38**).[38] Shares to be purchased must be fully paid-up and (unlike redemption) payment must be made at the time when the shares are purchased (s 691). The general requirement of payment on purchase is to prevent companies from oppressing shareholders by purchasing their shares so depriving them of their status as members but without actually paying over the proceeds. This requirement also resolves difficulties of timing and valuation. It had been thought that 'payment' had to be in cash, but in *BDG Roof-Bond Ltd v Douglas*[39] the court considered that a non-cash consideration may be agreed—the CA 2006 does not clarify this point. Payment may be made from distributable profits or the proceeds of a fresh issue made for the purposes of financing the purchase (s 692(2)), and a private company may purchase its own shares out of capital (s 692(1)), see **20-42**.

20-26 On purchase, (with the exception of treasury shares, see **20-38**), the shares are cancelled so reducing the company's issued capital by the nominal value of the shares purchased (CA 2006, s 706). Cancellation reduces the impact which purchase schemes can have within the company, for example, by ensuring that directors cannot exercise any voting rights in respect of those shares. Cancellation should increase the earnings of the remaining shares although this depends on factors such as the market's perception of the wisdom of redemption or purchase, the price paid and whether there has been a fresh issue of shares. Because of the requirement to establish a capital redemption reserve (s 733: see **20-35**), a reduction of capital does not occur save in the exceptional case where a private company purchases out of capital. If, having agreed to do so, a company fails to purchase shares, the company is not liable in damages in respect of any such failure.[40] Specific performance may still be available but not if the company shows that it is unable to meet the costs of purchasing the shares in question out of distributable profits.[41]

Off-market and market purchases

20-27 The scheme of purchase differs depending on whether the share purchases are 'off-market' or 'market' purchases as defined in CA 2006, s 693. A lower level of regulation of market purchases is appropriate in recognition of the fact that the market authorities[42] impose additional regulatory requirements which, coupled with the higher degree of publicity attaching to such purchases, are sufficient to deter any abuses.

20-28 A market purchase is made where the purchase is made on a recognised investment exchange (RIE) and subject to a marketing arrangement on the exchange,[43] i.e. where the shares are listed[44] or are capable of being dealt with on the RIE without a requirement for

---

[38] CA 2006, s 690. A listed company with a premium listing of equity securities, see **19-100**, is subject to additional constraints as to the manner in which it can conduct share buy-backs, the price it pays, the timing of purchases and the disclosure required, see LR 12.2 and LR 12.4. The Takeover Code, rule 9 may also be relevant, see Appendix 1 to the Code.   [39] [2000] 1 BCLC 401.

[40] CA 2006, s 735(2). See also n 36.

[41] CA 2006, s 735(3). As to the position where the company goes into winding up, see s 735(4)–(6).

[42] i.e. the UK Listing Authority, which is part of the FSA, and market operators such as the London Stock Exchange.

[43] CA 2006, s 693(3). 'Recognised investment exchange' means a body (other than an overseas investment exchange) which is a recognised investment exchange for the purposes of the FSMA 2000, Pt 18: CA 2006, s 693(5). The relevant RIEs for this purpose are the London Stock Exchange plc and Plus Stock Exchange plc. A list of RIEs is maintained by the FSA on its website.

[44] i.e. listed by the UKLA, the UK Listing Authority, which maintains the official list of securities, see FSMA 2000, s 74, see **19-100**.

permission for individual transactions.[45] An off-market purchase is where the purchase does not take place on an RIE or the purchase is on an RIE but the company's shares are not listed or traded on the exchange.[46]

20-29 As a general rule, private companies and public companies which are not publicly traded make off-market purchases while publicly traded companies normally make market purchases, but in some instances may transact off-market purchases.

20-30 In relation to an off-market purchase, the terms of a specific contract of purchase must be authorised in advance by the company by a special resolution.[47] In the case of a public company, the resolution must specify a date on which the authority to purchase is to expire and that date must not be later than five years after the date on which the resolution is passed.[48]

20-31 Where the resolution is a written resolution, a member who holds shares to which the resolution relates is not an eligible member, i.e. is not entitled to vote, so the resolution must be carried without his support.[49] Where the resolution is to be passed at a meeting, the resolution is not effective if any member of the company holding shares to which the resolution relates exercises the voting rights carried by any of those shares[50] in voting on the resolution and the resolution would not have been passed if he had not done so (CA 2006, s 695(3)). The special resolution is not validly passed, where a written resolution is used, unless a copy of the contract (if it is in writing) or a memorandum of its terms (if it is not) is circulated to the members at or before the time the resolution is sent or submitted to the members (s 696(2)(a)). The copy or memorandum must give the names of the members holding shares which are to be purchased.[51] Where a meeting is held, the copy or memorandum must be available for inspection by members of the company both at the company's registered office (for not less than 15 days prior to the meeting) and at the meeting itself (s 696(2)(b)).

20-32 A company may not make a market purchase unless the purchase has first been authorised by an ordinary resolution (CA 2006, s 701(1)).[52] The authority may be general or limited to the purchase of shares of any particular class or description and may be conditional

---

[45] CA 2006, s 693(3), (4). Purchases of shares in companies traded on AIM (the Alternative Investment Market, see **19-101**) are market purchases therefore.   [46] CA 2006, s 693(2).

[47] CA 2006, ss 693(1)(a), 694. The authority conferred by the resolution may be varied, revoked or from time to time renewed by a further special resolution: s 694(4). See *Dashfield v Davidson* [2008] BCC 222. Shareholder approval is sought because the funding of the purchase comes primarily from distributable profits and these are funds which could otherwise be distributed to all the shareholders so their approval is needed for a decision to use the funds for the benefit of some shareholders only. This potential disadvantage to all shareholders explains why the Listing Rules require listed companies which wish to purchase 15% or more of their shares to make a tender offer to all the shareholders of that class so that they all have the opportunity to participate, see LR 12.4.2. The FSA is proposing a change to that provision to make it clear that a listed company can purchase 15% or more of any class of its own equity shares, provided that the full terms of the share buyback are specifically approved by shareholders: see FSA, Amendments to the Listing Rules, Prospectus Rules and Disclosure and Transparency Rules (January 2012) CP 12/2, para 4.34.

[48] CA 2006, s 694(5).   [49] CA 2006, s 695(2).

[50] This is less restrictive than the position with respect to a written resolution where the member affected is entirely disenfranchised, whereas on a resolution at a meeting, a member is only restricted from exercising the votes attached to the shares to be acquired.   [51] CA 2006, s 696(3), (4).

[52] ABI Guidelines suggest additional obligations to those set out in s 701, namely that a company making a market purchase should obtain shareholder authorisation by a special resolution, rather than an ordinary resolution, and should renew that authority annually, rather than take it for a five-year period; also that the company should undertake to exercise an authority to purchase its own shares only if so to do would result in an increase in earnings per share and is in the best interests of shareholders generally.

or unconditional (s 701(1)). The authority must specify the maximum number of shares which may be acquired, determine both the maximum and minimum price which may be paid for the shares[53] and specify a date on which the authority is to expire which must in any event be not later than five years from the date when the resolution is passed (s 701(5)). Any resolution conferring, varying, revoking or renewing such an authority to purchase must be sent to the registrar of companies within 15 days after it is passed.[54] No question of disenfranchising any shares arises in this context since the authority is not specifically aimed at any particular shares but is a general authority.

Financing of redemption and purchase-back schemes

20-33 A crucial element in any redemption or purchase-back scheme is the source of the funding to pay for it. The risk to creditors is that capital is returned to the shareholders leaving a shell with inadequate assets to pay off the company's creditors in full. The legislation attempts to prevent that happening by providing that, save in the case of private companies which may redeem or purchase out of capital, companies must fund redemption or purchase-back:

(1) out of distributable profits;[55] or the proceeds of a fresh issue of shares made for the purpose of redemption or financing the purchase; and

(2) any premium payable on redemption or purchase must be paid out of distributable profits of the company, subject to certain exceptions.[56]

20-34 Essentially, the company must use funds (distributable profits) which could have gone to the shareholders anyway (usually in the form of dividends) or it must substitute new capital brought in by a fresh issue of shares for the capital which it is repaying. Neither has any impact on the company's creditors so there is no erosion of the capital maintenance doctrine. Furthermore, to ensure that this is in fact the case, the company must set up a capital redemption reserve fund which is one of the company's undistributable reserves (CA 2006, s 733(1)).

20-35 Where shares of a company are redeemed or purchased wholly out of the company's profits, the amount by which the company's issued share capital is diminished on cancellation of the shares redeemed or purchased must be transferred to the capital redemption reserve (s 733(2)).

20-36 If the shares are redeemed or purchased wholly or partly out of the proceeds of a fresh issue and the aggregate amount of those proceeds is less than the aggregate nominal value of the shares redeemed or purchased, the amount of the difference must be transferred to the capital redemption reserve; but this does not apply if the proceeds of the fresh issue are

---

[53] CA 2006, s 701(3). The price may be determined either by specifying a particular sum or providing a basis or formula for calculating the price in question without reference to any person's discretion or opinion: s 701(7). This is to ensure that the directors are not in a position to enter into transactions at varying prices depending on their relationship with the vendors.

[54] CA 2006, ss 701(8), 30(1). This is an exception to the general rule that ordinary resolutions do not have to be delivered to the registrar of companies.

[55] i.e. profits out of which the company could make a distribution within the meaning of CA 2006, s 830: s 736. The rules establishing what is a lawful distribution are set out in CA 2006, Pt 23, discussed at **20-84**.

[56] CA 2006, ss 687(2), (3), 692(2); the exceptions are where the shares redeemed or purchased back were originally issued at a premium in which case the proceeds of a fresh issue may be used to pay the premium to a limited extent: see ss 687(4), 692(3).

applied by the company in making a redemption or purchase of its own shares in addition to a payment out of capital.[57] Payments out of capital are discussed later.

20-37 The provisions of the Companies Act relating to the reduction of a company's share capital[58] apply as if the capital redemption reserve were paid-up share capital of the company, except that the reserve may be applied by the company in paying up shares to be allotted to members of the company as fully-paid bonus shares (CA 2006, s 733(5), (6)). Reduction of capital is discussed at **20-56**.

Treasury shares

20-38 Where companies purchase 'qualifying shares' out of distributable profits, they may hold those shares 'in treasury' rather than cancel them (CA 2006, ss 724(3), 706).[59] 'Qualifying shares' for these purposes are: listed shares, i.e. shares included on the official list maintained by the UKLA in accordance with the FSMA 2000, Pt 6 (see **19-100**); shares traded on AIM, the Alternative Investment Market (see **19-101**); shares listed in an EEA State; or shares traded on a regulated market.[60]

20-39 Once shares are held in treasury,[61] the voting rights attached to such shares are suspended and the company is prohibited from paying any dividend or making any other distribution to itself as a result of it holding treasury shares (CA 2006, s 726). The holding of treasury shares by nominees is not permitted and the fact that the company is holding the shares as treasury shares will be apparent as the company must be entered in the register of members as the holder of the shares (s 724(4)).

20-40 Treasury shares may be sold for cash by the company, transferred for the purposes of or pursuant to any employees' share scheme or cancelled.[62] The ability to sell the shares for cash gives the company flexibility to raise additional funds without the need for further allotments of shares but, as noted at **19-37**, any sale of treasury shares is subject to the pre-emption requirements. Details of any shares held as treasury shares must be given in the notes to the company's accounts.[63] Contravention of any of these provisions is an offence by the company and every officer in default (CA 2006, s 732).

Disclosure requirements

20-41 Within 28 days of any shares purchased being delivered to the company, a return must be delivered to the registrar of companies distinguishing between treasury shares and other shares and stating the number and nominal value of the shares and the date on which they

---

[57] CA 2006, s 733(3); in the latter case, it is accepted that there will be a reduction of capital.

[58] See CA 2006, ss 641–652.

[59] For the background to these provisions which were first introduced in 2003, see Morse, 'The Introduction of Treasury Shares into English Law and Practice' [2004] JBL 303.

[60] CA 2006, s 724(2). Regulated markets are markets so designated under the Markets in Financial Instruments Directive (2004/39/EC) (the Mifid Directive) and the FSA maintains the list of regulated markets for these purposes which is available on their website. The relevant regulated markets for this purpose are the London Stock Exchange and the Plus-listed market.

[61] There is no longer any cap on the number of shares which may be held in treasury. Previously, CA 2006, s 725(1) limited the number of shares which could be held in treasury to 10% of the nominal value of the company's issued share capital, reflecting the requirements of the Second EC Company Law Directive, since amended. Consequently, CA 2006, s 725 has been repealed.   [62] CA 2006, ss 727(1), 729(1).

[63] CA 2006, s 396; The Large and Medium-sized Companies and Groups (Accounts and Reports) Regulations 2008, SI 2008/410, Sch 1, Pt 3, para 47(1)(b).

were delivered to the company (CA 2006, s 707(1)). In the case of a public company, further details relating to the aggregate amount paid by the company for the shares and the maximum and minimum paid by the company for shares of each class purchased must be included (s 707(4)). A copy of any contract of purchase, or a written memorandum of its terms, must be kept at the company's registered office or other specified place for 10 years from the date of purchase and must be available for inspection by any member of the company and, if it is a public company, by any other person (s 702(2)–(6)). Details of any purchases must also be given in the directors' report.[64]

Private companies—redemption or purchase out of capital

20-42 Subject to any restrictions or prohibitions in its articles, a private company may redeem or purchase its own shares otherwise than out of distributable profits or the proceeds of a fresh issue of shares (CA 2006, s 709(1)). Permitting private companies in certain circumstances to redeem or purchase shares out of capital is something which potentially has a significant impact on creditors. It is unsurprising therefore that the statutory provisions surround such purchases with even more stringent requirements than those already noted.

20-43 First, to minimise the amount which may be paid out of capital, the company must first use any available distributable profits[65] and the proceeds of any fresh issue made for the purpose of redemption or purchase before resorting to capital with the amount then needed being described as 'the permissible capital payment'.[66] On the other hand, there is no requirement to have any available distributable profits or to have a fresh issue of shares.

20-44 Secondly, a payment out of capital is not lawful (CA 2006, s 713(1)) unless the following requirements are met:

- a directors' statement and auditor's report is required;
- the payment must be approved by special resolution;
- there must be public notice of the proposed payment;
- the directors' statement and auditor's report must be available for inspection before approval.

20-45 The company's directors must make a statement[67] specifying the amount of the permissible capital payment for the shares in question and stating that, having made full inquiry into the affairs and prospects of the company, they have formed the opinion:

(1) as regards its initial situation immediately following the date on which the payment out of capital is proposed to be made, that there will be no grounds on which the company could then be found unable to pay its debts;[68] and

---

[64] CA 2006, s 396; The Large and Medium-sized Companies and Groups (Accounts and Reports) Regulations 2008, SI 2008/410, Sch 7, Pt 2, para 9.

[65] Whether there are available profits is determined in this instance in accordance with CA 2006, s 712 rather than Part 23 which applies generally: s 711(2).

[66] CA 2006, s 710. See s 734(2), (3) as to the necessary transfers to, or reduction of, the capital redemption reserve.

[67] The statement must be in the prescribed form: CA 2006, s 714(5). The requirements are set out in The Companies (Shares and Share Capital) Regulations 2009, SI 2009/388, reg 14: the statement must be in writing, it must indicate that it is the directors' statement, it must be signed by each director, and must state whether the company's business includes that of a banking or insurance company.

[68] CA 2006, s 714(3)(a). In forming their opinion for these purposes, the directors must take into account all of the company's liabilities (including contingent or prospective liabilities): s 714(4).

(2) as regards its prospects for the year immediately following that date that, having regard to:

(a) their intentions with respect to the management of the company's business during that year; and

(b) the amount and character of the company's financial resources that will in their view be available to the company during that year, the company will be able to continue to carry on business as a going concern (and will accordingly be able to pay its debts as they fall due) throughout that year (CA 2006, s 714(3)).

20-46 This emphasis on solvency reflects the overriding concern that creditors must be protected from injudicious use of redemption or purchase schemes. Any director who makes this statement without having reasonable grounds for the opinion expressed in it is liable to imprisonment or a fine or both (CA 2006, s 715). More significant, however, is the potential liability where a company is wound up and it has made a payment out of capital and its assets prove insufficient for the payment of its debts and liabilities and the expenses of winding up.[69] If the winding up commenced within one year of the date on which the relevant payment out of capital was made, then the person whose shares were redeemed or purchased and the directors who signed the statement are, so as to enable the insufficiency to be met, liable to contribute to the company's assets.[70]

20-47 The person whose shares were so redeemed or purchased is liable to contribute an amount not exceeding so much of the relevant payment as was made by the company in respect of his shares and the directors are jointly and severally liable with that person to contribute that amount.[71] A director will be excused liability if he shows that he had reasonable grounds for forming the opinion set out in the declaration.[72] Presumably he will claim that he was justified in relying on the auditors who, after all, agreed with his opinion because annexed to the directors' statement must be a report by the company's auditor stating that:

(1) he has inquired into the company's state of affairs;[73]

(2) the amount specified in the statement as the permissible capital payment for the shares in question is in his view properly determined in accordance with CA 2006, ss 710–712; and

(3) he is not aware of anything to indicate that the opinion expressed by the directors in their statement as to any of the matters in s 714(3) (set out at **20-45**) is unreasonable in all the circumstances (s 714(6)).

20-48 Any payment out of capital must be approved by a special resolution.[74] Where a written resolution is used, a member who holds shares to which the resolution relates is not an eligible member, i.e. is not entitled to vote (CA 2006, s 717(2)). Where the resolution is passed at a meeting, the resolution is not effective if any member of the company holding shares to which the resolution relates exercises the voting rights carried by any of those

---

[69] See IA 1986, s 76(1).   [70] IA 1986, s 76(2).   [71] IA 1986, s 76(3)   [72] IA 1986, s 76(2)(b).

[73] A failure by an auditor to inquire to the extent that an auditor of reasonable competence would do means that the auditor is not in a position to say whether the directors' opinion is reasonable or not and, in consequence, the auditor cannot properly give an opinion for these purposes; if he does give an opinion in such circumstances, he is liable in negligence, see *Cook v Green* [2009] BCC 204 which concerned the equivalent auditor's statement then required for the purposes of financial assistance by a private company.

[74] CA 2006, s 716. The resolution must be passed on or within the week immediately following the date of the directors' statement required by s 714. The actual payment out of capital must be made no more than five and not later than seven weeks after the date of the resolution: s 723(1).

shares in voting on the resolution and the resolution would not have been passed if he had not done so (s 717(3)).

20-49 The resolution is also ineffective unless the required directors' statement and auditor's report (discussed above) are circulated with or before the written resolution is circulated to the members or the statement and report are available for inspection by members of the company at the meeting at which the resolution is passed (CA 2006, s 718(2), (3)).

20-50 Various disclosure requirements apply which are aimed at bringing the proposed payment to the attention of creditors who may wish to apply to the court for an order prohibiting payment (see **20-53**). Within the week immediately following the date of the resolution for payment out of capital, the company must cause to be published in the *Gazette* a notice:

(1) stating that the company has approved a payment out of capital for the purpose of acquiring its own shares by redemption or purchase (as the case may be);

(2) specifying the amount of the permissible capital payment and the date of the resolution;

(3) stating that the directors' statement and the auditor's report are available for inspection; and

(4) stating that any creditor of the company may at any time within the five weeks immediately following the date of the resolution apply to the court for an order prohibiting payment (CA 2006, s 719(1)).

20-51 A similar notice must be published in a national newspaper or a notice in writing to that effect must be given to each creditor (s 719(2)). A copy of the directors' statement and the auditor's report must also be sent to the registrar of companies at the same time (s 719(4)).

20-52 In recognition of the potential for abuse when companies are permitted to redeem or purchase back out of capital, provision is made in CA 2006, s 721 for an application by an objecting creditor or member to the court for cancellation of the resolution authorising payment out of capital. No such procedure is available in respect of purchase or redemption in any other instance.

20-53 An application must be within five weeks of the date on which the resolution was passed and may be made by any member of the company (other than one who consented to or voted in favour of the resolution) or by any creditor of the company.[75] No minimum shareholding or debt is required but the more insignificant the amounts, the less weight is likely to be attached to the objections. The difficulty for those objecting, particularly if they are members, is to persuade the court to set aside something which has been approved by a special resolution and without the votes of any member who holds shares to which the resolution relates. The courts in such circumstances tend to refuse redress, stating that the members know best and that it is not for the court to interfere in what is essentially a difference as to business policy.[76]

20-54 The jurisdiction of the court on any application is open-ended. The court may adjourn the proceedings in order that an arrangement can be made for the purchase of the interests of

---

[75] CA 2006, s 721(1), (2); notice of the application must also be given immediately to the registrar of companies: s 722(1).

[76] The position would not be dissimilar to that of shareholders trying to persuade the court not to confirm a reduction of capital sanctioned by special resolution. They have usually been unsuccessful. See **20-78**.

dissentient members or for the protection of dissentient creditors, as the case may be (CA 2006, s 721(3)). Without prejudice to such powers, the court must make an order on such terms and conditions as it thinks fit either confirming or cancelling the resolution. The court's order may, in particular, provide for the purchase by the company of the shares of any members and for the reduction of the company's capital accordingly.[77]

Purchase out of capital/reduction of capital

20-55 The Company Law Review recommended the retention generally of the provisions on redemption and purchase of own shares, subject to some technical improvements and one substantive change.[78] The CLR recommended the introduction of a simplified procedure for a reduction of capital on the basis of a special resolution and a declaration of solvency by the directors (see CA 2006, s 641), see **20-65**. The CLR considered that such a procedure would mean that there was no need to retain the procedure allowing for redemption or purchase out of capital.[79] The Government was persuaded, however, that there are sufficient differences between the two regimes to justify the retention of the power to purchase out of capital. The distinct elements of a purchase out of capital include that the directors' statement has to be backed up by an auditor's report, the requirement for publicity in the *Gazette* and a national newspaper, and the ability of a creditor to go to court to challenge the transaction. Those elements may in some circumstances provide greater reassurance for creditors than a reduction of capital on the basis of a solvency statement by the directors under s 641, hence the need for both procedures.

C Reduction of capital

The statutory framework

20-56 At the beginning of this chapter, we noted that the House of Lords in *Trevor v Whitworth*[80] had established the fundamental principle that there can be no return of capital by a company to its members other than on a proper reduction of capital duly sanctioned by the courts. The statute now allows for reduction in a number of ways, some of which we have already considered, such as a reduction of capital on a redemption or purchase of its own shares by a private company out of capital.[81] Creditors and members are protected in such cases by the extensive statutory provisions governing such schemes which were discussed at **20-42**. Reduction can also occur as a consequence of a court order for the purchase by the company of shares held by an objecting member under a variety of provisions[82] or as

---

[77] CA 2006, s 721(6). A copy of any order must be delivered to the registrar of companies: s 722(3).

[78] Company Law Review, *Final Report*, vol I (2001), para 10.6; *Completing the Structure* (2000), paras 7.16–7.19; *Company Formation and Capital Maintenance* (1999), paras 3.49–3.64 and Annex B.

[79] See *Modernising Company Law* (Cm 5553-I, 2002), para 6.5.

[80] (1887) 12 App Cas 409. The courts are alert to attempts to disguise what is in effect a return of capital to the shareholders, see *Aveling Barford Ltd v Perion Ltd* [1989] BCLC 626 (a sale of an asset, at a gross undervalue, to a company controlled by a shareholder did not hide the true nature of the transaction which was an unauthorised return of capital to that shareholder). See also Harman J in *Barclays Bank plc v British & Commonwealth Holdings plc* [1996] 1 BCLC 1 at 10–11, Ch D, aff'd on different grounds [1996] 1 BCLC 27, CA.

[81] Reduction does not occur in the case of redemption or purchase otherwise than out of capital for, in those instances, an amount equivalent to the amount redeemed or purchased must be transferred to the capital redemption reserve which, for most purposes, is treated as if it were share capital: CA 2006, s 733(6).

[82] For example, under CA 2006, s 98 (proceedings objecting to resolution for public company to be re-registered as private); s 721(6) (objection to redemption or purchase out of capital); s 759 (remedial order in

a result of forfeiture or surrender by members. For example, a public company may provide in its articles that shares may be forfeited for non-payment of calls in respect of sums remaining unpaid on the shares.[83]

20-57 In practice, the most important ways in which a limited company may reduce its share capital are set out in CA 2006, s 641(1), namely:

(1) in the case of a private company limited by shares, by special resolution supported by a solvency statement (ss 642–644);

(2) in any case, by special resolution confirmed by the court (ss 645–651).

20-58 The Company Law Review initially favoured the replacement of the procedure for reduction subject to court confirmation with the scheme based on a special resolution supported by a declaration of solvency.[84] Consultations showed that the finality which is given to disputes by a court confirmation is valued highly in practice, however, and so the Review concluded that the court-based procedure should be retained.[85]

20-59 These powers to reduce capital are subject to any restriction or prohibition contained in the company's articles[86] (CA 2006, s 641(6)) and, if the reduction of capital amounts to a variation or abrogation of class rights, additionally class consent will be required; that issue is discussed at **14-43**. Also, a private company cannot reduce capital by means of a solvency statement if the effect would be to leave the company without any member holding other than redeemable shares (s 641(2)). Otherwise, a company may reduce its share capital in any way,[87] but the most common methods of reduction are those identified in s 641(4) which provides that a company may:

(1) extinguish or reduce the liability on any of its shares in respect of share capital not paid up; or

(2) either with or without extinguishing or reducing liability on any of its shares,

(a) cancel any paid-up share capital that is lost or unrepresented by available assets; or

(b) repay any paid-up share capital in excess of the company's wants.

---

case of breach of prohibition of public offers by private company) or Part 30 (protection of members against unfair prejudice): s 659(2).

[83] See The Companies (Model Articles) Regulations 2008, SI 2008/3229, reg 4, Sch 3, arts 58–61 (public companies) and see CA 2006, ss 662–664. Forfeiture does not fall foul of the prohibition on a company acquiring its own shares: s 659(2)(c). Forfeiture provisions are penal provisions and must be construed strictly: *Johnson v Lyttle's Iron Agency* (1877) 5 Ch D 687, CA. A public company's articles also commonly provide for the surrender of shares in lieu of forfeiture: see SI 2008/3229, reg 4, Sch 3, art 62. A surrender of shares in a public company is governed by the same rules as those applying to forfeiture: CA 2006, s 662(1).

[84] Company Law Review, *Strategic Framework* (1999), paras 5.4.4–5.4.13; *Company Formation and Capital Maintenance* (1999), paras 3.27–3.35 and Annex B.

[85] Company Law Review, *Completing the Structure* (2000), paras 7.9–7.10; *Final Report*, vol I (2001), para 10.6.

[86] In public companies, the articles typically state that the reduction must not have the effect of reducing the share capital below the authorised minimum, see CA 2006, s 763 and **19-10**. Such a provision does not rule out a reduction by a company which momentarily reduces the company's capital to nil before following it with an increase in capital to above that minimum: *Re MB Group plc* [1989] BCLC 672. When a reduction does result in the capital of a public company falling below the authorised minimum, see CA 2006, ss 650, 651 which allow for expedited re-registration in that case as a private company.

[87] See *British & American Trustee Corpn v Couper* [1894] AC 399 at 410; *Poole v National Bank of China* [1907] AC 229 at 237–8; *Re Thomas de la Rue & Co Ltd* [1911] 2 Ch 361 at 365; *Ex p Westburn Sugar Refineries Ltd* [1951] 1 All ER 881 at 884.

Extinction or reduction of liability on shares not paid up

20-60 Reduction in this instance appears to involve risk to creditors for it extinguishes a liability (namely the obligation on the part of the holders of partly-paid shares to pay the amount due on those shares) which would be a valuable asset to the creditors in the event of a winding up, assuming that those shareholders were in a position to meet their liability on those shares. This category is of limited significance, however, for it is unusual for shares to be issued as partly-paid so there is rarely any question of there being any unpaid share capital outstanding, see **19-16**.

Cancellation of share capital lost or unrepresented by available assets

20-61 The cancellation of paid-up share capital which is lost or unrepresented by available assets appears to have an impact on creditors for it reduces the minimum level of assets which must be maintained by the company. However, reduction in this instance is usually a necessary exercise to restore reality to the company's accounts. If a company had at one time a paid-up share capital of £200,000 but, following trading losses, its net assets now amount only to £50,000, little is achieved by maintaining the figure of £200,000 in the accounts as the capital yardstick. A reduction of capital in such circumstances will also be crucial to the company's ability to make or resume dividend payments to its shareholders and it is important to appreciate the impact of the distribution rules in CA 2006, Pt 23, see **20-84**, in this context. The need under those distribution rules to have regard to accumulated profits and losses means that it will be necessary for the company to reduce its capital to cancel past losses so as to be in a position to resume the payment of dividends from current profits.

20-62 The court must be satisfied that the capital is lost and that that loss is permanent (so far as presently foreseeable) for, if it is not permanently lost, a cancellation of paid-up share capital may prejudice the interests of the creditors. In *Re Jupiter House Investments (Cambridge) Ltd*[88] where the loss could not be proved to be permanent,[89] the court confirmed the reduction subject to an undertaking by the company which ensured that if the loss of capital was in fact recovered, it would not be distributed to the shareholders as dividends but would be placed to a capital reserve. On the other hand, in *Re Grosvenor Press plc*[90] the court was loath to require such an undertaking, noting that there are already statutory safeguards[91] to protect the interests of future creditors and shareholders and there is no need, except in special circumstances, for the court to require a reserve to be set aside indefinitely. It suffices if the reserve is made undistributable as long as any creditor at the time of the reduction remains unpaid.[92]

Repay share capital in excess of company's wants

20-63 The repayment of paid-up share capital in excess of the company's needs poses no risk to creditors[93] and may simply reflect a shrinking of the company's activities. It might be noted that it is only in this instance that capital is actually returned to the shareholders.

---

[88] [1985] BCLC 222.

[89] The loss arose from defects in a substantial building which the company owned. The company had been advised that it had more than an even chance of recovering the loss by an action for damages against a third party.   [90] [1985] BCLC 286.

[91] Creditors and shareholders are protected by the publicity requirements surrounding a reduction of capital and the need for the company's accounts to give a true and fair view of the state of its affairs.

[92] [1985] BCLC 286 at 289.

[93] A reduction of capital by repayment is not a distribution for the purposes of CA 2006, Pt 23: see s 829(2)(b)(ii).

In the other instances of reduction noted earlier, either the capital has never been received or the capital is lost.

20-64 It is not necessary that the shareholders who are being paid off should actually receive cash. Non-cash assets may be used instead[94] and in that case there need not be an exact correlation between the capital reduced and the value of the assets transferred.[95] This may appear to offer some opportunity for abuse but the courts have indicated that the important matter is not how much is returned to the shareholders but how much is retained for the protection of creditors.[96] If what is offered to the shareholder is illusory, however, the court will refuse to confirm the reduction.[97]

Reduction supported by solvency statement

20-65 This procedure is only available to private companies and is subject to any restriction or prohibition in the company's articles. Also, a private company cannot reduce capital using this mechanism if the effect would be to leave the company without any member holding other than redeemable shares.[98] Some creditors may be uneasy about a procedure based on shareholder approval and a directors' solvency statement and there may be some pressure on companies to include restrictions or prohibitions in their articles.[99] Equally, it may be that an attempt to exercise the power will be a default trigger under loan agreements so in effect preventing the company from using the procedure.[100] In the absence of any restrictions, all that is required is a special resolution and a solvency statement in the prescribed form.[101]

20-66 Where a written resolution is used, a copy of the solvency statement must be sent or submitted to every member at the time when the proposed resolution is sent. If the resolution is passed at a meeting, the solvency statement must be available for inspection by members throughout the meeting. In either case, a failure to comply with this requirement does not affect the validity of the resolution (presumably because of the difficulty of unravelling these transactions if the non-compliance does not come to light for some time), but non-compliance is a criminal offence.[102]

20-67 The statement must be to the effect that each of the directors:[103]

    (1) has formed the opinion, as regards the company's situation at the date of the statement, that there is no ground on which the company could then be found unable to pay (or otherwise discharge) its debts; and

---

[94] *Ex p Westburn Sugar Refineries Ltd* [1951] 1 All ER 881; *Re Thomas de la Rue & Co Ltd* [1911] 2 Ch 361.

[95] In *Ex p Westburn Sugar Refineries Ltd* [1951] 1 All ER 881 at 885, Lord Reid made the point that this must be the position because in many cases it is impossible to make any exact valuation of the non-cash assets.

[96] See, for example, *Ex p Westburn Sugar Refineries Ltd* [1951] 1 All ER 881 at 884, per Lord Normand.

[97] *Re Thomas de la Rue & Co Ltd* [1911] 2 Ch 361.   [98] CA 2006, s 641(2).

[99] The drawback for the creditors is that the articles can be changed by a special resolution under CA 2006, s 21 so the protection afforded by a prohibition in the articles is limited.

[100] A prohibition or restriction on the exercise of the power by the company outside of the articles would not be effective: *Russell v Northern Bank Development Corp Ltd* [1992] BCLC 1016, but making an exercise a default event has the same practical effect.

[101] The solvency statement must state the date on which it is made and give the name of each director: CA 2006, s 643(3); and it must be in writing, be signed by each director, and indicate that it is a solvency statement for the purposes of s 642: SI 2008/1915, art 2.   [102] CA 2006, ss 642(2)–(4), 644(7).

[103] As to the requirement of 'each director', this includes de facto directors which may cause a problem, see *Re In a Flap Envelope Co Ltd* [2004] 1 BCLC 64 (a different context, but still relevant).

(2) has also formed the opinion:

    (a) if it is intended to commence the winding up of the company within 12 months of that date, that the company will be able to pay (or otherwise discharge) its debts in full within 12 months of the commencement of the winding up; or

    (b) in any other case, that the company will be able to pay (or otherwise discharge) its debts as they fall due during the year immediately following that date (CA 2006, s 643(1)).[104]

In forming those opinions (note the plural) for these purposes, the directors must take into account all of the company's liabilities (including contingent or prospective liabilities):[105] CA 2006, s 643(2).

20-68 This statement must be delivered to the registrar of companies within 15 days of the resolution being passed together with a copy of the resolution and a statement of capital (CA 2006, s 644(1)) and the reduction does not take effect until those documents are registered (s 644(4)), see also **20-82**. It is an offence for a director to make a statement and deliver it to the registrar without having reasonable grounds for the opinions expressed in it (s 643(4)).

20-69 The notable features of this procedure are: the absence of any requirement for an auditor's report to back up the directors' solvency statement; the absence of any publicity to alert creditors either through notification in the *Gazette* or by an advertisement in a national newspaper; and the absence of any mechanism for objections by shareholders or creditors. For these reasons, creditors may want companies to place restrictions or prohibitions in their articles to curtail the directors' freedom of action. The risk for the creditors is that the directors will take advantage of the scheme to return capital to the shareholders before the company later collapses to the detriment of the creditors. On the other hand, directors may be wary of giving solvency statements, given the criminal sanction which attaches to the giving of a statement without reasonable grounds for the opinions expressed in it, and they may prefer to have a supporting auditor's opinion, even though it is not a legal requirement. Despite the apparent simplicity of these procedures, business practice may dictate that it is not used as much as currently anticipated. Equally, once settled practice emerges, reduction of capital in this way may become routine, just as share buy-backs have become routine. A key practical issue which will encourage its use is that the reserve arising on a reduction, whether on the basis of a solvency statement or a reduction confirmed by the court, is to be treated as a realised profit and therefore

---

[104] There is no express requirement for the directors to make full inquiry into the affairs and prospects of the company, as is required by s 714(3) in the case of a purchase of own shares out of capital, but such a requirement is probably implicit in any case: see Hannigan & Prentice, *The Companies Act 2006, A Commentary* (2nd edn, 2009), para 8.12; also *Re In a Flap Envelope Co Ltd* [2004] 1 BCLC 64. A director could not have reasonable grounds for his opinion unless he has made such inquiries as he ought to make to enable him to express such an opinion: *Cook v Green* [2009] BCC 204 (concerning an auditor's report on a financial assistance scheme, but relevant in this context also).

[105] In *BNY Corporate Trustee Services Ltd v Eurosail-UK* [2011] 2 BCLC 1 the Court of Appeal examined the phrase 'contingent and prospective liabilities' in the context of the definition of inability to pay debts in IA 1986, s 123(2), see further at **24-127**, and the reasoning would be equally applicable here. The court ruled that, rather than taking contingent and prospective liabilities at their face value, a valuation exercise has to be done on the basis of commercial reality and fairness and the closer in time a future liability is to maturity, or the more likely a contingency which would activate a contingent liability, the more weight would be attached, determining these matters on a balance of probabilities.

distributable subject, in either case, to any contrary provision in the court order, the reso-lution for reduction or the company's memorandum or articles of association.[106]

Reduction subject to court confirmation

20-70 The alternative procedure (and the only option for public companies) is to pass a special resolution (CA 2006, s 641(1)(b)) and seek court confirmation of the reduction (s 645(1)) which order the court may make on such terms and conditions as it thinks fit,[107] subject to the position of the company's creditors having been safeguarded (s 648(1), (2)).

20-71 If the proposed reduction of capital involves either (a) diminution of liability in respect of unpaid share capital (which as noted is rare), or (b) the payment to a shareholder of any paid-up share capital, as would often be the case, there is a statutory procedure for objec-ting creditors (s 646) which applies unless the court otherwise directs, which it may do if it thinks it proper to do so (s 645(2), (3)); vice versa, the court can direct that the proced-ure for objecting creditors applies though the reduction does not fall into these categories (s 645(4)). Every creditor of the company who (a) at the relevant date fixed by the court (for settling the list of creditors) is entitled to any debt or claim that, if that date were the commencement of the winding up of the company, would be admissible in proof against the company[108] and (b) can show that there is a real likelihood that the proposed reduction would result in the company being unable to discharge his debt or claim when it fell due, is entitled to object to the reduction of capital (s 646(1)). What is meant by a 'real likelihood' in this context was considered by the court in *Re Liberty International Ltd*[109] where Norris J held that the section required the creditor to demonstrate a particular present assessment about a future state of affairs. In considering whether such a real likelihood has been shown the court looks first at the factual and, while looking to the future, the court will avoid the purely speculative. Secondly, he said, there is a temporal element: in general the more remote in time the contemplated event that would make payment fall due the more difficult it would be to establish the likelihood that the return of capital would itself result in inabil-ity to discharge the debt. Thirdly, showing a real likelihood required the objecting creditor to go some way up the probability scale, beyond the merely possible, but short of the prob-able. On the facts in this case, where there was evidence that the company had working capital for at least 18 months following the transaction, the creditors could not show a real likelihood that the proposed reduction of capital would result in the company being unable to discharge their debts as they fell due. Accordingly, the reduction was confirmed.

20-72 This limitation of the right to object to creditors who can show (the onus is on the creditor) that the proposed reduction will put at risk the due discharge of their claim is a change brought about from 1 October 2009 by amendments to the Second Company

---

[106] CA 2006, s 654(1) and The Companies (Reduction of Share Capital) Order 2008, SI 2008/1915, art 3(2)–(4).

[107] The court can confirm a resolution even if there is a factual error in it, provided that it is so insignificant that no one could be thought to be prejudiced by its correction: *Re Willaire Systems plc* [1987] BCLC 67. See also *Re European Home Products plc* [1988] BCLC 690 where a more significant error occurred but the court reluctantly confirmed the reduction as creditors were not affected and no shareholder regarded the mistake as being of such importance as to seek the court's refusal.

[108] In the absence of an exercise of discretion by the Pensions Regulator (to make a contribution notice or financial support direction against a company), the company was not at present liable to the pension scheme trustees or to the Pension Protection Fund and, in the absence of any liability on the part of the company, there were no pensions claims which were 'admissible in proof' for these purposes and no creditors 'entitled to object' under this provision: *Re Liberty International plc* [2010] 2 BCLC 665.

[109] [2010] 2 BCLC 665.

Law Directive.[110] Previously all creditors were entitled to object and it was standard practice for the court to dispense with the settling of the list of creditors as invariably the company would have reached an agreement with its creditors who would either have been paid off or have consented to the scheme subject to bank guarantees from the company covering the amounts due to them. In other words, the onus was on the company to reach an accommodation with its creditors. The position under CA 2006, s 646 now puts the onus on the objecting creditor to show to the court how he is at risk from any reduction. There had been concerns that the previous procedures gave creditors a degree of excessive protection[111] and the amendments to the Second Company Law Directive are designed to re-balance the position between the company and its creditors.

20-73 Where there are creditors so entitled to object, a list of creditors must be settled (CA 2006, s 646(2)) but the court may, if it thinks fit, dispense with the consent of an undischarged creditor on the company securing payment of his debt or claim (s 646(4)).

20-74 It is not clear that the changes have made much difference in practice. Strictly speaking, s 646(1) puts the onus on the creditors to establish their entitlement to object, but rather than arguing with creditors as to their entitlement, it may make more commercial sense to proceed as before by addressing the concerns of creditors through payment (though the debt is not yet due) or by means of agreements and guarantees so that the court can dispense with their consent under s 646(4).

20-75 Where the procedures are followed properly and the necessary special resolution passed, the court's role is little more than to endorse the company's plans which it can do once it is satisfied, as required by s 648(2), that every creditor entitled to object has either consented to the reduction, or his debt or claim has been discharged or has determined, or has been secured. The consent of the creditors having been secured, the shareholders usually have little interest in objecting other than in the context of a variation of class rights (see **14-43**). There are no specific statutory provisions dealing with the shareholders' position; instead it is for objecting shareholders (objecting in effect to being expelled from the company) to persuade the court not to confirm the reduction.

Role of the court

20-76 The court has a discretion whether or not to confirm a reduction[112] and the main question for the court is whether the proposed reduction is fair and equitable as between the different classes of shareholders,[113] given that the position of the creditors is protected by the procedures outlined at **20-71**.

---

[110] Directive 2006/68/EC amending Directive 77/91/EEC, OJ L 264/32, 25.09.2006, see art 9, implemented by SI 2009/2022 amending CA 2006, s 646.

[111] Company Law Review, *Strategic Framework* (1999), paras 5.4.10–5.4.12; *Company Formation and Capital Maintenance* (1999), para 3.31.

[112] *British & American Trustee Corpn v Couper* [1894] AC 399; *Re Thomas de la Rue Ltd* [1911] 2 Ch 361.

[113] *British & American Trustee Corpn v Couper* [1894] AC 399; *Re Thomas de la Rue Ltd* [1911] 2 Ch 361; *Poole v National Bank of China Ltd* [1907] AC 229; *Scottish Insurance Co Ltd v Wilsons & Clyde Coal Co Ltd* 1948 SC 360, aff'd [1949] AC 462, HL; *Ex p Westburn Sugar Refineries Ltd* [1951] 1 All ER 881. As long as creditors and shareholders are not prejudiced, wider public concerns do not influence the court and it is not concerned with any ulterior purpose for the reduction provided it is lawful. Thus reduction schemes for reasons of tax avoidance (as opposed to evasion) or to avoid some of the consequences of nationalisation have in the past been approved: *Ex p Westburn Sugar Refineries Ltd* [1951] 1 All ER 881.

20-77 Speaking generally, a reduction of capital need not be spread equally or rateably over all the shares of the company.[114] If there is nothing unfair or inequitable in the transaction, the shares of one or more shareholders may be extinguished without affecting other shares of the same or a different class.[115] However, a reduction which does not provide for uniform treatment of shareholders whose rights are similar is narrowly scrutinised.[116]

20-78 It is rare for there to be any difficulty about securing court confirmation which is seen as a purely routine matter. The scheme in question is always supported by a large majority of the shareholders (necessarily so, for the statute requires a special resolution) and raises issues of internal management and business judgement which are for the company to decide upon and not the courts.[117]

20-79 The approach of the courts was explained by Harman J in *Re Ratners Group plc*[118] as follows:

> 'The court has over the years established … three principles on which the court will require to be satisfied. Those principles are, first, that all shareholders are treated equitably in any reduction. That usually means that they are treated equally, but may mean that they are treated equally save as to some who have consented to their being treated unequally, so that counsel's word "equitably" is the correct word which I adopt and accept. The second principle to be applied is that the shareholders at the general meeting had the proposals properly explained to them so that they could exercise an informed judgment on them. And the third principle is that creditors of the company are safeguarded so that money cannot be applied in any way which would be detrimental to creditors.'

20-80 In most instances, the creditors, shareholders and the company are in complete agreement about the proposed reduction and the court's role is limited to endorsing their plans so even the presence of dissentient shareholders is unlikely to alter the court's willingness to approve a reduction scheme.

20-81 What has troubled the courts to a slightly greater degree in some of the cases has been a claim by preference shareholders that the effect of a proposed reduction of capital[119] is to vary or abrogate their class rights and so requires their consent before the reduction can be confirmed by the court. That issue is discussed in detail at **14-43**. It suffices to note here that, where the proposed reduction is in accordance with the class rights as

---

[114] *Re Agricultural Hotel Co* [1891] 1 Ch 396; *Re Floating Dock Co of St Thomas Ltd* [1895] 1 Ch 691; *Re London and New York Investment Corpn* [1895] 2 Ch 860; *British and American Trustee and Finance Corpn v Couper* [1894] AC 399.

[115] *British and American Trustee and Finance Corpn v Couper* [1894] AC 399 at 406, 415, 417, HL; *Bannatyne v Direct Spanish Telegraph Co* (1886) 34 Ch D 287, CA; *Re Direct Spanish Telegraph Co* (1886) 34 Ch D 307; *Re Thomas de la Rue & Co Ltd and Reduced* [1911] 2 Ch 361.

[116] In *Re Robert Stephen Holdings Ltd* [1968] 1 WLR 522, it was stated that the better practice in cases where one part of a class is to be treated differently from another part of the same class (unless all the shareholders consent) is to proceed by way of a scheme of arrangement under what is now CA 2006, Pt 26, as this affords better protection to a non-assenting minority. In this case the court did confirm the reduction despite its affecting shareholders of the same class in different ways but no shareholder appeared to oppose the confirmation.

[117] See *Poole v National Bank of China Ltd* [1907] AC 229 at 236, per Lord Loreburn '… it is no part of the business of a Court of justice to determine the wisdom of a course adopted by a company in the management of its own affairs'.

[118] [1988] BCLC 685 at 687. See also *Re Thorn EMI plc* [1989] BCLC 612. The other qualification on the court's discretion noted by Harman J in both of these cases was that the court must not be asked to confirm a reduction which is for no discernible purpose.

[119] Typically, a proposal for the reduction of capital by paying off the preference shares on the grounds of excessive capital.

they would apply on a winding up of the company, the reduction does not amount to a variation of class rights and the consent of the class to the reduction is not required.[120] Preference shareholders can avoid the danger of a restrictive interpretation of what constitutes a variation of their class rights by the courts by identifying in the terms of issue those matters (such as a reduction of capital) which are deemed to be a variation or abrogation of the rights attached to that class and which therefore are governed by the scheme for variation or abrogation laid down in CA 2006, s 630, see **14-50**. If a scheme of reduction does vary or abrogate class rights, despite the generality of the court's power to confirm (and some suggestions to the contrary in older cases),[121] the court will not confirm a reduction without the appropriate class consent having been obtained.[122]

Registration of court order

20-82 The registrar, on production of the court order confirming the reduction and the delivery of a copy of the order and of a statement of capital (approved by the court), registers the order and statement (CA 2006, s 649(1)) whereupon the resolution for the reduction of capital takes effect (s 649(3)(b)), except in the case of a reduction of share capital that forms part of a compromise or arrangement sanctioned by the court under Part 26 (arrangements and reconstructions) in which case the reduction takes effect (1) on delivery of the order and statement of capital to the registrar, or (2) if the court so orders, on the registration of the order and statement of capital (s 649(3)(a)). The registrar certifies the registration of the order and statement of capital and this certificate of registration is conclusive evidence that all the requirements with respect to the reduction of share capital have been complied with and that the company's share capital is as stated in the statement of capital (s 649(5), (6)).

20-83 Where the court makes an order confirming a reduction of a public company's capital which has the effect of bringing the nominal value of its allotted share capital below the authorised minimum, the registrar of companies must not register the order unless the court so directs, or the company is first re-registered as a private company.[123]

D Distributions to the members

Introduction

20-84 The most common type of distribution is a dividend, expressed as so many pence per share and paid to the shareholders according to the number of shares held by them, but the statutory rules on distributions (CA 2006, Pt 23, ss 829–853) are wider and apply to 'every description of distribution of a company's assets to its members, whether in cash or otherwise', subject to a limited number of exceptions (s 829(1)). Furthermore, the wide-ranging common law principle that distributions cannot be paid out of capital is expressly retained by the statute (s 851(1)).[124]

---

[120] *Re Saltdean Estate Co Ltd* [1968] 3 All ER 829; *House of Fraser v ACGE Investments Ltd* [1987] AC 387, HL.

[121] See *Re William Jones & Sons Ltd* [1969] 1 All ER 913.

[122] See *Re Northern Engineering Industries plc* [1994] 2 BCLC 704 at 713, CA.

[123] CA 2006, s 650. The authorised minimum is set at £50,000 or €57,100, the prescribed euro equivalent: s 763, see **19-10**.

[124] See, generally, Micheler, 'Disguised Returns of Capital—An Arm's Length Approach' (2010) CLJ 151.

20-85 The label which the parties give to a transaction is not determinative of whether it is a 'distribution' for these purposes.[125] In *Re Halt Garage (1964) Ltd*[126] the court found that sums paid to a director, at a time when the company was insolvent (and therefore had no distributable profits) and in excess of what the director was entitled to under the articles for holding office as a director, were a disguised gift of capital or payment of dividends in recognition of her co-proprietorship of the business. As such, they were ultra vires and void. In *Aveling Barford Ltd v Perion Ltd*[127] a sale of property by a company (which though solvent had no distributable profits) at a considerable undervalue (sale was at £350,000, independent valuation valued it at £650,000[128]) to another entity controlled by the company's sole beneficial shareholder was an unlawful distribution. As an unauthorised return of capital, it was ultra vires and void. In *Secretary of State for Business, Innovation and Skills v Doffman (No 2)*[129] a company paid £1.2m to an associated company for an option to purchase a property from that other company. The court found that the sum was very large for an option which only lasted 18 months; the figure was less a valuation of the option and more the figure of the 'surplus' cash which the first company had. There was no real prospect that the first company would ever exercise the option since there was no evidence of any way in which it could fund the exercise and in fact no attempt was ever made to exercise the option. In reality, the court found the payment of £1.2m represented a disguised return of capital to the shareholders at a time when the company had no distributable profits and the option was merely a device for transferring £1.2m out of the first company leaving it with no reserves and no way of meeting its own liabilities.[130]

20-86 Whether a transaction amounts to an unlawful return of capital to a shareholder is a matter of substance not form, requiring the court to enquire into the true purpose and substance of the impugned transaction, as the Supreme Court affirmed in *Progress Property Co Ltd v Moorgarth Group Ltd*.[131] In that case, a company had sold an asset (a shareholding in another company) to another company in the group (all were controlled by the same investor) for a sum which turned out to be a gross undervalue. The sale price had reflected the fact that, as a term of the sale, the vendor had been released from substantial liabilities which it was understood by all concerned it had incurred under certain indemnities. Later it was established that the vendor had no liability under those indemnities and there was no liability from which it could have been released so the purchase price was indeed too low. Hence the allegation that the sale was essentially a disguised return of capital to a shareholder since the purchasing shareholder obtained an asset the value of which greatly exceeded the price paid to the company.

20-87 The Supreme Court ruled that, in categorising a transaction, the court must look at the transaction objectively, but not relentlessly objectively, otherwise doubt would be cast on any transaction between a company and a shareholder, even if negotiated in good faith and at arm's length, whenever the company proved with hindsight to have got significantly the worse of the transaction.[132] In the case of a commercial transaction, there

---

[125] See *Progress Property Co Ltd v Moorgarth Group Ltd* [2011] 2 BCLC 332, SC; *Aveling Barford Ltd v Perion Ltd* [1989] BCLC 626 at 631; *Ridge Securities v IRC* [1964] 1 All ER 275.   [126] [1982] 3 All ER 1016.
[127] [1989] BCLC 626.   [128] The property was sold on six months later for £1,526,000.
[129] [2011] 2 BCLC 541 at [142]–[149].
[130] This case concerned a series of transactions between companies within a group where the directors (the subjects of these disqualification proceedings) transferred assets without regard to the rules prohibiting distributions and without regard to the interests of the separate legal entities; see other unlawful distributions at [97], [207], [213]–[215], involving gratuitous transfers of assets and the waiver of debts at a time when the companies had no distributable profits.   [131] [2011] 2 BCLC 332 at [27], per Lord Walker.
[132] [2011] 2 BCLC 332 at [24], while noting, at [26], an article by Micheler, 'Disguised Returns of Capital—an Arm's Length Approach' (2010) CLJ 151 who, because of the policy of creditor protection which underlies

must be a realistic assessment of all the relevant facts, including the motives and intentions of those involved and not just a retrospective valuation exercise in isolation from all other enquiries (i.e. the court is calling for a more sophisticated analysis than merely a calculation of what the company gave and what it received).[133] Applying that approach, a commercial transaction may be a genuine transaction, but a bad bargain in which case it stands, the court said, but it may be an improper attempt to extract value by the pretence of an arm's length sale, in which case it will be held unlawful.[134] On the other hand, the court seemed to accept that in the case of unlawful dividend (or equivalent) payments, an almost entirely objective analysis to determine whether the distribution is unlawful is possible and appropriate,[135] presumably because, in the absence of any disguise of the payment, the enquiry can be much more limited and the unlawful return of capital easier to objectively ascertain—looking simply at a payment to a shareholder in the absence of distributable profits. On the facts in *Progress Property Co Ltd v Moorgarth Group Ltd*,[136] looking at the commercial transaction between the parties, the court affirmed the Court of Appeal decision that there was no unlawful return of capital, rather an arm's length sale negotiated in good faith, though with hindsight the company had got a bad bargain.[137]

20-88 The distribution rules, whether statutory or common law, are an important component of the capital maintenance regime. The rules address concerns that, if the directors and shareholders are able to collude in the distribution of the company's assets to the members during the company's lifetime, the creditors will find the company stripped of its assets.[138] On liquidation, the creditors must be paid in full before any capital can be returned to the shareholders and an unlawful distribution of assets ahead of winding up defeats that priority.[139] Equally, the rules protect shareholders against dissipation of the company's assets by the directors for improper purposes in breach of duty.[140] Where a company wishes to return capital to its shareholders, it must do so via a purchase or redemption of shares or reduction of capital in accordance with the statutory schemes and not by way of an improper distribution of assets to the members.[141] In the much cited words of Pennycuick J in *Ridge Securities Ltd v IRC*:[142]

> 'A company can only lawfully deal with its assets in furtherance of its objects. The corporators may take assets out of the company by way of dividend or, with leave of the court, by way of reduction of capital, or in a winding up. They may of course acquire them for full consideration. They cannot take assets out of the company by way of voluntary

---

the doctrine of capital maintenance, favours and finds support in the authorities for an entirely objective approach without regard to the parties' intentions or knowledge, see at 170–5.

[133] [2011] 2 BCLC 332 at [29], [31] and see also at [24].   [134] [2011] 2 BCLC 332 at [29].

[135] [2011] 2 BCLC 332 at [28].   [136] [2011] 2 BCLC 332.

[137] Lord Mance commented that the suggestion that the transaction be re-categorised as an illegitimate distribution of capital was particularly artificial and unappealing, see [2011] 2 BCLC 332 at 345.

[138] See *It's a Wrap (UK) Ltd v Gula* [2006] 2 BCLC 634 at 641, per Arden LJ, and at 645 where Sedley LJ comments that the ability to recover unlawful dividends from the recipients is 'designed to protect those who have a prior call on a company's funds from the appropriation of them by those who control the company'. A creditor does not have *locus standi*, however, to seek an injunction to prevent an unlawful dividend, only a shareholder can do that: *Mills v Northern Railways of Buenos Ayres Ltd* (1870) 5 Ch App 621.

[139] See *It's a Wrap (UK) Ltd v Gula* [2006] 2 BCLC 634 at 641 where Arden LJ notes that any leniency to shareholders in receipt of an improperly paid dividend detracts from the protection available to the creditors.   [140] See *Bairstow v Queens Moat Houses plc* [2001] 2 BCLC 531 at 546, CA.

[141] See *Ridge Securities Ltd v IRC* [1964] 1 All ER 275 at 288; *Re Halt Garage (1964) Ltd* [1982] 3 All ER 1016.

[142] [1964] 1 All ER 275 at 288 (excessive interest on debentures amounted to a gratuitous distribution of the company's assets and was ultra vires and void).

disposition, however described, and, if they attempt to do so, the disposition is ultra vires the company.'

20-89 With regard specifically to dividends, being a common type of distribution, directors considering a dividend pay-out will want also to have regard to broader commercial issues which will vary depending on the size and type of the company. Many private companies are small family concerns where all the shareholders also act as the directors and profits may be distributed by way of directors' remuneration instead of by formal declaration of dividends. On the other hand, there may be tax savings to be made by paying dividends rather than paying national insurance contributions on salary so the question of dividends or salary has to be determined in the light of the individual's position. A further point of confusion in small private companies is that directors and shareholders often make withdrawals from the company without identifying clearly whether the payment is: (1) a dividend; (2) a loan from the company; or (3) remuneration.[143] Other difficulties can arise in private companies where profits are distributed by way of remuneration but not all of the shareholders are directors. This practice can be a source of internal tension, particularly if the company has amassed considerable reserves and the directors' remuneration is generous. In such cases, a persistent failure to pay dividends when funds are available, coupled with high levels of directors' remuneration, may amount to unfairly prejudicial conduct meriting relief under CA 2006, s 994 (see at **17-61**).

20-90 Shareholders in public companies are much less likely to be directors and they expect dividend payments to be made to the shareholders when distributable profits are available. For listed public companies, a failure to maintain an appropriate level of dividend pay-out each year can have an adverse effect on the company's share price and may expose the company to potential takeover bids. It is also likely to be unpopular with the company's institutional investors. Such market pressure for dividend payments is often criticised as contributing to the 'short-termism' problem in British companies. The argument is that it forces management to concentrate excessively on short-term strategies designed to give immediate shareholder returns and maintain the company's share price rather than on long-term planning which would be to the advantage of the company and the economy. Whether there is a short-termism problem as opposed to a perception problem and whether, if there is a problem, it should be attributed to shareholders' attitudes to dividends rather than managerial conduct (given the link between remuneration and short-term targets) continues to be much debated, see **5-59**. But, to some extent, that debate has moved on to a recognition of the need for a better engagement between companies and their shareholders which, given their predominance, essentially means between companies and their institutional shareholders, see **5-43**.

Statute, common law and directors' duties

20-91 The statutory distribution rules originated in the CA 1980 against a background of a common law principle which prohibits distributions to shareholders out of capital,[144] but the application of which to the payment of dividends was rather lax in some respects.[145] For example, the common law permitted dividends to be paid out of current trading profits

---

[143] See, for example, *Queensway Systems Ltd v Walker* [2007] 2 BCLC 577. Some of the problems are eased somewhat by the relaxation of the prohibitions on loans to directors by CA 2006, ss 197–214.

[144] *Re Exchange Banking Co, Flitcroft's Case* (1882) 21 Ch D 519.

[145] For an interesting account of the historical development of the dividend rules, see Yamey, 'Aspects of the Law relating to Company Dividends' (1941) 4 MLR 273.

without making good losses in fixed capital[146] or trading losses in previous years;[147] and allowed dividends to be paid out of an unrealised capital gain resulting from a bona fide revaluation of fixed assets;[148] and did not require companies to provide for depreciation.[149] Many of these legal rules were commercially unwise and contrary to good accounting practice, but the courts were reluctant to interfere with the directors' discretion as men of business.[150]

20-92 The statutory provisions are particularly useful therefore in constraining dividend abuse though, as noted at **20-84**, they apply more widely to 'any distribution' and operate along-side the common law which is expressly retained by CA 2006, ss 851 and 852. These sections continue the application of any rule of law, any provision in the articles or in any enactment restricting the sums out of which, or the cases in which, a distribution may be made. The result is the continued application of the common law prohibition on distribu-tions to the members out of capital[151] which has the important consequence that, where a company has distributable profits for the purposes of CA 2006, Pt 23, but those profits have been dissipated subsequent to the preparation of the accounts, the common law rule applies to prevent a distribution out of capital. Mostly, the application of the common law and the statute will give the same result, given that the statute requires distributions to be out of distributable profits, but a distribution which is lawful under the common law could still fall foul of the statute as, where the company's accounts are not properly prepared. A distribution to meet the requirements of the statute requires distributable profits, as defined by the statute, determined on the basis of accounts properly prepared as required by the statute. At common law, the question is merely whether, at the time of a distribution, it was made out of capital.

20-93 The statutory provisions work also within the general framework of the law which imposes other constraints on directors. Directors must exercise their powers for the purposes for which they are conferred (CA 2006, s 171) and have a duty to act to promote the success of the company for the benefit of the members having regard to the factors set out in s 172. That duty is of particular importance in this context because it includes an obliga-tion, in certain circumstances, to have regard to the interests of the company's creditors (s 172(3)), the circumstances being when the company is insolvent or of doubtful solvency (see **9-41**). The directors' duty to exercise care and skill (discussed in Chapter 10) is also relevant.[152] In that regard directors need to consider whether, whatever the position in terms of strict compliance with CA 2006, Pt 23, it is prudent to declare a dividend, given the company's trading position and funding needs.[153] In a situation where the company's position is one of doubtful solvency, or the effect of the dividend would be to render the company insolvent or doubtfully solvent (given the duty to have regard to creditors' inter-ests at that stage), a prudent director exercising care and skill would not recommend the payment of a dividend without ensuring that the company was in a position to meet the

---

[146] *Lee v Neuchatel Asphalte Co* (1889) 41 Ch D 1; *Verner v General & Commercial Investment Trust* [1894] 2 Ch 239.

[147] *Ammonia Soda Co v Chamberlain* [1918] 1 Ch 266; *Re National Bank of Wales Ltd* [1899] 2 Ch 629.

[148] See *Dimbula Valley (Ceylon) Tea Co Ltd v Laurie* [1961] Ch 353 at 371–3.

[149] *Lee v Neuchatel Asphalte Co* (1889) 41 Ch D 1; *Bolton v Natal Land & Colonization Co* [1892] 2 Ch 124.   [150] See *Lee v Neuchatel Asphalte Co* (1889) 41 Ch D 1 at 18, 21.

[151] *Re Exchange Banking Co, Flitcroft's Case* (1882) 21 Ch D 519. See also *Trevor v Whitworth* (1887) 12 App Cas 409.

[152] See, for example, *Re Loquitur Ltd, IRC v Richmond* [2003] 2 BCLC 442 at 489–90.

[153] See Tech 02/10, n 156, paras 2.4–2.5 which caution prudence when considering a distribution from profits arising from changes in the value of financial instruments considered to be volatile, even if the profits are deemed by accounting principles to be realised profits for these purposes.

claims of its creditors as they fall due.[154] The result is that directors considering distributions need to be alert to their fiduciary duties, the requirements of CA 2006, Pt 23 and the common law principle precluding distributions out of capital.

20-94 Distributions in breach of the common law prohibition or of the statutory requirements or requirements in the articles are ultra vires and void and cannot be ratified by the company in general meeting.[155] The liabilities of the directors and the shareholder recipients are discussed at **20-113**.

Distributions and distributable profits—CA 2006, Part 23

20-95 The basic rule is that a company may only make a distribution out of profits available for the purpose, determined by accounts which have been properly prepared in accordance with the Companies Act.[156] In Part 23, a 'distribution' means every description of distribution of a company's assets to its members,[157] whether in cash or otherwise, except distributions by way of:

(1) an issue of shares as fully or partly-paid bonus shares;

(2) the reduction of share capital by extinguishing or reducing the liability of any of the members on any of the company's shares in respect of share capital not paid up, or by repaying paid-up share capital;

(3) the redemption or purchase of any of the company's own shares out of capital (including the proceeds of any fresh issue of shares) or out of unrealised profits in accordance with the statutory provisions; and

(4) a distribution of assets to members of the company on its winding up (s 829).

20-96 The profits available for distribution are defined as the company's accumulated realised profits, so far as not previously utilised by distribution or capitalisation, less its accumulated realised losses, so far as not previously written off in a reduction or reorganisation of capital duly made (CA 2006, s 830(2)). Whether such sums exist must be determined by reference, essentially, to the company's last annual accounts and to specified items in those accounts,[158] the importance of which is discussed at **20-101**. Primarily the issue of whether there is a realised profit or loss is a matter of the application of accounting principles at the time the accounts are prepared.[159]

---

[154] See *Re Loquitur Ltd, IRC v Richmond* [2003] 2 BCLC 442 at 489–90.

[155] *Re Exchange Banking Co, Flitcroft's Case* (1882) 21 Ch D 519; *Precision Dippings Ltd v Precision Dippings Marketing Ltd* [1985] BCLC 385; *Aveling Barford v Perion Ltd* [1989] BCLC 626; *Bairstow v Queens Moat Houses plc* [2001] 2 BCLC 531, CA.

[156] CA 2006, s 830 and s 836. As discussed at **20-101**, a company's accounts play a crucial role in determining whether a company has profits for distribution for the purposes of CA 2006, Pt 23 and key technical guidance on the accounting issues is provided by the Institute of Chartered Accountants for England and Wales (ICAEW): see ICAEW, Tech 02/10, *Guidance on the Determination of Realised Profits and Losses in the Context of Distributions under the Companies Act 2006*, hereafter Tech 02/10.

[157] See *TXU Europe Group plc* [2012] BCC 363 (a payment proposed by supervisors of a CVA of a subsidiary company to the parent company where the payment was in respect of the parent company's shareholding and was described as an 'equity payment' was a distribution to the company's members for the purposes of CA 2006, Pt 23 and the conditions of Part 23 not being met, the proposed distribution would be unlawful).

[158] CA 2006, s 836(1). In some circumstances, initial or interim accounts may be used instead: see s 836(2).

[159] CA 2006, s 853(4), hence the importance of Tech 02/10, see n 156. References to profits and losses, except where the context otherwise requires, are to revenue or capital profits and losses made at any time: s 853(2).

20-97 It is only *realised* profits or losses which enter the equation, a requirement designed to prevent companies from relying on estimated or expected profits which might never materialise. In accounting terms, profits are treated as realised for these purposes only when 'realised in the form of cash or other assets, the ultimate cash realisation of which can be assessed with reasonable certainty'.[160] On the other hand, unrealised losses are not taken into account (save to the extent that they are reflected in the accounts) unless the company is a public company and the losses mean that the company's net assets are less than its called-up share capital and undistributable reserves (see **20-99**). Equally important, the amount of *accumulated* realised losses must be deducted before any distribution can be made which abrogates the common law rule that losses made in previous accounting periods did not have to be made good.[161] Accounting periods can no longer be regarded in isolation from one another, hence the need in many cases to write off losses by way of a reduction of capital (see **20-56)** before resuming the payment of dividends.

20-98 The decision in *Aveling Barford Ltd v Perion Ltd*,[162] noted at **20-85**, caused problems in practice for reconstructions involving intra-group transfers of assets which were commonly done at book value rather than market value. Post-*Aveling Barford* it was thought that such transactions were open to challenge as improper distributions unless the transferring company had distributable profits to cover the gap between the book value and the market value. The issue is addressed by CA 2006, s 845 which deals with distributions consisting of or including, or treated as arising in consequence of, the sale, transfer or other disposition by the company of a non-cash asset and which applies to distributions under the statute or distributions under the common law (s 851(2)).[163] For companies which have available profits, this provision determines the amount of the distribution (and therefore the amount which needs to be covered by those distributable profits). Where the amount of the consideration received by the company out of the transaction is not less than the book value of the asset, the amount of the distribution is zero (s 845(2)(a)). Where the amount of the consideration received by the company is less than the book value, the company needs distributable profits equal to the difference between the consideration received and the book value (s 845(2)(b)).[164] Where the amount received exceeds the book value of the asset, the profits available for distribution are increased by that amount (s 845(3)). These provisions apply only where the company has available profits; where the company has no distributable profits and makes a distribution of assets at an undervalue, it remains an unlawful distribution, as in *Aveling Barford Ltd v Perion Ltd*.[165]

20-99 In addition to having realised profits available for distribution (a requirement which precludes a payment out of capital), a public company must satisfy two further conditions

---

[160] Tech 02/10, n 156, para 3.3. See too *In Re Oxford Benefit Building & Investment Society* (1886) 35 Ch D 502 at 510: 'realised profits' must have its ordinary commercial meaning which, if not equivalent to 'reduced to actual cash in hand', must at least be 'rendered tangible for the purpose of division'. Tech 02/10, para 3.1, notes that it is apparent that the concept of a realised profit is intended to be dynamic, changing with the development of generally accepted accounting principles, as well as bringing within the definition profits which might not in ordinary language be called realised.

[161] See *Ammonia Soda Co v Chamberlain* [1918] 1 Ch 266; *Re National Bank of Wales Ltd* [1899] 2 Ch 629.

[162] [1989] BCLC 626; see also *Ridge Securities Ltd v IRC* [1964] 1 All ER 275.

[163] See the *Explanatory Notes to the Companies Act 2006*, paras 1151–1157 on the scope and application of CA 2006, s 845. On the application of s 845, see Tech 02/10, n 156, para 2.9B.

[164] To the extent that the book value represents an unrealised profit, it is treated as realised, for these purposes, see CA 2006, s 846.

[165] [1989] BCLC 626; see *Explanatory Notes to the Companies Act 2006*, para 1153.

before it makes a distribution.[166] These additional requirements ensure that, not only does a public company not make a distribution out of capital, but a public company must also maintain a cushion of assets sufficient to cover the amount of its share capital and undistributable reserves.[167] CA 2006, s 831(1) provides therefore that a public company may only make a distribution:

(1) if the amount of its net assets is not less than the aggregate of its called-up share capital and undistributable reserves, and

(2) if, and to the extent that, the distribution does not reduce the amount of those assets to less than that aggregate.[168]

20-100 This requirement ensures that, even if a public company has trading profits, it cannot pay a dividend if it has a deficit on its reserves. A company's undistributable reserves under the CA 2006 are:

(1) its share premium account;

(2) its capital redemption reserve;

(3) the amount by which the company's accumulated unrealised profits (so far as not previously utilised by any capitalisation) exceed its accumulated unrealised losses (so far as not previously written off in a reduction or re-organisation of capital duly made); and

(4) any other reserve which the company is prohibited from distributing by any enactment or by its articles.[169]

Justification by reference to accounts

20-101 All of these matters as to distributable profits are determined in accordance with the company's last individual annual accounts[170] circulated to the members in accordance with CA 2006, s 423, properly prepared in accordance with the requirements of the Act[171] and accompanied by an auditor's report unless the company has claimed exemption from audit.[172] The amount of the distribution is to be determined by reference to specified

---

[166] See CA 2006, s 831. Further requirements are also imposed on investment companies, see ss 832–834, as amended.

[167] These additional requirements reflect the Second Company Law Directive 77/91/EEC, art 15, OJ L 26, 31.01.1977, p 1. In response to criticisms that art 15 is unduly prescriptive, the European Commission pointed out that art 15 does not require non-distributable legal or statutory reserves, rather it recognises them if national law requires them. If there is no national law requirement, art 15 only requires that the net assets cover the amount of the called-up share capital and the Second Directive only requires a minimum share capital of €25,000 (art 6(1)), which the Commission notes is not a significant amount in this context. See DG Internal Market and Services, Position Paper on results of external study on the Feasibility of Alternative to the Capital Maintenance regime of the Second Company Law Directive (January 2008), pp 10–11.

[168] CA 2006, s 831(1) (modified for investment companies, see s 832). For this purpose, 'net assets' means the aggregate of the company's assets less the aggregate of its liabilities: s 831(2); and 'called-up share capital' is widely defined to include capital called up but not yet paid and capital to be paid on a specified future date: s 547. The redenomination reserve is treated as if it is paid-up share capital: see s 628(3).

[169] CA 2006, s 831(4); see s 669(1) for an example of an undistributable reserve.

[170] CA 2006, s 836(1); group accounts are not relevant for this purpose.

[171] CA 2006, s 837(1), or have been properly prepared subject only to matters that are not material for determining (by reference to s 836(1)) whether the distribution would contravene Part 23: s 837(2). Accounts so prepared must only be approved by the directors if they give a true and fair view of the state of the company's affairs: s 393. [172] CA 2006, s 837(3).

items in the accounts (profits, losses, assets and liabilities, provisions, share capital and reserves).[173]

20-102 In some circumstances, initial or interim accounts may be used instead and these accounts generally must be sufficient to enable a reasonable judgement to be made as to whether there are available profits.[174] Where a public company wishes to rely on initial or interim accounts, there are specific requirements as to form and content and the accounts must be delivered to the registrar of companies.[175] Interim accounts are particularly useful when the company's position has improved significantly since the last accounts and it wishes to make a distribution larger than would be possible under those accounts. Contravention of the accounting requirements in CA 2006, ss 837–839 means that the distribution is in contravention of Part 23 (s 836(4)).

20-103 The central importance of these accounting requirements in determining whether a distribution is lawful was highlighted by the decision in *Bairstow v Queens Moat Houses plc*[176] where the Court of Appeal emphasised that the consequence of the accounts not being properly prepared, or not giving a true and fair view as required, is that the distribution is unlawful. In this case, the accounts gave the misleading impression of significant profits when the company did not have distributable profits. The defendant directors argued that, while the company did not have distributable profits, there were profits available in wholly-owned subsidiary companies which might have been paid up to the parent company and any breach with respect to the accounts of the parent company was purely technical.

20-104 This argument was emphatically rejected by the Court of Appeal which emphasised that the statutory requirements as to proper accounts are an important part of the protection provided by the Act and are not to be regarded as a mere procedural formality. As the accounts in this case had been drawn up in breach of the statutory requirements, any distribution based upon them was an unlawful distribution and the directors were not entitled to go behind the accounts to argue that the company did have the required distributable profits.[177] The court held that the dividend was an unlawful distribution regardless of whether the company might have had distributable profits had the accounts been properly prepared. The point is clearly made in CA 2006, s 836(4) which provides that, if the accounting requirements are not complied with, 'the accounts may not be relied on for the purposes of this Part and *the* [emphasis added] distribution is accordingly treated as contravening this Part'.

20-105 Likewise in *Allied Carpets Group plc v Nethercott*[178] where the court found that the company had declared a dividend on the strength of accounts which did not give a true and fair view. The figures in the accounts for turnover and sales were inflated by a practice known as pre-despatching whereby sales were treated as realised once customers placed an order for carpet although the company's policy was that sales should only be booked to the accounts when the carpet had actually been fitted. Whether the company would have had distributable profits had the accounts been properly prepared was irrelevant

---

[173] See CA 2006, s 836(1). See also s 840 which deals with successive distributions on the basis of the same accounts and ensures that other distributions and financial assistance and other relevant payments from available profits already made on the strength of those same accounts are taken into account in determining whether there are sufficient profits for a further distribution.   [174] CA 2006, ss 838(1), 839(1).
[175] See CA 2006, ss 836(2), (3), 838(6), 839(7). For an example of interim accounts being used, see *Re Loquitur Ltd, IRC v Richmond* [2003] 2 BCLC 442.   [176] [2001] 2 BCLC 531, CA.
[177] [2001] 2 BCLC 531 at 544–5; *Inn Spirit Ltd v Burns* [2002] 2 BCLC 780 at 786.
[178] [2001] BCC 81.

and the company was entitled to summary judgment for £227,491 with respect to unlawful dividends received by a director who knew of the pre-despatching practice and knew therefore that the accounts were false.

20-106 The possibility that the distribution might have been made lawfully (if the accounts had been properly prepared) may influence the court, however, in terms of the remedy which it is willing to grant, for example by allowing relief for the directors under CA 2006, s 1157 (acted honestly and reasonably and ought fairly to be excused, see **13-53**) or by tailoring the remedy which the court is prepared to grant under IA 1986, s 212, see **6-58**), as in *Re Loquitur Ltd*.

20-107 In *Re Loquitur Ltd, IRC v Richmond*[179] a company failed to make appropriate provision in its accounts for a possible tax liability, though the company knew that the tax relief which the company was seeking was likely to be rejected by the Inland Revenue. A dividend of £5.9m was paid on the strength of those accounts to the company's parent company. On the company going into liquidation, the Inland Revenue successfully challenged the payment of the dividend under IA 1986, s 212 (misfeasance by directors). The court found that the failure to make provision for the possible tax liability meant that the accounts were improperly prepared and therefore the dividend was paid in contravention of the statutory requirements. The directors had acted in breach of their duty to have regard to the interests of their creditors and had failed to exercise appropriate care and skill in failing to retain sufficient assets to cover reasonably anticipated liabilities.[180] On that basis, the court did not think that the defendants as directors had acted honestly and reasonably in authorising and procuring payment of the dividend and they could not be granted relief under what is now CA 2006, s 1157. The court declined to order repayment of the entire amount of the dividend, however, and limited the order to the amount of the outstanding tax liability (exercising its discretion under IA 1986, s 212(3) to make such order for the purposes of s 212 as the court thinks just).[181] The court limited recovery in this way on the basis that, had the accounts been properly drawn up, it is likely that a substantial dividend could have been paid. Crucially, the court also considered that the subsequent insolvency of the company was not caused by the accounting failures, but by a disastrous fire at the company's premises.[182]

20-108 Another scenario is where profits are available and the accounts are properly prepared but the company makes an excessive distribution, for example the company has £100,000 available profits for distribution but makes a distribution of £180,000. The question then is whether the distribution is unlawful as to the entire amount or only to the amount in excess of the available profits. In *Re Marini Ltd, Liquidator of Marini Ltd v Dickenson*[183] the court concluded that the prohibition is on making a distribution other than out of profits available for distribution (CA 2006, s 830(1)). To the extent therefore that a distribution is out of such profits, it cannot be unlawful, a conclusion supported by s 847(1) which envisages a shareholder being required to return part of a distribution.

20-109 Unless the company has taken advantage of the audit exemption available to small companies, the auditor must have made his report on the accounts (CA 2006, s 837(3)). If the auditor has qualified his report, he must state in writing (either at the time of his report or subsequently) whether, in his opinion, the substance of the qualification is material for

---

[179] [2003] 2 BCLC 442.   [180] See [2003] 2 BCLC 442 at 489–90.
[181] See also *Re Paycheck Services 3 Ltd, Revenue and Customs Commissioners v Holland* [2011] 1 BCLC 141, SC, and the obiter comments therein as to the court's discretion under IA 1986, s 212, see at **13-56**.
[182] See [2003] 2 BCLC 442 at 490–1.   [183] [2004] BCC 172.

determining whether the proposed distribution would contravene Part 23 and a copy of that statement must have been circulated to the members of a private company and, in the case of a public company, laid before the company in general meeting before the distribution was made (s 837(4)).

20-110 The significance of this statement by the auditor was considered by the Court of Appeal in *Precision Dippings Ltd v Precision Dippings Marketing Ltd*.[184] In this case, no auditor's statement had been made although the accounts had been qualified. A dividend of £60,000 was paid by Dippings to its parent company, Marketing. Dippings later went into liquidation. The auditors at that stage (i.e. post-distribution) issued a written declaration to the effect that the qualification in their report did not affect the validity of the dividend payment. The liquidator of Dippings successfully sued to recover the amount of the dividend from Marketing. The court found that the accounting requirements, of which the auditor's statement forms part, are not mere procedural requirements but an important part of the scheme provided by the statutory provisions as a major protection for creditors.[185] The wording of the provision, 'must have stated', now CA 2006, s 837(4)(a), showed that the auditor's statement had to be available to the shareholders before the distribution was made. As it had not been so available, the statutory provisions had been contravened and the payment of the dividend was ultra vires and void.

Declaration and payment of dividends

20-111 Assuming that a company does have available profits as determined in accordance with the statutory provisions, the next question is whether this automatically entitles the shareholders to a dividend. The position is that it does so only if the articles expressly provide for the payment of a fixed dividend where the company has distributable profits.[186] More commonly, the articles will allow for the declaration of a dividend by ordinary resolution following a recommendation by the directors.[187]

20-112 Only when a dividend has been declared does it become payable and due to the members.[188] As a rule a dividend must be paid in cash, but the articles may allow for a non-cash distribution to be made[189] (e.g. in the form of additional shares). A dividend paid in the form of additional shares is known as a scrip dividend.

Consequences of unlawful distributions

20-113 An unlawful distribution, whether unlawful at common law for being out of capital, or unlawful because in breach of the statute (either no available profits and/or some breach of the accounting requirements), is ultra vires and void and cannot be ratified by the

---

[184] [1985] BCLC 385.   [185] [1985] BCLC 385 at 389.

[186] See *Evling v Israel & Oppenheimer Ltd* [1918] 1 Ch 101.

[187] See The Companies (Model Articles) Regulations 2008, SI 2008/3229, Sch 1, art 30 (private companies), Sch 3, art 70 (public companies); the resolution may decrease but not increase the amount to be distributed. Informal unanimous assent will suffice, but only if the shareholders know what they are assenting to, see *Queensway Systems Ltd v Walker* [2007] 2 BCLC 577.

[188] The declaration of the dividend creates an immediate debt: *Re Severn and Wye and Severn Bridge Ry Co* [1896] 1 Ch 559, unless it is expressed as payable at a future date, in which case a shareholder has no right to enforce payment until the due date for payment arrives: *Re Kidner, Kidner v Kidner* [1929] 2 Ch 121. In the case of an interim dividend which the board has resolved to pay, it is open to the board at any time before payment to review its decision and resolve not to pay the dividend: *Lagunas Nitrate Co Ltd v Schroeder & Co and Schmidt* (1901) 85 Law Times 22.

[189] See The Companies (Model Articles) Regulations 2008, SI 2008/3229, Sch 1, art 35 (private companies), Sch 3, art 76 (public companies); also *Wood v Odessa Waterworks Co* (1889) 42 Ch D 636.

company in general meeting;[190] likewise where a dividend is paid in breach of a restriction in the articles[191] or contrary to some other enactment.

20-114 Where an unlawful distribution has been made, the company may seek to recover the amount distributed under the statute or at common law and the latter option offers the greatest range of possibilities. There are two main targets for any action by the company: (1) the recipient of the unlawful distribution; and (2) the directors who authorised the unlawful distribution.[192] As the shareholder recipients, especially in larger public companies, are frequently unaware of the circumstances surrounding a distribution in the form of a dividend and rely on the directors to act properly, there is little likelihood of successfully pursuing the shareholders to recover unlawful dividends (other than shareholders who are also directors or where the shareholder is a parent company).[193] It is more likely, though still comparatively rare, for the company (usually because a liquidator or new board of directors is in place) to pursue recovery from the directors who authorised the improper payments. Another possibility is that a creditor, such as the Inland Revenue, may bring a claim for misfeasance under IA 1986, s 212 against directors who authorise improper dividends.[194] Disqualification is also a possibility.[195]

Liability of recipients

20-115 Where a distribution, or part of a distribution,[196] is made in contravention of the requirements of CA 2006, Pt 23, any member who, at the time of the distribution, knows or has reasonable grounds for believing that it is so made is liable to repay the distribution (or part of it, as the case may be) to the company.[197] This statutory liability is without prejudice to any obligation imposed apart from the statutory provisions on a member to repay a distribution unlawfully made to him,[198] i.e. as a knowing recipient of trust funds.[199] An

---

[190]   *Re Exchange Banking Co, Flitcroft's Case* (1882) 21 Ch D 519; *Precision Dippings Ltd v Precision Dippings Marketing Ltd* [1985] BCLC 385; *Aveling Barford v Perion Ltd* [1989] BCLC 626; *Bairstow v Queens Moat Houses plc* [2001] 2 BCLC 531, CA.   [191]   *Guinness plc v Saunders* [1990] BCLC 402, HL.

[192]   Where the accounts have not been prepared properly and do not give a true and fair view as required, the company may also bring an action for negligence against its auditors.

[193]   An interesting development is the pursuit by the Serious Fraud Office of dividends paid to parent companies by subsidiaries which are found to have acted corruptly. In January 2012 the SFO announced that, using powers under the Proceeds of Crime Act 2002, it had recovered £131,201 in dividends paid to a parent company by a subsidiary which subsidiary had pleaded guilty to corruption charges with respect to contracts in Iraq in breach of UN sanctions: see SFO Press Release, 'Shareholder agrees civil recovery by SFO in Mabey & Johnson', 13 January 2012.

[194]   For examples, see *Re Loquitar Ltd, IRC v Richmond* [2003] 2 BCLC 444; *Re Paycheck Services 3 Ltd, Revenue and Customs Commissioners v Holland* [2011] 1 BCLC 141.

[195]   See *Re AG (Manchester) Ltd, Official Receiver v Watson* [2008] 1 BCLC 321 where a director left all financial and strategic decisions to an inner group of directors (including her husband) and was content to take substantial dividends from the company regardless of how and whether they could be paid. The court found her abdication of responsibility in failing to act independently and in the interests of the company justified her disqualification for four years; see also *Secretary of State for Business, Innovation and Skills v Doffman* [2011] 2 BCLC 541 (directors disqualified on the ground of unfitness, most of the evidence against them related to unlawful distributions).

[196]   If the company has available profits and properly prepared accounts, but pays a dividend in excess of that amount, it is only the part in excess of the available profits that is in contravention of the Act and must be repaid to the company: see *Re Marini Ltd, Liquidator of Marini Ltd v Dickenson* [2004] BCC 172.

[197]   CA 2006, s 847(1), (2)(a). Where the distribution is made otherwise than in cash, the statutory liability is to pay to the company a sum equal to the value of the distribution at the time of the distribution: s 847(2)(b), but at common law a proprietary claim may lie against the recipient, see **13-36**.

[198]   CA 2006, s 847(3).

[199]   See *Bank of Credit and Commerce International (Oversea) Ltd v Akindele* [2000] 4 All ER 221, CA and the discussion at **13-36** as to liability on a 'knowing receipt' basis.

illustration of liability based on 'knowing receipt' can be found in *Precision Dippings Ltd v Precision Dippings Marketing Ltd*[200] where a dividend was paid by a company (Dippings) to its parent company (Marketing) and the directors of Dippings were the only directors and shareholders of Marketing. The Court of Appeal held that the payment of the dividend in breach of the statutory provisions was an ultra vires act of the company. Marketing, when it received the money, had notice of the facts and held the £60,000 dividend on constructive trust for the company which was entitled to repayment.[201]

20-116   The flexibility to proceed either under the statutory provision or the common law is necessary since, as discussed, it is possible for a distribution to a member to be valid under CA 2006, Pt 23 (there are available profits and the accounting requirements are met) so no statutory liability arises, but the payment is in breach of the common law (because, for example, at the time of the payment, the company's position has worsened) or the company's articles. Also the test of liability as a recipient is different under the statute and at common law.[202] Statutory liability arises where the shareholder knows the facts which lead to the conclusion that the distribution is in contravention of the Act, but it is not necessary that the member knows the legal rules and the consequences of those rules when applied to the facts.[203] Liability as a constructive trustee arises where the shareholder knows or ought to know that the distribution is unlawful.[204] Therefore, depending on the facts, one or other route may offer the best chance of recovery.

20-117   The statutory liability was considered by the Court of Appeal in *It's a Wrap (UK) Ltd v Gula*[205] where the focus was on the meaning of the requirement that the member 'knows or has reasonable grounds for believing' that the distribution is in contravention of the Act (now CA 2006, s 847(2)). The company had two members, a husband and wife, who were also the directors. The company made no profits during its brief (four years) existence but the directors each took dividends of £14,000 per annum as a tax-efficient alternative to receiving a salary from the company. On the company going into insolvent liquidation, the liquidator sought to recover £56,000 in total from them, but they were found not liable at first instance on the basis that the section required knowledge of the legal position. The Court of Appeal swiftly overruled the decision and confirmed that it is not necessary to show that the shareholders know the statutory provisions. It is enough that the shareholders know the facts which lead to the conclusion that the distribution does contravene the statutory provisions.[206] The defendants knew the company had no profits, therefore they knew of the contravention for the purpose of the statutory liability and they had to repay the sums which they had received.

---

[200] [1985] BCLC 385, CA.

[201]   See [1985] BCLC 385 at 390, per Dillon LJ, applying *Rolled Steel Products (Holdings) Ltd v British Steel Corpn* [1986] Ch 246, [1985] 3 All ER 52.

[202]   See Arden LJ in *It's a Wrap (UK) Ltd v Gula* [2006] 2 BCLC 634 at [12] who comments that the statutory remedy is more absolute and stringent than that at common law because it is tailor-made to facilitate the recovery of unlawful distributions whereas the remedy under the general law is an adaptation of the law of constructive trusteeship, but the need for some form of actual or constructive knowledge on the part of the shareholder is common to both forms of remedy; see also, at [52], per Chadwick LJ .

[203]   *It's a Wrap (UK) Ltd v Gula* [2006] 2 BCLC 634 at [50], per Chadwick LJ.

[204]   *Moxham v Grant* [1900] 1 QB 88; see also *Precision Dippings Ltd v Precision Dippings Marketing Ltd* [1985] BCLC 385; *Re Cleveland Trust plc* [1991] BCLC 424; *Allied Carpets Group plc v Nethercott* [2001] BCC 81. See *It's a Wrap (UK) Ltd v Gula* [2006] 2 BCLC 634 at [52] where Chadwick LJ notes that he does not think that the composite phrase 'knows or has reasonable grounds for believing' has the same meaning as 'knows or ought to know'.   [205]   [2006] 2 BCLC 634, CA.

[206]   [2006] 2 BCLC 634 at [50], per Chadwick LJ; see also [27], [35], per Arden LJ; at [39], per Sedley LJ.

Liability of directors

20-118 The statute deals with the liability of the recipient of an unlawful dividend, but does not address the liability of the directors for authorising or procuring the payment of the dividend which remains a matter for the common law. Once it is established that there has been an unlawful distribution, the extent of the liability of those directors who caused the distribution is clear. Directors are trustees of the company's assets and as such are jointly and severally liable for the full amount of any unlawful distribution of the company's assets to the shareholders, whether the company is solvent or insolvent and whether or not profits could have been available.[207] The classic authority is *Re Exchange Banking Co, Flitcroft's Case*[208] where the directors had been in the habit of including among the company's assets a number of debts which they knew to be bad. The effect was to give the appearance of profits when in fact there were none. The directors recommended and the general meeting approved the payment of dividends over a period of several years on the strength of those accounts. On the company going into insolvent liquidation, the court ordered the directors jointly and severally to repay the moneys improperly expended in this way.[209] The potential extent of this liability can be seen in *Bairstow v Queens Moat Houses plc*[210] where the company obtained a judgment for £78m against its former directors who, the court found, had deliberately (and dishonestly in certain cases) made unlawful dividend payments over a period of years. In this instance, the company sought to recover from the directors the entire amount paid to the shareholders.[211] There is no doubt then about the level of recovery—the entire amount of the unlawful distribution, regardless of loss or whether the distribution could have been made in a lawful manner, because of the directors' trustee-like responsibilities for the trust assets.[212]

20-119 More difficult is the basis on which the individual directors should be liable for having caused the improper payments. It is clear from the cases that liability can arise either because of actual knowledge of the improper payment or because of negligence, a failure to exercise care and skill,[213] which is why the directors in *Kingston Cotton Mill (No 2)*[214] and *Dovey v Cory*[215] escaped liability, not having been found to have breached the duty of care and skill as it was at that time, though higher standards of care and skill are expected of directors now (see discussion in Chapter 10). For example, a director who relies unduly

---

[207] *Re Exchange Banking Co, Flitcroft's Case* (1882) 21 Ch D 519; *Re Oxford Benefit Building & Investment Society* (1886) 35 Ch D 502; and see the discussion of directors' liabilities in Chapter 13. Directors who are liable for the entire amount of the distribution may seek an indemnity from the shareholders who received it: *Moxham v Grant* [1900] 1 QB 88.   [208] (1882) 21 Ch D 519.

[209] To the extent that a distribution is made in excess of available profits as determined by properly prepared accounts, any liability of the directors extends only to the repayment of that part which is unlawful: *Re Marini Ltd, Liquidator of Marini Ltd v Dickenson* [2004] BCC 172 at 193. The distinguishing feature from *Bairstow v Queens Moat Houses plc* [2001] 2 BCLC 531 at 546, CA is that profits were available in *Marini* whereas in *Bairstow* there were no profits in the company and, even if there might have been elsewhere in the group, they had not been paid up into the company.

[210] [2001] 2 BCLC 531, CA; *Re Denham & Co* [1884] LR 25 Ch D 752.

[211] As to whether the directors might have sought contribution from any shareholder recipients who had knowledge of the unlawful nature of the payments, see [2001] 2 BCLC 531 at 547–8; also *Moxham v Grant* [1900] 1 QB 88.

[212] See *JJ Harrison (Properties) Ltd v Harrison* [2002] 1 BCLC 162; *Re Lands Allotment Co* [1894] 1 Ch 616.

[213] See *Bairstow v Queens Moat Houses plc* [2000] 1 BCLC 549 at 559–60, ChD which contains a useful summation by Nelson J of the circumstances in which a director will be liable. The case was appealed on other grounds, see [2001] 2 BCLC 531, CA.

[214] [1896] 1 Ch 331 at 348.   [215] [1901] AC 477.

on others in breach of her duty to exercise residual supervision of the management of the company's affairs and who fails to apply her mind to whether a distribution is proper is in breach of her duty of care and skill.[216]

20-120   This issue of the directors' liability for improper dividends was discussed, obiter, in the Supreme Court in *Re Paycheck Services 3 Ltd, Revenue and Customs Commissioners v Holland*[217] where essentially improper dividends had been paid without appropriate provision for corporation tax. The case revolved around whether a director of a corporate director was a de facto director (see the detailed discussion at **6-13**) with responsibility for having declared the dividends. Obviously, once the Supreme Court found that the defendant was not a de facto director, the question of his liability for the improper dividends fell away, but Lord Hope had some interesting, though obiter, comments on Counsel's argument that any liability of a director for the repayment of unlawful dividends was based on negligence rather than a strict liability.

20-121   Lord Hope accepted that there were some authorities such as *Kingston Cotton Mill (No 2)*[218] and *Dovey v Cory*[219] which supported a liability based on a duty of care, but he considered that such authorities come to an end with *Dovey v Cory* and that thereafter the authorities, rightly in his view, say that the directors' obligation in respect of improperly paid dividends is to account to the company for the full amount of those dividends.[220] In his opinion, the better view in cases where it is accepted that the payment of the dividends is unlawful is that a director who causes their payment is strictly liable, subject to the possibility of relief under what is now CA 2006, s 1157, or the exercise of the court's discretion in terms of the order it makes under IA 1986, s 212.[221] Once a director is liable, Lord Hope agreed with the Court of Appeal that the remedy is not equitable compensation or damages for loss sustained, but restoration of the money paid out.[222] In this he agreed with Rimer LJ in the court below that the directors' trustee-like duties in respect of the company's assets require the directors to reinstate the full amount of the improper payment of dividends without any inquiry as to the loss said to be suffered by the company.[223]

20-122   There seems a degree of confusion of issues here. As noted, there is no doubt that directors who cause a misapplication of the company's funds are liable to reinstate the trust assets and that liability is strict in the sense that full reinstatement must be made without inquiry as to loss, etc. But the issue of whether the director caused the misapplication does require a finding of fault; though the threshold for fault is low, it is not limited to distributions in breach of trust, but arises also where there has been negligence. Hence, in most instances of an unlawful distribution, the directors will be liable; they caused the misapplication, either because they are active participants in the wrongdoing or because the wrongdoing is a consequence of a lack of care on their part. Given their obligations under CA 2006, Pt 23 and the higher standards now expected of directors as compared with the

---

[216] See *Re AG (Manchester) Ltd, Official Receiver v Watson* [2008] 1 BCLC 321 at [184]–[187]; *Queensway Systems Ltd v Walker* [2007] 2 BCLC 577; *Neville v Krikorian* [2007] 1 BCLC 1, CA.

[217] [2011] 1 BCLC 141.   [218] [1896] 1 Ch 331 at 348.   [219] [1901] AC 477.

[220] [2011] 1 BCLC 141 at [45]–[46]

[221] [2011] 1 BCLC 141 at [45]–[46], see discussion of relief under CA 2006, s 1157 and IA 1986, s 212, at **13-53** and **13-56,** respectively. See Ferran (2011) CLJ 321 for critical comment on Lord Hope's views. As discussed at **13-55**, the courts are unlikely to grant relief in respect of conduct which benefits shareholders to the detriment of creditors: see *Inn Spirit Ltd v Burns* [2002] 2 BCLC 780 at 787–8; *Re Loquitur Ltd, IRC v Richmond* [2003] 2 BCLC 442; *Re Marini Ltd, Liquidator of Marini Ltd v Dickenson* [2004] BCC 172 at 193; *Queensway Systems Ltd v Walker* [2007] 2 BCLC 577.   [222] [2011] 1 BCLC 141 at [48]–[49].

[223] [2009] 2 BCLC 309 at [98], per Rimer LJ, with whom Elias LJ agreed, at [125]. There was broad agreement in the Supreme Court with Rimer LJ, see [2011] 1 BCLC 141 at [49], per Lord Hope; at [124], per Lord Walker; at [146], per Lord Clarke.

era of *Dovey v Cory*, it will be relatively easy to establish a breach of duty by them. There may be scope for argument in non-dividend situations, i.e. the commercial transaction distribution cases, either that the transaction was not a distribution in the first place or, if it was, that the director was not implicated in the wrongdoing and there was no breach of the duty of care, in which case no liability would arise. But once a director has 'caused' an unlawful distribution, whether knowingly or carelessly, there is a strict liability to make good the entire misapplication, subject only to the court's discretion to grant relief either under CA 2006, s 1157, or in the appropriate case under IA 1986, s 212.

Alternative frameworks—solvency statements

20-123 The Company Law Review favoured only technical amendments to the statutory provisions on distribution rather than wholesale revision.[224] A more fundamental debate subsequently emerged at the European level (though influenced by developments here)[225] as to whether it was time to shift away from a statutory framework on distributions closely tied to the company's accounts and the determination of the existence of available profits under those accounts to a scheme based on directors' declarations of solvency (whereby if the directors certify that the company will remain solvent following a distribution, that should suffice). This approach, or variations thereof, is relied upon in other jurisdictions and the accounting profession seemed keen on such reform.[226] The issue arose as part of a broader debate, see **20-8,** as to whether the capital maintenance doctrine is obsolete and serves no practical purpose.

20-124 Against that backdrop, the European Commission launched an external assessment of the capital maintenance regime established by the Second Directive which was carried out by KPMG and published in early 2008.[227] KPMG were asked to consider in particular the impact of International Financial Reporting Standards (IFRS, which must be used for consolidated accounts and may be used for individual accounts) on distributions and whether an alternative regime would be better. On the distribution issues, the KPMG study concluded that the requirements of the Second Directive were modest in relation to the cushion required before a distribution might be made, the use of IFRS as such did not cause companies problems in terms of distributions, and that those jurisdictions which do rely on solvency statements frequently also impose a balance sheet test.[228] In the light of those findings, the Commission announced that 'no follow-up measures or changes to the Second Company Law Directive are foreseen in the immediate future'.[229] Subsequently, the momentum for changes to the rules governing distribution dissipated.

---

[224] See Company Law Review, *Final Report*, vol I (2001), para 10.6; *Completing the Structure* (2000), paras 7.20–7.23; *Company Formation and Capital Maintenance* (1999), paras 3.65–3.76 and Annex B; also *Capital Maintenance: Other Issues* (2000).

[225] See Rickford (ed), Reforming Capital: Report of the Interdisciplinary Group on Capital Maintenance' (2004) EBLR 919.

[226] See FEE Discussion Paper on Alternatives to Capital Maintenance Regimes, September 2007. FEE is an umbrella group for accountants in Europe representing 45 member bodies in 33 countries including all EU countries. For the views of a leading British proponent of a move to a solvency regime, see Rickford, 'Legal Approaches to Restricting Distributions to Shareholders: Balance Sheet Tests and Solvency Tests' (2006) 7 EBOR 135.

[227] KPMG, 'Feasibility Study on an alternative to the capital maintenance regime established by the Second Company Law Directive 77/91/EEC of 13 December 1976 and an examination of the impact on profit distribution of the new EU accounting regime', January 2008.

[228] See Schon, 'Balance Sheet Tests or Solvency Tests—or Both?' (2006) EBOR 181, who argues for the dual approach.

[229] Commission statement on the results of the external study on the feasibility of an alternative to the Capital Maintenance Regime of the Second Company Law Directive and the impact of the adoption of IFRS on profit distribution.

Certainly, the European Commission is unlikely to support any wholesale change from the current system in the absence of identifiable benefits from doing so. Also, to some extent, these issues have been overtaken by market developments and, given the financial crisis, the current demand is for tighter regulation of business and stronger accounting standards to prevent optimistic valuations and inappropriate distributions. There is likely to be little support for measures which are perceived (even if that perception might be erroneous) as reducing protection for creditors.

E Financial assistance by a company for the acquisition of its own shares

The problem with financial assistance

20-125 Financial assistance given by a company for the purchase of its own shares can arise in many circumstances but the classic abuse relates to the acquisition of a company by a bidder who borrows to fund the acquisition and then uses the company's assets once control has been secured to repay the funding. There are legitimate ways of carrying out this manoeuvre, as we shall see, but the concern is that, once the bidder has gained control, an element of asset stripping may occur to the detriment of the creditors.[230] Shareholders who have not had or taken the opportunity to exit from the company may also suffer as a consequence, though the primary concern here is creditor protection which is why these rules are linked to the capital maintenance rules discussed in this chapter. Concerns about the giving of financial assistance by a company for the purchase of its own shares date back to the 1920s. Though the statutory provisions have been restated on a number of occasions since their introduction in the Companies Act 1928, as Arden LJ noted in *Chaston v SWP Group plc*:[231]

> 'The general mischief, however, remains the same, namely that the resources of the target company and its subsidiaries should not be used directly or indirectly to assist the purchaser or financially to make the acquisition. This may prejudice the interests of the creditors of the target or its group and the interests of any shareholders who do not accept the offer to acquire the shares or to whom the offer is not made.'

20-126 The mischief can arise in the context of significant companies with substantial assets, but it may also arise in smaller companies where typically the existing shareholders/directors wish to exit the business but cannot find a purchaser with funds to acquire their shares. The temptation or solution, depending on your viewpoint, is to use the company's assets to assist a possible purchaser. The risk is that the shareholders'/directors' personal determination to exit leaves them indifferent or reckless to the consequences of using the company's assets to assist an impecunious purchaser. An example can be seen in *Re In A Flap Envelope Co Ltd*[232] where the directors of a company in financial difficulties sold their shareholding in the company to L. Some months later, when L had still not paid for the shares, it was agreed that the company would lend money to L to enable it to pay for the shares. L then paid the shareholders £355,000 approximately. Twelve months later the company collapsed owing £3.2m.

---

[230] See Report of the Company Law Committee (the Jenkins Committee) (Cmnd 1749, 1962), para 176; see *Re VGM Holdings Ltd* [1942] 1 All ER 224 at 225.

[231] [2003] 1 BCLC 675 at 686; for criticism of the view that this mischief requires rules on financial assistance, see Ferran (2004) CLJ 225.

[232] [2004] 1 BCLC 64.

The legislative response

20-127 Financial assistance was first made a criminal offence by the CA 1929. The current prohibition on the giving of financial assistance by companies for the purchase of their own shares is set out in CA 2006, ss 677–683 (previously CA 1985, ss 151–158).[233]

20-128 The provisions on financial assistance are wide-ranging and practitioners frequently complain of the additional expense and complexity involved in ensuring that innocuous transactions linked to the acquisition of companies do not fall foul of the prohibition, particularly given that it is a criminal offence. A further problem is that, while the potential for abuse in funding acquisitions in this way is clear, it is also clear that if this type of funding is not possible, then many perfectly acceptable acquisitions will not occur, giving rise to economic loss and stagnation. Recognising these difficulties, the Companies Act 1981 introduced a 'whitewash' procedure for private companies which enabled such companies to give financial assistance provided certain conditions were met (CA 1985, ss 155–158). The whitewash procedure was complicated and costly to execute in that it required a special resolution by the shareholders, a directors' statement (essentially as to the solvency of the company at the time of giving the assistance and for a year thereafter) backed up by an auditors' statement and objecting shareholders could apply to the court to block the assistance. Crucially, the financial assistance could only be given if the company had net assets which were not thereby reduced or, to the extent that they were reduced, the assistance was provided out of distributable profits (CA 1985, s 155(2)).

20-129 On a variety of occasions in the early 1990s, the Department of Trade and Industry consulted as to possible reform of the statutory provisions without any progress being made. In due course, the Company Law Review considered the issue and was highly critical of the statutory provisions (CA 1985, ss 151–158).[234] The Review recommended, therefore, that the provisions on financial assistance should not apply to private companies (so dispensing with the need for the whitewash procedure) and that such abuses as prompted the legislation (asset stripping essentially) should be addressed through directors' duties and the insolvency legislation.[235] Public companies would remain subject to the prohibitions in the light of the Second Company Law Directive. These recommendations were adopted in the CA 2006, ss 677–683.

20-130 Repealing the prohibition on financial assistance by private companies is seen by the Government as one of the key de-regulatory measures of the CA 2006. That said, the remaining provisions are still complex and wide-ranging and do apply to some extent to private companies (where they are part of a group with public companies) so the position still needs careful consideration. It must also be appreciated that, while the prohibition on the giving of financial assistance by private companies has been repealed, the broader protective rules discussed in this chapter, on distributions and reduction of capital, still apply as does the common law principle (*Trevor v Whitworth*[236]) prohibiting a return

---

[233] For a comprehensive account of the 1985 provisions, see Roberts, *Financial Assistance for the Acquisition of Shares* (2005).

[234] Company Law Review, *Final Report*, vol I (2001), para 2.30: 'These provisions are among the most difficult of the Act, and in many cases it is all but impossible for a company to assess whether a proposed course of action is lawful or not. The provisions are arbitrary in their effect on private companies, and innocuous transactions may be rendered unlawful by criminal law requirements that are often unenforceable and by civil sanctions of wide and damaging effect.'

[235] See Company Law Review, *Final Report*, vol I (2001), para 10.6; *Completing the Structure* (2000), paras 7.12–7.15; *Company Formation and Capital Maintenance* (1999), paras 3.41–3.48 and Annex B; *Strategic Framework* (1999), paras 5.4.20–5.4.25.

[236] (1887) 12 App Cas 409, HL.

of capital to shareholders.[237] Any transaction which involves giving financial assistance needs to be looked at carefully to ensure it does not fall foul of those other rules or principles, for example where it gives rise to a reduction in net assets which cannot be covered by distributable reserves. The possibility that a transaction might be challenged subsequently as a transaction at an undervalue under IA 1986, s 238 also needs to be borne in mind. Directors' fiduciary duties also come into play when the company is giving financial assistance and the directors need to consider carefully (and probably minute carefully) whether they are exercising their powers for a proper purpose (CA 2006, s 171) and to promote the success of the company (s 172). The duty of care and skill is also relevant (s 174) and possibly even the duty to avoid a conflict of interest (under s 175 or even s 177). Removing the prohibition does not therefore open up the way for freewheeling financial assistance of the type which perhaps some of the proponents of abolition envisaged.

20-131 The position with respect to public companies is unchanged by the CA 2006 because of the requirements of the Second Company Law Directive which initially provided that a public company may not advance funds, nor make loans, nor provide security with a view to the acquisition of its shares by a third party[238] before being amended to allow Member States to permit public companies to grant financial assistance up to the limit of the company's distributable reserves.[239] The relaxation is surrounded by onerous procedural requirements, however, including prior shareholder approval based on a detailed report to be presented to the general meeting and the creation of an undistributable reserve equal to the amount of the financial assistance. Therefore the UK decided not to implement this option so the prohibition of financial assistance by public companies remains. Public companies can take comfort, however, from evidence of a more pragmatic approach by the courts to financial assistance issues in recent years which respects genuine commercial transactions and seeks to constrain the prohibition to the mischief identified by Parliament, namely the risk to creditors of asset depletion from financial assistance.[240] The courts have emphasised the importance of looking at the overall commercial realities of a situation instead of allowing a narrow focus on whether technically a transaction may be classified as financial assistance, see **20-140**. Further, the courts are minded to limit the scope of the resulting illegality. In *Anglo Petroleum Ltd v TFB (Mortgages) Ltd*,[241] for

---

[237] In an attempt to allay concerns as to the extent to which the common law may still be relevant, an obscurely worded saving provision was included in The Companies Act 2006 (Commencement No. 5, Transitional Provisions and Savings) Order 2007, SI 2007/3495, art 9, Sch 4, para 52. The intention, apparently, is to ensure that private companies which are now released from the statutory prohibitions on financial assistance should not be subject to any residual common law restriction on financial assistance. The difficulty is that the common law restriction is a broader prohibition on a return of capital so the saving may prove pointless if it was intended to close off challenges on the basis of an improper return of capital. It does close off challenges on the grounds of improper financial assistance, but as the Department of Trade pointed out, that was the consequence of the repeal of the prohibition so far as it applied to private companies in any event. See the Explanatory Memorandum to the Fifth Commencement Order, para 7.

[238] Second Council Directive (77/91/EEC) [1977] OJ L 26/1.

[239] By Directive 2006/68/EC, OJ L 264/32, 25.09.2006. See criticism by Ferran 'Simplification of European Company law on Financial Assistance' (2005) 6 EBOR 93.

[240] For example, the courts have been alert to attempts by parties to evade their commercial obligations on the basis of spurious claims of illegal financial assistance, see *Dyment v Boyden* [2005] 1 BCLC 163, CA (tenant tried to have an onerous lease declared void for illegal financial assistance when the reality was that she had made a bad bargain and was paying an extortionate rent, see **20-144**); *Anglo Petroleum Ltd v TFB (Mortgages) Ltd* [2008] 1 BCLC 185, CA (borrower essentially tried to renege on a £15m loan and related guarantee by alleging illegal financial assistance when the reality was that its financial position had worsened and it was finding it difficult to make repayments, see **20-142**).

[241] [2008] 1 BCLC 185, CA.

example, the Court of Appeal noted obiter that, even if it had found illegal financial assistance in respect of the use of funds borrowed by the company, the loan agreement and associated charges and guarantees would not have been illegal. Those agreements did not necessitate any breach of the law, Toulson LJ said, and no reason of public policy required those perfectly ordinary commercial transactions to be struck down.[242] All of these elements show a concern to keep the prohibition within appropriate boundaries.

The prohibition on financial assistance

20-132 There are three prohibitions in all. First, where a person is acquiring or is proposing to acquire any shares in a public company, it is not lawful for the company or a company that is a subsidiary of that company[243] to give financial assistance directly or indirectly for the purpose of that acquisition before or at the same time as the acquisition takes place (CA 2006, s 678(1)). The first scenario then is the acquisition of shares in a public company where the financial assistance is given by that (public) company or by a subsidiary company (which may be a private or public company).

20-133 Secondly, where a person has acquired shares in a company and a liability has been incurred (by that or any other person) for the purpose of the acquisition, it is not lawful for that company or a company that is a subsidiary of that company[244] to give financial assistance directly or indirectly for the purpose of reducing or discharging the liability[245] if, at the time the assistance is given, the company in which the shares were acquired is a public company (CA 2006, s 678(3)). The second scenario covers the situation where shares have been acquired whether in a public or private company provided that at the time the assistance is given (again whether by a public or private company) to reduce or discharge the liability incurred on that purchase the company in which the shares are acquired is a public company.

20-134 Finally, where a person is acquiring or is proposing to acquire shares in a private company, it is not lawful for a public company that is a subsidiary of that company[246] to give financial assistance directly or indirectly for the purpose of that acquisition before or at the same time as the acquisition takes place (CA 2006, s 679(1)) or to give financial assistance directly or indirectly for the purpose of reducing or discharging a liability incurred for the purpose of the acquisition (s 679(3).[247]

20-135 There is no requirement that the assistance be given to the vendor or the purchaser of the shares; it may be given to a subsidiary or associated company or other person nominated by one of the parties, but it will still fall within the prohibitions, provided it is for the purpose of the acquisition.[248]

---

[242] [2008] 1 BCLC 185 at 202–3, CA.

[243] The prohibition applies only to subsidiaries registered in this jurisdiction and a foreign subsidiary of an English parent company can give financial assistance for the acquisition of the latter's shares: *Arab Bank plc v Merchantile Holdings Ltd* [1994] 1 BCLC 330, but see also at 335; *AMG Global Nominees (Private) Ltd v SMM Holdings Ltd* [2008] 1 BCLC 447. [244] See n 243.

[245] A reference to a company giving financial assistance for the purpose of reducing or discharging a liability incurred by a person for the purpose of the acquisition of shares includes its giving such assistance for the purpose of wholly or partially restoring his financial position to what it was before the acquisition took place: CA 2006, s 683(2)(b).

[246] See n 243.   [247] See n 245.

[248] *Chaston v SWP Group plc* [2003] 1 BCLC 675 at 689, CA. But see criticisms by Ferran, n 231, p 237 who argues that there is no need to extend the prohibition beyond assistance of benefit to purchasers, since that is the mischief at which the prohibition is aimed; also Look Chan Ho, 'Financial Assistance after Chaston and MT Realisations' (2003) JIBLR 424.

20-136 A breach of these provisions is a criminal offence and the company is liable to a fine and every officer in default is liable to imprisonment or a fine or both (CA 2006, s 680). The civil consequences are not dealt with in the statute and remain a matter for the common law, see **20-153**.

20-137 To establish liability, it is necessary to show that financial assistance was given and that it was given for the purpose of the acquisition or the reduction/discharge of a liability, as the case may be.[249]

The meaning of financial assistance

20-138 The legislation is broadly drafted to catch a wide variety of types of financial assistance, for example financial assistance given by way of gift, guarantee, security or indemnity, release or waiver or a loan, etc, all of which are listed in CA 2006, s 677(1). The requirement is that the transaction be of the type mentioned (and the terms used, indemnity etc, must be given their normal legal meaning) and also amount to financial assistance.[250] As Arden LJ pointed out in *Chaston v SWP Group plc*,[251] there is no requirement of detriment with regard to these elements, for example financial assistance via a loan could be on terms which are beneficial to the company.[252] Detriment is only required under CA 2006, s 677(1)(d) which includes 'any other financial assistance given by a company where the net assets[253] of the company are reduced to a material extent[254] by the giving of the assistance, or the company has no net assets'. As Ward LJ noted in *Chaston v SWP Group plc*,[255] these words are 'as wide as can be' and so have the potential to catch the unwary as a transaction which does not appear to be financial assistance in any of the more obvious ways (loans, guarantees etc) may fall foul of this element. On the other hand, CA 2006, s 677(1)(d) is necessary precisely to catch transactions which do not fall into the more obvious categories of financial assistance listed in the section, such as where a company purchases an asset at an overvalue for the purpose of putting the vendor of the asset in funds with which to acquire the company's shares.[256]

20-139 Drawing lines can be difficult, however, as noted earlier. For example, the payment of a debt owed by the company cannot be financial assistance for that is a mere discharge of a debt.[257] Likewise the grant of security in respect of a debt cannot amount to financial assistance,[258] but the payment off of a parent company's debt by a subsidiary in order to

---

[249] *Charterhouse Investment Trust Ltd v Tempest Diesels Ltd* [1986] BCLC 1 at 10, per Hoffmann J.

[250] *Barclays Bank plc v British & Commonwealth Holdings plc* [1996] 1 BCLC 1 at 38, CA.

[251] [2003] 1 BCLC 675 at 689.

[252] See Ferran, n 231 at 231 who agrees with Arden LJ as a matter of statutory interpretation, but see Look Chan Ho, n 248, who is more critical of this interpretation.

[253] 'Net assets' is defined as the aggregate of the company's assets less the aggregate of its liabilities (CA 2006, s 677(2)), meaning the actual rather than the book value of the assets and liabilities and in this case the liabilities must include provision as required by s 677(3): see *Re Uniq plc* [2011] EWHC 749 at [33], per David Richards J.

[254] There is no definition of material extent, but in practice a reduction of 1% would be considered material.   [255] [2003] 1 BCLC 675 at 694.

[256] See *Belmont Finance Corpn Ltd v Williams Furniture Ltd* [1980] 1 All ER 393, CA. See *Re Uniq plc* [2011] EWHC 749 at [39] where the court accepted that a payment made by the company to a purchaser of shares in the company in return for the purchaser taking on certain pension responsibilities of the company could not be financial assistance within s 677(1)(d) when the payment made (£79.9m) resulted in the company's release from liabilities for which a provision of £231m was shown in the company's accounts. See Leivesley [2011] JBL 725 on this case.

[257] *Armour Hick Northern Ltd v Armour Trust Ltd* [1980] 3 All ER 833; and see *Re Uniq plc* [2011] EWHC 749 at [39].

[258] *Anglo Petroleum Ltd v TFB (Mortgages) Ltd* [2008] 1 BCLC 185, CA.

facilitate an acquisition of the parent company's shares may constitute such assistance.[259] In *Chaston v SWP Group plc*[260] a subsidiary company agreed to pay certain adviser fees with respect to a report on the affairs of its parent company which report was carried out for the purpose of a proposed acquisition of the parent company's shares by another party and that was held by the Court of Appeal to be financial assistance for the purpose of the acquisition of the parent company shares.

20-140 The potential scope of the prohibition is wide, but the courts, starting with Hoffmann J in *Charterhouse Investment Trust Ltd v Tempest Diesels Ltd*,[261] have emphasised that, when deciding whether a transaction can properly be described as the giving of financial assistance by the company, the commercial realities of the transaction as a whole must be considered, bearing in mind, as Hoffmann J said, that the section is a penal provision and should not be strained to cover transactions which are not fairly within it. That view was endorsed most notably by the Court of Appeal in *Anglo Petroleum Ltd v TFB (Mortgages)*[262] where Toulson LJ crisply summed up the correct approach as follows: 'In cases where its application [the prohibition on financial assistance] is doubtful, it is important to remember its central purpose, to examine the commercial realities and to bear in mind that it is a penal statute.'

20-141 In *MT Realisations Ltd v Digital Equipment Co Ltd*,[263] a subsidiary company paid certain sums due under a secured loan to it from its parent company and those sums were used to pay off the liability incurred by the parent company in acquiring the shares in the subsidiary. In fact, for convenience, the sums were paid directly by the subsidiary to the vendor of the shares so it appeared that the subsidiary's funds were being used to pay liabilities arising on the acquisition of shares in the subsidiary. An allegation arose that this was illegal financial assistance. The Court of Appeal found that the commercial reality of this transaction was that (1) the subsidiary was not giving the parent company anything, (2) the parent company was exercising its entitlement as a secured creditor to require certain sums to be paid to it, and (3) as a matter of commercial convenience those sums were paid direct to the vendor rather than from the subsidiary to the parent to the vendor. As a matter of commercial reality and legal principle, the Court of Appeal held, such an agreement did not involve the subsidiary in giving financial assistance for the acquisition of its own shares.

20-142 A similarly robust approach is evident in *Anglo Petroleum Ltd v TFB (Mortgages) Ltd*.[264] In this case a company in financial difficulties (it owed £30m, unsecured, to its parent company) negotiated a reduction in that debt to £15m and gave a charge over its assets to secure the repayment of the £15m. At the same time, the parent company sold its entire shareholding in the company to K for £1 and K guaranteed to ensure that the company would repay the outstanding indebtedness. The court rejected a claim that the charge given to secure the repayment of the £15m was financial assistance for the acquisition of the shares by K. The court noted that it is well established that the repayment of a debt which is properly due from a company does not constitute financial assistance. If it is lawful for a company to repay its own indebtedness; the court held, it must also equally be lawful for the company to assist that repayment by providing security. In this case, the

---

[259] *Armour Hick Northern Ltd v Armour Trust Ltd* [1980] 3 All ER 833.   [260] [2003] 1 BCLC 675, CA.
[261] [1986] BCLC 1 at 10.
[262] [2008] 1 BCLC 185 at 191; see also *MT Realisations Ltd v Digital Equipment Co Ltd* [2003] 2 BCLC 117, CA; and *Chaston v SWP Group plc* [2003] 1 BCLC 675, CA.
[263] [2003] 2 BCLC 117.   [264] [2008] 1 BCLC 185, CA.

commercial reality was a restructuring of debt with a significant reduction in amount achieved in return for security.

20-143 K subsequently borrowed £15m from TFB to pay off the outstanding £15m to the original parent company and that TFB borrowing was secured on the company's assets. It was then alleged that this TFB borrowing and charge too was financial assistance since it was done to reduce or discharge a liability incurred in the acquisition by K of the shares. The Court of Appeal did not accept that this could be financial assistance. The issue is not where the money comes from,[265] but the use the company makes of it. The TFB loan and related security was ordinary commercial lending, even where, as here, the bank knows the purpose is to repay the original parent company. A bank cannot be expected to investigate whether that repayment might infringe rules of financial assistance. As noted, the Court of Appeal did not believe that public policy required those perfectly ordinary commercial transactions to be struck down,[266] a pragmatic position which gives considerable comfort to the parties. This approach is also consistent with the principle that, where an agreement is capable of being performed in alternative ways, one lawful and one in breach of the provisions on financial assistance, it is to be presumed that the parties intend to carry out the agreement in a lawful and not an unlawful manner.[267] A bank is entitled to expect a company to use borrowed funds in a legal and not illegal manner.

The purpose of the transaction

20-144 In addition to the assistance being financial assistance, the assistance must be given for the purpose of the acquisition or to reduce or discharge a liability incurred for the purpose of the acquisition.[268] In *Dyment v Boyden*[269] three individuals had been involved in running a nursing home together. As part of a deal to separate their various interests, A acquired all of the shares of B and C. This acquisition gave A total control of the company which ran the nursing home, but the freehold of the property from which the business was operated was controlled by B and C. They granted the company a lease of the premises at a very high rental. In subsequent proceedings, A tried to argue that the rental payments were linked to her acquisition of B and C's shares in the company and as such amounted to financial assistance given directly or indirectly for the purpose of that acquisition. The Court of Appeal found that the reason why the company entered into the lease was because the company needed the premises from which to conduct its business. The entry into the lease, the court said, could not be linked to A's acquisition of the shares.

20-145 In *Chaston v SWP Group plc*,[270] as noted at **20-139**, a subsidiary company paid fees with respect to a report drawn up about its parent company. The purpose of the arrangement was to facilitate the negotiations by a possible purchaser and to enable it to determine whether it wished to acquire the shares. As such, the court held, it was financial assistance given for the purpose of the acquisition of the shares.

20-146 Even if the assistance is given for the purpose of the acquisition etc, the prohibition does not apply if the company's principal purpose in giving that assistance is not to give it

---

[265] [2008] 1 BCLC 185 at 195.

[266] [2008] 1 BCLC 185 at 202–3, CA. To the extent that *Re Hill & Tyler Ltd* [2005] 1 BCLC 41 supports striking down a loan and security in these circumstances, it must be considered now to be of doubtful authority.

[267] *Neilson v Stewart* [1991] BCC 713. See also *Brady v Brady* [1988] 2 All ER 617, HL; *Parlett v Guppys (Bridport) Ltd* [1996] 2 BCLC 34.

[268] See *Charterhouse Investment Trust Ltd v Tempest Diesels Ltd* [1986] BCLC 1 at 10, per Hoffmann J.

[269] [2005] 1 BCLC 163.

[270] [2003] 1 BCLC 675. See also *Corporate Development Partners LLC v E-Relationship Marketing Ltd* [2009] BCC 295.

for the purpose of any such acquisition, or the giving of the assistance for that purpose is but an incidental part of some larger purpose of the company, and the assistance is given in good faith in the interests of the company (CA 2006, s 678(2)). A similar exemption applies where the financial assistance is for the purpose of reducing or discharging a liability incurred in the acquisition of shares (CA 2006, s 678(2)). The scope of this 'principal purpose' etc exception was construed in an unhelpfully narrow way, however, by the House of Lords in *Brady v Brady*.[271] In this case, assistance was given by a company to reduce or discharge a liability incurred for the acquisition of shares in the company in *prima facie* breach of the statutory prohibition. The transaction arose as part of an elaborate scheme for the division of a family business between two brothers. It was argued that this division of the business was the larger purpose, as required by the statute, and the financial assistance was only incidental to it.

20-147 The House of Lords adopted a restrictive interpretation of the provision, distinguishing between a *purpose* and the *reason* why a purpose is formed. The fact that a company in giving financial assistance has some more important reason for the transaction than the giving of financial assistance, Lord Oliver said, is not the same thing as the company having a 'larger purpose' as envisaged by this provision.[272] The *purpose* of the transaction in *Brady* was to assist in the financing of the acquisition of the shares although the *reason* for the transaction was to facilitate a break-up of the business.[273] The financial assistance in *Brady* was not incidental to a larger purpose, therefore, and was provided in breach of the statute.

20-148 The approach adopted by the House of Lords in *Brady* was driven by a concern that companies always have a variety of motivations and reasons for transactions and, if financial assistance can be justified as being part of wider corporate schemes, the section could be effectively nullified. The effect of this interpretation has been to limit the scope for applying this exception, but an example can be found in *Re Uniq plc*.[274] In this case, the court was asked to sanction a scheme of arrangement, but an issue arose as to whether the court could sanction it when an element of the scheme appeared to infringe the financial assistance provisions. Essentially, the company, the subject of the scheme, was to pay a significant sum of money, directly or indirectly, to fund Newco which in turn was to acquire shares in the company, hence the immediate appearance of financial assistance. As part of the scheme, the receipt of the moneys by Newco would result in the release of the company from extensive pension liabilities which would instead be assumed by Newco. Richards J found that the principal purpose of the payments to Newco was to obtain this release which was overwhelmingly in the interests of the company and the payments were made in good faith, hence the case did fall within the exception in s 678(2).

Exceptions to the prohibition on financial assistance

20-149 There are two categories of excepted transactions: (1) unconditional exceptions, and (2) conditional exceptions.

Unconditional exceptions

20-150 The prohibitions on the giving of financial assistance do not apply (CA 2006, s 681) to:

(1) a distribution of a company's assets by way of dividend lawfully made or a distribution in the course of the company's winding up;

---

[271] [1988] 2 All ER 617, HL. See also *Plaut v Steiner* (1988) 5 BCC 352.
[272] [1988] 2 All ER 617 at 633, HL.   [273] [1988] 2 All ER 617 at 633, HL.
[274] [2011] EWHC 749; and n 256.

(2) the allotment of bonus shares;

(3) a reduction of capital duly made in accordance with the statutory schemes;

(4) a redemption or purchase of shares made in accordance with the statutory provisions;

(5) anything done in pursuance of an order of the court under CA 2006, Pt 26 dealing with compromises and arrangements with creditors and members;[275]

(6) anything done under an arrangement made in pursuance of the statutory provisions enabling liquidators in winding up to accept shares as consideration for the sale of property; or

(7) anything done under an arrangement made between a company and its creditors which is binding on the creditors by virtue of the statutory provisions relating to such arrangements when made by a company about to be or in the course of being wound up.

20-151 As noted, the prohibition of financial assistance is essentially based on the need to protect creditors from the improper depletion of the company's assets.[276] All of the transactions and schemes mentioned in **20-150** are subject to statutory requirements designed to ensure the protection of creditors and prevent the misuse of assets and in a number of cases the schemes require the confirmation of the court. There is no need therefore to subject such transactions to the prohibition on financial assistance.

Conditional exceptions

20-152 This category provides exemptions for those companies where the lending of money is part of the ordinary business of the company[277] and exemptions designed to facilitate employees' share schemes.[278] A public company may rely on the exemptions in this category only if the company has net assets that are not thereby reduced by the giving of the assistance, or to the extent that those assets are so reduced, the financial assistance is provided out of distributable profits.[279]

Consequences of breach of the financial assistance provisions

20-153 Contravention of the provisions on financial assistance is a criminal offence (CA 2006, s 680) but the statute does not deal with the civil consequences which remain a matter for the common law.

The status of any agreement

20-154 An agreement to provide unlawful financial assistance is unenforceable by either party to it.[280] In *Heald v O'Connor*,[281] for example, where the financial assistance consisted of

---

[275] See *Re Uniq plc* [2011] EWHC 749 where Richards J noted that this power to sanction financial assistance as part of a scheme is not qualified by reference to any particular criteria, at [45], and, on the facts, he would approve the granting of certain indemnities and the payment of costs which would otherwise amount to financial assistance, being granted as they were by a company with respect to the acquisition of the company's shares by a third party as part of the scheme. He noted the restructuring would benefit both the creditors and members of the company and it was appropriate therefore to approve the indemnities etc which were necessary for the restructuring, at [46]. See also n 256.

[276] *Wallersteiner v Moir* [1974] 3 All ER 217 at 239, per Denning LJ.

[277] CA 2006, s 682(2)(a); see *Steen v Law* [1963] 3 All ER 770.

[278] CA 2006, s 682(b), (c), (d). For the definition of 'employees' share scheme', see s 1166.

[279] CA 2006, s 682(1)(b), (3)–(4).

[280] *Brady v Brady* [1988] 2 All ER 617, HL; *Plaut v Steiner* (1989) 5 BCC 352.   [281] [1971] 2 All ER 1105.

security given by the company for money lent to enable a person to purchase shares in the company, the court held that that security was unenforceable.[282] The court noted that such a result best furthers the policy of the legislation in that it deters potential lenders from lending money on security which might be held to contravene the statute.

20-155 If the illegal element of the transaction can be severed from the agreement, the court will do so.[283] In *Carney v Herbert*[284] the Privy Council took the view that the nature of the illegality in cases of financial assistance is not such as to preclude severance on the grounds of public policy and severance can take place provided that the financial assistance is ancillary to the overall transaction and its elimination would leave unchanged the subject-matter of the transaction.[285] In this case, the illegal financial assistance (in the form of mortgages) was severed from an agreement for the sale of shares which could then be enforced between the parties in the ordinary way.

20-156 Returning to *Anglo Petroleum Ltd v TFB (Mortgages) Ltd*,[286] see **20-142**, the Court of Appeal said, obiter, that, even if it had found illegal financial assistance in respect of the use of funds borrowed by the company from a third party, the loan agreement and associated charges and guarantees would not have been illegal. Those agreements did not necessitate any breach of the law, Toulson LJ said, and no reason of public policy required those perfectly ordinary commercial transactions to be struck down.[287] This is an important approach which narrows the range of transactions which can be struck down as illegal. The loan and the security is treated as ordinary commercial lending. The use which the company makes of the funds it borrows may amount to financial assistance, but that is a separate matter.

Breach of fiduciary duty

20-157 A director who authorises the giving of financial assistance in breach of the statutory provisions is in breach of his duties to the company.[288] As a trustee of the company's assets, the misapplication by a director of those assets is a breach of trust and the director is obliged to account for the full amount of the improper financial assistance.[289] A shareholder may seek an injunction to restrain the giving of financial assistance in breach of the statutory provisions or he may seek permission to bring a derivative action on behalf of the company to recover the sums expended.[290]

20-158 The involvement of third parties such as bankers is often crucial to the carrying out of an illegal financial assistance scheme and they may be liable either on the basis of 'dishonest assistance' in breach of fiduciary duty or 'knowing receipt' of company funds, see Chapter 13.

---

[282] *Victor Battery Co Ltd v Curry's Ltd* [1946] Ch 242 to the contrary effect is generally accepted to be wrongly decided: see *Selangor United Rubber Estates Ltd v Cradock (No 3)* [1968] 2 All ER 1073.

[283] *Herbert Spink (Bournemouth) Ltd v Spink* [1936] 1 All ER 597; *South Western Mineral Water Co Ltd v Ashmore* [1967] 2 All ER 953; *Carney v Herbert* [1985] 1 All ER 438, PC; *Neilson v Stewart* [1991] BCC 713, HL.

[284] [1985] 1 All ER 438, PC. [285] [1985] 1 All ER 438 at 446, PC. [286] [2008] 1 BCLC 185, CA.

[287] [2008] 1 BCLC 185 at 202–3, CA.

[288] See, for example, *Re In a Flap Envelope Co Ltd* [2004] 1 BCLC 64.

[289] See discussion in Chapter 13 of the liability of directors for beach of trust and see *JJ Harrison (Properties) Ltd v Harrison* [2002] 1 BCLC 162; *Rolled Steel Products (Holdings) Ltd v British Steel Corpn* [1985] 3 All ER 52; *Re Lands Allotment Co* [1894] 1 Ch 616.

[290] See *Smith v Croft* [1987] 3 All ER 909; the derivative action is discussed in detail in Chapter 18.

21

Loan capital–secured creditors and company charges

A Introduction to company charges

21-1 The majority of companies on the register of companies are private companies with very limited amounts of share capital.[1] It follows that if those companies are carrying on business to any significant level, it must be on the basis of other forms of funding and there are many other methods of financing to which companies may resort.[2] For example, they may obtain goods under hire-purchase agreements[3] or conditional sale agreements.[4] They may use factoring[5] and invoice discounting[6] to realise sums due to them by users of their goods or services. For many companies, though, the starting point is usually loan capital, typically in the form of straightforward commercial borrowing from high street banks and financial institutions.

21-2 Of course, when lending to a limited liability company, the lender is conscious of the need for security to cover the amount lent, knowing he cannot have recourse to the members to meet any deficiency on insolvency. On occasion, a lender may obtain personal guarantees from the directors, but personal guarantees are a poor substitute for security over tangible assets as the guarantor may not be good for the money when the lender needs to enforce the personal guarantee. The lender/creditor prefers therefore to look to security to protect its position in the event of the insolvency of the company. By security is meant that, in addition to the ability to sue the company for the discharge of the debt, the

---

[1] Of the 2,400,300 companies on the register at 31 March 2011 with an issued share capital, 1,858,500 (roughly 78%) had an issued share capital of up to £100: see Companies House, *Statistical Tables on Companies Register Activities 2010–11*, Table A6. These statistical tables are available on the Companies House website: www.companieshouse.gov.uk.

[2] See Law Commission, *Registration of Security Interests: Company Charges and Property other than Land* (Consultation Paper No 164), 2002, Ch 6 where there is a useful account of the other forms of financing which companies use and which the Commission describes as involving a type of quasi-security.

[3] A hire-purchase agreement is an agreement for the hire of goods under which the hirer is given the option to purchase the goods at a certain point when a certain number of payments have been made.

[4] A conditional sale agreement is an agreement for the sale of goods under which the property in the goods remains with the seller until payment of the price is completed.

[5] Factoring involves a factor taking over responsibility for collection of the debts due by customers to a company. The factor pays between 80–85% of the value of those invoices up front to the company, so assisting its cash flow, and pays the balance when the customer pays, in return for a fee set as a percentage (typically 0.75–2.5%) of turnover. Many of the high street banks operate specialist subsidiaries offering factoring services.

[6] Invoice discounting is very similar to factoring except that the discounter does not take over collection of the company's debts, but provides funds up front (again between 80–85% of the amount) for the company in respect of approved invoices in return for a fee set either as a flat monthly fee or as a percentage of turnover. Many of the high street banks operate specialist subsidiaries providing this service.

creditor is able to look to some property in which the company has an interest in order to enforce the discharge of the company's obligation to the creditor. At the same time as the lender seeks security, the company wants to be able to borrow without having to give such security to the lender that its ability to trade is affected by the constraints imposed by the security.[7] The company therefore wants freedom to trade, the lender wants security for its lending and the law needs to facilitate both the company and the lender.

Taking security

21-3 Central to the question of security is the issue of priority on insolvency. Obviously, if the company never becomes insolvent, no problem arises and the precise nature of the security obtained never becomes important. It is because the company may become insolvent that security must be sought and the type of security which is sought is dictated by the order of distribution of assets on insolvency. A creditor does not want a form of security which leaves the creditor in the queue behind several other creditors on insolvency. Therefore a creditor requires not just security but a form of security which gives sufficient prior claim to the assets on insolvency so that the creditor has some prospect of recovering the debt.

21-4 The order of distribution and winding up is discussed in detail in Chapter 24 and a broad overview suffices for our purposes here. On liquidation, the assets of the company fall into two categories, those secured to creditors, and the free assets. Those free assets form a common fund which, subject to the expenses of winding up and the rights of the preferential creditors (discussed later), are held on a statutory trust for the benefit of the unsecured creditors.[8] The secured creditors who, as we shall see, generally have fixed and floating charges over the company's assets, have rights *in rem* and they look to the secured assets for payment of their debts. They do not need to look to the common fund for repayment of their claims. However, the precise degree of priority depends on the nature of the security obtained and Parliament has intruded to establish a statutory priority for the payment of the expenses of winding up (and administration) and the preferential debts which has the effect, as we shall see, of eroding the quality of floating charges held by creditors where the free assets of the company are insufficient to meet these prior claims (as they often are).[9] The two categories of assets overlap in that a deficiency in the 'free' assets must be met by the realisations held by the floating chargeholder to the extent dictated by Parliament. The fixed chargeholder is unaffected by this statutory interference.

21-5 The standard devices used by a lender to obtain security are legal mortgages, fixed charges and floating charges. A mortgage needs no detailed description; it involves the transfer of legal ownership to the lender subject to the mortgagee's equity of redemption. In practice, since the Law of Property Act 1925, the form of legal mortgage of an estate in fee simple has been by a charge by deed expressed to be by way of legal mortgage. For various

---

[7] As Nourse LJ noted in *Re New Bullas Trading Ltd* [1994] 1 BCLC 485 at 487: 'He who lends money to a trading company neither wishes nor expects it to become insolvent. . . . But against an evil day he wants the best security the company can give him consistently with its ability to trade meanwhile.'

[8] See *Ayerst (Inspector of Taxes) v C & K (Construction) Ltd* [1975] 2 All ER 537; *Webb v Whiffin* (1872) LR 5 HL 711 at 721, 724.

[9] As Armour notes, one consequence of carving out a preference for certain claimants on insolvency is that the history of the floating charge (which is subject to these prior claims) is largely the story of the litigation ensuing from attempts by floating chargeholders to draft (at considerable cost) their charges in a way that defeats that statutory priority: see Armour, 'Should We Redistribute in Insolvency?' in Getzler & Payne, *Company Charges, Spectrum and Beyond* (2005).

reasons, the charge by deed has become the standard form of mortgage so that the terms 'mortgage' and 'charge' have become interchangeable.[10] With that statutory exception of a legal charge, all charges, whether fixed or floating, are equitable.

21-6 Usually it is clear that the parties have created a charge (though whether it is a fixed or a floating charge may be more problematic) but, in cases of doubt, it is a matter of construction whether the transaction gives rise to a charge. For example, if a contract gives a contracting party the right (on default by the other party) to sell machinery belonging to the other contracting party and to apply the proceeds of sale in discharge of the debts of the other party due under the contract, this provision creates a security interest, a charge, allowing one party to look to a particular asset or class of assets for the discharge of a debt.[11] The essence of an equitable charge, as Millett J explained, is that:[12]

> '...without any conveyance or assignment to the chargee, specific property of the chargor is expressly or constructively appropriated to or make answerable for the payment of a debt, and the chargee is given the right to resort to the property for the purpose of having it realised and applied in or towards payment of the debt.'

21-7 On the other hand, a contractual provision which merely allows one contracting party to use a machine belonging to that other party in order to complete works required by the contract does not confer any security interest and is not a charge at all.[13]

21-8 As to whether the charge created is a fixed or floating charge, the distinction between them was explained by Lord Macnaghten in *Illingworth v Houldsworth*[14] as follows:

> 'A specific charge...is one that without more fastens on ascertained and definite property or property capable of being ascertained or defined. A floating charge, on the other hand, is ambulatory and shifting in its nature, hovering over and so to speak floating with the property which it is intended to affect until some event occurs or some act is done which causes it to settle and fasten on the subject of the charge within its reach and grasp.'

21-9 A fixed (or specific) charge is typically taken over identified assets not commonly used or dealt with in the day-to-day business of the company. A fixed charge gives the holder of the charge an immediate proprietary interest in the assets subject to the charge which means that a fixed charge is inappropriate for assets which the company needs to deal with in the ordinary course of business.[15]

21-10 A floating charge is an equitable invention, first recognised by the Court of Appeal in *Re Panama, New Zealand & Australian Royal Mail Co.*[16] The classic description of the characteristics of a floating charge is that of Romer LJ in *Re Yorkshire Woolcombers Association*,[17] where he stated that a floating charge is:

---

[10] CA 2006, s 861(5) defines 'charge' for the purpose of Part 25 (Company Charges) as including 'mortgage'.

[11] See *Re Cosslett (Contractors) Ltd* [1999] 1 BCLC 205 at 216, CA; and sub nom *Smith (Administrator of Cosslett (Contractors) Ltd) v Bridgend County Borough Council* [2002] 1 BCLC 77 at 88–9, 91, HL.

[12] *Re Charge Card Services Ltd* [1987] BCLC 17 at 40, per Millett J; see also *Re Cosslett (Contractors) Ltd* [1999] 1 BCLC 205 at 215.

[13] See *Re Cosslett (Contractors) Ltd* [1999] 1 BCLC 205 at 215.   [14] [1904] AC 355 at 358.

[15] See *Agnew v IRC (Re Brumark)* [2001] 2 BCLC 188 at 192, PC, per Lord Millett.

[16] (1878) LR 5 Ch App 318; and see *Re Florence Land & Public Works Co, ex p Moor* (1878) 10 Ch D 530. See generally the valuable collection of essays in Getzler & Payne, *Company Charges, Spectrum and Beyond* (2005) (hereinafter Getzler & Payne), also Gough, *Company Charges* (2nd edn, 1996).

[17] [1903] 2 Ch 284 at 295, although Romer LJ did not say that all three elements must be present in order for the charge to be a floating charge.

(1) a charge on a class of assets of a company, present and future;

(2) that class is one which, in the ordinary course of the business of the company, would be changing from time to time; and

(3) by the charge it is contemplated that, until some future step is taken by or on behalf of those interested in the charge, the company may carry on its business in the ordinary way.

21-11 A floating charge is typically taken over the entire undertaking of the company,[18] meaning all of the company's assets, both present and future, including assets such as removable plant and equipment, tools, intellectual property rights, stock-in-trade, work in progress and book debts (i.e. sums due to the company by its debtors). These are circulating assets used in the normal course of business and they are constantly changing so they are not amenable to a fixed charge.[19] The hallmark of the floating charge is the freedom of the company to deal with the assets in the ordinary course of business without the need to obtain the consent of the chargee. The assets in this instance remain under the control of the chargor, not the chargee, so avoiding the 'restricting (and in some cases, paralysing) effect on the use of the assets of the company resulting from a fixed charge'.[20] The charge floats or hovers over the assets until some event occurs causing it to crystallise which can occur in a variety of ways.[21] As a matter of law, a floating charge crystallises on the appointment of a receiver or administrator, or when the company goes into liquidation (on a resolution being passed or a compulsory winding up ordered) or there is otherwise a cessation of business on the part of the company, for the effect of these circumstances is to bring to an end the company's freedom to carry on business in the ordinary way.[22] Equally, the charge document may prescribe situations where the charge crystallises which may or may not require the intervention of the chargee. For example, the charge may crystallise on the appointment by the chargee of an administrator under the charge, or on the company exceeding defined financial thresholds, or on the company making a disposition of its assets other than by way of sale in the ordinary course of business, or on the service of a notice by the chargee (a method approved in *Re Brightlife Ltd*).[23] Once the charge has crystallised, the chargor's freedom to deal with the assets comprised in the charge comes to an end and the charge becomes a fixed charge attached to the assets within the scope of the charge. Despite the charge becoming a fixed charge at this point, its priority vis-à-vis other claimants on insolvency is determined by the fact that, *as created*, it was a floating charge.[24]

---

[18] As Lord Millett explained in *Agnew v IRC (Re Brumark)* [2001] 2 BCLC 188 at 191, a charge on the 'undertaking' is taken to mean a charge on all the assets of the company, both present and future, including its circulating assets, i.e. assets that are regularly turned over in the course of trade.

[19] See *Re Spectrum Plus Ltd* [2005] 2 BCLC 269 at 304, per Lord Scott.

[20] *Re Keenan Bros Ltd* [1986] BCLC 242 at 245, per Walsh J (Irish S Ct).

[21] The nature of the chargee's interest ahead of crystallisation has been the subject of much debate (possibilities range from no interest, some form of present proprietary interest, which is probably the most generally accepted view, a modified defeasible fixed charge or a present equitable interest which may be overreached), see Goode, *Legal Problems of Credit and Security* (3rd edn, 2003), Ch 4; Turner, 'Floating Charges—A No Theory Theory' [2004] LMCLQ 319; Nolan, 'Property in a Fund' (2004) 120 LQR 108; also Worthington, 'Floating Charges: The Use and Abuse of Doctrinal Analysis' in Getzler & Payne, n 16, esp at pp 37–44 who admits that the question is of limited practical significant—her view is that it is a modified defeasible form of fixed charge. See too Ferran, *Principles of Corporate Finance Law* (2008), p 373 who admits that the lack of certainty on this issue does not appear to cause major practical problems.

[22] *Evans v Rival Granite Quarries* Ltd [1910] 2 KB 979; *Re Woodroffes (Musical Instruments) Ltd* [1985] BCLC 227. See also *National Westminster Bank plc v Jones* [2002] 1 BCLC 55, CA.   [23] [1986] BCLC 418.

[24] See IA 1986, s 251. See *Re Beam Tube Products Ltd, Fanshawe v Amav Industries Ltd* [2007] 2 BCLC 732 (floating charge as created was not converted by subsequent conduct of the parties into a fixed charge). The solution is to create a new charge.

21-12 The freedom of the chargor to deal with the assets in the ordinary course of business includes a freedom to create further fixed charges ranking in priority to the floating charge,[25] though the courts have restricted the ability to create subsequent floating charges. A second floating charge over all of the property comprised in the first charge and ranking *pari passu* with or in priority to that charge is incompatible with the first charge and ranks subject to it.[26] A subsequent floating charge can rank *pari passu* with or in priority to the first floating charge, however, where the first floating charge permits of such a charge and the second charge is over part only of the assets comprised in the original charge.[27]

21-13 The possibility that the chargor might grant subsequent charges over the assets within the reach of the floating charge (and so diminish its value) has resulted in the practice of including clauses in the charge document (the debenture), usually described as negative pledges, prohibiting the chargor from creating further fixed or floating charges ranking *pari passu* with or in priority to the current charge, but these clauses cannot bind a subsequent chargee for value without notice. Details of these clauses are often included by chargees in the particulars delivered to the registrar although they are not amongst the prescribed particulars and third parties cannot be affected by constructive notice of such extra-statutory material,[28] but they are affected by actual notice of the restriction if they search the register of charges. All chargees have constructive notice of prior registered charges.[29]

21-14 Where a high street bank provides funds to a company, therefore, the typical security package which the bank takes is: (1) a legal mortgage over the company's land or buildings; (2) a fixed charge over such of the company's plant, equipment, furniture and fittings as are not required in the day-to-day conduct of its business (and much ingenuity is expended on drafting charges which fall into this category since, as we shall see, it is the most effective type of charge); and (3) a floating charge over the entire undertaking of the company, meaning all the assets of the company not otherwise charged. In effect, the floating charge is often used as a catch-all final charge over anything else of value not yet encompassed by another charge. It will be appreciated that once a bank has secured this level of security, there is little security that the company can provide for subsequent creditors since, one way or another, every asset of any value has been appropriated to the payment of the bank borrowings.

21-15 In terms of enforcement, if the secured creditor has taken a legal mortgage of the company's property, land or buildings, the mortgagee is able to sell the property to recover the debts.[30] If the creditor has taken a fixed charge over the company's plant, equipment etc, the creditor has rights *in rem* with respect to those assets which are appropriated to the payment of that creditor's debts and do not fall into the pool of assets for the unsecured creditors. The chargee may take such steps to realise those assets as are permitted by the debenture which invariably provides for their sale to allow the chargee to be repaid. A

---

[25] *Wheatley v Silkstone Haigh Moor Coal Co* (1885) 29 Ch D 715.

[26] *Re Benjamin Cope & Sons Ltd* [1914] 1 Ch 800.

[27] *Re Automatic Bottle Makers Ltd* [1926] Ch 412.

[28] See *Siebe Gorman & Co Ltd v Barclays Bank Ltd* [1979] 2 Lloyd's Rep 142 at 159–60, overruled on other grounds, *Re Spectrum Plus Ltd* [2005] 2 BCLC 269, HL.

[29] *Wilson v Kelland* [1910] 2 Ch 306; see *Siebe Gorman & Co Ltd v Barclays Bank Ltd* [1979] 2 Lloyd's Rep 142 at 160, overruled on other grounds, *Re Spectrum Plus Ltd* [2005] 2 BCLC 269, HL. See generally Gough, *Company Charges* (2nd edn, 1996), Ch 23.

[30] Either under the express terms of the mortgage deed or under the Law of Property Act 1925, s 101.

floating charge, as noted, hovers over the assets within it and only subsequently attaches to those assets when the charge crystallises. Once the charge has crystallised, it becomes a fixed charge and the bank is entitled to realise the assets as provided for by the debenture which will usually provide for the appointment of an administrator: see **21-84**.

21-16 Finally, it should be noted that the document setting out the charge taken by a lender is called a debenture, though 'debenture' has many other meanings also. For these purposes, however, it is a document acknowledging an indebtedness which may be (and in this context is) secured by a charge or charges.[31] Hence a lender is often referred to as a debenture holder.

B Fixed and floating charges

21-17 The attraction of a floating charge for lenders, especially banks, was explained as follows by Lord Millett in *Agnew v IRC* (*Re Brumark*):[32]

> 'The floating charge is capable of affording the creditor, by a single instrument, an effective and comprehensive security upon the entire undertaking of the debtor company and its assets from time to time, while at the same time leaving the company free to deal with its assets and pay its trade creditors in the ordinary course of business without reference to the holder of the charge.'

21-18 It would seem then that the floating charge meets the two key objectives already noted: security for the lender, the chargee; and flexibility for the company, the chargor. However, the value of a charge lies in the ability of the chargee on insolvency to realise the assets charged to secure repayment of the debt without regard to the insolvency rules governing the distribution of the common fund of unsecured assets. The problem, noted at **21-4**, is that a floating charge is subject to the insolvency rules (priority is given to other claims) in a way that affects the possible recoveries by a floating chargeholder. This is one of the most important distinctions between fixed and floating charges.

21-19 A floating charge (but not a fixed charge) is subject to the prior claims of preferential debts (debts accorded statutory priority, though the categories accorded such priority have been much reduced: see **24-70**)[33] and is subject to the 'prescribed part' provision in IA 1986, s 176A, which ring-fences certain funds in favour of unsecured creditors: see **24-72**. The effect of the latter should be neutral for the chargeholder as the formula used

---

[31] See *Levy v Abercorris Slate & Slab Co* (1887) 37 Ch 260 at 264, per Chitty J.

[32] [2001] 2 BCLC 188 at 192. While the floating charge has played an important role in corporate financing for many decades, the prevailing academic view (with some support from practitioners) is that the time has come to abolish it and create a modern secured finance regime suitable for domestic purposes and for the role that English law plays in international commerce. See Goode, 'The Case for the Abolition of the Floating Charge' in Getzler & Payne, n 16; also Worthington, n 21, pp 45–9; Wood, 'A Review of *Brumark* and *Spectrum in an International Setting*' in Getzler & Payne, n 16, pp 149–50.

[33] See IA 1986, ss 40, 175, Sch B1, para 65(2); CA 2006, s 754. The priority accorded to preferential debts is not as important an issue as it once was as the preferential status accorded to certain categories of debts (for example, debts to Inland Revenue, Customs and Excise and social security contributions) was abolished by the Enterprise Act 2002, s 251 with effect from 15 September 2003 and the categories of preferential debt are now much reduced, see IA 1986, Sch 6. See Worthington, n 21, at p 46 who points out that there is little by way of defensible justification for discriminating between fixed and floating chargeholders in this way. Gullifer & Payne, 'The Characterization of Fixed and Floating Charges' in Getzler & Payne, n 16, suggest the justification lies in the all-embracing nature of a floating charge and the fact that the floating charge enables the company to continue to trade and incur fresh debt: see pp 79–81.

to determine the 'prescribed part' (which must go to the unsecured creditors) is meant to equate to the gain to the floating chargeholder from the reduction of the categories of preferential debts. The application of the prescribed part therefore is not necessarily to the disadvantage of the floating chargeholder, but the floating charge's subordination to the prior claims of the preferential debts is a disadvantage when compared to a fixed charge.

21-20 More significantly, a floating charge, but not a fixed charge, is subject, if the company is in liquidation, to the prior claims of the expenses of liquidation[34] (see **24-63**) and, if the company is in administration, to the prior claims of the expenses of administration[35] (see **23-114**). In so far as these claims cannot be met from the unencumbered assets of the company, the deficiency must be made up out of the proceeds of the floating charge.[36] The creditor with a floating charge has security, therefore, in that assets are appropriated to the charge once it crystallises (as discussed at **21-11**), but it is a form of security which is not as comprehensive as a fixed charge because it is subject to these other (usually substantial) claims being met.

21-21 One of the major advantages of having a floating charge was that, on crystallisation, the chargeholder could appoint an administrative receiver to realise the assets and pay off the debt. This was an entirely contractual process within the control of the chargeholder and with limited regard being paid to the interests of other creditors. The right to appoint administrative receivers in this way was abolished for the most part (there are some exceptional cases[37]) by the Enterprise Act 2002 (EA 2002) with respect to floating charges created on or after 15 September 2003.[38] For qualifying floating charges (as defined in IA 1986, Sch B1, para 14(2)) created subsequently, the appropriate enforcement mechanism is the appointment of an administrator whose role and functions are statutory and not contractual: see **21-84**. An administrator is an officer of the court (IA 1986, Sch B1, para 5) and has a duty to perform his functions in the interests of the creditors as a whole (IA 1986, Sch B1, para 3(2)). An administrator can also dispose of property subject to a floating charge without the consent of the chargee whereas, if the charge is fixed, the consent of the court is required (IA 1986, Sch B1, paras 70, 71), see **23-97**.

21-22 It is clear that the fixed charge is the superior charge but there are reasons why it is still worthwhile having a floating charge including:

(1) a qualifying floating charge is required if the lender is to secure valuable rights with respect to the appointment of an administrator and in terms of the choice of administrator.[39] This is very much a prime motivation for obtaining a floating charge. Administration is discussed in Chapter 23.

(2) a floating charge, when coupled with fixed charges, allows one chargee to have comprehensive security over all of the company's assets;

(3) a floating charge gives the chargee a measure of control over the company's business because, while the charge is in existence and especially when coupled with

---

[34] To the extent provided for by IA 1986, s 176ZA, inserted by CA 2006, s 1282, reversing the decision of the House of Lords in *Re Leyland Daf Ltd, Buchler v Talbot* [2004] 1 BCLC 218 which had itself reversed decades of established law and had decided that the floating charge realisations were not subject to the expenses of winding up: see **24-63**.

[35] To the extent provided for by IA 1986, Sch B1, para 99. A floating charge, unlike a fixed charge, is also open to challenge by an administrator or liquidator under IA 1986, s 245 (avoidance of certain floating charges) see discussion at **25-64**.

[36] See IA 1986, ss 40, 175; Sch B1, para 65(2); CA 2006, s 754.   [37] See IA 1986, ss 72B–72GA.

[38] See IA 1986, s 72A.   [39] See IA 1986, Sch B1, paras 14, 35–37.

fixed charges, the chargor typically is expected to provide up-to-date accounts to the lender so the lender is well placed to monitor its security;

(4) even if the floating charge is subject to the prior claims of preferential debts and the expenses of winding up/administration, the charge still has priority over the claims of the unsecured creditors (as noted at **21-19**, the position as between the floating chargeholder and the unsecured creditors should be essentially unchanged by the requirements of the prescribed part) and so the lender might as well take a charge for that purpose.

21-23 Notwithstanding these advantages, it is still the case that a fixed charge offers greater security than a floating charge and so much of the litigation in this area involves disputes between creditors as to their respective places in the queue to claim the company's assets on insolvency. For example, if Bank A can establish that it has a fixed charge over Asset X, it is able to appropriate that asset to the payment of its debt. On the other hand, if a liquidator or administrator can establish that the charge is a floating charge subject to the expenses of winding up or administration, then the bank's claim is subject to those expenses in the event that the unencumbered assets are otherwise insufficient to meet those expenses. Likewise, if the preferential creditors can establish that a charge is a floating charge, the preferential creditors have a prior claim to the floating charge realisations if the company's assets are otherwise insufficient to meet the preferential claims.

21-24 The distinction between fixed and floating charges also affects registration under CA 2006, s 860. All floating charges must be registered (s 860(7)(g)) but fixed charges need only be registered if they are over one of the specified classes of assets in s 860(7). Admittedly, s 860(7) encompasses most classes of charges but there are some significant exceptions, such as fixed charges over shares which are not registrable. As a failure to register a registrable charge renders the charge void (s 874), a creditor may need to argue that a charge is fixed and not within the registration requirements in the hope of escaping that invalidity.[40] Equally, liquidators have an interest in establishing that a particular arrangement is a registrable charge which is void for lack of registration so forcing a creditor to claim as an unsecured creditor. For a variety of reasons then the nature of a charge is of real significance and, unsurprisingly, most of the litigation focuses on this issue.

C The approach to categorisation

21-25 In determining the character of a charge, neither the intentions of the parties nor the terms which they use to describe the transaction are necessarily determinative. If the parties describe a charge as fixed when it is in fact floating then, as Millett LJ noted, 'their ill-chosen language must yield to the substance'.[41] Deciding whether a charge is a fixed charge or a floating charge is a two-stage process, as was established by the Privy Council in *Agnew v IRC*[42] (better known as *Re Brumark*). First, the court must construe the instrument of charge and seek to gather the intention of the parties from the language used in order to ascertain the nature of the rights and obligations which the parties intended

---

[40] See, for example, *Arthur D Little Ltd v Ableco Finance LLC* [2002] 2 BCLC 799 at 812.
[41] *Orion Finance Ltd v Crown Financial Management Ltd* [1996] 2 BCLC 78 at 84. See, for example, *Russell–Cooke Trust Co Ltd v Elliott* [2007] 2 BCLC 637 where the charge was described, oddly, as a floating deed, then as a floating charge, and then the document contained restrictions incompatible with a floating charge so leaving it to the court to determine the nature of the charge. In the light of the restrictions, the court decided it was a fixed charge.   [42] [2001] 2 BCLC 188.

to grant each other in respect of the charged asset. Once that has been determined, the second stage of the process is one of legal categorisation and it is a matter of law for the courts to determine whether the charge, as created, is fixed or floating. This approach was swiftly endorsed by the House of Lords in *Smith (Administrator of Cosslett (Contractors) Ltd) v Bridgend County Borough Council*[43] (hereinafter *Re Cosslett*). Lord Hoffmann noted that the intentions of the parties are relevant only to establish their mutual rights and obligations: whether such rights and obligations are characterised as a floating charge is a question of law.[44]

21-26 In *Re Cosslett* a contractor abandoned a contract for some works with a local council. In accordance with a standard condition contained in the contract, the council then entered the site, seized the contractor's equipment and obtained another contractor to complete the contract using that equipment. The contract conditions also permitted the council, on a default by the contractor, to sell the contractor's plant and apply the proceeds in discharge of the contractor's debts to the council. The equipment was ultimately sold by the second contractor with the consent of the council.

21-27 An initial issue was whether the clause entitling the council to sell the plant and apply the proceeds was a charge. At first instance, the court concluded that the charge was a fixed charge, for there was a further term in the contract which precluded the removal of the equipment from the site until such time as the contract was completed. Jonathan Parker J thought this restriction on the freedom of the chargor was inconsistent with the charge being a floating charge.[45] The Court of Appeal disagreed[46] and pointed out, first, that an unfettered freedom to carry on business is not essential to the existence of a floating charge. After all, floating charges commonly restrict the ability of the company to create further charges (see **21-12**). Secondly, the restriction on removal in this case had nothing to do with the security interest of the council, but was imposed to secure performance of the contract, and therefore did not affect the status of the charge as a floating charge, given that the equipment was not under the control of the chargee. That the charge was a floating charge was confirmed by the House of Lords where the case is reported as *Smith (Administrator of Cosslett (Contractors) Ltd) v Bridgend County Borough Council*,[47] Lord Hoffmann noting:[48]

> 'I do not see how a right to sell an asset belonging to a debtor and appropriate the proceeds to payment of the debt can be anything other than a charge. And because the property…(constructional plant, temporary works, goods and materials on the site) was a fluctuating body of assets which could be consumed or (subject to the approval of the engineer) removed from the site in the ordinary course of the contractor's business, it was a floating charge.'

21-28 In *Arthur D Little Ltd v Ableco Finance LLC*[49] the court had to determine the nature of a charge created by a company over its shareholding in a subsidiary company where the charge was described as a first fixed charge but the chargor company retained the right to receive dividends and to exercise voting rights with respect to the shares. The chargee asserted that the charge was fixed. The company's administrator argued that it was a

---

[43] [2002] 1 BCLC 77 at 89 (per Lord Hoffmann), at 91–2 (per Lord Scott), HL.
[44] [2002] 1 BCLC 77 at 89; and Lord Scott of Foscote at 91–2. See also *Arthur D Little Ltd v Ableco Finance LLC* [2002] 2 BCLC 799 at 812; *Queens Moat Houses plc v Capita IRG Trustees Ltd* [2005] 2 BCLC 199 at 208; *Re Beam Tube Products Ltd, Fanshawe v Amav Industries Ltd* [2007] 2 BCLC 732.
[45] See [1996] 1 BCLC 407, Ch D.   [46] [1999] 1 BCLC 205, CA.   [47] [2002] 1 BCLC 77, HL.
[48] [2002] 1 BCLC 77 at 88–9, HL.   [49] [2002] 2 BCLC 799.

floating charge. The court, looking at categorisation as a matter of law, concluded that the charge was fixed. The class of asset involved was not a body of fluctuating assets changing in the ordinary course of business: it was simply the company's shareholding in its subsidiary. There were no dealings in that asset by the chargor company in the ordinary course of business and the shares could not be disposed of, dealt with or substituted by the chargor company. It followed that the asset was under the control of the chargee not the chargor. The charge was a fixed charge and the ability of the company to receive dividends and exercise voting rights did not alter that characteristic.

21-29 Once the court has determined by a process of construction the contractual rights created between the parties, it is then for the law to determine the nature of the security arising. The focus, in particular, is on the third element of the description given by Romer LJ in *Re Yorkshire Woolcombers*,[50] set out at **21-10**, as to whether the chargor has continued freedom to deal with the assets charged in the ordinary course of business. This key issue of the control of the charged assets was central to a series of cases, all concerning book debts, which culminated in the landmark decisions of the Privy Council in *Agnew v IRC (Re Brumark)*,[51] and the House of Lords decision in *Re Spectrum Plus Ltd, National Westminster Bank plc v Spectrum Plus Ltd*.[52] These two cases provide the authoritative statement of the law as to the correct approach to categorisation and the essential characteristics of a floating charge and, more specifically, as to the nature of charges on book debts, an issue which had been the subject of much litigation.

Re Brumark

21-30 Book debts or, to use the modern term, receivables (i.e. sums due to the company and arising from goods or services supplied by the company in the course of its business) are a valuable asset, assuming they are not bad debts, for they represent an income stream for the company and therefore creditors are anxious to obtain security over them.[53] Equally, book debts are precisely the sort of assets where the company is anxious to preserve its freedom to control the assets to the greatest extent possible, given that book debts provide part of the company's cashflow. It is unsurprising therefore that considerable efforts have been expended on drafting charges over book debts in an attempt to meet these conflicting concerns.

21-31 In *Agnew v IRC, Re Brumark Investments Ltd*[54] (hereinafter *Re Brumark*) a company created in favour of its bank a fixed charge over all book debts of the company arising in its ordinary course of business. The proceeds of the book debts received by the company were excluded from the fixed charge unless the bank ordered (which it did not do) payment into an account which the company could not operate freely whereupon the

---

[50] [1903] 2 Ch 284 at 295.   [51] [2001] 2 BCLC 188, PC.   [52] [2005] 2 BCLC 269, HL.

[53] It is now accepted that a bank may take a charge over a credit balance in an account maintained by a customer with the bank: *Re BCCI (No 8)* [1998] 1 BCLC 68, so resolving the uncertainty which had arisen on this matter as a result of Millett J's conclusion to the contrary in *Re Charge Card Services Ltd (No 2)* [1987] BCLC 17 which had been affirmed by the Court of Appeal, see [1988] 3 All ER 702, but see Goode (1998) 114 LQR 178. Such a charge is not a charge on book debts: *Northern Bank Ltd v Ross* [1991] BCLC 504; *Re Brightlife Ltd* [1986] BCLC 418; *Re Buildhead (No 2) Ltd* [2006] 1 BCLC 9 at 31–2. See also *Re SSSL Realisations (2002) Ltd* [2005] 1 BCLC 1 at 19, a charge over a sum of money once it has been paid to a person is not a charge over the debt or other right by reason of which the sum of money has come to be paid.

[54] [2001] 2 BCLC 188, PC. See Oditah, 'Fixed Charges over Book Debts after Brumark' (2001) Insolv Int 49; Rumley & Jeffries, 'Brumark: Where are we now' (2003) Insolv Int 19; Pennington, 'The Interchangeability of Fixed and Floating Charges' (2003) Co Law 60; Tamlyn & Fennessy, 'Fixed and Floating Charges: Brumark' [2002] Insolv Law 56; Berg, 'Recharacterisation after Enron' [2003] JBL 205.

proceeds would be treated as being subject to the fixed charge. If the bank did not order the payment of proceeds into such an account, the proceeds were subject to a floating charge in favour of the bank.

21-32 A dispute arose between receivers appointed to the company and the preferential creditors as to the nature of the charge on the book debts which were uncollected at the time of the appointment of the receivers.[55] The New Zealand Court of Appeal held that the charge was a floating charge and so subject to the claims of the preferential creditors.[56] The court considered that where the chargor was free to collect the book debts, thus extinguishing them, and was free to deal with the proceeds in the normal course of its business, the charged book debts were not sufficiently under the control of the chargee to make the charge a fixed charge. The Court of Appeal also noted that '...we cannot see how the debate on whether book debts and their collected proceeds constitute separate security interests offers any new aid in determining whether a particular charge is fixed or floating'.[57] The matter was appealed to the Privy Council.

21-33 Giving the judgment of the Privy Council, Lord Millett outlined the two-stage process noted at **21-25**. The first step is the ascertainment of the rights which the parties intended to grant each other in respect of the charged assets. Then the court can embark on the categorisation of the charge which is a matter of law and not a matter determined by the description attached to a charge by the parties. If the rights granted are inconsistent with the nature of a fixed charge, the charge cannot be a fixed charge, however the parties choose to describe it. The question, Lord Millett said, is whether the intention is that the company should be free to deal with the charged assets and withdraw them from the security without the consent of the holder of the charge or, to put it another way, whether the charged assets are intended to be under the control of the company or of the chargeholder.[58] The fact that the company may be prohibited from assigning, factoring or charging the asset to anyone else is not sufficient to make a charge a fixed charge if the company retains the freedom to collect the asset in the ordinary course of business for its own benefit.[59]

21-34 As for the fact that different charges were assigned to the debts and the proceeds, Lord Millett stated, and this passage is central to the issues surrounding charges on book debts so it is useful to quote his exact words:[60]

> 'While a debt and its proceeds are two separate assets, however, the latter are merely the traceable proceeds of the former and represent its entire value. A debt is a receivable; it is merely a right to receive payment from the debtor. Such a right cannot be enjoyed in specie; its value can be exploited only by exercising the right or by assigning it for value to a third party. An assignment or charge of a receivable which does not carry with it the right to the receipt has no value. It is worthless as a security. Any attempt in the present context to separate the ownership of the debts from the ownership of their proceeds (even if conceptually possible) makes no commercial sense.'

21-35 The issue in the case of a charge on a debt then is who has control of the proceeds and the answer to that question determines the nature of the charge.[61] On the facts in *Re*

---

[55] The dispute arose subsequent to the decision of the English Court of Appeal in *Re New Bullas Trading Ltd* [1994] 1 BCLC 485, CA which had held that it was possible to draft a charge so as to create a floating charge over the proceeds of book debts once collected while retaining a fixed charge over the uncollected proceeds. The debenture in *Brumark* was modelled on that in *New Bullas*.

[56] See [2000] 1 BCLC 353.   [57] See [2000] 1 BCLC 353 at 364.   [58] [2001] 2 BCLC 188 at 200.

[59] [2001] 2 BCLC 188 at 201.   [60] [2001] 2 BCLC 188 at 204.

[61] See also *Re Beam Tube Products Ltd, Fanshawe v Amav Industries Ltd* [2007] 2 BCLC 732 at 742.

Brumark,[62] the company's freedom to collect and use the proceeds of the book debts for its own benefit was inconsistent with the nature of a fixed charge. The decision of the New Zealand Court of Appeal that the charge was a floating charge was confirmed.[63]

21-36 The Privy Council did not deny that a fixed charge might be created over book debts. This might be done where the chargee prohibits the company from realising the debts itself, whether by assignment or collection.[64] Moreover, it is not inconsistent with the fixed nature of a charge on book debts for the holder of the charge to appoint the company as its agent to collect the debts for its account and on its behalf. The Privy Council noted that a fixed charge had been created in *Re Keenan Bros Ltd*[65] by means of a requirement that funds collected by the company be paid into a blocked account with the chargeholder. The prior written consent of the bank was required for each withdrawal from that account. As the debts are not available to the company as a source of its cashflow, such an arrangement is inconsistent with the charge being a floating charge.[66] The Privy Council emphasised, however, that the account must be operated in practice as a blocked account.[67]

21-37 A decision of the Privy Council while highly persuasive is not binding on the English courts. The banks therefore took what in effect was a test case to the House of Lords in order to secure a definitive statement of the English position which shows how important these issues are to everyday banking arrangements with companies.

Re Spectrum Plus

21-38 In *Re Spectrum Plus Ltd, National Westminster Bank plc v Spectrum Plus Ltd*,[68] (hereinafter *Re Spectrum Plus*) the charge in question stated that:

> 'With reference to the book debts and other debts hereby specifically charged the company shall pay into the company's account with the bank all moneys which it may receive in respect of such debts and shall not without the prior consent of the bank sell factor discount or otherwise charge or assign the same in favour of any other person or purport to do so and the company shall if called upon to do so by the bank from time to time execute legal assignments of such book debts and other debts to the bank.'

21-39 Provided the overdraft limit was not exceeded, the company was free to draw on the account, a current account, for its business purposes. The company duly collected its book debts, paid them into the account and drew on the account as it wished. The company went into voluntary liquidation and the liquidators declined to hand over the collected book debts to the bank. The bank sought a declaration that the proceeds were the subject of a fixed charge in its favour. The issue is different here from in *Re Brumark* (which concerned the existence of two charges, one fixed and one floating) but the court is

---

[62] [2001] 2 BCLC 188, PC.　　[63] [2001] 2 BCLC 188 at 205.　　[64] [2001] 2 BCLC 188 at 204.

[65] [1986] BCLC 242 (Irish S Ct).　　[66] [2001] 2 BCLC 188 at 204.

[67] [2001] 2 BCLC 188 at 204. This comment has attracted considerable controversy as to the extent to which post-charge conduct affects the determination of the nature of the charge, see Atherton & Mokal, 'Charges over Chattels: Issues in the fixed/floating jurisprudence' (2005) 26 Co Law 10; Oditah, 'Fixed Charges and the Recycling of Proceeds of Receivables' [2004] 120 LQR 533; also Berg, 'The Cuckoo in the Nest of Corporate Insolvency: Some Aspects of the *Spectrum* Case' [2006] JBL 22 at 33–44. The pragmatic position seems to be that the courts do not have regard to post-agreement conduct when construing the debenture to identify the rights that the parties have agreed to confer on one another, but that the court does look at it in determining the categorisation issue.

[68] [2005] 2 BCLC 269, HL. There are numerous commentaries on the case, see in particular Baird & Sidle, 'Spectrum Plus: House Of Lords Decision—A Cloud With A Silver Lining?' (2005) 18 Insolv Int 113; Hare, 'Charges over Book Debts: The End of an Era' [2005] LMCLQ 440; Berg, n 67.

concerned with the same essential issue, the nature of a charge over the proceeds of a book debt.

21-40   At first instance, the court held that the charge was a floating rather than a fixed charge over book debts and that *Siebe Gorman & Co Ltd v Barclays Bank Ltd*[69] (where 25 years earlier Slade J held an identically worded charge to be a fixed charge and which wording was adopted by the banks thereafter) had been wrongly decided.[70] The Court of Appeal disagreed and held the charge to be a fixed charge. Lord Phillips considered that there were sufficient restrictions to put the bank in control of the proceeds and therefore the charge was fixed.[71] He also expressed a concern not to upset banking arrangements which have been in place for 25 years and which companies, banks and individual guarantors of company debts had relied upon.[72]

21-41   Allowing an appeal, their Lordships held[73] that the debenture, although expressed to grant the bank a fixed charge over the company's book debts, in law granted only a floating charge.[74]

21-42   As far as book debts are concerned,[75] the main speech is by Lord Scott who agreed with Lord Millett in *Brumark* that it is the third characteristic identified by Romer LJ in *Re Yorkshire Woolcombers Association*[76] (set out at **21-10**) that is the hallmark of the floating charge.[77] The essential characteristic of a floating charge, the characteristic that distinguishes it from a fixed charge, is that the asset subject to the charge is not finally appropriated as a security for the payment of the debt until the occurrence of some future event.[78] In the meantime the chargor is left free to use the charged asset and to remove it from the security. In any case where the chargor is free to remove the charged assets from the security, Lord Scott said, the charge should in principle be categorised as a floating charge for the assets would have the circulating, ambulatory, character distinctive of a floating charge.[79] Lord Walker too agreed that the crucial question is whether the chargor is free to deal with the book debts and withdraw them from the security without the consent

---

[69]   [1979] 2 Lloyd's Rep 142. The restrictions imposed in *Siebe* were a requirement that the chargor pay all moneys received in respect of such book debts into a designated bank account and a prohibition on the charging or assigning of those sums without the prior consent of the chargee. Additionally, and as a matter of construction of the debenture, Slade J considered that, while there was no express prohibition on the use by the company of the proceeds once collected, the debenture did restrict the company's access to those funds without the consent of the bank, see [1979] 2 Lloyd's Rep 142 at 159–60. These restrictions were such that, in Slade J's opinion, the charge was a fixed charge.   [70]   See [2004] 1 BCLC 335, Ch D.

[71]   [2005] 2 BCLC 30 at 58–9, CA, and see n 69, as to the restrictions.

[72]   [2005] 2 BCLC 30 at 59–60, CA.

[73]   [2005] 2 BCLC 269, HL. As noted, see n 75, the case was heard unusually by seven Law Lords, but on the book debts issues, only Lords Hope, Scott and Walker expressed a view. Lord Scott's judgment contains a particularly useful account of the development of the floating charge.

[74]   The fact that banking practice had relied on it being a fixed charge for a lengthy period was not relevant for, like any first instance decision, *Siebe Gorman* was always open to correction by the higher courts, see [2005] 2 BCLC 269 at 294, HL.

[75]   A further issue in the case was whether the House of Lords has power to deliver prospective rulings, applicable only to the future and whether, if so, the power should be exercised in the instant case. The significance of this issue resulted in the case being heard, unusually, by a panel of seven law lords. As for prospective overruling, their Lordships held that in a wholly exceptional case the interests of justice might require the House of Lords to declare that its decision was to operate only with prospective effect but the instant case did not fall into such an exceptional category.

[76]   [1903] 2 Ch 284 at 295: the third characteristic was that by the charge it is contemplated that, until some future step is taken by or on behalf of those interested in the charge, the company may carry on its business in the ordinary way.   [77]   [2005] 2 BCLC 269 at 308–9; also at 318, per Lord Walker.

[78]   See [2005] 2 BCLC 269 at 310.   [79]   See [2005] 2 BCLC 269 at 304.

of the bank.[80] This approach is entirely consistent with that in *Brumark* as to the issue of categorisation—the issue is whether the chargor has control of the asset such that it can be removed from the security without the consent of the chargee.[81]

21-43 In this case, the company was free to draw on the account pending notice by the bank terminating the overdraft facility, requiring immediate repayment of the indebtedness and turning the account into a blocked account. Their Lordships were agreed that the restrictions imposed in this case were not sufficient as the chargor remained free to draw on the proceeds of the book debts in the ordinary course of business. So long as the chargor could draw on the account, and whether the account was in credit or debit, the money was available to the chargor and the charge was a floating charge,[82] an outcome entirely consistent with *Brumark*. The decision in *Siebe Gorman & Co Ltd v Barclays Bank Ltd*[83] which had determined commercial practice in this area since 1979 was wrong and overruled.

Charges on book debts

21-44 The decisions in *Re Brumark* and *Re Spectrum Plus Ltd* end the long-running saga as to the precise nature of charges on book debts. A book debt and its proceeds are indistinguishable as the only value lies in the receipt and the nature of the charge is to be determined therefore by the control of the receipt. As it is practically impossible in most cases to give control to the chargee, charges on book debts will almost invariably be floating charges. The House of Lords did not deny that it is possible to create a fixed charge over book debts,[84] and it is open to the banks to alter their documentation to do so, but essentially to be a fixed charge the proceeds must be placed in a blocked account under the control of the chargee.[85] It will be appreciated that it is difficult to impose the level of control over the proceeds necessary for the charge to be classified as a fixed charge without paralysing the company's activities.[86] In *Re Keenan Bros Ltd*,[87] it will be recalled, the book debts were segregated in a designated account and were unusable by the chargor save with the prior written consent of the chargee.[88] Even where the chargee is a clearing bank, the degree of control required over the company's account is commercially impractical and unacceptable for most businesses. As Sir Roy Goode has said, 'for most practical purposes, the fixed charge on book debts is dead'.[89]

21-45 At one level, the decision was something of a blow for the banks since they had depended for more than 20 years on obtaining a fixed charge, so defeating the prior claims of the

---

[80] See [2005] 2 BCLC 269 at 323–4.

[81] See too *Re F2G Realisations Ltd* [2011] 1 BCLC 313 (floating charge where money in bank account was at the free disposal of the chargor company until certain events of default occurred).

[82] See [2005] 2 BCLC 269 at 312.   [83] [1979] 2 Lloyd's Rep 142.

[84] See Lord Hope on possible methods of creating a fixed charge on book debts, [2005] 2 BCLC 269 at 291.

[85] See *Re Beam Tube Products Ltd, Fanshawe v Amav Industries Ltd* [2007] 2 BCLC 732 (charge on book debts was a floating charge as proceeds were available to company and the fact that the parties did eventually set up a blocked account into which the proceeds were paid did not alter that categorisation).

[86] Although it is not impossible, see *William Gaskell Group Ltd v Highley* [1994] 1 BCLC 197.

[87] [1986] BCLC 242, (Irish S Ct).

[88] See Berg, n 67, at 44–6 who cautions that there is more to *Re Keenan* than their Lordships seem to have appreciated and therefore merely drafting a charge in the manner of *Re Keenan* will not necessarily guarantee that the charge is a fixed charge.

[89] See Goode, n 32. See *Re Beam Tube Products Ltd, Fanshawe v Amav Industries Ltd* [2007] 2 BCLC 732 (fixed charge over uncollected and floating charge over proceeds categorised as floating charge over proceeds).

preferential creditors who are the beneficiaries of the *Spectrum Plus* decision.[90] On the other hand, the outcome cannot have been surprising since the lower courts had been signalling for some time that inadequate constraints on the freedom of the chargor would mean that the charge was floating. For example, in *Re Brightlife Ltd*,[91] although there were some restrictions on the debtor company, it retained the freedom to collect in the debts and pay the proceeds into its bank account and to use them in the ordinary course of business and so the charge was a floating charge. In *Royal Trust Bank v National Westminster Bank plc*[92] there was a failure to require and control a designated account and so the charge was a floating charge. In *Re Double S Printers Ltd*[93] the chargee had no control over the debts or the proceeds and so the charge was a floating charge.

21-46 In any event, changed circumstances mean that the fixed charge issue is not as significant as it once was. The desire of the banks to have fixed rather than floating charges over book debts was fuelled mainly by a desire to defeat the statutory priority afforded to the preferential debts which were frequently substantial in size (especially the sums due to the Inland Revenue and Customs and Excise). The Enterprise Act 2002 abolished the main categories of preferential debts (including with respect to sums due to HMRC) leaving more limited preferential claims with respect to employees and some other claims: see **24-70**.[94] The result is that whether the charge is fixed or floating with respect to book debts is not as crucial an issue as it was previously.

21-47 While the claims of the preferential creditors have been significantly reduced, a floating charge is subject, however, to the prior claims of the expenses of winding up or administration. In view of that priority, a lender's preference would still be for a fixed charge. On the other hand, the holder of a qualifying floating charge has certain valuable rights and privileges with respect to appointing an administrator so there are some advantages in having a charge over book debts even it if is only a floating charge.

21-48 In any event, banks and other lenders do not rely on one type of security and so, while these decisions effectively prevent lenders from taking fixed charges on book debts, lenders will simply look to increase their protection in other ways, such as by taking fixed charges on other types of assets, or persuading companies to make increased use of factoring and/or invoice discounting which do not involve the creation of charges over the debts,[95] and perhaps, with regard to smaller companies, a greater insistence on personal guarantees from directors in respect of the company's borrowings.

---

[90] Indeed the Crown Departments (Inland Revenue, HM Customs and Excise and the Redundancy Payments Service) were quick to issue a statement reserving the right to challenge any distributions made or proposed to be made to chargeholders after the Privy Council decision based on charges which purport to be fixed charges but which in reality are floating charges. See 'Statement on behalf of HM Revenue & Customs and the DTI Insolvency Service (The Crown Departments) in light of the HL judgment in the case of National Westminster Bank Plc v Spectrum Plus Limited' (2005) 18 Insolv Int 159.

[91] [1986] BCLC 418; also *Re Pearl Maintenance Services Ltd* [1995] 1 BCLC 449 (no restrictions on the freedom of the chargor to realise the book debts and to use the proceeds in the ordinary course of business: the charge was a floating charge although described as fixed).   [92] [1996] 2 BCLC 682, CA.

[93] [1999] 1 BCLC 220. See *Re ASRS Establishment Ltd* [2000] 2 BCLC 631 (charge on escrow account fell within charge on 'debts and other claims' which was designated as a fixed charge but chargor was free to use the proceeds of the escrow account in the ordinary course of business: the charge was a floating charge); also *Re Chalk v Kahn* [2000] 2 BCLC 361.   [94] See IA 1986, Sch 6.

[95] As to factoring and invoice discounting, see nn 5 and 6.

Charges on other income-generating assets

21-49 The focus of *Re Brumark* and *Re Spectrum Plus* is clearly book debts so the issue then arises as to the implications, if any, for charges on other income-generating assets.[96] This issue centres to some extent on the decision of the Court of Appeal in *Re New Bullas Trading Ltd*[97] which had held that it was possible to create a floating charge over the proceeds of book debts once collected while retaining a fixed charge over the uncollected proceeds. The decision in *New Bullas* was much criticised on this 'two charges' point[98] and the Privy Council in *Brumark* had no doubt that *New Bullas* was wrongly decided.[99] Lords Scott and Walker in *Re Spectrum Plus* were also in agreement that it was wrongly decided.[100] Applying those decisions (*Brumark* and *Spectrum*) to the facts in *New Bullas*, there was no fixed charge in *New Bullas*, merely a floating charge over the proceeds of the debts. This does not mean that there cannot be fixed charges on income-generating assets. The problem in respect of book debts, as *Re Brumark* and *Re Spectrum Plus* now show and as the dictum from Lord Millett in *Brumark*, noted at **21-34** makes clear, is that while there are theoretically two assets (debts and proceeds), the debt is worthless as security without the proceeds so in effect the two assets are one asset—the receipt of the money due. Where there are distinct assets (Lord Millett gave the example in *Brumark*[101] of land generating rental income and which would also apply to other assets such as equipment and intellectual property rights which also generate income), then there can be distinct charges secured on the asset and on the income stream derived from the asset. The nature of those charges will be determined by the application of the two-step process already noted (see at **21-25**). There is no legal obstacle to having a fixed charge on the income stream, assuming the requisite control is in place though, as noted, that will often be impracticable and so the charge will be floating, but if the circumstances allow for control by the chargee, the charge can be fixed. In other words, *Re Brumark* and *Re Spectrum Plus*, in dictating that there is only one charge, are limited to charges on book debts and equivalent income streams where the asset and the proceeds of the asset are one and the same thing.[102]

Categorisation of charges

21-50 There is no doubt that there has been a concerted judicial effort to bring some clarity to this area which is of such practical importance to companies and their banks and other

---

[96] See Frome & Gibbons, 'Spectrum—An End To The Conflict Or The Signal For A New Campaign?' in Getzler & Payne, n 16, at pp 111–16 on this issue.   [97] [1994] 1 BCLC 485, CA.

[98] Most of the commentary was hostile, see Goode, 'Charges Over Book Debts: A Missed Opportunity' [1994] 110 LQR 592; Worthington, 'Fixed Charges Over Book Debts and Other Receivables' [1997] 113 LQR 562; Moss, 'Fixed Charges on Book Debts: Puzzles and Perils' (1995) Insolv Int 25; but not all: see Berg, 'Charges Over Book Debts: A Reply' [1995] JBL 433.   [99] [2001] 2 BCLC 188 at 205, PC.

[100] [2005] 2 BCLC 269 at 310 (Lord Scott), 322 (Lord Walker), HL.

[101] [2001] 2 BCLC 188 at 203, PC.

[102] See Worthington, n 21, at pp 37–44; and Wood, n 32, at p 147 who makes the point that the decision in *Brumark* (and now *Spectrum)* must be limited to book debts and does not apply to a broad range of income-generating assets since the House of Lords cannot have intended that in all cases charges over such assets should be floating charges. The position taken in *Re Atlantic Computer Systems plc* [1991] BCLC 606 at 625, CA and *Re Atlantic Medical Ltd* [1993] BCLC 386, Ch D (charges over the income from equipment sub-leases where the chargor was allowed continued use of the income were fixed charges) is undermined. They have always been the subject of criticism, see Goode, n 98; Oditah, n 54: 'odd decisions of questionable application'; Moss (1995) 8 Insolv Int 25, unless it is possible to regard the charges over the leases as involving rights greater than merely rights to the income stream, see Frome & Gibbons, n 96, at pp 113–15; *Arthur D Little Ltd v Ableco Finance LLC* [2002] 2 BCLC 799.

lenders. The law is now clearly articulated in *Agnew v IRC (Re Brumark)*, PC[103] and *Re Spectrum Plus Ltd, National Westminster Bank plc v Spectrum Plus Ltd*, HL,[104] which convey a single consistent message. The categorisation of a charge involves a two-step process—determining the parties' rights and categorising those rights as a matter of law. Whether a charge is a fixed or a floating charge depends on whether the intention is that the company should be free to deal with the charged assets and withdraw them from the security without the consent of the holder of the charge or, to put it another way, whether the charged assets are intended to be under the control of the company or of the chargeholder.[105] For most commercial lending to companies, that test can be applied and can provide a clear answer. Of course, there is still uncertainty as to the precise degree of control which makes a charge fixed rather than floating, for example the extent to which 'sweeping' arrangements from a blocked account to an account to which the chargor has access is compatible with a fixed charge[106] and uncertainty as to the precise application of *Brumark* and *Spectrum Plus* to complex securitisations.[107] Nevertheless, these issues do not appear to have given rise to practical difficulties and the position post-*Spectrum* (at least in so far as it can be gauged from the dearth of litigation now on these issues) would suggest that these decisions have brought certainty to a large swathe of the market and have not resulted in the sort of upheaval in lending practices nor the uncertainty in complex transactions such as securitisation which had been predicted.

D Registration of charges

Reform of registration requirements

21-51 The Company Law Review (CLR) initially consulted on the option of retaining the core charge registration requirements from the CA 1985 while updating and improving them,[108] though it subsequently put forward a more radical proposal to replace the

---

[103] [2001] 2 BCLC 188, PC.   [104] [2005] 2 BCLC 269, HL.

[105] [2001] 2 BCLC 188 at 200. The decision in *Queens Moat Houses plc v Capita IRG Trustees Ltd* [2005] 2 BCLC 199 appears difficult in this regard and must now be read in the light of *Re Spectrum Plus*. The court held that it was not inconsistent with a fixed charge for the chargor to have a contractual right to withdraw property from the charge and distinguished that right from the chargor's freedom to deal with the charged assets in the ordinary course of business which would make a charge a floating charge. But if the feature of the fixed charge, to quote Lord Walker in *Spectrum Plus* [2005] 2 BCLC 269 at 318, is that the asset is permanently appropriated to the payment of the sum charged and that assets can be released from the charge only with the active concurrence of the chargee, then it is difficult to see how the charge here can be a fixed charge if the property subject to it can be altered by the chargor unilaterally.

[106] A better arrangement may be a sweep from an open access account to a blocked account so the charge is floating on the proceeds paid into the open account but the chargor is required to sweep a certain percentage amount to a blocked account over which the chargee has a fixed charge. Of course, evidence that the chargee sweeps funds back from the blocked account to the open account would raise issues as to whether the accounts were all part of the same arrangement and subject to a single floating charge, but clearly there are permutations here for banks and companies to consider: see Oditah [2004] 120 LQR 533 at 540–1. The uncertainties and practicalities combined may mean that it is cheaper all round to settle for a floating charge.

[107] See Frome & Gibbons, n 96, at p 129 who conclude that the constraints on the SPV (special purpose vehicle) used for securitisation transactions are such that a court would consider the charge is fixed even though the chargor has some rights to use the income stream. See also Ferran, *Principles of Corporate Finance Law* (2008), pp 385–6.

[108] See CLR, *Modern Company Law for a Competitive Economy, Registration of Company Charges* (October 2000).

registration scheme with a system of 'notice filing'.[109] Given that it had not been possible to consult on that more radical proposal, the CLR recommended that the issue of registration be referred for consideration by the Law Commission.[110]

21-52 The Law Commission duly noted a variety of weaknesses in the statutory registration requirements such as: the statutory list of charges which require registration (now in CA 2006, s 860(7), see **21-57**) is outdated; the information provided to the registrar of companies is not always reliable or completely accurate with prudent searchers looking to the chargor company for further information; dual registration at Companies House and specialist registries is required in a number of cases such as for charges on land, aircraft and ships; and while a failure to register a registrable charge has consequences as against an administrator, liquidator or other creditors, registration itself is not a priority point and does not determine priorities. Several consultation papers and a final report making modest proposals for reform duly followed,[111] modest because in part practitioners were not convinced of the need for change, or at least that the disruption of change would be outweighed by the benefits.[112]

21-53 The Commission's final report concentrated on recommending the introduction of an electronic notice-filing system, akin to the systems in operation in the US and many Commonwealth countries, applying to all charges unless expressly excluded, with priority generally determined by the date of filing. The effect of a failure to register would be invalidity against an administrator or liquidator and a loss of priority against a subsequent secured creditor who filed. While the Government consulted further on whether to implement the Law Commission's recommendations,[113] specifically in terms of the economic benefits of so doing, there was little or no support for change and no progress was made, though a power to amend CA 2006, Pt 25 dealing with company charges by regulations was inserted in CA 2006, s 894.

---

[109] See CLR, *Modern Company Law for a Competitive Economy, Final Report*, vol 1 (July 2001), Ch 12.

[110] The Commission's terms of reference excluded any intrusion into insolvency law, however, a somewhat significant restriction when security issues by their very nature are most acute in the context of insolvency.

[111] The Law Commission published an initial consultation paper on registration of security interests, see Law Commission, *Registration of Security Interests: Company Charges and Property other than Land* (Consultation Paper No 164), 2002; followed by another consultation paper advocating radical reform of personal property security law including the abolition of the floating charge: see Law Commission, *Company Security Interests* (Consultation Paper No 176), 2004, but its final Report in 2005 contained more modest proposals: Law Commission, *Company Security Interests* (Law Comm No 296, Cm 6654). For a detailed account of the process and the proposals by the Law Commissioner with responsibility for the project, see Beale, 'Reform of The Law Of Security Interests Over Personal Property' in Lowry & Mistelis (eds), *Commercial Law: Perspectives and Practice* (2006); also Goode on how the proposals came to move from radical reform to something of a damp squib: see Goode, n 32, 16–20.

[112] The influential Law Society Committee on Company Law broadly welcomed the proposal for introducing a system of notice filing, but noted that the proposals were potentially very major reforms going well beyond the confines of company law and that it would be inappropriate to make such major changes to security law and transfer of title law in a Companies Act or by way of secondary legislation pursuant to a Companies Act. The Law Society Committee also commented that: '...it is fair to say that the present system has not come in for extensive criticism from those who use it. It works relatively well in practice although its interrelationship with the specialist title registries is somewhat unsatisfactory. In short, it is not an obstacle to the obtaining of credit and we doubt whether business would suffer if the present system (subject possibly to some limited amendment) were allowed to continue.' See Law Society Company Law Committee, *The Registration of Security Interests: Company Charges and Property other than Land* (October 2002), Memo No 448, para 12.2.

[113] See DTI, *Registration of Companies Security Interests (Company Charges)* (July 2005).

21-54 The Government has indicated that it now intends to exercise that power in 2012 or 2013. The changes to be made to the registration system have been outlined, but the regulations giving effect to the proposals were not available at the time of writing. The changes are therefore highlighted in the text as changes to be made by the 'proposed new scheme' which should be understood as a reference to the changes now proposed by the Government, the main elements of the proposed scheme being that:[114]

- there will be a single UK-wide scheme applicable to all companies incorporated under the CA 2006 or its predecessors;
- the requirement to register will apply to every charge granted by a UK-registered company over any of its property (wherever situated) subject to some limited exclusions;
- there will not be any change to the sanction of invalidity where a charge is not registered within 21 days of its creation (it will continue to be void as against the liquidator, an administrator and any creditor of the company);
- any person taking a charge over the company's property will be deemed to have notice of any previously registered charge; and
- it will be possible to register a charge electronically.

The most important elements are the application of the registration requirements to all charges so ending uncertainty over whether certain types of charges require registration, see **21-57**) and the possibility of electronic filing which will entail merely the filing of shorter particulars of the charge and a copy of the charge instrument.

The obligation to register

21-55 Particulars of charges of the type specified in CA 2006, s 860(7) created by a company registered in England and Wales must be delivered to the registrar of companies within 21 days of creation[115] and an unregistered charge is void to the extent prescribed by s 874 which is discussed at **21-67**.[116]

21-56 The object of registration is not to provide a comprehensive account of all of a company's charges but to warn unsuspecting creditors that the debtor company has charged its assets.[117] The register of charges is publicly available (CA 2006, s 885(6)) so enabling creditors taking security to appreciate to what extent the assets are already encumbered. The register also assists unsecured creditors because it allows them to appreciate the extent to which the assets are earmarked for other creditors in the event of insolvency.

21-57 Only charges included in CA 2006, s 860(7) must be registered[118] but those listed include practically all the forms of charges commonly given by companies, covering charges on

---

[114] See BIS, *Registration of Company Charges: Issues to be resolved before preparation of Draft Regulations* April 2011 (URN 11/862). The key preceding documents are BIS, *Registration of charges created by companies and limited liability partnerships, Proposals to amend the current scheme and relating to specialist registries*, March 2010 (URN 10/697); BIS, *Government Response, Consultation on Registration of Charges Created by Companies and Limited Liability Partnerships*, December 2010 (URN 10/1319); BIS, *Revised scheme for registration of charges created by companies and limited liability partnerships, Proposed revision of Part 25, CA 2006*, August 2011, URN 11/1108.

[115] As the charge must be created by the company, security interests arising by law, such as liens and pledges, are excluded from the registration requirements.

[116] For a comprehensive account of registration, see McCormack, *Registration of Company Charges* (3rd edn, 2009).   [117] See *Re Welsh Irish Ferries Ltd* [1985] BCLC 327 at 332.

[118] Certain financial collateral arrangements are exempt from registration under the CA 2006, Pt 25, see the Financial Collateral Arrangements (No. 2) Regulations 2003, SI 2003/3226, regs 3, 4(4), but the exemption

land, goods (encompassed by the obscurely worded s 860(7)(b)), book debts, goodwill, intellectual property and floating charges over the undertaking.[119] The full list in s 860(7) is:

(a) a charge on land (wherever situated) or any interest in it, but not including a charge for any rent or other periodical sum issuing out of the land;

(b) a charge created or evidenced by an instrument which, if executed by an individual, would require registration as a bill of sale;[120]

(c) a charge for the purpose of securing any issue of debentures;

(d) a charge on uncalled share capital of the company;

(e) a charge on calls made but not paid;

(f) a charge on book debts of the company;

(g) a floating charge on the company's undertaking or property;

(h) a charge on a ship or aircraft, or any share in a ship;

(i) a charge on goodwill, or on any intellectual property (CA 2006, s 860(7)).

21-58 A significant omission is charges on shares, particularly shares in subsidiary companies, which can be a valuable source of security.[121] Registration is required even if the property charged is situated abroad (CA 2006, s 866) and charges existing on property acquired by the company must also be registered (this latter requirement is likely to be made an optional feature of the proposed new scheme).[122] Under the proposed new scheme, see **21-54**, the requirement to register is intended to apply to any charge or mortgage[123] granted by a company registered in the UK over any of its property (wherever situated) unless expressly excluded by regulations under the Companies Act[124] or any other statute.[125]

21-59 The prescribed particulars and the instrument of charge must be delivered to the registrar of companies within 21 calendar days after the date of creation,[126] i.e. the date of

requires the collateral taker to have possession or control of the financial collateral and an ordinary floating charge (where necessarily the chargee does not have possession or control of the asset charged) does not fall within the scope of the exemption: *Re F2G Realisations Ltd* [2011] 1 BCLC 313, esp at [52]–[55], [59]–[63].

[119] There is an overlap between a number of the categories so, for example, a charge could be registrable because it falls within CA 2006, s 860(7)(f) or (g), i.e. as a charge on book debts and as a floating charge. Equally, notwithstanding the scope of the provision, some charges are not registrable, such as a fixed charge on a credit balance at a bank; or a fixed charge on shares; or a fixed charge on an insurance policy (see *Paul & Frank Ltd v Discount Bank (Overseas) Ltd* [1966] 2 All ER 922).

[120] The Bills of Sale Acts do not apply to companies: see *Online Catering Ltd v Acton* [2011] 1 BCLC 699.

[121] For an example, see *Arthur D Little Ltd v Ableco Finance LLC* [2002] 2 BCLC 799.

[122] CA 2006, s 862, assuming the charge is of a kind which, if it had been created by the company after the acquisition of the property, would require registration under s 860. A failure to register as required by this provision does not attract the statutory invalidity of s 874, but merely a fine: s 862(5).

[123] The requirement will also apply to any pledge under which the debtor has possession of collateral and attorns to the pledgee as if the pledge were a charge.

[124] The intention is that the regulations will exclude charges created by corporate members of Lloyd's; security taken by a landlord to secure liabilities of its tenant under a lease; charges over credit balances; and market charges.

[125] See BIS, *Registration of Company Charges: Issues to be resolved before preparation of Draft Regulations* April 2011 (URN 11/862), pp 7–8. An example of excluded charges would be charges governed by The Financial Collateral Arrangements (No. 2) Regulations 2003, SI 2003/3226.

[126] Under the proposed new scheme, the period for delivery of a charge will be 21 days beginning with the day after the day on which execution of the deed is completed by delivery (with a requirement that the particulars indicate if this date is not the same as the date of execution). If there is no instrument, the

execution of the charge.[127] The problem which this period creates is that anyone searching the register of charges with respect to the company and finding no charges cannot be sure that there are not charges which have been created but have not yet been registered. Searchers of the register must not rely therefore on the absence of charges and must ask the company to confirm that no other charges have been created which have yet to be registered.

21-60 It is the company's duty to deliver the particulars and the original charge instrument to the registrar of companies.[128] In practice, because of the consequences of non-delivery, practically all registrations are undertaken by the chargee (CA 2006, s 860(2)). Under the proposed new scheme the obligation to register will apply to any person who takes a registrable charge or security over property of a UK company.

21-61 There is no mechanism whereby subsequent variations in the terms of the charge, for example an increase in the secured moneys or a variation of priorities as between chargees, can be registered. In effect, the parties must register the variation under CA 2006, s 860, as if an entirely new charge has been created. While a little confusing, the practice at least has the merit that the variation appears on the company's public record. Under the proposed new scheme it will be possible for the chargee voluntarily to file an assignment of the charge and the addition of a negative pledge.

21-62 Following delivery of the prescribed particulars and the original instrument of charge, the registrar checks the accuracy of the particulars against the charge instrument. It is important that the particulars reflect the full extent of the charge so as to ensure that any person searching the public register is not misled as to the extent of the security, but it can be difficult for the registrar's staff to ensure that this is the case, given the nature of the documentation submitted by chargees. Indeed it is often difficult to deduce from the instrument delivered either the nature of the charge which the parties have purported to create or the assets which are the subject of the charge. It is the opaqueness of these documents which leads to so much litigation on these matters later and it is clear that few commercial lenders regularly review their standard documentation to ensure its continued appropriateness, both generally in terms of creating security, and specifically in the context of the company in question. For example, many lenders continue to claim fixed charges on book debts when it is clear post-*Re Spectrum Plus Ltd*[129] that the charges they have created are floating charges (though this may be as much through commercial inertia as any real expectation that such charges are fixed).

21-63 The proposed new scheme will simplify matters significantly by requiring the filing of brief prescribed particulars[130] and a certified copy of the charge instrument, so

---

period for delivery of a charge will continue to be 21 days beginning with the day after the day on which the charge was created, see BIS, *Registration of Company Charges: Issues to be resolved before preparation of Draft Regulations* April 2011 (URN 11/862).

   [127] CA 2006, ss 860(1), 870(1); and see The Companies (Particulars of Company Charges) Regulations 2008, SI 2008/2996. If because of errors in the particulars provided, the registrar is required to return the forms to the presenter for correction, re-submission must occur within the 21-day limit. If the registrar improperly rejects a form, for example, because of doubts as to whether the charge is within s 860(7), the charge is not invalidated as delivery will have occurred within the 21-day period. The 21-day period is extended where the charge is created outside of the UK over property situated outside of the UK: see s 870(2).

   [128] CA 2006, s 860(1). A registration fee of £13 is payable: The Companies (Fees) Regulations 2004, SI 2004/2621, Sch 4.   [129] [2005] 2 BCLC 269, HL.

   [130] The brief particulars are to be as follows: (a) the registered name and number of the company; (b) whether the charged assets are held in trust by the chargor; (c) the day on which execution of the deed was

removing the need for the registrar's staff to check the accuracy of the particulars against the instrument.

21-64 Once checked against the particulars, the original instrument is returned to the presenter together with a certificate of registration and an entry is made on the register of charges (CA 2006, s 869). The certificate is conclusive as to compliance with the registration requirements even if it is inaccurate.[131]

21-65 A copy of the instrument of charge must be available at the company's registered office or other specified location for inspection by any creditor or member (CA 2006, s 875 and this requirement will be retained under the proposed new scheme). The company must maintain a register of all charges (whether or not registrable under s 860) at the registered office or other specified place and that register is available for inspection by any person (s 877), but the new scheme will do away with this register in most cases.

21-66 There is no statutory requirement to notify the registrar of companies of the satisfaction or release of any charge. Companies which want to clear debts of their public record can make a statement under CA 2006, s 872, however, to the effect either that the debt for which the charge was given has been paid or satisfied in whole or in part, or that part of the property or undertaking charged has been released from the charge or has ceased to form part of the company's property or undertaking. On receipt of that statement, the registrar may enter on the register a memorandum of satisfaction to this effect. The new scheme continues the position that the filing of a satisfaction or release is voluntary but, where the filing is by the chargor, as a safeguard against fraudulent filing, there will have to be a statement explaining why it is not being made by the chargee.

Statutory invalidity for non-registration

21-67 The consequence of a failure to deliver the prescribed particulars within the required period means that the charge is void against the liquidator or administrator and any creditor of the company (CA 2006, s 874(1)), but it is a limited invalidity. The statute 'makes void a security; not the debt, not the cause of action, but the security, and not as against everybody, not as against the company grantor, but against the liquidator, [and now an administrator] and against any creditor'.[132] This statutory invalidity will continue under the proposed new scheme, see **21-54**.

21-68 The invalidity of the security is without prejudice to the obligation for repayment of the money secured by the charge and the money secured immediately becomes payable (CA

---

completed by delivery (with a requirement to indicate if this date is not the same as the date of execution); (d) whether the terms of the charge are expressed to extend to all the assets of the company. If not, whether any of the following assets are the subject of the charge: (i) land registrable at the Land Registry (ii) intangible property; (e) where the charge is expressed to extend to either all assets of the company or all the assets of a particular type of the company, then whether its terms prevent the chargor from creating any further security that will rank equally with or ahead of the charge: see BIS, *Registration of Company Charges: Issues to be resolved before preparation of Draft Regulations* April 2011 (URN 11/862), p 13.

[131] CA 2006, s 869(6)(b) and see *Re Mechanisations (Eaglescliffe) Ltd* [1966] Ch 20 (amount secured wrongly stated). The certificate is conclusive even if it shows the wrong date of creation of the charge, so that the charge may not have been delivered within the 21-day period: *Re C L Nye Ltd* [1970] 3 All ER 1061.

[132] *Re Monolithic Building Company* [1915] 1 Ch 643 at 667, per Phillimore LJ; and see *Re Cosslett Ltd* [2002] 1 BCLC 77 at 84: it is not void against the company when it is a going concern, but it is void when the company is in liquidation or administration. See also *Re F2G Realisations Ltd* [2011] 1 BCLC 313 (unregistered floating charge).

2006, s 874(3)). This liability to immediate repayment allows a creditor to insist on recovering his money once he has lost his security as a result of the failure to deliver the particulars within 21 days.

21-69 The nature of the statutory invalidity imposed by CA 2006, s 874(1) was considered by the House of Lords in *Smith (Administrator of Cosslett (Contractors) Ltd) v Bridgend County Borough Council*,[133] which was noted at **21-26**.

21-70 A council had contracted with a company (the contractor) to carry out coal washing on a particular site for the council. The terms of the contract allowed the council, in the event of default by the contractor, to enter the site, use the machinery of the contractor to complete the job and to sell the machinery and apply the proceeds to the liabilities of the contractor under the contract. When the company defaulted on the contract, the council duly entered the site, seized the contractor's machinery and obtained another contractor to complete the contract using that machinery. The council then permitted the second contractor to remove and sell the machinery. A variety of legal proceedings ensued, part of which concluded, as discussed at **21-27**, that the council's right to sell the machinery and apply the proceeds to the debt due by the contractor to the council amounted to a floating charge which charge was void for non-registration under what is now CA 2006, s 874.

21-71 The administrator then brought successful proceedings claiming damages from the council for conversion of the machinery by allowing the second contractor to remove it from the site. The Court of Appeal allowed an appeal by the council against that liability for conversion, finding that the contractual conditions as to the use of, and power to sell, the machinery etc (despite amounting to an unregistered floating charge void as against the administrator for non-registration under what is now CA 2006, s 874) remained valid as against the company and was the answer, the Court of Appeal said, to the conversion claim.[134]

21-72 On appeal to the House of Lords, their Lordships rejected this finding by the Court of Appeal as a narrow and arbitrary construction of what is now CA 2006, s 874(1) and reversed the decision. The statutory provision does not invalidate a charge against a company while it is a going concern but makes an unregistered but registrable charge void against a company acting by its liquidator or administrator, that is to say void against a company in liquidation or in administration.[135] The council could not therefore rely on its terms against the company or the administrator of the company. As the council's charge was void for non-registration, the council had no proprietary interest in the machinery and therefore allowing the second contractor to remove the equipment was a violation of the first contractor's right of possession. That was sufficient to amount to a conversion in respect of which the administrator could seek damages. The council's claim for damages for breach of contract by the contractor would have to be pursued in the liquidation of the contractor.[136]

---

[133] [2002] 1 BCLC 77.   [134] See [2000] 1 BCLC 775, CA.

[135] See [2002] 1 BCLC 77 at 84, per Lord Hoffmann.

[136] Counsel for the council attempted to secure some redress by claiming the benefit of some equitable set-off so as to set off the council's breach of contract claim against the administrator's claim for conversion. The House of Lords was robust in rejecting this possibility. Lord Scott noting that, given that the council's security was invalid because of a failure to comply with the statutory provisions as to registration, it was no part of equity to provide, via equitable set-off, an alternative security: see [2002] 1 BCLC 77 at 97.

21-73 This attempt by the Court of Appeal to ascribe a type of partial invalidity to the unregistered charge was, Lord Hoffmann said, 'a startling and unorthodox approach' to what is now CA 2006, s 874(1). He noted that the Court of Appeal may have been influenced in adopting that approach by its perception of the merits of the case. The local council found itself in a position where it had no security for the debts owed to it (which included a large amount advanced by the council to the contractor to enable the contractor to acquire the machinery in the first place) as its floating charge was void for non-registration and it was liable in conversion to the administrator.

Remedial measures in cases of non-registration

21-74 Where the required particulars have not been delivered to the registrar of companies and the 21-day period has elapsed so attracting the statutory invalidity, there are a number of options open to the company and the chargee. The main option is an application by either party to the court for registration out of time under CA 2006, s 873 and this step should be taken without delay once the failure to register is discovered.

21-75 Section 873 allows the court to extend the time for registration if satisfied that the omission to register a charge within the time required was accidental, or due to inadvertence or to some other sufficient cause, or is not of a nature to prejudice the position of creditors or shareholders of the company, or that on other grounds it is just and equitable to grant relief.[137] Even if the court's discretion does arise, the court may decide not to exercise it as where the application is made only after long delay.[138] But in general, the practice of the court is to exercise the power to extend the period for registration, subject to the proviso that registration is without prejudice to any rights acquired between the date of creation of the charge and the date of its actual registration,[139] so as to ensure that intervening creditors are not adversely affected.[140]

21-76 As an alternative to applying to the court, the chargee may attempt to remedy the situation by getting another charge executed by the company and registered before any third party intervenes.[141] This approach is a risky strategy for, if it fails, the court may look unfavourably on an application under CA 2006, s 873.[142] A further risk with executing a new charge is that if the company goes into insolvent liquidation or administration shortly thereafter, the new charge may be open to challenge as a vulnerable transaction under IA 1986, ss 239, 245 (discussed in Chapter 25).

---

[137] The final 'just and equitable' category allows for any reason, whether specified in the section or not, to be put forward: *Re Braemar Investments Ltd* [1988] BCLC 556 at 561. See also *Confiance Ltd v Timespan Images Ltd* [2005] 2 BCLC 693.

[138] See *Re Telomatic Ltd* [1994] 1 BCLC 90; *Victoria Housing Estates Ltd v Ashpurton Estates Ltd* [1982] 3 All ER 665.

[139] *Re Joplin Brewery Co Ltd* [1902] 1 Ch 79 (as modified following the decision in *Watson v Duff Morgan & Vermont (Holdings) Ltd* [1974] 1 All ER 794); and see *Victoria Housing Estates Ltd v Ashpurton Estates Ltd* [1982] 3 All ER 665 at 670 for the history of this proviso; and see *Barclays Bank plc v Stuart Landon Ltd* [2001] 2 BCLC 316.

[140] The extension may also be subject to the proviso in *Re L H Charles & Co Ltd* [1935] WN 15 allowing the company, through any liquidator subsequently appointed, to apply within a specified period (for example, 42 days) after the commencement of the winding up to discharge the order granting an extension of time and containing an undertaking by the applicant for late registration to abide by any order which the court may make.

[141] A process which may be fraught with difficulties: see *Re Telomatic Ltd* [1994] 1 BCLC 90.

[142] See *Victoria Housing Estates Ltd v Ashpurton Estates Ltd* [1982] 3 All ER 665 at 677 (the court should look askance at a chargee who deliberately defers his application in order to see which way the wind is going to blow).

21-77 Another possibility is that the chargee can seek immediate repayment of the sum secured (see CA 2006, s 874(3)) and this ability to demand immediate repayment of the entire amount may assist him in obtaining a new charge from the company. If the unregistered chargee succeeds in securing repayment before liquidation or administration, the charge is spent and there is nothing for the statutory invalidity to bite on.[143]

Priority as between charges

21-78 The registration of a charge as required by CA 2006, s 860 does not determine priorities as between successive chargees, save to the extent of the statutory invalidity affecting any unregistered charge.

21-79 Priority issues are determined at common law with the basic rules being that legal interests prevail over equitable, fixed charges over floating charges, and where the equities are equal, the first in time prevails. The position is then complicated by issues of notice and, in particular, the application of the doctrine of constructive notice. Anyone dealing with a company is deemed under the doctrine of constructive notice to have notice of its public documents including the articles of association which doctrine was extended, obiter, by *Wilson v Kelland*[144] to the register of charges but only to the extent that there is constructive notice of the existence of a registered charge and not of any special provisions contained in the charge[145] (this will remain the position under the proposed new scheme, see **21-54**).[146] It means, however, that successive chargees have notice of the preceding charges (assuming they are registered). The position with respect to the creation of further charges post the granting of a floating charge was discussed at **21-12**.

E Enforcement of a floating charge

Receivers, administrative receivers and administrators

21-80 The appointment of a receiver by the Court of Chancery was an ancient equitable remedy available to creditors whether secured or unsecured[147] but, in the modern business context, receiverships are associated particularly with a default by a corporate borrower on a secured loan.[148]

---

[143] *Mercantile Bank of India Ltd v Chartered Bank of India, Australia and China* [1937] 1 All ER 231; *Re Row Dal Construction Pty Ltd* [1966] VR 249 at 258; *NV Slavenburg's Bank NV v Intercontinental Natural Resources Ltd* [1980] 1 All ER 955.   [144] [1910] 2 Ch 306.

[145] See *Siebe Gorman & Co Ltd v Barclays Bank Ltd* [1979] 2 Lloyd's Rep 142 at 160, overruled on other grounds, *Re Spectrum Plus Ltd* [2005] 2 BCLC 269. See generally Gough, *Company Charges* (2nd edn, 1996), Ch 23.

[146] The proposal under the new scheme is that 'from the day following the appearance on the public register, the registration of a charge created by a company should constitute notice of the existence of the charge and, in the case of a floating charge, whether or not it has a negative pledge, to any person taking a charge over a company's property; any purchaser of receivables from the company; and any buyer or similar disponee of the company's assets unless those assets are of the kind regularly sold by the company in the course of its ordinary business', see BIS, *Registration of Company Charges: Issues to be resolved before preparation of Draft Regulations* April 2011 (URN 11/862), pp 9–10.

[147] The power to appoint a receiver is vested in the High Court, see the Supreme Court Act 1981, s 37. For an outline of the development of receivers, see Rigby LJ in *Gaskell v Gosling* [1896] 1 QB 669 at 691–3.

[148] See generally, Finch, *Corporate Insolvency Law: Perspectives and Principles* (2nd edn, 2009), Ch 8.

21-81 During the 19th century conveyancers realised the advantages in terms of costs and speed of providing for the appointment of a receiver as a contractual remedy under a debenture without the necessity of going to court. A *receiver*, strictly speaking, is appointed just to receive the rent or other income from property.[149] Over time, appointments of receivers for this purpose became the accepted practice, so much so that the power to appoint a receiver of income is now implied into mortgages by deed unless the parties provided otherwise and such receivers are known as LPA receivers and their powers are usually extended by deed to include powers to sell and manage the property.[150] If it is desirable for the receiver to manage the property or to carry on the debtor's business, the receiver must also be appointed under the terms of the debenture as a manager with appropriate powers and such a person is often referred to as a receiver and manager.[151] Again such powers are commonplace. The result is that the debenture commonly provides for the appointment of receivers with wide power to receive income, to manage the business and to sell the assets secured for the benefit of the chargee. In addition to receivers, and receivers and managers, the IA 1986, s 29(2) provides for a further category, administrative receivers, defined essentially as receivers appointed under a floating charge over all or substantially all of the company's property. Most appointments of receivers in recent years were appointment of administrative receivers, reflecting the prevalence of floating charges over all or substantially all the company's assets. The IA 1986 as amended by the EA 2002 now prohibits the appointment of administrative receivers, however, where the floating charge is created on or after 15 September 2003 (IA 1986, s 72A). To understand why this prohibition was imposed, it is necessary to understand how administrative receiverships operated prior to the EA 2002.

21-82 Essentially, administrative receivership worked in the following way. A secured creditor (typically a clearing bank with fixed and floating charges over the company and its undertaking) would appoint a receiver following a default by the corporate borrower. Appointment was purely a contractual issue requiring no assistance from the courts and the receiver's primary function was to realise sufficient of the company's assets comprised in the security to discharge the debt due to the secured creditor. The receiver had to decide quite quickly whether to continue the business in order to sell it as a going concern or to sell off the company's assets piecemeal. In theory, once the receiver completed his task of realising sufficient funds to satisfy his appointor, the company could continue trading. In practice, the receiver would commonly not realise sufficient funds even to pay his appointor in full and the company would go into liquidation. Moreover, as the appointment of a receiver did not impose a moratorium on other creditors enforcing their rights, his appointment usually galvanised other creditors into asserting their rights and remedies.

[149] The powers conferred by the LPA 1925 are limited in this way but they may be varied or extended by the mortgage deed: s 101(3).

[150] See Law of Property Act 1925, s 101(1)(iii). The use of LPA receivers can be quite effective where the borrower has properties which are generating rental income which the lender would like to secure to repay the mortgage interest at least, especially when it may be difficult to sell the property to recover the capital. The powers of an LPA receiver are usually increased by the terms of the deed and an LPA receiver need not be a qualified insolvency practitioner. For an overview, see CML Guidance Note, *The Role of the LPA Receiver* (February 2011).

[151] As to the distinction, see *Re Manchester and Milford Rly Co* (1880) 14 Ch D 645 at 653 where Jessel MR noted that: 'A "receiver" is a term which was well known … as meaning a person who receives rents or other income paying ascertained outgoings, but who does not … manage the property in the sense of buying or selling or anything of that kind. … If it was desired to continue the trade at all, it was necessary to appoint a manager, or a receiver and manager as it was generally called.'

For example, creditors might petition the court for a compulsory winding-up order or the members might resolve to put the company into voluntary liquidation.

21-83 There were obvious advantages to administrative receiverships, particularly for the appointor, most notably the ease and speed with which an appointment might be made once the borrower was in default and the focus on realising sufficient assets to satisfy the debt due to the debenture holder. But receiverships were frequently criticised precisely because of this focus on one secured creditor to the exclusion of other interests, in particular, the interests of unsecured creditors: see **23-3**. As a matter of policy, the Government decided their use should not be continued and its preference was for a collective process for the benefit of the creditors as a whole—administration.

21-84 The holder of a qualifying floating charge is prohibited then from appointing an administrative receiver of the company where the charge was created on or after the 15 September 2003.[152] It is still possible to appoint an administrative receiver under charges created prior to that date but creditors often prefer to appoint an administrator even where they have power to appoint an administrative receiver.[153] The right to appoint an administrative receiver is retained by IA 1986, ss 72B–72GA for specialist areas such as public–private partnership projects, utility projects and urban regeneration projects[154] but those specialist cases are beyond the scope of this work.

21-85 For a floating chargeholder outside of those specialist contexts, the means of enforcement is through the appointment of an administrator under the IA 1986, Sch B1, and it is possible to do so out of court in a manner very similar (in terms of speed and efficiency) to the appointment of an administrative receiver: see **23-48**. Administration is discussed in detail in Chapter 23 and it will be seen that an administrator is able to realise the assets quickly (see **23-85**) and to make distributions to secured creditors (see **23-91**) in a manner which can look very like administrative receivership. The process of enforcement may have changed, but the outcome may be very similar: see **23-121**.

---

[152] IA 1986, s 72A; SI 2003/2095.

[153] Figures for Great Britain show that the number of receiverships halved between 2003–04 (1,284) and 2007–08 (634), but rose again to 1,312 in 2010–11, reflecting the financial crisis, but the figures do not distinguish between administrative receivers and other types, such as receivers appointed under the Law of Property Act 1925; in 2007–08 there were 2,733 administrator appointments and that figure rose to 3,032 in 2010–12, see *Statistical Tables on Companies Registration Activities 2010–11*, Table C2,

[154] IA 1986, s 72A.

PART V

Corporate Rescue and Restructuring

22

Company voluntary arrangements

A Introduction

22-1 One of the most important options for those managing a company in financial difficulty is the ability to make binding compromises or arrangements with the creditors of the company. For any compromise or arrangement to work effectively, it is necessary for all the creditors to be bound by it. This can be achieved either by ensuring that the creditors unanimously agree to the plan (which is usually impractical) or by making use of statutory provisions which enable a specified majority to bind the minority.

22-2 One option might be to use the provisions governing schemes of arrangement (contained in CA 2006, Pt 26) but these complex provisions are time-consuming and expensive to operate especially with respect to identifying distinct classes of creditors who are entitled to separate meetings, see **26-90**. Schemes of arrangement are discussed in Chapter 26 and, though they are of value in a variety of situations, they are an inappropriate rescue mechanism for companies in financial difficulty other than in complex cases.

22-3 The option usually chosen is a company voluntary arrangement, invariably known as a CVA. There are two types of CVA: a CVA under Insolvency Act 1986, Pt 1 or a CVA with a moratorium governed by IA 1986, Sch A1. This chapter concentrates on the former with only a brief account of CVAs with a moratorium. The latter CVA was an innovation introduced by the Insolvency Act 2000 but it has proved unpopular (it is administratively burdensome and therefore expensive, see **22-39**). Most CVAs therefore remain CVAs under IA 1986, Pt 1 which suffer from the disadvantage of not having a moratorium but that is overcome commonly by preparing proposals for a voluntary arrangement in conjunction with the appointment of an administrator. There is a close link between administration and CVAs since, if a company in administration is to be rescued as a going concern (see **23-14**), this frequently means entering into a CVA with the company's creditors and most CVAs are entered into in the context of administrations. A particular attraction of a CVA (outside of administration) for the directors is that they retain control over the choice of nominee/supervisor who will conduct the CVA, they remain in post and, crucially, a nominee/supervisor under a CVA is not required to make reports as to the directors' conduct under the Company Directors Disqualification Act 1986. Even so, CVAs remain one of the least used insolvency procedures.[1]

---

[1] In 2010–11, for example, 742 companies (772 in 2009–10) went into a CVA compared with 2,827 (3,608) companies in administration and 17,098 (20,188) insolvent liquidations: see Companies House, *Statistical Tables on Companies Registration Activities 2010–11*, Table C2. See generally, Finch, *Corporate Insolvency law, Perspectives and Principles* (2nd edn, 2009), Ch 11, esp 495–9 for a discussion of the reasons why CVAs are unpopular, not least their costs). For proposals for reform (which have so far come to nothing), see the discussion at **23-118**.

B Company voluntary arrangements—IA 1986, Part I

Proposing an arrangement

22-4 A voluntary arrangement, defined as a composition in satisfaction of the company's debts, or a scheme of arrangement of its affairs, may be proposed:

(1) by the directors of the company (where the company is neither in administration nor in winding up); or

(2) by an administrator where the company is in administration; or

(3) by a liquidator where the company is being wound up (IA 1986, s 1(1), (3)).

22-5 In practice, proposals from liquidators are unusual[2] and CVAs are more commonly a matter for the directors or an administrator. Neither creditors nor members may initiate a voluntary arrangement. There is no requirement that the company is unable to pay its debts, but obviously the company must be in financial difficulty or anticipating financial difficulties for the directors to consider a voluntary arrangement.

22-6 The proposal must provide for a nominee to act either as trustee or otherwise for the purpose of supervising the implementation of the voluntary arrangement and the nominee must be a qualified insolvency practitioner or authorised to act as nominee in relation to the voluntary arrangement.[3]

22-7 Where the proposal is made by the directors (the company not being in liquidation or administration), they draw up and submit to the nominee a document setting out the terms of the proposed voluntary arrangement and a statement of the company's affairs and, in practice, they usually do this with the assistance of the nominee whom they will have approached already about the company's difficulties (IA 1986, s 2(3)). Having assisted them with drawing up their proposals and agreed to be the nominee, within 28 days of being given notice of the proposals[4] the nominee submits a report to the court stating whether, in his opinion, the proposed voluntary arrangement has a reasonable prospect of being approved and implemented,[5] whether meetings of the company and its creditors should be summoned to consider the proposal and, if so, stating the date, time and place where such meetings should be held (s 2(2)). His report is merely filed with the court and, unless there is an objection, there is no court hearing. The nominee proceeds to summon the required meetings and, with respect to creditors, the summons will extend to all creditors of whose claim and address the nominee is aware.[6]

22-8 Where the proposal for the CVA is put forward by a liquidator or an administrator and he is to act as the nominee, he proceeds to summon the necessary meetings of the members and the creditors at such time, date and place as he thinks fit without any need to notify the court (IA 1986, s 3(2)).

---

[2] For an example of a joint liquidation and CVA, see *Re Energy Holdings (No 3) Ltd* [2011] 1 BCLC 84.

[3] IA 1986, s 1(2); persons who are not qualified insolvency practitioners may be recognised by the Secretary of State as authorised to act as nominees and supervisors of CVAs (and IVAs): ss 389, 389A.

[4] The court can allow a longer period: IA 1986, s 2(2).

[5] There are some concerns as to the basis on which the nominee might reach this opinion, given that he will be unable to sound out the creditors as to whether they will approve the CVA for fear of sparking precipitate action by them.

[6] IA 1986, s 3(1), (3). The meetings must take place not less than 14 days from and not more than 28 days from the filing of the nominee's report with the court: IR 1986, r 1.9(1).

Approving an arrangement

22-9   The purpose of the meetings is to decide whether to approve the proposed voluntary arrangement, with or without modifications (IA 1986, s 4(1)). No proposal or modification can be approved which affects the right of a secured creditor of the company to enforce his security without the concurrence of the creditor concerned.[7] No proposal or modification can be approved under which any preferential debt of the company is to be paid otherwise than in priority to non-preferential debts, or other than on a pro-rata basis to other preferential debts, again without the concurrence of the preferential creditor concerned.[8] However, this requirement of priority for preferential debts does not preclude the payment of non-preferential creditors by third parties from their own funds.[9] The significance of preferential debts is much reduced in any event (see **24-70**). The agreement of the secured creditors, on the other hand, is crucial to the viability of any CVA, not least because the secured creditor is likely to be a bank which will need to provide funding to support the company during the CVA.

22-10   Apart from those limitations with respect to secured and preferential creditors, any proposal can be presented for approval, provided it meets the general requirement that it is a voluntary arrangement as defined in IA 1986, s 1(1), namely a composition in satisfaction of the company's debts or a scheme of arrangement of its affairs. In *Commissioners of Inland Revenue v Adam & Partners Ltd*,[10] the Revenue Commissioners sought a declaration that a proposal purportedly approved by the creditors was not a CVA within the meaning of the Insolvency Act. The scheme envisaged that preferential and unsecured creditors would receive no payments while the company's main secured creditor (its bank) would receive a better return than would otherwise be the case under any other procedure. The Court of Appeal agreed that the proposal did not amount to a composition of the company's debts which is an agreement between the compounding debtor and all or some of the creditors by which the compounding creditors agree with the debtor to accept from the debtor payment of less than the amount due to them in full satisfaction of the whole of their claims.[11] The court did accept, however, that the proposal was for a scheme of arrangement which is different from a composition and involves something less than the release or discharge of creditors' debts.[12] On its proper construction, the scheme involved a moratorium on the prosecution of claims by creditors, which moratorium did not prevent the Inland Revenue and other unsecured creditors from subsequently asserting their contractual rights as creditors of the company after the moratorium ended. The scheme had the requisite element of give and take as between the creditors to qualify as a 'scheme of arrangement'.

22-11   Typically, the agreement includes express terms precluding the commencement of proceedings by the CVA creditors against the company and/or the enforcement of their debts during the continuance of the agreement, provided the company is complying with the CVA. In the absence of an express term, the court may imply such a term in order to give

---

[7] IA 1986, s 4(3); as to the definition of 'secured creditor', see s 248.
[8] IA 1986, s 4(4); see s 386 and Sch 6.
[9] See *IRC v Wimbledon Football Club Ltd* [2005] 1 BCLC 66. If a third party chooses to pay certain non-preferential creditors out of his own funds, that is not a breach of IA 1986, s 4(4) conferring priority on preferential creditors. The creditors in this case were paid off by the buyer of the company's assets under a sale agreement and not under the CVA.
[10] [2001] 1 BCLC 222.   [11] See [2001] 1 BCLC 222 at 231.
[12] [2001] 1 BCLC 222 at 231, relying on Lightman J in *March Estates Ltd v Gunmark Ltd* [1996] 2 BCLC 1.

business efficacy to the agreement.[13] The proposal must also state how it is proposed to deal with the claims of unknown creditors (discussed at **22-17**).[14] Neither the supervisor (as the nominee becomes once the proposal is approved) nor the courts have any power to amend a CVA and so it is important that the arrangement contains an express power for its terms to be varied or altered which power will then limit the extent of any variation or alteration;[15] nor does the court have a power to direct a course of action by the supervisor which would involve a breach of the terms of the CVA other than to the extent that the terms of the CVA confer a power on the supervisor to depart from its terms.[16]

22-12   In *Prudential Assurance Co Ltd v PRG Powerhouse Ltd*[17] the court accepted that a CVA could operate to release third parties from obligations to the company. In this case, the claimant landlords were creditors of the insolvent company and the beneficiaries of guarantees (of rental payments due to them) given by the parent company of the insolvent company. The CVA allowed for the release of the company from its liabilities on the payment of 28p in the £1 to the creditors. The terms of the agreement required the claimants to treat the guarantees too as having been released and, the court said, the company (but not the parent) was entitled to enforce that obligation against the landlords. The court went on, however, to find the agreement was unfairly prejudicial to the landlord creditors, see **22-27**, but that does not detract from the court's acceptance that a CVA may release third parties from their obligations provided the agreement is not otherwise unfairly prejudicial.[18]

The voting rules

22-13   A significant advantage of a CVA is that there is no requirement for separate class meetings of creditors though, as can be seen from *Prudential Assurance Co Ltd v PRG Powerhouse Ltd*,[19] this can work to the disadvantage of a class of creditors who find themselves outvoted by other creditors with different interests.[20] There is just one meeting for creditors and one for members, with the meetings held on the same or different days, in either case with the creditors' meeting taking place first and the meetings must be held within seven days of each other.[21]

22-14   At the members' meeting, a majority of more than half in value of the ordinary shareholders is required in favour of the resolution and members vote according to the rights

---

[13] See *Johnson v Davies* [1998] 2 BCLC 252 (term implied that creditors would take no enforcement steps); *Sea Voyager Maritime Inc v Bielecki* [1999] 1 BCLC 133 at 149–51 (court considered that term might be implied to preclude commencement of proceedings); *Alman v Approach Housing Ltd* [2001] 1 BCLC 530 (strong grounds would be needed to imply term precluding commencement of proceedings).

[14] IR 1986, r 1.3(2)(fa).

[15] *Re Beloit Walmsley Ltd* [2009] 1 BCLC 584; see also *Re Alpha Lighting Ltd* [1997] BPIR 341, CA, noted Jones (1997) 10 Insolv Int 60; also *Raja v Rubin* [1999] 1 BCLC 621, CA; *Re Broome, Thompson v Broome* [1999] 1 BCLC 356.   [16] *Re Beloit Walmsley Ltd* [2009] 1 BCLC 584.

[17] [2008] 1 BCLC 289; and see Swain, 'Power Surge for Landlords' (2007) 20 Insolv Int 123.

[18] These releases, in the context of parent company guarantees of leases held by insolvent subsidiaries, being described as guarantee-stripping CVAs. As to this point, however, note the comment of Henderson J subsequently in *Mourant & Co Trustees Ltd v Sixty UK Ltd* [2011] 1 BCLC 383 at [71], '... although the possibility of "guarantee-stripping" in a CVA was established in the *PRG Powerhouse* case, and it has given rise to a good deal of debate among practitioners and academics, there is no subsequent reported case in which the court has had to consider whether and how a CVA might fairly effect a compromise of a landlord's claim against a guarantor of the tenant debtor'; see also at [88] on the obligations of the office-holder proposing such a CVA.   [19] [2008] 1 BCLC 289.

[20] A concern which may be met by making the consent of a class of creditors a term of the CVA, see Baird & Look Chan Ho, 'CVA—The Restructuring Trends' (2007) 20 Insolv Int 124.   [21] IR 1986, r 1.13(3), (4).

attached to their shares by the articles.[22] At the creditors' meeting, the proposal must be approved by a majority in excess of 75% in value of the creditors present (in person or by proxy) and voting on the resolution.[23] On other matters, a majority in excess of half in value is required.[24]

22-15   Each creditor who has notice of the creditors' meeting is entitled to vote and his vote is calculated according to the amount of his debt.[25] Secured creditors may not vote other than with respect to any element which is unsecured.[26] A creditor may vote in respect of a debt for an unliquidated amount and any debt where the value of the debt is unascertained and, for the purpose of voting only, the debt must be valued at £1 unless the chairman of the meeting agrees to put a higher value on it.[27] The result is that the creditor in respect of an unliquidated or unascertained debt becomes a creditor entitled to vote. A contingent creditor is also a 'creditor' for these purposes.[28]

22-16   This issue of entitlement to vote is crucial because a CVA which is approved binds every person entitled to vote at the creditors' meeting (whether or not he was present or represented at it) as if he were a party to the voluntary arrangement (IA 1986, s 5(2)). It is of crucial importance to the efficacy of the agreement that it should bind all the creditors as far as possible and it would be too easy for creditors to defeat a CVA merely by staying away from the meeting.[29]

22-17   A creditor is also bound even if for some reason he did not receive notice of the meeting and he is bound even if he is a creditor of whom the nominee was unaware and therefore was not someone to whom any notice was sent (IA 1986, s 5(2)). This latter point is an important change effected by the IA 2000 which is intended to make the binding effect of a CVA more extensive so that unknown creditors cannot undermine the agreement by appearing subsequently and pursuing their individual claims. Redress for the creditor who is bound but who was unaware of the CVA lies in his ability to go to court to challenge the approval of the CVA under IA 1986, s 6, see **22-23**.

22-18   The only creditors who are not bound are those who are not 'entitled to vote' and as entitlement to vote has been expanded, as noted at **22-15**, to include those with unliquidated debts and debts for unascertained amounts, the result is that only secured creditors are excluded and not bound by the CVA.[30] In practice, while not bound by it, the secured creditors must have indicated their support for the CVA, otherwise it is unlikely that the proposals would have come before a meeting of the creditors.

---

[22] See IR 1986, rr 1.18; 1.20.

[23] IR 1986, r 1.19(1); a majority in number of creditors is not required. 'Creditor' for these purposes includes a person entitled to a future or contingently payable debt, such as future payments of rent under an existing lease: *Re Cancol Ltd* [1996] 1 BCLC 100. If half in value of the creditors who are unconnected with the company vote against the resolution, the resolution is invalid, see IR 1986, r 1.19(4).

[24] IR 1986, r 1.19(2); and note the important constraint in r 1.19(4), see n 23.

[25] IR 1986, r 1.17(1), (2). The chairman determines the entitlement to vote and if he is in doubt as to whether to admit a claim, he must mark it as being objected to and allow the votes to be cast, subject to their being ruled invalid subsequently: see r 1.17A.   [26] IR 1986, r 1.19(3)(b).

[27] IR 1986, r 1.17(3). In *Doorbar v Alltime Securities Ltd* [1996] 1 BCLC 487 the Court of Appeal concluded that 'agrees' in this context does not require an agreement between the creditor and the chairman as to the estimated value, it simply means that the chairman must agree to place a value on the debt. See also *Re Newlands (Seaford) Educational Trust, Chittenden v Pepper* [2007] BCC 195.

[28] *Re T & N Ltd* [2006] 2 BCLC 374.

[29] See *Doorbar v Alltime Securities Ltd* [1996] 1 BCLC 487 at 497 on this point.   [30] See IA 1986, s 4(3).

22-19 The chairman of the meetings must report the result of the meetings to the court within four days[31] (though it is merely a report and there is no need to seek court approval) and he must send the report to every person who was sent notice of the meetings.[32] Once appointed, the supervisor (the title now given to the nominee) must forthwith send a copy of the chairman's report to the registrar of companies.[33]

22-20 Finally, it is an offence for an officer of the company for the purpose of obtaining the approval of the members or creditors to a proposal for a voluntary arrangement to make any false representations or fraudulently do or omit to do anything, even if the proposal is not approved (IA 1986, s 6A).

22-21 A decision to approve a CVA has effect if it is taken by the meeting of the company and the creditors or if it is taken by the creditors' meeting (IA 1986, s 4A(2)). In other words, the CVA has effect as long as the creditors approve it, even if the members reject it. If that happens, a member may apply to the court which may order the members' decision to have effect instead of a decision of the creditors or it may make such order as it thinks fit (s 4A(3)–(6)). It is unlikely that the court would overrule the decision of the creditors' meeting given that, without their commitment to the company and the proposed arrangement, it would be very difficult to make a CVA work effectively. In the light of this ability of the creditors to overrule the members' meeting, it might be asked whether there is any point in holding the members' meeting. The reason why it is still appropriate to hold a members' meeting is that the company is not necessarily insolvent and the members retain a residual interest in its assets. It is appropriate therefore that they should be able to express their views at a meeting, even if the creditors' interests prevail.

22-22 If the CVA is approved by the appropriate meetings, the voluntary arrangement takes effect as if made at the creditors' meeting. It binds every person entitled to vote at that meeting (whether or not he was present or represented at it) or who would have been so entitled if he had had notice of it, as if he were a party to the voluntary arrangement (IA 1986, s 5(2), see **22-17**). As noted, this outcome explains the importance of establishing a creditor's entitlement to vote, see **22-15**.

Challenging the approval

22-23 Anyone entitled to vote at the members' meeting or the creditors' meeting (or who would have been entitled to vote at the creditors' meeting if he had had notice of it), or the nominee, or the liquidator or administrator (if the company is being wound up or is in administration) may apply to the court under IA 1986, s 6 on one or both of the following grounds:[34]

  (1) that a voluntary arrangement which has taken effect[35] unfairly prejudices the interests of a creditor, member or contributory of the company;

  (2) that there has been some material irregularity at or in relation to either of those meetings.

---

[31] IA 1986, s 4(6); also IR 1986, r 1.24(3).

[32] IR 1986, r 1.24(4). Typically, the chairman is the nominee but he may need to nominate another, see IR 1986, r 1.14.   [33] IR 1986, r 1.24(5).

[34] Note the important time-limits within which this application must be made, essentially within 28 days of the report of the meetings being filed with the court, but with greater flexibility for a creditor who was unaware of, but who is bound by, the CVA: IA 1986, s 6(3); also s 6(7).

[35] i.e. has effect under IA 1986, s 4A which provides that the approval of the CVA takes effect either on the approval of both meetings or the approval of the creditors' meeting.

22-24 If the court is satisfied as to either of these grounds, it may revoke or suspend any decision giving effect to the CVA or any decision taken by a meeting where there has been a material irregularity and it may give directions to any person for the summoning of further meetings (IA 1986, s 6(4)–(6)).

22-25 The unfair prejudice must be to the interests of creditors as creditors and not in any other capacity[36] and the unfair prejudice complained of must be caused by the terms of the arrangement itself.[37] As any CVA which leaves a creditor in a less advantageous position than before the CVA is prejudicial, the question for the court will usually be whether it is unfairly prejudicial.[38] Important guidance as to the scope of this jurisdiction is found in *Prudential Assurance Co Ltd v PRG Powerhouse Ltd*[39] where Etherton J identified certain principles which should govern the court's approach to what is unfair prejudice in this context.[40] On the facts in *Powerhouse*, see **22-12**, the position was that, without the CVA, the landlords were in a position to rely on a guarantee of the rent due to them which had been given by the parent company of the insolvent company; within the CVA, they were obliged to treat the guarantees as having been released and could expect a dividend of 28p in the £1.

22-26 Etherton J noted that it is common ground that there is no single and universal test for judging unfairness in the context of IA 1986, s 6. The court must consider all the circumstances, including, in particular, the alternatives available and the practical consequences of a decision to confirm or reject the arrangement.[41] Unfairness may be assessed by a comparative analysis from a number of different angles, including vertical and horizontal comparisons[42] (a vertical comparison is with the position on winding up[43] and a horizontal comparison is with other creditors or classes of creditors). Another helpful comparison is with the position if, instead of a CVA, there had been a formal scheme of arrangement under CA 2006, Pt 26 (compromise or arrangement between a company and its creditors or members), while recognising that these are different processes.[44] Differential treatment of creditors is a relevant factor for the court to consider but it does not necessarily mean unfair prejudice.[45]

22-27 Returning to the facts in *Powerhouse*, under this CVA all the creditors, other than the landlords, were to be paid in full. In substance, the court said, the landlords' claims were to be discharged at a fraction of their value in order that other creditors would be paid in full.[46] While the authorities clearly show that there may be circumstances in which a CVA may properly provide for one set of creditors to be paid in full while others receive only a fraction of the sums due to them, the unusual feature of this case, the court said, was that

---

[36] *Doorbar v Alltime Securities Ltd* [1996] 1 BCLC 487; *Sea Voyager Maritime Inc v Bielecki* [1999] 1 BCLC 133; *Sisu Capital Fund Ltd v Tucker* [2006] BCC 463.   [37] *Sisu Capital Fund Ltd v Tucker* [2006] BCC 463.

[38] *Prudential Assurance Co Ltd v PRG Powerhouse Ltd* [2008] 1 BCLC 289 at [72].

[39] [2008] 1 BCLC 289.

[40] See [2008] 1 BCLC 289 at [74]–[96].

[41] [2008] 1 BCLC 289 at [74]; and see *Re a debtor (No 101 of 1999)* [2001] 1 BCLC 54 at 63; *Sisu Capital Fund Ltd v Tucker* [2006] BCC 463 at [71].   [42] [2008] 1 BCLC 289 at [75].

[43] He noted that a comparison with a winding up is always a useful starting point and a highly material comparison, see [2008] 1 BCLC 289 at [77], citing *Re T & N Ltd* [2005] 2 BCLC 488 at [82].

[44] [2008] 1 BCLC 289 at [76], [91]–[95], citing *Re T & N Ltd* [2005] 2 BCLC 488 at [81].

[45] [2008] 1 BCLC 289 at [86]–[89]; and see *Re a debtor (No 101 of 1999)* [2001] 1 BCLC 54; *Re a debtor (No 87 of 1993) (No 2)* [1996] 1 BCLC 63 at 86, per Rimer J; *Re a debtor (No 259 of 1990)* [1992] 1 All ER 641 at 643. Equally, the prejudice may arise from failing to distinguish between creditors, as where creditors with interests under the Third Party (Rights Against Insurers) Act 1930 were not treated differently from other creditors: see *Sea Voyager Maritime Inc v Bielecki* [1999] 1 BCLC 133.   [46] [2008] 1 BCLC 289 at [105].

on a winding up the landlords would still have had the benefit of the valuable guarantees of the parent company, whereas the other unsecured creditors would receive nothing.[47] In other words, the court said, the landlords were the class of creditors that would suffer least in the event of an insolvent liquidation of the company, but they were the group most prejudiced by the CVA.[48] In effect, the votes of those unsecured creditors who stood to lose nothing from the CVA and had everything to gain from it swamped the votes of the landlords who were significantly disadvantaged by it.[49] The court was satisfied that the CVA unfairly prejudiced the interests of the claimants as creditors of the company and the approval of the proposal was set aside.

22-28   The approach adopted in *Powerhouse* was applied in *Mourant & Co Trustees Ltd v Sixty UK Ltd*[50] where, on the facts, the High Court was very critical of an attempt to use a CVA to release a solvent parent company from rent guarantees given in respect of an insolvent subsidiary company which was in administration. Setting aside the CVA, Henderson J found the terms of the release were unfairly prejudicial and the administrators' conduct in proposing a CVA of the type involved here was open to criticism. In this case, the effect of the CVA essentially was that the solvent parent company guarantor was to be released from all liability under the guarantees upon payment of a sum of £300,000 to the land-lords, the £300,000 being said to represent 100% of the lessee company's estimated liability to the applicants on surrender of the leases, calculated on the basis of advice received and certain assumptions. The proposal was approved at a creditors' meeting. Henderson J thought the facts were very similar to *Powerhouse,* the only essential difference being that the landlords were offered the full amount of the value placed on their rights.[51] Applying the principles identified by Etherton J in *Powerhouse,* it was unreasonable and unfair in principle to require the landlord to give up the guarantees.[52] At a time of market uncertainty it would be difficult, if not impossible, to determine what sum would fairly compensate the landlord for the loss of the right to enforce the terms of a lease against a guarantor and, in the absence of a compelling justification, a landlord should not be forced to accept a sum which was based on numerous assumptions (for example about the landlord's ability to re-let the premises) which might or might not prove to have been well-founded.[53] To adopt such a procedure, in circumstances where the solvency of the guarantor was not in issue, Henderson J thought, was to undermine the basic commercial function of the guarantee and to force the landlord to accept a commercially inferior substitute for it.

22-29   Returning to the facts in *Mourant*, the ability to enforce the terms of the existing leases against the guarantor for a further seven and a half years was a most valuable right, and there was no sufficient justification for requiring any of the guaranteed landlords to accept a sum of money in lieu.[54] Even if that conclusion was wrong, on the evidence, a figure in the region of £1m was the least that could have been fairly regarded as appropriate. The position was made worse by the fact that £300,000 was not, in fact, a genuine estimate of the value of the applicants' claim, but had instead been dictated to the administrators

---

[47] [2008] 1 BCLC 289 at [106].   [48] [2008] 1 BCLC 289 at [107].   [49] [2008] 1 BCLC 289 at [108].
[50] [2011] 1 BCLC 383.
[51] [2011] 1 BCLC 383 at [77]. That apart, Henderson J said, the similarities were striking: 'on a winding up, the applicants would still have had the benefit of the guarantees, and there was no reason to doubt the ability of Sixty SpA (the parent company) to honour them (see below); the guaranteed landlords would have formed a separate class for the purposes of a formal scheme of arrangement under s 899 of the 2006 Act, and would clearly have vetoed any such scheme; and the CVA was passed by the votes of the unsecured creditors, who stood to lose nothing from the CVA and whose votes inevitably swamped those of the guaranteed landlords.'
[52] [2011] 1 BCLC 383 at [77].   [53] [2011] 1 BCLC 383 at [77].   [54] [2011] 1 BCLC 383 at [77].

by the parent company.[55] The administrators had allowed the parent company to dictate the offer to be made to the landlords, secure in the knowledge that the CVA would be passed by a large majority of unsecured creditors who would be paid in full and that the landlords would then face lengthy and expensive court proceedings before the CVA could be overturned.[56] In all the circumstances, the court thought it was abundantly clear that the CVA was fatally flawed and had to be set aside.[57] Where the challenge under IA 1986, s 6 is on the grounds of a material irregularity, it is necessary to establish both elements: irregularity and materiality.[58] Where the irregularity is the non-disclosure of information, the question is whether the revelation of the truth would have made a difference to the way in which the creditors would have considered the terms of the CVA and whether there was a substantial chance (which does not have to be beyond 50%) that they would not have approved the CVA as presented.[59]

Implementing the arrangement

22-30 On approval of the scheme, the nominee becomes the supervisor (IA 1986, s 7(2)) and he sets about the implementation of the CVA. Typically he holds any funds in his possession on trust for the CVA creditors pursuant to the terms of and for the purposes of the voluntary arrangement.[60] A supervisor may apply to the court for directions if necessary (s 7(4)), but the court has no power to give directions or to authorise a supervisor of a CVA to breach such a trust, for example, to allow a distribution to a wider class of creditor than the CVA creditors.[61] Any creditor or any other person dissatisfied by the conduct of the supervisor may apply to the court which may confirm, reverse or modify any act or decision or give the supervisor directions or make such other order as it thinks fit (s 7(3)).

Terminating the arrangement

22-31 A CVA may be completed either at the end of a specified period or earlier if all the payments required by the CVA have been made. Equally, it may not prove possible to proceed with the CVA and it may be necessary to terminate the agreement, typically because the company has failed to maintain the level of payments to creditors required by the CVA. In that case, the supervisor can petition for winding up or for an administration order.[62] Indeed while the CVA is continuing, it is possible that the members will resolve to place the company into voluntary liquidation, even if that has the effect of breaching

---

[55] [2011] 1 BCLC 383 at [78].   [56] [2011] 1 BCLC 383 at [79], [87]–[90].

[57] [2011] 1 BCLC 383 at [86]. Indeed the judge considered that this was a CVA 'which should never have seen the light of day', stressing the duty of administrators in such circumstances to maintain an independent stance and only to propose a CVA if they are satisfied that it will not unfairly prejudice the interests of any creditor, member or contributory of the company, see at [86]. His final act was to direct that the judgment be sent to the professional body governing the administrators in this case, see at [90].

[58] *HMRC v Portsmouth Football Club Ltd* [2011] BCC 149.

[59] *HMRC v Portsmouth Football Club Ltd* [2011] BCC 149; *Re Trident Fashions plc (No 2)* [2004] 2 BCLC 35.

[60] *Re NT Gallagher & Son Ltd* [2002] 3 All ER 474; see also *Welburn v Dibb Lupton Broomhead* [2003] BPIR 768, CA.   [61] *Re Beloit Walmsley Ltd* [2009] 1 BCLC 584.

[62] IA 1986, s 7(4); and the supervisor may then be appointed as the liquidator: s 140(2). Typically, a CVA provides that the supervisor must petition for the compulsory winding up of the company if the company is not complying with the CVA.

the arrangement; likewise a non-CVA creditor may petition the court for the compulsory winding up of the company.[63]

22-32   Following completion (or termination) of the CVA, the supervisor must send notice to this effect within 28 days to all the creditors and members bound by the CVA together with a copy of a report drawn up by him and summarising all receipts and payments by him.[64] Notice must also be given within the 28-day period to the registrar of companies and to the court (IR 1986, r 1.29).

22-33   The effect on the CVA if the CVA is terminated by the company going into liquidation was the subject of a number of conflicting first instance decisions[65] which differed as to whether the trust in favour of the CVA creditors continued or whether the supervisor had to hand over any assets of the company in his control to the liquidator which assets were then freed from any trust for the creditors under the CVA and became subject to the statutory trust arising on compulsory liquidation, see **24-47**.

22-34   The matter was resolved by the Court of Appeal in *Re NT Gallagher & Son Ltd*.[66] The company in this case entered into a CVA in 1995 before going into a creditors' voluntary winding up in October 1997. The company's assets were a claim against a principal customer (for £2.3m); a claim against another company for £350,000; and realisable assets of £98,000. Its total liabilities were just over £5m of which £2.5m were post-CVA liabilities. The liquidators sought a direction as to whether sums retained by the supervisors of the CVA (some £570,000), the benefit of the cause of action against the principal customer and the other assets, were held on trust for the sole benefit of the CVA creditors or were available for distribution to all the creditors of the company in accordance with the statutory scheme applicable on winding up. The Court of Appeal reached the following conclusions.

22-35   Where a CVA provides for moneys or other assets to be paid to or transferred or held for the benefit of the CVA creditors, this creates a trust of those moneys or assets for those creditors, but which assets are the subject of the trust depends on the terms of the arrangement. On the facts in this case, the sums retained by the supervisors and the claim against the principal customer were the subject of the CVA trust but the other realisable assets were not.

22-36   The effect of the liquidation of the company on the trust created by the CVA depends on the provisions of the CVA which can, and should, provide for what is to happen to the assets on the termination of the CVA. If the CVA provides what is to happen on liquidation, effect must be given thereto. If the CVA does not so provide, the trust continues notwithstanding the liquidation and must take effect according to its terms. The court thought that to conclude otherwise would run counter to the general law which left trusts of assets not held for a company unaffected by its liquidation. Furthermore, as a matter of policy, in the absence of any provision in the CVA as to what should happen to trust assets on liquidation of the company, the applicable default rule should be one that furthered rather than hindered what might be taken to be the statutory purpose of IA 1986, Pt I.

---

[63] See *Re Arthur Rathbone Kitchens Ltd* [1997] 2 BCLC 280; *Re Excalibur Airways Ltd* [1998] 1 BCLC 436.

[64] IR 1986, r 1.29. In the case of termination, the report must explain why the CVA has been terminated.

[65] The authorities are considered in *Re NT Gallagher & Son Ltd* [2002] 2 BCLC 133 at 143–6.

[66] [2002] 2 BCLC 133, CA.

22-37 The Court of Appeal acknowledged the possibility that there may be post-CVA creditors who are unaware of the CVA and its terms,[67] but it thought that in practice there is likely to be a considerable overlap between CVA and post-CVA creditors and, in any event, no one is forced to become a creditor of a company without making such inquiries as are thought appropriate to ascertain the financial position of the company. The court considered that Parliament plainly intended to encourage companies and creditors to enter into CVAs so as to provide creditors with a means of recovering what they were owed without recourse to the more expensive means provided by winding up or administration while giving companies the opportunity to continue to trade. If the trust was terminated, trust assets under the CVA which happened not to have been distributed before the liquidation would become available to the post-CVA creditors as well as CVA creditors which would be a disincentive to creditors to agree to a CVA and to keep it in operation. Furthermore, since the liquidation of the company brought the CVA to an end, though not the trust created thereunder, it was only just that the CVA creditors should be able to prove in the liquidation for so much of their debt as remained after payment of what had been or would be recovered under the trust.

22-38 This ruling by the Court of Appeal acts as an incentive for creditors to enter into CVAs, given this ring-fencing of the CVA assets in the hands of the supervisor on liquidation. Equally, however, it may make it difficult to ensure continued support by post-CVA creditors and may therefore make continued trading while in a CVA more difficult.

C Company voluntary arrangement with a moratorium

22-39 As noted the IA 1986 was amended by the IA 2000 to allow directors wishing to propose a CVA to obtain a moratorium from actions against the company by creditors so making it easier to negotiate a CVA.[68] Where the directors wish to proceed in this way, the CVA is governed by IA 1986, Sch A1. In practice the scheme has proved unpopular. The advantage of the moratorium is outweighed by the relative complexity (and resulting costs) of the scheme. The necessary publicity attached to the moratorium also renders the process unsuitable for companies where publicity given to financial difficulties will drive their customers away and render future trading impossible. The onerous obligations and possible liabilities which attach to the supervisor also make it unattractive. Finally, the scheme was overtaken by the reforms to administration effected by the EA 2002 which allow in particular for the speedy appointment of out of court of administrators (see **23-19**) and companies in administration benefit from a moratorium.

22-40 The first limitation on use of the CVA with a moratorium is that many classes of companies are excluded or ineligible[69] leaving as eligible companies essentially small private companies which meet two out of the three criteria for 'small' in CA 2006, s 382. The requirements are that the company has a turnover of not more than £6.5m; a balance sheet total of not more than £3.26m; and the number of employees must not exceed 50. Additionally, the company must not be a holding company of a group of companies which does not qualify as a small group or a medium-sized group in respect of the last financial year of the company before the date of filing of the required documents.[70] The company

---

[67] Despite the existence of the CVA being reported to the registrar of companies by the supervisor: see IR 1986, r 1.24(5).   [68] IA 1986, s 1A.

[69] See IA 1986, Sch A1, paras 2–4.

[70] IA 1986, Sch A1, para 3(4). A group qualifies as small or medium-sized if it qualifies as such under CA 2006, s 383(2)–(7) (small) or s 466(2)–(7) (medium): Sch A1, para 3(5).

must not be in administration or being wound up; there must not be an administrative receiver or a provisional liquidator in place or a voluntary arrangement in effect in relation to the company; and there must not have been an administrator appointed or a failed CVA in the previous 12 months.[71]

Obtaining a moratorium

22-41 Where the directors of a company wish to obtain a moratorium, they must submit to the nominee a document setting out the terms of the proposed voluntary arrangement and a statement of the company's affairs and any other information requested by the nominee.[72] It is an offence for an officer of the company for the purpose of obtaining a moratorium or an extension of a moratorium to make any false representations or fraudulently do or omit to do anything.[73] The nominee in turn must submit to the directors a statement indicating whether in his opinion:[74]

(1) the proposed voluntary arrangement has a reasonable prospect of being approved and implemented;

(2) the company is likely to have sufficient funds available to it during the proposed moratorium to enable it to carry on its business; and

(3) meetings of the company and its creditors should be summoned to consider the proposed voluntary arrangement.

22-42 If the nominee supports the proposed voluntary arrangement, the directors must file with the court:

(1) a document setting out the terms of the proposed voluntary arrangement;

(2) a statement of the company's affairs;

(3) a statement that the company is eligible for a moratorium;

(4) a statement from the nominee that he has given his consent to act; and

(5) a statement from the nominee that, in his opinion the proposed voluntary arrangement has a reasonable prospect of being approved and implemented, and the company is likely to have sufficient funds available to it during the proposed moratorium to enable it to carry on its business, and that meetings of the company and its creditors should be summoned to consider the proposed voluntary arrangement (Sch A1, para 7(1)).

22-43 The moratorium comes into force when these documents are filed by the directors with the court.[75] When a moratorium comes into force, the directors must notify the nominee[76] and the nominee must advertise that fact,[77] and notify the registrar of companies, the company and any petitioning creditor of the company of whose claim he is aware, of

---

[71] See IA 1986, Sch A1, para 4(1).
[72] IA 1986, Sch A1, para 6(1). The nominee must be a qualified insolvency practitioner or someone authorised to act as nominee in relation to the voluntary arrangement: s 1(2). The statement of affairs must contain such particulars of the company's creditors and of its debts and other liabilities and of its assets as is prescribed by IR 1986, r 1.37.   [73] IA 1986, Sch A1, para 42.
[74] IA 1986, Sch A1, para 6(2). In forming his opinion, the nominee is entitled to rely on the information submitted to him by the directors unless he has reason to doubt its accuracy: para 6(3).
[75] IA 1986, Sch A1, para 8(1).   [76] IA 1986, Sch A1, para 9(1).
[77] i.e. in the *London Gazette* and a newspaper: see IR 1986, r 1.40(2).

that fact.[78] Every invoice, order for goods or services, business letter or order form which is issued by or on behalf of the company and all the company's websites must contain the nominee's name and a statement that the moratorium is in force for the company.[79]

Duration and effect of the moratorium

22-44 The moratorium ends at the end of the last day on which the meetings of the company and its creditors (summoned by the nominee) are first held,[80] and the nominee has 28 days from the date of filing of the documents securing the moratorium to call those meetings. The moratorium may last 28 days therefore, but it may be shorter as where, for example, the meetings are held much earlier in the 28-day period and decide to approve a voluntary arrangement[81] or reject the agreement.[82] The meetings summoned may resolve that the moratorium be extended but the moratorium may not be extended for more than two months from the date of the meeting.[83] The moratorium comes to an end if the nominee withdraws his consent to act or the court so orders.[84] When a moratorium comes to an end, the nominee must advertise that fact forthwith and notify the court, the registrar of companies, the company and any creditor of the company of whose claim he is aware, of that fact.[85]

22-45 The restrictions arising under the moratorium are very similar to those which apply on a company going into administration (see the detailed discussion at **23-62**). The standard restrictions apply: no petition (other than public interest petitions) may be presented for the winding up of the company;[86] no administration application may be made in respect of the company: and no administrator may be appointed out of court (IA 1986, Sch A1, para 12(1)). No other steps may be taken to enforce any security over the company's property, or to repossess goods in the company's possession under any hire-purchase agreement, except with the leave of the court and subject to such terms as the court may impose; and no other proceedings and no execution or other legal process may be commenced or continued, and no distress may be levied, against the company or its property except with the leave of the court and subject to such terms as the court may impose.[87]

22-46 Various restrictions are imposed on the company's activities during the period of the moratorium, such as a restriction on the ability to raise credit and limitations on the power to dispose of any company property other than in the ordinary course of business.[88] Transactions entered into in breach of these restrictions remain valid,[89] but the company is liable to a fine and any officer of the company who authorises or permits the contravention, without reasonable excuse, is liable to imprisonment or a fine, or both.[90]

---

[78] IA 1986, Sch A1, para 10(1); and see IR 1986, r 1.40(3). A 'petitioning creditor' means a creditor by whom a winding-up petition has been presented before the beginning of the moratorium, as long as the petition has not been dismissed or withdrawn; see IA 1986, Sch A1, para 10(2).

[79] IA 1986, Sch A1, para 16(1).   [80] IA 1986, Sch A1, para 8(2).   [81] IA 1986, Sch A1, para 8(7).

[82] IA 1986, Sch A1, para 8(6)(c).

[83] IA 1986, Sch A1, para 32(2) and, if the meetings are held on separate dates, the extension is from the date when the last meeting is held. The nominee must set out the expected costs of the extension and the meetings must approve those expected costs otherwise the moratorium comes to an end: see para 32(4), (5). If a decision is taken to extend the moratorium by either the company and the creditors or by the creditors, the extension takes effect and the nominee must notify the registrar of companies and the court: para 34(1).

[84] See IA 1986, Sch A1, paras 8(6)(b), 25(4).   [85] IA 1986, Sch A1, para 11; and see IR 1986, r 1.42.

[86] IA 1986, Sch A1, para 12(4), (5).

[87] IA 1986, Sch A1, para 12(1); and see the limitation on enforcement in para 13(5).

[88] IA 1986, Sch A1, paras 17(1), 18(1), (2), 19(1).   [89] IA 1986, Sch A1, para 15(2).

[90] See IA 1986, Sch A1, paras 17(3), 18(3), 19(3).

Role of the nominee during the moratorium

22-47　During a moratorium, the nominee must monitor the company's affairs[91] and he must withdraw his consent to act if, at any time during a moratorium, he forms the opinion that:

(1) the proposed voluntary arrangement no longer has a reasonable prospect of being approved or implemented; or

(2) the company will not have sufficient funds available to it during the remainder of the moratorium to enable it to continue to carry on its business; or

(3) he becomes aware that, on the date of filing of the documents with the court, the company was not eligible for a moratorium; or

(4) the directors fail to provide him with the necessary information to carry out his monitoring obligations (IA 1986, Sch A1, para 25(2)).

22-48　If the nominee withdraws his consent to act, the moratorium comes to an end and he must notify the court, the registrar of companies, the company and any creditor of the company of whose claim he is aware, of his withdrawal and the reason for it.[92]

22-49　Any creditor, director or member of the company, or any other person affected by a moratorium, who is dissatisfied by the conduct of the nominee during the moratorium, may apply to the court either during the moratorium or after it has ended.[93] Additionally, where there are reasonable grounds for believing that as a result of any act etc of the nominee during the moratorium, the company has suffered loss, but the company does not intend to pursue any claim it may have against the nominee, any creditor may apply to the court during the moratorium or after it has ended.[94] The court may order the company to pursue any claim against the nominee, authorise any creditor to pursue such a claim in the name of the company, or make such other order as it thinks fit, unless the court is satisfied that the act etc of the nominee was in all the circumstances reasonable.[95] For the nominee, the combination of the obligation to monitor with the risk of potential challenge and liability under these provisions is a significant deterrent to use of this form of CVA.

Role of the directors during the moratorium

22-50　The onerous obligations imposed on nominees arise in part out of concerns that unscrupulous directors might use the 28-day moratorium, given that they remain in control of the company, to deal with the assets in an unacceptable way—hence the requirement that the nominee has an ongoing responsibility for monitoring the conduct of the company's affairs during the moratorium and his obligation to withdraw his consent to act in certain cases, so bringing the moratorium to an end.[96] Additionally, provision is made for creditors

---

[91]　IA 1986, Sch A1, para 24(1). The directors must submit to the nominee any information necessary to enable him to comply with this monitoring obligation which he requests from them: para 24(2). In forming his opinion, the nominee is entitled to rely on the information submitted to him by the directors unless he has reason to doubt its accuracy: para 24(3).
[92]　IA 1986, Sch A1, para 25(4), (5); see also IR 1986, r 1.44.　　[93]　IA 1986, Sch A1, para 26(1), (2).
[94]　IA 1986, Sch A1, para 27(1), (2).　　[95]　IA 1986, Sch A1, para 27(3).
[96]　See IA 1986, Sch A1, paras 24, 25(2), (4).

and members to challenge the conduct of the directors in court and the civil remedies are bolstered by a number of criminal offences.[97]

22-51   A creditor or member of the company may apply to the court during or after the moratorium for an order on the ground that the company's affairs are being or have been managed by the directors in a manner which is unfairly prejudicial to the interests of its creditors or members generally, or of some part of its creditors or members (including at least the petitioner), or that any actual or proposed act or omission of the directors is or would be so prejudicial.[98] The court has wide powers on any such application to make any appropriate order.[99]

Approving an arrangement

22-52   Where a moratorium is in force, the nominee must summon meetings of the company and its creditors (i.e. every creditor of whose claim the nominee is aware) as he thinks fit and not later than 28 days after the date on which the moratorium came into force.[100] The meetings must decide whether to approve the proposed voluntary arrangement (with or without modifications).[101] As with CVAs without a moratorium, no proposal or modification may affect the rights of secured or preferential creditors without their consent.[102] The voting requirements are similar in most respects also to those discussed at **22-13**. After the conclusion of either meeting, the chairman of the meeting must report the result of the meeting to the court within four days[103] and, immediately after reporting to the court, must give notice of the result of the meeting to every person who has sent notice of the meeting.[104]

22-53   A decision to approve the CVA or an extension to the moratorium or a decision to bring the moratorium to an end has effect if it has been taken by the meeting of the company and the creditors or if it has been taken by the creditors' meeting.[105] Where a decision approving a voluntary arrangement has effect,[106] the CVA takes effect as if made at the creditors' meeting and binds every person who was entitled to vote at that meeting (whether or not he was present or represented at it), or would have been so entitled if he had had notice of it, as if he were a party to the voluntary arrangement.[107] Following approval, any petition for the winding up of the company (other than a public interest petition) presented before the beginning of the moratorium, must be dismissed by the court.[108] If, when the moratorium comes to an end, no CVA has been approved, one or more creditors may present a

---

[97]   See IA 1986, Sch A1, para 41, also IA 1986, s 7A which makes further provision for the prosecution of these offences and in particular imposes an obligation on the nominee or supervisor where it appears a criminal offence may have been committed to report that matter to the appropriate authority (the Secretary of State).   [98]   IA 1986, Sch A1, para 40(2), (3).

[99]   Including an order regulating the management by the directors during the remainder of the moratorium; requiring them to do or refrain from doing any act; summoning a meeting of the creditors or members or bringing the moratorium to an end, see IA 1986, Sch A1, para 40(4), (5).

[100]   IA 1986, Sch A1, para 29(1), (2); IR 1986, r 1.48.   [101]   IA 1986, Sch A1, para 31(1).

[102]   IA 1986, Sch A1, para 31(4), (5).   [103]   IR 1986, r 1.54(2) applying r 1.24(3)–(5).

[104]   IA 1986, Sch A1, para 30(3); see IR 1986, r 1.24(4) which applies: r 1.54(3)(b).

[105]   IA 1986, Sch A1, para 36(2).

[106]   i.e. the CVA is agreed at a meeting of the company and of the creditors or a meeting of the creditors: IA 1986, Sch A1, para 36(2).   [107]   IA 1986, Sch A1, para 37(1), (2).

[108]   IA 1986, Sch A1, para 37(4), and subject to para 37(5).

petition for winding up the company on that ground,[109] i.e. without establishing that the company is unable to pay its debts.

22-54 As is the case with a CVA without a moratorium, it is possible to challenge the approval of a CVA by applying to the court on the grounds that the CVA unfairly prejudices the interests of a creditor, member or contributory of the company and/or that there has been some material irregularity at or in relation to the meetings:[110] see **22-23**.

Implementing the arrangement

22-55 Where a voluntary arrangement approved by one or both of the meetings has taken effect, the implementation of the CVA is as discussed at **22-30**. The nominee becomes the supervisor of the voluntary arrangement[111] and, on approval of the CVA, he must send a copy of the chairman's report of the result of the meetings to the registrar of companies.[112] Once in post, the supervisor sets about the implementation of the CVA and he holds any funds in his possession on trust for the CVA creditors pursuant to the terms of the voluntary arrangement.[113]

Terminating the arrangement

22-56 The CVA may come to an end through completion or termination and the supervisor must send notice to this effect within 28 days to all the creditors and members bound by the CVA, together with a copy of a report drawn up by the supervisor and summarising all receipts and payments by him.[114] Notice must also be given to the registrar of companies and to the court.[115] Where the company goes into liquidation, the effect on the CVA creditors and assets held by the supervisor is as discussed at **21-33** et seq.

---

[109] IA 1986, ss 122(1)(fa), 124(3A).
[110] IA 1986, Sch A1, para 38(1), (2); and see the time-limits within which this application must be made: para 38(3).
[111] IA 1986, Sch A1, para 39(1), (2).   [112] IR 1986, r 1.54(2) applying r 1.24(5).
[113] *Re NT Gallagher & Son Ltd* [2002] 2 BCLC 133, CA.
[114] IR 1986, r 1.29. In the case of termination, the report must explain why the CVA has been terminated.
[115] IR 1986, r 1.29.

23

Corporate rescue–administration

A Introduction

Background–rescue and the Cork Committee

23-1 The origins of administration lie in the recommendation of the Cork Committee on Insolvency Law that provision should be made to enable a person called an administrator to be appointed to an insolvent but potentially viable company with all the powers normally conferred upon a receiver and manager under a floating charge including power to carry on the business of the company and to borrow for that purpose.[1] The intention was to provide a breathing-space, free from the pressure of creditors' claims, which would enable the administrator to consider whether the business could be rescued and/or to negotiate with creditors regarding any possible arrangement or compromise of the company's debts.

23-2 Administration was introduced by the Insolvency Act 1985 and consolidated in the Insolvency Act 1986, Pt 11, before being entirely recast and reformed by the Enterprise Act 2002 as a result of a decade of discussion as to the role, purpose and structure of administration.[2] The current administration provisions of general application are set out in IA 1986, Sch B1 which was inserted by the EA 2002.[3]

23-3 The background to the enactment of the EA 2002 was that, after much consultation, the Government had concluded that administrative receivership should cease to be a major insolvency procedure (discussed at **21-84**) and there should be wholesale reform of the administration regime.[4] Essentially, the Government's concerns with respect to

---

[1] *Report of the Review Committee on Insolvency Law and Practice*, Cmnd 8558 (1982), para 497. The Cork Committee envisaged administration as being a secondary procedure to administrative receivership and of use primarily where, for whatever reason, an administrative receiver could not be appointed: see para 503. In practice, administration has evolved in a very different way to that envisaged by Cork.

[2] See Insolvency Service, *The Insolvency Act 1986, Company Voluntary Arrangements and Administration Orders, A Consultative Document* (October 1993); *A Review of Company Rescue and Business Reconstruction Mechanisms* (September 1999); *A Review of Company Rescue and Business Reconstruction Mechanisms, Report by the Review Group* (May 2000).

[3] There are special administration regimes for other specific sectors such as investment banks, but those regimes are beyond the scope of this work.

[4] DTI, 'Productivity and Enterprise—Insolvency: A Second Chance' (Cm 5234, 2001) (hereinafter 'Productivity and Enterprise'). Much valuable work on the evaluation of the EA 2002 reforms has been conducted for the Insolvency Service by insolvency expert Dr Sandra Frisby: see Frisby, 'The Pre-Pack Progression: Latest Empirical Findings' (2008) 21 Insolv Int 154; also Frisby, *Report on Insolvency Outcomes—Presented to the Insolvency Service* (2006) and *Interim Report to the Insolvency Service on Returns to Creditors from Pre- and Post-Enterprise Insolvency Procedures* (2007) which reports formed the basis, with other studies, for the Insolvency Service's *Evaluation Report on the Enterprise Act 2002—Corporate Insolvency Provisions* (January 2008). See generally Finch, 'Corporate Rescue Processes, the Search for Quality and the Capacity

the appointment of administrative receivers related to issues such as the extent to which that procedure provided adequate incentives to maximise economic value; whether there was an adequate level of transparency and accountability to a range of stakeholders; unease with the fact that the administrative receiver's principal obligations were towards his appointor even though receivership impacted substantially on the interests of the unsecured creditors; and the fact that administrative receiverships fitted badly into international law which generally emphasises collective procedures.[5] The Government's view was that on the grounds of both equity and efficiency the time had come to:[6]

> 'tip the balance firmly in favour of collective insolvency procedures—proceedings in which all creditors participate, under which a duty is owed to all creditors and in which all creditors may look to an office-holder for an account of his dealings with the company's assets'.

23-4 It was therefore decided that administrative receivership should cease to be a major insolvency procedure and there should be a statutory restriction on the right to appoint an administrative receiver (other than with respect to certain transactions in the capital markets).[7] Instead, a floating chargeholder would be able to petition for an administration order and, in some cases, to petition without notice and, given this shift to administration as the main rescue procedure, that procedure would be reformed to ensure it operated effectively.[8] Overall, the Government believed that the result would be a procedure which would be as flexible and cost-effective as administrative receivership, but with an administrator owing a duty to act in the interests of all creditors, with unsecured creditors having an opportunity for input and participation and the process being subject to the oversight and direction of the court in a public and transparent way.[9] The Government subsequently updated its proposals to make provision for out-of-court routes into administration.[10] Before turning to examine the statutory scheme in IA 1986, Sch B1 in detail, it is necessary to consider the development of pre-pack administrations.

Pre-pack administrations

23-5 One of the more controversial aspects of administration in recent years has been the emergence of the 'pre-pack' as a standard administration mechanism.[11] A pre-pack is a pre-packaged sale of the business agreed before the company enters administration and executed immediately thereafter. The business is transferred to the purchaser (often the existing management) and the company in administration is left as a shell consisting of its liabilities and the proceeds of sale which are then distributed by the administrator, usually to the secured creditor who was party to the negotiation of the pre-pack. There is a mismatch between this pre-pack process and the legislation 'on the books'[12] which is the subject of the remainder of this chapter. The statutory scheme envisages a

---

to Resolve' [2010] JBL 503 who looks at the evolution of 'rescue' over the decades since the Cork Committee Report. Also, Finch, 'Corporate Rescue: Who is interested?' [2012] JBC 190.

[5] See *Productivity and Enterprise*, n 4, paras 2.2–2.3.   [6] *Productivity and Enterprise*, n 4, para 2.5.
[7] *Productivity and Enterprise*, n 4, para 2.5.   [8] *Productivity and Enterprise*, n 4, paras 2.8, 2.10.
[9] *Productivity and Enterprise*, n 4, para 2.12.
[10] See Insolvency Service, *An Update on the* Corporate *Insolvency Proposals* (14 January 2002).
[11] For a useful summary of the concerns raised by pre-packs, see *Re Kayley Vending Ltd* [2011] 1 BCLC 114 at [6]–[12].
[12] As one commentator put it, pre-packs are invisible in the insolvency legislation, see Davies, 'Pre-pack—He who pays the piper calls the tune' Recovery (Summer 2006), p 16; also Walton, 'Pre-Packaged Administration—Trick or Treat' (2006) 19 Insolv Int 113.

process taking place over weeks and months with an administrator first being appointed, then drawing up proposals to be considered, discussed and approved by the creditors within the breathing space of a moratorium preventing a free-for-all amongst the creditors, before the business is either rescued or sold in keeping with the statutory purposes of administration discussed at **23-12**. The pre-pack process, which the Insolvency Service believes accounts for about 30% of all administrations, is quite different from the statutory scheme. It involves:

- a sale being agreed (after discussions involving the management, the main creditor or creditors, typically the holder of the floating charge, and an insolvency practitioner);

- an administrator being appointed (usually out of court by the directors or the major creditor);

- the immediate sale of the business (frequently to the management), executed instantly on the appointment of the administrator,[13] without any creditors' meeting being called or any proposals being approved (as the administrator is entitled to do, see **23-85**) and with the creditors informed after the event;

- finally, the proceeds of sale are distributed by the administrator and as typically there will not be any funds or only very limited funds for distribution to the unsecured creditors, the administrator files a notice with the registrar and the company is dissolved under Sch B1, para 84, see **23-111**.

23-6 The arguments in favour of pre-packaged administration are that it offers precisely the sort of rapid, solution-driven, process which is required when a company is in financial difficulties and does so without the business being visibly in an insolvency process so maximising value.[14] The focus is on 'rescuing' those elements of the business which can be salvaged and on preserving brands and employment. The speedy sale and the fact that the administration itself is short enables costs to be reduced. The reality in many instances is that there will be nothing left for unsecured creditors and there are no willing purchasers other than the existing management for whom a pre-pack is an opportunity to salvage something from the situation.[15] Also, as we shall see, aggrieved creditors are not without means of redress, as discussed at **23-98**.

23-7 However, pre-packs are controversial and have attracted a considerable amount of critical comment including adverse media coverage.[16] Broadly, the issue is whether this process is compatible with the spirit of informed creditor participation, particularly for

---

[13] Sales to the directors when the company is in administration do not require shareholder approval under CA 2006, s 190: see s 193(1).

[14] Indeed its attractions are such that companies have re-located to this jurisdiction in order to take advantage of the process, see *Re Hellas Telecommunications (Luxembourg) II SCA* [2010] BCC 295; *Re European Directories (DH6) BV* [2012] BCC 46.

[15] See Frisby, *Report to the Association of Business Recovery Professionals, A Preliminary Analysis of pre-packaged administrations* (August 2007), p 46 who found a demonstrable trend towards pre-pack sales to connected persons, but also that pre-packs perform better than business sales in preserving employment, p 71.

[16] See generally Finch, 'Pre-packaged Administration and the Construction of Propriety' (2011) 11 J Corp L Studies 1; Haywood, 'Pre-pack administration' (2010) Insolv Into 17; Xie, 'Regulating Pre-pack Administrations' [2010] JBL 513; Walton, 'Pre-appointment Administration Fees—Papering over the Cracks in Pre-packs?' (2008) 21 Insolv Int 72; Kastrinou, 'An Analysis of the Pre-pack Technique and Recent Developments in the Area' (2008) 29 Co Law 259; Frisby, *Report to the Association of Business Recovery Professionals, A Preliminary Analysis of Pre-packaged Administrations* (August 2007); Qi, 'The Rise of Pre-Packaged Corporate Rescue on Both Sides of the Atlantic' (2007) 20 Insolv Int 129; Finch, 'Pre-packaged Administrations: Bargains in the shadow of insolvency or shadowy bargains?' [2006] JBL 568.

unsecured creditors, which underlies the modernisation of the administration regime by
the Enterprise Act 2002, as outlined at **23-4**. The necessary secrecy, while a deal to sell the
business is being negotiated, combined with the apparent speed of the sale, raises the suspicions of creditors as to the relationship between the administrators and the purchasers
who are often members of the existing management (the so-called 'phoenix' pre-pack).[17]
Linked to the particular concern about connected parties' sales would be concerns as to
whether true market value was secured and whether other purchasers might have been
willing to offer a higher price and this concern persists even though independent valuations are standard.[18] There are also concerns as to whether, given the speed involved, the
administrator can be said to be acting in accordance with the purposes of administration
laid down in Sch B1, para 3 (see **23-12**) and about the conflict of interest between his pre-
administration role in advising the company on its difficulties and his post-appointment
role which requires him to act in the interests of the creditors as a whole.

23-8 The initial response to these concerns was the introduction of Statement of Insolvency
Practice 16 (SIP 16) which insolvency practitioners are expected to comply with (non-
compliance may give rise to disciplinary proceedings by their authorising bodies).[19] SIP
16 came into effect on 1 January 2009 and it sets out detailed requirements as to the extensive information which must be disclosed to creditors in all cases where there is a pre-pack
sale. The information to be disclosed to the creditors (SIP 16, para 9) includes:

- the extent of the administrator's involvement with the company prior to his appointment as administrator;
- any alternative courses of action that were considered;
- an explanation of why it was not appropriate to continue trading and sell the business as a going concern;
- whether efforts were made to consult major creditors;
- details of the assets involved, the consideration for the transaction, the terms of payment, the identity of the purchaser and any connection between the purchaser and
  the directors, shareholders or secured creditors of the company.

This information must be provided in all cases unless there are exceptional circumstances
and, if the sale is to a connected party, it is noted that it is unlikely that considerations of
commercial confidentiality would outweigh the need for creditors to be provided with
this information (SIP 16, para 10). Unless it is impracticable to do so, this information
should be provided with the first notification to creditors (SIP 16, para 11). It is stressed
that practitioners appointed to advise the company need to bear in mind the nature and
extent of their role in the pre-appointment period when regard must be had to the interests of the company and any duties which may be owed to creditors (SIP 16, paras 5–6).
The directors should be encouraged to take independent advice (SIP 16, para 5) and the

---

[17] Insolvency Service figures for 2009 and 2010 showed 79% and 72% of pre-pack sales were to parties
connected with the insolvent company, see Insolvency Service, *Report on the Operation of SIP 16 for 2010*
(2010), p 12.

[18] Though independent valuations are used, a perception of a 'stitch-up' can remain: see Frisby, *Report on
Insolvency Outcomes—Presented to the Insolvency Service* (2006), p 70.

[19] Statement of Insolvency Practice 16, *Pre-Packaged Sales in Administration*. Essentially, SIPs are statements of the standards expected of insolvency practitioners, drawn up and approved by the Joint Insolvency
Committee (JIC) which is made up of representatives of the bodies responsible for the authorisation and
regulation of insolvency practitioners and The Insolvency Service (part of BIS) and then adopted by the
authorising bodies.

administrator, in any case where a pre-packaged sale has been undertaken, must hold a creditors' meeting as soon as possible after his appointment (SIP 16, para 11). As administrators, they are reminded of the need to bear the statutory purposes of administration in mind and that they should be able to demonstrate that they have acted in the interests of the creditors as a whole and in making a distribution to secured or preferential creditors have avoided unnecessarily harming the interests of the creditors as a whole (para 7).

23-9   Initial reviews by the Insolvency Service of the operation of SIP 16[20] resulted in additional guidance to practitioners in October 2009 stressing the importance of providing creditors with a detailed explanation and justification of why a pre-packaged sale was undertaken so that they can be satisfied that the administrator has acted with due regard for their interests. The importance of timely information was also emphasised meaning that, in the majority of cases, SIP 16 information should be sent to creditors within a few days of the practitioner's appointment or upon completion of the sale. In all but the most exceptional of cases, SIP 16 information should be sent to creditors within 14 days of the completion of the sale. A further review of the second year of operation (2010) of SIP 16 found improvements in disclosure but also that approximately one-quarter of all reports were still non-compliant, the main problems being issues associated with the timeliness of the disclosure and insufficient information on valuations, marketing and asset details. In March 2010, the Insolvency Service launched a consultation seeking views on how confidence in pre-packaged sales could be improved[21] and a year later announced that further measures would be introduced, via statutory instrument, particularly addressing sales to a connected party.[22] In particular it was proposed (and clarified in subsequent draft regulations) that administrators would be required to give three business days' notice to creditors where they propose to sell a significant proportion of the assets of a company or its business to a connected party (defined to include a secured creditor) in circumstances where there had been no open marketing of the assets. This requirement was to apply not just to pre-packs but to any sales to connected parties in an administration where there had been no open marketing of the assets. It was also intended that the administrators would provide a statement of their opinion that the purpose of the administration would be achieved by a pre-pack sale and would achieve a better result for the creditors than anything else. Additional information about the sale would be filed at Companies House. However, in January 2012, a Ministerial Statement indicated that in keeping with Government policy to reduce regulation of small businesses, these proposals will not now be taken forward.[23] This reversal was somewhat surprising and is something of a triumph for those who argued that the requirement for three days' notice, in particular, would make pre-packs unworkable and make rescues more difficult. In the current economic climate, the Government found that concern persuasive and so, instead, there will be further consultation to consider how the existing regime might be made to work better so as to improve transparency and confidence in pre-pack administrations.

---

[20] See Insolvency Service, *Report on the First Six Months' Operation of Statement of Insolvency Practice 16* (June 2009); *Report on the Operation of Statement of Insolvency Practice 16, July to December 2009* (December 2009); *Report on the Operation of Statement of Insolvency Practice 16, January to December 2010* (2010).

[21] See Insolvency Service, *Consultation/Call for Evidence, Improving the transparency of, and confidence in, pre-packaged sales in administrations* (March 2010).

[22] See Ministerial Statement, *Improving Transparency and Confidence in Pre-Packaged Sales in Administration (Pre Packs)*, 31 March 2011; published at the same time as a summary of responses to the consultation of the same name, see n 21, see Insolvency Service Summary of consultation responses, March 2011.   [23] Ministerial Statement, 'Pre-packaged Sales in Insolvency', 26 January 2012.

Judicial attitudes to pre-pack administration

23-10 The general judicial attitude has been supportive of pre-packs with the court facilitating the process by interpreting the legislation as allowing sales of a company's assets ahead of a creditors' meeting, see **23-85.** The courts had also accepted that, on an application for an administration order, the court has a discretion to order that the proposed administrators' pre-appointment costs (in negotiating the pre-pack) be treated as an expense of the administration pursuant to IA 1986, Sch B1, para 13(1)(f),[24] a matter now addressed by the Insolvency Rules 1986, see **23-114.** These are two key component of pre-packs—the ability to sell the business without the creditors' consent and the possibility of having pre-appointment costs treated as an expense in the administration (ensuring that insolvency practitioners will be willing to act). At the same time, the courts have tried to balance their acceptance of the pre-pack process by reinforcing where possible the disclosure requirements of SIP 16 (see **23-8**) when an application is made for an administration order (see **23-30**). In *Re Kayley Vending Ltd*[25] the court noted that, in the exercise of its discretion to make an administration order, it must be alert to see, so far as it can, that the pre-pack procedure is at least not being obviously abused to the disadvantage of creditors. If it is, or may be, the court may conclude that it is inappropriate to give the pre-pack the apparent blessing conferred by making an administration order.[26] In reaching its decision, the court said it is likely to be assisted by the provision of information in relation to the pre-pack transaction and its background. It is likely therefore that in most cases the information required by SIP 16 should be supplied to the court as part of the application for an administration order in keeping with the obligation under IR 1986, r 2.4(2)(e), to provide information likely to assist the court.[27]

23-11 While the courts have generally been supportive of the process, or at least have not placed obstacles in its way, an issue which has the potential to limit business sales (and this applies generally to administration, not just to pre-packs) is whether the sale can be effected without the application of the TUPE Regulations, i.e. without the purchaser having to take on the employees of the former business as a result of the application of the Transfer of Undertakings (Protection of Employment) Regulations 2006, SI 2006/246 (TUPE). Recently, the Employment Appeal Tribunal (EAT) ruled that a sale by an administrator does attract the application of TUPE and therefore any contracts of employment of employees assigned to the undertaking transferred will pass to the transferee and any dismissal for the sole or principal reason of the transfer will automatically be unfair.[28] The EAT accepted that there is a mismatch between the ostensible primary purpose of administration (see **23-12**)—to rescue a company as a going concern—and the uses to which it is commonly put in the case of a pre-pack sale of the company's assets which can

---

[24] See *Re Kayley Vending Ltd* [2011] 1 BCLC 114 (in the exercise of this discretion, the court may make the costs order sought where the court is satisfied that the balance of benefit arising from the incurring of these pre-appointment costs is in favour of the creditors generally rather than the management as potential purchasers of the business). See also *Re Johnson Machine & Tool Co Ltd* [2010] BCC 382.

[25] [2011] 1 BCLC 114.   [26] [2011] 1 BCLC 114 at [24].

[27] [2011] 1 BCLC 114 at [21, [24]. See *Re Halliwells LLP* [2011] 1 BCLC 345 where the court, in making an administration order, was influenced by the evidence of a fully compliant SIP 16 statement, giving a detailed exposition of why the pre-pack in that case was appropriate, the marketing which had been undertaken, and a complete explanation of the terms materially affecting the consideration paid, see at [22].

[28] *OTG Ltd v Barke* [2011] BCC 608. The EAT disapproved of the earlier EAT decision in *Oakland v Wellwood (Yorkshire) Ltd* [2009] IRLR 250, widely considered to be wrong, which had concluded to the contrary. See also *Spaceright Europe Ltd v Baillavoine* [2012] IRLR 111 (dismissal of managing director by administrator unfair although it took place a month before a sale was agreed and before the eventual transferee was identified—it was connected with the transfer and his dismissal was unfair).

look very like liquidation. There is an exemption from the application of TUPE in liquidation proceedings so the point is relevant to the application of TUPE, but the EAT said the exemption essentially focuses on the character of the proceedings when instituted. Administration might lead to liquidation but, when instituted, the primary objective of administration is to rescue the company as a going concern (see **23-12**). It cannot be said at the moment of institution of any administration proceedings that their object is to liquidate the assets hence the exemption does not apply and a sale by an administrator does attract the application of TUPE. The Court of Appeal subsequently confirmed that the liquidation exception does not apply to administration and, on administration, a business transfer will fall within TUPE and dismissals of employees for the sole or principal reason of the transfer will be automatically unfair.[29] Therefore, administrators and purchasers of a business from an administrator must assume that the employees will transfer to the new business on the same terms as they were previously employed. These decisions may have a dampening effect on business sales in administration generally, not just in pre-pack administrations, as often purchasers will not wish to take on the expense of the employees of the former business.

B The purpose of administration

23-12   The 'purpose of administration' is a term of art spelt out in IA 1986, Sch B1, para 3(1) as follows:

> 'The administrator of a company must perform his functions with the objective of—
>
> (a) rescuing the company as a going concern, or
>
> (b) achieving a better result for the company's creditors as a whole than would be likely if the company were wound up (without first being in administration), or
>
> (c) realising property in order to make a distribution to one or more secured or preferential creditors.'

23-13   In order to address concerns that administrators appointed by a floating chargeholder would have little regard to Sch B1, paras 3(1)(a) and (b) and would merely proceed under para 3(1)(c) to make distributions to the secured and preferential creditors in a manner little different from the appointment of an administrative receiver, the statute lays down a hierarchy as between these objectives. The administrator must perform his functions with the objective specified in para 3(1)(a) unless he thinks either that it is not reasonably practicable to achieve that objective or that the objective specified in para 3(1)(b) would achieve a better result for the company's creditors as a whole (para 3(3)). The administrator may perform his functions with the objective specified in para 3(1)(c) only if he thinks that it is not reasonably practicable to achieve either of the objectives in paras 3(1)(a) or (b), and he does not unnecessarily harm the interests of the creditors of the company as a whole (para 3(4)). There is some flexibility as between paras 3(1)(a) and 3(1)(b) and it is a commercial decision for the administrator (who must be a qualified insolvency practitioner, Sch B1, para 6) as to how to proceed. In practice, administrators always seek to achieve one or more of these purposes and the most common purpose given is para 3(1)(b). Throughout the administrator must perform his functions as quickly and efficiently

---

[29] *Key2Law (Surrey) LLP v De'Antiquis* [2012] IRLR 212.

as is reasonably practicable (para 4)[30] and he must perform his functions in the interests of the creditors of the company as a whole (para 3(2), subject to para 3(4)). The intention is to create an appropriate balance between the need for the administrator to have flexibility to act to maximise economic value and the Government's view that collective procedures in the interests of all the creditors is the right approach.

Rescuing the company as a going concern

23-14 This option envisages the company continuing as a going concern with all or a significant part of its business. This option is likely to involve the creditors agreeing to the company entering a CVA (discussed in Chapter 22) or a scheme of arrangement (discussed in Chapter 26).[31] This use of administration as a 'wrapper' for a CVA can be a useful option on occasion for companies in difficulties, though the number of companies entering CVAs remains small, see **22-3**.[32]

Achieving a better result than on a winding up

23-15 On occasion, there are circumstances where continued trading for a short period is advantageous, for example to complete an order so ensuring a higher return to the creditors. The Explanatory Notes to the Enterprise Act 2002 suggest that this option would be relevant where there is no financing available and so the administrator can quickly reach the conclusion that rescue is not possible or where the time-scale for rescue is too long in terms of realising economic value.[33] The idea here is that the administrator has the flexibility to sell part of the business as a going concern while accepting that this is not possible with all of the business. The aim is to maximise the economic value of the assets.[34]

Realising property for preferential and secured creditors

23-16 The other options must be exhausted before the administrator considers this possibility and even then this option must be exercised in a way which does not unnecessarily harm the interests of the creditors of the company as a whole (Sch B1, para 3(4)). In these cases, the business is not viable and it is just a case of selling the assets that are available and

---

[30] This provision was added at a late stage to the legislation. The Government intention had been that administration would be a rapid procedure. For example, the Government had intended that proposals should be put to creditors by the administrator within 28 days of his appointment, but this period was lengthened during the Parliamentary debates to 10 weeks. Likewise, the Government had intended that an administration should be completed within three months, but this period was lengthened during debate to 12 months. Imposing a duty on the administrator to act quickly and efficiently is an attempt to counterbalance these longer time-limits.

[31] The *Explanatory Notes to the Enterprise Act 2002*, paras 647, 649, indicate that a proposal that would result in a 'shell' company remaining after all the assets have been sold would not be considered a rescue for these purpose. Seeking administration merely to sell the company's assets at a better price (possibly) than may be achieved by a receiver under the Law of Property Act 1925 is not a 'rescue as a going concern' for these purposes so as to justify an administration order: *Doltable Ltd v Lexi Holding plc* [2006] 1 BCLC 384.

[32] See Baird & Chan Ho, 'CVAs—The Restructuring Trend' (2007) Insolv Int 124.

[33] See *Explanatory Notes to the Enterprise Act 2002*, paras 648, 650.

[34] For example, in *Re Logitext UK Ltd* [2005] 1 BCLC 326, administration would give a better return possibly than liquidation when funding was available in an administration but not in a liquidation for the investigation of whether company assets had been improperly transferred away and might be recovered.

seeing how many creditors can get paid.[35] Issues such as the timing of the realisation of assets, the manner of sale and the identity of the purchasers will be important, given the requirement not to unnecessarily harm the interests of the creditors of the company as a whole. In *Re Halliwells LLP*[36] the court made an administration order in respect of a large law firm. The court found that it was not reasonably practicable to rescue the firm, given its size, nor to achieve a better result for the creditors than if the firm had been wound up, but administration would enable the administrators to realise property in order to make a distribution to one or more secured or preferential creditors. In this instance, the plan was to sell parts of the business through a pre-pack arrangement, but a court order for administration was required because the would-be purchasers of those parts of the business wanted to ensure that certain debts owed by the firm to members of the firm were repaid.[37] The court accepted that these payments to what were essentially certain unsecured creditors were undoubtedly preferences but were driven by necessity to maximise the returns of the administration, as the secured creditor acknowledged. In the circumstances, therefore, the court considered that the payments did not unnecessarily harm the interests of the creditors as a whole.[38]

23-17 Administrators are anxious to be seen to be acting in accordance with these statutory purposes and to explain (as they are required to do) to the creditors the options which they have taken (Sch B1, para 49, see **23-76**). Administrators are also mindful that creditors may apply to the court for relief on the ground that the administrator has acted or is proposing to act in a way which is unfairly harmful to their interests (see **23-98**) or that the administrator has not acted as quickly and as efficiently as he ought (Sch B1, para 74, see **23-100**) and that actions for misfeasance may be brought (Sch B1, para 75, see **23-102**) and for their removal from office (Sch B1, para 88). This jurisdiction to order the removal of the administrator is wide, but there must be a good ground or cause for doing so, though it need not involve misconduct or personal unfitness on the part of the administrator.[39] The court will have regard to, but not be bound by, the wishes of the majority of creditors.[40] In *Clydesdale Financial Services Ltd v Smailes*[41] the court did order the removal of the administrators where they had been involved in the negotiations for the sale of the business prior to their appointment and so, when legitimate questions arose as to whether that sale was at an undervalue, the court held that they were not in a position to conduct an independent review and should be replaced. In this case a significant body of major creditors representing a majority of the creditors in value wanted the administrators removed. In *Coyne v DRC Distribution Ltd*,[42] while the application to remove the administrators fell away when the company was put into compulsory winding up, the Court of Appeal was highly critical of their conduct in failing to challenge the disposal, before their appointment, of part of the company's assets by the director who appointed them. The court ordered that the administrators personally and the director jointly and severally pay the creditor's costs of that removal application. On appeal, the Court of Appeal confirmed the order. The administrators had not acted expeditiously or with the necessary robustness of purpose and it was right, the court said, that they be penalised in costs.

---

[35] See *Explanatory Notes to the Enterprise Act 2002*, paras 651–652.   [36] [2011] 1 BCLC 345.
[37] The purchasers were other law firms which were going to hire these members of Halliwells and did not want any risk of their being made bankrupt as a consequence of the firm's failure to pay outstanding debts to them as bankruptcy would prevent them working as solicitors.   [38] [2011] 1 BCLC 345 at [7], [23].
[39] *Finnerty v Clark, Re St George's Property Services (London) Ltd* [2012] 1 BCLC 286; see also *Sisu Capital Fund Ltd v Tucker* [2006] BCC 463 at [88]; *Clydesdale Financial Services Ltd v Smailes* [2011] 2 BCLC 405 at [15].   [40] *Clydesdale Financial Services Ltd v Smailes* [2011] 2 BCLC 405 at [15], [30].
[41] [2011] 2 BCLC 405.   [42] [2008] BCC 612, CA.

23-18   At the same time, the courts are anxious not to second-guess the commercial decisions of the administrators which are not matters for the courts.[43] In *Finnerty v Clark, Re St George's Property Services (London) Ltd*[44] the Court of Appeal refused an application for removal of the administrators by the major unsecured creditors (who were the directors and shareholders of the company) who wanted the administrators to challenge the rate of interest levied by the main secured creditor as an extortionate credit transaction (see IA 1986, s 244). The administrators refused and an application was made for their removal under Sch B1, para 88. The court said that the administrators had taken a commercial decision not to bring legal proceedings to challenge the interest rate and they had done so competently, without bias, and with the benefit of independent legal advice. The mere hope that another administrator might reach a different decision was not a good ground for their removal. The application was refused, the court noting that the creditors could have pursued other options, such as seeking directions from the court, rather than seeking to remove the administrators from office.[45]

C The appointment of an administrator

23-19   There are three routes into administration. An administrator may be appointed (Sch B1, para 2):[46]

    (1) by administration order of the court under para 10;

    (2) by the holder of a floating charge under para 14;

    (3) by the company or its directors under para 22.

23-20   There are certain general restrictions on the appointment of an administrator (for example, with respect to certain banking and insurance companies: Sch B1, para 9). More broadly, no administrator may be appointed:

- where the company is already in administration (Sch B1, para 7);

- where the company is in liquidation by virtue of a resolution for voluntary winding up, except on an application to the court by the liquidator;[47]

- where the company is in compulsory liquidation by virtue of a court order, except on an application to the court by the holder of a qualifying floating charge or the liquidator.[48]

23-21   An administrator, however appointed, is an officer of the court[49] and must be a qualified insolvency practitioner (Sch B1, para 6). In the absence of special circumstances, the

---

[43] See *Re T & D Industries plc* [2000] 1 BCLC 471; *Re CE King Ltd* [2000] 2 BCLC 297.
[44] [2012] 1 BCLC 286.   [45] [2012] 1 BCLC 286 at [42].
[46] In practice the majority of appointments are out of court. The Insolvency Service, *Evaluation Report on the Enterprise Act 2002—Corporate Insolvency Provisions* (January 2008), hereinafter *Insolvency Service Evaluation Report* (2008), noted that of the sample of administrations reviewed for the purposes of the evaluation, 30% were by court order and 70% were out-of-court appointments of which 70% were made by the directors and only 18% by floating chargeholders (see para 3.3). It was also noted that many of the appointments by directors may well be instigated by chargeholders who prefer not to make the appointment directly so as to avoid any adverse publicity (see para 3.10).
[47] IA 1986, Sch B1, paras 8(1)(a), 38.   [48] IA 1986, Sch B1, paras 8(1)(b), 37, 38.
[49] IA 1986, Sch B1, para 5; and therefore subject to the rule in *Ex p James* (1874) 9 Ch App 609 as to the high standards of conduct expected of officers of the court; see *Re Collins & Aikman Europe Ltd* [2007] 1 BCLC 182 (administrators should honour undertakings given to foreign creditors); also *Re British American*

administrator owes his duties to the company and not to the creditors, individually or collectively.[50]

The interim moratorium

23-22 In certain circumstances prior to the formal appointment of an administrator, an interim moratorium precluding actions against the company by creditors and others applies (Sch B1, para 44). The moratorium ensures that the status quo is preserved regarding the company's assets pending the granting or dismissal of the administration application or the appointment or otherwise of an administrator. If there is an administrative receiver of the company when the administration application is made, the interim moratorium does not begin to apply until the person by or on behalf of whom the receiver was appointed consents to the making of the administration order (Sch B1, para 44(6)).

23-23 An interim moratorium applies where:

(1) an application for an administration order has been made to the court;

(2) a qualifying floating chargeholder has filed with the court a copy of a notice of intention to appoint an administrator;[51]

(3) the company or the directors have filed with the court a copy of a notice of intention to appoint an administrator.[52]

23-24 The extent of the moratorium is set out in Sch B1, paras 42 and 43 and once the company is in administration, the moratorium continues: see **23-61**. Essentially the moratorium means that the company cannot be placed in winding up (save on a public interest petition), security cannot be enforced, goods cannot be repossessed, leases forfeited or legal processes instituted without the permission of the court (Sch B1, para 44(5)).

23-25 The interim moratorium does not prevent and the permission of the court is not required for:

(1) the presentation of a winding-up petition on public interest grounds;[53]

(2) the appointment of an administrator by a qualifying floating chargeholder;

(3) the appointment of an administrative receiver; or

(4) the carrying out by an administrative receiver (whenever appointed) of his functions (Sch B1, para 44(7)).

23-26 Obviously, categories (3) and (4) become increasingly obsolete with the passage of time since administrative receivers can only be appointed under floating charges created before 15 September 2003 (IA 1986, s 72A) and, see **21-84**; even when such a charge exists, an administrative receiver may not be appointed. The important provision is (2) which

---

Racing (Holdings) Ltd [2005] 2 BCLC 234; but the rule in *Ex p James* cannot be used to justify distributions of the company's assets in a way that is incompatible with the company's interests and the interests of any preferential creditor: *Re Farepak Food & Gifts Ltd* [2007] 2 BCLC 1.

[50] *Kyrris v Oldham* [2004] 1 BCLC 305, CA.

[51] In many cases, the qualifying floating chargeholder will be able to appoint without the need for an interim moratorium and therefore will not file a notice of intention to appoint an administrator, see **23-51**.

[52] IA 1986, Sch B1, para 44(1)–(4). See *Re Business Dream Ltd* [2012] BCC 1150.

[53] i.e. petitions for winding up on public interest grounds under IA 1986, ss 124A, 124B, by the Secretary of State or under FSMA 2000, s 367 by the Financial Services Authority: IA 1986, Sch B1, para 42(2), (3).

allows a qualifying floating charge to 'trump' a proposed appointment by making their own appointment of an administrator, see **23-48**.

23-27 The duration of this interim moratorium depends on the route into administration which is being pursued. If the administrator is to be appointed by the court, the interim moratorium applies where an administration application has been made and the application has not yet been granted or dismissed or the application has been granted but the administration order has not yet taken effect.[54]

23-28 If the administrator is to be appointed by a qualifying floating chargeholder, the interim moratorium applies from the time when a copy of the notice of intention to appoint is filed with the court until the appointment of the administrator takes effect[55] or the period of five business days beginning with the date of filing expires without an administrator being appointed (Sch B1, para 44(2), (3)).

23-29 If the administrator is to be appointed by the company or the directors, the interim moratorium applies from the time when a copy of the notice of intention to appoint is filed with the court until the appointment of the administrator takes effect[56] or the period of 10 business days beginning with the date of filing expires without an administrator being appointed (Sch B1, para 44(4)).

Appointment of an administrator by the court

23-30 An application to the court for an administration order (an administration application) may be made by:

(1) the company;

(2) the directors of the company;

(3) one or more creditors of the company;[57]

(4) the designated officer for a magistrates' court;[58]

(5) a combination of persons listed in (1)–(4).[59]

23-31 The members have no right to apply for an administration order other than by a resolution of the company. The directors are given the right to apply because of their potential liability for wrongful trading under IA 1986, s 214, see **25-18**.[60] While the holders of qualifying floating charges are able to appoint an administrator out of court, for all other creditors, the only method of appointing an administrator is through an application to the court.

---

[54] IA 1986, Sch B1, para 44(1). An administration order takes effect in accordance with para 13(2), either at the time appointed by the order or, if no time is appointed, when the order is made. If the time appointed by the order is at some point in the future, this provision ensures that the interim moratorium continues until that time.

[55] An appointment in this case takes effect in accordance with IA 1986, Sch B1, para 19.

[56] An appointment in this case takes effect in accordance with IA 1986, Sch B1, para 31.

[57] Defined IA 1986, Sch B1, para 12(4) to include contingent and prospective creditors.

[58] See IA 1986, Sch B1, para 12(1)(d)—an application in this case is made in exercise of the power conferred by the Magistrates' Courts Act 1980, s 87A (fine imposed on company).

[59] IA 1986, Sch B1, para 12(1); note that an application cannot be withdrawn without the permission of the court: para 12(3).

[60] An important defence to that liability is for the directors to show that they took every step to minimise potential loss to creditors: IA 1986, s 214(3). Such a step might be applying for the appointment of an administrator.

23-32 In practice, a creditor who does not have a qualifying floating charge would not usually have any sufficient interest in putting the company into administration though an example can be found in *Hammonds v Pro-Fit USA Ltd*.[61] In this case, a firm of solicitors was owed a significant sum for advisory work for a company. While negotiations were underway as to payment of the debt, certain intellectual property rights were transferred by the company to an associated company. The negotiations collapsed and the firm applied to the court for an administration order. The company disputed the debt and cross-claimed alleging negligent advice. Among the issues for the court was whether the firm could be a 'creditor', given any damages that might be awarded on the cross-claim. The court held that a person may be a 'creditor' for these purposes even if the debt is bona fide disputed or there is a cross-claim. Crucially, the court considered that there is no need to follow the practice which applies in relation to winding-up petitions which normally means that a winding-up petition would be dismissed in such circumstances. That practice arose, the court said, because of the very serious consequence of bringing a company's life to an end by winding up whereas the consequences of an administration order are not so drastic. On the evidence, the company was or was likely to become unable to pay its debts, for even if the company was able to pay its debts as they fell due, it was likely (in the sense of more probable than not) that it would be unable to do so in the foreseeable future. Though the court did not think this was a compelling case for an administration order, an administration order would enable the administrator to investigate the circumstances of the transfer of the intellectual property rights and whether the transaction was at an undervalue. Therefore the court would exercise its discretion to make an administration order subject to the respondent being given the opportunity to obtain a surrender of the rights which had been transferred.

23-33 In addition to the categories of applicant noted at **23-30**, a liquidator may apply for an administration order (Sch B1, para 38). This power is included in order to give maximum flexibility to rescue a company, should that appear possible, even if a liquidation of the company has been initiated. Previously there was no method of reversing out of a liquidation, but now if a liquidator considers that it is possible that administration is a more appropriate process, he may apply to the court for an administration order. A supervisor of a company voluntary arrangement may also apply for an administrator to be appointed,[62] as may the Financial Services Authority (Financial Conduct Authority from 2013) in certain circumstances.[63]

Conditions which must be met for court to order administration

23-34 For an administration order to be made, the court must be satisfied that the company is or is likely to become unable to pay its debts (Sch B1, para 11(a)),[64] and that the administration order is reasonably likely to achieve the purpose of administration (Sch B1, para 11(b), see **23-12**).[65] The court's jurisdiction to make such an order is also subject to the EC Regulation

---

[61] [2008] 2 BCLC 159.   [62] IA 1986, s 7(4)(b); Sch A1, para 39(5).   [63] See FSMA 2000, s 359.

[64] Whether a company is unable to pay its debts is determined in accordance with IA 1986, s 123, i.e. it must be proved to the satisfaction of the court that the company is either cash-flow insolvent (unable to pay its debts as they fall due) or balance sheet insolvent (after taking into account its contingent and prospective liabilities, the value of its assets is less than the amount of its liabilities): Sch B1, para 111(1); see the detailed discussion at **24-26** of the meaning of s 123.

[65] The application to the court must include the matters referred to in IR 1986, rr 2.2–2.4 including details of the company's financial position and, as noted at **23-10**, a compliant SIP 16 statement if a pre-pack sale is involved.

on Insolvency Proceedings (see **24-3**) which limits the court's power to open main proceedings to cases where the debtor's centre of main interests is in the UK.[66]

23-35 These thresholds were considered by Lewison J in *Re AA Mutual International Insurance Co Ltd*[67] where he concluded that it is necessary for the company to show both that it is more probable than not (likely) that it is or will become unable to pay its debts, and that there is a real prospect (reasonably likely) that an administration order would achieve the purpose of the administration, in this case a better result for the company's creditors as a whole than was likely if the company were wound up. In this instance, as the company (an insurance company) had no income coming in because it no longer wrote any new business, the court thought it was more probable than not that the company's liabilities would exceed its assets within a short space of time. The company had also established to the court's satisfaction that there was a real prospect of achieving a better result for the creditors through an administration than a winding up. Administration would save the ongoing costs of run-off and the prospective costs of dealing with threatened arbitration proceedings, it would provide a moratorium against other claims, it would facilitate the preparation of a scheme of arrangement and it would possibly enable the company to enter into a commercial arrangement with the Financial Services Compensation Scheme on more advantageous terms. For those reasons, the court made an administration order.

23-36 While it is a precondition for making an administration order that there is a real prospect that an administration order would achieve one of the purposes of administration (see **23-12**), it is not strictly necessary for an applicant or prospective administrator to identify in advance with certainty which of those objectives it is intended to be attained, merely that the prospective administrator considers that one of those objectives would be achieved if the prior objective or objectives proves not to be possible.[68] In practice, it is common for more than one of the options to be put forward so as to give the administrator maximum flexibility.

23-37 Once satisfied that the required thresholds are met, it is for the court in the exercise of its discretion to make an order.[69] For example, an administration order was made in *Re DKLL Solicitors*[70] (involving an insolvent partnership) in the face of opposition from the Inland Revenue because the court was entitled in the exercise of its discretion to take into account not merely the interests of the partnership's creditors, but the fact that the proposed sale of the partnership (which was to be the purpose of the administration) was likely to save the jobs of the employees and would result in minimum disruption to the affairs of the partnership's clients. Likewise in *Hammonds v Pro-Fit USA Ltd*,[71] see **23-32**, while the court did not think the case for an administration order was too compelling, the court did decide in favour of an order because it would allow a transfer of assets by the company to be investigated. On the other hand, in *Doltable Ltd v Lexi Holdings plc*[72]

---

[66] See EC Regulation 2000/1346, art 3. See, for example, *Re Collins & Aikman Europe Ltd* [2007] 1 BCLC 182 where administration orders were made in England in respect of companies in Spain, Sweden, Germany, Belgium, Italy and the Netherlands.

[67] [2005] 2 BCLC 8 at 13.   [68] *Hammonds v Pro-Fit USA Ltd* [2008] 2 BCLC 159.

[69] *Re Harris Simons Construction Ltd* [1989] BCLC 202; also *Re Imperial Motors (UK) Ltd* [1990] BCLC 29 (order refused because on balance it was not a suitable case: petitioning creditor was fully secured); see also *Re Arrows Ltd (No 3)* [1992] BCLC 555. In approaching this issue, the interests of secured creditors carry less weight than those of other creditors: *Re Consumer & Industrial Press Ltd* [1988] BCLC 177.

[70] [2008] 1 BCLC 112.   [71] [2008] 2 BCLC 159.

[72] [2006] 1 BCLC 384.

the court did not think it appropriate to make an order where the substance of the matter was a dispute between the company and a secured creditor over the terms on which the creditor was proposing to sell the company's only asset.

Position with respect to administrative receiverships

23-38 As soon as is reasonably practicable after the making of an administration application, the applicant must notify: (1) any person who has appointed an administrative receiver or who is or may be entitled to appoint an administrative receiver; and (2) any holder of a qualifying floating charge who is or may be entitled to appoint an administrator out of court.[73]

23-39 If the company is already in administrative receivership, the court must dismiss an administration application in respect of the company unless the person by or on behalf of whom the receiver was appointed consents to the making of an administration order, or the security under which the receiver is appointed would be liable to be released or discharged or avoided under various provisions[74] (Sch B1, para 39). If the company is not yet in administrative receivership, anyone entitled to do so may proceed to appoint an administrative receiver following the making of the administration application for, as noted at **23-25**, the interim moratorium which arises on the making of an administration application does not prevent the appointment of an administrative receiver.[75] If an appointment is made by the time of the court hearing, the administration application must be dismissed. As noted, these rights are of diminishing significance as it is not possible to appoint an administrative receiver under a floating charge created on or after 15 September 2003 (IA 1986, s 72A).

23-40 Once an administration order is made, no administrative receiver may then be appointed (Sch B1, para 41(1)). These are mutually exclusive procedures and a company can be in administrative receivership or administration but it cannot be in both at the same time.[76]

Special rights of floating chargeholders on application to the court

23-41 Various special rights are conferred on floating chargeholders to balance the loss of the right to appoint an administrative receiver under a floating charge created on or after 15 September 2003.

23-42 First, a qualifying floating chargeholder who has the option of appointing out of court may prefer the security of a court order and therefore provision is made for an administration application to court by the floating chargeholder (Sch B1, para 35).[77] In this instance, the court may make an administration order whether or not satisfied that the company is or is likely to become unable to pay its debts provided the floating chargeholder satisfies the court that an appointment could be made out of court (Sch B1, para 35(2)).

23-43 Secondly, where the administration application is made by someone other than a qualifying floating chargeholder, the chargeholder can intervene and apply to the court for the

---

[73] IA 1986, Sch B1, para 12(2); and see also IR 1986, r 2.7.

[74] i.e. under IA 1986, ss 238–240, 245—transaction at an undervalue, preferences and avoidance of certain floating charges. [75] IA 1986, Sch B1, para 44(1), (5), (7).

[76] See also IA 1986, Sch B1, paras 17(b), 25(c).

[77] A court-based appointment may be preferable and necessary where there is an international element to the insolvency, though out-of-court administration appointments are recognised as insolvency proceedings for the purposes of the EC Insolvency Regulation 2000/1346.

appointment of his choice of administrator and not the person chosen by the applicant (Sch B1, para 36(1)). In that case, the court must grant that application by the floating chargeholder unless the court thinks it right to refuse because of the particular circumstances of the case (Sch B1, para 36(2)).

23-44 This provision was controversial because this presumption in favour of the floating chargeholder's nominee is seen as enabling banks via administration to remain much in the same position as before—the appointment of their nominee to recover their money—despite the restriction on the appointment of administrative receivers.[78] There are a variety of mechanisms in the legislation designed to ensure that these concerns are misplaced:

(1) the administrator is an officer of the court and must be a qualified insolvency practitioner (Sch B1, paras 5, 6); as such he is subject to high standards of conduct;

(2) the administrator is constrained in his conduct of the administration by the specified purpose of administration as expressed in Sch B1, para 3, see **23-12**;

(3) the administrator must explain his conduct to the creditors and in particular he must explain why he has not pursued the objective of rescuing the company as a going concern or achieving a better result for the creditors as a whole than would have been likely on a winding up (Sch B1, para 49(2));

(4) the administrator must perform his functions in the interests of the creditors as a whole (Sch B1, para 3(2));

(5) an administrator is open to challenge by creditors who feel their interests have been unfairly harmed by his conduct and to actions for misfeasance (Sch B1, paras 74, 75, see **23-98**) and to removal from office (Sch B1, para 88, see **23-17**).

23-45 Thirdly, a qualifying floating chargeholder may apply to the court for an administration order where the company has gone into compulsory winding up (Sch B1, para 37), despite the general restriction on appointing an administrator in such circumstances (Sch B1, para 8(1)(b)). If the court makes an administration order, it will make such consequential provision dealing with the winding up as is necessary, including the discharge of the winding-up order (Sch B1, para 37(3)).

Powers of court

23-46 The court's powers on an administration application, see **23-30**, are to make an administration order or to dismiss the application, to adjourn it, or to make an interim order or any other order which the court thinks appropriate[79] (Sch B1, para 13(1)). The court may also treat the application as a winding-up petition and make any order which it could make on such a petition.[80] Where an administration order is made, the court appoints the administrator and, as noted at **23-43**, a qualifying floating chargeholder can intervene to secure his choice of administrator unless the court thinks it right to refuse because of the particular circumstances of the case (Sch B1, para 36).

23-47 Any petition for the winding up of a company must be dismissed on the making of the administration order unless the petition is a public interest petition.[81] Any administrative

---

[78] See IA 1986, s 72A.

[79] Sch B1, para 13(1). An order can be made with retrospective effect: *Re G-Tech Construction Ltd* [2007] BPIR 1275; *Re Derfshaw Ltd* [2011] BCC 631.

[80] i.e. such order as might be made under IA 1986, s 125: Sch B1, para 13(1)(e).

[81] IA 1986, Sch B1, para 40(1), (2). As to public interest petitions: see n 53.

receiver must vacate office and any receiver of part of the company's property must vacate on being asked to do so by the administrator.[82]

Appointment of administrator by holder of floating charge

23-48 The holder of a qualifying floating charge in respect of a company's property may appoint an administrator out of court (Sch B1, para 14(1)), but not if the company is already in administration,[83] or is in liquidation,[84] or if a provisional liquidator has been appointed,[85] or if an administrative receiver is in office.[86] There is no requirement in this instance that the company is or is likely to become unable to pay its debts. The important concepts of a 'qualifying floating charge' and the 'holder of a qualifying floating charge' are defined in detail in IA 1986, Sch B1, paras 14(2) and (3).

23-49 A 'qualifying floating charge' is a charge created by an instrument which:

(1) states that Sch B1, para 14(2) applies to a floating charge; or

(2) purports to empower the holder of the floating charge to appoint an administrator of the company; or

(3) purports to empower the holder of the floating charge to make an appointment which would be the appointment of an administrative receiver (Sch B1, para 14(2)).

23-50 A person is a 'holder of a qualifying floating charge' if he holds one or more debentures of the company secured:

(1) by a qualifying floating charge which relates to the whole or substantially the whole of the company's property;[87]

(2) by a number of qualifying floating charges which together relate to the whole or substantially the whole of the company's property; or

(3) by charges or other forms of security which together relate to the whole or substantially the whole of the company's property and at least one of which is a qualifying floating charge (Sch B1, para 14(3)).

23-51 In order to exercise this power to appoint, the floating charge on which the appointment relies must be enforceable (Sch B1, para 16) in the sense that some default or other event must have occurred which, under the terms of the charge, allows for its enforcement. The holder must give at least two business days' written notice to the holder of any prior qualifying floating charge of his intention to appoint an administrator or the holder of a prior qualifying floating charge must consent in writing to the making of the appointment (Sch B1, para 15(1)).[88]There is no requirement to give advance notice of the appointment to the

---

[82] IA 1986, Sch B1, para 41. Of course, the court could only have made an administration order in this situation if the person entitled to appoint the administrative receiver consented to the order or if the charge under which the receiver was appointed was open to challenge: see Sch B1, para 39.

[83] IA 1986, Sch B1, para 7.

[84] IA 1986, Sch B1, para 8. If the company is in compulsory liquidation, the holder of a qualifying floating charge can still make an application to the court for an administration order under para 37: para 8(1)(b), (3).   [85] IA 1986, Sch B1, para 17(a).

[86] IA 1986, Sch B1, para 17(b).

[87] If a chargeholder has a charge which relates only to part of the company's assets, as a creditor he may apply to the court for an administration order under IA 1986, Sch B1, para 22: see **23-30**.

[88] A prior floating charge is one within IA 1986, Sch B1, para 15(2), namely, one created first or one treated as having priority because of an agreement to which the holder of each floating charge was party. A junior floating chargeholder can secure an interim moratorium (see **23-22**) by filing a notice of intention to appoint

company. This ensures that floating chargeholders are able to act with the same degree of speed which was a feature of appointments of administrative receivers.[89]

23-52 A person who appoints an administrator under this procedure must file with a court a notice of appointment[90] which must include a statutory declaration by or on behalf of the person making the appointment that the person is the holder of a qualifying floating charge; that each floating charge relied on in making the appointment is or was enforceable at the date of appointment and that the appointment is in accordance with Sch B1.[91] The appointment takes effect when the person appointing has filed these documents with the court.[92] Any outstanding winding-up petition (other than a public interest petition) is suspended following the appointment of an administrator out of court by a qualifying floating chargeholder.[93]

23-53 The notice of appointment must identify the administrator and be accompanied by a statement by him that he consents to the appointment; that in his opinion the purpose of administration (as defined in Sch B1, para 3, see **23-12**) is reasonably likely to be achieved; and the statement must give details of any prior professional relationship which the administrator has had with the company.[94]

23-54 There is some potential for disputes surrounding the process since the time of appointment is of some importance and, as the notice of appointment and other documents must meet certain requirements, there may be challenges as to their effectiveness and as to whether the appointment has taken effect. In order to minimise confusion on this issue, the floating chargeholder appointing an administrator out of court is required to notify the administrator as soon as it is reasonably practicable that the notice of appointment etc has been filed with the court and a copy of the notice of appointment must be sent to any person who has made an administration application to court and to the court to which the application has been made.[95]

Appointment of administrator by company or directors

23-55 The company by an ordinary resolution or the directors[96] may appoint an administrator out of court under IA 1986, Sch B1, para 22, but not if the company is already in adminis-

---

(para 44(2), (3)) which allows some breathing space for the chargeholders to consult together as to how to proceed.

[89] In the event of an invalid appointment, the appointor may be ordered by the court to indemnify the administrator against loss, Sch B1, para 21, but the administrator is likely to require an indemnity in any event as a term of his appointment.

[90] IA 1986, Sch B1, para 18(1). The notice and any accompanying documents must be as prescribed by IR 1986, r 2.16(2) and the statutory declaration must be made no more than five business days before filing: IR 1986, r 2.16(3); IA 1986, Sch B1, para 18(5), (6). As to penalties for false statements in a statutory declaration, see para 18(7). A failure to serve a copy of the notice of intention to appoint in the prescribed form prevents the interim moratorium coming into effect: see IA 1986, Sch B1, para 44(2), (3).

[91] IA 1986, Sch B1, para 18(2).

[92] IA 1986, Sch B1, para 19. Given the importance of filing the notice of appointment, it is possible to file notice of the appointment by fax outside of court opening hours, see IR 1986, r 2.19.

[93] IA 1986, Sch B1, para 40(1)(b), (2).

[94] IA 1986, Sch B1, para 18(3); IR 1986, r 2.3(5); to prevent undue investigation and therefore expense, the administrator in making his statement is entitled to rely on information provided by the directors unless he has reason to doubt its accuracy: Sch B1, para 18(4).   [95] See IA 1986, Sch B1, para 20; IR 1986, r 2.18.

[96] Either the directors acting unanimously or by a majority: see IA 1986, Sch B1, para 105, but any decision must be taken in conformity with the constitutional requirements of the company: *Minmar (929) Ltd v Khalatschi* [2011] BCC 485.

tration, or is in liquidation,[97] or essentially if in the past 12 months the company was put into administration by the company or the directors or during that period the company has unsuccessfully pursued a CVA.[98] The intention is to prevent the directors switching between these procedures to the detriment of creditors who constantly find that some form of moratorium is in place affecting their rights. While an appointment out of court cannot take place in these cases, an application to the court for an administration order under Sch B1, para 12 is still possible (see **23-30**). Also, the company or the directors may not look to appoint an administrator out of court under Sch B1, para 22 if a petition for winding up has been presented and not yet disposed of;[99] an administration application has been made to the court and is not yet disposed of; or an administrative receiver is in office (Sch B1, para 25).

23-56 A person who proposes to make an appointment under Sch B1, para 22 must give at least five business days' written notice to any floating chargeholder who is or may be entitled to appoint an administrative receiver or to appoint an administrator out of court.[100] No appointment may be made unless this required notice has been given and the period specified has expired or the recipient of the notice has consented in writing to the appointment (Sch B1, para 28(1)). In practice, the company will have consulted the floating chargeholder about the appointment in advance.

23-57 A person who gives notice of intention to appoint must file a copy of the notice with the court as soon as is reasonably practicable.[101] That filing sets running a period of 10 business days beginning with the date on which the notice of intention to appoint is filed within which an appointment of an administrator by the company or directors must take place (Sch B1, para 28(2)). Once the notice of intention to appoint is filed with the court, the interim moratorium applies (Sch B1, para 44(4)), see **23-22**.

23-58 Once the appointment is made, the appointor must file with the court a notice of appointment including a statutory declaration made not more than five business days before the filing by or on behalf of the person making the appointment that the company/directors are entitled to make an appointment under these provisions; that the appointment is in accordance with IA 1986, Sch B1; and that, as far as the person is reasonably able to ascertain, the statements made and information given in the statutory declaration filed with the notice of intention to appoint remain accurate.[102]

---

[97] IA 1986, Sch B1, paras 7 and 8.   [98] IA 1986, Sch B1, paras 23, 34.

[99] The presentation of a winding-up petition takes place when the petition is delivered to the court for filing notwithstanding that that date might be well in advance of the date when the petition is sealed and issued by the court for service which makes it difficult for those considering making an appointment to know whether there is a pending petition: see *Re Blights Builders Ltd* [2008] 1 BCLC 245 (administrators' appointment invalid as a winding-up petition had been presented and had not been disposed of).

[100] IA 1986, Sch B1, para 26(1); and notice of the intention to appoint must be given to those persons prescribed by IR 1986, r 2.20(2). The notice must be in the prescribed form and identify the proposed administrator: IA 1986, Sch B1, para 26(3). In the event that there are no persons to whom notice must be given under this provision: see para 30. A particular problem has arisen as to whether, on an appointment made by the directors, notice must be given to the company, as appears to be required by IR 1986, r 2.20(2)(d), with the result that a failure to give such notice renders the appointment a nullity, as appears to be required by IR 1986, r 28, see Palser, 'Appointing Administrators Out of Court' (2011) 24 Insolv Int 113. It is expected that the Court of Appeal will be required to resolve these issues on an appeal from *Re Care Matters Partnership Ltd* [2011] BCC 957 where the conflicting issues are set out; see also *Minmar (929) Ltd v Khalatschi* [2011] BCC 485.   [101] IA 1986, Sch B1, para 27(1); IR 1986, r 2.22.

[102] IA 1986, Sch B1, para 29(1), (2), (5); IR 1986, rr 2.23–2.24. For the criminal penalties for a false statement in a statutory declaration, see Sch B1, para 29(7).

23-59 The notice of appointment must identify the administrator and be accompanied by a statement by him that he consents to the appointment; that in his opinion the purpose of administration (as defined in Sch B1, para 3, see **23-12**) is reasonably likely to be achieved and the statement must give details of any prior professional relationship which the administrator has had with the company.[103]

23-60 The appointment of an administrator under these powers takes effect when the requirements as to the filing with the court of the notice of appointment (and accompanying documents) are satisfied (Sch B1, para 31). In order to minimise confusion on this issue, the person appointing is required to notify the administrator as soon as it is reasonably practicable that the notice of appointment etc has been filed with the court.[104] If before the requirements as to the filing of the notice of appointment are satisfied, the company enters into administration by virtue of a court order or an appointment out of court by a qualifying floating chargeholder, the appointment by the company/directors under Sch B1, para 22 does not take effect (Sch B1, para 33).

D The company in administration

23-61 As noted, one of the key elements of administration is the moratorium on the enforcement of creditors' rights and other processes. It is essential to the continuation of business by the administrator that he should have the right to use the property of the company free from interference by creditors and others.[105] In particular, the intention is to prevent a litigation free-for-all by creditors with administrators feeling obliged to compromise on weak claims because the cost of defending them to a conclusion would be difficult to justify.[106] The effect of the moratorium is that owners of property, and charges over property, are disabled from exercising their proprietary rights unless the administrator consents or the court gives permission.[107]A moratorium is just that, however, a moratorium on the enforcement of the creditor's right and it does not affect the substantive rights of the creditor.[108]

23-62 Once the company is in administration, the extent of the moratorium is governed by IA 1986, Sch B1, paras 42 and 43 which provide that:

(1) no resolution may be passed or order made for the winding up of the company, other than on public interest petitions;[109]

(2) no step may be taken to enforce security over the company's property;[110]

---

[103] IA 1986, Sch B1, para 29(3); IR 1986, r 2.3(5); to avoid unnecessary investigation and expense, the administrator may rely on information provided by the directors unless he has reason to doubt its accuracy: Sch B1, para 29(4).

[104] See IA 1986, Sch B1, para 32; IR 1986, r 2.26(2); it is an offence to fail to comply without reasonable excuse.   [105] See *Bristol Airport plc v Powdrill* [1990] BCLC 585 at 594.

[106] See Laddie J in *Holdenhurst Securities plc v Cohen* [2001] 1 BCLC 460 at 463–4.

[107] *Re Atlantic Computer Systems plc* [1992] 1 All ER 476 at 488, CA, per Nicholls LJ.

[108] *Barclays Mercantile Business Finance Ltd v Sibec Developments* [1992] 2 All ER 195.

[109] IA 1986, Sch B1, para 42; as to public interest petitions, see n 53.

[110] IA 1986, Sch B1, para 43(2). 'Security' is defined as 'any mortgage, charge, lien or other security': s 248(b)(ii). In *Bristol Airport plc v Powdrill* [1990] 2 All ER 493, CA, 'security' was held to include the exercise of a statutory lien, in this case the right of an airport to detain aircraft for unpaid airport charges under the Civil Aviation Act 1982; see also *Re Sabre International Products Ltd* [1991] BCLC 470 (enforcement of a lien). 'Property' is defined in IA 1986, s 436 as including money, goods, things in action, land and every

(3) no step may be taken to repossess goods in the company's possession[111] under any hire-purchase agreement;[112]

(4) a landlord may not exercise a right of forfeiture by peaceable re-entry in relation to premises let to the company;[113]

(5) no legal process (including legal proceedings, execution, distress and diligence) may be instituted or continued against the company or property of the company;[114]

except in cases (2)–(5) with the permission of the court or the consent of the administrator.[115]

23-63 Two issues related to the moratorium have particularly concerned the courts: (1) the scope of the prohibition on instituting or continuing a 'legal process'; and (2) the nature of the court's discretion to grant permission to persons to act against the company despite the moratorium.

Restriction on legal process

23-64 The restriction on any 'legal process' extends to any legal or quasi-legal proceedings, such as arbitration proceedings,[116] tribunal proceedings[117] or adjudication procedures.[118] It is not limited to proceedings by creditors.[119] It can include proceedings brought by a

---

description of property wherever situated and also obligations and every description of interest, whether present or future or vested or contingent, arising out of, or incidental to, property.

[111] In *David Meek Plant Ltd, Re David Meek Access Ltd* [1994] 1 BCLC 680, the court found goods to be 'in the company's possession under a hire-purchase agreement' although the hire-purchase agreement had terminated: it was sufficient that the possession was attributable to or derived from a hire-purchase agreement at some time, not necessarily one still subsisting; see also *Re Atlantic Computer Systems plc* [1992] 1 All ER 476, CA: equipment held by a company on hire-purchase was in the company's possession for these purposes whether the equipment remained on the company's premises, was entrusted to others for repair, or was sub-let by the company as part of its trade with others. See also *Fashoff (UK) Ltd v Linton* [2008] 2 BCLC 362 as to whether goods obtained subject to a retention of title clause had remained in the constructive possession of the company in administration.

[112] IA 1986, Sch B1, para 43(3). A hire-purchase agreement is defined as including a conditional sale, a chattel lease and a retention of title agreement: para 111(1): see *Re City Logistics Ltd* [2002] 2 BCLC 103.

[113] IA 1986, Sch B1, para 43(4). Earlier litigation had established that such a right of a landlord did not amount to the enforcing of security over the company's property and therefore the permission of the court was not required by the landlord: see *Re Lomax Leisure Ltd* [1999] 2 BCLC 126. That position has now been reversed.

[114] IA 1986, Sch B1, para 43(6). See *Re Olympia & York Canary Wharf Ltd* [1994] BCLC 453 (legal process means a process which requires the assistance of the court and does not extend to the service of a contractual notice which renders time of the essence or terminates a contract by reason of the company's anticipatory breach). Despite the prohibition on the institution of legal processes, an administration does not stop time running for limitation purposes: *Re Maxwell Fleet and Facilities (Management) Ltd* [2000] 1 All ER 464.

[115] IA 1986, Sch B1, para 43; the court's permission may be conditional, see para 43(7).

[116] *Bristol Airport plc v Powdrill* [1990] BCLC 585 at 600.

[117] Such as an industrial tribunal: see *Carr v British International Helicopters Ltd* [1994] 2 BCLC 474.

[118] Such as those brought under the Housing Grants Construction and Regeneration Act 1986: see *A Straume (UK) Ltd v Bradlor Developments Ltd* [2000] BCC 333.

[119] In so far as *Air Ecosse v Civil Aviation Authority* (1987) 3 BCC 492 took the contrary view, it has not been followed by the English courts: see *Environment Agency v Clark (Re Rhondda Waste Disposal Ltd)* [2000] BCC 653 at 678.

competitor[120] and it applies to criminal proceedings against the company.[121] In all these cases, the permission of the court or the administrator is required.

23-65 On the other hand, a direction by a rail regulator against a rail company is not a legal process or proceeding for these purposes for the regulator performs a broader role than that required of a judicial or quasi-judicial decision-maker and does not act as a result of a legal process against the company.[122] If the regulator subsequently needs the court's assistance to enforce his direction, this would be a legal process requiring the consent of the court or the administrator. Equally, an application for the late registration of a charge is not within the mischief aimed at although such applications are subject to the court's discretion in any case.[123]

Setting aside the moratorium–the permission of the court

23-66 In *Royal Trust Bank v Buchler*[124] the court noted that its discretion to grant leave under IA 1986 s 11(3) (now a requirement for the permission of the court under IA 1986, Sch B1, para 42) is a general discretion which requires the court to have regard to all the relevant circumstances. Having regard to those circumstances, it could be appropriate for a secured creditor to be given leave to enforce its security even if no criticism could be made of the administrator. In this case, the property at the centre of the dispute between the secured creditor and the administrator was an office block. After months of fruitless efforts by the administrator to find tenants for the property, the creditor wanted to appoint a receiver to sell the property, with or without tenants, before the value of the property (and therefore its security) deteriorated further. As the property would realise more money if sold as fully let, the administrator wanted more time to find tenants.

23-67 Weighing up the conflicting interests, the court decided that appointing a receiver would result in additional costs and further reduce the net proceeds available to the creditors. On the other hand, the administration in this case had gone on for a long time and it was therefore reasonable to require the administrator to return to court in two months if he had not by then achieved a binding contract of sale when a further application by the creditor could be considered.

23-68 Many of the main issues with regard to the release of a security holder from the constraints of the moratorium were considered at length by the Court of Appeal in *Re Atlantic Computer Systems plc*[125] and the guidance provided therein has proved very influential. In this case, the company in administration supplied computers on sub-lease to end-users. The company in turn obtained the computers either on hire-purchase or on lease from finance companies ('the funders'). Throughout the period of administration the end-users had continued to pay the rentals due under the sub-leases, but the administrators had not paid any sums due to the funders under the leases. The funders wished to ascertain, *inter alia*, whether the equipment could be repossessed by the funders and whether, if the court's leave was required to do so, it would be granted.

---

[120] See *Biosource Technologies Inc v Axis Genetics plc* [2000] 1 BCLC 286 (competitor company precluded without consent of administrator or permission of the court from taking proceedings against company in administration for the revocation of a patent held by that company).

[121] *Environment Agency v Clark (Re Rhondda Waste Disposal Ltd)* [2001] BCC 653.

[122] *Re Railtrack plc, Winsor v Bloom* [2002] 2 BCLC 755.

[123] *Re Barrow Borough Transport Ltd* [1989] BCLC 653.   [124] [1989] BCLC 130.

[125] [1992] 1 All ER 476, CA.

23-69 In addressing these issues, the Court of Appeal used the opportunity to set out the following general observations regarding cases where leave is sought to exercise existing proprietary rights, including security rights, against a company in administration:[126]

- It is for the person seeking permission to make out his case.

- Leave should normally be given to a lessor of land or the hirer of goods (a 'lessor') to exercise his proprietary rights and repossess his land or goods where that is unlikely to impede the achievement of the purpose for which the administration order was made (now to be read in the light of the statutory purpose of administration, set out at **23-12**).[127]

- In other cases, the court has to carry out a balancing exercise, balancing the legitimate interests of the lessor and the legitimate interests of the other creditors of the company.[128]

- In carrying out the balancing exercise, great weight is normally to be given to the proprietary interests of the lessor and an administration for the benefit of unsecured creditors should not be conducted at the expense of those seeking to exercise their proprietary rights, save to the extent that this is unavoidable and even then this will usually be acceptable only to a strictly limited extent.

- Therefore, leave will normally be granted if significant loss would be caused to the lessor by a refusal; but if substantially greater loss would be caused to others by the grant of leave, or loss which is out of all proportion to the benefit which leave would confer on the lessor, that may outweigh the loss to the lessor caused by a refusal.

- In assessing these respective losses, the court will have regard to matters such as: the financial position of the company, its ability to pay the rental arrears and the continuing rentals, the administrator's proposals, the period for which the administration order has already been in force and is expected to remain in force, the effect on the administration if leave were given, the effect on the applicant if leave were refused, the end result sought to be achieved by the administration, the prospects of that result being achieved, and the history of the administration so far.

- If leave is refused, it may commonly be on terms, for example, that the administrator pay the current rent which should be possible, since if the administration order has been rightly made the business should generally be sufficiently viable to hold down current outgoings.

- The comments were mainly directed to the situation where a lessor of land or the owner of goods seeks to repossess his land or goods because of non-payment of rentals but a broadly similar approach would be applicable on many applications to enforce a security. On such applications, an important consideration will often be whether the applicant is fully secured. If he is, delay in enforcement is likely to be of less prejudice than in cases where his security is insufficient.

23-70 Returning to the facts in *Re Atlantic Computer Systems plc*,[129] the court found that the administrators wanted to remain in possession of the computers partly in order to renego-

---

[126] [1992] 1 All ER 476 at 500–2, CA.

[127] Undue delay in seeking leave is itself sufficient to justify a refusal of permission since delay is contrary to the objectives of the legislation and a delay may also mean that an order of the court at a late stage is likely to impede the purpose of the administration: *Fashoff (UK) Ltd v Linton* [2008] 2 BCLC 362.

[128] See also *Royal Bank Trust v Buchler* [1989] BCLC 130. The conduct of the parties may also be relevant to the issue of whether leave should be granted: *Bristol Airport plc v Powdrill* [1990] 2 All ER 493, CA.

[129] [1992] 1 All ER 476, CA.

tiate the arrangements between the company and the funders which negotiations would be conducted in circumstances where the funders were not in a position to rely on their full rights. The court concluded that it was never intended that administration should strengthen the administrators' hands in negotiations with property owners who could not assert their full rights because of the moratorium and accordingly the court would grant leave to the funders to enforce their rights.[130]

23-71 In *Somerfield Stores Ltd v Spring (Sutton Coldfield) Ltd*[131] a tenant sought the court's permission to continue a claim for a new tenancy (an entitlement under the Landlord and Tenant Act 1954 unless the landlord was going to redevelop the property) against a landlord in administration. The administrators objected saying that they needed time to put together a scheme of redevelopment of the property which would defeat the claim for the tenancy. Citing *Atlantic Computer Systems*, the court noted the need to balance the right of the administrators to proceed with an orderly administration in accordance with the purpose of the administration and the right of the applicant to have its application for a new tenancy determined. Here the purpose of the administration was to make a distribution to the secured creditor, nothing else was possible, and even if the administrators succeeded on a redevelopment plan, only the secured creditor would benefit. Delaying a decision on the new tenancy in circumstances where the company could not as presently situated oppose the tenancy in the hope that the administrators might come up with a scheme which would be to the advantage of the secured creditor and defeat the claim for the new tenancy was not acceptable, the court said. In balancing the rights involved, the court had to have regard to the purpose of the administration, but it was not necessary for the purpose of the administration to go so far as to improve the position of the secured creditor over the interests of the third party who had a right to a new tenancy.[132] The court therefore gave permission for the tenancy claim to proceed.

23-72 In a different context, in *Environment Agency v Clark (Re Rhondda Waste Disposal Ltd)*[133] the Court of Appeal overruled a refusal by the trial judge to grant permission to the Environment Agency to bring a criminal prosecution against a company in administration. The Court of Appeal concluded that the trial judge had given too much weight to the interests of the company's creditors and insufficient interest to the wider public interest in the prosecution, including the Agency's concerns that any criminal liability should not be evaded by a company going into administration. In the event of a conviction, the court was obliged to fix any fine taking into account the financial circumstances of the company.

23-73 On the other hand, in *Re David Meek Plant Ltd, Re David Meek Access Ltd*[134] leave to repossess goods on hire-purchase to a company in administration was refused, the court having balanced the interests of those leasing creditors against the legitimate interests of the other creditors. To have allowed repossession would have ensured that the administration would be abortive and that would deprive the creditors of the opportunity of considering proposals designed to achieve a more advantageous realisation of the assets than would have been the case in a winding up. In *AES Barry Ltd v TXU Europe Energy Trading Ltd*[135] the court held that only in very exceptional circumstances would the court allow a creditor whose claim was simply a monetary one a right to take proceedings, a position confirmed in *Unite the Union v Nortel Networks UK Ltd.*[136]

---

[130] [1992] 1 All ER 476 at 498–9, CA.   [131] [2010] 2 BCLC 452.   [132] [2010] 2 BCLC 452 at [13].
[133] [2001] Ch 57, CA.   [134] [1994] 1 BCLC 680.   [135] [2005] 2 BCLC 22.
[136] [2010] 2 BCLC 674—the court refused permission for employees to bring claims for unfair dismissal, breach of contract and discrimination before an employment tribunal. The court noted that, although the

E The role and powers of the administrator

23-74 As soon as is reasonably practicable after his appointment (by whatever route),[137] the administrator must send a notice of his appointment to the company and publish a notice of his appointment.[138] He must obtain a list of the company's creditors;[139] send a notice of his appointment to the registrar of companies within seven days;[140] call on officers or employees of the company for a statement of the affairs of the company;[141] and take custody or control of all the property of the company (Sch B1, para 67). While the company is in administration, every business document issued by or on behalf of the company or the administrator and all the company's websites must state the name of the administrator and that the affairs, business and property of the company are being managed by him.[142]

23-75 The administrator effectively replaces the directors in the management of the business, given that all power to manage the business is vested in him (Sch B1, para 59(1)).[143] The directors do not vacate office and remain subject to their usual range of duties including their statutory obligations to file documents with the registrar of companies.[144] A company in administration or an officer of a company in administration may not exercise a management power, however, without the consent of the administrator which consent may be general or specific.[145]

Proposals to creditors

23-76 Once appointed, the administrator must make a statement setting out proposals for achieving the purpose of administration and also indicating how it is proposed that the administration will end (a requirement which means that from the outset the administrator needs to be focused on an expeditious process[146] with a definite end in prospect).[147] A copy of this statement must be sent to the registrar of companies and to every creditor of

enforcement of those rights are suspended, the claims of creditors do not disappear. The suspended rights are replaced by a right under IR 1986, r 2.72 to submit a claim in writing to the administrator which would be dealt with in accordance with the Insolvency Rules.

[137] His appointment takes effect according to the manner in which it is made: see IA 1986, Sch B1, paras 13(2), 19, 31.

[138] His appointment must be published in accordance with the requirements of IR 1986, r 2.27, essentially in the *Gazette* and in one appropriate newspaper: IA 1986, Sch B1, para 46(2).

[139] He is required to send a notice of his appointment to each creditor of whose claim and address he is aware: IA 1986, Sch B1, para 46(3), but the court may direct that this requirement does not apply: para 46(7)(a).

[140] IA 1986, Sch B1, para 46(4); and to those persons prescribed by IR 1986 r 2.27(2). This notice to the registrar must be sent before the end of seven days beginning with the date of the order appointing him or the date of his receiving notice of his appointment: para 46(6).

[141] IA 1986, Sch B1, para 47; IR 1986, r 2.28(2).

[142] IA 1986, Sch B1, para 45(1). 'Business document' is defined in para 45(3).

[143] As a consequence, the administrator owes his duties to the company in the manner that the directors do: see *Kyrris v Oldham* [2004] 1 BCLC 305, CA.

[144] The administrator also has power to remove any director of the company and to appoint any person to be a director of it, whether to fill a vacancy or otherwise: IA 1986, Sch B1, para 59(1).

[145] IA 1986, Sch B1, para 64(1). A management power is defined as a power which could be exercised so as to interfere with the exercise of the administrator's powers: para 64(2).

[146] An administration terminates automatically after one year unless the period is extended by consent of the creditors or order of the court: IA 1986, Sch B1, para 76.

[147] IA 1986, Sch B1, para 49(1), (3). The contents of the statement are prescribed by IR 1986, r 2.33. The rules anticipate that the purpose of the administration may be achieved before the proposals are sent to the creditors: see r 2.33(6).

whose claim and address the administrator is aware and to every member of the company of whose address he is aware as soon as reasonably practicable after the company enters administration,[148] but in any event not later than the end of eight weeks commencing with the company entering administration.[149]

23-77 The proposals must take into account the purpose of administration as set out in IA 1986, Sch B1, para 3, see **23-12**. Most importantly, the proposals may not include any proposal which affects the rights of a secured creditor without his consent; likewise, no proposal may provide for the payment of preferential debts other than in priority to non-preferential debts or other than on a pro-rata basis to other preferential debts without the consent of the preferential creditor.[150] As discussed at **23-7**, this process of consultation with creditors is effectively short-circuited in the case of a pre-pack administration, as is the requirement to hold an initial creditors' meeting. In that case, where the administrator intends to apply to the court or file a notice under Sch B1, para 80(2) (see **23-106**) for the administration to cease at a time before he has sent a statement of his proposals to creditors, he must, at least seven business days before he takes such a step, send to all creditors of the company (so far as he is aware of their addresses) a report containing the information which would otherwise be required in a statement of proposals.[151]

Initial creditors' meeting

23-78 This statement by the administrator of his proposals must be accompanied by an invitation to an initial creditors' meeting (Sch B1, para 51(1)). An initial creditors' meeting need not be held (Sch B1, para 52(1)) where the administrator thinks that:

    (1) the company has sufficient property to enable each creditor to be paid in full;

    (2) the company has insufficient property to enable a distribution to be made to unsecured creditors other than in accordance with the rules governing the prescribed part under IA 1986, s 176A(2) (see **24-72**); or

    (3) neither of the objectives specified in IA 1986, Sch B1, para 3(1)(a) (rescue) and (b) (better realisation than on a winding up) can be achieved (see **23-12**).

23-79 If an initial creditors' meeting is to be held, it must be held as soon as is reasonably practicable after the company enters administration but not later than the end of 10 weeks beginning with the company entering administration (Sch B1, para 51(2)).[152]

23-80 The administrator must present a copy of his proposals to the meeting which may approve or reject the proposals[153] but approval with modifications is only permissible if the administrator consents to each modification.[154] For the proposals to be accepted, they must be accepted by a majority in value of the creditors present and voting, in person or

---

[148] As to when a 'company enters into administration', see IA 1986, Sch B1, para 1(2)(b).

[149] IA 1986, Sch B1, para 49(4), (5). The time period may be varied and extended by the court or administrator in accordance with Sch B1, paras 107, 108. It suffices for these purposes if the administrator publishes a notice undertaking to send a copy of his proposals to any member who applies in writing: see para 49(6).

[150] IA 1986, Sch B1, para 73, unless the proposal is for a CVA or scheme of arrangement which would require the consent of the secured or preferential creditors in any event.   [151] IR 1986, r 2.33(6).

[152] The time period can be varied or extended by the court or the administrator under IA 1986, Sch B1, paras 107, 108.

[153] If a creditors' meeting is not held, approval of the proposals is assumed under IR 1986, r 2.33.

[154] IA 1986, Sch B1, paras 51(3), 53(1).

by proxy.[155] Any resolution is invalid if those voting against it include more than half in value of the creditors to whom notice of the meeting was sent and who are not, to the best of the chairman's belief, persons connected with the company.[156]

23-81 After the meeting, the administrator must as soon as is reasonably practicable report any decision taken to the court and to the registrar of companies and to the prescribed persons[157] but there is no hearing and, in particular, no requirement for the court to approve the proposals. The remedy of any creditor or member who feels aggrieved by the approval of the proposals is to apply to the court to challenge the administrator's conduct (see **23-98**).

23-82 If the administrator subsequently wishes to revise his proposals and he thinks that the proposed revision is substantial, he is required to go through this process again and to present the revised proposals to the creditors and have them approved and then to report the matter to the court.[158]

23-83 If the report is that the creditors have failed to approve the proposals or the revised proposals, as the case may be, the court may provide that the appointment of the administrator shall cease, or may adjourn the hearing, or may make an interim order, or may make an order on any winding-up petition which had been suspended once the company had gone into administration;[159] or it may make any other order that it thinks appropriate (Sch B1, para 55(2)).[160]

23-84 Apart from the initial creditors' meeting, the administrator may call a meeting of creditors at any time (Sch B1, para 62) and must call a meeting of creditors if requested by creditors whose debts amount to at least 10% of the total debts of the company (Sch B1, para 52(2))[161] or if directed to hold a creditors' meeting by the court (Sch B1, para 56).[162] The creditors may also decide to set up a creditors' committee and the committee may require the administrator to attend before it and to provide it with information as to the exercise of his functions (Sch B1, para 57).

---

[155] IR 1986, r 2.43(1). Votes are calculated according to the amount of the creditor's debt as at the date of administration, deducting any amounts paid in respect of the debt after that date: r 2.38(4). A secured creditor is entitled to vote only in respect of the balance of his debt after deducting the value of his security as estimated by him: r 2.40(1). As to the powers of the chairman to give an estimated minimum value to an unliquidated or unascertained debt, see r 2.38(5) and *HMRC v Maxwell* [2011] 2 BCLC 301.

[156] IR 1986, r 2.43(2).   [157] IA 1986, Sch B1, para 53(2); IR 1986, r 2.46.

[158] IA 1986, Sch B1, para 54. See the suggestion by Neuberger J in *Re Dana (UK) Ltd* [1999] 2 BCLC 239 that the original proposals should include a streamlined mechanism to get around the potentially cumbersome need for more meetings. Matters are made easier now by the ability to use correspondence (including electronic communication) in place of meetings, see IA 1986, Sch B1, paras 58, 111.

[159] i.e. under IA 1986, Sch B1, para 40(1)(b).

[160] The court may authorise the implementation of the proposals even in the face of the opposition of the majority creditor, see *Re Structures & Computers Ltd* [1998] 2 BCLC 292; also *Re DKLL Solicitors* [2008] 1 BCLC 112 at 119.

[161] See IR 1986, r 2.37. The creditors must act quickly and a request to hold a meeting must be made within 12 days of the administrator's proposals being sent out. The creditors are liable for the costs (and must give security for the costs) unless the meeting resolves otherwise.

[162] Equally, any matter which might be dealt with at a creditors' meeting may be dealt with by correspondence (including electronic communication) and a requirement to hold a meeting (including the requirement to hold the initial creditors' meeting) may be satisfied by correspondence instead of by an actual meeting: IA 1986, Sch B1, paras 58, 111; also IR 1986, r 2.48.

Disposals ahead of the initial creditors' meeting

23-85 Although the initial creditors' meeting is supposed to approve the administrator's pro-posals, it may happen that the administrator must decide at short notice whether to accept an offer for the company's business. Whether he could do so ahead of the initial meeting was the subject of much debate until Neuberger J in *Re T & D Industries plc*[163] took a robust line concluding that the administrator could dispose of assets without the leave of the court unless the administration order provided otherwise. In his view, this power was necessary in order to avoid unnecessary delay and expense. To preclude sales would be inconsistent with the policy of administration which is meant to provide a more flexible, cheaper and comparatively informal alternative to liquidation.[164] That position was confirmed by Lawrence Collins J in *Re Transbus International Ltd*[165] and the mat-ter is now settled. An administrator (however appointed) has a power of sale ahead of a creditors' meeting and neither the sanction of the creditors nor a direction from the court is required. This position is consistent with the underlying policies of expeditious administration with minimum court involvement. It is also essential to the use of pre-pack administration as discussed at **23-5**. While a sale is permissible, this does not mean that the conduct of the administrator is not open to challenge, for example as unfairly harming the creditors (IA 1986, Sch B1, para 74) or misfeasance (Sch B1 para 75), see at **23-98**.

Managing the business

23-86 An administrator may do anything necessary or expedient for the management of the affairs, business and property of the company (Sch B1, para 59(1))[166] and a person who deals with the administrator in good faith and for value need not inquire whether the administrator is acting within his powers (Sch B1, para 59(3)). In exercising his functions, the administrator acts as the company's agent which is bound by and liable for his acts (Sch B1, para 69).

23-87 The administrator has the powers set out in IA 1986, Sch 1 (Sch B1, para 60) which are derived from the wide powers commonly provided by debenture for administrative receivers and include *inter alia* and without prejudice to the generality of his powers to manage the company's affairs:

- the power to take possession of, collect and get in the property of the company (Sch 1, para 1);
- the power to sell or otherwise dispose of the property of the company (Sch 1, para 2);
- the power to raise or borrow money and grant security (Sch 1, para 3);
- the power to bring and defend any action or other legal proceedings (Sch 1, para 5);
- the power to make any payment which is necessary or incidental to the performance of his functions (Sch 1, para 13);
- the power to carry on the business of the company (Sch 1, para 14).

23-88 An administrator may call a meeting of the members of the company at any time (Sch B1, para 62). An administrator has the same powers as a liquidator to challenge transactions

---

[163] [2000] 1 BCLC 471.   [164] See [2000] 1 BCLC 471 at 477, 483–4.   [165] [2004] 2 BCLC 550.
[166] The power to manage the company's affairs extends to the company's pension scheme since such a scheme is integrally connected with the management of the staff of the company: *Denny v Yeldon* [1995] 1 BCLC 560.

at an undervalue or preferences,[167] extortionate credit transactions and certain floating charges,[168] all of which are discussed in Chapter 25. The administrator has no power
to seek contributions to the company's assets with respect to fraudulent or wrongful
trading,[169] however, but he does have to report on whether the directors' conduct may
merit their disqualification.[170]

23-89 In carrying out his functions, it has to be borne in mind that an administrator, however
appointed, is an officer of the court (Sch B1, para 5). Moreover, in managing the company's affairs etc, the administrator must act in accordance with any proposals or revised
proposals approved by the creditors (Sch B1, para 68(1)). An administrator may apply
to the court for directions in connection with his functions and he must comply with
any directions given.[171] The court may only give directions if: no proposals have been
approved by the creditors;[172] the directions are consistent with any proposals which have
been approved; the court thinks the directions are required by changed circumstances;
or the court thinks the directions are desirable because of a misunderstanding about
proposals or revised proposals (Sch B1, para 68(3)). The courts are anxious to stop administrators making unnecessary use of the power to seek directions in order to ensure that
their decisions are free from legal challenge.[173] Seeking directions adds to the costs of the
administration and may unnecessarily delay matters.

23-90 An administrator is not personally liable on any contracts entered into during the
administration as he acts as the company's agent (Sch B1, para 69), but priority is
accorded to debts or liabilities arising out of any contract entered into by an administrator, see **23-115**. The appointment of an administrator in itself has no effect on existing contracts of the company and, subject to the need to obtain the consent of the court
or administrator for proceedings, see **23-66**, any right to specific performance, lien,
set-off, rescission or injunction available against the company before administration
continues to be available against the company in administration.[174] In practice, contracts often provide for termination on one of the parties going into administration.
Likewise the appointment of an administrator as such has no effect on contracts of
employment, but administrators will frequently need to reduce the workforce and so
dismissals may follow. For contracts of employment adopted by the administrators,
priority is also accorded to certain sums arising with respect to such contracts, as is
discussed at **23-116**.

Distributions to creditors

23-91 A particular problem for administrators prior to the reforms effected by the EA 2002
was that there was no general power to make distributions to creditors and creative
schemes had to be devised which allowed for payments to be sanctioned as ancillary matters to the discharge of the administration.[175] The legislation now specifically
provides that an administrator may make a distribution to a creditor of the company,

[167] IA 1986, ss 238, 239.   [168] IA 1986, ss 244, 245.   [169] i.e. under IA 1986, ss 213, 214.
[170] Company Directors Disqualification Act 1986, s 7(3)(c).   [171] IA 1986, Sch B1, paras 63, 68(2).
[172] i.e. because the initial creditors' meeting has not been held.
[173] See comments by Neuberger J in *Re T and D Industries plc* [2000] 1 BCLC 471 at 478.
[174] *Astor Chemicals Ltd v Synthetic Technology Ltd* [1990] BCLC 1. See also *Re P & C and R & T (Stockport)
Ltd* [1991] BCLC 366.
[175] See *Re Lune Metal Products Ltd* [2007] 2 BCLC 746, an 'old' case which reviews the mechanisms which
were used to get around these problems.

subject to the application of IA 1986, s 175 (preferential debts) as it applies on a winding up.[176] Where the creditor is neither secured nor preferential, the permission of the court is required (Sch B1, para 65).[177] This provision has proved invaluable in the light of the way in which administration has developed with it now being common for the administrator to seek permission to make a distribution to unsecured creditors (where funds are available for that purpose) and then to have the company dissolved expeditiously by notice to the registrar in accordance with Sch B1, para 84, discussed at **23-111**.[178] The breadth of the jurisdiction to make distributions under Sch B1, para 65, can be seen from decisions such as *Re HPJ UK Ltd*[179] where the court accepted that the power is wide enough to allow a distribution to a specified creditor (HMRC in this case) in full satisfaction of all claims even though this was not a rateable distribution. The crucial considerations were that the creditors unanimously approved of the distribution and the court considered the distribution to be important in attaining the objectives of the administration in the interests of the creditors as a whole. In *Re MG Rover Belux SA*[180] the court was willing to authorise a distribution (to Belgian creditors) otherwise than in accordance with the priorities which would apply under English law, when a distribution in this way was in the interests of the creditors as a whole.

23-92   In addition, an administrator may make a payment to any creditor if he thinks it is likely to assist achievement of the purpose of administration (Sch B1, para 66).[181] In *Re Collins & Aikman Europe SA*,[182] following the opening of main insolvency proceedings in England, the administrators were anxious to preclude the opening of secondary proceedings in other countries which would have impeded the achievement of the purpose of the administration. The administrators therefore gave undertakings to creditors in those other jurisdictions that, if they desisted from opening secondary proceedings, their respective financial positions as creditors under local law would be respected, so far as possible, in the English administration. On seeking directions to this effect, the court considered that the payments could be regarded as being properly made if the administrators reasonably thought them to be 'likely to assist achievement of the purpose of administration' within Sch B1, para 66. On the facts, the administrator did so consider and the court could direct that they should honour their undertakings.

Selling the business

23-93   In selling the business, the administrator owes a duty to the company to take reasonable care, judged by the standard of the ordinary skilled insolvency practitioner, to obtain the best price that the circumstances permit, including a duty to take reasonable care in choosing the time at which to sell the property.[183]

---

[176] The relevant date for determining the amount of preferential debts is the date when the company entered administration: IA 1986, s 387. The preferential debts are those debts set out in IA 1986, Sch 6.

[177] Once permission has been granted, the administrator must adhere to the detailed rules governing distributions laid down in IR 1986, rr 2.68–2.105 which include (in r 2.85) rules on set-off broadly similar to those applicable in liquidation (see **24-58**), the difference being that the set-off rule only applies if the administrator makes a distribution to unsecured creditors.

[178] See, for example, *Re Ballast plc* [2005] 1 BCLC 446.   [179] [2007] BCC 284.

[180] [2007] BCC 446.

[181] There is an uncertain overlap between this provision and IA 1986, Sch 1, para 13 (power to make any payment which is necessary or incidental to the performance of the administrator's functions).

[182] [2007] 1 BCLC 182.   [183] *Re Charnley Davies Ltd (No 2)* [1990] BCLC 760.

Dealing with charged property

23-94 A matter of concern for secured creditors or creditors with proprietary rights is the power of an administrator to deal with certain assets as if the company has an unencumbered title to them. This power is thought necessary particularly if the administrator wishes to sell the business as a going concern. There are two categories of powers, depending on whether the administrator needs the consent of the court.

23-95 With an order of the court, an administrator may dispose of assets subject to a security other than a floating charge as if the property were not subject to the security or he may dispose of goods in the possession of the company under a hire-purchase agreement (which includes under a retention of title agreement)[184] as if the rights of the owner were vested in the company; in each case, the court must think that the disposal would be likely to promote the purpose of administration in respect of the company.[185] The court's order will be conditional on the application of the net proceeds of the disposal (or market value, if higher) towards discharging the sums secured by the security or payable under the hire-purchase agreement.[186]

23-96 In considering whether or not to consent to the disposal of charged property, the court's approach is similar to that considered at **23-66** in relation to the granting of permission for actions otherwise restrained by the moratorium. The court will balance the prejudice felt by a secured creditor if an order is made against the prejudice that would otherwise be felt by those interested in the promotion of the purpose of administration.[187] But the burden of proof lies on the administrators to satisfy the court that it would be appropriate to interfere with the rights of the secured creditors to conduct their own sale at a time of their choosing and, in particular, the court must be satisfied that the sale of the assets unencumbered by the security interest would be likely to promote the purpose of the administration and that the net proceeds would be paid towards discharging the secured debts.[188]

23-97 An administrator may dispose of or take action relating to property which is subject to a floating charge as if the property were not subject to the charge.[189] Where such property is disposed of, the chargeholder has the same priority in respect of property which directly or indirectly represents the property disposed of as he had in respect of that property.[190] There is no need to obtain the consent of the creditor or the court in this instance. Of course, since the proceeds of the property disposed of may be used by the administrator to meet the expenses of administration (see **23-114**), there may be no property to which the interest of the floating chargeholder can transfer. The existence of this power is one

---

[184] Defined IA 1986, Sch B1, para 111(1).

[185] IA 1986, Sch B1, paras 71(2), 72(2). A copy of any order made by the court under these provisions must, within 14 days starting with the date of the order, be sent by the administrator to the registrar of companies: paras 71(5), 72(4). [186] IA 1986, Sch B1, paras 71(3), 72(3).

[187] See *Re ARV Aviation Ltd* [1989] BCLC 664; *Re Capitol Films Ltd, Rubin v Cobalt Pictures Ltd* [2011] 2 BCLC 359.

[188] *Re Capitol Films Ltd, Rubin v Cobalt Pictures Ltd* [2011] 2 BCLC 359 at [35]–[36] (on the facts in this case, there was no basis for giving consent—there was uncertainty as to the identity of the assets being sold and concerns about the price and the purchaser—who was an associate of the director of the company in administration). Note also that the court concluded in this case that the application by the administrators for an order under IA 1986, Sch B1, para 71, allowing disposal, was irrational and misconceived and ordered that the secured creditors who opposed the application should have their costs against the administrators on an indemnity basis, see at [96].

[189] IA 1986, Sch B1, para 70(1). As to whether a charge is fixed or floating, see Chapter 21.

[190] IA 1986, Sch B1, para 70(2), (3).

reason why the debenture holder needs to consider carefully whether he wants to prevent the appointment by others of an administrator and instead appoint an administrative receiver, if that option is available to him, or perhaps to appoint an administrator out of court. A creditor who objects to a disposal by an administrator can challenge the conduct of the administrator.

Challenging the administrator's conduct

Unfairly harm

23–98 Any creditor or member of a company in administration may apply to the court claiming that:

(1) the administrator is acting or has acted so as unfairly to harm the interests of the applicant (whether alone or in common with some or all other members or creditors); or

(2) the administrator proposes to act in a way which would unfairly harm the interests of the applicant (whether alone or in common with some or all other members or creditors) (Sch B1, para 74(1)).

23–99 The wording of this provision (unfairly harm) was altered from 'unfairly prejudicial' in the 'old' provision which latter term is well established in the context of shareholder remedies (see CA 2006, s 994 and Chapter 17). This welcome distancing of this quite distinct provision from that remedy may also suggest a lowering of the threshold. The harm required is harm to the interests of the creditor or member arising from the actions of the administrator and it must be unfair to the creditor.[191] An order can be made under this provision whether or not the action complained of is within the administrator's powers under Sch B1 or was taken in reliance on a court order allowing for the disposal of property of a creditor (Sch B1, para 74(5)).

Inefficient

23–100 It will be recalled that an administrator is under an obligation to perform his functions as quickly and efficiently as is reasonably practicable (Sch B1, para 4), see **23-13**. To provide an incentive to adhere to that obligation, a creditor or member of a company in administration may apply to the court claiming that the administrator is in breach of this requirement (Sch B1, para 74(2)).

23–101 The court may take a variety of steps on an application on either of these grounds including granting relief, dismissing the application, adjourning the hearing, making an interim order or any other order it thinks appropriate; but an order must not impede or prevent the implementation of a voluntary arrangement or a scheme of arrangement or any proposals approved by the creditors.[192] The range of possible orders includes requiring an administrator to do or not to do a specified thing or requiring a creditors' meeting to be held for a specified purpose (Sch B1, para 74(4)).

---

[191] See *Re Lehman Bros, Four Private Investment Funds v Lomas* [2009] 1 BCLC 161 (where administrators were acting in accordance with their obligations under IA 1986, Sch B1, the court thought it was difficult to see how an unwillingness on the administrators' part to devote more time and resources than they had already done to answering questions put to them by a particular group of creditors, directed to eliciting information about assets in which the creditors claimed an interest, could be said to be unfair, even if the refusal to provide the information sought was potentially harmful).

[192] IA 1986, Sch B1, para 74(3), (4), and (6).

Misfeasance

23-102 The court, on the application of the Official Receiver, an administrator or liquidator, or a creditor or contributory of the company may examine the conduct of an administrator (Sch B1, para 75(1), (2)). The grounds for such an investigation are allegations that the administrator has misapplied or retained or become accountable for money or other property of the company, or has breached a fiduciary or other duty in relation to the company, or has been guilty of misfeasance (Sch B1, para 75(3)). The court may order the administrator to repay or account for money to the company, to pay interest, and to contribute a sum to the company's property by way of compensation for breach of duty or misfeasance (Sch B1, para 75(4)). This provision is an improvement on the previous position which required the company to go into liquidation before a misfeasance action could be brought against an administrator.

F Ending administration—exit routes

23-103 The appointment of an administrator ceases at the end of the period of one year beginning with the date on which it takes effect, but the period may be extended by the court for a specified period on the application of the administrator.[193] The creditors may extend the administrator's term of office (once) for a specified period not exceeding six months by consent, defined as the consent of each secured creditor and more than 50% of the unsecured creditors who respond to the request to give consent.[194] An extension by consent cannot be given after an extension has been ordered by the court.

Termination of administration

23-104 An administrator must apply to the court to bring the administration to an end if he thinks the purpose of administration cannot be achieved; or that the company should not have entered administration; or if required to do so by a creditors' meeting (Sch B1, para 79(2)). The administrator must also apply to the court to bring an administration to an end where he has been appointed by the court and he has achieved the purpose of administration.[195]

23-105 Additionally, a creditor can apply to the court to have an administration stopped if he or she considers that the appointment was made for an improper motive (Sch B1, para 81). The court may also order that the appointment of an administrator is to cease where a winding-up order is made on a public interest petition.[196]

23-106 Where the administrator has been appointed out of court, i.e. by a qualifying floating chargeholder or by the company or directors, and he considers that the purpose of

---

[193] IA 1986, Sch B1, para 76(1), (2); and the court may do so even if the period has already been extended by order or consent: para 77(1). The *Insolvency Service Evaluation Report* (2008), n 46, found that 80% of administrations within the sample reviewed were completed within one year and the remainder within 18 months and so these findings would suggest that the time parameters set by the Act are suitable: see *Evaluation Report*, para 3.5.

[194] IA 1986, Sch B1, paras 76(2)(b), 78(1). It may be that only the consent of preferential and secured creditors is required: see para 78(2).

[195] IA 1986, Sch B1, para 79(3). On the hearing of the application, the court may adjourn the hearing, dismiss the application, make any interim order, or make any order it thinks appropriate: para 79(4).

[196] IA 1986, Sch B1, para 82; equally, the court may order that the administrator remain in post, see para 82(3). As to a public interest petition, see n 53.

administration has been sufficiently achieved, he may file a notice with the court and the registrar of companies and his appointment ceases on that filing.[197]

Administration to voluntary winding up

23-107 An administrator can end the administration and convert to a voluntary winding up where the administrator thinks that the secured creditors have received all that they are likely to receive (remember the administrator can make distributions to secured and preferential creditors) and there is money available for the unsecured creditors (Sch B1, para 83).[198]

23-108 This conversion option is available even to an administrator appointed by court order and it is not necessary in that case first to obtain a court order terminating the administration.[199] Whether it is appropriate to convert the administration to voluntary winding up (i.e. whether the circumstances exist for the use of the procedure) is a matter for the administrator[200] and the administrator is not subject to any objective test when so deciding.[201]

23-109 The administrator must send the appropriate notice to the registrar of companies and a copy of this notice is filed with the court and sent to each of the company's creditors of whom he is aware (Sch B1, para 83(5)). Once the notice is registered by the registrar of companies, the administrator's appointment ends and the company moves into a creditors' voluntary winding up as if a resolution for winding up had been passed on the date of registration of the notice (Sch B1, para 83(6)).[202] The administrator becomes the liquidator unless the creditors choose to appoint someone else (Sch B1, para 83(7)). It is the registration of the notice from the administrator which causes the appointment of the administrator to cease to have effect and the operative date is the date of registration and the Parliamentary intention is that the company passes from administration to winding up without any hiatus.[203]

23-110 A particular problem under the old law related to the position of the preferential creditors who were disadvantaged if the company went from administration into voluntary rather than compulsory liquidation for reasons to do with the date at which the pref-

---

[197] IA 1986, Sch B1, para 80(1)–(3). The administrator must send a copy of this notice to every creditor of whom he is aware: para 80(4), (5).

[198] Even if this mechanism is not available (because the administrator does not think he can make a distribution to unsecured creditors), an administrator can seek an order under IA 1986, Sch B1, para 79, that the administration end at a specified time, that time being the passing of a resolution for the company to go into a creditors' voluntary liquidation so allowing a seamless passage from administration to a CVL in this way: see *Re T M Kingdom Ltd* [2007] BCC 480.   [199] *Re Ballast plc* [2005] 1 BCLC 446.

[200] *Re Ballast plc* [2005] 1 BCLC 446. The Insolvency Service found that this ability to convert from administration to a creditors' voluntary liquidation was one of the most marked consequences of the reforms effected by the EA 2002, with the result that the lines between the two processes have blurred: see *Insolvency Service Evaluation Report* (2008), n 46, paras 3.6 and 3.8, also noting that administration is often a terminal event with few companies emerging from the process as 'active' companies, see para 3.7. See also n 235.

[201] *Unidare plc v Cohen* [2006] 2 BCLC 140.

[202] A notice sent but not registered before the administration automatically ended (one year having elapsed, Sch B1, para 76) is still effective for these purposes for the crucial requirement is that it is sent by an administrator before his appointment ceases to have effect: *Re E Squared Ltd* [2006] 2 BCLC 277.

[203] *Re E Squared Ltd* [2006] 2 BCLC 277. See Todd, 'Administration Post-Enterprise Act—What are the Options for Exits' (2006) 19 Insolv Int 17 who comments that this mechanism makes 'for a very slick exit indeed' with no need to advertise the liquidator's appointment or to hold a creditors' meeting and with the administrator becoming liquidator (though he can later be replaced). As to the date of registration, see *Re Globespan Airways Ltd* [2012] EWHC 359.

erential debts were calculated. Various contorted schemes were devised to address this difficulty,[204] but the issue has been resolved, for the date for determining the relevant preferential debts, even if the company subsequently goes into liquidation, is now the date on which the company enters administration (IA 1986, s 387).

Administration to dissolution

23-111   If the administrator thinks that the company has no property or no remaining property which might permit a distribution to its creditors, he must send a notice to that effect to the registrar of companies (Sch B1, para 84) and this requirement applies to administrators appointed by the court and out of court.[205] On receipt of this notice, the registrar must register it and three months after the filing, the company is deemed dissolved. As under Sch B1, para 83 above, this option is entirely a matter for the administrator, even an administrator appointed by court order, and it is not necessary to obtain a court order terminating the administration.[206]

23-112   The nature of the obligation imposed on the administrator by Sch B1, para 84 was considered in *Re GHE Realisations Ltd*[207] where the court held that once the administrator 'thinks' that the company has no further assets (regardless of whether the company had assets which had previously been distributed) he is under a duty to serve a notice under Sch B1, para 84(1), subject always to the option of making an application under para 84(2) for the court to disapply para 84(1). In other words, para 84 is not limited to the scenario where the company never had any assets for distribution.

Vacation of office

23-113   An administrator can resign his office by giving the required notice (Sch B1, para 87), he can be removed from office by the court (Sch B1, para 88, see **23-17**), and he must vacate his office if he ceases to be qualified to act as an insolvency practitioner (Sch B1, para 89).

G Administration expenses and liabilities

23-114   Where a person ceases to be an administrator,[208] his remuneration and any expenses are charged on and payable out of property of which he had custody or control immediately before he ceased to be the company's administrator and are payable in priority to any security which, as created, was a floating charge (Sch B1, para 99(1)–(3)). This provision gives the administrator's claim for remuneration and expenses priority over the claims of the holder of a floating charge. The detailed mandatory rule as to administration expenses is set out at IR 1986, r 2.67 which mimics r 4.218 in respect of liquidation expenses. Rule 2.67 lists the order of priority governing the payments of the expenses of the administration[209] and the most significant categories are r 2.67(a), expenses properly

---

[204]   See, for example, *Re Mark One (Oxford St) plc* [2000] 1 BCLC 462.
[205]   *Re Ballast plc* [2005] 1 BCLC 446.   [206]   *Re Ballast plc* [2005] 1 BCLC 446.
[207]   [2006] 1 All ER 357.
[208]   Although strictly speaking the Insolvency Act envisages these payments being made when the administration ceases, in fact the administrator will pay these expenses as they arise in the course of the administration: see *Powdrill v Watson* [1994] 2 BCLC 118 at 142.
[209]   The court may alter the priority if the assets are insufficient to pay all of the expenses in the administration, see IR 1986, r 2.67(2), (3).

incurred by the administrator in performing his functions in the administration of the company; r 2.67(f), necessary disbursements;[210] r 2.67(h), the administrator's remuneration and unpaid pre-appointment costs; and r 2.67(j), corporation tax. The issue of what is an expense in administration (or in liquidation, see **24-63**) continues to exercise the courts. In *Goldacre (Offices) Ltd v Nortel Networks UK Ltd*[211] it was held that where an administrator elects to use leasehold premises for the benefit of the administration, any liability incurred while the property is so used is payable in full as an administration expense.[212] Meanwhile the Court of Appeal ruled in *Bloom v The Pensions Regulator*[213] that sums due under certain directions and notices issued by the Pensions Regulator under the Pensions Act 2004 against companies in administration,[214] though they did not give rise to a provable debt in the administration, are payable as a necessary disbursement by an administrator within IR 1986, r 2.67(f). While the Court of Appeal agreed that this conclusion gave rise to difficulties and anomalies which had been identified in the court below,[215] there was an equal or greater anomaly, the court said, in treating these liabilities as not payable as an expense, and not as provable debts, in which case they would disappear into a black hole which cannot have been the intention of Parliament when enacting the Pensions Act 2004. It is understood that the decision is under appeal to the Supreme Court. The question of pre-appointment expenses had been controversial[216] and it is an important issue in the context of the extensive use of pre-packs, discussed at **23-5**, where a great deal of work is done pre-appointment by the person who subsequently becomes the administrator. On occasion those costs have been allowed, as a discretionary matter, on an application for an administration order, see **23-10**. The position is now governed by the Insolvency Rules 1986 which allow pre-appointment costs to be an expense in the administration in certain circumstances.[217] Essentially, the pre-appointment costs must be approved by the creditors' committee (if there is one), or by a resolution at a meeting of creditors, or (if the administrator makes a statement that the company has insufficient property to enable a distribution to be made to unsecured creditors other than by virtue of the prescribed part) by approval of the secured or preferential creditors. Ultimately, if the creditors do not reach a decision or the administrator is dissatisfied with the amount, the administrator may apply to the court.[218]

23-115 Priority over both the administrator's remuneration and the expenses of the administration and the claim of a floating chargeholder is given in respect of any sum payable in

---

[210] See *Re Trident Fashions Ltd, Exeter City Co v Bairstow* [2007] 2 BCLC 455 (business rates payable in respect of occupied property were 'necessary disbursements' falling within IR 1986, r 2.67(1)(f) and therefore administration expenses; likewise with respect to unoccupied premises), but SI 2008/386 now exempts companies in administration from rates on unoccupied premises.   [211] [2010] 2 BCLC 248.

[212] Crucially, the court also ruled that the liability to pay the full quarter's rent falls due on each quarter day and it is not to be apportioned to the amount of time the administrators use the premises so if they vacate a day into the quarter, the entire rent for that quarter is still payable as an administration expense, see at [20]. See too *Re Luminar Lava Ignite Ltd* [2012] EWHC 951.   [213] [2012] 1 BCLC 248.

[214] Essentially notices or directions requiring these companies to make payments to an employer's underfunded pension scheme—the employer usually being other companies in the same group.

[215] [2011] BCC 277, Briggs J acknowledged that classifying these payments as necessary disbursements and therefore an expense in the administration is likely to prove unfair to the creditors of the company which receives the direction or notice from the Pensions Regulator.

[216] See Walton, 'Pre-Appointment Administration Fees—Papering Over the Cracks in Pre-Packs' (2008) 21 Insolv Int 72.

[217] IR 1986, r 2.67A. Note that a statement as to pre-administration costs must be included in the administrator's proposals for achieving the purpose of administration, see IR 1986, r 2.33(ka).

[218] IR 1986, r 2.67A(5).

respect of debts or liabilities arising out of a contract entered into by the former administrator before he ceased to be the administrator (Sch B1, para 99(4)).[219] This provision
creates a statutory charge in favour of these claimants which attaches to any property of
which the administrator had custody or control immediately before he ceased to be the
administrator and, if that property is insufficient to meet all of those claims, the claimants must be paid *pari passu.*[220]

23-116 This super-priority, as it is often called, for contractual liabilities extends to any liability
arising out of a contract of employment adopted by the former administrator before he
ceased to be the company's administrator.[221] For this purpose, the administrator is not
to be taken to have adopted a contract of employment by reason of anything done within
14 days of his appointment; and no account is taken of any liabilities by reference to anything done before the adoption of the contract and no account is taken of a liability to
make a payment other than wages or salary.[222] 'Salary' for these purposes does include an
employer's liability to pay PAYE and National Insurance Contributions to the Revenue
since these payments are part of a salary and liability for them can only arise when a salary payment is made to an employee. Therefore such sums have priority over the payment
of the administrator's remuneration and expenses of administration.[223] But payments in
lieu of notice and protective awards,[224] redundancy and unfair dismissal payments[225] and
wrongful dismissal awards[226] are not wages or salary for these purposes and therefore do
not benefit from the statutory super-priority on insolvency. The courts are anxious not to
take such a wide construction of 'wages or salary' as to undermine the rescue culture by
making administration more expensive.[227]

23-117 The result is that, in administration, claims are to be ranked as follows: (1) secured creditors with fixed charges in relation to their security (subject to the costs of realisation);
(2) debts and liabilities arising from contracts entered into by the administrator and
liabilities for 'wages or salary' arising under contracts of employment adopted by the

---

[219] This 'super-priority' does not extend to expenses incurred under contracts entered into by the company prior to administration: *Centre Reinsurance International Co v Freakley* [2007] 1 BCLC 85 (expenses
incurred by a company's insurers in administering and handling claims by employees under an insurance
policy were not recoverable as such expenses did not represent a debt payable or a liability incurred under a
contract entered into by the administrators in carrying out their functions for these purposes).

[220] *Re Spread Betting Media Ltd* [2008] 2 BCLC 89; in these circumstances the court, in the exercise of
its inherent jurisdiction, may order that the administrators be paid a reasonable sum out of the available
funds.

[221] IA 1986, Sch B1, para 99(5). These provisions originated in the IA 1994: see *Re a company (No 005174
of 1999)* [2001] 1 BCLC 593 at 597–8.

[222] IA 1986, Sch B1, para 99(5); and 'wages or salary' are defined in para 99(6) to include contributions to
an occupational pension scheme. See *Powdrill v Watson* [1995] 2 All ER 65, HL.

[223] *Inland Revenue Commissioners v Lawrence* [2001] 1 BCLC 204, CA.

[224] *Re Huddersfield Fine Worsteds Ltd* [2006] 2 BCLC 160. An exception is made with respect to one limited category of payments in lieu of notice, where an employer, having given notice to an employee, decides
not to require the employee to work his notice and pays the wages attributable to the notice period in a lump
sum (so-called 'garden leave'). Such payments are 'wages' since they are payments in lieu of the wages which
would have been payable had the notice been worked and, as such, are entitled to super-priority over the
expenses of the administration.   [225] *Re Allders Department Stores Ltd* [2006] 2 BCLC 1.

[226] *Re Leeds United AFC Ltd* [2008] BCC 11. If a payment is not referable to an obligation of an employee
under a subsisting contract of employment to render his services, it does not fall within the ordinary meaning of the word 'wages'. Any payment on account of an employee's claim for damages for breach of contract
is not a payment of 'wages' in the ordinary meaning of that word.

[227] *Re Huddersfield Fine Worsteds Ltd* [2006] 2 BCLC 160 at 190–1, CA; *Re Allders Department Stores Ltd*
[2006] 2 BCLC 1.

administrator; (3) the expenses of administration including the administrator's remuneration; (4) preferential claims,[228] though this is a much less significant category now, see
24-70; (5) claims under a floating charge (subject to the application of the prescribed part
under IA 1986, s 176A, see **24-72**); and (6) unsecured creditors.[229]

H Concluding issues

Reform

23-118 In the wake of the financial crisis, the Insolvency Service consulted in 2010 as to whether
a new restructuring moratorium might be introduced,[230] but a Ministerial Statement[231]
in 2011 accepted that the urgency of the case for introducing such a moratorium is not
as great as previously thought and that existing mechanisms such as schemes of arrangement and administration have proved effective. It has been decided therefore that the
Insolvency Service will continue to consider issues surrounding restructuring and company rescue, but it is clear that there are no plans for changes to the existing regimes at this
stage.[232]

The role of liquidation

23-119 As noted, it is common for administrators either to convert an administration into a
creditors' voluntary liquidation or to make a distribution to unsecured creditors and then
file notice for dissolution under Sch B1, para 84.[233] In other words, the process either
becomes a liquidation or is conducted as a liquidation followed by dissolution and the
issue is whether there is some abuse of process involved in this development.[234] On the
one hand, it is difficult to see a risk of abuse—the administrator is a licensed insolvency
practitioner, as is a liquidator; the administrator has power to challenge vulnerable transactions and must report on whether the directors are unfit and should be disqualified,
as does a liquidator. The expenses of administration as set out in IR 1986, r 2.67 mirror
those set out for liquidation in IR 1986, r 4.218. The requirement to set aside a prescribed
part for unsecured creditors applies in administration and liquidation. In other words, in
some ways the processes are very similar so it may not matter very much which route is

---

[228] IA 1986, s 175 is applied in administration by virtue of Sch B1, para 65.

[229] Paid on a *pari passu* basis, if there are insufficient funds, see IA 1986, Sch B1, r 2.69.

[230] See Insolvency Service, *Proposals For A Restructuring Moratorium*—a consultation (July 2010); also
an earlier consultation from the Insolvency Service entitled *Encouraging Company Rescue* (2009) which
focused on whether greater use might be made of Company Voluntary Arrangement (CVA) procedures as a
route for the restructuring of a company's affairs with a view to extending to medium and large-sized companies the option of a CVA with a moratorium.

[231] See Ministerial Statement, *Consultation On Proposals For A Restructuring Moratorium*, 11 May
2011.

[232] For a discussion of the evolution of 'rescue' through from the Cork Committee to pre-pack admin-
istration and beyond and the difficulties in quantifying 'rescue', see generally Finch, 'Corporate Rescue
Processes, the Search for Quality and the Capacity to Resolve' [2010] JBL 503; Finch, 'Corporate Rescue in a
World of Debt' [2008] JBL 756.

[233] In 2010–11, 1,384 administrations were converted into a creditors' voluntary liquidation, in 2009–10
the figure was 1,623; see *Statistical Tables on Companies Registration Activities 2010–11*, Table C2.

[234] See Keay, 'What Future for Liquidation in Light of the Enterprise Act Reforms?' [2005] JBL 143; Frieze,
'The Company in Financial Difficulties: The Alternatives' (2008) 21 Insolv Int 124 at 126.

used. On the other hand, there are concerns that administrators are using the process as a way of increasing their fees by having the company go into administration first and then into liquidation when objectively it might have been evident that the purpose of administration cannot be achieved and the company should have gone straight into liquidation with lower costs to creditors.[235] In a liquidation a liquidator has a duty to investigate the causes of collapse (though the extent to which this happens in a voluntary liquidation is debatable) and the directors' conduct may be open to greater scrutiny. For example, a liquidator, but not an administrator, can bring a claim for wrongful trading or fraudulent trading under IA 1986, ss 213, 214, see **25-8**. A director also has to face a creditors' meeting in a creditors' voluntary liquidation (IA 1986, s 99(1)) but can avoid this process in an administration.

The demise of administrative receivership

23-120 Though the demise of administrative receivership might have been expected, the financial crisis has brought a resurgence in their use where that option is still open to lenders, i.e. because they have a qualifying floating charge created before 15 September 2003.[236]

The position of the unsecured creditor

23-121 One of the intended strengths of administration is that it is a collective procedure conducted in the interests of the creditors as a whole in comparison to the time when an administrative receiver could conduct a receivership with little or no regard to the interests of other creditors. As mentioned, the rise of the pre-pack administration (see **23-5**) and the ability, even when there is no pre-pack, for an administrator to sell assets without the need for the consent of the creditors or a direction of the court (see **23-85**) has meant that the unsecured creditors are in many ways as sidelined under this process as they were under administrative receiverships.[237] That situation might be tolerable if it could be shown that returns to the unsecured creditors have improved, but the limited evidence on shareholder returns is mixed.[238] Essentially, it seems that secured and preferential creditors have maintained, if not improved, their levels of returns on

[235] See Mumford & Katz, 'Study of Administration Cases' (2007) 20 Insolv Int 97 at 102 who found that while the majority of cases studied by them were situations where the company had been properly put into administration, they found that in 29% of the cases studied, there were greater doubts about why the company was in administration rather than liquidation, but those 29% of cases involved smaller companies which amounted to only 3% by asset value of the companies surveyed. The Insolvency Service view is that, if there are concerns about the appropriateness of some administrations, that is a matter for the regulatory body of the relevant administrator to consider: see *Insolvency Service Evaluation Report* (2008), n 46, para 3.8.

[236] The number of receiverships (GB) was 552 in 2006–07 (compared to 3,536 administrations); in 2009–10, there were 1,526 receiverships (3,879 administrations); in 2010–11, there were 1,312 receiverships (3,032 administrations): see *Statistical Tables on Companies Registration Activities 2010–11*, Table C2, but the receivership figures do not distinguish between administrative receivers and receivers appointed under the Law of Property Act 1925.

[237] See Walton, 'Pre-Appointment Administration Fees—Papering Over the Cracks in Pre-Packs' (2008) 21 Insolv Int 72.

[238] See Mumford & Katz, 'Study of Administration Cases' (2007) 20 Insolv Int 97 at 102 who believe that administration is likely to produce a result at least equal to that achievable in a creditors' voluntary liquidation.

administration compared to administrative receiverships, but ordinary unsecured creditors have yet to see much improvement in returns to them from administration[239] (though their position may have improved because of the prescribed part, see **24-72**).[240]

[239] See early research by Frisby, *Preliminary Analysis*, n 15, who found that the average return to secured creditors in pre-packs was 42% and in business sales the average return was 28%; the equivalent figures for preferential creditors were 13% and 38%; and for unsecured creditors were 1% and 3%: see pp 53–7.

[240] See *Insolvency Service Evaluation Report* (2008), n 46, para 3.10; Frisby, *Report on Insolvency Outcomes—Presented to the Insolvency Service* (2006), p 73; Frisby, *Interim Report to the Insolvency Service on Returns to Creditors from Pre- and Post-Enterprise Insolvency Procedures* (2007). Also note that while realisations may have increased in administration compared to receiverships, there is evidence of higher costs as well: see Armour, Hsu and Walters, 'The Impact of the Enterprise Act 2002 on Realisations and Costs in Corporate Rescue Proceedings, A Report Prepared for the Insolvency Service' (2006), paras 3.4–3.5.

24

Liquidation and dissolution— winding up the insolvent company

A Introduction

24-1 Winding up is a term commonly associated with the ending of a company's existence. In fact, winding up or liquidation (the terms are synonymous) is the process by which the assets of the company are collected in and realised, its liabilities discharged and the net surplus, if there is one, distributed to the persons entitled to it.[1] Only when this has been done is the company's existence finally terminated by a process known as dissolution. A company may be wound up though it is solvent, for example, because a business project has come to an end or because members of a family business wish to retire or, sometimes, because of internal disputes; more commonly a company is wound up because it is insolvent and this chapter concentrates on the winding up of insolvent companies. Prior to winding up, a company may have been in some other insolvency process, for example, it may come to liquidation via administration (and remember also that an administration can in some ways look very like a liquidation where there is a distribution to secured creditors followed by speedy dissolution, see **23-111**) or via a company voluntary arrangement which has failed. A company may go directly then into liquidation or it may be that winding up is preceded by some other form of insolvency proceeding.

The legislative framework

24-2 The core insolvency legislation is the Insolvency Act 1986 while the procedural rules are contained in the Insolvency Rules 1986. Many insolvencies now involve a cross-border element. This factor raises many issues, the most basic being the need to decide which jurisdiction should govern any insolvency process. Essentially, the choice is between territorialism (each jurisdiction acts with regard to assets within its jurisdiction), universalism (one jurisdiction assumes responsibility for all the assets and liabilities wherever located) or, more pragmatically, a modified universalism which involves identifying the jurisdiction best placed to deal with the insolvent entity while recognising the sovereign right of other jurisdictions to manage aspects of the insolvency process within their territories in respect of assets and liabilities located there.[2]

---

[1] See IA 1986, ss 107, 143(1).

[2] See the discussion in *Re HIH Casualty and General Insurance Ltd*; *McMahon v McGrath* [2008] 3 All ER 869, HL; also *Rubin v Eurofinance* [2011] 2 BCLC 473 at [61]–[62]; *Cambridge Gas Transport Corp v Official Committee of Unsecured Creditors of Navigator Holdings Ltd* [2007] 2 BCLC 141.

24-3 The European framework addressing these issues is the EC Regulation on Insolvency Proceedings (Council Regulation (EC) No 1346/2000)[3] which has direct effect and is an integral element of our insolvency law. The aim of the Regulation is to improve the efficiency and effectiveness of insolvency proceedings having cross-border effect, but it does not attempt to harmonise insolvency procedures throughout the EU and generally the applicable law is the national law of the state in which proceedings are opened. The Regulation applies only when the debtor has his centre of main interests within the EU (other than Denmark) and it deals only with procedures, assets and creditors within the EU.[4]

24-4 The insolvency proceedings within the UK which are affected by the EC Regulation (and which therefore can only be opened in accordance with the rules laid down by the EC Regulation) and which enjoy automatic recognition and enforcement under the EC Regulation are:

(1) compulsory winding up[5] and creditors' voluntary winding up with confirmation of the court[6] (discussed later); and

(2) voluntary arrangements and administration (discussed in Chapters 22 and 23, respectively).

The EC Regulation does not apply to receiverships, winding up on the just and equitable ground (a shareholder remedy) or members' voluntary winding up (company is not insolvent).

24-5 The main advantage of the EC Regulation is that it establishes a clear structure for the commencement and recognition of insolvency proceedings where there is a cross-border element involving business in more than one Member State. Essentially, the Regulation provides for main proceedings, territorial proceedings and secondary proceedings (see art 3). Main proceedings may be opened in the Member State where the debtor has his 'centre of main interests' which is presumed, in the case of a company, to be the place of the registered office, but that presumption can be rebutted if factors which are both objective and ascertainable by third parties establish that the actual position is different.[7] Territorial proceedings may be opened in any Member State where the debtor has an

---

[3] OJ L 160/1, 30.06.2000, which came into effect on 31 May 2002 throughout the EU (with the exception of Denmark) and applies to relevant insolvency proceedings (see **24-4**) opened on or after that date; see generally Moss, Fletcher and Isaacs, *The EC Regulation on Insolvency Proceedings: A Commentary and Annotated Guide* (2nd edn, 2009); Goode, *Principles of Corporate Insolvency Law* (4th edn, 2011). A revision of the Regulation is expected in 2012–13.

[4] The EC Regulation also confers jurisdiction on the courts of a Member State to open insolvency proceedings in relation to a company incorporated outside the Community if the centre of the company's main interests is in that Member State: *Re BRAC Rent-a-Car International Inc* [2003] 1 BCLC 470.

[5] In *Re Marann Brooks CSV Ltd* [2003] BPIR 1159 Patten J thought, obiter, that the Regulation has no application to winding up petitions brought by the Secretary of State on public interest grounds under IA 1986, s 124A.

[6] A creditors' voluntary winding up does not require confirmation by the court but a liquidator in such a winding up may apply to the court for a confirmation order for the purposes of the EC Regulation: see IR 1986, r 7.62.

[7] *Interedil Srl v Fallimento Interedil Srl* [2011] BPIR 1639, noted Moss (2011) 24 Insolv Int 126; *Re Eurofood IFSC Ltd* (C-341/04) [2007] 2 BCLC 151. An extensive jurisprudence now exists on the meaning of 'centre of main interests' ('comi') since that determines which Member State has jurisdiction for main proceedings. See Moss, Fletcher and Isaacs, *The EC Regulation on Insolvency Proceedings: A Commentary and Annotated Guide* (2nd edn, 2009), para 8.85; Goode, *Principles of Corporate Insolvency Law* (4th edn, 2011) Ch 15; Wessels, 'Comi, Past, Present and Future' (2011) Insolv Int 17; Mevorach, 'European Insolvency Law in a Global Context' [2011] JBL 666.

establishment,[8] but such proceedings are restricted to the assets situated in that Member State. Where the territorial proceedings are commenced after the opening of main proceedings, the proceedings are described as secondary proceedings and they must be winding up rather than rescue proceedings. Where main proceedings are opened in the UK (which can only be if the debtor's centre of main interests is in the UK) and there are no secondary proceedings elsewhere in the EU, the liquidator may deal with all the assets wherever situated in the EU. If secondary proceedings are opened elsewhere in the EU, the liquidator in the main proceedings cannot deal with assets in those Member States (art 18).

24-6 Main proceedings are effective in all Member States as long as no territorial proceedings have been opened (art 17) and the liquidator appointed in the main proceedings is able immediately to exercise his powers in other Member States in accordance with the general law of that Member State (art 18) and is required to furnish only a certified copy of his appointment in order so to act (art 19). To ensure that all concurrent proceedings are properly co-ordinated, the liquidators in the main proceedings and in the secondary proceedings have a duty to co-operate and communicate with each other (art 31).

24-7 The UK has given effect, by the Cross-Border Insolvency Regulations 2006,[9] also to the UNCITRAL Model Law on Cross-Border Insolvency Proceedings. This Model Law (in the manner of the EU Regulation) does not seek to unify the substantive and procedural law on insolvency of the adopting States. It simply seeks to ease the access of foreign representatives and creditors to the courts and insolvency procedures of Great Britain and is particularly valuable in the context of UK/US insolvencies.[10] The Model Law entitles a foreign representative to apply directly to the courts to commence insolvency proceedings and to participate in such a proceeding once commenced. The Model Law also addresses specific issues such as the recognition of foreign proceedings, co-ordination of proceedings concerning the same debtor, rights of foreign creditors, the rights and duties of foreign representatives, and co-operation between national authorities. In the event of a conflict between the application of the Model Law and the EC Regulation, the Regulation prevails.

B Voluntary winding up

Resolution of the company

24-8 In practice, voluntary winding up is the most common form of winding up.[11] The advantage of proceeding in this way is that there is no court involvement so costs and time-scales

---

[8] Defined in the EC Regulation as 'any place of operations where the debtor carries out a non-transitory economic activity with human means and goods': EC Regulation 1346/2000, art 2(h), OJ L 160, 30.06.2000, p 1.

[9] SI 2006/1030. See generally Mevorach, 'On the Road to Universalism' (2011) EBOR 517; Goode, *Principles of Corporate Insolvency Law* (4th edn, 2011), Ch 16; Fletcher, 'The UNCITRAL Model Law in the United Kingdom' (2007) 20 Insolv Int 138; McCormack, 'Comi and Comity in UK and US Insolvency Law' (2012) 128 LQR 140.

[10] See, for example, *Rubin v Eurofinance SA* [2011] 2 BCLC 473 also see *Larsen v Navios International Inc* [2012] 1 BCLC 151.

[11] In 2010–11, out of 18,130 insolvencies, 11,806 were creditors' voluntary liquidations (CVLs) and 1,384 were administrations which converted to CVLs; there were 4,940 compulsory liquidations and 3,526 members' voluntary liquidations: see Companies House, *Statistical Tables on Companies Registration Activities 2010–11*, Table C2. All figures for Great Britain.

may be reduced and the nomination of the liquidator is a matter for the members and/or the creditors.

24-9   A voluntary winding up begins with a resolution passed by the members. Typically, a special resolution is required (IA 1986, s 84(1)(b)), but an ordinary resolution is sufficient in the unusual case where the articles limit the duration of the company (s 84(1)(a)). Five business days' notice of the intention to pass a resolution for voluntary winding up must be given to a floating chargeholder which gives the chargeholder an opportunity to appoint an administrator instead (s 84(2A)): see **23-48**.

24-10   A copy of the resolution for winding up must be forwarded to the registrar of companies within 15 days of being passed (IA 1986, s 84(3)); and the company must give notice of the resolution by advertisement in the *Gazette* (s 85(1)). A voluntary winding up, whether a members' voluntary or a creditors' voluntary (see below), is deemed to commence at the time of the passing of the resolution for voluntary winding up (s 86). From that commencement, the company ceases to carry on its business, except so far as may be required for its beneficial winding up (s 87(1)).

Declaration of solvency—members' voluntary winding up

24-11   If in the five weeks immediately preceding the date of the resolution to wind up the company, or on the date of the resolution but before it is passed, the directors or a majority of the directors make a statutory declaration of solvency, the winding up is a members' voluntary winding up (IA 1986, ss 89, 90).

24-12   The statutory declaration must be to the effect that the directors have made a full enquiry into the affairs of the company and have formed the opinion that the company will be able to pay its debts in full (together with interest) within such period, not exceeding 12 months from the date of the commencement of the winding up (i.e. the date of the passing of the resolution for winding up),[12] as may be specified in the declaration.[13]

24-13   The advantage to the directors in making such a declaration is that it enables the appointment of the liquidator by the members. The risk in doing so is that if the declaration is made by a director without reasonable grounds, he commits a criminal offence and, if the debts are not paid in full within the specified time, that raises a rebuttable presumption that the director did not have reasonable grounds for making the declaration.[14]

24-14   If it turns out that the declaration is erroneous and the liquidator appointed by the members is of the opinion that the company will be unable to pay its debts in full within the 12-month period, he must summon a meeting of creditors within 28 days (IA 1986, s 95(1), (2)). As from the day of that meeting, the situation is treated as if no declaration of solvency was made and the winding up becomes from that date onwards a creditors' voluntary winding up.[15]

---

[12] IA 1986, s 86.

[13] IA 1986, s 89(1). The statutory declaration must be delivered to the registrar of companies within 15 days after the resolution for winding up is passed: s 89(3). Failure to do so gives rise to criminal penalties.

[14] IA 1986, s 89(4), (5). See Simmons, 'The Statutory Declaration of Solvency—Voluntary Winding Up of Companies—Members or Creditors' (1996) 9 Insolv Int 33.

[15] IA 1986, s 96. The general meeting already held and the creditors' meeting under s 95 are treated as if they were the meetings required under s 98 in the case of a creditors' voluntary winding up: s 96(b).

No declaration of solvency–creditors' voluntary winding up

24-15 If the directors do not make a statutory declaration of solvency, the winding up is a creditors' voluntary winding up (IA 1986, s 90). In this case, in addition to the meeting of members called to pass a resolution for the company to go into liquidation, as outlined at **24-8**, a meeting of creditors must be summoned to take place not more than 14 days after the members' meeting (s 98(1)(a)). The directors must lay before that meeting a statement as to the company's affairs showing, in particular, the company's assets, debts and liabilities and one of the directors must preside at the creditors' meeting (s 99(1)).

Appointing a liquidator

24-16 Having passed a resolution for voluntary winding up, the members or the creditors proceed to appoint a liquidator. In a members' voluntary winding up, the members at their meeting to pass the resolution for winding up must appoint a liquidator (IA 1986, s 91(1)). In a creditors' voluntary winding up, the creditors may appoint a liquidator[16] and, if desired, a liquidation committee.[17] In all liquidations (compulsory or voluntary) a liquidator, apart from the official receiver acting in a compulsory liquidation, must be a qualified insolvency practitioner.[18]

24-17 Where there is no liquidator appointed for whatever reason, the court may appoint (IA 1986, s 108). In that situation, the directors' powers to deal with the company's assets pending the appointment of a liquidator are essentially restricted to the preservation of the assets.[19] Likewise, in a creditors' voluntary winding up, if the members' meeting has nominated a liquidator prior to the creditors' meeting being held, that liquidator has power only to protect and preserve the company's property or to dispose of perishable items and he otherwise requires the consent of the court to act (s 166(2),(3)).

24-18 Once appointed, the liquidator must publish in the *Gazette* and deliver to the registrar of companies a notice of his appointment (IA 1986, s 109). The company ceases to carry on business and all the directors' powers cease[20] although, in a voluntary winding up, they are not automatically removed from office.[21]

C Compulsory winding up

24-19 A compulsory winding up requires a court order and the court's jurisdiction to make such an order is subject to the EC Regulation on Insolvency Proceedings which limits the court's power to open main proceedings to cases where the debtor's centre of main

---

[16] IA 1986, s 100(1); the members' meeting may already have nominated a liquidator but, in the event of a conflict, the creditors' choice prevails: s 100(2). Objectors may apply to the court for an appointment in place of the creditors' choice: s 100(3).

[17] IA 1986, s 101. A liquidation committee essentially oversees the conduct of the liquidation and consists of creditors' (and possibly members') representatives, see IR 1986, rr 4.151–4.172A.

[18] IA 1986, ss 230(1)–(5); ss 389–393; and see the Insolvency Practitioners Regulations 2005, SI 2005/524.

[19] IA 1986, s 114; and see *Re a company (No 006341 of 1992), ex p B Ltd* [1994] 1 BCLC 225.

[20] See IA 1986, s 91(2) (members' voluntary winding up), except so far as the company or the liquidator sanctions their continuance; s 103 (creditors' voluntary winding up), except so far as the liquidation committee or the creditors sanction their continuance.   [21] *Madrid Bank Ltd v Bayley* (1866) LR 2 QB 37.

interests is in the UK and territorial proceedings to cases where the debtor possesses an establishment within the UK (see **24-5**).[22]

Petitioners for a winding-up order

24-20   The vast majority of petitions for winding up are presented by creditors,[23] but a petition can be presented by, amongst others, the company, its directors and contributories (essentially members).[24] Equally, provision is made for public interest petitions, for example by the official receiver where there are concerns as to the conduct of a voluntary winding up;[25] by the Secretary of State;[26] and by the Financial Services Authority.[27] As noted at **24-1**, it is possible that the company has been the subject of some other insolvency process already, hence provision is made for petitions for a winding-up order by a supervisor of a company voluntary arrangement (CVA);[28] by an administrator;[29] and by a liquidator appointed in main proceedings in another Member State under the EC Insolvency Regulation.[30]

24-21   A contributory (essentially a member) is not entitled to present a winding-up petition unless either the number of members is reduced below two (except where the company is a single member company)[31] or the shares held by him were originally allotted to him or have been held by him for at least six months during the 18 months before the commencement of the winding up or have devolved to him through the death of a former holder.[32] This provision is designed to prevent individuals from purchasing shares with a view to winding up a company, though a six-month period seems inadequate for this purpose. Additionally, a contributory must establish an interest in the winding up. For example, a partly paid-up shareholder who remains liable to contribute the amount unpaid on his shares in the event of the company being wound up has an interest. For a fully paid-up member to establish that he has a tangible interest in the winding up, he must show a *prima facie* probability of surplus assets remaining after the creditors have been paid.[33]

Grounds for compulsory winding up

24-22   The process of obtaining a winding-up order begins with a petition based on one of the grounds set out in the IA 1986, s 122(1). Some of these grounds are relevant to solvent

---

[22] See IA 1986, s 117(7); EC Regulation, art 3.

[23] A creditor may petition even though the company is in voluntary winding up: IA 1986, s 116.

[24] IA 1986, s 124(1). 'Contributory' encompasses members of the company as well as others not registered as members but who are liable to contribute to the assets of the company: see IA 1986, s 79.

[25] See IA 1986, s 124(5).

[26] i.e. under IA 1986, ss 122(1)(b), (c) or 124A. As to the exercise of the court's discretion in public interest petitions, see *Secretary of State for Business, Enterprise and Regulatory Reform v Amway (UK) Ltd* [2011] 2 BCLC 716 (in an exceptional case, the court can refuse to make an order and accept undertakings from the company as to its future conduct though the Secretary of State has refused to accept the undertakings); also *Secretary of State v Charter Financial Solutions Ltd* [2011] 2 BCLC 788.

[27] See Financial Services and Markets Act 2000, s 367.

[28] IA 1986, s 7(4)(b); Sch A1, para 39(5)(b).   [29] IA 1986, Sch 1, para 21; Sch B1, para 60.

[30] IA 1986, s 124(1).   [31] IA 1986, s 124(2)(a).

[32] IA 1986, s 124(2)(b). Where the *locus standi* of a contributory to petition is disputed, the court will consider all the circumstances, including the likelihood of damage to the company if the petition is not dismissed, in deciding whether first to require the petitioner to seek the determination of his status outside of the winding up petition: *Alipour v Ary, Re a company (No 002180 of 1996)* [1997] 1 BCLC 557, CA; and see *Alipour v UOC Corp* [2002] 2 BCLC 770.

[33] *Re Rica Gold Washing Co* (1879) 11 Ch D 36; *Re Expanded Plugs Ltd* [1966] 1 All ER 877; *Re Othery Construction Ltd* [1966] 1 All ER 145; *Re Bellador Silk Ltd* [1965] 1 All ER 667.

companies, for example where a petition is brought for winding up on the just and equitable ground which is essentially a shareholder remedy.[34] For insolvent companies, the ground relied on is that the company is unable to pay its debts (s 122(1)(f)) and, in such cases, the petition is invariably brought by a creditor.[35]

Company is unable to pay its debts

24-23 The circumstances in which a company is deemed to be unable to pay its debts are set out in IA 1986, s 123 and include a failure to meet a statutory demand (s 123(1)(a)), a failure to satisfy a judgment against the company (s 123(1)(b)) and a general ground of being unable to pay its debts as they fall due (s 123(1)(e)). Reliance on a failure to meet a statutory demand is a straightforward way to show that the company is insolvent since it merely requires that the facts about the statutory demand be established, but there must be due compliance with all the procedural requirements of a statutory demand.[36] Section 123(1)(e) allows a creditor, without serving a statutory demand or attempting to enforce a judgment, to satisfy the court by suitable evidence of the company's inability to pay (the cash-flow test). Failure to pay an undisputed debt, despite repeated requests, must *prima facie* mean an inability to pay and a winding-up order may be sought by a creditor.[37] A company is not entitled to have the petition struck out, or prevent it being issued, merely because it is in fact solvent.[38]

24-24 If the debt is due and is undisputed, the petition proceeds to hearing and adjudication in the normal way, but it is an abuse of process and the petition will be struck out if the debt is bona fide disputed and the petition is being used as a means of pressurising the company.[39] A petition may also be dismissed if the company has a genuine and serious cross-claim for an amount which exceeds the petitioner's debt and which the company has been

---

[34] i.e. under IA 1986, s 122(1)(g): see **18-74**. Other grounds include that the company has resolved by a special resolution to be wound up by the court; that the company is a public company and has not been issued with a trading certificate under CA 2006, s 761; that the company has not commenced business within one year of incorporation or has suspended its business for a whole year: IA 1986, s 122(1)(a), (b), (d).

[35] Additionally, a creditor (only) may petition for winding up where a company voluntary arrangement with a moratorium comes to an end without a voluntary arrangement being approved: IA 1986, ss 122(1)(fa); 124(3A); the advantage of using this option is that the creditor does not have to establish that the company is unable to pay its debts.

[36] A creditor to whom the company is indebted in a sum exceeding £750 then due must have served on the company, by leaving it at the company's registered office, a written demand (in the prescribed form) requiring the company to pay the sum so due and the company must for three weeks thereafter have neglected to pay the sum or to secure or compound for it to the reasonable satisfaction of the creditor. As to the detailed requirements concerning this statutory demand, see IR 1986, rr 4.4–4.6. The demand must be for a liquidated amount. A demand must be for a debt 'then due' and a contingent debt when the contingency has not happened has not fallen due: *JSF Finance & Currency Exchange Co Ltd v Akma Solutions Inc* [2001] 2 BCLC 307.

[37] *Taylors Industrial Flooring Ltd v M & H Plant Hire (Manchester) Ltd* [1990] BCLC 216, CA; *Cornhill Insurance plc v Improvement Services Ltd* [1986] BCLC 26. The courts will not allow a winding-up petition to enforce what is essentially a small debt and in effect impose a minimum debt of the amount required for a statutory demand: see Fletcher, *The Law of Insolvency* (4th edn, 2009), para 21-006.

[38] *Cornhill Insurance plc v Improvement Services Ltd* [1986] BCLC 26.

[39] See *Re MCI WorldCom Ltd* [2003] 1 BCLC 330; *Re a company (No 0012209 of 1991)* [1992] 2 All ER 797; *Stonegate Securities Ltd v Gregory* [1980] 1 All ER 241; *Mann v Goldstein* [1968] 2 All ER 769. If the debt is disputed, the petitioner may not actually be 'a creditor' and therefore lacks *locus standi* to bring a petition: see *Re Bayoil SA* [1999] 1 BCLC 62 at 66, CA.

unable to litigate, subject to the court's residual discretion to consider whether there are any special circumstances which might make it inappropriate to dismiss the petition.[40]

24-25 This long-established approach of dismissing the petition where the debt is bona fide disputed is a rule of practice only, however, and it must give way to exceptional circumstances which make it desirable that the petitioner should proceed.[41] In particular, the court will have regard to whether the petitioner would otherwise be without a remedy, whether injustice would result, whether there is some other sufficient reason for allowing the petition to proceed or whether there is a likelihood of damage to the company if the petition is not dismissed.[42]

24-26 The three methods of establishing an inability to pay debts (statutory demand, unsatisfied judgment and inability to pay debts as they fall due, see **24-23**) are based on petitioning creditors who have debts that are immediately due and payable. But petitions may also be brought by contingent or prospective creditors.[43] It might be the case that a creditor has lent money to a company which is not due to be repaid until some date in the future but the creditor is concerned that the present financial position of the company suggests it will not be able to repay the debt when payment is due. Such a creditor may rely on the balance sheet test in IA 1986, s 123(2), to show that the company is insolvent and should be wound up. IA 1986, s 123(2) provides that:

> 'A company is also deemed unable to pay its debts if it is proved to the satisfaction of the court that the value of a company's assets is less than the amount of its liabilities, taking into account its contingent and prospective liabilities.'

24-27 The Court of Appeal gave a detailed analysis of that section in *BNY Corporate Trustee Services Ltd v Eurosail-UK 2007-3BL plc*.[44] The case is of particular significance because, in many financial transactions, the balance sheet insolvency test set out in IA 1986, s 123(2) is specified as an event of default. Hence the decision is important, not just in the statutory context of winding-up petitions, but in the commercial context of contractual definitions of acts of default. The facts of the case (a complex bondholder dispute arising out of the collapse of Lehman Brothers) are irrelevant, the general interest lies in the proper approach to the interpretation and application of s 123(2). The main judgment was given by Lord Neuberger MR and he started by rejecting the proposition that the section requires a mechanical and artificial assessment merely of the figures as extracted from the company's accounts.[45] On that basis, he said, many companies would be balance sheet insolvent and at the risk of being wound up by a creditor.[46] In his view, and Toulson and Wilson LJJ agreed, the purpose of s 123(2) and the reason why it is included in addition to

---

[40] *Re Bayoil SA* [1999] 1 BCLC 62, CA; *Montgomery v Wanda Modes Ltd* [2002] 1 BCLC 289; *Re VP Developments Ltd* [2005] 2 BCLC 607. The significance of the 'inability to litigate' requirement was doubted in *Montgomery v Wanda Modes Ltd* as not forming part of the ratio of *Bayoil*. Park J noted that there is nothing objectionable in a company which has refrained from pursuing a claim which it believed it has against another party, later deciding to pursue that cross-claim if the other party threatens it with winding-up proceedings; he thought it would be undesirable for companies to be penalised for refraining from litigating a claim or if parties were to be encouraged to litigate possible claims sooner rather than later; see also *Re a debtor (No 87 of 1999)* [2000] BPIR 589 to the same effect and on which Park J relied.

[41] *Re GBI Investments Ltd* [2010] 2 BCLC 624; *Parmalat Capital Finance Ltd v Food Holdings Ltd* [2009] 1 BCLC 274, PC; *Alipour v Ary, Re a company (No 002180 of 1996)* [1997] 1 BCLC 557, CA; *Brinds Ltd v Offshore Oil NL* (1986) 2 BCC 98, 916; *Re Claybridge Shipping Co SA* [1997] 1 BCLC 572, (CA, 1981).

[42] *Re GBI Investments Ltd* [2010] 2 BCLC 624 at [80]–[90]; *Alipour v Ary, Re a company (No 002180 of 1996)* [1997] 1 BCLC 557, CA; see also *Re Claybridge Shipping Co SA* [1997] 1 BCLC 572, (CA, 1981).

[43] IA 1986, s 124(1); IR 1986, r 13.12(3).   [44] [2011] 2 BCLC 1.   [45] [2011] 2 BCLC 1 at [44].

[46] [2011] 2 BCLC 1 at [44], 47.

s 123(1)(e) (the cash-flow test) is, as Professor Sir Roy Goode had identified, to cover a case where, although it could not be said that a company 'is [currently] unable to pay its debts as they fall due' (either because it has no debts which are currently payable, or because it has, or can achieve, the cash flow to pay such debts), it is, in practical terms, clear that it will not be able to meet its future or contingent liabilities', having reached the point of no return.[47] If provision is not made for a company to be wound up when it has reached the point of no return, then current and short-term creditors would in effect be paid at the expense of the future or contingent creditors, as Professor Sir Roy Goode had explained.[48] Therefore, in Lord Neuberger's view, s 123(2) can only be relied on by a future or contingent creditor of 'a company which has reached "the end of the road", or in respect of which the shutters should be "put up", imprecise, judgement-based and fact-specific as such a test may be'.[49] Declining to give further guidance, Lord Neuberger concluded that the court will have to determine the question of whether the company has reached that point of no return on the balance of probabilities with a firm eye both on commercial reality and on commercial fairness.[50] On the facts in the case, it had not been established that the company at the heart of the dispute had reached the point of no return and therefore it was not insolvent.[51] It is thought that the clear rejection of a mechanistic approach and the reluctance to give guidance as to how to determine whether the point of no return has been reached means that, in future, it will be difficult for a contractual party, with any certainty, to invoke balance sheet insolvency as a default event or as triggering some other contractual process or remedy and, likewise, difficult for a creditor to petition for winding up on this basis. Given the commercial significance of the ruling, an appeal is pending.

The court's discretion to make a winding-up order

24-28 Having grounds for the presentation of a petition does not necessarily entitle the creditor to a winding-up order, though if the creditor has standing and the court is satisfied that the company is unable to pay its debts, a winding-up order should follow unless there is some special reason why it should not be made.[52] Winding up is a collective or class remedy, however, and an order may be refused if the petitioner is merely seeking to obtain some private advantage,[53] but if the purpose of the petition is legitimate, it does not matter that the motive of the petitioner is malicious.[54]

24-29 There may well be differences of opinion among the creditors as to whether a compulsory winding up is appropriate in which case the court can direct meetings to be held to

---

[47] [2011] 2 BCLC 1 at [48]–[49], [115], [121]. See also *Re Cheyne Finance plc* [2008] 1 BCLC 741 at [51].

[48] See Goode, *Principles of Corporate Insolvency Law* (4th edn, 2011), para 4-23.

[49] [2011] 2 BCLC 1 at [58].

[50] [2011] 2 BCLC 1 at [61], [62]. It is not enough to take the future and contingent liabilities at face amount, a valuation exercise will be needed, at [60], [117]. The starting point would be the company's latest audited accounts, but it would be necessary to take other factors into account and adjust the figures accordingly, at [65], [68].

[51] The court took into account the fact that the company had substantial assets, its liabilities had to be met over a relatively long period of time and there was potential for significant changes in values since they depended on currency fluctuations, see [2011] 2 BCLC 1 at [80].

[52] See *Re Demaglass Holdings Ltd* [2001] 2 BCLC 633; *Re Lummus Agricultural Services Ltd* [2001] BCLC 137. But see *Re Minrealm Ltd* [2008] 2 BCLC 141 where the court adjourned the petition to await the resolution of unfairly prejudicial proceedings.

[53] *Re a Company (No 001573 of 1983)* [1983] BCLC 492.

[54] *Bryanston Finance Ltd v De Vries (No 2)* [1976] 1 All ER 25, CA; *Re a Company (No 001573 of 1983)* [1983] BCLC 492.

ascertain the creditors' wishes (IA 1986, s 195). A particular aspect of this clash of opinions is where a company is already in voluntary winding up and the court is asked to substitute a compulsory winding-up order for that voluntary process. Again, the court takes account of the wishes of the majority of the creditors and where the majority oppose the making of a compulsory winding-up order, the onus is on those seeking the order to show good reason why it should be granted.[55] The court looks carefully at the quality of the creditors on either side as well as the quantity and where some of the creditors are also shareholders or directors of the company or their associates, their views may be given less weight or disregarded altogether.[56] Principles of fairness and commercial morality are taken into account and may require that the creditors secure the independent scrutiny of the company's affairs which is a consequence of a compulsory winding-up order.[57]

24-30   On the making of the winding-up order and by virtue of his office, the official receiver becomes the liquidator.[58] If the official receiver considers it worthwhile, or if 25% in value of creditors request it, the official receiver calls separate meetings of creditors and of members for the purpose of choosing a person to be the liquidator of the company in his place.[59] Each meeting may nominate a liquidator and, in the event of different nominations, the creditors' nominee is appointed.[60] If no meetings are held or no nominations made, the official receiver remains as liquidator.[61]

D Consequences of winding-up order

24-31   In the case of a compulsory winding up, the winding up is deemed to commence at the time of the presentation of the petition, unless the company had passed a resolution for voluntary winding up prior to the presentation of the petition, in which case the winding up is deemed to commence at the date of the passing of the resolution.[62] In a compulsory winding up, the directors are automatically dismissed from office on the making of the order,[63] the employment of all employees is terminated, and the liquidator takes the company's property into his custody and control (IA 1986, s 144).[64]

---

[55] *Re JD Swain Ltd* [1965] 2 All ER 761; *Re Gordon and Breach Science Publishers Ltd* [1995] 2 BCLC 189. It may be more appropriate in some cases simply to apply under IA 1986, s 171 for the appointment of a different liquidator: see *Re Inside Sport Ltd* [2000] 1 BCLC 302.

[56] *Re Demaglass Holdings Ltd* [2001] 2 BCLC 633; *Re Lummus Agricultural Services Ltd* [2001] BCLC 137; *Re Falcon (R J) Developments Ltd* [1987] BCLC 437.

[57] *Re Lowerstoft Traffic Services Ltd* [1986] BCLC 81; *Re Palmer Marine Surveys Ltd* [1986] BCLC 106; *Re Gordon and Breach Science Publishers Ltd* [1995] 2 BCLC 189.

[58] IA 1986, s 136(1), (2). The court also has power to appoint a provisional liquidator prior to the making of the winding-up order: see s 135. Three copies of the winding up order are sent to the official receiver; one copy is served by him on the company at its registered office and one copy is sent to the registrar of companies and the order is notified in the *Gazette* and advertised in a local paper: IR 1986, r 4.21.

[59] IA 1986, s 136(4), (5).   [60] IA 1986, s 139(2), (3).

[61] The Secretary of State may appoint a replacement liquidator on the application of the official receiver or following the failure of the meetings to appoint: IA 1986, s 137(1)–(3).

[62] IA 1986, s 129. Presentation of the petition takes place when the petition is delivered to the court for issue, not when it is issued: *Re Blights Builders Ltd* [2008] 1 BCLC 245.

[63] *Measures v Measures* [1910] 2 Ch 248.

[64] Note also IA 1986, s 132 which provides that where a winding-up order is made by the court, it is the duty of the official receiver to investigate the causes of the failure (if the company has failed) and, generally, the promotion, formation, business, dealings and affairs of the company, and to make such report (if any) to the court as he thinks fit.

Dispositions of the company's property

24-32 A compulsory winding up commences with the presentation of the petition but there is a risk that property which should be available to the creditors may be disposed of in the period (which may be quite lengthy) between the presentation of the petition and the making of the winding-up order. To preserve such property for the creditors, any disposition of the company's property and any transfers of shares or alteration in the status of the company's members after the commencement of a compulsory winding up is void, unless the court otherwise orders (IA 1986, s 127).[65] The value of this provision is that it enables liquidators subsequently to challenge certain dispositions with a view to recovering assets for the benefit of the creditors generally. Equally, the court's discretion to validate transactions offers some relief for those dealing with a company in this situation. The application of s 127 is therefore of considerable practical importance (its application is limited to compulsory winding up).

24-33 In exercising this discretion to validate dispositions, the court looks to see if the disposition was made bona fide to assist the company,[66] such as the repayment of or the grant of security for loans made to the company after the commencement of winding up.[67] But the court generally refuses to validate payments which have the effect of preferring pre-insolvency creditors[68] unless the payment confers a benefit on creditors generally.[69] It is open to the company or any creditor to apply to the court to validate a transaction in advance of it taking place and this is particularly useful where the company carries on business in the period between the presentation of a winding-up petition and the making of a winding-up order. In such circumstances, the court adopts the same general approach and takes into account the benefit to the creditors generally of keeping the business going with a view to selling it as a going concern.

24-34 The application of IA 1986, s 127 is limited to where there is 'a disposition of the company's property'. In *Hollicourt (Contracts) Ltd v Bank of Ireland*[70] the Court of Appeal considered the position regarding payments out of a company's bank account. In this case, after the presentation of a petition for the winding up of the company, the bank continued to operate the company's bank account for a period of three months, having overlooked the advertisement of the petition. The bank debited the company's account, which was in credit throughout, with payments in favour of third parties totalling £156,200. The liquidator commenced proceedings against the bank seeking repayment by the bank of the moneys paid out on the basis that the payments were 'dispositions' of the company's property within IA 1986, s 127 and void.

24-35 The Court of Appeal held that IA 1986, s 127 only invalidated dispositions by the company of its property to the payees of the cheques. It enabled the company to recover the amounts disposed of from the payees but not from the bank. The purpose of s 127, the court said, is to prevent the directors of a company, when liquidation is imminent, from disposing of the company's assets to the prejudice of its creditors and to preserve those assets for the benefit of the general body of creditors. The policy promoted by s 127 is not

---

[65] See IA 1986, s 88 (which applies in a voluntary winding up) to similar effect, but it is limited in application to transfers of shares and alterations in the status of the company's members.

[66] *Re J Leslie Engineering Co Ltd* [1976] 2 All ER 85.

[67] *Re Steane's (Bournemouth) Ltd* [1950] 1 All ER 21; *Re Clifton Place Garage Ltd* [1970] 1 All ER 353, CA.

[68] *Re Civil Service and General Store Ltd* (1887) 57 LJ Ch 119.

[69] *Re A I Levy (Holdings) Ltd* [1963] 2 All ER 556.

[70] [2001] 1 BCLC 233, CA; see Hare, 'Banker's Liability for Post-Petition Dispositions' (2001) CLJ 468.

aimed at imposing on a bank restitutionary liability to a company in respect of payments made by cheque in favour of creditors in addition to the unquestioned liability of the payees of the cheques. The section impinged on the end result of the process of payment initiated by the company, i.e. the point of ultimate receipt of the company's property in consequence of a disposition by the company. The statutory purpose is accomplished, the court said, without any need for the section to impinge on the legal validity of intermediate steps, such as banking transactions, which are merely part of the process by which dispositions of the company's property are made.[71]

24-36 Though not necessary to its decision (the account in *Hollicourt* was in credit throughout), the Court of Appeal made the point that, even if the payments had been made out of an overdrawn account (as in *Coutts v Stock*[72]), the outcome would have been the same in respect of a claim for recovery against the bank. The court thought that this result has the very real practical advantage of not requiring what could be a complex analysis of whether payments were made out of an account which was in debit or in credit.[73] This approach also avoids the risk that the banks are the deep pockets pursued by liquidators rather than the payees in respect of whom the liquidators had an undoubted claim.

24-37 These cases concerned payments *out* of a company's bank account. Payments by a company *into* an overdrawn account with its bank with the resulting reduction in its indebtedness to the bank is a disposition requiring consent[74] while a payment into an account which is in credit simply results in an adjustment of the records between the company and its bank and is not a disposition of the company's property for these purposes.[75] Where a bank seeks a validation order with respect to payments into an overdrawn account, the essential question is whether the payments into the account are in the ordinary course of business and whether they are likely to be for the benefit of the creditors generally, but where there is no real benefit to the creditors generally, merely a reduction in the amount owed to the bank, a validation order will not be made.[76] To do so would breach the *pari passu* principle and result in the bank's pre-liquidation debt being repaid to the detriment of the other creditors.[77]

Control of legal proceedings and enforcement of remedies

24-38 When a winding-up order is made, all pending proceedings are automatically halted and no new proceedings may be commenced except by the leave of the court under IA 1986, s 130(2).[78] In practice, the court allows the enforcement of rights by secured creditors[79] (since such proceedings cannot adversely affect the position of unsecured creditors), but

---

[71] [2001] 1 BCLC 233 at 239.   [72] [2000] 1 BCLC 183.

[73] [2001] 1 BCLC 233 at 242.

[74] *Re Gray's Inn Construction Co Ltd* [1980] 1 All ER 814, CA; although this case was much criticised in *Hollicourt (Contracts) Ltd v Bank of Ireland* [2001] 1 BCLC 233, CA, on this point it remains valid; see also *Re Tain Construction Ltd* [2003] 2 BCLC 374.

[75] *Re Barn Crown Ltd* [1994] 4 All ER 42.   [76] *Re Tain Construction Ltd* [2003] 2 BCLC 374.

[77] *Re Tain Construction Ltd* [2003] 2 BCLC 374.

[78] Distress (essentially taking possession of goods in satisfaction of a debt) is an 'action or proceeding' within s 130(2) and requires court consent: *Re Memco Engineering Ltd* [1985] BCLC 424; *Herbert Berry Associates Ltd v IRC* [1978] 1 All ER 161, HL. Distress is defined at IA 1986, s 436.

[79] *Re David Lloyd & Co, Lloyd v David Lloyd & Co* (1877) 6 Ch D 339, CA and *Re Aro Co Ltd* [1980] 1 All ER 1067, CA (secured creditors enforcing security); *Re Coregrange Ltd* [1984] BCLC 453 (creditor suing for specific performance). A freezing order over assets, without more, does not constitute a security for these purposes, for it does not impose an obligation to satisfy any judgment debt out of those frozen assets: *Flightline Ltd v Edwards* [2003] 1 BCLC 427, CA.

in relation to other matters the court must decide whether there is any sensible point in allowing the proceedings to continue and what is right and fair in the circumstances of the particular case.[80] Once a winding-up order has been made, IA 1986, s 128(1) appears to render void any enforcement of a remedy (attachment, sequestration, distress or execution) after the commencement of the winding up.[81] It is invariably treated, however, as also subject to the court's discretion under s 130(2) to allow the enforcement to continue.[82] The court has a broad and unfettered discretion to do what is right and fair in the circumstances of the particular case, but it must not allow the individual creditor the benefit of enforcing the judgment if this will prejudice the equal treatment of creditors generally.[83] On the other hand, the court has allowed an individual creditor to succeed where the debtor forced,[84] tricked[85] or persuaded[86] the creditor to abstain from enforcing a judgment sometime before the winding up commenced.

E The role and powers of a liquidator

24-39 Duties owed by liquidators are owed to the company and not to individual contributories or creditors.[87] When carrying out his functions, the liquidator acts as an agent of the company.[88] Any contracts entered into by him are entered into by the company and the liquidator incurs no personal liability unless the terms of the contract show that he is undertaking a personal liability.[89] Title to the company's assets is not automatically vested in the liquidator but remains vested in the company unless, exceptionally, the court so orders (IA 1986, s 145).

---

[80] *New Cap Reinsurance Corp Ltd v HIH Casualty & General Insurance* Ltd [2002] 2 BCLC 228, CA; see also *Bourne v Charit-Email Technology Partnership LLP* [2010] 1 BCLC 210. Leave will not be given if the issues can conveniently be decided in the winding up: *Craven v Blackpool Greyhound Stadium and Racecourse Ltd* [1936] 3 All ER 513, CA; *Re Exchange Securities and Commodities Ltd* [1983] BCLC 186; but will be given if the issues are better decided by an action: *Currie v Consolidated Kent Collieries Corpn Ltd* [1906] 1 KB 134, CA.

[81] This provision is limited to compulsory winding up and there is no directly equivalent provision with respect to voluntary winding up, but the liquidator would apply to the court for directions under IA 1986, s 112 with a view to the court exercising its discretion as to whether to permit execution following the commencement of the winding up. If proceedings have already resulted in a judgment against the company, but enforcement of that judgment has not been completed prior to the commencement of the winding up, the proceeds of an execution etc cannot be retained by the creditor against the liquidator unless the court orders otherwise, see IA 1986, s 183, which applies to compulsory and voluntary winding up.

[82] *Re Lancashire Cotton Spinning Co, ex p Carnelly* (1887) 35 Ch D 656, CA. If distress is in progress at the commencement of the winding up but not completed, the courts will allow it to continue unless there is something inequitable in allowing the distraining party to have the fruits of the distress. See *Re Memco Engineering Ltd* [1985] BCLC 424; *Herbert Berry Associates Ltd v IRC* [1978] 1 All ER 161, HL; *Re Bellaglade Ltd* [1977] 1 All ER 319. The Tribunals, Courts and Enforcement Act 2007 prospectively abolishes the common law right to distrain for arrears of rent instead there is a limited right for the recovery of rent arrears due under a lease of commercial premises only: see ss 71 and 72, but these provisions are not in force.

[83] *New Cap Reinsurance Corp Ltd v HIH Casualty & General Insurance* Ltd [2002] 2 BCLC 228, CA; *Re Aro Co Ltd* [1980] 1 All ER 1067, CA; *Roberts Petroleum Ltd v Bernard Kenny Ltd* [1983] 1 All ER 564, HL; *Re Grosvenor Metal Co Ltd* [1950] Ch 63.   [84] *Re London Cotton Co* (1866) LR 2 Eq 53.

[85] *Armorduct Manufacturing Co Ltd v General Incandescent Co Ltd* [1911] 2 KB 143, CA.

[86] *Re Grosvenor Metal Co Ltd* [1950] Ch 63; *Re Suidair International Airways Ltd* [1950] 2 All ER 920; *Re Redman (Builders) Ltd* [1964] 1 All ER 851.

[87] See *Lomax Leisure Ltd v Miller* [2008] 1 BCLC 262; IR 1986, r 4.182(3).

[88] A liquidator in a compulsory winding up is an officer of the court: IA 1986, s 160.

[89] *Stewart v Engel* [2000] 2 BCLC 528; *Stead, Hazel & Co v Cooper* [1933] 1 KB 840; *Re Anglo-Moravian Hungarian Junction Rly Co, ex p Watkin* (1875) 1 Ch D 130, CA.

24-40   The basic duty of the liquidator in all types of liquidation is to wind up the company's affairs, to collect in and realise the company's assets and to make distributions to the creditors in accordance with the statutory scheme with any surplus being returned to the shareholders.[90] To assist in these tasks, an extensive array of powers are conferred on a liquidator by IA 1986, Sch 4, some of which require the sanction of the court or creditors before exercise. The power to pay any class of creditors in full, to reach any compromise with any creditors and to bring any legal proceedings under certain provisions of the IA 1986[91] require sanction before being exercised in any type of winding up (Sch 4, Pt I). The power to bring or defend any action or other legal proceeding in the name and on behalf of the company and the power to carry on the business of the company so far as may be necessary for its beneficial winding up also require sanction if it is a compulsory winding up, but not if it is a voluntary winding up (Sch 4, Pt II). Finally, regardless of the type of winding up, a wide variety of other powers are listed in Sch 4, Pt III, such as the power to sell any of the company's property and including the power to do all such other things as may be necessary for winding up the company's affairs and distributing its assets and no sanction is required in these cases. In a compulsory winding up, the sanction needed is that of the court or the liquidation committee if one has been appointed.[92] In the case of a creditors' voluntary winding up, the sanction required is of the court or the liquidation committee or of a meeting of the company's creditors if there is no committee.[93] In a members' voluntary winding up, the sanction required is a special resolution of the company.[94]

24-41   When deciding whether to sanction the exercise of a power, the decision for the court or the liquidation committee is not whether the liquidator is acting bona fide and reasonably, but whether the interests of those creditors or contributories who have a real interest in the assets of the company in liquidation are likely to be best served by permitting the company to enter into the proposed transaction.[95] A liquidator can assign a cause of action available to the company as it forms part of the company's 'property' which can be sold.[96]

24-42   A particularly useful power which a liquidator has is the power of disclaimer. Disclaimer is a means by which a liquidator can terminate certain future obligations of the company

---

[90] IA 1986, ss 91(1), 100(1), 107 (voluntary winding up); s 143(1) (compulsory winding up).

[91] In particular, whether in a compulsory or voluntary winding up, sanction is required for the exercise of power to bring legal proceedings under IA 1986, ss 213, 214, 238, 239, 242, 243, or 423 (provisions allowing actions to be brought to recover assets or seek contributions to the company's assets), see the discussion in Chapter 25.

[92] IA 1986, s 167(1). Consent should be sought first from the liquidation committee and application to the court made if consent is refused or given subject to conditions that the liquidator will not accept. The liquidator should tell the committee of his application to the court so that their views may be heard as well: *Re Consolidated Diesel Engine Manufacturers Ltd* [1915] 1 Ch 192. A creditor or contributory of the company is entitled to be heard on an application by a liquidator for the sanction of the court: *Re Greenhaven Motors Ltd* [1999] 1 BCLC 635, CA.   [93] IA 1986, s 165(2)(b).

[94] IA 1986, s 165(2)(a).

[95] *Re Barings plc (No 7)* [2002] 1 BCLC 401; *Re Greenhaven Motors Ltd* [1999] 1 BCLC 635, CA.

[96] *Guy v Churchill* (1889) 40 Ch D 481 at 485, per Chitty J; see also *Norglen Ltd v Reeds Rains Prudential Ltd* [1998] 1 BCLC 176 at 182–3, HL. But the 'property' must be property of the company at the commencement of the litigation and it does not include property which only arises after the liquidation and is recoverable by the liquidator pursuant to his statutory powers, such as the fruits of a wrongful trading action under IA 1986, s 214: *Re Oasis Merchandising Services Ltd, Ward v Aitken* [1997] 1 BCLC 689, CA. This entitlement to assign in this way is an exemption from the rules of champerty, which exemption is conferred because the statutory powers of liquidators place them in a privileged position. See *Norglen Ltd v Reeds Rains Prudential Ltd* [1998] 1 BCLC 176 at 182.

or disclaim ownership of unsaleable assets and he can exercise the power to disclaim onerous property notwithstanding that he has taken possession of the property, endeavoured to sell it or otherwise exercised rights of ownership in relation to it.[97] Any person sustaining loss or damage as a consequence of the operation of a disclaimer has a statutory right to compensation (s 178(6)).[98]

24-43 Disclaimer is effected by the liquidator serving a notice[99] and the effect of a disclaimer is to terminate, as from the date of the disclaimer, the rights and liabilities of the company in the property disclaimed (IA 1986, s 178(4)(a)). But, it does not, except so far as is necessary for the purposes of releasing the company from any liability, affect the rights or liabilities of any other person.[100] There is no time-limit within which the liquidator must decide whether to disclaim property, but any person with an interest in the property can serve a notice on the liquidator requiring the liquidator to disclaim within 28 days or lose the right to do so (s 178(5)). The court can interfere with a disclaimer only if it is exercised in bad faith or the liquidator's decision is perverse.[101]

24-44 To assist liquidators to get a complete picture of the company's affairs, liquidators have extensive powers to inquire into the company's dealings and to seek the court's assistance by summoning persons to appear before it, or requiring persons to submit affidavits or produce books, documents or other records relating to the company (ss 235, 236). In a compulsory winding up, the liquidator may summon general meetings of the creditors or contributories for the purpose of ascertaining their wishes and, in some circumstances, he can be compelled to call such meetings (s 168(1), (2). He may also apply to the court for directions in relation to any particular matter arising in the winding up.[102]

24-45 In a compulsory liquidation, individual contributories or creditors may apply to the court to control the exercise or proposed exercise of any of the liquidator's powers (IA 1986, s 167(3)). There is no equivalent provision with respect to voluntary liquidation, but an application to the court may be made under IA 1986, s 112(1) by any contributory or any creditor to determine any question arising in the winding up. Furthermore, in a compulsory winding up, any person aggrieved by an act or decision of the liquidator may apply to the court under s 168(5) which may confirm, reverse or modify the act or decision complained of and may make such order as it thinks fit.[103] The court will not interfere with the business decisions of a liquidator, however, and it is necessary to establish that the

---

[97] IA 1986, s 178(2). 'Onerous property' is defined as: (1) any unprofitable contract; and (2) any other property of the company which is unsaleable or not readily saleable or is such that it may give rise to a liability to pay money or perform any other onerous act: s 178(3). It is a necessary feature of an 'unprofitable contract' that it imposes future obligations (i.e. obligations yet to be performed), the performance of which might be detrimental to creditors by prejudicing the liquidator's obligation to realise the company's property and pay a dividend to the creditors within a reasonable time: *Re SSSL Realisations (2002) Ltd* [2007] 1 BCLC 29, CA. 'Property' is defined in IA 1986, 436 and extends to a waste disposal licence under the Environmental Protection Act 1990 which may be disclaimed by a liquidator: *Re Celtic Extraction Ltd* [1999] 2 BCLC 555, CA.   [98] See *Re Park Air Services plc* [1999] 1 BCLC 155, HL.

[99] For the rules as to the notice, see IR 1986, rr 4.187–4.194.

[100] IA 1986, s 178(4)(b); and see *Hindcastle Ltd v Barbara Attenborough Associates Ltd* [1996] 2 BCLC 234, HL; *Capital Prime Properties plc v Worthgate Ltd* [2000] 1 BCLC 647.

[101] *Re Hans Place Ltd* [1993] BCLC 768.

[102] IA 1986, s 168(3) (compulsory winding up); s 112 (voluntary winding up).

[103] Applications under IA 1986, s 168(5) may be brought by creditors or contributories or persons directly affected by the exercise of a power given specifically to a liquidator and who otherwise would not be able to challenge the exercise of that power: *Mahomed v Morris* [2000] 2 BCLC 526, CA.

liquidator has acted mala fide or in a way in which no reasonable liquidator would have acted.[104]

24-46 Individual contributories or creditors may use the summary misfeasance procedure under IA 1986, s 212 to ask the court to compel the liquidator to restore property to the company or compensate it for breach of duty. The power to make such an application continues after the winding up is completed and notwithstanding the release of the liquidator from all liability connected with the liquidation,[105] but any application in these circumstances requires the court's consent (s 212(4)).

F The anti-deprivation rule, proof of debts and set-off

Overview

24-47 On liquidation all the assets of the company form a common fund which, subject to the expenses of the winding up and the rights of the preferential creditors, are subject to a statutory trust for the benefit of all the unsecured creditors.[106] Secured creditors look not to the statutory trust but to their security for payment of the sums due to them but, if that security takes the form of a floating charge, the sums realised by that charge are subject to the prior claims of the expenses of winding up (so far as the general assets are insufficient to meet those expenses), the claims of the preferential creditors and the need to set aside the 'prescribed part' (a percentage of the realisations of the floating charge set aside for the general body of creditors), all of which are discussed later. Unsecured creditors are restricted to claiming against any 'free' assets of the company, i.e. assets not appropriated to any security, and that pool of assets must be distributed *pari passu* (a fundamental principle of insolvency law)[107] which requires that all creditors participate in the pooled assets in proportion to the size of their claim and where the assets are insufficient to meet all the claims, they abate proportionately.[108] For example, if there are three unsecured creditors who are owed £100,000 (A), £200,000 (B) and £300,000 (C) and £240,000 remains available for distribution by the liquidator, A gets £40,000, B gets £80,000 and C £120,000. While the *pari passu* principle is the fundamental basis for the distribution of assets on insolvency, its application is limited to unsecured creditors (and preferential creditors in the event of a deficiency in meeting their claims) and it is precisely in order to avoid its application that creditors look for security and other mechanisms to remove themselves from the common pool.[109] In an attempt to limit the scope for defeating the *pari passu* distribution rule which applies to the common fund, there are some rules affecting the composition of the fund and the claims which can be made against it which need to be considered.

---

[104] See *Re Greenhaven Motors Ltd* [1997] 1 BCLC 739; *Re Edennote Ltd, Tottenham Hotspur plc v Ryman* [1996] 2 BCLC 389, CA.

[105] IA 1986, ss 173(4), 174(6).

[106] See *Ayerst (Inspector of Taxes) v C & K (Construction) Ltd* [1975] 2 All ER 537; *Webb v Whiffin* (1872) LR 5 HL 711 at 721, 724.

[107] See *Re HIH Casualty and General Insurance Ltd; McMahon v McGrath* [2008] 3 All ER 869, HL.

[108] IA 1986, s 107; IR 1986, r 4.181.

[109] See Goode, *Principles of Corporate Insolvency Law* (4th edn, 2011), Ch 7; Finch, *Corporate Insolvency Law: Perspectives and Principles* (2nd edn, 2009), Chs 14 and 15; Mokal, *Corporate Insolvency Law* (2005), Ch 4.

Establishing the estate—the anti-deprivation rule

24-48 Clearly it is important that an insolvent company should not be able to remove or prevent the removal of assets from its estate at the point of insolvency so leaving the creditors to claim against a smaller estate.[110] This rule is known now as the anti-deprivation rule and its origins can be traced to the 19th century. Often cited in this regard is the dictum of Cotton LJ in *Ex p Jay, re Harrison*[111] that 'there cannot be a valid contract that a man's property shall remain his until his bankruptcy, and on the happening of that event shall go over to someone else, and be taken away from his creditors'. The anti-deprivation rule was the subject of lengthy consideration recently by the Supreme Court in *Belmont Park Investments Pty Ltd v BNY Corporate Trustee Services Ltd.*[112]

The case arose out of the collapse of Lehman Brothers and the facts are complex but, in essence, the issue was that various investors (noteholders) claimed certain assets held as security by a trustee in circumstances where the investors' claim to the assets was in competition with a claim to the assets by a related insolvent swap counterparty (LBSF, one of the Lehman companies). The terms of the investment agreement provided that, on an event of default, the prior claim of LBSF to the assets would flip so as to give the investors prior claim to the assets. LBSF argued that the effect of 'the flip' was to deprive it (an insolvent company) of valuable assets on insolvency and so it infringed the anti-deprivation rule, a view rejected by the High Court and the Court of Appeal, each of which held that the anti-deprivation rule was not infringed in these circumstances. The Supreme Court affirmed the lower court decisions with five of their Lordships endorsing the judgment of Lord Collins who provided a detailed analysis of the development and scope of the rule.[113] The key points made by Lord Collins were that:

- The policy behind the anti-deprivation rule is clear: the parties cannot, on bankruptcy, deprive the bankrupt of property which would otherwise be available for creditors, but the rule is not triggered by deprivation for reasons other than insolvency.[114]

- The anti-deprivation rule is too well-established to be discarded[115] despite the detailed provisions set out in modern insolvency legislation, all of which should be taken to have been enacted against the background of the rule.[116]

- Despite statutory inroads, party autonomy is at the heart of English commercial law, particularly in the case of complex financial instruments.[117] It is desirable that, so far as possible, the courts give effect to the contractual terms which parties have

---

[110] There is an overlap with the rule of *pari passu* distribution (discussed at **24-75**), see *Belmont Park Investments Pty Ltd v BNY Corporate Trustee Services Ltd* [2012] 1 All ER 505 at [1], [9], [14].

[111] (1880) 14 Ch D 19 at 26.

[112] [2012] 1 All ER 505, aff'g the ruling of the Court of Appeal which is reported as *Perpetual Trustee Co Ltd v BNY Corporate Trustee Services Ltd* [2010] 1 BCLC 747, aff'g [2009] 2 BCLC 400. On the Supreme Court ruling, see Fletcher (2012) Insolv Int 25; Worthington (2012) 75 MLR 78; on the Court of Appeal ruling, see Goode (2011) 127 LQR 1. See also *Money Markets International Stockbrokers Ltd v London Stock Exchange Ltd* [2001] 2 BCLC 347; *Lomas v JFB Firth Rixson* [2012] EWCA Civ 419 at [80]–[100].

[113] Lord Mance agreed with the conclusion but not with the analysis put forward by Lord Collins.

[114] [2012] 1 All ER 505 at [104].

[115] In the Court of Appeal Patten LJ had queried whether the rule was needed any longer in the light of the IA 1986, see [2010] 1 BCLC 747 at [171]–[172].

[116] [2012] 1 All ER 505 at [101]. See Fletcher, n 112, who notes the judicial determination not to deliver any game-changing pronouncements in this eagerly awaited judgment and the insistence that it is now for the legislature to change this rule. He also noted that realistically the prospect of any such reform must be considered very remote, at 27.   [117] [2012] 1 All ER 505 at [103].

agreed. In line with that approach, it is possible to give the policy behind the anti-deprivation rule a common sense application which prevents its application to bona fide commercial transactions which do not have as their predominant purpose, or one of their main purposes, the deprivation of the property of one of the parties on bankruptcy.[118] Lord Collins noted that there is an impressive body of authority that, in the case of the anti-deprivation rule, a deliberate intention to evade the insolvency laws is required, though not in the sense of finding a subjective intention.[119] Finally, the source of the asset—who funded its acquisition (which the High Court and Lord Neuberger in the Court of Appeal thought important)—is an important and sometimes decisive factor when concluding that a transaction is a commercial one entered into in good faith and outside the scope of the anti-deprivation rule.[120]

24-49 In the instant case, the court had to look at the substance of the matter which was that LBSF had had a security interest, the content and extent of which had altered by an act of default (insolvency proceedings in the US). The transaction in question had been a complex commercial transaction. There had never been any suggestion that those provisions had deliberately been intended to evade insolvency law. That was obvious in any event from the wide range of non-insolvency circumstances capable of constituting an event of default under the swap agreement. The fact that, in certain circumstances, the change in priority would lead to a (possibly unanticipated) benefit to the investors and to the loss of LBSF's security rights in the assets did not alter the position. The anti-deprivation principle is essentially directed to intentional or inevitable evasion of the principle that the debtor's property is part of the insolvent estate and, applying the principle in a commercially sensitive manner, taking into account the policy of party autonomy and the upholding of proper commercial bargains, these 'flip' provisions did not infringe the principle.[121] Overall, the approach of the Supreme Court is to endorse the rule while offering commercial parties considerable freedom to contract around it, as long as there is a commercial purpose to the transaction and the parties are not starting from a position of a deliberate intention to contract out of the insolvency legislation.[122]

24-50 A more routine application of the anti-deprivation rule can be seen in *Folgate London Market Ltd v Chaucer Insurance plc*.[123] In this case, a truck company commenced proceedings against a broker in negligence after it transpired that the company did not have insurance coverage in respect of an accident involving a third party. The company and the broker entered into a settlement agreement whereby the broker agreed to pay 85% of any claim which the company had to pay to the third party, but the broker would be released from its obligations under the settlement on the insolvency of the company. The truck company went into administration and the administrators assigned all interest in the settlement agreement to the company's insurers (the claimant) which sought and obtained an order striking down these settlement provisions as offending the anti-deprivation rule. On appeal, the Court of Appeal held that the commercial objective of this provision in the settlement agreement, properly construed, was an attempt to provide that, while the company's right to payment and the broker's obligation to pay would survive so long as the payment accrued exclusively to the benefit of the company, they were to be extinguished

---

[118] [2012] 1 All ER 505 at [104].   [119] [2012] 1 All ER 505 at [78]–[79].
[120] [2012] 1 All ER 505 at [98].   [121] [2012] 1 All ER 505, at [106] [108]–[114].
[122] Worthington, see n 112, at 121, criticises the focus on intention and comments that the ruling 'effectively eliminates the insolvency-triggered deprivation limb of the anti-deprivation principle, certainly for complex financial deals involving sophisticated parties'.
[123] [2011] BCC 675, aff'g [2010] 2 BCLC 440 where the case is reported as *Mayhew v King*.

if such payment would instead be available for the company's creditors generally in the event of its insolvency. It was settled law, the court said, that a purported contracting out of insolvency legislation is contrary to public policy and therefore this provision was void. As Lord Collins noted in *Belmont Park Investments*,[124] this case was a blatant attempt to deprive a party of property in the event of liquidation.

24-51 Finally, note that one area where the anti-deprivation rule is not engaged is in the context of licences and leases which determine on insolvency. Rather than viewing these transactions as a contracting out contrary to the anti-deprivation rule, the position is better viewed as one whereby the company has a determinable interest in an asset which determines on insolvency in accordance with the terms of its grant.[125] The termination does not remove from the insolvent estate property in which the company ever had an unfettered interest, the company's interest always was limited by the terms on which it was granted and therefore the rule has no application.[126]

24-52 The result of the anti-deprivation rule and its invalidation of any removal of assets from the pool on insolvency is that creditors go to great lengths prior to this point to ensure that assets are available to meet their claims outside of the common fund. Indeed, in many cases, these devices ensure that there are no unencumbered assets available to the unsecured creditors. The mechanisms involved include, for example, taking security over the assets (even if a floating charge is subject to some prior claims) or retaining title to the goods so that those assets never become part of the company's assets on liquidation and are not swept into the common fund for *pari passu* distribution. A clause in a sale of goods contract preventing property in the goods passing to the purchaser until payment of debts due to the supplier ensures that such goods remain in the ownership of the supplier pending payment and do not form part of the assets of the company available to any unsecured creditors in a winding up.[127]

24-53 Another useful mechanism for some creditors is a trust. It is only property to which the company is beneficially entitled that is available to its creditors so, if the company holds property on trust for others, that property is not available to the company's creditors.[128] This has led to the use of the trust as a means of protecting unsecured creditors, especially where customers make advance payments to a company when the company is already in some financial difficulty.[129] By holding such customer sums on trust, they are protected from the claims of the creditors of the company in the event of insolvency. The use of such trusts is relatively common now and disputes tend to centre on whether the three certainties (of intention, subject matter and objects) required of any trust are present.[130] As

---

[124] [2012] 1 All ER 505 at [104].

[125] While this carve out for licences and leases is criticised, it is too well established now, as Professor Sir Roy Goode notes, to be dislodged other than by legislation, see Goode (2011) 127 LQR 1 at 8. See discussion in *Butters v BBC Worldwide Ltd* which is reported as a joined appeal in *Perpetual Trustee Co Ltd v BNY Corporate Trustee Services Ltd* [2010] 1 BCLC 747 at [84]–[88].

[126] See *Perpetual Trustee Co Ltd v BNY Corporate Trustee Services Ltd* [2010] 1 BCLC 747 at [146], per Patten LJ.

[127] See *Aluminium Industries Vaassen v Romalpa Ltd* [1976] 2 All ER 552; *Clough Mill Ltd v Martin* [1985] BCLC 64.

[128] See *Barclays Bank Ltd v Quistclose Investments Ltd* [1968] 3 All ER 651, HL; also *Carreras Rothmans Ltd v Freeman Matthew's Treasure Ltd* [1985] 1 All ER 155.

[129] For a valuable account of the advantages and disadvantages of using trusts in this way, see Ellis & Verrill, 'Twilight Trusts' (2007) 20 Insolv Int 151.

[130] See *Re Kayford Ltd* [1975] 1 All ER 604; *Re Lewis's of Leicester Ltd* [1995] 1 BCLC 428; *Re Holiday Promotions (Europe) Ltd* [1996] 2 BCLC 618; *Re Fleet Disposal Services Ltd, Spratt v AT & T Automotive*

these trusts are often hastily constructed as financial problems mount, it is not unusual for there to be issues as to whether they have been correctly constituted and disputes as to whether moneys have been properly assigned to the trust fund.[131] Another way in which unsecured creditors may escape from the pool is if they are in a position to benefit from the doctrine of set-off which is discussed at **24-58**.

Establishing the liabilities—proof of debts and set-off

24-54 Contrary to what might be supposed, the administration of an insolvent debtor's estate does not involve the payment and discharge of all the debts owing by the debtor. Instead, it is only those debts which are provable in the insolvency and which are proved which will receive any payment.

Submission of proofs

24-55 The rules specifying which debts are provable and the procedure to be followed in establishing a claim are contained in the Insolvency Rules 1986.[132] All claims by creditors are provable as debts against the company whether they are present or future, certain or contingent, ascertained or sounding only in damages (IR 1986, r 12.3(1)). The debt may be a debt to which the company is subject at the date on which the company goes into liquidation[133] or it may be a debt which arises after the company goes into liquidation provided that it is in respect of an obligation incurred before that date.[134] Thus a contractual promise, entered into before going into liquidation, to pay a sum of money at a date occurring after the company has gone into liquidation gives rise to a provable debt. Any liability in tort is a debt provable in the winding up if either (1) the cause of action has accrued at the date on which the company goes into liquidation; or (2) all the elements necessary to establish the cause of action exist at that date except for actionable damage.[135] The liquidator is given power to estimate the value of contingent liabilities or debts of an uncertain amount.[136]

24-56 In a compulsory winding up, creditors are required to submit a written claim and the document by which a creditor seeks to establish his claim is known as his 'proof'.[137] In a voluntary winding up, it is for the liquidator to decide whether he requires written

---

Services Ltd [1995] 1 BCLC 345; *Re Sendo International Ltd* [2007] 1 BCLC 141; *Re Farepak Food & Gifts Ltd* [2007] 2 BCLC 1. *Re BA Peters plc* [2010] 1 BCLC 142.

[131] For an example of the value of having customer funds held on trust, see *Re Lehman Brothers International (Europe) (No 2)* [2011] 2 BCLC 184 (court found statutory trust in that case imposed in respect of client money immediately the money was received from or on behalf of the client regardless of when it was segregated in a client account).   [132] IR 1986, rr 4.73–4.94.

[133] IR 1986, r 13.12(1)(a). A company goes into liquidation if it passes a resolution for voluntary winding up or an order for its winding up is made by the court at a time when it has not already gone into liquidation by passing such a resolution: IA 1986, s 247(2).   [134] IR 1986, r 13.12(1)(b).

[135] IR 1986, r 13.12(2). This rule was substituted by SI 2006/1272 to redress the problems created by the decision in *Re T & N Ltd* [2005] EWHC 2870, [2006] 2 BCLC 374 where the court held that future asbestos claims were not provable debts for the purposes of winding up because the cause of action had not accrued by the liquidation date. See Toube, 'Future Contingent Claims' (2008) 21 Insolv Int 12 for the background to the change.

[136] IR 1986, r 4.86. In cases of difficulty, application may be made to the court for assistance: IA 1986, s 168(3), (5). See *Revenue and Customs Commissioners v Maxwell* [2011] 2 BCLC 301 as to how estimates might be made—in that case in the context of an administration and determining the value of a debt for voting purposes, but useful also in this context of a liquidator estimating the amount of a debt.

[137] IR 1986, r 4.73(1), (3).

proofs[138] and in practice he will require the submission of proofs. The liquidator examines the proof and may admit all or part of the debt or may reject it.[139] Parties aggrieved by his decision may apply to the court.[140] The liquidator has four months from the last date for proving to declare a dividend which he must do, provided he has sufficient funds (IR 1986, r 4.180), unless he has cause to postpone or cancel the dividend (r 11.5). But the liquidator is not personally liable in respect of a dividend and there is no relationship of debtor and creditor between the liquidator and any creditor.[141] If a liquidator fails to pay a declared dividend, an aggrieved creditor can apply to the court for an order directing payment.[142]

24-57 In the case of secured creditors, if they are content to rely solely on their security they do not submit a proof of debt at all. Alternatively, they may realise their security and prove for any unsecured balance, or surrender their security and prove for the whole amount.[143]

Set-off

24-58 A further restriction on the amount for which creditors may prove arises from the application of the set-off rule in IR 1986, r 4.90 where, before the company goes into liquidation, there have been mutual credits, mutual debts or other mutual dealings (subject to certain exclusions, r 4.90(2)) between the company and any creditor of the company proving or claiming to prove for a debt in the liquidation.[144] In that case, an account must be taken of what is due from each party to the other in respect of the mutual dealings and the sums due from one party must be set off against the sums due from the other (r 4.90(3)). Set-off is mandatory and creditors are not allowed to contract out of their right of set-off.[145] Set-off is automatic and self-executing as at the date of the winding-up order[146] with the original claims extinguished and only a net balance remaining.[147]

24-59 The provisions on insolvency set-off are intended 'to promote speedy and efficient administration of the assets so as to enable a distribution to be made to creditors as soon as possible and in a manner which achieves substantial justice between the parties to the set-off and, so far as practicable, equality in the treatment of creditors'.[148] In practice, set-off benefits creditors for, instead of having to prove with other unsecured creditors for the whole of their debt (i.e. having to claim against the pooled assets and possibly risk not being paid at all), creditors can set off debts which they owe to the company and prove or pay only the balance.[149] Creditors will therefore seek to acquire rights of set-off, but there must be mutual credits, mutual debts or other mutual dealings giving rise to

---

[138] IR 1986, r 4.73(2).   [139] IR 1986, r 4.82.   [140] IR 1986, r 4.83.
[141] *Lomax Leisure v Miller* [2008] 1 BCLC 262.   [142] See *Lomax Leisure v Miller* [2008] 1 BCLC 262.
[143] IR 1986, r 4.88(1), (2). As to the liquidator's right to redeem the security at the creditor's valuation, see r 4.97.
[144] IR 1986, r 2.85 sets out the equivalent set-off rule in administration which applies if the administrator gives notice that he intends to make a distribution to creditors.
[145] *National Westminster Bank Ltd v Halesowen Presswork and Assemblies Ltd* [1972] 1 All ER 641, HL; *Stein v Blake* [1995] 2 All ER 961, HL, noted Berg [1997] LMCLQ 49; *MS Fashions Ltd v Bank of Credit and Commerce International SA (No 2)* [1993] 3 All ER 769, Ch D, CA.
[146] *MS Fashions Ltd v Bank of Credit and Commerce International SA (No 2)* [1993] 3 All ER 769 at 775.
[147] *Re Bank of Credit and Commerce International SA (No 8)* [1997] 4 All ER 568, HL, aff'g [1996] 2 All ER 121, CA; *Stein v Blake* [1995] 2 All ER 961, HL. Any balance can be assigned by the party entitled to it: *Stein v Blake*.   [148] *Re Kaupthing Singer & Friedlander Ltd (No 2)* [2011] 1 BCLC 12 at [32], per Etherton LJ.
[149] See *Stein v Blake* [1995] 2 All ER 961, HL. This is a bankruptcy case, but the principles are essentially common to winding up and bankruptcy. Any balance due to the company is not discounted to its current value in the way that a future debt is discounted for the purpose of set-off, see *Re Kaupthing Singer & Friedlander Ltd (No 2)* [2011] 1 BCLC 12 (administration case, but the equivalent rule applies in liquidation).

set-off which must have occurred before the company went into liquidation (IR 1986, r 4.90(1)). 'Mutual debts' does not in itself require anything more than commensurable cross-obligations between the same people in the same capacity and the origin of the debt (whether contract, statute, tort, voluntarily or by compulsion) is immaterial.[150] 'Mutual dealings' merely requires that there should be 'dealings' (in an extended sense which includes the commission of a tort or the imposition of a statutory obligation) giving rise to commensurable cross-claims.[151]

24-60 Set-off is strictly limited to mutual claims existing at the time of liquidation[152] and there can be no set-off of claims by third parties, even with their consent. The issue of third party claims was considered in several banking cases where companies had borrowed from and therefore were debtors of an insolvent bank and their controlling shareholders and directors were also depositors with the bank. The question was whether the depositors' claims against the bank could be set off against the banks' claims against the companies. Without set-off, the bank liquidators were entitled to claim the entire debt from the companies while the depositors would have to prove in the liquidation for their deposits with little hope of recovery. In *MS Fashions Ltd v Bank of Credit and Commerce International SA (No 2)*[153] the bank advanced money to a company and repayment was guaranteed by a director who had a deposit account with the bank. As between himself and the bank, the director was expressed to be a principal debtor. It was held that the company director, as a principal debtor, could rely on the right of set-off to reduce or extinguish the debt owed to the bank by him and his company by the amount standing to his credit in his own deposit account with the bank. The key point, however, was that under the terms of this particular loan, the director was deemed to be the principal debtor.

24-61 In *Re Bank of Credit and Commerce International SA (No 8)*[154] the House of Lords considered this issue of third party deposits.[155] In this case the bank had lent money to a company on the security of a deposit made with the bank by the company's controlling shareholder. A charge was granted over the deposit but the charge did not contain any promise by the shareholder to pay what might be due from the company to the bank. The liquidators sought directions as to whether the bank could claim repayment of the loan from the company and leave the depositor to prove in the liquidation or whether it was obliged to set off the loan against the deposit and treat the company as discharged to that extent. The House of Lords held that set-off was limited to mutual claims existing at the date of the winding-up order and there could be no set-off of claims by third parties, even with their consent, as to do so would be to allow parties by agreement to subvert the fundamental principle of *pari passu* distribution of an insolvent company's assets.[156] There was no mutuality between the depositor and the bank which would permit the

---

[150] *Re West End Networks Ltd, Secretary of State for Trade and Industry v Frid* [2004] 2 BCLC 1, HL. The mutual debts must have existed before the company went into liquidation and the company cannot seek to create a set-off after that date: see *Hague v Nam Tai Electronics Inc* [2007] 2 BCLC 194 at 198, PC; and see IR 1986, r 4.90(2)(a).

[151] *Re West End Networks Ltd, Secretary of State for Trade and Industry v Frid* [2004] 2 BCLC 1, HL (there was mutuality and therefore set-off was permissible when a company had a claim against Customs & Excise for a VAT credit and there was a claim against the company by the Secretary of State with respect to redundancy payments). See also *Manson v Smith* [1997] 2 BCLC 161, CA; *Re a company (No 1641 of 2003)* [2004] 1 BCLC 210; *Smith (Administrator of Cosslett Contractors Ltd) v Bridgend County BC* [2002] 1 BCLC 77 at [35].   [152] The time of liquidation is defined in IA 1986, s 247(2), see n 133.

[153] [1993] 3 All ER 769.

[154] [1997] 4 All ER 568, HL; aff'g [1996] 2 All ER 121, CA; see Calnan (1998) 114 LQR 174; Goode (1998) 114 LQR 178. See also *Tam Wing Chuen v Bank of Credit and Commerce Hong Kong Ltd* [1996] 2 BCLC 69, PC.

[155] The third parties were the beneficial owners of the companies.   [156] [1997] 4 All ER 568 at 573.

sum owed by the bank to the depositor (i.e. the amount of the deposit and interest) to be set off against the amount owed by the company to the bank. The depositor did not owe anything to the bank (not having taken on any personal liability for the borrower's debt) but had simply created an effective charge over the deposit in favour of the bank.[157] *MS Fashions Ltd v Bank of Credit and Commerce International SA (No 2)* was distinguishable on the basis of the very unusual security documents executed by the depositor in that case which resulted in the depositor being personally liable to the bank and so the bank's liability to the depositor and the depositor's liability to the bank in that case did constitute mutual dealings falling to be set off under IR 1986, r 4.90.[158] Here there was no such mutuality.

G The order of distribution

23-62 On winding up, secured creditors look to realise their security outside of the liquidation[159] while the fund available for distribution in the liquidation is disbursed in the following order: (1) the expenses of liquidation; (2) the preferential debts; (3) the claims of the floating chargeholder from which must be deducted the prescribed part if the charge was created on or after 15 September 2003; (4) the unsecured creditors on a *pari passu* basis (and their fund is swelled by the amount set aside under the prescribed part).

The expenses of winding up

24-63 Section 115 of the IA 1986 provides that all expenses properly claimed in the winding up, including the remuneration of the liquidator, are payable out of the company's assets in priority to all other claims.[160] Section 176ZA further provides that the expenses of winding up have priority over any claims to property comprised in or subject to any floating charge and must be paid out of such property to the extent that the assets of the company available for payment of general creditors (excluding any sum set aside under the prescribed part provisions: see **24-72**) are insufficient to meet the expenses of winding up.[161] Preferential creditors also have priority over the claims to property of a floating chargeholder and are entitled to be paid out of such property to the extent that the assets of the company available for payment of general creditors are insufficient to meet the preferential debts (s 175(2)).[162] The result is that the expenses of winding up and the preferential debts must be paid in priority to the claims of the floating chargeholder and, to the extent that the assets available to the general creditors are inadequate for this purposes, these prior claims must be met out of property subject to the floating charge.

24-64 Obviously, given the priority accorded to expenses of the winding up, if extensive costs can be recovered as expenses, then less will be available to pay the floating chargeholder and ultimately the general unsecured creditors. Creditors have an interest therefore in

---

[157] [1997] 4 All ER 568 at 574, 576, 577.   [158] See [1997] 4 All ER 568 at 574;

[159] As a practical matter the secured creditor may ask the liquidator to realise the assets and charge the costs of realisation against those assets.

[160] The company's assets for this purpose include the proceeds of any legal action taken by a liquidator in his own name or on behalf of the company or arising from any arbitration or other dispute resolution procedure: IR 1986, r 4.218(2)(a).

[161] Inserted by CA 2006, s 1282, overruling *Re Leyland Daf, Buchler v Talbot* [2004] 1 BCLC 281, HL, and applicable to liquidations post-6 April 2008, subject to certain transitional provisions; see Fletcher, 'CA 2006, Reversal of *Leyland Daf*' (2007) 20 Insolv Int 30.

[162] A point reinforced by IA 1986, s 176ZA(2)(b)(ii).

what is an expense of the winding up, both in terms of whether they can bring their claim within that category and secure priority and, vice versa, whether they can prevent undue depletion of such funds as are available by challenging whether a particular cost is indeed an expense of the winding up.

24-65 The issue of what amounts to an 'expense of the winding up' was for many years a hotly disputed matter, both as to what constituted an 'expense' and as to the order of priority to be accorded *inter se*. The position was clarified initially by the decision of the House of Lords in *Re Toshoku Finance UK plc*[163] and by subsequent changes to the key provision which is IR 1986, r 4.218 which identifies 18 classes of debts as expenses of the winding up and sets out the order of priority in which they must be paid.

24-66 In *Re Toshoku Finance UK plc*[164] the House of Lords reviewed the operation of IR 1986, r 4.218 and concluded that the rule is a definitive statement of what counts as an expense of the liquidation. It is a complete statement of liquidation expenses, subject only to the qualifications contained in the rules themselves and subject to the principle, which Lord Hoffmann described as the principle in the *Lundy Granite* case,[165] which allows liabilities incurred before the liquidation in respect of property afterwards retained by the liquidator for the benefit of the insolvent estate to be treated as expenses in the winding up (such as liabilities arising under a pre-existing lease). To that limited extent, benefit of the estate is a relevant issue, but it is irrelevant to the payment of an item expressly provided for by IR 1986, r 4.218.[166] The only power reserved to the court is that conferred by IA 1986, s 156 which gives the court in a compulsory winding up a discretion to rearrange the priorities of the listed expenses *inter se*.[167]

24-67 The result is that IA 1986, s 115 determines the priority of expenses of winding up as against other claims and IR 1986, r 4.218 determines both what is an expense and the order of priority of expenses *inter se*.[168] Turning to r 4.218, two of the most important categories of debts identified therein are:

- expenses properly chargeable or incurred by the official receiver or the liquidator in preserving, realising or getting in any of the assets of the company or otherwise in the preparation or conduct of any legal proceedings, arbitration or other dispute resolution procedures which he has power to bring or defend whether in his own name or the name of the company or relating to the settlement or compromise of any action or dispute to which the proceedings or procedures relate (r 4.218(3)(a)(ii)); and

- any necessary disbursements by the liquidator in the course of his administration (r. 4.218(3)(m)).

24-68 In relation to IR 1986, r 4.218(3)(a)(ii) the issue of legal costs had been controversial with creditors concerned that such realisations as the liquidator might have in hand should not be 'wasted' on litigation by the liquidator against the former directors on grounds such as wrongful trading (IA 1986, s 214: see **25-18**) or transactions at an undervalue or preferences (IA 1986, ss 238, 239: see **25-37, 25-50**). Liquidators for their part were anxious to pursue possible claims, but not if the costs were not permissible as an expense

---

[163] [2002] 1 BCLC 598, HL.   [164] [2002] 1 BCLC 598, HL.
[165] *Re Lundy Granite Co* (1871) 6 Ch App 462.
[166] In reaching this conclusion the House of Lords rejected the so-called liquidation expenses principles as expressed in *Re Atlantic Computers plc* [1992] Ch 505 at 519–23 to the effect that all expenses incurred post-liquidation were payable provided they were incurred for the benefit of the insolvent estate.
[167] See also IR 1986, r 4.220(1).   [168] *Re Toshoku Finance UK plc* [2002] 1 BCLC 598.

in the winding up, as the courts in fact confirmed.[169] The issue is resolved by IR 1986, r 4.218(3)(a)(ii) which expressly allows litigation costs to be recoverable as an expense in the winding up. Creditor concerns about 'wasteful' litigation are met by the requirement imposed by IA 1986, Sch 4, Pt 1 that a liquidator who wishes to exercise his power to bring proceedings under IA 1986, ss 213, 214, 238, 239, 242, 243 or 423 (all provisions allowing actions to be brought to recover assets or seek contributions to the company's assets) requires the sanction of the court or liquidation committee or creditors (depending on the type of winding up, see **24-40**). In other words, a balance has been struck. A liquidator cannot go off on a frolic of his own running up litigation expenses without consent, but where proceedings are duly sanctioned, the expenses are an expense in the winding up within IR 1986, r 4.218(3)(a)(ii). A further limitation is that litigation expenses which exceed £5,000 are only recoverable out of floating charge realisations where approval or authorisation of such litigation expenses has been granted in accordance with IR 1986, rr 4.218A to 4.218E (i.e. by the preferential creditor or chargeholder with a claim to the realisations or by the court).[170]

24-69 As for necessary disbursements under IR 1986, r 4.218(3)(m), which was the actual issue in *Re Toshoku Finance UK plc*,[171] specifically the company's liability to corporation tax, the liquidators argued that payment was not required for the liquidation expenses principle meant that a liability need only be met if it arose as a result of a step taken with a view to, or for the purpose of, obtaining a benefit for the insolvent estate. Applying the analysis set out at **24-66**, the House of Lords rejected this argument. As this tax liability is expressly made an expense in the winding up by r 4.218, issues of benefit to the estate are irrelevant and the court has no discretion to decide other than that the tax liability is a post-liquidation liability which the liquidators are bound to discharge.[172] As noted, expenses in administration (IR 1986, r 2.67) mimic those here in respect of liquidation and therefore the ruling in *Bloom v The Pensions Regulator*,[173] see **23-114**, that sums due under certain directions and notices issued by the Pensions Regulator under the Pensions Act 2004 against companies in administration,[174] though they did not give rise to a provable debt in the administration, are a necessary disbursement by an administrator and payable as an expense in administration, would equally be applicable here and, in an appropriate case, amount to a necessary disbursement in liquidation.

Preferential debts

24-70 Preferential debts are debts (sometimes described as Crown debts) which Parliament has decided should be paid in priority to all other debts other than the expenses of winding up (IA 1986, s 175). The categories of debts which qualify as preferential debts are set out in IA 1986, Sch 6. Preferential debts rank equally amongst themselves and must be paid in full unless the assets are insufficient to meet them in which case they abate in equal

---

[169] See *Re Floor Fourteen Ltd, Lewis v IRC* [2001] 2 BCLC 392, CA; *Re R S & M Engineering Ltd, Mond v Suddards* [1999] 2 BCLC 485; *Re M C Bacon Ltd (No 2)* [1999] 2 BCLC 485.

[170] IR 1986, r 4.218(2)(b); see IR 1986, rr 4.218A–4.128E as to the procedure for obtaining that approval or authorisation.   [171] [2002] 1 BCLC 598, HL.

[172] The position on corporation tax has been modified since the case and it is not a necessary disbursement any more within IR 1986, r 4.218(3)(m) but is specifically provided for as r 4.218(3)(p).

[173] [2012] 1 BCLC 248.

[174] Essentially notices or directions requiring these companies to make payments to an employer's underfunded pension scheme—the employer usually being other companies in the same group.

proportions.[175] In so far as the assets available for payment of general creditors are insufficient for the payment of the preferential debts, the preferential debts have priority over the claims of and must be paid out of the property subject to the floating charge.[176]

24-71 The categories of preferential debts are now much reduced[177] and preferential status is accorded only to contributions due by employers to certain occupational and state pension schemes and certain limited amounts due as remuneration of employees.[178]

The floating chargeholder—the prescribed part

24-72 The floating chargeholder is entitled to be paid once the liabilities in respect of the expenses of winding up and the preferential debts have been met. As noted, the categories of preferential debts have been reduced with the intention of releasing funds to benefit unsecured creditors and so hopefully save such creditors from insolvency themselves. To ensure this outcome, it was necessary to provide a mechanism whereby the sums released from Crown preference did not merely increase the returns to the floating chargeholder but would percolate down to the unsecured creditor. The mechanism used is the 'prescribed part' imposed by IA 1986, s 176A which is that part of the estate of a company which must be set aside for unsecured creditors out of sums which would otherwise be available to the holders of a floating charge.[179] The percentage share of the company's assets which must be set aside in this way for unsecured creditors is:[180]

(1) where the company's net property does not exceed £10,000 in value, 50% of that property;

(2) where the company's net property exceeds £10,000 in value, 50% of the first £10,000 in value; and 20% of that part of the company's net property which exceeds £10,000 in value, subject to a maximum of £600,000.

24-73 The prescribed part only applies to floating charges created on or after 15 September 2003 (IA 1986, s 176A(9)). It is possible to disapply the requirement to set aside the prescribed part if the net property amounts to less than £10,000 and the office-holder thinks that the cost of making a distribution to the unsecured creditors would be disproportionate to the benefits (s 176A(3)). It is also possible for the prescribed part to be disapplied as part of a company voluntary arrangement or a scheme of arrangement (s 176A(4)) or by court

---

[175] A creditor owed preferential and non-preferential debts must exercise any right of set-off proportionately against each class of debt: *Re Unit 2 Windows Ltd* [1985] 3 All ER 647.

[176] See IA 1986, s 175(2)(b), see also s 176ZA(2)(b). 'Floating charge' is defined in s 251. Note also that in a compulsory winding up where distress is levied in the three months before a winding-up order, the preferential debts constitute a first charge on the proceeds of the distress: s 176(2),(3). This does not apply in a voluntary winding up: *Herbert Berry Associates Ltd v IRC* [1978] 1 All ER 161, HL.

[177] The Enterprise Act 2002, s 251 removed the preference afforded to categories of claims payable to the Inland Revenue, Customs and Excise and certain social security contributions. Also retained as preferential, but of limited practical relevance, are certain levies on coal and steel production: IA 1986, Sch 6, para 15A.

[178] Employees are entitled to claim as a preferential debt wages or salary for services rendered in the four months before winding up but up to a maximum amount of £800 per employee; IA 1986, Sch 6, paras 9–12; The Insolvency Proceedings (Monetary Limits) Order 1986, SI 1986/1996, art 4. In addition, all accrued holiday remuneration has priority and is not counted towards the £800 limit: IA 1986, Sch 6, para 10. See also Employment Rights Act 1996, ss 186, 189.

[179] The prescribed part applies in liquidation, administration, provisional liquidations and receiverships: IA 1986, s 176A(1); and it is not subject to the expenses of winding up: see IA 1986, s 176ZA(2)(a).

[180] See The IA 1986 (Prescribed Part) Order 2003, SI 2003/ 2097, art 3. See generally Keay, 'The Prescribed Part: Sharing around the Company's Funds' (2011) Insolv Int 81. The Insolvency Service found no support for any amendment of the level of the prescribed part, see Ministerial Statement, 20 December 2011.

order (s 176A(5)) where costs are disproportionate to the benefits.[181] In *Re International Sections Ltd*[182] the court suggested that disapplication orders should be exceptional for, in these sorts of situations, small dividends will often be the case irrespective of the costs of making any distribution. Here a significant, albeit relatively small, sum would remain for distribution once the costs were catered for and the court refused to make a disapplication order saying that it would not be right to deprive the unsecured creditors of what remained.[183]

24-74 A fixed or floating chargeholder with a shortfall in their security cannot be classed as unsecured creditors so as to participate in the prescribed part which is held for the benefit of unsecured creditors alone. In *Re Airbase (UK Ltd), Thorniley v Revenue and Customs Comrs*[184] and in *Re Permacell Finesse Ltd*[185] the courts rejected such claims concluding that, as a matter of construction of IA 1986, s 176A and as a matter of policy, secured creditors are precluded from participation in the prescribed part with respect to a shortfall. But there is no policy reason and nothing in the statute to prevent a floating chargeholder surrendering totally their security and then participating as an unsecured creditor in the prescribed part carved out of realisations of chargeholders with priority to them.[186] The relevant time for determining the matter is when the claim is made against the prescribed part and a floating chargeholder who surrenders his entire security after the commencement of the winding up may participate in the prescribed part.[187]

Unsecured creditors—the *pari passu* principle

24-75 As noted, unsecured creditors must be paid in accordance with the principle of *pari passu* distribution that all creditors participate in the pooled assets in proportion to the size of their claim and, where the assets are insufficient to meet all the claims, then they abate proportionately.[188] The *pari passu* rule is designed to ensure equal treatment applies but, in fact, as Professor Milman noted, the application of the rule may simply secure an equality of misery,[189] given the widespread use of various mechanisms (i.e. security, trusts and retention of title clauses) which mean that the pooled assets will usually be insubstantial and quite inadequate to meet the claims of the unsecured creditors. The position is alleviated somewhat by the prescribed part, as discussed at **24-72**. Also, a liquidator may be able to swell the assets available to the unsecured creditors by challenging transactions entered into by the company prior to winding up on the grounds, for example, that they

---

[181] The power to disapply the prescribed part is a power to disapply it in its entirety or not at all: *Re Courts plc* [2009] 2 BCLC 363 (court refused to disapply the prescribed part in a way which would have allowed the 37 largest creditors (with claims in excess of £28,000) to take the prescribed part in its entirety while leaving the remaining 260 creditors (claims below that amount) to receive nothing. See also *Re Hydroserve Ltd* [2008] BCC 175.   [182] [2009] 1 BCLC 580.

[183] The company had 66 known unsecured creditors to whom £230,613 was owed. The prescribed part amounted to £6,731.09, with the estimated costs amounting to £3,332, leaving a maximum balance of £3,409.09 available for distribution which would result in each of the unsecured creditors receiving a dividend of 1.48 pence in the pound.   [184] [2008] 1 BCLC 437.

[185] [2008] BCC 208.

[186] *Re PAL SC Realisations 2007 Ltd, Kelly v Inflexion Fund Ltd* [2011] BCC 93. The chargeholder was third behind two other chargeholders and their claims would wipe out all the available assets so the chargeholder would recover nothing; the chargeholder once it had surrendered its security would be able to claim against the prescribed part and given the level of its claim would gain about 73% of the prescribed part which was estimated to be in the region of £317,000. In those circumstances, it made sense to surrender the security.

[187] [2011] BCC 93 at [44].   [188] IA 1986, s 107; IR 1986, r 4.181.

[189] See Milman, 'Priority Rights on Corporate Insolvency' in Clarke (ed), *Current Issues in Insolvency Law* (1991), p 77.

were transactions at an undervalue or preferences or by seeking a contribution from the company's directors alleging wrongful trading: all these issues are discussed in Chapter 25. As noted at **24-40**, a liquidator needs the sanction of the court or the creditors to bring litigation under these provisions so as to ensure that the company's assets are not further depleted by the pursuit of what turn out to be pointless claims.

24-76 It should be noted that there is nothing to prevent an unsecured creditor with a claim against the pooled assets from agreeing as a matter of contract to subordinate his claim until such time as all other unsecured creditors are paid, for such an agreement does not have the effect of shrinking the pool of assets available to the creditors.[190] In *Re SSSL Realisations (2002) Ltd* [191] the Court of Appeal concluded that if a group of companies enters into a subordination agreement (that no group company will prove for an inter-company debt in the liquidation of any group company until a principal creditor was paid in full), it is commercially important that the group companies be held to that agreement when the very circumstances which it addressed (insolvent group companies) arise.[192]

Deferred debts

24-77 Certain debts are deferred by statute until all the other debts of the company have been paid. Thus interest on all proved debts, whether or not the debt was an interest-bearing debt, from the company going into liquidation until the date of actual payment, is deferred until the payment of all debts, but any surplus then remaining must be applied in paying interest before being applied for any other purpose.[193] Another deferred debt is where a company has contracted to redeem or purchase some of its own shares (see Chapter 20) and the company has not completed the transaction by the time of the commencement of the winding up. The company may be compelled to complete the bargain but only after all other debts and liabilities of the company (other than any due to members in their character as such) have been paid, see **20-24**.[194] A further deferred payment is any debt or liability due to a member in his character of a member whether by way of dividends, profits or otherwise (IA 1986, s 74(2)(f)). A sum is due to a member of a company 'in his character of a member' if the right to receive it is based on a cause of action founded on the statutory contract between the members and the company imposed by CA 2006, s 33 and such other provisions of the Act as confer rights or imposed liabilities on members.[195] A member having a cause of action independent of the statutory contract is then in no worse a position than any other creditor. Debts due to members in other capacities such as trade creditors or lenders rank, therefore, alongside similar debts due to non-members. Finally, the courts do have a power, however, to defer payment of debts due from the company to persons found liable for fraudulent or wrongful trading in relation to it until all other debts owed by the company (and interest) have been paid (s 215(4)).

[190] See *Re Maxwell Communications Corp plc (No 2)* [1994] 1 BCLC 1; Nolan, 'Less Equal than Others: *Maxwell* and Subordinated Unsecured Obligations' [1995] JBL 485; also *Re British & Commonwealth Holdings (No 3) plc* [1992] BCLC 322.   [191] [2007] 1 BCLC 29, CA.

[192] [2007] 1 BCLC 29 at 59, CA.

[193] IA 1986, s 189(1), (2); for the purposes of interest under this provision, all debts rank *pari passu* and it makes no difference, for example, whether the debt was preferential: s 189(3).

[194] CA 2006, s 735(4)–(6).

[195] *Soden v British and Commonwealth Holdings plc* [1997] 2 BCLC 501, HL.

Shareholders

24-78 It is only on a solvent winding up that there can be any return of capital or surplus to the shareholders and the priorities as amongst the shareholders and classes of shareholders are discussed in Chapter 14, see **14-19**. On an insolvent liquidation, there will be insufficient funds to pay the creditors in full and therefore there will be no funds remaining for the shareholders who lose their capital, but their losses are limited to that amount and they bear no responsibility for payments to creditors (assuming they have not given personal guarantees to any creditor), hence the attraction of limited liability.

H Dissolution of the company

Dissolution after winding up

24-79 After completion of the winding up process, the company is removed from the register of companies, a process known as dissolution, and it ceases to exist. In both compulsory and voluntary liquidation, dissolution occurs automatically three months after the registration by the registrar of companies of the liquidator's final return at Companies House.[196] An official receiver acting as the liquidator in a compulsory liquidation may apply to the registrar for early dissolution of the company where the realisable assets are insufficient to cover the expenses of winding up and the affairs of the company do not warrant further investigation. In that case, the company is dissolved three months after the application for early dissolution.[197] On being dissolved, any property of the company is deemed to be *bona vacantia* and vests in the Crown (CA 2006, s 1012).

Striking companies off the register of companies

24-80 In practice, the majority of companies that are dissolved in England and Wales each year are not formally wound up at all. Instead, they cease to exist when the registrar of companies strikes them off the register as defunct. The registrar has power to do this where the registrar has reasonable cause to believe that a company is not carrying on business or is not in operation (CA 2006, s 1000(1)).[198] Many of the companies targeted will have failed to file annual returns and accounts which may suggest that the company has ceased trading.

24-81 Alternatively, any company may apply to be struck off the register on payment of the appropriate fee (currently £10). This procedure is governed by CA 2006, s 1003–1011 and is designed to enable companies quickly and inexpensively to be dissolved and removed from the register. The application for striking off must be made by the company's directors or a majority of them (s 1003(2)). Elaborate provision is made for notifying members, creditors and interested parties (via the *Gazette* and otherwise) of the application to be struck off (ss 1003(3), 1006).

---

[196] IA 1986, s 201(1), (2) (voluntary winding up); s 205(1), (2) (compulsory winding up).

[197] IA 1986, s 202(2), (5).

[198] The registrar may also strike off a company under this procedure where the company has gone into liquidation but no liquidator is acting or the final returns have not been delivered: see CA 2006, s 1001.

Restoration to the register

24-82 An application may be made to the court for an order restoring a company to the register where the company has been dissolved or deemed dissolved on liquidation or administration or has been struck off either by the registrar of companies or following an application for striking off (CA 2006, s 1029(1), (2)). The registrar of companies is able also to restore companies to the register when they have been struck off as defunct by the registrar,[199] see CA 2006, ss 1024–1028.

---

[199] Company Law Review, *Final Report*, vol 1 (2001), para 11.19.

25

Directors' liabilities and vulnerable transactions on insolvency

A Introduction

25-1 In addition to the formal processes of dealing with an insolvent company (liquidation, administration etc), the collapse of the company is also the time when the conduct of the directors of the company is reviewed.[1] Generally, the emphasis is on civil remedies and recoveries for creditors. There are a small number of provisions (essentially IA 1986, ss 206–211) which create criminal offences[2] as does CA 2006, s 993 (fraudulent trading) although the number of prosecutions under these provisions is low. On the civil side, redress for breach of duty by directors is available through the summary action for misfeasance (IA 1986, s 212) while particular types of trading are targeted for civil recoveries, namely fraudulent trading (s 213) and wrongful trading (s 214). A liquidator or administrator may also seek to challenge certain transactions which took place in the run-up to liquidation or administration, for example, on the basis that they were transactions at an undervalue (s 238) or intended to prefer a particular creditor (s 239). The phoenix syndrome, i.e. continuing to trade using the name by which the insolvent company was known or a name which is so similar as to suggest an association with that company attracts criminal and civil liabilities (ss 216, 217). More broadly, the overall conduct of the directors is reviewed in order to determine whether disqualification is an appropriate response.

25-2 With the exception of disqualification proceedings (and even there the numbers are modest), limited use is made of these provisions because of the investigative difficulties which liquidators face in trying to bring cases against directors and also because of a lack of funding to pursue these matters. A liquidator or administrator requires the sanction of the court or liquidation committee or creditors (depending on the circumstance) to bring proceedings under IA 1986, ss 213, 214, 238, 239, see **24-40**. If duly sanctioned to bring proceedings, the costs are liquidation expenses within IR 1986, r 4.218 and payable in priority from the assets of the company, but subject to a requirement that the secured or preferential creditors must consent to litigation expenses in excess of £5,000: see **24-68**. Though claims are limited by these funding difficulties, the provisions are thought to

---

[1] A number of the provisions, e.g. IA 1986, ss 206–211, apply to 'officers' which includes a director, manager or secretary (see CA 2006, s 1173, applied by IA 1986, s 251), but our discussion focuses primarily on directors. See generally Goode, *Principles of Corporate Insolvency Law* (4th edn, 2011), Chs 13, 14; Finch, *Corporate Insolvency Law* (2nd edn, 2009), Ch 16.

[2] The offences under the IA 1986 relate mainly to offences committed by officers of the company in the course of or just prior to winding up and they range from fraudulently removing the company's property, to destroying or falsifying entries in the company's books, to failing to co-operate and assist the liquidator in a winding up.

have some deterrent value and provide liquidators with some negotiating weapons when dealing with directors of insolvent companies. When claims are brought, they are often brought on multiple grounds so it is not uncommon to find allegations of misfeasance, wrongful trading, transactions at an undervalue and preferences all in the one case.[3]

B Misfeasance procedure—IA 1986, s 212

25-3 The misfeasance provision is a procedural mechanism whereby actions may be brought, typically by liquidators (though the section is wider than that and it is possible for a claim to be brought by a creditor) typically against directors (again the section is wider than that) with a view to holding them liable for a breach of duty to the company.[4] The section provides 'a summary procedure in a liquidation for obtaining a remedy against delinquent directors without the need for an action in the name of the company. It does not create new rights and obligations'.[5]

25-4 The section enables the court, on the application of the official receiver, the liquidator, or any creditor, or a contributory with the leave of the court,[6] to examine the conduct of any officer[7] of the company to see if they have misapplied or retained or become accountable for money or other property of the company or been guilty of any misfeasance or breach of fiduciary or other breach of duty to the company (so negligence is included).[8] The court may order the person to repay, restore or account for the money or property or to make such contribution to the assets of the company (payment is to the company and not to the applicant) as the court thinks just (IA 1986, s 212(3)).

25-5 The court's power under IA 1986, s 212(3) is discretionary, but the extent of this discretion is unclear and was the subject of conflicting views, obiter, in *Re Paycheck Services 3 Ltd, Revenue and Customs Commissioners v Holland*[9] in the Court of Appeal and the Supreme Court though there was, at least, a degree of unanimity that the discretion cannot be used to reduce a director's liability to nothing.[10] It is a discretion as to the order that should be made once liability has been established and the section is not intended to replicate or extend the court's power to grant relief against liability under CA 2006, s 1157,[11] see **13-53**.

---

[3] Note that there is difference between misfeasance claims (where sums recovered form part of the general assets of the company and so are capable of being caught by a prior floating charge) and sums recovered pursuant to IA 1986, ss 213 or 214, 238, 239 which are held by the office-holder on behalf of the creditors of the company and do not form part of the assets subject to the floating charge, see **25-29**; where there are concurrent claims, see *Re Idessa Ltd, Burke v Morrison* [2012] 1 BCLC 80 at [128]. See also *Earp v Stevenson* [2011] EWHC 1436.

[4] In a compulsory winding up, a liquidator can only bring a misfeasance claim with the sanction of the court or the creditors: IA 1986, Sch 4, Pt II, para 4, see **24-40**.

[5] *Cohen v Selby* [2001] 1 BCLC 176 at 183, per Chadwick LJ; see also *Re DKG Contractors Ltd* [1990] BCC 903; and generally Doyle, 'Misfeasance Proceedings: Chasing the Delinquents' (1994) 7 Insolv Int 25, 35; Oditah, 'Misfeasance Proceedings against Company Directors' [1992] LMCLQ 207.

[6] IA 1986, s 212(5).

[7] 'Officer' includes director: IA 1986, s 251; and includes de facto directors: see *Re Paycheck Services 3 Ltd, Revenue and Customs Commissioners v Holland* [2011] 1 BCLC 141 at [55]; *Re Idessa Ltd, Burke v Morrison* [2012] 1 BCLC 80.

[8] See *Re Barton Manufacturing Co Ltd* [1998] 1 BCLC 740; *Re D'Jan of London Ltd, Copp v D'Jan* [1994] 1 BCLC 561; also *Re Welfab Engineers Ltd* [1990] BCLC 833.

[9] [2011] 1 BCLC 141, SC, affirming [2009] 2 BCLC 309.

[10] [2011] 1 BCLC 141 at [49], per Lord Hope; [2009] 2 BCLC 309 at [108]–[110], per Rimer LJ with whom Lords Walker and Clarke agreed, see [2011] 1 BCLC 141 at [124], [146].

[11] [2009] 2 BCLC 309 at [103], per Rimer LJ, with whom Lords Walker and Clarke agreed at [2011] 1 BCLC 141 at [124] and [146], respectively.

It enables the court to adjust the remedy to the circumstances of the particular case[12] and allows 'the delinquent director to submit that the wind should be tempered' on the particular facts.[13]

25-6 On the facts in *Re Paycheck Services 3 Ltd*, the company had paid unlawful dividends. At first instance, the court found the director liable, declined to award relief under what is now CA 2006, s 1157 and ordered under IA 1986, s 213(3) that the director's liability to make restitution should be limited to the amount of tax outstanding on the unlawful payments. The Revenue Commissioners were the applicants under s 212. The discussion of liability became moot when the higher courts agreed that the individual was not a de facto director after all (see **6-15**) and therefore could not be liable to repay the unlawful dividends. However, the majority in the Court of Appeal (Ward and Elias LJJ) agreed that the order made (limiting the director's obligation to repay) would have been appropriate. Rimer LJ disagreed saying that the correct approach is to decide whether the director is liable, then whether he is entitled to relief under what is now CA 2006, s 1157 and then to make a fair order under IA 1986, s 212 reflecting the wrong committed—paying unlawful dividends—and the refusal of relief under s 1157.[14] In Rimer LJ's view, the appropriate order would have required the repayment of the full amount of the unlawful dividends. Having refused relief under CA 2006, s 1157, there was no basis, Rimer LJ said, for reintroducing relief and giving effect to it by using IA 1986, s 212. In the Supreme Court, Lords Clarke and Walker agreed with Rimer LJ.[15] But Lord Hope in the Supreme Court preferred the view of the majority in the Court of Appeal and agreed that, in the exercise of its discretion under IA 1986, s 212(3), it was open to the court to limit the award to what was required to make up the deficiency of a particular creditor where the misfeasance claim was made by a party other than the liquidator.[16] The approach of Rimer LJ is to be preferred. A director who is liable to reinstate the company's assets and who is refused relief under CA 2006, s 1157 (which relief requires him to have acted honestly and reasonably) should not be able, by the back door of IA 1986, s 212, to obtain what he could not obtain under CA 2006, s 1157. The purpose of IA 1986, s 212(3) is to temper the relief where that is required by the circumstances, such as where otherwise there might be a windfall to an undeserving party (for example, the repayment to the company of the amount paid in unlawful dividends by a director might result in a windfall to the very shareholders who had received the dividends), but should not otherwise be used to relieve a director of liability.

25-7 Any recoveries on the grounds of misfeasance are in respect of pre-existing rights of the company and are therefore capable of being charged or assigned by the liquidator.[17] Such recoveries (as an asset of the company) are subject to the claims of a floating chargeholder (i.e. where the charge is over the whole of the undertaking, as is commonly the case, the

---

[12] [2011] 1 BCLC 141 at [124] and [146], per Lords Walker and Clarke, agreeing with Rimer LJ at [2009] 2 BCLC 209 at [110]; *Re Loquitar Ltd* [2003] 2 BCLC 442 at [245].

[13] *West Mercia Safetywear Ltd v Dodd* [1988] 2 BCLC 250 at 253, per Dillon LJ; *Re Paycheck Services 3 Ltd* [2011] 1 BCLC 141 at [51], [124], [146]; [2009] 2 BCLC 309 at [110].

[14] [2009] 2 BCLC 309 at [103], [110]–[112].　　　[15] [2011] 1 BCLC 141 at [124] and [146].

[16] [2011] 1 BCLC 141 at [49], [51], approving [2009] 2 BCLC 309 at [133]–[134], [143]. There was a degree of agreement that recovery of the full amount would have been appropriate had the claim been brought by a liquidator or the official receiver, see [2009] 2 BCLC 309 at [143], per Ward LJ and, in the Supreme Court, at [2011] 1 BCLC 141 at [49], per Lord Hope.

[17] *Re Oasis Merchandising Services Ltd* [1997] 1 BCLC 689.

recoveries fall within the grasp of the charge)[18] and subject to the prior payment of the expenses of winding up (see **24-63**) and the preferential debts (see **24-70**).

C Fraudulent and wrongful trading

Fraudulent trading

25-8 Liability for fraudulent trading is imposed on persons knowingly a party to the carrying on of any business of a company with intent to defraud creditors of the company, or creditors of any other person, or for any fraudulent purpose.[19]

25-9 There are two aspects to fraudulent trading:[20]

- a civil liability in IA 1986, s 213 which applies when the company is in the course of winding up when a liquidator (only) may apply for a declaration that any persons knowingly parties to the carrying on of the business in the manner stated are to be liable to make such contribution to the company's assets as the court thinks proper;[21]

- a criminal offence contained in CA 2006, s 993 which applies regardless of whether the company is in winding up.

Civil liability

25-10 This civil liability is less important now in the light of the provision on wrongful trading in IA 1986, s 214 (based on negligence), see **25-18,** and any liquidator interested in seeking civil recoveries is likely to look to that provision so avoiding the difficult task of establishing an intent to defraud. On occasion, recourse to s 213 is useful, however, because it applies to a wider category of respondents ('any persons')[22] whereas s 214 applies only to directors or shadow directors.

25-11 A distinction must be drawn between an individual creditor who is defrauded in the course of the carrying on of the business of the company—he has his individual remedy under the general law—and fraudulent trading.[23] Fraudulent trading requires that the business of the company has been carried on with intent to defraud creditors of the company. If that is the position, liability arises, even if then only one creditor is shown to have been defrauded.[24] The power to order a contribution is compensatory and not penal[25] as the penal position is preserved in CA 2006, s 993 and Parliament could not have intended that the civil power would be used to punish a wrongdoer.[26] The principle on which the

---

[18] This is not the case with recoveries, for example, for wrongful trading, see **25-29**, and so the court will take into account the differing positions in cases where a liquidator claims, as is common, on a number of grounds, see, for example, *Re Idessa Ltd, Burke v Morrison* [2012] 1 BCLC 80 at [128].

[19] The word 'creditor'…in its ordinary meaning, denotes one to whom money is owed, whether that debt can presently be sued for is immaterial: *R v Smith (Wallace Duncan)* [1996] 2 BCLC 109, CA.

[20] See generally Keay, *Company Directors' Responsibilities to Creditors* (2007), Chs 3–6.

[21] In a creditors' voluntary liquidation or a compulsory winding up, a liquidator can only bring a claim under this section with sanction of the court or the creditors: IA 1986, Sch 4, Pt I, para 3: see **24-40**.

[22] See *Re BCCI (No 15), Morris v Bank of India* [2005] 2 BCLC 328.

[23] *Morphitis v Bernasconi* [2003] 2 BCLC 53, CA.

[24] *Re Gerald Cooper Chemicals Ltd* [1978] 2 All ER 49; *Morphitis v Bernasconi* [2003] 2 BCLC 53, CA.

[25] *Re BCCI (No 15), Morris v Bank of India* [2005] 2 BCLC 328 at 356, CA; *Re Overnight Ltd, Goldfarb v Higgins* [2010] 2 BCLC 186.

[26] *Morphitis v Bernasconi* [2003] 2 BCLC 53, CA.

contribution power should be exercised is that the contribution to the assets in which the company's creditors will share in the liquidation should reflect (and compensate for) the loss which has been caused to those creditors by the carrying on of the business with an intent to defraud.[27] Where there are several respondents, the court may order that they be jointly and severally liable, but equally may make a separate assessment of the contribution to be made by each.[28]

25-12 Any sums recovered by the liquidator are impressed with a statutory trust in favour of the unsecured creditors (rather than for the creditor(s) defrauded).[29] Recoveries do not form part of the assets of the company so as to fall within the grasp of any floating charge[30] for they arise post the commencement of the winding up as a result of the exercise of a statutory power by a liquidator, but they are subject to the prior claims of the expenses of the winding up, see **24-63,** and any preferential debts, see **24-70.**

Criminal offence

25-13 Fraudulent trading is also a criminal offence under CA 2006, s 993 and prosecutors find it useful because of the wide variety of company frauds which may fall within its scope, assuming that it is possible to establish an intent to defraud to the criminal burden of proof. On the other hand, it may prove of diminishing importance as the Fraud Act 2006 offers prosecutors a range of open-ended fraud provisions which may be more suitable in a given case.

25-14 The section applies not just to the carrying on of the business of the company with an intent to defraud creditors, but to the carrying on of business for any fraudulent purpose.[31] Provided the business has been carried on with an intent to defraud, it suffices even though only one creditor has been defrauded,[32] although most cases would involve a pattern of fraudulent trading by the defendant.

25-15 The type of conduct commonly involved includes the obtaining of credit from suppliers with no intention of paying for those goods; persuading customers to place large deposits with no intention of supplying the goods; obtaining credit from banks and factors by false invoices or accounts; falsifying accounts to show inflated profits; and trading to defraud the Inland Revenue. But the mere granting of a preference to a creditor is not, without more, fraudulent trading.[33]

---

[27] *Morphitis v Bernasconi* [2003] 2 BCLC 53, CA; *Re Overnight Ltd, Goldfarb v Higgins* [2010] 2 BCLC 186.

[28] *Re Overnight Ltd, Goldfarb v Higgins* [2010] 2 BCLC 186 (that is the position under IA 1986, s 214, see **25-19,** and given the similar wording in immediately adjacent statutory provisions, the court said no distinction in approach should be drawn between ss 213 and 214).

[29] *Re Esal (Commodities) Ltd* [1997] 1 BCLC 705, CA.

[30] *Re Oasis Merchandising Services Ltd, Ward v Aitken* [1997] 1 BCLC 689 at 698–700, CA.

[31] See *Re Overnight Ltd, Goldfarb v Higgins* [2010] 2 BCLC 186 (as the company's business could only have been carried on at a loss had it not been for a VAT fraud, it could be readily concluded that the company's business was carried on with intent to defraud a creditor or with a fraudulent purpose); R v *Kemp* [1988] QB 645, CA (victims here were not creditors but customers of the company who were induced to accept worthless goods which they were duped into buying); *Re Sarflax Ltd* [1979] 1 All ER 529 (distributing the proceeds of the realisation of assets could constitute carrying on business); also *Re Augustus Barnett & Son Ltd* [1986] BCLC 170.

[32] *Morphitis v Bernasconi* [2003] 2 BCLC 53, CA; *Re Gerald Cooper Chemicals Ltd* [1978] 2 All ER 49.

[33] *R v Sarflax* [1979] 1 All ER 529.

25-16   The essence of fraudulent trading is dishonesty[34] and it is not enough to show that the company has continued to trade while insolvent (although such conduct may give rise to liability for wrongful trading, discussed below). Instead the conduct must 'involve actual dishonesty, involving, according to current notions of fair trading among commercial men, real moral blame'.[35] Although this is a strict standard, it will clearly be satisfied where directors allow a company to incur credit when they have no reason to think the creditors will ever be paid.[36] It will also be established, as the Court of Appeal made clear in *R v Grantham*,[37] where credit is incurred at a time when the directors have no good reason to think funds will become available to pay the creditors when their debts become due or shortly thereafter.

25-17   Liability extends beyond directors to any persons 'knowingly parties to the carrying on of the business' with intent to defraud which will include those exercising at least some positive role in the management of the business.[38] Creditors can be party to fraudulent trading if they accept money knowing it has been procured by carrying on business with intent to defraud creditors and for the very purpose of paying their debts.[39] Third parties who are involved in and who assist and benefit from the offending business, or the business carried on in an offending way, and do so knowingly and therefore dishonestly do fall, or at least can fall, within the provision.[40] A company secretary who merely carries out the administrative functions of such an office, however, is not concerned in the management of the company or in carrying on its business.[41]

Wrongful trading

25-18   The difficulties in establishing the intent to defraud necessary to give rise to liability for fraudulent trading led the Cork Committee to recommend the introduction of a provision for wrongful trading under which civil liability could arise without proof of fraud or dishonesty and without requiring the criminal standard of proof.[42]

25-19   IA 1986, s 214 allows a liquidator (only) of a company in the course of winding up to apply where certain conditions are met for an order that a director (including a shadow director) make such contribution[43] to the company's assets as the court thinks proper.[44] The conditions are that:

---

[34]   The ordinary criminal law test of dishonesty as laid down in *R v Ghosh* [1982] 2 All ER 689 applies.

[35]   *Re Patrick and Lyon Ltd* [1933] Ch 786 at 790, per Maugham J. See *R v Cox, R v Hedges* [1983] BCLC 169.   [36]   *Re William C Leitch Bros Ltd* [1932] 2 Ch 71.

[37]   [1984] 3 All ER 166, CA.

[38]   See *Re BCCI (No 15), Morris v Bank of India* [2005] 2 BCLC 328, CA (bank knowingly party to the carrying on of business with intent to defraud when general manager of London branch of the bank was party to that fraudulent trading, see **3-100**). Someone who orchestrates, organises or can seize control of the business concerned is within the provision: *Re BCCI, Banque Arabe v Morris* [2001] 1 BCLC 263; see also *Re Overnight Ltd, Goldfarb v Higgins* [2010] 2 BCLC 186 (company secretary had the requisite knowledge when he deliberately chose not to make enquiries about what he must have realised appeared to be dishonest transactions).

[39]   *Re Gerald Cooper Chemicals Ltd* [1978] 2 All ER 49.

[40]   *Re BCCI, Banque Arabe v Morris* [2001] 1 BCLC 263.

[41]   *Re Maidstone Building Provisions Ltd* [1971] 3 All ER 363. Cf the role of the company secretary in *Re Overnight Ltd, Goldfarb v Higgins* [2010] 2 BCLC 186.

[42]   See the Cork Committee Report (Cmnd 8558, 1982), Ch 44.

[43]   The declaration by the court is for the recovery of a sum of money although there is nothing to preclude the liquidator from accepting property to satisfy that liability: see *Re Farmezier Products Ltd* [1997] BCC 655, CA, aff'g [1995] 2 BCLC 462.

[44]   IA 1986, s 214(1), (7). An administrator has no power in this regard; see Keay, n 20, p 125. Relief is not available under CA 2006, s 1157, see **13-53**; *Re Produce Marketing Consortium Ltd* [1989] 3 All ER 1. Once

- the company has gone into insolvent liquidation;[45] and
- at some time before the commencement of the winding up, the director knew or ought to have concluded that there was no reasonable prospect that the company would avoid going into insolvent liquidation (s 214(2)).

Section 214(4) provides that the facts which a director of a company ought to know or ascertain, the conclusions which he ought to reach and the steps which he ought to take are those which would be known or ascertained, or reached or taken, by a reasonably diligent person having both:

(1) the general knowledge, skill and experience that may reasonably be expected of a person carrying out the same functions as are carried out by that director in relation to the company, and

(2) the general knowledge, skill and experience that that director has.

25-20 As discussed in Chapter 10, IA 1986, s 214(4) was taken to set the standard of care and skill for directors in all contexts and not just in relation to wrongful trading, hence it is replicated now in CA 2006, s 174 as one of the general duties of directors. As noted at **10-10**, the standard imposed by IA 1986, s 214(4) is an objective minimum standard, that of a reasonably diligent person who has accepted the office of director, set in the context of the functions undertaken, with that objective minimum standard capable of being raised in the light of the particular attributes of the director in question.[46]

The 'twilight' zone

25-21 The most difficult issue in applying IA 1986, s 214 is identifying the point in time when directors acting to the standard required by s 214(4) knew or ought to have concluded there was no reasonable prospect of avoiding insolvent liquidation. Of course, there is something of an overlap between s 214 and a director's duty to have regard to creditors' interests in cases of insolvency or doubtful solvency as required by CA 2006, s 172(3), discussed at **9-42**.[47] As discussed in the context of CA 2006, s 172(3), directors are subject to a variety of obligations in terms of maintaining financial records and preparing accounts which should help them appreciate at any given time the company's financial position. Proper regard to their duties of care and skill should also ensure that they are well informed about the company's financial position (see **9-51**). The purpose of IA 1986, s 214 is in effect to force them to act on that knowledge or risk a personal liability under this provision, but often whether out of optimism or 'head in the sand' blindness, directors fail to act until too late with disastrous consequences for the company's creditors.[48]

---

found liable, the court can also make a disqualification order under CDDA 1986, s 10. As to wrongful trading generally, see Keay, n 20, Chs 7–10. For a broader perspective on the difficulty in balancing directors' duties to shareholders and to creditors in the vicinity of insolvency, see Davies, 'Directors' Creditor—Regarding Duties in Respect of Wrongful Trading Decisions in the Vicinity of Insolvency' (2006) 7 EBOR 301.

[45] Defined IA 1986, s 214(6): a company goes into insolvent liquidation for these purposes if it goes into liquidation at a time when its assets are insufficient for the payment of its debts and other liabilities and the expenses of the winding up.

[46] See *Re Brian D Pierson (Contractors) Ltd* [2001] 1 BCLC 275 at 302.

[47] See Davies, n 44, at 329 who notes that the duty plays a useful supplementary role to IA 1986, s 214.

[48] See, for example, *Roberts v Frohlich* [2011] 2 BCLC 625 at [112]; directors in that case exhibited 'wilful blind belief' and 'reckless belief' that something would turn up though the company was balance sheet and cash-flow insolvent.

25-22 In *Re Cubelock Ltd*[49] the question was whether the directors were liable for wrongful trading from the beginning of trading as the company was balance sheet insolvent (assets insufficient to meet its liabilities) from the outset. The court rejected the claim, noting that it is common for companies to trade in this manner in the initial months of business.[50] The issue for the purpose of IA 1986, s 214 is whether the directors continued trading after a point in time when they either knew or on any realistic view ought to have known that there was no reasonable prospect of avoiding insolvent liquidation. In *Official Receiver v Doshi*,[51] for example, a director who knew that his company could only continue to trade as a result of fraudulent invoicing ought to have concluded that there was no reasonable prospect that the company would avoid going into insolvent liquidation. In *Re The Rod Gunner Organisation Ltd, Rubin v Gunner*[52] the court agreed that the directors were entitled for a period of approximately six months (March to September 1998) to accept assurances from a new chief executive that he would be able to raise funds to deal with the company's pressing financial needs but, as he repeatedly failed to make good on his promises, the court said, no reasonably diligent director would have continued to give him the benefit of the doubt. By October 1998 they ought to have known that there was no reasonable prospect that the company would avoid going into insolvent liquidation and they were liable for wrongful trading, the company only having gone into liquidation in June 1999. In *Roberts v Frohlich*[53] the directors of a property development company continued on for a year after a point where the court said the most rudimentary accounts would have shown the company to be balance sheet and cash-flow insolvent with immediate liabilities mounting and restricted access to bank finance and with attempts at attracting new investment having collapsed. The directors' hope that 'something might turn up' was groundless and they ought to have concluded that there was no realistic prospect of the company avoiding insolvent liquidation.[54] In *Re Idessa Ltd, Burke v Morrison*[55] the company continued to trade for more than two years after the date when the contract which was its main source of income came to an end, a period of time during which the directors continued to draw salary and expenses on a grand scale and when the company was at all times balance sheet insolvent. The court held the directors liable for wrongful trading from the date of the loss of the contract.

25-23 A more specific issue regarding the level of knowledge required was canvassed in *Re Continental Assurance Co of London plc*[56] which involved the collapse of a small insurance company in 1992. Large and unexpected losses had arisen which came to the board's attention in June 1991. The liquidators sought contributions to the company's assets from the directors on the grounds of wrongful trading and/or misfeasance. In particular, it was alleged that the company applied inappropriate accounting policies which showed the company to be solvent when, had an appropriate accounting policy been adopted by the company, the directors would and should have appreciated that the company was insolvent and they should have taken steps to stop trading.[57]

---

[49] [2001] BCC 523. See also *Re Hawkes Hill Partnership Ltd* [2007] BCC 937.

[50] Cf *Singla v Hedman* [2010] 2 BCLC 61 at [96]–[100], [107] (a sole director who committed his company to onerous contractual obligations at a time when it had £2 of share capital and no funding in place ought to have known at the date of the contract that there was no reasonable prospect of the company avoiding insolvent liquidation, given it had no means of honouring its obligations—the director had nothing more than a speculative hope that things would work out). [51] [2001] 2 BCLC 235.

[52] [2004] 2 BCLC 110. Cf *Hawkes Hill Partnersship Ltd* [2007] BCC 937.

[53] [2011] 2 BCLC 625 at [94], [112]–[113]. [54] [2011] 2 BCLC 623 at [111]–[113].

[55] [2012] 1 BCLC 80; see also *Earp v Steverson* [2011] EWHC 1436.

[56] [2007] 2 BCLC 287.

[57] In fact, the court concluded that, even if an alternative accounting approach had been taken, the company was solvent in June 1991: see [2007] 2 BCLC 287 at 399.

25-24 The court found that for the directors to have reached these conclusions would have required of them knowledge of accounting concepts of a particularly sophisticated nature. Park J rejected any idea that IA 1986, s 214(4) imposes such an unrealistically high standard of skill. On the facts, he found that the directors had taken a wholly responsible and conscientious attitude both to the company's position and to their own responsibilities as directors at all times from and after the first crisis board meeting in 1991 when major and unexpected losses were reported to them. The directors did not ignore the question of whether the company could properly continue to trade; on the contrary, the court found that they considered it directly, closely and frequently.[58] They were entitled, the court said, to have regard to the accounts before them and to the opinion of the finance director and the auditors that the company was solvent. They did not just accept in an unquestioning way the figures which were put before them, but questioned the executive directors closely and at length on them and were satisfied with the explanations given.[59] Overall, the court considered that the way in which the directors reacted to the financial crisis which blew up in the middle of 1991 was entirely appropriate. There was no liability either on the ground of wrongful trading or on the ground of misfeasance.[60]

25-25 In deciding when the point in time is reached—when the directors knew or ought to have known that there was no reasonable prospect of avoiding insolvent liquidation—the courts are torn between ensuring that the statutory provision does impose an element of pressure on directors, as Parliament intended, so that they do not continue to display inappropriate optimism in the face of mounting losses for the creditors. On the other hand, the courts are anxious not to judge commercial situations with hindsight[61] and take such a strict approach that cautious directors, for fear of wrongful trading, rush too soon to put their companies into administration or liquidation.

25-26 Even if it is established that a director knew or ought to have concluded that insolvent liquidation could not be avoided (and the onus is on the liquidator or administrator to establish that), the director has a defence if he can satisfy the court (and the onus is on the director in this regard) that, after that point in time was reached, he took every step with a view to minimising the potential loss to the company's creditors as he ought to have taken (IA 1986, s 214(3)). Having said that, the threshold set is high ('every step').[62] In *Re Brian D Pierson Ltd*[63] the court noted that it is not sufficient for these purposes for a director to claim that he continued to trade with the intention of trying to make a profit. The provision is intended to apply, the court said, to cases 'where, for example, directors take specific steps with a view to preserving or realising assets or claims for the benefit of creditors, even if they fail to achieve that result, and it does not cover the very act of wrongful

---

[58] *Re Continental Assurance Co of London plc* [2007] 2 BCLC 287 at 360.

[59] *Re Continental Assurance Co of London plc* [2007] 2 BCLC 287 at 404.

[60] See Keay, n 20, p 98 who criticises the emphasis placed by Park J on the need for some blameworthy behaviour by the directors when the section does not require the establishment of any wrongdoing. The issue, Keay says, is merely whether the directors should have concluded that there was no reasonable prospect of avoiding insolvent liquidation. It can be argued that the court is not so much looking to establish blameworthiness but merely using that measure as a device to determine whether the directors should have concluded there was no reasonable prospect of avoiding insolvent liquidation.

[61] See *Re Idessa Ltd, Burke v Morrison* [2012] 1 BCLC 80 at [112]–[114], [119]–[121]; and see *Re Hawkes Hill Publishing Ltd* [2007] BCC 937.

[62] As Goode points out, this may mean no more than 'every reasonable step' when read with 'reasonably diligent person', see Goode, *Principles of Corporate Insolvency Law* (4th edn, 2011), para 14-44. Directors who continue to pay themselves improper salaries and expenses after the point in time when they ought to have concluded that there was no reasonable prospect of avoiding insolvent liquidation have not taken 'every step', see *Re Idessa Ltd, Burke v Morrison* [2012] 1 BCLC 80.   [63] [2001] 1 BCLC 275.

trading itself'.[64] Equally, it is difficult to know what practical steps would convince the court that the director took 'every step', but presumably steps such as attempting to secure additional financing, reaching agreements with creditors, taking professional advice, and working closely with the company's bank would all be steps which the court would accept as steps designed to protect the creditors' interests. Cautious and risk-adverse directors may consider that the only appropriate step is to put the company into administration, liquidation etc, but that is not what the legislation necessarily demands though, obviously, it may be the only practical step in many instances.

Extent of any liability

25-27 Once liability is established, the extent of any contribution to the company's assets is a matter for the court's discretion and the aim here is primarily compensatory rather than penal to ensure that any depletion of the assets attributable to the period of wrongful trading is made good.[65] On the issue of the quantum of liability for wrongful trading, the section offers no guidance and to that extent imposes no limits, but there is much of interest in the obiter comments of Park J in *Re Continental Assurance Co of London plc.*[66] Although Park J concluded that the directors had acted perfectly properly in that case in continuing to trade (see **25-22**), having heard argument on the issue of quantum, he thought it proper to deal with the issue in some detail. In his view, the quantum of liability can be summed up as one of an increase in net deficiency reflecting the loss to the company of the continued trading between the date when the company should have been put into liquidation and the date of actual liquidation.[67] But even then there must be a connection between that increase and the conduct of the directors which resulted in the wrongful trading. Park J was anxious not to describe this as an issue of causation,[68] nevertheless he thought that there must be some nexus between the wrongfulness of the directors' conduct and the losses which the liquidator seeks to recover. For example, the company might incur losses during the period of wrongful trading as a result of bad weather which had nothing to do with the directors' conduct.[69] He considered that the proper principle would be that liability should be limited to those consequences which are attributable to that which made the act wrongful. Furthermore, in his view, the starting point for liability under IA 1986, s 214 is that it is a several liability (i.e. a personal liability of the director) and not a joint and several liability, for it is plain that the focus of the section is on the individual director and his conduct and the contribution he ought to make and not on the joint conduct of the board as a whole.[70] Of course, the court in the exercise of its discretion may order that the liability be joint and several.[71]

---

[64] [2001] 1 BCLC 275 at 308.
[65] *Re Produce Marketing Consortium Ltd (No 2)* [1989] BCLC 520 at 553–4; see also *Re Purpoint Ltd* [1991] BCLC 49. The court has the power to defer debts owing from the company to any person found liable for wrongful trading: IA 1986, s 215(4).   [66] [2007] 2 BCLC 287.
[67] [2007] 2 BCLC 287 at 294, 296, 413. See *Re Idessa Ltd, Burke v Morrison* [2012] 1 BCLC 80; also *Re Bangla Television Ltd, Valentine v Bangla Television Ltd* [2010] BCC 143 (at a time when company hopelessly insolvent and the directors knew or ought to have known that the company could not avoid insolvent liquidation, directors committed the company to a transfer of its assets for no consideration so giving rise to a straightforward increase in the net deficiency of the company (by £250,000) for which amount the directors were jointly and severally liable).
[68] Park J noted that Chadwick LJ had been content in *Cohen v Selby* [2001] 1 BCLC 176 at 183–4 to assume that it may not be necessary to establish a causal link between the wrongful trading and any particular loss.
[69] Citing *Re Brian D Pierson (Contractors) Ltd* [2001] 1 BCLC 275, see in particular at 310.
[70] But see Prentice, 'Corporate Personality, Limited Liability and the Protection of Creditors' in Grantham & Rickett (eds), *Corporate Personality in the 20th Century* (1998) at pp 122–3.
[71] See *Re Continental Assurance* [2007] 2 BCLC 287 at [382]–[390]; *Re Brian D Pierson (Contractors) Ltd* [2001] 1 BCLC 275 at 311; *Re Idessa Ltd, Burke v Morrison* [2012] 1 BCLC 80 at [129] (given equal degrees of

25-28 Park J's position was endorsed in *Re Marini Ltd*[72] where the court agreed that, before any question of invoking the powers of the court could arise, it has to be shown that the company at the date of actual liquidation was in a worse position than it would have been in if trading had ceased earlier. The appropriate comparison, the court said, was between the net deficiency in the assets of the company as at the date at which it was contended that trading should have ceased and the day on which trading did in fact cease. The appropriate test was not whether new debt had been incurred after the first date, or whether cash had been paid out after that date; the only proper question was whether, on a net basis, it was shown that the company was worse off as a result of the continuation of trading.[73]

25-29 Any recoveries obtained under this provision, being property which arises only after the liquidation of the company and which is recoverable only by the liquidator pursuant to his statutory powers, is held by him on a statutory trust for distribution to the company's unsecured creditors.[74] These sums are not subject therefore to the claims of the holder of a floating charge over all the undertaking of the company. The contribution recovered goes to meet the claims of all the unsecured creditors rather than specifically the claims of creditors whose debt arose in the period of wrongful trading. The recoveries are subject, however, to the prior claim of the expenses of winding up which include litigation costs incurred by the liquidator, see **24-63**, and preferential debts, see **24-70**. Though the floating chargeholder does not benefit directly from the recoveries, the chargeholder benefits indirectly in that the floating charge realisations are subject to the prior claims of the expenses of winding up and preferential debts to the extent that the general assets of the company are insufficient (IA 1986, s 176ZA). If the recoveries from wrongful trading swell the general assets, there is less need to have resort to the floating charge realisations so to that extent the floating chargeholder benefits.

25-30 To judge by the level of reported cases, there has been limited use of IA 1986, s 214 though there is anecdotal evidence of advisers in large companies advising frequently on the potential liability for wrongful trading despite the fact that claims for wrongful trading are rare and unlikely to succeed where the directors have behaved responsibly (as is made clear in *Re Continental Assurance*,[75] discussed at **25-23**).[76] While directors would be concerned about the potential (unquantifiable) civil liability, though they have insurance cover, directors of such companies are concerned particularly about the reputational damage involved if they were to be sued for wrongful trading following the collapse of their company. For smaller companies,[77] the issues are different but equally pressing in that a personal liability would wipe out the advantages of having incorporated in the first place. Given that in these companies the directors are likely also to be shareholders and employees, a significant personal liability as directors on top of the loss of whatever capital they have contributed (which admittedly may be small) and the loss of their employment is a matter of some concern to them and they are very unlikely to have insurance

---

involvement in the management of the company and therefore the wrongful trading, the court ordered that the directors' liability be joint and several).

[72] [2004] BCC 172 at 197–8; noted Spence (2004) 17 Insolv Int 11.

[73] On the facts in *Re Marini*, there was little evidence to support that allegation and the wrongful trading claim was dismissed.

[74] *Re Oasis Merchandising Services Ltd, Ward v Aitken* [1997] 1 BCLC 689 at 698–700, CA; see Keay, n 20, pp 104–6.   [75] [2007] 2 BCLC 287.

[76] See Keay, n 20, Ch 10 who summarises the many defects of the provision and points out that it needs to be redrafted and refocused if it is to prove useful.

[77] Keay, n 20, makes the point that the reported cases where liability has been imposed have been exclusively small closely held companies.

cover. For that reason, directors of small companies also show some awareness of this potential liability.

D Prohibition on the re-use of company names

25-31 When a company has gone into insolvent liquidation, its directors may be tempted to set up another company immediately under the same or a similar name or may already have several other companies incorporated, all with similar names. The business then continues much as before, a practice often referred to as the phoenix syndrome. The second company frequently operates from the same premises, commonly using the same assets acquired in a fire sale from the liquidator and exploiting what remains of the former company's goodwill. Not surprisingly, existing creditors are aggrieved by these practices and the public concerned about the ability of such 'rogue' directors to operate in this fashion.[78]

25-32 The phoenix syndrome is governed by IA 1986, s 216 which renders the re-use of the name of a company which has been wound up insolvent a criminal offence in certain circumstances.[79] Any directors concerned (and others) may incur personal liability under s 217 for debts incurred during the period of the offence,[80] though little use appears to be made of this provision.

The prohibition

25-33 Where a company has gone into insolvent liquidation,[81] it is an offence (except with the leave of the court or in such exceptional circumstances as laid down in the Insolvency Rules 1986, rr 4.226–4.230) for a director or shadow director of the company who was in post any time in the 12 months preceding the liquidation:

(1) to be a director of, or in any way directly or indirectly be concerned or take part in the promotion, formation or management of, any other company known under a prohibited name; or

(2) in any way, directly or indirectly, be concerned or take part in the carrying on of a business carried on (otherwise than by a company) under a prohibited name (IA 1986, s 216(1), (3)).

25-34 A prohibited name is a name by which the company was known[82] in the 12 months preceding liquidation or a name which is so similar to it as to suggest an association with

---

[78] The problem has been reduced since the IA 1986 required liquidators to be licensed insolvency practitioners so collusive deals to pass over assets are much less likely though the Company Law Review took the view that the phoenix problem remains significant. See Company Law Review, *Final Report* (July 2001), paras 15.55–15.77; also Milman, 'The Phoenix Syndrome' [2001] Insol L 199. See generally Carter, 'The Phoenix Syndrome—The Personal Liability of Directors' (2006) 19 Insolv Int 38.

[79] It is an offence of strict liability: *R v Cole, Lees, Birch* [1998] 2 BCLC 235. Any misuse of the name is a factor to be taken into account in disqualification proceedings: *Re Migration Services International Ltd* [2000] 1 BCLC 666.

[80] See *First Independent Factors Ltd v Mountford* [2008] 2 BCLC 297; *First Independent Factors Ltd v Churchill* [2007] 1 BCLC 293; *Ricketts v Ad Valorem Factors Ltd* [2004] 1 BCLC 1, CA.

[81] For these purposes, a company goes into insolvent liquidation if it goes into liquidation at a time when its assets are insufficient for the payment of its debts and other liabilities and the expenses of the winding up: IA 1986, s 216(7).

[82] i.e. including business names as well as the company's registered name.

that company (IA 1986, s 216(1), (3)).[83] The prohibition on the use of the name lasts for five years (s 216(3)). The penalty for contravention is imprisonment or a fine (s 216(4)) and section 217 imposes a personal liability for all the debts and other liabilities incurred by a company when a person, in contravention of s 216, is involved in the management of the company or when a person acts or is willing to act on the instructions of a person whom he knows to be acting in contravention of s 216.[84] Liability therefore extends beyond the director or shadow director acting in breach of s 216 to persons who act on their instructions. Liability is joint and several with the company for the relevant debts (s 217(4), (5)). A claim may be brought by any creditor for a declaration that the directors are personally liable for the relevant debt or debts and recovery is by the applicant for the debt owed to him. An assignee of a debt may bring proceedings and it makes no difference to the legitimacy of the debt which is the basis of a s 217 claim whether the debt was acquired before or after the defunct company went into liquidation.[85]

25-35 The emphasis in the provision is on the use of the company name. The prohibition is on the re-use of the name or a similar name by a director or shadow director. It does not prevent those directors from being directors of another company as long as that company does not use a prohibited name nor does it stop another company from using the name as long as the directors and shadow directors have no connection with that company. The intention is to prevent any exploitation by the directors of any remaining goodwill in the insolvent company, but these sections do not address concerns about the ability of individuals to set up again in business following an earlier insolvency. That problem is addressed through disqualification which is discussed at **25-69**.

The exceptions

25-36 As noted, the prohibitions apply save where re-use of the name is permitted with the leave of the court or in three exceptional cases prescribed in the IR 1986. The first case essentially allows directors to continue to act when a successor company acquires the whole or substantially the whole of the business from the liquidator and notice is given to the creditors that the director will be acting in that capacity in the successor company (IR 1986, r 4.228). The second case is where the court which winds up the insolvent company gives a director leave to use a prohibited name (IR 1986, r 4.229).[86] The third excepted case is set out in IR 1986, r 4.230. A former director can continue to act in the affairs of

---

[83] As to whether a name suggests an association with another company, the question is whether the similarity between the two names is such as to give rise to a probability that members of the public, comparing the names in the relevant context, would associate the two companies with each other, whether as successor companies or as part of the same group: see *First Independent Factors Ltd v Mountford* [2008] 2 BCLC 297.

[84] Liability is limited to the debts and liabilities incurred in carrying on business or part of the business under a prohibited name: *Glasgow City Council v Craig* [2009] 1 BCLC 742 (prohibited name related to restaurant business, company using prohibited name ran a restaurant and separate wine bar and used the prohibited name only in the restaurant business; the directors who were personally liable under IA 1986, s 217 for involvement in a company using a prohibited name were liable only for debts incurred in running the restaurant business and not the wine bar). See also *R v Weintroub* [2011] EWCA Crim 2167 where confiscation orders were made under the Proceeds of Crime Act 2002, s 76 (confiscation of benefits received from criminal conduct) in respect of directors convicted of breach of IA 1986, s 216—the Court of Appeal ruled that the amount of the benefit which could be recovered was the benefit which the directors received from acting as directors when prohibited from doing so, i.e. the full amount of salary and dividend received by them—and not some proportion attributable to the misuse of the name.

[85] *First Independent Factors Ltd v Mountford* [2008] 2 BCLC 297; *Ricketts v Ad Valorem Factors Ltd* [2004] 1 BCLC 1, CA.

[86] See *Penrose v Official Receiver* [1996] 1 BCLC 389; followed in *Re Lightning Electrical Contractors Ltd* [1996] 2 BCLC 302.

an established company even though it is known by a prohibited name provided that that company has been using that name for at least a year before the insolvent company went into liquidation and the company was not a dormant company (i.e. inactive) during that time.[87] This exception addresses the situation where a director may have numerous companies all with quite similar names and, when one becomes insolvent, he wishes to continue his business activities as a director of or be involved in the management of the others. As the other companies are known by prohibited names, were it not for this exemption, he would be caught by the prohibition.

E Avoidance of transactions prior to winding up

Transactions at an undervalue—IA 1986, s 238

25-37 Section 238 essentially allows a liquidator or administrator to challenge a transaction previously entered into by the company as being at an undervalue and the court is able to make such order as it thinks fit for restoring the position to what it would have been if the company had not entered into the transaction. There is considerable similarity between IA 1986, s 238 and IA 1986, s 423 (transactions defrauding creditors) and therefore a certain cross-over between the authorities on these provisions. There are a number of differences to note, however, between the provisions.[88] Essentially, s 423 is applicable in a broader range of circumstances; it is not dependent on the company being in liquidation or administration and there is no time period limiting the review of the transaction, unlike the two-year limit in s 238. Secondly, applications under s 423 can be by the liquidator or the administrator but also, with the leave of the court, by any victim of the transaction.[89] Thirdly, it must be shown under s 423(3) that the company's intention was to put assets beyond the reach of the claimant or otherwise prejudice a claimant.

25-38 The key questions under IA 1986, s 238 are:

- has the company gone into administration or liquidation?

- did the company enter into a transaction at an undervalue with any person[90] within the period of two years ending with the onset of insolvency?[91] and

- was this transaction at a time when the company was unable to pay its debts[92] or did it become unable to pay its debts in consequence of the transaction?[93] This requirement is presumed when the transaction is entered into by the company with a connected person.[94]

---

[87] It is sufficient for the purpose of IR 1986, r 4.230 that either the registered name or a trading name of the established company is a prohibited name. In either circumstance, if the company is 'known by' a prohibited name during the relevant period, a director is entitled to rely on r 4.230: *ESS Production Ltd v Sully* [2005] 2 BCLC 547, CA.

[88] See generally Stubbs, 'Section 423 of the Insolvency Act in Practice' (2008) 21 Insolv Int 17.

[89] IA 1986, s 424(1)(a); see *National Bank of Kuwait v Menzies* [1994] 2 BCLC 306, CA.

[90] The provision applies to any person wherever resident and an application may be made against a person resident abroad with no place of business in the UK and who does not carry on business within the jurisdiction, provided that the defendant has a sufficient connection with England for it to be just and proper to make an order against him, despite the foreign element: *Re Paramount Airways Ltd* [1992] 3 All ER 1, CA.

[91] The expression 'the onset of insolvency' is defined in detail in IA 1986, s 240(3).

[92] Within the meaning of IA 1986, s 123, see discussion at **24-23**.   [93] IA 1986, s 240(2).

[94] IA 1986, s 240(2). The precise definition of persons connected with the company is complex: see IA 1986, ss 249 and 435 but broadly it includes any directors or shadow directors of the company: ss 249(a), 251; and their families, partners and associated companies: s 435(2), (3), (6), (8).

An undervalue arises if:

(a) the company makes a gift to that person or otherwise enters into a transaction with that person on terms that provide for the company to receive no consideration; or

(b) the company enters into a transaction with that person for a consideration the value of which, in money or money's worth, is significantly less than the value, in money or money's worth, of the consideration provided by the company.[95]

25-39 In determining whether there is a transaction at an undervalue, the court starts by identifying the relevant transaction and the consideration for that transaction.[96] The issue is whether the consideration provided by the transferee is 'significantly less' than the value provided by the transferor company. On this point, a comparison must be made between the value obtained by the company and the value of the consideration provided by the company,[97] though it may be difficult to assess the relative weight of the consideration provided when the transaction may already be several years old by the time the liquidator has an opportunity to review it. Both the consideration provided and received must be measurable in money or moneys' worth; both must be considered from the company's point of view and a comparison must be made between two figures representing the actual value of the consideration.[98]

25-40 The issue of the transaction and the nature of the consideration to be valued was considered by the House of Lords in *Phillips v Brewin Dolphin Bell Lawrie Ltd*.[99] The company carried on business as stockbrokers and its assets included computer equipment which it held on lease. A purchaser wished to acquire part of the company's business for £1.25m. For commercial and tax reasons, the transaction was structured into two elements, one the sale of the business via a wholly owned subsidiary of the company with the purchaser buying the shares in the subsidiary for a nominal £1 and taking on the costs of certain redundancy payments. Another company associated with the purchaser leased the computer equipment from the company on an annual rent. The company was wound up and the liquidator contended, as against the purchaser and the associated company, that the share sale agreement was a transaction at an undervalue within the meaning of IA 1986, s 238.

25-41 The trial judge held that the equipment lease was not part of the consideration which was limited to the £1 and the redundancy payments (worth approximately £325,000) and, since the *prima facie* value of the business sold was £1.05m, the transaction was at an undervalue, a decision affirmed by the Court of Appeal.[100] An appeal was dismissed, but the House of Lords disagreed with the lower courts as to the nature of the transaction. In the view of Lord Scott, the transaction was clear—the sale of shares in return for agreements by the purchaser and the associated company. It was plain that, apart from the consideration under the share sale agreement, the sub-lease agreement also formed part

---

[95] IA 1986, s 238(4). See *Re Taylor Sinclair (Capital) Ltd* [2001] 2 BCLC 176 where the court considered that, with the exception of gifts which are expressly included, a transaction must have an element of dealing between the parties.

[96] *National Westminster Bank plc v Jones* [2002] 1 BCLC 55, CA (a s 423 case).

[97] *Re MC Bacon Ltd* [1990] BCLC 324.

[98] *Re MC Bacon Ltd* [1990] BCLC 324. See the difficulties in valuing the consideration received by the company in *Lord v Sinai Securities Ltd* [2005] 1 BCLC 295.

[99] [2001] 1 BCLC 145; noted by Parry [2001] Insolv Law 58; Moss [2001] 14 Insolv Int 29; see also Mokal and Ho, 'Consideration, Characterisation, Evaluation: Transactions at an Undervalue after *Phillips v Brewin Dolphin*' (2001) JCLS 359.

[100] See [1999] 1 BCLC 714, CA.

of the consideration. The key issue was the value of that consideration. On the facts, the sub-lease provided no value since the company was not entitled to sub-lease the equipment in this way and it had been repossessed shortly after the agreement had been entered into. Therefore, while the lease was part of the consideration, it added nothing of value to the agreement. It followed that the company had entered into a transaction, namely the share sale agreement, at an undervalue and that the amount of the undervalue was £725,000, i.e. £1,050,000 (the value of the asset sold) less £325,000 (the value received and which had been paid in respect of redundancies).[101]

25-42 The value of the asset sold by the company (in this case, the value of the shares in the subsidiary), Lord Scott noted, is *prima facie* not less than what a reasonably well-informed purchaser is prepared to pay in an arm's length negotiation.[102] As for the value of the consideration received, where the value of any consideration is speculative (as in the case of the lease agreement here), it is for the party who relies on that consideration to establish its value.[103]

25-43 This willingness of the House of Lords to treat the lease agreement and the share sale agreement as one transaction is of practical importance since there may be, as here, good business and taxation reasons for dividing the consideration into a number of separate, though linked, transactions, not all of them necessarily with the company. By treating the combined elements as the transaction, this approach maximises the consideration provided and lessens the possibility of there being an undervalue unless, as here, some element of the consideration is of doubtful value. At the same time, the policy of the legislation is upheld by the finding that those who provide speculative consideration must establish its value and, where they cannot, the result will be recovery by the liquidator.

25-44 A debatable point is whether the creation by a company of a charge over its assets in favour of a creditor is a transaction at an undervalue. In *Re MC Bacon Ltd*[104] Millett J ruled against such a conclusion. In his view the creation of a charge could not amount to an undervalue as it does not deplete the company's assets and neither the granting of the debenture nor the consideration received by the company in granting the charge can be measured in money or money's worth.[105] Arden LJ makes the point in *Hill v Spread Trustee Co Ltd*[106] that the grant of a charge could be for no consideration (and therefore would be within IA 1986, s 238(4)(a) even if the application of s 238(4)(b) is ruled out, see **25-38**) as where a charge is granted to a creditor who is not in fact pressing for repayment so there is no forbearance as consideration (as there was in *Re MC Bacon Ltd*).[107] Equally, Arden LJ queried why the value of the creditor's right to have recourse to the security and to take priority over the other creditors should be left out of account.[108] Professor Goode makes the point that a charge in these circumstances should be challenged as a preference and not as an undervalue since the creditor benefits from being able to look to the assets secured rather than being left to claim as an unsecured creditor.[109] As Millett J noted, the creation of the security adversely affects the rights of other creditors in the event of insolvency.[110]

---

[101] [2001] 1 BCLC 145 at [32].   [102] [2001] 1 BCLC 145 at [30].   [103] [2011] 1 BCLC 145 at [27].
[104] [1990] BCLC 324.   [105] [1990] BCLC 324 at 341; *Re Mistral Finance Ltd* [2001] BCC 27.
[106] [2007] 1 BCLC 450 at 473, 485.
[107] The bank exercised forbearance in that case by not calling in its overdraft and honouring cheques and it provided fresh advances to the company: see [1990] BCLC 324 at 340.
[108] See [2007] 1 BCLC 450 at 485.
[109] See Goode, *Principles of Corporate Insolvency* Law (4th edn, 2011), para 13-38.
[110] [1990] BCLC 324 at 340.

The order of the court

25-45 Section 241 lists a wide variety of orders which the court may make in the context of restoring the company to the position it would have been in had the company not entered into the transaction at an undervalue, including orders requiring property to be vested back in the company and requiring any person to make payments to the administrator or liquidator in respect of benefits received by him from the company.[111] The power is very wide and extends to recovery from any person who has received a benefit from the company unless that person can show (and the onus is on him) that he acted in good faith and for value.[112] In *Phillips v Brewin Dolphin Bell Lawrie Ltd*,[113] discussed at **25-40**, as the transaction could not be reversed, the court ordered the purchaser of the shares to pay the amount of the undervalue to the liquidator. In *National Westminster Bank plc v Jones*[114] the court ordered that a suspect transfer of assets be reversed so as to place assets back in the ownership of an individual who was subject to various outstanding mortgages.

25-46 The court's discretion extends to not making any order, as happened in *Re MDA Investment Management Ltd*,[115] even though there was a clear transaction at an undervalue. The company's business had been sold for £2.41m, but the company had only received £1m since the rest of the consideration had been diverted by a director, in breach of duty, to a partnership of which he was a partner. The company was in insolvent liquidation and therefore an order to restore the company to the position prior to the transactions would have been positively detrimental to the company since the company would have been in an even worse position if it had not entered into the transaction at all (at least it had received £1m).

25-47 The court's concern is with the company and it is less concerned with protecting the position of the other party to the transaction. In *Lord v Sinai Securities*[116] Hart J noted that it is arguable that the court's primary and possibly only concern is the restoration of the company's position. The position of the counterparty needs to be considered by the court as a general matter of discretion, but the court is not obliged to ensure that his position is restored in every particular to the status quo before the transaction. There will be many cases where that is simply impossible.

25-48 The court will not make an order if it is satisfied that the company entered into the transaction in good faith and for the purpose of carrying on its business and at the time it did so there were reasonable grounds for believing that the transaction would benefit the company (IA 1986, s 238(5)). For example, a sale of an asset at what appears, with hindsight, to be an undervalue may be explicable as having been the best option available to the company at that time when it was undergoing serious cash-flow difficulties which could only be solved by an expeditious sale. The onus of proof in this regard is on those opposing the court's order.[117]

25-49 Any recoveries obtained under this provision, not being property of the company, but property which arises only after the liquidation of the company, and which is recoverable

---

[111] There is a presumption of the interest being acquired or the benefit received other than in good faith in the circumstances outlined in s 241(2A), (3)–(3C); but sub-transferees acquiring interests or benefits in good faith and for value are protected: IA 1986, s 241(2).

[112] See IA 1986, s 241(2), (3); also *Re Sonatacus Ltd* [2007] 2 BCLC 627.

[113] [2001] 1 All ER 673, HL.   [114] [2002] 1 BCLC 55, CA.   [115] [2004] 1 BCLC 217.

[116] [2005] 1 BCLC 295.

[117] *Re Barton Manufacturing Co Ltd* [1999] 1 BCLC 740 (a considerable volume of evidence will be needed to convince the court of the bona fides of a gift made by the company in these circumstances).

only by the liquidator pursuant to his statutory powers is held by him on a statutory trust for distribution to the company's unsecured creditors,[118] but subject to the expenses of winding up, see **24-63** and any preferential debts, see **24-70**.

Preferences—IA 1986, s 239

25-50 One of the main objectives in the winding up of an insolvent company (see **24-47**) is to ensure the equal treatment of creditors. To help achieve this the court is given a power to set aside, on the application of a liquidator or administrator, transactions or arrangements entered into by the company which have the effect of preferring a creditor or creditors ahead of other creditors.

25-51 A preference can arise, for example, where an unsecured creditor is paid by the company in circumstances where this is done to ensure that on insolvency the creditor is not left to claim against the pooled assets with the risk of non-payment which that entails; or where the company at the eleventh hour gives security to an unsecured creditor for the same reason; or where the directors ensure that the company pays those creditors whose debts are personally guaranteed by the directors.[119] The rules on preferences do not stop companies from paying their creditors as insolvency looms, but the company has to show that the transaction was as a result of ordinary commercial considerations.

25-52 Section 239 sets out in some detail what constitutes a preference and there are a variety of conditions which must be satisfied:

- the company must have gone into administration or liquidation;[120]
- the company must have given a preference to a person;
- the preference must have been given within the period of six months ending with the onset of insolvency[121] or, in the case of a connected person, within the period of two years ending with the onset of insolvency;[122]
- at the time of giving the preference, the company must have been unable to pay its debts[123] or it must have become unable to pay its debts in consequence of the preference;
- there must have been a desire on the company's part to prefer that person; and there is a presumption of a desire to prefer in the case of a connected person.[124]

---

[118] *Re Oasis Merchandising Services Ltd, Ward v Aitken* [1997] 1 BCLC 689 at 698–700, CA.

[119] Such conduct may also merit disqualification on the grounds of unfitness, see *Re Sykes (Butchers) Ltd, Secretary of State for Trade and Industry v Richardson* [1998] 1 BCLC 110 (director caused the company to reduce its bank overdraft which he had personally guaranteed instead of settling the claims of the company's trade creditors). As to the relationship between s 239 and CA 2006, s 172(3), see *GHLM Trading v Maroo* [2012] EWHC 61.

[120] IA 1986, ss 239(1), 238(1).

[121] The expression 'the onset of insolvency' is defined in detail in IA 1986, s 240(3).

[122] IA 1986, s 240(1). 'Connected person' is defined expansively in IA 1986, s 249; and see also s 435 and n 94. See *Re Thirty-Eight Building Ltd* [1999] 1 BCLC 416 as to connected persons—trustees of a pension scheme which was the recipient of large sums of company money in circumstances which would otherwise amount to a preference but which had been received more than six months prior to the insolvency were not connected persons due to the exception in IA 1986, s 435(5)(b), despite the fact that four of the five trustees were beneficiaries of the trust and were connected persons—the presence of a fifth independent trustee and the fact that they acted collectively meant they were not connected persons; see also [2000] 1 BCLC 201.

[123] Within the meaning of IA 1986, s 123. There is no presumption with respect to this element of this provision, unlike under IA 1986, s 238, see s 240(2).

[124] IA 1986, s 239(6); save where the person is connected by reason only of being an employee of the company.

25-53 A company gives a preference to a person if:

- that person is one of the company's creditors or a surety or guarantor for any of the company's debts or other liabilities; and

- the company does anything or suffers anything to be done which (in either case) has the effect of putting that person into a position which, in the event of the company going into insolvent liquidation, will be better than the position he would have been in if that thing had not been done (IA 1986, s 239(4)).[125]

25-54 A key element in establishing the existence of a preference is that there is a desire to prefer that creditor on an insolvent liquidation (IA 1986, s 239(5)). Whether there was such a desire must be considered by reference to the date of the decision to give a preference[126] and where the preference is in favour of a connected person, there is a presumption of a desire to prefer, unless the contrary is shown (s 239(6)).

25-55 The requirement of a desire to prefer was considered in *Re MC Bacon Ltd*[127] where a liquidator applied to the court to set aside, as a preference, a debenture granted by the company to its bank. The company had gone into insolvent liquidation in August 1987 (the onset of insolvency) with an estimated deficiency as regards unsecured creditors of £329,435. At that date, the company's overdraft at the bank stood at £235,530. This overdraft was secured by a debenture granted by the company in May 1987, i.e. within the six months prior to the onset of insolvency at a time when the company was unable to pay its debts. The court emphasised that a key element in the test of what is a preference is that the company acted out of a positive wish to improve the creditor's position in the event of its own insolvent liquidation. There is no need for direct evidence of the requisite desire; its existence may be inferred from the circumstances of the case. The mere presence of the requisite desire is not sufficient by itself, it must have influenced the decision of the company to enter into the transaction. But it is sufficient if it is one of the factors which operated on the minds of those who made the decision and it need not have been the only factor or even the decisive one.[128] Here the company did not positively wish to improve the bank's position, its only concern was that the bank should not call in the overdraft and force the company to stop trading. When the company gave the security to the bank, it did so out of a desire to continue trading. The debenture was not therefore void as a preference.

25-56 Given the need to establish a desire to prefer in this way, it is not surprising that the preference provisions operate most effectively with respect to connected persons where the liquidator is assisted by the statutory presumption of a desire to prefer.[129] In that situation, the alleged beneficiary must satisfy the court that, on the balance of probabilities, the

---

[125] The effect of the preference must be to benefit the recipient in one of these capacities, as a creditor, surety or guarantor, and if his position in those capacities has not been improved, then there is no preference: see *Re Oxford Pharmaceuticals Ltd, Wilson v Masters International Ltd* [2009] 2 BCLC 485. If there is no change of position, there is no preference: *Re Hawkes Hill Publishing Ltd* [2007] BCC 937.

[126] *Re Stealth Construction Ltd* [2012] 1 BCLC 297; *cf Wills v Corfe Joinery Ltd* [1997] BCC 511. A desire to prefer is insufficient if, on the facts, no actual preference occurred, see *Lewis v Hyde* [1997] BCC 976, PC (on the equivalent New Zealand provision).

[127] [1990] BCLC 324, Ch D; *Re Hawkes Hill Publishing Ltd* [2007] BCC 937. See Fletcher [1991] JBL 71.

[128] [1990] BCLC 324 at 335–6, Ch D; see also *Re Living Images Ltd* [1996] 1 BCLC 348; also *Re Oxford Pharmaceuticals Ltd, Wilson v Masters International Ltd* [2009] 2 BCLC 485 at [82], preference when desire to prefer was in some way an influencing factor in certain payments from a subsidiary to a parent company.

[129] IA 1986, s 239(6). 'Connected person' is defined in IA 1986, s 249 and s 435 and see n 94. The statutory presumption may be rebutted, see for example *Re Brian D Pierson* [2001] 1 BCLC 275 at 298; *Re Fairway Magazines Ltd, Fairbairn v Hartigan* [1993] 1 BCLC 643 at 649–50.

alleged preferor was acting solely by reference to proper commercial considerations in having made the payment.[130]

25-57 Certainly, preferences given to connected persons just prior to the collapse of the company are the precise types of transaction which the Cork Committee thought should be challenged.[131] A typical example can be seen in *Re Exchange Travel (Holdings) Ltd*[132] where in July 1990 the company repaid loans made by the directors to the company of £200,000 (approximately) before going into administration in September 1990 with a deficiency running into millions of pounds. The courts have little difficulty in finding such repayments to be preferences and the transactions will be reversed leaving the directors to claim as unsecured creditors in the liquidation with no real prospect of recovering the sums due to them.

25-58 Similarly, in *Wills v Corfe Joinery Ltd*[133] repayment of directors' loans by the company (on 2 February 1995) just prior to ceasing to trade (on 6 February 1995) constituted a preference. The payments were made at a time when other creditors were pressing, employees were being made redundant and so, the court asked, why did the directors choose to pay these creditors? 'In the absence of evidence to show that it was purely for commercial reasons, there is nothing to rebut the statutory presumption [of a desire to prefer] and, indeed, everything to support that statutory presumption.'[134]

25-59 Another common scenario is where a director ensures that a particular creditor gets paid because the director has personally guaranteed that debt. In *Re Agriplant Services Ltd*,[135] S was a director of A Ltd which hired equipment from C Ltd and S personally guaranteed any indebtedness arising from that equipment hire. S ensured that A Ltd paid £20,000 to C Ltd two weeks before A Ltd was placed in voluntary liquidation. The court held that the £20,000 payment constituted a preference given to the creditor and to the director since it had the effect of improving the position of the creditor and the director (as a contingent creditor under his guarantee)[136] in the event of the insolvent liquidation of the company. The director tried to persuade the court that the payment was motivated by the commercial needs of A Ltd, namely the need to keep machinery on site so that A Ltd could continue in operation. The court found, however, that his main motivation was his own personal guarantee of that indebtedness. The director clearly had a desire to prefer himself, Jonathan Parker J noted, but it was only by improving the position of the creditor on an insolvent liquidation of the company that his own position under the guarantee could be improved. The payment was therefore a preference in relation to the creditor and the director. The court ordered the creditor to repay the £20,000 to the company with interest and ordered the director to pay the creditor £20,000 pursuant to his guarantee so that the position was restored to what it would have been on insolvency—i.e. the director would have had to meet the creditor's claim under his guarantee.

25-60 In *Re Sonatacus Ltd*[137] the company made a payment of £50,000 to C Ltd at a time when the company was insolvent or it became insolvent as a consequence of the payment. The payment arose because C Ltd had lent £65,000 to a director of the company who had then lent the money on to the company. The company therefore owed its director £65,000 and

---

[130] *Re Oxford Pharmaceuticals Ltd, Wilson v Masters International Ltd* [2009] 2 BCLC 485.
[131] See the Cork Committee Report (Cmnd 8558, 1982), paras 1257–1258.   [132] [1996] 2 BCLC 524.
[133] [1997] BCC 511.
[134] [1997] BCC 511 at 517, per Lloyd J. See also *Re DKG Contractors Ltd* [1990] BCC 903 (payments of £417,763 to one of the directors in the 10 months before liquidation).   [135] [1997] 2 BCLC 598.
[136] See IA 1986, s 239(4), see **25-53**.   [137] [2007] 2 BCLC 627.

he owed C Ltd. The Court of Appeal held that the payment to C Ltd constituted a preference to the director (the director was the creditor) since the company was in effect repaying a loan by him to the company. C Ltd in turn had received a benefit from the preference given by the company to the director and an order could be made against it for recovery of the benefit under IA 1986, s 241(1)(d). It could only retain the benefit if the benefit had been received in good faith (s 214(2)). In the instant case, the evidence fell short of establishing that C Ltd had received the money in good faith and the onus was on C Ltd to establish its good faith. The controller of C Ltd knew of the financial difficulties of the company which is why he had been reluctant to lend directly to the company. He must have known, the court found, that it was likely that the repayment had been made by the company at a time when it was insolvent or at the least he must have shut his eyes to that possibility. Accordingly, C Ltd was liable to repay £50,000 to the liquidator.

25-61 Where the court is satisfied that a preference has been given, the court may make such order as it thinks fit for restoring the position to what it would have been if the company had not given that preference.[138] Typically the court orders the repayment by the creditor (whether a third party or a director) of the amount received. For example, the directors in *Re Exchange Travel (Holdings) Ltd*[139] were ordered to pay the amounts received by them back to the liquidator leaving them to claim as unsecured creditors for the amounts of directors' loans due to them from the company, see **25-57**. Where the preference amounts to the payment of a sum of money to a creditor, the obvious starting point to any relief is that the recipient creditor should be ordered to repay the money but orders against a third party should only be made as part of the process of restoration of the company's position where the third party is in possession of assets applied in making the preference or has otherwise benefited in monetary terms from the payment in some direct and tangible way.[140]

25-62 Any recoveries obtained under this provision, being property which arises only after the liquidation of the company and which is recoverable only by the liquidator pursuant to his statutory powers, are held by him on a statutory trust for distribution to the company's unsecured creditors[141] and are not available to a holder of a floating charge, but they are subject to the expenses of winding up, see **24-63**, and any preferential debts, see **24-70**.

Extortionate credit transactions—IA 1986, s 244

25-63 Liquidators and administrators may challenge an extortionate credit transaction (i.e. where the company is a party to a transaction for, or involving, the provision of credit to the company) entered into by the company in the three years before the company went into administration or liquidation (IA 1986, s 244(1), (2)). The test of whether a transaction is extortionate is whether, having regard to the risk accepted by the person providing the credit, the terms of it require grossly exorbitant payments in respect of the provision of the credit or it otherwise grossly contravenes ordinary principles of fair dealing (s 244(3)).[142] It is presumed, unless the contrary is proved, that a transaction with respect

---

[138] IA 1986, s 239(3). The range of orders the court can make is the same as in relation to a transaction at an undervalue: s 241(1), discussed at **25-45**. The court may make an order against only some of the parties involved: see *Re Agriplant Services Ltd* [1997] 2 BCLC 598 at 610. See also *Hawkes Hill Publishing Ltd* [2007] BCC 937.

[139] [1996] 2 BCLC 524.

[140] *Re Oxford Pharmaceuticals Ltd, Wilson v Masters International Ltd* [2009] 2 BCLC 485.

[141] *Re Oasis Merchandising Services Ltd, Ward v Aitken* [1997] 1 BCLC 689 at 698–700, CA.

[142] The test for 'extortionate' in a commercial transaction where the interest rates are spelled out at the outset is a very stringent one: *White v Davenham Trust Ltd* [2011] BCC 77, at [47]-[50] (case involved a high

to which an application is made under this provision is or was extortionate (s 244(4)). It is for those who seek to uphold the transaction to show that it is or was not an extortionate credit transaction. If the office holder's challenge is successful, the court's powers extend to setting aside the whole or part of any obligations created by the transaction, varying any of its terms or requiring the creditor to repay any sums to the liquidator.[143]

Avoidance of floating charges—IA 1986, s 245

25-64 Section 245 is designed to invalidate floating charges given close to insolvency which simply secure past indebtedness and provide no new benefits to the company.[144] The effect of the invalidity is to deprive the creditor of the security which he thought he had obtained and to prevent the substitution of a secured debt for an unsecured debt. Only the charge is rendered void, the underlying debt remains valid and, if the debt is repaid before winding up, the fact that the charge would have been void in the winding up does not affect the repayment.[145] In appropriate circumstances, it may be possible to challenge the repayment as a preference.

25-65 A floating charge is invalid and open to challenge by a liquidator or administrator under IA 1986, s 245 if the charge was created within the 12 months ending with the onset of insolvency[146] and at the time, or as a result of the transaction, the company was unable to pay its debts.[147] Where the charge was created in favour of a person connected with the company, the relevant period is extended to two years before the onset of insolvency and it is irrelevant whether or not the company was unable to pay its debts at the time.[148] Even if these conditions are satisfied, the floating charge is nevertheless valid to the extent that money is paid or goods or services are supplied to the company or any debt of the company is reduced or discharged at the same time as, or after, the creation of the charge (s 245(2)).

25-66 In *Power v Sharp Investments Ltd*[149] the board of a company (Shoe Lace Ltd) resolved in March 1990 to grant a debenture to its parent company, Sharp. The debenture granting a fixed and floating charge was duly executed on 24 July 1990 in respect of sums of money which had been advanced by Sharp in April, May, June and finally on 16 July 1990. A petition for winding up was presented on 4 September and the company was compulsorily wound up on 20 November. The liquidator challenged the validity of the charge in the light of IA 1986, s 245.

25-67 The Court of Appeal found that there was insufficient contemporaneity between the prior payments made by the debenture holder and the execution of the charge so as to bring it within IA 1986, s 245(2) which requires the consideration to be paid at the same time as, or after, the creation of the charge. The words were clearly included by the legislature, the court said, for the purpose of excluding from the exemption the amount of moneys paid to the company before the creation of the charge even though they were paid in

risk commercial transaction with interest rates of 3% per month in the event of default; arguable, however, that a substantial increase in the interest rate on default is a penalty clause - here the rate effectively doubled on default - and unenforceable at common law).

[143] IA 1986, s 244(4). One of the functions of this section is to prevent companies in effect preferring a creditor by agreeing artificially high rates of interest on the creditor's debt. If arrears of interest are allowed to build up, the creditor's proof of debt is artificially increased. See the Cork Committee Report, (Cmnd 8558, 1982), 1379–1381.

[144] For the background to this provision, see the Cork Committee Report, (Cmnd 8558, 1982), paras 1551–1556.   [145] *Mace Builders (Glasgow) Ltd v Lunn* [1987] Ch 191, CA.

[146] The 'onset of insolvency' is defined in detail in IA 1986, s 245(5).

[147] IA 1986, s 245(2), (3)(b), (4).   [148] IA 1986, s 245(2), (3)(a).   [149] [1994] 1 BCLC 111, CA.

consideration for the charge. On any other construction, these words would be mere sur-plusage.[150] Sir Christopher Slade concluded that:[151]

> '…no moneys paid before the execution of a debenture will qualify for the exemption under the subsection [i.e. under s 245(2)] unless the interval between payment and execution is so short that it can be regarded as minimal and payment and execution can be regarded as contemporaneous.'

As the court noted, 'it is always open to the lender not to lend until the charge has actually been executed; that must be the prudent course'.[152] This situation is distinguishable, the court said, from the case where the promise to execute a debenture creates a present equitable security and moneys are advanced in reliance upon it. In that case, the delay between the advances and the execution of the formal instrument of charge are immaterial as the charge has already been created and is immediately registrable so that other creditors have the opportunity of learning of its existence.[153]

25-68 The fresh sums received must be received by the company and it is insufficient if sums are advanced by the third party to the company's bank to reduce the company's overdraft which the third party has guaranteed. The money paid direct to the bank never becomes freely available to the company and thus is not paid 'to it' within the meaning of the section.[154]

F Disqualification of directors

Legislative framework and purpose

25-69 Disqualification is governed by the Company Directors Disqualification Act 1986,[155] as amended, and the purpose of the CDDA 1986 was stated succinctly by Lord Woolf MR in *Re Blackspur Group plc, Secretary of State for Trade and Industry v Davies*[156] as follows:

> 'The purpose of the 1986 Act is the protection of the public, by means of prohibitory remedial action, by anticipated deterrent effect on further misconduct and by encouragement of higher standards of honesty and diligence in corporate management, from those who are unfit to be concerned in the management of a company.'

That the protection of the public (broadly defined to include all relevant interest groups, such as shareholders, employees, lenders, customers and other creditors)[157] is the key consideration is evident from the wording of the statute itself which authorises an application for disqualification (and the acceptance of a disqualification undertaking) where it appears that it is expedient in the public interest for the director to be disqualified

---

[150] [1994] 1 BCLC 111 at 122, CA.   [151] [1994] 1 BCLC 111 at 123, CA.
[152] [1994] 1 BCLC 111 at 123, CA, quoting Hoffmann J at first instance, see [1992] BCLC 636, Ch D; see also *Rehman v Chamberlain* [2011] EWHC 2318.
[153] [1994] 1 BCLC 111 at 122, CA and see n 152.
[154] *Re Fairway Magazines Ltd, Fairbairn v Hartigan* [1993] 1 BCLC 643; see Prentice (1993) 109 LQR 371; also *Re Orleans Motor Co Ltd* [1911] 2 Ch 41.
[155] On disqualification, see generally Walters and Davis-White, *Directors' Disqualification and Insolvency Restrictions* (3rd edn, 2009); Finch, *Corporate Insolvency Law: Perspectives and Principles* (2nd edn, 2009), pp 716–40; Williams, 'Disqualifying Directors: A Remedy Worse than the Disease?' [2007] 7 JCLS 213; Hicks, 'Director Disqualification: Can it Deliver?' [2001] JBL 433.
[156] [1998] 1 BCLC 676 at 680.
[157] See *Re Tech Textiles Ltd, Secretary of State for Trade and Industry v Vane* [1998] 1 BCLC 259 at 268; also *Hill v Secretary of State for the Environment, Food and Rural Affairs* [2006] 1 BCLC 601 at 608 (the 'public' consists of, or at least includes as a primary class, those who might extend credit to the company).

(CDDA 1986, s 7).[158] Disqualification is not a criminal matter, but a civil proceeding and disqualification is not intended as a punitive measure, though there is a punitive element to the proceedings. Removing the privilege of trading through a limited liability company does involve a substantial interference with the freedom of the individual[159] and carries a degree of stigma for anyone who is disqualified.[160] On the other hand, there are approximately 2.4 million companies on the register, each of which must have at least one director, so the numbers actually being disqualified (approximately 1,400 per annum) are very small and likely to remain so.[161] Nevertheless, as the enforcement of directors' duties through actions by the company or derivative claims by shareholders is unusual, as discussed in Chapter 18, disqualification proceedings do provide a measure of indirect enforcement. Its importance must not be overstated, however, for this is enforcement without any personal liability on the part of the director to account for any gains or make good any losses arising from any breach of his duties.

Grounds for disqualification

25-70 While the CDDA 1986 provides for a wide variety of grounds on which disqualification orders may be made,[162] in practice almost all disqualification orders or undertakings are made under CDDA 1986, s 6 (duty of court to disqualify unfit directors of insolvent companies)[163] and unfitness is discussed at **25-81**.

The disqualification order or undertaking

25-71 A disqualification order is an order made against a person that for a period specified in the order, he shall not be a director of a company, act as receiver of a company's property or in any way, whether directly or indirectly, be concerned or take part in the promotion, formation or management of a company unless (in each case) he has the leave of the court, and he shall not act as an insolvency practitioner (CDDA 1986, s 1).[164] The courts take a broad approach to the prohibition on being 'concerned in the management of a company' which is widely cast in order to make it impossible for a disqualified person to be part of

---

[158] See *Secretary of State for Trade and Industry v Gray* [1995] 1 BCLC 276 at 288; see also *Re Lo-Line Electric Motors Ltd* [1988] 2 All ER 692 at 696; also *Re Sevenoaks Stationers (Retail) Ltd* [1991] 1 BCLC 325 at 329; *Re Westmid Packing Services Ltd, Secretary of State for Trade and Industry v Griffiths* [1998] 2 BCLC 646 at 654–5; *Re Barings plc (No 5)* [1999] 1 BCLC 433 at 482.

[159] See *Re Lo-Line Electric Motors Ltd* [1988] 2 All ER 692 at 696, per Browne-Wilkinson V-C; also *Re Crestjoy Products Ltd* [1990] BCLC 677 at 681.

[160] *Re Westminster Property Management Ltd, Official Receiver v Stern* [2000] 2 BCLC 396 at 423, per Henry LJ.

[161] The latest statistics in the Insolvency Service Annual Report and Accounts 2010–11, p 30, show 1,437 disqualifications in 2010–11, up from 1,388 disqualifications in 2009–10.

[162] Other possible grounds include where a person is convicted of an indictable offence in relation to a company (CDDA 1986, s 2); persistent default in respect of filing documents with registrar of companies (s 3); fraudulent trading or other fraud (s 4); where an investigation shows a person to be unfit (ss 1A, 8); infringement of competition law (ss 9A–9E); where civilly liable under s 213 (fraudulent trading) or s 214 (wrongful trading) (s 10).

[163] The Insolvency Service no longer provides a detailed breakdown of disqualification statistics in terms of the section of the CDDA relied on, but previous records showed that 90% of disqualifications were under CDDA 1986, s 6 (unfit directors of insolvent companies) and there is no reason to think that that position has changed.

[164] See also The Companies (Model Articles) Regulations 2008, SI 2008/3229, reg 2, Sch 1, art 18 (Ltd), reg 4, Sch 3, art 22 (Plc) which provide that a director ceases to be a director as soon as he is prohibited from being a director by law.

the management and central direction of a company's affairs.[165] The court cannot pick and choose elements of the prohibitions in CDDA 1986, s 1 to apply in a particular case, but must order that the person be disqualified from any of these activities for the set period.[166]

25-72 A disqualification undertaking has an identical effect to a disqualification order and undertakings are agreed between a director and the Disqualification Unit of the Insolvency Service without the need to involve the courts.[167] Undertakings are possible only in cases of disqualification on the grounds of unfitness on insolvency and unfitness identified after an investigation of a company (CDDA 1986, s 1A(1)). The use of undertakings enables non-contentious cases to be dealt with expeditiously so hastening the commencement of the disqualification period (to the advantage both of the public and the disqualified director) and reducing the burden of costs on the disqualified director, but there is no obligation on a director to offer an undertaking nor on the Secretary of State to accept it and disputed cases are still a matter for the courts. Nevertheless, most disqualifications now are the subject of undertakings rather than court orders.[168] Once made or given, the order or undertaking is notified to the registrar of companies for entry on the register of disqualified directors which is open to inspection by the public (CDDA 1986, s 18).

25-73 Undischarged bankrupts are automatically disqualified from acting as directors or in the promotion, formation or management of a company without the leave of the court (CDDA 1986, s 11) and, even after the discharge of their bankruptcy, unfit bankrupts may be subject to bankruptcy restriction orders (BROs) or bankruptcy restriction undertakings (BRUs) which are very similar in effect to disqualification orders or undertakings. It is an offence for a person to act as a director of a company, or directly or indirectly to take part in or be concerned in the promotion, formation or management of a company, without the leave of the court, at a time when (1) he is an undischarged bankrupt or (2) a BRO or BRU is in force in respect of him (CDDA 1986, s 11). An undischarged bankrupt or a bankrupt subject to a BRO so acting is also civilly liable for the debts of the company incurred when so acting (CDDA 1986, s 15), (see **25-92**).

The period of disqualification

25-74 The period of disqualification varies depending on the grounds for disqualification. In most cases, the maximum period is 15 years[169] and, where the court makes a disqualification

---

[165] *R v Campbell* [1984] BCLC 83. See *Hill v Secretary of State for the Environment, Food and Rural Affairs* [2006] 1 BCLC 601 (undischarged bankrupt who was the effective manager running a company and who made two important contracts on its behalf affecting its future activities was a person concerned in the management of a company).

[166] *R v Cole* [1998] 2 BCLC 234, CA; *Re Gower Enterprises Ltd (No 2)* [1995] 2 BCLC 201.

[167] The background and purpose of the changes to allow for undertakings is described by Chadwick LJ in *Re Blackspur Group plc (No 3), Secretary of State for Trade and Industry v Davies (No 2)* [2002] 2 BCLC 263 at 287–90; see also *Re INS Realisations Ltd, Secretary of State for Trade and Industry v Jonkler* [2006] 2 BCLC 239 at 247.

[168] The Insolvency Service Annual Report and Accounts year on year show a relatively consistent 80% of disqualifications are by undertakings, see for example, the Annual Report for 2010–11, p 30. A consequence is far fewer reported disqualification cases and so fewer opportunities for the court to consider and comment on directors' conduct and fitness for office.

[169] CDDA 1986, ss 2(3)(b), 4(3), 6(4), 8, 10. Where a person is disqualified for persistent default, or on conviction of an indictable offence by a court of summary jurisdiction, or on conviction of summary offences in relation to returns to the registrar of companies, the maximum period of disqualification is five years: ss 3(5), 2(3)(a), 5(5).

order on the grounds of unfitness in the case of insolvency, there is a minimum period of disqualification of two years.[170] In *Re Westmid Packing Services Ltd, Secretary of State for Trade and Industry v Griffiths*[171] Lord Woolf MR noted that in truth the fixing of the period of disqualification is little different from any sentencing exercise. The period of disqualification should be fixed, he said, by starting with an assessment of the correct period to reflect the gravity of the offence and then allowing for any mitigating factors.[172] A director may appeal against his disqualification and the Secretary of State may (and does) appeal against the length of disqualification imposed by the court.[173] A person subject to a disqualification undertaking may apply to the court to reduce the period for which the undertaking is in force but this jurisdiction does not extend to annulling or rescinding the undertaking from the start.[174]

Leave to act despite being disqualified

25-75 The statute expressly provides that a disqualified person (whether disqualified by order or by undertaking) may apply for leave to act (other than to act as an insolvency practitioner).[175] The court's discretion to grant leave is unfettered by any statutory condition or criterion.[176] On an application for leave, the court has to balance the protection of the public and any practical need that the applicant should be able to act as a director of a particular company.[177] In carrying out this balancing task, the court must pay attention in particular to the nature of the defects in company management which led to the disqualification and ask itself whether, if leave were granted, a situation might arise in which there would be a risk of recurrence of those defects.[178] The court must also bear in mind the legislative policy of disqualifying unfit directors to minimise the risk of harm to the public and that objective must not be undermined by the approach of the court to the issue of leave.[179]

[170] CDDA 1986, s 6(4). In *Re Sevenoaks Stationers (Retail) Ltd* [1991] BCLC 325, at 328, the Court of Appeal identified three brackets of periods of disqualification for the purposes of CDDA 1986, s 6, essentially two to five years where the case is not very serious, six to 10 years for serious cases which do not merit the top bracket and over 10 years for particularly serious cases. Reference to these brackets is standard practice when determining the period of disqualification.   [171] [1998] 2 BCLC 646.

[172] [1998] 2 BCLC 646 at 655; also *Re Bradcrown Ltd, Official Receiver v Ireland* [2001] 1 BCLC 547 at 551. See *Re Normanton Wells Properties Ltd, Official Receiver v Jupe* [2011] 1 BCLC 191 at [21], a substantial or significant return to creditors might be a mitigating factor.

[173] See, for example, *Secretary of State for Trade and Industry v McTighe (No 2)* [1996] 2 BCLC 477 (eight and four-year periods increased to 12 and six years respectively).

[174] *Re Blackspur Group plc (No 4), Eastaway v Secretary of State for Trade and Industry* [2006] 2 BCLC 489 at 508. See also *Re INS Realisations Ltd, Secretary of State for Trade and Industry v Jonkler* [2006] 2 BCLC 239 at 253–4 (jurisdiction to reduce period of undertaking to be used sparingly and only where there are special circumstances).

[175] CDDA ss 1(1), 17. As to an application for leave, see *Secretary of State for Trade and Industry v Collins* [2000] 2 BCLC 223, CA.

[176] *Re Dawes & Henderson (Agencies) Ltd (No 2)* [1999] 2 BCLC 317.

[177] *Re Barings plc (No 4), Secretary of State for Trade and Industry v Baker* [1999] 1 BCLC 262 at 269. See *Re Tech Textiles Ltd, Secretary of State for Trade and Industry v Vane* [1998] 1 BCLC 259 at 269; see also *Secretary of State for Trade and Industry v Barnett* [1998] 2 BCLC 64 at 72; *Re Dawes & Henderson (Agencies) Ltd (No 2)* [1999] 2 BCLC 317 at 326.

[178] *Re Barings (No 4), Secretary of State for Trade and Industry v Baker* [1999] 1 BCLC 262 at 269; *Re Dawes & Henderson (Agencies) Ltd (No 2)* [1999] 2 BCLC 317 at 325.

[179] See *Re Tech Textiles Ltd, Secretary of State for Trade and Industry v Vane* [1998] 1 BCLC 259 at 267; *Re Barings plc (No 4), Secretary of State for Trade and Industry v Baker* [1999] 1 BCLC 262 at 269.

25-76 The court may grant leave subject to certain conditions,[180] typically restricting the director to acting in a named company or companies, limiting the roles which the individual may undertake and imposing conditions as to the composition of the board in the company in question.[181] A failure to observe the conditions of leave means that the director is acting without leave and in breach of his disqualification order[182] which is a criminal offence and leaves him open to potential personal liability (see discussion at **25-92**).

Grounds for disqualification—Unfit directors of insolvent companies

25-77 As noted, most disqualification orders or undertakings are made under CDDA 1986, s 6 (duty of court to disqualify unfit directors of insolvent companies). If it appears to an official receiver, liquidator, administrator or administrative receiver (collectively referred to as the office-holder) that in the case of a person who is or has been a director[183] or shadow director[184] of a company which has become insolvent (whether while he was a director or subsequently) that his conduct as a director of that company (either taken alone or taken together with his conduct as a director of any other company or companies) makes him unfit to be concerned in the management of a company, he must forthwith report the matter to the Secretary of State.[185] In practice, this means he must report to the Disqualification Unit which is part of the Insolvency Service which in turn is an executive agency of the Department for Business, Innovation and Skills.

25-78 A company 'becomes insolvent' for these purposes if:

(1) the company goes into liquidation[186] at a time when its assets are insufficient for the payment of its debts and other liabilities and the expenses of the winding up;

(2) the company enters administration; or

(3) an administrative receiver of the company is appointed (CDDA 1986, s 6(2)).

25-79 Having considered the report, if it appears to the Secretary of State (i.e. the Disqualification Unit) that it is expedient in the public interest[187] that a disqualification order under CDDA 1986, s 6 should be made against any person, an application may be made by the Secretary of State to the court for a disqualification order.[188] Before this occurs, the Disqualification

---

[180] See *Secretary of State for Trade and Industry v Collins* [2000] 2 BCLC 223 at 235; *Re Tech Textiles Ltd, Secretary of State for Trade and Industry v Vane* [1998] 1 BCLC 259.

[181] See, for example, *Re Dawes & Henderson Ltd* [1999] 2 BCLC 317 at 328; *Re Gibson Davies Ltd* [1995] BCC 11.

[182] *Re Brian Sheridan Cars Ltd, Official Receiver v Sheridan* [1996] 1 BCLC 327.

[183] The word 'director' in this context includes a de facto director: *Re Lo-Line Electric Motors Ltd* [1988] 2 All ER 692; *Re Kaytech International plc, Secretary of State for Trade and Industry v Kaczer* [1999] 2 BCLC 351. A corporate director may be disqualified: see *Official Receiver v Brady* [1999] BCC 847.

[184] CDDA 1986, s 6(3C). As to shadow directors, see **6-17**.

[185] CDDA 1986, s 7(3); and see The Insolvent Companies (Reports on Conduct of Directors) Rules 1996, SI 1996/1909.

[186] Defined by IA 1986, s 247, incorporated by CDDA 1986, s 22(3), as the time when the company passes a resolution for voluntary winding up or the time of the court order in the case of a compulsory winding up.

[187] The question whether it is expedient in the public interest to commence and thereafter to pursue applications for disqualification is a matter for the Secretary of State and not for the court: *Re Blackspur Group plc, Secretary of State for Trade and Industry v Davies* [1998] 1 BCLC 676 at 680; *Re Barings plc (No 3), Secretary of State for Trade and Industry v Baker* [1999] 1 BCLC 226 at 252; and see *Re Blackspur Group plc (No 3), Secretary of State for Trade and Industry v Davies (No 2)* [2002] 2 BCLC 263 at 287, per Chadwick LJ.

[188] CDDA 1986, s 7(1). Except with the leave of the court, an application for a disqualification order under CDDA 1986, s 6 must not be made after the end of two years beginning with the day on which the company became insolvent: CDDA 1986, s 7(2). The two-year time period runs from the happening of the first of the

Unit will give notice to the director (under CDDA 1986, s 16) of the intention to proceed under s 6 and this notice will draw his attention to the possibility of his offering a disqualification undertaking rather than having the matter determined by the court.[189]

25-80 Following the application by the Secretary of State or official receiver, the court must make a disqualification order for a minimum period of two years and a maximum of 15 years if it is satisfied that the conduct of that person as a director of that company makes him unfit to be concerned in the management of a company.[190]

The court's approach to the issue of unfitness

25-81 A review of reported cases where disqualification proceedings have been brought under CDDA 1986, s 6 (unfitness in cases of insolvency) reveal a very similar fact scenario in each case.[191] Often the director has been associated with a number of companies which have gone into insolvent liquidation over a relatively short period of time. The allegations of unfitness typically include that the director caused or permitted the company to trade to the detriment of its creditors; that the company continued trading while insolvent, usually by means of pursuing a policy of paying only those creditors who pressed; and that Crown debts were retained to finance continued trading (these grounds are discussed in more detail later). Despite the financial difficulties, the directors continue throughout the period to obtain significant personal benefits by way of remuneration and frequently by misappropriating corporate assets and opportunities. Examples of the type of misconduct commonly featured in the cases include the granting of preferences to themselves and to family and friends,[192] the transfer or use of the company's assets for inadequate consideration or without security for the sale price[193] and undisclosed conflicts of interest resulting in personal gain.[194]

25-82 It is clear that many of the allegations suggest breaches of a director's duties, though in this context the conduct is usually described in terms of a failure to meet the required standards of competence and probity.[195] For example, trading in disregard of creditors' interests is a failure to act as required by CA 2006, s 172(3), while managerial incompetence and inertia is a failure to exercise care and skill as required by s 174, and the continued receipt of excessive personal benefits and the misappropriation of corporate assets involves breaches of the no-conflict rule set out in s 175.

---

events specified (going into liquidation, administration etc) in CDDA 1986, s 6(2): *Re Tasbian (No 1) Ltd* [1991] BCLC 56, CA.

[189] As to the content of this s 16 notice, see *Re Surrey Leisure Ltd, Official Receiver v Keam* [1999] 1 BCLC 731. [190] CDDA 1986, s 6(1), (4).

[191] See, for example, *Re Amaron Ltd, Secretary of State for Trade and Industry v Lubrani* [2001] 1 BCLC 562, aff'g [1997] 2 BCLC 115; *Re Galeforce Pleating Co Ltd* [1999] 2 BCLC 704; *Re Landhurst Leasing plc, Secretary of State for Trade and Industry v Ball* [1999] 1 BCLC 286.

[192] See *Secretary of State for Trade and Industry v Gray* [1995] 1 BCLC 276; *Re Living Images Ltd* [1996] 1 BCLC 348; *Re Sykes (Butchers) Ltd, Secretary of State for Trade and Industry v Richardson* [1998] 1 BCLC 110.

[193] *Secretary of State for Trade and Industry v McTighe (No 2)* [1996] 2 BCLC 477; *Re Keypak Homecare Ltd* [1990] BCLC 440; *Re Normanton Wells Properties Ltd, Official Receiver v Jupe* [2011] 1 BCLC 191.

[194] *Re Dominion International Group plc (No 2)* [1996] 1 BCLC 572; *Re Godwin Warren Control Systems plc* [1993] BCLC 80. See *Secretary of State for Business, Enterprise and Regulatory Reform v Sullman* [2009] 1 BCLC 397 at [100]–[106], [116] (extraction of personal gains by directors must be subject to the most rigorous application of the standards of fit conduct).

[195] See *Re Landhurst Leasing plc* [1999] 1 BCLC 286 at 344; *Secretary of State for Trade and Industry v Gray* [1995] 1 BCLC 276 at 286.

25-83 A finding of breach of duty is neither necessary (had it been so, the section would not be defined in terms of 'unfitness') nor of itself sufficient for a finding of unfitness, however, as was explained by Jonathan Parker J in *Re Barings plc (No 5), Secretary of State for Trade and Industry v Baker (No 5)*,[196] a point specifically endorsed by the Court of Appeal.[197] Clearly, a director may be guilty of misfeasance or breach of duty without that breach necessarily meaning that he is unfit and should be disqualified.[198] Equally, a director may be unfit, though no breach of duty is established, but his conduct fails to reach an acceptable level of commercial probity.[199] In particular, unfitness by reason of incompetence may be established without proof of a breach of duty, as where a respondent shows himself so completely lacking in judgement as to justify a finding of unfitness, notwithstanding that he has not been guilty of misfeasance or breach of duty.[200] Lewison J agreed on this point in *Secretary of State for Trade and Industry v Goldberg*[201] while acknowledging that the court must be very careful before holding that a director is unfit because of conduct that does not amount to a breach of any duty (whether contractual, tortious, statutory or equitable).

25-84 Just as it is not necessary to show a breach of duty (though there commonly is a breach), it is not necessary to show dishonesty,[202] though often that element is present,[203] and unfitness may be shown by conduct which is merely incompetent. Where there is no dishonesty of any kind, however, because of the serious nature of a disqualification order, the burden on the Secretary of State is to satisfy the court that the conduct complained of demonstrates incompetence of a high degree.[204]

25-85 The burden of proof is on the applicant for the disqualification order and to the civil standard of the balance of probabilities and it is for the Secretary of State to establish the matters on which the allegations of unfitness are based and for the court to be satisfied that the conduct alleged is sufficiently serious to warrant disqualification.[205]

---

[196] [1999] 1 BCLC 433 at 486.

[197] See [2000] 1 BCLC 523 at 535. See too *Secretary of State for Business, Enterprise and Regulatory Reform v Sullman* [2009] 1 BCLC 397, at [30].

[198] See, for example, *Re Deaduck Ltd, Baker v Secretary of State for Trade and Industry* [2000] 1 BCLC 148.

[199] See *Secretary of State for Business, Enterprise and Regulatory Reform v Sullman* [2009] 1 BCLC 397 at [30], [43], [103]–[106], as Norris J noted, at [82], 'fit conduct entails as much an assessment of the commercial realities of managing a business as an appreciation of legal nicety'.

[200] *Re Barings plc (No 5)* [1999] 1 BCLC 433 at 486.   [201] [2004] 1 BCLC 597.

[202] See *Secretary of State for Trade and Industry v Goldberg* [2004] 1 BCLC 597 at 611.

[203] See, for example, *Re Bunting Electric Manufacturing Co Ltd, Secretary of State for Trade and Industry v Golby* [2006] 1 BCLC 550 (finance director dishonestly acting in his personal interests in breach of duty to the company).

[204] *Re Barings plc (No 5), Secretary of State for Trade and Industry v Baker (No 5)* [1999] 1 BCLC 433 at 483–6; endorsed on appeal, [2000] 1 BCLC 523 at 535, CA, but the degree of incompetence required should not be exaggerated. See also *Re Sevenoaks Stationers (Retail) Ltd* [1991] 1 BCLC 325 at 337: incompetence or negligence 'in a very marked degree' is enough to render a director unfit, but it need not be 'total' incompetence.

[205] *Secretary of State for Trade and Industry v Swan* [2005] BCC 597 at 606, per Etherton J. Care must be taken in formulating the allegations which suggest unfitness: *Official Receiver v Key* [2009] 1 BCLC 22 (a lengthy disqualification might have been imposed if the charges had been properly formulated—public entitled to expect that all charges which the claimant has a reasonable prospect of establishing against a defendant will be included in order that the period of disqualification will be commensurate with the conduct alleged).

25-86 Overall, the question for the court to decide, taking a broad brush approach,[206] is whether the conduct complained of,[207] viewed cumulatively and taking into account any extenuating circumstances accompanying the conduct in question, has fallen below the standards of probity and competence appropriate for persons fit to be directors of companies trading with the privilege of limited liability.[208] In considering the director's conduct, the court must have regard to CDDA 1986, Sch 1,[209] but the Schedule is not exhaustive,[210] and the court is entitled to take into account any misconduct that shows unfitness.[211]

Failure to have regard to creditors' interests

25-87 As discussed in Chapter 9, the duty of directors to act to promote the success of the company is subject to an obligation to have regard to the interests of the company's creditors in situations of insolvency or doubtful solvency, see CA 2006, s 172(3) and the discussion at **9-41**. Breaches of that obligation, often described in disqualification proceedings as trading while insolvent to the detriment of the creditors, are central usually to the allegations of unfitness in most disqualification proceedings brought under CDDA 1986, s 6, given that it is a pre-condition of that section that the company must have become insolvent (see **25-77**).

25-88 A common problem in these cases is that the directors continue to trade after a point in time when the company's financial position is hopeless instead of putting the company into insolvent liquidation and so the continued trading is unwarranted and at the creditors' risk. Merely trading while the company is insolvent is insufficient, as the Court of Appeal stressed in *Secretary of State v Creggan*,[212] it must be established that, in addition to causing the company to trade while insolvent, the director knew or ought to have known that there was no reasonable prospect of meeting creditors' claims.

25-89 The courts are alert to and very critical of such trading without a reasonable prospect of meeting creditors' claims. In *Secretary of State for Trade and Industry v Collins*[213] the directors (who were disqualified for periods of seven to nine years) caused the company

---

[206] See *Secretary of State for Trade and Industry v Goldberg* [2004] 1 BCLC 597 at 611; *Re Westmid Packing Services Ltd, Secretary of State for Trade and Industry v Griffiths* [1998] 2 BCLC 646 at 658; *Secretary of State for Business, Enterprise and Regulatory Reform v Sullman* [2009] 1 BCLC 397 at [114], [118], also at [71] where Norris J noted that 'the essential simplicity of the question', whether the director's conduct renders him unfit, must remain at the forefront of the court's consideration.

[207] 'The reason for disqualification can only be a person's 'conduct as a director.' 'Conduct' encompasses both acts and omissions. The phrase 'as a director' means 'in his capacity as a director'... Even if the case is based on allegations of dishonesty, the dishonesty in question must be dishonesty 'as a director.': *Secretary of State for Trade and Industry v Goldberg* [2004] 1 BCLC 597 at [46], per Lewison J.

[208] *Secretary of State for Trade and Industry v Gray* [1995] 1 BCLC 276 at 284; *Re Barings plc (No 5), Secretary of State for Trade and Industry v Baker (No 5)* [1999] 1 BCLC 433 at 483; endorsed on appeal, [2000] 1 BCLC 523 at 535, CA; also *Secretary of State for Business, Enterprise and Regulatory Reform v Sullman* [2009] 1 BCLC 397 at [118] (inviting the public to deal with the company on a false basis in a material particular falls below the standard of commercial probity which the law is entitled to expect of a limited liability company).   [209] CDDA 1986, s 9.

[210] *Re Barings plc (No 5), Secretary of State for Trade and Industry v Baker (No 5)* [1999] 1 BCLC 433; *Re Migration Services International Ltd, Official Receiver v Webster* [2000] 1 BCLC 666 (breach of IA 1986, s 216—misuse of company name—may be taken into account even though not mentioned in the Schedule).

[211] *Re Amaron Ltd, Secretary of State for Trade and Industry v Lubrani* [2001] 1 BCLC 562, aff'g [1997] 2 BCLC 115.

[212] [2002] 1 BCLC 99 at 101, CA; and see Chadwick J in *Secretary of State for Trade and Industry v Gash* [1997] 1 BCLC 341 at 348–9.

[213] [2000] 2 BCLC 223. See also *Secretary of State for Trade and Industry v McTighe (No 2)* [1996] 2 BCLC 477; *Re Living Images Ltd* [1996] 1 BCLC 348; *Official Receiver v Stern (No 2)* [2002] 1 BCLC 119, CA; *Secretary of State for Trade and Industry v Hollier* [2007] BCC 11.

to continue to trade to September 1994 when they knew by November 1993 that there was no reasonable prospect of avoiding insolvent liquidation. The company was eventually compulsorily wound up with a deficiency of £11.3m. In *Re Amaron Ltd, Secretary of State for Trade and Industry v Lubrani*[214] the directors (who were disqualified for three years) unreasonably continued to trade for 21 months after the time when they knew the company was making losses on an increasingly large scale.[215] On the other hand, in *Secretary of State for Trade and Industry v Gill*[216] the court rejected any suggestion of unfitness where directors continued to accept customer deposits to facilitate ongoing trading while they searched for a commercial solution to the company's difficulties. The key difference was that, while the company did subsequently go into liquidation, the court accepted that at all material times there was a reasonable prospect of avoiding insolvency.

25-90   A common scenario is that in a group situation, or where there are related businesses, the directors disregard the interests of the creditors of an individual company in the interests of the overall business in clear breach of their duty to promote the success of that individual company. For example, in *Re Mea Corporation Ltd, Secretary of State for Trade and Industry v Aviss*[217] directors were disqualified for periods ranging from seven to 11 years, in essence, for causing or allowing each of three companies to trade to the detriment of creditors. At a time when those companies were under increasing pressure from creditors and were each insolvent, the directors allowed such cash as was available to be paid out to other companies in which one of the directors had a substantial personal interest in disregard of the interests of the creditors of the individual companies. In *Secretary of State for Business, Innovation and Skills v Doffman*[218] the court was particularly critical of two directors who disregarded the separate interests of individual companies within a group of companies in which they were the sole shareholders and transferred assets between the companies without regard to the interests of the transferor.

25-91   Another common scenario is that, as the company's financial position worsens, the directors adopt a deliberate policy involving some decision, conscious or unconscious on their part, of paying only those creditors who press for payment or those who are essential to the continued operation of the company.[219] In effect, they operate a policy of unfair discrimination between creditors.[220] In *Re Sevenoaks Stationers (Retail) Ltd*[221] the Court of Appeal held that the adoption of such a policy, of itself, merits a finding of unfitness and disqualification.[222] The directors are taking unfair advantage of the forbearance on the part of the creditors not pressing for payment and are trading at those creditors' expense while the company is in financial difficulty. If the evidence does not suggest a deliberate policy, but rather a general uncaring and dismissive attitude to the company's creditors, then an allegation of unfair discrimination will not be made out,

---

[214] [2001] 1 BCLC 562, aff'g [1997] 2 BCLC 115.   [215] See [2001] 1 BCLC 562 at 566.

[216] [2006] BCC 725.

[217] [2007] 1 BCLC 618 at 635, 643. See too *Re Genosyis Technology Management Ltd, Wallach v Secretary of State for Trade and Industry* [2007] 1 BCLC 208; *Secretary of State for Trade and Industry v Goldberg* [2004] 1 BCLC 597 (director disqualified for, *inter alia*, allowing company moneys to be used for the purpose of other businesses connected with the controller of the company in disregard of the corporate personalities and interests of the companies involved).   [218] [2011] 2 BCLC 541.

[219] *Re Verby Print for Advertising Ltd, Fine v Secretary of State for Trade and Industry* [1998] 2 BCLC 23 at 39; *Official Receiver v Key* [2009] 1 BCLC 22.

[220] See *Re Verby Print for Advertising Ltd, Fine v Secretary of State for Trade and Industry* [1998] 2 BCLC 23; *Official Receiver v Dhaliwall* [2006] 1 BCLC 285.   [221] [1991] 3 All ER 578.

[222] [1991] BCLC 325 at 337. See *Re Hopes (Heathrow) Ltd, Secretary of State for Trade and Industry v Dyer* [2001] 1 BCLC 575; *Re Structural Concrete Ltd, Official Receiver v Barnes* [2001] BCC 578; *Secretary of State for Trade and Industry v McTighe (No 2)* [1996] 2 BCLC 477 at 486–7f.

though it may be possible to establish that trading has been at the risk of or to the detriment of the creditors.[223] Where the period during which the non-pressing debts have accrued is short, or where the amount outstanding is not a substantial proportion of the company's total deficiency, the court may be reluctant to conclude that there was a policy of non-payment.[224] A related issue is the non-payment of Crown debts (i.e. sums sue to HM Revenue and Customs in respect of PAYE, National Insurance and VAT receipts) which often account for a significant proportion of the deficiency on liquidation. Initially the courts regarded the non-payment of Crown debts as particularly culpable,[225] but in *Re Sevenoaks Stationers (Retail) Ltd*[226] the Court of Appeal rejected this approach. The issue is the significance of that non-payment and whether it is part of a deliberate decision by the directors only to pay those creditors who press for payment and to retain sums which should have been paid to creditors (be they the Crown or otherwise) to fund the company's continued trading.[227] As noted, that discrimination in itself is evidence which justifies a finding of unfitness.

Consequences of acting while disqualified

25-92　It is a criminal offence punishable by imprisonment or a fine or both for a person to act in breach of a disqualification order or undertaking or while an undischarged bankrupt or subject to a bankruptcy restriction order or undertaking (CDDA 1986, ss 11 and 13). A civil liability applies under CDDA 1986, s 15 whereby any disqualified person who, in contravention of a disqualification order or undertaking, is involved in the management of a company may incur personal liability for the debts of the company contracted at that time. The liability also applies to any person who is involved in the management of the company and who acts or is willing to act on instructions given without leave of the court by a person whom he knows at that time to be disqualified.[228] This liability has a significant deterrent effect by making it risky for a co-director to act with a disqualified person in the management of a company.

25-93　The effect of CDDA 1986, s 15 was considered in *Re Prestige Grindings Ltd, Sharma v Yardley*[229] where the court held that it confers on each creditor a direct statutory right of action against the disqualified director in respect of the debt owed to the creditor by the company, but the right must be exercised by individual creditors and it is not open to a liquidator to use the section as a representative of all the creditors. On the facts here, the Inland Revenue and Customs as an individual creditor was able to claim the debt due to it by the company from the two directors on the grounds of one of them acting while disqualified and the other acting on the instructions of someone whom he knew to be disqualified. Likewise in *Inland Revenue Commissioners v McEntaggart*[230] where an undischarged bankrupt who acted as a director was liable for the company's debts due to

---

[223] See *Official Receiver v Key* [2009] 1 BCLC 22 at [75], where the court was critical of the failure of the OR to bring charges other than a charge of a policy of unfair discrimination (which policy could not be found on the facts) where there was evidence of trading in disregard of creditor interests and the payment of preferences to connected persons which, had they been alleged, might have resulted in a lengthy period of disqualification.

[224] See *Official Receiver v Key* [2009] 1 BCLC 22 at [64]; *Re Verby Print for Advertising Ltd, Fine v Secretary of State for Trade and Industry* [1998] 2 BCLC 23 at 39.

[225] See *Re Lo-Line Electric Motors Ltd* [1988] 2 All ER 692 at 698, per Browne-Wilkinson V-C.

[226] [1991] BCLC 325.

[227] [1991] BCLC 325 at 337. See also *Re GSAR Realisations Ltd* [1993] BCLC 409 at 412, per Ferris J; *Re Verby Print for Advertising Ltd, Fine v Secretary of State for Trade and Industry* [1998] 2 BCLC 23.

[228] As to whether they are willing so to act, note the presumption in CDDA 1986, s 15(5).

[229] [2006] 1 BCLC 440.　　[230] [2006] 1 BCLC 476.

the Revenue. The court noted that, in effect, CDDA 1986, s 15 imposes a collateral liability on the part of the disqualified directors for the debts of the company. Furthermore, as liability is in respect of recovery of a debt by a third party, it is not open to the director to seek relief under CA 2006, s 1157 which allows the court to grant relief where a director has been held liable to the company for negligence, default, breach of duty or breach of trust (see **13-53**). To have a direct claim in this way is valuable, but there is little evidence of many creditors being in a position to take advantage of this direct liability. Apart from this (occasional) civil liability, in practice, there is little policing of disqualification orders and undertakings once they have been put in place. Such enforcement action as occurs is likely to arise only when the conduct of the disqualified director has been brought to the attention of the Secretary of State in some way, such as where a further venture collapses or a member of the public complains.

26

Corporate takeovers and reconstruction

A Introduction

26-1 In this chapter we examine aspects of the regulation of takeovers and mergers. The conventional meaning of 'takeover' is the acquisition by one company (the bidder) of sufficient shares in another company (the target) to give the bidder control of the target company. In the Takeover Code (see **26-15**), the bidder company is described as the offeror company and the target company is described as the offeree company. 'Merger' means the uniting of two companies, but as this is possibly done through an acquisition by one company of a controlling holding of shares in another, it is not surprising that the terms 'takeover' and 'merger' have become almost synonymous. 'Merger' is often used to describe a recommended takeover bid rather than a hostile one, i.e. one opposed by the board of the offeree company, and often it will be a combination of two companies of similar sizes and the consideration will be shares in the merged entity. Essentially takeovers involve bids for publicly traded companies. In the case of private companies and public companies which are not publicly traded a sale of the company is normally a matter for private negotiation rather than a formal takeover bid.

26-2 Takeovers are the means by which business expansion occurs. Companies may seek vertical integration (i.e. takeovers of companies at different stages in the production process) or horizontal integration (takeovers of companies at the same stage of the production process) or seek to diversify, as in the case of conglomerates. Takeovers tend to be associated in the public mind with aggressive or predatory management. In practice, a management that wishes to expand a company's business may have a choice of doing so via organic growth or through an acquisition or merger and may choose the latter simply because of the advantage it offers in terms of shorter time-scales.

26-3 As with any major investment decision, there may be a variety of motives for a company making a takeover bid for another company.[1] For example, a company may be concerned about its access to raw materials or vital components and thus seek a merger with one of its suppliers. It may be concerned to safeguard outlets for its products and so seek to merge with or take over one of its distributors or dealers. A company may want to diversify its activities by taking over a company in a completely different field. Equally, companies may be motivated less by economic considerations and more by financial or fiscal ones of improving the appearance of their balance sheet or reducing their liability to tax. Directors too may be motivated in part by personal 'empire-building' rather than any grand corporate strategy.

---

[1] For a readable account of the issues from a business perspective, see Moeller & Brady, *Intelligent M&A* (2007).

26-4 More broadly, for many years, there has been a debate (mainly conducted by economists) about whether takeovers and mergers are generally beneficial or harmful to the overall economy.[2] The economic argument in favour of takeovers essentially is that the business synergies arising from the deal result in efficiency gains and lower costs as the new management extracts higher value from the company's assets. Takeovers thus enable less productive or less efficient management to be replaced by more efficient management and it is in this way that takeovers are said to form part of the market for control of corporate assets.[3] Even an unsuccessful takeover bid, or the mere threat that a takeover bid could be made, acts as a discipline and a spur to efficiency by ensuring that management make the most productive use of resources under their control. Finally, takeovers offer shareholders the opportunity to recover a premium on their investment.

26-5 On the other hand, it is argued that there is little evidence that hostile bids perform a disciplining function (and often little evidence of prior underperformance by the target) and, even when there is a disciplining effect, it is argued that a takeover is a costly way of dealing with an underperforming incumbent management, occurring in only a random and opportunistic way, and requiring significant fees to advisers who may in fact be instrumental in initiating many takeovers.[4] The critics of takeovers would argue that improved corporate governance mechanisms (such as better board monitoring, better informed non-executive directors and more active investors) could be used to address underperforming management in a less expensive and disruptive way.[5] Fears have also been expressed that takeovers, or the threat of takeovers, far from leading to productive use of assets, compel managements to concentrate too much on short-term profitability to boost the share price and ward off a takeover while avoiding long-term investment and innovation.[6] There is also controversy as to the motivation of the offeror company's management in pursuing a bid and the cost of the bid to the offeror company's shareholders (much of the evidence suggests that these shareholders may be the losers in any takeover bid).[7] Offeror shareholders do have an opportunity to have their say on acquisitions

---

[2] See generally Romano, 'A Guide to Takeovers: Theory, Evidence and Regulation' in Hopt & Wymeersch (eds), *European Takeovers—Law and Practice* (1992); also Cranston, 'The Rise and Rise of the Hostile Takeover' in the same volume; Fairburn & Kay (eds), *Mergers and Merger Policy* (1989); Chiplin & Wright, *The Logic of Mergers* (1987).

[3] See Bradley, 'Corporate Control: Markets and Rules' (1990) 53 MLR 170; Fairburn & Kay (eds), *Mergers and Merger Policy* (1989), Introduction; Jensen and Ruback, 'The Market for Corporate Control' (1983) 11 J of Fin Econ 5; Manne, 'Mergers and the Market for Corporate Control' (1965) 73 J of Pol Econ 110.

[4] Franks & Mayer, 'Hostile Takeovers and the Correction of Management Failure' (1996) 40 J of Fin Econ 163; also Franks, Mayer and Renneborg, 'Managerial Disciplining and the Market for (partial) Corporate Control in the UK' in McCahery et al (eds), *Corporate Governance Regimes: Convergence and Diversity* (2002).

[5] See Moerland, 'Alternative Disciplinary Mechanisms in Different Corporate Systems' (1995) 26 J of Econ Behaviour & Organization 17; Coffee, 'Institutional Investors as Corporate Monitors: Are Takeovers Obsolete' in Farrar (ed), *Takeovers, Institutional Investors and the Modernization of Corporate Laws* (1993); Baums, 'Takeovers versus Institutions in Corporate Governance in Germany' in Prentice & Holland (eds), *Contemporary Issues in Corporate Governance* (1993); Marsh, *Short-termism on Trial* (1990).

[6] There are renewed concerns as to whether the pressure which takeovers exert on target company management contributes to problems of short-termism in UK companies, see BIS, *A Long-term Focus for Corporate Britain, A Call for Evidence* (October 2010), Ch 6; also Kay review, *Review of UK Equity Markets and Long-Term Decision Making,* launched by BIS in 2011 (examining the mechanisms of corporate control and accountability provided by UK equity markets and their impact on the long-term competitive performance of UK businesses). The Kay review provided an interim report in February 2012 and its final report is expected in July 2012.

[7] See Moerland, 'Alternative Disciplinary Mechanisms in Different Corporate Systems' (1995) 26 J of Econ Behaviour & Organization 17 at 29, 30.

where the offeror company has a Premium Listing of equity shares, see **19-100** as the Listing Rules require shareholder approval of major transactions (including a takeover) and the need to seek shareholder approval can act as a constraint on acquisitive boards.[8]

An offer for shares

26-6   A takeover bid in the form of an offer for shares is an offer made by the offeror company to the offeree company's shareholders to acquire their shares. The offeror may offer cash for those shares, or shares in the offeror company, or a combination of cash and shares.

A scheme of arrangement

26-7   The other standard mechanism used to effect a takeover or merger or reconstruction is a scheme of arrangement under court supervision. Appendix 7 to the Takeover Code (introduced in 2007, given the increasing use of schemes) specifically addresses how the Takeover Code applies to a takeover effected by a scheme. Essentially, the aim is that the Takeover Code should apply in the usual way with necessary modifications to accommodate a court-based scheme. The decision as to whether to proceed with a contractual offer or a scheme of arrangement depends on a variety of factors such as whether the approach is hostile or friendly (a hostile approach normally cannot proceed under a scheme, for the assistance of the offeree board is required to convene the various meetings required by a scheme) and the time-scale envisaged (a scheme may prove quicker in some circumstances than a bid). There may well be taxation issues (stamp duty is usually less on a scheme) and even political considerations (particularly if there are cross-border elements) where jurisdictions may have a preference as to the manner in which control changes hands. The major attraction of using a scheme is that the 75% approval required for a scheme binds all the members (or the creditors in a reconstruction, as the case may be) (CA 2006, s 899(3)). The disadvantages of schemes relate to the complexity of the class meetings required—if the classes are constituted improperly, the court will refuse to sanction the scheme (see **26-99** et seq)—and the costs involved, given the court involvement.

B The regulatory framework

26-8   The regulatory framework is found in the Takeover Code administered by the Takeover Panel and the Companies Act 2006, Pts 26–28, which together reflect the pre-existing

---

[8] Hence, from time to time, there are examples of offeror boards withdrawing bids once they realise that their shareholders are not likely to approve the transaction, see, for example, 'G4S chief admits error as ISS deal collapses', Financial Times, 1 November 2011. BIS sought views on whether this requirement for shareholder approval should be extended to shareholders of acquiring companies in all cases, but found no support for an extension beyond the requirements of the Listing Rules. A practical problem is that many offerors will not be UK companies and therefore to impose the requirement only on UK companies would place them at a competitive disadvantage, see BIS, *A Long-term Focus for Corporate Britain, A Call for Evidence* (October 2010), para 6.8, and BIS, *Summary of Responses* to that consultation (March 2011), paras 80–84. Likewise the Takeover Code Committee, in reviewing the Code in 2010, considered extending protections to offeror shareholders, see PCP 2010/2, n 65, section 7, but considered that this would constitute a major expansion of the Takeover Panel's role (the principal focus of the Takeover Code being the protection of the offeree shareholders) and therefore accepted the view of the majority of respondents who opposed any such change, see RS 2010/22, n 65, paras 4.7–4.11.

domestic position and also the requirements of the Takeover Directive.[9] The Takeover Directive was under negotiation from 1989 (albeit intermittently) before being adopted in 2004 and coming into force on 20 May 2006.[10] The European Commission considered it important to secure a Takeover Directive to ensure that shareholders of listed companies, especially minority shareholders, throughout the internal market should enjoy equivalent safeguards in the event of a change of control. The Takeover Directive was seen also as a key element in the integration of financial markets and specifically included in the Financial Services Action Plan which aimed to ensure a single financial market.

26-9 The Takeover Directive applies to takeover bids for securities of a company governed by the law of a Member State where all or some of the securities are admitted to trading on a regulated market in the EU (art 1). The Directive is a minimum standards Directive laying down a framework of principles as well as detailed rules as to the conduct of the bid, disclosure requirements etc. The impact of the Directive is reduced by a variety of Member State opt-outs which were necessary to secure the adoption of the Directive. In particular, Member States are allowed to opt out of two important provisions, art 9 on frustrating action by company boards and art 11, the breakthrough provision (the detail of these provisions is discussed at **26-52** and **26-53** respectively).[11] Nevertheless, given the history of the Directive, it was an achievement merely to have secured a framework for the conduct of takeovers throughout the EU. The real merit of the Takeover Directive may lie therefore in providing those Member States with little experience of takeovers with a framework for their domestic regulation rather than requiring them to devise a regulatory system for themselves.

26-10 In the UK, initially, there were concerns about the effect which the Takeover Directive would have on the position of the Takeover Panel and on the Panel's decision-making and rule-making powers. One of the often identified strengths of the Takeover Code is the flexibility inherent in the requirement to adhere to the spirit of the Code rather than rigid adherence to rules and the ability to change the Code quickly to meet changing market practices and it was not clear that that flexibility could be retained under the Directive. There were also concerns about the potential loss of speed of decision-making by the Panel and possible limits on the discretion of the Panel, within the framework of the General Principles, to grant dispensations from the Code.[12] Now it is clear that the adoption of the Directive did not have any significant impact on takeover practices in the UK and the Panel has reported that the overall picture, post-implementation of the Directive, is one of business as usual.[13]

The Companies Act 2006

26-11 The regulatory framework for takeovers is provided by CA 2006, Pts 26–28:

---

[9] 13th EC Directive on Company Law Concerning Takeover Bids, Directive 2004/25/EC, OJ L 142, 30.04.2004, p 12 ('the Takeover Directive').

[10] The first proposal for a Takeover Directive was put forward by the European Commission in 1989: see OJ C 64/8 14.03.1989. It was revised in 1990: see OJ C 240/7, 6.09.1990; in 1996: see Com (95) 655, 7.02.1996; in 1997, see OJ C 378, 13.12.97; followed by a new proposal in 2002, see OJ C 45 E, 25.02.2003, p 1.

[11] See Clarke, 'Articles 9 and 11 of the Takeover Directive and the Market for Corporate Control' [2006] JBL 355.

[12] For the background to implementation of the Takeover Directive, see the Explanatory Memorandum to SI 2006/1183, the interim regulations which implemented the Directive pending the commencement of the CA 2006; also DTI, *Implementation of the European Directive on Takeover Bids, A Consultative Document* (2005), URN 05/511.

[13] See Takeover Panel, Annual Report for 2006–07, p 9 which noted that there were no signs that the independence of the Panel, its constitution or its efficacy had been adversely affected by implementation.

- Part 26, ss 895–901, deals with schemes of arrangement which, while of wider application, can be used to effect a takeover, see **26-82**.

- Part 27 deals with mergers and divisions of public companies. This Part implements the Third and the Sixth Company Law Directives which address mergers and divisions of public companies within a single Member State.[14] They are of limited significance in this jurisdiction since they apply to mergers by way of the transfer of assets and liabilities from one company to another, whereas acquisition by the purchase of the shares in the entity rather than the underlying assets is the mechanism commonly used here. The package is completed by the Tenth Company Law Directive[15] which facilitates mergers of companies from different Member States and was implemented by the Cross-Border Mergers Regulations 2007.[16] These matters are not considered further in this chapter (though some cross-border mergers effected under these regulations will be subject to the Takeover Code which is the subject of this chapter).[17]

- Part 28 implements the Takeover Directive and, for the first time, places the Takeover Panel on a statutory footing as the designated supervisory authority for the purposes of the Directive, but, as we shall see, apart from this necessary implementation of the Directive and the statutory underpinning of the regulatory activities of the Panel, the Government has been content to leave the content of the Code and its application very much to the Panel as before.

Other regulatory issues

26-12   Quite apart from company law issues, takeovers provide the context in which issues of market abuse or manipulation may arise, for example through improper financial assistance (contrary to CA 2006, s 678, see **20–125**) given to effect a share support scheme to boost the offeror company's share price.[18] The price of the offeror's shares can be crucial if the consideration being offered to the offeree company's shareholders includes shares in the offeror. Many of these price-support schemes and other manipulations of the markets ahead of or during a bid fall within the market abuse provisions of the Financial Services and Markets Act 2000 which is policed by the Financial Services Authority (FSA)[19] (to be replaced from 2013 by the Financial Conduct Authority). The Panel and the FSA work closely together[20] and regard is had by the FSA to the extent to which the behaviour under

---

[14] Third Company Law Directive 78/855/EEC concerning mergers of public limited liability companies, now codified as Directive 2011/35/EU, OJ L 110/1, 29.04.2011; Sixth Company Law Directive 82/891/EEC concerning the division of public limited liability companies, OJ L 378/47, 31.12.1982.

[15] Directive 2005/56/EC on cross-border mergers of limited liability companies, OJ L 310/125.11.2005.

[16] See The Companies (Cross-Border Mergers) Regulations 2007, SI 2007/2974.

[17] See Takeover Panel Practice Statement No 18 on the application of the Takeover Code to transactions effected pursuant to these regulations.

[18] For an example of a share support scheme on a massive scale, see DTI, *Guinness plc, Investigation under ss 432(2) and 442 of the Companies Act 1985* (1997); also *Panel Report on the various hearings and appeal by Guinness: Takeover Panel, Guinness plc/The Distillers Company plc* (1989); [1989] JBL 520.

[19] See *FSA Handbook, Market Conduct Rules*.

[20] For example, the FSA will not normally make public the fact that it is or is not investigating a particular matter, or any of the findings or conclusions of an investigation. However, it may make an announcement that it is not investigating a particular matter where the matter in question has occurred in the context of a takeover bid, and the FSA has not appointed, and does not propose to appoint, investigators, and considers (following discussion with the Takeover Panel) that such an announcement is appropriate in the interests of preventing or eliminating public uncertainty, speculation or rumour: *FSA Handbook, Enforcement Guide*, para 6.2.

scrutiny complies with the Takeover Code although it is not determinative as to whether it amounts to market abuse. The FSA will not take action against a person over behaviour which (1) complies with the Takeover Code and (2) falls within the safe harbours provided by the FSA Code of Market Conduct which states that behaviour so conforming does not amount to market abuse.[21] In any case where the FSA is of the opinion that any potential exercise of its enforcement powers[22] may affect the timetable or the outcome of a takeover bid, the FSA consults the Takeover Panel before taking any steps to exercise its powers and the FSA is required to give due weight to the Panel's views.[23] Where the Takeover Panel is in a position to require appropriate redress, the FSA will not generally exercise its own powers to seek restitution.[24]

26-13 Takeovers also present the ideal occasion for insider dealing, as information before and during a bid is highly price-sensitive inside information which can have a dramatic effect on the share prices of the companies involved, especially the offeree company. Individuals who have inside information from an inside source are subject to prohibitions on dealing in price-affected securities, encouraging another person to deal, and communicating the inside information to another person, all of which are offences in the circumstances set out in Part V of the Criminal Justice Act 1993. These broader dimensions to the regulation of takeovers therefore also need to be borne in mind.

26-14 Finally, any takeover or merger may raise competition issues, either nationally or at the EU level. Competition issues are beyond the scope of the work and readers are referred to the specialist works on competition law.

C The Takeover Panel

Composition and role

26-15 Set up in 1968, the Takeover Panel is an independent body which issues and administers the City Code on Takeovers and Mergers,[25] hereinafter the Takeover Code. As the Introduction notes, the Takeover Code is not concerned with the financial or commercial advantages or disadvantages of a takeover, nor with matters such as competition policy.[26] The Code is designed principally to ensure shareholders are treated fairly and are not denied an opportunity to decide on the merits of a takeover and that shareholders in the offeree company of the same class are afforded equivalent treatment by an offeror. The Code provides an orderly framework within which takeovers are conducted[27] and it is also designed to promote, in conjunction with other regulatory regimes, the integrity of the financial markets. It is not the purpose of the Code either to facilitate or impede takeovers. The Code is said to represent the collective opinion of those professionally

---

[21] See FSMA 2000, s 120; as to the safe harbours with respect to the Takeover Code, see *FSA Handbook*, MAR 1.10.3–1.10.6.

[22] i.e. under FSMA 2000, s 380 (injunctions and restitution), s 381 (injunctions in cases of market abuse).

[23] *FSA Handbook, Enforcement Guide*, para 10.3(11).

[24] *FSA Handbook, Enforcement Guide*, para 11.3(6).

[25] At the time of writing, the current edition is the 10th edition of the Takeover Code published in September 2011 and the full text (300 pages long) is available on the Panel's website: www.thetakeover-panel.org.uk. See generally, Weinberg & Blank on *Takeovers and Mergers* (5th edn) (a looseleaf work); The Takeover Code developed out of the Notes for Amalgamations of British Businesses issued in 1959 by the Issuing Houses Association. For the historical background, see Johnston, *The City Takeover Code* (1980).

[26] Takeover Code, Introduction, para 2(a).   [27] Takeover Code, Introduction, para 2(a).

involved in the field of takeovers as to appropriate business standards and as to how fairness to shareholders and an orderly framework for takeovers can be achieved.[28]

26-16 The Panel is the designated supervisory authority for the purposes of the Takeover Directive and it is obliged to make rules as required by the Directive. Though the requirement to implement the Takeover Directive has meant putting the Panel on a statutory footing, the Panel remains an unincorporated body and it is not a statutory body constituted by the statute (CA 2006, s 942).[29] This approach to implementation of the Takeover Directive is designed to give effect to the Directive without unduly impinging on the manner in which the Panel operates (see **26-22)**. The Panel has up to 35 members, up to 22 of whom are appointed by the Panel. The remaining members are nominated by major financial and business institutions.[30] The Panel has overall responsibility for the policy, financing and administration of the Panel's functions and for the functioning and operation of the Code.[31] The Panel has a number of committees, one of which is the Code Committee with responsibility for rule-making and for keeping the Code under review and for consulting on, making and issuing amendments to the Code.[32]

26-17 The day-to-day work of takeover supervision and regulation is carried out by the Panel Executive which operates independently of the Panel.[33] The Panel Executive is available for consultation and may give guidance and rulings on the interpretation, application or effect of the Code.[34] The Executive or the Panel may take active steps to regulate the conduct of a bid while it is in progress, for example by requiring announcements or clarifications from the parties.

26-18 Rulings of the Executive are subject to review by the Hearings Committee which is a committee of the Panel (CA 2006, s 951(1)). The Hearings Committee can also be convened where the Executive wishes to refer a matter to the Committee without itself giving any ruling where it considers that there is a particularly unusual, important or difficult point at issue. Disciplinary proceedings may be instituted by the Executive before the Hearings Committee where it considers that there has been a breach of the Code or of a ruling of the Executive or of the Panel.[35] The Takeover Appeal Board is an independent body which hears appeals against rulings of the Hearings Committee (CA 2006, s 951(3)). The chairman and deputy chairman of the Appeal Board must usually have held high judicial office

---

[28] Takeover Code, Introduction, para 2(a). The courts may on occasion look to the Takeover Code to identify what is good practice on a particular matter: see *Fiske Nominees Ltd v Dwyka Diamond Ltd* [2002] 2 BCLC 108.

[29] See *Explanatory Notes to the Companies Act 2006*, paras 1180–1181.

[30] The bodies represented include: the Association for Financial Markets in Europe (three representatives); the Association of British Insurers; the Association of Investment Companies; the Association of Private Client Investment Managers and Stockbrokers; the British Bankers' Association; the Confederation of British Industry; the Institute of Chartered Accountants in England and Wales; the Investment Management Association; and the National Association of Pension Funds.

[31] Takeover Code, Introduction, para 4(a). The Panel must publish an annual report: CA 2006, s 963.

[32] Takeover Code, Introduction, para 4(b).

[33] CA 2006, s 942(3); Takeover Code, Introduction, para 5. Headed by a Director General, the Executive is staffed by a mixture of employees and secondees from City organisations, investment banks, accountancy and law firms.

[34] Takeover Code, Introduction, para 5. The Executive issues Practice Statements from time to time. Any person in doubt as to whether a proposed course of conduct is in accordance with the Takeover Code must consult the Executive in advance and legal or other professional advice on the interpretation or application of the Code is not an appropriate alternative to obtaining a ruling from the Executive: Takeover Code, Introduction, para 6(b). [35] Takeover Code, Introduction, para 7(a).

and are appointed by the Master of the Rolls. The Appeal Board may confirm, vary, set aside, annul or replace a contested ruling.[36]

26-19 The Panel is the designated supervisory authority for the purpose of the Takeover Directive with power to make rules[37] and it must make rules giving effect to the Directive.[38] The Panel has retained its traditional flexibility in that it may permit derogations from the rules in particular cases and with regard to any circumstances (CA 2006, s 944(1)(d)), subject to the Panel giving reasons for any derogation or modification of a rule and provided, in the case of a transaction and rule subject to the requirements of the Directive, that the General Principles (see **26-31**) are respected.[39]

26-20 In addition to making rules, the Panel may give rulings on the interpretation, application and effect of the rules (CA 2006, s 945(1)) and, for the first time, the rulings of the Panel have binding effect (s 945(2)). The rules may confer power on the Panel to give directions to restrain a person from acting or continuing to act in breach of the rules or to restrain a person from doing or continuing to do a particular thing, pending determination of whether that conduct is or would be a breach of the rules; and otherwise to secure compliance with the rules (s 946). Failure to comply with the rules or with a direction of the Panel may attract sanctions under s 952, see **26-25**.

26-21 The Panel has significant powers to require by notice in writing the production of such documents and information as it may reasonably require in connection with the exercise of its functions (CA 2006, s 947), subject to an exception regarding documents or information covered by legal professional privilege (s 947(10)) and subject to the privilege against self-incrimination (s 962). There are restrictions on the onward disclosure of information obtained by the Panel (other than with the consent of the person or business in question) backed up by criminal sanctions (ss 948–949), subject of course to a wide range or permitted disclosures to facilitate the carrying out by the Panel of any of its functions (CA 2006, s 948(3)).

Challenging the Panel

26-22 One of the concerns with the implementation of the Takeover Directive and the designation of the Takeover Panel as the supervisory authority was that this might expose the Panel to greater legal challenge. In order to reduce the possibilities of tactical or nuisance litigation, the Takeover Directive makes it clear (in art 4(6)) that it is for the Member States to designate judicial or other authorities responsible for dealing with disputes and to regulate whether and under which circumstances parties to bids are entitled to bring administrative or judicial proceedings. The position in the UK, laid down in *R v Panel on*

---

[36] Takeover Code, Introduction, para 8.

[37] CA 2006, ss 942(2), 943(2). This general power to make rules is expressed very broadly in s 943(2). In particular, rules may be made with regard to any matter similar to a matter provided for by the Panel as it operated prior to the passing of the CA 2006: s 943(3).

[38] CA 2006, s 943. See the *Explanatory Notes to the Companies Act 2006*, paras 1180–1188: the specified articles of the Takeover Directive in respect of which rules must be made are the general principles (art 3.1), jurisdictional rules (art 4.2), matters relating to protection of minority shareholders, mandatory bid and equitable price (art 5), contents of the bid documentation (art 6.1–6.3), time allowed for acceptance of the bids and publication of the bid (arts 7 and 8), obligations of the management of the target company (art 9) and other rules applicable to the conduct of bids (art 13). The Government decided that the Panel would not make rules with regard to art 11 (barriers to takeover), arts 15 and 16 (squeeze-out and sell-out provisions) and art 10 (information to be published by companies in the annual reports), it being preferable to deal with these matters in the CA 2006.   [39] Takeover Code, Introduction, para 2(c).

Take-overs and Mergers, ex p Datafin plc[40] is that judicial review is possible, but only once a bid is completed and only with a view to a declaration as to how future bids might be conducted[41] so as to enable the Panel not to repeat any error or to relieve individuals of any disciplinary consequences of an erroneous decision.[42]

26-23   A similarly pragmatic approach was taken recently by David Richards J in *Re Expro International Group plc*[43] which concerned a takeover effected through a scheme of arrangement which, as noted at **26-7**, is governed by Appendix 7 of the Takeover Code. The court refused to delay court sanction of a scheme to see whether another bid might emerge for the company. Richards J said he was concerned that there should, if possible, be a common approach to the conduct of bids, whether they are structured as an offer or as a scheme. He did not think it desirable that the court procedure involved in a scheme should allow in an undesirable level of uncertainty which the provisions of the Code have successfully reduced or eliminated in the case of ordinary offers. Under the Takeover Code rules, the prospective bidder had been asked by the Panel to 'put up or shut up' (see **26-36**) and having failed to put up in accordance with that requirement, the court was not willing to open up the whole situation again by adjourning the application for sanction of the scheme. The Panel subsequently noted that 'on this evidence it does not appear that there is any current likelihood of the courts playing a more active role in determining the outcome of offers'.[44]

26-24   In implementing the Takeover Directive, a number of measures were included specifically to limit the scope for tactical litigation by:[45]

(1) providing initially for appeals from decisions of the Executive to go to the Hearings Committee and from there to the Takeover Appeal Board chaired by a former member of the judiciary before there is recourse to the courts, see **26-18**;

(2) excluding any new right of action for breach of statutory duty for a breach of the Panel's rules (CA 2006, s 956);

(3) protecting concluded transactions from challenge for breach of the Panel's rules (CA 2006, s 956(2) provides that any contravention of a rule-based requirement does not make any transaction void or unenforceable or affect the validity of any other thing);

(4) exempting the Panel and its individual members, officers and staff, from liability in damages for things done in the discharge of the regulatory functions of the Panel, save in the case of bad faith (CA 2006, s 961).

---

[40]   [1987] 1 All ER 564, CA; noted Hilliard (1987) 50 MLR 372; (1987) 103 LQR 323; See Hilliard, 'The Take-over Panel and the Courts' (1987) 50 MLR 372 at 377: '...a Panel subject to review the scope of which is so hedged about with qualification that any notion of substantive supervision is illusory'. See also Lord Alexander, 'Judicial Review and City Regulators' (1989) 52 MLR 640.

[41]   Though the emphasis in that case on the Panel's lack of legal authority has been overtaken by the CA 2006.

[42]   [1987] 1 All ER 564 at 579, CA. See also *R v Panel on Takeovers and Mergers, ex p Guinness plc* [1989] 1 All ER 509, CA: the test is whether something has gone wrong with the Panel's procedure so as to cause real injustice and require the intervention of the court. Panel's decision not to adjourn a hearing of a concert party allegation could be criticised, but overall the conduct of the Panel had been fair and had not caused injustice. See also *R v Panel on Takeovers and Mergers, ex p Fayed* [1992] BCLC 938; noted Morse, 'Panel disciplinary hearings and judicial review' [1992] JBL 596.   [43]   [2010] 2 BCLC 514.

[44]   See Takeover Panel, *Annual Report for 2007–08*, p 14.

[45]   See the Explanatory Memorandum to SI 2006/1183, para 47, see n 12. See generally Mukwiri, 'The Myth of Tactical Litigation in UK Takeovers' (2008) JCLS 373; Ogowewo, 'Tactical Litigation in Takeover Contests' [2007] JBL 589.

Sanctions for breach of the Takeover Code

26-25 The rule-making powers of the Takeover Panel extend to rules conferring power on the Panel to impose sanctions on a person who has acted in breach of the rules or failed to comply with a direction given by the Panel (CA 2006, s 952). The rules may confer a power on the Panel to order a person to pay such compensation as it thinks just and reasonable, but it is a limited power to order compensation only where the rule which has been breached requires the payment of money (CA 2006, s 954(1)).

26-26 In addition to acting to provide redress for shareholders, the Panel may also consider disciplinary action as appropriate.[46] The Panel Executive may deal with the matter if the person agrees to the facts and the action proposed by the Executive, or the matter may go to the Hearings Committee.[47] If the Hearings Committee finds a breach of the Code or of a ruling of the Panel, it may issue a private statement of criticism or a public statement of censure, though only a handful of statements are issued in any year.[48] The controversial takeover of Cadbury by Kraft in 2010 did prompt a public statement of censure where Kraft made a number of statements as to the continued operation of one of Cadbury's UK factories. The issue had been the subject of much public debate in circumstances where, because it was a hostile takeover, Kraft was not able to verify the facts surrounding the statements.[49] Within days of completing the takeover, Kraft had to concede that it was not possible to reverse Cadbury's earlier decision to close the factory having discovered that Cadbury had already spent £100m on a new facility in Poland to which production would be transferred. The Panel Executive accepted that Kraft had an honest and genuine belief that it could keep the factory open, but given it did not know the details of Cadbury's plans, the Panel concluded that it should not have made the statements in the form in which it did. Kraft's belief, no matter how well-intentioned, was not a belief which Kraft had a reasonable basis for holding.[50] The Panel Executive therefore concluded that Kraft was deserving of public censure for not meeting the standards of care and accuracy required by Code rule 19.1 with respect to statements made during the course of an offer. Rule 19 emphasises that every document or statement published or made during the course of an offer must be prepared with the highest standards of care and accuracy.

26-27 In addition to statements of criticism or censure, the Hearings Committee may suspend or withdraw or make conditional any exemption, approval or other special status

---

[46] Takeover Code, Introduction, paras 10, 11(b). The available sanctions are all sanctions which the Panel was able to impose prior to the commencement of CA 2006, Pt 28. If the Panel wishes to adopt any new sanctions, it can only do so in accordance with the procedure set out in s 952(3): s 952(2). These limitations on the power to devise new sanctions were added to the legislation to meet concerns expressed by the House of Lords Delegated Powers and Regulatory Reform Committee, see 9th Report, Session 2005–06, HL Paper 86, para 15; 680 HL Debs, GC307, 28 March 2006.   [47] Takeover Code, Introduction, para 11(a).

[48] In 2010–11, the Panel issued five private statements of criticism and one public statement of censure; in the preceding year the corresponding figures were nine and none: see Takeover Panel, *Annual Report for 2010–11*, p 15. For examples of public criticism, see Takeover Panel Statement 2007/29, *iSoft Group plc* and Statement 2007/06, *Plusnet plc*, available at www.thetakeoverpanel.org.uk, although as Morse notes: 'the whole concept of "public" criticism in this context is a highly specialised one': see Morse, 'Assessing the Impact of the Takeover Panel's Takeover Code Committee—Takeover Code reform institutionalised?' [2003] JBL 314 at 325.

[49] See Takeover Panel Statement, 2010/14, 'Kraft Foods Inc Offer for Cadbury plc' (May 2010).

[50] Interestingly, the Panel did not think that the failures of Kraft's financial advisers (to make further enquiry of Kraft as to the basis of its belief that it could keep the UK factory open) were sufficient to merit public censure.

which the Panel has granted or it may report the offender to a UK or overseas regulatory authority or professional body (most notably the FSA) so that authority or body can consider whether to take disciplinary or enforcement action.[51] Also, the Hearings Committee may publish a Panel Statement indicating that the offender is someone who, in the Hearings Committee's opinion, is not likely to comply with the Code.[52] The rules of the FSA and certain professional bodies oblige their members not to act for that person in a transaction subject to the Takeover Code (so-called 'cold-shouldering').[53] It is a feature of the Code that it applies to a wide variety of professionals involved in bids including company advisers, especially financial advisers, and the directors of companies subject to the Code, all of whom are expected to be aware of and to comply with their responsibilities under the Code.[54] It is the professionals and the directors who must operate in the London marketplace who are most susceptible to the Panel's disciplinary powers and who would be most concerned about any possible cold-shouldering.

26-28   The Panel alone may apply to the court for a court order to secure compliance with any rule-based requirement or any disclosure requirement[55] (CA 2006, s 955). The court will only make an order if it is satisfied that there is a reasonable likelihood that a person will contravene a rule-based requirement or has contravened a rule-based requirement or a disclosure requirement.

D The conduct of takeovers under the Takeover Code

Application of the Code

26-29   The Takeover Directive applies to takeover bids for securities of a company governed by the law of a Member State where all or some of the securities are admitted to trading on a regulated market in the EU;[56] the reach of the Takeover Code is wider, as discussed at **26-30**. A key issue when the Takeover Directive was being negotiated was which supervisory authority would have control of the bid in circumstances where a company might have its registered office in one Member State while admitted to trading on a regulated market in another Member State. The compromise reached is to allow for shared jurisdiction in certain circumstances. A further jurisdictional issue was whether it was appropriate

---

[51] The FSA enforcement powers are extensive and include public censure, fines, prosecutions, the removal of authorisation, the imposition of injunctions and orders for restitution: see *FSA Handbook, Enforcement Guide.*

[52] See Takeover Code, Introduction, para 11(b)(iii). This sanction will normally remain effective for a specified period. The Takeover Panel's website contains only two examples of cold-shouldering, one in 1992, the other in 2010. The latter concerns three individuals 'cold-shouldered' for a period of three years as a result of a finding that they acquired shares in a company as members of a concert party in a deliberate attempt to circumvent the mandatory rule provisions (see rule 9) and further declined to assist the Panel in its investigation of the circumstances of the share acquisition; see the details in the Takeover Appeal Board decision 2010/1.   [53] See *FSA Handbook* MAR 4.3.3–4.3.5.

[54] Takeover Code, Introduction, para 3(f).

[55] A disclosure requirement is defined as any requirement to disclose documents or information under CA 2006, s 947, see **26-21**. The unusual wording ('rule-based requirement') was criticised in the Parliamentary debates, but the Government stated that it was 'perfectly functional' and that it was clear that this requirement includes any decisions or rulings of the Panel made pursuant to the rules: 680 HL Debs, GC313, 28 March 2006.

[56] A regulated market is a market within the meaning of the Markets in Financial Investments Directive, Directive 2004/39/EC, (Mifid), art 47, OJ L 145, 30.04.2004, p1.

for what might be described as company law issues to be determined by any state other than the state of incorporation. On this issue the solution devised by the Takeover Directive is to draw a distinction between bid issues to do with consideration and procedures[57] and employee and company law issues to do with information, voting control and frustrating action by directors, with the latter issues, in keeping with the core rule of private international law, remaining subject to the law of the state of incorporation (art 4(2) (e)). Consideration and procedural matters then are subject to the rules of the Member State of the competent authority supervising the bid. Employee and company law issues are matters for the Member State in which the offeree company has its registered office. This distinction drawn between 'consideration and procedural issues' and 'employee and company law' matters is not very clear, but has not given rise to difficulties to date.

26-30 These elaborate jurisdictional requirements are reflected in the Takeover Code which also has to allow for the traditional jurisdiction of the Panel which extends to bids for all public companies (not just those publicly traded) and even to some private companies. The Code essentially applies to (and therefore the Panel has jurisdiction):[58]

(1) all offers (not falling within paragraph (3) below) for companies (including SEs see **2-45**) which have their registered offices in the UK, the Channel Islands or the Isle of Man if any of their securities are admitted to trading on a regulated market in the UK or on any stock exchange in the Channel Islands or the Isle of Man;

(2) all offers (not falling within paragraph (1) above or paragraph (3) below) for public and private companies (including SEs)[59] which have their registered offices in the UK, the Channel Islands or the Isle of Man and which are considered by the Panel to have their place of central management and control in the UK.

In either of these cases, the Code is concerned with regulating takeover bids and merger transactions of the relevant companies, however effected, including by means of statutory merger or a scheme of arrangement.[60]

(3) Shared jurisdiction—UK and other EEA registered and traded companies. The Code also applies to offers for the following companies:[61]

---

[57] Bid issues are matters relating to the consideration offered in the case of a bid, in particular the price, and matters relating to the bid procedure, in particular the information on the offeror's decision to make a bid, the contents of the offer document and the disclosure of the bid.

[58] See Takeover Code, Introduction, para 3. As the Code Committee has noted, 'broadly, the Code applies by reference to the offeree company's country of registration, regardless of the nationality of the offeror and regardless of the offeror's legal form,' see PCP 2010/2, n 65, para 7.3.

[59] Private companies only if their securities have been listed or traded or marketed or been the subject of a public offer during the 10 years prior to the date on which an announcement is made of a proposed or possible offer for the company: see Takeover Code, Introduction, para 3(a)(ii).

[60] Takeover Code, Introduction, para 3(b). The Takeover Code is also concerned with regulating other transactions (including offers by a parent company for shares in its subsidiary, dual holding company transactions, new share issues, share capital reorganisations and offers to minority shareholders) which have as their objective or potential effect (directly or indirectly) obtaining or consolidating control of the relevant companies, as well as partial offers (including tender offers) to shareholders for securities in the relevant companies.

[61] 'Offers' in this context means only any public offer (other than by the company itself) made to the holders of the company's securities to acquire those securities (whether mandatory or voluntary) which follows or has as its objective the acquisition of control of the offeree company: Takeover Directive, art 2; Takeover Code, Introduction, para 3(b). 'Control' is a matter to be defined by each Member State and is defined in the Takeover Code as 'an interest, or interests, in shares carrying in aggregate 30% or more of the voting rights of a company, irrespective of whether such interest or interests give de facto control'. See Takeover Code, Definitions.

(a) a company which has its registered office in the UK whose securities are admitted to trading on a regulated market in one or more Member States of the European Economic Area (EEA) but not on a regulated market in the UK.

In cases within this category, the Code applies in respect of 'employee information and company law matters'; 'consideration and procedural matters' are governed by the rules of the Member State supervising the bid.

(b) a company which has its registered office in another Member State of the EEA whose securities are admitted to trading only on a regulated market in the UK.[62]

In this case, the Code applies in respect of 'consideration and procedural matters' and 'employee information and company law matters' are governed by the rules of the Member State where the offeree company has its registered office.

General Principles

26-31 The Takeover Code is based upon a number of General Principles which are also set out in art 3 of the Directive (though their origin was the Takeover Code which has long been based on a series of General Principles). The General Principles are expressed in broad terms and they are essentially statements of standards of commercial behaviour which are applied by the Panel in accordance with their spirit to achieve their underlying purpose.[63] The General Principles are:

(1) All holders of the securities of an offeree company of the same class must be afforded equivalent treatment; moreover, if a person acquires control of a company, the other holders of securities must be protected.

(2) The holders of the securities of an offeree company must have sufficient time and information to enable them to reach a properly informed decision on the bid; where it advises the holders of securities, the board of the offeree company must give its views on the effects of implementation of the bid on employment, conditions of employment and the locations of the company's places of business.

(3) The board of an offeree company must act in the interests of the company as a whole and must not deny the holders of securities the opportunity to decide on the merits of the bid.

(4) False markets must not be created in the securities of the offeree company, of the offeror company or of any other company concerned by the bid in such a way that the rise or fall of the prices of the securities becomes artificial and the normal functioning of the markets is distorted.

(5) An offeror must announce a bid only after ensuring that he/she can fulfil in full any cash consideration, if such is offered, and after taking all reasonable measures to secure the implementation of any other type of consideration.

(6) An offeree company must not be hindered in the conduct of its affairs for longer than is reasonable by a bid for its securities.

26-32 These principles can be expressed as the following broad propositions: treat all shareholders of the offeree company in an equivalent way; give the shareholders time to reach an informed judgement; directors must remember that it is for the shareholders to decide on

---

[62] For the position if the securities are admitted to trading on more than one regulated market, but are not admitted to trading on the regulated market where the company has its registered office, see Takeover Code, Introduction, para 3(a)(iii)(C). [63] Takeover Code, Introduction, para 2(b).

the bid; there must be no market abuse, no offers if the offeror cannot afford the deal and no laying siege to the offeree company.

The rules governing takeover bids

26-33   In addition to the General Principles, the Takeover Code contains a series of rules (currently 38) with extensive accompanying notes—the latest (2011) edition of the Code runs to 300 pages. The rules must be interpreted in order to achieve their underlying purpose and the spirit as well as the letter of a rule must be observed.[64] The 2011 Code reflects a number of significant amendments made following a review of the Code[65] initiated by the Code Committee (see **26-16**) in response to the debate concerning the regulation of takeovers which was sparked by the contentious takeover of Cadbury plc by Kraft Foods in 2010. The subsequent changes to the Code were intended, essentially, (a) to reduce the perceived tactical advantage which hostile offerors had acquired over the boards of offeree companies (needing only over 50% to gain control and with short-term investors willing to sell out) and to redress the balance in favour of the offeree company[66] and (b) to improve the offer process and to take more account of persons affected by takeovers in addition to offeree company shareholders, especially employees, and in that regard to improve communication between the board of the offeree company and the company's employee representatives.[67] Critics would argue that one consequence may be to give the offeree company's board too much power with respect to potential offers (in particular the ability to agree an inducement fee with a white knight when a hostile offer is already on the table, see **26-60**) and that the changes may act ultimately to the disadvantage of shareholders in the offeree company. Meanwhile, a broader debate about the contribution of takeovers to the UK economy continues.[68]

Announcements and secrecy

26-34   As noted, General Principle 4 emphasises the importance of preventing false markets and a key obligation in that regard is the timely release of announcements relating to a possible offer for a company.[69] Prior to any announcement of an offer or a possible offer,

---

[64] Takeover Code, Introduction, para 2(b).

[65] The review process started with a public consultation paper, 'Review of Certain Aspects of the Regulation of Takeover Bids' (June 2010), PCP 2010/2, followed by a Code Committee response statement (same title) RS 2010/22. There followed a further public consultation paper, PCP 2011/1 (March 2011), (same title), setting out the detailed amendments to the Code required to implement RS 2010/22, followed by a further Code Committee response statement, RS 2011/1, July 2011 (same title). Given the significance of the changes, the Code Committee intends to review the operation of the amendments, looking at a period of at least 12 months, post-implementation, depending on the level of bid activity during the period, see RS 2011/1, para 1.13. See, generally, Clarke, 'Reviewing Takeover Regulation in the Wake of the Cadbury Acquisition – Regulation in a Twirl' [2011] JBL 299.

[66] See RS2010/22, n 65, paras 3.1–3.2 which sets out the factors which the Committee believes gave the offeror a tactical advantage (for example, the long drawn out virtual bid, their destabilising effects, the pressure to agree deal protection measures) etc.

[67] See RS 2011/1, n 65, para 1.2; PCP 2011/1, n 65, para 1.1.

[68] In addition to the Code Committee's review, the HC Business, Innovation and Skills Committee reviewed the Cadbury/Kraft deal and its aftermath, see 9th Report, Session 2009–10, 'Mergers, Acquisitions and Takeovers: the Takeover of Cadbury by Kraft' (HC 234) and the Government's Response, CM 7915, July 2010. The Government followed up on the 'long-term' issues highlighted in the HC report with further consultations and review, see BIS, *A Long-term Focus for Corporate Britain, A Call for Evidence* (October 2010), Ch 6; also the Kay review, *UK Equity Markets and Long-Term Decision Making* which is expected to report in 2012, see n 6.

[69] See Panel Practice Statement No 20, *Rule 2, Secrecy, Possible offer announcements and pre-announcement responsibilities*, para 1.1.

it is crucial that all concerned treat the information surrounding the offer as secret (rule 2.1(a)) for information regarding a pending takeover bid is highly price-sensitive and provides significant opportunities for insider dealing. As the Panel has noted, if secrecy is maintained, it should be possible for offer preparations to be conducted in private without an announcement of a possible offer being required.[70]

26-35   An announcement of an offer is required when a firm intention to make an offer is notified to the board of an offeree company by or on behalf of an offeror, irrespective of the attitude of the board to the offer (rule 2.2(a)) or when an obligation to make a mandatory bid arises (rule 2.2.(b), see **26-65** on mandatory bids). Additionally, an announcement of a possible offer may be required where there are rumours about a bid or untoward movement in the offeree's share price in which case the offeree board, if it has already been approached, must make the announcement (rule 2.2(c)). Likewise, if there is rumour and speculation or untoward price movement etc and there is reason for concluding that it is the potential offeror's actions which have led to this situation,[71] but the board of the offeree company has not been approached, then the offeror must make an announcement, as it must where discussions of a possible offer are to be extended beyond a very restricted number of persons (other than those who need to know in the parties concerned or their immediate advisers)[72] so secrecy will be impossible to maintain (rule 2.2 (e)).

'Put up or shut up'

26-36   As noted at **26-33**, the Code was reviewed in 2011 and that review concluded, *inter alia*, that there was a need for a rebalancing of the Code in favour of the board of the offeree company to reduce the advantages which 'hostile' offerors (i.e. those not recommended by the board of the offeree company from the outset) were perceived to have over the board of the offeree company.[73] Concerns had already arisen and been partially addressed as to the length of time during which the offeree board and company were in effect under siege and destabilised by 'virtual' bids where offerors made 'possible offer' announcements subject to pre-conditions, creating uncertainty for boards, shareholders and markets as to whether an offer would then actually materialise. In response, the Panel had devised a regime involving the issuing of a 'put up or shut up' notice, following a request to do so from the offeree company, setting a time frame within which the potential offeror had to announce either a firm intention to make an offer or that it did not intend to make an offer.[74] That 'put up or shut up' regime has now been modified and formalised in the Code. Now any announcement which commences an offer period must identify any potential offeror with which the offeree company is in talks or from which an approach has been received (and not unequivocally rejected).[75] This announcement automatically[76]

---

[70]   See Statement No 20, n 69, para 2.1.

[71]   Takeover Code, rule 2.2(d); and see rule 2.4 on the announcement of a possible offer and see rule 2.5(c) on pre-conditions to a possible offer.

[72]   The general position is that a proposed offer can be discussed with up to six 'persons' before an announcement is required under rule 2.2.   [73]   See RS 2011/1, n 65, para 1.2.

[74]   A description of the practice which had developed in respect of possible offers can be found in PCP 2010/2, n 65, paras 8.4–8.22.

[75]   Takeover Code, rule 2.4(a). The announcement must identify all potential offerors if there are more than one at the time when the requirement to make an announcement arises; and see RS 2011/1, n 65, para 2.12. A potential offeror can avoid being named by 'downing tools', see note 4 on rule 2.2, but then that offeror cannot return to the table for a period of six, or possibly, three months.

[76]   It was thought that making the matter automatic would mean that the offeree board could not be pressurised into a different time frame and that a standard deadline avoids endless discussions between the parties and the Panel as to the appropriate deadline, see RS 2011/1, n 65, para 2.29.

sets in train a standard 28-day period after which the potential offeror must announce a firm intention to make a bid, or state that it has no intention to bid in which case it is bound by that statement for a period of six months (rule 2.6(a)), or an extension to the period is requested by the offeree board. It is expected that the Panel will normally consent to a request for an extension from the board of the offeree company, though it will not make a decision on the matter until close to the deadline (rule 2.6(c)).[77] Once any offeror announces a firm intention to make an offer, the 28-day period lapses for those other potential offerors (rule 2.6(b))[78] and they have in effect until day 50 of that first bid to announce their intentions.[79] Once an announcement setting in train the 28-day period has been made, there is no need to publicly identify any subsequent potential offerors who emerge unless they are identified specifically in rumour and speculation so that an announcement is then required in respect of them, or the offeree company makes a statement about the existence of a new potential offeror, in which case that subsequent announcement must identify the new potential offeror.[80]

26-37 The Code Committee made these changes regarding identification of possible offerors and the automatic 28-day period despite critics who argued that the changes would deter offerors from making approaches who would not want to be associated with a 'failed' bid if they are subsequently unable to make a firm offer within the 28-day period. It was argued also that the time period was so short that it might prevent offerors (particularly private equity bidders) from being in a position to proceed with an offer and so it would have the effect of depriving shareholders of possible bids.[81] The Code Committee was undeterred, noting the importance of removing the tactical advantage of anonymity that potential offerors often enjoy over offeree companies and the importance that shareholders and other market participants attach to the identity of the potential offeror.[82] The Code Committee also considered that the changes will incentivise potential offerors to improve and maintain secrecy surrounding their plans precisely so as not to trigger the 28-day period before they are ready to proceed and this outcome will have the additional benefit of helping to minimise leaks of price-sensitive information.[83] Additionally, the Code Committee thought that the short time frame will discourage potential offerors from making premature approaches to the offeree so reducing the siege effect[84] and, if the offeree board is supportive (which hands some negotiating power to the board of the offeree company), it will be straightforward for a potential offeror to get an extension

---

[77] The board of the offeree company may ask for different extensions for different offerors and may decline to ask at all so there is some scope here for the offeree board to exert some pressure on potential offerors. In order to prevent all potential offerors from making their approach conditional on the offeree board agreeing to seek an extension, the Code Committee suggested that the Panel should only decide on an extension at a time close to the deadline and in the light of the status of the negotiations between the parties at that time, see RS 2011/1, n 65, para 2.34.

[78] The Code Committee explained that in the situation where there is a firm intention to make an offer, the uncertainty created by a virtual bid falls away and there is no need for the 28-day period to be maintained, see RS 2011/1, n 65, para 2.28.   [79] See Takeover Code, note 3 on rule 2.6.

[80] The result will be differing 28-day periods applicable to different potential offerors, see RS 2011/1, n 65, para 2.31–2.32.

[81] RS 2011/1, n 65, paras 2.4, 2.19; The Code Committee conceded that two-thirds of respondents to the consultation paper opposed this change, see paras 2.3, 2.18; also RS 2010/22, n 65, paras 5.5–5.11.

[82] RS 2010/22, n 65, paras 5.5–5.11, also RS 2011/1, paras 2.5, 2.7.

[83] See RS 2011/1, n 65, paras 2.5, 2.11, 2.26; also RS 2010/22, n 65, para 5.7.

[84] See RS 2011/1, n 65, para 2.11; the Code Committee believes that 28 days is an appropriate period to bring the 'virtual bid' to an end, given the disruption it causes and that the offeror does not have the support of the offeree board, see paras 2.25, 2.26; also RS 2010/22, n 65, para 5.7.

to the 28-day period.[85] Of course, if the offeree company board is not willing to seek an extension, and the potential offeror is not able to announce a firm intention to proceed at the end of the 28 days, then costs have been incurred, but the offeror must retire from the contest for at least six months. There is an exemption from the requirement to identify potential offerors and from the application of the 28-day period if the offeree company has commenced a formal sale process[86] (the exemption lasts so long as the potential offeror is participating in the sale process) which might give offeree companies an incentive to take this route in some circumstances rather than wait for an approach.[87]

A firm intention to make an offer

26-38 An offeror or its advisors must notify a firm intention to make an offer first to the board of the offeree company or to its advisers and the board of the offeree or its advisers must make an immediate announcement when a firm intention to make an offer is notified to the board.[88] The content of the announcement of a firm intention to make an offer is prescribed in detail and must indentify the offeror (rule 2.7(c)). Once an offeror has announced a firm intention to make an offer, the offeror must proceed to make the offer unless, and in accordance with rule 13 governing pre-conditions, the offer was subject to pre-conditions which have not been met (rule 2.7(b)). This restriction on the right to withdraw is imposed in order to prevent offerors making opportunistic bids based on particular market conditions or attempting to manipulate the market with no intention of carrying through a bid. The Panel will not normally give consent to the withdrawal of a bid merely because market conditions have altered and the offer is now at an unrealistically high price. Parties can include a material adverse change clause which allows the offer to be withdrawn in certain limited circumstances. The Panel's practice is that, to invoke such a clause, the offeror must demonstrate that the relevant circumstances are of very considerable significance striking at the heart of the purpose of the transaction, but the test does not require the offeror to demonstrate frustration in the legal sense.[89]

Financing the bid—the price—the costs

26-39 If, in the three months prior to the commencement of the offer period, the offeror purchases shares in the offeree company, the offer to shareholders of the same class must be on no less favourable terms, unless the Panel otherwise agrees (rule 6.1). Likewise, if, during the offer, the offeror buys shares at above the offer price, the offer price for all must be correspondingly increased (rule 6.2). An offeror must be sure that it is able to fund the offer and, to avoid any distortion of the market or the misleading of the shareholders, an offeror should announce a firm intention to make an offer only after the most careful and responsible consideration and only when the offeror has every reason to believe that it can and will continue to be able to implement the offer and responsibility in this connection also rests on the financial adviser to the offeror (rule 2.7). Considerably more disclosure is required now by an offeror of its funding arrangements, irrespective of whether the offer is for cash or shares (previously, less information was required in the case of a

---

[85] See RS 2011/1, n 65, para 2.26.
[86] See RS 2010/22, n 65, para 5.8; and RS 2011/1, n 65, paras 2.39–2.41.
[87] See Takeover Code, note 2 on rule 26.   [88] See Takeover Code, rule 1(a); rules 2.2–2.3.
[89] See Panel, Practice Statement No 5, *Rule 13.5(a) – invocation of conditions*. The issue of material adverse change (MAC) clauses was reviewed by the Panel in the context of an offer by WPP Group Plc for Tempus Group plc when the Panel rejected an attempt by WPP Group plc to rely on the terrorist attacks on the US on 11 September 2001 as triggering a MAC clause: see the Panel Statement 2001/15, *Offer by WPP Group Plc for Tempus Group plc*, 6 November 2001. The Practice Statement clarifies the Panel's practice in the light of the Panel Statement in the WPP case.

cash offer). As the Code Committee has acknowledged, financing issues concern wider constituencies than just the offeree company shareholders.[90] Detailed disclosure is therefore required in the offer document as to how the offer is to be financed and the source or sources of financing together with the amount of each debt facility, the names of the principal financing banks, the interest rates, any security provided, a summary of the key covenants and any refinancing requirements (rule 24.3(f)).[91] The offeror company will also have to include a statement of the effect of full acceptance of the offer on its earnings, assets and liabilities (rule 24.3(a)(vi)).

Publicity and information to shareholders and employees

26-40 The essential obligations with respect to the publication of each offer document and offeree board circular are that:

(1) they are sent to every shareholder and person with information rights and made readily available to employee representatives or employees (rule 24.1(a), rule 25.1(a));

(2) they are published on the same day on a website and an announcement made via a regulatory information service that they have been so published (rule 24.1(b), rule 25.1(b)).

Employee interests

26-41 One of the main changes in the 2011 Takeover Code is the increased prominence given generally to employee interests.[92] As soon as an offer period commences[93] (and not just when a formal bid is made) a copy of the relevant announcement must be made readily available to the employee representatives (broadly defined)[94] or, if there are none, to the employees themselves (rule 2.12(a)). At that time the representatives or the employees must be informed of their right to have an opinion on the effects of the offer on employment appended to the offeree board's response circular when published[95] and of their right to have the offeree company meet the costs reasonably incurred in obtaining advice required for the verification of information contained in the representatives' opinion (rule 2.12.(d)).[96]

---

[90] See PCP 2011/1, n 65, para 6.1; RS 2011/1, n 65, para 6.7; also PCP 2010/2, n 65, para 5.10; and RS 2010/22, n 65, paras 5.29–5.32.

[91] See also Takeover Code, rule 26 which requires certain offer-related documents to be available on a website of the relevant party for the duration of the offer including any documents relating to the financing of the offer. The Code Committee noted that this level of financial information is needed to assist the reader in analysing the balance sheet and debt of the combined group following the completion of the proposed transaction: RS 2011/1, n 65, para 6.23.

[92] See RS 2010/22, n 65, paras 5.33–5.39; also RS 2011/1, n 65, para 8.1; PCP 2011/1, n 65, section 7.

[93] See Takeover Code, Definitions: An offer period will commence when the first announcement is made of an offer or possible offer for a company, or when certain other announcements are made, such as an announcement that a purchaser is being sought for an interest in shares carrying 30% or more of the voting rights of the company or that the board of the company is seeking potential offerors.

[94] See Code, Definitions: an employee representative is: (a) a representative of an independent trade union, where that trade union has been recognised by the offeror or the offeree company in respect of some or all of its employees; and (b) any other person who has been elected or appointed by employees to represent employees for the purposes of information and consultation.

[95] Though little use is made of this provision by employees, see PCP 2010/2, n 65, para 5.19.

[96] The limits to the costs for which the company is responsible are explained in note 1 on rule 25.9 and see RS 2011/1, n 65, para 8.16, but obviously there is some potential here for significant additional costs to be added to the bill.

26-42   Once a formal offer is made and an offer document is sent to the shareholders, that offer document must disclose the offeror company's intentions vis-à-vis the offeree company and the continued employment of its employees and management including any material change in the conditions of employment; its strategic plans for the offeree company and their likely repercussions on employment and the locations of the offeree company's places of business; and its intentions with regard to any redeployment of the fixed assets of the offeree company (rule 24.2(a)).[97] The Code Committee has suggested that this information should be as detailed as possible on the basis of information known to the offeror at the time the statement is made which will include knowledge of the fundamental business rationale for seeking to acquire the offeree company.[98] Crucially, the offeror company must make a negative statement if it has no plans regarding these matters or if it considers that its strategic plans for the offeree will have no repercussions on employment, etc (rule 24.2(b)). Furthermore, any statement on these matters, whether in the offer document or in any other statement or document made during an offer period, will be expected to hold true for a period of at least one year from the date on which the offer period ends (or a shorter[99] or longer period specified in the statement) unless there has been a material change of circumstances (note 3 to rule 19.1). The Code Committee notes that it would expect the Panel to investigate any complaint from an interested person of any breach of this requirement with the normal disciplinary steps to follow if the Panel finds a breach.[100] Indeed, a rare public censure was issued to Kraft Foods in this type of situation, as discussed at **26-26**, an outcome which is likely to have a salutary effect on offerors and their advisers in future.

26-43   In addition to the information on the offeror's intentions so far as they affect the employees, the content of the offer document is prescribed in great detail by rule 24.3 and it must include details of a website where the offeror company's audited consolidated accounts for the past two financial years are published and this financial information is incorporated by reference into the offer document. Subsequent documents (whether from the offeror or the offeree) must contain details of any material changes in information previously published by or on behalf of the relevant party during the offer period (rule 27).[101]

26-44   The response circular is crucially important if the board of the offeree company is to dissuade the shareholders from accepting the offer and it must set out the opinion of the offeree board on the offer and its reasons for forming its opinion and must include its views on: (i) the effects of implementation of the offer on all the company's interests, including, specifically, employment; and (ii) the offeror's strategic plans for the offeree company and their likely repercussions on employment and the locations of the offeree company's places of business as set out in the offer document (rule 25.2).[102] In formulating

---

[97] The offeror is also required to disclose its intentions with regard to the maintenance of existing trading facilities for the offeree company's relevant securities which may be of importance to the shareholders in the offeree company: rule 24.2(a)(iv).

[98] See RS 2011/1, n 65, para 7.8, which notes that a general statement is not likely to be satisfactory in the context of a recommended offer.

[99] The Code Committee notes that, if a very short period is specified, readers will draw their own conclusions, see RS 2011/1, n 65, para 7.13.

[100] See RS 2011/1, n 65, para 7.17.

[101] The Code Committee has indicated that it intends to consult in due course on amending rule 27 to require parties to disclose material changes promptly and on a continuing basis, not just when a subsequent document is sent to shareholders and persons with information rights, see RS 2011/1, n 65, para 3.11.

[102] Where a takeover bid has been made, the directors must provide sufficient information to enable shareholders to make an informed decision and they must refrain from giving misleading advice or exercising their fiduciary powers in ways which would prevent shareholders from making an uninhibited choice:

its response to any offer, of course, the board will be guided by its obligations under CA 2006, s 172 to promote the success of the company for the benefit of the members as a whole, see Chapter 9.[103] The board is required to obtain competent independent advice on the offer and the circular must include the substance of this advice (rule 3.1).[104] The Code Committee noted that a perception had arisen (wrongly) in the market that the offeree board was required to consider the offer price as the determining factor in deciding whether to recommend an offer. The Code Committee has emphasised and the Code now states that the Code does not limit the factors that the board of the offeree company is able to take into account, in particular it is not limited to the interests of the current shareholders, and there is no requirement to consider the price to be the determining factor.[105] The offeree board circular must contain particulars of all service contracts of any director or proposed director of the offeree company with the company or any of its subsidiaries (rule 25.5).

26-45 Both the offer document and the offeree board circular now must contain comprehensive disclosure of the fees being expended on advisers to the bid which will give shareholders a better understanding of how much the bid is costing the respective companies and also will indicate whether, as is often alleged, advisers are driving some transactions because of the scale of fees involved. In addition to the aggregate fees and expenses expected to be incurred in relation to an offer, there must be a breakdown of the aggregate amount as between different types of advisers, for example, financial, legal, accounting and public relations advice and, in the case of an offeror, there must be an estimate of the fees and expenses expected to be incurred in relation to the financing of the offer (rule 24.16(a)).[106]

26-46 In the case of a takeover bid for a company that has securities carrying voting rights admitted to trading on a regulated market in the UK, criminal sanctions apply where there are failures to comply with the rules governing either the offer document or the response document. In the case of a non-compliant offer document, an offence is committed by the offeror and by any director or officer who knew that the offer document did not comply (or was reckless as to whether it did so) and failed to take reasonable steps to ensure that it did comply with the requirements of the rules (CA 2006, s 953(1)–(3)). In the case of a non-compliant response document, an offence may be committed by the directors or officers of the offeree company who knew that the response document did not comply (or was reckless as to whether it did so) and failed to take reasonable steps to ensure that it did comply with the requirements of the rules (s 953(4)).

Re a Company [1986] BCLC 382; *Dawson International plc v Coats Paton* plc [1989] BCLC 233; *Gething v Kilner* [1972] 1 All ER 1166.

[103] Where the directors must only decide between rival bidders, the interests of the company must be the interests of the current shareholders, as the future of the company will lie with the successful bidder: *Heron International Ltd v Grade* [1983] BCLC 244 at 265.

[104] See also rule 3.3. as to disqualified advisers, also Practice Statement No 21, *Rule 3 – Independent Advice*.

[105] See Takeover Code, note to rule 25.2; also RS 2010/22, n 65, paras 5.21–5.22; PCP 2011/1, para 4.3. It is not the case that the board must inevitably be under a positive duty to recommend and take all steps within its power to facilitate whichever is the highest offer: *Re a Company* [1986] BCLC 382.

[106] See RS 2011/1, n 65, para 5.13. As some of the fees will be variable, and will therefore change from the published information, the Code also requires a material increase (more than 10%) in fees from the published figures to be disclosed to the Panel which will decide whether public disclosure is required in all the circumstances (rule 24.16(c), (d)).

26-47 The criminal sanction is deliberately limited to these two documents and applies only with respect to takeover bids as defined in CA 2006, s 953(1), i.e. takeovers within the Takeover Directive. The imposition of criminal sanctions in these circumstances was the subject of much debate in Parliament, but the Government's view was that these provisions were necessary in order to implement art 17 of the Directive which requires Member States to put in place sanctions which are effective, proportionate and dissuasive.[107] In the Government's view, the sanctions available to the Panel (see **26-25**) are inadequate for this purpose. In particular, there was a concern that there might be serious or deliberate misstatements in the documentation that might only come to light some time after the bid had been completed and in respect of which sanctions of the Panel would be inadequate.[108] Imposing a criminal liability is an appropriate way of closing that loophole, the Government said, especially given that the documentation is not only of direct concern to shareholders, but also to employees and others affected by the bid. In the Government's view, this is a carefully targeted offence aimed specifically at those who fail to comply with the bid documentation rules and it provides them with an incentive to take the task of drawing up these documents seriously.[109]

The timetable

26-48 General Principle 2 provides that the shareholders of an offeree company must have sufficient time and information to enable them to reach a properly informed decision on the bid. There are two guiding principles as far as the timetable of an offer is concerned: first that the duration of a bid should be limited; secondly, that the shareholders should have time for consideration and to obtain advice and information. It is important that the offer process is not so drawn out that uncertainty is created in the market and the management of the offeree company is distracted from the management of the business. This position is sometimes described as the siege principle—an offeree company must not be hindered in the conduct of its affairs for longer than is reasonable by a bid for its securities: General Principle 6. Once an offer is referred to domestic or European competition authorities, the offer period usually ends and a new offer period only begins when the competition process has ended and the offeror is allowed to proceed.[110] The Takeover Code requires that a bid be open for acceptances for not less than 21 days and for not more than 60 days, but the timetable may be extended, subject to the 'siege principle'.[111]

26-49 The timetable under the Takeover Code runs from the posting of the offer document, known as Day 1, which normally must be within 28 days of the announcement of a firm intention to make an offer (rule 24.1). The board of the offeree company must give advice (the response circular) to their shareholders by the end of Day 14, i.e. within 14 days of the publication of the offer document (rule 25.1). To ensure shareholders in the offeree company have time to consider the offer and are not rushed into acceptance, an offer must remain open for at least 21 days following the date on which the offer document is published so Day 21 is the first possible closing date for the offer (rule 31.1). After Day 39 there must be no further announcements by the board of the offeree company of any material new information (including trading results, profit or dividend forecasts, assets valuations or proposals for dividend payments or for any material acquisition or disposal) without

---

[107] See 680 HL Debs, GC 304–5, 28 March 2006. [108] See 680 HL Debs, GC 305, 28 March 2006.
[109] See 680 HL Debs, GC 305, 28 March 2006.

[110] Takeover Code, rule 12.2. A new offer proceeds only if the offer or potential offeror indicates within 21 days of being allowed to proceed that it does wish to proceed, otherwise the offer lapses (rule 12.2(b)(ii)).

[111] The respective periods in the Takeover Directive, art 7, are not less than two weeks and not more than 10 weeks, which also may be extended.

the consent of the Panel (rule 31.9) and Day 46 is the last date for revision of the offer by the offeror (rule 32.1(c)). Day 60 is the last possible closing date and no offer may be left open for more than 60 days without the consent of the Panel which may be granted, for example, if a competing offer is announced or the board of the offeree company consents to an extension (rule 31.6).[112]

26-50 At the end of Day 60, the offeror announces whether it has received sufficient acceptances. The offeror must secure acceptances for at least 50% of the voting rights to secure control and, if it is a voluntary bid, it may have stipulated (and usually does stipulate) that it requires 90% acceptances. If the offeror has secured the requisite level of acceptances, the offer goes unconditional as to acceptances and must be left open for a further 14 days (rule 31.4). Except with the consent of the Panel, the consideration for the offer must be posted within 14 days of the offer becoming unconditional (rule 31.8).

26-51 Where an offer has not become unconditional by Day 60 and has therefore lapsed, the offeror may not announce another offer or possible offer for the offeree company during the next 12 months nor acquire any shares which would oblige it to make a mandatory offer (see **26-65**), nor make any statement which raises or confirms the possibility that an offer might be made for the offeree company, except with the consent of the Panel (rule 35.1). This restriction can be of crucial importance to a company which has successfully resisted an unwelcome bid as it secures for it a breathing space before the offeror can return. The Panel will normally grant a dispensation from this restriction where, for example, the new offer is recommended by the board of the offeree company or the new offer follows the announcement by a third party of a firm intention to make an offer for the offeree company or the Panel determined that there has been a material change of circumstances (note (a) on rule 35.1).

Board neutrality

26-52 In a bid situation there is a clear conflict of interest between the board and the shareholders of the offeree company. The shareholders have an economic interest in receiving any available offers for their shares but the directors (who commonly lose their positions following a successful takeover) have an interest in warding off takeovers or in favouring takeovers from bidders who may have links to the directors or who make promises to them with respect to their positions. The directors may hinder other bidders who might be willing to offer a higher price for the shares. It is important therefore to limit the ability of directors to erect defences against takeovers save where they have the consent of the shareholders to do so.

26-53 Article 9(2) of the Takeover Directive provides that from the time when the board of the offeree company receives information that a bid is to be made until the result of the bid is made public or the bid lapses, the board of the offeree company must obtain the prior authorisation of the general meeting of shareholders before taking any action (other than seeking alternative bids) which may result in the frustration of the bid. In particular, the specific authorisation of the shareholders is required before the board issues any shares which may result in a lasting impediment to the offeror in acquiring control over the

---

[112] An accepting shareholder is entitled to withdraw his acceptance from the date which is 21 days after the first closing date of the initial offer (normally 42 days from the offer being made), if the offer has not by such date become or been declared unconditional as to acceptances, to the date when the offer is declared unconditional as to acceptances (rule 34.1).

offeree company. This article is designed to ensure that if a company is to be insulated from takeover bids, it is as a consequence of decisions taken by the shareholders and not by the directors. Further, as regards decisions taken before the board receives information that a bid is to be made, but not fully implemented, shareholder approval is also required where the matter in question does not form part of the normal course of the company's business and its implementation may result in the frustration of the bid.[113] The crucial importance of the board's role is underlined by General Principle 3 which provides that the board of an offeree company must act in the interests of the company as a whole and must not deny the holders of securities the opportunity to decide on the merits of the bid.

26-54   Article 9(2) is one of the optional articles of the Directive, however, and a number of Member States have chosen to opt out of this provision.[114] The UK opted into art 9 as it is consistent with the long-established position on frustrating action established by rule 21 of the Takeover Code.[115] Rule 21 provides that during the course of an offer, or even before the date of the offer if the board of the offeree company has reason to believe that a bona fide offer might be imminent, the board must not without the approval of the shareholders in general meeting:

'(a) take any action which may result in any offer or bona fide possible offer being frustrated or in shareholders being denied the opportunity to decide on its merits; or

(b) (i) issue any shares or transfer or sell, or agree to transfer or sell, any shares out of treasury;[116]

  (ii) issue or grant options in respect of any unissued shares;

  (iii) create or issue, or permit the creation or issue of, any securities carrying rights of conversion into or subscription for shares;

---

[113] See Takeover Directive, art 9(3). To facilitate the seeking of shareholder approval, a Member State may adopt provisions for the calling of meetings on short notice, but no shorter than two weeks: art 9(4).

[114] See generally Clarke, 'Articles 9 and 11 of the Takeover Directive and the Market for Corporate Control' [2006] JBL 355; also Gatti, 'Optionality Arrangements and Reciprocity in the European Takeover Directive' (2005) 6 EBOR 553. See Gerner-Beuerle, Kershaw and Solinas, 'Is the Board Neutrality Rule Trivial? Amnesia about corporate law in European Takeover Regulation' (2011) EBL Rev 559 who essentially argue that the board neutrality rule is probably unnecessary since Member States' corporate law already adequately controls board power.

[115] The European Commission's initial review of the implementation of the Takeover Directive found that 18 Member States had imposed or were expected to impose the board neutrality rule, but that for only one of these States was this a new requirement. Further, five of these Member States had introduced a reciprocity requirement, see n 114 so implementation had increased the management's powers to take frustrating action: see SEC (2007) 268, 21.02.2007, para 2.1.3(b).

[116] Directors are subject to various constraints in any event on their powers to allot shares including the proper purpose duty imposed by CA 2006, s 171(b): see Chapter 8. Statutory constraints on allotments are discussed at 19–30. As to the redemption or purchase of its own shares, note rule 37.3 which provides that, during the course of an offer, or even before the date of the offer if the board of the offeree company has reason to believe that a bona fide offer might be imminent, no redemption or purchase by the offeree company of its own shares may be effected without the approval of the shareholders at a general meeting. The notice convening the meeting must include information about the offer or anticipated offer. Where it is felt that the redemption or purchase is in pursuance of a contract entered into earlier or another pre-existing obligation, the Panel must be consulted and its consent to proceed without a shareholders' meeting obtained.

    (iv) sell, dispose of or acquire, or agree to sell, dispose of or acquire, assets of a material amount;[117] or

    (v) enter into contracts otherwise than in the ordinary course of business.'[118]

26-55 These restrictions on the actions which may be taken by the board without shareholder approval are imposed in order to prevent the board of an offeree company making the company unattractive to the offeror by disposing of the assets which the offeror most wishes to acquire or by increasing significantly the costs involved in dispensing with the incumbent management should the bid be successful. Directors are not prevented from seeking alternative bidders, so-called 'white knights', nor do these constraints prevent companies putting defensive measures in place before any bid is under contemplation. Increasingly companies have an in-built defence mechanism in the form of an unfunded pension deficit which makes a takeover prohibitively expensive for a bidder who may be required to make good that deficiency.

26-56 In the US, more exotic variations of these frustrating devices are described as 'poison pills'[119] and the courts here had a rare opportunity to consider the validity of so-called 'poison pill' arrangements in *Criterion Properties plc v Stratford UK Properties LLC*.[120] In this case, a managing director had his company enter into an agreement with a substantial shareholder (Oaktree) which amounted to a 'poison pill', i.e. a device designed to ensure that any would-be bidder for the company would be deterred from proceeding.[121] The effect of the agreement was to require the company to buy out Oaktree at a very high price in the event of any change of control of the company or certain changes in board personnel, including the removal from the board of the managing director who drew up and executed the agreement on behalf of the company. The managing director was sacked subsequently and the issue arose as to whether the agreement could be enforced against the company. In the Court of Appeal, Carnwath LJ commented briefly on the extent to which a 'poison pill' arrangement is permissible in English law. He agreed with counsel that it may be legitimate, depending on the circumstances, for the board to exercise its power to issue shares in order to deter a takeover which would cause serious economic harm to the company.[122] He also noted, however, that the gratuitous disposition of the company's assets for this purpose had never been upheld by any reported authority, whether in the US or the Commonwealth. Without having to determine the extent to which 'poison pills' limited to seeing off a particular predator might be permissible in English Law, the agreement in this case, he thought, went far beyond anything which could be justified for the purpose of deterring an unwelcome predator and could not be a reasonable exercise of the board's powers in the interests of the company.

26-57 On appeal to the House of Lords, their Lordships decided that the lower courts had wrongly focused on the role and knowledge of Oaktree and the case was remitted for trial on the issue identified by their Lordships as crucial, namely whether the directors who signed the agreement had authority, actual or apparent, to do so, see **8-63**. It was not necessary

---

[117] The Panel normally considers relative values of 10% or more as being of a material amount, but the amount could be less if the asset is of particular significance to the company: see Note 2 on rule 21.1.

[118] Entering into or amending a director's service contract is regarded as entering into a contract other than in the ordinary course of business if the new or amended contract or terms constitute an abnormal increase in the emoluments or a significant improvement in the terms of service: note 5 on rule 21.1.

[119] See Herzel & Shepro, *Bidders and Targets, Mergers and Acquisitions in the US* (1990), Ch 8.

[120] [2006] 1 BCLC 729, HL overruling [2003] 2 BCLC 129, CA. See Clarke, 'Regulating Poison Pill Devices' (2004) JCLS 51.

[121] As the agreement was entered into at a time when there was neither an offer nor a potential offer for the company, the provisions of the Takeover Code requiring shareholder approval did not come into play.

[122] See [2003] 2 BCLC 129 at 139.

therefore for their Lordships to consider the validity of a poison pill, but it is clear from Lord Scott's judgment that he was very doubtful that it could be permissible. First, he noted that whether it is open to a board of directors of a public company to authorise the signing on the company's behalf of a 'poison pill' agreement intended to deter outsiders from making offers to shareholders to purchase their shares is an issue of considerable public importance. Secondly, he queried whether directors could possibly have apparent authority to enter into an agreement which consisted of a contingent divesting of company assets which would not only deter an unwanted predator but also the most desirable of predators and which would have entrenched the chairman's and the managing director's continuance in their then offices.[123] Clearly, Lord Scott was very doubtful that such agreements, or at least such far reaching agreements, could be valid. That view is impliedly accepted by all concerned in takeovers and it is very unusual for companies here to adopt poison pill agreements. They would be contrary in any event to the spirit of General Principle 3 that the board must not deny the shareholders the opportunity to decide on the merits of the bid.

26-58   The Code draws attention to the responsibility of the board as a whole to monitor the conduct of a bid.[124] Directors of an offeror and the offeree company must always, in advising their shareholders, act only in their capacity as directors and not have regard to their personal or family shareholdings or to their personal relationships with the companies. It is the shareholders' interests taken as a whole, together with those of employees and creditors, which should be considered when the directors are giving advice to shareholders.

Deal protection measures—inducement fees and other offer-related arrangements

26-59   A particular issue in the takeover context is whether directors can agree with an offeror to recommend their bid and not to solicit other bids and not to co-operate with any other offeror that might emerge. While there was some initial uncertainty as to the position, its resolution appears from the decision of the Court of Appeal in *Fulham Football Club Ltd v Cabra Estates plc*[125] (a non-takeover case, see **10-47**). The court distinguished between directors fettering their discretion, which is prohibited,[126] and directors exercising their discretion in a way which restricts their future conduct, which is permissible, assuming that the exercise of that discretion can be justified as being in the interests of the company. It is therefore possible to enter into a lock-out agreement, but the directors must be able to justify that decision as being (in the language of CA 2006, s 172) to promote the success of the company. Given other potential offerors, a lock-out agreement is unlikely to be in the interests of the company, i.e. in the interests of the current shareholders which lie in the company being on the market for any bidder.[127] It is not their interests as sellers of their shares but their interests as members in an open market for corporate control which, of course, impacts on the value of their shares as any competing offer will necessarily be for a higher price. A lock-out agreement is therefore possible in theory, but any attempt to enforce it is likely to result in considerable debate as to whether the directors acted to promote the success of the company in entering into it and they will only do so if they leave open the possibility of recommending an alternative offer which, of course, weakens the 'lock-out' in the first place. Bidders had turned therefore to a whole range of break and inducement fees and other deal protection measures such

---

[123] [2006] 1 BCLC 729 at 740, HL.   [124] See Takeover Code, Appendix 3.
[125] [1994] 1 BCLC 363, CA; noted Griffiths (1993) JBL 576.
[126] *Motherwell v Schoof* (1949) 4 DLR 812 (Alta SC); *Selangor United Rubber Estates Ltd v Cradock (a bankrupt) (No 3)* [1968] 2 All ER 1073.   [127] See *Heron International Ltd v Grade* [1983] BCLC 244.

as exclusivity agreements as a method of ensuring the support of the offeree board or at least the payment of financial compensation for the withdrawal of that support.[128] A break or inducement fee is a contractual agreement whereby the offeree company agrees to pay the offeror a fee in the event of certain circumstances arising which result in the failure of the offeror's bid, such as the endorsement by the offeree board of a competing bid. These fee arrangements diminish the assets secured by the successful offeror (as a significant sum has to be paid to a failed bidder) and in effect transfer the risk of a failed bid from the (ultimately unsuccessful) offeror to the offeree company. The argument in favour of these arrangements essentially is that they bring bidders to the table since the potential offeror does not run the risk of having incurred significant irrecoverable costs in the event that the deal cannot be completed.

26-60 Following the Code review in 2011, however, the Code Committee recommended and the Code now includes a prohibition, except with the consent of the Panel, on any offer-related arrangements between the offeree company and any person acting in concert with it and any offeror or any person acting in concert with it during an offer period or when an offer is reasonably in contemplation (rule 21.2(a)). This has been a controversial change to the Code, but was justified by the Code Committee out of concerns that these deal protection measures had become standard 'packages' which offeree boards felt compelled to accept with little or no room for negotiation and that they impacted detrimentally on offeree shareholders by deterring other bidders from making an offer or led to offers being on less favourable terms that would otherwise have been available.[129]

For these purposes, 'offer-related arrangement' is widely defined as any agreement, arrangement or commitment in connection with an offer, including any inducement fee arrangement or other arrangement having a similar or comparable financial or economic effect (rule 21.2(b)). The offeror may seek commitments from the offeree board, however, as to (i) the confidentiality of information provided to the offeree company during the offer; (ii) the non-solicitation of the offeror's employees, customers or suppliers; (iii) the provision of information or assistance for the purpose of obtaining any official authorisation or regulatory clearance, (iv) irrevocable commitments and letters of intent (and these are likely to assume greater practical importance given that potential bidders can no longer enter into break fee or inducement fee arrangements); (v) arrangements imposing obligations only on the offeror or persons acting in concert with it; and (vi) agreements relating to any existing employee incentive arrangement.[130] Most significantly, there is an exemption from the general prohibition for an inducement fee arrangement (only) entered into with a subsequent offeror (a so-called 'white knight') after a non-recommended bid for the company is announced, but subject to a limit on the inducement fee or fees in aggregate (if inducement fee arrangements are entered into with more than one competing offeror) of normally not more in aggregate than 1% of the value of the offeree company and payable only if an offer becomes wholly unconditional (note 1 on rule 21.2). There is also an exemption where the offeree board puts the company up for sale for, in that case,

---

[128] For a detailed account of the offer-related arrangements which concerned the Code Committee, see PCP 2010/2, n 65, section 9 which explains the nature, development and use of these arrangements prior to the review of the Code in 2011.

[129] See PCP 2010/2, section 9; RS 2010/22, paras 5.12–5.20; n 65 above.

[130] The latter was added since they involve either the issue of shares or the payment of bonuses and it should be possible for the offeror and the offeree company to reach an agreement as to how these arrangements are to work so that all can have certainty as to the continued operation of the incentive agreement, see RS 2011/1, n 65, para 3.9.

the company is seeking a purchaser and may need or want to tie in an offeror through an inducement fee arrangement[131] (note 2 on rule 21.2).

26-61 As regards bids implemented via a scheme of arrangement where previously detailed implementation agreements containing comprehensive deal protection measures were commonly entered into, the Code allows the parties to the offer to include timing conditions within the scheme (as to a long-stop date by which the scheme must become effective and specific dates by which the shareholder meetings and court sanction hearing must be held, subject to the agreement of the parties to extend these dates) so giving the offeror some reassurance as to the timely progression of matters (Appendix 7, section 3(b)). While this option is useful, it is more limited in reach than the previously common implementation agreement so schemes may prove less popular in future. These conditions must be given prominent reference in the offeror's announcement of a firm intention to make an offer and the offeree company must implement the scheme in accordance with the expected timetable, but that timetable may cease to apply in certain circumstances, for example, if the board of the offeree company withdraws its recommendation of the scheme or seeks the adjournment of the scheme meetings (Appendix 7, section 3(f)).

26-62 Finally, there must be disclosure in the offer documentation of any offer-related arrangements which are permitted by rule 21.2 or are the subject of a dispensation by the Panel in accordance with rule 21.1 so as to enable the Panel and interested persons to see that the arrangement does not go further than is permitted (note 4 on rule 21.2).

Break-through provisions

26-63 There were concerns that imposing a requirement of board neutrality in the Takeover Directive would mean that companies in their Member States would be exposed to hostile takeovers while companies in other Member States with protective mechanisms (such as restrictions on the transfer of shares and on the exercise of voting rights) which are equally protective of incumbent management are not so exposed. The High Level Group of Company Law Experts, set up by the European Commission, considered that the solution to this lack of a level playing field lay in the introduction of 'break-through' provisions, i.e. provisions which break through structural defensive mechanisms and prevent them from operating to defeat an offeror.[132] Hence art 11 of the Takeover Directive contains a break-through provision, the effect of which is that certain restrictions on the transfer of securities and on voting rights, in certain defined circumstances, can be set aside so as to allow an offeror to 'break through' to gain control of a company. However, Member States may opt out of the break-through provision in art 11[133] and practically all have done so.[134]

---

[131] The Committee did not recommend the addition of an exemption to cover the situation where a company is in serious financial distress and might need to enter into an inducement agreement. The Committee thought it would be appropriate for the Panel to deal with that scenario through its general power of dispensation rather than provide a specific exemption, see RS 2011/1, n 65, para 3.22.

[132] See *Report of the High Level Group of Company Law Experts on Issues Related to Takeover Bids* (10 January 2002, Brussels), Ch 1.

[133] A Member State which opts out of art 11 must still give companies in that Member State the option of making use of such break-through provisions (art 12). In keeping with those obligations, in the UK companies may opt in (and subsequently opt out) of art 11 by way of a special resolution (CA 2006, ss 966–972).

[134] The European Commission found that, as at January 2007, only three Member States (Estonia, Latvia and Lithuania) had opted into art 11 and imposed on their companies a requirement to adhere to the break-through provision; see *Report on the Implementation of the Directive on Takeover Bids*, SEC (2007) 268, 21.02.2007, para 2.1.4.

Transparency requirements

26-64 As part of the effort to restrict the use of defensive measures by boards and companies, or at least to alert the market to the existence of defensive measures, article 10 of the Takeover Directive imposes extensive disclosure requirements which must be addressed in the directors' report.[135] These disclosure requirements are designed to bring greater transparency to the market and apply to all companies registered in the UK which have voting shares admitted to trading on a regulated market at the end of the relevant financial year and they apply annually regardless of whether or not the company is subject to a takeover bid.[136] The disclosure required focuses in particular on disclosure of the capital structures and mechanisms that could hinder an offeror in securing control of the company, such as restrictions on share transfer and on voting rights and the existence of cross-holdings. It also requires identification of the holders of any shares with special control rights and the disclosure of any agreements between shareholders that can affect voting or transfer rights that are known to the company (though the company is frequently unaware of these agreements). Disclosure is also required of any agreements between the company and its directors or employees providing for compensation for loss of office or employment (whether through resignation, purported redundancy or otherwise) that occurs because of a takeover bid.[137] The company must disclose any rules that the company has about appointment and replacement of directors, or amendment of the company's articles of association and the powers of the company's directors including, in particular, any powers in relation to the issuing or buying back by the company of its shares.[138] The company must disclose any significant agreements to which the company is a party that take effect, alter or terminate upon a change of control of the company following a takeover bid and the effects of any such agreements (there is an exemption if disclosure of the agreement would be seriously prejudicial to the company).[139] In other words, disclosure must be made of poison pill-type agreements (discussed at **26-56**) so that a potential offeror can see whether there are arrangements in place which would make it prohibitively expensive or difficult to take over the company.

E Protection of minority shareholders

Mandatory bids

26-65 As part of the insistence on equivalent treatment of shareholders, it has always been a fundamental principle underlying the Takeover Code that a shareholder should have a right to exit from the company by selling his shares on a change of control of the company.[140] Accordingly, in some circumstances there is a mandatory bid requirement (i.e. a requirement for a general offer for all the remaining shares of the company) governed by rule 9 although provision is made for some dispensations from this general requirement.[141] If an offeror acquires or enhances a controlling stake in a company, a

---

[135] See CA 2006, s 416(4); SI 2008/410, reg 10, Sch 7, Pt 6, paras 13, 14.

[136] See SI 2008/410, reg 10, Sch 7, Pt 6, para 13(1).

[137] See SI 2008/410, reg 10, Sch 7, Pt 6, para 13(2)(k).

[138] See SI 2008/410, reg 10, Sch 7, Pt 6, para 13(2)(h), (2)(i).

[139] See Takeover Directive, art 10(1)(j); SI 2008/410, reg 10, Sch 7, Pt 6, para 13(2)(k).

[140] See generally Jennings, 'Mandatory Bids Revisited' (2005) JCLS 37.

[141] See Takeover Code, Notes on Dispensations from Rule 9. For example, a mandatory bid is not required where there is an independent vote at a shareholders' meeting approving an issue of new shares (known as the 'whitewash procedure') as consideration for an acquisition or cash subscription which would otherwise

similar offer must be extended to all shareholders. The price paid for control is thus extended to all shareholders and control is effectively treated as an asset of the company, reflected in the value of each share, rather than as an asset of the controlling shareholder. All the shareholders share in the premium paid by the offeror and can exit from the company on a change of control.

26-66 The Takeover Directive also includes a requirement for a mandatory bid for all holdings so allowing the minority shareholders to exit the company at an 'equitable price' on a change of control. The threshold at which the mandatory bid is triggered by the acquisition of voting rights by a person and those acting in concert with him is a matter for the Member State in which the offeree company has its registered office.[142] The 'equitable price' which must be paid is defined by the Takeover Directive (art 5(4)): it must be the highest price paid for the same securities by the offeror, or by persons acting in concert with him, over a period of between six and 12 months (as the Member State decides) prior to the bid, with the possibility of an adjustment to that price by the supervisory authority in exceptional circumstances.[143] As noted, it is for Member States to set the level at which a mandatory bid is required and while a number of Member States have set it at 30%, a number have set substantially higher figures.[144]

26-67 A mandatory bid is required by the Takeover Code when:[145]

(1) any person acquires an interest in shares which (taken together with shares in which persons acting in concert with him are interested) carry 30% or more of the voting rights of a company; or

(2) any person, together with persons acting in concert with him, is interested in shares which carry not less than 30% of the voting rights of a company but not more than 50% of such voting rights and such person, or any person acting in concert with him, acquires an interest in any other shares which increases the percentage of shares carrying voting rights in which he is interested (rule 9).[146]

26-68 Mandatory offers must be for cash or with a cash alternative at not less than the highest price paid by the offeror or persons acting in concert with it for shares of that class in the preceding 12 months (rule 9.5). Mandatory bids may not include any conditions other than a requirement for acceptances in respect of shares carrying more than 50% of the voting rights of the company and a provision that the bid will lapse automatically on reference to the competition authorities.[147] These restrictions as to the conditions which may be attached to a mandatory bid are designed to prevent the offeror defeating the purpose

---

trigger a mandatory bid, or where a 30% holding is acquired in the context of a rescue operation, or on the enforcement by a creditor of security for a loan, or through inadvertent mistake and where the holding is then reduced below 30% in a manner which is satisfactory to the Panel.

[142] See Takeover Directive, art 5(1), (3). See Wymeersch, 'The Mandatory Bid: A Critical View' in Hopt & Wymeersch (eds), *European Takeovers—Law and Practice* (1992).

[143] Consideration payable may be securities (provided they are admitted to trading on a regulated market which ensures they are liquid securities) or a Member State may require cash, at least as an alternative and, in some circumstances, a cash alternative must be provided: see Takeover Directive, art 5(5).

[144] See *Report on the Implementation of the Directive on Takeover Bids*, SEC (2007) 268, 21.02.2007, Annex 2 which shows about 12 Member States setting 30–33% as the trigger requirements with some States on 40%, some on 50% and Poland on 66%.

[145] Partial bids, i.e. bids for shares carrying over 30% but less than 100% of the voting rights of a company, are discouraged and cannot be made without the Panel's consent: see rule 36.

[146] If a person already owns over 50%, he may continue to acquire shares without making a general offer since strengthening a controlling stake which is already over 50% is not regarded as affecting the minority shareholder to the same extent.   [147] Takeover Code, rule 9.3, 9.4.

of rule 9 by attaching conditions to the offer which would make acceptance unattractive to the shareholders. These limitations also make a mandatory bid unattractive to the bidder as he cannot insist on 90% acceptances which is important if statutory powers to acquire minority holdings are to be used. In fact, few mandatory bids are made, as offerors take care to ensure that they do not find themselves in a position where a mandatory bid is required.[148]

Squeeze-out and sell-out rights

26-69 Where an offer or makes an offer for the shares in another company, it may be content simply to acquire sufficient shares to give it control of the offeree company. But, in many circumstances, the offeror will want to acquire 100% of the shares in the offeree company. Since 1929, there has been a specific statutory procedure, now contained in CA 2006, ss 974–991, whereby an offeror, whose offer has been accepted by holders of 90% or more of the shares to which the offer relates, can compulsorily acquire the remaining shares (squeeze-out) unless the court upholds an objection by a dissenting shareholder and, vice versa, a minority shareholder can demand to be bought out (sell-out). The purpose of these provisions is to facilitate the acquisition by an offeror of 100% of the shares in a target company so enabling the offeror to operate the subsidiary as a wholly-owned subsidiary without regard to minority shareholders. Equally, the provisions facilitate the exit of minority shareholders from a target company so enabling such shareholders to avoid the problems arising from being locked into a company under new control. The Takeover Directive in arts 15 and 16 also makes provision for squeeze-out and sell-out rights which allow:

- an offeror to require the remaining shareholders to sell their holdings to him at a fair price[149] when he has secured a set level of acceptances (to be determined by each Member State[150] and to be on the acquisition of between 90% and 95% of the capital);[151] and

- a minority shareholder to require an offeror to acquire his shares at a fair price when the offeror has secured 90–95% of the capital, again the threshold to be determined by each Member State.[152]

---

[148] The Annual Reports of the Takeover Panel consistently show only a very small number of mandatory bids. In 2010–11, 91 formal offer documents were sent to shareholders of which only nine involved mandatory bids; in 2009–10, 88 offer documents, only 10 involving mandatory bids; in 2008–09, 101 offer documents, only five involving mandatory bids.

[149] A Member State must ensure a fair price and the same form of consideration as offered in the bid: Takeover Directive, art 15(5).

[150] See *Report on the Implementation of the Directive on Takeover Bids*, SEC (2007) 268, 21.02.2007, Annex 4, which shows the thresholds chosen by the Member States, the majority of whom have opted for a 90% threshold.

[151] The High Level Group favoured compulsory powers to acquire minority shareholders on a variety of grounds noting that minority shareholders can impose disproportionately high costs on bidders, for example, by preventing full integration of the bidder and target companies, by 'free-riding' on the success of the new owners and by demanding extortionate prices for their shares, see *Report of the High Level Group of Company Law Experts on Issues Related to Takeover Bids*, 10 January 2002, Brussels, para 3.1.

[152] The High Level Group favoured sell-out powers for minority shareholders on a variety of grounds noting that, after a takeover bid, the majority shareholder may be tempted to abuse his dominant position; minority shareholders cannot obtain appropriate compensation by simply selling their shares in the market; the sell-out right is an appropriate mechanism to counter the pressure on shareholders to tender in the takeover bid; and the sell-out right is a fair counterpart for the squeeze-out right conferred

Application of compulsory acquisition powers

26-70 The statutory scheme for compulsory acquisition applies where an offeror has made a takeover offer to acquire all the shares,[153] or where there is more than one class of shares, all of the shares of one or more classes of shares, in a company (other than those already held at the date of the offer by the offeror or its associates);[154] and the offer must be on the same terms for all the shares of the same class.[155] Two important time-limits are imposed:

(1) the offeror must, by virtue of acceptances of the offer, have acquired or unconditionally contracted to acquire not less than 90% in value of the shares to which the offer relates (and for this purpose the offeror need only bring into the calculation shares which are actually in issue (i.e. allotted) at the relevant time),[156] and, where the shares are voting shares, not less than 90% of the voting rights carried by those shares (CA 2006, s 979(2));[157]

(2) once the offeror has secured such acceptances, he has three months from the date when he reached the 90% threshold to notify dissentient shareholders that he wishes to exercise his statutory powers to acquire their shares;[158] or in the case of a takeover which is not subject to the Takeover Directive, within a period of six months of the date of the offer if this is earlier than the period ending three months after the end of the offer (see s 980(2), (3)).

26-71 Assuming no application is made to the court by dissenting shareholders within six weeks of receiving the notice of acquisition (see CA 2006, s 986, and discussion at **26-73**), the offeror is entitled and bound to acquire the shares at the end of six weeks from the date of the notice on the terms of the offer (s 981(2)). The offeror sends a copy of the notice to the target company and pays to it the consideration for the shares to which the notice relates (s 988(6)). That consideration is held on trust for payment to the former shareholders who have now been compulsorily acquired by the offeror. At this point, the company removes the names of those former members from the share register and enters the name of the offeror on the register as the holder of those shares.[159]

on the majority shareholders: see *Report of the High Level Group of Company Law Experts on Issues Related to Takeover Bids* (10 January 2002, Brussels), para 3.2.

[153] The bidder must make an offer and not merely an invitation to treat: see *Re Chez Nico (Restaurants) Ltd* [1992] BCLC 192. An offer can be for all the shares in a company although it is not communicated to or is impossible or difficult to accept by some shareholders by reasons of the laws of another jurisdiction, provided the conditions set out in CA 2006, s 978 are met; and see *Winpar Holdings Ltd v Joseph Holt Group Plc* [2001] 2 BCLC 604.

[154] CA 2006, ss 975, 977. In ascertaining the offeror's position at the start of the bid, shares which he has conditionally or unconditionally contracted to acquire are treated as shares already held by the offeror: s 975(1), but shares which are the subject of irrevocable undertakings do count towards the 90% calculation: s 975(2).

[155] CA 2006, s 974(1), (3); and see s 976(2): an offer can be treated as being on the same terms even if the offeror agrees to pay more depending on dividend rights or pays different but equivalent consideration to shareholders in countries outside the UK. [156] CA 2006, s 979(5).

[157] The second element, 90% of the voting rights carried by those shares, was introduced to implement the Takeover Directive, art 15. In practice, this makes little difference in this jurisdiction where most shares carry voting rights so anyone holding 90% of the shares will have 90% of the voting rights, but other Member States have more varied voting structures.

[158] CA 2006, s 980(2). The notice given must also be sent to the company accompanied by a statutory declaration by the offeror stating that the conditions for giving notice have been satisfied: s 980(4). See *Re Chez Nico (Restaurants) Ltd* [1992] BCLC 192 (lateness in complying with requirement re statutory declaration does not nullify the whole procedure). [159] CA 2006, s 981(7), (8).

26-72 Obviously it is essential to many offerors to get to the necessary 90% acceptances (which is why it is a common condition in a takeover bid) but various matters need to be borne in mind when considering whether an offeror has crossed that threshold and the statute has a variety of provisions which help with the calculations. The first problem is where the offeror continues to buy shares in the offeree company in the market during the period of the offer. The difficulty here is that shareholders who sell during the bid are people who might otherwise have accepted the offer, thus making it harder to obtain a 90% acceptance of the actual offer as a result. This problem is resolved by providing that shares acquired during the offer by the offeror or its associates can be treated as acceptances of the offer provided that the consideration does not exceed the offer price or, if it does, that the offer price is correspondingly increased.[160] Another issue is whether raising the offer amounts to a new offer and so acceptances have to be counted of the new offer only. The answer is that a revised offer is not a fresh offer as long as the original offer allowed for revision and for acceptance of previous terms to be treated as acceptance of revised terms.[161] Another problem in the calculation is that some of the shareholders to whom the offer has been made will prove to be untraceable and those people may make all the difference in determining whether the offeror has 90% acceptance of the bid. This issue can be dealt with by the court which, provided certain conditions are met, may make an order authorising compulsory notices to be given.[162]

Objecting shareholders

26-73 A shareholder who receives a notice from an offeror of the intention to acquire the holder's shares has six weeks in which to apply to the court asking it to disallow the acquisition or to specify terms different from those in the offer (CA 2006, s 986). The court may not reduce the consideration payable to below the consideration offered in the bid, but a shareholder may apply to the court for consideration higher than that offered in the bid in exceptional circumstances (s 986(4)). A shareholder who decides to apply to the court must promptly notify the offeror and in turn the offeror is required, at the earliest opportunity, to notify other shareholders who are not a party to the application that proceedings have been initiated. Once an application is made, the offeror cannot proceed to enforce the compulsory acquisition notices already given until the application is resolved (s 986(2)).

26-74 The courts are unsympathetic generally when faced with challenges to the procedure by minority shareholders and are much swayed by the fact that 90% of the shareholders think the offer is acceptable. The onus is on the dissenters to convince the court that the offer for their shares is unfair.[163] The test is whether the offer is fair to the shareholders as a body without reference to the particular circumstances of the applicant to the court, so it will not be relevant that the dissenting shareholders will be forced to sell at a loss,[164] nor is it sufficient to show that the scheme was open to criticism or capable of improvement.[165]

---

[160] CA 2006, s 978(8), (10).

[161] CA 2006, s 974(7); and see *Re Chez Nico (Restaurants) Ltd* [1992] BCLC 192.

[162] CA 2006, s 986(9), (10).

[163] *Re Grierson, Oldham and Adams Ltd* [1967] 1 All ER 192; *Re Sussex Brick Co Ltd* [1960] 1 All ER 772n; *Re Press Caps Ltd* [1949] 1 All ER 1013; *Re Hoare & Co Ltd* (1933) 150 LT 374. It will be helpful if the dissenters can show substantial non-compliance with the Takeover Code: see *Re Chez Nico (Restaurants) Ltd* [1992] BCLC 192. See Morse [1992] JBL 316.

[164] *Re Grierson, Oldham and Adams Ltd* [1967] 1 All ER 192; where the shares are quoted on the Stock Exchange and the offer price is above the market price, that raises a presumption that the price is fair. See also *Re Press Caps Ltd* [1949] 1 All ER 1013.

[165] *Re Grierson, Oldham and Adams Ltd* [1967] 1 All ER 192; *Re Sussex Brick Co Ltd* [1960] 1 All ER 772n.

26-75 The onus of proof is reversed if those accepting are in effect the offerors. In *Re Bugle Press Ltd*[166] the 90% acceptances in the offeree company came from two persons who owned all the shares in the offeror company and it was held that the onus of proof was on them to show positively that the offer was fair rather than on the dissenter to show the offer was unfair. Since they produced no evidence at all, the court refused to allow the compulsory acquisition of the dissenter.

26-76 In *Fiske Nominees Ltd v Dwyka Diamonds Ltd*[167] also the court agreed that, while the onus is on those objecting to the compulsory acquisition notice to establish affirmatively that the offer to acquire their shares is unfair, the court will look at factors such as the relationship between the bidder and those accepting the offer. In any event, the court has a discretion as to the order which may be made. It may order that the shares should not be acquired, or permit acquisition but on different terms, or dismiss the application so that the compulsory notice stands and the shares may be acquired on the terms of the offer.

26-77 In *Fiske* the transaction was not subject to the Takeover Code, but the court looked to the Code as evidence of good practice. For an offer to be fair, it must be made in sufficient detail to enable the offeree to make an informed decision. By the standards of the Code, insufficient information had been provided to the shareholders as to the value of the consideration which would be provided for the shares and the offer was not fair. Furthermore, given that there was a connection between the accepting shareholders and the offeror, the fact that 90% had accepted the offer could not be given any real weight, still less decisive weight. The defendants were not entitled to acquire the objectors' shares on the terms of the offer, but the court did order that the defendants purchase the shares on different terms, in this case at a price to be determined by an independent valuer.

26-78 Another interesting case on these compulsory acquisition powers is *Re Greythorn Ltd*[168] where a minority shareholder opposed a compulsory acquisition notice which the offeror then purported to withdraw. The shareholder wished to continue her application to the court arguing that, while she did not accept compulsory acquisition on the terms of the offer, she did wish her shares to be acquired on terms to be determined by the court.[169] The court concluded that not only has the court the discretion to set different terms for the purchase of the shares, it also has the power to require the offeror to implement such terms; otherwise the applicant and the court are engaged in a fruitless exercise. The court further considered that an offeror has no right to withdraw a compulsory acquisition notice once served, but having given notice is entitled and bound to acquire the shares (CA 2006, s 981(2)). The court noted that, had Parliament intended to confer such a right of withdrawal, it would have done so expressly.

26-79 Of course, if a compulsory acquisition notice cannot be withdrawn once served, but the shareholder who is the subject of the notice may persuade the court to order that the shares be acquired on terms other than those offered by the offeror, the result may not be to the liking of the offeror. In *Fiske Nominees Ltd v Dwyka Diamonds Ltd*,[170] noted at **26-76**, instead of being able to insist on a share-for-share offer, the offeror was required to acquire the minority's shares for cash at a price determined by an independent valuer. There are therefore tactical issues to be considered by an offeror before deciding to

---

[166] [1960] 3 All ER 791, CA; see also *Re Chez Nico (Restaurants) Ltd* [1992] BCLC 192 at 207.
[167] [2002] 2 BCLC 123.   [168] [2002] 1 BCLC 437.
[169] The Takeover Code rule 35.3 prohibits an offeror who holds more than 50% of the voting rights from offering within six months of the closure of any previous offer for the company more favourable terms to any shareholder in that company than those available under the offer provision.   [170] [2002] 2 BCLC 123.

activate the compulsory acquisition mechanism; equally, a minority shareholder must decide whether to accept the terms on offer or whether to apply to the court in the hope of securing different terms. Of course, a minority shareholder may find that the offeror takes no steps to utilise these compulsory acquisition powers, in which case the minority may choose to activate the process under CA 2006, s 983.

Right of minority to be bought out

26-80 Those shareholders who do not accept the takeover bid may decide subsequently that they may not wish to remain as minority shareholders in the company given its new controllers. The statute therefore allows them to insist on being bought out by the offeror at the price paid to the other shareholders or on such other terms as may be agreed or the court may fix.[171]

26-81 This right to be bought out by the offeror arises where the offeror has made a takeover offer for all the shares (or all the shares of a class) in a company and, before the offer expires, the offeror and its associates own at least 90% in value of those shares (or the shares of that class) and 90% of the voting rights carried by those shares or by that class of shares.[172] In these circumstances, any shareholder who has not accepted the offer may require the offeror to acquire his shares. To ensure that the minority are aware of this option, within one month of these conditions being satisfied, the offeror must give those shareholders notice of their right to sell, specifying a closing date not less than three months after the expiry of the offer.[173] This right to sell out may be exercised either within the period of three months from the end of the offer or, if later, three months from the notice given to the shareholder of his right to exercise sell-out rights.

F Schemes of arrangement—CA 2006, Part 26

Introduction

26-82 As noted at **26-7**, it is quite common to effect an agreed takeover by way of a scheme of arrangement and there are various advantages noted there to using a scheme rather than a takeover bid. The decision as to whether to proceed with a straight bid or a scheme of arrangement depends on a variety of factors but is dictated normally by whether the approach is hostile or friendly. It is only possible to proceed by way of a scheme if the offeror has the approval of the board of the offeree company because the board's co-operation is needed in calling the various meetings required under a scheme. Any offer for a company effected through a scheme of arrangement is still within and subject to the Takeover Code which expressly applies to takeovers and mergers effected by means of a scheme and which is modified to accommodate schemes as set out in Appendix 7 to the Code.[174]

26-83 A typical scheme of arrangement effecting a transfer of control provides for the cancellation of the shares in the target company and the capitalisation of the reserve arising on the cancellation of those shares to pay up new shares in the target to be allotted, credited as fully-paid,

---

[171] CA 2006, ss 983, 985; and see s 986(3) where an application may be made to the court by either the shareholder or the offeror to determine the terms on which the offeror must acquire the shares.

[172] CA 2006, s 983(2)–(4). This 90% threshold is not limited to 90% arising from acceptances of the bid.

[173] CA 2006, s 984(3).   [174] Takeover Code, Introduction, para 3(b).

to the bidder. In consideration of the allotment of the target company's shares to the bidder, the bidder allots fully-paid shares in the bidder company to the shareholders of the target company. The result is that the target company becomes a subsidiary of the bidder company and the target company's shareholders become shareholders in the bidder company.[175] Equally, a scheme may be used to merge two companies into a new third company.

26-84 Schemes of arrangements are also commonly used to restructure insolvent companies where a scheme may be used in conjunction with the appointment of an administrator or where a provisional liquidator is in place. The major attraction of using a scheme is that the 75% approval required for a scheme binds all the members or the creditors, as the case may be (CA 2006, s 899(3)). This ability to reach a binding settlement in this way is invaluable as it enables 100% of creditors to be bound though only a majority agree. Schemes are particularly valuable in large and complex insolvencies and much use is made of schemes, for example, in respect of insolvent insurance companies where there may be a wide range of claimants and reinsurers involved and multiple group companies, some solvent and some insolvent.[176] Schemes have also been used extensively in respect of mass tort claims especially asbestos claims which have involved an indeterminate number of claimants (actual and contingent) against large groups with activities in many jurisdictions.[177]

A compromise or arrangement with members or creditors

26-85 Where a compromise or arrangement is proposed between a company and its creditors, or any class of them, or between the company and its members, or any class of them, the court may on the application of the company or any creditor or member (or a liquidator or administrator as the case may be) order a meeting of the creditors or class of creditors, or of the members of the company or class of members, to be summoned in such manner as the court directs (CA 2006, ss 895, 896).[178] Each class affected by the proposed scheme must approve the scheme by a majority in number representing 75% in value of those present and voting either in person or by proxy (s 899(1)). Once sanctioned by the court, the scheme becomes binding on all the creditors or class of creditors, or members or class of members, as the case may be (s 899(3)),[179] and it becomes effective upon a copy of the court order being delivered to the registrar of companies (s 899(4)). The court may not sanction a compromise or arrangement between a public company and its creditors or members or any class of them which falls within CA 2006, Pt 27 (mergers and divisions of public companies) unless the relevant requirements of Part 27 are complied with in addition to the requirements of Part 26 (s 903).[180] Though binding the members or creditors to

---

[175] See, for example, *Re BTR plc* [2000] 1 BCLC 740.

[176] See, for example, *Re Sovereign Marine & General Insurance Co Ltd* [2007] 1 BCLC 228.

[177] See the Turner & Newall asbestos claims; see *Re T & N Ltd (No 2)* [2006] 2 BCLC 374; *Re T & N Ltd (No 3)* [2007] 1 BCLC 563; also *Re Cape plc* [2007] 2 BCLC 546 (also asbestos claims).

[178] A scheme may apply to only some of a company's creditors: *Re PT Garuda Indonesia* [2001] All ER (D) 53 (Oct), Ch D.

[179] Any agreement entered into pursuant to the court's order is binding even though it might otherwise be ultra vires and void: *British and Commonwealth Holdings plc v Barclays Bank plc* [1996] 1 All ER 381, CA.

[180] In particular there are additional disclosure and valuation requirements and, most importantly, the court may not sanction a scheme unless a majority in number representing 75% in value of each class of members of every pre-existing transferee company concerned in the scheme, present and voting, agree to the scheme: CA 2006, s 907(1) (mergers), s 922 (division).

the same extent as if they had made a contract, a scheme is not a contract, but a statutory procedure subject to court approval.[181]

26-86 A scheme must be between the company (either through its board or by a majority of the members in general meeting) and the members or creditors (including secured creditors).[182] 'Company' for the purposes of the section includes any company capable of being wound up under the IA 1986 (CA 206, s 895(2)(b)), i.e. any registered or unregistered company including a foreign company[183] and the question in respect of a foreign company is simply whether the court should exercise its discretion to sanction a scheme in relation to such a company. To do this, there must be a sufficient connection with this jurisdiction and it can be sufficient that the company's creditors or the class of them the subject of the scheme have chosen English law (including a choice of English jurisdiction) to govern their relationship with the company.[184] 'Arrangement' is interpreted widely by the courts which are anxious not to restrict a provision which Parliament has not limited.[185] However, this liberal approach must not obscure the requirement that it has to be an arrangement with creditors or members, as the case may be, and the word is given context by the parties to it.[186]

26-87 In *Re Lehman Brothers International (Europe) Ltd*[187] the Court of Appeal held that the court has no jurisdiction to sanction a scheme for persons having proprietary claims against the company in respect of which the scheme was proposed. As Patten LJ noted, as a matter of ordinary language, a creditor is someone to whom money is owed.[188] A proprietary claim to assets held by a company is not a claim in respect of a debt or liability owed by the company and a person holding a proprietary claim is not a creditor of the company in any conventional sense of the word. An arrangement between a company and its creditors means an arrangement which deals with their rights *inter se* as debtor and creditor and does not include rights which persons have over their own property held by the company which never becomes part of the company's assets. Proprietary claims to those trust assets cannot be the subject of a scheme of arrangement. Generally, 'creditor' is to be construed widely in keeping with the purpose of the statutory provisions which is to encourage arrangements which avoid liquidation and facilitate the financial rehabilitation of the company and it therefore includes contingent creditors such as future tort claimants.[189]

---

[181] *Kemp v Ambassador Insurance Co* [1998] 1 BCLC 234 at 238, PC; also *Re Cape plc* [2007] 2 BCLC 546 at [77]–[78] (not being a contract, a scheme is not subject therefore to the Unfair Contract Terms Act 1977).

[182] *Re Savoy Hotel Ltd* [1981] 3 All ER 646; see *Re T & N Ltd (No 3)* [2007] 1 BCLC 563 at [46]–[50] as to what is an 'arrangement' for these purposes.

[183] See *Re Rodenstock Gmbh* [2011] EWHC 1104 at [56]. Nothing in the EC Judgments Regulation or the EC Insolvency Regulation narrows the jurisdiction of the court to sanction a scheme of arrangement; see also *Re Primacom Holdings Gmbh* [2012] EWHC 164.

[184] *Re Rodenstock Gmbh* [2011] EWHC 1104; *Re Drax Holdings Ltd* [2004] 1 BCLC 10.

[185] See *Re T & N Ltd (No 3)* [2007] 1 BCLC 563 at [53].

[186] *Re Lehman Brothers International (Europe)* [2010] 1 BCLC 496 at [61], per Patten LJ.

[187] [2010] 1 BCLC 496.

[188] [2010] 1 BCLC 496 at [59]. He went on: 'Given that "creditor" is not defined in the legislation, it is inconceivable that Parliament should have used the word in the 2006 Act in any but its literal sense.'

[189] *Re T & N Ltd (No 2)* [2006] 2 BCLC 374; and actual or potential claimants for contribution with an accrued right to claim contribution under the Civil Liability (Contribution) Act 1978 are creditors for these purposes: *Re T & N Ltd (No 3)* [2007] 1 BCLC 563, but see comments by Neuberger LJ in *Re Lehman Brothers International (Europe)* [2010] 1 BCLC 496 at [83], that this decision in *Re T & N Ltd (No 3)* is near the outer limits of the scope of CA 2006, s 895.

26-88 A compromise and an arrangement are separate concepts and an arrangement need not involve a compromise or be confined to a case of dispute or difficulty.[190] An arrangement or compromise involves some element of give and take, some element of accommodation on each side,[191] and while an arrangement often alters rights between the company and the creditors or members, it need not alter the rights provided that overall the scheme constitutes an arrangement.[192] Where members or creditors give up all their rights and receive no benefit, there is no compromise or arrangement,[193] but when the scheme forms an integral part of a restructuring which confers substantial benefit on the members bound by the scheme, then it is artificial to confine the analysis of whether the situation amounts to a compromise or arrangement just to the terms of the scheme.[194]

26-89 There are three distinct stages to a scheme of arrangement:

(1) the application to the court for an order convening the necessary meeting or meetings of members or creditors, as the case may be (the convening hearing, CA 2006, s 896);

(2) the holding of the meetings for approval by the requisite majority; and

(3) the application to the court for the sanctioning of the scheme under s 899 (the sanction hearing).

Identifying the classes

26-90 If the class meetings are improperly constituted, the court will refuse to sanction the scheme[195] so objectors to a scheme will often allege that the class meetings were incorrectly composed. Equally, the courts are aware of the importance of schemes of arrangement to the resolution of very real practical difficulties in many cases of insolvency and reorganisation and they are anxious that objectors should not be able to rely on unrealistic distinctions so as to thwart the approval of the scheme. As Neuberger J noted in *Re Anglo American Insurance Co Ltd*,[196] unless a practical approach is adopted to this question, there is a danger that 'one could end up with virtually as many classes as there are members of a particular group'. The position is governed now by the Court of Appeal ruling in *Re Hawk Insurance Co Ltd*[197] where the scheme concerned an insolvent insurance company. The scheme had been approved unanimously at a single meeting of the scheme creditors, but the court at first instance declined to sanction the scheme as it was not satisfied that the scheme creditors constituted a single class, though no creditor appeared to oppose the scheme. On appeal, the Court of Appeal held that it is settled law that in determining whether creditors fall into separate classes, the test to be applied is that of Bowen LJ in *Sovereign Life Assurance Co v Dodd*[198] to the effect that a class consists

---

[190] *Re Guardian Assurance Co* [1917] 1 Ch 431; *Re T & N Ltd (No 3)* [2007] 1 BCLC 563 at 583.

[191] *Re Savoy Hotel Ltd* [1981] 3 All ER 646; *Re NFU Development Trust Ltd* [1973] 1 All ER 135; a compromise requires some settling of a controversy or some difficulty: see *Sneath v Valley Gold* (1893) 1 Ch 477 at 491, per Fry LJ. See also CA 2006, s 895(2). A scheme used to effect a takeover bid is not a compromise, but it is an arrangement between the company and its members because it involves a change in the membership of the company: *Re T & N Ltd (No 3)* [2007] 1 BCLC 563 at 583.

[192] *Re T & N Ltd (No 3)* [2007] 1 BCLC 563.   [193] *Re NFU Development Trust Ltd* [1973] 1 All ER 135.

[194] *Re Uniq plc* [2011] EWHC 749 at [24].

[195] See, for example, *Re British Aviation Insurance Co Ltd* [2006] 1 BCLC 665.   [196] [2001] 1 BCLC 755.

[197] [2001] 2 BCLC 480. See Moss, 'Hawk Triumphant: A vindication of the modern approach to classes in s 425 schemes' [2003] 40 Insolv Int 41.

[198] [1892] 2 QB 573 at 583, CA (holders of matured insurance policies constituted a different class from holders of unmatured policies); also *Re United Provident Assurance Co Ltd* [1910] 2 Ch 477 (partly-paid shares and fully-paid shares are different classes requiring separate meetings).

of 'those persons whose rights are not so dissimilar as to make it impossible for them to consult together with a view to their common interest'. But Chadwick LJ stressed that:[199]

> 'When applying Bowen LJ's test to the question "are the rights of those who are to be affected by the scheme proposed such that the scheme can be seen as a single arrangement; or ought it to be regarded, on a true analysis, as a number of linked arrangements?" it is necessary to ensure not only that those whose rights really are so dissimilar that they cannot consult together with a view to a common interest should be treated as parties to distinct arrangements—so that they should have their own separate meetings—but also that those whose rights are sufficiently similar to the rights of others that they can properly consult together should be required to do so; lest by ordering separate meetings the court gives a veto to a minority group.'

26-91 The Court of Appeal ruled that the scheme would be sanctioned, the lower court having fallen into error in concluding that the creditors fell into more than one class. Neither the rights released or varied nor the new rights given under the proposed scheme were so dissimilar as to make it impossible for the creditors to consult together with a view to their common interest. That common interest lay in a simple, inexpensive and expeditious winding up of the company's affairs without the need for a formal liquidation. Chadwick LJ stressed that it is important that Bowen LJ's test should not be applied in such a way that it becomes an instrument of oppression by a minority and the protection for any shareholder who feels aggrieved at the composition of the meeting lies in the requirement that the court must sanction a scheme.[200] As noted in *Re BTR plc*,[201] 'Parliament has recognised that it is for the court…to hold the ring between different interests; and to decline to sanction a scheme if satisfied that members having one interest have sought to take advantage over those having another.'

26-92 In assessing the rights of creditors for the purpose of establishing the classes of creditors in a particular scheme the court has to consider, as David Richards J explained in *Re T & N Ltd (No 3)*,[202] (a) the rights of creditors in the absence of the scheme and (b) any new rights to which the creditors become entitled under the scheme. If there is a material difference between the rights of different groups of creditors under (a) or (b), they may constitute different classes.[203] Richards J went on to say that in considering the rights of creditors which are to be affected by the scheme, it is essential to identify the correct comparator. In the case of rights against an insolvent company, where the scheme is proposed as an alternative to an insolvent liquidation, it is their rights as creditors in an insolvent liquidation of the company while in a company which is solvent and will continue in business, the creditors' rights against the company as a continuing entity are the appropriate comparator.[204]

26-93 If any class of creditor or contributories are not affected by a scheme, either because their rights are not altered or because they have no economic interest in the company, the company need not consult or include them in the scheme, it being established that a company is free to select the creditors with whom it wishes to enter into an arrangement.[205] In *Re Bluebrook Ltd*[206] a company was balance sheet insolvent and a scheme was drawn up with its senior creditors which involved a sale of the business to a new company and

---

[199] [2001] 2 BCLC 480 at 519. See also *Re BTR plc* [1999] 2 BCLC 675 at 682.
[200] [2001] 2 BCLC 480 at 519.   [201] [2000] 1 BCLC 740 at 748.   [202] [2007] 1 BCLC 563.
[203] [2007] 1 BCLC 563 at [86].
[204] [2007] 1 BCLC 563 at [87]. See also *Re Cape plc* [2007] 2 BCLC 546 at [36]; *Re British Aviation Insurance Co Ltd* [2006] 1 BCLC 665.   [205] *Re Tea Corpn Ltd* [1904] 1 Ch 12; *Re Bluebrook Ltd* [2010] 1 BCLC 338.
[206] [2010] 1 BCLC 338.

a debt/equity swap for those senior creditors in the new company. The junior creditors would be left behind in the insolvent old company. On a challenge to the scheme by the junior creditors, the court accepted that, on an appropriate going concern valuation of the company,[207] there was no possibility of the senior claims being met and therefore no possibility of the junior creditors having any economic interest remaining in the company. The scheme did not affect their rights, therefore, and they had no economic interest so their consent was not required.[208]

26-94   The onus is on the company to ensure that the meetings are properly constituted according to the rights of the members or creditors, as the case may be, and the court will not sanction a scheme where separate meetings have not been held for those with different substantive rights. There remains a risk, therefore, that the company may not correctly identify the classes for which separate meetings are required and so, at the later stage, it will find that the court will not sanction the scheme. But that risk has been reduced by a change of practice on these matters following the decision in *Re Hawk Insurance Co Ltd*.[209]

26-95   In *Re Hawk Insurance Co Ltd* Chadwick LJ had commented on the need to re-examine the (then) established practice of the court not to decide on the composition of the classes but to leave it to the company (or liquidator etc) to determine which meetings needed to be called, with the risk that an erroneous decision as to the composition of the meetings would result in the court subsequently refusing to sanction the scheme with all the delay and expense which that would entail.[210] This message was duly noted by the lower courts which began to consider the issue of the composition of the meetings to a greater degree than previously. For example, in *Re Equitable Life Assurance Society*[211] Lloyd J agreed that it was appropriate for the court to attempt to formulate a *prima facie* view as to whether the class or classes put forward by the company were appropriate while emphasising that this could only be a provisional conclusion and was subject to contrary submissions when the court was asked subsequently to sanction the scheme.[212]

26-96   The effect is to require the company and its advisers at a preliminary stage to focus their efforts on identifying the classes correctly in order to satisfy the court that it should order the convening of meetings. The greater the focus at that stage, the more likely it is that the company will have identified the classes correctly. These changes were reflected in a 2002 Practice Statement (*Companies: schemes of arrangement*) which clarifies the approach taken by the courts on scheme applications so as to enable issues concerning the composition of classes of creditor and the summoning of meetings to be identified and if appropriate resolved early in the proceedings.[213] Essentially, the responsibility for the composition of the classes remains with the applicant who must draw the attention of the

---

[207] The court agreed that, in assessing the fairness of the scheme, the appropriate method of valuation was a going concern valuation rather than using a break-up valuation (the company was capable of trading profitably), using real world judgements as to what was likely to happen rather than relying on a range of mechanistic probability calculations: see [2010] 1 BCLC 338 at [35], [40], [45], [52]. Cf *Re Mytravel Group plc* [2005] 2 BCLC 123 at [55]–[58].

[208] [2010] 1 BCLC 338 at [25], [51]–[52]; *Re Tea Corpn Ltd* [1904] 1 Ch 12. This ability to deal with junior creditors in this way is one of the attractions of an English scheme of arrangement and explains why foreign companies are interested sometimes in using a scheme to reorganise their affairs; see for example *Re Rodenstock Gmbh* [2011] EWHC 1104, see **26-86**. Another possibility is for the foreign company to change its 'comi' and use an English administration to achieve a restructuring, see **23-6**, but that is likely to be much more complex and expensive than using a scheme of arrangement.

[209] [2001] 2 BCLC 480.   [210] [2001] 2 BCLC 480 at 513.   [211] [2002] BCC 319.

[212] See also *Re Telewest Communications plc (No 1)* [2005] 1 BCLC 752.

[213] The full text of the Practice Statement is set out at [2002] 3 All ER 96.

court to any issue as to composition which may arise. Indeed, any issue which goes to the jurisdiction of the court to sanction a scheme or which would otherwise lead the court to refuse to sanction the scheme should be raised at this stage.[214] The applicant must take all steps reasonably open to it to notify any person affected by the scheme which gives parties an opportunity to make representations as to the composition of the meetings.[215] While creditors who consider that they have been unfairly treated are still able to appear and raise objections at the hearing to sanction the scheme, the court will expect them to show good reason why they did not raise their concerns at an earlier stage. In other words, the company must expend greater effort in determining the composition of the classes and objectors must make their case earlier, while not excluding the possibility of a challenge to the scheme at the subsequent sanction hearing. The courts are anxious to eliminate as much as possible the risk of a successful challenge at the sanction stage when the company has already been put to a great deal of expense in advancing the scheme. In practice, once the court has formed a *prima facie* view as to the correct composition of the class meetings, it may prove difficult to challenge that conclusion at the sanction stage save in cases of significant substantive error. The result is greater commercial certainty with some concerns (probably overstated) that this certainty has been achieved at the expense of minority protection.

The meetings of the class

26-97 The notice calling the meeting must be accompanied by a statement explaining the scheme,[216] disclosing any material interests of the directors and whether the arrangement affects them differently from others with a similar interest (CA 2006, s 897(1), (2)). If there is any material alteration to the circumstances after the notice is sent, a further communication is required, otherwise there is a risk that the court may not approve the scheme, for those voting must be informed as to the issues before them.[217] Save where a class consists of only one member, a meeting must be attended (whether in person or by the use of technology) by more than one person and the court has no jurisdiction to sanction a scheme which provides for a class meeting of creditors to be constituted by the attendance of one creditor.[218] It is possible for a person to fall into two classes and properly attend each meeting.[219]

26-98 Each class affected by the proposed scheme must approve the scheme by a majority in number representing 75% in value of those present and voting either in person or by proxy (CA 2006, s 899(1)).[220] The passing of the resolution represents a threshold which

---

[214] See *Re T & N Ltd (No 3)* [2007] 1 BCLC 563 at 574, per David Richards J.

[215] See *Re British Aviation Insurance Co Ltd* [2006] 1 BCLC 665 (requirements as to notification are not absolute and do not apply if there are good reasons, such as time and expense, why they should not apply).

[216] The statement must explain how the scheme affects the creditors or shareholders commercially and the extent of the information required depends on the facts of the particular case: see *Re Heron International NV* [1994] 1 BCLC 667; *Re Allied Domecq plc* [2000] 1 BCLC 134.

[217] *Re Jessel Trust Ltd* [1985] BCLC 119; *Re Minster Assets plc* [1985] BCLC 200: the role of the court is to be satisfied that no reasonable shareholder would have changed his decision as to how to act on the scheme if the information had been disclosed: *Re Heron International NV* [1994] 1 BCLC 667; *Re Allied Domecq plc* [2000] 1 BCLC 134.   [218] *Re Altitude Scaffolding Ltd; Re T&N Ltd* [2007] 1 BCLC 199.

[219] *Re Alabama, New Orleans, Texas and Pacific Junction Rly Co* [1891] 1 Ch 213, CA; *Re Cape plc* [2007] 2 BCLC 546 at 555.

[220] Depending on the circumstances a low turn out in terms of numbers or value may be a matter of concern to the court which will want to see that the class to be bound by the scheme was fairly represented at the meeting: *Re Uniq plc* [2011] EWHC 749 at [22]–[23] (only approximately some 15% of shareholders turned out to the meeting, but as the company had an unusually large number of shareholders with very

the company must surmount, but it must then be given effect to by the sanction of the court which acts, as Parliament envisaged, as a check or balance on the majority.[221]

The sanction of the court

26-99 Once the meetings have been held, a further application is made to the court for the court to sanction the scheme.[222] In approaching the question of sanction, the courts have been content to endorse on numerous occasions the following statement in *Buckley on the Companies Acts* which explains the role of the court in these terms:[223]

> 'In exercising its power of sanction the court will see, first, that the provisions of the statute have been complied with,[224] second, that the class was fairly represented by those who attended the meeting and that the statutory majority are acting bona fide and are not coercing the minority in order to promote interests adverse to those of the class whom they purport to represent, and thirdly, that the arrangement is such as an intelligent and honest man, a member of the class concerned and acting in respect of his interest, might reasonably approve.[225] The court does not sit merely to see that the majority are acting bona fide and thereupon to register the decision of the meeting, but, at the same time, the court will be slow to differ from the meeting, unless either the class has not been properly consulted, or the meeting has not considered the matter with a view to the interests of the class which it is empowered to bind, or some blot is found in the scheme.'

26-100 In practice, the courts are reluctant to interfere if a proper majority has approved the scheme and typically the scheme is approved by a majority considerably in excess of the required 75% so it would be unusual for a scheme to be refused sanction at this stage.[226] In *Re British Aviation Insurance Co Ltd*[227] the court did refuse to sanction a scheme because the class meetings had not been correctly constituted, but also because, in any event, the court did not think the scheme was fair to creditors, though beneficial to the company and its shareholders.

---

small numbers of shares, this turnout was neither a surprise nor a concern to the court). See also *Re British Aviation Insurance Co Ltd* [2006] 1 BCLC 665 at [114]–[117].

[221] See *Re BTR plc* [2000] 1 BCLC 740 at 747, per Chadwick LJ.

[222] The court can approve a scheme which is to be binding after liquidation and can approve a scheme, exceptionally, which involves a departure from the rules as to mutual credit and set-off in insolvency: *Re Anglo American Insurance Co Ltd* [2001] 1 BCLC 755. The court's approval may be subject to undertakings; see *Re Osiris Insurance Ltd* [1999] 1 BCLC 182; *Re Allied Domecq plc* [2000] 1 BCLC 134.

[223] This statement was approved by Plowman J in *Re National Bank Ltd* [1966] 1 All ER 1006 at 1012, and has subsequently been cited and applied by the courts on numerous occasions, see *Re Allied Domecq plc* [2000] 1 BCLC 134 at 142; *Re RAC Motoring Services Ltd* [2000] 1 BCLC 307 at 321; *Re BTR plc* [1999] 2 BCLC 675 at 680; *Re Osiris Insurance Ltd* [1999] 1 BCLC 182 at 188.

[224] The court may sanction a scheme despite there being a clear error in the special resolution altering the company's share capital as part of the scheme when it was clear from the accompanying circular that an error had been made and the chairman of the meeting had notified the meeting of the correct position before the vote on the resolution: *Re Uniq plc* [2011] EWHC 749 at [29].

[225] Applying the test laid down by Maugham J in *Re Dorman, Long & Co Ltd, South Durham Steel and Iron Co Ltd* [1934] Ch 635 at 657. See also *Re Alabama, New Orleans, Texas and Pacific Junction Rly Co* [1891] 1 Ch 213, CA.

[226] Which is why the rejection of the scheme at first instance in *Re Hawk Insurance Co Ltd* [2001] 2 BCLC 480, when it had been unanimously approved by the creditors, was so exceptional. For a rare example of a case where the court did refuse to sanction a scheme although it had been approved by the requisite majority, see *Re NFU Development Trust* [1973] 1 All ER 135 (the court concluded that the scheme properly examined was a scheme which no member voting in the interests of the members as a whole could reasonably approve). [227] [2006] 1 BCLC 665.

26-101 An issue which has concerned the courts is whether the court has jurisdiction to sanction a scheme of arrangement between a company and its creditors which affects or varies claims which creditors of the company have against third parties. The issue was addressed in *Re La Seda de Barcelona*[228] where the scheme was entered into by a parent company with its creditors. It was a term of the scheme that a subsidiary company, A Ltd, would be released from any obligations which it might have been subject to as a guarantor of loans made by the creditors to the parent company and also that A Ltd would also release any claims which it had against the parent company and other companies in the group. A Ltd was not a party to the scheme. The court sanctioned the scheme, accepting that the release was part of the give and take between the scheme creditors and the parent company which benefited the scheme creditors because A's release of its claims against the parent and other group companies improved the financial position of the parent and those other companies.[229] This was also the position of David Richards J in *Re T & N Ltd (No 3)* where he considered that the court could sanction an arrangement between a company and its creditors which affected the ability of third party claimants to make a claim against those creditors (insurers) where those third party claims were closely linked to their rights against the company.[230]

26-102 In *Re Cape plc*[231] David Richards J held that the court has jurisdiction to sanction a scheme of arrangement which contains provision for future amendment either of the scheme itself or of agreements and other documents to be made pursuant to the scheme, but that there are strong reasons why in most cases the court is unlikely to sanction a scheme with provisions for future amendments. The reasons for not sanctioning would include the need for creditors and the court to know with clarity and certainty the terms of the arrangement and how they will affect creditors. On the other hand, in some unusual contexts, such as in this case where the scheme was to deal with asbestos-related claims which are likely to continue for 40 to 50 years, there was a clear case for some flexibility.

26-103 In *Re National Bank Ltd*[232] the question arose as to whether, if a scheme of arrangement involves the compulsory elimination of minority shareholders, the court should impose a 90% acceptance level (which would apply if compulsory acquisition powers were to be used following a takeover bid, see **26-70**) as a condition for approving the scheme. Plowman J rejected the argument stating that these statutory schemes are quite distinct.[233] Jonathan Parker J in *Re BTR plc*[234] agreed with this approach noting that Parliament had clearly intended that a scheme of arrangement should be available as a means of effecting a binding compromise between a company and its members and that it should be available as an alternative to the use of compulsory acquisition following a takeover offer.[235] Likewise in *Re TDG plc*[236] the court rejected the complaint of an objecting shareholder that he was to be bound by a scheme and bought out in circumstances where the scheme, while it had the support of the necessary majorities, was supported by far fewer than the 90% which

---

[228] [2011] 1 BCLC 555.   [229] [2011] 1 BCLC 555 at [19]–[22].

[230] [2007] 1 BCLC 563 While agreeing with this decision, Lord Neuberger, in *Re Lehman Brothers International (Europe)* [2010] 1 BCLC 496 at [83], noted that the decision was near the outer limits of the scope of CA 2006, s 895 (as to what is a scheme which is capable of sanction).   [231] [2007] 2 BCLC 546.

[232] [1966] 1 All ER 1006; see also *Singer Manufacturing Co v Robinow* 1971 SC 11 in which the offeror company, which already owned 92% of the shares in the offeree company, used a scheme of arrangement with its lower acceptance level requirement to compulsorily acquire the remaining 8% of shares, rather than comply with the conditions for compulsory acquisition discussed at **26-70**.   [233] [1966] 1 All ER 1006 at 1013.

[234] [1999] 2 BCLC 675 at 684.

[235] [2000] 1 BCLC 740 at 747, per Chadwick LJ. In so far as Templeman J suggested to the contrary in *Re Hellenic and General Trust Ltd* [1975] 3 All ER 382, that case must be regarded as of doubtful validity on this point.   [236] [2009] 1 BCLC 445.

would have been required to buy him out had the matter progressed as a takeover. The court noted that how matters might have progressed under a takeover offer was not to the point. The company was entitled to proceed by way of a scheme and the members were protected by the checks and balances in the statutory provisions governing schemes.[237] Here on the facts the court could and would sanction the scheme.

26-104 When the scheme being sanctioned is for the purposes of, or in connection with, a reconstruction or amalgamation and the transfer of the whole or part of one or more companies' businesses to another company, the court has extensive powers under CA 2006, s 900 to make such ancillary orders as are necessary.[238] The court can by order transfer not only the whole or any part of a company's undertaking or property but also its liabilities (s 900(2) (a)). In cases where the company is solvent and there is no risk to creditors, the courts will transfer the liabilities by court order. It has been held that property rights which are not assignable by law cannot be transferred[239] nor can functions which are personal to the company concerned[240] so these restrictions limit the use of s 900 orders. But the former rule, that contracts of employment could not be transferred[241] has been reversed and they are automatically transferred when the undertaking or part thereof is transferred whether the transfer is effected by sale or by some other disposition or by operation of law.[242]

G Reconstruction in the course of voluntary liquidation

26-105 A reconstruction may also be effected under IA 1986, s 110, whereby a liquidator may be authorised (in a members' voluntary winding up, by special resolution; in a creditors' voluntary winding up, by a special resolution of the members and with the sanction of the court or the liquidation committee, see s 110(3)(b)), to sell the whole or part of the company's business or property to another company in return for shares (or other consideration)[243] in that other company which are then distributed among the members of the company in liquidation.[244]

26-106 In its simplest form, where one company transfers its business to a new company, this is called reconstruction. Historically, this was usually done either because the new company had wider or different objects than the old company or to change the rights of different classes of shareholders by giving them shares with altered rights in a new company. But this provision can be used to effect a merger by putting one company into liquidation and transferring its business to the other in return for shares in that other or by putting two companies into liquidation and transferring their businesses to a third company which issues shares to the two liquidators for distribution to the shareholders in the two com-

---

[237] See generally Payne, 'Schemes of Arrangement, Takeovers and Minority Shareholder Protection' (2011) JCLS 67.

[238] In *Re Mytravel Group plc* [2005] 2 BCLC 123, Mann J held that the essence of a reconstruction is that substantially the same shareholders should be involved in both the old and the new companies. Here as 4% by value of the shareholding in the new company was held by 100% of the shareholders in the old, the case was not one in which there was a substantial identity between the two bodies of shareholders in the new company and the scheme did not fall within what is now CA 2006, s 900 (CA 1985, s 427). The case was appealed to the Court of Appeal but there was no appeal on this point.

[239] *Re L Hotel Co Ltd and Langham Hotel Co Ltd* [1946] 1 All ER 319 at 320 (an order under this provision can only transfer such property as could be transferred by an act *inter partes*).

[240] See *Re Skinner* [1958] 3 All ER 273.

[241] *Nokes v Doncaster Amalgamated Collieries Ltd* [1940] 3 All ER 549, HL.

[242] Transfer of Undertakings (Protection of Employment) Regulations 2006, SI 2006/246.

[243] See IA 1986, s 110(2), (4).   [244] IA 1986, s 110 (1), (2), (3)(a).

panies now in liquidation. Equally, businesses may use this type of scheme where they are demerging, i.e. splitting off their businesses into more discrete units.[245]

26-107 The sale or arrangement is binding on all the members of the company[246] subject to the right of any members who did not vote for the resolution to give notice in writing to the liquidator, within seven days after the passing of the resolution, requiring the liquidator either to abstain from carrying out the resolution or to purchase their interest at a price to be determined by agreement or arbitration.[247] Effectively, therefore, the dissenters have to be paid off under this scheme or, more commonly, agreement will already have been reached with them as to the manner of their exit. This does not mean that shareholders who neither assent nor give formal notice of dissent are bound to take the shares in the transferor company. They may instead forfeit their interest in the company altogether[248] or the scheme may provide for the shares of such shareholders to be sold and the proceeds paid to them.[249]

26-108 The consideration received by the liquidator must be distributed among the shareholders entitled to it strictly in accordance with their respective rights as shareholders.[250] In other words, although their rights as shareholders in the new company may be very different from their rights in the old company, the shares in the new company must somehow be distributed in a way that exactly reflects the rights of shareholders in the old company.

26-109 The sale or arrangement agreed to by the special resolution is also binding on the creditors of the old company.[251] They are not transferred with the business to the new company but remain creditors of the old company and they must look to the liquidator of the old company to retain sufficient assets or to realise sufficient of the consideration received from the transferee company to be able to pay them.[252] If they doubt whether the liquidator will be able to pay them, their remedy is to petition for the compulsory liquidation of the company. If an order for winding up is made within a year of the special resolution being passed, the resolution is not valid unless sanctioned by the court (IA 1986, s 110(6)). Liquidators will therefore usually make adequate provision for creditors since they will not want to run the risk of the whole transaction being invalidated as would be the case if the special resolution were invalidated.

26-110 It will be apparent that any transaction that could come within the IA 1986, s 110 could in principle come within a scheme of arrangement as well.[253] The courts have held, however, that the special protection afforded to dissenting shareholders (of compelling the liquidator to buy them out or drop the transaction) must be made available to dissenting shareholders if a similar scheme is effected under a scheme of arrangement.[254] Where the company is transferring only part of its undertaking or assets and is continuing in existence with the remaining assets rather than going into liquidation so that IA 1986, s 110 would not apply, there is no necessity for dissenting shareholders to be given a cash option.[255]

---

[245] As to the use of IA 1986, s 110 schemes for demergers, see Dwyer, 'Section 110 Reconstructions in Private Equity Transactions' [2002] 13 ICCLR 295.   [246] IA 1986, s 110(5).

[247] IA 1986, s 111(1), (2). A shareholder may also be able to halt the transaction by obtaining a winding-up order: s 110(6); see *Re Consolidated South Rand Mines Deep Ltd* [1909] 1 Ch 491 (where scheme is eminently unfair).

[248] *Re Bank of Hindustan, China and Japan Ltd, Higgs's Case* (1865) 2 Hem & M 657; *Burdett-Coutts v True Blue (Hannan's) Gold Mine* [1899] 2 Ch 616, CA.

[249] *Fuller v White Feather Reward Ltd* [1906] 1 Ch 823.   [250] *Griffith v Paget* (1877) 6 Ch D 511.

[251] *Re City and County Investment Co* (1879) 13 Ch D 475, CA.

[252] *Pulsford v Devenish* [1903] 2 Ch 625.

[253] Further, a reconstruction by way of a merger or division of a public company could be effected under CA 2006, Pt 27, without liquidation.   [254] *Re Anglo-Continental Supply Co Ltd* [1922] 2 Ch 723.

[255] *Watt v London & Northern Assets Corpn* [1898] 2 Ch 469, CA.

Index